VOLUME TWO

THE STRUGGLE AGAINST THE BOMB

RESISTING THE BOMB

A History of the World Nuclear Disarmament Movement, 1954–1970

LAWRENCE S. WITTNER

Stanford University Press, Stanford, California, 1997

Stanford University Press, Stanford, California
© 1997 by the Board of Trustees of the Leland Stanford Junior University
Printed in the United States of America
CIP data appear at the end of the book

In memory of Jack and Marjie Wittner

The Stanford
Nuclear Age Series

Conceived by scientists, delivered by the military, and adopted by policymakers, nuclear weapons emerged from the ashes of Hiroshima and Nagasaki to dominate our time. The politics, diplomacy, economy, and culture of the Cold War nurtured the nuclear arms race and, in turn, have been altered by it. "We have had the bomb on our minds since 1945," E. L. Doctorow observes. "It was first our weaponry and then our diplomacy, and now it's our economy. How can we suppose that something so monstrously powerful would not, after forty years, compose our identity? The great golem we have made against our enemies is our culture, our bomb culture—its logic, its faith, its vision."

The pervasive, transformative potential of nuclear weapons was foreseen by their creators. When Secretary of War Henry L. Stimson assembled a committee in May 1945 to discuss postwar atomic energy planning, he spoke of the atomic bomb as a "revolutionary change in the relations of man to the universe." Believing that it could mean "the doom of civilization," he warned President Truman that this weapon "has placed a certain moral responsibility upon us which we cannot shirk without very serious responsibility for any disaster to civilization."

In the decades since World War II that responsibility has weighed heavily on American civilization. Whether or not we have met it is a matter of heated debate. But that we must meet it, and, moreover, that we must also prepare the next generation of leaders to meet it as well, is beyond question.

Today, over half a century into the nuclear age the pervasive impact of the nuclear arms race has stimulated a fundamental reevaluation of the role of nuclear armaments and strategic polices. But mainstream scholarly work in strategic studies has tended to focus on questions related to the development, the deployment, and the diplomacy of nuclear arsenals. Such an exclusively managerial focus cannot probe the universal revolutionary changes about which Stimson spoke, and the need to address these changes is urgent. If the academic community is to contribute imaginatively and helpfully to the increasingly complex problems of the nuclear age, then the base of scholarship and pedagogy in the national security–arms control field must be broadened. It is this goal that the Stanford Nuclear Age Series is intended to support, with paperback reissues of important out-of-print works and original publication of new scholarship in the humanities and social sciences.

Martin J. Sherwin
General Editor

Preface

> The great tragedies of history often fascinate people with
> approaching horror. Paralyzed, they cannot make up their minds
> to do anything but wait. So they wait, and one day the Gorgon
> devours them. But I should like to convince you that the spell
> can be broken . . . , that strength of heart, intelligence, and
> courage are enough to stop fate and sometimes reverse it.
>
> Albert Camus, 1956

How should we account for the fact that, since 1945, the world has avoided nuclear war? The conventional explanation is that nuclear weapons have "deterred" it. This variant on the idea of "peace through strength" sounds plausible enough, at least on the surface. And yet it fails to account for some important developments. Since 1945, nuclear powers have not waged nuclear war against non-nuclear powers. Sometimes, as in the case of the United States in Vietnam or the Soviet Union in Afghanistan, they suffered military defeat rather than resort to nuclear war. Why? Moreover, if national security is guaranteed by possession of nuclear weapons, it is hard to understand why countries should bother with nuclear arms controls or disarmament. Why sign a partial test ban treaty? A nonproliferation treaty? An antiballistic missile treaty? Strategic arms limitation treaties? Furthermore, numerous nations quite capable of developing nuclear weapons have not done so. Why?

These unresolved questions suggest that something is missing from the conventional explanation.

This study argues that the missing ingredient is the largest grassroots struggle in modern history, one that mobilized millions of people in nations around the globe: the world nuclear disarmament movement. To make this claim is not to insist that deterrence has never "worked." It may have, on some occasions. People are sometimes dissuaded from violent behavior by the threat of violent reprisal. But the threat of violence is not the only reason for peaceful behavior. Similarly, nuclear deterrence is insufficient to explain some of the major developments of the nuclear age. Indeed, as this book will illustrate, the history of nuclear arms controls without the nuclear disarmament movement is like the history of U.S. civil rights legislation without the civil rights movement.

Curiously, I began this study with a different operating assumption from the one implied in these last comments. Specifically, I believed that—because the Bomb had not been banned—the nuclear disarmament movement had failed. And I wanted to understand why. While doing the research, however, I began to see that the movement had been more effective than I had imagined. I turned from asking "Why is the Bomb still with us?"—a question that does not address the complexity of historical events—to exploring subtler changes in public consciousness and public policy. As I hope this altered assumption indicates, I do not desire to foster a myth about the omnipotence of the nuclear disarmament movement. Instead, I am trying to discover the truth about a very important issue. And the truth seems to be that public pressure helped curb the nuclear arms race and prevent nuclear war.

This conclusion challenges the traditional wisdom about international behavior. In the fields of international relations and diplomatic history, a "Realist" paradigm has long held sway, despite challenges from a variety of perspectives. According to its proponents, the interests of the nation-state—and specifically its struggles for power with other nation-states—set the tone for international relations. Readers of this book will observe that I do not deny the allure of serving the "national interest," particularly for policymakers. But the "Realist" emphasis misses the mark when it comes to other actors, who are sometimes driven by quite different concerns and who, in these instances, bring countervailing pressure to bear on national leaders. In short, although state-centrist pressures certainly exist, there are also global integrationist pressures, and the resulting direction of public policy appears to be a compromise between them.

While pondering the degree to which they find this book a credible challenge to orthodox assumptions, readers should keep in mind that it is part of a trilogy, *The Struggle Against the Bomb*. Volume 1, *One World or None*, covers the period up to 1953. This volume, *Resisting the Bomb*, runs from 1954 to 1970. And volume 3, still untitled, will span the years since then. A more condensed history, I believed, would not do justice to an antinuclear campaign that operated in dozens of nations, involved millions of people, and has already lasted for more than half a century. Nor would it provide a thorough analysis of the response of policymakers to these efforts. Consequently, this study has three parts, and I accept the responsibility for that.

In most ways, however, *Resisting the Bomb* is a collective enterprise. Not only do historians stand on the shoulders of their predecessors, but they lean heavily on their contemporaries. I am particularly grateful to the American Philosophical Society, which helped fund the extensive research necessary for this project. Furthermore, numerous archivists guided me to important documents and manuscript collections. Although their very substantial number makes it impossible to list them all here, Wendy Chmielewski and the staff of the Swarthmore College Peace Collection deserve special commendation. In addition, many persons provided me with copies of key documents, printed materials, or useful information, including Graham Barker-Benfield, Gregory Bell, Ruth Benn, Iris Berger, Donald Birn, Claude Bourdet, Nancy Bramson, Pat Broudy, April Carter, Blanche Wiesen Cook, Matthew Evangelista, Peter Goodwin, Ruzanna Ilukhina, Glenn Inghram, Sheila Jones, Anne Kjelling, Raisa Kuznetsova, Elsie Locke, Tom Milne, David Patterson, Linus Pauling, Michalis Peristerakis, Alexander Pikhovkin, Murray Polner, Colin Pritchard, Michael Randle, Marion Sarafis, Joseph Sarfoh, David Schalk, Dhirendra Sharma, Ralph Summy, Richard Taylor, E. P. Thompson, Chikara Tsuboi, Peter van den Dungen, Günter Wernicke, Patricia West, Dan White, Mary Woodward, Kasei Yoshida, and Nigel Young. Others, among them my friends George Berger, Charles Nadler and Hanna Weston, David and Mary-Margaret Patterson, and Michael Weinberg, put me up (and put up with me) during research trips in their vicinity.

Many other persons made important contributions. My daughter, Julia Wittner, and my student Randal Angiel served as research assistants at different stages of the project and performed admirably. In addition, Robert Frost, Deborah Neuls, Harriet Temps, and, especially, Gerald Zahavi helped me frequently with computer, Fax, E-mail, and other modern gadgetry that went beyond my limited technological abilities. Moreover, I could not possibly have translated the mass of materials necessary for this book without the help of Gertrude May Ahders, Randal Angiel, Thomas Conley, Elisabeth Egetemeyr, Hans Fenstermacher, Nadieszda Kizenko, Anne Marfey, Adonios Mikrakis, Thomas Reimer, Svetlana Salikova, Bernadette Schempers, Andrei Streke, Raphael Sulkovitz, Theresa Verderber, Maria Wemple, John Wolcott, and Joseph Zimmerman. I am also grateful to the people who have read and commented on portions of the manuscript, including Irwin Abrams, Harriet Hyman Alonso, Graham Barker-Benfield, Donald Birn, Martin Ceadel, Muriel Duckworth, Frances Early, Lloyd Gardner, Dee Garrison, Sheila Jones, Bruce Kent, Kay Macpherson, Joseph Rotblat, and Martin Sherwin. My former student Donald Drewecki prepared the index. From the inception of this project, Martin Sherwin (the series editor) and Muriel Bell and Ellen Smith (of Stanford University Press) were enthusiastic supporters, and their assistance with this volume is greatly appreciated.

Finally, I owe a great debt to my partner, Dorothy Tristman, who understands the importance—indeed, the necessity—of meaningful work.

L.S.W.

Contents

32 pages of photographs follow page 334

Men and women, stand together!
Do not heed the men of war.
Make your minds up now or never.
Ban the Bomb forever more.

Campaign for Nuclear Disarmament
marching song, 1958

The Gathering Storm, 1954–56

We are speaking . . . as human beings . . . whose
continued existence is in doubt.

Russell-Einstein Manifesto, 1955

Beginning in 1954, a rising sense of uneasiness about nuclear weapons emerged around the world. An earlier surge of antinuclear activity, launched by the shock of the Hiroshima and Nagasaki bombings, had been promoted with some effectiveness by atomic scientists, pacifists, world government advocates, and *hibakusha* (Japanese survivors of the atomic bomb). Yet after the late 1940s it had ebbed dramatically, as Cold War divisions, exhaustion, and controversies ignited by Communist-led peace campaigns undermined the appeal of nuclear disarmament.[1] Starting in 1954, however, the rapid development of the hydrogen bomb—a weapon with a thousand times the power of the bomb that had destroyed Hiroshima—began to revive the idea that humanity was teetering on the brink of disaster. Atmospheric nuclear weapons tests, particularly, stimulated public concern. They scattered clouds of radioactive debris around the globe and, furthermore, symbolized the looming horror of a U.S.-Soviet nuclear war. Deeply disturbed by this turn of events, many of the early critics of the Bomb renewed their calls for nuclear arms control and disarmament—measures which appealed to ever larger sections of the public.

Ominous Developments, 1954–56

Although the U.S. government had tested the world's first thermonuclear device in 1952 and the Soviet Union had made its own thermonuclear breakthrough the following year, not until 1954 did nuclear testing deeply impress itself on public consciousness. The turning point was the first U.S. H-Bomb test, conducted by the Atomic Energy Commission (AEC) on March 1, 1954. It occurred at Bikini atoll, located in the Marshall Islands, a United Nations trust territory in the Pacific. The AEC had staked out a danger zone of fifty thousand square miles (an area roughly the size of New England) around the test site. But the blast proved to be more than twice as powerful as planned and generated vast quantities of highly radioactive debris. Within a short time, heavy doses of this nuclear fallout descended on four inhabited islands of the Marshall grouping—all outside the danger zone—prompting U.S. officials to evacuate 28 Americans working at a U.S. weather station and 236 Marshallese. Thanks to their rapid escape, the Americans went relatively unscathed. But the Marshall Islanders, who were not removed from their radioactive surroundings for days, soon developed low blood counts, skin lesions, hemorrhages under the skin, and loss of hair.[2] Over time, the islanders also suffered a heavy incidence of radiation-linked illnesses, notably thyroid cancer and leukemia.[3]

Much of this might have gone unnoticed by the outside world had there not been a further incident. About eighty-five miles from the test site—and also outside the official danger zone—radioactive ash from the H-Bomb explosion showered a small Japanese fishing boat, the *Lucky Dragon*. By the time the ship had reached its home port of Yaizu two weeks later, the twenty-three crew members were in an advanced stage of radiation sickness, with skin irritations and burns, nausea, loss of hair, and other afflictions. The Japanese government promptly hospitalized the ailing fishermen and destroyed their radioactive cargo. As the disturbing news spread across Japan, a panic swept that nation. Although most of the crew recovered, the ship's radio operator, Aikichi Kuboyama, died during hospital treatment in September.[4]

In the midst of a growing international furor, U.S. officials sought to reassure the public that all was as it should be. On March 31, in a statement read at President Dwight Eisenhower's press conference, Lewis Strauss, the AEC chair, maintained that "at no time was the testing out of control." The U.S. personnel were in good shape, he said, and the Marshall Islanders appeared "well and happy." The Japanese fishermen, to be sure, seemed to be experiencing some problems, but these, Strauss insisted, were minor. "The blood count of these men is comparable to that of our weather station personnel," he contended, and the skin lesions "are thought to be due to the chemical activity of the converted material in the coral rather than to radioactivity." In any case, he implied, the Japanese alone bore the responsibility for their ailments, for the *Lucky Dragon*, he stated falsely, "must have been well within the danger area." The only discomforting observation came during the question period, when Strauss remarked that an H-Bomb could be made "as large as you wish . . .

large enough to take out a city." Asked "how big a city?" the AEC chair responded: "Any city."[5]

Despite the ominous portents, the nuclear arms race continued. In early 1955, the AEC conducted tests of atomic bombs in Nevada, and later that year the Soviet Union set off hydrogen blasts on its territory, raising radioactivity levels over large areas and rekindling popular anxieties. In the spring of 1956, the AEC commenced Operation Redwing, a new series of nuclear explosions at its Pacific test site. Questioned by the Senate Armed Services Committee, General James M. Gavin, U.S. Army chief of research and development, predicted that a Soviet thermonuclear attack on the United States would kill millions of Americans and leave large regions uninhabitable. U.S. retaliation against the Soviet Union, he observed, would spread death and radiation across Asia to Japan and the Philippines—unless, of course, the winds blew the other way, in which case a U.S. nuclear attack on eastern Russia could eventually kill hundreds of millions of Europeans. In June 1956, the same month that Gavin's testimony was released to the press, a study by the U.S. National Academy of Sciences contended that the fallout produced by nuclear weapons testing thus far did not add substantially to the risks of cancer. But the Academy warned that *any* amount of radiation caused genetic damage.[6]

Nuclear testing represented the tip of a potential iceberg, for both the U.S. and the Soviet governments showed a clear willingness to use nuclear weapons when it suited their purposes. In late October 1953, the U.S. National Security Council secretly resolved that in the event of hostilities with the Soviet Union or China "the United States will consider nuclear weapons to be as available for use as other munitions." On January 12, 1954, in a speech before the Council on Foreign Relations, Secretary of State John Foster Dulles publicly unveiled the administration's new plan for "massive retaliation." Henceforth, he declared, the U.S. government's defense strategy would "depend primarily upon a great capacity to retaliate, instantly, by means and at places of our choosing." Determined to obtain public "acceptance of the use of atomic weapons as 'conventional,'" Eisenhower stated at his press conference of March 16, 1955, that in a battlefield situation the U.S. government would employ tactical nuclear weapons "just exactly as you would use a bullet or anything else."[7] Soviet officials, while rejecting the inevitability of nuclear war, also showed few qualms about waging it. Speaking at the Twentieth Communist Party Congress in February 1956, Premier Nikita Khrushchev warned that if "the imperialists" unleashed a war, the Soviet Union was prepared to give them "a smashing rebuff." That November, during the Suez crisis, he threatened the British and French governments with the prospect of nuclear annihilation.[8]

Some Important Signs of Dismay

As might be expected, international peace organizations found these develop-ments deeply disturbing. Horrified by the thermonuclear buildup, worldwide pacifist bodies—the War Resisters' International (WRI), the International Fel-lowship of Reconciliation (International FOR), and the Women's International League for Peace and Freedom (WILPF)—renewed their earlier demands for an end to the nuclear arms race. In 1955, the WILPF's international executive called on its national branches to mobilize public opinion against nuclear weapons. The following year, opposition to nuclear weapons testing provided the major topic of discussion during the WILPF's international congress.[9] Within the world federalist movement, too, the hydrogen bomb generated strong apprehensions. Meeting in September 1954, the World Association of Parliamentarians for World Government, with representatives from twenty-one countries, warned that "rival nations are now engaged in the most dangerous arms race of all time. . . . A war fought with nuclear weapons would annihi-late whole countries, and indeed threaten the existence of human life." That same month, leaders from these and other peace groups attended a meeting of the loosely knit International Liaison Committee of Organizations for Peace (ILCOP), which called for an end to nuclear testing and a program of "drastic disarmament."[10]

The escalating nuclear arms race also sparked concern within international religious bodies. Although the World Council of Churches, the major Protes-tant federation, steered clear of the pacifist program championed by small an-tiwar denominations like the Society of Friends, its August 1954 world assem-bly at Evanston, Indiana, called for the elimination and prohibition of nuclear weapons. The world body also recommended that nations pledge to refrain from use of the Bomb and that the United Nations enforce this pledge. A year later, in Switzerland, the Central Committee of the World Council of Churches endorsed the U.N. General Assembly's call to limit atomic energy to peaceful purposes. In July 1956, the executive committee of the world body's Commis-sion of the Churches on International Affairs argued that "tests of nuclear weapons should be discontinued under international agreement as soon as pos-sible," an idea reiterated by the Central Committee the following month. "Pro-vision must be made to safeguard both the health of the people and the security of the nations," that body declared. "The churches should continue insistently to press for an adequate system of disarmament."[11]

Statements from the Catholic Church during these years touched on similar themes. Pope Pius XII devoted much of his 1954 Easter message to a critique of "new, destructive armaments, unheard of in their capacity of violence," which "could cause the total extermination of all life." He asked: "When will the rulers of nations understand that peace does not exist in an exasperating and costly relationship of mutual terror?" That September, in an address to the World Medical Association, he argued that nations should strive to avoid nuclear war "by all means," for it could result in "the pure and simple annihilation of human life." Calling attention to the dangers of nuclear testing during 1955, the pope warned of "the increased density of radioactive products in the atmosphere" and "the horrors of monstrous offspring." Although Pius XII's strong anticommunism and acceptance of nuclear deterrence blunted the impact of these and other pronouncements, he used his Christmas message that year to promote an international agreement to ban nuclear testing and outlaw the use of nuclear weapons.[12]

The Role of Bertrand Russell

The famed mathematician and philosopher Bertrand Russell served as a key figure in the reviving struggle against the Bomb. Appalled by the prospect of nuclear war, Russell had become a leading proponent of world government in the years after World War II. With the inception of the scramble for the H-Bomb in the 1950s, he grew increasingly outspoken. "I felt I *must* find some way of making the world understand the dangers into which it was running blindly, head-on," he recalled. Writing in mid-June 1954 to the British Broadcasting Corporation, Russell proposed that he deliver a radio address focused on the weapons issue. Although BBC officials wanted to sandwich his talk between cheerier messages from a journalist and an athlete, eventually Russell prevailed and, on December 23, delivered his somber message, "Man's Peril." The question now confronting the world, he noted, was: Were human beings "so destitute of wisdom, so incapable of impartial love, so blind even to the simplest dictates of self-preservation," that they would carry out "the extermination of all life on our planet?"[13]

Russell's message attracted considerable attention, including the praise of the distinguished French nuclear physicist, Frédéric Joliot-Curie. As president of the Communist-led World Peace Council and of its scientific counterpart, the World Federation of Scientific Workers, Joliot-Curie had launched slashing attacks on the nuclear policies of Western nations in the postwar era. But his pro-Soviet position, in the context of the Cold War, had left him with little credibility outside Communist circles. Consequently, he now approached the non-Communist Russell and urged him to endorse the plan of the World Federation of Scientific Workers for a world conference of scientists that would stress "the dangers facing humanity."[14] Cautious about becoming involved in a Communist-led enterprise but impressed by the potential of an agreement that spanned the political gap, Russell replied that although a conference at this point would be premature, he favored a public statement about the dangers of nuclear weapons by a small group of the world's most eminent scientists, representing "all shades of opinion."[15]

Without waiting for Joliot-Curie's reply, Russell wrote to the revered American physicist, Albert Einstein, on February 11, 1955, to promote this idea. "Eminent men of science ought to do something dramatic to bring home to the public and governments the disasters that may occur," he argued. It was "wholly futile to get an agreement prohibiting the H-bomb," Russell stated, for "such an agreement would not be considered binding after war had broken out." Instead, "the thing to emphasize is that war may well mean the extinction of life on this planet," thereby helping to convince citizens and governments alike that in the nuclear age nations must find a route to peace. Einstein, who had agitated vigorously against nuclear weapons since their inception, responded that he agreed "with every word" of Russell's letter; "something must be done" that "will make an impression on the general public as well as on political leaders."[16] After conferring at length with Joliot-Curie and incorporating his suggestion for a future conference among scientists, Russell prepared a revised version of his "Man's Peril" address and began gathering signatures.[17]

Despite these auspicious beginnings, the task proved difficult. Five important non-Communist scientists in the West refused to sign the statement, in most cases on the basis of their strong anti-Communist sentiments.[18] Moreover, Einstein, Russell's most valuable collaborator in the venture, died after a short illness on April 13. Nevertheless, in one of the last acts of his life, the American physicist sent a letter endorsing the wording, and it reached Russell later that day.[19] Finally, the key Communist signer, Joliot-Curie—on whom Russell had relied for obtaining signatures from Communist nations—began to argue that Russell's statement was only a "draft" and to insist on rewording it to accommodate wars within nations and other items in line with Communist policy. Eventually, Joliot-Curie even produced his own statement for Russell to endorse. On June 17, Russell responded in exasperation that given Einstein's death he could not make any significant changes in his statement. Although he had hoped "to build a bridge between opposing camps," he and Joliot-Curie might have to issue separate messages.[20] At the last moment, after additional attempts to alter the wording, Joliot-Curie agreed to endorse Russell's statement if his objections were recorded in footnotes. Soviet and Chinese scientists did not sign at all.[21]

To Russell's delight, his frustrating efforts now culminated in a very successful event. Booking the largest room in London's Caxton Hall for July 9,

1955, he invited representatives from the press, magazines, radio, and television networks. The physicist Joseph Rotblat, a pioneer in the British struggle against nuclear weapons and, at the time, executive vice president of Britain's Atomic Scientists' Association, agreed to chair the meeting. On the day of the event, a hall packed with emissaries of the mass media listened as Russell summarized the background of the statement and of its impressive list of signers. Aside from Einstein and Russell, they included Percy Bridgman and Hermann Muller of the United States; Cecil Powell and Rotblat of Britain; Hideki Yukawa of Japan; Joliot-Curie of France; Max Born of Germany; and Leopold Infeld of Poland.[22] In the shadow of the Bomb, they declared, "We have to learn to think in a new way. We have to learn to ask ourselves, not what steps can be taken to give military victory to whatever group we prefer, for there no longer are such steps." Rather, "the question . . . is: What steps can be taken to prevent a military contest of which the issue must be disastrous to all parties?" Although the meeting began with some skepticism on the part of the press, the message quickly captured its imagination, as did the dramatic news of Einstein's deathbed endorsement of the venture. Consequently, what now became known as the Russell-Einstein Manifesto received very widespread and favorable coverage.[23]

As Russell proceeded with these activities, two German scientists also launched an international appeal. Max Born, a physicist who had found refuge in Britain during the Nazi regime, had returned to his native Germany to live quietly among Quaker pacifists. Awarded the Nobel Prize for physics in 1954, he conceived the idea of inducing Nobel laureates in physics and chemistry to sign a statement along the lines of Russell's BBC broadcast of December 1954. Born was assisted by Otto Hahn, a leading chemist and pioneer in nuclear fission research.[24] In early 1955, working with German physicists Werner Heisenberg and Carl Friedrich von Weizsäcker, they drafted an appeal which they circulated among participants in a July 1955 conference of Nobel laureates at Mainau, Germany. Signed by eighteen participants at the gathering,[25] this Mainau Declaration, released on July 15, expressed their "horror" that "science is giving mankind the means to destroy itself." Although peace might be preserved temporarily by fear of nuclear weapons, "we think it is a delusion if governments believe they can avoid war for a long time" through such fear. Therefore, "all nations must come to the decision to renounce force as a final resort of policy. If they are not prepared to do this they will cease to exist." Issued only six days after the dramatic Russell-Einstein Manifesto, the Mainau Declaration—which drew the signatures of fifty-two Nobel laureates within a year—attracted far less public attention. Even so, it bolstered the confidence of nuclear critics and enhanced their credibility.[26]

A Furor in Japan

Among all nations, Japan clearly underwent the greatest turmoil over the development of the H-Bomb. Not only had the Japanese people been the first to suffer the horrors of nuclear war, but now—thanks to the Bikini Bomb tests of March 1954—they were nuclear victims again. The arrival of the *Lucky Dragon* at its home port, Yaizu, along with its irradiated Japanese crew and cargo, touched off a furor all across the nation. Nuclear fallout—or, as the Japanese called it, "the ashes of death"—became a household term. Terrified of being poisoned by radioactive fish, hundreds of tons of which were destroyed by the Japanese government, consumers shunned this staple of the Japanese diet. A May 1954 poll by the *Asahi Shimbun* found that only 11 percent of respondents wanted to "cooperate with American H-Bomb tests to protect the security of the free nations." Another poll revealed that 78 percent of respondents opposed all nuclear testing under any circumstances; only 2 percent unconditionally approved it.[27] That same month, determined "to protect the lives and the happiness of all mankind," middle-class housewives of the Suginami ward in Tokyo began a petition campaign against H-Bombs. This "Suginami Appeal," carried in their shopping baskets, blossomed into a nationwide movement and, by the following year, had attracted the signatures of 32 million people—about a third of the Japanese population. Meanwhile, the Yaizu city council passed a resolution urging the United States to ban atomic and hydrogen bombs, an action repeated in most villages, towns, and cities throughout the country.[28]

Some of this resistance to the Bomb emerged from Japan's traditional antinuclear constituency. Immediately after the *Lucky Dragon* incident, the Japanese WILPF section appealed for a halt to nuclear testing and to the manufacture of nuclear weapons. Like the Japanese FOR, the WILPF assisted with the mass petition drive, and it followed up in October with a call for "a ban on the A-bomb and H-bomb."[29] Scientists, too, played a prominent role in the antinuclear effort. "The scramble we see around us for the production of ever bigger and more fearful atomic weapons cannot but leave us in despair," observed an April 1954 declaration by the Science Council of Japan. "We believe we are voicing the common feeling of the people of all the world in sincerely appealing for the suspension of the atom and hydrogen bomb experiments, the abolition of mass-destructive nuclear weapons, and the establishment of really effective international control of atomic energy." Assailing the nuclear arms race, the venerated physicist Hideki Yukawa warned that the Bomb was "threatening to become the cancer that will destroy mankind."[30]

Among the survivors of the atomic bombings, the pace of antinuclear activism quickened. Organized during these years in Hiroshima, Nagasaki, and nationwide, *hibakusha* associations agitated not only for medical treatment and other relief measures but for an end to the nuclear arms race.[31] Both Hiroshima and Nagasaki constructed peace parks, including exhibit halls within them, to memorialize their residents annihilated by the atomic bomb and to further the cause of peace. In 1955, the first year of their operation, Hiroshima's Peace Memorial Museum and Nagasaki's International Cultural Hall drew some 336,000 visitors, and the numbers climbed steadily thereafter. On August 6, 1954, a record turnout of 20,000 people attended Hiroshima's yearly Peace Memorial Ceremony, presided over by Mayor Shinzo Hamai. With the appearance of the hydrogen bomb, he noted, "the whole human race has come to be exposed to the ever-increasing menace of its total extinction." Consequently, "we make this appeal to the entire world: Let all wars be outlawed and all atomic energy placed under an appropriate control. And to the consecrated souls of our fallen citizens, we humbly pledge ourselves that with renewed determination we shall pursue the way leading to the establishment of peace."[32]

The Japanese antinuclear movement soon spread far beyond the *hibakusha* and other early opponents of the Bomb. On August 6, 1955, thousands of delegates, mostly Japanese, convened in Hiroshima for the First World Conference Against Atomic and Hydrogen Bombs. Among the sponsors were Tetsu Katayama (a former prime minister and Socialist Party leader), Saburo Yamada (president, Japan Academy of Science), Tamaki Uemura (president, Japan YWCA), the Reverend Benkyo Shiio (president, All-Japan Buddhist Association), Shozo Murata (president, International Trade Promotion Commission), and Hamai. The first evening session, in the Peace Memorial Park, drew thirty thousand people. Conference participants listened to the grim stories of the *hibakusha*, sang of resistance to the Bomb, and responded with thunderous applause to the proclamation of the Hiroshima Appeal, which demanded aid to atomic bomb victims and the abolition of nuclear weapons. In September, building on this success, organizers of the event established the Japan Council against Atomic and Hydrogen Bombs (Gensuikyo), which soon had local affiliates all across the country.[33]

Gensuikyo became one of Japan's most important and enduring mass movements. Much of its activist base came from the powerful Socialist Party and its trade union affiliate, Sohyo. Some also came from the smaller Communist Party. Nevertheless, Gensuikyo and its work did not immediately take on a left-wing tone,[34] for antinuclear sentiments enjoyed a broad popularity in Japanese life. Surveyed in January 1956, 55 percent of Japanese respondents favored (and only 9 percent opposed) banning nuclear weapons even if it meant leaving "anti-Communist powers militarily weaker than the Communist powers." That June, 86 percent of Japanese polled expressed disapproval (and only 5 percent approval) of U.S. nuclear tests.[35] Sponsors of the Second World Conference against Atomic and Hydrogen Bombs, held in August 1956 in Nagasaki, represented every political party and a broad array of organizations, including women's associations, religious and scientific bodies, unions, and pacifist groups. A pacifist participant from overseas recalled that in addition to the gathering at Nagasaki Gensuikyo arranged meetings at Tokyo and Osaka stations with twenty to thirty thousand people in attendance, as well as many smaller events. Governors and mayors gave banquets for the foreign delegates, while press conferences and interviews occurred on an almost daily basis. Everywhere she went she encountered the slogan: "Ban the Bomb."[36]

Antinuclear Stirrings in the United States

Although the reaction to the advent of thermonuclear weapons was far milder in the United States, here, too, concern about the H-Bomb was rising. The Bikini tests of 1954, with their vast destructive power and radioactive fallout, proved particularly unsettling. Urging a pause in nuclear testing, the liberal *Nation* asked for some "hard political thinking" while people were still "able to think." The normally apolitical *Scientific American* opined that the H-Bomb had "become too big to be entrusted any longer to the executive sessions of rulers in Washington." In a widely reprinted letter to the *New York Times*, the writer Lewis Mumford suggested an end to experiments with these "horrifying weapons of destruction." At the same time, novels and films focusing on the Bomb began to proliferate, thereby casting an alarming perspective on the future. In October 1956, disturbed by reports that nuclear testing added deadly strontium-90 to milk ingested by children, leaders of women's groups in St. Louis demanded an investigation of radioactive contamination in their city. That June, warning that "these fiendish instruments of annihilation" would soon "be beyond any known means of control," the *Washington Post* called for a nuclear test ban treaty.[37]

Some of the most spirited opposition to nuclear weapons came from American pacifists. Although weakened by the early Cold War and its chilling effects on criticism of U.S. military policy,[38] pacifist groups drew on their limited resources for sharp, repeated attacks on the Bomb. The FOR circulated Mumford's statement and a petition calling for the abandonment of H-Bomb tests to its twelve thousand members and, through them, to thousands of other Americans. In a *New York Times* advertisement headed "We Dissent, Mr. President," the WILPF deplored the program of Pacific H-Bomb tests and warned that the Bomb threatened "the continued existence of mankind."[39] Pacifist pamphlets assailed nuclear war and associated military measures. "'Civil Defense' is a fraud," charged the FOR. "Against the weapons of modern global war there is no defense!" Instead, it diverted attention "from the realization that we cannot have both war and survival."[40] On June 15, 1955, in New York City, twenty-seven men and women from the War Resisters League (the U.S. section of the WRI), the FOR, and the Catholic Worker movement—mobilized largely by A. J. Muste and Dorothy Day—publicly refused to take shelter during a nationwide civil defense drill. Arrested, tried, and convicted, they returned annually thereafter to engage in nonviolent resistance to preparations for nuclear war.[41]

Like the pacifists, the remnants of the postwar atomic scientists' movement constituted a key component in the reviving struggle against the Bomb. Determined as ever to avert nuclear catastrophe, Leo Szilard raised disarmament issues with political leaders, in newspapers like the *New York Times*, and in movement publications like the *Bulletin of the Atomic Scientists*. Nevertheless, more interested in a Cold War political settlement than in halting nuclear testing, Szilard was temporarily out of step with the campaign he had helped create.[42] By contrast, the chair of the Federation of American Scientists (FAS) told the Senate Subcommittee on Disarmament in June 1956 that his organization favored "a worldwide ban on further tests of nuclear weapons." Such a measure would provide "a preliminary step toward complete and universal disarmament," as well as limit nuclear proliferation, reduce international tensions, allay worldwide fears of radioactive fallout, and provide savings for "worthwhile projects." The FAS issued similar public statements later that year.[43] Polled again in October about a test ban, members of the FAS Council, Executive Committee, and Advisory Panel endorsed it by a vote of 38 to 1. Many activist scientists, convinced that a test ban was technologically and politically feasible, felt they had reached a turning point. W. A. Higinbotham, an FAS leader since its inception, thought the possibilities for peace and disarmament "better than any time since 1946."[44]

Another traditionally antinuclear group, the world federalists, seemed to play little role in this wave of concern about the Bomb; the reality, though, was more complex. Having suffered precipitous losses in membership, mass media coverage, and grassroots activism during the early 1950s, the world government movement had little public visibility thereafter. Even more important, many of the movement's most prominent leaders became active in nuclear disarmament campaigns, thereby muting its voice still further. In the 1940s, most had turned to advocacy of One World because of the menace of atomic war. But, by the mid-1950s, the Cold War had made world unity seem like a utopian

vision, at best a distant goal. By contrast, banning the Bomb—or, at least, halting nuclear testing—appeared to be a feasible project, as well as one with immediate relevance. Consequently, dedicated proponents of world government like Einstein, Russell, and Rotblat, while retaining their globalist convictions, gravitated to the struggle against the Bomb.[45]

One of America's leading advocates of world government, Norman Cousins, illustrates this tendency. Horrified by the atomic bombing of Japan, Cousins, the liberal editor of the *Saturday Review of Literature*, used his magazine to deepen popular awareness of nuclear dangers. He also initiated a "moral adoption" program to assist the orphaned children of Hiroshima. In September 1953, when Cousins visited the stricken city to deliver funds raised for the project, the Reverend Kiyoshi Tanimoto, a prominent *hibakusha* who worked closely with him, suggested a related idea. Would it not be possible, Tanimoto wondered, to bring some of the girls disfigured by bombing scars to the United States for plastic surgery? Eventually, Cousins and Tanimoto arranged it, and on May 5, 1955, twenty-five "Hiroshima maidens" set out for New York City for surgery at Mt. Sinai Hospital. The American press gave the venture reasonably good coverage, at least in part because it avoided issues of guilt and focused instead on practical, benevolent action to heal the horrors of war. But from the standpoint of the sponsors—and from that of most Japanese—the visit of the "Hiroshima maidens" had obvious antinuclear implications.[46] Indeed, in August 1956, Cousins and others from the *Saturday Review* held an intense meeting with scientists at Washington University, in St. Louis, to discuss the issue of radioactive fallout. Scientific studies, they found, pointed to the radioactive contamination of milk and to the accumulation of radioactive strontium in bone and tissue, especially in the bodies of children. "We came away from that meeting," Cousins recalled, "with an enlarged understanding of the need to bring nuclear testing under control."[47]

Religious organizations, too, played an important role as critics of the Bomb. Pacifist denominations, of course, were particularly prominent. In joint advertisements in the *New York Times* and other newspapers, the American Friends Service Committee (AFSC), the Brethren Service Committee, and the Mennonite Central Committee called for the outlawing of nuclear weapons. Beneath a drawing of a cross and a nuclear mushroom cloud, their statement compared these "two crosses: one standing for redemptive love and forgiveness, for the acceptance of suffering, for hope, for life; the other for hatred and massive retaliation, for the infliction of suffering, for fear, for death." Non-pacifist religious bodies, usually of a liberal persuasion, also pressed for nuclear disarmament. At its 1954 annual meeting, the American Unitarian Association unanimously supported "a pact which would renounce the use of . . . the

A-bomb and the H-bomb" and provide for "an across-the-board fool-proof plan for universal disarmament under effective controls." In 1956, the General Conference of the Methodist Church, citing the "possible deleterious hereditary effects of atomic radiation," called for "discontinuance of nuclear explosions by all nations." It also emphasized the need for world disarmament under international authority. That same year, the Commission on Justice and Peace of the Central Conference of American Rabbis championed "an international agreement to govern or abolish the testing of nuclear weapons" and the banning of "atomic energy . . . as an instrument of international warfare."[48]

Opinion surveys of the time indicated substantial public uneasiness about nuclear weapons, combined with increasing support for nuclear disarmament. Between 1954 and 1956, polls found that from 60 to 63 percent of American respondents thought that in the event of a world war the United States would be attacked with hydrogen bombs. Indeed, 57 percent told interviewers that they believed that in these circumstances there was a fair or good chance that their own communities would be attacked.[49] Not surprisingly, arms control and disarmament treaties enjoyed considerable popularity. Between 1949 and 1955, backing for an international agreement to avoid first use of nuclear weapons rose from 68 percent to 74 percent. Asked in July 1955 if they favored an agreement among all major nations to reduce armaments, 67 percent of Americans responded affirmatively.[50] Meanwhile, the willingness of Americans to use the Bomb declined. Between 1949 and 1955 support for employing the atomic bomb in the event of a Soviet invasion of Western Europe sagged from 50 to 44 percent. Furthermore, between April 1954 and October 1956 support for calling off U.S. hydrogen bomb tests rose from 20 to 24 percent, while opposition dropped from 71 to 56 percent.[51]

The nuclear testing issue became intertwined with U.S. electoral politics in 1956, when Adlai Stevenson, the Democratic presidential candidate, brought it into his campaign. On April 21, speaking before the American Society of Newspaper Editors, Stevenson proposed halting H-Bomb testing and challenging other nations to do the same. This would "reflect our determination never to plunge the world into nuclear holocaust" and "would reaffirm our purpose to act with humility and a decent concern for world opinion." Sharp retorts from the press and the president led Stevenson to shelve the issue for a time,[52] but he revived it on September 5, when, in a speech to the American Legion, he warned that "there is not peace—real peace—while more than half of our federal budget goes into an armaments race . . . and the earth's atmosphere is contaminated from week to week by exploding hydrogen bombs." Despite slashing counterattacks from the Republicans—including Vice President Richard Nixon, who charged the Democratic standard-bearer with propounding "catastrophic nonsense"—Stevenson pressed forward with his call to end nuclear testing. On October 15, in a nationwide television broadcast entirely devoted to the issue, he promised to make a nuclear test ban his "first order of business" as president.[53] The issue seemed to give the Stevenson campaign new momentum, inspiring a flood of favorable mail and endorsements from prominent scientists. But the Soviet government's public praise of Stevenson's proposal served as what *Newsweek* called "a political kiss of death." At the least, it neutralized any political advantage Stevenson might have derived from the nuclear issue.[54]

Although Stevenson sincerely favored a halt to nuclear testing,[55] his decision to press the issue in his campaign did not develop in a vacuum. In 1955, responding to Stevenson's query about "how to seize the peace initiative" from the Republicans, his aide Thomas Finletter had suggested that he attack the Republican administration for bringing the nation twice "to the brink of total atomic war" and that he strongly state "the case for disarmament." Stevenson's willingness to do so was reinforced by the pleas for nuclear disarmament of religious groups and leaders, distinguished scientists, and the one Democratic holdover on the AEC—pleas referred to by the Democratic candidate in his speeches. Although some campaign staffers feared that the nuclear testing issue would hurt Stevenson at the polls, others favored his raising it, at least in part because they were impressed by the enthusiastic applause it generated at campaign rallies.[56] Moreover, Stevenson felt considerable respect for the leaders of the atomic scientists' movement, some of whom he employed as top advisers and speech writers.[57] He also had a close personal relationship with Norman Cousins. As the campaign progressed, Stevenson repeatedly drew on Cousins for advice and campaign speeches. One of them apparently served as the basis for a nuclear disarmament address Stevenson delivered to eighteen thousand people at a Madison Square Garden rally.[58] According to Stevenson, Cousins was his "constant counsellor and conscience."[59]

Uneasiness in Britain

As in the United States, peace and disarmament activists in Britain reacted strongly against this latest surge in the arms race. Russell's dire warnings about the H-Bomb received the plaudits of leading world federalists, among them Henry Usborne, who proposed that as "a first step" toward survival, all nations other than the United States and the Soviet Union renounce the manufacture of nuclear weapons.[60] Drawing on his immense prestige, Russell repeatedly highlighted the perils of the Bomb, arguing that humanity's survival could be ensured only by "avoiding war."[61] Britain's pacifist leaders and groups were particularly active as nuclear critics. Messages or resolutions from the FOR, the WILPF, the Society of Friends, and other organizations roundly condemned nuclear weapons and nuclear testing. Working together, they organized small anti-H-Bomb demonstrations in London.[62] In mid-1955, the National Peace Council—which brought together numerous pacifist and peace-oriented reform groups—voted unanimously to launch a campaign to push the British government toward "a policy of unilateral renunciation of the manufacture of the H-bomb."[63]

Actually, British pacifists were already organizing an innovative venture along these lines. In December 1951, several members of the Non-Violence Commission of the Peace Pledge Union—the British section of the WRI—had established Operation Gandhi, a project whose goals included "stopping . . . the manufacture of atomic bombs in Britain." On January 11, 1952, the group conducted a sit-down outside the War Office in London in which thirteen members were arrested. Tried and convicted, they assailed Britain's conversion into "one of the chief atom bomb bases of the world" and announced plans to combat it through promotion of "non-violent resistance." In March, they held a small, legal demonstration at the Atomic Energy Research Establishment at Aldermaston, where they carried posters reading "No more war," "Atomic secrecy breeds fear," and "Atom bombs disgrace democracy." In June, they staged a combined poster walk and civil disobedience action at the U.S. atomic bomber base at Mildenhall in East Anglia. Renamed the Non-Violent Resistance Group in the summer of 1952, the organization engaged in similar ventures—all on a small scale and with minimal public impact—in subsequent years. In 1955, Hugh Brock, the group's leading light, became editor of the Peace Pledge Union's newspaper, *Peace News*, but younger activists like Michael Randle and April Carter were coming to the fore as leaders of the new direct action movement.[64]

New constituencies, too, were speaking out against the Bomb. Departing from its traditional silence on nuclear weapons, the British Council of Churches, at its April 1954 meeting, expressed dismay at the radioactive fallout generated by U.S. nuclear tests in the Pacific. Although many religious leaders, particularly Anglicans, showed few qualms about the nuclear arms race, a number of important prelates did criticize Britain's development of the H-Bomb. They included the bishops of Exeter and of Chichester, who appealed to the British government to discontinue nuclear testing and declared that use of the hydrogen bomb would be immoral.[65] Meanwhile, Britain's trade unions began to criticize the weapon. Representing a million British workers, delegates at the May 1954 conference of the Amalgamated Engineering Union passed a resolution calling for "a total ban on the H-bomb." Prominent scientists also demanded action. H. W. Massey, president of the Atomic Scientists' Association, declared that an international agreement on nuclear weapons had become "urgently necessary."[66]

The H-Bomb issue also stirred a current of concern within the Labour Party. In the aftermath of the Bikini Bomb tests of 1954, Labour introduced a parliamentary resolution calling on the Conservative government to press for a summit meeting that would end nuclear testing. Although Prime Minister Winston Churchill eventually rallied his party's legislators to defeat the resolution, the Labour Party's leadership continued to express misgivings about nuclear testing and about the destructive effects of nuclear weapons. In addition, more than a hundred Labour M.P.'s demanded an immediate halt to the weapons tests. Civilization could still "be saved," declared former prime minister Clement Attlee, "but only if the peoples of the world are roused to action."[67] In early March 1955, when Churchill defended his government's decision to build the H-Bomb, he again encountered sharp criticism from antinuclear elements in the Labour Party. On March 10, Sir Richard Acland, a prominent Labour M.P., startled political observers by resigning his parliamentary seat, thus clearing the way for him to fight a by-election focused on the nuclear weapons issue. "I have sinned," he told the House; "I should have protested, or protested much more vigorously, not merely against the H-bomb today, but against the A-bomb and the strategic bomber force." Overtaken by a general election in May 1955, Acland's one-man crusade was defeated. Furthermore, the Labour Party's executive joined the Conservatives in endorsing Britain's manufacture of the H-Bomb. Nevertheless, the division in Labour's ranks over the issue was illustrated that spring, when sixty-two Labour M.P.'s, led by Aneurin Bevan, defied party policy and voted against Britain's production of the weapon.[68]

Meanwhile, small-scale antinuclear organizations emerged. Initiated by Labour M.P. Fenner Brockway, a Hydrogen Bomb National Campaign sprang up in late April 1954, with the Reverend Donald Soper as chair and other clergy (e.g. Canon John Collins) and Labour M.P.'s (e.g. Anthony Greenwood, Sidney Silverman, and Anthony Wedgwood Benn) in leading roles. During the balance of the year, the campaign held poster demonstrations in Whitehall, addressed a few small meetings, and circulated a petition—eventually signed by half a million Britons—calling for internationally negotiated nuclear disarmament. Then, facing financial and other difficulties, it faded rapidly from sight.[69] In early 1955, though, the Golders Green Women's Co-operative Guild, in North London, convened a meeting of local groups to discuss "the banning of the H-Bomb." This resulted, that July, in the formation of a Golders Green Joint Committee for the Abolition of Nuclear Weapons and, that December, in the establishment of a Hampstead Joint Committee for the Abolition of Nuclear Weapons, headed by Arthur Goss, a Quaker peace activist. With both groups working smoothly together, Gertrude Fishwick, a retired civil servant who had organized the Hampstead group, now approached the National Peace Council about sponsoring a meeting to discuss the testing of nuclear weapons. Held in London on November 29, 1956, the gathering of about sixty activists voted enthusiastically to establish a nationwide organization to work for the abolition of nuclear testing.[70]

These stirrings both reflected and encouraged antinuclear opinions in the broader society. To be sure, a March 1955 Gallup poll found that 54 percent of British respondents supported British manufacture of the H-Bomb, while only 32 percent opposed it. But most Britons resisted the idea of using such a weapon. In May 1954, 24 percent of British respondents told pollsters that they opposed employing atomic bombs under any circumstances and another 42 percent favored their use only "if an aggressor used or threatened to use them first." In February 1955, a U.S. government survey reported that 71 percent of Britons opposed (and only 10 percent supported) employing nuclear weapons against an invasion of Western Europe by conventional forces. That April, a Gallup poll found that 78 percent rejected using the H-Bomb against a non-nuclear power and that 67 percent opposed first use of the weapon against a nuclear power. The figures remained virtually the same in October.[71]

Nuclear testing also aroused considerable antipathy. In December 1955, a poll found that 52 percent of British respondents thought the United Nations should try to stop the testing of H-Bombs; only 29 percent disagreed. According to a U.S. intelligence report, when the U.S. government announced its plans for nuclear testing in 1956, "the press as a whole expressed varying degrees of repugnance to the idea," with considerable "concern for the possible genetic effects of radiation." In April 1956, a secret U.S. government study brought the disconcerting news that Britons were almost evenly divided on the U.S. nuclear testing program. In September 1956, another poll reported that 72 percent of British respondents thought that the party receiving their vote should support an "international agreement to stop H-bomb tests."[72]

Indeed, as a secret U.S. government study noted, a total ban on atomic weapons exerted "a powerful attraction" in Britain. In April 1954, asked their opinion of an "agreement to ban the atom and hydrogen bomb," 74 percent of British respondents thought it desirable, and only 15 percent undesirable. Fourteen months later, another secret study found that support for the abolition of nuclear weapons had climbed to 80 percent of Britons, while opposition had dipped to 14 percent.[73]

Anxiety in West Germany

Public debate over nuclear issues also grew in the Federal Republic of Germany. In 1953, with the arrival of the first U.S. nuclear weapons to be based on West German soil, atomic cannon, the German Social Democratic Party (SPD) warned that Germany might become a nuclear battlefield. Use of these weapons, an SPD defense expert told the Bundestag's Defense Committee, would cause "massive destruction of the surrounding area." After NATO's 1954 field exercise, Battle Royal, which took place in the Federal Republic and involved atomic weapons, SPD leader Carlo Schmid asked angrily: "Hasn't anyone done any thinking at all about civilian losses caused by the use of such atomic weapons?" U.S. and Soviet H-Bomb tests that year also produced a sense of shock. Horrified by the nuclear explosions and intrigued by the pope's critique of them, Pastor Martin Niemöller, a leader of the fight against German rearmament, initiated conversations between German religious leaders and nuclear physicists and appealed to the Council of the Evangelical Church to speak out against nuclear testing. Similarly, Max Born, appalled by "the production of ever more horrible bombs," set out to "arouse the consciences" of his fellow scientists.[74]

Antinuclear activism accelerated thereafter. In late June 1955, a month after the Federal Republic regained formal sovereignty, NATO held a major combat exercise, Carte Blanche, in Western Europe. Within West Germany, the press gave widespread coverage to the simulated results: 335 atomic bombs dropped between Hamburg and Munich, with some 5.2 million Germans immediately killed or wounded and countless others thereafter facing nuclear fallout. Shock and fear swept the nation. Angry citizens held public meetings. Pacifist groups issued apocalyptic warnings. Focusing on Carte Blanche and its implications, the SPD charged that a European conflict fought with nuclear weapons would end in "collective suicide." Meanwhile, German unions—traditionally aligned with the SPD—also took up the nuclear issue. Asked, after the Suez crisis, what would have happened had the Soviet Union made good its threat of nuclear war, most Germans responded that their country would have "become a desert."[75]

Opinion surveys reinforce this picture of widespread and growing popular distaste for nuclear weapons. Asked in September 1955 what they thought about atomic tests, 71 percent of West German respondents called them dangerous or very dangerous; only 11 percent said they were not so dangerous or harmless. Secret U.S. government polls found that between April 1954 and April 1956 approval for U.S. nuclear testing dropped gradually from 37 to 26 percent of West German respondents. By contrast, disapproval of U.S. testing rose from 35 to 59 percent.[76] The same trend developed with respect to the combat use of nuclear weapons. Between April 1954 and September 1955, the proportion of West German respondents favoring use of nuclear weapons to defend West Germany against a non-nuclear attack by the Soviet Union dropped from 22 to 15 percent, while the opposition rose from 60 to 65 percent. Even in the event of a nuclear attack on Western Europe, a February 1955 poll reported, only a bare majority—51 percent—favored nuclear retaliation, and 37 percent did not.[77] Not surprisingly, then, in the Federal Republic banning the Bomb had what the U.S. government conceded was "overwhelming appeal." In June 1955, 88 percent of survey respondents reported that they would support an agreement to ban the Bomb outright.[78]

Opposition in France

On the surface, at least, French resistance to the nuclear arms race was more restrained. The only major critique of nuclear weapons to appear in these years pertained to the development of a French Bomb. In July 1954, with pressure mounting to start work on French nuclear weapons, more than a third of the scientists, engineers, and technicians employed by the Atomic Energy Commission sent a lengthy petition to François Perrin, the French AEC high commissioner, urging him to keep France's atomic energy program limited to peaceful purposes. It assailed the idea that nuclear weapons were necessary for national defense and argued that France's national prestige would not be enhanced by possession of the Bomb. In March 1955, a French nuclear armament program also drew the fire of the Socialist Party's executive committee and parliamentary group. By contrast, the announcement of U.S. plans for nuclear testing in 1956 received very little attention in the French press and attracted almost no editorial comment.[79]

Even so, French opinion was coalescing against the Bomb. In April 1956, a secret U.S. survey reported, 56 percent of French respondents opposed U.S. nuclear testing, while only 15 percent supported it. When the French were asked about Soviet nuclear testing, the figures came out roughly the same: 51 percent opposed and 15 percent in favor.[80] The use of nuclear weapons also inspired little popular enthusiasm. In October 1954, only 10 percent of respondents in this NATO nation supported a Western nuclear response to a non-nuclear attack.[81] Overall, the French showed widespread support for abolishing nuclear weapons. Asked in February 1955 what they thought of banning the Bomb, 87 percent expressed approval and 6 percent disapproval. That June, approval fell slightly to 86 percent, but disapproval dropped to 3 percent. Asked that month if they favored an atomic ban if it left "Western military forces weaker than the Communist forces," 44 percent of French respondents said yes, 25 percent no. Even the proposal for a French Bomb encountered stiff resistance. A July 1956 Gallup poll found the French lining up in opposition by nearly two to one.[82]

Malaise in Italy

In yet another large NATO nation, Italy, sentiments were roughly the same. As a 1956 U.S. intelligence report concluded, "like their Western European neighbors, most Italians are keenly aware of the existence of atomic weapons and would prefer to see them banned." The trend was clear as early as April 1954 when, in an apparent effort to deflect criticism of nuclear weapons by the powerful Communist and Socialist parties, the directorate of the governing Christian Democratic Party unanimously adopted a resolution appealing to the world to renounce violence in international affairs, to promote disarmament, and to employ atomic energy for peaceful purposes. When the Russell-Einstein Manifesto appeared, the Italian press gave it a sympathetic response. The Christian Democratic *Il Popolo* commented approvingly that the scientists had reduced the problem to its "essence of life or death."[83]

Polls of the time indicate the breadth of antinuclear attitudes among Italians. Queried in April 1956 about U.S. nuclear testing, only 25 percent of Italian respondents favored it, as compared to 38 percent who opposed it. Opinions of Soviet nuclear tests were even more negative. Asked about using atomic weapons against enemy cities in the event of a conventional attack on Western Europe, only 5 percent of Italian respondents approved; 75 percent disapproved. Even when asked if they favored the use of tactical atomic weapons on enemy troops at the front line "if it were the only way to stop an enemy at the threshold instead of being overrun," only 32 percent of the Italian respondents did, and 38 percent did not. Moreover, banning nuclear weapons had great appeal in Italy. Polled in February 1955, 80 percent of Italian respondents favored the idea and only 6 percent opposed it. Four months later, another poll found that support for a ban had risen to 85 percent. Asked in June 1955 if they favored banning nuclear weapons if that left the West militarily weaker than Communist nations, Italians responded affirmatively by a ratio of more than two to one.[84]

Rising Concern in the Nordic Countries

Although the Nordic countries remained somewhat off the path of the U.S.-Soviet confrontation—without nuclear weapons and (in the case of Sweden and Finland) without Cold War alliances—they also showed signs of uneasiness about the nuclear arms race. Swedes and Finns took a particularly somber view of the hydrogen bomb. Polled in July 1954, only 26 percent of Swedish respondents said that the new weapon made a world war less likely, compared to 35 percent who thought the reverse. In Finland, the corresponding figures were: less likely, 21 percent; more likely, 28 percent. Meanwhile, in Norway, pacifist groups made substantial membership gains, and a poll in late 1955 found that although 32 percent of Norwegians viewed atomic energy as a boon, 43 percent regarded it as a curse.[85] In Denmark, the pacifist organization No More War (Aldrig mere Krig) called in mid-1956 for Danish withdrawal from NATO in light of the fact that "the risks which Denmark incurred by joining . . . have become so overwhelming." Meeting in June 1956, a gathering of Social Democratic women from Denmark, Finland, Norway, and Sweden issued a strong declaration against nuclear weapons.[86]

Criticism of nuclear weapons grew particularly lively in Sweden. In part this reflected a response to the unnerving U.S. nuclear tests on Bikini. In their aftermath, Social Democratic gatherings and statements highlighted the menace of the nuclear arms race. On April 4, 1954, a mass meeting sponsored by Stockholm's labor organization appealed to the Swedish government "to take energetic action to promote international control of atomic weapons." The following year, forty-three women's organizations—warning of genetic damage to future generations—presented a petition to the U.N. General Assembly calling for a halt to nuclear testing.[87]

The nuclear issue took on additional salience, however, when, in 1954, the commander-in-chief of the Swedish armed forces issued a report calling for Sweden's acquisition of tactical nuclear weapons. The Conservative Party promoted procurement of the weapons and the Liberal Party suggested upgrading Sweden's capability to produce them. But the governing Social Democratic Party divided sharply over the nuclear issue, as did the Swedish press. Peace organizations lined up against providing Sweden with a nuclear capability, and eventually the powerful Social Democratic women's federation, led by Inga Thorsson, adopted a similar stance. At their ninth national convention, in May 1956, the Social Democratic women passed a resolution contending that obtaining nuclear weapons from a superpower would compromise Sweden's political position, that making the nation a strategic target would undermine its military position, and that threatening to use such weapons would subvert its ethical position.[88]

Elsewhere in Non-Communist Europe

Signs of misgivings about nuclear weapons also emerged in other West European countries. In April 1955, the Dutch Association of Scientific Workers sponsored a meeting in Utrecht, "The Dangers of Nuclear Weapons," attended by hundreds of persons. The following year, a Dutch Committee for the Abolition of Atom Bomb Experiments issued a petition, signed by more than a hundred scientists and other prominent figures, highlighting the dangers of radioactive contamination and calling on the Dutch government to work for the abolition of nuclear testing.[89] Although the overall peace movement remained weak, an April 1956 poll found that whereas 41 percent of Dutch respondents supported U.S. nuclear tests, 43 percent did not. Moreover, Dutch sentiment ran two to one against Soviet nuclear tests.[90] In neighboring Belgium, although the newspapers tactfully avoided comment on the resumption of U.S. nuclear testing, a poll that December reported that a slight plurality of the people surveyed (47 percent) favored an immediate ban on the production of atomic weapons, before controls were developed.[91] Meanwhile, in Austria, surveys disclosed a strong popular desire to abolish nuclear weapons. Polled in June 1955, Austrians favored banning the Bomb by a ratio of over twenty to one.[92]

Antinuclear agitation also emerged in Switzerland. In 1954, three French-speaking cantons in that country (Geneva, Vaud, and Neuchatel) adopted resolutions calling for nuclear arms control and disarmament. That same year, Switzerland's French cantons provided the major base for the Chevallier initiative, a mass petition sparked by the journalist Samuel Chevallier to cut Switzerland's military budget by 50 percent and redirect the money to social programs. According to the U.S. embassy, a "sense of helplessness in face of the nuclear armaments programs of the Big Powers" provided a key factor behind the eighty-five thousand signatures collected on the petition. When the Swiss government declared the initiative void, a new Chevallier initiative emerged in 1956, this time drawing strong support in the German-speaking portion of the country. Although it, too, failed to affect public policy, largely thanks to the Soviet invasion of nearby Hungary,[93] Swiss antinuclear sentiment continued to grow. Prominent Protestant and Roman Catholic church activists joined forces that year to form a nationwide body, Swiss Action Against the Atomic Danger. Arguing that the Swiss government should work to induce the great powers to halt tests of nuclear weapons and, eventually, renounce their use, the group appealed for support from everyone opposed to "the atomic peril."[94]

Opposition in the Soviet Union

Although political repression sharply limited the possibilities for overt agitation within the Soviet Union, here too, negative attitudes about nuclear weapons began to emerge. In large part, this reflected the vast destructiveness of the hydrogen bomb. The first Soviet H-Bomb test, recalled Andrei Sakharov, soon to become one of the weapon's sharpest critics, "made me more aware of the human and moral dimensions of our work." Even Igor Kurchatov, the physicist directing the Soviet Bomb project, was profoundly shaken. Asked what was the matter, he told a friend: "That was such a terrible, monstrous sight! That weapon must not be allowed ever to be used." Meanwhile, dismayed by the dangers of nuclear fallout, Sakharov and other Bomb project scientists prevailed upon military authorities to undertake an unprecedented mass evacuation of residents of the Soviet test site region in Kazakhstan. In 1955, he suggested to Marshal M. I. Nedelin, a crusty military commander chosen to direct the buildup of the Soviet Union's strategic missile forces, that it would be a catastrophe if thermonuclear weapons were ever used—advice the military official did not appreciate. Other scientists, though, privately agreed with Sakharov.[95]

The critical attitudes developing among Bomb project scientists reflected other factors as well. Ironically, the Soviet regime's dire need for top-rate scientists, especially physicists, to work on the building of the Bomb protected them from the worst abuses of the totalitarian state. Indeed, they lived on an island of relative freedom, where they sometimes discussed political issues. As the physicist Viktor Adamsky recalled: "We . . . were not dissidents, neither were we heroes. It was just that we were fortunate and had the chance to discuss anything we wanted freely." Furthermore, they were influenced by the antinuclear ventures of scientists elsewhere, including the Russell-Einstein Manifesto. Soviet scientists read about them in the *Bulletin of the Atomic Scientists*, to which the project's library subscribed. "That magazine," Adamsky recalled, "gave coverage of social and moral problems encountered by American scientists who worked in the same field as us, which made them our overseas colleagues. . . . Getting to know, via that magazine, how freely the American scientists could discuss professional, as well as political matters . . . was very . . . thought-provoking."[96]

This trend toward politicization accelerated with the death of Joseph Stalin in January 1953 and the advent of a more liberal regime, headed first by Georgii Malenkov and, later, by Khrushchev. "You could now live without hysteria" and no longer needed to fear arrest on the most arbitrary charges, recalled Yuri Orlov, a dissident physicist. "Anyone who has not skated on that surrealist rink will never comprehend how enormously liberated people were by Khrushchev's turn to elementary legality." Some scientists, driven by moral concerns, resisted assignment to the nuclear weapons program. A few others, like the physicist Lev Landau, took the opportunity to resign, convinced—correctly, as it turned out—that he would not be called to account for it. For the most part, however, the scientists continued their work and, at the same time, felt freer to question its consequences. Accorded considerable respect by the government, they began to travel to the West and to become involved with many of the same issues as scientists elsewhere.[97]

Their growing independence was exemplified by the antinuclear stance of Peter Kapitza. An eminent physicist and probably the best-known Soviet scientist, Kapitza had been under house arrest during Stalin's final years, only to be rehabilitated afterward by Khrushchev and reinstated as director of the prestigious Institute of Physical Problems. "We wanted Kapitsa . . . to work on our nuclear bomb project," Khrushchev later recalled, but "he refused to touch any military research. He even tried to persuade me that he couldn't undertake military work out of some sort of moral principle." On a later occasion, Khrushchev tried again. "Comrade Kapitsa, why won't you work on something of military significance?" The Soviet Union, Khrushchev claimed, "simply must push ahead with defense research. Otherwise, we'll be choked to death, smashed to pieces, trampled in the dust." According to the Soviet leader, Kapitza replied coolly that he refused "to have anything to do with military matters."[98]

In 1956, Kapitza wrote an article for the Soviet journal *New Times* in which he remarked pointedly that he did not work in the area of nuclear physics and, moreover, professed his desire to "make a contribution . . . toward the prevention of an atomic war." Addressing Russell's contention that banning the Bomb would not be of great benefit "so long as the danger of war exists," Kapitza observed that the abolition of war, while admirable, "has a slow course," and a war might stop progress toward better relationships among nations. Therefore, "despite the imperfect means of control, any measures and treaties for disarmament, and for banning the production and testing of nuclear bombs, must be welcomed and supported in all ways." In this friendly piece, so different from the vicious diatribes against Russell that the Soviet press had carried in the Stalin years, he gently reminded the British philosopher of the saying that "the better is enemy of the good." Skeptics can point to the fact that this argument meshed nicely with the official Soviet position. Yet given Kapitza's challenges to Soviet authorities in other contexts, the concern about nuclear weapons he expressed in his private life, and the reasonableness of this stance, it seems likely that he believed what he wrote.[99]

Furthermore, in secret, Soviet scientists made a strong case against the Bomb to the Soviet government. In late March 1954, four senior physicists from the Bomb project (including Kurchatov) prepared a startling report on the dangers of the H-Bomb. Sent to Soviet party leaders in the aftermath of the Bikini Bomb tests, it warned that thermonuclear explosions enabled nations "to increase, practically to an unlimited extent, the explosive energy contained in a bomb." This would lead not only to the "devastation of the warring countries" but also to "poisoning the atmosphere and the surface of the globe with radioactive substances." Within only a few years, "the stockpiles of atomic explosives will be sufficient to create conditions under which the existence of life over the whole globe will be impossible." Consequently, "mankind faces an enormous threat of the termination of all life on Earth." Alluding to recent events—including the *Lucky Dragon* incident—and to the fact that "defense against such weapons is practically impossible," the scientists concluded that the concern of "the world community" was "entirely understandable." Indeed, there was no alternative to a "complete ban on the military utilization of atomic energy."[100]

Protest in Australasia

In Australia—a nation close to the U.S. nuclear test site in the Pacific and even closer to the British test sites at Monte Bello and Maralinga—opposition to the Bomb grew particularly intense. On April 8, 1954, an overflow crowd of four thousand people packed an anti-H-Bomb meeting at Sydney's Town Hall to hear speeches by four prominent and respected Australians. One of them, Marc Oliphant (director of the School of Physics at the Australian National University), warned that both sides in the Cold War would soon "stand armed to the teeth with enough weapons to blow to pieces all the cities, centers of civilization, and industries of the world." In a military conflict, he predicted, "hundreds of millions of people would be killed" and civilization destroyed.[101] Meanwhile, on a smaller scale, pacifist groups like the Society of Friends and the WILPF agitated vigorously against nuclear testing and nuclear weapons. In 1955, the WILPF reprinted Russell's "Man's Peril" address, adding to it the injunction: "Remember Hiroshima! Everyone MUST act!" It called for the "immediate cessation of all experiments in destructive atomic explosions," the "banning of production of all weapons of mass destruction," and the "scrapping of all existing stocks of such weapons."[102] Pacifist groups kept up a particularly sharp attack on proposals to test nuclear weapons either within Australia or in its vicinity, a position which enjoyed popular appeal. In 1956, a Gallup poll found that 60 percent of Australians opposed such tests. The following January, another poll found that 66 percent of Australians questioned wanted all nuclear tests halted by international agreement.[103]

In neighboring New Zealand, antinuclear sentiment was also on the rise. The March 1954 Bikini Bomb tests drew extensive press coverage which, though usually restrained, provided an unsettling picture of the new weapon's destructiveness. Expressing "grave concern at the insane lengths to which men are going in their efforts to perfect weapons for mass destruction," the international relations committee of the Presbyterian Church passed a resolution requesting the government to indicate what action it would take in view of widespread public dismay. By 1956, nuclear testing had become a major public issue. That September, two antinuclear petitions were presented to New Zealand's parliament. One of them, organized by the Society of Friends, drew the backing of the Federation of Labour, the National Council of Women, and the National Council of Churches. Signed by some of Auckland's most prominent citizens, it called for an immediate suspension of nuclear testing. The petition also demanded that the New Zealand government refuse to assist other powers in conducting such tests, criticize nuclear testing at British Commonwealth and U.N. meetings, and take active steps to secure a ban on the further manufacture and testing of nuclear weapons. Although a government spokesperson proclaimed the indivisibility of New Zealand's security with Britain and the United States, he acknowledged that public opinion favored a nuclear test ban.[104]

Reaction in the Third World

Outcries against nuclear weapons also came from the Third World, particularly from nuclear-sensitive Asia. In 1954, a public meeting in Mavelikara, India, resolved that since use of nuclear weapons "would mean the annihilation of human culture and human society," it called on "the great powers" to assure the world "that they would not under any circumstances manufacture, store or use" them and on the United Nations "to take immediate and effective steps for the banning of these weapons." The statement was signed by leaders of churches and of the Indian FOR. The following year, more than a hundred Indian parliamentarians issued an appeal to ban, "under the supervision of the United Nations," the production of nuclear weapons.[105] Reacting to British plans for nuclear testing in the Pacific in the fall of 1956, newspapers in Ceylon asked why the people of their country should "be made guinea pigs" without their consent. The Ceylonese may have been thinking of the Marshall Islanders, who had already joined the chorus of protest. In April 1954, a small group of Marshallese sent a petition to the United Nations, which had ultimate jurisdiction over the Pacific Trust Territory used by the United States for its nuclear tests. Documenting how these tests had inflicted sickness on their people and had led to their removal from Eniwetok, Bikini, Kwajalein, and other islands, they appealed for an immediate halt to nuclear testing.[106]

Problems and Progress

Although a wave of antinuclear sentiment began to rise around the world in the years from 1954 to 1956, its momentum as yet remained limited. Fearful of their adversaries in the Cold War, millions of people believed that their security rested on possession of nuclear weapons. Certainly this was true in the United States, where powerful forces fiercely resisted any limitations on America's nuclear options. *Time* magazine warned that the Communists "conduct their experiments in aggression not on remote Pacific Ocean atolls" but on the people of Europe and Asia. "Not tuna, but men and women by the millions, were deliberately killed or contaminated by terror." *U.S. News & World Report* insisted that there was "not a word of truth in scare stories" about deformed babies. Even many scientists, especially those employed by the AEC, denied that nuclear fallout constituted a danger. Furthermore, the press generally avoided the nuclear testing issue, focusing instead on the appealing concept, developed by the government, of "Atoms for Peace." In 1954, a poll found that 54 percent of American respondents thought the H-Bomb made war *less* likely. According to a 1955 survey, 55 percent of Americans favored using atom bombs (and 44 percent H-Bombs) in the event of "a war with Red China."[107]

Nor were these pro-nuclear views confined to the United States. Surveyed in July 1954, majorities or pluralities of respondents in Australia, Canada, and Britain agreed that the H-Bomb made war less likely. Similarly, in 1955, U.S. government-sponsored polls found that pluralities or majorities in five of eight West European nations surveyed—Belgium, Britain, Denmark, France, and Italy—considered atomic energy more of a boon than a curse.[108] Most tellingly, within Western nations and Japan there was a substantial falling off in public support for nuclear disarmament if it left the West militarily weaker than the Communist bloc. Indeed, under these circumstances, pluralities of West Germans, Austrians, and Britons opposed nuclear disarmament. Similarly, polls found that support for the use of nuclear weapons rose substantially in Western nations if the alternative was the overrunning of Western Europe or if Communist nations employed them first.[109] Although comparable polls are not available for Communist nations, it seems likely that they would lead to the same conclusion: the appeal of nuclear disarmament declined in proportion to perceived threats to national security.

Nevertheless, these factors should not obscure the widespread and growing unpopularity of nuclear weapons during these years. In the four largest West European NATO countries—Britain, France, West Germany, and Italy—reported a June 1955 poll, a plurality of respondents (40 percent) favored a ban on nuclear weapons even if it left Communist nations stronger than non-Com-

munist nations. The same was true in Japan.[110] Moreover, polls found that between August 1955 and April 1956 attitudes toward atomic energy grew more
negative among the citizens of numerous nations, including Britain, France,
West Germany, and Italy. In these four countries, respondents claiming that
atomic energy would prove a boon slipped from 38 to 36 percent, while those
believing it would prove a curse rose from 29 to 38 percent. By 1956, negative attitudes toward atomic energy also prevailed in the three other nations
surveyed by U.S polls—the Netherlands, Finland, and Japan.[111] Just as striking, in the spring of 1956, polls reported that disapproval of U.S. nuclear
weapons testing outweighed approval in four of the five NATO nations surveyed: France, West Germany, Italy, and the Netherlands. Only in Britain did a
plurality express approval of the U.S. nuclear testing program—by a slim 2
percent.[112]

Furthermore, the storm was only beginning.

International Appeals, 1957–58

> I had no choice but to speak out. . . . Those who can
> must bark out against atomic tests and atomic war like
> dogs in the African night.
>
> Albert Schweitzer, 1958

As public concern grew about the nuclear arms race, prominent humanitarian, scientific, and religious leaders issued calls for an end to nuclear weapons testing and to preparations for nuclear war. Some of these individuals felt uneasy about entering the realm of politics and public policy. But a sense of looming world catastrophe heightened their determination to act. As the major powers accelerated their testing programs, more nuclear explosions occurred in 1957 and 1958 than in all the preceding years combined. By the end of 1958, the United States, Soviet, and British governments had exploded an estimated 307 nuclear weapons, the vast majority of them in the atmosphere.[1] Meanwhile, to annihilate enemy cities more efficiently, the major Cold War adversaries raced to perfect new delivery vehicles for these weapons—intercontinental ballistics missiles—and the United States deployed nuclear weapons on the territory of many of its NATO allies. Furthermore, additional countries (including France and China) began to develop their own nuclear weapons capability and missile technology. Consequently, by 1957–58 the situation seemed alarming enough to convince even many normally reticent individuals to place their great public renown behind the movement to halt the nuclear arms race.

Albert Schweitzer's Message

Perhaps the best-known among these individuals was Albert Schweitzer. Born in 1875 in Alsace, then part of Germany, Schweitzer carved out careers as a distinguished musician, philosopher, and—in the jungles outside Lambaréné, in French Equatorial Africa—as a medical missionary. In 1924, bidding farewell to Europe, he returned to his African hospital to work selflessly thereafter as a physician. Gradually, in the ensuing decades, Schweitzer gained international fame as a great humanitarian and proponent of reverence for life. In 1952, he was awarded the Nobel Peace Prize. By the mid-1950s, then, Schweitzer enjoyed enormous worldwide esteem. In December 1956, a Gallup poll found that, among Americans, he was the fourth most admired man in the world.[2]

Schweitzer's humanitarianism, together with his international renown, led Norman Cousins to approach him about the issue of nuclear weapons. Urged by the head of the Schweitzer Fellowship and by Schweitzer's London publishers to travel to Lambaréné to rescue the aging physician's unpublished manuscripts from destruction in the jungle, Cousins had agreed to undertake the task in January 1957. But he went with an additional motive: to inspire Schweitzer to speak out against the nuclear arms race. Although Schweitzer loathed nuclear weapons and, moreover, was a friend of Einstein and Russell and an admirer of their antinuclear ventures, he had rarely commented publicly on the nuclear issue, largely because he believed that he should avoid involvement with politics. Yet Cousins thought the possibility existed that if encouraged, Schweitzer might take a stand on "an overriding moral question" like preparations for nuclear war. The political leaders of nations, trapped by traditional assumptions about national security, remained unable to confront the nuclear menace. But "a man like Albert Schweitzer might enable people to see the need for fashioning allegiances to each other as members of the human commonwealth."[3]

Visiting Lambaréné in January 1957, Cousins engaged in lengthy discussions on the nuclear issue with Schweitzer. Cousins emphasized the dangers of nuclear testing, but went beyond this, as he recalled, to argue that "nuclear experimentation did not exist in an otherwise placid world. . . . What we had most to fear was not merely the tests themselves . . . but a saturation of tensions resulting in all-out nuclear war." As Cousins had surmised, Schweitzer disliked involving himself with political issues and, moreover, underrated his worldwide renown. Nonetheless, he was also deeply concerned about the nuclear arms race. Eventually, albeit with some reluctance, he agreed that the time had come to speak out. "The leaders of the world today have to act in an unprecedented way if the crisis is to be met," he told Cousins. "Therefore, they must be strengthened in their determination to do the new and bold things that must be done." And they "will act only as they become aware of a higher responsibility that has behind it a wall of insistence from the people themselves." Pondering the matter, he concluded: "I have no way of knowing whether I can help in this," but "perhaps I may be justified in trying."[4]

Although Cousins was the catalyst in recruiting Schweitzer into the nuclear disarmament movement, the doctor from Lambaréné charted his own course of action. Rejecting Cousins's idea of a broad statement addressing the dangers of war and the need for developing a system of world law, Schweitzer argued that "the place to take hold is with the matter of nuclear testing." The issues involved were not complicated, he believed, and "a ban on testing requires no intricate system of enforcement. All peoples are involved," he pointed out; "therefore, the matter transcends the military interests of the testing nations." Furthermore, "if a ban on nuclear testing can be put into effect, then perhaps the stage can be set for other and broader measures related to the peace." Subsequently, Schweitzer also rejected Cousins's suggestion for a conference of world leaders and arranged his own plan for disseminating his statement. "A message by radio can be heard over the whole world," he told Cousins, and he had found the perfect broadcaster: "Radio Oslo . . . city of the Nobel Peace Prize!" It would impart to his statement a "completely neutral," nonpartisan tone. Drawing on his close contacts with Nobel officials and Norwegian radio, Schweitzer arranged to have his message read over Radio Oslo in numerous languages and then transmitted to additional radio stations around the world.[5]

Schweitzer's "Declaration of Conscience," broadcast over Radio Oslo on the night of April 23, 1957, provided a sharp critique of nuclear testing, coupled with an appeal to the people of the world to bring it to an end. Observations of the effects of nuclear weapons explosions thus far, he argued, led to the conclusion that their accompanying radiation "represents a danger to the human race—a danger not to be underrated—and that further explosions of atomic bombs will increase this danger to an alarming extent." Furthermore, "not our own health only is threatened by internal radiation, but also that of our descendants." Thus "we are forced to regard every increase in . . . radioactive elements by atomic bomb explosions as a catastrophe for the human race, a catastrophe that must be prevented." Humanity "must muster the insight, the seriousness, and the courage to leave folly and to face reality." Statesmen talked of stopping nuclear tests, he noted, but never quite managed to do so. Only when public opinion demanded it would they "reach an agreement to stop the experiments." This halt to nuclear explosions, he predicted, "would be like the early sunrays of hope which suffering humanity is longing for."[6]

Broadcast in some fifty nations and covered in countless newspapers, Schweitzer's message had a substantial impact on world opinion. In Italy and India, it attracted widespread public attention. In West Germany, nearly all newspapers commented at length on Schweitzer's statement and warned against continued nuclear tests. In Norway, it produced what the U.S. ambassador called a "striking reaction," with thousands of people adding their names to Schweitzer's declaration. Within a brief time, the pope endorsed Schweitzer's appeal and the West German Bundestag voted to ask the nuclear powers to suspend nuclear testing while they negotiated an arms control agreement. In Sweden, Schweitzer's message became a topic of vigorous discussion in women's clubs throughout the country.[7] Meanwhile, in the United States, peace and disarmament publications ran condensed versions, hundreds of prelates used it as the subject of sermons, and Oregon Senator Richard Neuberger read it on the floor of the U.S. Senate. Publishing the "Declaration" in full, the *Saturday Review* received orders for seventy-five thousand reprints.[8] At the White House, officials logged in a large quantity of correspondence from concerned citizens. That June, the Democratic Party's titular leader, Adlai Stevenson, traveled to Lambaréné to confer with Schweitzer.[9]

Some reaction to Schweitzer's appeal was considerably less enthusiastic, particularly in the United States. No American radio station broadcast the "Declaration of Conscience," and among the popular print media, the only significant attention to it came from the *Saturday Review*. Most U.S. newspapers simply ignored the message, while some disparaged it. In an editorial headlined "Pull in Your Horns, Doc," the New York *Daily News* attacked Schweitzer's "long-winded epistle" for repeating "the stale Communist propaganda about how nuclear fall-out is a fearful danger." Readers, the editors suggested, should "laugh off this Schweitzer manifesto." No doubt many did.[10]

Schweitzer, however, had become a relentless crusader against the Bomb. Arriving at the physician's jungle headquarters, Stevenson found him thoroughly committed to the antinuclear struggle. The first item in the Democratic Party leader's notes on their meeting was: "Must stop nuclear testing." Stevenson later told the outside world that Schweitzer "considered this the 'most dangerous' period in history" and had expressed his pleasure at a recent appeal by scientists for a nuclear test ban. Discussing the issue with Cousins, Schweitzer told him that November to "count on me for everything that I will be able to do to propagate the movement." The following month, he joined other Nobel laureates in signing an antinuclear petition. In February 1958, he wrote to Kaare Fostervoll (director of Norwegian radio) and Gunnar Jahn (head of the Nobel Prize Commission) about the possibility of doing additional radio broadcasts on the nuclear question. Initially, they resisted, but they yielded after reading the addresses he prepared. Schweitzer confided to Cousins: "The text is intended for Europe, where we have to keep the NATO generals from forcing launching pads and nuclear weapons on the governments."[11]

Accordingly, Schweitzer had another three radio addresses—each of which he researched and drafted laboriously, in longhand—translated and delivered over Radio Oslo on April 28, 29, and 30, 1958. Far more sweeping than his first message, delivered a year before, they stressed the need to end nuclear testing, the dangers of nuclear war, and the necessity for "negotiations at the highest level." He also attacked the "reassurance propaganda" disseminated by physicist Edward Teller and other government scientists. In this fashion, Schweitzer reached the listeners of another hundred radio stations and readers of numerous newspapers and magazines around the world. Moreover, drawing on his publishers, he had these appeals printed in book form in numerous nations under the title *Peace or Atomic War?* Writing to Cousins on May 17, the eighty-three-year-old Schweitzer remarked that he was "still very tired by the work on the three appeals. . . . My eyes have suffered from this. Sometimes now they refuse to work. Also my hand is exhausted and refuses sometimes to serve me. However, more important is that the appeals catch the attention of people and awake them."[12]

Cousins's gamble, then, paid off handsomely. Enlisted in the cause, Schweitzer showed an unwavering determination to foster nuclear disarmament. "Despite all the political happenings," he told Cousins in late 1958, "the nuclear question demands prior attention." That October, one of their mutual friends, Erica Anderson, reported from Lambaréné that Schweitzer persisted in devoting himself to an "avalanche of correspondence in connection with the atomic question," although, to her regret, he preferred writing letters on the subject to appearing on television. Meanwhile, Schweitzer's popularity continued to grow. In December 1958, a Gallup poll reported that, among Americans, his standing had risen to the third most popular man in the world.[13]

The Emergence of the Pugwash Movement

Less flamboyant, but also an influential factor in spurring concern about nuclear weapons, was the revival of the international scientists' movement. Divided and debilitated by the early Cold War, it began to show signs of renewed life after the demise of Stalin and the onset of hydrogen bomb testing. Accordingly, in the spring of 1954, the Federation of American Scientists and the British Atomic Scientists' Association (ASA) polled their leaders on the desirability of organizing an International Conference on Science and World Affairs. Eugene Rabinowitch, editor of the *Bulletin of the Atomic Scientists*, explained that "the successful development of thermonuclear weapons makes the role of science in human affairs an even more urgent subject for scientists to consider than it was before, and calls for a new stock-taking and, if possible, concerted educational activity of scientists of good will everywhere." To the delight of Rabinowitch and Joseph Rotblat, who handled matters in Britain, considerable support for the conference idea existed within both groups, as well as among a few French scientists to whom the subject was broached. By October 1954, the ASA had agreed to establish study groups to prepare the groundwork for a conference.[14]

These initiatives were soon overtaken by other events. In the spring of 1955, the World Association of Parliamentarians for World Government, head-quartered in London and working closely with Bertrand Russell, began sketching out its own plan to convene an international conference of scientists. This plan gathered momentum in July 1955 thanks to the announcement of the Russell-Einstein Manifesto, which also called for an international conference of scientists to appraise the perils of the nuclear arms race. Asked for assistance by the World Association, Rotblat and Rabinowitch managed to organize a small gathering in London from August 3 to 5 to prepare the agenda for the London Conference. Rabinowitch recalled that "it was largely improvised and was attended by only a few scientists—and not the most representative ones." Rabinowitch was the only participant from the United States. Even so, the London meeting and the Russell-Einstein appeal provided important stepping-stones toward a more impressive event. In an unprecedented display of concern across Cold War barriers, four Soviet scientists, led by Academician Alexander Topchiev, joined their British and American counterparts by attending the London Conference, at which participants established study commissions to prepare for a future meeting. Russell also began to turn his efforts toward convening an international conference on the nuclear issue.[15]

Nevertheless, despite the momentum provided by the Russell-Einstein Manifesto and the subsequent London Conference, the world gathering of scientists did not materialize for another two years. One obstacle it faced was the nature of its leadership. As late as September 1955, Russell had not been wholly convinced that such a conference was necessary or that, as a non-scientist, he was the proper person to organize it. Even after he threw himself into the task, serious problems remained. To prepare for the conference, Russell secured the assistance of Cecil Powell, Eric Burhop, and Rotblat. Powell and Burhop, however, were leaders of the Communist-dominated World Federation of Scientific Workers (WFSW), which also handled much of the early correspondence for the meeting. Unhappy about this close association with the WFSW and determined to keep the conference an independent, nonaligned venture, Russell gradually shifted primary responsibility to Rotblat, who conducted most of the organizational work at his University of London office.[16]

The venue also provided a source of difficulties. Thanks to support from Indian scientists and from India's prime minister, Jawaharlal Nehru, New Delhi was chosen as the conference site and, in June 1956, Russell dispatched invitations for a conference there in January 1957. But funding problems and the ensuing Suez crisis put travel plans in jeopardy, and prompted the organizers to consider another location. Eventually, they seized on an offer from Cyrus Eaton, a wealthy Cleveland industrialist and admirer of the Russell-Einstein Manifesto, to cover the transportation and living costs for a meeting of scientists to be held at a conference center he had built in Pugwash, Nova Scotia.[17]

The first Pugwash Conference on Science and World Affairs met from July 6 to 10, 1957, with participants from ten Western, Eastern, and nonaligned countries. Nineteen of the participants were scientists, sixteen of them physicists; the exceptions were Anton Lacassatne (a physician), Brock Chisholm (a psychiatrist who formerly headed the World Health Organization), and David Cavers of Harvard (a lawyer who specialized in atomic energy and disarmament issues). Given his advanced age, Russell did not attend, but kept in touch with the gathering by telephone. In his place, Powell presided over the meeting. The scientists included many who had previously spoken out on nuclear disarmament issues—Marc Oliphant of Australia, Hans Thirring of Austria, Powell and Rotblat of Britain, Hideki Yukawa of Japan, Paul Doty, Hermann Muller, Rabinowitch, Szilard, and Victor Weisskopf of the United States—as well as three important scientists from the Soviet Union: Topchiev (an organic chemist and general secretary of the Soviet Academy of Sciences), A. M. Kuzin (a biophysicist), and Dimitri Skobeltzyn (a pioneer in cosmic ray research and the Soviet representative on the scientific and technical advisory group during the U.N. atomic energy control negotiations of the 1940s).[18]

Naturally, the previously forbidden contact among leading scientists of "enemy" nations imparted to the meeting an atmosphere of excitement and even danger. Nor was there total agreement on the major issues discussed: (1) the hazards of atomic energy; (2) the control of nuclear weapons; and (3) the social responsibility of scientists. Nevertheless, the Pugwash meeting was infused by a general sense of respect, goodwill, and common purpose that united participants across Cold War barriers. Reflecting on the gathering some weeks later, Rabinowitch wrote that it confirmed his belief "that all scientists—including those from the other side of the Iron Curtain—have a common language and can discuss fruitfully even controversial political matters."[19]

This general accord was reflected in a statement signed by twenty of the twenty-two Pugwash participants and subsequently released to the press. There had been a "high degree of unanimity . . . among all the members of the Conference on fundamental aims," it declared. "We are all convinced that mankind must abolish war or suffer catastrophe; that the dilemma of opposing power groups and the arms race must be broken; and that the establishment of lasting peace will mark the opening of a new and triumphant epoch for the whole of mankind." Most of the statement dealt with the need to cope with the dangers of nuclear weapons, and it made specific proposals along these lines. They included the observation that "the prompt suspension of nuclear bomb tests could be a good first step" toward reducing international tensions and curbing the arms race. Rebellious as ever, Leo Szilard promoted a different approach. Accordingly, he became one of the two dissenters from the final conference statement. But, like the other participants, he delighted in the give and take among scientists from different lands at the Pugwash gathering and even helped to draft statements he refused to sign.[20]

Although the Pugwash conference of July 1957 did not attract the same widespread popular attention in the West that the Russell-Einstein Manifesto of 1955 and the Schweitzer appeals of 1957 and 1958 had attracted, it did have a public impact there and, especially, in other parts of the world. In various nations, scientific journals reprinted the conference statement, while scientific and lay groups adopted its recommendations. At least initially, newspapers and magazines in the United States and Britain gave the event rather limited coverage, although, as Powell noted, it was "seriously treated," especially by the *New York Times*. Lauding the Pugwash meeting as "a great step forward," Rabinowitch wrote a thorough account of it for the *Bulletin of the Atomic Scientists* and encouraged others to do the same in other scientific journals. In the Soviet Union, the Academy of Sciences formally endorsed the conference statement and large gatherings of scientists met in its support. The statement also received a good deal of publicity in China.[21]

Originally, Russell and the other organizers had felt that one conference would be sufficient; but the Pugwash approach proved so successful that it was decided to institutionalize it. At the conference, the participants themselves chose a continuing committee, chaired by Russell and with four additional members: Powell, Rabinowitch, Rotblat, and Skobeltzyn. After conversations with additional scientists, they met at Rotblat's London office from December 18 to 20, 1957, to consider future activities. Szilard and Carl von Weizsäcker, a leader of concerned German scientists, also attended the meeting. After what Rotblat recalled as "intense discussion," they agreed that future Pugwash gatherings should have three goals: "to influence governments, to form a channel of communication among scientists, and to educate public opinion." Even so, in line with the views of British and American scientists, who had been polled by Rabinowitch and Rotblat, they decided to emphasize small, private meetings that would study specific problems in depth, with the goal of influencing decision-makers. Cold War partisanship and divisive statements would be avoided. In 1958, they held two Pugwash conferences, a small one at Lac Beauport, Canada, and a somewhat larger one at Kitzbühel, Austria. Both focused on the dangers of the nuclear age. Cyrus Eaton helped fund the former, while Hans

Thirring secured local foundation support for the latter. Rotblat, who continued to handle most of the organizational work, became secretary-general of the Pugwash conferences in 1959. Russell remained the titular head of the movement, although his involvement with it gradually diminished.[22]

These and subsequent Pugwash conferences—a total of twenty-one by the end of 1971—met their organizers' expectations in varying degrees. Given the relative indifference of the mass media, compounded by the routine exclusion of the press and by the determination of the conference organizers to avoid public controversy, the Pugwash conferences received limited publicity. Consequently, they affected public opinion very little. But the Pugwash conferences did have a major impact on scientists, who became aware of them through personal participation, word of mouth, and professional journals. In 1959, when Pugwash officials polled thirty-five thousand scientists on the early work of the conferences and the related issue of the social responsibility of scientists, Soviet scientists expressed approval by an overwhelming margin and Western scientists showed their support by a ratio of two to one. Furthermore, among the participants were many influential atomic scientists, including a number who were serving (or who would serve) as arms control and disarmament advisers for their respective governments. For this reason, the Pugwash conferences not only became important meeting places for scientists of East and West, but, gradually, informal channels for international communications and negotiations about nuclear weapons.[23]

The Pauling Petitions

Scientists were mobilized against the arms race with far greater public fanfare by Linus Pauling. An eminent scientist at the California Institute of Technology and author of the classic study, *The Nature of the Chemical Bond*, Pauling had been awarded the 1954 Nobel Prize for chemistry. Pauling was also a well-known critic of the Bomb, and since its inception had been a prominent participant in both nonaligned and Communist-led nuclear disarmament ventures.[24] His best-known crusade began in 1957, when he traveled to St. Louis to address a Washington University honors convocation on the subject of science and the modern world. On May 14, the day before his speech, Pauling discussed it with Barry Commoner—a biologist at the university and a key figure in local nuclear disarmament activities[25]—and hatched the idea of a plea by American scientists for an international agreement to end nuclear testing. Addressing the convocation the following day, Pauling spoke movingly of the Schweitzer appeal and the test ban issue, declaring that "no human being should be sacrificed to the project of perfecting nuclear weapons that could kill hundreds of millions of human beings, could devastate this beautiful world in which we live." The enthusiastic response to this address, coupled with the many questions from the audience concerning what could be done, convinced Pauling to move ahead with the scientists' appeal. Assisted by Commoner and Edward Condon, a Washington University physicist, Pauling drafted an antitesting petition and distributed it to scientists at more than a hundred institutions. Within ten days, it had been signed by about two thousand of them. In early June, Pauling released this "Appeal by American Scientists" to the press and dispatched a copy to President Eisenhower.[26]

Although a great public relations success for the nuclear disarmament movement—both in the United States and, as Schweitzer reported, in Europe[27]—the Appeal by American Scientists produced mixed feelings within the American scientific community. Many scientists, whatever their personal views, disliked taking a public stand on a matter of political controversy. Beyond this, moreover, some scientists remained uncertain as to the extent of the health hazards generated by nuclear weapons tests. For the most part, biologists took the dangers of radioactive fallout very seriously, and this apparently accounted for the fact that a large number signed the appeal, including some very eminent geneticists. Among them were Hermann Muller, a Nobel Prize winner, and Laurence Snyder, president of the American Association for the Advancement of Science. Less certain about the health hazards of nuclear testing, physicists tended to be more standoffish. Some, indeed, argued vociferously that there were no dangers at all. For its part, the Federation of American Scientists did not formally support the petition because it did not discuss the necessity for an adequate inspection system. Even so, many FAS members signed as individuals. And some, like Rabinowitch, who decided not to do so because of disagreement with the petition's wording, personally favored a nuclear test ban.[28]

Pauling himself was delighted with the results of the Appeal by American Scientists, which he had run on a shoestring basis, and soon expanded it into a worldwide operation. On June 8, 1957, he had been asked by a reporter if scientists from other countries could sign the appeal, and he had responded affirmatively. A month later, he received a letter endorsing the petition from 40 Belgian scientists at the Free University of Brussels. With other scientists also writing to him along these lines, Pauling decided that September to solicit signatures overseas. Accordingly, he hired a secretary and, again aided by Commoner and Condon, dispatched five hundred letters, enclosing the American petition, to prominent scientists in other lands. Although the signature-gathering varied dramatically from country to country, depending on the zeal of the collectors, by January 13 Pauling had received the signatures of 9,235 scientists, from forty-six countries. On that date, he presented the petition to Dag Hammarskjold, secretary general of the United Nations. In July, he sent the U.N. official a supplementary list, bringing the total to 11,038 scientists, from forty-nine nations. They included 37 Nobel laureates, as well as more than a fifth of the members of the U.S. National Academy of Sciences, 95 Fellows of the Royal Society of London, and 216 members of the Soviet Academy of Sciences.[29]

Launched on his new career as an apostle of a nuclear test ban, Pauling resigned his administrative post at Cal Tech to enter the political fray. Throughout 1958, he clashed repeatedly with Teller, the leading scientific proponent of nuclear testing, in magazines, in books, and on television. To Teller's claim that nuclear tests did not endanger present or future generations, Pauling retorted that "the man who gives the order to test a superbomb is dooming 15,000 children to a defective life." Nuclear tests thus far, he charged in his 1958 book, *No More War!*—fifteen hundred copies of which he mailed to influential people, including every member of the U.S. Congress—"will ultimately produce about 1 million seriously defective children and about 2 million embryonic and neonatal deaths."[30] Clear, articulate, and self-confident, Pauling proved an extraordinarily effective champion of a nuclear test ban. Although some scientific critics of radioactive fallout, including Muller, considered Pauling's claims—as well as Teller's—to be exaggerated, they acknowledged that their movement benefited greatly from his enormous energy and popular appeal.[31]

Religious Bodies

By contrast to Schweitzer and the scientists, international religious bodies played a very low-key role in the growing protest against the nuclear arms race. Although they occasionally issued public pronouncements, there seemed to be little if any follow-up on the grassroots level. "The church is slow," Schweitzer complained to an interviewer in 1958, in an apparent reference to his Protestant brethren. Schweitzer had even less use for organized Catholicism. Writing to Cousins on May 17 of that year, he suggested leaving the pope entirely out of their antinuclear plans. "He may be a good man," Schweitzer observed, "but he is no fighter. Or did you ever read anywhere that he condemned the atomic and H bombs in the name of Christian religion?" And Pius XII did continue his ambivalent relationship to the Cold War and the nuclear arms race, as did the official Catholic peace movement, Pax Christi. At Pax Christi's Mariazell congress in the summer of 1957, the questions of atomic weapons, their legitimacy, and their use did not appear on the program.[32]

Nevertheless, through occasional public statements, international religious bodies did voice support for nuclear arms control and disarmament. On August 5, 1957, the Central Committee of the World Council of Churches, the major Protestant federation, reaffirmed its backing of the 1954 Evanston appeal that called for an international agreement, including provisions for inspection and control, to prohibit atomic and hydrogen bombs. Now, moreover, it went beyond that to "urge that as a first step governments conducting [nuclear] tests should forego them, at least for a trial period, either together, or individually in the hope that the others will do the same, a new confidence be born, and foundations be laid for reliable agreements." The Catholic church, too, publicly called for reversing the arms race. In his Christmas message of December 22, 1957, Pius XII declared that "the divine law of harmony in the world strictly imposes on all rulers of nations the obligation to . . . reduce armaments under a system of effective inspection." That same year, Josei Toda, the president of the Soka Gakkai—an international Buddhist society dedicated to the dignity of life—issued a declaration that assailed nuclear weapons as an "absolute evil" and called for their prohibition. If the antinuclear activities of world religious organizations remained limited, their attitude toward the Bomb reinforced the mood of public dismay.[33]

The Rise of
Ban-the-Bomb Movements

Japan, Britain, and the
United States, 1957–58

> To hell with all the humbug
>   and to hell with all the lies
> To hell with all the strontium
>   continuing to rise
> To hell with all the Charlies
>   with a gift for compromise
> If they won't ban the H-bomb
>   now.
>
>   Student song, Britain, 1958

During 1957 and 1958, the pent-up public frustration at the spiraling nuclear arms race—heightened by the international appeals of these years—spilled over into the formation of vigorous, mass-based, nuclear disarmament organizations. Since 1945, of course, small groups of atomic scientists, pacifists, world government advocates, and *hibakusha* had helped spotlight the dangers of nuclear weapons. But except for the emergence of Gensuikyo in Japan, it was not until the late 1950s that powerful, nonaligned, citizens' organizations, focused exclusively on ridding the world of nuclear weapons, made their appearance around the world. These new citizens' groups sometimes differed in their approaches from country to country and within countries. Nevertheless, their goals were remarkably similar. Repelled by nuclear testing, nuclear weapons, and the prospect of nuclear war, they sought to free the world from the danger of nuclear annihilation. In the parlance of the time, they were determined to "ban the Bomb."

Japan's Resistance to Atomic and Hydrogen Bombs

Of all nations, as a U.S. intelligence report noted in early 1957, Japan was "most sensitive to developments respecting nuclear weapons." Behind this sensitivity lay the terrible Japanese experience with nuclear war,[1] as well as the vigorous antinuclear activities of key constituencies. Japanese pacifist organizations, such as the local WILPF group, pressed for the abandonment of plans for nuclear testing. Calling attention to "the menace of nuclear weapons," the revered religious pacifist Toyohiko Kagawa urged all the world's people "to do their utmost to ban A and H bombs."[2] Japanese scientists, too, played an important role in the antinuclear struggle. On February 28, 1957, more than 350 of them issued a public appeal to their British colleagues, asking them to help convince the British government to cancel plans for forthcoming nuclear tests at Christmas Island. Nuclear testing, they declared, was "the worst sort of crime against all human beings." Later that year, 1,141 Japanese scientists signed Linus Pauling's antitesting petition.[3] Students, too, became increasingly involved in antinuclear ventures. In May 1957, the Zengakuren (National Federation of Student Self-Government Associations) launched boycotts of classes and massive public rallies against nuclear weapons with the participation of an estimated 350,000 students at more than 200 universities.[4] Although opposition to nuclear weapons transcended party lines, it remained strongest in the Socialist Party, which—together with its close ally, Sohyo, the Japanese labor federation—continued to serve as a major source of backing for Gensuikyo.[5]

Throughout 1957 and 1958, Gensuikyo was certainly the leading force behind the mobilization of Japanese sentiment against nuclear weapons. Although some Japanese pacifist groups remained aloof from the antinuclear organization, it constituted the most broadly based and powerful peace group in Japan's history. Gensuikyo's advisory committee included prominent Japanese politicians, religious leaders, businessmen, scientists, and academics, as well as the presidents of the Japan YWCA, the labor federation, and the Federation of Japanese Women's Organizations. Staging peace walks and petition campaigns, it also sponsored numerous rallies against nuclear testing, some of them nationwide. Every August, usually in Hiroshima or Tokyo, Gensuikyo sponsored a World Conference Against Atomic and Hydrogen Bombs with thousands of participants. Although the World Conference remained an overwhelmingly Japanese affair that issued lengthy declarations with little impact on other nations, it provided an important forum within Japan for continued agitation against nuclear weapons.[6]

Japanese public opinion seemed remarkably receptive to Gensuikyo's antinuclear appeals. In May 1957, the U.S. ambassador remarked glumly that the "US position on nuclear testing has virtually no support from [the] Jap[anese] public." In their "present emotional mood," the Japanese were "unwilling to support anything less than unconditional and immediate suspension of all nuclear tests." This was no exaggeration. Polling the Japanese population in June 1957, the U.S. Information Agency found that 91 percent of respondents viewed nuclear tests as either "dangerous" or "very dangerous." Only 2 percent thought they were "not so dangerous," and no one considered them "harmless."[7] In July, the *Asahi Shimbun* reported that 88 percent of the public thought nuclear tests "horrible"; only 6 percent disagreed. That same month, a poll found that 89 percent supported the Japanese government's appeal for a worldwide ban on the manufacture and testing of nuclear weapons.[8]

Greatly disturbed by this situation, U.S. officials waited expectantly for the tide to turn, but without any luck. In February 1958, the U.S. embassy reported hopefully that "the vigor and emotion of Japanese opposition has appeared to diminish in recent months." Only weeks later, however, after the Soviet Union had announced a halt to its own nuclear tests, a new wave of intense criticism swept over Japan. Newspapers issued slashing condemnations of nuclear testing, with the *Yomiuri Shimbun* denouncing the U.S. government's forthcoming series as "diabolical." By contrast, observed the U.S. embassy, "no one has failed to welcome [the] Soviet action as at least [a] step forward." By November 1958, according to polls, 78 percent of the Japanese population considered H-Bomb explosions harmful to the health of future generations—up two points from the previous year.[9]

Nor did the Japanese seem much happier about other uses of atomic energy. In June 1957, a poll found that only 5 percent supported (and 76 percent opposed) arming U.S. forces in Japan with atomic weapons. Although the Tokyo government moved gradually to develop its own military forces, extraordinarily few Japanese wanted them equipped with nuclear armaments. In 1959, a leading specialist on Japanese politics reported that over the past few years both national and regional surveys demonstrated "almost unanimous rejection of nuclear weapons for the Japanese Self-Defense Force." Indeed, in July 1957, 87 percent of the Japanese surveyed told pollsters that they favored a complete ban on atomic and hydrogen bombs.[10] In July 1958, a poll found that 91 percent of the population favored establishing a worldwide organization to ensure that no nation could produce nuclear weapons. Despite considerable publicity for the wonders of the "peaceful atom," the idea had limited appeal in Japan. Asked in the fall of 1957 if they thought atomic energy would prove more of a boon or a curse to humanity, only 28 percent predicted that it would be a boon.[11]

Britain and the Campaign for Nuclear Disarmament

Throughout 1957, the public outcry against nuclear weapons increased in Britain, often linked to the first British H-Bomb tests, scheduled for Christmas Island that May. Responding to a plea from the National Christian Council of Japan, the British Council of Churches—by a narrow margin—voted to condemn the British nuclear tests. In March, the United Nations Association added itself to the chorus calling for test suspension.[12] Inside Parliament the Labour Party offered a resolution to postpone the tests pending a new effort at an international test ban agreement; meanwhile, outside it, the party sponsored protest meetings against the Conservative government's implacable decision to push forward with them.[13] Nor did the public furor ease after conclusion of the tests that June. To the consternation of some of its leaders, the Atomic Scientists' Association released a study, prepared by its radiation hazards committee, highlighting the dangers of strontium-90. This added to the impact of Linus Pauling's "Appeal by American Scientists," which peace periodicals helped to publicize. A few months later, at its annual conference, the Trades Union Congress unanimously passed a resolution calling for an end to nuclear weapons production and testing.[14]

Soundings of popular sentiment also revealed substantial opposition to public policy. That April, a Gallup poll found that although 41 percent of Britons approved of their government's proposed H-Bomb tests, 44 percent did not. In June, another poll reported that 50 percent of respondents thought Britain should hold no further nuclear tests. Four months later, when Britons were queried about new British tests scheduled for that winter, 57 percent expressed disapproval. Asked, in January 1958, if the Western countries should halt nuclear weapons tests for at least a few years if the Soviet Union agreed to do so, 74 percent of British respondents responded favorably and only 15 percent unfavorably.[15]

Against this backdrop, a National Council for the Abolition of Nuclear Weapon Tests (NCANWT) developed throughout the country. Sparked by the London meeting called by the National Peace Council the previous November, the NCANWT was officially launched in early February 1957, with Quaker pacifist Arthur Goss as chair, Sheila Jones (a physicist) as secretary, and Peggy Duff (a veteran Labour Party activist) as chief of staff. It urged the British government to call off its Christmas Island tests, thereby giving "a moral lead to Russia and America to reach agreement on the banning of all further tests." In an attempt to sway public opinion, the NCANWT persuaded a group of eminent figures to sign on as sponsors, including John Boyd Orr, Benjamin Britten, Ritchie Calder, Edith Evans, E. M. Forster, Alexander Haddow, Julian Huxley,

Compton Mackenzie, Henry Moore, Herbert Read, Bertrand Russell, Donald Soper, and Michael Tippett. Protesting against the British nuclear experiments, the NCANWT organized a dramatic march of two thousand women that May. Carrying black sashes and banners, they paraded through the driving rain to London's Trafalgar Square. The NCANWT also circulated petitions, held public meetings, and published antinuclear literature. By the end of 1957, it had established more than a hundred local chapters throughout Britain. Women comprised about two-thirds of the NCANWT members.[16]

Meanwhile, the direct action wing of the movement also acquired a public presence. Convinced that the more conventional tactics of the NCANWT would not stop the Christmas Island tests, an Emergency Committee for Direct Action against Nuclear War—composed of prominent pacifists and a few non-pacifists, including Russell—announced plans to have Harold and Sheila Steele, two elderly Quaker pacifists, disrupt the event by sailing into the test site. Although the Bomb testing began before the sailing could be arranged, the plans received widespread publicity. In Japan, Harold Steele spent several weeks addressing meetings and giving television, press, and radio interviews. That fall, when he returned to Britain, about thirty of the project's supporters and members of the Non-Violent Resistance Group, which had carried out civil disobedience actions against nuclear weapons in preceding years, met with him and organized the Direct Action Committee Against Nuclear War (DAC). Its first project, they decided, would be a protest march, in the spring of 1958, to the Atomic Weapons Research Establishment, at Aldermaston.[17]

Throughout 1957, the growing opposition to nuclear testing was paralleled by a heightened concern over the dangers of nuclear war. In part, this resulted from the British government's own pronouncements, for in its Defence White Paper of that year, it admitted frankly that defending Britain against nuclear bombing was hopeless. At the same time, it proposed to rely heavily on nuclear weapons, including their employment in response to a conventional attack. Many Britons did not find this entirely reassuring.[18] Polls reported large majorities opposing both the establishment of U.S. missile bases in their country and NATO plans to defend Europe from a conventional attack through nuclear war.[19] In April 1957, Commander Stephen King-Hall, a retired naval officer and respected former member of Parliament, began to argue for the establishment of a royal commission to evaluate nonviolent resistance as an alternative defense strategy. In November, former U.S. diplomat George Kennan stirred further dismay when, in the Reith lectures, he told Britons of the stark dangers of nuclear confrontation between East and West.[20]

Those looking to the Labour Party as an agent of change received a severe jolt that fall. A considerable degree of antinuclear sentiment existed within

Labour's ranks—particularly within its left wing, headed by the charismatic Aneurin Bevan—and its parliamentary representatives were far more likely than their Tory counterparts to look askance at nuclear testing, missile bases, and the prospect of nuclear war. Indeed, a revived Labour H-Bomb Campaign, emerging from the rank and file, held an antinuclear rally in Trafalgar Square in September 1957. With a large number of antinuclear resolutions on the agenda for the party's fall 1957 conference at Brighton, hopes were high among critics of the Bomb for Labour's outright repudiation of nuclear weapons. Nevertheless, when antinuclear forces rallied behind a resolution calling for a Labour commitment not to manufacture nuclear weapons, the party leadership secured its resounding defeat. The most poignant moment came when Bevan—a leading critic of the Bomb but now apparently determined to uphold his credibility as the prospective foreign secretary in a new Labour government—swung behind the party leaders, arguing that British renunciation of nuclear weapons would "send a British Foreign Secretary . . . naked into the conference chamber" and drive Britain into a "diplomatic purdah."[21]

Outraged by government policy and the apparent collapse of Labour opposition, J. B. Priestley, one of Britain's best-known playwrights, produced a stinging response in the November 2 *New Statesman*. In a reference to Bevan, Priestley observed that although "independent action by this country, to ban nuclear bombs, would involve our foreign minister in many difficulties, most of us would rather have a bewildered and overworked Foreign Office than a country about to be turned into a radio-active cemetery. Getting out of the water may be difficult, but it is better than drowning." As for the Conservative government, it was leading Britain not into "anything recognisable as a war," but into "universal catastrophe and apocalypse, the crack of doom into which Communism, western democracy, their way of life and our way of life, may disappear." Britain's "bargaining power is slight; the force of our example might be great. . . . Alone, we defied Hitler; and alone we can defy this nuclear madness into which the spirit of Hitler seems to have passed, to poison the world. There may be other chain-reactions besides those leading to destruction; and we might start one." The British people, he concluded, seemed to be waiting for "something great and noble. And this might well be a declaration to the world that . . . one power able to engage in nuclear warfare will reject the evil thing for ever."[22]

Priestley's article proved the catalyst for the most dramatic upsurge of social protest in modern Britain. Unable to handle the ensuing flood of letters to the *New Statesman*, the editor, Kingsley Martin, turned them over to the NCANWT. Even so, Martin, Priestley, and a few others now began to gravitate toward the idea of a broadly based, nationwide campaign, not merely against nuclear testing, but against nuclear weapons themselves. The NCANWT was moving in the same direction. Responding to a poll of the NCANWT membership, its executive committee voted to expand its focus to nuclear disarmament. Starting in late December 1957, leaders of the NCANWT joined with cultural and intellectual luminaries at the homes of Martin and, later, Canon John Collins of St. Paul's Cathedral, to hammer out strategies for a powerful disarmament campaign. In late January, they agreed to form a new organization, with Russell as president, Collins as chair, and Peggy Duff of the NCANWT as organizing secretary.[23] The NCANWT thereupon turned over all its assets and chapters to the new group, formally constituted on January 27, 1958, as the Campaign for Nuclear Disarmament (CND).[24]

Taking over the NCANWT's arrangements for a large meeting in London on February 17, 1958, CND used the occasion to make its public debut. On the evening of the event, some five thousand people filled Central Hall, Westminster, and four overflow meeting halls to hear impassioned speeches on behalf of nuclear disarmament by Russell, Collins, Priestley, King-Hall, Michael Foot (a leader of the Labour left), and A. J. P. Taylor (a prominent historian). Accepting the position of campaign chair, Collins contended that "the question of whether we arm ourselves with nuclear weapons is, perhaps, the supreme moral issue of our day." Priestley and Taylor, particularly, emphasized the need for Britain's renunciation of nuclear weapons, an idea that inspired great enthusiasm among those assembled.[25] Responding to frenzied applause, Taylor proposed that just as the suffragettes had disrupted political meetings by shouting "Votes for Women," so advocates of nuclear disarmament should wreck the meetings of every politician favoring nuclear weapons by crying "Murderer." At the conclusion of the gathering, about a thousand participants surged downtown for an antinuclear protest on the steps of the prime minister's office.[26] Delighted by the vigor of the public response, CND's leaders considered the launching of their movement, in Russell's words, an "outstanding success."[27]

The enthusiasm shown at the meeting also convinced CND's leaders to make the clear-cut, uncompromising demand for Britain's unilateral nuclear disarmament a centerpiece of their campaign. CND's initial policy statement had been rather ambiguous on this matter, but it now adopted a revised declaration of policy that clarified its stance. In response, a few members of the executive committee resigned, including the representative of the United Nations Association. Even so, unilateralism was quite popular among CND's founders, including Russell. That March, he explained that he favored "unilateral nuclear disarmament for Britain whose nuclear contribution is in any case unimportant." It was not worth discussing the unilateral nuclear disarmament of the United States or of the Soviet Union, for that was "an academic proposition."

In fact, Russell continued for a time to argue that the only long-term solution to the nuclear dilemma lay in world government. Like Priestley, however, he believed that in the meantime Britain could help reduce tensions and light the way to a saner world.[28]

During the balance of 1958, CND flourished. More than 250 meetings similar to that at Central Hall were held up and down the country, often featuring Canon Collins, Taylor, and a local speaker or two. Many drew large crowds and raised substantial sums of money. In addition, CND organized a Combined Universities CND to stimulate antinuclear activity on the campuses, a Film Group to make movies of CND events, and an Architect's Group to hold exhibitions. That June, the CND Women's Group held a large, very successful public meeting in London, and that December it organized a deputation that met with women members of Parliament. Although, thanks to a private arrangement with Russell, Joseph Rotblat resigned from the CND executive committee to devote himself to the Pugwash movement, he helped put together a CND Scientists' meeting that September. CND also devoted a large amount of time to wooing the Labour Party, a task officially assigned to CND's Labour Advisory Committee. Naturally, the campaign produced vast quantities of literature, including 412,000 CND leaflets; hundreds of thousands of reprints of speeches or articles by Russell, Priestley, Taylor, and others; and many thousands of posters and bumper stickers. Although CND could claim 270 local groups by the end of the year, the new movement was less a membership drive than a moral crusade. Taylor recalled how, after listening to one of his CND speeches, his former teacher told him: "God spoke through you tonight." In response, Taylor burst into tears.[29]

CND's crusading fervor became especially apparent during the Aldermaston march. Although conceived and organized by the Direct Action Committee, the 1958 march, scheduled for Easter, eventually secured CND's support and participation. As plans for the event took shape in early 1958, Gerald Holtom, an artist from Twickenham, convinced the march organizers to adopt a new and rather eerie symbol: a circle encompassing a broken cross. The drooping cross, he explained, contained the semaphore signals for the *n* and *d* of "nuclear disarmament." But the emblem also symbolized human despair in a world facing the looming threat of nuclear catastrophe. That April, some 5,800 marchers braved the rain for a rally in Trafalgar Square before thousands set out on the fifty-two-mile march to the nuclear weapons facility at Aldermaston.[30] Although pointless on the face of it, this four-day march through the chilling rain by large numbers of well-dressed, earnest citizens—many bearing the nuclear disarmament symbol, in its stark, funereal black and white—provided a powerful demonstration of public resolve to halt the nuclear arms race. Bayard Rustin, an American pacifist and civil rights activist who addressed the crowd of 8,000 that surged into Aldermaston, was so struck by the event that it led him to propose and organize the 1963 March on Washington. CND was impressed, too; it immediately adopted the nuclear disarmament symbol and, in subsequent years, staged Aldermaston marches of increasing size and intensity.[31]

Despite this brief venture in cooperation between CND and the DAC, the two organizations usually pursued very different approaches. From the beginning, CND's leadership had opted for a constitutionalist course, with its strategy centered on converting the Labour Party; therefore, it would not endorse civil disobedience but, rather, leave it to the DAC.[32] For a time, this division of labor worked reasonably well. During the balance of 1958, as CND sought to rally public opinion and build a basis for parliamentary action, the DAC— led by Michael Randle (chair), Hugh Brock (vice chair), April Carter (secretary), and Pat Arrowsmith (field organizer)—expanded the direct action wing of the nuclear disarmament campaign. DAC projects included a week's vigil by 31 people that April at Aldermaston; ten weeks of picketing at Aldermaston that summer by about 150 people, mostly under 35 years of age, including a sit-in by 27 of them; and nonviolent obstruction of missile base construction that fall and winter by 70 to 80 people at North Pickenham. Thanks to intensive discussions and campaigns in these locales, the DAC won some sympathy among workers and their unions. Small numbers of workers even resigned their jobs. But the DAC encountered stiffer resistance from government authorities. At Aldermaston, the director refused to meet with picketers, and at North Pickenham 30 people blocking missile base construction received two-week prison terms.[33]

The launching of a mass movement for nuclear disarmament had considerable appeal within several key constituencies. Taking the purist position that nuclear disarmament fell short of total disarmament, two important pacifist groups—the Peace Pledge Union (PPU) and the British FOR—refused to endorse CND. Nevertheless, some of their leaders and many of their members became stalwarts of the new movement. The PPU's newspaper, *Peace News*, covered the nuclear disarmament campaign so ardently that Sybil Morrison— one of the leading critics within the PPU—resigned as chair of the newspaper's board in protest. Indeed, one study of CND activists found that 46 percent described themselves as absolute pacifists.[34] CND also drew considerable support from young people, especially those attending colleges and universities. Breaking the mold of conventional politics through the moral purity of unilateral nuclear disarmament and the excitement of the Aldermaston march, CND appealed strongly to the idealism and daring of the younger generation.[35] Sometimes this group overlapped with another important (albeit smaller) CND constituency, the burgeoning New Left. Disgusted by the rigidities of Stalinism and the suppression of the Hungarian rebellion, a group of young intellectuals brought to the nuclear disarmament campaign an independent Marxist perspective. Meanwhile, another group of young radicals, connected with the *Universities and Left Review*, scrapped Marxism entirely and turned eagerly to the revolt against nuclear weapons as the cutting edge of social change.[36]

The churches and the Labour Party also provided important sources of support for the nuclear disarmament campaign. Although the hierarchies of most of the churches—and particularly that of the Church of England—took a dim view of CND and of Britain's abandonment of the Bomb,[37] the Quakers, Unitarians, and Methodists officially endorsed them. Furthermore, some church leaders (e.g. Canon Collins) and many rank-and-file Christians played significant roles in the new movement.[38] Within the Labour Party, too, opinions were sharply divided on unilateral nuclear disarmament. The party leadership, in particular, strongly opposed CND. Commenting tartly on the new campaign, one of Labour's wheelhorses dismissed Russell contemptuously as "a superannuated philosopher." But renouncing the Bomb had a strong appeal to the party's left wing and to its grassroots activists. Thus, even though CND sought to project a nonpartisan image, a clear majority of its supporters came from the Labour Party. Indeed, no other political party had much attraction for the CND leadership or the rank and file.[39]

Throughout 1958, the British public continued to show a deep aversion to nuclear weapons and a growing support for the unilateralist position of CND. In February 1958, a Gallup poll found that 64 percent of British respondents opposed using the H-Bomb to respond to a Soviet conventional attack on Western Europe. That November, another Gallup poll found that 47 percent of Britons, if confronted with the alternative of waging nuclear war against the Russians, favored (and only 25 percent opposed) coming to terms with them "at any price." By roughly the same percentages—and bolstering this attitude—Britons believed that their nation could not survive a nuclear war. Naturally, then, nuclear disarmament had considerable appeal. In March 1958, a poll found that 72 percent of Britons supported (and only 10 percent opposed) internationally enforced nuclear disarmament. Halting nuclear testing was even more popular. That November, a poll reported that 76 percent of British respondents favored (and only 7 percent opposed) an international agreement to halt nuclear tests on a year-to-year or permanent basis. Although unilateral measures had less backing, they also drew significant support. In May 1958, 43 percent of Britons favored halting British and U.S. nuclear tests immediately and another 19 percent favored stopping them after the current round;

only 28 percent opposed the idea.[40] According to Gallup polls, Britain's unilateral renunciation of the Bomb was supported by 22 percent of respondents in February, 25 percent in April, and 30 percent in September. Opposition over this period fell from 58 to 47 percent.[41] If CND still had some distance to go before it spoke for most Britons, it was clearly making progress.

America's Quest for a Sane Nuclear Policy

In the United States, pacifist groups increasingly concentrated their efforts on nuclear issues. "These are times when, not only the morality, but the very sanity of society is brought into question," wrote Clarence Pickett, secretary emeritus of the American Friends Service Committee. "We are relying on means of defense which threaten to defend nothing and destroy everything." As they had in the past, the Friends, Mennonites, and Brethren issued strong statements condemning the nuclear arms race and calling on religious bodies to oppose it. During 1957, the AFSC and the WILPF presented the White House with petitions against nuclear testing signed by more than 37,000 Americans. The AFSC petition contended that "the stopping of nuclear tests would go a long way toward halting the spread of the nuclear arms race to other nations. It would stop the increasing danger from radioactive fall-out. It would be a dramatic moral act which would ease tensions and create the political climate for positive steps to peace."[42] Meanwhile, leaders of the FOR conferred with Japanese officials on halting nuclear testing and the arms race, appealed to the U.S., British, and Soviet governments to stop nuclear testing unilaterally, and circulated antinuclear statements among the clergy. In November 1957, the FOR, the WILPF, the War Resisters League, and other pacifist groups joined to sponsor a "prayer and conscience vigil" in Washington, protesting the continued manufacture and testing of nuclear weapons. This event initiated a period of concerted effort among them around the nuclear weapons issue. By February 1958, they had put into circulation more than 150,000 petitions calling for the cancellation of forthcoming U.S. Bomb tests in the Pacific.[43]

American scientists were also becoming increasingly restive. In June 1957, the Federation of American Scientists proposed a ban on the testing of large nuclear weapons. And, in February 1958, it again urged an international agreement prohibiting all nuclear testing. According to the FAS, this measure would limit nuclear proliferation, allay fears of radioactive fallout, and help establish "a more favorable atmosphere for subsequent negotiation of the many political and military problems requiring resolution."[44] A few leading critics of the Bomb, like Szilard and Muller, remained unenthusiastic about a nuclear test ban, which they felt skirted more fundamental issues.[45] Furthermore, a substantial number of more hawkish scientists refused to consider any curbs on America's nuclear options. The most prominent among them, Edward Teller, argued vociferously that the medical and genetic hazards of nuclear testing were insignificant. Nevertheless, the tide of scientific opinion was running against him. Influential journals such as *Science* and *Scientific American* joined. the *Bulletin of the Atomic Scientists* in issuing warnings about radioactive fallout. At congressional hearings in 1957, even the AEC's scientists conceded that fallout might cause cancer and would certainly produce some level of genetic damage.[46]

Sensing that the moment was ripe for a breakthrough on the testing issue, American peace activists moved to make it the centerpiece of a major campaign. In April 1957, Lawrence Scott, Peace Secretary of the American Friends Service Committee in Chicago, began efforts to establish a broadly based Committee to Stop H-Bomb Tests. Eventually, Scott prevailed on Clarence Pickett and Norman Cousins to organize a meeting for this purpose. Convened on June 21 at New York City's Overseas Press Club, the gathering drew twenty-seven well-known Americans, including prominent writers, clergy, business executives, and scientists. Pickett opened the meeting by stating that "something should be done to bring out the latent sensitivity of the American people to the poisoning effect of nuclear bombs on international relations and on humanity." During five hours of ensuing discussion, participants proved uninterested in creating a new organization; instead, they decided to support the launching of an ad hoc effort to focus American opinion on the dangers of nuclear testing.[47] The group selected a steering committee, which met that summer and considered policy statements by Socialist leader Norman Thomas, a committee member. Meanwhile, Homer Jack, a Unitarian minister who served as the committee secretary, distributed a disarmament newsletter, organized a clearinghouse for local committees opposing nuclear tests, and established contact with Britain's NCANWT. "The normal drive for survival has been put out of action by present propaganda," observed Erich Fromm, an eminent psychoanalyst and supporter of the new venture. "We must . . . try to bring the voice of sanity to the people." Adopting the idea, the group called itself the National Committee for a Sane Nuclear Policy.[48]

The National Committee for a Sane Nuclear Policy—or SANE, as it came to be known—made its debut on November 15, 1957, with an advertisement in the *New York Times*. Written largely by Cousins and signed by forty-eight prominent Americans,[49] the ad contended that "we are facing a danger unlike any danger that has ever existed. In our possession and in the possession of the Russians are more than enough nuclear explosives to put an end to the life of man on earth." Sadly, "our approach . . . is unequal to the danger," for "the slo-

gans and arguments that belong to the world of competitive national sover-
eignties . . . no longer fit the world of today or tomorrow." When, through their
rivalries, nations acted to destroy the "natural rights" of the planet's inhabitants, "whether by upsetting the delicate balances on which life depends, or
fouling the air, or devitalizing the land, or tampering with the genetic integrity
of man himself, then it becomes necessary for people to restrain and tame the
nations." Calling for the immediate suspension of nuclear testing by all countries, SANE argued that this action would both halt radioactive contamination
and provide "a place to begin on the larger question of armaments control."
The great "challenge of the age," it maintained, is to move beyond the traditional interests of the nation-state to "a higher loyalty"—loyalty "to the human
community."[50]

SANE's advertisement, as its newsletter recalled, "started a movement."
By the end of the year, some 2,400 enthusiasts had written to SANE's over-
whelmed national office, and citizens in various parts of the country had
reprinted the ad in twenty-three newspapers with a total circulation of over
three million. In New York City, a local SANE leader reported, the popular response "has exceeded our highest expectations. . . . Meetings have been held,
petitions filed, community leaders visited, literature distributed, newspaper ads
published, and essential organizational steps taken at an ever-accelerating rate."
"When was the last time a Friends, or a Federalist, or an AAUN meeting pulled
1500 to 2000 people?" mused Trevor Thomas, SANE's first executive secretary. "These turnouts, though, are not unusual when a well-known speaker is
talking about 'a sane nuclear policy.'" SANE had "stepped into a vacuum that
no other committee or association had filled," he concluded.[51] Given the "elec-
trifying" response at the grassroots, a SANE leader recalled, a new membership group "came spontaneously into being." Thus, despite the caution of its
founders, by the summer of 1958 SANE had become a national organization,
with some 130 chapters and 25,000 members. Holding press conferences, arranging television interviews, and churning out literature on nuclear testing,
SANE had become America's largest, most visible, and most influential peace
group.[52]

Sustaining SANE's remarkable momentum proved a formidable challenge.
Cousins later wrote that he and Pickett, now SANE's co-chairs, were "flabber-
gasted" to find themselves "with a national membership organization on our
hands." To keep SANE afloat financially, Cousins borrowed against his stock in
the *Saturday Review*; the poet Lenore Marshall also made substantial contributions. SANE ran a series of new advertisements on the dangers of nuclear
testing, beginning with one on March 24, 1958, proclaiming: "No Contamination without Representation." Although SANE failed to persuade Hubert

Humphrey, chair of the U.S. Senate Subcommittee on Disarmament, to introduce into Congress a SANE-drafted resolution calling for a testing moratorium
under international supervision, the Minnesota Democrat did put questions to
the AEC prepared by Cousins and promise hearings on nuclear testing. In a
speech of June 4, 1958, he also lauded SANE on the floor of the U.S. Senate.
"The objectives of the committee are honorable and directed toward the attain-
ment of a just and enduring peace," he declared. SANE had "done much to encourage a constructive and thoughtful discussion of the problems inherent in
the development of nuclear weapons testing."[53]

Although SANE began with a focus on halting all nuclear testing, in 1958
the organization gradually extended its purview to securing nuclear disarmament. This broadened goal—comparable to the shift during the same period in
Britain from the aims of the NCANWT to those of CND—reflected the fact
that, above all else, SANE's leaders were determined opponents of nuclear
weapons. Pickett was a staunch pacifist and, not surprisingly, he advocated
halting the testing of nuclear weapons as "a first step in the direction of disarmament."[54] SANE's two leading non-pacifists, Norman Cousins and Norman
Thomas, had long been nuclear disarmament proponents.[55] Indeed, since the
inception of the Eisenhower administration, Thomas had been badgering Secretary of State Dulles to halt the drift toward nuclear war "through universal,
controlled disarmament." In December 1957, Cousins told Schweitzer that "the
danger of contamination from radioactive fallout is great, but an even greater
danger is represented by the fact that the world situation is getting out of control." Writing to the head of SANE's Los Angeles chapter the following June,
Cousins argued that "a cessation of testing . . . does not represent the be-all and
end-all of world peace and nuclear sanity. A truly sane nuclear policy will not
be achieved until nuclear weapons are brought completely under control."[56]
Thus, after the great powers began a moratorium on nuclear testing in late
1958, SANE's activists moved toward realization of their broader goals.[57]

As in Britain, some advocates of nuclear disarmament turned to nonviolent
direct action. This, too, developed out of Lawrence Scott's efforts of early 1957
to organize a campaign against nuclear testing. In April, he recalled, it was decided "to separate the educational and conventional action"—which became
the basis for SANE—"from the satyagraha or Gandhian type of action." Scott
chose to remain with the Gandhian current, although he continued to hope for
"some organic and spiritual relationship between the two aspects within a
larger movement of Creative Truth." Later that spring, with the support of pacifist groups, Scott established Non-Violent Action Against Nuclear Weapons
(NVAANW), which laid plans for direct action at the U.S. government's nuclear testing site in Nevada. On August 6, 1957, the anniversary of the Hiro-

shima bombing, about thirty-five pacifists—watched warily by AEC security
police, local deputy sheriffs, and state police, whom NVAANW had informed
of its plans—gathered outside the gates of the AEC Bomb project for a prayer
vigil. Eleven of them, including Scott, crossed over onto the military property
and were immediately arrested. Others, led by the pacifist A. J. Muste, remained for an all-night vigil at the gates. Here, the next morning, they observed
the AEC's latest nuclear device explode with a blinding flash and a gray and
pink cloud of radioactive debris rising from behind the mountains. One participant called it "a nightmare come true."[58]

NVAANW's best-known venture was the voyage of the *Golden Rule*.
Among the pacifists arrested at the Nevada test site was Albert Bigelow, a lieu-
tenant commander in the U.S. Navy during World War II who, with the bombing of Hiroshima, had concluded "that morally war is impossible." In 1952, a
month before he became eligible for his pension, he resigned from the U.S.
Navy reserve. Thereafter, he invited two of the "Hiroshima maidens" to live in
his home. On January 8, 1958, Bigelow and three other pacifists recruited by
NVAANW wrote to President Eisenhower of their plan to sail a thirty-foot vessel, the *Golden Rule*, into the U.S. nuclear testing zone in the Pacific. "For
years we have spoken and written of the suicidal military preparations of the
Great Powers, but our voices have been lost in the massive effort of those responsible for preparing this country for war. We mean to speak now with the
weight of our whole lives." In a press release, they explained that although
many Americans knew that "no vital risk is involved" in halting nuclear testing,
"we stand benumbed, morally desensitized by ten years of propaganda and fear.
How do you reach men when . . . they feel no horror? It requires, we believe,
the kind of effort and sacrifice we now undertake." They hoped their act would
"say to others: Speak Now."[59]

A remarkable string of events ensued. Captained across stormy seas by
Bigelow, the *Golden Rule* arrived in Honolulu, where a federal court issued an
injunction barring the rest of its voyage. After pondering the legal ramifica-
tions, the four pacifists decided: "We would sail—come what may." Overtaken
by U.S. authorities on the journey to Eniwetok, they were arrested, tried, convicted, and placed on probation. Not easily subdued, they set sail again. Once
more, they were arrested, tried, convicted, and—this time—imprisoned. Meanwhile, Earle Reynolds, an American anthropologist previously employed by
the AEC in Japan, arrived in Honolulu with his wife, Barbara, and their two
children on board the fifty-foot sailing ship, *Phoenix*. Intrigued by the furor
over the *Golden Rule*, the Reynolds family attended the local trial and, eventually, concluded that the AEC had misinformed the public about the dangers of
radioactive fallout, had illegally restricted entry into the test zone, and lacked

constitutional authority to explode nuclear weapons in the Pacific. "We all felt strongly that the men of the *Golden Rule* were both morally and legally right," wrote Reynolds. Consequently, determined to complete the voyage of the *Golden Rule*, they set sail for Eniwetok. On July 1, Reynolds went on the radio to announce that the *Phoenix* was entering "the U.S. nuclear test zone as a protest against nuclear testing. Please inform appropriate authorities." The U.S. Coast Guard boarded the *Phoenix* the following day, arrested Reynolds, and returned him for trial in Hawaii, where he was convicted and sentenced to a prison term.[60]

These well-publicized events unleashed an enormous surge of energy. Picket lines sprang up around federal buildings and AEC offices across the nation, including those in Boston, Philadelphia, New York, Washington, Chicago, Los Angeles, and San Francisco. Signs proclaimed: "Stop the tests, not the *Golden Rule*." In San Francisco, 432 residents—proclaiming that they were guilty of "conspiring" with the crew members—petitioned the U.S. attorney to take action against them. Most of the people involved in the protests had never participated in a demonstration before, and relatively few were pacifists. Reynolds, out on bail before a higher court ruled in his favor—and, implicitly, in favor of his imprisoned predecessors—went on a speaking tour that included 58 major talks, 20 other meetings, 21 radio programs, and 8 television appearances. He spoke to live audiences totaling some 10,000 people at 26 colleges, 4 high schools, and 22 churches.[61] Although SANE did not sponsor the voyages, it expressed its warm enthusiasm to the participants and planners. SANE also dispatched telegrams to assorted political leaders declaring that it joined the *Golden Rule*'s crew members "in protesting against [the] unrightful use of [the] Pacific Ocean for nuclear weapons testing, and against [the] Atomic Energy Commission's exercise of authority which it does not rightfully possess, thus perpetuating [the] spirit of lawlessness which promotes war."[62] Privately, Cousins helped finance the voyage of the *Golden Rule* and, publicly, he lauded its voyage and that of the *Phoenix* in the *Saturday Review*.[63]

During 1958, the direct actionists also organized some lesser-known ventures. That April, they sponsored a Walk for Peace under the slogan "Stop the A-Bomb Testing." Beginning in Philadelphia and New Haven and culminating at the United Nations in New York City, it drew more than seven hundred participants on its final day. Meanwhile, as a counterpart to the voyage of the *Golden Rule*, a pacifist delegation—including Scott of NVAANW and Bayard Rustin of the War Resisters League—began a journey to the Soviet Union to appeal to its people and government for a unilateral halt to nuclear testing. After several weeks of fruitless waiting in Helsinki for the promised Soviet visas, they issued a strong statement that May, condemning the policies of the Soviet government.[64] In August, attempting to halt the building of a nuclear missile base in Cheyenne, Wyoming, pacifists distributed leaflets among the workers and repeatedly sat down in front of construction trucks. Military authorities ordered them removed, arrested, and, in one case, crushed under the wheels.[65]

Having launched a startling campaign of nonviolent resistance to nuclear war, activists took stock of their successes and made plans for the future. Against the backdrop of internal controversy over the wisdom of the confrontation at Cheyenne,[66] the major pacifist groups decided to reorganize their direct action efforts. Consequently, in September 1958, representatives from these groups agreed to close down NVAANW and to replace it with a more tightly structured Committee for Nonviolent Action (CNVA). The sponsoring groups—the FOR, the WILPF, the War Resisters League, and the Friends Peace Committee of the Philadelphia Yearly Meeting—would have seats on its executive committee, and no civil disobedience project would be conducted by CNVA without the unanimous consent of these groups. George Willoughby, a Quaker active in the *Golden Rule* project, became CNVA's first chair. Nevertheless, with antinuclear fervor imparting an urgency and momentum to direct action projects, CNVA—like SANE—took on a life of its own, and its leading voice became that of another religious pacifist, the increasingly radical A. J. Muste.[67]

Not all Americans, of course, welcomed the advent of ban-the-Bomb activism. Outside the Northeast, the Middle West, and the Pacific Coast, relatively few people joined SANE or provided it with funding. Furthermore, many large organizations and opinion leaders remained aloof. Sometimes, in fact, they responded venomously. In New York City, the Reverend Daniel Poling denounced a SANE march against nuclear testing as part of the "most insidious and far-reaching menace of atheist Communism." Ridiculing the peace group's efforts, the New York *Daily News* claimed that when it came to nuclear weapons tests SANE's leaders were "as nutty as so many fruitcakes." In Honolulu, Bigelow recalled, the newspapers at first maintained that the crew of the *Golden Rule* was "sincere but misguided," and later shifted to the contention that they were "playing into the hands of the Communists." At Cheyenne, a carload of local residents physically assaulted the demonstrators. "If you were my daughter," an irate woman told one of the pacifists, "I'd kill you." Taking aim at SANE in April 1958, *Time* condemned "the folks who listened to the horror stories without listening to evidence on fallout, to say nothing of survival" for "stepping up the pressure as the crucial Eniwetok tests drew nigh." According to the magazine, "this was what the sworn enemies of religion, liberty and peace itself were telling them to do." The chair of the House Committee on Un-American Activities, Representative Francis Walter, argued that behind the seemingly innocent facade of the antinuclear movement lay "the black hand of the Communist conspiracy."[68]

Even so, there were signs that the popular tide was turning. In June 1957, the AEC reported to the White House that it had received such a flood of mail concerning the dangers of nuclear testing that it had been compelled to develop a new form letter to reply to it.[69] Published in the summer of 1957, Nevil Shute's grim novel, *On the Beach*, which recounted the story of how nuclear war and radioactive fallout brought an end to life on earth, sold 100,000 copies in the first six weeks. In September, some forty newspapers with a circulation of eight million began to serialize it. Although fundamentalist Christian groups continued to champion the U.S. nuclear buildup, the National Council of Churches, at its December 1957 General Assembly, warned that "the accelerating arms race which now grips our world may lead directly to a war which will destroy civilization" and called on the U.S. government to seek workable nuclear arms control agreements. The following June, the General Board of the NCC reiterated these concerns and demanded a "frank disclosure" of the reasons for and dangers of nuclear tests. That same month, a commission of the Central Conference of American Rabbis asked for "the immediate abandonment of the testing of nuclear weapons. . . . Governments simply have no moral right . . . to impose pain, crippling, and death upon innocent human beings."[70]

Ending nuclear testing had particular appeal among Democrats and, especially, liberals. Continuing to press the issue, Adlai Stevenson restated the case for halting H-Bomb testing in a *Look* magazine article in February 1957. That July, when he visited with Albert Schweitzer, Stevenson told reporters: "I am in complete agreement with my old friend, Doctor Schweitzer, on the question of suspending hydrogen bomb tests."[71] To the dismay of the AEC, the Joint Committee on Atomic Energy, chaired by Democratic Senator Clinton Anderson of New Mexico, announced in March 1957 that it would hold hearings "to educate the Committee and the public" about the hazards of radioactive fallout. Anderson clashed with Strauss frequently, and in 1958 assailed the latter's claim that Bomb tests were needed to develop "cleaner" weapons. In July 1957, the maverick Republican senator from Oregon, Wayne Morse, introduced a congressional resolution calling for immediate cessation of nuclear weapons testing. "The halting of nuclear-bomb testing is absolutely essential," he wrote to a disarmament activist in St. Louis. "It is essential not only because of the radiation hazards it threatens, but also as a first and essential step toward disarmament and peace." In 1958, the nation's leading liberal organization, Americans for Democratic Action, called on the U.S. government to halt nuclear testing and to press for the development of an inspection system.[72]

Polls of the time confirm the fact that public opinion strongly favored a test ban and, more broadly, nuclear disarmament. Although support for a unilateral halt to U.S. nuclear testing stood at only 29 percent in April 1958, support had risen and opposition had fallen over the previous four years.[73] Moreover, support for a multilateral nuclear test ban stood at 63 percent of U.S. respondents in April 1957. Even in January 1958, amid fears for U.S. national security aroused by the recent Soviet launching of *Sputnik*, polls found that 49 percent of the nation still backed (and only 36 percent opposed) a U.S.-Soviet nuclear test ban.[74] This continued support for a nuclear test ban treaty[75] was hardly surprising, for polls in both 1957 and 1958 revealed that—despite official claims as to the harmlessness of radioactive fallout from nuclear tests—about half the population considered it a health hazard. Moreover, Americans were not driven merely by "fear of fallout."[76] Instead, very substantial numbers desired an end to the nuclear arms race. A March 1958 poll by the American Institute of Public Opinion found that 70 percent of the American public favored "setting up a world-wide organization which would make sure—by regular inspections—that no nation, including Russia and the United States, makes atom bombs, hydrogen bombs, and missiles."[77]

Revival and Decline

"Is there a pacifist revival going on today?" asked *Liberation*, an American pacifist magazine, in May 1958. "Many signs," it noted, "indicate that there is: the outpourings of thousands in protest against nuclear tests in Great Britain and Western Germany, the unexpected support given in the United States to the voyage of the *Golden Rule* and to the Walk for Peace, the work of . . . SANE," and "the protest actions taken by scientists here and in Europe." These were "some of the indications that the rigid attitudes and thought-patterns" of the past are "beginning to give way." Indeed, during these years, traditional critics of militarism had considerable justification for taking heart, for the rising tide of antinuclear sentiment did augur well for realization of their goals. "There is a feeling of lift and hope," reported the American FOR in 1958. "The achievement of peace has become no simpler, but there are signs that the apathy is lifting, and that we are finding more and more allies."[78]

Nevertheless, the burgeoning antinuclear activism of 1957–58 also masked an important trend. Ban-the-Bomb organizations clearly mobilized broader sectors of society than could those with a more deeply rooted critique of international violence. But greater popularity came at the price of muting more thoroughgoing alternatives.[79] To be sure, pacifist leaders continued to make the case for nonviolent approaches to conflict resolution. Meanwhile, world government advocates championed the development of world law.[80] Nevertheless, they had clearly lost the initiative to antinuclear activists and, in some cases—like that of Britain's Peace Pledge Union and America's United World Federalists—their membership dwindled.[81] The same phenomenon occurred on the leadership level. Some of the most eminent world federalists—like Russell and Cousins— assumed the top posts in nuclear disarmament campaigns. And although they remained committed to world government,[82] they became less useful in pro- moting it. "This is one of the real problems that arises from the existence of the Sane Nuclear Policy Committee," the president of United World Federalists told Cousins in the summer of 1958.[83] Thus, even as the emphasis on banning the Bomb transformed peace activism into a mass movement in Japan, Britain, and the United States, it began to overshadow alternative routes to a peaceful world or, for that matter, to nuclear disarmament.

The Rise of
Ban-the-Bomb Movements

Elsewhere, 1957–58

> We *must* do something! We must do it *now*!
>
> Anti-Atoombom-Actie, 1957

In 1957–58, lively ban-the-Bomb campaigns also appeared in other parts of the world. Spurred on during these years by the most obvious manifestations of the arms race—the diffusion of nuclear weapons and their testing in the atmosphere—activists succeeded in launching grassroots, antinuclear movements in Western Europe, North America, the Pacific region, and portions of the Third World. Meanwhile, public opinion—influenced by these movements and, at the same time, bolstering them—grew ever more hostile to nuclear weapons. Even in the unpromising territory of the Soviet Union, growing fears of nuclear catastrophe, combined with the example of protest efforts elsewhere, helped foster the development of antinuclear activity. The result, by late 1958, was the emergence of a nuclear disarmament campaign that although not a powerful presence in all nations, had become in many places an increasingly visible and important phenomenon.

West Germany

In the Federal Republic of Germany, a mass mobilization against the Bomb was sparked by government plans to acquire nuclear weapons. Speaking before the German Defense Committee in March 1957, NATO's military commander, General Lauris Norstad, contended that "if we want to defend ourselves in the event of a general war, then we must do it with atomic weapons." At roughly the same time, Chancellor Konrad Adenauer and Defense Minister Franz Josef Strauss talked publicly of arming the Bundeswehr with tactical nuclear weapons supplied by the United States. In private conversations with

Christian Democratic Party leaders, Strauss—who had served as minister of atomic affairs in 1955–56—took a more independent line, implying that Germany should develop its own nuclear weapons. Responding publicly in early April to queries about the government's intentions, Adenauer referred vaguely to an array of possibilities. "Tactical atomic weapons" were "basically nothing but the further development of artillery," he commented. They were "practically normal weapons" and "we cannot dispense with having them for our troops." As for "the large-yield weapons . . . this whole development is in flux. Great Britain announced last week that it intends to become a nuclear power. . . . We Germans cannot halt this process. We must adapt to the developments." Unilateral "renunciation of these weapons," he argued, would be ridiculous.[1]

On April 12, 1957, responding to these statements and to the arrival of U.S. medium-range missiles, a group of Germany's top physicists issued a declaration of protest. Since the fall of 1956, some of them had been secretly communicating with Strauss, attempting to dissuade him from producing or stationing nuclear weapons in Germany. Now, worried that both projects had been launched, they responded with a public message of protest, the Göttingen Manifesto. Written by Carl Friedrich von Weizsäcker and signed by eighteen of West Germany's most eminent physicists, including four Nobel Prize winners (Born, Hahn, Heisenberg, and Max von Laue), the Manifesto argued that "tactical atomic bombs have the same destructive effects as normal atomic bombs." Moreover, "since tactical atomic weapons are today available in large numbers, their destructive effect would be on the whole much larger" than the bomb that obliterated Hiroshima. Hydrogen bombs, of course, could destroy entire nations, including "the whole population of the German Federal Republic." A small country like their own, they contended, could "protect itself best and promote world peace by renouncing explicitly and voluntarily the possession of atomic weapons of any kind." Accordingly, none of the signers would take part "in the production, the tests, or the application of atomic weapons."[2]

The Göttingen Manifesto created a furor in West Germany. Because of the signers' great prestige, the press gave their statement widespread coverage, praising the "Göttingen 18" as courageous, determined scientists. Although Christian Democratic journals attacked these "sorcerer's apprentices" for addressing political matters beyond their competence, the opposition parties praised them lavishly and hammered away at the nuclear weapons issue. Seeking to dampen the controversy, government leaders met with a delegation of the Göttingen scientists on April 17. On this occasion, Adenauer pleaded for "unanimity of the West," while Strauss argued that the Bonn government did not intend to build nuclear weapons or to have direct control over those stationed in West Germany. Adenauer prepared a joint communiqué for the press, stressing areas of agreement. But the physicists were only partially appeased by what they had heard, for they desired West Germany's total renunciation of nuclear weapons. Therefore, they amended the statement to read that their "primary goal" was to have the Federal Republic "take an initiative that would help protect the world" from a "threatening catastrophe."[3] In fact, they believed that they had secured a partial victory by convincing the government to renounce production of nuclear weapons.[4]

Although the physicists now retreated from the political limelight, the opposition parties—the Social Democratic Party (SPD) and the much smaller Free Democratic Party (FDP)—intensified their attack on the government's nuclear policy. In part, this represented a logical extension of the Social Democrats' antimilitarist tradition, most recently their opposition to German rearmament. But with the approach of a general election, it also reflected their recognition of the political opportunities. In the spring of 1957, polls found that 81 percent of the population opposed further nuclear testing, 88 percent favored an international agreement on nuclear weapons, and 56 percent felt nuclear weapons heightened the dangers for Germany in the event of a European war. On the sensitive issue of equipping German troops with nuclear weapons, polls reported opposition ranging from 64 to 72 percent of the population.[5] That May, in sharp Bundestag debates, the Social Democrats, led by party chair Erich Ollenhauer, pressed for an appeal to the great powers to halt test explosions, for withdrawal of permission to foreign nations to deploy nuclear weapons in Germany, and for the scrapping of plans to equip West German forces with nuclear weapons. Defending the administration's record, Strauss argued evasively that it had "not up to this moment requested equipping the Bundeswehr with nuclear weapons." Adenauer, too, sought to defuse the nuclear issue by denying its immediacy. Controlled by the Christian Democrats, the Bundestag rejected all the antinuclear measures proposed by their rivals.[6]

Much the same pattern ensued in the hotly contested parliamentary election campaign. Demanding that the Federal Republic renounce nuclear armaments, the SPD also called for the withdrawal of all foreign nuclear weapons deployed on German territory. One SPD campaign poster showed a tank firing atomic missiles under Adenauer's face. Another depicted the head of a corpse, disfigured by radiation, with the slogan: "Atomic armament begets mass death." In a television broadcast beginning with scenes of an atomic explosion and the ruins of Nagasaki, an SPD narrator explained that just as the SPD had once warned that Hitler would plunge the country into ruin, so it was now sounding a modern alarm. Dispatched to every household, a letter by Ollenhauer charged that a Christian Democratic victory would lead to "our living

under the atom bomb and perhaps dying by it." By contrast, an SPD government would "see that atomic energy is used only for peaceful purposes." Although differing at some points with the SPD, the Free Democrats also took a
sharply antinuclear approach. In September 1957, however, the election results
proved a sharp disappointment to the opposition parties. Adenauer's Christian
Democrats won a smashing victory, drawing an absolute majority of the vote—
the first party to do so in Germany's electoral history.[7]

Even so, the outcome of the election could hardly be construed as an endorsement of plans to nuclearize West Germany. Uncertain, especially at the
outset of the campaign, about the effects of the opposition's call for nuclear
disarmament, Adenauer and the Christian Democrats repeatedly dodged the
nuclear question and focused instead on the growing sense of comfort, safety,
and contentment in postwar West Germany. If the opposition came to power,
he implied, it would sacrifice the nation's well-being through dangerous experiments. This proved an effective appeal. Analyzing the election results, the
U.S. ambassador reported that West Germany "had become one of [the] great
'have' nations of [the] world, and well-filled stomachs combined with [a] sense
of relative security vis-a-vis [the] outside world, left most Germans unwilling
to risk what they had by experimenting with [an] uncertain future under [a]
changed government." Although of limited assistance in these circumstances,
the SPD's antinuclear stand may have improved the party's fortunes somewhat,
for, between 1953 and 1957, the SPD share of the vote did grow, from 28.8 to
31.8 percent.[8] In December 1957, an opinion poll reported that, despite the
Adenauer landslide, only 19 percent of West Germans favored arming the Bundeswehr with atomic weapons.[9]

Against this backdrop, the SPD renewed its nuclear critique in the Bundestag. Attacking plans to equip the nation's armed forces with nuclear
weapons, Ollenhauer charged that November that they would further increase
international tensions. In December, attempting to influence West Germany's
role at a forthcoming NATO conference, the SPD Bundestag faction introduced
a motion, supported by the FDP, to have the government press for an end to
nuclear testing and the proliferation of nuclear weapons, renounce atomic
weapons for the Bundeswehr, reject missile bases on its territory, and promote
negotiations for the creation of "an atom-free zone in Europe." Although Adenauer again sidestepped these issues, in March the confrontation became direct, for the victorious Christian Democrats were now determined to use their
Bundestag majority to dispose of the nuclear question. A bitter and vituperative debate ensued, concluding on March 25, 1958, after a forty-hour marathon
session, with a solid endorsement of Adenauer's nuclear policy, including the
plan to arm the Bundeswehr with U.S. nuclear weapons.[10]

Determined to keep the issue alive, opponents of nuclear weapons pressed forward with a dramatic, extraparliamentary campaign, the Struggle Against Atomic Death (Kampf dem Atomtod). Launched on March 10, 1958, with a demand that the Federal Republic reject participation in the nuclear arms race, it erupted into a mass movement after the Bundestag approved Adenauer's atomic armaments program later that month. As the Struggle Against Atomic Death spread across West Germany in the spring and summer, over half a million Germans took part in more than a hundred antinuclear rallies. Protesting the Bundestag's decision, 150,000 people demonstrated in Hamburg, 40,000 in Hannover, 30,000 in Frankfurt, 25,000 in Bremen and in Bielefeld, 20,000 in Karlsruhe, 15,000 in Ulm, 11,000 in Dortmund, and 10,000 in Munich. Groups of professors and physicians issued antinuclear appeals. Writers and artists signed resolutions against government policy. Students demonstrated at the universities.[11] Polls found that 52 percent of the population thought a strike justified in order to block the nuclear armament of their country. In fact, antinuclear strikes did break out at about twenty factories, one involving twenty thousand workers. Although the German trade union federation, the DGB (Deutscher Gewerkschaftsbund), resisted calls for a general strike, it provided the antinuclear campaign with considerable financial and other assistance. The massive Hamburg rally owed its success in part to the labor movement's decision to organize a citywide work stoppage one hour before closing time, thus making it easier for workers to participate in the event. West Germany's unions also displayed antinuclear slogans at their traditional May Day rallies.[12]

Although prominent intellectuals, members of the clergy, and leading liberals spoke at these antinuclear demonstrations, the muscle behind the Struggle Against Atomic Death came from the SPD and its ally, the DGB. With the exception of the new movement's Bavarian wing—the Committee against Atomic Armaments (Komitee gegen Atomrüstung), headed by the author Hans Werner Richter—and of complementary efforts by small pacifist groups, the SPD and the DGB dominated the campaign.[13] As before, the central role of the SPD reflected a blend of principle and opportunity. Polls that April and June continued to show that nearly two-thirds of the population opposed arming West German troops with nuclear weapons. Admittedly, the Bundestag had taken a crucial decision in March; but it still seemed possible to reverse it and to garner popular support along the way. That May, to offset charges that it had no interest in the nation's defense, the SPD declared its support for the establishment of small, mobile, well-equipped (but non-nuclear) armed forces. Meanwhile, it announced that to give voice to the country's antinuclear majority, it would sponsor antinuclear referenda and run antinuclear campaigns in state elections, scheduled for the latter part of 1958.[14] Some SPD and DGB officials harbored doubts about this approach. But, for the most part, it was popular with the party leadership and with the party rank and file.[15]

The Struggle Against Atomic Death enjoyed less support in the broader society. Germany's Protestants, located overwhelmingly in the Evangelical Church (EKD), were fiercely divided over nuclear issues. One faction, the Church Brethren, whose dissenting role had begun with resistance to the Nazi regime, pushed hard for the EKD's outright repudiation of nuclear weapons. Another wing of the church, however, championed nuclear deterrence. On April 30, 1958, after a particularly heated debate, the EKD's synod adopted a compromise resolution. "The antagonism among us over our judgment of nuclear weaponry is very deep," it acknowledged, and participants could only "ask God to lead us to a common understanding and decision through His words." The result was that although many Protestant church leaders—like Martin Niemöller, Gustav Heinemann, and Helmut Gollwitzer—played key roles in the antinuclear campaign, the EKD as a whole remained apart from it.[16] The campaign also received minimal support from the Free Democrats. As the voice of a relatively comfortable, middle-class constituency, the FDP hesitated to tie its fortunes to an extraparliamentary venture that might even touch off a general strike. Consequently, although the party remained opposed to arming the Bundeswehr with nuclear weapons and leading Free Democrats spoke at antinuclear rallies, it did not endorse the Struggle Against Atomic Death. The same was true of the German Physics Society. In October 1958, the three-thousand-member body issued a grave warning about the atomic arms race. But despite the fervent participation in the campaign of some of its luminaries, such as Max Born, it steered clear of a political role.[17]

More conservative forces in German life—the ruling Christian Democratic Party, the Catholic Church, big business, and, for the most part, the press—adopted a stance of dogged opposition to the antinuclear movement. That stance gained added credibility during 1958 thanks to some particularly provocative moves by the Soviet government. After executing Hungarian reformer Imre Nagy at mid-year, Kremlin officials undermined the antinuclear campaign still further that November by demanding West Berlin's demilitarization and by threatening West Germany with nuclear annihilation.[18]

The failure of the Struggle Against Atomic Death to mobilize the nation's antinuclear majority became increasingly apparent as the year wore on. By June, participation in antinuclear rallies was dwindling, and the following month the federal courts dealt the campaign's strategy a heavy blow by ruling that the proposed referenda were unconstitutional. Meanwhile, gearing up for the state elections, Adenauer and the Christian Democrats launched a powerful counteroffensive. Sometimes, they claimed that they could promote nuclear disarmament more effectively than could the Social Democrats. On other occasions, they charged that their opponents would deliver the nation to Communism. That July, in the first and largest state election, held in North Rhine-Westphalia, the Christian Democrats won a resounding victory, drawing a majority of the vote. Although the Social Democrats also improved their standing at the polls, observers considered the election a sharp defeat for the SPD's antinuclear strategy.[19] This assessment was reinforced in the coming months, when the SPD won election victories in Hesse and in Berlin, where nuclear weapons did not figure as a significant issue. The lesson seemed clear. As one scholar has observed: "The majority preference was to concentrate on personal affairs, not to question too deeply into these matters of national security."[20]

These sharp setbacks had a devastating effect on the antinuclear campaign. Convinced by the disappointing election results that further opposition to nuclear weapons was pointless, the SPD and the DGB withdrew their support from the Struggle Against Atomic Death. Although that movement limped along into the last months of 1958, it could not survive without the resources of its most powerful backers. Soon, it disappeared entirely.[21]

Nevertheless, antinuclear activities and sentiments in West Germany did not come to an end. Pacifist groups, particularly, had been energized by the antinuclear campaign and now focused their efforts more sharply on nuclear weapons. Within Protestant ranks, the Church Brethren assumed an important role and new groups of a pacifist nature, such as Action for Reconciliation (Aktion Sühnezeichen), were born.[22] Combined with Schweitzer's latest appeal and other nuclear disarmament agitation during 1958, this helped maintain a very high level of antinuclear feeling within West Germany. In July 1958, a poll reported, 92 percent of the population favored (and only 1 percent opposed) the establishment of a worldwide organization to prevent the manufacture of nuclear weapons. In October, 63 percent of West Germans surveyed viewed atomic energy as a curse. That November, 64 percent of West German respondents indicated that they considered nuclear tests harmful to future generations—up from 60 percent a year before. Indeed, some seventeen thousand citizens of the Federal Republic signed petitions that fall calling for a ban on nuclear testing. Thus, although West Germany's tumultuous struggle of 1957–58 ground to a halt, a smaller-scale antinuclear campaign voiced the sentiments of a substantial portion of the population.[23]

Scandinavia

Concern about nuclear weapons also acquired new momentum in Scandinavia, where nuclear testing stirred considerable antipathy. Reporting from the region

in May 1957, a *New York Times* correspondent declared that "just about everybody" wanted to see an end to nuclear weapons tests. In Norway's cities, "people have been standing by hundreds in queues awaiting a chance to sign a public round-robin saying simply: 'We think Albert Schweitzer is right.'" Asked
later that year if they believed that H-Bomb tests imperiled future generations,
76 percent of respondents in Norway, 65 percent in Sweden, and 39 percent in
Denmark answered affirmatively. Stockholm's *Dagens Nyheter* asked rhetorically: "Who is there who would not like to see the abolition of these tests?"
Actually, some people did not want an end to nuclear testing, but their numbers were comparatively few. Surveying public attitudes, a June 1958 Gallup
poll found that 82 percent of respondents in Oslo favored a halt to U.S. nuclear
tests, as did 55 percent in Copenhagen, and 53 percent in Stockholm.[24]

In Sweden, opposition to nuclear weapons was heightened by proposals to
make that country a nuclear power. In a report delivered in October 1957, the
commander-in-chief of the Swedish armed forces renewed his call for equipping the Swedish military with tactical nuclear weapons. A fierce debate ensued,
dividing all of Sweden's political parties except the Conservatives (who supported the proposal) and the Communists (who opposed it).[25] The confrontation
within the governing Social Democratic Party was particularly intense, with the
powerful Social Democratic Women's Organization, led by Inga Thorsson, arguing strongly against nuclear weapons for Sweden on the grounds that they
would invite a nuclear attack and would destroy future generations. Portions of
the Social Democratic and labor press also adopted a sharply critical stance.[26]
Pacifists, religious leaders, and prominent intellectuals assailed nuclear weapons
in public meetings, in newspapers, and on the radio. Curiously, the world federalists endorsed a Swedish development program, a position that led to the collapse of their prestige and support.[27] Meanwhile, a citizens' petition against
Swedish nuclear weapons gathered ninety-five thousand signatures, which were
presented to the prime minister in February 1958. That same month, the Social
Democratic Women's Organization issued its own antinuclear pamphlet.[28]

Some of the developing resistance movement took the form of a ban-the-
Bomb organization. As debate deepened over the nuclear issue, a group of
twenty-one intellectuals—mostly authors, journalists, and artists—launched the
Action Group Against a Swedish Atomic Weapon (Aktionsgruppen mot svenska atomvapen, AMSA) in June 1958. Arranging meetings, rallies, and discussions on the subject of the Bomb throughout the country, AMSA reached a
broad audience and had particular appeal among young people. The new group
also published a newsletter, *Mot svensk atombomb* (*Against a Swedish Atomic
Bomb*), edited by one of the campaign's best-known leaders, the writer Barbro
Alving. Since most of AMSA's executive committee members were pacifists,

AMSA not only championed a nuclear-free Sweden, but sharply criticized conventional military measures. Adopting an idea popularized by Per Anders Fogelström (another AMSA leader) and Roland Morell in their influential pamphlet, *I stället för atombomb* (*Instead of an Atom Bomb*), AMSA contended that Sweden should scrap its military role in the world and become a source of medical and technical assistance to developing countries. Irked by AMSA's pacifist approach, the Social Democratic Party distanced itself from the group, as did the Social Democratic Women's Organization, which continued to advocate a conventional military defense. Nevertheless, AMSA's antinuclear campaign, together with the efforts of others, contributed to a remarkable turnabout in public opinion. Between June 1957 and October 1959, support for building a Swedish atomic bomb fell from 40 to 29 percent, and opposition grew from 36 to 51 percent.[29]

Although no comparable ban-the-Bomb group emerged in Denmark during 1957–58, opposition to nuclear weapons intensified in that nation. At its April 1957 annual convention, No More War (Aldrig mere Krig), the Danish WRI group, passed a resolution appealing to Danes to "refuse the offer of American guided missiles." It also urged the Danish government to take an active role in eliminating testing and production of nuclear weapons. Popular views did not differ substantially. Polled in October 1957, 54 percent of the Danish population thought other nations should accept a Soviet offer to simply suspend nuclear tests for two years; only 20 percent disagreed. Secretly, the U.S. embassy in Denmark warned the State Department that "it would be counterproductive at this time to attempt [to] pressure [the] Danes" to accept NATO nuclear weapons, for "public opinion here is not yet prepared for this step." In May 1958, when a NATO conference convened in Copenhagen, antinuclear activity surged. One antinuclear protest, on May 5, attracted a crowd of from eight to ten thousand people, who filled Copenhagen's Town Hall.[30]

Nuclear disarmament activity also flourished in Norway. In response to Schweitzer's appeal to halt nuclear testing, a petition endorsing it drew 225,000 signatures (out of a population of 3.5 million) by late June 1957, when it was submitted to the parliament. That same year, the governing Labor Party's general congress unanimously resolved that nuclear weapons tests should be immediately halted in all countries and—in a clear challenge to NATO policy—"that atomic weapons should not be placed on Norwegian territory." In 1958, the Norwegian WILPF branch sponsored a public lecture on the dangers of nuclear weapons by Professor Kathleen Lonsdale of Britain in the Nobel Hall and called on the government to work through the United Nations to prohibit nuclear testing on the high seas. That June, it joined with other groups in holding a demonstration in Oslo against the testing of nuclear weapons. Beginning with a silent procession from University Square, the demonstration ended with a mass gathering at the Stortorvet, a large open space in the city, where the gathering heard speeches by author Finn Havrevold and WILPF president Marie Lous-Mohr. Peace activity, only recently held in disrepute, gained substantial credibility, and Norwegian Broadcasting arranged programs featuring representatives of the FOR, the WRI, the WILPF, and the world federalists.[31]

Opinion surveys of the time confirm the impact of antinuclear ideas and activities. Asked in October 1957 if other nations should accept the Soviet proposal to suspend H-Bomb tests for a two-year period, Norwegians supported the idea by 62 to 18 percent. In November 1957, after pointing out that Britain had reduced its armed forces and put more emphasis on nuclear weapons for national defense, Gallup pollsters asked Norwegians if they would like to do the same. In response, 50 percent said no and only 27 percent yes. Talk about the "peaceful" uses of the atom was common enough in the 1950s, but Norwegians seem not to have been greatly impressed. Queried in October and November 1957 concerning whether they thought atomic energy would prove "more of a boon or more of a curse to mankind," 51 percent of Norwegians predicted it would be a curse and only 16 percent a boon—the lowest level of support in the ten nations surveyed.[32]

Switzerland

Swiss activists developed a particularly vigorous antinuclear campaign. During 1957 and early 1958, the Swiss press reported intermittently on enthusiastic support among Swiss military officers and some government leaders for the arming of Swiss military forces with atomic weapons. Alarmed by these developments and inspired by the Struggle Against Atomic Death in neighboring West Germany, a gathering of some 120 individuals associated with churches, unions, cultural institutions, and the sciences convened in Bern on May 18, 1958. Here they organized the Swiss Movement Against Atomic Armaments (Schweizerische Bewegung gegen die atomare Aufrüstung), with the goal of launching a popular referendum that would add a ban on atomic weapons to the Swiss constitution. As the Swiss Movement gathered momentum, pro-nuclear forces launched a powerful counterattack. Addressing a meeting of the Swiss Officers Association on June 8, the chief of the Army General Staff issued an immediate and unequivocal call for nuclear weapons. On July 11, the Federal Council announced that it had ordered the military to study the problems involved in Switzerland's atomic armament. "To safeguard our independence and to protect our neutrality the army will have to be given the most effective weapons," it declared, and "among those belong atomic weapons."

Meanwhile, on June 27, a group of 53 Swiss intellectuals issued a statement at Geneva pleading for Swiss renunciation of nuclear weapons. In August, the U.S. embassy reported that nuclear weapons had become "a predominant issue" in Swiss politics.[33]

Support for the Swiss Movement was limited and uneven. For the most part, the press exhibited considerable hostility, as did the other mass media. On the very day the Swiss Movement began, the *Neue Züricher Zeitung* issued a "Warning about a Dangerous Campaign." Labor unions, in general, were also wary. On the other hand, the Swiss Movement did have substantial strength among pacifists and within the Protestant churches. In late 1958, a poll of the Swiss Association of Reformed Clergymen, to which most pastors of the Swiss Church belonged, found that 407 of the 937 who responded opposed atomic armaments for Switzerland. Furthermore, the Swiss Movement drew on many prominent figures in Swiss intellectual life, including the scientists Gerhardt Wagner, Leopold Ruzicka, and M. Rossel and the theologians Willi Kobe and Fritz Lieb. Karl Barth, one of the world's leading theologians and a founder of the Swiss Movement, frequently used his considerable prestige to rally opponents of nuclear weapons and to condemn what he called "the ungodly and nefarious growth of atomic armament."[34]

Although none of Switzerland's political parties endorsed the Swiss Movement, it did have considerable strength within the Social Democratic Party. Indeed, Fritz Giovanoli, a Social Democratic member of parliament, presided at the Swiss Movement's founding conference and Social Democrats comprised about a third of those in attendance. Attempting to stave off party endorsement of the Swiss Movement, a group of thirty-five prominent Social Democrats and union leaders issued a statement on June 8, 1958, criticizing the campaign against nuclear armaments and urging party members not to join it. At its June 21 meeting, the party's central committee, uneasy about the division within its ranks, rejected a resolution of endorsement and, instead, followed the leadership's recommendation to delay a decision until a special party conference that October. At that gathering, the party president narrowly prevailed over the Giovanoli faction, defeating endorsement of the Swiss Movement. Nevertheless, to secure this victory, the leadership made significant concessions to the party's antinuclear wing. They included supporting a plan to launch a separate initiative to make it obligatory to hold a popular referendum on all atomic armament decisions of the Federal Council. Furthermore, as the Swiss Movement's campaign gathered momentum, many Social Democrats participated in it as individuals.[35]

Despite the difficulties it experienced at rallying mainstream support, the Swiss Movement carried on widespread and often effective agitation against nuclear weapons. It distributed Albert Schweitzer's call for nuclear disarmament and at public meetings staged by proponents of nuclear weapons engaged them in sharp debate. In October 1958, the Swiss Movement began a petitioning campaign to gather the fifty thousand signatures necessary to put its antinuclear referendum on the ballot. It also widely distributed an antinuclear leaflet, *Appeal to the Swiss People.* Contending that atomic weapons were not armaments in the conventional sense, but means of extermination, the Swiss Movement leaflet argued that the struggle against such weapons must be waged in places where people were in a position to conduct it honestly and effectively: in their own countries. Although the antinuclear campaign generated unusually strong public reactions, both supportive and hostile, the petition drive swept forward without major difficulty.[36]

The Netherlands and Belgium

The Netherlands also experienced an upsurge of antinuclear protest, often linked to nuclear testing. In February 1957, the Dutch Reformed Church appealed to the Dutch government to work toward the abolition of nuclear tests. Later that year, a Dutch committee, Stop Atom Bomb Tests (Stopzetting Atoombomproeven), issued a petition along similar lines, signed by some 650 doctors. Meanwhile, the local FOR group, Church and Peace (Kerk en Vrede), ran a special issue of its magazine *Militia Christi* on Albert Schweitzer's antinuclear appeal of that year and distributed a pamphlet urging a halt to nuclear weapons tests to some 220,000 people.[37] That November, in conjunction with a report on radioactivity by the Royal Academy, Dutch scientists participating in the study called for a suspension of nuclear testing. Within both Protestant and Catholic church groups, the nuclear weapons issue became a source of serious contention.[38]

Two new organizations took the lead in rallying Dutch antinuclear sentiment. Founded in May 1957, shortly after Schweitzer's first message on Radio Oslo, the Albert Schweitzer Committee Against Nuclear Weapons pressed for an end to nuclear testing and production. Later that year, anxious to unite previously disparate groups and individuals around resistance to the nuclear menace, peace activists established Anti-Atom Bomb Action (Anti-Atoombom-Actie, AAA). It advocated an end to nuclear tests, a ban on the manufacture of nuclear weapons, and the destruction of existing stockpiles. Determined to avoid being pushed in a "particular political or religious direction," AAA barred leaders of political parties, clergy, and military personnel from membership. Each supporter, it contended, should canvass at least ten friends and acquaintances. "We can all do something!" it told concerned Dutch citizens. "We *must* do something! We must do it *now*!"[39]

Numerous signs appeared that antinuclear agitation was having some effect. In October 1957, a poll reported, 61 percent of the Dutch population favored accepting the Soviet offer to suspend nuclear tests. The following month, another poll found that 59 percent of Dutch respondents thought H-Bomb explosions endangered the health of future generations (compared to only 12 percent who disagreed). As one Dutch writer has noted, among many members of the population the Bomb was replacing the Soviet Union as a symbol of evil. Attempting to bring antimilitary ideas into the political arena, a group of activists from The Third Way (De Derde Weg), a pacifist group, sought to convince the Dutch Labor Party, which already drew the backing of many pacifists, to place some of them on its electoral list. When the Labor Party refused, they bolted in 1957, launching the Pacifist Socialist Party. Few observers thought the new group, dominated by activists from The Third Way and Church and Peace, had much of a future. Nevertheless, the Pacifist Socialist Party entered a provincial election in northern Holland in March 1958 and, unexpectedly, captured two legislative seats. Thereafter, the cause of nuclear disarmament had an official voice in Dutch politics.[40]

Although antinuclear activism was less prominent in Belgium, the movement here also emerged as an important phenomenon. By early 1958, a provisional Belgian National Committee against the Nuclear Peril had appeared, with three local committees in existence and others in formation. Federal Union, a world government organization which served as the secretariat for the group, reported in November of that year that eight antinuclear committees had been formed in the provinces, where frequent lectures on nuclear issues were now delivered. "An atomic world war," Federal Union warned in a widely used pamphlet, would not only produce "monstrous injustice, but also a collective suicide of humanity." One local group, the Antwerp Initiative Committee for Halting Nuclear Weapons Testing, although composed of only 60 members, distributed substantial quantities of antinuclear material throughout that city in 1958 and helped garner the signatures of some 150,000 Belgians on a petition calling for a ban on nuclear weapons tests.[41] In the fall of that year, a poll found that Belgians favored the Soviet proposal to suspend H-Bomb tests by 62 to 18 percent. Moreover, between 1957 and 1958, the percentage of Belgians considering nuclear tests harmful rose from 60 to 71 percent.[42]

Ireland

The antinuclear campaign also took hold in Ireland. In May 1957, a group of prominent scientists and union leaders addressed a public meeting in Dublin that called for an end to nuclear testing and for the banning of nuclear weapons throughout the world. The Aldermaston march in neighboring Great Britain, however, proved the immediate spur to action. Connor Farrington, a writer and broadcaster, participated in the march and brought back a very enthusiastic account of it to Ireland's pacifist and antinuclear circles. This led to the formation of an Irish Campaign for Nuclear Disarmament (CND) later that year. The aim of the new group, it announced, was "to press for the immediate suspension of nuclear tests and to give active support to all policies which may further the ultimate aim of nuclear disarmament and the removal of the causes of war." Irish CND quickly obtained the support of many prominent persons in the sciences, arts, and literature. It also distributed leaflets on the effects of nuclear weapons and picketed the embassies of the nuclear powers, carrying posters reading: "Stop Nuclear Bomb Tests Now." In December, Irish CND held its first large public meeting, chaired by the mayor of Dublin. Amid speeches on the dangers of nuclear testing and nuclear war, the group's secretary, B. de Courcy Ireland, sketched out plans to place appropriate lecturers in the schools and to make antinuclear films available in Dublin and in Ireland's towns and villages.[43]

France

France continued to present a curious paradox: a country in which strong antinuclear attitudes coexisted with a weak antinuclear movement. Asked in September 1957 if they thought nuclear explosions endangered the health of future generations, 73 percent of French respondents answered affirmatively (as compared to only 7 percent who disagreed). A month later, 76 percent of the French surveyed told pollsters that they favored accepting the Soviet proposal for the suspension of nuclear tests. Nor was the French distaste for nuclear weapons limited to nuclear testing. In the spring of 1958, 75 percent of French respondents described themselves as "very anxious" or "quite anxious" about the prospect of nuclear war. Furthermore, from 1956 through 1958, polls consistently found substantially larger numbers predicting that nuclear energy would prove a curse rather than a boon.[44] Not surprisingly, a March 1958 poll reported that 85 percent of the French public favored the establishment of an international organization to ensure that no nation made atomic or hydrogen bombs.[45] Even so, unlike many of its neighbors, France exhibited few signs of active resistance to nuclear weapons,[46] largely—it seems—because leading peace activists were preoccupied with opposing France's fierce colonial war in Algeria.[47]

There were, however, some important exceptions. The French WILPF section and a group of 150 scientists, many of them quite eminent, issued strong antinuclear statements.[48] On April 11, 1958, following a French study conference on nonviolent action, eighty-two participants entered the French atomic research laboratories at Marcoule and staged a nonviolent sit-down outside the administration building to protest the possible manufacture of nuclear weapons by France. Led by Lanza del Vasto (a disciple of Gandhi), André Trocmé (a Protestant clergyman and FOR leader), and Robert Barrat (the former secretary general of the Catholic Center of French Intellectuals), the group was composed primarily of members of the Community of the Ark, an interreligious, Gandhian ashram established in France by del Vasto. Local and military police carried or dragged participants to another building in the nuclear complex, but they refused to depart until after a lengthy discussion of nuclear war with officials and guards. "Today we appear to be mad, but tomorrow perhaps it will be recognized that we are the ones who are sane," remarked Magda Trocmé.[49] That June and July, members of the Community of the Ark conducted a fifteen-day, anti-Bomb fast in front of the Palace of Nations, in Geneva, the site of an international scientific conference on nuclear arms controls.[50]

Greece

An antinuclear movement was also emerging in Greece. In May 1957, Greek newspapers published the text of an appeal for the cessation of all nuclear weapons tests, signed by sixty-two prominent Greek personalities. They included scientists, authors, political leaders, and industrialists. "Continued nuclear tests threaten to undermine the health of this and future generations," they declared, and, in conjunction with the growing deployment of nuclear weapons, "tend to carry mankind to universal destruction." Furthermore, they argued that Greece should reject nuclear bases on its territory, thus precluding its becoming "a target for . . . reprisals." Distraught U.S. officials on the scene appealed to the signers to repudiate the petition, but met with little success. Indeed, some signers suggested that a unilateral halt to U.S. tests would earn the United States "worldwide gratitude." The following April, when residents of Athens were surveyed on nuclear testing, 71 percent stated that the United States should simply cease nuclear testing.[51]

Elsewhere in Non-Communist Europe

Although relatively little antinuclear activism developed in the balance of non-Communist Europe, the public there exhibited signs of substantial uneasiness about nuclear weapons. In Italy, pollsters reported that, in the fall of 1957, 62 percent of the population thought nuclear tests harmful to future generations

and that 48 percent of Italians favored the Soviet proposal to halt nuclear testing, while only 29 percent did not. Between April 1956 and October 1958, Italians viewing atomic energy as a boon fell from 32 to 28 percent, while those
viewing it as a curse rose from 31 to 42 percent.[52] Among Austrians surveyed
in November 1957, 67 percent said they believed H-Bomb explosions endangered the health of future generations; a year later, 78 percent took that position. In October 1957, 70 percent of Austrians favored the Soviet proposal to
halt nuclear tests. Queried about atomic energy in October and November
1957, 52 percent of Austrians polled considered it a curse.[53] Even in Spain,
where critics of the military faced severe reprisals by the right-wing dictatorship, antinuclear attitudes were rife. Surveyed in November 1957, 42 percent of
the residents of Madrid opposed (and only 26 percent favored) equipping U.S.
forces in Spain with atomic weapons. The same poll found that 50 percent
viewed atomic energy as a curse, and only 25 percent as a boon. Similar attitudes prevailed in Cadiz.[54]

Australia and New Zealand

Although Australia lay thousands of miles from Europe's Cold War confrontations, nuclear testing in the Pacific—and particularly at two sites in South Australia, Emu Field and Maralinga, used by the British—gave the nuclear arms
race considerable immediacy. In February 1957, the WILPF group, the
Women's Christian Temperance Union, and the Aboriginal Rights Council
sponsored a public meeting in Melbourne that highlighted the dangers of nuclear testing for aboriginal residents of these regions. Another local conference
that October, in Adelaide, also warned of contamination by radioactive fallout.
The Australian Council of Trade Unions, as well as the one major union outside it, the Australian Workers' Union, protested strongly against any nuclear
tests in the Pacific and, particularly, on Australian soil. Meanwhile, in March
1957, at its national conference in Brisbane, the Labor Party joined the foes of
nuclear testing. Herbert Evatt, its distinguished elder statesman, argued that "ab-
surd risks are being taken by Britain, Russia, and the USA. . . . Either we go on
until we reach the point of self-destruction, or we organize for peace." In October 1957, a poll found that 50 percent of Australian respondents agreed (and 38
percent disagreed) with the Soviet proposal to suspend nuclear testing.[55]

Australian opposition to nuclear testing and to nuclear weapons escalated
during 1958. Some 360 Australian scientists signed the Pauling petition appealing for an end to nuclear testing. One of them, Marc Oliphant, the eminent
physicist who had attended the first Pugwash conference, served as a keen
critic of the nuclear arms and an organizer of future Pugwash contingents from

Australia.[56] In the spring of 1958, exhibits in Melbourne, Perth, Sydney, and Adelaide of the "Hiroshima Panels" by artists Iri Maruki and Toshiko Akamatsu drew large crowds and sympathetic editorials in major newspapers. For its part, the Labor Party, growing ever friendlier to the organized peace movement, decided to conduct a nationwide campaign against nuclear weapons. In mid-July, citing the Labor Party stand and "an unusually large number of news articles" raising concern about nuclear fallout, including prominently featured items by Russell and Schweitzer, the U.S. consul in Sydney reported glumly that public sentiment was "hardening in opposition to further atomic weapons' testing."[57] Admittedly, a poll in April 1958 indicated that among sixteen nationality groups Australians constituted the only one (other than Americans) to oppose a unilateral halt to nuclear testing by the United States.[58] Nevertheless, surveys also revealed that between November 1957 and November 1958 the percentage of Australians who thought that H-Bomb tests endangered future generations rose from 46 to 57 percent.[59]

Nuclear testing in the Pacific also provided the spur for an antinuclear campaign in New Zealand. In early 1957, a leading pacifist, Lincoln Efford, reported widespread "apprehension concerning the H-Bomb and similar weapons," but relatively little activism.[60] Determined to mobilize popular sentiment against the nuclear arms race, the small WILPF group, the Christian Pacifist Society, and the Society of Friends organized a public meeting that spring at the Auckland Town Hall that drew a remarkably large turnout of sixteen hundred people. The gathering called on the New Zealand government to work through British Commonwealth meetings and the United Nations to end nuclear testing. This provided the momentum for a petition drive, during the ensuing parliamentary election campaign, demanding that the government devote its energies to halting nuclear testing and persuading the British government to give a lead to the nations of the world by repudiating the manufacture of nuclear weapons. Pacifist groups set up petitioning tables, encouraged ministers to display the petition in churches and to deliver antinuclear sermons, distributed the message on postcards, stirred up a flurry of antinuclear letters in the press, and embarked on door-to-door canvassing. Eventually, they gathered the signatures of eleven thousand people. Meanwhile, the Labor Party, impressed by the upsurge of antinuclear sentiment, announced its opposition to all future tests of nuclear weapons.[61]

By 1958, New Zealand's nuclear disarmament campaign was well under way. Encouraged by the mass meeting, the petition campaign, and the formation of CND in Britain, groups focusing on the nuclear weapons issue appeared in Auckland, Dunedin, Christchurch, and Wellington. Meanwhile, pacifist organizations continued their antinuclear emphasis. Together with the new groups, they helped establish a loose nuclear disarmament association, the Movement against Further Testing, Manufacture, and Use of Nuclear Weapons, headed by Robert Chapman, a historian at Auckland University. In terms of constituency, the campaign had its greatest appeal among church members and intellectuals. Typically, the most powerful of the new groups, the Dunedin Society for the Prevention of Nuclear Warfare, drew on the clergy, university faculty, and other professionals for its leaders. Like the campaign's founders, many activists were pacifists, but—with dismay about the nuclear arms race spreading rapidly throughout the broader society—an increasing number were merely concerned citizens.[62]

Canada

In another British Commonwealth nation, Canada, activism remained on a smaller scale. Responding to Schweitzer's appeal of April 1957 to rouse world opinion against nuclear testing, the FOR, the WILPF, and the Church Peace Mission did sponsor a public meeting on the issue that June in Toronto. When the gathering recommended continued efforts to educate the Canadian public on the testing question, the three groups formed a Toronto Committee Opposing the Testing of Nuclear Bombs. Its first major activity was the circulation of a statement which urged "vigorous action to effect a ban on the testing of nuclear bombs anywhere in the world." The statement also called attention to Canada's role in supplying uranium for the production of U.S. nuclear weapons. But little seems to have come of these and other efforts. Canada's pacifist groups were quite small and, furthermore, the nation was far removed from the growing nuclear confrontation in Europe and from the controversial nuclear testing sites of the Pacific.[63]

Even so, the pace of antinuclear activity quickened in 1958. On Easter Sunday of that year, members of the FOR, the WILPF, and the Society of Friends staged a parade through Toronto, protesting nuclear tests and distributing peace literature. They followed up with a rally on May 11 in Queen's Park which, despite rain, drew three hundred people bearing antinuclear placards. The three city newspapers gave good coverage to both events. Similarly, in Vancouver, the FOR sponsored its first open air demonstrations—staging an antinuclear poster walk through a local park, a parade through the university campus, and a motorcade to outlying towns to place wreaths on cenotaphs on Hiroshima Day. As elsewhere, the growing dissent often went beyond the testing issue to other aspects of the nuclear arms race. In June, James S. Thomson, Moderator of the United Church of Canada, called on his nation to make "a clear and unequivocal renunciation of all reliance on the use of mass destructive weapons." Two months later, a gathering of three hundred delegates representing pacifist groups condemned the maintenance of military bases on Canadian soil "which, in the event of a conflict, would automatically embroil this country in a nuclear war."[64]

The Third World

Latin America seemed particularly distant from the nuclear arms race and this factor—combined with the curbs placed on citizen activism by right-wing military dictatorships and more immediately pressing issues like widespread poverty—limited nuclear dissent in this region. Occasionally, to be sure, a prominent individual spoke out. In early 1957, questioning the drift "to universal suicide," Victor Haya de la Torre, leader of Peru's Aprista Party, declared that "we speak too much of which country has the more nuclear bombs, too much in military terms of power." Even so, popular protest against the nuclear arms race remained minimal. Returning from a visit to Latin America in the spring of 1958, two leading American pacifists reported that "general opinion is not stirred up by fear of atomic bombs and fallout. They seem a remote danger concerning which South America can do little or nothing."[65]

Nevertheless, fragmentary polling data indicates that considerable public uneasiness lurked below the surface. Surveyed in the fall of 1957, residents of Brazil's two largest cities, Rio de Janeiro and Sao Paulo, favored acceptance of the Russian proposal to suspend H-Bomb testing by 45 to 24 percent. An estimated 55 percent of Brazilians of the time considered nuclear tests harmful to future generations; a year later, the figure stood at 60 percent. In line with these views, a fall 1957 poll of the residents of Rio de Janeiro and São Paulo found that 43 percent considered atomic energy a curse, 24 percent a boon. Among residents of Mexico City, the corresponding figures were 60 percent and 26 percent. In April 1958, when residents of Montevideo, Uruguay, were asked if they favored a unilateral halt to U.S. nuclear testing, 59 percent responded affirmatively. Only 18 percent opposed the idea.[66]

The distaste for nuclear weapons in the underdeveloped nations of Africa, the Middle East, and Asia appears to have been considerably greater. Although nuclear disarmament organizations had not, as yet, emerged within these nations, their proximity to the Pacific testing grounds and, for the most part, their nonaligned status in the Cold War encouraged antinuclear sentiment. According to a *New York Times* dispatch from India in May 1957, "the banning of atom and hydrogen bomb tests has become such a lively issue in this country that hardly a day passes without some reference to it by political leaders, scientists and the press." Newspapers were "almost unanimous in opposing the bomb tests," the dispatch reported. One of India's most revered elder statesmen, Chakravarti Rajagopalachari, called for his nation to leave the British Commonwealth if Britain did not halt nuclear testing. Lauding the Göttingen declaration, C. V. Raman, a Nobel Prize–winning physicist, declared that scientists should be willing to starve rather than work on nuclear weapons.[67] In the spring of 1958, a poll found that 90 percent of the people questioned in New Delhi thought that the United States should unilaterally halt nuclear testing—the highest level in the sixteen countries surveyed. That July, a Gallup poll concluded that 78 percent of its Indian respondents favored—and only 1 percent opposed—the establishment of a worldwide organization to ensure that no nation could make atomic or hydrogen bombs.[68]

Opposition in the Third World to the nuclear arms race sometimes represented an extension of the strong anti-imperialist sentiments of that region, large parts of which still lay under colonial control or provided the nuclear testing sites for the Western powers. When the French government began publicly to discuss nuclear testing in the Sahara, protest against the idea grew dramatically in French West Africa. In July 1958, Emile Zinsou, a Dahomey senator and leader of the Party of African Reform, told the official French news agency that "we are absolutely opposed to the choice of the Sahara as the place for the French atomic bomb testing." Later that month, at the party's first congress, held in Cotonou, it called on France to "renounce" its plans for the atomic tests. Other organizations in French West Africa also condemned French nuclear programs, including the African Independence Party and the General Union of Workers of Black Africa. Seydou Diallo, a member of the labor federation's executive committee stated: "We do not want our continent to be a second Hiroshima." The proposed French tests, he declared, were "the criminal initiative of the imperialists who believe they are the masters of African soil."[69]

The Soviet Union

Although curbs on civil liberties continued to block the development of an opposition movement in the Soviet Union, the Pugwash conferences encouraged a growing respect for nuclear disarmament among Soviet scientists. Through their participation in these conferences, Soviet scientists traveled abroad and met privately, away from the glare of publicity and the blare of propaganda, with their Western counterparts. Here they had the opportunity for a relatively candid discussion of the dangers of the nuclear arms race and what might be done about it. Consequently, as the Soviet dissident Zhores Medvedev noted, the Pugwash conferences "raised the consciousness of Soviet scientists about their role in society and in the world." Of course, Soviet scientists could not engage in foreign travel without the approval of their government; and, therefore, participants tended to come from the Soviet nuclear establishment. Moreover, wary of government disapproval and anxious to exercise influence within official channels, these scientists remained discrete. Even so, Topchiev and other Soviet participants struck Western observers as genuinely interested in securing a nuclear arms control treaty, especially a ban on nuclear testing.[70]

Other developments also indicated the emergence of Soviet scientific concern, albeit within officially approved channels. Presented with Linus Pauling's petition calling for an international agreement to end nuclear testing, more than two hundred Soviet scientists signed it during late 1957. Meanwhile, a group of Soviet scientists produced articles that sharply condemned nuclear testing and, particularly, nuclear fallout. Because these activities—like the Pugwash conferences—were consonant with official Soviet policy—there is no reason to take the sincerity of every participant at face value. On the other hand, some of these scientists undoubtedly meant what they said. More than three decades later, Andrei Sakharov looked back with pride on an antinuclear article he had published in 1958. Focused on the radiation effects of nuclear testing, it argued that every one-megaton detonation would produce ten thousand victims. It concluded: "Each and every nuclear test does damage. . . . Furthermore, posterity has no way to defend itself from our actions. Halting the tests," he wrote, "will directly save the lives of hundreds of thousands of people, and it also promises even greater benefits, reducing international tension and the risk of nuclear war, the fundamental danger of our time."[71]

The genuine aversion to nuclear testing felt by at least some Soviet scientists is illustrated by secret efforts to stop the Soviet Union's test program. In 1957, alarmed by what Sakharov had told him about the effects of nuclear tests in the Semipalatinsk region, the physicist Zhores Takibayev sent a petition to Khrushchev protesting Soviet explosions there—a venture that earned him an official reprimand.[72] Although, for unrelated reasons, the Soviet government did announce a halt to nuclear testing in the spring of 1958, orders came from the government to resume testing in the fall. Considering this "completely unacceptable, both politically and morally," Sakharov prepared proposals for extending the Soviet moratorium and developing means other than nuclear testing for measuring the efficiency of Soviet nuclear devices. In September 1958, he made his case to Kurchatov, the top scientist in the Soviet nuclear weapons program. According to Sakharov, Kurchatov "listened closely to what I had to say," expressed his "basic agreement," and traveled to Yalta in an effort to convince Khrushchev that he should adopt these proposals. The Soviet premier, however, proved implacable, and plans moved forward for a new round of Soviet nuclear tests.[73]

Although Kurchatov now desisted from this effort to halt Soviet nuclear testing, Sakharov persevered. As Khrushchev recalled, "A day or two before the resumption of our testing program, I got a telephone call from Academician Sakharov," who "said he had a petition to present. The petition called on our government to cancel the scheduled nuclear explosion and not to engage in any further testing, at least not of the hydrogen bomb." Sakharov declared: "As a scientist and as a designer of the hydrogen bomb, I know what harm these explosions can bring down on the head of mankind." According to Khrushchev, "Sakharov went on in that vein, pleading with me not to allow our military to conduct any further tests. He was obviously guided by moral and humanistic considerations. I knew him and was profoundly impressed by him. Everyone was. He was, as they say, a crystal of morality among our scientists." Sakharov "hated the thought that science might be used to destroy life, to contaminate the atmosphere, to kill people slowly by radioactive poisoning." Committed to test resumption, Khrushchev sought to convince the scientist of the error of his ways. But Sakharov remained obdurate. As Khrushchev recalled: "My arguments didn't change his mind, and his didn't change mine."[74]

How should one account for these daring—and potentially dangerous—attempts by scientists to block Soviet nuclear testing? Kurchatov, one of his colleagues later remarked, had developed "a kind of guilt complex" about his nuclear weapons work. Deeply disturbed by the effects of the H-Bomb since the Bikini tests and the ensuing protests,[75] the Soviet physicist was ready by 1958 to challenge official priorities. As for Sakharov, he was, indeed, "a crystal of morality" and, as some have suggested, may also have had recent Soviet nuclear disasters on his mind.[76] Nevertheless, his own explanation of his conduct emphasizes other factors. Noting that beginning in 1957 he felt "responsible for the problem of radioactive contamination from nuclear explosions," Sakharov attributed this to "the influence of statements on this subject made throughout the world by such people as Albert Schweitzer, Linus Pauling, and others." On another occasion, he remarked that among those writers whose works he had consulted when preparing his 1958 critique of nuclear testing, "Albert Schweitzer left a lasting impression on me." Still elsewhere, he declared his indebtedness to Einstein, Russell, and others concerned about "the fate of mankind."[77] As Edward Teller concluded—much to his chagrin—Sakharov's antinuclear activities reflected the effectiveness of the worldwide struggle against the Bomb at propagating its message, even within the relatively closed confines of the Soviet Union.[78]

Nonaligned Versus Aligned Movements, 1954–58

We . . . know how to protect ourselves from
false friends who wish to exploit this serious
question for their own ends.

Berlin Action Committee Against
Atomic Death, 1958

In the period from 1954 to 1958, two very different types of disarmament movement organized antinuclear activities and, at times, clashed. One type, exemplified by CND and SANE, reflected a thoroughgoing revulsion to nuclear testing and to nuclear war and, for this reason, refused to temper its critique of the nuclear arms race by favoring the interests of either Cold War camp. Although most nuclear disarmament activism in these years was of this nonaligned variety, some had a more partisan motivation. Anxious to stave off a nuclear war against Communist nations and to hobble Western military efforts, Communist-led organizations—most notably, the World Peace Council and its national affiliates—played their own role in the antinuclear campaign. Given the considerable resources available to them from Communist governments and Communist parties, their efforts were sometimes quite substantial. Nevertheless, the fundamental one-sidedness of the Communist-led peace movement, as well as its Machiavellian tactics, sharply alienated nonaligned peace groups. Consequently, despite occasional Communist calls for "unity," nuclear disarmament efforts could hardly have been more divided. Indeed, the two movements—while superficially working toward the same goals—remained rivals and, at times, strong antagonists.

Toward a Nonaligned International

Opposition to the worldwide nuclear arms race led naturally to efforts by nonaligned groups that transcended national lines. Pacifist organizations, of course, already had their own international networks, which they employed increasingly for the antinuclear campaign. In March and April 1957, John Swomley of the American FOR discussed with representatives of the Japanese FOR, the British FOR, the American Friends Service Committee, and other groups the possibility of sailing a protest vessel into the British nuclear testing zone. Although this idea was abandoned, the following month, in an effort to encourage countries to stop nuclear testing unilaterally, Swomley contacted pacifist leaders in the United States, West Germany, and Britain about forming an international delegation to meet with heads of government. In addition, he hoped they might spark mass meetings in Britain, Japan, the United States, and the Soviet Union. Peace activist groups in many lands also maintained a loose connection through the International Liaison Committee of Organizations for Peace (ILCOP). Fostering communication between such groups and occasionally developing them where none existed, ILCOP held international conferences every August, usually on means for reducing international conflict. ILCOP's 1958 conference, in Denmark, sought to call attention to the "common interests" of the great powers, such as "the need to avoid a war which none could win and few survive," "the need to restrict the possession of nuclear weapons," and "the need to reduce the ruinous and wasteful expenditure of money and resources involved in the present arms race."[1]

Because these channels of communication failed to meet the urgent needs of the new antinuclear movements for information, materials, speakers, and other resources, they quickly established a working relationship with one another. In late 1957, Britain's National Council for the Abolition of Nuclear Weapon Tests and America's SANE began a direct exchange of information on their activities, and this liaison was maintained thereafter by CND and SANE. During the spring of 1958, Cousins met with Russell and Canon Collins in London to share views on their nuclear disarmament organizations. Expressing his "hope that co-operation between your Campaign and the Campaign in Britain can be maintained and increased," Collins reported soon thereafter that he was recruiting prominent sponsors of SANE for speaking assignments in Britain. Cousins, in turn, featured Russell's statements in the *Saturday Review* and urged CND to bring additional pressure for nuclear disarmament to bear on the Macmillan government. SANE did reject an appeal for funding from its fledgling French counterpart, but this reflected SANE's financial difficulties rather than any qualms about the new group, which it welcomed wholeheartedly. Informed of plans for a rally in Frankfurt, West Germany, organized by the Struggle Against Atomic Death, CND dispatched a strong message of support.[2]

Indeed, as newspapers, radio, and television carried stories on antinuclear

activities around the world, sympathizers in diverse lands drew ideas and inspiration from overseas. Greatly impressed by the French civil disobedience
action at Marcoule, Britain's Direct Action Committee adapted it to the situation at Aldermaston, where protesters occupied the forecourt of the nuclear
plant for a week in the summer of 1958. Similarly, proponents of nonviolent
action from the United States and Britain swapped ideas on how to develop a
protest in the Soviet Union comparable to the Pacific campaign that culminated
in the sailing of the *Golden Rule*. In a letter published in the Irish press during
April 1958, peace activists in that country lauded "the protests being made in
England, America, Germany and elsewhere" and appealed to their compatriots
"to give every support" to them. Meanwhile, the nuclear disarmament symbol,
created for the first Aldermaston march, spread rapidly around the globe.[3]

The growing internationalization of the movement was also exemplified
when in April 1958 well-known critics of nuclear weapons from numerous
countries commenced a lawsuit in the United States to bar the AEC from conducting further nuclear weapons tests. Among them were Russell and Kathleen
Lonsdale of Britain, Pauling and Norman Thomas of the United States, Martin
Niemöller of West Germany, Toyohiko Kagawa of Japan, André Trocmé of
France, and Michael Scott of South Africa. In the suit, they argued that "no
power has been delegated to Congress by the Constitution to enact legislation
as a result of which the atmosphere will be contaminated and the lives and
progeny of the population damaged." Pauling, who played a major role in initiating the lawsuit, announced at a press conference that the signers planned
similar legal action against the governments of Britain and the Soviet Union.
Although a U.S. federal judge rejected the antinuclear case that July, it provided a further indication of an emerging global alliance.[4]

With need and sentiment coalescing across national boundaries, leading activists took the first steps toward developing an international, nonaligned, nuclear disarmament organization. Sponsored by several of the new antinuclear
groups, a European Congress Against Nuclear Weapons was planned for July 5
and 6, 1958, in Basel, Switzerland. The conference, chaired by Russell and
sponsored by prominent intellectuals and political leaders, was to be attended
by delegates from Belgium, Britain, France, the Netherlands, Sweden, Switzerland, and West Germany. Several days before its scheduled convocation, however, the gathering was blocked by action of the Swiss government.[5] Even so,
the momentum behind international activity remained strong. Consequently,
West Germany's Struggle Against Atomic Death and Bavaria's Committee
Against Atomic Weapons joined Britain's CND in planning another conference
of the European movements, to be held the following January.[6]

The Communist-Led Antinuclear Campaign

During these years, the powerful Communist-led peace movement trumpeted many of the same themes advanced by nonaligned activists. In the aftermath of the Bikini Bomb tests of 1954, the World Peace Council (WPC) and its scientific counterpart, the World Federation of Scientific Workers, called for the cessation of nuclear tests and the banning of nuclear weapons. The question posed by nuclear war, contended Frédéric Joliot-Curie, the WPC president, "is whether humanity will accept the ruin and the destruction, the death of hundreds of millions of people, the sufferings of the survivors, the probable birth of monsters—and even the possibility of the annihilation of all life on this planet."[7] Meeting in Vienna in January 1955, the WPC launched the Vienna Appeal, opposing "any government that prepares for atomic war" and demanding that "the nuclear powers abolish all the atomic weapons they have in their possession and cease to produce them immediately." According to the WPC, 660 million people eventually signed this statement. In 1956, attempting to influence scientists, the World Federation of Scientific Workers published a pamphlet on radioactive fallout, *Unmeasured Hazards*, which achieved a circulation of about 120,000.[8]

Despite the obstacles introduced by the illness of Joliot-Curie and the death of his wife, Irène, in 1956,[9] the Communist-led disarmament campaign proceeded apace. In April 1957, Joliot-Curie delivered a message over French radio that emphasized the dangers of nuclear radiation and lauded the Göttingen appeal by German scientists. That June, more than four hundred delegates, guests, and observers attended a meeting of the WPC in Colombo, Ceylon. Representing Communist-led peace groups in seventy nations, the gathering called on the U.N. secretary general to bring together the United States, Britain, and the Soviet Union "to conclude an immediate agreement to stop all tests of nuclear weapons." In late 1958, *Scientific World*, the magazine of the World Federation of Scientific Workers, ran a special issue on the dangers of nuclear weapons, warning of the effects of nuclear tests in peacetime and of nuclear weapons in war. Before its appearance—but after a visit to the Soviet Union, where he met with Khrushchev and with leaders of the Soviet peace movement—Joliot-Curie finally succumbed to illness. He was succeeded as WPC president by another eminent physicist and staunch Communist, J. D. Bernal. In his book *World Without War*, published that year, Bernal lauded the WPC as "a kind of Parliament of Man, attempting, and with some success, to influence governments to halt their conflict, to negotiate, to disarm, and to ban all nuclear weapons."[10]

Within numerous nations, WPC affiliates and other Communist-led groups emphasized the nuclear weapons issue. Nuclear tests "must be stopped," insisted the Canadian Peace Congress, and "the H-bomb must be outlawed." Responding to an appeal by the WPC, the Reverend James Endicott, leader of the Canadian organization, delivered speeches on such subjects as: "Disarmament—How to Get it Started Now."[11] In Greece, where a WPC branch—the Greek Committee for International Detente and Peace (EEDYE)—was established in 1955, it went beyond assailing Greece's role in NATO to stress the importance of nuclear disarmament.[12] Throwing its efforts behind the Struggle Against Atomic Death, the West German Peace Committee changed its slogan in 1958 to "Down with atomic armament for the Federal Army!" In Stockholm, according to the U.S. embassy, the Communist *Ny Dag* averaged "at least [a] page of H-bomb comment and photos per day." Initiated by another WPC affiliate, the All-India Peace Council, numerous Communist-choreographed peace congresses convened in India, where they, too, hammered away at the need to resist nuclear weapons.[13]

Motives and Behavior in the Communist-Led Campaign

Communist parties and the organizations they controlled had strong incentives to engage in antinuclear activities. Ever since the late 1940s, when they had launched the World Peace Council, Communist leaders had been haunted by the fear that the United States would initiate a nuclear war against the Soviet Union or other Communist states. In the context of the escalating Cold War, this seemed a definite possibility, particularly given Washington's new doctrine of "massive retaliation." By the mid-1950s, with its superior nuclear stockpile and delivery system, the West was better suited than its Communist adversary to wage a nuclear war. Conversely, the Soviet Union and China—with their substantial advantages over the West in ground forces—seemed likely to fare better in a "conventional" military conflict. Moreover, under Khrushchev's leadership, the Soviet government grew increasingly interested in some kind of nuclear arms control agreement, which antinuclear pressures in the West seemed likely to facilitate. Finally, by directing their own antinuclear campaign, Communist leaders could depict the Soviet Union as a peace-loving nation, channel recruits to their parties, and seize the initiative from the nonaligned movement, which showed a disturbing proclivity to criticize not only Western military measures, but Communist ones as well.[14]

Although many non-Communists participated in the activities of the WPC and its affiliates, these organizations remained under the firm control of Communist parties, usually that of the Soviet Union. This Communist domination guaranteed them lavish funding and ready-made, often substantial, constituencies. On the other hand, it left them with a minimum of independence. In May 1957, for example, shortly before the WPC's world conference convened in Colombo, the Central Committee of the Communist Party of the Soviet Union met to decide policy for the meeting. It not only appropriated substantial funding for the conference—$80,000, to be paid by the Soviet Peace Committee— but dictated the position to be taken by the Soviet delegates, who would set the tone for the meeting. These Soviet delegates, the Central Committee decided, would work out steps for a major international campaign against nuclear testing and add to it demands for a ban on nuclear weapons. In addition, they would be instructed to have the conference avoid apportioning blame equally to the East and West for nuclear testing. Furthermore, they would be told to support a proposal to convoke a conference that made disarmament and banning nuclear weapons central themes.[15]

As an organizational subsidiary of world Communism, the Communist-led peace movement remained thoroughly aligned with the policies of Communist nations. In March 1955, Kuo Mo-jo, chair of the China Peace Committee, an affiliate of the WPC, helped launch the campaign in China for the Vienna Appeal with a sizzling attack on the "atom-maniacs in the United States." He contrasted the U.S. plan "to use atomic weapons against peaceloving peoples" with the nuclear weapons policy of the Soviet Union, which "wants to see them destroyed," and of the Chinese government, "which shall be using atomic energy for peaceful purposes." In fact, the Chinese Bomb project began two months before, and neither Kuo nor other leaders of the China Peace Committee ever criticized it. Similarly, a delegate from the Polish Committee of Defenders of Peace rather incongruously used the occasion of a massive WPC conference that June (the World Convention of Peace-Loving Forces) to laud the formation of the Warsaw Pact. This Soviet–East European military alliance, he explained, "defends the cause of peace all over the world." In East Germany, the German Peace Council worked to popularize what it called "the rational peace policy of the USSR" and of its own government. It wanted the entire nation to understand that "the aims of the peace movement are identical with those of the state leadership."[16] Certainly, the movement labored to avoid any divergence!

The starkest evidence of the Communist-led movement's Cold War partisanship surfaced in 1956. That November, after sharply attacking the Anglo-French invasion of Suez, the WPC dodged criticizing the Soviet Union's bloody military conquest of Hungary. "On this question," read the WPC's official statement, "serious divergences and . . . opposing theses have not permitted the formulation of a common opinion." Although troubled by the Soviet invasion, Endicott considered it less significant than the Suez invasion and French policy in Algeria, which he termed "fifty times worse." Indeed, in some countries, leaders of the Communist-led peace movement vigorously defended the Soviet government's Hungarian venture. The Reverend Hewlett Johnson, a British stalwart of the movement, condemned the British for "naked aggression" at Suez, but argued that "politically, the situation is different in Hungary." The British "were attempting to put the clock back to imperialism and colonialism, whereas the action of the Soviet Union was to prevent its being put back to fascism." In Communist nations, where WPC affiliates were simply arms of the state, the peace committees carefully avoided any criticism of the Soviet government. Ignoring other issues raised by the invasion, the Polish Committee of Defenders of Peace attacked the attempts of "reaction" to "exploit the Hungarian tragedy in order to spread hatred and aggravate the atmosphere of the cold war."[17]

Similarly, the top leaders of the World Peace Council looked askance at political independence. To the end of his life, Joliot-Curie remained a dedicated Communist and supporter of the Soviet Union. In July 1956, addressing a convention of the French Communist Party in the aftermath of Khrushchev's devastating revelations about Stalin, Joliot-Curie noted that "recent events have provoked appeals and invitations on the part of some intellectuals. . . . 'Free yourselves,' they say to the Communist intellectuals, 'free yourselves, if only with a cry.' But from what are we supposed to free ourselves? I never felt freer in all my life!" Certainly, "mistakes have been made. . . . But these are matters which concern neither the doctrine of Marxist Leninism nor the socialist system."[18] His successor as WPC president, J. D. Bernal, although a brilliant intellectual, also had an unshakable faith in Communist rectitude. A recipient of the Stalin Peace Prize, Bernal contended at the time of the Soviet dictator's death that Stalin "combined as no man had before his time, a deep theoretical understanding with unfailing mastery of practice." Not surprisingly, Bernal continued the WPC's unbroken pattern of Soviet partisanship.[19]

Although the WPC's endorsement of official Communist policy was a foregone conclusion, a major conflict developed in its ranks over which Communist policy to endorse. At the WPC's 1957 conference in Colombo, Joliot-Curie's personal representative, Emmanuel d'Astier de la Vigerie, stressed the movement's themes of abolition of nuclear tests, disarmament, and peaceful coexistence. But the delegations from China, India, Latin America, and Africa objected to this emphasis and insisted on giving priority to what they called national liberation struggles. The vice chair of the China Peace Committee, Liao Cheng-chih, told Endicott that China was determined to spearhead a "diametrically opposed line" in the WPC. The most important issue before them was not disarmament, he insisted, but armed struggle against U.S. aggression.

Anxious to block this trend and a possible split in the organization, the Soviet secretary, Valentine Sorokin, suggested that WPC affiliates in the northern hemisphere should work on curbing the arms race and those in the southern should combat Western imperialism. This compromise was accepted by key leaders at the WPC headquarters in Vienna after the meeting. Nevertheless, it broke down soon thereafter, for the Soviet Peace Committee recalled Sorokin and replaced him with Viktor Chkhikvadse, who reverted to Soviet insistence on disarmament as the WPC priority.[20] Whatever the issues before the World Peace Council, the interests of Communist governments remained primary.

On the face of it, the Communist-led movement reacted enthusiastically to the upsurge of nonaligned nuclear disarmament activism that characterized the years from 1954 to 1958. The British Peace Committee, a WPC affiliate, passed a resolution in early 1958 declaring that it welcomed the formation of CND and that it had urged its local groups to provide the new group with "every possible support." The *Daily Worker*, organ of the British Communist Party, gave the 1958 Aldermaston march more extensive and enthusiastic coverage than did any other national newspaper.[21] Preparing for the WPC's 1958 conference, Joliot-Curie invited Bertrand Russell to help organize it and, later, to submit a short statement on peace.[22] Similarly, Professor Kaoru Yasui, the pro-Communist director general of Gensuikyo, wished SANE leaders "a full success in their timely powerful undertaking." He also urged SANE and other nonaligned groups to send delegates to the World Conference Against Atomic and Hydrogen Bombs. Writing to SANE on behalf of the WPC in late 1958, Bernal remarked that the movement against nuclear testing "has so far not been strong or united enough" to secure an international agreement. "How much stronger and more effective this public pressure would be," he argued, "if a combined effort were made by all who really want to put an end to the tests." He therefore urged SANE to suggest "some form of common action."[23]

Nevertheless, the "unity" called for by Communist leaders remained strictly on their own terms. In France, where Trocmé, Barrat, and del Vasto were known for their anti-Communist sentiments, *l'Humanité*—the Communist newspaper—ignored the pacifist occupation of the Marcoule atomic center. In Sweden, the Communist *Ny Dag* reversed the tactic, but not the goal, by crediting the Communists with initiating the struggle against the Bomb. In West Germany, a large number of Communists attended an April 1958 meeting of the Berlin Action Committee Against Atomic Death, which they repeatedly disrupted by shouting, including demands for a general strike. Their shouting became so obnoxious that the SPD's Willy Brandt, mayor of the city, stood up, turned to the crowd, and called out: "If [the] Communists do not keep quiet, we will throw them out of here." Some left, but others remained and disrupted the gathering still further. When a local labor leader made some remarks critical of Communism, they became so abusive that he broke off his address, left the hall, and resigned from the antinuclear group.[24]

Below the surface, the Communist Party also responded coolly to CND in Britain. Not only did it throw its influence against unilateralism in several key unions, but it expelled party members who participated in the Aldermaston march. From the party's standpoint, by championing unilateralism, CND had taken an adventurist position. This "maximalist" demand, the party insisted, would divide the broader peace movement. In addition, members of CND did not necessarily oppose NATO and made no distinction between the alleged virtues of Soviet nuclear weapons and the evils of the Western variety. More-over, CND was largely a middle-class movement, whereas, according to the party, the "crucial" issue was "the degree to which the working class and its allies are active in the fight for peace." Finally, and perhaps most significant, CND was simply too large, feisty, and independent to be transformed into a creature of Soviet foreign policy. As British historian E. P. Thompson recalled, "The public reason" for British Communists' rejection of CND "was their op-position to unilateralism as 'sectarian' or adventurist. The real reason was that they could not abide sharing in any movement which they could not manipulate or control."[25]

The determination of Communist parties to control the movement was il-lustrated by their gradual takeover of Gensuikyo. Although Yasui denied that Gensuikyo was becoming a proponent of East bloc foreign policy,[26] this was just what was happening as the Japanese Communist Party tightened its grip on the organization. Dominated by delegates from WPC affiliates, the Third World Conference Against Atomic and Hydrogen Bombs, held in August of 1957, produced a declaration that, if not totally pro-Communist, was clearly anti-American.[27] By the time of the Fourth World Conference, in August of 1958, the trend was unmistakable. At one point, André Trocmé rose and—amid noisy efforts to prevent him from speaking—protested against the proposed passage of a resolution dealing with colonialism, the Middle East, and military alliances. He pointed out that none of these items was germane to the purpose of the conference. Conversely, the drafting committee had scuttled a recom-mendation made by three subcommittees calling for international control over the production and stockpiling of nuclear weapons. Trocmé was supported by Soji Okada, head of the delegation from the Japanese Socialist Party, and by the Yugoslav delegate. In the face of this challenge, chaos reigned on the con-vention floor. Meanwhile, to cut off any possibility of Trocmé's amending the resolution, the meeting's chair, James Endicott—a wheelhorse of the WPC—

used his power to force an immediate vote. Eventually, Trocmé recalled, when a group of pacifist delegates voted against the final conference declaration, they did so "under a shower of insults."[28]

Response of the Nonaligned Movement

Despite these difficulties, some elements in the nonaligned peace movement favored cooperation with Communist-organized peace campaigns. In June 1958, at the invitation of Joseph Hromadka and other church leaders in Czechoslovakia, a small group of Western church leaders began to participate in a series of Christian Peace Conferences in Prague. Although these gatherings drew considerably larger delegations from Soviet bloc nations and received little attention in the West, they provided a forum for discussion of ways and means to moderate international tension and, especially, to curb the nuclear arms race. They also generated appeals for nuclear disarmament to U.S. and Soviet leaders.[29]

Of all the leaders of the nonaligned movement, the best-known advocate of cooperation with Communist-led peace movements was Linus Pauling. Arguing that the broadest possible constituency should be mobilized against the nuclear arms race, Pauling staunchly supported nonaligned participation in Communist-led peace ventures. Although Pauling resigned as a vice president of the World Federation of Scientific Workers, he took this action, he remarked, "because I did not want to be handicapped in my activities by associations of any sort and . . . because I felt that I had not been effective in that office." He encouraged others, however, to participate and also served as a sponsor of Gensuikyo's controversial 1958 World Conference Against Atomic and Hydrogen Bombs. As late as 1990, Pauling continued to maintain that he supported "all peace movements, even those conducted by communists."[30]

Among nonaligned peace activists, however, this remained the position of no more than a very small minority. Attempting to distance itself from the WPC, the International Liaison Committee of Organizations for Peace stated in a 1953 leaflet that "ILCOP has no association with the World Peace Council or any of its national affiliates." In 1956, the German section of the War Resisters' International released a statement condemning the failure of the WPC and of its local affiliate, the West German Peace Committee, to respond to Soviet H-Bomb tests. "Are Russian atomic and hydrogen bombs less dangerous than the American variety?" it asked pointedly. In Sweden, AMSA discouraged its members from participating in the Communist-led peace movement and adopted a chilly attitude toward the Communist-dominated Peace Committees. Responding in July 1958 to two of its local branches which inquired about sending delegates to a forthcoming WPC conference in Stockholm, Britain's CND urged them not to participate.[31]

The situation was much the same elsewhere. Taking a stand against those whom it viewed as false friends, the Swiss Movement Against Atomic Armaments rejected any collaboration with the Swiss branch of the Communist Party. In New Zealand, the founders of the Dunedin Society for the Prevention of Nuclear Warfare were deeply suspicious of their country's WPC affiliate, the New Zealand Peace Council. According to Mary Woodward, a founder of New Zealand's nonaligned nuclear disarmament movement, all of its groups sought "to avoid any political bias in considering the work for peace"—bias that "had so often earned those quotation marks" around the word.[32] In the United States, pacifist groups studiously avoided coalition ventures with Communist-controlled organizations, and SANE repeatedly rebuffed the WPC's appeals for cooperative activity. American peace activists "should not cooperate with the World Council for Peace," Homer Jack told A. J. Muste in October 1958, but should themselves help organize a world peace conference on nonaligned principles.[33]

This rejection of cooperation with the Communist-led peace movement was typified by the stance of Bertrand Russell. In 1957, the British philosopher complained that although he and other non-Communists deplored Western aggression, "we find that our Communist colleagues are not equally willing to criticize Communist Governments." In early 1958, Russell declined Joliot-Curie's invitation to serve on a planning committee for the WPC's forthcoming world conference in Stockholm, although he did dispatch a short message to the conference on the necessity for nuclear arms controls and, eventually, world government.[34] In July 1958, startled to find that he was listed as a conference sponsor, disgusted by Soviet intervention in Hungary (including the murder of two of that nation's leaders), and convinced that the WPC was "reverting towards Stalinism," Russell sent a stiff letter to the WPC:

I am writing to you to withdraw my name as one of the Sponsors of the forthcoming Congress in Stockholm and generally as a supporter of the World Council of Peace. The policy of this body is more pro-Communist than I can agree with. Those in the West who think as I do are always willing to condemn what we consider bad actions by Western Governments, but I do not observe that the World Council for Peace is prepared to condemn actions by Communist States which all non-Communists consider worthy of condemnation. I should like to see the Congress at Stockholm pass a resolution to the effect that men who have been given safe-conducts should not be treacherously executed by those who had granted the safe-conduct. Failing this kind of action, I cannot regard your organization as impartial, and I must therefore sever all connection with it.

Informed of Russell's letter, CND executive committee promptly endorsed it.[35]

Similarly, most of the nonaligned movement was dismayed by the growing Communist control of Gensuikyo. The War Resisters' International sent
warm greetings to Gensuikyo's 1955 and 1956 World Conferences Against
Atomic and Hydrogen Bombs, but its enthusiasm and that of other nonaligned
organizations cooled thereafter.[36] Most nonaligned peace groups declined to
send delegations, and the small numbers of nonaligned activists who did participate brought back discouraging reports. Representing the nascent SANE
group at the 1957 World Conference in Tokyo, Homer Jack felt "deep disappointment." The gathering was "more one-sided" and "more pro-Moscow"
than he had feared. After two days, he began asking himself: "What am I doing
here?" He concluded that "pacifists should amass their energies and their
funds" for a nonaligned conference "and give no more heed to Communist
fronts or those conferences such as that in Tokyo, which are, at best, united
fronts."[37] Although some pacifists suggested that Gensuikyo organize "a truly
representative conference" in 1958, rather than one predisposed to "a single
political tendency,"[38] many nonaligned organizations had lost interest in participating. Furthermore, those nonaligned activists who attended felt deeply
alienated by the experience. Trocmé reported: "It was upsetting to see how
skilled maneuverers, under the cover of a struggle against nuclear weapons,
would . . . sow fear and hatred against the West alone."[39]

Communist Decline, Nonaligned Advance

In the midst of repeated rebuffs from nonaligned peace groups, the Communist-led peace campaign also suffered the devastating effects of a sharp crisis
within the world Communist movement. During 1956, Khrushchev's revelations of Stalin's crimes combined with the Soviet invasion of Hungary to foster
widespread disillusionment with Communism, including mass resignations
from Communist parties. At the same time, the WPC's double standard in dealing with the Hungarian issue sharply discredited that body. In Britain, where
both the British Peace Committee and Communist Party leaders felt betrayed
by the Hungarian invasion, normally pro-Soviet activists hardly knew which
way to turn. Indeed, the head of the British Peace Committee actually sought
out pacifist leaders for advice. In Sweden, the Communist-led Peace Committees tottered toward collapse. In Italy, the Socialist Party—allied with the Communists since World War II—withdrew from the Communist-controlled Peace
Partisans.[40]

Throughout much of the world, the reaction was the same. Torn by fierce
dissension over events in Hungary, the Canadian Peace Congress declined in
membership, staff, and activities. Endicott gloomily informed a leader of the

Soviet Peace Committee that "many of the peace fighters in the West have ceased, for the time being, to trust Soviet leadership." Meanwhile, the New Zealand Peace Council, sharply divided over the Hungarian invasion and over the subsequent hypocrisy of the WPC, began to disintegrate.[41] Within the friendly confines of Communist states, of course, the Communist-led peace movement survived unscathed. And even in some Third World countries, far from the bloodbath in Hungary, Communist-led movements could safely ignore the furor elsewhere.[42] Nevertheless, within Western nations especially, the traumatic events of 1956 sharply undermined the strength and influence of the Communist-led peace movement. Once able to dominate public discussion of peace and disarmament, the WPC declined into a marginal force in many parts of the world.[43]

In a number of ways, nonaligned groups benefited from the weakening of Communist parties and of the Communist-led peace movement. Most significantly, this trend freed them—at least in part—from the stigma nonaligned peace activities had acquired in the West during previous years thanks to their association in the popular mind with Communism.[44] Wherever Communism became a negligible phenomenon, it ceased to serve as a credible pretext for dismissing that nation's mass peace movement. Furthermore, substantial numbers of people who left Communist parties or WPC affiliates—often because they favored a more balanced critique of the Cold War—now joined nonaligned peace organizations. According to E. P. Thompson, some ten thousand members of the British Communist Party resigned in disillusionment in 1956 and 1957. Many of them had been active in early peace ventures and, with the founding of CND in 1958, flocked to its ranks. Thompson and other young intellectuals clustered around the *New Reasoner* were among them.[45]

Much the same phenomenon occurred elsewhere. Abandoning the Canadian Peace Congress in the wake of the Hungarian invasion, some members found a more congenial home in the Society of Friends, the FOR, the WILPF, or other peace groups. In Denmark, a group of former Communists, homeless for a time, organized the neutralist Socialist People's Party in 1958.[46] In Japan, the Zengakuren—the national federation of student government associations—had been largely controlled by the Japanese Communist Party from 1952 to 1955. But rapid shifts of the party line, student participation in antimilitary activity, Soviet suppression of the Hungarian revolt, and Communist Party attacks on Zengakuren leaders led to a complete break between the two groups. Although the Zengakuren leaders viewed themselves as building a revolutionary movement—more revolutionary than the Communists, whom they now denounced as tools of Moscow—for a time they became an important component of Japan's nonaligned peace movement.[47]

Nevertheless, the rise of nonaligned peace movements and the decline of their Communist competitors also created a major problem for the former: that of Communist participation. Particularly in countries lacking a substantial Communist-led peace movement, Communist parties sought to exert influence by encouraging their members to join nonaligned peace groups.[48] As civil libertarians, nonaligned activists frequently defended the civil and political rights of Communists, even when this was a very unpopular position in the broader society.[49] Furthermore, the presence of a few Communist members in their own groups rarely perturbed them. But they were concerned by the prospect that substantial Communist participation or capture of the top leadership posts would lead to Communist control. And this, in turn, would discredit their groups and, worst of all, alter their fundamental objectives. Thus, in an early appeal to Russell, the National Council for the Abolition of Nuclear Weapon Tests sought to reassure him that it was not "a left-wing organization. The only bias on the Executive Committee is in favour of the Society of Friends," which held three of the seven executive committee positions. Furthermore, "in order to preserve our independence, the Council has . . . declined donations . . . from bodies . . . who are proscribed by the Labour Party as being Communist dominated."[50]

The position taken on Communist participation by nonaligned groups and their leaders varied from country to country. In New Zealand, the leaders of the Dunedin Society for the Prevention of Nuclear Warfare, although setting no policy as to Communist membership, worked to keep Communists out of positions in which they could act as representatives of the group. In Britain, Russell privately suggested that Communists stay clear of CND, arguing that "we wish in our actions to stand only for peace, and not, except unavoidedly, to further the interests of either East or West." Sweden's AMSA adopted a tougher approach. Determined to avoid charges of Communist domination, the group decided at the outset to limit membership to non-Communists.[51] In the United States, WILPF chapters were torn by fierce conflicts over the question of Communist participation, with the organization's leadership and much of its membership feeling threatened both by Communist takeover and right-wing attack.[52]

In the United States, of course, the issue of Communism was particularly virulent, for the Soviet Union—the great hope of so many Communists—was also the United States's great enemy on the world scene. Writing to SANE's executive director, Trevor Thomas, in June 1958, Cousins argued that SANE

must develop a razor-sharp vigilance against the danger of Communist infiltration or control. The issue of nuclear testing . . . provides an attractive sphere of action for Communism. Naturally, the Communist Party would like to recoup some of its prodigious losses in recent years by exploiting an issue with such dramatic import and impact. Moreover, the issue of nuclear testing provides Communism with a chance to damage the United States in its relations with the rest of the world.

Clearly, "the easiest way for our committee to lose its standing and—even more serious—to lose its objective is to be accurately identified with an element of Communist control." In addition, he and his co-chair, Clarence Pickett, had "an overriding obligation to the people on the committee who repose their trust in us to protect them against damaging associations." Conceding that "several situations which could be potentially harmful—one in New York, one in Oregon, and one in Missouri"—were "under control," he still thought Thomas should give his "central attention" to this "vitally important problem."[53]

But how, exactly, was SANE to deal with the issue? Nonplussed, Thomas confessed that it would not be easy. The organization was loosely structured and there were "no mechanics for chartering local groups," he pointed out. In two cases where suspicion arose of Communist infiltration, "we were able to remedy it before any serious dimension developed." Searching for "a middle ground between the extreme of, say, requiring an anti-communist oath, or, on the other hand, having no structure for control and responsibility," Thomas preferred to "rely on the integrity and good sense of most people, recognizing that the batting average will be less than 100%." There would have to be "*some* method of seeking out reliable leadership," although he did not specify what it should be. Cousins apparently remained dissatisfied, for that summer he went so far as to ask the FBI to furnish him with the names of Communists infiltrating SANE's local committees. Ironically, the FBI refused its assistance.[54] And there the situation remained, at least for the time being.

By late 1958, then, although the nonaligned movement had supplanted the World Peace Council as the major champion of nuclear disarmament in many parts of the world, it viewed itself as waging a struggle on two fronts. On one front lay the recalcitrant nuclear powers, determined to press ahead with further development of nuclear weapons, and also their many potential imitators. On the other lay the Communist-led peace movement—weakened for the moment by world Communism's severe losses, but potentially capable of either breathing new life into shaken WPC affiliates or capturing control of the new, nonaligned movements themselves. Lavishly funded by Communist governments and fervently supported by Soviet sympathizers, the Communist-led peace movement remained a force to be reckoned with. Gensuikyo's slide into Cold War partisanship provided a powerful example of the fate that might befall the flourishing nonaligned campaign. If, at times, leaders of the nonaligned movement overestimated the danger of a Communist takeover, there was some basis for their concern.

Policymakers and Protest

Governments Confront the Movement, 1954–58

> It is most important that we should find some way of organizing and directing an effective campaign to counter the current agitation against this country's possession of nuclear weapons.
>
> Harold Macmillan, 1958

Around the world, governments watched the development of the nuclear disarmament movement with considerable interest and, sometimes, with great concern. Here, after all, was a volatile political force—one that might alter the very cornerstone of modern national security policies and, thereby, have a substantial impact on international relations. In general, governments reacted to it in light of their own attitudes toward nuclear weapons and the Cold War. If they were anxious to limit or contain the nuclear arms race on both sides of the "iron curtain," they encouraged the new movement as an adjunct to their own disarmament efforts. If they sought to pressure their rivals into backing away from nuclear confrontation and accepting some measure of arms control, they tried to manipulate the new movement accordingly. And if they were committed to the nuclear buildup of their own nations, they worked to discredit antinuclear activism and to soothe popular anxieties about nuclear testing and nuclear war.

Neutral and Nonaligned Nations

Nonaligned nations were the sharpest and most frequent critics of the Bomb. Addressing the Indian parliament on April 2, 1954, in the aftermath of the disastrous U.S. H-Bomb tests at Bikini, Prime Minister Jawaharlal Nehru noted "the deep and widespread concern in the world about these weapons and their dreadful consequences." Destruction, he argued, "threatens to . . . overtake us on its march to its sinister goal. We must seek to arrest it and avert the dire end it threatens." Pending progress on the prohibition of such weapons, he called for an immediate "standstill agreement" on stopping nuclear tests, "full publicity" by the nuclear powers and the United Nations on "the extent of the destructive power and the known effects of these weapons," and "active steps by states and peoples of the world," whom, he hoped, would "express their concern and add their voices and influence . . . to arrest the progress of this destructive potential, which menaces all alike." Two days later, Premier Ali Sastroamidjojo of Indonesia, speaking for his neutralist nation, appealed to the nuclear powers to halt their H-Bomb tests and supported Nehru's proposal to place the issue on the agenda at a conference of South Asian prime ministers opening in Colombo, Ceylon, at the end of the month. Throughout the rest of the year, Nehru and other leaders of nonaligned nations kept up the attack.[1]

This critique of nuclear weapons by nonaligned nations acquired an institutional form through the organization of an Afro-Asian Conference in Bandung, Indonesia. Convening in late April 1955, the Bandung conference drew two thousand delegates from twenty-nine nations. The conference call, issued in Bogor, Indonesia, by five Asian governments, noted their "grave concern" at "the destructive potential of nuclear and thermonuclear explosions for experimental purposes," which threatened not only their countries, but "the world." At the conference, Sir John Kotelawala of Ceylon charged that the great powers were "hag-ridden by the demon of progress, the monsters their scientists have created." African and Asian nations could serve "as mediators in the dispute between the giants of communism and anti-communism which, if fought out to an end, will deluge the world in blood and leave the earth infected with atomic radiation." A final conference statement declared that "disarmament and the prohibition of the production, experimentation, and use of nuclear and thermonuclear weapons of war are imperative to save mankind and civilization from . . . wholesale destruction." Pending prohibition of the manufacture of nuclear weapons, the conference "appealed to all the powers concerned to reach agreement to suspend [nuclear weapons] experiments."[2]

Naturally, governments of nonaligned nations frequently felt a kinship with the nonaligned nuclear disarmament movement. When news of Albert Einstein's death reached the Bandung conference, numerous delegates were deeply moved. Choosing antinuclear Hiroshima as the site for an address to thirty thousand people in October 1957, Nehru expressed his hope that nuclear explosions would be stopped "and that the terrible scourge and fear of warfare with atomic weapons will also be banned and ended." May the key to Hiroshima, he said, "prove a key to the heart of people all over the world, moving them to compassion, moving them to discard fear and to live in friendship and cooperation with each other." In May 1958, Yugoslavia's president, Josip Broz

Tito, congratulated Bertrand Russell on the second Pugwash conference and assured him that he held "in high esteem the endeavors being made by scientists who are in the present grave international situation displaying a strong feeling of responsibility for the fate of mankind." He was "confident such efforts will help the responsible political factors in the world perceive that peace, and thereby the existence of all of mankind, depends above all on eliminating the danger of use of weapons of mass destruction and on the policy of peaceful solution of outstanding international problems." That September, the Austrian government hosted a Pugwash gathering in Vienna, addressed by the nation's president, Russell, and other participants. The next day, the conference resumed in the City Hall auditorium, with some ten thousand people present.[3]

Sometimes, relations did not proceed this smoothly. Little enthusiasm, for example, existed for the efforts of the World Peace Council. Nehru believed, as he told Norman Cousins, that "so-called peace conferences and congresses, usually organized by Communists and their friends, do more harm than good" in terms of mobilizing public opinion. "They have patently political objectives in view and they irritate many people outside their fold," he noted. The Austrian government, too, took a dim view of Communist-led peace ventures, and in 1957 closed down the WPC's world headquarters in Vienna.[4] Even nonaligned groups encountered rebuffs on occasion. On July 1, 1958, with the Swiss government intrigued by the possibility of acquiring atomic weapons, the Swiss Federal Council banned the holding of the European Congress Against Nuclear Weapons in Basel. The head of the Federal Department of Justice and Police argued that the meeting had been banned in order to prevent interference with Swiss national defense policy. Although Russell issued a public protest, the government refused to respond to Russell or to other critics of the decision.[5]

Usually, however, the nuclear disarmament movement received a warm welcome from nonaligned and neutral governments and, particularly, from the government of India. Writing to Russell in January 1955, India's foreign minister, V. K. Krishna Menon, assured the British philosopher of his "deep sense of gratitude" for "your work in the cause of peace." Indeed, he added, "the Prime Minister has recently referred to your suggestions generally in some of his talks and even the other day in the private session of the Bogor Conference." Later that year, at Russell's suggestion, the Indian government authorized a study on the consequences of nuclear war.[6] For a time, in fact, it seemed that the Indian government would sponsor the international scientific gatherings that became the Pugwash conferences. Although Russell eventually turned elsewhere for support, Nehru continued his keen interest in this venture. In April 1958, when the British philosopher sent the Indian prime minister a number of papers from a recent Pugwash meeting, Nehru responded that he considered them "of great importance" and would bring them "to the notice of our nuclear scientists here." He added a suggestion that they be made available in book form. Concluding, Nehru expressed his "deep admiration for the lead you have given in this matter which is of the most vital importance to the world."[7]

Nehru also encouraged the antinuclear activities of Norman Cousins and, through him, the efforts of Albert Schweitzer. Responding in February 1957 to a letter from the American editor that recounted his crucial meeting with Schweitzer at Lambaréné, Nehru declared enthusiastically that he doubted "if there is anyone in the world today whose opinion can carry more weight in these matters than Dr. Schweitzer. No one can accuse him of partiality, and whatever he says will at least command world attention. I welcome, therefore, his intention to try his utmost to deal with the present crisis." Returning repeatedly to the proposed appeal by Schweitzer, Nehru insisted that "he is the man who might bring some light into closed minds." Cousins, in turn, passed along Nehru's fulsome message to the diffident Schweitzer, who moved forward with plans for his first radio broadcast. In a lengthy letter to Cousins that March, Nehru strongly endorsed the idea, declaring that he agreed "entirely . . . that Oslo will be the right and appropriate place for an appeal by Dr. Schweitzer, and it would certainly add to the value of that appeal . . . if it was made under the auspices of the Nobel Committee." That June, following Schweitzer's appeal, Nehru told Cousins that he was "sure that Schweitzer's statement has helped" create "a far greater realization all over the world of the effect of these test explosions." He added: "Pressure must come from awakened and, where possible, organized public opinion." Thus he suggested that Schweitzer "follow up his broadcast."[8] Eventually, Schweitzer did.

Communist Bloc Nations

In the aftermath of Stalin's death, the rise to power of a new generation of Soviet leaders, combined with further Soviet progress in developing nuclear weapons, led to a sudden fluidity in Moscow's nuclear weapons policy. On March 12, 1954, shortly after the disastrous Bikini H-Bomb tests and very likely in response to a description by Kurchatov of the nuclear peril, Premier Georgii Malenkov publicly warned that war in the nuclear age "would mean the destruction of world civilization." A week later, *Red Star*, the Soviet Army newspaper, provided the most realistic account of a nuclear explosion ever published in the Soviet press and described the enormous losses that nuclear war would produce. Other Soviet leaders, however, challenged this gloomy prognosis, so out of line with the traditional notion of Communist triumph. Condemned at a Central Committee meeting that April by V. M. Molotov and Nikita Khrushchev, Malenkov publicly recanted his heresy. Nor was this enough for his party enemies, who attacked his statement again at the January 1955 Plenary meeting of the Central Committee. The following month, they had him demoted.[9] According to Khrushchev, Malenkov's talk about thermonuclear destruction had been "theoretically mistaken and politically harmful." It encouraged "feelings of hopelessness about the efforts of the peoples to frustrate the plans of the aggressors."[10] Molotov, the Soviet foreign minister, took an even harsher tack. "A communist should not speak about the 'destruction of world civilization,'" he insisted, "but about the need to prepare and mobilize . . . for the destruction of the bourgeoisie."[11]

Yet Malenkov's fall from power did not foster much greater equanimity about nuclear war. Gradually securing control of the party and governmental apparatus, Khrushchev adopted a position on the issue only modestly more optimistic than that of his predecessor. Rejecting Malenkov's stark picture of universal destruction, he talked instead of nuclear war's vast devastation. If attacked, Khrushchev insisted gamely, the Soviet Union would fight back and prevail. Nevertheless, he emphasized that the enormous destructiveness of nuclear weapons made a major war unthinkable and better relations with the West an objective necessity. As early as 1954, he began to speak of "peaceful coexistence" as the basis for Soviet foreign policy. Toward this end, he encouraged the friendly, if vacuous, "summit" meeting with Western leaders in 1955 at Geneva, where Soviet and U.S. officials commiserated about the catastrophic nature of nuclear war. Furthermore, even as he continued to trumpet Marxism-Leninism as the panacea for the world's ills, Khrushchev argued that the Soviet Union did not need or want war to assure its survival and triumph.[12]

But to what extent did Khrushchev favor nuclear disarmament? Like his Western counterparts, Khrushchev was fascinated by nuclear weapons and missiles. Although he considered nuclear war disastrous and unnecessary, the possession of nuclear weapons, by contrast, would enable the Soviet Union to deter foreign aggression, exercise substantial influence in world affairs, and cut spending on conventional arms.[13] Consequently, to avoid nuclear war or the prospect that the United States might take a substantial lead in the nuclear arms race while, at the same time, preserving his nation's nuclear arsenal, Khrushchev began to press for nuclear stability and restraint. In this context, some kind of nuclear arms controls looked appealing. At the 1955 Geneva conference, Soviet officials reiterated their interest in a nuclear test ban. A few months before, they even adopted a new disarmament position. But, as Soviet diplomat Anatoly Dobrynin later recalled, his government's insistence on complete disarmament was "nothing more than a good piece of propaganda." Indeed,

"Soviet leaders, and Khrushchev in particular, strongly doubted the effectiveness of practical steps toward disarmament at that stage of the arms race. . . . Their minds were not ready for it."[14]

Once contemptuous of nuclear weapons, China's leaders grew more enthusiastic about them during the 1950s. "The atom bomb is a paper tiger which the U.S. reactionaries use to scare people," Mao Zedong told a journalist in 1946. "Of course, the atom bomb is a weapon of mass slaughter, but the outcome of war is decided by the people, not by . . . new types of weapon." Nonetheless, this faith in the triumph of "people's war" began to erode during the Korean conflict, when China suffered enormous combat casualties. In conversations with Khrushchev, Mao still insisted that China's superior manpower could prevail over the West's nuclear weapons, a contention which the Soviet leader thought ridiculous. But Washington's threats of nuclear war with China over Korea, Taiwan, and the offshore islands, coupled with its talk of "massive retaliation," ultimately convinced China's leaders that U.S. "nuclear blackmail" could only be offset by developing a Chinese Bomb. On January 15, 1955, Mao presided over a meeting of Chinese leaders that finally gave the go-ahead for a Chinese nuclear weapons project.[15]

Given their ambivalent attitudes toward nuclear weapons, governments of Communist bloc nations encouraged antinuclear efforts in a selective, self-serving fashion. In East Germany, where the authorities billed Marxism-Leninism as "the peace concept par excellence," the ruling Communist party denounced pacifism for undermining the resistance of the masses to Western imperialism. On the other hand, it took a far more favorable view of ventures under its control. Addressing a congress of the East German Communist party in April 1954, amid the growing furor over U.S. nuclear testing in the Pacific, party boss Walter Ulbricht declared that "our first demand is the removal of all atomic weapons from West Germany." He entrusted the task of developing the appropriate movement in the Federal Republic to the delegation from the West German Communist Party. In China, the government threw itself enthusiastically behind the Communist-organized ban-the-Bomb campaign in early 1955, producing mountains of literature designed to stir up the population against the dangers of nuclear weapons, or at least the weapons produced by the Western powers. China's own nuclear weapons program remained unmentioned. Delighted with the pro-Communist slant of Gensuikyo's 1958 World Conference, the Peking government presented the organization with 7.5 million yen for its relief fund.[16]

Recognizing the significance of nonaligned nuclear disarmament activities in Western nations, Communist governments sometimes portrayed them quite favorably, though rarely very accurately. Devoting enormous attention to the

Göttingen appeal by West German scientists, the East German press used it to make the regime's case that the Western powers were preparing to launch an atomic war, a convenient pretext for its own military buildup. In a radio and television presentation of April 16, 1957, East German defense minister Willi Stoph warned that unless the Federal Republic halted its preparations for nuclear war, East Germany would be forced to take countermeasures. Local readers did not get a chance to see the actual Göttingen appeal, for *Neues Deutschland*, the official government organ, published a bowdlerized version that omitted embarrassing phrases, including the signers' support for "the freedom that is today safeguarded by the Western world against Communism." In a similar fashion, the East German press lauded a West Berlin march against atomic death in April 1958, but distorted its character by exaggerating Communist participation and by making it appear that the demonstrators shared the East German government's policy positions.[17]

Soviet policymakers, too, adopted a self-serving approach to antimilitary pressures. Determined to maintain the Soviet public's Cold War militance, Kremlin leaders blocked writers from publishing books with a mordant view of war. Similarly, Soviet officials vetoed publication of the grim analysis of nuclear war by Kurchatov and his colleagues. The government-controlled mass media ridiculed pacifism, depicting it as bizarre and crankish. "Soviet military ideology has nothing in common with pacifism," *Red Star* told readers in 1957; instead, it relies on "constant vigilance and preparedness for victorious defense of the socialist countries against the attacks of imperialism."[18] Andrei Sakharov recalled that, in November 1955, when he toasted a gathering of Bomb project officials with his hope that Soviet nuclear weapons would always explode "over test sites and never over cities," the room "fell silent, as if I had said something indecent." Finally, Marshal Mitrofin Nedelin arose and responded with a lewd story, evidently designed to bolster martial spirits and to put such subversive ideas in their place.[19]

Nevertheless, as they observed the burgeoning of nonaligned antinuclear sentiment in non-Communist nations, Soviet officials began to develop respect for it as a factor that could restrain Western belligerence and promote nuclear arms controls. In 1954, diplomats at the Soviet embassy in Washington sent reports to the Soviet Foreign Ministry emphasizing the growing concern of U.S. allies and public opinion about the threat of nuclear war. The following January, a staff member at the embassy compiled a history of the movement for a nuclear test ban for use by the Foreign Ministry. Reviewing the arguments for an end to nuclear testing, the report stressed the work of peace activists and others in countries allied to the United States, especially Britain and Japan. Similar analyses began to make their way into Soviet publications. In September 1958, a key article contended that, in the United States, a new political tendency was developing—that of "realism." Its adherents, the article maintained, did not seek war with the Soviet Union and would agree to arms control measures. To support this proposition, the article cited Norman Cousins, George Kennan, and Senators Humphrey and Morse, among others.[20]

Khrushchev, particularly, took the nuclear disarmament movement seriously. In 1952, Stalin had warned ominously that the West European peace movement could not prevent a new war. By contrast Khrushchev stressed the importance of what he called "peace forces" to bolster his 1956 contention that war with the West was not inevitable.[21] During 1956, in an unusual move, Khrushchev allowed Kurchatov to travel to Britain "to establish useful contacts with the Western scientific community." In 1958, he personally authorized the publication of Sakharov's articles assailing nuclear testing. He also argued that the people's desire for peace was isolating aggressive forces in the imperialist camp. That May, when the ailing Joliot-Curie met privately with Khrushchev, the two men spent hours discussing the importance of creating a world climate favorable to disarmament and peace. The Soviet leader stated his belief that government behavior could be strongly influenced by public opinion and, more remarkably, that a peace movement did not necessarily have to identify fully with Soviet foreign policy.[22]

Reversing the venomously hostile behavior characteristic of the Stalin years,[23] the Soviet government began to court leaders of the nonaligned disarmament movement. Bertrand Russell, once condemned as a fascist warmonger in Soviet periodicals, found his messages on nuclear disarmament and world government printed therein, accompanied by approving editorial comments. Following his dramatic petition against nuclear testing, Linus Pauling was named a full member of the Soviet Academy of Sciences.[24] In an apparent gesture of deference to Szilard, soon after he mentioned at a Pugwash conference that Edward Teller's mother and sister were being detained in Hungary against their wishes, they were allowed to emigrate to the United States. Cousins had applied repeatedly for a visa to visit the Soviet Union without success—or even a response—in the past. He even hired a lawyer to try to facilitate the process, but to no avail. In 1958, however, he was suddenly admitted to the Soviet Union for a lecture tour.[25]

Moscow's growing interest in nonaligned nuclear disarmament activism was exemplified by its backing of the Pugwash conferences. Although the Soviet government had blocked the participation of Soviet scientists in a similar venture in 1948,[26] Kremlin officials were considerably more agreeable a decade later. They facilitated the attendance of top Soviet scientists at the 1957 and 1958 Pugwash meetings, apparently encouraged their informal discussions with

American scientists, and—to judge from the endorsement of the first conference statement by the Soviet Academy of Sciences—approved of the results.[27]
In fact, behind the scenes, Soviet officials felt somewhat uneasy about the Pugwash gatherings. They chose conference participants carefully and, even then,
kept them under close scrutiny.[28] Shortly before the first Pugwash conference
and, continuing for a time after it, top Soviet party officials secretly planned to
organize their own conference of scientists that could be used to support the
Soviet position at the forthcoming meeting of the U.N. General Assembly.[29]
Nevertheless, the Kremlin dropped the idea and, convinced of the value of the
Pugwash arrangements, continued to support them. In mid-1958, Khrushchev
sent a warm letter of thanks to conference host Cyrus Eaton, stressing "the
great importance" he attached to "the efforts of scientists of countries of the
world to remove the terrible threat of nuclear war hanging over humanity."
Their opinion "on this pivotal problem," the Soviet leader assured him, "is of
deep interest to the Governments of the different countries."[30]

Even so, this admiration for nonaligned disarmament sentiment remained
largely confined to its appearance in nations outside the Communist bloc.
Khrushchev recalled that when Peter Kapitza, perhaps the leading Soviet physicist, rejected his appeal to "work on something of military significance," he
came away with an impression of Kapitza that was "not at all favorable."
Khrushchev was also irked by Kurchatov's efforts in 1958 to block resumption
of Soviet nuclear testing. According to Sakharov, the Soviet leader "was extremely displeased and . . . from then until Kurchatov's death a year and a half
later," Khrushchev no longer trusted him. As for Sakharov, Khrushchev recalled that "he went too far in thinking that he had the right to decide whether
the bomb he had developed could ever be used in the future." Rejecting
Sakharov's 1958 appeal for an end to Soviet nuclear testing, Khrushchev stated
that "as the man responsible for the security of our country, I have no right to
do what you're asking. For me to cancel the tests would be a crime against our
state. . . . We can't risk the lives of our people again by giving our adversary a
free hand to develop new means of destruction. . . . To agree to what you are
suggesting would spell doom for our country."[31]

Consequently, there were limits to Soviet encouragement of antinuclear
sentiment. In fairness to Khrushchev, it should be emphasized that his belief
in the danger of disarmament was thoroughly in line with traditional statecraft
and was no more bloodthirsty than the beliefs of his Western competitors. In
fact, it rather resembled them. Moreover, none of the maverick scientists faced
any disciplinary action by the Soviet state for their unorthodox activities—although Kurchatov spared himself this possibility by changing his stance, telling
the Twenty-first Communist Party Congress, in 1959, that Western nuclear pol-

icy "forced our country to resume tests." But, symptomatically, when Linus Pauling proposed to begin legal proceedings against the individuals in the United States, Britain, and the Soviet Union responsible for the continuation of nuclear testing, Soviet party officials looked askance at the idea. Outlining a campaign focused on the health hazards of nuclear testing in August 1958, Boris Ponomarev of the Central Committee's International Department noted that it would "be directed above all at the capitalist countries in order not to allow the populations in the socialist states to become frightened."[32]

Uneasy lest antinuclear sentiment get out of hand, the Soviet government continued to lean heavily on its traditional, one-sided propaganda operations. Through its direction and funding of the World Peace Council and its branches, the Kremlin promoted ventures that placed Soviet nuclear policy in the best possible light. The party's central committee scrutinized (and authorized) the most detailed activities in this regard, including the junkets of foreign "peace partisans" to the Soviet Union.[33] It also awarded the munificent Stalin Peace Prizes (soon renamed the Lenin Peace Prizes) for appropriate service to the cause. Meanwhile, the Soviet press churned out articles with headlines like "Soviet Union's New Contribution in Struggle for Banning Atomic and Hydrogen Weapons." News stories continued to display a Cold War, Manichaean flavor. "On the one hand, countries of the North Atlantic bloc, headed by the U.S.A., are intensifying the arms race," *Pravda* insisted. "On the other hand, democratic countries, headed by the U.S.S.R., . . . are waging a constant fight to ban all weapons of mass destruction." A *Pravda* editorial insisted that the Warsaw Pact nations were "consistent advocates of . . . the banning of atomic weapons."[34]

Western Bloc Nations

Fearing Communist military power, many Cold War allies of the United States turned eagerly to nuclear weapons as the solution to their national security dilemmas. According to the minutes of a NATO foreign ministers meeting on December 13, 1956, the British argued that NATO could not "afford to have old arms vis-à-vis Soviet capabilities," and this necessitated "tactical atomic weapons." The Dutch contended that NATO's "shield forces are too weak and [the] only way to strengthen them is with atomic weapons." The West Germans wanted "tactical atomic weapons . . . available down to [the] divisional level." For their part, the Italians and the Greeks expressed approval of the new weapons, with the French observing that "everyone [is] aware that nuclear weapons are required . . . if Europe [is] not to be overrun."[35] Although the leaders of Norway, Denmark, Japan, Australia, and New Zealand did not encourage the deployment of nuclear weapons on their territory, they seemed happy enough to be sheltered under the Western nuclear umbrella. Indeed, the Australian government provided the testing sites for British nuclear weapons.[36]

Furthermore, key NATO nations sought to push beyond nuclear-sharing arrangements toward an independent nuclear weapons capability. Having already developed the atomic bomb as a means of safeguarding Britain's security and influence, the British government moved to develop the H-Bomb as well. In July 1954, when Churchill made the crucial decision, he told the British Cabinet that "we could not expect to maintain our influence as a world power unless we possessed the most up to date nuclear weapons."[37] The French government, too—unsure of the extent of U.S. support and determined, above all, to restore France's standing as a great power—began a nuclear weapons development program in late 1954.[38] Despite the West German government's 1955 treaty commitment not to produce nuclear weapons, Defense Minister Franz Josef Strauss showed a keen interest in moving ahead on just these lines. The nuclear ambitions of France and West Germany became so apparent that, in April 1957, the leading U.S. arms control official predicted that unless a test ban treaty were negotiated, "the production and testing of nuclear weapons by France and the Federal Republic of Germany" would occur within a year. In late 1957 and 1958, Strauss played an important role in securing a French-German-Italian agreement on common development of armaments, including nuclear weapons.[39]

Combat use of the weapons remained quite another matter. When Eisenhower declared in 1953 that the atomic bomb had to be treated as just another weapon of war and that if hostilities resumed in Korea, the United States might employ it to good effect, Churchill grew apoplectic. Such action, he protested, might touch off World War III and "the destruction of all we hold dear." Dulles complained that British officials "were almost pathological in their fear of the H-Bomb." On the other hand, British leaders embraced the idea of nuclear deterrence. Churchill told Eisenhower that the threat to retaliate against a Soviet nuclear attack by killing forty to sixty million Russians would lead to "the end of nuclear war." Or, as he stated publicly in March 1955, with H-Bombs in the hands of the three great powers, "by a process of sublime irony," the world may reach a point where "safety will be the sturdy child of terror and survival the twin brother of annihilation."[40] The leaders of NATO governments in Western Europe shared this position. West Germany's chancellor, Konrad Adenauer, combined an uneasiness about waging nuclear war with an unwavering faith in the efficacy of nuclear deterrence.[41]

Not surprisingly, then, nuclear disarmament had little appeal to the governments of NATO nations. Indeed, as NATO countries increased their nuclear capabilities and decreased their conventional forces, nuclear deterrence became increasingly vital to their defense. In his memoirs, Macmillan complained of "the hopelessness of our position should the 'bomb' be effectively 'banned,' and Western Europe with its tiny armies left to face the overwhelming conventional forces of the Soviet Union." Adenauer objected not only to nuclear disarmament, but to Western talk of it, claiming that such public discussion was "raising peoples' hopes" and would "increase neutralization sentiment in the Federal Republic." Commenting on the North Atlantic Council meetings of early May 1957, Dulles reported that "if the point of view reflected here were to be controlling, there would not be a chance . . . of any disarmament at all."[42]

Even so, the Western bloc could hardly ignore the growing resistance to the Bomb. "Our Allies are seriously concerned about the impact of the slogan 'Ban the Bomb,'" reported Harold Stassen, Eisenhower's adviser on arms control issues. "Public opinion in Europe has been enamoured with the slogan." In West Germany, Adenauer felt considerable alarm at the opposition to his pro-nuclear position by the bulk of public opinion and great concern at the issuance of the Göttingen and Schweitzer appeals. Schweitzer's prestige was "very great in Germany," the chancellor remarked ruefully, for he spoke "almost with the authority of the Bible."[43] In Italy, the government was "under considerable pressure from Italian public opinion to support moves in the direction of banning nuclear bomb production and tests," a U.S. government report warned. In Norway, the prime minister conceded that the 1957 Schweitzer Appeal had "tremendous significance in a world frightened by the awesome threat of atomic war." A year later, the Norwegian Foreign Office secretly informed the U.S. embassy that it was "disturbed" about the latest Schweitzer broadcasts. Thanks to "the public fear of the effects of radiation," an Australian diplomat acknowledged, his government, too, faced difficulties justifying nuclear weapons tests.[44] In Japan, the government felt thoroughly intimidated by anti-nuclear sentiment.[45]

The British government considered itself besieged. Shortly after the *Lucky Dragon* incident, Churchill told Eisenhower that "there is widespread anxiety here about the H-bomb and I am facing a barrage of questions . . . about the March 1 explosion." Although the prime minister loyally defended U.S. nuclear testing and U.S. possession of the Bomb, the situation continued to worsen. On January 31, 1956, at a conference of top British and U.S. officials, the British foreign secretary warned that there was "a considerable and growing body of public opinion in the U.K. in favor of some form of regulation" of nuclear testing. "It was comprised not of fellow-travellers but of a broad section of middle-of-the-road opinion. The government had to decide whether to be dragged along behind or to take an initiative themselves." The following day, the British returned to this point, noting that "a steady build up of public feeling on this subject was to be expected. This would not come only from the left but from middle of the road opinion and from the churches." In early 1957, the prime minister complained to the Americans that he was "receiving questions every week" regarding nuclear testing and "underneath it all there was a strong feeling in Britain that nuclear tests should in some way be limited." He stressed that "this matter of nuclear test limitation" had become "an important domestic political issue."[46]

"It is difficult now to realize the genuine anxiety about nuclear arms, amounting almost to hysteria, which had started to develop," the new prime minister, Harold Macmillan, recalled years later. "Processions, demonstrations and deputations began to pursue me in and out of season. Deputations of worthy intellectuals" met with him repeatedly. "As young boys and girls began to organize marches from Aldermaston, I began to realize how profound and how widespread was the concern, and how easily it could be exploited." For example, "the dangers of allowing the Opposition to exploit the position were considerable." Referring bitterly to Aneurin Bevan of the Labour Party, Macmillan wrote in his diary that "he thinks the H-bomb can be an electoral winner for the Socialists" and "I fear that he is right." The prime minister confided to one of his associates: "I wonder . . . whether all this propaganda about the bomb has really gone deeper than we are apt to think. This, combined with Suez, has drawn away from us that wavering vote with vague Liberal and nonconformist traditions which plays such an important role because it is still the no-man's land between the great entrenched parties." "The bomb," he noted gloomily, "presents many features useful to the agitator. It has an appeal for the mother, the prospective mother, the grandmother, and all the rest, and every kind of exaggeration or mis-statement is permissable."[47]

Viewing the emergence of the nuclear disarmament movement with alarm, Western bloc leaders groped for means to combat it. Under enormous pressure from its antinuclear public, the Japanese government remained by far the most accommodating, treating pacifists with courtesy and going so far as to send greetings to the first World Conference Against Atomic and Hydrogen Bombs.[48] Other governments, though, were more combative. In an apparent attempt to discredit the Pauling petition against nuclear testing, the French proposed that the participants in the North Atlantic Council gather derogatory information on petition signers in their respective countries. "Considerably concerned" over Schweitzer's 1958 radio addresses, the Norwegian Foreign Office made the text available to Edward Teller and Willard Libby, two leading U.S. advocates of the Bomb criticized in the broadcasts, and invited their response. According to the U.S. embassy, the Foreign Office would then attempt to "have [their] comments broadcast on Norwegian Radio." Exactly how the Norwegian government would handle this remained "uncertain," for it "desires [the] implication [to be] avoided [that] Libby and Teller [are] being invited to comment, which [the] Foreign Office considers would be [an] improper act [on] its part."[49]

Although the Canadian government publicly termed the Russell-Einstein Manifesto "a timely reminder" that "warrants the most careful examination,"[50] it did not show much sympathy for the ensuing Pugwash conferences. During the planning of the first Pugwash gathering, in 1957, the Canadian Cabinet discussed the issue and, in the aftermath of the meeting, reached negative conclusions. "While a number of participants . . . were selected for their repute in the scientific fraternity and not because of possible communist sympathies," the Canadian government secretly informed the British, "a communist-front organization (the World Federation of Scientific Workers) was nevertheless well represented, and subsequently enjoyed some success in using the gathering for its own propaganda purposes. . . . It is to be expected that increased efforts will be made by the communists to exploit any pronouncement issued by a future conference." With this—plus British government hostility to the gatherings—in mind, the Canadian Cabinet referred the matter to the minister of justice. His office, in turn, sought to persuade Cyrus Eaton to postpone the date of the 1958 conference and defer applying for visas. Eaton, however, proved stubborn, and threatened that if Canadian authorities caused difficulties, he would change the venue of the gathering to the West Indies and stir up embarrassing publicity about the move. Uneasy at this prospect, Canadian officials drew back from attempts to derail the second Pugwash conference.[51]

Without abandoning its suspicion of the 1958 Pugwash meeting, the Canadian government adopted subtler measures to influence it. The Canadians notified the British that they agreed with them "that it would be desirable for the Western members of the sub-committee of the [Commonwealth] Disarmament Commission to exchange information about the activities of Mr. Eaton and Lord Russell, and to reach some understanding on a common attitude towards any conference which they may arrange this year." They further agreed that "at least until more is known about the composition and agenda of such a conference, the Western attitude should be one of skepticism." Meanwhile, adopting yet another British proposal, the Canadian government decided that although arranging for some scientists "to argue the Western viewpoint is . . . a matter of considerable delicacy," it would "obviously be advantageous" to have a favorable delegation "who have been briefed." Therefore, should one or more of the Canadian scientists "be persons in whom the Canadian government has confidence, it will try to arrange an appropriate political briefing."[52]

The West German government also worked to contain nuclear disarmament activities. Enraged by the Göttingen declaration, Adenauer confided to Christian Democratic leaders that its call for West German renunciation of nuclear weapons was "the silliest thing I have ever heard."[53] Publicly, he assailed it as an "unrealistic proposal" that would mean the dissolution of the entire Western defense system. Communist nations, he charged, were overjoyed by the declaration. Other top Christian Democrats secretly referred to its issuance as a "grave setback" and "a black day" for their party. At their lengthy meeting with five of the dissident scientists, Adenauer and other top government officials alternately lectured and cajoled them about the imperatives of a nuclear defense. The situation was tense. "During an adjournment to the garden," Otto Hahn recalled, "Strauss gave me a thorough telling-off. I could see from the Communists' 'yells of triumph' what I had gone and done." Although Hahn and other Göttingen signers felt that they had stood their ground against the government steamroller, Adenauer privately boasted to U.S. officials that he had forced the scientists to retreat. According to one U.S. official, Adenauer said that he "had succeeded in convincing them of the error of their conclusions but that, like most scientists, they did not have the courage to reverse themselves in public."[54]

Adenauer also sought to have Schweitzer reverse his position. In May 1957, when Lewis Strauss implied that a gullible Schweitzer had been manipulated by Cousins into making his 1957 appeal, Adenauer seized on this point and pressed Strauss "to obtain a retraction from Schweitzer." Strauss dodged the suggestion, but Adenauer—as the meeting's record indicates—"reverted to the great prestige of Albert Schweitzer and how important it would be to get him to admit inaccuracies in his statement. He felt that millions of people had developed fears as a result of the Schweitzer statement." Strauss responded that the U.S. government had "no present means of contacting Albert Schweitzer" and turned quickly to another issue, but Adenauer was not easily deflected. "Concerned" about this "most unfortunate" incident, the chancellor said "it would be desirable" to have Schweitzer "clarify his statement." In fact, Schweitzer had no intention of changing his position, although he recognized Adenauer's discomfort. "He can bear only people who speak according to his opinion," the missionary noted. Antinuclear opinion "creates great worries in him. . . . And in me he sees the big enemy, who . . . contributes to this public opinion."[55]

There were other enemies as well. Although the Christian Democratic government's competitive attitude toward its leading rival, the Social Democratic Party, was hardly surprising, the level of enmity was remarkably high. Through their antinuclear campaign, charged Franz Josef Strauss, the SPD and the

Communists had finally achieved "unity of action." Adenauer, too, contended that SPD policy would destroy NATO and "result in the communization of Europe." For the most part, the government respected the civil liberties of campaigners for nuclear disarmament, but not universally. Charging that the Munich Anti-Atom Committee had been soliciting funds without a valid permit, government authorities had the police search and seize materials in that group's office.[56]

British policy toward nuclear disarmament activism also evinced a remarkable degree of hostility. After the Atomic Scientists' Association produced reports emphasizing the radiation dangers of the H-Bomb and strontium-90, the irate government brought enough pressure to bear on the organization to ensure that similarly controversial statements would no longer be issued—a factor that led to the group's demise. Meanwhile, Nehru's calls for a halt to nuclear testing and for progress on disarmament stirred considerable irritation in official ranks, as did the antinuclear activities of Linus Pauling. In 1958, the Home Office initially refused to grant the American chemist a visa that would enable him to speak at a CND scientists' meeting in London.[57] That May, Prime Minister Macmillan responded tartly to a letter from Russell and an enclosed petition, signed by 618 British scientists, calling for an international agreement to end nuclear testing. Emphasizing the differences between the petition and Russell's letter, which had called on Britain to follow the Soviet Union's lead by halting nuclear testing, Macmillan insisted that Britain could not "simply . . . abandon its contribution to the nuclear deterrent."[58]

The British government also adopted an adversarial approach toward the Pugwash conferences. Convinced that "the Communists" wanted to use the 1958 conference "to secure support for the Soviet demand for the banning of nuclear weapons and thus embarrass Western governments," the British Foreign Office initially sought to play down the meeting by promoting an attitude of skepticism toward it. Nevertheless, the Foreign Office maintained that if—despite these efforts—the conference were held, Western governments should "take whatever steps are open to them to arrange that . . . some of those who participate in it are adequately briefed to argue the Western viewpoint."[59] With this in mind, when the Canadian government failed to torpedo the gathering and, furthermore, Rotblat asked J. D. Cockcroft of the Atomic Energy Authority for his views on who might be invited, Cockcroft and the Foreign Office arranged for the invitation and briefing of the scientist George Thomson. Although Thomson could not attend the entire gathering, he and the Foreign Office agreed that Charles Darwin would be a useful replacement. According to the Foreign Office, Darwin "had a word with us about the agenda." Eventually, one British diplomat noted, "the 2nd Pugwash conference . . . passed off quietly enough, and not too unsuccessfully from our point of view. . . . Departments are now studying the conference papers."[60]

Despite the benign outcome, the British government remained wary. Learning of plans for the third Pugwash gathering, in Vienna, the British Foreign Office warned of the possibility "that this will be more dangerous from our point of view than its predecessors." Communist participants might launch "a major propaganda drive against nuclear weapons," a U.N. commission's report seemed "likely to strengthen the campaign against nuclear tests," and the Austrian president might lend the conference his support. Furthermore, "the organizing committee consists of Lord Russell and Professor Rotblat, both of whom are organizers of the Campaign for Nuclear Disarmament, Professor Powell, who is a Vice President of the World Peace Council, a Russian, and an American, [Eugene] Rabinowitch, who is a critic of U.S. government policy." In these circumstances, the British government regarded the Pugwash meetings as verging on "Communist front gatherings."[61]

Government suspicions mounted to intense hostility in the case of the Campaign for Nuclear Disarmament. In mid-February 1958, the Foreign Office closely scrutinized CND's founding meeting, noting the "variety of political views" and promising a full analysis once its counterintelligence division produced a list of Communists among the participants. On March 3, citing the receipt of hundreds of antinuclear letters, as well as balloting on nuclear disarmament at Oxford and London Universities, the same official warned that "the Campaign for Nuclear Disarmament and allied activities are pressing their case with increasing vigour and success. If we are to maintain the effectiveness of the deterrent and are not to be pushed into disarmament which is either unilateral or unbalanced and not properly controlled, it seems that considerably more will have to be done than hitherto." That same day, in a memo on the "Anti H-Bomb Campaign," the undersecretary of state warned that it "could prove most damaging to the foreign and defense policies of Her Majesty's Government if it were to gain sufficient momentum." As this was a matter "of great urgency," it was necessary "to discuss the appropriate measures for dealing with this development at the highest level."[62]

In fact, discussions at the highest level had already begun in connection with the proposed Aldermaston march. Appraising the demonstration in a memo to Macmillan on February 21, the home secretary, Reginald Butler, noted that he had told Sir Edwin Plowden, chair of the Atomic Energy Authority, that "we ought to take this quite seriously," including "what protective action might be taken at Aldermaston and elsewhere." Five days later, at the prime minister's request, Butler and Plowden met with Macmillan to hammer out a strategy. According to the record of the meeting, Butler "said that the police had the matter in hand" and "did not anticipate great trouble." Furthermore, he did not think the demonstrators had the legal right to "peaceful picketing." Plowden "was not afraid of any disaffection among the workers at Aldermaston," but nonetheless thought he should arrange for the issuance of "instructions to the workers." Macmillan "considered whether he might write to the Archbishop of Canterbury asking him to warn the local clergy not to help the demonstrators, but it was generally agreed that this course would not be very useful." Thereafter, relying on the discussions at this meeting, Plowden told local police officials that the demonstrators had no right to picket, that they were to be kept from using sound vans, and that they were to be barred from walking on the approach road or meeting on the Authority's property.[63]

As the date of the Aldermaston march neared, government planning grew more intense. On March 17, the Aldermaston March Committee added to the distress of the authorities by requesting a site, located on the Aldermaston Housing Estate, where the marchers could "assemble in an orderly manner." Although some distance from the nuclear weapons plant, this site was located on land owned by the Atomic Energy Authority. Reversing his earlier position and arguing that "any meeting held in the vicinity of our establishment to protest against the manufacture of nuclear weapons cannot but be discouraging to the morale of the Authority's staff," Plowden suggested that permission be denied. Macmillan initially thought "it would be wiser to allow this meeting on the space proposed, if it will not be a nuisance."[64] But, eventually, he agreed to bar the marchers from meeting on any land owned by the Authority. The prime minister also prepared the final draft of the statement, issued over Plowden's name, that was distributed to members of the Aldermaston staff. Calling attention to the forthcoming meeting of "advocates of unilateral abandonment of nuclear weapons," it urged employees to "behave with dignity and restraint."[65]

Even though—as Butler reported to Macmillan—"the march to Aldermaston was a peaceful affair which gave rise to no trouble,"[66] the government continued to treat CND and its ventures with disdain. When April Carter, on behalf of the Aldermaston marchers, asked for the opportunity to have a deputation meet with Authority officials, Plowden and Macmillan rejected the request. For its part, the Foreign Office had little use for what one official termed CND's "'holier than thou' approach."[67] In October 1958, CND groups at Greenwich and Blackheath invited the government to send a speaker on nuclear issues to a public meeting they had organized, but the Foreign Office spurned the idea. Years later, Macmillan depicted the new organization as composed of "the more extreme and excitable members of the public," whose fears "the Soviet government exploited . . . with considerable skill."[68]

In addition to opposing antinuclear groups directly, numerous governments sought to counter their influence through management of public opinion. Meeting in November 1954 with Eisenhower, Japanese Prime Minister Shigeru Yoshida declared that because "the Communist peace offensive was being stepped up in Asia," the "free nations" would have "to take the propaganda offensive." Later that day, Yoshida confided to Dulles that he had established a special Cabinet committee to wage the propaganda battle within Japan. Actually, however, the government strategy was less confrontational than cooptive. For example, Japanese officials issued numerous protests against nuclear weapons testing designed primarily to soothe domestic public opinion. On May 3, 1956, a U.S. official explained that the "chief purpose" of the latest Japanese representations against U.S. nuclear tests "is to create a feeling in the minds of the Japanese, particularly opposition members of the Diet [Japan's parliament], that they are actively struggling with this problem and to demonstrate that they are fully responsive to Japanese public opinion." The Japanese ambassador explained that "this is largely a public opinion matter inside Japan."[69] The next day, secretly apologizing for delivering a note calling for a halt to U.S. nuclear testing—and, "off-the-record," expressing his disagreement with it—the Japanese chargé d'affaires depicted it as an attempt to woo parliament and public opinion. Meanwhile, as the U.S. ambassador observed, the Japanese government was doing "everything it can to encourage [the] Japanese press to play down Japanese [public] protest on US nuclear tests."[70]

Much the same pattern continued in 1957–58. Explaining his government's recent critique of nuclear tests, the Japanese foreign minister told Dulles and other U.S. officials in September 1957 that "the Japanese people, old and young, are very sensitive on this question." Therefore, "the Japanese government was placed in a position where it had to lodge a protest" against nuclear testing. "The psychological situation in Japan compels the government to stand for disarmament . . . and against the manufacture and use of all nuclear weapons." He added: "If the question of nuclear testing would be handled awkwardly or unfortunately, the very existence of the [governing] Liberal-Democratic Party might be endangered. Japan has therefore concluded that it had to make a unilateral proposal for the banning of nuclear tests." Similarly, in February 1958, after yet another Japanese government statement deploring nuclear testing, the U.S. ambassador reported that the prime minister secretly told him that it had been "imperative from a domestic political viewpoint" for the Japanese government "to make [the] protest, but that he had not wished to handle it in such [a] way that it would start [a] dispute" with the United States. According to the U.S. embassy, the Japanese government had "developed a compromise position directed at mollifying public opinion without . . . seriously embarrassing relations with the West whose position on nuclear weapons testing many Conservative leaders privately acknowledged as eminently sound and even desirable." By expressing popular fears and framing them "in the most moderate terms which are politically feasible," the Japanese government "has, in effect, become the principal moderating influence on the public."[71]

Other leaders of Western bloc nations also worked to pacify public opinion. In the aftermath of the controversial Bikini H-Bomb tests, the New Zealand government told the press that it was studying their radioactive effects. Privately, the minister of external affairs assured the U.S. ambassador that his government's action "stemmed more from political necessity than from any actual apprehension about the after-effects of the explosion." "With so much talk going on," he explained, "the government politically was not in a position to ignore the matter." At roughly the same time, "in order to counteract" antinuclear agitation, the Italian government laid the groundwork for what the foreign minister called "an all-out campaign to explain American thermo-nuclear policy."[72] The Canadian government, too, sought to develop a satisfactory public relations program. According to a U.S. government report on a 1955 NATO meeting, Lester Pearson, Canada's minister for external affairs, lauded "nuclear strength" as the key to peace while, at the same time, stressing the need to "counter Commie propaganda." Therefore, "however effective [the] nuclear deterrent," NATO leaders "must satisfy [the] public . . . that [a] search continues for alternative means [of] keeping [the] peace." This would "call [the] bluff [of the] professional peace propagandists, who [are] prepared [to] disarm us to [the] last atom bomb." Similarly, at a NATO meeting of February 6, 1958, "there was general recognition [of the] public anxiety over nuclear tests." Consequently, a statement was authorized "to convince public opinion" of NATO's desire to end nuclear testing.[73]

In West Germany, where antinuclear protest raged, Adenauer and his Christian Democratic Party did their best to foster the belief that—despite the nation's nuclear buildup—his government stood foursquare behind nuclear disarmament. In campaign speeches and Bundestag addresses throughout 1957–58, Adenauer asserted his total support for general, controlled disarmament. On August 28, 1957, he promised that, in the event of his party's election victory, it would be "the supreme goal" of his government "to employ the entire political and moral weight of the German nation to work for the success of the London disarmament negotiations."[74] Replying to the antinuclear campaign of the Social Democrats, one of his party lieutenants proclaimed that "the entire German people are opposed to atomic death." The Christian Democrats further developed this theme when—in an obvious riposte to their political rivals—they announced their own Campaign Against Atomic Death in All the World.[75]

However well this approach worked among Germans, it did not fool out-side observers. In the spring of 1957, worried that an end to the London disar-mament negotiations would seriously jeopardize his reelection, Adenauer se-cretly urged U.S. government officials not to break off the talks until after the West German elections. Thereafter, when it came to nuclear weapons, they never doubted his willingness to sacrifice principle for political expediency. Noting that Adenauer had taken the unusual stand of welcoming the Soviet de-cision to suspend nuclear testing in early 1958, the U.S. ambassador wrote this off as "obviously . . . a sop to public opinion. . . . There is no question but that this was a purely tactical move on the Chancellor's part." A month later, re-porting Adenauer's "stress on disarmament," the U.S. embassy again catego-rized it as "a tactical maneuver. After having taken the unpopular decision to equip the German army with atomic weapons, the Chancellor believed some palliative was necessary for German public opinion." With his eye on state elections in which the Social Democrats were relying heavily on the antinu-clear theme, Adenauer "apparently believes that by aggressively taking a posi-tive stand on disarmament he can in large measure reduce the effect of the Op-position's campaign." Indeed, Adenauer "finds general disarmament a conve-niently broad goal in which to take refuge."[76]

If this was the high road toward winning public support, there was also a low one. Mobilizing opposition to the Göttingen appeal, Adenauer arranged for an "enlightenment campaign" by three prominent intellectuals: Pascual Jordan (a physicist), Karl Jaspers (a philosopher), and Helmut Thielicke (a theologian). Jordan was a particularly bizarre character, who viewed radioactive poisoning as nature's answer to the "threatening overpopulation of the earth." The Göt-tingen physicists, he charged, had no competence whatsoever to appraise the nuclear situation, and they had issued an "extreme, one-sided" statement "in sensational form." Meanwhile, Adenauer worked to convince the public of the utter villainy of his political competitors. On August 1, turning the tables, he charged that Social Democratic policy was threatening the London disarma-ment negotiations. At the end of the month, he publicly accused the SPD of "stabbing the London disarmament talks in the back" and, at the same time, working to turn Germany into a Soviet satellite.[77]

Just as determined as its allies to keep public opinion in line, the British government tightly controlled the release of information. In July 1954, recog-nizing that its decision to proceed with an H-Bomb program would offend the consciences of "substantial" numbers of Britons, the British Cabinet opted to keep its plans secret. A Cabinet committee argued that "the man in the street" was "apt to be . . . fearful about comparatively mysterious forces like radioac-tivity" and would "be confused by conflicting scientific opinions." Later that year, the government began pressuring the BBC to keep a full discussion of the H-Bomb off the air. Churchill explained that he did not want disturbing information reaching into "millions of humble homes." In early 1956, the Cabinet decided to avoid an early announcement of British test plans, lest it "stimulate political controversy on the general question of nuclear tests."[78] Much the same attitude prevailed in early 1957, when the home secretary suggested government publication of a pamphlet on civil defense measures against radioactive fallout. "Publication of our pamphlet before our tests will only increase the anti–H-bomb agitation," one of Macmillan's aides objected. The prime minister agreed, delaying the appearance of the pamphlet until late 1958.[79] In October 1957, when a fire broke out at the Windscale plutonium plant in Cumbria, spreading radioactive contamination throughout the region, Macmillan ordered the rewriting of the accident report to conceal the true gravity of the incident.[80]

In early 1958, Lord Hailsham suggested a debate in the House of Lords to clear up the misunderstanding about nuclear fallout; but, for similar reasons, the government dodged it. The home secretary tartly responded: "We certainly don't want such a debate in the Commons. Ergo, we don't want to encourage a debate in the Lords." Hailsham persisted, leading Alec Douglas-Home, the Commonwealth secretary, to tell Macmillan that he had "considerable doubts as to the wisdom of staging a debate." The "reasoned analysis" of the experts "would attract less attention than the examples of strontium percentages in children, cows, sheep and pastures which would be gleefully trotted out by those who are always looking for a good platform to do so and are waiting to stir up the public to put more pressure on the government to abandon tests."[81]

Given these concerns, it was also important to keep nuclear critics from disseminating their views. In April 1954, during an appearance on the BBC's *Panorama* program, Rotblat had minimized the hazards of radioactive fallout produced by H-Bombs. In subsequent months, though, he concluded that the radiation effects were far greater. Learning of Rotblat's plans to publish his new findings, British officials worked hard to dissuade him. Cockcroft warned that the Americans would consider this one more example of a British scientist releasing classified nuclear data. As Rotblat's information was not based on classified material, he decided to deal with this objection by citing a published U.S. government report. From the standpoint of British officials, this was a most unsatisfactory concession, and they were furious at the appearance of his article on radiation dangers in the March 1955 issue of the *Atomic Scientists' Journal* and in the May 1955 issue of the *Bulletin of the Atomic Scientists*. When *Panorama* scheduled Rotblat for another program that August, the BBC—under government pressure—barred his discussing the radiation effects of thermonuclear weapons. In these circumstances, Rotblat refused to participate.[82]

Recognizing, however, that the nuclear issue could not be entirely avoided, the British government sought to put the best face possible on its activities. In March 1955, responding to questions from Parliament, Churchill stated that the British government agreed with the estimate of the U.S. Atomic Energy Commission that all nuclear tests thus far had released radioactive material with the effect of no more than one chest x-ray per person—a statement that might hold up if nuclear fallout spread evenly around the globe, which it did not. In March 1957, as the day approached for the explosion of Britain's first H-Bomb, the foreign secretary secretly warned that "the more extreme elements of public opinion, both at home and abroad," were "mobilizing in opposition." Considering "means of allaying public disquiet," he and the Cabinet agreed on a number of measures. In May 1957, when the government exploded its thermonuclear weapon—in the midst of Japanese, Labour Party, and other protests—it claimed that it had taken meticulous safety precautions and, indeed, had exploded a "clean" Bomb. "Fall-out was insignificant," the British government insisted, "and a survey after a few hours showed very little contamination even below the point of the burst."[83]

Even so, given the continued popular distaste for nuclear weapons, the British government recognized the political necessity of appearing to favor nuclear disarmament. In September 1955, "to allay the fear" that the West was "giving up the quest for a control system which would include the elimination of nuclear weapons," the British government floated the idea that a committee of scientists be appointed to study the issue of inspection and control of nuclear weapons. As an apparent followup, during a meeting at the White House among top U.S. and British officials on January 31, 1956, Foreign Secretary Selwyn Lloyd suggested that it might "be advisable to designate a small group to look into the question of the feasibility of limiting tests," for "the work of such a group might prove to be a useful 'cold war' exercise." The two nations would not "lose anything, even though the result is a determination that limitation is not practical," for it "would put the West in a better posture vis-à-vis public opinion."[84]

On February 1, 1956, Prime Minister Anthony Eden returned to the issue, inquiring—according to government records—"whether, as a move in the cold war, the United States and the United Kingdom could make some offer in regard to an agreement to limit, control, or restrict testing. He pointed out how this would help the domestic United Kingdom political situation in view of the widespread apprehension about radiation effects." The foreign secretary chimed in that "the problem had two aspects—one, convincing the public that there was no harm in the testing, and two, convincing the public that it would be impractical to limit testing." The British government "would like to be able to say that they had studied the issues carefully, had compared notes with the Americans, and had found that the control of tests was impractical." Misunderstanding the British, Lewis Strauss retorted that "if we had acceded to critics in the early 1950s we would be in a bad case now, with fewer weapons and less capable ones." Patiently, Eden explained "that he had no idea of suggesting cessation of testing but merely hoped that we could say something publicly about looking into the possibilities of test regulation." Otherwise, there was a "danger of loss of public support in the United Kingdom" for its testing program.[85]

Throughout 1957, the British government continued its efforts to recapture public support. In March, citing the importance of the nuclear issue in Britain's domestic politics, Macmillan welcomed Eisenhower's proposal to say something positive in their conference communiqué about not testing nuclear weapons beyond the limits of safety. That December, in the context of new Soviet disarmament proposals, the foreign minister suggested relieving Western embarrassment by taking "the political offensive" in this area. "Worried about signs of change in thinking from 'unexpected' people," Macmillan stressed "the need of a constructive counterattack" by proposing "further disarmament negotiations" along Western lines. As the Russians would probably reject inspection, "this would call their bluff" and leave the Western powers as the apparent champions of nuclear disarmament.[86]

Sometimes, British government officials adopted a more aggressive strategy, spearheading a public attack on the antinuclear movement. In a radio broadcast of April 29, 1957, the British foreign secretary argued that "a good deal of the agitation against our tests really does come from the Communist sources which want to prevent Great Britain emerging as a third nuclear power." Addressing the House of Lords that May, Lord Cherwell charged that none of "the ring leaders of this campaign . . . seems to worry very much about the Russian tests." The *Daily Worker* "has been in the forefront of the movement," he said, but "a variegated lot of scientists have also given tongue. Some seem to be ordinary fellow travellers; some are emotional pacifists; some appear to be publicity mongers, and some are just honestly misguided." He added that "this sort of thing becomes particularly obnoxious since various universally respected figures like the Pope and Dr. Schweitzer have been persuaded to intervene. How they could allow themselves to be taken in by the inaccurate propaganda of the friends of Russia is hard to understand."[87]

It took the founding of CND, however, to convince the British government to give top priority to coordinating its own propaganda campaign. Four days after CND's inaugural meeting, in the midst of plans for the first Aldermaston march, the home secretary suggested to Macmillan that "some counter-propaganda would put this pacifist proposal in its true light." At the Foreign Office, one anxious official remarked that "the Ministry of Defense are themselves considering what more can be done, but it may be that the Foreign Office also should press for more action. . . . Probably what is needed is not more statements by Ministers, but by independent scientists and military commentators." Another recommended "briefing a few 'trusty' correspondents" and "getting them . . . on the B.B.C." It was necessary to have "the government's position . . . stated as repeatedly and widely as the thesis of the Nuclear Disarmers."[88] Convinced that the situation was serious, Macmillan promised Plowden in mid-March to do his best to "steady public opinion" on the nuclear question. Later that month, with the prime minister's approval, the home secretary arranged a meeting which brought together Macmillan, Plowden, Sir Norman Brook, and himself to discuss "how we can better organize the anti-antinuclear campaign."[89]

As a follow-up to the gathering, Macmillan sent a memo on March 24 to the member of his Cabinet in charge of public relations—Charles Hill, chancellor of the Duchy of Lancaster. The memo read:

It is most important that we should find some way of organizing and directing an effective campaign to counter the current agitation against this country's possession of nuclear weapons. This is a question on which the natural emotions of ordinary people would lead them to be critical of the government's policy, and to accept without question or reason the arguments which our opponents use. . . .

The question is how to . . . exploit the differences between those who oppose our policy.

Mr. Butler has been asked by the B.B.C. to take part in a discussion on this in Panorama in a week's time, and I have asked him to accept. . . . Could we not get the I.T.A. [Independent Television Authority] to take the initiative, but perhaps in a more positive way, by finding suitable people who would speak in support of the U.K.'s possession of nuclear arms? Sir Ivone Kirkpatrick ought to enjoy working out a plan for this.

There are no doubt many other ways in which we could press the campaign. . . . Can we persuade some influential publicists to write articles? Are there any reliable scientists? Or Church of England Bishops? . . .

Will you please look into this question, in consultation with the Conservative Central Office, and let me have a report as soon as possible.[90]

Responding to the prime minister's directive, Hill developed a very vigorous program. In a memo to Macmillan of April 2, he reported: "Active steps are being taken to identify the intellectuals, Churchmen, scientists and others who support the government in the controversy over this country's possession of nuclear bombs." Once identified, these persons "will be discreetly approached with a suggestion that they should give expression to their views in one way or another. The B.B.C. and the program companies will be confidentially informed and the suggestion made that these people should be invited to give expression to their views on sound and television." Meanwhile, "Canon Mortlock, Treasurer of Chichester Cathedral, and Sir Kenneth Grubb, both of whom I have seen, are helping in the theological field." Macmillan scrawled on the memo: "This is good."[91]

On April 22, 1958, Hill reported new progress in the "H-bomb campaign" to Macmillan. "Steps have been taken to gather together a group of distinguished churchmen and Conservative backbenchers to organize the public expression of support for the government's attitude," he wrote. Canon Mortlock and William Deedes "are convening a meeting within the next few days to start the ball rolling. The next step will be a larger meeting to which selected bishops and Members of both Houses will be invited. The objective is a steady stream of spoken, printed and broadcast contributions. With the confidential help of Sir Henry Willink and others," Hill was "considering how best to secure parallel action by scientists and other intellectuals." Once again the prime minister expressed his satisfaction at the measures taken.[92]

In May, Hill worked hard—and with some effect—to counter the petition, drafted by Russell and signed by British scientists, criticizing nuclear weapons testing and calling for an immediate international agreement to ban it. "The press reaction to the Russell letter and petition was better than I feared," Hill reported happily to Macmillan on May 7. "After consulting Sir Harold Himsworth, I put out a good deal of guidance on Thursday night, at a special meeting of the Lobby and through other contacts." As a result, "Friday's press played the story down, giving as much prominence to your letter as to Russell's effort. The Sunday press ignored the petition," while "the supplementary Russell letter aroused little interest in yesterday's press."[93]

Hill also visited and had "a long talk" with Lord Adrian, former president of the Royal Society and then master of Trinity College, where Russell's antiwar statements had resulted in his dismissal from his lectureship decades before. Adrian agreed that "the moderate view"—as Hill put it—"seldom finds expression and he gave me the impression that he will help to stimulate such expression." Hill "thought it best not to press him too hard and he promised to think over what I said." Meanwhile, Hill was "continuing such personal contacts in Cambridge, Oxford and London" in the hope of stimulating pro-government statements. Unfortunately, he added, "there is little chance of organized action. Many dons prefer to smile indulgently at those who have fallen for Russell and leave it at that." On the other hand, work with the press was proving rather efficacious, and "we are more than usually busy 'killing' stories."[94]

Throughout 1958, much British government effort continued to go into assuring the public that nuclear fallout was really quite harmless. The Foreign

Office responded to the flood of mail opposing nuclear testing with soothing responses that downplayed the radiation hazards.[95] Meanwhile, fearful that a forthcoming U.N. study dealing with nuclear radiation would heighten opposition to its nuclear testing program, the government developed an extensive program to manage public response to it.[96] From the official standpoint, the program proved a success. On August 13, Hill reported to the prime minister that "the publicity exercise on the United Nations radiation report went reasonably well," thanks to the statements of three experts. "There was a welcome emphasis on man-made radiation other than Hydrogen-bomb tests. At least, the press promptly passed to other things." Nevertheless, there remained "a danger that the publication of the Medical Research Council's comments . . . may 'reactivate' the subject and with this is mind, my office is keeping in touch with the M.R.C.'s press section."[97] In Britain, as elsewhere, containing the movement had become a full-time occupation.

Policymakers and Protest

The U.S. Government Confronts the Movement, 1954–58

> At the bottom of the disturbance there is a kernel
> of very intelligent, deliberate propaganda.
>
> Lewis Strauss, 1958

The burgeoning nuclear disarmament movement proved particularly irritating to the U.S. government. Engaged in a nuclear buildup as part of its "New Look" national security policy, the Eisenhower administration deeply resented challenges to its role in the nuclear arms race. Of course, the United States had a long tradition of civil liberties, freedom of association, and citizen participation in public affairs. Nevertheless, in the context of a bitter Cold War struggle against the Soviet Union and its Communist allies, U.S. officials felt considerable alarm as public sentiment began to shift against nuclear weapons. Consequently, during the mid- to late 1950s, they had little tolerance for organizations or individuals fostering antinuclear ideas, at home or abroad. Where they could, they took action against the critics. In addition, they developed a formidable propaganda program to bring public opinion into line with Washington's view of the world.

U.S. Policymakers and the Bomb

From the advent of the Eisenhower administration, nuclear weapons provided the centerpiece of its national security policy. Anxious to perfect the H-Bomb and to construct intercontinental ballistic missiles that could deliver nuclear warheads against Communist targets, the administration sponsored an extensive buildup of the U.S. nuclear arsenal. Its "New Look" replaced conventional military forces with nuclear striking power and facilitated highly publicized threats of "massive retaliation" against Communist aggression.[1] Furthermore, key U.S. policymakers championed not only the maintenance of nuclear weapons as a deterrent, but their use in combat. At a National Security Council (NSC) meeting in August 1953, the new chair of the Joint Chiefs of Staff (JCS), Admiral Arthur Radford, complained that the United States was "holding back on their use because of our concern for public opinion" and that they should be employed "in the event of a major conflict." According to the records of an NSC meeting two months later, Dulles "repeated his often-expressed view that somehow or other we must manage to remove the taboo from the use of these weapons." The following spring, he told the North Atlantic Council that the United States "considers that the ability to use atomic weapons as conventional weapons is essential for the defense of the NATO area. . . . Such weapons must now be treated as in fact having become conventional."[2]

This emphasis on employing nuclear weapons continued to serve as a central component of the Eisenhower administration's national security policy. In November 1954, Secretary of Defense Charles Wilson secretly reported that the nation's top military leaders had concluded that "NATO forces in Europe can provide a successful forward defense only through the integrated use of atomic weapons from the outset of hostilities." Early the following year, after discussing the matter with the president, Dulles again declared that the United States would use nuclear weapons in the event of a war. In 1956, Eisenhower informed Radford that if a war "grew to anything like Korea proportions, the action would become one for use of atomic weapons." Ten days later, in meetings with military leaders, Eisenhower remarked that, in "local wars," he favored use of "tactical atomic weapons," an action which he did not think would "trigger off a big war."[3] Moreover, if a "big war" occurred, Eisenhower had every intention of drawing on the full power of the U.S. nuclear arsenal. The United States, he argued, must be willing to "push its whole stack of chips into the pot."[4]

These considerations fed into NSC 5707/8, the official statement of U.S. national security policy. Signed by the president on June 3, 1957, the document declared: "It is the policy of the United States to place main, but not sole, reliance on nuclear weapons; to integrate nuclear weapons with other weapons in the arsenal of the United States; to consider them as conventional weapons from a military point of view; and to use them when required to achieve national objectives." In addition, "the United States should continue efforts to persuade its allies to recognize nuclear weapons as an integral part of the arsenal of the Free World and the need for their prompt and selective use when required."[5]

On a number of occasions, the administration gave serious consideration to launching nuclear attacks. In February 1953, Eisenhower and the NSC discussed the possibilities of using atomic bombs against Chinese troops in Korea.

Dulles helped scotch this idea by noting what he called the "Soviet success to date in setting atomic weapons apart from all other weapons," although he added that the U.S. government "should try to break down this false distinction." The idea was revived in December, when the JCS, initially supported by Eisenhower, argued that if the Chinese Communists resumed hostilities in Korea, the United States should respond with a full-scale nuclear war against China. Dulles objected strongly to this proposal, insisting that it would lead to war with the Soviet Union and horrify U.S. allies—a contention bolstered when the idea was broached to the startled British and French governments. Consequently, in January 1954, the NSC adopted a compromise position. In the event of a new Communist attack in Korea, the United States would undertake "offensive air operations employing atomic weapons against military targets in Korea, and against those military targets in Manchuria and China" used to support the Communist attack.[6]

The administration continued serious planning for nuclear war during the French crisis at Dien Bien Phu, Indochina, in 1954,[7] and again during the 1955 crisis over China's offshore islands. "If we defend Quemoy and Matsu," Dulles stated bluntly, "we'll have to use atomic weapons. They alone will be effective against the mainland airfields." Moreover, he thought there was "at least an even chance that the United States will have to go to war." On March 15, 1955, the secretary of state announced publicly that the United States was ready to employ tactical nuclear weapons in the event of war in the Formosa Straits. Queried about this nuclear threat at his press conference the following day, Eisenhower declared: "Yes, of course they would be used." He saw "no reason why they shouldn't be used just exactly as you would use a bullet or anything else." When asked if the United States itself would not be destroyed in a nuclear war, the president replied coolly: "Nobody in war or anywhere else ever made a good decision if he was frightened to death."[8]

Given the increasing dependence of U.S. policymakers on nuclear weapons, nuclear disarmament had little appeal. In secret planning meetings, Defense Department officials argued that unless war itself were eliminated, nuclear disarmament was unwise and should not be promoted by the United States. Writing to Eisenhower in mid-1955, Defense Secretary Wilson "strongly" endorsed the views of U.S. military leaders that "dealing with arms regulation in advance of the settlement of the major political issues" would endanger U.S. national security.[9] Dulles, who brought to his post of secretary of state a long-term skepticism about arms control and disarmament, adopted a similar position, arguing that "only after considerable progress" had been made toward settling other issues with the Soviet Union "would there appear to be any likelihood of securing an agreed disarmament program which would safeguard our interests."

In early 1954, he told the British that it was "impossible to devise any adequate system of inspection and control until the Soviet system itself was changed." Therefore, "any discussion of abolition or control of atomic weapons at this time . . . probably had significance only in the propaganda field." Speaking to Japanese officials in the summer of 1955, Dulles argued that nuclear weapons "are here to stay," and "even if it were possible to abolish them, as the Soviet Union would like to do, it is doubtful whether abolition would be desirable." He stated bluntly: "If atomic weapons were banned, the chief deterrent against Communist aggression would vanish."[10]

Other key U.S. officials also had little interest in promoting nuclear disarmament. The new chair of the U.S. Atomic Energy Commission (AEC), Lewis Strauss—or "the Admiral," as he liked to be called—exercised immense influence over U.S. nuclear policy, invariably in the direction of accelerated military activity. An inveterate foe of disarmament, Strauss argued that "the only thing that retires a weapon is a superior weapon." In early 1956, he maintained that "this nonsense about ceasing tests (that is tantamount to saying ceasing the development) of our nuclear weapons plays into the hands of the Soviets."[11] Despite his own military background, Eisenhower lacked this unwavering commitment to the Bomb and occasionally expressed his wistful hope that it could be banished from international affairs. But he also argued—as he did in early 1954 at a meeting with Dulles, Strauss, and other top national security officials—that "in the present state of world affairs," it was "impossible that any effective agreement toward this end could be worked out." Indeed, the record of this same gathering indicated general agreement that the U.S. government "would not be drawn into any negotiations" for "the control or abolition of nuclear weapons."[12]

The Pressures of Public Opinion

At the same time, U.S. officials felt hard-pressed by the rising tide of antinuclear sentiment. On March 29, 1954, three days after the disastrous U.S. H-Bomb test at Bikini, Dulles made a frantic telephone call to Strauss, warning him of "the tremendous repercussions these things have. . . . The general impression around the world is [that] we are appropriating [a] vast area of the ocean for our use. . . . There is panic re[garding] the fish being contaminated. . . . Some feel the British Isles could be wiped out, and so they better make a deal on the best terms possible with the Russians." Something had to be done to "moderate [the] wave of hysteria. It is driving our Allies away from us. They think we are getting ready for a war of this kind. . . . They might go into the Soviet-proposed agreement that we will each agree not to use" the

Bomb. So shaken was Strauss by the furor that, within administration circles, he began to contend that, to further embarrass the United States, the Russians might "fill the oceans all over the world with radioactive fish. It would be so easy to do!"[13]

Confronted by reports of a "strong world-wide reaction to the test programs and numerous official suggestions that they be halted," top U.S. policymakers held frequent crisis conferences. According to the record of one, an NSC meeting of May 6, 1954, Dulles suggested that the administration might want to propose an international moratorium on nuclear testing, which "would place us in a much better position from the point of view of propaganda and our posture vis-à-vis the free world." Eisenhower expressed "with great emphasis the necessity we were under to gain some significant psychological advantage in the world. Everybody seems to think that we're skunks, saber-rattlers and warmongers." Although Strauss and Wilson opposed even considering such an idea, Nixon rejoindered that the United States was "taking a 'hell of a licking' on the propaganda front. An offer of this sort would certainly help." Dulles lamented that "we are losing ground every day in England and in other allied nations because they are all insisting we are so militaristic. Comparisons are now being made between ours and Hitler's military machine." Speaking with what the minutes called "great conviction," Dulles "insisted that we could not sit here in Washington and develop bigger bombs without any regard for the impact of these developments on world opinion." Taking the side of the secretary of state, the president opined that the world was "much more terrified now" than at the outset of the nuclear arms race.[14]

From the administration's standpoint, the situation went from bad to worse. A National Intelligence Estimate of June 14, 1955, appraising "the effects of increasing nuclear capabilities on public attitudes and national policies," concluded that "there is increased public pressure on governments to find some means of international disarmament, and especially some means of insuring that nuclear weapons will not be used in war." Furthermore, "as nuclear capabilities further increase, and the possibilities of mutual devastation grow, the tendencies to caution and compromise presently discernible in non-Communist countries will probably be accentuated. Aversion to risks of war, pressures for disarmament, and fear of general war will almost certainly be more marked than now." When CIA director Allen Dulles read these conclusions to the NSC meeting of July 14, 1955, the president remarked glumly that "the people of the world" were "getting thoroughly scared of the implications of nuclear war" and "running for cover as fast as they could go."[15]

These observations seemed to be borne out in the following years. A February 1956 memorandum by the NSC Planning Board declared that "increasing

U.S. and Soviet nuclear capabilities have produced growing apprehension about the catastrophic nature of general nuclear war." That same month, the secretary of state told an NSC meeting "that we must . . . realize that today the world is afraid of nuclear war and its consequences, and that this state of mind led many people and many governments . . . to go for superficial panaceas . . . such as the 'ban the bomb' idea." The United States, "as the last best hope of the world for our way of life," would have to explain why these panaceas" will not work, and then to provide affirmative, saleable, understandable, and workable substitutes for such panaceas as 'ban the bomb.'" Despite the ensuing U.S. government explanations, however, Dulles fretted about the opposition to U.S. nuclear weapons of the Asian "masses" and Strauss worried about the antinuclear attitudes of Americans.[16]

Nailing Stevenson, Placating the Pope

The administration reacted with considerable hostility to Adlai Stevenson's call for a halt to nuclear testing. Although some State Department officials argued, in April 1956, that a private briefing might lead the Democrat to "keep quiet on this subject," Dulles adamantly vetoed the idea. The administration wanted no rapprochement with Stevenson. In early October, when the Democratic candidate renewed his critique of nuclear testing, Strauss insisted that the time had come to "nail him." Stevenson's election, the AEC chair told Eisenhower, "would seriously endanger our country. We can make this clear to the public." Indeed, nuclear testing could "be made into the most telling issue of the campaign."[17] Intensely angered by the broaching of the testing issue, Eisenhower publicly assailed Stevenson for his antinuclear stand. Privately, the president dismissed him contemptuously as "that monkey."[18] Meanwhile, Strauss lined up prominent scientists to endorse the president's policy and to criticize the Democratic candidate. When an occasional scientist refused to lend himself to this enterprise, Strauss filed a caustic memorandum recording this perfidy.[19]

The attack on Stevenson picked up steam after October 18, when Soviet premier Nikolai Bulganin secretly sent a letter to Eisenhower criticizing the administration's position on nuclear testing and implicitly endorsing that of the Democratic candidate. Dulles told Strauss that he was indignant at the note's tone and content, but Strauss responded that he "regarded it as in the nature of a windfall in view of the headway which Stevenson had made with the issue during the campaign." Indeed, "if carefully handled, the note could be turned to considerable advantage." Strauss worked with Dulles and, later, with the president and other administration officials, helping to produce a withering public response. Attacking the Soviet Union for interfering in U.S. politics, Eisenhower's rebuttal—together with Bulganin's letter—helped to undermine Stevenson's campaign. Several days later, Eisenhower assailed Stevenson more directly, charging that the Democrat advocated "disarmament without inspection." Peace, the president maintained, necessitated U.S. possession of "the most advanced military weapons."[20]

U.S. officials adopted a more conciliatory approach toward Pope Pius XII. In June 1955, contending that the pope's statements on disarmament "have been possibly of more help to the neutralists in Europe than to American foreign policy," several AEC officials proposed to Strauss that he arrange to call on the pontiff in Rome to promote the U.S. position on nuclear weapons.[21] This suggestion gathered momentum after the pope deeply embarrassed Strauss and the AEC by using his December 1955 Christmas message to call for an end to nuclear testing. Complaining that Thomas Murray, a holdover Democratic commissioner on the AEC, was "the source of the pope's misunderstanding," Commissioner Willard Libby drafted a soothing memo for Pius XII, arguing that his Christmas message had overstated the radiation hazards. Although the State Department remained uneasy about this approach or a visit to Rome, Strauss was determined to persist. In mid-January 1956, he dispatched the memo to the Vatican with Monseigneur Sheehy, a prelate whom he considered "a very good friend in the hierarchy."[22]

The AEC's wooing of the papacy continued throughout 1956. On April 17, Strauss finally visited the pope at the Vatican and discussed with him at great length the nuclear weapons issue. In contrast to the U.S. "endeavor to end" the arms race, Strauss declared, the Soviet Union not only accelerated its development of nuclear weapons, but worked "to weaken the free world by clever propaganda designed to induce us, unilaterally, to abandon atomic armament. . . . One of the methods they employ against the United States is an exaggerated description of the results of the testing of weapons by us." Furthermore, "a propaganda argument largely used by the Communists and repeated by those whom they have duped, is to the effect that these tests have endangered human life by reason of the radioactivity which they have produced. It is this, in particular, upon which I wish to reassure Your Holiness," he said. That day, and in follow-up communications sent to the Vatican for the rest of the year, Strauss insisted that nuclear tests produced a "very small fraction of the normal radioactive background in which we all live." This increased radioactivity, he insisted, was entirely harmless from the standpoint of human health and genetics. According to Strauss, the pope told him that his work was "important and valuable and that it had . . . his blessing."[23]

The Subversive Dr. Schweitzer

U.S. officials had greater difficulty formulating a strategy to deal with Albert Schweitzer. Given Schweitzer's remarkable popularity, U.S. political leaders had paid court to him for years. In January 1955, Eisenhower sent greetings to Schweitzer on his eightieth birthday. "Your spirit and work have been an example and inspiration to all of us," the president wrote in this message, also distributed as a White House press release. That same month, Dulles told Schweitzer that his "contributions to the peoples of the world" were "indelibly written into the annals of our civilization." For this reason, Schweitzer's public call for an end to nuclear testing, delivered through his 1957 radio broadcast, was particularly galling. As Strauss told an AEC committee that spring, Schweitzer's appeal was "a body blow to the testing program."[24]

Naturally, in the view of administration officials, everything possible had to be done to counteract its damaging effects. Libby, on whom Strauss leaned heavily when dealing with nuclear critics, prepared a public rebuttal to Schweitzer. Carefully crafted and tactfully deferential to the revered missionary, it contrasted the "extremely small" risks from atmospheric nuclear testing with "the terrible risk of abandoning the defense effort which is so essential under present conditions to the survival of the Free World." In the United States, Libby's letter attracted far more attention than did the "Declaration of Conscience." Overseas, the AEC response also secured wide distribution, due to the vigorous efforts of the U.S. Information Agency (USIA).[25]

Behind the scenes, AEC officials were simmering. In a memo to Libby of April 26, 1957, Everett Holles, the AEC's public relations director, noted that Cousins—who was "hostile toward all of our studies and statements regarding fall out"—had complained to CBS about the limited coverage given Schweitzer's declaration by the American mass media. "It is a curious coincidence," Holles remarked acidly, "that the New York Daily Worker on Friday accused the radio-TV networks of 'suppressing' the Schweitzer story." Fortunately, though, the Communist action had backfired, for it had "influenced the networks, or at least CBS, to give minimum regard to Cousins' agitation." The AEC, however, also played a role in the CBS decision to drop the issue. The network had asked if it could count on the AEC, including Libby, for cooperation if it decided to set aside a time for a special program on the Schweitzer statement. Holles, however, declined to answer, noting only that "since Dr. Libby had made a respectful, scientific reply to Schweitzer I was not sure that he would want to carry on the matter over the air."[26]

Other U.S. government agencies also went to work on the Schweitzer case. That July, the Central Intelligence Agency presented the State Department with copies of four letters Schweitzer had written to Gunnar Jahn and to Kaare Fostervoll, director of Radio Oslo, regarding arrangements for the release of his appeal. The State Department later shared these letters with Strauss and other officials at the AEC. Given the CIA's subsequent refusal to declassify these letters or the accompanying memo, it remains unclear how the CIA obtained copies of Schweitzer's private correspondence. Schweitzer, however, believed that people—in his opinion, journalists—were tampering with his personal mail at the post office in Lambaréné, a conclusion echoed by his biographer. Consequently, Schweitzer eventually advised both Jahn and Fostervoll to address all correspondence pertaining to his antinuclear activities to a member of his hospital staff.[27]

U.S. officials viewed Schweitzer's radio broadcasts of late April 1958 as particularly nefarious. Obtaining copies of Schweitzer's address a few days in advance of the broadcasts, the U.S. ambassador to Norway claimed that it "generally supports [the] Soviet propaganda line." Although, in a subsequent telegram, she revised her message to delete this phrase, she later warned that "large portions of the talks are critical of the United States, and in many instances coincide with the Soviet line." Once again, there was consternation at the AEC, with the commissioners rallying around the idea of having Schweitzer rebutted "by a distinguished public figure with a large popular following." Libby agreed to prepare the script.[28] On May 2, Dulles reported that the Schweitzer talks had been "reviewed by interested agencies." Although it would "be unwise for government officials [to] answer Schweitzer directly," he argued, private scientists should "challenge his remarks," perhaps in the *Bulletin of the Atomic Scientists*. U.S. officials also agreed that it would be "counter productive" for "anyone to stimulate any reports to [the] effect [that] Schweitzer's broadcasts were ghost written." In Norway, however, at the request of the AEC, the U.S. ambassador investigated this appealing possibility. Drawing on information provided by a friendly local radio official, she cabled on May 12 that Schweitzer had sent Jahn his talks "in manuscript form, handwritten in 'old fashioned' German" and that they were subsequently translated by Norwegian radio. Apparently, then, there were no foreign agents at work—or, at least, none employed by countries other than the United States—just the determined, eighty-three-year-old Schweitzer.[29]

Even so, U.S. officials searched zealously for evidence of Communist subversion or other malfeasance. On May 2, 1958, just two days after the broadcasts concluded, Strauss had the FBI launch an investigation of the Schweitzer Fellowship, the U.S.-based organization that had raised thousands of dollars over the years to maintain Schweitzer's hospital at Lambaréné. In three separate reports, J. Edgar Hoover concluded that the Fellowship was just what it purported to be: a charitable organization that funded this humanitarian work and nothing more.[30]

Meanwhile, cognizant of Schweitzer's latest appeal but unaware of Washington's attitude toward him, the U.S. consul general in the Congo, James Green, reported in late May that he would be visiting Schweitzer in June. Would the State Department want him to "deliver greetings" from Eisenhower or Dulles or to "summarize current thinking [on] suspension [of] nuclear testing"? In response, Acting Secretary of State Christian Herter warned that Schweitzer's articles and speeches had been "highly critical [of] United States nuclear test policy" and had been "closely adhering [to the] Communist line. Your visit would probably not convince [the] aging Schweitzer [of] his error and might provide ammunition for [a] declaration [that a] United States official [was] trying [to] bring pressure [to] bear on him." Therefore, Herter advised Green to "exercise extreme caution and under . . . no circumstances discuss nuclear policy or disarmament." Furthermore, there would be "no message of greeting from [a] high United States official."[31]

Despite these admonitions, when Green visited Lambaréné in mid-June, he engaged in extensive discussions with Schweitzer about nuclear testing and nuclear weapons—discussions he justified by pointing out that Schweitzer was the one who had introduced the subjects. In these conversations, summarized in a lengthy memo to the State Department, Green found Schweitzer "extraordinarily alert," eloquent, and quite sincere. When discussing the terrible effects on nature produced by years of nuclear weapons explosions, tears came to the doctor's eyes. Green concluded, unhappily, that "although the Department understandably resents the fact . . . that Dr. Schweitzer is giving support to the Communist line, it should not be concluded that Dr. Schweitzer has any sympathy for Communism or any desire to support the Soviet Union against the Free World. On the contrary," Green argued, Schweitzer was "acting on the basis of deep humanitarian convictions. These convictions happen—unfortunately—to coincide with current Soviet policy."[32]

Scientists and Public Affairs

U.S. officials also resented the activities of the atomic scientists' movement. The *Bulletin of the Atomic Scientists* "has not been objective," Strauss complained in 1953—a jeremiad he repeated throughout the decade. Berating the *Bulletin*'s editor, Eugene Rabinowitch, in the spring of 1957, Strauss denounced the journal's "hypocritical attitude . . . of pretending to be objective" while publishing articles that portrayed U.S. nuclear policy in an unfavorable light.[33] Eisenhower, too, complained about "the extent to which scientists have suddenly become military and political experts." Scientists, the State Department told planners for the second Pugwash conference, should examine scientific issues but not political ones. Brooding on the issue in late 1958, Strauss argued that "scientists have an inescapable desire to become involved in domestic and international politics and . . . the prestige which they enjoy as scientists gives their political views a weight beyond their real worth." They were "as frequently wrong as other men, but apt to be wrong in more critical areas and where the damage from being wrong is more irreparable."[34]

Convinced that many leading atomic scientists had the "wrong" political attitudes, U.S. officials sometimes gave them rather rough treatment. Beginning an investigation of Albert Einstein in 1950, the FBI gathered fifteen hundred pages of material on his political activities, including articles he had written for the *Bulletin of the Atomic Scientists* and other publications on nuclear arms controls and world government. Not until the scientist's death in 1955 did the FBI close the Einstein case. In 1956, the State Department decided that the "political views" of Marc Oliphant, Australia's most famous physicist and critic of nuclear weapons, were sufficiently dangerous to deny him a visa to enter the United States for a scientific meeting. The following year, the British government, under pressure from U.S. security officials, mysteriously refused to renew the consultancy at Harwell of the physicist Rudolf Peierls, a former president of Britain's Atomic Scientists' Association. When Peierls reapplied years later, his consultancy was restored.[35]

The most famous U.S. "security" case of the decade involved Robert Oppenheimer, a leading U.S. physicist who had chaired the AEC's General Advisory Committee from 1946 to 1952. Shortly after taking office, Strauss ordered Oppenheimer's security clearance revoked and had the AEC attorney draw up a list of charges against Oppenheimer that included the contention that the physicist had "strongly opposed the development of the hydrogen bomb." To remove the implications of disloyalty that now surrounded his name, Oppenheimer decided to appeal the action. A hearing ensued before the AEC's Personnel Security Board, which ultimately ruled against him. Prominent among the Board's contentions was its finding that Oppenheimer's lack of enthusiasm for the H-Bomb was "sufficiently disturbing" to raise doubts whether his reappointment "would be clearly consistent with the best interests of security." In June 1954, the AEC voted to uphold the Board's decision, but downplayed the H-Bomb issue and focused instead on Oppenheimer's alleged character defects. Although the administration later denied that Oppenheimer's views had anything to do with purging him from government service, Strauss confided at the time to the FBI that if the AEC lost its case against the scientist, the nation's atomic energy program would fall into the hands of "left-wingers" and scientists.[36]

The AEC's insistence on making agreement with the administration's nuclear policy the test of loyalty flared up again the following year, in the case of Hermann Muller. A Nobel Prize–winning geneticist and renowned specialist on the effects of radiation, Muller was asked by scientists at the AEC to present a paper on the genetic effects of radiation at a U.N. Conference on the Peaceful Uses of Atomic Energy scheduled for August 1955. On April 25, 1955, however, he alarmed U.S. government officials by presenting a paper at the National Academy of Sciences on the genetic dangers of radiation. In this paper, Muller argued that the demands of national security justified the testing of nuclear weapons, but also stated that explosions of such weapons caused genetic damage and, therefore, great care should be taken to guard against exposure to the radiation they produced. In early June, within days of this paper's publication in the *Bulletin of the Atomic Scientists*, Strauss ordered Muller's new paper withdrawn from the U.N. conference agenda. In late July, the AEC finally informed Muller that his paper had been rejected, blaming this on U.N. officials. Muller, though, attended the gathering anyway, and—when word of his treatment leaked out—received a prolonged, standing ovation from his outraged scientific colleagues.[37]

Although Muller contended that the paper had been canceled because its conclusions were "disagreeable to one or more persons influential in the A.E.C.," U.S. officials staunchly denied this. In September, after a *Washington Post* reporter phoned the AEC about the incident, a Commission press statement declared that Muller's invitation had been withdrawn because his paper contained "material referring to the nonpeaceful uses of atomic energy, namely, the bombing of the Japanese city of Hiroshima." Few took this explanation seriously, for Muller's paper—subsequently published in the *Bulletin of the Atomic Scientists*—referred to the bombing of that city very briefly and in the context of radiation effects. In fact, a chronology of events secretly prepared by the AEC reveals that, in early June, AEC officials decided that the real question at issue was "the loyalty of Dr. Muller."[38]

But what, exactly, did that mean? Libby, a fierce anti-Communist, told Muller's biographer years later that he had been horrified by evidence gathered by the FBI that Muller had held Communist views decades before. Therefore, he did not want the geneticist to represent the United States at the U.N. conference. Libby also knew, though, that for some time Muller had been a bitter critic of Communism, including Soviet genetics policy under Trofim Lysenko. Would Muller's past have mattered if he were not making embarrassing statements about radiation? At the time, Libby secretly told Strauss that Muller's paper was "out of bounds." The AEC, said Libby, had "pointed to the fact" that radiation from tests is "small . . . compared to normal dosages and therefore the prophets of doom had better check their reasoning." But "Muller apparently hasn't noticed this." Strauss, too, worried about the policy implications of Muller's work. Referring in his memoirs to a figure who must have been Muller, Strauss wrote that the "statements of a very distinguished geneticist, who contended that damage caused by even the smallest increase in radiation could result in an accumulation of undesirable mutations in the human race," had produced "the most disquieting opposition to the test program." Indeed, even Muller's reference to the Hiroshima bombing probably triggered alarm bells in the minds of U.S. officials, for—in their view of things—who would mention it except a subversive? As in the Oppenheimer case, AEC officials easily conflated dissent with disloyalty.[39]

Although the Oppenheimer and Muller cases received considerable attention, the AEC's vendetta against Ralph Lapp went largely unnoticed. Beginning in 1949, Lapp—a physicist once employed by the Manhattan project and other U.S. government agencies—became a popular writer on nuclear issues. His revelations about U.S. nuclear policy, coverage of the *Lucky Dragon* incident, and, particularly, his criticism of the AEC, made him *persona non grata* in official circles. Together with the journalist Stewart Alsop, he was chided in 1952 by AEC chair Gordon Dean, who told them of his "deep concern about their writings in this field."[40] Lapp's activities obsessed Strauss, who—apparently with the assistance of FBI surveillance operations—even read the physicist's private mail.[41] In June 1955, the AEC chair sent a lengthy report on Lapp's purported journalistic indiscretions and other alleged "security" lapses to Senator Clinton Anderson, chair of the Congressional Joint Committee on Atomic Energy. That same month, Strauss also helped block the appearance of a story by Lapp in the *New York Times*.[42] Moreover, at Strauss's request, his special assistant, Manuel Dupkin, reviewed the transcript, word for word, of Lapp's statements on a "Face the Nation" television and radio broadcast, only to report his "regret that I cannot find a single thing which Dr. Lapp said which was not . . . permissible." That summer, however, Dupkin did manage to convince the managing director of the Uranium Association of America not to hire Lapp as a technical adviser.[43]

In the following years, the AEC continued its efforts to destroy Lapp's credibility and his livelihood. In October 1956, Strauss suggested that "in view of Governor Stevenson's citation of Ralph Lapp as his great scientific authority on weapons tests, fallout, etc.," Libby "give consideration as to whether or not some scientists might not characterize him for the fraud he is." Meeting with Rabinowitch in April 1957, Strauss complained that the *Bulletin of the Atomic Scientists* "published articles by Lapp, who . . . was simply a pamphleteer living on sensationalism."[44] The following month, the Commission's staff prepared a long list of embarrassing questions to be addressed to the physicist when he appeared before U.S. Representative Chet Holifield's Special Subcommittee on Radiation on June 5. Subsequently, Bryan LaPlante, who handled congressional relations for the AEC, reported gleefully to Strauss that "our friends—Cole, Hickenlooper, and Van Zandt—did a beautiful job on Dr. Lapp (with the info)." Lapp "was properly 'drawn & quartered' and very much discredited." Nevertheless, the physicist did not fade away. In July, citing another letter critical of nuclear testing, Dupkin exploded to Strauss: "Here is Lapp again. All of our troubles from Lapp are our own fault; we should have done a long time ago what I asked you to do. Everett [Holles] feels strongly about this, too. How about considering my plan again?" Unfortunately, Dupkin's "plan" and Strauss's response can only be conjectured.[45]

From the standpoint of U.S. officials, if Lapp was a thorn in the flesh, Linus Pauling was a dagger to the heart. Unlike virtually all other leading U.S. critics of the Bomb, Pauling actually had associated with Communist-led peace campaigns (as well as with non-Communist ones) and this fact—combined with the extraordinary effectiveness of his antinuclear activities—made him a leading target of the U.S. government. Insisting that Pauling followed "the Communist Party line," the State Department denied him a passport to travel abroad for scholarly purposes on three occasions, only to retreat in embarrassment after late 1954, when Pauling received the Nobel Prize in Chemistry.[46] AEC officials, too, were venomously hostile, circulating reports on Pauling drawn up by the House Committee on Un-American Activities and keeping watch lest Pauling obtain a security clearance. The appearance of Pauling's Appeal by American Scientists on June 3, 1957, was the final straw. At his press conference two days later, Eisenhower stated caustically: "Scientists that seem to be out of their own field of competence are getting into this argument, and it looks like almost an organized affair." Listeners took this to mean that the president considered Pauling and other critics of the Bomb integral parts of a Communist conspiracy, an assumption that helped trigger a wave of public attacks along these lines.[47]

Actually, the president's comments reflected a high-level conspiracy against Pauling. The day after Pauling's petition appeared, Strauss reported to a confidant on his efforts "to offset the propaganda from Pauling, Mueller [sic] and their followers," citing in this regard an article in *U.S. News & World Report*, which charged that the test ban movement was "Communist-inspired." That same day, AEC staff members also arranged for Republican legislators to place in the *Congressional Record* a newspaper article that denounced Pauling as "an old hand" at promoting Communist front campaigns. On the day of Eisenhower's press conference, Strauss gave the president a brief memo providing the basis for his subsequent remarks. It included the observations that the scientific "pressure has at least the earmarks of organization," that "many of those opposed to testing are out of their fields of scientific competence," and that "they include many who have publicly urged our unilateral disarmament years before the fall-out issue was raised."[48] Actually, only that day did Strauss tell Libby to "get the list of signers to the Pauling petition and mark those who are out of their fields of competence," and not until a week later did the AEC inform the White House press secretary that "many" of the two thousand signers of the Pauling petition were not specialists in the field. The fact that the AEC's conclusions preceded its investigation, however, did not faze Strauss, who also saw to it that Pauling's petition to the president received no more than a perfunctory response.[49]

The AEC and its allies kept up the drumbeat against Pauling in the following months. In July 1957, Representative Sterling Cole—one of the Republicans Strauss frequently provided with useful tidbits—publicly charged that although U.S. nuclear weapons were "humane," the Communist attempts to fan the "flames of misconception" were becoming "astonishingly" successful. Writing to the chair of the Republican Party that September, Strauss deprecated the signers of the Pauling petition and, especially, its initiator. Pauling, declared Strauss, was "a man whose affiliations have been notably with the extreme Left," and the petition, "of course, received a very wide circulation throughout the world by all Communist publications." Several days later, acting on a confidential tip from a friendly FBI agent, Strauss held up an unclassified research contract on which Pauling was scheduled to serve as the senior investigator.[50] In early 1958, Edward Teller, writing in *Life* magazine, assailed Pauling's worldwide petition. Never quoted or discussed in detail, its statements were described as "at best half-truths" which "are misleading and dangerous. If acted upon, they could bring disaster to the free world." Nuclear test radiation "need not necessarily be harmful," Teller argued, "indeed, may conceivably be helpful."[51]

Meanwhile, other government bodies joined the campaign against Pauling. On June 6, 1957, the Senate Internal Security Subcommittee announced that it was subpoenaing Pauling to inquire into the role of Communist organizations in his petition drive. However, when Pauling publicly responded that he would welcome a chance to discuss the dangers of nuclear weapons, the subcommittee retreated. On June 19, 1957, J. Edgar Hoover provided the White House with a report, "Communist Exploitation of Radiation 'Fall-Out' Controversy," prepared the previous week. In his cover letter, Hoover placed Pauling at the top of the list of those "familiar names in the field of science frequently associated with communist front activities" who are "creating fear, misunderstanding, and confusion in the minds of the public on this issue." The following year, the FBI produced another report for the White House on the Communist role in the fallout controversy. Bolstered by citations of *Reader's Digest*, it charged that "precisely because the tests are in this Nation's vital interest, communist propagandists have sought to magnify the danger of fall-out to an alarming degree." Pauling, the report charged, "has an extensive record of communist front activity," and "a number of the individuals in the United States and abroad who signed the petition have similar records." Pauling twice tried to meet with Eisenhower to discuss his petitions, but—not surprisingly—was rebuffed.[52]

The Perils of Pacifism

The administration also regarded pacifist agitation against the Bomb as a subversive activity. In the spring of 1954, when the St. Louis WILPF chapter wrote to the president to protest atmospheric nuclear testing and to advocate disarmament efforts through the United Nations, the White House promptly alerted the FBI. In July 1957, Non-Violent Action Against Nuclear Weapons notified the AEC of its plans to protest nuclear tests at the Nevada test site, and this, too, led top AEC officials—including Strauss—to pass along the names and information to the FBI for investigation. The FBI, of course, had long been hot on the trail of pacifist troublemakers—planting informers at their meetings, gathering antinuclear literature, and leaking derogatory information about them. After the 1955 civil defense protest in New York City, Hoover made an unsuccessful attempt to have the Justice Department prosecute the Catholic Worker movement for sedition. In 1957, citing the WILPF's criticism of nuclear testing and its call for disarmament agreements, Hoover informed the U.S. attorney general and the AEC's director of security that the women's group constituted a potential threat to U.S. internal security.[53] Alerted that November by the Washington police department to plans by the WILPF, the War Resisters League, and the FOR to hold a "Prayer and Conscience Vigil" of five to fifteen people in the nation's capital to protest the development and use of nuclear weapons, Hoover fired off a memo on this to the attorney general, the State Department, the AEC, the Secret Service, the intelligence agencies of the armed forces, and to the special assistant to the president for national security affairs. The Defense Department also fretted about the Prayer and Conscience Vigil, especially the fact that the pacifist participants were distributing copies of a mildly antiwar speech by a U.S. Army general.[54]

FBI reports on pacifist activities were not always totally disparaging, but usually had a negative twist. On January 30, 1958, Hoover informed the White House and the attorney general of plans by the American Friends Service Committee to launch a petition campaign urging the U.S. government to halt nuclear tests scheduled for later that year. Hoover correctly identified the AFSC as "a pacifist organization whose members strive for peace and good will among all nations." At the same time, he warned that its national director, Norman Whitney, had signed a number of petitions in cases involving subversives, including a "Christmas amnesty petition for Smith Act prisoners." Similarly, the FBI never quite managed to deny the pacifist motivations of the FOR; it merely charged that the group's secretary, A. J. Muste, had "long fronted for Communists."[55]

In these circumstances, administration officials gave pacifists a wide berth. Attempting to meet with the president in 1954 for a discussion of H-Bomb testing, a small delegation representing the Society of Friends had no success.[56] In December 1957, when Albert Bigelow was asked by the New England office of the AFSC to present a petition to the president calling for an end to nuclear testing, the Friends Committee on National Legislation tried repeatedly, and unsuccessfully, to arrange an appointment for Bigelow with some responsible person at the White House. Arriving in Washington, Bigelow phoned the White House five times to arrange such an appointment. Each time he spoke with a secretary who said she would call him back as soon as she had arranged it. She never did. In response to his last phone call, she suggested he leave the petition with a policeman outside the White House gate. Bigelow was "deeply troubled by the incident" and, as it turned out, for good reason. A White House aide, Maxwell Rabb, had deliberately arranged the rebuff. He later explained: "I suspected that, while this group is a well-known and respected agency, it was doing pro-Communist work, probably unwittingly."[57]

The full dimensions of the pacifist menace became apparent in early 1958, as Bigelow and other activists announced their plans to sail the *Golden Rule* into the U.S. nuclear testing zone in the Pacific. The secretary of state, the AEC, and U.S. Navy officers immediately began conferring on how to counter the threat. The U.S. commander-in-chief in the Pacific warned that this group of "Communists or misguided humanitarians" hoped "either to stop tests by preventing us from firing . . . or if we did fire and killed a few people, that the result, publicity wise, would create additional anti-atomic test support." Dulles worried, on the one hand, that closure of a large area on the high seas would "have serious international repercussions," while, on the other, too lenient a policy toward protesters might encourage participation by Japanese antinuclear groups. Eventually, the administration decided to have the AEC issue a regulation proscribing entry to the test zone by U.S. citizens and to press the Japanese government to deter participation by Japanese groups. Meanwhile, U.S. intelligence agencies swapped data on Bigelow, including information on his private telephone conversations and legal plans.[58]

Consequently, when the encounter occurred, U.S. officials acted promptly and decisively. Arresting the crew of the *Golden Rule*, the government sent them to jail for sixty days. Earle Reynolds, who unexpectedly took up their cause and sailed his ship, the *Phoenix*, into the test zone, received a two-year jail term. Reynolds never served it, however, because an appeals court eventually threw out the AEC regulation as invalid. Appearing on a "Face the Nation" broadcast over CBS television on May 4, 1958, Strauss commented: "At the bottom of the disturbance there is a kernel of very intelligent, deliberate propaganda. I can't put my finger on it—I can't identify it. But we see that a great deal of money is being spent on it." Asked if there were not some genuine pacifist motivation, too, the AEC chair conceded reluctantly: "There is a certain amount of pacifist sentiment in it." But, he added, "when this comes at a time after the Russians have finished their tests and we are about to begin ours . . . it runs up a signal that warrants inquiry."[59]

To Strauss's dismay, antinuclear activists had some inquiries for him. Only a few days after his television comments, a group of pacifists picketing the new AEC headquarters at Germantown, Maryland, walked into the lobby of the building and asked to speak with the commissioners. Until they had that opportunity, they announced, they would remain there and, furthermore, would conduct a fast. To avoid the adverse publicity that seemed likely to result from arrests, the AEC decided to let them stay and even to provide them with cots, blankets, a telephone, and restrooms. Although the pacifists praised the AEC for its generosity, they continued to assert that they would not leave before meeting with the commissioners. Finally, after a week, Strauss—perhaps realizing that a Red revolution was not imminent—agreed to talk with them. The ensuing conversation, which focused on the hazards of nuclear testing, was polite, even amicable, although there was no meeting of minds. Strauss recalled that, at the end of the encounter, the pacifists "said some friendly words, admonished me to beat swords into plowshares, and departed." Strauss found them "respectable, terribly earnest, and completely impractical." In his memoirs, he did not call them subversives, though he did portray them as hypocrites.[60]

Norman Cousins and SANE

Assisted by allies on the White House staff, Strauss also reacted with hostility to Norman Cousins. In 1951–52, Eisenhower and Cousins had exchanged warm letters.[61] Moreover, Cousins's editorship of a major magazine, the *Saturday Review*, provided him with some degree of access to the new president. Nevertheless, since nuclear-related matters were invariably referred to Strauss, the AEC chair managed to undercut Cousins's influence. In August 1956, when Cousins wrote twice to Eisenhower about the nuclear issue, Strauss apparently played a role in drafting Eisenhower's cool response to the first letter and in the decision to ignore the second.[62] In January and February 1957, Cousins twice sought to arrange a meeting with the president to report on his conversations with Schweitzer, only to have the White House staff deliberately sabotage the project.[63] When Cousins sent a lengthy letter to the president questioning him about the derogatory statement made at his June press conference about the Pauling petition, Strauss warned Eisenhower that a serious answer would establish a bad precedent and a potentially dangerous "exchange of correspondence with the publisher of a magazine." Accordingly, the president chose the route of a perfunctory response, accompanied by a story from *U.S. News & World Report* implying that critics of nuclear testing were allies or dupes of the Soviet Union.[64]

Although Cousins kept trying, the pattern continued. On June 27, 1957, the *Saturday Review* editor proposed that Eisenhower hold a discussion of nuclear testing with a group of distinguished scientists who, unlike the men with whom the president had recently met, were not participants in the government's nuclear weapons program. Eisenhower liked the idea, but Strauss objected vehemently to the president's giving way to Cousins's "fall-out propaganda." Such a meeting would undermine "very eminent men who are devoting their talents and reputations to a vital, though presently unpopular, service to the government," Strauss insisted. Furthermore, "with a few exceptions, the persons he has proposed are individuals who . . . endorsed Adlai Stevenson's position on atomic weapons." Consequently, Eisenhower rejected this proposal as well.[65] On July 15, Cousins tried once more, this time pointing to recent correspondence he had had with Nehru emphasizing the widespread opposition in Asia to nuclear testing. Would not the president make "an historic speech which is directed to all peoples in their status as fellow human beings rather than as members of this or that nation"? This brought an end to the correspondence. Working together, Strauss and the president's secretary decided to stop acknowledging receipt of Cousins's letters. "He writes to me too," Strauss noted, adding mockingly: "What a busy man!"[66]

Cousins's major venture, the National Committee for a Sane Nuclear Policy, also made no headway with the administration. In July 1957, Norman Thomas wrote to the president, informing him that "a rather notable group of persons" had met recently to seek "some first step" toward "universal, controlled disarmament" and had concluded that the "minimum first step" was "monitored suspension of nuclear tests." Thomas now proposed a meeting with some of them: "at least one outstanding scientist, two or three leading churchmen, Charles E. Wilson, Clarence Pickett, Norman Cousins, and myself." Although Eisenhower was willing to speak with them, Dulles vetoed the idea, contending that publicity about the meeting might undermine disarmament discussions then under way.[67] In November, Cousins sent the president a letter enclosing the copy for SANE's first newspaper advertisement, and soon thereafter, Thomas proposed that the president meet with SANE's leaders at the White House. Typically, Thomas was shunted off to see Strauss, with whom he conferred in February 1958. The AEC chair told Thomas about "the impossibility of a foolproof monitoring of tests" and the allegedly small risk from fallout, while Thomas continued to argue that "the advantages of . . . monitoring suspension of tests outweigh the disadvantages."[68]

Although this meeting and its follow-up seemed cordial enough, below the surface the chill ran deep. In 1958, the FBI began extensive investigations of SANE's national organization and local chapters. These investigations never concluded that SANE was anything other than a citizens' organization promoting international agreements for nuclear disarmament. Nevertheless, the FBI warned that American Communists were interested in infiltrating the new group because its antimilitary work allegedly paralleled the party line. Meanwhile, Strauss channeled useful information on the purported need for continued nuclear testing to Victor Lasky, a right-wing journalist affiliated with the American Committee for Liberation. In April 1958, Lasky reported to Strauss that he and other patriots had met at the Waldorf Towers "to discuss how we can combat the propaganda of the Committee for a Sane Nuclear Policy—the Linus Pauling–Norman Thomas–Norman Cousins outfit which appears to have tremendous funds at its disposal." Working with C. D. Jackson (recently the administration's expert on psychological warfare) and Theodore Streibert (the former director of the USIA), they were putting together a statement to be signed by influential persons emphasizing "the necessity of continued U.S. nuclear testing."[69]

The Foreign Threat

Increasingly aware of foreign antinuclear activities, the U.S. government regarded them with an attitude that ranged from suspicion to enmity. A world leader like Nehru, of course, could not be easily dismissed, and, at the United Nations, Henry Cabot Lodge Jr., the U.S. ambassador, avoided a direct rebuff to the Indian prime minister's 1954 call for a standstill in nuclear testing. Nehru's suggestion, he said tactfully, "is entitled to respectful attention."[70] On the other hand, U.S. officials deliberately ignored protests against nuclear testing from overseas groups regarded as Communist-led. Sometimes, indeed, they directly challenged such groups. In Italy, "perturbed about the effect of Communist propaganda" against the Bomb, U.S. officials told their Italian counterparts of their hope that "we would all work together to set up effective counterpropaganda."[71]

Attitudes toward nonaligned disarmament groups fell somewhere in between. Interested in reaching "the *New Statesman*'s audience and the many in Europe who share its leftist views," Dulles produced a lengthy statement for that British publication. This came in response to Bertrand Russell's "Open Letter to Eisenhower and Khrushchev," which had appeared in the November 23, 1957, issue.[72] Thereafter, however, U.S. diplomats submitted such negative appraisals of the burgeoning nuclear disarmament campaign in Britain that the door closed on any further efforts to court this constituency. Having met with a small antinuclear delegation, an official of the U.S. embassy in London was not impressed. It consisted of pacifists, leaders of the Aldermaston march, and "pacifist or extreme left-wing Labour MPs." The embassy concluded: "There is little doubt of the earnestness of many members" of CND, the Direct Action Committee, and similar groups, but "with the possible and rather marginal exceptions of Lord Russell and J. B. Priestley, none of the leaders of these organizations has national standing or reputation." From Glasgow, where disturbing signs of antinuclear activism had appeared, the U.S. consul general commented reassuringly that "the thinking people" still believed "that the only difference between conventional weapons and nuclear ones really is a question of degree."[73]

In West Germany, where the antinuclear campaign seemed for a time capable of toppling the Adenauer government, U.S. officials took it more seriously, although no more sympathetically. Even before that campaign's inception, U.S. officials had regarded the antimilitary stance of the Social Democrats with dread. In 1956, U.S. Ambassador James B. Conant reported that an election victory by the Social Democrats and the Free Democrats the following year "would be really disastrous" and could "only be regarded with horror."[74] When these two parties and other groups embraced antinuclear issues in 1957, the U.S. government did what it could to ensure Adenauer's re-election. "The Chancellor is . . . perplexed about how to handle during the election period the atomic problem," Dulles told Eisenhower in early May 1957. "The issue is being exploited by the Socialists, and the scientists and the churchmen, particularly Evangelical, are making life difficult for him." Therefore, Dulles had suggested to Adenauer that it "would be a good idea if we could have stationed at our Embassy for the next few weeks someone knowledgeable in these matters who could help meet the emotional appeals which are becoming the battle cry of his political opposition." Adenauer had "warmly welcomed" the suggestion, and Dulles urged Eisenhower to speak to Lewis Strauss about making appropriate arrangements. The president apparently did so, for at a meeting later that month with Adenauer, Strauss told the Chancellor that an AEC official would travel to Bonn to assist him and that he could also draw on the services of an AEC representative in Paris.[75]

U.S. government partisanship continued during West Germany's ensuing parliamentary election campaign. On September 2, 1957, with the elections only two weeks off, Dulles suggested to Stassen that "before we agreed to any complete break" in the London disarmament negotiations, "the matter be discussed with Adenauer." Although Adenauer wanted to avoid a breakdown of the talks for domestic political reasons, measures to prolong them "should not seemingly be related to the German elections." Shortly thereafter, when the Christian Democrats triumphed at the polls, Dulles confided that Adenauer's "great victory was indeed a matter of much satisfaction to us." The new U.S. ambassador, William Bruce, reported happily that the SPD's failure to benefit from its "atomic death" theme "seems to reflect a healthy recognition of [the] fact that atomic weapons are one of [the] unpleasant facts of life" with which Germans would have to live.[76]

Unfortunately, the Social Democrats failed to share this healthy recognition, leading to further recriminations by U.S. officials. The "atomic weapons issue" was "not taken lightly" by the German public, Bruce lamented in March 1958, and the "SPD will undoubtedly be able [to] keep its emotional Campaign Against Atomic Death in [the] spotlight." Nevertheless, the "clear and courageous stand" of the government was garnering popular support, unlike the position of the Social Democrats, with their "demagogic speeches" and "transparent" tactics. That April, the U.S. consul general in Hamburg warned that "by means of scare tactics and emotional appeals, the anti-atomic weapon issue is being kept before the public constantly"; there was "a continuous barrage of propaganda in SPD controlled newspapers and neutralist publications." Reporting on the SPD convention in late May, the U.S. embassy characterized it as "a discouraging spectacle," indicative of the SPD's "largely negative and opportunistic course." The embassy found it "noteworthy that among the new members of the [party's] executive committee is Gustav Heinemann, outspoken neutralist and pacifist. He . . . can be expected to add his negative influence in foreign policy." Indeed, "the SPD showed itself discouragingly ready to abide by its long-standing sterile opposition policies," including placing "all its eggs in the anti-atomic basket."[77]

From the standpoint of U.S. officials, the most serious threat emerged in Japan. With the *Lucky Dragon* incident, the U.S. ambassador reported, the "government and people cracked." A "period of uncontrolled masochism ensued, as [the] nation aided by [an] unscrupulous press, seemed to revel in [its] fancied martyrdom." This "breakdown," he argued, "was triggered by [a] small group [of] Japanese scientists and doctors, many of whom were fuzzy-minded leftists, pacifists, neutralists. . . . All of them had vistas of nation-wide publicity at home and world-wide scientific prominence as exclusive proprietors of [the] world's first hydrogen-bomb patients." Although an "assessment of [the] lasting damage done by [the] incident must be incomplete," the "position of neutralists, pacifists, feminists, and professional anti-Americans . . . has been strengthened." According to Dulles, who forwarded this message to the president, Eisenhower found it "of great interest and value from [the] standpoint of policy formulation." Nine days later, the acting secretary of state added his own warnings. "The Japanese are pathologically sensitive about nuclear weapons," he told the president. "They feel they are the chosen victims."[78]

Strauss, characteristically, assumed that a situation like this could only result from a Communist plot. The *Lucky Dragon*, he told the White House press secretary, was really a "Red spy outfit," part of a "Russian espionage system." At the AEC chair's request, the CIA conducted a special investigation of this possibility. Reporting back to Strauss on April 29, 1954, the CIA declared that "our inquiry indicates that there is no evidence, direct or otherwise, that the ship was in or near the danger area for the purpose of observing or recording the explosion." Indeed, "the ship and its crew were neither equipped nor qualified for such activities." In addition, "there was no evidence, direct or otherwise, of a propaganda purpose; rather . . . the evidence indicates that the ship had a legitimate fishing mission and its presence in the area was not unusual." Finally, there was no evidence "that Communist propaganda exploitation was planned beforehand"; even the Japanese Communist Party was "caught off guard by the incident."[79] Nevertheless, Strauss continued to maintain, as he did as late as 1966, that the *Lucky Dragon*'s exposure to fallout "was no accident," for the captain of the ship "was in the employ of the Russians."[80]

In this context, U.S. officials consistently worked at cross purposes with the Japanese antinuclear movement. Although Dulles agreed to meet with an opponent of nuclear testing who was dispatched as a special envoy of the Japanese government, he and other U.S. officials deliberately kept aloof from citizens' antinuclear efforts. Responding to letters criticizing nuclear testing from a Nagasaki peace group and from the Japanese labor federation, the State Department insisted that nuclear explosions were vital for the "defense of the Free World." For its part, the AEC brushed off Japanese complaints about radioactive contamination by stressing its "pride" in "the high degree of safety with which the American nuclear tests have been conducted."[81] Meanwhile, behind the scenes, Strauss told authors to ignore the contention of the "propa-

gandists" that a crew member of the *Lucky Dragon* had died of radiation exposure. Learning of plans by a Hiroshima peace group to invite the pilot of the
plane that had dropped the first atomic bomb to the 1958 World Conference
Against Atomic and Hydrogen Bombs, the State Department had the U.S. Air
Force pressure him to decline the offer.[82]

Managing Public Opinion

From the standpoint of administration officials, it was essential not only to contain nuclear disarmament activism, but to win the battle for public opinion. "No
national strategy to meet the Soviet threat can be successful without the support of the American people," the NSC insisted in early 1955. "During a time
of increasing Soviet atomic power, the determination of U.S. citizens to face
the risks involved in carrying out such national strategy will be of increasing
importance." Similarly, Dulles argued in 1956 that when it came to the nuclear
arms race, the U.S. government would have to give "highest regard to world
opinion." Concerned with the "world-wide public relations problems" faced
by U.S. nuclear weapons policy, the AEC proposed a major gearing up of "U.S.
propaganda."[83]

One way to influence public opinion was to limit the information released
about U.S. nuclear weapons policy. Conferring with the AEC chair on May 27,
1953, Eisenhower suggested that "thermonuclear" be left out of AEC press releases and speeches. "Keep them confused as to 'fission' and 'fusion,'" the
president advised. That same day, at a meeting of the NSC, Robert Oppenheimer—not yet purged from government service—proposed what he called a
"policy of candor": having the president enlighten the public as to the dangers
of the nuclear era. But this idea had little appeal. Defense Secretary Wilson argued that "the proposal was more likely to frighten people than to reassure
them," a position seconded by Treasury Secretary George Humphrey. The acting secretary of state warned that such a statement would "intensify" the "increasing feeling among Western European peoples that anything was better
than atomic warfare." Taking the floor once again, Wilson argued that this was
not "the right moment to acquaint the American people with the facts." Given
these concerns, "Operation Candor" and similar proposals made little headway.
At another NSC meeting that October, the president stated that although he was
quite willing to employ nuclear weapons, he could not speak bluntly about the
matter. "Nothing would so upset the whole world as an announcement at this
time by the United States of a decision to use these weapons," he explained.[84]

The same administration emphasis on avoiding discussion of unpleasant
realities emerged in the context of a report, "The Human Effects of Nuclear

Weapons Development," prepared by social scientists under the direction of the Civil Defense Administration. At an NSC meeting in November 1956, Eisenhower expressed his pleasure at the report's concrete proposals for readying the U.S. public for nuclear war. But others mounted a strong counterattack. In February 1957, Strauss insisted that "the only thing we could expect from the kind of large-scale propaganda program recommended . . . would be, on the one hand, panic among our people, and, on the other, terrific pressure" to embark on a large, useless fallout shelter program. George Humphrey argued that "it would do no good for the Administration to scare the public to death," while Dulles contended that the program would create "a mob psychology which would compel us against our better judgment to accept a dangerously faulty disarmament program or else to undertake a vast and costly shelter program." The secretary of state warned against "creating a world opinion that might force us to do things which we do not want to do." By August 1957, Eisenhower, too, had concluded that "if we attempted to inform the public on the human effects of nuclear weapons by dramatic actions, we would create hysteria." Therefore, the NSC did no more than approve a much watered-down version of the program.[85]

Anxious about the public response to nuclear weapons, U.S. officials frequently sought to conduct their operations under a blanket of secrecy. At a conference with the president in March 1956, Undersecretary of State Herbert Hoover Jr. spoke out against allowing the U.S. press to cover the event. "Every bit of emphasis and publicity on tests," he maintained, "brings closer the time when we will be faced with the necessity of discontinuing them or losing our allies." In the spring of 1958, the administration kept its nuclear test series in the Pacific entirely secret. The American people did not learn of it until May 7, nine days after it had begun, when U.S. Representative Charles Porter of Oregon forced its disclosure.[86] Even USIA polls on foreign attitudes toward nuclear weapons remained under cover. The director of the USIA polling remarked of a 1955 survey: "The confidential character of our sponsorship is important. This questionnaire . . . would be embarrassing to us if its U.S. sponsorship were publicized by anti-American elements."[87]

From the standpoint of U.S. officials, statements on the hazards of fallout could prove particularly embarrassing. In 1954, Admiral Paul Foster of the AEC warned that release of a public report in this regard would undermine support for the administration's defense strategy in both Europe and the United States. Although Foster thought a televised fireside chat by Eisenhower might strike a happy balance between hysteria and reality, Wilson strenuously objected to any presidential discussion of fallout hazards. Meanwhile, the State Department opposed release of an AEC report on fallout, arguing that it would

stimulate pacifism, especially in Germany, and lead to additional tensions between the United States and Japan. The AEC report received two further setbacks in February 1955. The deputy director of the Bureau of the Budget contended that "one certain consequence" of its release would be "an increased
demand for the banning of atomic weapons." Moreover, the president of the
Coca Cola Company, whom Eisenhower considered the "best public relations
man" in the country, cautioned that it would create adverse reaction in foreign
lands. When the AEC finally issued a statement, on February 15, 1955, it was
deliberately limited and—to minimize popular fears—distorted.[88]

Release of an international study promised to be even more counterproductive. A U.N. investigation of fallout, warned the assistant secretary of defense, "would place the United States in a position of recognizing and admitting that its weapons tests are endangering the lives and health of the peoples of
other countries." This was no idle fear, for pressure was growing in the General
Assembly for some kind of international study. To counter this threat, in May
1955 Lodge proposed that the U.S. government ask the world organization to
collect and disseminate national studies. This would "divert attention from our
own tests . . . and at the same time avoid the pressures that are increasingly
building up for a moratorium on tests." Noting that Sweden intended to propose U.N. action to investigate the radioactive effect of nuclear tests and that
India planned to raise this question in the U.N. Disarmament Commission,
Dulles supported this idea, for it "would be in our interest to take the initiative
in the UN on this subject and guide it in a direction not harmful to us." Strauss,
however, responded that "any report by an international body . . . would undoubtedly be adverse to our possession of nuclear weapons." Indeed, making
"an investigation on an international scale would lead us into dangerous paths
where demands for cessation of nuclear tests and the disclosure of information
concerning our weapons would possibly result." Realizing that Strauss had
misunderstood him, Lodge explained that the United Nations would not conduct an "investigation" or render a "judgment," but merely gather national
studies, including one commissioned by the AEC. Eventually, then, even
Strauss approved Lodge's modest proposal.[89]

It would have been particularly embarrassing if full information about radiation hazards had been available to Americans. During the 1950s, the AEC
conducted seven major nuclear test series at its Nevada test site, with nearly a
hundred atmospheric nuclear explosions. Thanks to changing wind currents,
poor weather forecasting, or general carelessness, nearly 30 percent of the radioactive debris drifted over the towns to the east, which housed a population
of some 100,000 people. Residents of St. George, Utah, recalled that a "pink
cloud" would hang over them, sometimes for more than a day, while they

worked amid the fallout, walked in it, breathed it, washed their clothes in it, and ate it. "Even the little children ate the snow," recalled one resident. "They didn't know it was going to kill them later on." During subsequent decades, leukemia and cancer rates soared in the counties adjoining the nuclear test site, as they did among the 250,000 U.S. soldiers exposed to U.S. nuclear tests, among the 600,000 American workers in nuclear weapons plants and laboratories, and among the hundreds of thousands of Americans living in communities adjacent to these plants. At the Nevada test site, miners recovered instruments from tunnels strewn with radioactive debris. Workers, without respirators to shield their lungs, cleaned up radioactive rubble at ground zero. "What did we know?" a former miner, afflicted with cancer of the bone marrow, asked years later. "We believed it was safe. They even told us we could take our clothes home, with all that stuff on it," to "wash . . . with the family clothes."[90]

Although U.S. officials did not know everything about the insidious effect of nuclear fallout, they knew a great deal more about it than they admitted at the time. During 1953, for example, the AEC commissioners grew so alarmed at the high levels of radioactivity produced by their recent nuclear tests that they ordered special studies of the deaths of thousands of nearby sheep and of other disturbing phenomena. But safety monitors, some of whom found startling levels of radioactivity, were told by an AEC official: "Let's cool it—quiet it down." Otherwise, "there might be repercussions and they might curtail the program which, in the interest of national defense, we can't do." Accordingly, reports were changed, readings lowered. AEC commissioners devoted themselves to dealing with the "public relations aspects of the tests." Some officials did propose that the AEC consider alternatives to continental testing, but Strauss—concerned that he might lose the ability to conduct further tests in Nevada—prevailed on Eisenhower to continue the test series there. Moreover, when local ranchers brought suit against the government for damage to their herds, the AEC convinced the court that the sheep had died from natural causes. Some twenty-seven years later, after the AEC's own secret studies were released and brought before the same judge, he reversed his earlier decision, citing "conduct by the government that amounted to a species of fraud upon this court." He concluded that this fraud was perpetrated for the purpose of "advancing the perceived interests of the United States in the unimpeded testing of nuclear weapons."[91]

The AEC continued its cover-up in subsequent years. During the nuclear test series of 1955, some newspapers and politicians from the area, growing restive, suggested for the first time that it might be a good idea to explode nuclear weapons elsewhere, perhaps in the Pacific. Meeting on February 23,

1955, the AEC commissioners were deeply concerned. "This will set the weapons program back a lot to go to the Pacific," remarked Libby. "People have got to learn to live with the facts of life, and part of the facts of life are fallout." Strauss quipped, sarcastically: "It is certainly all right, they say, if you don't live next door to it." "Or live under it," the AEC general manager chimed in. Commissioner Murray, usually at odds with his Republican colleagues, set the AEC's course for the future: "We must not let anything interfere with this series of tests—nothing." And nothing did. Although Strauss secretly conceded that the nuclear tests "apparently always plaster" St. George with fallout, they continued, with the usual soothing assurances from government experts. On March 10, 1955, the day after the explosion of a large nuclear device, a local newspaper carried a headline reading: "Fallout? 'Not Enough to Worry About,' Says AEC." Testifying at congressional hearings on April 15, Strauss maintained that "so far as we are aware, no civilian has ever been injured as a result of these tests."[92]

The "downwinders," then, received little candor or, for that matter, consideration, from the administration. In 1980, a congressional study concluded that the U.S. government had "failed to give adequate warning to the residents living downwind from the test site regarding the dangers posed by the radioactive fallout," that "the radiation monitoring system established by the government . . . was deficient," and that the government "falsely interpreted and reported radiation exposure rates so as to give an inaccurate estimate of the hazards." In addition, the report noted, the government "knowingly disregarded evidence which questioned the accuracy of the government's measurements of radioactivity emitted from the test site as well as the adequacy of the then-employed radiological safety standards," and that exposure to radioactive fallout "was, more likely than not, responsible for the serious adverse health effects suffered by the downwind residents."[93]

U.S. officials also recognized that nuclear fallout posed a threat to the health of the overall population. As the U.S. Justice Department finally conceded in November 1985, during a civil suit before a federal district court in California, "the government has been aware of the hazards of radiation since the inception of the nuclear weapons program." During 1957, the AEC's advisory committee on biology and medicine produced a report for the commission that noted that, since 1954, the strontium-90 content of the soil had grown markedly. In addition, the strontium-90 concentration in milk had "increased steadily with time." Nuclear testing, the AEC committee estimated, would contribute to a small increase in leukemia deaths and would cause genetic damage to the world's population that, over the course of time, could "be large in absolute terms." Indeed, at the very time that government specialists labored at convincing the public that fallout was relatively harmless, they were working to perfect a nuclear weapon that would kill enemy soldiers through radiation.[94]

Determined to reassure an uneasy citizenry, U.S. officials generated a plethora of distorted information. From all the nuclear tests likely in a human being's life span, they argued, that person would absorb less radiation than from a luminous dial on a wrist watch. The AEC asserted that the danger from U.S. nuclear tests was "no worse than having a tooth x-rayed." In an article put together in cooperation with the AEC, one popular magazine noted that "some experts believe that mutations usually work out in the end to improve species." Meanwhile, just in case a few doubts lingered, Commissioner Libby announced the good news that the AEC was studying the use of special fertilizers to neutralize radioactivity in the soil and special pills to lessen the body's absorption of strontium-90 in case of a nuclear attack. "Fallout is nothing more than particles of matter in the air," noted a 1955 civil defense pamphlet. And although these particles are radioactive, "RADIOACTIVITY IS NOTHING NEW. . . . THE WHOLE WORLD IS RADIOACTIVE." Americans could take shelter from a nuclear war by hiding in "an old-fashioned storm cave or root cellar," which one could stock with food "as Grandmother did." In civil defense training films, Americans would emerge from their shelters a short time after a nuclear attack with their clothes only slightly crumpled. A calm father figure would urge his family to "wait for orders from the authorities and relax."[95]

Naturally, government officials made every effort to steer the mass media in the right direction. The AEC kept a watchful eye on the press, producing stories with a pro-nuclear slant. Assisted by the AEC, *U.S. News & World Report* turned out articles like its 1955 classic, "The Facts about A-bomb 'Fall-out': Not a Word of Truth in Scare Stories over Tests." In May 1958, Strauss wrote to the editor of the *Richmond Times Dispatch*, complaining about the "substantial" amounts of money spent by nuclear disarmament groups—60 cents for postage in the case he cited—on mailing material to newspapers. "There is probably a Pulitzer Prize waiting for some reporter who will discover whether or not the pump is being primed from Soviet sources," the AEC chair suggested helpfully. The following month, when Strauss discussed a forthcoming U.N. report on radiation with his British counterpart, the AEC chair proposed that they "take positive action to try to guide press comments on to the right lines."[96]

Sometimes, government officials covered unpalatable realities with clearcut lies. Despite the fact that the *Lucky Dragon* had been sailing outside the official danger zone for the 1954 Bikini tests when it was showered with nuclear fallout, U.S. officials continued to assert that it was located inside—a contention repeated in the memoirs of Eisenhower and Strauss.[97] When the Japanese government reported that the ship's radio operator died of "radiation sickness," U.S. officials stubbornly insisted that he died of hepatitis. Although Japanese doctors pointed out that the autopsy revealed radioactive elements in his liver and bone marrow, the AEC and the Defense Department continued to maintain that U.S. nuclear testing was not responsible. In March 1958, amid hot debates over the feasibility of detecting nuclear tests, the AEC announced that its latest underground nuclear explosion could not be detected beyond 250 miles from the site. When protests ensued, the AEC was forced to concede that, in actuality, the test had been detected some 2,300 miles away.[98]

Given the Eisenhower administration's determination to put a positive spin on its nuclear activities, the USIA assumed an increasingly significant role. In 1955—at the initiative of the State Department, the CIA, the NSC, and the president—the USIA launched an extensive series of public opinion polls in foreign nations, designed to elicit everything from popular attitudes toward the use of nuclear weapons to "emotional blocks or repressions" related to the Bomb. Subsequently, these polls, their findings, and their significance for public policy were discussed at the highest levels of power.[99] Appealing for support of the new agency early that year, Eisenhower explained: "We are trying to convince the people in the world that we are working for peace and not trying to blow them to kingdom come with our atom and thermonuclear bombs." Although Eisenhower prided himself on cutting government spending, in late 1955 he called for a 50 percent increase in funding for the USIA. "I know that we Americans recoil by nature from the idea of 'propaganda,'" he told GOP congressional leaders. "But it is a necessity in the present kind of struggle."[100]

The USIA was certainly in the thick of the fray. In the last half of 1954, the USIA reported, it used its massive worldwide apparatus to emphasize "more heavily America's devotion to peace and the need for unity and strength to maintain it." The USIA also sought "to expose the 'peaceful coexistence' slogan as a barren promise" by developing a "global theme designed to convince people abroad that the U.S. stands and works for peace." At USIA cultural centers, "influential Japanese speakers and newspapermen," assisted by USIA films and publications, "helped counter anti-Americanism aroused by the contamination of fishermen and fish by hydrogen and ash fallout." In 1955, the USIA "made a major effort to counter" the "widespread fear of nuclear warfare in Western Europe" and "to reduce the undesirable effects of neutralist sentiments of Nehru . . . and other leaders of uncommitted countries." Attempting to overcome the "mixed emotions regarding the use of atomic weapons against Asiatic peoples," the USIA made particular efforts in Japan, where it "undertook special programs to develop Japanese confidence in U.S. policies" and "developed" favorable "editorial opinion . . . in important Japanese publications." In 1956, the USIA followed up with "an intensive campaign . . . to increase the acceptability of atomic energy to the Japanese public." During the 1957 disarmament negotiations in London, the USIA put additional staff on the job "to make the United States position as clear and persuasive as possible." Although "the Soviets won at least momentary propaganda advantage by use of the simple 'ban the bomb' formula," the USIA planned in the year ahead to "give top priority" to the disarmament issue.[101]

One of the largest USIA propaganda ventures—the "Atoms for Peace" campaign—began under other auspices in 1953. Determined to take an aggressive role in opinion formation, the Eisenhower administration recruited C. D. Jackson, a vice president of *Time* magazine who specialized in psychological warfare. Jackson tried his hand at drafts of speeches for the president on nuclear issues, but Eisenhower rejected them, complaining that "we don't want to scare the country to death." In passing, however, Jackson mentioned "peaceful uses" of the atom, and this idea became the centerpiece for a dramatic proposal by the president. Addressing the United Nations on December 8, 1953, Eisenhower proposed donating a specific quantity of fissionable material to a U.N. agency for "peaceful" purposes. As Jackson noted, this "Atoms for Peace" speech provided "a direct challenge to the Soviets' near monopoly of 'peace' propaganda." Accordingly, he generated a blizzard of mass media commendation for it around the world. U.S. government agencies launched an enormous propaganda effort around "Atoms for Peace," for—as one report stated—it distracted "popular attention . . . from the image of a United States bent on nuclear holocaust" and focused it instead on "technological progress and international cooperation."[102]

The USIA waged a vast propaganda campaign along these lines. Throughout 1954, it reported, "major 'Atoms for Peace' exhibits in Berlin, Italy and Belgium capped USIA's continuing press, radio and film campaign to popularize the president's atom-pool proposal. A five-truck Italian exhibit was seen by nearly 2,000,000." Throughout the Near East, South Asia, and Africa, the program "was exploited through press placement, radio broadcasts, film shows, exhibits and information center activities." In Latin America, "Atoms for Peace" provided "the central positive theme" of the USIA's program. There was an "elaborate exhibit entitled 'Atoms for the Benefit of Mankind' developed under AEC guidance and displayed at Sao Paulo, Brazil," with 500,000 persons ultimately attending it. "A color film of the exhibit was prepared for general distribution. A separate panel exhibit on the same theme was provided to each Latin American post." The following year, noted the USIA, "the 'Atoms for Peace' program continued in high gear." Three million people in twenty-five European cities attended the mobile U.S. exhibits during the first half of the year and, in Britain, the USIA published a new magazine, *Atoms for Peace Digest*, for distribution to opinion leaders. Meanwhile, the USIA's "Atoms for Peace" exhibit "toured the main cities of India with marked success" and, in Japan, "a remarkable placement of material on the peaceful uses of atomic energy was achieved." In Latin America, "press, radio, and motion picture materials in this field were steadily augmented and increased publicity was built upon the visits of Latin American journalists and students to atomic installations in this country." In Honduras and Mexico, the USIA staged "atomic information weeks."[103]

Within the United States, a variety of groups propounded the message of the "peaceful" atom. The AEC developed new teaching materials and impressive traveling exhibits for high schools. Edward Teller trumpeted Project Plowshare, an AEC program of nuclear explosions to "make deserts bloom," cut through mountains, gouge out harbors, and blast a new canal across Panama. "We will change the earth's surface to suit us," the government physicist promised. Meanwhile, the mass media and other corporations joined this love affair with the atom. General Electric, which profited handsomely from its nuclear operations, promoted the alleged wonders of nuclear energy through its extensive "opinion leader advertising series" in American magazines, its widely viewed television programs, and—in the schools—through its animated color film, *A is for Atom*, which reached about two million students a year. Walt Disney's *Our Friend the Atom*, which began running in schools and on television in 1957, showed how a menacing giant was turned into a faithful servant who wielded the "magic power" of radioactivity, portrayed as glittering pixie-dust. David Sarnoff, chair of RCA, told readers of *Fortune* that, by 1980, every home would have its own nuclear power plant. The Atomic Industrial Forum did such useful public relations work for the government that White House aides lauded it as a valuable "cold-war weapon."[104]

The administration's announcement of its search for a "clean" Bomb provided yet another means of giving its nuclear program a positive image. In 1956, attempting once again to offset public fears about fallout from U.S. nuclear testing, Strauss began to argue that such testing would soon lead to the development of weapons with far lower radioactivity. "The current series of tests," he declared that July, "has produced much of importance not only from a military point of view, but from a humanitarian aspect." This angered Senator Anderson, for—as he recalled—"I knew the military was ordering production of heavily radioactive, or 'dirty' weapons, on the grounds that they would be deadlier in war." Furthermore, routine modification of hundreds of existing weapons was enhancing their radioactivity. And, finally, as he remarked years later, "I knew that Strauss didn't care about getting them clean at all."[105]

The Menace of the Maidens

Given the administration's desire to avoid criticism of its nuclear weapons program, its response to the visit to the United States for plastic surgery of the Hiroshima Maidens—the twenty-five young women badly disfigured and socially stigmatized by atomic bomb scars—was thoroughly predictable. In early 1954, State Department officials maintained that "from a political and public relations point of view," it was "highly advisable" that the Maidens "not come as a group" and not stay any longer in the United States than the time necessary for their treatment at Mt. Sinai Hospital. Although these injunctions were apparently forgotten or disregarded as the project gathered momentum, the publication of a story about the forthcoming visit of the Maidens in an April 1955 issue of the *Saturday Review* revived old anxieties and triggered an investigation of the sponsor of the visit, the Hiroshima Peace Center Associates, by the State Department's Security Office.[106] From Kobe, the U.S. consul questioned whether the Maidens' visit was in keeping with "our worldwide efforts to deemphasize the destructive effects of nuclear weapons." A growing panic began to steal over Washington officialdom. "My main concern was that this project might lend fuel to the public opinion in favor of outlawing the atomic bomb," Assistant Secretary of State Walter Robertson later admitted. After all, the sight of the bomb-scarred Maidens might "point up the horrors of atomic warfare."[107]

Nevertheless, State Department officials sprang into action too late to affect the course of events. In late April and early May 1955, the Maidens, the Reverend Kiyoshi Tanimoto (organizer of the project in Japan), and accompanying doctors, journalists, and interpreters received visas for travel to the United States. Approached by the president of the *Nippon Times*, which agreed to co-sponsor the venture, General John Hull of the U.S. Army Far East Command himself investigated the situation and, then—convinced of the humanitarian nature of the project—arranged for the entourage to fly to the United States in a U.S. Air Force plane. By contrast, the State Department grew increasingly jittery. As one official later remarked, "the entire issue went right to the top, and hours were spent discussing it." Determined to block the project, the State Department tried at the last moment to cancel the plane's departure. But when General Hull ignored State's order, the plane took off on the first lap of the journey. That left State Department officials in an embarrassing bind. As one of them recalled: "The reaction to cancelling the free ride for the girls, since the plane had started out, would have been too great, so they let it continue."[108]

The arrival of the Maidens in the United States, on May 9, 1955, aggravated official uneasiness about the venture's antinuclear implications. Two days later, appearing on the American television program, *This Is Your Life*, Tanimoto described the ordeal of Hiroshima and two of the Maidens expressed their gratitude to the people of the United States for providing them with medical assistance. Anxious messages flashed back and forth between Washington and Japan. On May 12, the U.S. embassy in Tokyo reported that the embassy and the USIA "share [the] Washington concern lest [the] Hiroshima girls project generate unfavorable publicity." Tanimoto "may well try to take advantage of [the] trip to raise funds for [the] Hiroshima Memorial Peace Center, his pet project." Although the embassy did "not believe he is [a] Red or Red-sympathizer . . . he can easily become [a] source of mischievous publicity." Similarly, the U.S. consul at Kobe contended that Tanimoto "appears to be anti-Communist and [is] probably sincere in his efforts to assist the girls." Even so, "in his desire to enhance his own prestige and importance he might ignorantly, innocently, or purposefully lend himself to or pursue a leftist line." For a time, recalled a State Department official, "it almost seemed that this had become one of the biggest international issues facing the government."[109]

The report of the State Department's Security Office, produced in early August 1955, helped to heighten official paranoia. Drawing on the Security Office's own files, as well as on those of the FBI, the House Committee on Un-American Activates, and assorted military intelligence agents in the United States and Japan, the report provided a remarkably hostile evaluation of the leaders of the Hiroshima Peace Center Associates and of the Hiroshima Maidens project. Norman Cousins had "been associated . . . with several 'left of center' groups since 1945," most notably the World Federalists and the American Civil Liberties Union. John Hersey "has been cited on numerous occasions by the House Committee of [*sic*] Un-American Activities from 1946 to recent date for left-wing activity, support or sponsorship of causes identified as Communist front activities." There was also the novelist Pearl Buck, whose security file "contains a number of items indicating that her political sympathies have paralleled those of the Communist line." Tanimoto, who had once addressed the Hawaiian branch of the United World Federalists, was a founder of the "No More Hiroshima" movement, which had participated in the Hiroshima Peace Festival. In a cover letter, an official of the Security Office charged that Tanimoto was "at least a liberal." Upon receipt of the report, the undersecretary of state's office dispatched it in August 1955 to top department officials with a strong endorsement, calling particular attention to the pages "which highlight the propaganda advantage to the communist line" of the Hiroshima Maidens project.[110]

Despite its fears, however, the U.S. government ultimately made the best of the situation. The Hiroshima Maidens project, after all, had gone too far for the State Department to do much about it and, moreover, did not seem to be generating a tidal wave of ban-the-Bomb sentiment. Instead, the project provided a practical route toward Japanese-American reconciliation. "There's a great sense of relief," one State Department official told Cousins that summer. "Some of the people here who imagined all sorts of disasters are beginning to take a different view of it." Indeed, it "seems surprising that the project took on the size it did in our discussions." Although the president refused a request for a meeting with the Maidens, the project ultimately received an official commendation. Reporting Eisenhower's great pleasure at its "splendid work," Sherman Adams, the assistant to the president, declared that "all those in Japan and in the United States who participated in this undertaking should take satisfaction in their contribution toward strengthening the bonds of friendship between our two countries."[111]

Buried, but not entirely forgotten, lay the U.S. government's fierce animosity toward this venture, as well as toward numerous others with antinuclear implications.

Governments Change Policies, 1954–58

The new thermonuclear weapons are tremendously
powerful; however they are not . . . as powerful as is
world opinion today.

Dwight Eisenhower, 1958

Although numerous governments perceived the nuclear disarmament movement as a threat to their national security policies, they could not entirely dis-
miss it, either. Admittedly, efforts to control or blunt the impact of antinuclear
agitation had some effect. Millions of people retained the belief that their governments knew best how to protect them, even in the new and dangerous nuclear age. And yet a disturbing number of people seemed to have lost this faith.
Many—including some of the most eminent individuals of their time—were
beginning to agitate, to criticize, and to demonstrate against nuclear weapons
programs. And behind them loomed far larger numbers of people—those who
never demonstrated, but nonetheless showed up in the polls as substantial majorities horrified by nuclear weapons and by the prospect of nuclear war. As
popular pressures grew, government officials began to realize that, despite their
best public relations efforts, it was impossible to contain the demand to control the nuclear arms race. Some compromise was inevitable. Accordingly,
slowly and with great reluctance, numerous governments began to alter their
nuclear policies.

The Intransigents

Some governments, of course, remained intransigent, especially if, like the
French, they were determined to maintain their great power status and were
well-insulated from public opinion. Pressured by military leaders, the French
government continued its secret studies of the military applications of nuclear
power. In April 1958, Premier Félix Gaillard gave the official go-ahead for the

building of nuclear weapons. Shortly thereafter, when the armed forces—angered by what they considered the government's restrained prosecution of the Algerian war—overturned the Fourth Republic and put into power a government headed by Charles de Gaulle, the decision was made public. At a press conference in October 1958, de Gaulle declared that France had the means of providing itself "with nuclear weapons and the day is approaching when we, in our turn, will carry out tests." Against the backdrop of U.S., Soviet, and British nuclear weapons programs, "France will not accept a position of chronic inferiority." From de Gaulle's viewpoint, nuclear weapons were necessary not only for France to ensure its own defense, but to guarantee its independence in world affairs. With the Bomb, de Gaulle argued, "France was once more in control of her own destiny." Ostensibly, the French government still supported the total abolition of nuclear weapons. In practice, however, it plunged ahead with its nuclear program and opposed all plans—such as a nuclear test ban—that would deprive it of the opportunity to join the nuclear club.[1]

The Chinese government, too, remained intensely committed to developing the Bomb. Keenly aware of U.S. nuclear threats and uncertain to what degree it could trust the defense guarantees of its Soviet ally, the Peking government gave the highest priority to its fledgling nuclear weapons program. In October 1957, that program took a key step forward when the Soviet and Chinese governments signed the New Defense Technical Accord, in which the Russians agreed to supplement the nuclear assistance they had thus far rendered the Chinese by supplying them with a prototype atomic bomb, missiles, and useful technical data. When, that same month, the Soviet government sent the world's first artificial satellite, Sputnik I, hurtling into space, Mao Zedong grew hopeful that the tide had turned against the United States. "The East wind," he assured Chinese students, now "prevails over the West wind." The world had reached a "turning point," in which the "socialist forces are now overwhelmingly superior to the imperialist forces." Even so, China was determined to have its own Bomb. Addressing a delegation from Japan, Mao declared that although the best situation for the world would be the total absence of nuclear weapons, the worst would be a nuclear monopoly by the United States and the Soviet Union.[2]

The Chinese government's attitude toward nuclear war remained rather ambiguous. Mao, at least, displayed a remarkable equanimity about the consequences of a nuclear showdown. A nuclear war with the "maniacs" might kill half to two-thirds of China's population, he conceded, but good Communists should not despair. Such a war would ensure the "total elimination of capitalism" and bring about "permanent peace." According to Khrushchev, in November 1957 Mao shocked a world gathering of Communist Party leaders with a speech whose gist was:

We shouldn't fear war. We shouldn't be afraid of atomic bombs and missiles. No matter what kind of war breaks out—conventional or thermonuclear—we'll win. As for China, if the imperialists unleash war on us, we may lose more than three hundred million people. So what? War is war. The years will pass, and we'll get to work producing more babies than ever before.

Nevertheless, China's Central Military Commission, chaired by Mao, resolved in mid-1958 that China was "developing nuclear weapons in order to warn our enemies against making war on us, not in order to use nuclear weapons to attack them." Furthermore, China's government desired to "reach agreement on nuclear disarmament."[3] Given the Chinese leadership's belief that it could defeat the West in a conventional war, it may well have found the idea of nuclear disarmament appealing.

The British government, although buffeted by antinuclear pressures to a far greater extent than the Chinese, also remained committed to a nuclear buildup. Shortly after taking office as prime minister in early 1957, Harold Macmillan decided to make substantial cuts in conventional forces and to base Britain's future security primarily on nuclear weapons. "We must rely on the power of the nuclear deterrent or we must throw up the sponge," the prime minister argued. In friendly talks with Eisenhower and other U.S. officials that March, Macmillan outlined Britain's new military policy, which reminded the president of his own "New Look" strategy. At the meeting, representatives of the two governments agreed on a plan whereby the Americans would supply the British with intermediate-range ballistics missiles for use with U.S. nuclear warheads. Although the British were delighted to obtain these missiles, at the heart of Macmillan's national security policy lay the development of Britain's own nuclear weapons. The program for a British Bomb, begun by his predecessors, reached an impressive fruition that May, when the British government exploded its first H-Bomb, at Christmas Island. Macmillan claimed that "it cleared the atmosphere in the political sense, even if it may have polluted it physically to a small degree."[4]

Naturally, then, the British government had little interest in nuclear disarmament. "Europe could never be protected by conventional means alone," Macmillan wrote in his memoirs; rather, "the nuclear deterrent" provided "the only ultimate defense." For this reason, he "had always opposed nuclear disarmament unless this was accompanied by conventional disarmament on a scale which would result in a reasonable balance between East and West." Or, as he told the chancellor of the exchequer in January 1958: "There have been repeated proposals for the abolition of nuclear armaments, atom bombs and hydrogen bombs." But "suppose that we worked out an agreement for the abolition of such weapons" and "that as a result of such agreement we found ourselves virtually defenseless before the greatly superior weight of Russian conventional arms. . . . If that happened, wouldn't we bitterly regret the loss of our nuclear deterrent?" The answer, he felt, was clear: "We daren't let our revulsion from the idea of the H-bomb deprive us of our best guarantee of safety from attack." On other occasions, Macmillan made much the same point.[5]

For similar reasons, the British government also looked askance at nuclear arms controls. At a Cabinet meeting of April 10, 1956, members argued that "it was important that no international agreement prohibiting or limiting the manufacture of nuclear weapons should come into force until we ourselves had adequate stocks of these weapons." Regarding nuclear testing as crucial to the development of their nuclear strength, British officials opposed any measures that would restrict it. In April 1957, the British government withdrew its acceptance of the compulsory jurisdiction of the International Court of Justice to preclude the possibility that the Court might issue an injunction barring its forthcoming nuclear tests. Later that year, when the Soviet Union and the United States seemed near an agreement on a nuclear test ban, the British government registered its strong objections. According to the U.S. ambassador, Macmillan said that he "would never sign an agreement which would permanently relegate the U.K. to a third rate stature as a power without nuclear weapons." Lauding Britain's nuclear "progress," Macmillan wrote in his diary: "To stop now would be like giving up 'in the straight.'" With the concurrence of the Cabinet, plans went forward for a new round of British nuclear tests in 1958.[6]

On the other hand, beset by antinuclear opinion, the British government groped for policies that might alleviate public restlessness. According to the record of a British Cabinet meeting in July 1956, the foreign secretary strongly supported the prime minister's suggestion that he put some "practical proposals" to the U.S. government for nuclear testing limitations. "Public anxiety was growing, and the government would be expected to take some fresh initiative before very long." Six days later, the U.S. State Department's top atomic energy official noted that the British government was "torn between a desire to become a first-class nuclear power" and "a desire to meet the broad opposition to thermonuclear testing which has developed in the U.K."[7] In September, the foreign secretary and the minister of defense teamed up to argue that "there is undoubtedly growing pressure in this country and elsewhere for the abolition of all tests of nuclear weapons. However much this pressure may be based on loose thinking or ignorance, it is very real and is an important factor in international and domestic affairs." Accordingly, they argued for an agreement among the atomic powers to limit the fission yield of nuclear tests. The following month, this proposal became the center of Cabinet discussion, with the defense minister observing that "public opinion was disturbed" at the possibility that nuclear tests "would . . . become a danger to human life." Therefore, to allay popular anxiety and, at the same time, provide for the continued testing of British nuclear weapons, he suggested that Britain propose limiting testing by fissionable yield. The Cabinet agreed.[8]

During the following year, Macmillan became bogged down in a public exchange of disarmament proposals with Bulganin—proposals that he regarded as propaganda exercises, but which were fraught with too much public significance to ignore. Noting "the British public's growing apprehension as to the dangers of nuclear warfare," Macmillan resolved that "I must try . . . to make at least some indent upon the Iron Curtain, partly in the hope of some genuine détente and partly to satisfy public opinion at home."[9]

By 1958, as a British disarmament official recalled, "the pressure of public opinion against nuclear testing had . . . become a serious factor; no British government could afford to appear to drag its feet." This was particularly true after the Soviet Union's unilateral suspension of testing on March 31. According to the record of a meeting with U.S. government officials on June 9, Macmillan raised "the broad question: could we go on testing nuclear weapons indefinitely?" Soon the report of the U.N. Radiation Committee would appear, and "some of its contents would help the agitators and critics to make a strong case against continued tests. So the first thing to decide was whether we could continue testing." Macmillan warned, though, that if the Western powers did suspend tests, "it would be hard to start them again." On July 8, he went so far as to suggest to the foreign secretary the possibility of "an agreement to suspend tests as from January 1 for a period of two years," to be accompanied by progress toward an agreement on a detection system. Macmillan added: "It seems to me that we will not be able to stand up against the pressure in the [U.N. General] Assembly and public opinion here after the medical report of the United Nations."[10]

So strong was the British government's desire to improve its nuclear arsenal, however, that it refused to give way to public opinion or even to growing pressure from the U.S. government. Although, in late March, Macmillan realized that the Russians might unilaterally suspend nuclear testing, he told Eisenhower that Britain would not accept a halt to nuclear tests without knowing "the help we can count on from you." Indeed, the crux of the issue for the British rapidly became whether the U.S. atomic energy act would be amended to provide them with the nuclear information they would lose by forgoing nuclear testing. Without this assurance of American assistance, British officials planned to stand firm against any interference with their testing program.[11] Lacking definite assurance from Washington along these lines, Macmillan urged Eisenhower as late as August 21 to resist acceptance of the Soviet proposal for the suspension of nuclear testing. British nuclear tests would not be completed until mid-October, observed the prime minister. Furthermore, the Russians should be made to pay the "price" of international control.[12]

Believers and Converts

Nonaligned nations, particularly those from the increasingly self-conscious Afro-Asian bloc, remained the sharpest critics of the nuclear arms race. In a note delivered to the British government in the spring of 1957, the Indonesian ambassador expressed his government's condemnation of British plans for nuclear weapons tests at Christmas Island. The Indonesian parliament, it observed, sought "to prevent every atom bomb test." Moreover, the Bandung conference of Afro-Asian nations viewed disarmament, as well as the prohibition of the production, testing, and use of nuclear weapons, as "imperative to save mankind and civilization from the fear and prospect of wholesale destruction." In a joint declaration the following month, the prime ministers of Ceylon and India formally urged "immediate suspension" of nuclear weapons testing by the Soviet Union, the United States, and Britain. Nuclear explosions had "already proved injurious" to people in countries near the test sites, "dangerously polluted the world's air and water, and threatened the present and future generations with . . . known and unknown risks." Meanwhile, the Indian government repeatedly raised objections in the U.N. Trusteeship Council to U.S. government use of the Marshall Islands, a trust territory, for nuclear weapons tests. "These islands, be they inhabited by Micronesians or Americans or anybody else," insisted V. K. Krishna Menon, "are homelands of the people who are there, and to regard them as proving grounds is contrary to the conception of sacred trust."[13]

Among all Afro-Asian leaders, India's prime minister, Jawaharlal Nehru, remained the most vigorous and persistent critic of the Bomb. Delivering a major address in April 1957, he renewed his appeal for a nuclear test ban. The following month, on a visit to Ceylon to celebrate the 2,500th anniversary of the birth of the Buddha, Nehru once more called for a halt to nuclear tests, to save the world from "extinction." Touching on Buddhist values, he argued that "we should go deep and try to divert the mind of mankind in another direction," in which people do "not think of military might and destruction but in terms of compassion, human freedom, and human cooperation." In public addresses before large crowds over the following days, Nehru came back again and again to the contrast between nuclear weapons explosions and the "spirit" of Buddhism. At the same time, however, he emphasized that he was speaking as a "politician" and not as a "saint"; if war among the great powers occurred, "we go down with it." In subsequent months, Nehru continued his crusade against the arms race. According to a *New York Times* dispatch from India in February 1958, Nehru made "the danger from nuclear tests and nuclear weapons a recurrent theme in his speeches" and had government scientists draw up reports on the hazards of nuclear explosions. Writing in the preface to one report, Nehru argued that a nuclear war would seriously affect unborn generations. And, to some degree, nuclear tests were already spreading "this evil thing" over the world.[14]

Meanwhile, the Swedish government also began to turn against the Bomb. For officials in Stockholm, this represented an important policy shift. In 1957, Sweden had the technological capacity for a nuclear program, the armed forces and opposition parties championed the development of Swedish nuclear weapons, and the Social Democratic government was split on the issue. "The nuclear weapons problem," recalled Prime Minister Tage Erlander, was "my most difficult political decision. In 1958, though, the Social Democrats began gravitating toward a policy that they could live with: postponing action on developing a Swedish nuclear defense. Behind the new policy, Erlander noted, lay the influence of nuclear critics, his determination to avoid a split in Social Democratic ranks, and his conclusion that Swedish nuclear weapons entailed "risks for our neutrality." In addition, he believed that "we ought to support the efforts going on to prohibit nuclear weapons. Nobody would trust us if we made Swedish nuclear weapons." Consequently, with the Social Democrats championing a postponement policy and more conservative parties consoling themselves that nuclear weapons remained a possibility, the Riksdag voted in July 1958 to delay a resolution of the issue. The Swedish government then added its voice to the antinuclear refrain. That fall, Foreign Minister Östen Undén, speaking before the U.N. General Assembly, called for a treaty to ban nuclear testing.[15]

The Middle-of-the-Roaders

In other nations, such as Japan, official inclinations to support U.S. nuclear policies were offset by popular antinuclear pressures. On repeated occasions, the Japanese government issued public protests against the nuclear tests of the United States, Britain, and the Soviet Union.[16] To be sure, Japanese officials secretly assured the U.S. State Department that such protests were sops to domestic antinuclear sentiment and should not be taken seriously. At the same time, however, they recognized that they had been forced to deliver them and, thus, embarrass their U.S. ally.[17] Furthermore, pressed by unanimous parliamentary resolutions calling for a nuclear test ban, Japanese officials did make efforts to secure it. Meeting with U.S. State Department officials in Washington in June 1957, Prime Minister Nobusuke Kishi told Dulles that "the Japanese are very serious about this matter" and that it was his "fervent hope" that "some arrangement could be arrived at to prohibit all nuclear tests." That September, the Japanese government submitted an antitesting resolution to the United Nations.[18]

On related policy issues, too, the Japanese government accommodated itself to public opinion. Japan, after all, had the scientific and technological capacity to produce nuclear weapons, and, in 1956, U.S. officials predicted that Japan would soon be manufacturing them. But that prognosis did not reckon with the political barrier erected by Japanese antinuclear sentiment. In May 1957, when Kishi declared that he did not believe the Japanese constitution barred the maintenance of nuclear weapons for defense, this stirred up a political firestorm. Consequently, he quickly added that he had no intention of providing Japanese forces with nuclear arms or of reversing his opposition to the U.S. government's stationing of nuclear units in Japan.[19] The following year, the Japanese foreign minister warned U.S. officials that the introduction of nuclear weapons into his country was a political "hot potato."[20] Indeed, during the late 1950s, as the electoral majority of the conservatives shrank and the dovish (albeit divided) opposition grew in strength, Japan's rulers were careful to avoid moves that would cost them support at the polls. And no move seemed more likely to do so than embracing nuclear weapons. In 1957, as another concession to antinuclear sentiment, the government backed legislation to provide free medical treatment to victims of the 1945 atomic bombing.[21]

Although more in line with Western nuclear policy, the governments of Australia and New Zealand also showed signs of straying from the fold. In the aftermath of the disastrous Bikini H-Bomb experiments and the resulting furor, the Australian government told the British that it would no longer allow thermonuclear tests on Australian soil. By contrast, the New Zealand government assisted the British with the resulting tests at Christmas Island, arguing that it would be dangerous for Western nations to stop testing until there was a verifiable agreement on the means of proceeding to comprehensive disarmament. But as a concession to uneasy public opinion, New Zealand officials began monitoring air, water, and soil in New Zealand and its island territories for radioactivity. Furthermore, in August 1957, when the British sought to make their testing program more palatable by indicating that nuclear weapons would be made available for the defense of the SEATO area, including Australia and New Zealand, Prime Minister Keith Holyoake announced that although his National Party would continue to support the Western testing program, New Zealand did not wish to acquire nuclear weapons or to serve as "a storage base for them." When the Labour Party swept to power later that year, it continued most of the National Party's defense program, but took another step in the antinuclear direction by issuing the government's first clear call for a ban on nuclear testing.[22]

Even within the NATO alliance, there were indications that some governments, at least, were becoming uneasy about nuclear weapons programs. In mid-1957, as the U.S. government laid plans to provide its NATO allies with intermediate-range ballistic missiles, the Danish government indicated that it would not accept the weapons. Later that year, after the successful Soviet launching of an intercontinental ballistics missile and two earth satellites, the U.S. government came to regard the deployment of missiles in NATO's forward bases, such as Denmark and Norway, as increasingly desirable. Nevertheless, at a NATO heads of government meeting that December, the Danish and Norwegian delegations sharply rejected placement of missiles in their countries, at least in peacetime.[23] The Norwegian action reflected the governing Labor Party's recent decision to oppose nuclear weapons on Norwegian territory; the Danish decision, too, rested on domestic controversy over the weapons.[24] Furthermore, Canada's prime minister, John Diefenbaker, stressed that the new missile placement went "beyond" past NATO agreements "into [a] new field and requires careful study." Ultimately, only Italy and Turkey agreed to accept the new missiles on their territory.[25]

NATO countries also showed a new interest in nuclear disarmament. Disarmament was "very important to Canada," Diefenbaker told the December 1957 gathering, "especially [the] safeguarded cessation [of] nuclear testing." Although the Greek government argued that NATO should not appear "to plead with [the] USSR to discuss disarmament," since that "might give [the] impression [of] weakness and fear," most other nations argued that new disarmament efforts had to be made, if only to keep "public opinion" in line. These pressures escalated in early 1958. According to a report on a NATO meeting in early February, Canada and Belgium indicated that they were sticking to NATO's position on the inseparability of halting nuclear tests and a general disarmament agreement "only because of [the] position [of] other NATO partners. They were not entirely convinced, however, and would not oppose [a] short term, independent" test suspension. Indeed, there was a "general recognition" at the meeting of the "public anxiety over nuclear tests." Paul Henri Spaak of Belgium remarked that the "clean Bomb" argument was "not well accepted by [the] European population." Underscoring this point, the Norwegians complained that it was "poor consolation for people in areas of [fallout] concentration to know that [the] statistical overall average is low." The Belgians warned that if the forthcoming U.N. report on health hazards from nuclear testing found any risk, "Western insistence on continued testing would receive [an] unfavorable public reaction."[26]

With the Soviet government's announcement of March 31, 1958, that it was halting nuclear tests unilaterally, pressures for changing Western policy intensified. According to a U.S. government account of a NATO meeting on April 2, "Norway called attention to [the] Soviet declaration" and declared that NATO "could not let much time pass" before reviewing its policy on nuclear tests. Although the U.S. government reiterated its publicly stated rationale for continued testing, "Canada supported Norway," arguing that it was "useful" for NATO to "consider [the] pros and cons on cessation of tests." Anxious to safeguard their own testing programs, France and Britain rejoindered that the Soviet action was "phony" and hypocritical. But Canada insisted that although the public "realized [the] Soviet action was [a] maneuver," it "still did not understand why tests needed to be continued." Returning to the fray, Norway again urged a prompt reappraisal of NATO's position on nuclear testing. After the meeting, a member of the Norwegian delegation explained to the U.S. delegation that his government wanted NATO to "go into not only [the] question of [the] presentation [of the] Western position to [the] public," but the issue of "continuation of tests." Later that month, Norwegian diplomats renewed their pressure, citing their "great concern over public reaction" to nuclear testing.[27]

The Soviets Make Their Move . . . Toward "Peace"

Soviet policy, too, showed important signs of change. At the Twentieth Communist Party Congress of February 1956, Khrushchev emphasized that war was not "fatalistically inevitable" and, furthermore, that there was no reasonable alternative to peace. "Either peaceful coexistence or the most destructive war in history," he stated; "there is no third way." Officially endorsed by the party gathering, "peaceful coexistence" seemed likely to provide the Soviet Union with at least two substantial benefits. First, as Khrushchev had argued, it would help to avert a disastrous war with the West. In addition, by bolstering the contention of Soviet propaganda that Moscow followed a "peace-loving policy," it would have a strong appeal to the many people around the world horrified by the prospect of nuclear war. To be sure, the Kremlin continued a vigorous program of nuclear testing and spurred the development, in 1957, of Soviet intercontinental ballistics missiles. Khrushchev stressed in his memoirs that "we wanted to exert pressure on American militarists—and also influence the minds of more reasonable politicians—so the United States would start treating us better." But, he added, "we had no intention of starting a war. We stood firm on . . . peaceful coexistence. We only wanted to deter the Americans' threats, their aggressiveness, and their attempts to terrorize us."[28]

Khrushchev's profession of peaceful intentions takes on added weight in the context of a major power struggle that erupted within the Soviet leadership during 1957. With Khrushchev's position weakened by the uprisings that broke out in Poland and Hungary in the fall of 1956, his rivals united in June 1957 in an attempt to remove him as party secretary. Speaking before the Central Committee plenum, Molotov took the lead in denouncing Khrushchev's policy of "peaceful coexistence." In turn, Anastas Mikoyan, Khrushchev's ally, assailed Molotov as "a dyed-in-the-wool conservative" who wanted to "turn around our foreign policy, [which is] aimed at the relaxation of international tension." Ultimately, the Khrushchev forces emerged victorious, purging Molotov and other leaders of the "anti-party group" from the Central Committee. Khrushchev became premier in March 1958; meanwhile, his rivals dropped out of sight, although their views remained much the same. Even decades later, Molotov continued to fulminate against peaceful coexistence, "the very idea" of which "draws people toward a pacifist way of thinking." Under peaceful coexistence, Molotov charged, "we are, as it were, begging for peace." "For Bolsheviks," that was "unseemly."[29]

The Soviet Union's new national security policy also prompted a split with its Chinese allies. Viewing Mao's slogan "imperialism is a paper tiger" as "incredible," Khrushchev grew increasingly alarmed at what he considered the Chinese leader's cavalier attitude toward nuclear war. In November 1957, when Mao brushed off the consequences of such a conflict in his speech before world Communist leaders, Khrushchev found his comments "deeply disturbing." During a recess in the meeting, Polish and Czech leaders expressed a similar indignation. Khrushchev recalled: "Everybody except Mao was thinking about how to avoid war. Our principal slogan was 'On with the Struggle for Peace and Peaceful Coexistence.' Yet suddenly here came Mao Tse-tung, saying we shouldn't be afraid of war." In early 1958, as Soviet doubts grew over the reliability of the Chinese leadership, Khrushchev made a decision to postpone shipment of the prototype atomic bomb to the Chinese.[30]

Meanwhile, Soviet officials showed a new seriousness about nuclear arms control. Scrapping their sweeping, propagandistic disarmament proposals, they began to bargain in earnest. In April 1957, chief U.S. negotiator Harold Stassen reported that Soviet responses to U.S. positions "have been quite different" from those of the past. "There has been a lack of recrimination . . . and a more sensible approach to procedures than before." The Soviet proposal for a cessation of nuclear tests "appears to be motivated in part by a real concern over the prospective spreading of the nuclear weapons into the control of additional governments, and the consequent danger that developments not initiated by either the US or USSR might involve the USSR in a nuclear war in which they would suffer great casualties." Later that month, Stassen again reported that there were "important indications of a changing attitude on the part of the Soviets," who seemed "to be ready for more inspection than heretofore" and concerned that "'irresponsible' powers"—interpreted by U.S. officials to mean West Germany and China—might use nuclear weapons to trigger a U.S.-Soviet war.[31]

During the balance of 1957, developments pointed in the same direction. Writing to Macmillan in May, Eisenhower told him that the Russians "probably are worried by the prospect of the spread of nuclear weapons," the "coming of ballistic missiles," and "the burden of their military forces." That June, in an important concession to the Western position, the Soviet negotiator at the London disarmament talks, Valerian Zorin, announced that the Soviet Union would accept a nuclear test ban with international control and supervision. Meeting in October with Dulles, Soviet foreign minister Andrei Gromyko renewed pressure for a nuclear test ban, arguing that it "would lead to a better atmosphere between our countries and a better world atmosphere."[32] As one Sovietologist has argued: "The burden of available evidence suggests that the Kremlin sought at least a de facto cessation of nuclear testing as early as 1957 and probably would have agreed to a comprehensive test ban treaty then, provided intervention by international inspection would be kept to a low level." After all, such a test ban seemed likely to improve relations between Washington and Moscow, inhibit U.S. advances in nuclear weapons technology, and prevent the acquisition of nuclear weapons by West Germany and China.[33]

Why, then, did a test ban remain elusive? In the absence of full Soviet documentation on the issue, an answer cannot be provided with any certainty. Even so, one reason appears to have been the U.S. government's insistence on accepting such a ban only as part of a broader disarmament package that would prohibit the manufacture of nuclear weapons. As Zorin complained in August 1957, "the most important question" remained "the link between a suspension of testing and other parts of a disarmament agreement." Zorin—and Gromyko, too—pushed U.S. officials hard that year to sever the connection, but without success.[34] A second issue dividing the two superpowers was the U.S. demand that any arms control agreement provide for extensive inspection of Soviet territory as a means of verification. This, too, Soviet leaders resisted at every turn. The reason for both Soviet positions appears to have been that Soviet nuclear strength lagged substantially behind that of the United States. Therefore, a ban on nuclear weapons production would have locked the Soviet Union into an inferior position. Moreover, extensive U.S. inspection would have revealed Soviet weakness. Even U.S. officials recognized this on occasion, though usually after the fact. In 1956, Admiral Radford observed that one reason the Russians rejected Eisenhower's earlier "Open Skies" proposal was that "they did not want us to see how little they had."[35]

Indeed, the Kremlin went to great lengths to hide military weakness behind a facade of strength. In 1955, the number of advanced bombers on display at a Soviet air show startled Western intelligence experts. Only years after the event did they learn that, to exaggerate their military might, Soviet leaders had put every advanced bomber they possessed in the air and may even have circled them around for a second run. In September 1957, pointing to the Soviet Union's development of intercontinental ballistics missiles, *Red Star* stressed "the significance of this outstanding achievement for strengthening the defensive capacities of the Soviet state." Similarly, for all Khrushchev's talk of "peaceful coexistence," he had the curious habit of boasting of enormous military power, including a massive H-Bomb that "could melt the Arctic ice cap and send oceans spilling all over the world." This hyperbole may have come easily to Khrushchev, given his coarse, peasant style. But it seems likely to have been calculated, based on a desire to impress his enemies. Significantly, a word commonly used for "deterrence" in Russian is "ustrashenie," which means "terrorization." Certainly, during these years, Soviet leaders never lost an opportunity to boast of their military strength or to hide the reality of their weakness.[36]

Nevertheless, by early 1958, the Soviet government was ready for a daring move: a unilateral suspension of nuclear tests, publicly announced on March 31. Behind the Soviet moratorium, which remained uninspected and of indefinite duration, lay not only the continuing Soviet desire for a nuclear test ban, but a new confidence—based on its successful missile tests and space exploration of late 1957—that the outside world regarded it as at least the equal of the West in military strength.[37] In addition, as one Soviet Foreign Ministry memo argued, the Soviet initiative would serve the "goal of increasing pressure on the USA and England" by mobilizing international public opinion in favor of a test ban.[38] This factor apparently played a very significant role in government thinking, for—despite the fact that the Soviet Union completed a nuclear test series just before the March 31 announcement—the unilateral moratorium served Soviet diplomatic interests better than it did military ones. Indeed, key scientists were not told of the leadership's decision until too late to complete important work on the Soviet nuclear program. Moreover, Soviet military experts appear to have opposed the suspension of nuclear tests.[39]

Therefore, the Soviet government's announcement was, in large part, just what Western analysts considered it—a shrewd propaganda ploy designed to enlist world public opinion behind the Soviet effort to force the United States and Britain to halt nuclear testing.[40] And it worked.

The U.S. Government Becomes "Boxed . . . In"

Irked, even infuriated by antinuclear pressures, U.S. officials increasingly recognized that they set limits to public policy. The use of nuclear weapons, particularly, became harder and harder to justify. In April 1955, Eisenhower insisted to Dulles that the United States had to avoid a firm commitment to defend Quemoy and Matsu. Their successful defense, he explained, would "require counteraction against the mainland of China," and "we have ample forewarning of the adverse character of world reaction that would follow any such action on our part, especially if we felt compelled to use atomic weapons. . . . Public opinion in the United States would . . . become further divided" and "we would be isolated in world opinion." On January 24, 1956, U.N. Ambassador Lodge lamented that "communist propaganda has . . . 'given the atomic bomb a bad name,' and to such an extent that it seriously inhibits us from using it." Two days later, Dulles complained to an NSC meeting that although the United States should stick to "a position which . . . would enable us to use nuclear weapons" in a conventional war begun by the Soviet Union, it was "approaching" a situation in which "our allies will not permit us to have recourse to nuclear weapons except to retaliate for their use by the Soviets."[41]

At NSC meetings in 1956, the use of nuclear weapons became a heated point of contention. Addressing a February 27 meeting, Radford called for greater flexibility in the employment of nuclear weapons for small wars. But, according to the minutes, Eisenhower countered that "the use of nuclear weapons would raise serious political problems in view of the current state of world opinion." Eisenhower "did not say that world opinion was right in its views about the use of nuclear weapons in small wars," but "it was nevertheless a fact." When treasury secretary Humphrey retorted that "we have got to use nuclear weapons in the event of a future war," Dulles responded that "we must choose between having all the military flexibility we wished and losing all our allies." Stassen chimed in that he agreed with Dulles, who thereupon "added a warning of the terrible repercussions which we would experience if we had recourse to the use of nuclear weapons against the colored peoples of Asia." That May, Eisenhower complained to another NSC meeting that Korea, Formosa, and other countries "do not wish to be defended by nuclear weapons." Indeed, "our allies are absolutely scared to death that we will use such weapons." The president maintained that "in the defense of the United States itself we will certainly use nuclear weapons, but to use them in other situations will prove very difficult."[42]

In fairness to U.S. officials, it is important to note that a few of them felt genuinely ambivalent about full-scale nuclear war. Although willing to risk a nuclear showdown with the Soviets under exceptional circumstances, Eisenhower remained very uneasy about the prospect. As the record of another NSC meeting during 1956 indicates, "he feared some of our thinking overlooked a transcendant consideration—namely, that nobody can win a thermonuclear war." Or, as he wrote to a friend later that year, "we are rapidly getting to the point that no war can be won. War implies a contest." But "you get to the point that [a] contest is no longer involved and the outlook comes close to destruction of the enemy and suicide for ourselves." Thus, the "usefulness" of nuclear weapons "becomes concentrated more and more in their characteristics as deterrents" rather than in their employment as "instruments with which to obtain victory."[43] Dulles, too, gradually lost faith in the utility of the nuclear option. According to Strauss, in April 1958 he expressed the view "that U.S. military strategy . . . necessitated a review and revision. He said that while he had been the father of the massive deterrent, he had reached the conclusion that . . . with the early approach of mutual deterrents by both the USSR and the U.S., some new approach to the international political problem was needed."[44]

Yet public pressures constituted a crucial ingredient in their thinking, particularly when it came to smaller-scale nuclear engagements. Countering ambitious proposals by Strauss and the Defense Department for nuclear war-fighting, Dulles told an NSC meeting in May 1957 that "world opinion was not yet ready to accept the general use of nuclear weapons in local conflicts. If we resort to such a use of nuclear weapons we will, in the eyes of the world, be cast as a ruthless military power, as was Germany." Furthermore, each of the State Department's assistant secretaries opposed such employment of nuclear weapons "because of the disastrous effect of such a policy on public opinion" in their regions. Dulles predicted, hopefully, "that all this would change at some point in the future, but the time had not yet come." Losing patience with Dulles's caution, Radford objected that the government had "adopted the essentials of this policy as far back as 1953." Defense Secretary Wilson supported him strongly, adding that there was "no real way of avoiding resort to new military power once such power appears in the world." Dulles, though, insisted that the United States must not "get out of step with world opinion." With Eisenhower in apparent agreement, the NSC adopted national security guidelines that downplayed resort to nuclear war and emphasized conventional military action.[45]

Antinuclear opinion had less impact on the U.S. government's deployment of nuclear weapons. Committed to upgrading NATO's military forces in Western Europe, the Eisenhower administration moved rapidly to arm its allies with tactical nuclear weapons. As the missile race progressed during the first half of 1957, the administration arranged with the British government to provide it with intermediate-range ballistics missiles (IRBMs) and established stockpiles of nuclear weapons in Western Europe. Furthermore, in the aftermath of Soviet success at launching Sputnik, the administration laid plans to offer IRBMs to all NATO nations, under dual control.[46] Admittedly, growing antinuclear agitation in these countries made the administration uneasy about these plans. According to the minutes of an NSC meeting on December 12, 1957, Dulles complained that "there was a good deal of discussion being generated by the opposition parties in the various NATO governments with respect to the question of where to deploy these missiles. Indeed, there was a real danger that this could become a serious political issue."[47] Nevertheless, Dulles made the offer later that month at the NATO heads of government meeting.[48]

For national security reasons, the Eisenhower administration was far less enthusiastic about nuclear proliferation. Stassen began to sound the alarm in 1956, warning that if current trends continued, France, Japan, West Germany, and China would develop independent nuclear capabilities. The Defense Department and (apparently) Strauss took a more relaxed view of the matter, with the Joint Chiefs of Staff arguing that "nuclear weapons in the hands of our Allies should strengthen our alliances." But Eisenhower, the State Department, and the CIA showed some dismay, insisting that the dissemination of nuclear weapons entailed "serious risks for US security." Discussing the issue with a Japanese diplomat in April 1957, Dulles stated that the U.S. government was "concerned about the spread of atomic weapons" because it "could put the weapons into irresponsible hands."[49] Even so, the administration found little that it could do to halt the trend. Although it tried to dissuade the French from developing nuclear weapons—through admonitions and offers to place U.S. missiles in France, under dual control—it feared that more vigorous opposition might inflame nationalist passions and jeopardize NATO. Ultimately, the U.S. government watched helplessly as France and other nations moved forward with their nuclear weapons programs.[50]

Popular pressures did underlie the administration's growing flirtation with arms control and disarmament measures. In the spring of 1954, shocked by the worldwide protest unleashed by the *Lucky Dragon* incident, Dulles convinced Eisenhower to launch a study to determine if the U.S. government should agree to Nehru's proposal for a moratorium on nuclear testing. Within a short time, though, a State-Defense-AEC committee concluded that the military benefits of continuing U.S. nuclear testing more than offset the major "propaganda advantage" to backing a test ban.[51] Public opinion also inspired deferential gestures to disarmament. Discussing the disarmament talks among the great powers which took place in March 1955 under U.N. auspices, Lodge recalled that they were held as "a response to a public demand that the governments 'do something' and surely did not reflect a readiness by the parties to agree or even seriously to negotiate." That same month, as a further sign of the administration's sensitivity to public uneasiness about the arms race, Eisenhower appointed Stassen as his special assistant on disarmament. "Should the United States forego the search for disarmament," Stassen told the Cabinet, "the impact on world opinion would be terrible."[52]

In reality, Stassen proved less interested in disarmament than in modest arms control measures. That June, in a report to Eisenhower, Stassen argued for providing the public with "forthright information on the impossibility of secure elimination of nuclear weapons." Rejecting any reference to "a distant prospect of complete elimination of nuclear weapons," Stassen argued that it merely bolstered "communist 'ban the bomb' propaganda." In July, an administration planning paper for the forthcoming Geneva conference—which presumably reflected Stassen's input on armaments questions—noted that a key U.S. goal was "a leveling and control of armaments, which will build-in US atomic superiority and protect against evasions and surprise by carefully planned and implemented supervision." On September 16, Stassen met with the president to discuss what his notes called "the Ban-the-Bomb Psychological Problem," which included both the "position of our allies" and "United States public opinion." Opposed to banning nuclear weapons, the president's top disarmament adviser championed far more cautious measures. According to Dulles, Stassen told him in late December 1955 that his planning group had come to the conclusion "that any substantial disarmament would not really be in the interest of the United States."[53]

Dulles, however—keenly concerned about public opinion—insisted on *discussing* disarmament. The United States needed its nuclear arsenal, he wrote in a memo of June 29, 1955, but "the frightful destructiveness of modern weapons creates an instinctive abhorrence to them and a certain repulsion against the strategy of 'massive retaliatory power.'" Furthermore, "natural humanitarian instincts" and other factors "combine to create a popular and diplomatic pressure for limitation of armament that cannot be resisted by the United States without our forfeiting the good will of our allies and the support of a large part of our own people." Consequently, "we must . . . propose or support some plan for the limitation of armaments." Addressing the NSC the following day, Dulles insisted that the U.S. government "make some positive move in the direction of disarmament." If it failed to do so, it "would lose very important assets, such as the support of our allies and the right to use bases in allied countries." Others argued ferociously against this. At an NSC meeting on October 13, Radford insisted that "it was certain that atomic and nuclear weapons would be used eventually in future wars" and that the NSC had already "in effect agreed that the attempt to ban nuclear weapons was essentially unrealistic." In reply, Dulles granted the validity of the admiral's remarks, but observed that he did "not feel able, from the standpoint of public relations, to stand up and say to the entire world that nuclear weapons are here to stay forever."[54]

The degree to which popular distaste for nuclear weapons was beginning to color U.S. policy proposals became evident in early 1956. At an NSC meeting on January 26, Dulles attacked Stassen's modest arms control plan, arguing that "from the standpoint of world opinion, there would be widespread doubt" whether it was "genuine, sincere, or adequate. . . . It would not be looked upon as an honest U.S. effort to reduce the level of armaments and to mitigate the horrors of atomic war." Although Stassen argued that it should be possible to "sell" his program, Eisenhower joined Dulles in expressing doubts. How was the United States going to provide Stassen's proposals with "some real appeal, both to our own people and to the people of the world?" the president asked. In this connection, he cited Dulles's concern for winning the "support of world public opinion," noting "the enormous importance of the psychological and public relations aspect." Dulles now joined in, asserting that he agreed with the Joint Chiefs of Staff on "the unlikelihood of achieving any genuine international agreement with people such as the Soviets." But this, in turn, meant that "anything we do in this area should be of such a character as to ensure the good will and support of our allies. . . . Disarmament proposals are probably an operation in public relations," and "until we can achieve good faith on the part of the Russians" there would be no disarmament. "Nevertheless, we must seem to strive for it or else we shall be isolated in the world."[55]

With Dulles's support for disarmament limited to appearances, the only serious policy debate within the administration focused on arms control measures. In early 1956, leading administration officials, including Dulles, argued forcefully against a nuclear test ban. Addressing Hubert Humphrey's disarmament subcommittee of the Senate Foreign Relations Committee that January, Stassen insisted that nuclear testing was "essential" to U.S. national security and that the Soviet Union was exploiting the issue for propaganda purposes. Strauss argued that past tests had produced great benefits for the United States and that further tests would result in the production of still better weapons. Nevertheless, by mid-1956—in the midst of growing public furor over nuclear testing, including the Democratic presidential candidate's call for halting it—Stassen came around to the position that a test ban treaty was worth pursuing, although only as part of a comprehensive arms control and disarmament arrangement. Eisenhower, particularly, liked the idea. At an NSC meeting on September 11, 1956, he ordered a new study of the matter, pointing to "the rising concern of people everywhere over the effect of radiation from tests, of their reaction each time a test was reported, and their extreme nervousness over the prospective consequences of any nuclear war."[56]

But other officials fiercely resisted nuclear arms control measures. In a memo to the defense secretary, the Joint Chiefs of Staff insisted that the United States should "avoid the regulation of nuclear weapons, their means of delivery or tests, except as a part of the final phase of a comprehensive disarmament agreement"—a situation they regarded as virtually impossible and, furthermore, not particularly desirable. At the NSC meeting of September 11, 1956, Radford questioned "the practicality of ever achieving a reliable inspection system" and insisted that "the size of the U.S. [nuclear] stockpile has a vital bearing on the probability of our winning a global war. . . . The U.S. needs large stockpiles of nuclear weapons . . . all over the world." As he told Stassen that year, "if we worry about world opinion we will go 'down the drain.'" Strauss, too, adopted an uncompromising position. The United States should hold nuclear tests "whenever an idea has been developed which is ready for test," he told the president. At the September 11 meeting, the AEC chair expressed doubts "whether the U.S. could ever stop testing nuclear weapons to detect deterioration" and "to effect improvements." Meeting with top administration officials in May 1957, he warned that if the United States yielded "to the pressure of so-called world opinion," it would give "color to the propaganda now current concerning the alleged danger from fall-out" and would make it very difficult to ever resume nuclear testing.[57]

Dulles was more ambivalent. In August 1956, pointing to "the general growth of world opinion against tests" and to the fact that "public opinion, including US opinion, has become increasingly concerned with effects on health and genetics arising from radiation," the State Department went so far as to suggest a unilateral halt to U.S. tests of nuclear weapons of more than one hundred kilotons. The following spring, Dulles defended Stassen's call for a testing moratorium by insisting that "public opinion is powerful and it is hard not to fulfill expectations." In June 1957, he even confided to US officials his fear that, given the pressure of public opinion and the great costs of military priorities, unless progress in disarmament were made soon, several countries, including the United States, might begin to disarm unilaterally. Nonetheless, he told Japanese officials that same month that it was impossible for the U.S. government to accept a test ban separate from a broad-ranging (and probably impossible) agreement on disarmament. When, in September 1957, Stassen proposed a more flexible U.S. position, decoupling a test ban treaty from the comprehensive disarmament package, Dulles grew irate. In a stinging retort to Stassen, Dulles wrote that his proposals "reinforce the fear, held by many both here and abroad, that you feel that some agreement between the United States and the Russians is so sought by world public opinion that we should if necessary make such an agreement on Russia's terms. But world public opinion, now largely emotional, should not be our guide. We should try to guide it."[58]

Eisenhower proved just as fickle. On June 24, 1957, Strauss ushered in three top scientists from the government's nuclear weapons program—Teller, Ernest Lawrence, and Mark Mills—to see the president. Lauding "clean" nuclear weapons, Lawrence argued that to forgo their development would be a "crime against humanity." Teller raved about plans to use "clean thermonuclear weapons" to "produce steam," "modify the flow of rivers, and perhaps even to modify the weather." According to the record of the meeting, Eisenhower "said that no one could oppose the development program they had described." Even so, "we are . . . up against an extremely difficult world opinion situation and he did not think that the United States could permit itself to be 'crucified on a cross of atoms.'" There was not only "the question of world opinion . . . but an actual division of American opinion . . . as to the harmful effects of testing." In response, Strauss assured the president that nuclear testing was harmless and Teller cast aspersions on the Pauling petition. Despite the self-interested, even fantastic, nature of this presentation, Eisenhower was greatly impressed by it and, as Dulles noted, consequently "seemed to question the wisdom of any suspension of testing." Accordingly, that October, when Stassen pleaded with the president to decouple the test ban from other aspects of the government's program—arguing that a "historic moment" had arrived for a U.S.-Soviet test ban treaty—Eisenhower sided with Strauss, Dulles, the Joint Chiefs of Staff, and the defense secretary. Nuclear tests were necessary, and Stassen was not. Asked by Eisenhower to resign, Stassen did so in early 1958.[59]

Public pressures for a test ban, however, were not so easily dismissed. Thanks to the furor raised by the Soviet launching of Sputnik, in November 1957 Eisenhower appointed James R. Killian, president of the Massachusetts Institute of Technology, his special assistant for science and technology. Among his other duties, Killian headed up a reconstituted President's Science Advisory Committee (PSAC). Until this bureaucratic shift, Strauss, Teller, and other nuclear zealots provided Eisenhower with most of his advice on the technical aspects of nuclear issues. Now, however, the president came under the influence of a more representative body of American scientists, some of whom shared the views of the Federation of American Scientists.[60] The PSAC held meetings on nuclear test issues and, as Killian recalled, "the growing world-wide criticism of nuclear testing in the atmosphere by the United States and the fear of fallout from these tests provided an atmosphere of urgency for these early discussions." Ultimately, the PSAC concluded that a test ban detection system was quite feasible and, furthermore, that such a ban would be to the military advantage of the United States. At an NSC meeting on January 6, 1958, when Dulles bemoaned the battering the United States was taking at the United Nations over its nuclear tests, Killian spoke up and reported the PSAC's conclusions. Both Dulles and Eisenhower reacted with delight. Ordering an NSC study of nuclear testing detection, the president remarked that public opinion was now driving U.S. nuclear policy.[61]

So powerful were the outside pressures becoming that Dulles, increasingly taking on Stassen's role within the administration, now began a fight for a uni-lateral halt to U.S. nuclear testing. Learning, through the CIA, that the Soviet Union was about to announce a unilateral suspension of tests on the completion of its current series, the secretary of state called together Defense Department and AEC officials for a crisis meeting on March 23, 1958. Here he revealed a statement he had prepared for the president to issue, announcing that, after the U.S. nuclear test series later that year, Eisenhower did not intend to authorize any further nuclear testing. If this statement were released before the Soviet announcement, declared Dulles, "it would make a great diplomatic and propa-ganda sensation to the advantage of the United States." Aghast at this proposal, Strauss and Undersecretary of Defense Donald Quarles fiercely resisted it. But Dulles planned to press for the unilateral moratorium before the president and other top national security officials the following day.[62]

At the March 24 meeting, the pro-testing forces within the administration emerged triumphant, although only after a bitter dispute. Conceding that a nu-clear test moratorium represented an important shift in the U.S. position, Dulles nonetheless championed it forcefully, observing: "I feel desperately the need for some important gesture in order to gain an effect on world opinion." Re-plying to continued objections from Strauss, Dulles maintained that the State Department must "think in terms of all means of conducting the international struggle" and that the United States was "losing the struggle for world opin-ion." Typically, Eisenhower remained indecisive. It was "intolerable" that cur-rent policy did not have "an advantageous impact on world opinion," he said. Moreover, the American people were "scared" of "these tremendous weapons." Testing was "not evil," but "the fact is that people have been brought to be-lieve that it is." And yet, in the face of fierce resistance from the Defense De-partment and the AEC, Eisenhower failed to change the course of U.S. policy.

As a sop to Dulles, he promised to keep "searching for ideas to stem and turn the tide of propaganda success."[63]

Thereafter, however, it became increasingly difficult to continue nuclear tests. On March 31, the Soviet government announced its unilateral moratorium—an enormous propaganda success for that nation and a disaster for the United States. With their halt to nuclear testing, recalled one U.S. arms control official, "the Russians boxed us in." Meeting with reporters on April 9, Eisenhower told them that if technical reports from his scientific advisers proved favorable, he would support a test ban. In fact, he added, he might even suspend testing unilaterally. On April 10, Dulles wrote secretly to Macmillan: "We are under mounting pressure here to suspend testing after the present series is over. It is not . . . irresistible pressure, but it is appreciable."[64] One week later, the PSAC turned in a report to the president arguing that a test ban "would be to our overall advantage." Meanwhile, the administration's most inveterate foe of a test ban, Lewis Strauss, handed in his resignation as AEC chair, effective at the end of June. Strauss recognized that his reappointment would not clear the U.S. Senate, a fact at least partially attributable to his strident insistence on nuclear testing and his vituperative attacks on its critics.[65]

Taking charge of the situation, Dulles appointed a group of individuals well regarded by the president as an advisory committee on nuclear testing and held a meeting with them on April 26. Predictably, Strauss insisted—as he recalled—that halting testing was "a phoney issue which had been whipped up by the Soviets with the assistance of some disingenuous people in our own country and of some others who knew very well what they were doing." Killian, however, came out strongly for a test ban, pointing to its feasibility and to its advantages. Dulles argued forcefully that "unless we could make some affirmative gesture in the very near future looking to arms reductions, we might lose as allies Japan and Germany and even the U.K." He doubted whether the government's "further refinement of nuclear weapons" was worth a pariah status on the world scene. On April 30, Dulles reported to the president that there was "a consensus" among the advisers that the U.S. government should offer to suspend nuclear tests, pending the development of an inspection system. They believed that "only by concrete actions can we counteract the false picture, all too prevalent abroad, of the United States as a militaristic nation." If U.S. nuclear testing continued, "the slight military gains" would "be outweighed by the political losses, which may well culminate in the moral isolation of the United States." The following morning, the president telephoned Dulles, expressing his agreement that, unless the United States took positive action, it was going to be isolated.[66]

Thereafter, Dulles proved unyielding. Meeting with British officials on June

9 regarding the suspension of nuclear tests, he argued, according to a meeting record, that "the attitude of world opinion about any nation helped to determine the degree of its security. . . . We had to recapture some ground." Later that month, he received word that, unless the United States accepted test suspension, it would be "clobbered" at the forthcoming U.N. General Assembly session. On July 4, the British ambassador noted, Dulles told him that he "thought that in face of public pressure we would have to suspend tests for a specific period."[67] Conferring with Eisenhower that August, Dulles declared that "the opinion of peoples throughout the world is sharply opposed to the continuance of nuclear testing because of their fears over the injury nuclear fallout would bring to them and the yet-unborn generations." Whether such fears "are justified or not . . . doesn't matter. The fact is there's no denying the adverse state of world opinion." Consequently, "if the United States did not announce its readiness to cease nuclear testing, the Soviet Union having already done so, world public opinion would ascribe aggressive intent to the United States which would be definitely harmful to this country."[68]

By this point, too, Eisenhower was determined to change course. On August 12, when he met with Teller and other officials—including Strauss's successor as AEC chair, John McCone—the president reacted skeptically to their enthusiastic reports about recent weapons tests. According to the minutes of the meeting, he remarked that "the new thermonuclear weapons are tremendously powerful; however, they are not . . . as powerful as is world opinion today in obliging the United States to follow certain lines of policy." Six days later, the president overruled the objections of Defense Department and AEC officials to his plans for the suspension of nuclear testing, insisting that "our world situation requires that we achieve the political benefits of this action."[69] Receiving the unwelcome news from McCone, Strauss—now a private citizen—went to the White House and discussed the issue with Eisenhower. Deeply disturbed, Strauss argued that "I felt about Communism as I did about sin—that there was no compromise with it, and that the arms race between good and evil had been going on for centuries and that there would never be an end to it." The president, however, demurred, and Strauss left feeling that they had experienced "a permanent fundamental disagreement." Meeting with the French foreign minister the following day, Eisenhower told him that the suspension of nuclear testing was necessary because the United States appeared "in the eyes of the world as a 'warmonger.'"[70]

Accordingly, on August 22, 1958, with the latest U.S. nuclear testing series at an end, Eisenhower publicly announced that, as of October 31, the United States would suspend nuclear testing for the following year. He called on the nuclear powers to begin test ban negotiations on that date and promised that, with establishment of an inspection network and "satisfactory progress" toward arms control, the U.S. government would renew the test suspension yearly. Nevertheless, instead of bringing nuclear testing to an end, Eisenhower's announcement provoked a surge of nuclear explosions by the governments of the Soviet Union, Britain, and the United States, each apparently determined to maximize its military gains in the final months of nuclear freedom. In late October, as the AEC detonated explosion after explosion, a wind shift sent radioactive clouds scudding toward Los Angeles, bringing radiation in that city to 120 times its normal level. Although the mayor appealed to the U.S. government to call off the final tests, the AEC—insisting that the fallout blanketing the city was "harmless"—completed the series. By its end, there had been at least 125 atomic and hydrogen bomb tests conducted by the United States, 44 by the Soviet Union, and 21 by Britain. Even so, on October 31, 1958, for the first time since the grim inaugural of the nuclear era in 1945, nuclear explosions had ceased around the world.[71]

And What of Disarmament?

By late 1958, then, the world had taken its first steps to halt the nuclear arms race. But, for the most part, this constituted the beginning of arms control—a rationalizing and stabilizing of the military environment. Disarmament remained considerably more problematic. Dulles, whose lengthy career spanned decades of war and international strife, wrote to Adenauer in June 1958: "When there is not imminent danger, governments feel justified in taking some chances" with disarmament. "But when there is a high degree of political tension . . . when 'cold war' is being aggressively waged under conditions which make violent outbreaks likely, and when 'cheating' could have fatal consequences, then governments do not like to take chances." Or, as he told the German ambassador the preceding November: "History indicates that one does not obtain disarmament unless there is confidence." Curiously, only weeks before, Soviet foreign minister Gromyko had said almost the same thing to him. The Soviet Union could not accept an aerial inspection system, Gromyko explained, because "there is a lack of confidence between our two countries."[72] And, given the limits of the traditional international system, both had a good point. But they did not go further and ask: How might this confidence be fostered? Certainly it would not come from the Cold War and the arms race! Consequently, although antinuclear groups helped generate some remarkable changes in public policy, the road to disarmament stretched far off beyond the distant horizon.

The Movement Crests

Britain, Canada, Australia, and New Zealand, 1958–65

> Here, on the historic field of Runnymede, on the
> Aldermaston March, 1963, we . . . demand:
>> Freedom from . . . the nightmare of senseless
> statesmanship which relies on the balance of terror.
>> The right of our children to live, uncrippled by
> nuclear poisons.
>> The right of every individual to say "I shall not
> be party to nuclear murder."
>
> British CND, 1963

Despite the 1958 moratorium on nuclear weapons testing, the nuclear disarmament movement continued its dramatic advance. In part, this reflected the fact that many activists regarded the halting of nuclear testing as only the first step toward global sanity. Roused from politics as usual by the spiraling nuclear arms race, many concerned citizens wanted nothing less than to ban the Bomb. Their determination was reinforced by the disastrous Paris "summit" conference of 1960, the fruitless nuclear arms control negotiations among the great powers at Geneva, and by the 1962 Cuban missile crisis, during which the world teetered eerily on the brink of nuclear war. Furthermore, even the testing moratorium proved evanescent. France began atmospheric nuclear testing in 1960, the Soviet Union resumed atmospheric nuclear testing in 1961, the United States and Britain reverted to underground testing in 1961 and to atmospheric testing in 1962, and China began its first nuclear tests in 1964. As the great powers made nuclear testing, intercontinental ballistics missiles, and preparations for nuclear war ever more prominent features of their "national security" programs, popular resistance to the Bomb grew to unprecedented proportions.

Britain

During 1959 and 1960, the antinuclear campaign in Britain flourished as never before. Religious groups like Christian Action and the Friends Peace Committee organized mass meetings on nuclear disarmament. Eminent scientists rallied to the antinuclear cause. Thousands of citizens turned out in far-flung cities for "Ban the Bomb" demonstrations.[1] Meanwhile, the Direct Action Committee—led by young activists Pat Arrowsmith, Hugh Brock, April Carter, and Michael Randle—organized a brief strike at the missile factories in Stevenage, picketed missile sites in Suffolk and the East Midlands, nonviolently obstructed the nuclear missile base at Harrington, and addressed rallies of workers at key aircraft factories around the country.[2] But it was the Campaign for Nuclear Disarmament that generated a mass constituency for the movement. "CND prospered beyond our wildest dreams," recalled Canon Collins. "Everything seemed to be going our way." Around the country, "groups sprang up like mushrooms; campaign meetings . . . were held in towns and country places; the youth of the country, to the envy of churches and the political organizations, were flocking to our aid and finding in CND a cause, a purpose which at last seemed to make some sense of life." CND's nuclear disarmament symbol "became as well known as the Union Jack and, if to some it was the mark of crankiness, to thousands the world over it became a sign of sanity and hope."[3]

Certainly, CND acquired enormous momentum. Although no membership figures were kept, by 1960 CND had over 450 local groups. Tens of thousands of Britons participated in their activities, and with an enthusiasm that greatly magnified their influence. In 1959, at the suggestion of CND leader Jacquetta Hawkes, it was decided to have CND reverse the course of the previous year's mass march and walk from Aldermaston to London. This would serve as a symbol of CND's immediate political goal—changing the policy of the British government—and, at the same time, enhance the movement's sense of growth, camaraderie, and élan.[4] Conducted over the Easter weekend, the 1959 Aldermaston march—with Collins heading up the wet and bedraggled crew—mustered thousands of marchers and drew 20,000 to the culminating rally. In 1960, 10,000 began the march at Aldermaston and, by the fourth and final day, 40,000 marchers, in a column six miles long, swept into the nation's capital. At their final destination, Trafalgar Square, a crowd estimated at from 60,000 to 100,000 people gathered behind nuclear disarmament banners from unions, churches, political parties, universities, and regions throughout Britain. Observers agreed that it was the largest and most significant popular rally held in that nation since the Chartist demonstrations of 1848.[5]

Nuclear disarmament sentiment also had a powerful impact on the Labour

Party. In 1959, an election year, the party explicitly committed itself to immediately halting all British nuclear tests and to working for an agreement among
all nations other than the United States and the Soviet Union to renounce nuclear weapons. The "Non-Nuclear Club" proposal, particularly, was designed to
head off a split in the party between unilateralists and multilateralists, for a
number of key unions, including the powerful Transport and General Workers
Union, had lined up behind CND's demand for Britain's unilateral nuclear disarmament.[6] In the aftermath of Labour's electoral defeat that fall, the pressure
heightened to revise its defense policy. Additional unions—some of them angry
at party leader Hugh Gaitskell because of his equivocating stance on domestic
issues—endorsed unilateralist resolutions, while forty-three Labour M.P.'s
backed a unilateralist motion in Parliament. In July 1960, the party came out
against Britain's role as an independent nuclear power.[7] That October, as the
Labour Party's annual conference convened at Scarborough, nuclear disarmament demonstrators flooded through the streets of the town, adorned by CND
banners, and key unions lined up behind unilateralism. Fighting back ferociously, Gaitskell denounced the "pacifists, neutralists, and fellow-travellers"
whom he claimed were destroying the Labour Party. The delegates, however,
rejected the leadership's appeals, adopting a resolution calling for "the unilateral renunciation of the testing, manufacture, stockpiling and basing of all nuclear weapons in Great Britain."[8]

Nevertheless, CND proved unable to consolidate this stunning victory. After a vigorous campaign by Gaitskell and his allies, the Labour Party reversed
its position on unilateralism at its fall 1961 conference.[9] Unlike CND and most
of its supporters within the Labour Party—who pamphleteered and held large
rallies in an attempt to keep Labour on track[10]—Gaitskell had an insider's
knowledge of the party apparatus, which served him to good effect. In addition, leading unions wanted to heal the bitter division in the party opened by
defense issues, and key figures proposed compromise positions that muddied
the waters. Indeed, even the victors in the intra-party battle continued to oppose Britain's role as an independent nuclear power. Moreover, following
Gaitskell's death in January 1963, the ascendancy to the party leadership of the
more accommodating Harold Wilson—who brought nuclear critics into his
shadow cabinet and implied that he would scrap some of the Tories' nuclear
plans—led CND's allies within the party to downplay unilateralism in an attempt to further the chances for party unity and, they hoped, electoral victory.
The result was that although Labour did win the 1964 elections, it did so without adopting a unilateralist platform or other solid commitments to CND.[11]

CND's difficulties with the Labour Party were exacerbated by a growing
rift within its own ranks. From the outset, the young militants of the Direct Ac-

tion Committee had no faith in CND's Labour strategy. Convinced that time was limited and that the Bomb could be banned only by a profound transformation of British life, they championed a series of daring, if small-scale, civil disobedience projects, for which they sought CND support.[12] In January 1959, however, the CND executive committee voted to neither "publicly repudiate nor formally associate itself with actions involving civil disobedience." Two months later, at CND's first annual conference, CND leaders helped defeat a resolution by Pat Arrowsmith that would commit CND to a civil disobedience campaign.[13] Over time, however, impatience burgeoned among the movement's rank and file. Angry letters arrived at CND headquarters from individuals and groups charging the leadership with holding back the movement. Russell, too, was growing restless. A supporter for years of nuclear disarmament ventures, including both CND and the DAC, the octogenarian philosopher, like the impatient young, felt a keen sense of frustration. By the summer of 1960, it seemed to him "as if Pugwash and C.N.D. and the other methods that we had tried of informing the public had reached the limit of their effectiveness."[14]

In this context, Ralph Schoenman, an American graduate student at the London School of Economics, set off an explosion in the ranks of the movement. Meeting with Russell that summer, he convinced the CND president that the time had come to organize a massive campaign of civil disobedience that would galvanize public opinion and compel the beleaguered British government to abandon the Bomb. On September 16, Russell—assisted by the Reverend Michael Scott, a minister active in the anti-apartheid movement—mailed out confidential letters to prominent personalities, declaring his belief that "the effectiveness of our Campaign is becoming dependent upon its endorsing a program of civil disobedience" and urging them to join a "Committee of 100" to implement this program.[15] Inadvertently, the press learned of the mailing and, on September 28, began publicizing a distorted version of the activity. This embarrassed both Russell and the CND executive committee, which had known nothing about it. Besieged by the press, Collins sought to distance CND from the Committee of 100, thereby offending Russell. Although CND's leaders tried to patch things up, this proved impossible. Russell, indignant at his presumed mistreatment by Collins, resigned as CND president, much to the distress of CND's members who—as Peggy Duff noted—"did not want to choose between the president and the chairman. They wanted them both." The resulting "chaos," she recalled, "remained with us a long time."[16]

Meanwhile, the Committee of 100 captured the spotlight. Launched at a meeting in October 1960, it secured the backing of some of Britain's most outstanding cultural luminaries. As Schoenman observed, the Committee hoped to create "waves" of "mass resistance" that would "obstruct" the centers of government power "to the point where the authorities have to give way." The Committee of 100 launched its first action on February 18, 1961, when a crowd it estimated at some five thousand people, led by Russell and Scott, staged a sit-down outside the Ministry of Defense, in downtown London. According to the Committee, the demonstrators demanded "the immediate scrapping" of the agreement to bring Polaris nuclear missiles to Britain and declared that they could "no longer stand aside while preparations are being made for the destruction of mankind." Somewhat to the distress of Russell and Schoenman, the police took no action on this occasion.[17] But, on April 29, as some twenty-five hundred demonstrators marshaled by the Committee attempted to march to a scheduled sit-down at Parliament Square, thousands of police blocked their way. Frustrated but nonviolent, the demonstrators sat down en masse, and the police made 826 arrests. At last, the struggle was joined. That August, Russell declared that "governments can be stopped in their mad folly" only "by a vast movement of protest in which all sane men and women must take part. . . . Action must be now or it may be too late."[18]

With the emergence of the Committee of 100 as the exemplar of mass civil disobedience, the DAC terminated its own activities. But the decision was not an easy one. Riding the tide of popular revolt against the Bomb, the DAC had begun to mobilize substantial support. In the spring of 1961, assailing the installation of the U.S. government's nuclear-armed Polaris submarine fleet at Holy Loch, Scotland, the DAC sponsored a mass march from London to Glasgow. Along the way, it sparked big union rallies and drew substantial crowds. Arriving at the submarine site, the demonstrators launched a small flotilla toward the fleet's supply ship, while thousands of others gathered on the beach to obstruct passage by the sailors. It was the group's largest, most dramatic venture yet.[19] Moreover, the Committee of 100 lacked the pacifist, Gandhian orientation of the DAC. Schoenman did not respect the DAC's appeal to individual conscience. Its leaders, in turn, considered him enormously energetic, but a "very difficult" person. Arrowsmith thought he might be a government agent. Nonetheless, the pull of the new, exciting Committee of 100, with its enormous potential, proved irresistible. The DAC's Michael Randle became the Committee's first secretary and other DAC leaders also assumed major posts. In June 1961, citing the duplication of effort between the two groups, the DAC voted to disband and turn over its Holy Loch operations to the Committee of 100.[20]

For a brief time, it seemed that the Committee of 100's daring campaign might just succeed. In July 1961, the Committee announced a new wave of mass civil disobedience against preparations for nuclear war that would culminate, in mid-September, with large-scale action in London and at Holy Loch. Determined to forestall these events, the government arrested more than a third of the Committee members, charging them with violating the Defense of the Realm Act, a law dating back to 1361. At his trial, Russell declared: "We . . . are prepared to suffer imprisonment because we believe that this is the most effective way of working for the salvation of our country and the world." Moreover, "while life remains to us, we will not cease to do what lies in our power to avert the greatest calamity that has ever threatened mankind." When the judge sentenced the eighty-nine-year-old philosopher—like others who refused to desist in their activities—to two months in prison, the action drew headlines around the world and outraged even many persons not ordinarily sympathetic to the Committee of 100. On September 17, the day of the planned sit-down at Parliament Square—an event now officially banned by the government under the Public Order Act—upwards of 12,000 people arrived. Barred by police from entering the area, they eventually occupied Trafalgar Square. Many were from CND, which viewed the government's crackdown as an attack on the movement's civil liberties. The police hardly knew what to do, but eventually arrested 1,314 demonstrators (including Collins) in London and another 351 sit-downers at Holy Loch.[21]

After delivering this stunning rebuke to the government's authority, however, the Committee of 100 lost momentum. To be sure, it protested the resumption of nuclear testing by the Soviet Union and, later, by the United States.[22] Furthermore, it spun off smaller-scale committees among dockworkers, steelworkers, and miners, as well as in thirteen regions throughout Britain, and they began waging campaigns on a local basis.[23] Nevertheless, outside of London, the Committee of 100 simply lacked the numbers necessary to conduct civil disobedience on a mass scale. In December 1961, still dizzy with its triumph at Trafalgar Square, the Committee sought to hold massive demonstrations at seven widely scattered military bases, only to draw, by charitable estimates, some seven thousand people.[24] Although Russell and the Committee issued sharp and well-publicized statements during the Cuban missile crisis, activists came away with a dispiriting sense that they had not affected the course of events.[25] Meanwhile, arrests and government persecution began to take their toll. To head off the military base demonstrations, the government arrested all six staff members of the Committee, charging them with violations of the Official Secrets Act. Five were sentenced to eighteen months in prison, and the sixth to one year. These stiff jail terms not only deprived the Committee of their services for a crucial portion of its history, but had an intimidating effect on the movement.[26]

Furthermore, the Committee's disdain for authority caused serious problems. As early as that spring, some Committee of 100 activists—having failed to convince the Committee to support a civil disobedience action at the end of

CND's Aldermaston march—went ahead and organized the venture anyway. In the confusion of the moment, it immediately disintegrated into two competing, disorderly activities.[27] At the end of the year, the Committee secretary informed Russell that Committees of 100 were "springing up all over the place, some of which do not seem to understand their responsibilities." "Should each Committee be entirely responsible, particularly legally, for each mass action?" she wondered. Indeed, "what, in your view, constitutes a Committee of 100"? In 1963, a small group within the Committee, "Spies for Peace," disrupted the Aldermaston march by leading breakaway demonstrations to previously secret sites, designed to serve as seats of government in the event of a nuclear war.[28] Russell was inclined to take a rather latitudinarian view of the chaos in the Committee's ranks, including the decision of one committee staffer, Pat Pottle, to go into hiding rather than accept arrest for his part in the military base demonstrations.[29] Nevertheless, even Russell eventually lost patience with his creation. To the dismay of many of his supporters, in early January 1963 Russell notified the Committee of 100 that he was resigning as its president. The Committee remained in existence for a few more years, but with far less impact or influence.[30]

By contrast, CND continued to serve as a powerful source of agitation for nuclear disarmament. Although badly shaken by the breakaway of the Committee of 100,[31] CND grew into one of the world's largest, most vigorous peace movements. By 1961, it could point to more than eight hundred local groups, more than twenty persons on its national headquarters staff, and an additional six persons working full-time as regional organizers. Special CND sections— often holding their own meetings and publishing their own literature—existed for Women, Students and Youth, Christians, Teachers, Scientists, and other professional groups. Founded in 1961, *Sanity*, a monthly newspaper published by CND, soon had 45,000 subscribers.[32] CND organized demonstrations of unprecedented size in diverse parts of the British isles, including Glasgow and Belfast.[33] The yearly Aldermaston march remained the largest and best publicized, with an estimated 150,000 people attending the culminating rally in 1962. Although attendance fell off in 1963—perhaps a reflection of the sense of futility engendered by the Cuban missile crisis—the gathering nonetheless provided an impressive display of antinuclear sentiment. The 1963 Aldermaston march had banners which read like a map of Britain, as well as those of dozens of Labour Party branches. Every major union and professional group sported a contingent, and delegations from numerous countries marched in its international section. Struck by the youthful energy and dynamism of the CND marchers, a BBC reporter quipped that they "may well be the only people left alive in Britain today."[34]

Throughout the early 1960s, CND channeled these energies in a variety of directions. To some degree, it still attempted to win the support of the Labour Party, although with diminishing effectiveness. Furthermore, without ever endorsing civil disobedience, it sought to remain on friendly terms with Russell and the Committee of 100.[35] When the Soviet government resumed nuclear testing in 1961, CND immediately dispatched a protest delegation to the Soviet embassy in London, held a March of Shame, and had Kingsley Martin raise the issue with diplomats at the Belgrade conference of nonaligned nations. After the U.S. government resumed nuclear testing, CND and other antinuclear groups maintained continuous picket lines outside both the U.S. and Soviet embassies.[36] CND's supporters demonstrated at the embassies again—as well as throughout Britain—in October 1962, during the Cuban missile crisis. Arguing that "the present Cuban crisis arises directly out of the international arms race," CND urged the closure of "all nuclear bases on the territory of other nations," condemned the U.S. blockade, and called on the British government to "demand assurances from the U.S. government that there will be no invasion or armed attack upon Cuba."[37] CND also organized door-to-door and other kinds of educational campaigns and, in 1961, began to advocate a new kind of foreign policy for Britain—"positive neutralism," which entailed leaving NATO and embracing nonalignment.[38]

For the most part, however, CND continued to hammer away at its critique of the Bomb. In April 1964, when it replaced the yearly Aldermaston march with a rally at Trafalgar Square, it told the assemblage:

We say, as we have always said, that nuclear weapons are morally abominable, militarily useless and economically ruinous; that the thought and threat of using them belongs to the dead past. . . .

Today we reaffirm all that we proclaimed and argued when our movement was born. We work now, as we worked then, for a national policy that will reject the threat of mass destruction as a principle; that will renounce the bomb without equivocation or deceit. . . .

. . . We work now, in the honored and welcome company of men and women all over the world who believe in creation and not destruction—in reason and not folly—in life and not death.

This, on Easter Monday 1964, is our statement, and to this we hold. From this we shall not be moved.[39]

In a number of ways, the constituency of Britain's antinuclear movement departed from that nation's political norms.[40] Promoting moral idealism rather than class or economic interests, the new movement—despite its flirtation with the unions and the Labour Party—did not attract a substantial number of blue-collar workers. Nor did it have much appeal to those elements of the middle or upper classes engaged in commercial pursuits. Instead, it drew heavily on socially concerned, organizationally active, and politically avant garde portions of the middle class, usually located in the human welfare and creative professions: teaching, social work, health care, the church, journalism, art, literature, theater, architecture, and scientific research. On university campuses, CND chapters became some of the largest, most powerful student groups. Provided with considerable autonomy by its parent organization, Colleges and Universities CND eventually claimed 150 chapters. Nuclear disarmament sentiment also swept like a storm through British intellectual and cultural life, emerging with the support of many of the nation's most celebrated artists, writers, musicians, and directors. They included John Osborne, Doris Lessing, Arnold Wesker, Benjamin Britten, Michael Tippett, Robert Bolt, Shelagh Delaney, Vanessa Redgrave, Iris Murdoch, Alan Sillitoe, Compton Mackenzie, Mervyn Jones, Alex Comfort, Herbert Read, Henry Moore, and Kenneth Tynan.[41]

The middle-class, intellectual tone of the movement caused some uneasiness on the Left. Uncomfortable with the movement's constituency and program, the British Communist Party remained aloof until 1960. The Trotskyists, too, though early enthusiasts, were impatient with the movement's moral emphasis. CND, they claimed, should "wage this campaign not in any abstract, humanitarian, above-class way, but as a frankly socialist campaign, with the industrial workers in the lead." Otherwise, the Aldermaston marches would do no more than provide "a yearly catharsis for the middle-class conscience, an act of ritual mortification and sacrifice, till one day good miraculously triumphs over evil." Only the younger, university-oriented New Left, casting off Marxist orthodoxy, felt at ease with the movement and developed an important role in it. With some success, they blended a critique of what E. P. Thompson called "the nuclear reign of terror" with a new, radical approach to British politics and foreign policy.[42]

Whatever the movement's moral emphasis cost it on the tiny Marxist-Leninist Left, it more than made up among persons with a religious orientation. Although the British Council of Churches, including the dominant Anglican Church, never endorsed Britain's unilateral renunciation of the Bomb, in 1963 it did urge Britain to express its "willingness to forego the claim to independent nuclear action" and did assail the Western policy of first use of nuclear weapons. Furthermore, some Anglican church leaders (e.g. Collins, Scott, and the Reverend Donald Soper) played a prominent part at the movement's national level, and others served as leaders of CND's local organizations. The movement had much greater popularity among followers of the Free Churches—Methodists, Presbyterians, Baptists and, especially, Quakers—and among Catholics. Such support flowed not only from the movement's moral approach, but from the religious, sacrificial aspects of its marches, fasts, and vigils—particularly the Aldermaston march, with its Easter setting and its strong overtones of pilgrimage. Eschewing civil disobedience and other dramatic gestures, Christian CND—established by Francis Jude of the Friends Peace Committee—sponsored discussions in the churches, organized antinuclear pilgrimages to cathedral towns, and published antinuclear literature. In 1964, a Whitsuntide pilgrimage of Christian CND marched with "The Complaint of Canterbury" before it, accusing the church of failing because of its own unbelief.[43]

Women played an important role in the movement. On the surface, this did not seem to be the case, for the national leadership of CND and of the Committee of 100 was predominantly male. Moreover, at least one survey of Aldermaston marchers, in 1963, found that men comprised two-thirds of the assemblage. Nevertheless, at a time when women had virtually no role in mainstream British politics, they constituted some of the key leaders of the Direct Action Committee (e.g. April Carter and Pat Arrowsmith) and of CND (e.g. Peggy Duff, Olive Gibbs, Jacquetta Hawkes, and Antoinette Pirie). Duff, a veteran political agitator, served as CND's secretary and chief organizer from 1958 to 1967. Gibbs, succeeding Collins as chair of CND in 1964, served in this capacity until 1967. CND's Women's Group emphasized women's roles as mothers, defending their children against radioactive fallout and nuclear war. This maternalist focus, rather than feminism, also provided the basis for two new women's organizations. In November 1961, a group of mothers in London decided to stage a protest at the U.S. and Soviet embassies against the resumption of atmospheric nuclear testing. Some eight hundred people turned out, leading to the formation of Women Against the Bomb. That same month, a writer and mother of young children, alarmed by threats of nuclear war over Berlin, published a letter in the *Guardian* asking what women should do. Within four days, a thousand letters arrived in response, leading to the formation of the Voice of Women. In 1962, these organizations and others, including the British WILPF section, established the Liaison Committee for Women's Peace Groups, which mobilized women's peace protest for years thereafter.[44]

The movement also had a strong appeal to the young. Provided with its own organizer and office space by CND, the Youth Campaign for Nuclear Disarmament became a powerful, semiautonomous force, with 250 local groups. It organized its own demonstrations, produced its own literature, published its own newspaper, ran its own conferences, and swelled the ranks of the movement. A survey of Aldermaston marchers in 1963 found that more than half were under twenty-six years of age. Many, in fact, were teenagers. Although most young activists had at least one parent who shared their views, they did tend to see the Bomb (and assorted social injustices) as evidence of the overall political bankruptcy of the older generation. Conversely, antinuclear protest—especially its demonstrations, marches, and civil disobedience actions—provided them with an unorthodox, exciting means of breaking with conventional politics and its bureaucratized forms. Not surprisingly then, nuclear disarmament activism helped spawn a rambunctious "youth culture" that scandalized more conventional members of British society and even some of the middle-aged stalwarts of CND. "They were slightly crazy," Duff recalled fondly, "but not so crazy as the world they were trying to change."[45]

Despite the impressive size and appeal of Britain's nuclear disarmament movement, it struggled with some significant problems. One of these had to do with public relations. Although the Committee of 100's early sit-downs were well attended and well publicized, they alienated many Britons. In October 1961, a Gallup poll found that 61 percent of the public disapproved of "the direct action of sitting-down against H-bombs." That December, noting that public support for unilateralism had slumped from 30 to 21 percent, the British Institute of Public Opinion concluded that the Committee of 100 demonstrations had produced "powerful support for their opponents." Writing in CND's newspaper, the Reverend Soper complained, with some justice, that civil disobedience "is debilitating the real argument about banning the Bomb."[46] In addition, the movement's occasionally strident pronouncements—most notably Russell's bitter denunciations of Western leaders—offended just those Britons to whom moderate critics of the Bomb like Sir Richard Acland sought to appeal: "a very large percentage of our 'middling people.'" In late 1962, at a CND executive committee meeting, Collins initiated a discussion of the Campaign's "public image" and suggested that the leadership "discuss seriously measures to improve it." But, in fact, the situation went from bad to worse. Unwaveringly hostile, the nation's press lavished attention on the movement's growing unruliness and unconventionality, including the embarrassing "Spies for Peace" incident.[47]

The movement also faced difficulties with respect to program. Duff and other leaders recalled that the demand for unilateral action gave the movement a "sharp cutting edge," enabling it to avoid sinking into the morass of insincere great power discussions of disarmament.[48] Even so, she observed, "unilateralism became a sort of religion," with little room for alternative approaches to banning the Bomb. And millions of Britons preferred nuclear disarmament through international measures. Ironically, even some of the movement's most prominent leaders—notably, Russell—were convinced globalists. Occasionally, CND published materials along these lines, including Frank Beswick's *Towards World Government*, promoted by *Sanity* as showing "how closely world government and disarmament interrelate." A sociological study found that when Aldermaston marchers were questioned about how they would like to see the world organized, a majority favored "a world government and the disappearance of national borders."[49] Nonetheless, the movement made Britain's unilateral action the centerpiece of its campaign, thereby writing off the substantial antinuclear sentiment that remained outside its ranks.[50] Furthermore, as the years passed and additional nations acquired nuclear weapons, even some early supporters of Britain's renouncing the Bomb felt it no longer had the same political relevance.[51]

Certainly, CND made little headway with popularizing Britain's unilateral nuclear disarmament. Between 1958 and 1963, polls reported, support for unilateralism varied from roughly one-fifth to one-third of the population. With the exception of a decline in support in late 1960 and 1961, the zenith of activity by the Committee of 100, the unilateralist tide lacked any consistent direction.[52] Nor did the movement have much greater success with convincing the public to oppose the stationing of Polaris submarines at Holy Loch. Between November 1960 and March 1964, public approval of the idea grew from 44 to 49 percent, while disapproval fell from 36 to 33 percent.[53]

Nevertheless, this focus on the limited appeal of unilateralism provides a very incomplete picture of the movement's impact on British public life. Although the movement rallied only a minority of the population, it mobilized this minority in a very dramatic way, making the Bomb an issue of great salience. Britain's newspapers were filled with stories about nuclear weapons and the protests against them. *Punch*, the comic weekly, ran a constant stream of Bomb-related cartoons. One showed a man saying: "I had the most ghastly nightmare: I dreamed I was red and dead." Another portrayed a man stating: "Just the same as gas—they'll never use it," as a vast mushroom cloud loomed behind him. Promoting a fallout shelter, one cartoon character remarked: "This is the de luxe model, and of course, if anything should go wrong, it makes the perfect family mausoleum." Substantial majorities of the population told pollsters that they worried about nuclear weapons—some a little and some a great deal. Asked, in October 1961, if they would prefer "fighting an all-out nuclear war" to "living under communist rule," only 21 percent of Britons chose the former.[54]

Nuclear testing continued to provide a focal point of popular discontent. In June 1959, when pollsters—after stating that "very little progress has been made" in the disarmament talks at Geneva—asked Britons if they thought the West should resume nuclear tests, 66 percent rejected the idea. In the immediate aftermath of the Soviet resumption of nuclear testing in the fall of 1961, 64 percent of Britons polled still opposed the resumption of Western nuclear testing. Even by April 1962, only 25 percent of Britons supported U.S. resumption of atmospheric nuclear testing; 56 percent opposed it. That December, asked their opinion of "Britain's decision to explode another nuclear device," only 27 percent expressed approval and 57 percent disapproval. In early 1962, 82 percent of Britons told pollsters that the party drawing their vote should support proposals to negotiate an "international agreement to stop H-bomb tests"; only 8 percent demurred.[55]

Furthermore, overwhelming majorities of Britons genuinely wanted to ban the Bomb. They strongly opposed proliferation of nuclear weapons, even to France (65 percent, with only 17 percent in favor), and consistently expressed a desire to rid the world of nuclear weapons. To be sure, in March 1958, with CND just beginning its activities, a poll found that 72 percent of Britons already favored internationally enforced nuclear disarmament. But that sentiment grew. In August 1962, as a Gallup poll indicated, 82 percent of Britons favored an agreement among all countries to eliminate the Bomb. Early the following year, 84 percent of survey respondents supported the worldwide abolition of nuclear weapons, leaving opposition at only 9 percent. As a new British musical group, the Beatles, toured the United States in March 1964, young Paul McCartney, appearing on television, blithely told millions of viewers what they already believed: "Ban the Bomb."[56] If the movement had failed to win Britons to its unilateralist strategy, it had helped to make its goal—a nuclear-free world—an inescapable part of public opinion.

Nor was this the movement's only accomplishment. Having shattered popular complacency about nuclear weapons, the movement also forced the issue of the Bomb into the political arena. As a somewhat overenthusiastic CND report of 1964 noted:

Our greatest achievement was to put the issue of nuclear arms and disarmament into the center of politics. We forced on the Labour Party an exhaustive and agonizing debate on the nuclear issue. . . . We so changed the public mood that whereas in 1957 it was possible for the government to carry out a massive series of tests, in 1961 the existence of world wide opposition had become a factor to be reckoned with, and by 1963, a partial Treaty had been signed. We so changed the public mood that it was possible, in 1964, for a Conservative government to make the retention of the independent nuclear force a major issue of the election, and to lose it.

Furthermore, and perhaps most important, CND—and, to a lesser extent, the proponents of civil disobedience—provided a model for the development of nuclear disarmament movements in nations around the world. In this sense, at least, Britain really did lead the way.[57]

Canada

Initially, the movement in Canada developed with a somewhat different orientation. In April 1959, after preliminary correspondence with Norman Cousins and SANE, Mary Van Stolk of Edmonton founded a community group, the Committee on the Control of Radiation Hazards. Her decision to act resulted, in part, from the fact that her husband, Dr. Jan Van Stolk, had worked at Lambaréné when Albert Schweitzer had written his "Declaration of Conscience."[58] Through the efforts of Mary Van Stolk, the Edmonton group became increasingly focused on halting the testing of nuclear weapons and, in September, sponsored a well-attended lecture in that city by Linus Pauling. Traveling across Canada and talking to prominent clergy, businessmen, academics, politicians, and other well-known figures, Van Stolk persuaded them to form a national committee. Chaired by Hugh Keenleyside, head of the British Columbia Power Commission and former director-general of the U.N. Technical Assistance Administration, the Canadian Committee for the Control of Radiation Hazards (CCCRH) issued its first press release that winter. Although the CCCRH called for "intensified research" on radiation hazards and for efforts to minimize them, its key demand was the "immediate cessation of nuclear tests by all countries, enforced by inspection, preferably under the United Nations."[59]

The Canadian government's announcement, in late 1959, that it planned to purchase Bomarc missiles from the United States, presumably to be fitted with nuclear warheads, launched the CCCRH on its career as a full-fledged ban-the-Bomb organization. Throughout 1960, CCCRH leaders addressed the nuclear issue in increasingly broad terms—a process helped along by the collapse of the Paris summit conference and by the great popularity of an antinuclear book, *Peacemaker or Powdermonkey*, by James Minifie, a Canadian newspaper correspondent in Washington.[60] In the spring of 1961, the CCCRH began circulating a petition calling on the government to reject nuclear weapons for Canada. The petition soon had some very eminent endorsers, including prominent educators, well-known authors, powerful newspapers, provincial legislatures, and the Canadian Labor Congress. Meanwhile, in Toronto and elsewhere, local affiliates and sympathetic groups organized mass meetings against nuclear weapons, featuring leaders of the American and British movements. In October 1961, when the CCCRH presented Canada's prime minister with the petition, it had 141,000 signatures; eventually, the number topped 200,000.[61] Although the CCCRH's actual membership, located primarily in the nation's large urban centers, was far smaller, by early 1962 the group claimed a respectable fourteen local branches and had perhaps eight thousand members. Recognizing that the organization had evolved into a popular movement similar to Britain's CND, delegates at the CCCRH's February 1962 national convention voted unanimously to rename it the Canadian Campaign for Nuclear Disarmament.[62]

Canadian CND inherited not only the CCCRH's local branches, but the chapters of Combined Universities CND, a youth group that had been developing independently since 1959. Shocked by the Canadian government's Bomarc decision, university students in Montreal began petitioning against it. On Christmas Day 1959, having adopted the name Combined Universities CND, they staged an antinuclear protest in Ottawa, Canada's first youth demonstration of the postwar era. Like the CCCRH, Combined Universities CND did not advocate unilateral nuclear disarmament by the United States, but by Canada, arguing—like its British model—that this country, "by its example, can give moral and political leadership to the world." The group supplemented this unilateralist program with a broad critique of the Bomb:

We affirm our conviction that nuclear arms are wholly evil; that, short of war, their very existence imperils present and future generations; and that, in the event of war, nations which condone their use will be committing suicide and will be guilty of the murder of the rest of mankind.

And we declare our aim—to secure their total abolition.

Inspired by these sentiments, students flocked to the new group on campuses from Newfoundland to British Columbia.[63]

By 1961, Combined Universities CND, chaired by young Dimitri Roussopoulos, was a flourishing operation. That September, it demonstrated against Soviet resumption of nuclear testing, arguing that "the further poisoning of our health, the damaging of our children, and [of] countless generations to come, is nothing short of . . . criminal. . . . No one has the right to do these things." Indeed, "the conduct of the great powers is an affront to the dignity of ordinary people all over the world." In addition, Combined Universities CND staged a three-day antinuclear vigil at the parliament building, established close contacts with activists in Britain and the United States, and began publishing a lively journal, *Our Generation Against Nuclear War*.[64] Providing a send-off in the first issue, Russell stated that "the movement for nuclear disarmament in Canada has already shown itself vigorous and forthright, and has roused the admiration of us in Britain who are engaged in the same task." In early 1962, when Combined Universities CND became the youth affiliate of Canadian CND, it brought new dynamism and strength to the parent group, including twenty-one university chapters with some seven thousand members.[65]

The heightening nuclear arms race also inspired the development of a substantial women's peace movement. In May 1960, when the Paris summit conference collapsed, Lotta Dempsey, a newspaper columnist for the *Toronto Star*, wrote an article urging collective action by women against the threat of nuclear war. Following up, leaders of the Toronto Committee for Disarmament (later the local branch of Canadian CND), chaired by Rabbi Abraham Feinberg, agreed to present the idea to a mass meeting the group had scheduled for June 10. When the gathering enthusiastically endorsed this approach, activists launched the Voice of Women (VOW) on July 28, 1960, with the dynamic Helen Tucker of the Toronto Committee as its first president. Although VOW attracted a goodly share of Quaker pacifists and other experienced political activists, it initially gave the appearance of a rather mild, respectable organization, for it drew many well-dressed, middle-class women, including the wives of prominent politicians. Like VOW's British counterparts, with which it was not affiliated, it took a traditional view of women's role. One of its early brochures declared: "VOW believes that women, as the givers of life, are particularly concerned about survival of children and have special responsibility for preserving life." Tucker argued that women were driven by "maternal urges to feed, to protect and to love"—characteristics "of creation not destruction." In line with these assumptions, VOW supported "universal controlled disarmament" and opposed the acquisition of nuclear weapons by additional nations, as well as the resumption of nuclear testing.[66]

For the new women's organization, the early 1960s proved a hectic time. As two of its leaders recalled: "The activity and women-hours of volunteer work were prodigious. Groups were formed, campaigns-of-the-week planned, plebiscites for peace collected, letters written to M.P.s, to Cabinet ministers, to mayors, to newspapers, to organizations, to women in other countries." In addition, vigils were held, "delegations sent, press conferences arranged, radio and television shows produced, public meetings held. To finance it all, members gave theatre parties, coffee parties, teas, auctions; they donated baby bonus checks, published cookbooks and greeting cards, held bazaars and canvassed their communities." Within a year, VOW had five thousand members, with an impact far greater than these numbers imply. In September 1962, it organized an International Conference of Women for Peace in Montreal. VOW also collected thousands of baby teeth to test for strontium-90, dispatched a delegation to the Geneva disarmament conference, and championed a peaceful settlement of the Cuban missile crisis. In September 1962, when VOW members assembled for the group's second annual meeting, it had almost doubled in size over the past year. For their new president, they elected Thérèse Casgrain, a prominent Quebec reformer and recent New Democratic Party candidate for parliament. As her successor, Kay Macpherson, recalled, Casgrain was "an enchanting mixture of grand dame and peacenik."[67]

A number of smaller groups rounded out Canada's nuclear disarmament movement. During 1961–62, a tiny Committee of 100 emerged briefly in Montreal and Toronto, but never attracted the interest or support generated by its British counterpart.[68] In addition, a group of French Canadians, previously active in Canadian CND or in Combined Universities CND, decided that they could better reach their compatriots in French-speaking Canada by founding an independent—albeit friendly—organization, the Movement for Nuclear Disarmament and Peace (Le Mouvement pour le Désarmement Nucléaire et la Paix). Launching the venture in November 1962, they claimed some eight hundred members in Quebec within a year.[69] Although organized pacifism in Canada remained fairly weak, the small FOR group did cooperate with the CCCRH. Moreover, the Quakers and Mennonites entered the nuclear debate, with the Quaker peace center on Grindstone Island serving as an important training camp for student activists.[70] Finally, the small but influential world federalist movement, although uncomfortable with unilateralist proposals, took a strong antinuclear stand. In 1960, the president of the Winnipeg branch of the World Federalists of Canada estimated that most of his members were also members of the local CCCRH group. Two years later, at the suggestion of the national federalist group, delegates from eleven Canadian peace and disarmament organizations met, established a loose coalition, and—to "hasten general disarmament under international control"—urged that Canada refuse to accept nuclear weapons.[71]

Throughout 1962, Canada's peace and disarmament organizations worked together, producing an unprecedented outpouring of popular concern about nuclear weapons. Adopting yet another British tactic, they staged Easter marches that year in Montreal, Toronto, Ottawa, Winnipeg, Vancouver, Edmonton, Calgary, and elsewhere, drawing some ten thousand people. Sponsorship of the demonstrations or speakers at their culminating rallies came from Canadian CND, VOW, the FOR, the World Federalists, the Society of Friends, and from assorted universities, churches, and unions.[72] Addressing a campaign rally in late May, Prime Minister John Diefenbaker was shocked to find the hall "filled with cries of 'Ban-Ban-Ban the Bomb.'" During the Cuban missile crisis, most of these groups joined together again to produce a stinging public indictment of the Soviet missile emplacement and of the U.S. blockade of Cuba. In November, Canadian CND and Combined Universities CND held a mass lobby of parliament in which M.P.'s were urged to reject Canadian possession of nuclear weapons, to oppose nuclear proliferation, to demand an immediate end to nuclear testing by all powers, and to initiate U.N. resolutions to maintain the Third World as a nuclear-free zone.[73]

Inevitably, the nuclear issue found its way into Canadian politics. The Conservative government's acquisition of Bomarc and later weapons systems seemed to portend the arrival of nuclear warheads, a plan promoted by the military and by the minister of defense. On the other hand, Howard Green, appointed minister of external relations in 1959, believed firmly in nuclear disarmament and, accordingly, strongly opposed Canada's acquisition of nuclear weapons. Furthermore, all the opposition parties (the Liberals and two smaller rivals, the New Democratic Party and the Social Credit Party) adopted an antinuclear stance. Impressed by these factors and, especially, by the surge of antinuclear sentiment, Diefenbaker began to hedge on the nuclear warheads. In 1961, he assured a CCCRH spokesperson that they would not be installed in peacetime. After the Cuban missile crisis, however, polls reported that a majority of the public favored acquiring nuclear weapons. Moreover, the split over the question widened within Conservative ranks. These factors—as well as a trip to the United States to confer with U.S. government officials—convinced Lester Pearson, head of the Liberal Party, to reverse his previous position and, in January 1963, to come out strongly in favor of the weapons. This Liberal turnabout, reinforced by a U.S. State Department press release denouncing the Canadian government's nuclear policy and by the resignation of the minister of defense, led to the passage in parliament of a vote of no-confidence in Diefenbaker's minority government and to the calling of elections for mid-April.[74]

Convinced, in the words of Canadian CND, that the centrality of the nuclear issue made this "the most important election in Canadian history," Canada's antinuclear movement threw itself into the ensuing campaign. Canadian CND branches brought their antinuclear message to the public by organizing public meetings, interviewing candidates, producing and distributing literature, holding radio, television, and public forums, and by running newspaper advertisements. In Toronto, the local CND group distributed an antinuclear arms statement signed by ninety-six ministers, sent a CND fact sheet to provincial weeklies and dailies, placed an advertisement in the *Daily Star*, and conducted a last-minute "blitz leafletting" with seventy-five thousand pieces of antinuclear literature.[75] The apostasy of Pearson and the Liberals, of course, came in for a great deal of criticism by Canada's nuclear disarmament groups, including VOW. In turn, Marion Pearson, wife of the Liberal leader, resigned as an Honorary Sponsor of VOW, charging that, by vigorously opposing nuclear arms for Canada, the women's organization had changed *its* position! Steering clear of party endorsements, Canadian CND called on Canadians to "resolutely oppose Canada's involvement in the spread of nuclear arms and warheads. This would be a major constructive contribution both to general disarmament and world peace."[76]

The April 1963 elections dealt a very serious setback to the movement. To be sure, Pearson's Liberals, though victorious, drew only 41 percent of the vote—a small increase over 1962, when they had lost—leading most commentators to conclude that Canadians had not rallied behind the call for nu-

clear weapons. Indeed, one leader of the Liberal Party claimed that its pro-nuclear stand had prevented it from winning a majority, for a number of attractive young Liberal candidates, including Pierre Trudeau, had bitterly denounced Pearson's turnabout and withdrawn from the party in protest.[77] Nevertheless, Pearson was able to form a minority government and lay plans to
bring nuclear weapons to Canada. These plans were sharply attacked in parliament by Tommy Douglas, head of the New Democratic Party, who proposed a
resolution that condemned Canada's acquisition of nuclear arms as "lessening
the chances for nuclear disarmament and increasing the danger of nuclear war."
After what the press described as an evening of high drama, the resolution was
defeated, 124 to 113. On December 31—a date chosen, some claimed, to minimize public attention—the government installed nuclear weapons in Ontario.
Ten days later, they were deployed in Quebec.[78]

Although badly shaken by these defeats, the movement did not collapse.
Canadian CND, the hardest hit of the disarmament organizations, did undergo
a serious loss of morale, focus, and leadership. Nevertheless, it continued to
organize parliamentary lobbying days, distribute antinuclear literature, arrange
for talks by prominent individuals, and sponsor demonstrations, albeit on a
smaller scale than in the past.[79] Combined Universities CND also persisted in
its antinuclear efforts. In late June 1964, it helped organize a sit-down of nearly
a hundred students outside the Bomarc base at La Macaza, Quebec. Removed
thirty-one times by guards, sometimes quite brutally, the protesters kept up
their nonviolent occupation for forty-eight hours. In 1965, activists in British
Columbia also initiated a campaign of nonviolent resistance against nuclear
weapons which, in 1971, culminated in the establishment of a new international
organization, Greenpeace.[80] Meanwhile, VOW—although losing some members and respectability thanks to its uncompromising stance during early
1963—continued its operations. It held antinuclear Mother's Day vigils and
dispatched a delegation to a NATO meeting at the Hague, where it joined
women from other nations protesting plans for a multilateral nuclear force. In
late 1964, VOW sent another antinuclear delegation to Paris, where Casgrain
and Macpherson, along with participants from other countries, found themselves thrown into a local jail after they sought to deliver a protest letter to
NATO's secretary-general.[81]

As in other countries, the impact of the nuclear disarmament movement on
public opinion cannot be measured with any precision, but it appears to have
had some effect. Between December 1961 and June 1963—the period of the
movement's greatest activity—Gallup polls found that support for arming
Canada's forces with nuclear weapons fell from 61 percent to 49 percent.[82] Furthermore, although polls reported overwhelming opposition to unilateral nu-

clear disarmament by the West, a survey in the winter of 1962–63 estimated that 92 percent of voters favored "general disarmament with proper safeguards" and that 85 percent thought "all nations should stop nuclear testing." Indeed, Gallup polls found that, between 1958 and September 1962, Canadians favoring a halt to U.S. nuclear tests rose from 41 to 47 percent and those favoring continuation fell from 45 to 39 percent. Asked, in the winter of 1962–63, if "the West should take all steps to defeat Communism, even if it means risking nuclear war," 42 percent of Canadian voters said "yes," but 47 percent said "no." That same poll found that 44 percent had never heard of the "Ban the Bomb Movement." But this did not mean that they were not influenced by its message. Furthermore, another 36 percent declared that they approved of the movement and only 20 percent said they did not.[83]

Australia

A nuclear disarmament movement on the British model also made its debut in Australia. Although efforts to form a Committee of 100 apparently came to naught,[84] activists interested in establishing an Australian CND had better luck. Inspired by the British campaign and uncomfortable with the Old Left leadership and conventional tactics of the established peace movement, a group of young intellectuals in Melbourne formed Victorian CND in 1960. It called on the Australian government to renounce any involvement in Western nuclear strategy, to work for a test ban treaty, and to pledge never to develop its own nuclear weapons. Activists at the University of Melbourne established a campus chapter, which served as the core of the broader group. In 1962, other CND groups emerged in Sydney, Perth, and Brisbane, providing the heart of CND organizations in the states of New South Wales, Queensland, and Western Australia. These groups were widely dispersed across Australia's vast territory and, furthermore, remained rather small. Indeed, in late 1962, Western Australia CND attracted only thirty to fifty people to its monthly meetings and had fewer than three hundred persons on its mailing list. Even at the height of their activity, in 1962–63, Australia's CND groups lacked the widespread participation of comparable movements in Britain and Canada. Nevertheless, they had enough strength, vitality, and potential to hold a convention in Sydney, in December 1963, and establish a nationwide CND.[85]

The constituency, activities, and program of Australian CND resembled its overseas counterparts. Appealing particularly to the youthful, educated middle class, CND drew heavily on teachers, students, assorted professionals, and young housewives. Many were supporters of the Labor Party or had avant garde political and social views. In downtown Brisbane, young people gathered on Sunday afternoons before a huge CND banner, where they played guitars, sang folk songs, and attracted small, youthful crowds to listen to antinuclear speakers. At the University of Sydney, the CND group protested against the resumption of Soviet and U.S. nuclear testing, proclaiming: "End all tests, East and West." Queensland CND sponsored discussion nights and showed films on the Hiroshima bombing, on current nuclear dangers, and on Britain's Aldermaston march. Kenneth McNaughton, a young teacher and chair of the Western Australia CND group, told the press that his movement's goal was to have people stop "looking at things only in the light of military advantage" and begin thinking about the consequences of nuclear war. Although the different regional groups sometimes emphasized different items, their program usually boiled down to having Australia refuse to possess, manufacture, or use nuclear weapons; ban nuclear bases on its territory; and ban nuclear tests on its territory.[86]

Unlike British CND, however, Australian CND faced competition from a larger, established peace movement. Recognizing its isolation in public life, the Communist-dominated Australian Peace Council had held a series of national conferences to broaden its constituency and appeal. The conferences of 1953 and 1956 met with little success along these lines. In November 1959, however, a conference in Melbourne—the Australian and New Zealand Congress for International Cooperation and Disarmament—made a partial breakthrough, for it drew the support of leading clergy, intellectuals, and union leaders. Although some pro-Soviet leaders retained their positions in the ANZ Congress, the new organization spawned by the gathering, it took a more even-handed approach than had past ventures. In 1961, the ANZ Congress condemned Soviet resumption of nuclear testing. Three years later, it criticized nuclear tests undertaken by China. Nevertheless, residual distrust of Communist-influenced peace organizations, combined with the disdain of the young for the group's unobtrusive activities and bland pronouncements, led most of the new generation of activists to seek out the more independent, youthful, and exciting CND. The ANZ Congress and its 1964 successor, the Australian Congress for International Cooperation and Disarmament, although increasingly nonaligned in orientation, remained confined largely to socially active clergy and left-wing trade unionists.[87]

Other key constituencies added to the demand for nuclear disarmament. Concerned scientists formed Pugwash branches in Melbourne, Sydney, and Adelaide. The FOR staged vigils outside churches to challenge the conscience of Australians on the subject of nuclear war. The *Peacemaker*, organ of the Federal Pacifist Council, gave a good deal of attention to the nuclear question and to CND. Eschewing a sectarian approach, a *Peacemaker* editorial commented that "this Campaign for Nuclear Disarmament seems worthy of support as a step in the right direction."[88] Although women's peace activism made less headway in Australia than it did in Britain and Canada, the WILPF group circulated a petition against nuclear testing in the southern hemisphere. Moreover, in late 1964, Australian women launched a Committee Against Atomic Testing in Sydney. Supported by women's peace groups in Sweden, Canada, the United States, and elsewhere, it originally planned to have women sail into the French nuclear testing site in the Pacific. Eventually, a somewhat different strategy emerged, in which women, some with babies in their arms, boarded an antinuclear launch that met French warships arriving in Australia. On the departure of the French fleet, local craft displayed signs reading: "No French Tests," "Sign the Treaty Against the Bomb," and "Ban the Bomb."[89]

Working together, antinuclear activists gave the issue of the Bomb enhanced visibility in Australian life. In April 1962, local CND and ANZ Congress groups—in uneasy harness—sponsored "Aldermaston Solidarity" marches in Melbourne and Sydney, drawing roughly two thousand participants to each event. Organizers developed the Australian movement's "radial walk," in which demonstrators marched from assorted suburbs to converge at a downtown rally, thus covering an H-Bomb's area of destruction. Along the way, marchers placed memorial wreaths at cenotaphs, met with public officials, and distributed large numbers of antinuclear leaflets. Young people, prominent in these events, favored a somewhat bohemian style and sang Aldermaston songs, including Australian variations.[90] That August, activists organized a "Peace Rally" in Canberra, with more than a thousand demonstrators marching through the city and visiting the embassies of the nuclear powers. They also delivered a petition, with 205,000 signatures, that called on the government to adopt the proposal of Arthur Calwell, leader of the Labor opposition, to make the southern hemisphere a nuclear-free zone, to assure the United Nations of Australia's willingness to sign an agreement not to acquire or deploy nuclear weapons, and to assist in securing a test ban treaty.[91] In the spring of 1963, activists organized another round of antinuclear marches, as more than three thousand people turned out for a radial march in Sydney and smaller crowds participated in Melbourne and Perth. Easter marches continued in 1964 and 1965.[92]

Although the Australian movement had some influence on the broader society, this remained limited. Individual clergy spoke out at times on nuclear questions and, in September 1961, the executive committee of the Australian Council of Churches did issue pleas to the governments of Australia and Britain "to pursue vigorously courses of action which will lead to the cessation of nuclear weapons testing and the resumption of negotiations of international

agreements." Nevertheless, with the exception of the Quakers, Australia's religious denominations exhibited little sustained public involvement with these
issues.[93] The movement had somewhat greater impact on the Labor Party,
which, during the early 1960s, not only championed a nuclear-free zone in the
southern hemisphere, but questioned the building of a United States–Australian
communications base with nuclear implications in West Australia. By contrast,
Prime Minister Robert Menzies denounced the nuclear-free zone proposal as
"suicidal" and excoriated Labor for raising questions about the base. In the
1963 elections for the House of Representatives, the political parties emphasized foreign and defense policy issues, an unusual phenomenon in recent Australian politics. When the governing conservatives emerged victorious, the Labor Party—convinced that its position on defense issues had hurt it at the
polls—quietly scuttled its nuclear dissent.[94]

Actually, Labor had less reason to retreat from antinuclear positions than
it thought. Surveys found that when it came to voting, issues of foreign and defense policy mattered less to Australians than did the much vaguer issue of Labor's fitness to govern. Moreover, most Australians strongly disliked the Bomb.
Although surveys in the spring of 1963 found that advocates of an inspected
nuclear test ban outnumbered supporters of an uninspected test ban by more
than three to one, the overwhelming majority of Australians favored an end to
nuclear testing. Furthermore, queried that spring about their attitudes toward
"a worldwide agreement to abolish all nuclear arms," 81 percent of Australian
respondents favored it and only 10 percent opposed it. Indeed, Australian attitudes toward nuclear weapons did not differ substantially from those in nuclear-sensitive Britain.[95]

New Zealand

Inspired by events in Britain and, to a lesser extent, the United States, a Campaign for Nuclear Disarmament also sprang up in New Zealand. In 1959 and
1960, the loosely affiliated nuclear disarmament groups in Auckland, Christchurch, Dunedin, and Wellington held conventions that, in response to enthusiasm among activists for merger, led to the formation of New Zealand CND.
Two key figures in the development of the new organization were Mary Woodward (a Quaker), who became national secretary, and Elsie Locke (a social reformer and writer). Determined to go beyond vague talk of disarmament, New
Zealand CND eventually hammered out a position that rejected New Zealand's
acquisition or use of nuclear weapons, opposed its nuclear defense by other
countries, promoted its role in fostering the abolition of nuclear testing and nuclear weapons, and pressed it to support the formation of a nuclear-free zone in

the southern hemisphere. During the early 1960s, New Zealand CND expanded rapidly. By early 1963, it claimed some seventeen hundred members throughout the country, including ten branches in major population centers. New Zealand CND had become the nation's largest, most vital peace organization.[96]

New Zealand CND members not only revved up their spirits by watching films of the British Aldermaston march, but, in 1961, began staging their own. On these four-day hikes, CNDers—mostly young—carried the nuclear disarmament message to the people and, sometimes, to the politicians. During the Easter march of 1962, both the prime minister and the leader of the Labour opposition met with the marchers en route for surprisingly amiable conversations. Some eight hundred people gathered for that year's final rally, held before the parliament building, in Wellington.[97] To dramatize Nevil Shute's grim depiction of the consequences of nuclear war, the 1963 Easter march proceeded along beaches and coastal roads—past Maori settlements where singers and guitarists entertained the demonstrators and a Maori mayor called on the world "to rid itself of these bombs." When the demonstrators, bearing aloft their "March for Life" banner, finally poured through the gates surrounding the parliament grounds, with loudspeakers blaring "The H-Bomb's Thunder" and "We Shall Not Be Moved," a surge of emotion engulfed the throng. This time, a thousand people attended the culminating rally on the parliament steps—a small event by British standards, but the largest open-air political gathering in New Zealand since the Second World War.[98]

New Zealand CND organized other antinuclear activities as well. After the Soviet Union announced resumption of nuclear testing, it staged a twenty-four-hour vigil, an action repeated when the United States followed the Soviet example. CND also held demonstrations to protest French and Chinese nuclear testing, declaring: "No matter which nation owns it, the Bomb can never be the way to peace, only to disaster."[99] During the Cuban missile crisis, CND dispatched telegrams to the U.S. and Soviet embassies urging them to use moderation and accept mediation. It also held public vigils in numerous cities around the theme of "Messrs. K, Hands Off Humanity!"[100] In 1963, with French nuclear tests looming in Polynesia, CND circulated a petition calling on the government of New Zealand to "take the necessary steps" to bring about an international agreement for a nuclear-free zone in the southern hemisphere. Eventually, 80,238 people, including political and religious leaders, signed it—a very impressive number in those days.[101] Furthermore, together with other groups, CND organized annual Hiroshima Day demonstrations. In 1962, there were Hiroshima Day marches or outdoor meetings in four of New Zealand's cities, with the Auckland march drawing twelve hundred people. New Zealand CND also generated literature on disarmament, published a newsletter, lobbied politicians, distributed antinuclear songbooks and tapes, sponsored films and plays about the Bomb, and held youthful encampments on the beach.[102]

Although CND remained in the forefront of New Zealand's nuclear disarmament activities, it had some useful allies. The Society of Friends, a strong supporter of CND's efforts, provided meeting houses that often served as sites for discussions of nuclear issues or for CND meetings. In a letter of protest to President Kennedy, the New Zealand Christian Pacifist Society asked him how he justified the U.S. resumption of nuclear testing "in view of your own strongly-expressed moral condemnation of the Russians for polluting the atmosphere with fall-out." The small WILPF section joined CND's nuclear-free zone campaign, participated in Hiroshima Day marches, and called on the New Zealand government to promote disarmament.[103] As early as 1962, Ormond Burton, one of the aging stalwarts of the New Zealand Christian Pacifist Society, had called for civil disobedience against preparations for nuclear war, but actual planning only began to take shape in 1964. Against the backdrop of preparations for French nuclear testing, Robert Stowell organized an independent Committee for Resolute Action against French Tests (CRAFT), with branches in Auckland and Wellington. CRAFT urged New Zealand's government to take antinuclear action, and—in the event that the government failed to respond—urged activists to sail their own vessels into the test zone. CND leaders, though, were not enthusiastic about this approach, and it did not become a movement tactic until years later.[104]

As in other countries, the antinuclear movement had a strong appeal to particular constituencies. Intellectuals and church members provided New Zealand CND with its major base of support during the early years, and they were joined in later years by large numbers of students. Not surprisingly, youthful activists constituted a substantial percentage of participants in New Zealand's Easter marches and other outdoor demonstrations. But they also became effective fundraisers and stalwarts of the movement. At its height, Youth CND had seven branches. Looking back on his activist days, one participant recalled that in its quest "for a world free of nuclear weapons and nuclear threat," CND effectively "harnessed moral and youthful fervor."[105] Women, too, flocked to CND and to allied women's groups. Although the Voice of Women, a spinoff of the Canadian group, failed to take root, Women for Peace distributed a CND pamphlet, *Dr. Spock writes to N.Z. Parents*, to women's groups and joined CND in co-sponsoring panels on such subjects as "Your Child and the Bomb." The North Shore Women's Peace Group (of Auckland) demonstrated in a local shopping area, carrying banners reading: "Peace and Security for the World's Children: End the Nuclear Arms Race." Driven by these kinds of maternal concerns—particularly protecting children against rising levels of stron tium-90—women's disarmament activism flourished.[106]

Although antinuclear agitation had a radical, insurgent flavor, together with the most flagrant aspects of the ongoing nuclear arms race it did stir up widespread resistance to the Bomb among New Zealanders. In 1962, when renewed U.S. testing in the Pacific lit up the skies over New Zealand, letters of protest flooded the press.[107] Increasingly concerned about nuclear testing, the New Zealand Federation of Labour publicized a report linking the growing rate of leukemia to rising levels of strontium-90 in milk. In August 1963, CND's petition for a nuclear-free zone in the southern hemisphere was debated in parliament, where—after drawing strong support from the Labour Party—it was unanimously referred to the government for "most favorable consideration." Although the governing National Party remained dubious about the idea of a nuclear-free zone, Labour now adopted it as official party policy. Nearby French nuclear tests seemed especially dangerous and unnecessary. The National Council of Churches urged the prime minister to press France to abandon its testing program, the Federation of Labour proposed a boycott of French goods, and sections of the Labour Party supported the proposal to send a New Zealand frigate to the test site. The following year, when CND circulated an Open Letter to French President Charles de Gaulle, calling for an end to French nuclear testing, it was signed by 406 organizations, including 96 church groups, 87 women's organizations, and 65 unions. They ranged from the Church of England, to branches of the Federated Farmers, to the Southland Oyster Openers' Union.[108]

Recognizing that it had helped unleash popular concerns about immediate issues, particularly about nuclear testing, New Zealand's nuclear disarmament movement nonetheless took a broad view of its work and of its larger significance. Assessing the situation in August 1964, CND's leadership declared:

Just as we, in considering the actions of a man like [Adolf] Eichmann, wonder how the community could allow such things to happen, so would any future generations wonder how our community could allow a nuclear war to happen. Then, as now the only defense we have is the human conscience. . . .

We hope that the C.N.D. may continue to provide an expression of human conscience . . . towards a more peaceful world.[109]

Proclaimed by islanders in a remote portion of the South Pacific, they were sentiments that, increasingly, reverberated around the globe.

The Movement Crests

Western Europe, 1958–65

To accept use of nuclear weapons as a solution
to conflicts is a crime against humanity.

Carl Scharnberg, 1961

The struggle against the Bomb also reached unprecedented proportions in
Western Europe. Outraged by the escalating nuclear arms race, mass nuclear
disarmament movements emerged or escalated their activities across sizable
portions of the Continent. In most nations, they constituted the largest, most
dynamic protest campaigns to appear since the turbulent 1930s. Issues differed,
of course, from country to country. In Sweden, Switzerland, and France, movements confronted government proposals for independent nuclear weapons programs. In other nations, antinuclear groups recognized that the deployment of
NATO missiles made their countries potential nuclear battlefields. Still others
faced the danger of radioactive contamination through nuclear testing or of national obliteration through a Europe-wide nuclear war. Nevertheless, despite
differing circumstances, the forms of public protest were remarkably similar
and the programs of the movements, whether unilateralist or multilateralist,
came down to the same demand: nuclear disarmament. Waging dramatic campaigns against the Bomb throughout most of Western Europe, these mass
movements heightened popular revulsion at nuclear weapons and made nuclear
disarmament an issue of great political significance.

The Nordic Countries

In Denmark, where antinuclear sentiment had simmered for years, it finally
boiled over into a full-scale campaign on the British model. Starting in September 1958, a small, low-key organization, the Committee for Information About
Nuclear Armaments (Komiteen for Oplysning om Atomfaren), distributed liter-

ature and sponsored public meetings on the nuclear issue.[1] Meanwhile, in August 1959, and again in January 1960, the pacifist No More War picketed the unloading of NATO nuclear missiles at Århus harbor. Encountering two British CND activists in Denmark during early 1960, Carl Scharnberg—a No More War member and a teacher at a local high school—accepted their invitation to attend Britain's Aldermaston march that spring. Scharnberg returned from Britain enthusiastic about what he had seen and, in April, convinced No More War to initiate a similar movement in Denmark.[2] Founded in June 1960, and drawing on pacifists and non-pacifists, it called itself the Campaign Against Atomic Weapons (Kampagnen mod Atomvåben, KmA). Scharnberg became the secretary and guiding light of KmA, which was designed to serve as something new in Danish public life: a grassroots, people's movement, without formal structure or connections to political parties. That October, KmA launched its first antinuclear march, from Holbæk (a Nike missile site) to Copenhagen, where it culminated in a rally of more than five thousand people.[3]

In the following years, KmA made protest against nuclear weapons a prominent feature of Danish life. Staging Easter marches from Holbæk to Copenhagen, KmA drew twenty thousand antinuclear demonstrators in 1961 and thirty thousand in 1962—very substantial turnouts for such a small nation. The participation in the 1961 event of the government's minister of ecclesiastical affairs, Bodil Koch, brought considerable attention from the mass media. The 1962 event also generated a great deal of publicity, including a half hour's coverage on television, another half hour on the radio, and, as organizers noted, "good reports and pictures" in the press.[4] In addition, KmA organized separate protests against the nuclear weapons tests of the French, Soviet, and U.S. governments. None drew fewer than a thousand people, and the largest—a march through Copenhagen against Soviet plans for the explosion of a fifty-megaton Bomb—attracted five thousand.[5] In the spring of 1963, KmA launched a march of thousands through southern Jutland in an attempt to join antinuclear demonstrators across the West German border at Flensburg. Although the march was halted by West German soldiers, some Danes managed the border-crossing by bus. That August, KmA held Hiroshima Day demonstrations in forty-five town squares around the country, with activists standing silently under antinuclear banners.[6]

KmA also developed a very widespread public education campaign. It produced vast quantities of antinuclear literature, including the pamphlet *If War Comes*, which it distributed to an estimated 70 percent of Danish households. To reach the large numbers of young people who flocked to Denmark every summer, it circulated a multilingual leaflet calling on "the youth of the world" to "demand the cessation of nuclear tests in both east and west" and "an international ban on production, storage and use of nuclear weapons."[7] Criticized, at times, for working outside the framework of the political parties, KmA responded by developing a campaign to influence the general elections of September 1964. After sending an antinuclear booklet to thirteen hundred parliamentary candidates, KmA followed up by having activists attend virtually all campaign meetings and direct questions to the candidates about nuclear disarmament. The climax to the venture was reached when, during the television time allotted to the governing Social Democratic Party, a young KmA member, sporting his nuclear disarmament pin, questioned the prime minister on what he planned to do about the nuclear menace.[8]

Despite its unusual tactics and assertiveness, KmA championed a position that did not depart dramatically from the policy of the government. Unlike its British counterpart, the Danish movement operated within a country that was nuclear-free. Although NATO missiles were deployed within Denmark, the governing Social Democratic Party had pledged to keep the nuclear warheads outside the country, at least in peacetime. For its part, KmA avoided calling NATO into question, but instead demanded: (1) no nuclear weapons on Danish territory under any circumstances; (2) full disclosure of information about nuclear weapons; and (3) a more independent foreign policy, including support for international agreements banning the production, testing, stockpiling, and use of nuclear weapons. In late 1963, KmA added a demand for a Nordic nuclear weapon–free zone. In this fashion, KmA blended unilateralism with internationalism.[9] A survey of Danish Easter marchers in 1965 found that only 24 percent thought that unilateral disarmament was "the most effective way to peace." Conversely, on October 24, 1962, KmA staged a demonstration of fifteen thousand people in support of a stronger United Nations. Surveys found that a large plurality of KmA supporters favored the establishment of a world government.[10]

Who participated in Denmark's KmA? Although from thirty to seventy KmA groups operated in most parts of the country between 1961 and 1967, this loosely structured organization had no official membership and, consequently, kept no membership statistics. In 1965 some twelve thousand people subscribed to the KmA journal, *Kampagne Orientering.* But this figure underestimates participation, for the 1961 and 1962 Easter marches attracted substantially larger numbers. Indeed, by 1967 KmA had sold an estimated 150,000 nuclear disarmament buttons. Virtually all observers agree, however, that KmA was predominantly a movement of the young intelligentsia. A British account of the October 1960 march that launched KmA reported that a large proportion of demonstrators "were young students, teachers and intellectuals." A sociological study of the Easter marchers of 1965 concluded that most ranged from eighteen to twenty-three years of age, attended educational institutions, and came from urban areas. Moreover, they possessed a high level of information about foreign policy issues, and their participation in the march was "part of a broad spectrum" of social concerns. Of course, a focus on lengthy marches probably biases findings toward youth. Substantial numbers of older pacifists from No More War and other groups also took part in KmA ventures, as did housewives with babies and occasional blue-collar workers. Even so, the movement drew very heavily on students and other young intellectuals.[11]

Denmark's political parties treated the burgeoning nuclear disarmament movement with considerable respect, and only the Conservative Party dissociated itself from KmA on principle. Although the governing Social Democratic Party never showed much enthusiasm for KmA, the movement did have the support of some of its leaders, such as Koch and Århus mayor Bernard Jensen. When Conservatives questioned the participation of Koch, a Cabinet minister, in the rally that concluded KmA's 1961 Easter march, the Social Democratic prime minister retorted that he found her presence perfectly appropriate. Party leader Jens Otto Krag told an interviewer some years later that he had "no doubt that the Campaign Against Atomic Weapons influenced the Social Democrats."[12] In 1962, at the invitation of KmA, all the political parties, including the Conservatives, sent speakers to the rally that concluded the Easter march. In addition, KmA had the solid backing of the pacifist-oriented Socialist People's Party. Making its debut in the nationwide elections of 1960, the new party won eleven seats in parliament. In 1964, it won ten. With KmA demonstrating in the streets, a peace party competing for votes at the polls, and surveys registering minimal support among Danes for Europe's acquisition of NATO nuclear weapons, none of the larger parties advocated the deployment of nuclear weapons in Denmark.[13]

The antinuclear campaign developed along similar lines in Norway. A contingent of Norwegians participated in Denmark's October 1960 demonstration against nuclear weapons and, the following month, a group of them launched their own organization, Protest Against Nuclear Weapons (Protest mot Atomvåpen). The new group, popularly known as "The 13" after its founders—all prominent figures in academic, labor, church, or women's organizations—concentrated on convincing the political parties not to station nuclear weapons in Norway. On March 19, 1961, The 13 staged antinuclear rallies in several Norwegian towns and cities. The Oslo rally drew ten thousand people, the largest turnout for a demonstration in Norway since the war. Soon thereafter, The 13 submitted an antinuclear petition to parliament, signed by 223,000 Norwegians, nearly 10 percent of the country's adult population. When both the governing Labour Party and the parliament voted to oppose installation of nuclear weapons in Norway in peacetime, The 13—satisfied that their work was done—terminated operations in May 1961.[14]

This did not end nuclear weapons protest in Norway, however, for another organization, Action for Nuclear Disarmament (Aksjon for Atomavrustning), moved to fill the vacuum. Founded in early 1961 by ten intellectuals—and, therefore, popularly known as "The 10"—the new group began with a broad antinuclear agenda. Consequently, it not only supported the activities of The 13, but petitioned the Norwegian parliament to press the United Nations to have nuclear weapons declared contrary to international law, staged public protests against French and Soviet nuclear testing, demonstrated against nuclear weapons deployment by NATO, and distributed hundreds of thousands of antinuclear leaflets. Inspired by the British Committee of 100, The 10 had a direct action emphasis and plans for rapid mobilization of small groups for "lightning actions." There were no provisions for membership. Nevertheless, the group did more to stage protest demonstrations than to foster civil disobedience. In October 1961, condemning Soviet nuclear testing, it did organize a sit-down of four hundred people outside the Soviet embassy; but, at the suggestion of the police, they departed after ninety minutes. At the same time, lacking prominent leaders or a constituency outside of Oslo, The 10 proved unable to attract large crowds to their events. In the fall of 1961, one of The 10's major activities, a symbolic peace march between the U.S. and Soviet embassies, drew only eight hundred people.[15]

The antinuclear efforts of The 13 and of The 10 received significant support from Norway's other peace organizations. The small Norwegian Pugwash group, comprised of physicists and chemists, produced numerous articles and delivered lectures on nuclear disarmament issues. The WILPF section made the campaign against deployment of nuclear weapons in Norway its top priority, while the FOR group publicized the dangers of radioactivity and warned of other types of nuclear catastrophe. In 1962, a small branch of Women's International Strike for Peace began demonstrating against nuclear testing and promoting demands for nuclear disarmament.[16] The largest of the pacifist groups, the WRI section (Folkereisning mot Krig), helped initiate Norway's antinuclear campaign and called for a peaceful settlement of the Cuban missile crisis. WRI activists also occupied key positions in the ventures of The 10, as did activists from other organizations. Pacifist participants in the broader antinuclear campaign recognized that, to some extent, it diverted energies from their own groups and concerns. At the same time, they believed that action against the nuclear arms race was imperative and that it provided them with an important means of outreach to the broader society. Indeed, thanks to its high-profile role in the antinuclear crusade, the WRI group recruited a new generation of activists.[17]

Determined to build an effective, nationwide movement, pacifists and other activists launched a new organization, the Campaign Against Atomic Weapons (Kampanjen mot Atomvåpen, KmA), in October 1962. The 10 wound up their operations, and KmA took over direction of antinuclear agitation. In the spring of 1963, KmA organized an Easter march, starting from Eidsvoll, Tonsberg, and Sarpsberg and culminating in Oslo. Funding came from the sale of a KmA literary magazine, *Solverv*. Slogans for the march included: "Yes to Life"; "Suicide is no Defense"; "No to NATO Nuclear Power"; and "No to Polaris." In the spring of 1964, KmA held another Easter march, this time with the slogan: "The Nordic countries—an atom-free zone." The turnout for both marches was rather thin, however, and it was clear that, despite efforts at renewal, the antinuclear movement had peaked in 1960–61. Organized in the aftermath of parliament's crucial decision to reject the stationing of nuclear weapons in Norway and of the shocking resumption of nuclear testing by the great powers, KmA never developed the immediacy or the momentum of the early movement. Within a short time, it dissolved.[18]

Fragmentary evidence suggests that Norway's nuclear disarmament campaign drew on a constituency roughly similar to that of its neighbors. In addition to the important role played by intellectuals and pacifists, substantial numbers of college and high school students gravitated to the movement, with the populations of entire schools addressing critiques of nuclear testing to Kennedy and Khrushchev. Women also participated in disproportionate numbers. Condemning the resumption of nuclear testing, the Norwegian section of Women's International Strike for Peace told Kennedy that "the responsibility of all women . . . is to protect the foundations of life." In 1964, comparing members of Norway's peace and disarmament organizations to members of the general population, a sociological study found them better educated, more likely to be involved in organizational activities, more likely to speak up at meetings, more likely to write letters to newspapers, and more satisfied with their jobs and incomes. Their interests and views also departed from the norm, for they were not only more hostile to nuclear weapons, but more interested in foreign affairs and domestic politics and more supportive of international cooperation and of the United Nations.[19]

Although short-lived, the antinuclear campaign had clear reverberations in Norwegian public opinion and politics. Newspaper reaction to the movement was sometimes quite hostile. But letters condemning nuclear war flooded the press and public approval of nuclear weapons sank to marginal levels. According to polls, between January 1961 and May 1962 support for stationing nuclear weapons in Norway fell from 11 to 8 percent, while opposition grew from 56 to 57 percent.[20] Before the public upsurge, the Norwegian Labor Party remained divided on the nuclear issue and, in the fall of 1960, expelled some party members associated with *Orientering*, a left-wing journal championing the antinuclear cause. Nonetheless, the issue came to a head at the Labor Party's conference in the spring of 1961, when it wrote into its election program the provision opposing deployment of nuclear weapons in Norway during peacetime. This came too late to head off a party split, with left-wing dissidents and the *Orientering* group moving to establish the Socialist People's Party. Adopting a strong antinuclear platform, the new party entered parliamentary elections that fall. It won two seats, thus giving it the balance of power between Labor and its conservative rivals. Hard-pressed, the Labor Party adopted a resolution at its May 1963 congress proclaiming that it had "always been and is a peace movement."[21]

Meanwhile, in neighboring Sweden, the Action Group Against a Swedish Atomic Bomb (AMSA) heightened its agitation against the military's proposal that the nation develop nuclear weapons. During 1959 and 1960, AMSA dispatched antinuclear speakers to hundreds of meetings, widely distributed its journal *Mot svensk atombomb*, sent a Swedish contingent to Denmark's first Easter march, and organized an anti–H-Bomb exhibit in Stockholm visited by more than twenty thousand people. Led by Barbro Alving, Elsa Cedergren, Per Anders Fogelström, and Bertil Svahnström, among others, AMSA could count on an estimated fifteen thousand participants. Although the governing Social Democrats, after lengthy deliberation, supported no more than extended research on how to defend the nation against nuclear attack, AMSA remained suspicious of this approach. Fearing that it would provide the basis for the development of nuclear weapons "behind the back and against the will of the Swedish people," AMSA continued its antinuclear campaign.[22]

The initiative, however, passed to a new organization, the Campaign Against Nuclear Weapons (Kampanjen mot Atomvapen, KmA). Launched in August 1961 with Svahnström—a pacifist journalist—as chair, KmA had a much broader antinuclear mandate than AMSA did. It quickly staged marches in Stockholm and Göteborg around the themes of halting nuclear testing, banning nuclear weapons, and securing general disarmament.[23] Preferring nuclear disarmament marches at Whitsun rather than Easter, KmA organized them in 1962, 1963, and 1964. Although the 1962 Whitsun march drew three thousand people to the culminating rally, in Stockholm, most of KmA's marches and torchlight parades—held not only in Stockholm, but in Malmö, Göteborg, Lund, and other urban areas—were much smaller affairs. During 1962–63, KmA sponsored the nationwide showing of a photo exhibit, "Hiroshima Today," by the well-known photographer, Christer Strömholm. Furthermore, with the cooperation of some of Sweden's most famous painters, KmA organized an art exhibit, "War and Peace," at a gallery in the center of Stockholm. KmA also distributed substantial quantities of literature, including such pamphlets as Svahnström's *The Atomic Weapons Question in Sweden* and *The Danger of War*, the scientist Filip Stenson's *The World at the Turning Point*, Axel Sors's *The Christian Case Against War and Atomic Weapons*, Linus Pauling's *Peace or Annihilation* (based on a speech he delivered in Stockholm in 1959), and AMSA's *Shall Sweden Have the Atom Bomb?*[24] In March 1964, KmA hosted a conference of four hundred delegates from the Nordic countries on making their region a nuclear-free zone.[25]

For the most part, Sweden's traditional peace groups worked closely with the antinuclear campaign. Although some world federalists criticized AMSA's approach as one-sided, the Swedish WILPF group voted in 1959 to support AMSA's stand against employing nuclear weapons for Sweden's defense. The pacifist journal *Freden* published articles by AMSA leaders and, in 1959, Svahnström became its editor. The oldest and largest of the peace groups, the Swedish Peace and Arbitration Society (Svenska Fredoch Skiljedomsföreningen, SFSF), provided AMSA with office space, took on some of its work, and added Cedergren and Fogelström to its executive board.[26] Fogelström, a well-known author and antinuclear activist, became chair of SFSF in 1963. When the great powers began a new round of nuclear tests, Sweden's peace groups subjected them to withering criticism. The Soviet government had participated in the Nuremberg trials "when the Nazi leaders were punished for their crimes against humanity," SFSF told the Soviet embassy, but was there "any principal moral difference between exterminating people by gas or by radiation?"[27]

Other constituencies also played an important part in Sweden's antinuclear campaign. A group of intellectuals was responsible for the formation of AMSA and, thereafter, many writers, teachers, and students lent their support to the movement. Nuclear disarmament proved popular at institutions of higher education such as the University of Lund, where a ban-the-Bomb group organized lectures, photo exhibits, films, and literature tables. Pressing the Social Democratic Party to reject Sweden's production of nuclear weapons, the party's student group published an anthology of antinuclear writings.[28] Whether or not they were students, young people often felt a keen sense of outrage at the nuclear arms race. When the Soviet Union announced plans to test a fifty-megaton Bomb in 1961, the Social Democratic youth group issued a public protest against "this insanity." Meanwhile, a Youth Campaign for Nuclear Disarmament grew rapidly.[29] Although wary of peace groups because they criticized conventional defense measures, the powerful Social Democratic Women's Organization played a crucial part in the antinuclear campaign. At its conventions, in meetings with party leader and Prime Minister Tage Erlander, and in published articles, Inga Thorsson, the group's president, sharply rejected any role for nuclear weapons in Sweden. Around the country, local branches applauded this stand, which eventually expanded into demands for worldwide nuclear disarmament.[30]

In their attempts to turn public opinion against nuclear weapons, activists scored one of their greatest victories in Sweden. According to Swedish opinion polls, in 1957, when public debate began over Sweden's building of the Bomb, a plurality of the population (40 percent) supported the idea. In the ensuing years, however, this situation gradually reversed itself until, by 1969, 69 percent of Swedes opposed the development of a Swedish Bomb and only 17 percent supported it. Commenting on this remarkable shift in popular attitudes, two Swedish scholars have concluded that antinuclear activism "had a strong impact on public opinion."[31]

Given these developments, it was hardly surprising that Sweden's political tide turned against nuclear weapons. At the outset of the nuclear debate, when the military and the Conservatives championed a nuclear defense, only the Communist Party took a clearcut antinuclear stand. Disarmament activists formed their own antinuclear party, the Progressive Union, but it fared very poorly at the polls and soon collapsed.[32] Nevertheless, the surge of opposition to nuclear weapons had a major effect on the existing parties. Although the Conservative press continued for a time to charge that nuclear critics were undermining the nation's defense morale, the ruling Social Democrats, worried about their election prospects, were determined to reach some agreement on the nuclear question within their own ranks. Accordingly, in November 1959, the party's atomic weapons committee issued a report stating that the government should take no position concerning the development of nuclear weapons and, thus, no action to build them, pending a later review. Meanwhile, debate continued within the Social Democratic Party until, by the mid-1960s, the opponents of a Swedish Bomb had triumphed.[33]

Finland also experienced an antinuclear upsurge, although in a somewhat different form. In this nation, endeavoring to cement good relations with its powerful Soviet neighbor, the Peace Union and other nonaligned groups remained on unusually good terms with the Communist-led Peace Committees. Working together, they sponsored two disarmament marches in the fall of 1961, culminating in Helsinki and Turku. Over a thousand people participated in each, with some four thousand attending the final meeting in Helsinki. In addition, many Finns campaigned for the establishment of a Nordic nuclear-free zone, an idea that gained increasing respectability after it was proposed in May 1963 by Finnish President Urho Kekkonen. About one hundred of the delegates at the March 1964 conference in Stockholm on making the Nordic countries a nuclear-free zone came from Finland, including university faculty, leaders of unions, and members of parliament.[34]

Finland's best-known antinuclear ventures, however, emerged under other sponsorship. Neither the aging leadership of the Peace Union nor the Communist leadership of the Peace Committees held much appeal for the rising student generation, which, in the summer of 1963, declared its independence by launching the Committee of 100. Starting at the University of Helsinki and spreading quickly to universities throughout Finland, the Committee of 100 became the dominant force among politically active students. The name, however, was misleading, for although largely pacifist and committed to symbolic acts of protest against the nuclear arms race, the Committee of 100 did not sponsor civil disobedience. Instead, it behaved like a youthful CND—organizing demonstrations (the first in the universities since the war), popularizing unilateralism, questioning civil defense, fostering peace research, and, above all, promoting disarmament. The national radio and television stations, largely controlled by young people, gave the movement a great deal of attention, and nuclear weapons became a subject of serious debate in Finnish life. Moreover, thanks to the fact that many founders of the Committee of 100 went on to become prominent journalists, academics, leaders of political parties, members of parliament, and government ministers, its influence persisted long after its formal demise.[35]

West Germany

In the immediate aftermath of the tumultuous campaign of the Struggle Against Atomic Death, nuclear disarmament activism in West Germany entered a lull. In 1959, the powerful Evangelical Church issued the Heidelberg Theses, which acknowledged the coexistence of differing views on the Bomb within the church. Thereby, it enabled German Protestants to live in good conscience with nuclear weapons while respecting the rights of those who criticized them. Even more damaging to the movement was the jettisoning of the nuclear issue by the Social Democratic Party (SPD), until then the mainstay of West Germany's antinuclear campaign. The SPD's electoral defeats of 1957–58 led to an internal shake-up, in which the reformists (Willy Brandt, Fritz Erler, Carlo Schmid, and Herbert Wehner) triumphed. Dropping Marxism and pacifism, they transformed the SPD from a "workers' party" into a "people's party," with a broad, nonideological program. This turn to pragmatic politics, designed to groom the Social Democrats as a credible alternative to the governing conservatives, was symbolized by the SPD's Bad Godesberg conference of 1959. Henceforth, the

SPD would act as a defense critic "from within" and would not attack what it considered irrevocable decisions, such as the deployment of nuclear weapons in West Germany.[36]

With the electoral route closed to antinuclear forces, activists began extraparliamentary efforts along the lines of Britain's Aldermaston marches. When the press revealed the fact that, in December 1959, atomic weapons had been tested by German troops in Bergen-Hohne, a small group of religious pacifists in Hamburg decided to organize an Easter march to the area. Led by two teachers, Hans-Konrad Tempel and Helga Stolle, they contacted the local chapters of the WRI and the German Peace Society, which proved enthusiastic. Nevertheless, to avoid having the action labeled either pacifist or—if pro-Soviet groups took part—Communist, the Committee for the Easter March decided that the planning of the event, as well as participation in it, would be by individuals rather than organizations. On April 18, 1960, after a three-day march, about a thousand demonstrators, mostly pacifists, rallied in Bergen-Hohne, close to the remains of a former concentration camp—a site chosen for symbolic purposes. Speakers at the rally emphasized that the protest was directed against the nuclear policies of both East and West.[37]

In the years that followed, the Easter March of Nuclear Weapons Opponents (Ostermarsch der Atomwaffengegner) blossomed into a mass movement. The second march, in the spring of 1961, drew 7,500 participants to twelve feeder marches and 23,000 to the culminating rally. During 1962 and 1963, the numbers jumped again, to 50,000 participants. By 1964, Easter marches were occurring in almost every major West German city and town—the biggest of them in Dortmund, Stuttgart, Munich, Frankfurt, Bremen, Mannheim, and Hamburg—with a total participation of more than 100,000 people. In subsequent years, the marches grew still larger, with 150,000 turning out for an estimated eight hundred events in 1967.[38] These West German marches resembled their counterparts elsewhere, with masses of youthful demonstrators sporting nuclear disarmament pins and singing antinuclear songs, including Britain's "The H-Bomb's Thunder" and America's "Down by the Riverside." The rhetoric was also similar. "The peace of the world, the existence of the human race are still mortally threatened," read the call to the 1962 march. "We will not become silent, as long as our lives are threatened by nuclear weapons."[39] Over time, the sponsors renamed their venture the Campaign for Disarmament (Kampagne für Abrüstung), developed additional activities, and adopted a more sharply political critique of West German nuclear policy. Meanwhile, its operations continued to generate a remarkable upsurge of grassroots, extraparliamentary activity.[40]

Although the massive Easter marches constituted West Germany's most dramatic display of antinuclear sentiment, numerous others were in evidence. Responding to the government's distribution of a reassuring civil defense pamphlet (*Everybody Has a Chance*), Bavaria's Committee Against Atomic Weapons (Komitee gegen Atomrüstung) produced 200,000 copies of a grim rebuttal. Nuclear testing also provided a focal point for activism, and in September 1961 its Munich affiliate protested against test resumption by the Soviet and U.S. governments. During the Cuban missile crisis, the Working Committee of German Peace Organizations joined the Easter march organizers in condemning the provocative acts of both sides and expressing support for mediation by the United Nations.[41] In addition, West Germany had its own Committee of 100 (Komitee der Hundert). Following up on pacifist-organized sit-downs outside nuclear weapons facilities from 1959 through 1961, the Committee of 100, inspired by Russell's work in Britain, began a campaign of small-scale actions in 1962—creating some of the same problems for the Easter march movement that its British equivalent caused for CND.[42]

German scientists constituted a less vigorous, but more socially acceptable, wing of the movement. In the fall of 1959, antinuclear physicists formed the Federation of German Scientists (Vereinigung Deutscher Wissenschaftler, VDW). Like the Federation of American Scientists, on which it was modeled, the VDW was formally devoted to heightening public awareness of the consequences of scientific innovation. But, as Born noted privately, its founders intended to use the new group to press the West German government to abandon plans for nuclear armaments. Within a short time the VDW had recruited three hundred members, including most of West Germany's leading physicists, and had become that country's branch of the Pugwash movement.[43]

Like its counterparts in other nations, West Germany's antinuclear movement drew largely on a middle class, intellectual, socially concerned, and youthful constituency. In 1964, the call to the Easter march was signed by 1,100 ministers, 400 professors and teachers, 400 authors and artists, and almost 300 lawyers and jurists. Although 450 union members also signed the call, the 1964 demonstration—like others held during the 1960s—did not receive the backing of the DGB, West Germany's trade union federation, or of any of its constituent unions. The strongest endorsement from within the labor movement came from the DGB youth section, yet another sign of the movement's appeal to the young.[44] Indeed, the Easter marches drew the enthusiastic backing of socialist, environmentalist, student, and other youth groups, which contributed heavily to their mass participation. The call to the 1967 march was signed by 1008 representatives of youth and student organizations.[45] In addition, particularly in the early, more isolated days of the movement, pacifist groups like the WRI and the FOR played crucial roles and provided some of its best-known leaders, including Tempel, Andreas Buro, Heinz Kloppenburg, and Martin Niemöller.[46]

But despite the movement's strength at the grassroots, it had little impact at the higher levels of power. The three parties represented in the Bundestag—the Christian Democrats, the Social Democrats, and the Free Democrats—evinced considerable hostility to the Easter marches and other antinuclear protests. Condemning the Easter march campaign as "biased against Western defense measures," the SPD officially warned its members "against participation in or support for the movement." On occasion, local SPD officials joined their conservative rivals in banning nuclear disarmament rallies. Although many SPD members simply ignored the party's strictures against the disarmament campaign, antinuclear groups had no success in changing the SPD's position on the nuclear issue, particularly after it formed a coalition government with the Christian Democrats in 1966.[47] In addition, the provocative statements and actions of the East German and Soviet governments inflamed West Germany's volatile anti-Communism. Finally, the press generally either ignored or defamed the Easter march movement. Tempel confided to Bertrand Russell that the movement faced a "very difficult situation" in West Germany, including "pressure from the authorities," "lack of prominent sponsors," "undue propaganda from the communist press," and "the reactions of our hysterical public."[48]

Nevertheless, activists did carve out an important space in West Germany's public life. By building a mass-based, extraparliamentary movement, they set in motion forces that, in later years, would put West German politics—including the SPD—on a new course.[49] Moreover, against considerable odds, they helped maintain remarkably widespread public opposition to nuclear weapons. In September 1963, although all major political parties supported the government's policy of arming West German forces with NATO nuclear weapons, a poll found that 38 percent of respondents still thought that Adenauer's successor should "renounce nuclear weapons for the Bundeswehr." Earlier that year, asked about West Germany "having its own nuclear force," West Germans opposed the idea by a ratio of seven to one. Although NATO plans called for a nuclear response to a conventional military attack, most West Germans considered the idea quite repellent. A survey in February 1963 found that only 7 percent approved (and 75 percent disapproved) of the use of atomic weapons on enemy soldiers at the front lines in such circumstances.[50] Furthermore, in mid-1961, polls found that 71 percent of West German respondents favored (and only 18 percent opposed) a nuclear test ban. Finally, queried in early 1963 about the movement's central goal—worldwide abolition of nuclear weapons—84 percent of West Germans polled supported the idea; only 4 percent expressed disagreement.[51]

The Netherlands and Belgium

From 1958 to 1960, protest against nuclear weapons grew steadily in the Netherlands. Calling on the leaders of the United States, the Soviet Union, and Britain to end nuclear tests forever, the Albert Schweitzer Committee Against Nuclear Weapons also gathered 65,373 signatures on a petition opposing the establishment of nuclear bases in Holland. In late 1959, the Stop Atom Bomb Tests committee presented a petition to the Dutch government, signed by nine hundred prominent citizens, urging it to press for a nuclear test ban treaty. In addition, it sent a letter of protest to the French government, arguing that France's nuclear tests would increase international tensions, undermine relations between Africa and the West, and end the temporary moratorium on testing by the great powers. Meanwhile, Anti-Atom Bomb Action, which participated in the Stop Atom Bomb Tests committee, carried on its own antinuclear agitation.[52] Most dramatically, the new Pacifist Socialist Party (PSP) entered the parliamentary elections of 1959 and—campaigning under the slogan, "Socialism without atom bombs"—drew 100,000 votes, giving it two seats in the House of Commons.[53]

Beginning in the 1960s, protest marches became a prominent symbol of Dutch resistance to the Bomb. Dazzled by the massive Aldermaston march of 1960 in Britain, speakers at that year's PSP congress asked why nothing similar was happening in the Netherlands. In response, that November the party leadership organized the Committee for Peace (Comité voor de Vrede), under the direction of the PSP's Hans Bruggeman. Securing the backing of Church and Peace, The Third Way, ANVA, and small, left-wing socialist groups, the Committee for Peace staged its first event on January 1, 1961—an antinuclear march through the streets of Amsterdam of about a thousand people. With some fifty local groups in the process of formation, the Committee joined its foreign counterparts that Easter by holding a march from Amersfoort to Amsterdam. Drenched by a driving rain, only 2,000 demonstrators reached their destination. Nor were any of the subsequent marches, held annually on New Year's Day and Easter, of vast dimensions. In 1962, the culminating rally drew 4,000 people; in 1963, 1,500; in 1964, 5,000. The Committee also held two demonstrations in October 1961—one against Soviet nuclear tests and the other against U.S.—and each drew about 2,500 participants. Rallies featured speeches by antinuclear leaders, Dutch versions of Aldermaston songs, and slogans such as "Don't prepare or test nuclear weapons," "No nuclear rocket bases," and "All out for international nuclear disarmament."[54]

Other antinuclear activities also accelerated. Protesting the Soviet resumption of nuclear testing, Anti-Atom Bomb Action sent a deputation to the Soviet embassy. It also organized a mass leafleting campaign throughout the Netherlands, distributing 185,000 copies of its first antinuclear leaflet and 250,000 copies of its second. Entering the parliamentary elections in the summer of 1963, the antinuclear PSP made the greatest gains of any Dutch party. With its vote expanding from 100,000 to 180,000, it doubled its representation in the lower house and, for the first time, captured two seats in the upper house.[55] In November 1961, civil disobedience made its debut. Inspired by a newspaper photo of Bertrand Russell at a London sit-down, forty students from the Hague Montessori school staged an antinuclear protest by occupying one of the busiest downtown squares in that city, thereby paralyzing traffic. One of the participants, seventeen-year-old Noel van Duyn, was so impressed by their success that he organized the Ban-the-Bomb Group (Ban-de-Bom Groep) to shock adults out of their acquiescence in preparations for nuclear war. Although startling Ban-the-Bomb actions spread to Amsterdam, Harlem, Leyden, and Rotterdam, the most notorious probably occurred at the Hague, in June 1962, when 123 young activists sought to raise a Ban-the-Bomb flag, adorned with the nuclear disarmament symbol, at the royal palace.[56]

Like their counterparts abroad, antinuclear scientists focused their efforts on elite opinion. The Netherlands Society of Scientists (Verbond van Wetenschappelijke Onderzoekers), although concerned about a broad array of social issues, repeatedly warned of the dangers of nuclear weapons. With some 570 members and its own monthly journal, the organization provided an important base of support for the smaller Pugwash group, with which it shared members. The Pugwashers gave radio talks, held press conferences reporting on the international gatherings, and arranged for the publication in Dutch of books dealing with nuclear weapons. Expressing its "grave concern" about the nuclear arms race and the limited information on nuclear weapons and civil defense that the Dutch government provided to its citizens, the Pugwash group published open letters to the Dutch parliament and government in February and June 1962. According to the head of the Dutch Pugwash Committee, several of its members maintained personal contacts with advisers to the government and the statement of the seventh Pugwash conference "met with considerable interest" from Holland's Royal Academy of Sciences.[57]

Indeed, antinuclear attitudes began to permeate powerful institutions in Dutch life. To be sure, none of the larger social structures—the churches, the unions, the major political parties—officially joined the protest campaign.[58] The Dutch Labor Party, determined to prove its trustworthiness to more conservative partners in the nation's coalition government, staunchly defended the installation of NATO nuclear weapons. Nevertheless, the competition of the PSP strengthened the hand of a growing antinuclear faction within the Labor

Party, which henceforth voted in parliament against military increases. At the party congress of January 1963, 12 percent of the delegates supported a proposal advocating Holland's nuclear disarmament as a first step toward banning the Bomb worldwide. Meanwhile, in October 1962, the synod of the Dutch Reformed Church issued a report sharply rejecting the use (but not the possession) of nuclear weapons on moral grounds. In addition, after 1963, the Catholic church, influenced by the papal encyclical *Pacem in Terris*, also began to take disarmament more seriously. In 1966, acting together, the Protestant and Catholic churches established the Inter-Church Peace Council (Interkerkelijk Vredesberaad, IKV). Authorized to study the issues of war and peace, develop an action program for the churches, and take public positions on issues, IKV gradually began to assume the functions of a peace and disarmament movement.[59]

In neighboring Belgium, mass marches provided a clear sign of growing antinuclear sentiment. Inspired by CND's activities in Britain, the National Federation of Initiatives for a Belgian Contribution to International Détente (Fédération nationale des initiatives pour une contribution belge à la détente internationale) sponsored a march of youthful nuclear opponents from Mol (site of Belgium's atomic research facility) to Antwerp in April 1960, drawing four thousand people to the culminating rally. By November 1962, at the instigation of the National Federation, a variety of peace, left-wing, and religious groups had joined together to organize what was billed as Belgium's first Easter march. As a result, on March 24, 1963, brandishing signs denouncing nuclear testing and nuclear weapons, more than ten thousand people—mostly young— thronged the center of Brussels. Senator Henri Rollin, a prominent figure in the Socialist Party, presided over the final rally. Another antinuclear march, in 1964, attracted a crowd estimated at seventeen thousand. Nevertheless, though impressive in size, these demonstrations remained sharply divided and, therefore, muffled in impact. Serious tensions existed between non-Communists and Communists, Young Socialists and the Socialist Party, freethinkers and religious believers, and Flemings and Walloons. To paper over these differences, the organizing committee sometimes banned all but very general, multilateralist slogans. Nevertheless, unilateralists consistently defied the organizers, and relationships remained stormy.[60]

Sometimes, though, the nuclear peril inspired greater cohesion. Belgium's small Committee for Non-Violent Action attracted a good deal of favorable attention when, in November 1961—to protest the resumption of nuclear testing—it held silent vigils outside the Soviet and U.S. embassies. That same month, dismayed by this new surge in the arms race, Belgium's League of Large Families took the initiative in organizing a broadly based, humanitarian campaign against nuclear weapons: the May 8 Movement. By the following spring, it had secured the support of mainstream women's organizations and the three major labor federations for its program of ending nuclear testing, limiting atomic energy to peaceful purposes, and fostering disarmament under international control. In response to its call, on May 8, 1962—the anniversary of the end of World War II in Europe—half the population of the country reportedly took part in a fifteen-minute work-stoppage. Bearing antinuclear placards, young people in Brussels chanted: "We want disarmament! We want peace!" Others surged into the streets to halt traffic. Heartened by support from most political parties, the Catholic hierarchy, and public opinion, the May 8 Movement continued its antinuclear protests until 1966.[61]

Neutral Nations: Switzerland, Austria, and Ireland

From 1958 to 1963, the newly formed Swiss Movement Against Atomic Armaments focused on its campaign to block the equipping of the Swiss armed forces with nuclear weapons. Petitioning for a nationwide referendum to revise the nation's constitution to ban nuclear arms, the Swiss Movement gathered the signatures of 73,339 citizens by March 1959. Having thereby ensured the vote, the Swiss Movement began a vigorous effort to undermine the widespread notion that Switzerland's defense depended on the acquisition of tactical nuclear weapons. It held two thousand public meetings, produced five hundred articles for the press, published a bimonthly *Atombulletin*, and distributed three million antinuclear leaflets. Against this grassroots campaign, with neither formal membership nor dues, stood the government, the military, the Catholic church, most political parties, and most of the press. The Social Democrats, the unions, and the Protestant churches were divided on the referendum, although a third of the country's Protestant pastors signed a statement supporting it. On March 31, 1962, Switzerland's voters—all male, as women lacked the vote—defeated the referendum, 65 to 35 percent.[62] The following May, a somewhat more moderate referendum—to change the constitution to require a popular vote before arming the nation with nuclear weapons—was sponsored by the Social Democrats and supported by the Swiss Movement. But this, too, went down to defeat, 62 to 38 percent.[63]

Despite this loss at the polls, the movement had not done badly. Although some activists felt discouraged, winning the support of roughly two-fifths of the electorate was a significant accomplishment for a grassroots, anti-establishment campaign. Moreover, in some areas, the Swiss Movement had done much better. Both referenda swept to victory in Switzerland's French and Italian cantons. And even in the German-speaking ones, the source of the movement's difficulties, it provoked an unprecedented debate over nuclear weapons. Furthermore, the nation's most prominent intellectuals endorsed the antinuclear campaign, giving resistance to the Bomb a prestige it had hitherto lacked. Finally, though a majority of voters had rebuffed the Swiss Movement's attempt to bar Switzerland from acquiring nuclear weapons, they had not endorsed acquisition, either. And the government made no further moves in this direction.[64]

Moreover, the Swiss Movement helped develop a broader antinuclear campaign. In early 1960, it staged a demonstration outside the French embassy in Bern to protest French testing in the Sahara, and the following year it organized protests against the resumption of Soviet nuclear tests. It also sponsored Hiroshima "Remembrance Days" in 1960 and 1961.[65] Largely preoccupied with the referenda, the Swiss Movement farmed out the job of organizing Easter marches to its youth group, which plunged ahead by announcing a march, from Lausanne to Geneva, in mid-April 1963. Under the slogan "Against the atom bomb—for a politics of peace," the march was designed "to support proposals for general and controlled disarmament" and to "awaken" public opinion "to the sense of struggle." About five hundred people walked the full seventy kilometers, with some one thousand converging, on Easter Sunday, for a vigil at the Palace of Nations in Geneva. The following year, another youth march took the same route, with some seven hundred participants increasing to an estimated sixteen hundred by the time of the Geneva rally. Their signs read "Nuclear-Free Zone in Central Europe," "Destroy Atomic Stockpiles," and "No Atomic Arms for Switzerland." The marchers—mostly of student age—received a generally friendly reception, even from the police.[66] Until 1967, Easter marches were an annual fixture of Swiss life, with the Swiss Movement evolving into the equivalent of the West German Easter march campaign: a youthful, vaguely radical, extraparliamentary opposition.[67]

In neighboring Austria, the antinuclear movement developed on a smaller scale, probably because the nuclear danger seemed less imminent. Thanks to the State Treaty of 1955, which brought the four-power occupation of that nation to an end, Austria accepted a status of permanent neutrality and also agreed to a ban on weapons of mass destruction. Some activists, like the physicist Hans Thirring, who became a Socialist member of parliament in 1957, championed unarmed neutrality as a route toward global disarmament. In June 1960, Thirring and other concerned scientists organized the Federation of Austrian Scientists (Vereinigung Österreichischer Wissenschaftler), modeled on the Federation of German Scientists. Designed to mobilize university researchers behind disarmament, it made some progress along these lines: sponsoring a lecture by Philip Noel-Baker, publicizing the Pugwash conferences, and opposing government plans for upgrading civil defense measures. Nevertheless, the organization remained very small, and Thirring enraged some legislators when he denounced civil defense as "a metastasis of the cancer tumor, the armed forces."[68] In 1962, however, inspired by activism elsewhere, the Austrian Union of Socialist High School Students began to adorn its uniforms with the nuclear disarmament symbol and to adopt the slogan: "Fight against atomic death." Finally, on December 19, 1962, a small group of activists staged an antinuclear parade through the streets of Vienna, thereby providing Austria with its first modern peace march.[69]

The December 1962 demonstration, combined with contagious examples abroad, launched Austria's nuclear disarmament movement. In early 1963, a group of intellectuals and young people, led by journalist Robert Jungk and philosopher Gunther Anders, organized the Austrian Easter March Committee (Österreichisches Komitee für den Ostermarsch). Preparing for a march that April, the committee distributed two leaflets. The first, a call to the march, described antinuclear activity in other countries and urged Austrians to do their part. The second, *The Struggle Against Atomic Death*, featured warnings by twelve leading Austrian scientists about the dangers of nuclear fallout and nuclear war and emphasized that even neutral countries like Austria could not escape their effects. On April 15, the Easter march began with six hundred people in Mödling and concluded with some sixteen hundred in Vienna. Organizers emphasized their "opposition to nuclear tests," to "the further spread of nuclear weapons," and to the "deception of the public about the dangers of the arms race." They urged "initiatives by Austria as a neutral country to bring about a reduction in international tension and mistrust." Subsequently, the committee, renamed Action for Peace and Disarmament (Aktion für Frieden und Abrüstung) and headed by Jungk, distributed additional antinuclear literature and sponsored annual Easter marches, usually drawing between one and three thousand participants. Representatives of pacifist groups, the Socialist youth group, and other sympathetic organizations served on its executive committee.[70]

In another small, neutral nation, Ireland, the movement found itself in the unusual position of championing some of its government's policies, including Ireland's disarmament proposals at the United Nations. Nevertheless, the combination of an escalating nuclear arms race and a flourishing CND in neighboring Britain contributed to the steady growth of the newly formed Irish CND. From 1959 through early 1962, it canvassed door to door, sponsored public meetings in Dublin, Limerick, and Belfast, publicized its efforts among debating societies and clubs, encouraged student antinuclear activities, protested the resumption of Soviet nuclear testing, and dispatched contingents to Britain's Aldermaston and Holy Loch marches. Raising money from sales of paintings and books donated by sympathetic artists and writers, Irish CND distributed large quantities of antinuclear literature. This included the pamphlet *You Believe in the Deterrent?* which portrayed the devastation that would result from the dropping of an H-Bomb on Ireland.[71]

Thereafter, Irish CND stepped up its activities. It led protests against new U.S. and Soviet nuclear tests, held a motorcade through Dublin on Hiroshima Day, produced a devastating critique of Ireland's civil defense program, and—during the Cuban missile crisis—launched a protest march that resulted in arrests (with charges quickly dropped). It also held a meeting of some nine hundred people at the Metropolitan Hall, Dublin, on the virtues of Irish neutrality and, in October 1962, sponsored a conference in that city titled "The World Without the Bomb." In Limerick, the local CND branch held a "flag day," during which its members sold flags on the streets (to raise money for the cause) and distributed antinuclear leaflets (to promote it). Because the event happened to coincide with the Cuban missile crisis, it acquired unusual immediacy. A participant recalled that ordinary people did not seem to think about nuclear disarmament or believe that it concerned them, "one way or another. But . . . if information is handed to them they are immediately interested." Drawing on the proceeds of their flag sale to produce more leaflets, Limerick activists returned on the weekend after Easter and handed out another five thousand. According to one participant, they were "widely read and discussed in pubs and shops."[72]

Pacifists played an important part in Ireland's antinuclear campaign. At a celebration it sponsored in 1960, the Irish Pacifist Movement, the Irish section of the WRI, launched a large, helium-filled balloon emblazoned with a message to Khrushchev and Eisenhower: Ban the hydrogen bomb! In 1962, the group's chair, Ciaran Mac an Fhaili, debated the morality of nuclear weapons in a Sunday newspaper and, later, contested that question with a U.S. embassy official on Radio Eireann. That fall, the Irish Pacifist Movement proclaimed that the Cuban missile crisis revealed what could happen if a nation like Ireland allowed foreign nuclear bases on its territory.[73] Rejecting the argument of some British pacifists that cooperation with CND would dilute their pacifist message, the Irish Pacifist Movement worked closely with Irish CND. It provided CND with petitioning booths at its events, featured the nuclear disarmament group in its newsletter, and declared that reports on the Aldermaston march left pacifists "buoyed up with hope." In April 1961, the two organizations jointly sponsored a public meeting, "Polaris and You."[74]

Although pacifists provided a core constituency for Ireland's nuclear disarmament campaign, it reached considerably beyond them. Meeting in May 1962, the general synod of the Church of Ireland—the Protestant body for the entire island—called on Britain to "give a moral lead to the nations of the world" by halting nuclear weapons tests. Many Catholics were active as well, taking heart from the papal encyclical *Pacem in Terris*. Politically, CND appears to have been on friendly terms with the Labour Party and with those whom it called "radical Republicans" in the larger Fianna Fail Party.[75] Young people, however, provided CND with its greatest single source of support. On March 1, 1961, students from all of Ireland's colleges and universities took part in a preliminary Aldermaston march. Meeting in Dublin the following year, representatives of Northern and Southern Irish students' groups merged the two bodies into a unified organization, Irish Students' CND. They continued to provide a large proportion of CND activists, as did an overlapping group, Irish Youth CND. According to *The Banner*, the CND newspaper, Irish Youth CND held "a very successful meeting" in Dublin in June 1963. Peace ballads alternated with speeches by CND president Peader O'Donnell and others, who contended that the youth of the world were rising up against war and mass destruction.[76]

The Southern Tier: France, Italy, and Greece

The French government's nuclear weapons program provided a spur to antinuclear activism in France. In the summer of 1959, thirty leading French scientists appealed to their government to seek an international agreement forbidding the testing, production, and use of nuclear weapons. And with the onset of French nuclear testing in the Sahara, in February 1960, concern among scientists grew. The small Pugwash group initiated a research project on problems of disarmament and, that March, ninety members of the science faculty at the University of Paris sent a message to President de Gaulle contending that the French atomic program should be limited to peaceful purposes.[77] That same month, to protest the government's nuclear tests, a new organization, the French Direct Action Committee Against Atomic Armament, staged a silent march to the French atomic weapons station near Bruyères. Some 150 people, led by pacifists André Trocmé and Lanza del Vasto, took part.[78] Resistance to nuclear weapons also spread to new constituencies, as Corsicans, including local officials, protested government plans to hold underground nuclear tests on their island.[79]

Until 1963, the only broadly based antinuclear organization to emerge in France was the French Federation Against Atomic Armament (Fédération française contre l'armament atomique). In early November 1958, Norman Cousins had asked Trocmé to gather French signatures on the disarmament appeal directed to the Geneva conference. Having secured the backing of hundreds of prominent writers and public figures—including Jean-Paul Sartre, Simone de Beauvoir, François Mauriac, Daniel Mayer, and Antoine Lacassagne—the organizers decided to use the momentum generated to form a mass organization on the model of SANE or CND. Toward this end, Claude Bourdet—a longtime peace activist and influential editor of *France-Observateur*—invited representatives of sympathetic social, religious, scientific, and youth groups to a luncheon and meeting at his house later that month. Enthusiastic about launching an antinuclear campaign, those present agreed to form a broadly based organization. In April 1959, about twenty groups with varying ideological and religious allegiances launched the new French Federation, with Trocmé and Alfred Kastler (a prominent physicist) chosen as co-presidents.[80] The organization had a very successful public debut in Paris on May 25, when a group of distinguished speakers—including Albert Chatelet, dean of faculty at the Sorbonne, who chaired the meeting—addressed an overflow crowd in a hall seating a thousand people.[81]

Although leaders of the French Federation viewed it as part of a worldwide campaign for nuclear disarmament, they also recognized that the French nuclear weapons program had reached a crucial point. On July 14, 1959, Trocmé and Kastler dispatched an appeal to de Gaulle, warning that the testing of a French Bomb would alienate Africa, impress neither the United States nor the Soviet Union, and "unleash a new atomic arms race" among additional nations. Conversely, by renouncing the Bomb France would contribute to "that moral progress" that "can alone answer the questions posed by technological progress." In October, the French Federation launched a nationwide appeal urging France to abandon nuclear testing and to support the initiative of the International Red Cross to abolish nuclear weapons. Signed by more than four hundred prominent academics, scientists, physicians, writers, and religious leaders, the appeal was delivered to the government on December 1 and published soon thereafter. On February 13, 1960, the day of the first French nuclear test, the French Federation proclaimed: "Today France is able to arm itself with atomic weapons. We demand that our country give other peoples an example of confident and generous good will, by voluntarily renouncing weapons of terror, and thus renew hope of a humane peace which alone can make world disarmament possible."[82]

To the disappointment of its founders, the French Federation did not become a mass movement. It did hold additional meetings, participate in some demonstrations, and generate antinuclear literature. But it lacked organizational coherence and mass participation. Indeed, it remained a federation of small, disparate organizations without individual membership. Beyond the elite university milieu, it had little strength or visibility.[83] Some of its weakness resulted from the rather cautious approach adopted by its leadership. Fearful of

alienating popular sentiment, Kastler chided Bourdet for urging African nations to oppose France's nuclear tests and the French Federation refused to
support the Sahara protest.[84] More fundamentally, though, the Algerian war
continued to preoccupy the nation and most of its peace constituency.[85] In this
context, as Bourdet recalled, the French Federation failed to develop "a very
real existence."[86]

One of the French Federation's component organizations, Non-Violent
Civic Action (Action Civique Non-Violente), filled some of the space left vacant in French public life by the absence of a powerful ban-the-Bomb group.
Forged around nuclear issues in September 1962, the organization drew on
France's small pacifist constituency. Although modeled loosely on America's
Committee for Nonviolent Action and cooperating closely with Britain's Committee of 100, Non-Violent Civic Action did not unleash a wave of civil disobedience but, rather, a round of publications and marches calling for unilateral nuclear disarmament. Later that fall, it issued an appeal titled "Yes to
Peace, No to the Bomb." Comparing the possession and use of nuclear weapons to crimes committed by the Nazis, the appeal urged the French to refuse
to participate in preparations for nuclear war and, instead, to foster understanding and cooperation among all people.[87] In March 1963, Non-Violent
Civic Action staged a small antinuclear march in Lyons in which it distributed
five thousand leaflets and carried banners reading "Against all bombs, both
West and East." The organization sponsored similar activities thereafter. In
1966, Non-Violent Civic Action staged a silent vigil in front of government
buildings to protest the construction of nuclear missile silos in the Haute
Provence.[88]

By early 1963, with the long, exhausting Algerian war at an end, French
peace activists—and particularly those on the Left—were ready for another try
at building a mass-based antinuclear movement. Inspired by an international
gathering of nonaligned peace groups that January, Bourdet mobilized his small
Unified Socialist Party behind creating a French counterpart to CND. However,
Jules Moch, a former minister of the interior and leader of the mainstream Socialist Party, had somewhat different ideas, for he preferred a movement focused exclusively on opposition to de Gaulle's nuclear striking force, the *force
de frappe*. Consequently, two groups announced their debut that March: Bourdet's Movement Against Atomic Armament (Mouvement contre l'armement
atomique, MCAA) and Moch's League Against the Force de Frappe (Ligue
contre la Force de Frappe). More grassroots-oriented than its rival, Bourdet's
MCAA began with a major publicity campaign in Paris, in which students put
up 3,000 posters and distributed 200,000 leaflets explaining the new organization. "We do not want supporters of the Atlantic Alliance, nor of the Soviet

bloc, nor of the French striking force," Bourdet declared. Or, as Jean Rostand, an eminent biologist and the first president of the MCAA, insisted: "The threat to all humanity caused by the existence of atomic bombs is so monstrous, so disproportionate to any other we have ever known . . . such a senseless defiance to our species' instinct of self-preservation, such an insult to the spirit of civilization" and "a dishonor to the science which gave it birth," that no compromise was possible.[89]

Although it vowed "absolute opposition to any kind of atomic weaponry," the MCAA did decide to give priority to the gathering struggle against the *force de frappe*. This enabled it to work in alliance not only with Moch's League and Non-Violent Civic Action, but with previously uninvolved groups and, thereby, mobilize unprecedented displays of antinuclear sentiment. During November 1963, the MCAA helped pull together some forty organizations—including the major union federations, the left-wing parties, the national students union, and peace groups—for an estimated sixty antinuclear demonstrations throughout France. In Paris, where the city council—under the prodding of Bourdet, a council member, and other sympathizers—went on record against French nuclear weapons by an overwhelming majority, 25,000 demonstrators turned out for a rally that condemned de Gaulle for his refusal to support the atmospheric test ban treaty and for his nuclear weapons program.[90] Subsequently, the MCAA, the League, and their allies sponsored massive Easter marches. According to its supporters, the 1964 march drew more than 100,000 demonstrators, and its successors (which continued, on a decentralized basis, through 1968) were also impressive events.[91] Along the way, the MCAA grew into an organization of ten thousand members, with some forty chapters located in France's metropolitan centers.[92]

Although the French press largely ignored the nuclear issue until mid-1959, when the government proclaimed its nuclear intentions, a lively debate began thereafter and continued until late 1964. Hubert Beuve-Méry, editor of the centrist *Le Monde*, took a dim view of nuclear weapons—indeed, he promised the French Federation his full cooperation with its work—and, consequently, that influential newspaper often raised questions about them. Bourdet's more left-leaning *France-Observateur* also made the case against nuclear weapons, as did *Liberation*. Many other newspapers, however, found them more appealing. After France's first nuclear explosion, Raymond Aron applauded the development in the conservative *Le Figaro*, although he objected to de Gaulle's plan for a strictly national defense. *La Croix*, a Catholic daily, lauded the French Bomb for providing what it claimed was a new respect for France. Except among the Communists, Soviet nuclear weapons had little appeal. In the fall of 1961, when the Soviet Union resumed nuclear testing, the moderate Left

Paris-Jour declared: "Whatever genuine or faked fears the USSR may allege to have caused its tests, the whole world will join in indignation to shout to Khrushchev: 'Enough, stop this diabolical game which risks blowing up our planet.'"[93]

In the French debate over nuclear weapons, the antinuclear movement generally succeeded in denying de Gaulle's government majority support for the *force de frappe*. According to a Gallup poll of July 1959, the French public split 37 percent in favor and 38 percent opposed to France's building its own Bomb. But the successful nuclear explosion of February 1960 and the government's subsequent ballyhoo as to France's revived glory seem to have inspired a turnabout. In March 1960, a Gallup poll found that 67 percent of French respondents thought that France's possession of atomic bombs would give it "an important trump in international affairs." In July 1962, supporters of a French atomic force outnumbered opponents by 39 to 27 percent; in January 1963, by 42 to 31 percent. But, in July 1963, shortly after the launching of France's mass nuclear disarmament movement, public attitudes reverted to 37 percent support and 38 percent opposition. By March 1964, 49 percent of poll respondents opposed a French nuclear defense force, while only 39 percent supported it.[94]

French attitudes were even more antinuclear on other issues. In a June 1961 opinion survey, 67 percent of the French people questioned said they supported a nuclear test ban. In August 1963, polls found that the French public favored France's adherence to the recently signed partial test ban treaty, even if it interrupted France's own nuclear armament program, by a ratio of three to one. In subsequent years, consistent majorities expressed their disapproval of France's nuclear weapons tests.[95] Global disarmament had still greater appeal. Surveyed in the summer of 1961, 76 percent of French respondents said they strongly favored a disarmament agreement between the Western powers and the Soviet Union, 17 percent said they favored it somewhat, and only 4 percent pronounced themselves against it. In early 1963, 95 percent of the French people polled said they desired "the abolition of nuclear weapons throughout the world." Indeed, by a ratio of two to one, French respondents favored banning nuclear weapons even if that left "the Western military forces weaker than the Communist forces."[96]

From 1960 to 1966, during the fierce parliamentary debate over the *force de frappe*, in which the government eked out a narrow legislative victory, all of the non-Gaullist parties came out against it. Their views ranged from abandoning it to accepting it only within the context of a European or Atlantic defense system. In the presidential race of 1965, the two major challengers, Jean Lecanuet and François Mitterand, both assailed the *force de frappe*. Lecanuet called for placing France's defense within a European framework, coordinated with the Americans. Mitterand, a rising star in Socialist ranks, proposed replacing construction of the French nuclear force with a policy of nonproliferation, adherence to the 1963 test ban treaty, and international disarmament. The Socialists, in fact, were undergoing an important shift on the nuclear issue. In July 1959, a Socialist national congress had voted in favor of France's development of nuclear weapons. But many Socialist leaders, union supporters, and rank-and-file activists were caught up in the MCAA and other antinuclear campaigns of the 1960s, and this set party policy on a new course. In 1972, the new direction triumphed with the adoption of the Socialist-Communist Common Program, which pledged that when the parties came to power, they would renounce the *force de frappe*, end French nuclear testing, add France to those nations ratifying the partial test ban and nonproliferation treaties, and support further efforts at internationally supervised nuclear disarmament.[97]

Italy's relative silence on the nuclear issue was broken in late 1960, when a professor of pedagogy, Aldo Capitini, announced a mass march "for the brotherhood of peoples." A well-known pacifist, social critic, and Gandhian, Capitini believed that, given the unprecedented dangers, his Center for Nonviolence in Perugia should organize "a peace march on the lines of the English ones." The march route ran twenty-six kilometers from Perugia to Assisi, the birthplace of St. Francis, patron of peace and of the poor. Although pacifists played a key role in organizing the event, significant help also came from labor unions, cooperative associations, and municipal councils. All groups, including the Communists, were invited to participate, contingent on leaving their banners behind and carrying those with messages prepared by the Center—"We are on the Verge of the Abyss: Enough War," "No More Nuclear Tests," "Disarmament of the West and East," and others of this kind. On September 24, 1961, thousands of persons turned out for the march, which ended with a very impressive assemblage of twenty-five thousand—including peasants, intellectuals, mayors, workers, and police (who joined the demonstration en route). Addressing the crowd, Capitini declared that the time was "ripe for a great turnabout of humanity," in which the people wrested the "huge destructive forces" from "the hands of a few decision-makers!"[98]

Elsewhere in Italy, other antinuclear elements were stirring. In the fall of 1961, when the Soviet Union resumed nuclear testing, students in eight cities and towns staged protest marches. Inspired by Britain's CND, an Italian Committee for Nuclear Disarmament (Comitato Italiano per il Disarmo Atomico, CND), located since 1960 in Milan, organized an antinuclear march of ten thousand in that city on October 28, 1961. Thereafter, CND staged a march at Piacenza and, in April 1962, again in Milan. Sponsored by the three trade union federations, previously at odds over politics, Milan's 1962 antinuclear march drew an estimated five thousand people.[99] Meanwhile, the mayor of Florence, Giorgio La Pira, convinced that humanity stood on an "apocalyptic ridge," hosted international conferences at the Palazzo Vecchio. Warning of universal death if fierce global rivalry continued, La Pira worked to replace it with a culture of cooperation. In April 1962, he called on President Kennedy to "put an end to the nuclear explosions which cause such damage and profound disturbance to . . . the world." Pacifist groups like the FOR, encouraged by La Pira and, more broadly, by a new openness to nonviolence in Italian life, held interfaith meetings and participated in antinuclear marches.[100]

Gradually, much of this scattered activity came under Capitini's direction. In the aftermath of the march from Perugia to Assisi, his Center for Nonviolence formed the Nonviolent Movement for Peace (Movimento nonviolento per la pace), a group that seems to have had little existence outside the Perugia Center. Committed to total pacifism, the Nonviolent Movement called for immediate efforts toward disarmament, unilateral if necessary, including the establishment of demilitarized zones and the removal of missile bases.[101] In the spring of 1962, the Center sponsored a second antinuclear march, to Cortona (in southern Tuscany), which drew fifteen thousand people. But soon thereafter it turned over the leadership of marches to yet another organization launched by Capitini. Recognizing that opposition to the Bomb had spread far beyond his own pacifist circle, Capitini had invited the leaders of all Italian groups interested in peace and social justice to a series of meetings in Florence in early 1962. Out of these meetings emerged the Council for Peace (Consulta per la Pace), drawing on a broad range of groups and chaired by Capitini. It planned to organize additional peace walks, hold seminars for study and discussion, press for the legal recognition of conscientious objectors, and form a Committee of 100. Absorbing Italian CND and other groups, the Council for Peace staged further antinuclear marches and meetings, some of very substantial size, thereby providing peace and disarmament activism with heightened visibility in Italian life.[102]

The Italian movement drew on a rather different constituency than its counterparts in northern Europe. Although prominent intellectuals often played leading roles as speakers and organizers, the movement had very substantial working-class and peasant participation at the grassroots, at least in part because of its backing by the mass-based Socialist and Communist parties. Men far outnumbered women at events, a fact that probably reflected women's limited role in Italian public life. The tiny Protestant and Jewish religious groups (and particularly their youth movements) often backed antinuclear agitation, but—although individual Catholics also participated—the giant Catholic church staunchly supported the military policies of the ruling Christian Democrats.

Beginning in 1963, however, antinuclear forces began to make some headway in Catholic ranks. The church's apparent support for the harsh punishment of a conscientious objector led Fr. Ernesto Balducci, a noted Catholic philosopher, to come to the young man's defense. In an age of nuclear weapons, Balducci declared, the Catholic "has not only the right but the duty to desert" from the military. Prosecuted for this statement, Balducci was sentenced to eight months in prison. But the ferment caused by his trial and, later, by the publication of *Pacem in Terris*, helped open the Catholic church to antimilitary currents, including the cause of nuclear disarmament.[103]

These developments contributed to a widespread revulsion against nuclear weapons among Italians. In the face of NATO battle plans calling for a nuclear response to a conventional invasion of Western Europe, a poll in June 1962 found that only 8 percent of respondents approved (and 78 percent disapproved) use of atomic weapons on enemy soldiers at the front lines in these circumstances. By the following February, approval for such use stood at only 5 percent, disapproval at 85 percent.[104] Conversely, nuclear disarmament proposals had great popularity. In July 1961, 69 percent of Italians polled said they favored a nuclear test ban, as compared to only 7 percent who did not. A year later (and ten months after the Soviet Union had resumed nuclear testing), a slight plurality of Italians (40 to 39 percent) considered the recent U.S. resumption of nuclear testing unjustified. Most tellingly, a poll in February 1963 found that 96 percent of Italian respondents favored the abolition of nuclear weapons throughout the world, and that only 1 percent did not. Asked if they favored banning nuclear weapons if that left "Western military forces weaker than the Communist forces," a slight plurality (36 percent) said "yes."[105]

Nevertheless, antinuclear forces had difficulty charting a clear course through the murky waters of Italian politics. During the late 1950s, the ruling Christian Democrats supported the installation of nuclear missiles in Italy, just as the opposition Socialists and Communists opposed them. But, in fact, government secrecy and the vagaries of Italian politics muted popular debate. Starting in 1953, the Socialists—under their revered leader, Pietro Nenni—had begun to back away from their postwar alliance with the Communists and to seek out areas of agreement with the Christian Democrats. Finally, in 1963, the Socialists joined the Christian Democrats in forming a Center-Left government. In this context, neither party wanted to damage their relationship by discussing the controversial nuclear issue.[106] Communist endorsement of the antinuclear movement also proved a mixed blessing, for although the Italian Communists ran the most liberal and independent Communist Party in the world, as well as one of the largest,[107] such support inevitably raised suspicions among non-Communists. Even many antinuclear activists felt uncomfortable with the

Communist embrace. Only the tiny Radical Party, which adopted a pacifist, antinuclear stance in 1963, was thoroughly in tune with the movement.[108]

In Greece, too, the antinuclear movement encountered difficulties carving out a nonaligned space in that nation's highly charged political life. Forced underground since the bloody civil war of the late 1940s, the Communist Party participated in politics through the United Democratic Left (EDA), a Popular Front–style political party, and in peace campaigns through the Greek Committee for International Detente and Peace (EEDYE), an affiliate of the World Peace Council. Although EEDYE, like EDA, drew on a constituency that ranged substantially beyond party members, its pro-Soviet orientation and aging leadership had little appeal for a new generation of activists.[109] As news of Easter marches elsewhere, accompanied by thousands of nuclear disarmament pins, flowed into Greece, Michalis Peristerakis, a law student at the University of Athens, decided to form a nonaligned peace group. During the Cuban missile crisis, he distributed a leaflet announcing this intention and asking young people of all political persuasions to join him. EEDYE criticized the formation of an independent organization, but students responded with alacrity and, within a short time, the Bertrand Russell Youth Committee for Nuclear Disarmament was born. Its first major activity—also opposed by EEDYE—was an Aldermaston-style march, from Marathon to Athens, to be held in April 1963.[110]

The Marathon march of 1963 triggered some of the stormiest events in modern Greek history. The conservative government of Constantine Caramanlis, viewing the antinuclear march as an incitement to revolution, officially banned it. In a democratic society like Greece, the government explained, protest marches were unnecessary. On April 21, the day the march was to begin, Greek police arrested some two thousand people, physically assaulting many of them. About three hundred were injured, including Russell's secretary. The only person to complete the march was Grigoris Lambrakis, an independent parliamentary deputy, spared arrest by his parliamentary immunity. A doctor who had scandalized the Greek medical profession by holding mixed medical-political clinics at which he treated poor patients free of charge, Lambrakis had also acquired fame as an Olympic athlete. Excited by CND's work in Britain, Lambrakis had broken with EEDYE, championed the nonaligned movement, and participated in the 1963 Aldermaston march, bearing the banner for Greece. And with the completion of his dramatic, one-man Marathon march, he emerged as the symbol of Greece's nuclear disarmament movement. A month later, leaving an antinuclear gathering in Salonika, he was murdered by right-wing vigilantes, secretly mobilized for the task by leaders of the Greek armed forces.[111]

The murder of Lambrakis by what Greeks called the "parallel government" generated a tidal wave of protest. When Greece's King Paul and Queen Frederika made a state visit to Britain soon thereafter, CND publicly denounced them, thousands demonstrated against them, and the Committee of 100 scrawled "Tyranny" all over the walls of London. On May 28, 1963, despite efforts by the Greek government to limit the turnout at Lambrakis' funeral, it erupted into the largest peace demonstration in world history. Athens came to a standstill. Construction workers went out on strike for the day, and the rest of the city deserted its desks or workshops. As the funeral procession of 500,000 people moved through Athens behind the coffin of Lambrakis, cascades of flowers rained down on it from the houses and shops along the route. Nuclear disarmament emblems appeared everywhere—on the silk banner borne by the Bertrand Russell Youth Committee, in the form of huge floral wreaths, and on the plain gray stone that marked the grave of Lambrakis. To millions of Greeks it had become a cherished symbol of resistance, second only to one other that emerged from the tragic events of 1963: Z ("He lives!").[112]

Despite the upsurge of support for the Greek antinuclear campaign, it faced some daunting problems. The Bertrand Russell Youth Committee never established a strong, efficient organization and, indeed, occasionally leaned on EEDYE and the youth group of EDA for assistance. As in Italy, the participation of the traditional Left helped make Greek disarmament events less bohemian and more socially integrated than in northern Europe, but at the price of relying to some degree on Communist-oriented organizations. Furthermore, given the weakness of the pacifist and nonaligned traditions in Greece, even the Bertrand Russell Youth Committee had difficulty staking out its position on disarmament. As of late 1963, it did not know where it stood on unilateralism, although it did favor world nuclear disarmament and the removal of nuclear bases from Greek soil.[113] And, finally, there remained the unremitting hostility of the authorities, especially the armed forces.

Nevertheless, in the aftermath of the Lambrakis assassination, the antinuclear movement held the initiative. Although police harassed participants in a Hiroshima Day gathering organized by the Bertrand Russell Youth Committee,[114] the government's popular support and moral authority were crumbling. Deeply embarrassed by the Lambrakis affair and other scandals, the Caramanlis government resigned. In the ensuing elections, held in November 1963, the Center Union Party—which had denounced Caramanlis as "the moral perpetrator of Lambrakis' murder"—emerged triumphant, ushering in an era of reform in Greek politics.[115] In the ensuing years, with a relatively liberal, sympathetic government in power, the antinuclear movement flourished. In 1964, a new Marathon march—sponsored by all of Greece's peace groups—began with

70,000 people and concluded with an estimated 250,000, bearing the nuclear disarmament symbol on flags, on pennants, on banners, on buttons, on brooches, and even on eyeglasses. Released from the repressive climate of the past, the crowds burst into dance, song, and poetry. The 1965 Marathon march proved even more successful, drawing half a million people.[116] Only recently banned, Greece's antinuclear marches had become the largest in the world.

The Movement Crests

Japan and the United States, 1958–65

> We demand of governments that nuclear weapons
> tests be banned forever, that the arms race end, and
> that the world abolish all weapons of destruction.
>
> Women Strike for Peace, 1962

During the late 1950s and early 1960s, nuclear disarmament activism played
an important role in the public life of Japan and the United States. Despite
widening political divisions within the ranks of Japan's antinuclear movement,
it waged a massive and spirited campaign against the Bomb. Few doubted that
it remained Japan's largest, most effective social movement. Furthermore,
given Japan's early victimization in nuclear war and relatively minor participation in the Cold War, antinuclear activists had little difficulty convincing the
public, mainstream groups, and political parties that they should oppose the
nuclear arms race. Facing very different circumstances, the American movement had substantially greater obstacles to overcome before winning public acceptance. Thus, while some elements took a radical pacifist approach, most
opted for a measured, multilateral strategy. Hammering away at nuclear testing and other salient features of the nuclear arms race, critics of the Bomb developed a lively, increasingly visible protest campaign in the United States, ri-
valed in size and intensity only by the simultaneous upsurge of the civil rights
movement. They also began to acquire some political influence. Consequently,
by the mid-1960s, both the American and Japanese antinuclear movements had
established themselves as major pressure groups, spurring powerful demands
for nuclear disarmament in their respective countries.

Japan

Although a political crisis within Japan's most significant antinuclear organization, Gensuikyo, dealt a serious setback to antinuclear efforts in Japan,[1] it

continued to exercise great influence in the nation's public life. In 1959, Gensuikyo's director-general, Kaoru Yasui, estimated that "about ten million people" participated in its Pilgrimage to Hiroshima, a nationwide demonstration in support of the Fifth World Conference Against Atomic and Hydrogen Bombs. These massive world conferences continued as well, designed—in the words of Gensuikyo's call to the 1960 conclave—to "strengthen every move toward a total ban on nuclear weapons" and to secure "general and complete disarmament." With the resumption of nuclear testing by the Soviet Union and the United States, Gensuikyo announced a three-month action campaign to petition for general disarmament, as well as to foster activities against nuclear weapons tests and military bases. Furthermore, it promised to work in support of Japan's peace constitution, to seek relief for atomic victims, and to press for the establishment of nuclear-free zones. Drawing on disparate elements of Japan's antinuclear population, Gensuikyo's activities were quite varied. In the spring of 1962, as a protest against nuclear testing, Gensuikyo paired a sitdown in front of Hiroshima's atomic bomb memorial by two of its revered leaders with a rally by irate fishermen at a coastal town.[2]

More traditional sources of antimilitary sentiment also contributed—albeit on a lesser scale—to Japan's antinuclear campaign. The small FOR, WILPF, and world federalist groups added their voices to others criticizing nuclear testing, protesting Japan's use as a nuclear base and pressing for nuclear disarmament.[3] Within the ranks of the Japan Science Council, the Pugwash conferences and their antinuclear conclusions stirred substantial support, leading to smaller disarmament conferences among scientists in Japan. One of these meetings, held in Kyoto in early May 1962, produced a forceful critique of nuclear testing and nuclear weapons that received front page coverage in all Japan's major newspapers. The Science Council also publicly opposed the government's plan to admit nuclear-powered submarines to Japanese ports.[4] As before, survivors of the Hiroshima and Nagasaki bombings remained key participants in the movement. The Japan Confederation of Hibakusha Organizations petitioned the government for legislation to improve the living conditions and health care of the survivors. Meanwhile, with local government backing, large memorial ceremonies, infused with an antinuclear message, continued annually at the bombing sites.[5]

The antinuclear campaign drew large numbers of recruits from Japan's radical student movement. Claiming to speak for some 350,000 students (more than half of Japan's university population), the Zengakuren promoted some of Japan's fiercest resistance to the Bomb. During the spring of 1962, the Zengakuren organized demonstrations by thousands of Japanese students against the resumption of U.S. atmospheric nuclear testing. Later that year, on Hiroshima Day, Zengakuren activists unfurled a banner in Moscow's Red Square denouncing Soviet nuclear tests. Simultaneously, they led massive antinuclear demonstrations outside the Soviet embassy in Tokyo. "Soviet nuclear tests do not contribute to peace at all," they declared, but only to "an endless nuclear armament race." Dogmatically Marxist, Zengakuren leaders had little use for capitalism, "petty bourgeois pacifists," or for Communist parties. Instead, they sought to develop "a workers' anti-war movement" in Japan and an alliance with student and other militantly antiwar groups abroad. The working class, they insisted, rejected both "imperialism and Stalinism" and should serve as "the central pole of the people's struggle." Although substantial portions of the Japanese public, including many workers, looked askance at the sectarianism, disrespect for authority, and occasional violence of the Zengakuren, these student radicals did swell antinuclear demonstrations and provide them with a militant, uncompromising tone.[6]

Even many of the nation's mainstream institutions adopted an antimilitary, antinuclear stance. Japanese teachers had their students read tragic stories of nuclear destruction, labor unions endorsed disarmament organizations and campaigns, university presidents condemned nuclear testing, and most newspapers and magazines opposed military programs on the part of their government and others. Although the sharp criticism of U.S. nuclear testing by the Japanese press led to charges that it was anti-American, Soviet nuclear policies met with no friendlier a reception. When the Soviet Union resumed atmospheric nuclear testing in the fall of 1961, Japanese newspapers quickly dismissed the Kremlin's contention that the tests were necessitated by the aggressive actions of the United States and added that nothing could justify poisoning the air for future generations. In late October, the *Asahi Shimbun*, the *Mainichi Shimbun*, the *Yomiuri Shimbun*, the *Sankei Shimbun*, and the *Tokyo Times* gave banner headlines to the Japanese government's protest against Soviet plans to test a fifty-megaton Bomb. The *Mainichi Shimbun* editorialized: "This is preposterous! . . . Bombs of this size . . . will rain heavy volumes of radioactive matter on the earth, endangering the health of mankind. Such a test must be halted." The *Nihon Keizai Shimbun* declared: "The voices calling for the cessation of the Soviet testing of the 50 megaton superbomb . . . have been the sincere protestation of all nations of the world."[7]

Given the antimilitary, antinuclear consensus in Japan, tumultuous protests erupted during negotiations for the revision of the Japan–United States Security Treaty. One of the heaviest charges leveled by critics was that it would turn Japan into a U.S. nuclear base. In March 1959, thirteen organizations—including Gensuikyo, the Socialist Party, and Sohyo (Japan's major labor federation)—established a People's Congress to Block the Security Treaty Revision. Conflict with the Japanese government intensified thereafter, reaching a peak in the spring of 1960, when activists launched wave after wave of protest demonstrations outside the gates of parliament. In mid-June, the Zengakuren broke through the gates to hold a demonstration within, where helmeted police assaulted them with truncheons. Later that evening, some four thousand students returned to protest the killing that day of a Tokyo University student. Again the police attacked, using truncheons and tear gas, injuring more than a thousand students and other demonstrators, and leaving much of the nation in a state of shock. Eventually, the government did force a revised Security Treaty through the conservative-dominated parliament, but only after inflaming national passions to such a point that President Eisenhower canceled his scheduled visit to Japan and Japanese Prime Minister Kishi resigned in humiliation.[8]

Visits by U.S. nuclear-powered warships—which, despite U.S. government denials, many feared might also be nuclear-armed—inspired storms of protest in Japan. In March 1963, an estimated 30,000 demonstrators turned out in the ports of Kobe, Sasebo, and Yokosuka for demonstrations protesting the proposed entry of U.S. nuclear submarines. On June 23 of that year, about 70,000 Japanese trade unionists and students held similar demonstrations in Yokosuka and Sasebo. When in November 1964 the first nuclear submarine, the *Sea Dragon*, finally docked in Japan, at the U.S. naval base in Sasebo, it sparked nationwide demonstrations. An estimated 2,000 people protested in Sasebo, 12,000 in Tokyo, and 27,000 in twenty-three other Japanese cities. This, too, failed to halt official U.S.-Japanese military cooperation. Nevertheless, it provided yet another indication of how fiercely many Japanese resisted any hint of accommodation with nuclear weapons.[9]

Although some Japanese condemned the antinuclear movement, they usually came from ultranationalist, right-wing groups with a marginal role in Japanese life. After Gensuikyo began agitating against the Security Treaty, the major conservative party, the misnamed Liberal Democrats, denounced it as "a spurious peace movement" and boycotted the Fifth World Conference Against Atomic and Hydrogen Bombs. Even so, the Liberal Democrats announced that they were forming their own nuclear disarmament organization. Ultrarightist groups provided more straightforward and vigorous opponents. During the conference, they dropped hostile leaflets from an airplane on Hiroshima's peace memorial ceremony. In addition, they attacked world conference delegates with bamboo poles and tossed liquid starch on them. On June 15, 1960, with the Security Treaty controversy at its zenith, right-wing extremists assaulted antitreaty demonstrators, mostly women, outside the parliament building, leaving more than sixty persons injured. That same year, a right-winger who had helped disrupt the Hiroshima conference went on to assassinate the chair of Japan's Socialist Party.[10]

These desperate attacks did little to stem the tide of antinuclear opinion. According to a USIA poll in the spring of 1963, 71 percent of Japanese respondents supported nuclear disarmament and only 1 percent opposed it. Furthermore, by a ratio of nearly two to one, the Japanese favored a U.S.-Soviet agreement to ban nuclear testing even if it did not permit "as much checking in both countries as the U.S. requests in order to verify that the agreement is kept." For years, pollsters did not even bother to ask about Japan's acquisition of nuclear weapons. And when they did, in the late 1960s, the results were thoroughly predictable. In December 1967, a nationwide survey found that only 14 percent of those questioned would consider themselves safer if Japan possessed nuclear arms. A June 1969 poll reported that 16 percent of Japanese respondents favored the acquisition of nuclear weapons, compared to 72 percent who did not. In December 1970, another nationwide survey found opposition to the nuclear armament of Japan slipping somewhat to 67 percent, but support falling even further, to 7 percent. That same year, a poll reported that even among the 16 percent of the population that favored expansion of Japan's armed forces, only a fourth approved of nuclear arms, and over half opposed them. In terms of age, the elderly were the most sympathetic to the acquisition of nuclear weapons, while students and young people expressed the greatest resistance.[11]

Furthermore, Japanese opinion on security issues remained strikingly antimilitary. Admittedly, polls found rising (and, eventually, overwhelming) support for maintaining the Self Defense Forces—the lightly armed military established by the government in violation of Article 9 of the constitution, which banned war and armed forces. But surveys also found very little backing for expanding the Self Defense Forces. Indeed, such backing declined from 19 percent to 15 percent between 1960 and 1963. Surveys also reported that, between 1952 and 1962, opposition to any revision of Article 9 rose from 32 to 60 percent. How, then, should Japan's security be maintained? Asked this question in 1968 by the *Tokyo Shimbun*, 50.7 percent of the Japanese surveyed replied that Japanese security should be guaranteed either "by the United Nations" or "by a policy of unarmed neutrality." Only 16.7 percent favored "maintaining the Security Treaty with the United States" and 15.1 percent "strengthening the Self Defense Force." Negative attitudes toward the Security Treaty were undoubtedly reinforced by its association with U.S. nuclear weapons. In an *Asahi Shimbun* poll at the end of 1968, 67 percent of those surveyed contended that the U.S. nuclear umbrella endangered Japan, as compared to only 12 percent who believed that it enhanced Japan's safety.[12]

This antinuclear sentiment had a major impact on Japanese politics. All four opposition parties took a strong antinuclear stand, and the largest of them, the

Socialist Party, served as a mainstay of the antinuclear movement. In January 1959, the Socialists formally adopted a policy of "positive neutrality"—by which they meant nonparticipation in military blocs, nonparticipation in the Cold War, moves to relax international tensions, and peaceful coexistence with all countries—as well as a new emphasis on nuclear disarmament. Surveying Socialist members of the parliament in 1962–63, pollsters reported that 92 percent considered the nuclear arms race "a very big threat," 92 percent thought the Soviet Union's resumption of nuclear testing in 1961 was "completely impermissible," and 95 percent favored Japanese neutrality. Even the governing Liberal Democrats, considerably more conservative and, for the most part, more hawkish than their opponents, hesitated to challenge Japan's antinuclear consensus. Until 1959, and the heated controversy over the Security Treaty, their national leaders sent annual greetings to the Hiroshima world conferences, while local leaders participated in Gensuikyo. Thereafter, although they presented a much frostier demeanor to the antinuclear movement, they nevertheless steered clear of anything that smacked of a pro-nuclear approach. In late October 1961, when the lower house of the Japanese parliament voted on a resolution calling for an immediate end to all nuclear testing, the measure passed unanimously.[13]

The United States

During these years, SANE remained America's largest, best-known antinuclear organization. Although membership never expanded much above (or fell much below) the twenty-five thousand attained by late 1958, the number of chapters grew to some 150, reaching beyond the original urban core on both coasts to outlying areas like Grand Forks, North Dakota, and Lincoln, Nebraska.[14] Hollywood SANE, headed by Steve Allen and Robert Ryan, mobilized disarmament sentiment in the entertainment industry, drawing on the support of Janet Leigh, Tony Curtis, Anthony Quinn, Jack Lemmon, Shirley MacLaine, Gregory Peck, Marlon Brando, and numerous other movie stars. Within national SANE, "the two Normans"—Cousins and Thomas—exercised effective leadership, although ultimate power resided in the board of directors. Most immediate decisions were made by Homer Jack, the Unitarian minister who—anxious to "jump with both feet into the real world"—became SANE's executive director in 1960. That spring, SANE put together an overflow rally at Madison Square Garden. Nearly twenty thousand people turned out for speeches by Cousins, Thomas, Eleanor Roosevelt, United Auto Workers president Walter Reuther, Michigan governor G. Mennen Williams, and others. At the end of the event, near midnight, Thomas, Reuther, and singer Harry Belafonte led an antinuclear march of five thousand persons to the United Nations.[15]

SANE threw much of its effort behind the campaign for a test ban treaty. In August 1958, when Eisenhower agreed to a moratorium on nuclear testing, SANE complimented him on his "wise and courageous action." Even so, it recognized the need to sustain public pressure if the ensuing Geneva disarmament talks were to reach fruition. That October, SANE ran an advertisement headed "To the Men at Geneva" and signed by a galaxy of its supporters, including Cousins, Pickett, Roosevelt, Muller, and Martin Luther King Jr. of the United States; Schweitzer of Gabon; Kagawa of Japan; Born and Niemöller of West Germany; François Mauriac and André Trocmé of France; Carlos Romulo of the Philippines; Russell, Collins, and Lord Boyd-Orr of Britain; Gunnar Myrdal of Sweden; and Trygve Lie of Norway. Asserting that no people in history "have had a bigger or nobler chance to serve their own age and all other ages to come," they called for "the permanent internationally inspected ending of nuclear weapons tests." SANE also circulated the ad as a petition, and—within nine days—gathered the signatures of sixty thousand Americans.[16] To support a comprehensive test ban, SANE organized large rallies at New York's Carnegie Hall and at similar sites in Cleveland, Chicago, Los Angeles, and other cities. Recognizing the division over nuclear issues within the Eisenhower administration, Cousins argued that an outpouring of public sentiment "may be decisive."[17]

Despite this emphasis on nuclear testing, SANE consistently widened its scope. In mid-1959, Pickett reported that a number of SANE leaders favored expanding the organization's mandate to opposing nuclear proliferation and all use of nuclear weapons—"a step toward a general peace movement." Thomas argued privately and publicly for tackling the issue of general disarmament. Noting the connection between weapons and global diplomacy, Erich Fromm favored the creation of a "committee for a sane foreign policy."[18] In response, a SANE conference in October 1959 broadened the organization's goals to include "comprehensive disarmament, a strong U.N. capable of enforcing world law, and the transition to a peacetime economy." In subsequent years, SANE's objectives expanded still further to include scrapping the U.S. civil defense program and finding solutions to the Berlin, Cuba, and Vietnam crises. SANE emphasized that it was "not unilateralist," but believed "in phased, inspected disarmament made by mutual agreement among all nations." Nevertheless, it did support "political and military initiatives by the U.S. to break the present impasse and to dramatize our desire to convert the arms race into a peace race." Championing "the educative, political, legislative" route to disarmament, SANE did not advocate civil disobedience.[19]

Operating within these parameters, SANE fostered a storm of activities. In the spring of 1959, it inaugurated the first substantial American peace demonstrations since the 1930s, patterned (it noted) "after the Aldermaston March." None of these, however, reached the massive proportions of the demonstrations in Britain and in some nations on the Continent. SANE's Hiroshima Day march of 1960, conducted in New York City, was a lively and impressive event, but drew only about three thousand people.[20] SANE captured far more public attention with its creative advertisements, designed without charge by the firm of Doyle, Dane, and Bernbach. Calling attention to the health hazards of nuclear fallout, one well-known ad featured a bottle of milk with a skull and crossbones—a source of much distress to the dairy industry. The most famous of them, headed "Dr. Spock is Worried," was widely published in April 1962 in an attempt to forestall the resumption of U.S. nuclear testing. In it, the famous pediatrician, recently recruited to SANE, looked glumly down at a child at play and declared:

I *am* worried. Not so much about the effect of past tests but at the prospect of endless future ones. As the tests multiply, so will the damage to children—here and around the world.
    Who gives us this right?[21]

SANE also assailed the resumption of Soviet nuclear testing—issuing press statements deploring the action, mobilizing its national board for a protest visit to the Soviet U.N. mission, and challenging the Soviet Peace Committee to condemn Soviet government policy.[22]

    SANE engaged in a broad range of other activities as well. It opened a Washington office for lobbying purposes; pressed for the establishment, and later the expansion, of the U.S. Arms Control and Disarmament Agency; and called for alternatives to nuclear war during the Berlin crisis. Turning to the United Nations, it became an active nongovernmental organization and provided the eighteen powers negotiating at Geneva with a library of books on disarmament. In addition, it endorsed candidates for election, sponsored a tour of the United States by CND's Canon Collins, and organized a seminar on U.S. relations with China.[23] During the Cuban missile crisis, SANE called on the Soviet government to stop arms shipments to Cuba and the U.S. government to suspend its blockade. As a solution to the problem, it favored closing down missile bases in Cuba and Turkey, with a U.N. guarantee of these countries' security. Although criticizing the Soviet Union "for recklessly extending the Cold War by setting up missile bases in Cuba," SANE joined other peace groups in demonstrating against a U.S. invasion of that nation. It called on President Kennedy to give "unqualified support" to U.N. Secretary General U Thant's proposal to mediate the conflict.[24]

    Although SANE never managed to acquire the broad-based, "mainstream" status that some of its founders had envisaged, it did help foster a popular climate for nuclear disarmament. Prominent Americans participated in its activities, tens of thousands of Americans joined it, and—through ads, publicity, and local events—most Americans heard at least part of its antinuclear message. If SANE made few inroads at the center of U.S. life, and even fewer among conservatives, it did have a significant impact on liberals, particularly on liberal intellectuals and other portions of the educated middle class. When Cousins and Pickett stepped down as co-chairs in early 1963, they were succeeded by two other liberal professionals, Spock and Harvard historian H. Stuart Hughes. In place of income, which—at about $100,000 per year—lagged far behind its ambitions, SANE relied heavily on the commitment, eloquence, and political skills of its leaders and members; in place of connections, intelligence and hard work. Although these ingredients remained insufficient to capture the broad middle ground in American life, they did—in conjunction with SANE's moderate stance—provide this peace group with an unusual measure of influence.[25]

Far less influential, but considerably more dramatic, was the civil disobedience campaign of the Committee for Nonviolent Action (CNVA). In 1959, CNVA launched Omaha Action, designed to call attention to the construction of an intercontinental ballistics missile base near that city. After a week's day and night vigil, activists—led by A. J. Muste, CNVA's chair—began climbing over the gates, as a crowd of incredulous local citizens and television crews stood watching. Eventually, sixteen persons were arrested and given six-month sentences.[26] The following year, CNVA took action against the launching of Polaris missile-carrying submarines at New London, Connecticut. More than fifty CNVA activists employed small boats with names like the *Henry David Thoreau* and the *World Citizen* to try to reach the nuclear-armed vessels and, ultimately, succeeded in boarding three of them. Many received jail sentences.[27] Although participants in both ventures sought to win the sympathy of local citizens and workers on the projects through antinuclear leaflets and meetings, they met a chilly reception in Omaha and a lukewarm one in New London.[28] Furthermore, few Americans seemed interested in joining a civil disobedience campaign. Even some key CNVA leaders criticized Omaha and Polaris Action for emphasizing obstructionism rather than an "appeal to the heart."[29] Nevertheless, through these small-scale, startling ventures, CNVA succeeded in heightening the salience of the nuclear issue and in promoting the idea of nonviolent resistance to nuclear war.[30]

CNVA also launched some dramatic transnational ventures. In December 1960, CNVA kicked off a San Francisco to Moscow Walk for Peace. Calling on the governments of all nations to disarm unilaterally, the marchers hiked and distributed leaflets across the United States, Western Europe, Eastern Europe, and the Soviet Union, before arriving ten months later, with thirty-one walkers from nine countries, in Moscow's Red Square. In 1963, deeply disturbed by the ongoing Cuban crisis, CNVA began a Quebec-Washington-Guantanamo Walk for Peace—a venture that, thanks to its racially integrated nature and to the U.S. ban on travel to Cuba, fizzled out in Southern jails.[31] As U.S. and Soviet nuclear testing resumed in the early 1960s, CNVA dispatched protest vessels to the test sites. In 1962, the U.S. government arrested the crew of *Everyman I* only fifteen miles outside San Francisco, but *Everyman II*, departing from Honolulu, succeeded in sailing through the U.S. Pacific test zone before U.S. authorities, hamstrung for days in securing a court injunction, hauled its crew members off to prison. To protest Soviet nuclear testing, CNVA launched *Everyman III* from London in September and, the following month, the forty-eight-foot ketch arrived at Leningrad. Refusing to allow antinuclear leafletting, Soviet officials gave the crew the choice of sailing away or being towed out to sea. The crew then began to sink *Everyman III* in the harbor, but anxious Soviet authorities managed to seize the ship and tow it away.[32]

The largest civil disobedience actions against nuclear war were not organized by CNVA, but grew out of earlier ventures. Ever since 1955, small groups of pacifists had courted arrest by refusing to take shelter in New York City during yearly civil defense drills. With the approach of the 1960 drill, two young mothers, Mary Sharmat and Janice Smith, organized a Civil Defense Protest Committee to broaden resistance efforts. Consequently, on May 3, 1960, as the sirens sounded, approximately two thousand New Yorkers staged antinuclear demonstrations at scattered sites. In City Hall Park, where some one thousand protesters gathered, half of them defied the authorities by standing their ground and refusing to take shelter. Although the police made twenty-six arrests, seemingly at random, the remaining demonstrators—including large numbers of women with baby carriages—remained good natured and immovable. At the all-clear siren, they cheered and sang "America the Beautiful." As the War Resisters League newsletter reported, it was the largest civil disobedience peace action in modern American history.[33] The following April, during the next nationwide civil defense drill, twenty-five hundred protesters turned out in City Hall Park and similar demonstrations erupted at universities, colleges, high schools, and other public places across the country. "Civil defense fosters war by offering a false sense of security," argued the Civil Defense Protest Committee. "The only defense is peace."[34]

Until 1961, in line with the gender norms of the era, almost all leaders of America's antinuclear activities were men; but this situation changed dramatically with the appearance of a new organization, Women Strike for Peace (WSP). On November 1, 1961, WSP startled observers by staging women's antinuclear protests in sixty cities, with participants alleged to number fifty thousand.[35] The new movement began the previous September when, in the context of renewed Soviet Bomb testing, a handful of Washington women resolved to take action against the accelerating nuclear arms race.[36] Through word of mouth, telephone calls, and contacts in PTA, church and temple groups, and the established peace organizations, they mobilized a women's constituency which burst onto the public scene that November. In small towns and cities across the country, thousands of women picketed public facilities, issued antinuclear press releases, and told public officials: "End the Arms Race—Not the Human Race." Furthermore, impressed by their success at mobilizing so many women and at garnering widespread, largely favorable publicity in the press, activists decided to maintain their organizational network. By the following June, as WSP prepared for its first national conference, it claimed to number "well over 100,000 people in approximately 145 groups throughout the country." In fact, WSP never developed a coherent national organization or formal membership, and these figures are probably exaggerations. Even so, it tapped enormous energy and talent among American women, thousands of whom joined eagerly in its campaign for nuclear disarmament.[37]

In the aftermath of its successful "strike," WSP engaged in a whirlwind of activities, many of them linked to securing a nuclear test ban. Condemning the resumption of Soviet and U.S. Bomb tests, WSP demanded of Khrushchev: "Will you not renounce this futile method, which can defend nothing, and which, even without war, is poisoning our planet?" To press its case, it organized numerous visits by WSP delegations to congressional representatives and administration officials, picketed the White House, published vast quantities of literature, and dispatched fifty WSP activists (including Coretta Scott King) to Geneva to talk with every delegation at the seventeen-nation disarmament conference. "General and complete disarmament under effective international control has been accepted in principle as a goal by both the U.S. and the U.S.S.R.," one WSP leader announced in early 1963. "But we women urge an immediate beginning, with a test-ban treaty, before it is too late." Repeatedly, WSP emphasized nuclear testing's adverse effects on children's health. Adopting the program begun by the St. Louis Committee for Nuclear Information, WSP urged women to have their children's lost baby teeth tested for strontium-90. Thereafter, WSP suggested, they should mail the teeth, with the lab report, to their senators. WSP also helped focus popular attention on the radioactive contamination of milk and, in early 1962, threatened a boycott of milk if the U.S. government resumed atmospheric nuclear testing.[38]

WSP took on other nuclear issues as well. The Berkeley WSP group turned out a thousand women to protest the California legislature's consideration of civil defense programs. When the federal government began distributing millions of brochures promoting domestic fallout shelters, WSP urged citizens to mail them back to President Kennedy with a letter calling for a more positive approach. WSP also championed economic conversion, making the argument that military spending was bad for the economy. In 1962, despite a reluctance to deal with "hot spots" rather than long-term issues, WSP spoke out in the midst of the Cuban missile crisis, condemning both Soviet provocation and the U.S. blockade. In 1964, WSP dealt with a lesser-known issue when it organized a massive women's rally and conference at the Hague against the NATO plan for a multilateral nuclear force. Although this stand put WSP in the position of opposing the nuclear program of only one side in the Cold War, on most occasions it was careful to take a balanced approach and to stress that it was not unilateralist.[39]

WSP's leaders and the press portrayed WSP as a rebellion of unsophisticated, middle-class, "housewives," but the reality was far more complex. To be sure, a study done by sociologist and WSP leader Elise Boulding in 1962 found that a majority of WSP activists surveyed were married, middle-class mothers who did not work outside the home. Nevertheless, they were far better educated than most women in the United States; 65 percent had an undergraduate or graduate degree, and only 9 percent had not attended college. Some 41 percent had been active in race relations, civil liberties, peace, or civic groups, or in political parties, and 62 percent of their husbands were then active in the peace movement. Dagmar Wilson, WSP's beloved founder and leading light, billed herself as a "housewife" who longed to return to her "pots-and-pans and PTAs." In fact, though, she was a prize-winning children's book illustrator and veteran peace activist. Indeed, all of WSP's Washington organizers belonged to SANE and some to WILPF—although they were put off by what they considered the excessive hierarchy and timidity of these groups. Even so, WSP leaders liked to play on their image as typical suburban wives and mothers, both because it enhanced their respectability and because they genuinely believed in the "feminine mystique." Indeed, taking their maternal responsibilities quite seriously, they concluded that it was imperative to save their children—and the world—from nuclear destruction.[40]

That WSP embraced nuclear disarmament activism on a maternalist rather than a feminist basis was not surprising. The women's rights movement had declined to a very small, marginal phenomenon by the early 1960s. Furthermore, nuclear weapons challenged women's traditional values, such as abhorrence of violence and nurturance of life. Not surprisingly, then, over the course of the New York City civil defense protests, women became the key leaders and—often accompanied by their children—grew from a minority to a substantial majority of the demonstrators. Admittedly, men often outnumbered women at peace protests. At a February 1962 antinuclear demonstration in Washington by thousands of American college students, only about 40 percent of the participants were female. Attending demonstrations, though, was "unfeminine." Even many WSP activists reported that they never participated in demonstrations or, if they did, disliked doing so.[41] But more women than men had negative views of war and the Bomb. A 1961 study of American college students found that only 45 percent of the females, as compared to 60 percent of the males, believed that pacifism was an impractical philosophy in the contemporary world. Conversely, the women were more than twice as likely as the men to favor unilateral disarmament. The authors of the study concluded that "male students are much more disposed to accept nuclear war than are female students." Similarly, a December 1961 Gallup poll reported that more women than men believed the current level of fallout in the air "dangerous to people." The following month, asked if the United States should resume nuclear testing, as the Soviet Union had, 50 percent of the women (but only 37 percent of the men) opposed the idea.[42]

Just as WSP provided the central rallying point for the women's peace constituency, so the Student Peace Union (SPU) emerged as the leading voice of antinuclear college students. In early 1959, the Chicago office of the American Friends Service Committee sponsored a small gathering of students from seven Midwestern college campuses. Concerned with facilitating communication and cooperation among young people working for peace, they organized the SPU, chiefly among pacifist and Socialist students.[43] The organization grew slowly but steadily thereafter and, in August 1960, held a planning meeting in Nyack, New York, to chart its future direction. Here it adopted a statement of purpose, proclaiming the SPU's belief "that war can no longer be successfully used to settle international disputes and that neither human freedom nor the human race itself can endure in a world committed to militarism." The SPU would work for a society ensuring "both peace and freedom" and for a peace movement "free of commitment to the existing power blocs." After discussing unilateral and multilateral approaches to nuclear disarmament, the SPU adopted a compromise stance, calling for "American unilateral initiatives" toward "world-wide disarmament."[44] Although the SPU's official membership never grew very large—reaching perhaps five thousand at its zenith—this was no measure of its impact on college campuses. Riding the crest of student concern about the nuclear arms race, the SPU had more than a hundred chapters or affiliates by the spring of 1962. By mid-1963, its national co-chair, Philip Altbach, claimed some two hundred, as well as twelve thousand subscribers to its monthly *Bulletin*.[45]

Determined to transform the campus and national political climate, the SPU plunged into a broad array of activities and, along the way, introduced the nuclear disarmament symbol into American life.[46] Local groups held peace marches, sponsored talks by proponents of disarmament (including sociologist Kenneth Boulding, economist Seymour Melman, and pacifist David McReynolds), gathered ten thousand signatures on a May 1960 "Petition to the Summit," and organized a Students Speak for Peace Day on over a hundred campuses. In the five months after the formation of the Washington University SPU chapter, it staged six demonstrations and raised enough money to build a peace library of three hundred volumes and twenty periodicals. Staffed by student volunteers, the SPU national office in Chicago churned out enormous quantities of literature designed for college students, including an estimated one million pieces from the spring of 1961 to the spring of 1962.[47] The SPU also publicized the dangers of nuclear fallout and condemned both the Soviet and U.S. governments for their resumption of nuclear testing. Such tests, it charged, were "the latest in a long series of acts by the two countries which demonstrate that the primary interest of the two power blocs is in strengthening and increasing their military influence irrespective of the welfare of the majority of the world's people." During the Cuban missile crisis, it again denounced the two nations for "provocative" behavior and, in addition, sponsored demonstrations calling for a peaceful resolution of the conflict.[48]

With the SPU in the lead, nuclear disarmament activism among American students burgeoned dramatically in the early 1960s. At Berkeley, three thousand students turned out for speeches by prominent advocates of disarmament, including Linus Pauling. Large numbers of students on New York City campuses publicly refused to participate in civil defense drills. In December 1960, over a thousand students at Harvard demonstrated for peace and disarmament under the leadership of a campus group, Tocsin. Multi-issue organizations like Students for a Democratic Society (SDS) emerged, defining themselves as opponents of racial bigotry and "the Bomb."[49] Much of this activity fed into the largest student peace demonstration yet held in Washington, when, in February 1962, roughly five thousand students—mobilized by the SPU, Student SANE, SDS, and Tocsin—descended on the nation's capital. Demanding that the U.S. government halt plans to resume nuclear testing, they picketed the White House on a round-the-clock basis, demonstrated at the Soviet embassy, held a large rally at the Washington monument, and met with members of Congress and administration officials. Their picket signs read: "Let us call a truce to terror" and "Neither Red nor Dead, but alive and free." During the 1950s, observers had talked of a "silent generation," but the pendulum was now swinging the other way. "I don't know what's got into the students," a Cornell University administrator complained to the press. "They seem to be demonstrating up here all the time."[50]

Even so, campus peace activists were not typical American students. Although, like most students of the era, they tended to choose male leaders,[51] in other ways they departed dramatically from the norm. A 1962 study of the nation's college students found that 72 percent thought that the United States should "run any risk of war . . . to prevent the spread of Communism," that 44 percent thought peace demonstrations harmful to the American people, and that only 6 percent advocated unilateral disarmament. But resistance to war was considerably higher among liberals, females, and male nonconformists. These findings are reinforced by a study of the Washington demonstrators of February 1962, which reported that a majority "came from politically liberal families." Indignant at governmental insensitivity to radioactive fallout and to the loss of life in nuclear war, they seemed "highly moralistic" and committed to an "uncompromising humanism." Two-thirds majored in the humanities or social sciences, with their career plans centered in teaching, social service, and research. Of those students with previous experience in social or political action (72 percent), about half had participated in civil rights activities. The authors, like analysts since that time, concluded that the development of the civil rights movement had a profound impact on American students—unleashing social activism, showing that it could be effective, and channeling it into forms of nonviolent protest. Indeed, like their counterparts in other lands, America's student peace activists were driven by a broad social idealism and a determination to act on it.[52]

Although overshadowed by newer, better publicized, and larger groups like SANE, WSP, and the SPU, America's traditional pacifist organizations played a lesser, but nonetheless significant, role in the antinuclear movement. The FOR hammered away at the nuclear arms race and its prime mover, the Cold War. "Each side, in its own way, is playing with fire," the religious pacifist group charged. Active in the campaign against civil defense drills, the War Resisters League also mobilized its members for Hiroshima Day rallies, Polaris Action, and for the San Francisco to Moscow Walk for Peace.[53] The American Friends Service Committee—in addition to putting resources into groups like the SPU—produced a series of peace pamphlets by leading intellectuals (*Beyond deterrence*), organized antinuclear film and discussion programs, and arranged lecture tours by prominent speakers.[54] For its part, the WILPF organized antinuclear demonstrations and protest marches, letter writing campaigns, probes of civil defense practices in the schools, investigations of strontium-90 in milk supplies, and a meeting of Soviet and American women at Bryn Mawr College. Calling for unilateral initiatives toward disarmament, the WILPF lobbied members of Congress and testified before the platform committee of the 1960 Democratic national convention.[55] Activists from these groups flocked to the more prominent antinuclear organizations, where some held key positions.[56] But—despite losses of members to the new groups (especially from the WILPF to WSP)—most grew in size and influence, probably because of the overall upsurge of protest against the Bomb.[57]

The atomic scientists' movement, while lower key than the newer groups, also played an important part in the antinuclear campaign, particularly through its impact on elite opinion. In 1960, the 2,500-member Federation of American Scientists (FAS) publicly stressed the "urgency" of securing "a test-ban agreement among the three major powers." When the Soviet Union broke the testing moratorium in late 1961, the FAS opposed the resumption of atmospheric nuclear testing by the United States. "The U.S. and the USSR already have sufficient weapons to destroy each other," it argued, "and further 'improvements' in nuclear weapons will not alter this situation significantly." Moreover, U.S. restraint would underscore the U.S. commitment to disarmament, limit nuclear fallout, and "strengthen international efforts to obtain a more stable world." In early 1963, the FAS added a call for the U.S. government to adopt a "no first strike" policy.[58] Meanwhile, Eugene Rabinowitch, editor of the movement's preeminent journal—the *Bulletin of the Atomic Scientists*, with a circulation that had climbed to thirty thousand—confessed that although he had been "skeptical" about the significance of a test ban, he now considered it "a matter of major importance." Committed to "the building of a world community" as a precondition for disarmament, Rabinowitch had been horrified by the Cuban missile crisis and driven to the conclusion that a "first step" was imperative. Accordingly, he now used the *Bulletin* to champion a test ban agreement as "a significant demonstration of the community of interests of the two nuclear superpowers."[59]

Individual scientists also applied themselves to the nuclear question. Most, like Hans Bethe and Ralph Lapp, continued to emphasize the need for a test ban treaty as a first step toward more comprehensive arms control and disarmament.[60] Leo Szilard, as usual, proved more idiosyncratic. Dismissing the idea of a test ban, he argued, instead, that the world would have to learn to "live with the Bomb," at least for a time. But this meant that it was imperative to find means for avoiding nuclear war. Along these lines, he sent frequent advice to Eisenhower and Kennedy, met and corresponded at length with Khrushchev, and proposed a series of ingenious schemes and ideas. These included the establishment of a "hot-line" between Washington and Moscow, a nuclear build-down to "minimum deterrence," and a "no first use" policy. In 1961, he published a whimsical book, *The Voice of the Dolphins*, which included a fanciful story relating how these intelligent creatures saved the world from nuclear destruction. Presenting an American safety razor as a gift to Khrushchev, Szilard joked that he would be happy to provide the Soviet leader with additional blades, "as long as there is no war."[61]

Among the scientists, the best-known for his antinuclear activities was certainly Linus Pauling. The renowned chemist barnstormed around the world denouncing nuclear weapons and issued public protests against the renewal of Soviet and U.S. nuclear testing. The Soviet resumption of tests, he told the press, "compares with the consignment of Jews to the gas chambers."[62] Shortly before attending a dinner for Nobel laureates at the White House, Pauling picketed the mansion in the cause of nuclear disarmament. Together with his activist wife, Ava Helen Pauling, he circulated a new petition opposing nuclear proliferation, which drew two hundred thousand signatures.[63] A contentious individual, Pauling sharply criticized other leaders of the scientists' crusade—including Rabinowitch and "the scurvy crowd in Chicago"—and sought to have two of them (Rabinowitch and Bentley Glass) purged from the Pugwash leadership for what he considered personal affronts. Even so, Pauling remained a towering figure in the struggle against the Bomb. In recognition of his antinuclear efforts, he was awarded the Nobel Peace Prize in 1963.[64]

Other intellectuals fostered a growing peace research movement. In 1957, a group of prominent social scientists had launched the *Journal of Conflict Resolution* at the University of Michigan and, in ensuing years, this became an important focal point for academic attempts to cope with issues raised by the nuclear arms race. Their ranks were bolstered when, in 1960, another group of social scientists—led by Erich Fromm, Jerome Frank, and David Riesman—launched the Committees of Correspondence. Critical of nuclear deterrence but non-pacifist, they sought to cut through the impasse represented by "Red or Dead" thinking.[65] Working along these lines, Charles Osgood and Seymour Melman produced influential books urging a U.S. policy of unilateral, tension-reducing measures that would encourage the Soviet Union to take similar steps—what Melman called "the Peace Race." One year later, Merle Curti, Edwin Bronner, Frederick Tolles, and other historians concerned with encouraging research on alternatives to war established the Conference on Peace Research in History, which became an affiliate of the American Historical Association.[66]

Although the United World Federalists (UWF) formally placed disarmament high on its agenda, in reality it adopted a rather subdued role in the struggle against the Bomb. Concentrating on what it considered the more fundamental issue of global governance, the UWF focused its energies on revising the U.N. charter.[67] Furthermore, the UWF's leaders sought to maintain its respectability by avoiding demonstrations and other "eyebrow-raising" activities. Even so, many members wanted to do more. At the UWF's 1962 national convention, the policy committee made no recommendation on nuclear testing, arguing that it was not related to world federation. But rank-and-file delegates rebelled, arguing that nuclear testing was a symptom that had to be treated before the disease of international anarchy could be successfully addressed. Eventually, the gathering condemned nuclear testing as a "major source of tension and . . . a serious detriment to the objective of peace through world law."[68] The UWF found SANE particularly appealing, for not only was SANE's best-known leader, Norman Cousins, a very prominent world federalist, but federalists like Homer Jack and Donald Keys held the major staff positions. Moreover, both groups were multilateralist and, in addition, SANE's public statements constantly played on the theme of subordinating national loyalties to the interests of the world community. These factors—plus the potential power of an organization fashioned out of SANE's twenty-five thousand members and the UWF's fifteen thousand—led the two groups to begin merger talks in 1963. Two years later, however, with the incompatibilities apparent, the discussions came to an end.[69]

Despite the collapse of the SANE-UWF merger attempt, most American nuclear disarmament groups cooperated quite closely. In the fall of 1961, prodded by Norman Thomas and others to develop a coordinating body and, at the same time, draw more mainstream organizations into the peace movement, they established Turn Toward Peace (TTP). Headed by Sanford Gottlieb and Robert Pickus, the TTP did pull together the major antinuclear groups, as well as some liberal unions, veterans groups, and religious organizations, in a loose national clearinghouse, with peace centers established on a local basis. The TTP sought to foster American initiatives toward the establishment of "a disarmed world under law," and its projects included the unprecedented student mobilization against nuclear testing of February 1962. Although personal and political differences led to the demise of the TTP in late 1963,[70] many of the participating groups worked together on numerous occasions. In the fall of 1961, when the Soviet Union resumed nuclear testing and the U.S. government announced plans to follow, a broad range of peace groups and their leaders issued protests.[71] They also cooperated closely during the Cuban missile confrontation. On October 26, forty peace leaders issued a joint statement on the crisis through SANE's office. The following day, SANE, WSP, and the SPU held a demonstration in front of the White House, followed by a rally and the dispatch of delegations to Soviet and U.S. officials. Leaders of the three groups also cabled to the Cuban president, urging that he suspend installation of missile bases "in the spirit of U Thant's mediation proposals." On October 28, calling for a peaceful settlement of the crisis, more than twenty peace groups joined for a rally at Dag Hammarskjold Plaza, outside the U.N. building.[72]

Joint demonstrations provided a common way for America's nuclear disarmament groups to show their collective strength. Although America's Easter marches never matched those of Britain in size or intensity, they did help convince the press that antinuclear activism was an important phenomenon. With SANE providing most of the muscle for the first Easter marches, in 1961, they drew an estimated 25,000 Americans in various parts of the country—the largest peace demonstrations for a generation.[73] An estimated 20,000 Americans participated in the 1962 Easter marches and, although the numbers for 1963 are fragmentary, there were reportedly substantial turnouts in New York City (several thousand), Los Angeles (3,000), Chicago (1,400), Detroit, Philadelphia, Minneapolis, Miami, San Francisco, and Austin. On October 28, 1962, during the Cuban missile crisis, peace groups staged America's largest open-air demonstration for peace up to that time, turning out 10,000 people for their joint rally at the United Nations. The leaders of SANE worried that demonstrations with unilateralist themes or unpopular images that were highlighted by the press did more to alienate than attract the general public. At the least, however, the onset of large peace demonstrations showed the seriousness with which many Americans took the nuclear arms race and heightened its salience as a public issue.[74]

During this period of antinuclear upsurge, America's major religious groups did comparatively little to encourage it. Although sermons on the dangers of nuclear testing and nuclear war were frequent in the tiny, liberal Unitarian and Universalist churches, this was hardly the case in the large Protestant denominations. To be sure, in the early 1960s the official pronouncements of the Episcopal church began to raise important questions about the morality of nuclear war, and the national conferences of the Methodist church went even further in stressing "the suicidal quest for military supremacy" and the necessity for disarmament. But these remained lofty generalities without significant follow-up. As Cousins privately complained: "The Church . . . manages to express its concern now and then but it has not made any dramatic connection with the problem; it has not made peace the central and overriding objective."[75] The Catholic church remained even more standoffish. Tiny pacifist groups like the Catholic Worker and a newer organization, PAX, founded in 1962 at the initiative of Eileen Egan, sought to foster nuclear disarmament sentiment within Catholic ranks. But the Catholic Association for International Peace, the official church body dealing with nuclear and defense issues, remained impervious to criticism of nuclear war.[76] Symptomatically, the religious orientation of the student antinuclear demonstrators of February 1962 differed dramatically from that of most Americans. In a nation where the vast bulk of the population attended the major Protestant or Catholic churches, 51 percent of the demonstrators had no religious preference, 20 percent were Jewish, and 14 percent were affiliated with liberal Protestant sects (e.g. Unitarian and Quaker); only 13.5 percent came from other Protestant groups and a mere 0.5 percent were Catholic.[77]

The mass media also provided the struggle against the Bomb with limited assistance. Spurred to some measure of social concern by the public protests and by SANE's sprightly ads, some magazines—including women's journals, the *New Yorker*, *Consumer Reports*, and *Playboy*—carried alarming stories on radioactive contamination, especially of milk. The antinuclear effort also gained appreciably when filmmaker Stanley Kramer turned the best-selling novel *On the Beach* into a powerful, influential movie.[78] But, for the most part, the mass media refused to publish the writings of nuclear critics and did little to question government policy. In 1961, *Life* ran a lengthy article assuring readers that 97 out of 100 Americans would survive a nuclear war if only they built bomb shelters. An appreciative letter from President Kennedy accompanied the story, as did a plethora of how-to-do-it pictures, with captions such as: "Family in the Shelter, Snug, Equipped and Well Organized." When SANE ran its "Dr. Spock Is Worried" ad, *Time* dismissed it as "Sane, but less than realistic." Indeed, *Time* vigorously attacked what it called "the illusions of a small but hardy Western breed: the ban-the-bomb campaigners, who are dedicated to the dubious proposition that any political fate is preferable to the horror of atomic war ('I'd rather be Red than dead')." Like many conservative publications, *Time* liked to tag antinuclear campaigners with the slogan "Better Red than Dead"—although, in fact, they never used it. To drive the point (or the image) home, *Time* added that the movement was "covertly but vigorously backed by local Communists."[79]

America's antinuclear campaign had some very ferocious opponents. Veterans' groups and other "patriotic" organizations sharply assailed Norman Cousins and other leading critics of the Bomb. Arriving to deliver nuclear disarmament talks in diverse cities, Steve Allen found himself confronted with picket signs reading: "Steve wants to crawl on his knees to the Kremlin" and "Is Steverino yellow?" In an article published in *Foreign Affairs*, nuclear analyst Henry Kissinger warned that a nuclear test ban would lead to "an increased campaign to outlaw nuclear weapons altogether." A few years later, he secretly told the British government that, at the September 1962 Pugwash conference, wily Russian scientists had hoodwinked their American counterparts and that the attendance of some of Kennedy's scientific advisers had been "especially irresponsible."[80] The best-known defender of America's nuclear options remained Edward Teller, who argued that thanks to what he insisted was Soviet cheating during the testing moratorium of 1958–61, the Soviet Union had acquired a "decisive advantage." Writing in the *Saturday Evening Post* in February 1962, Teller assailed the "alarmists" whose allegedly hysterical statements had led to this sad state of affairs and might soon lead to worse. "Fallout from nuclear testing is not worth worrying about," he assured readers. Indeed, "it might be slightly beneficial."[81]

Public opinion in the United States, though considerably more pro-nuclear than in other nations, found this line of argument unconvincing. In November 1959, a Gallup poll reported that 77 percent of American respondents wanted "the agreement to stop testing H-bombs" extended. To be sure, a June 1961 survey found that 55 percent of Americans favored U.S. test resumption, and the figure rose to 59 percent that September. But the former question stressed that "no permanent agreement" had been reached, and the latter that the Soviet Union had already resumed nuclear testing. Furthermore, in the unpromising context of Soviet atmospheric nuclear testing, support for resuming U.S. atmospheric tests remained remarkably weak. In November 1961, opponents outnumbered supporters of U.S. tests in the atmosphere by 45 to 44 percent. As late as January 1962, Americans—told that "last fall Russia resumed testing of nuclear bombs with a series of tests in the atmosphere"—split 46 percent in favor and 43 percent opposed to sanctioning similar action by the United States. Only in March 1962, after President Kennedy announced his decision to resume atmospheric nuclear testing, did a majority (66 percent) finally support the idea.[82] Back in 1955, popular support for a nuclear test ban treaty stood at no more than 20 percent, but the idea gained substantial popularity thereafter. In 1963, immediately after the signing of the atmospheric test ban treaty, 61 percent of the American respondents who had heard of the action supported Senate ratification, as compared to only 18 percent who opposed it. By September, when the treaty was voted on by the Senate, public approval reached 80 percent.[83]

Large numbers of Americans also felt uncomfortable with the possession of nuclear weapons and the prospect of nuclear war. In June 1961, asked about the chance of a world war breaking out in which atomic bombs would be used, 59 percent told pollsters that they were either fairly worried or very worried. Queried, in August, about what they thought their chances were of surviving "an all-out nuclear war," 83 percent responded "just 50–50" or "poor"; by February 1963, the figure had risen to 89 percent.[84] Admittedly, fear of Communism sometimes overcame other fears. Given the choice of "fighting an all-out nuclear war or living under communist rule," an overwhelming majority of Americans polled favored nuclear war.[85] But when it came to less threatening situations, Americans showed less belligerence. Even in the fall of 1967, as they grew frustrated with the Vietnam War, a clear plurality (48 percent) told pollsters that they rejected the idea of using "atomic weapons and bombs if the military believes we should." Asked, in September 1960 and August 1963, about a disarmament agreement with the Soviet Union, a plurality (46 percent on each occasion) expressed its approval.[86]

Given the substantial public concern about the nuclear arms race, leading politicians began to stake out antinuclear positions. On March 27, 1959, Senator Humphrey introduced a resolution supporting U.S. efforts to negotiate a test ban, including "an adequate inspection and control system." The measure was unanimously adopted by the Senate on April 30. Although touted by Humphrey as strengthening the hand of the Eisenhower administration in its dealings with the Russians, the resolution had the effect of making it more difficult for the administration to break off negotiations, and this may have been Humphrey's motive. Only a week before, campaigning for the Democratic presidential nomination, he spoke out publicly against using the atmosphere "as a rubbish dump for radioactive debris." By this time, the Minnesota senator had a close working relationship with Norman Cousins, as well as a sense of the nuclear issue's political potential. Recalling his decision to make nuclear disarmament "a primary matter" in his campaign, Humphrey observed that the nation "was more ready" than in the past for a discussion of the subject, "filled as we were with a fear of nuclear holocaust." Although Nelson Rockefeller, entering the Republican presidential race that fall, called for the resumption of underground nuclear testing, Senator John Kennedy, a leading aspirant for the Democratic nomination, declared that the United States should extend its moratorium "indefinitely." A week later, Vice President Nixon said that the U.S. government should refrain from nuclear testing as long as the disarmament negotiations continued at Geneva. Closing ranks behind Kennedy and Humphrey, the Democratic Advisory Council declared on December 19 that it supported continuation of the testing moratorium as "a first step toward disarmament and the relaxation of tensions."[87]

As the presidential race heated up in 1960, the leaders of both parties continued to voice support for nuclear disarmament. Two of the Democratic presidential hopefuls—Humphrey and Adlai Stevenson—sent messages of greeting to SANE's Madison Square Garden rally of May 1960. Nominated by the Republican Party with a platform pledged to a test ban with adequate safeguards, Nixon maintained that U.S. nuclear tests should not be resumed as long as any chance existed of obtaining a treaty along these lines. Kennedy, the Democratic nominee, in a major statement of October 9, declared that he opposed resumption of underground nuclear testing. Furthermore, he pledged that, if elected, his government would not be the first to resume atmospheric testing, for that would "contaminate the air that all must breathe and thus endanger the lives of future generations." He would also pursue "vigorous" test ban negotiations at Geneva and "earnestly seek an overall disarmament agreement." Although other aspects of the presidential race—particularly Kennedy's call for a rapid missile buildup—did not bring much cheer to the antinuclear movement, the center of gravity in U.S. politics was clearly shifting.[88]

Recognizing the importance of national politics, as well as their potential strength, nuclear disarmament activists groped toward an electoral strategy during the early 1960s. In the 1962 midterm congressional elections, more than twenty "peace candidates" ran campaigns, with assistance from SANE, student activists, and regional groups organized for the occasion, such as Political Action for Peace (New England), Voters for Peace (New Jersey and Chicago), Californians for Liberal Representation, and Platform for Peace (Seattle). The best-known of the races featured peace candidate, Harvard historian, and SANE leader H. Stuart Hughes waging an independent campaign for the U.S. Senate seat from Massachusetts against Democrat Edward Kennedy and Republican George Cabot Lodge. On election day, the results were mixed. Despite their energy and commitment, the third party candidates fared poorly. Even Hughes—whose campaign had amassed 150,000 signatures on his nominating petition and had fielded 3,000 volunteers—ultimately drew only 2.7 percent of the vote. By contrast, the major party peace candidates did rather well, with a number either winning victories or increasing their vote over that drawn in past races. Taking note of this, SANE and some of the regional groups concluded that, henceforth, the peace movement should concentrate its electoral resources exclusively on candidates of the major parties.[89]

This decision meshed well with the strategy of the most successful peace politics group, the Council for a Livable World. Having survived a bout of cancer—during which he supervised his treatment—Leo Szilard leaped back into public life in late 1961, when he began traveling from college to college with an alarming talk, "Are We on the Road to War?" In the speech, Szilard proposed the creation of an organization, directed by leading proponents of disarmament, that would encourage citizens to contribute 2 percent of their income to peace candidates for Congress. Reaching thousands of faculty, students, and others with this message, Szilard managed to raise substantial amounts of money (although only after scrapping the 2 percent idea) and, by June 1962, to form an entity to disburse it, the Council for Abolishing War. Concentrating on Senate races, it contributed over $20,000 to that of George McGovern (a fifth of his campaign funding), over $10,000 to that of Joseph Clark, and smaller amounts to the campaigns of Wayne Morse, Jacob Javits, and Frank

Church—all of whom won. In McGovern's race, decided by a few hundred votes, the Council claimed to have been a crucial factor. Having emerged as the nation's most effective peace PAC, the new organization adopted Szilard's dolphin as its logo and, in the winter of 1962, began calling itself the Council for a Livable World. Although Szilard's whirlwind of antinuclear activities finally came to a halt in mid-1964, when he succumbed to a heart attack, the Council remained an enduring monument to his crusade against the Bomb.[90]

By the early 1960s, then, as disarmament groups and public opinion began to make their mark on the nation's politics, the movement started to develop a constituency in the U.S. Congress. In the House, liberals like Robert Kastenmeier drew on peace groups for information about nuclear programs. In the Senate, Humphrey and a small band of others pressed for greater efforts to curb the arms race. With his White House influence enhanced by Kennedy's election, the Minnesota senator secured administration support for the establishment of the first U.S. government body to focus on disarmament: the Arms Control and Disarmament Agency. The Council for a Livable World identified seven incumbent senators that it wanted to back in the 1964 elections, and in early 1965 Gottlieb identified another six who "generally support the views of SANE." They included not only Clark, McGovern, and Church, but such rising political leaders as Eugene McCarthy, Albert Gore, and Edmund Muskie. All were liberal Democrats. Many others joined them on occasion in backing arms control and disarmament measures. In early 1963, Humphrey startled observers by persuading Senator Thomas Dodd, one of the more hawkish members of the Armed Services Committee, to co-sponsor a resolution affirming Senate readiness to accept a treaty banning nuclear tests in the atmosphere and in the oceans. Thirty-two senators soon joined them.[91] If U.S. disarmament groups had not yet secured respectability, important parts of their message had.

The Movement Crests

*Third World and Communist
Nations, 1958–65*

> There is an immediate relationship between the
> persistent terror of imminent nuclear war and the
> political and economic subjugation of the peoples
> of Africa and Asia.
>
> Kenneth Kaunda, 1961

By the early 1960s, nuclear disarmament activism—though usually on a much
smaller scale—was also emerging in Third World and Communist countries.
Given more immediately pressing concerns of poverty, colonialism, and dictatorship, the economically underdeveloped nations of Africa, Asia, and Latin
America did not normally provide fertile territory for peace movements. Usually, when nonviolent resistance campaigns did develop in some of these areas, they focused on ending social injustice or political violence.[1] Totalitarian
governments gave Communist states an even more forbidding terrain for peace
or antinuclear activities. Consequently, in the mid-1960s, pacifist organizations
like the War Resisters' International and the Women's International League for
Peace and Freedom had very few affiliates in the Third World and none in
Communist nations.[2] Nevertheless, so compelling was the sense of nuclear crisis that gripped the world in the late 1950s and early 1960s that, even in these
regions, forces arose to demand an end to preparations for nuclear war.

Africa

Africa's most dramatic antinuclear campaign emerged in the context of plans
for the explosion of France's first atomic bomb. In January 1959, Britain's Direct Action Committee first broached the idea of dispatching an international
protest team to the test site. That summer, as French government plans crystallized for a Bomb test in the Sahara, at Reggan, Algeria—a nation then locked

in a fierce war of independence against France—the DAC moved forward with the project. Meanwhile, African leaders and organizations began to protest bitterly against the heightened dangers of nuclear fallout on their continent and at France's latest display of colonialist arrogance. The Moroccan government offered the protest leaders the use of its country as a staging area, and this would have provided a relatively short route to the test site. But traveling from Morocco would also have enhanced the likelihood of being shot by French forces, deported, or handed over to the French government, or of becoming uncomfortably associated with the National Liberation Front, Algeria's revolutionary movement.[3]

Ghana, which had attained independence in 1957, seemed a much better base. Anti-French feeling ran high in Ghana thanks to France's ruthless war in Algeria and to its mistreatment of Guinea when the latter had opted for independence from France. Furthermore, under the leadership of Kwame Nkrumah, Ghana seemed committed to anti-imperialism and antimilitarism, as well as to the nonalignment proclaimed at the Bandung Conference of 1955. Even better, with the assistance of an American pacifist, Bill Sutherland, a Ghana Council for Nuclear Disarmament had been launched in August 1959. Organized the previous month as the Ghana Anti-Atom Committee, Ghana CND had a semi-official status rather different from its overseas counterparts. It enjoyed strong support from some of the nation's leading public figures, as well as from the Ghana Federation of Women, the Ghana Bar Association, and the Ghana Medical Association. If the leaders of Ghana CND were suspiciously influential, they were also sincere. The most prominent among them, Agbeli Gbedemah, Ghana's minister of finance, was also the president of the World Association of World Federalists. Given these advantages, the protest organizers opted for Ghana as the staging area.[4]

This proved a fruitful choice. With the support of the Direct Action Committee and America's Committee for Nonviolent Action, leading Western pacifists—including Michael Randle, A. J. Muste, and Bayard Rustin—flew to Accra, where they engaged in intense planning meetings with the leaders of Ghana CND. As foreign protest team members entered the country, they received very substantial support. Radio Ghana publicized their activities and they addressed numerous mass meetings, attended by tens of thousands of people. Arriving in Accra to head up the project, the Reverend Michael Scott was met at the airport by an enormous crowd, which hoisted him on its shoulders. On October 18, churches throughout the nation held a day of prayer for nuclear disarmament. Pleading for financial assistance over Radio Ghana, CND's Gbedemah raised six thousand pounds within twenty-four hours. After addressing the All-African Trade Union Federation in November 1959, the protest team received its official backing and its secretary called on all African workers to demonstrate against the French nuclear tests. Meanwhile, additional African leaders pledged their support, including the president of the Basutoland National Congress Party, who flew to Accra to join the protest team.[5] Rustin—withdrawn from the project when Martin Luther King Jr. and A. Philip Randolph pleaded for his help organizing civil rights protests in the United States—later remarked that this was the most significant pacifist venture with which he had ever been associated. It developed, he noted, "in an atmosphere where most of Africa was already aroused and was waiting for a project round which it could rally. . . . It tied together . . . militarism and political freedom in a way that people could understand and respond to."[6]

The journey to the test site posed greater difficulties. On December 6, 1959, a protest team of nineteen people (twelve from Ghana and the balance from Nigeria, Basutoland, Britain, the United States, and France) set out in two Land Rovers and a truck for Algeria, 2,100 miles away. In the words of the DAC's April Carter, they hoped "to arouse the conscience of the French people and the people of other nuclear powers; to stimulate further active opposition in Africa; and to halt the bomb tests—or at least to embarrass the French government." Three days later, sixteen miles inside French-controlled Upper Volta, French soldiers blocked their passage. Accordingly, they withdrew into Ghana. A reconstituted team entered Upper Volta on December 17, only to be barred once again by French troops. This time the protesters adopted a more confrontational approach—staging a sit-in at the barrier, holding vigils, distributing leaflets (despite threats of arrest), and broadcasting through loudspeakers to local residents. On January 8, four team members set off on foot, but troops with rifles and Bren guns arrested them, impounded the team's vehicles, and returned the team under armed guard to Ghana. A third protest team set out on January 17, slipped into Upper Volta on foot, and hitched rides with friendly truck drivers until French authorities apprehended it about sixty-six miles north of the border. With team members scattered about or in the process of being deported, their equipment confiscated, and all possible routes into Upper Volta under round-the-clock surveillance by French troops, protest organizers gave up the attempt to reach the Sahara test site.[7]

By this point, however, their mission was at least partly accomplished. During the team's attempts to reach Reggan, small demonstrations—including fasts, picketing, and leafleting—broke out in Upper Volta, Ghana, Nigeria, Britain, West Germany, and the United States. Groups of Nigerians and Iraqis volunteered to take part in future missions. As the test date approached, mass demonstrations erupted in Tunis on January 25 and in Tripoli on January 31. In Rabat, Morocco, two thousand people protested outside the French embassy, despite a government ban on demonstrations. In Paris, some five hundred African students from French Community nations gathered to present an antitesting petition to Premier Michel Debré. After the bomb test, Ghana CND released a statement declaring: "France, by exploding her bomb, has joined the nuclear club and resigned from the club of human decency and respect for the rights of others." Ghana CND would "continue to use every non-violent means to awaken the peoples of Africa to the dangers of what the French are doing." As Randle noted, the project had given "new impetus to the ideas of non-violence and direct action" in Africa, particularly with respect to nuclear weapons.[8]

In the aftermath of the expedition and the first round of French nuclear tests, Scott convinced Nkrumah to organize a conference that would bring together leaders of overseas peace groups with representatives of Africa's independent governments, liberation movements, and union federations to develop ongoing forms of peace activism. Held from April 7 to 9, 1960, this Conference on Positive Action for Peace and Security in Africa represented, as Sutherland noted, "the height of influence of the world pacifist movement on the African liberation struggle." Pacifist representatives at the event included Asadevi Aryanayyakum (one of Gandhi's close associates), Tomiko Kora of Japan, Muste and a substantial contingent of Western peace activists, and Ralph Abernathy (King's top aide in the Southern Christian Leadership Conference). Although advocates of armed struggle, among them the eloquent Frantz Fanon, also influenced the conclusions of the conference, it did help consolidate African opinion against the Bomb. By a unanimous vote, the conference applauded the contribution made by the Sahara protest team to the liberation of Africa, urged the development of larger-scale action against French nuclear tests, and—in this connection—called for the establishment of training centers for "positive nonviolent action."[9]

Things did not pan out as well thereafter. To be sure, a day after the conference ended, Nkrumah met with Muste and other pacifists, telling them of his desire to have work started immediately on the protest project, to have a training center established in Accra, and to have Sutherland and Randle work full-time on the project and for the training center. He also said that he would make $28,000 immediately available for these purposes. But opportunities for the protest and for the training center soon dwindled. Distracted by international events, Nkrumah did not follow through. In July, when he did act, he set up the Kwame Nkrumah Institute with two components—one to train party and union leaders and the other to provide training in "positive action." Meanwhile, the Sahara protest organizers grew increasingly worried that the center would not reflect their principles. Tightening the reins of government power, Nkrumah moved toward curbing civil liberties and repressing the opposition. Moreover, the officials directing the center seemed hostile to nonviolent resistance and likely to divert the institution to promoting armed struggle in Algeria or South Africa. In the fall of 1960, when Randle and Sutherland suggested a plan of coordinated protests against French nuclear testing, it was ignored. Eventually, Randle returned to Britain to lead the Committee of 100, and plans for turning Ghana into a stronghold of disarmament activism came to an end.[10]

But Ghana was not the only possibility along these lines. For some time, Western peace activists had been impressed by the Gandhian fervor of Kenneth Kaunda, the leader of Northern Rhodesia's independence movement, and he proved eager to work with them. In a statement prepared for the Committee of 100, Kaunda declared that "the day-to-day threat of total annihilation is an outrage to the conscience and sanity of all. . . . The peoples of the world must resist." He was joined by James Gichiuru, president of the Kenya African National Union, who announced that he and his party associated themselves "completely with your Committee of 100. . . . We look forward to the day when the great nations turn their attention from this destructive armaments race and face realities by diverting money spent on armaments to aid the under-developed countries of the world."[11] In February 1962, at the fourth annual conference of the Pan-African Freedom Movements of East and Central Africa (PAFMECA), in Addis Ababa, strong pressures developed to rally around a program of violent revolution, but Kaunda—elected PAFMECA's president—strongly opposed them. "Africa must not add to the violence of the West which already threatens the very existence of mankind," he insisted. "We must find another way or we perish." Kaunda and other African leaders favoring nonviolence ultimately secured a conference resolution approving the use of "many methods" in the struggle for liberation.[12]

These debates reflected the maturing of specific pacifist projects. By the time of the Addis Ababa conference, Rustin, Sutherland, and Scott were working closely with Kaunda. The African leader favored reviving the plan for establishing a training center in nonviolent resistance. Furthermore, in the context of colonialist opposition to granting universal suffrage in British-ruled Northern Rhodesia, he decided to back their idea of holding an international freedom march in the region to demonstrate solidarity with the struggle of the indigenous peoples for self-government. Since 1960, led by the WRI, overseas peace activists had been developing a World Peace Brigade (WPB), largely around the issue of direct action against nuclear war. Formally launched on January 1, 1962, under the leadership of Scott, Muste, and Jayaprakash Narayan (of India), the WPB cooperated closely with Kaunda and his political allies on organizing the freedom march. But the march never took place, for authorities in London, apparently embarrassed by the plans, acted to convince the white settler government in Northern Rhodesia to scrap the discriminatory election rules. In these new circumstances, Kaunda won the national elections, and his country, renamed Zambia, secured its national independence.[13]

The results of these dramatic events did not meet the high expectations of overseas peace groups. Kaunda and Julius Nyerere, the sympathetic president of neighboring Tanganyika, did act in March 1962 to set up a nonviolence training center, employing Sutherland and other pacifists, at Dar es Salaam. But the center never had adequate support or a clear focus and closed its doors a year later. Subsequently, although Kaunda offered the American Friends Service Committee the opportunity to set up a nonviolence center in Zambia, it never materialized. Meanwhile, as Kaunda assumed the responsibilities of a head of state and as the tempo of violent revolution increased in southern Africa, he gradually discarded his pacifist views. Once more, antinuclear activists found themselves with powerful friends and a reservoir of public sympathy, but without a solid, broadly based movement.[14]

Although nuclear disarmament activism in Africa never achieved the organizational success it had in Western Europe, it did make some headway. In December 1962, a small group of botany professors at Fourah Bay College established Sierra Leone CND. The new group announced its intention to cooperate with allied organizations in Africa and around the world in the fight against the production and testing of nuclear weapons.[15] Nuclear disarmament efforts also emerged in South Africa. In June 1959, determined to end nuclear weapons tests, activists established a Mothers' Anti-Atomic Bomb Organization in Pretoria, led by the writers Susan Kruger and Sanet te Groen. At the beginning of 1962, students at Witwatersrand University began their own campaign against the Bomb—showing films, sponsoring talks, and calling for nuclear disarmament activities at other universities. Pacifists from South Africa's WRI and FOR branches also assailed nuclear weapons, though their outspoken opposition to apartheid limited their effectiveness. In 1963, the South African government arrested the chair of the FOR, the Reverend Arthur Blaxall, on charges of violating the Suppression of Communism Act.[16]

Furthermore, a modest degree of disarmament activism persisted in Ghana. Responding to the Soviet government's resumption of nuclear testing, the National Union of Ghana Students protested the action, just as it did the later U.S. plan for resumption of atmospheric tests. In June 1962, with the financial assistance of Nkrumah's government, an assembly on disarmament convened in Accra around the theme, "The World Without the Bomb." Among the hundred participants from Western, Communist, and nonaligned countries were delegates from fourteen African nations. At the close of the event, the conference established a small secretariat in Ghana, the Accra Assembly, under the direction of Frank Boaten.[17] Henceforth, the Accra Assembly protested to de Gaulle against further French nuclear tests, sponsored a "Peace Week" in Ghana (with films, radio programs, and a broadcast by Nkrumah), and prepared proposals for the denuclearization of Africa. It also sent delegates (usually Boaten) to represent Africa at international meetings of disarmament leaders. Boaten warned, though, that "the question of independence and racial discrimination is still the paramount problem for the peoples and governments of Africa."[18]

Although polling organizations stayed clear of Africa, secret U.S. government studies in the early 1960s found strong public opposition to nuclear weapons. In January 1961, one report observed that Africans "deplore nuclear testing in the Sahara and hope to avoid . . . other 'Cold War' impingements upon African soil. They desire an East-West accommodation which would reduce the danger of a hot war and perhaps divert development funds in their direction." The following year, another study noted that Africans showed "widespread and often vehement opposition to nuclear testing—one of the few essentially non-African events on which there was near unanimity. They feared nuclear fallout and felt that testing perpetuated world tensions and heightened the risk of war." Naturally, "Africans were greatly annoyed and disappointed by the Soviet resumption of testing," felt that even underground U.S. testing was "reprehensible," and—in areas outside French control—reacted to the French nuclear tests with "a storm of protest." In addition, they strongly opposed the use of nuclear weapons and demanded nuclear disarmament. The report concluded that most Africans "favored an end to nuclear testing, a ban on the use of nuclear weapons in war, and disarmament among the Great Powers." They "tended to view the arms build-up, particularly in nuclear weapons, as a Cold War maneuver on the part of powerful nations who scorned the legitimate concerns of other peoples."[19]

The Near and Middle East

Nuclear weapons also met substantial resistance in the Near and Middle East. As France made plans for its nuclear tests in the Sahara, the *Cyprus Times* noted that, in this context, the soothing reassurances of the French premier were "like dropping poison in someone's food and telling him that he won't be able to taste it." When the Soviet Union resumed nuclear testing in the fall of 1961, the Cairo press ran stories headlined: "Entire World Opposes Nuclear Explosions," "UAR Opposes Nuclear Tests," and "Explosion of Terrible Russian Nuclear Bomb Arouses World Denunciation." Assailing the Soviet Union's explosion of "its terrible 50-megaton bomb," Cairo Radio warned that "if no effective positive attempts are made to ease international tension . . . the world will be threatened with annihilation." When the USIA surveyed public reaction in the Middle East to Kennedy's March 1962 announcement that the U.S. government would resume atmospheric nuclear testing, it found "over-all opposition." Opinion polls in the region were few, but a secret U.S. government survey in early 1963 reported that 77 percent of respondents in Teheran favored the abolition of nuclear weapons; only 4 percent opposed the idea.[20]

Although nonaligned peace activism remained weak in this area of mass poverty and authoritarian governments, it did emerge on occasion. In early 1961, during one of Turkey's surges of democracy, the National Union of Turkish Students organized a panel discussion on the nuclear issue before a large audience in Istanbul. At the end of the meeting, the gathering passed a resolution calling for the abolition of nuclear weapons, which appeared thereafter on the first page of almost all national newspapers. In the following years, Turkish criticism of nuclear weapons grew, with left-wing magazines and the new Turkish Labor Party taking the lead. Under the formal sponsorship of the Algerian Peace Committee, a Conference for the Denuclearization of the Mediterranean met in Algiers during the summer of 1964. But this gathering appears to have been largely a venture of Algeria's new government and without much participation by nonaligned peace activists.[21]

Antinuclear activism also developed, gradually, in Israel. Although pacifist groups operated in that country, for some time they focused their efforts on improving Arab-Israeli relations and, to a lesser degree, on defending conscientious objection to military service.[22] In late 1960, however, the Israeli government publicly disclosed its development of a plutonium-producing reactor—for peaceful purposes only, the prime minister insisted—and this sparked considerable talk within Israel and abroad about the advent of the "atomic age," including nuclear weapons, in the Middle East. One of the more striking discussions of the issue occurred in Tel Aviv during January 1961, sponsored by the newspaper *Ma'ariv*. Nahum Goldmann, president of the World Zionist Organization, declared that he did not think "any country," including Israel, had "the moral right to produce an atomic bomb." He also denied that nuclear weapons would improve Israel's security situation. Although Yigal Yadin, the former chief of staff of the Israeli army, took a different tack, the rector of Hebrew University of Jerusalem (Ephraim Auerbach) and one of the nation's leading poets (Avraham Shlonsky) both cited moral and security reasons to argue against Israel's development of nuclear weapons. Later that year, the Soviet government's resumption of nuclear testing heightened antinuclear feelings. The nation's press sharply denounced the Soviet action, and some newspapers demanded an end to all nuclear testing.[23] That October, small groups of protesters began demonstrating before the Soviet and U.S. embassies.[24]

These developments, coupled with the suspicious resignation of six out of seven members of Israel's Atomic Energy Commission, led in late 1961 to the formation of the Committee for Nuclear Disarmament of the Arab-Israeli Region. Formed by prominent scholars and scientists, many of them well informed on Israel's political and security problems, the Committee argued that the injection of nuclear weapons into the Middle East would be a disaster. In April, the Committee issued a statement, "On Nuclear Weapons in the Middle East," signed by the eminent Israeli pacifist Martin Buber and sixteen faculty members from Hebrew University and the Haifa Institute of Technology. Declaring that "the development of nuclear weapons in this part of the world" would "constitute a danger to Israel and to the peace of the Middle East," the Committee called on the Israeli public "to act while there is still time against this terrible eventuality" by joining in three demands. These were to "refrain from military nuclear production, if possible by mutual agreement," to request the United Nations "to supervise the region in order to prevent military nuclear production," and to see to it that "the countries of the Middle East avoid obtaining nuclear arms from other countries."[25]

Although the Committee for Nuclear Disarmament never developed into a mass movement, it did wage a low-key campaign. It held small protest meetings, issued pamphlets, published books, and produced additional antinuclear statements which it published in Israel's Hebrew and English language press. In addition to academics from Hebrew University and the Haifa Institute of Technology, the Committee drew into its ranks students, doctors, lawyers, and other elements of the concerned middle class—perhaps sixty people at any one time.[26] Much of its publicity and support came from the journal *New Outlook*, founded in July 1957 by the Jewish-Arab Association for Peace and Equality. Although *New Outlook* initially focused on "a peaceful and constructive solution to the problem of Israel-Arab relations," in the early 1960s it gave increasing attention to nuclear dangers. Members of the Committee for Nuclear Disarmament and other antinuclear intellectuals published sophisticated critiques of nuclear weapons in its monthly issues. Calling attention to the U.N. secretary general's letter to non-nuclear countries about their readiness to refrain from producing, acquiring, and storing nuclear weapons, Simha Flapan, *New Outlook*'s editor, argued that "the people of Israel must answer with an unqualified and unequivocal 'yes.'" Otherwise, the Middle East would be dragged "into the whirlpool of a nuclear armaments race."[27]

Other Israelis also participated in antinuclear efforts. In mid-1962, with both the United States and the Soviet Union engaged in atmospheric nuclear testing, small protest demonstrations again erupted outside both the Soviet and U.S. embassies. From Jerusalem, Martin Buber announced that whoever first stopped nuclear tests would "not only be more rightful, but more mightful."[28] In 1963, Ichud, Buber's small pacifist group, sponsored ads warning the people of the Middle East that a new war meant "death and destruction not only of the soldiers at the front, but also of you and your children . . . on both sides of the borders." Largely echoing the demands of the Committee for Nuclear Disarmament, with which it enjoyed good relations, it urged the people of Israel to call for U.N. supervision "of all atomic and rocket plants in the Arab States and in Israel" and an embargo by the great powers on arms shipments to the region. The leaders of Ichud also arranged for Bertrand Russell to write to the heads of state in the Middle East, appealing to them to accept international control of their nuclear facilities. In April 1964, Israelis conducted their first Easter peace march, walking to the Jordanian border with disarmament banners in Hebrew, Arabic, and English. Turned back by the authorities, they held a peace vigil on Mount Zion.[29]

Despite the limited size of Israel's antinuclear movement, it had a significant impact on the nation's politics. With the appearance of the Committee for Nuclear Disarmament, some of the leading figures of the major parties, both within the governing coalition and within the opposition, expressed their support for its approach. One coalition party, the left-wing Mapam (United Workers Party), immediately adopted the Committee's program for a nuclear-free Middle East as its official policy. During a Knesset debate, Mapam's leader called for an Israeli government initiative to prevent the spread of nuclear weapons to the region. Within the Labor Party, the most powerful component of the governing coalition, opinions were more divided, with the dominant figures favoring development of the Bomb to offset Arab military superiority in a crisis situation. But a group of influential Labor Party leaders, including Golda Meir and Yigal Allon, thought that arming Israel with nuclear weapons would increase the probability of an Arab first strike. This consideration, among others, led Allon to support the Committee for Nuclear Disarmament. By 1967, the Allon group had secured control of the Labor Party.[30]

Asia

Antinuclear attitudes also pervaded the nonindustrialized countries of Asia. In 1960, the Philippine Federation of Christian Churches, a Protestant organization, appealed to its nation's political leadership to oppose nuclear testing, which it argued was "diametrically opposed to Jesus' teaching of love, friendship, and reconciliation." A Committee of 100 flared up briefly in Pakistan, and leading Polynesians vehemently condemned French plans to begin nuclear testing on Moruroa Atoll.[31] Popular dismay, moreover, far outran these few resistance efforts. Polled in March 1959, 71 percent of Filipino respondents told interviewers that they thought atomic energy held more fear than hope for humanity. When the Soviet Union resumed nuclear testing in 1961, it provoked sharp press criticism in the Philippines, Malaya, and Thailand. And, although the Filipino and Thai press generally supported the U.S. government's later decision to resume nuclear testing, that decision—as the USIA noted—generated "overall opposition throughout most of South Asia."[32] Most South Asians, reported the U.S. agency, strongly desired disarmament and held the United States and the Soviet Union "almost equally responsible for the failure to achieve any accord." According to pollsters, in early 1963 support for the worldwide abolition of nuclear weapons stood at 76 percent in Bangkok (with 15 percent opposed), 79 percent in Saigon (with 2 percent opposed), and 84 percent in Singapore (with 7 percent opposed).[33]

For a time, India continued its role as a bastion of resistance to the Bomb. In the immediate aftermath of Soviet resumption of H-Bomb tests, 69 percent of New Delhi residents surveyed declared their opposition to U.S. test resumption. The following spring, when a member of the Lok Sabha, India's parliament, suggested sailing a protest vessel into the Pacific testing zone, 250 people immediately volunteered for the mission. Although the plan never reached fruition, it was supported by a number of prominent Indians.[34] Meanwhile, pacifist groups like the FOR and the WILPF condemned nuclear testing and called for the banning of nuclear weapons.[35] In fact, however, these groups remained small, while the larger Gandhian movement, with deeper roots in Indian life, devoted itself to quelling India's domestic violence rather than to addressing international issues. Nor did Indian scientists go as far as their overseas counterparts in criticizing nuclear weapons development. Even so, by late 1961, Gandhian leaders like Jayaprakash Narayan and Siddharaj Dhadda were discussing with Western peace leaders the prospect of developing a nuclear disarmament campaign along the lines of the mass movements in Europe and the United States.[36]

Ultimately, Gandhian efforts went into organizing an Anti-Nuclear Arms Convention, held in New Delhi during June 1962. Horrified by the great power resumption of nuclear testing, the Gandhi Peace Foundation, established in 1959 by India's foremost leaders, invited "some of the leading scientists and thinkers in the world" to lay plans "for complete disarmament and immediate cessation of all nuclear tests." Nearly a hundred people attended the event, among them prominent overseas peace activists (e.g. Muste, Danilo Dolci, and Niemöller), leading Gandhians, and the country's top political leadership (the prime minister, the president, the vice president, and leaders of the major parties). Opening the meeting, Rajendra Prasad, the former president of India, proposed that his country take the lead in disarmament by announcing that it was disarming unilaterally. This might reverse the whole trend of world affairs, he argued, starting a chain reaction against the drift toward nuclear war. Some delegates, mostly government officials, politely disagreed with Prasad's proposal, but most supported the idea. Furthermore, the convention adopted a package of measures to avert "a nuclear war and an immeasurable catastrophe." Although the convention was virtually ignored in the Western press, every Indian newspaper gave it front-page coverage.[37]

The Anti-Nuclear Arms Convention, its delegates resolved, was "only a beginning," for they dedicated themselves anew to "work for peace in the spirit of truth and nonviolence." And, indeed, the convention had agreed on an ambitious program for the future. It included making common cause with movements throughout the world to halt the nuclear arms race, assisting the United Nations to play a more active role in fostering disarmament, dispatching a deputation to appeal to the heads of government of the nuclear powers, increasing worldwide peace education programs, encouraging the nonviolent direct action campaigns of the *Everyman* and of the World Peace Brigade, urging India and other nations to give "serious study and consideration" to Prasad's call for unilateral disarmament, and linking efforts for disarmament with attempts to build a more just and cooperative world order. Some of these proposals were soon implemented. An Indian delegation—including R. R. Diwaker (chair of the Gandhi Peace Foundation) and Chakravarti Rajagopalachari (a distinguished veteran of the Indian independence struggle)—met that fall with President Kennedy, Prime Minister Macmillan, and Soviet and French government leaders on issues of nuclear testing and disarmament.[38]

For the most part, however, the Gandhian foray into the antinuclear crusade remained stillborn, for armed border clashes between India and China, beginning that October, sent political shockwaves through India. Viewing the Chinese as the aggressors, much of the Indian population was swept up in a surge of patriotism. Nehru reflected glumly on his past disdain for military force, remarking: "We were living in an artificial world of our own creation." Nor were the Gandhians immune to this trend. Although not directly endorsing military action, the Sarva Seva Sangh, the People's Service Organization which represented the Gandhian movement, proclaimed that the war had "been forced upon India" and that the nation's defense effort should be supported. To avoid causing offense, the Shanti Sena, the Gandhian Peace Army, softened its pledge denouncing war as a crime. Rajendra Prasad, who had recently argued for India's unilateral disarmament, declared that India must "meet bullets with bullets." Naturally, these developments undermined resistance to nuclear weapons. Visiting India in December 1962, an American pacifist reported that hc "met no one who felt that if China developed a nuclear weapon, India could afford to be without one."[39]

Despite this major setback, antinuclear agitation continued in India, albeit at a slower pace. Launched in December 1961 by J. J. Singh and a host of Gandhians, a campaign to gather a million Indian signatures on a petition demanding an end to nuclear testing achieved success by the fall of 1963.[40] Meanwhile, to ease tensions between India and China, the World Peace Brigade, at the invitation of the Shanti Sena, began a Delhi-Peking Friendship March. Starting at the Gandhi Memorial on March 1, 1963, thirteen participants—from India, other parts of Asia, Africa, Latin America, and Europe—began the four-thousand-mile journey on foot. They announced that "no good can come to any one from armaments, much less from war; no problems can be solved by such means, especially in this atomic age." Instead, through their example, they hoped to help "establish friendly relations between the people of India and China."[41] In 1965, the FOR joined with clergy, students, teachers, social workers, and business leaders in calling for support of the Indian government's nonnuclear policy. It petitioned against India's acquisition of nuclear weapons and urged other nations to limit the use of atomic energy to peaceful purposes.[42]

By the mid-1960s, although principled opponents of nuclear weapons had lost ground in Indian society and politics—at least relative to their hegemonic position until early 1962—they had not been vanquished, either. In December 1962, the militant nationalist Jana Sangh Party went on record favoring India's development of nuclear weapons, and the idea gained increasing respectability in other parties as well, particularly after the first Chinese nuclear tests, in 1964. But this remained a minority current, with the dominant forces in the ruling Congress Party, the pro-Western Swatantra Party, and the Communist Party, as well as among Socialists and Gandhians, opposed to launching an Indian nuclear weapons program. The idea of retaining an Indian nuclear option, in the event that the great powers failed to curb their own nuclear arms race, was somewhat more popular. India, many felt, should not be asked to forgo nuclear weapons indefinitely while its neighbors went ahead strengthening their nuclear weapons capabilities. Against this backdrop, worldwide nuclear disarmament retained substantial popularity, at both the political and the popular level. Polled in early 1963 as to the abolition of nuclear weapons, 72 percent of New Delhi residents favored the idea and only 3 percent opposed it.[43]

Latin America

Of all Third World regions, Latin America showed least concern about the nuclear arms race. Bertrand Russell speculated that "Latin Americans, perhaps, have enjoyed the illusion that the Cold War could not so directly affect them because of their distance from the United States and the Soviet Union." The USIA tended to agree. "On balance," it reported secretly in early 1961, "Latin Americans are more concerned with economic, cultural and ideological leadership issues than with those of a military and scientific nature." In general, they did not feel "immediately involved in the East-West struggle."[44] Consequently, Latin America remained almost entirely devoid of the organizationally based antinuclear activity that characterized Western Europe, North America, and some portions of Africa, the Middle East, and Asia. In Peru, a group of university students and, in Brazil, a pacifist young men's group proclaimed their opposition to nuclear weapons. In Argentina, the governing council of the University of Buenos Aires called on all powers to halt nuclear testing. Campaigning for the presidency of Chile in 1964, the Socialist Salvador Allende assailed the nuclear arms race in an attempt "to save humanity from destruction." But none of these ventures provided a base for substantial organizational activity.[45]

Even so, there existed widespread distaste for nuclear weapons throughout Latin America. When the Soviet Union resumed nuclear testing, there was (with the exception of the Communist press) universal condemnation in the mass media. In Argentina, *La Prensa* denounced Khrushchev's "strategy of terror," and *El Mundo* implored the Soviet government to call off its planned fifty-megaton bomb test. Brazil's *O Jornal* condemned the Soviet test series as "a plan of psychological terrorism." According to the USIA, as the Soviet tests continued, "the fear of the possible effects of fallout began to assume nearly hysterical proportions." And with this growth of fear, "criticism was even directed at a hypothetical US resumption of atmospheric testing. There were frequent cries of 'a plague on both your houses.'"[46] Admittedly, by the time the U.S. government announced its own resumption of atmospheric testing, most of the Latin American press had come around to support it, contending that Washington had been forced into this decision by Soviet policy. But there remained considerable public opposition to nuclear testing and to the Bomb. Asked, in early 1963, what they thought of abolishing nuclear weapons worldwide, 90 percent of the residents of Caracas, 87 percent of the residents of Mexico City, 84 percent of the residents of Buenos Aires, and 65 percent of the residents of Rio de Janeiro expressed approval.[47] If Latin Americans did not take to the streets to demand nuclear disarmament, they nevertheless liked the idea.

The Soviet Union

In the Soviet Union, scientists continued to play a key role in antinuclear efforts. Their public critique of the Bomb, of course, sometimes coincided with

government policy. Welcoming overseas scientists to the first Pugwash conference in Moscow, in November 1960, Topchiev cited Khrushchev's policy of
"peaceful coexistence" as justification for avoiding the "military conflicts which
in our age are fraught with dreadful consequences." After the Soviet Union resumed nuclear testing, Topchiev dutifully defended the action before a Pugwash gathering in London.[48] Nevertheless, Western scientists believed that
many of their Soviet counterparts at the Pugwash conferences—notably Lev
Artsimovich, Peter Kapitza, Vladimir Kirillin, Igor Tamm, and Topchiev—quite
sincerely favored disarmament. Artsimovich, recalled Bernard Feld, "stood out
for the depth of his concerns with . . . nuclear arms control." Franklin Long
characterized him as a physicist with a "great commitment" to peace and to disarmament. Rotblat recalled that, at Pugwash conferences, Artsimovich publicly
opposed the party line, going so far as to demand that Vladimir Pavlichenko,
the KGB agent on the scene, keep quiet. Even Topchiev, who publicly pressed
for Pugwash participation in a meeting of the World Peace Council, privately
told Rotblat that he was glad the British scientist squelched the idea.[49]

British officials were also impressed by the commitment and sincerity of
Soviet Pugwash participants. In a secret report he filed shortly after the September 1961 Pugwash conference, Solly Zuckerman, the science adviser to the
British Defense Ministry, commented that Soviet scientists "may have been
under direction, but they were not actors. They appeared to be immensely sincere and serious, and genuine in their fears that the West was ready and anxious
to launch a war against the Soviet Union." By September 1963, reported B. T.
Price, another Defense Ministry official, the Russian attitude was "very largely
one of free-and-easy social interchange. Tension seemed gone out of their relationship with the West." Indeed, "they spoke on occasions about internal disagreements within their delegation" and "about the irritation they felt with
Pavlichenko." They even became playful. "What is the difference between capitalism and communism?" one asked. "Under capitalism," he explained, "man
exploits man; under communism it is vice versa."[50]

Even before this relative liberalization, Soviet scientists took some principled actions. Yuri Smirnov, who worked on the Soviet Union's fifty-megaton
Bomb test, resigned from the nuclear project shortly thereafter, convinced that
nuclear weapons "in the hands of conflicting parties were not able to solve any
problems . . . and could only be fatal." In the Supreme Soviet debate of January
1960, Kurchatov was the only speaker to back up Khrushchev's strong advocacy of a nuclear test ban. Late that year, as Khrushchev's star and hopes for a
test ban waned, Topchiev published an article in a Soviet journal that advocated ceasing nuclear tests as a "practical step toward reducing the danger of
war." At a time when the Soviet government line was to equate verification

measures with Western espionage, Topchiev argued that verification of a test ban agreement was quite feasible. Artsimovich, who began attending Pugwash conferences in 1962, became an important proponent of verification, coming up with the idea of the so-called "black box" to check fulfillment of test ban obligations. As another Soviet Pugwash participant, Sergei Kapitza, recalled years later, political realities blocked Soviet scientists from assuming the public role played by many of their Western counterparts; but, within channels, they did work for arms control and disarmament.[51]

Furthermore, some Soviet scientists grew increasingly outspoken, including his father, Peter Kapitza. In 1959, the elder Kapitza joined Tamm and Artsimovich in a bitter attack, published in *Pravda*, on journalistic coverage of science in the Soviet Union. Writing in the *Ekonomicheskaya Gazeta* in 1962, Kapitza assailed the tendency to judge the truth of scientific discovery by applying Marxian dialectics.[52] Although much of Kapitza's protest activity reflected his desire to protect science from political dogma, he also showed a strong interest in promoting nuclear disarmament. Long a critic of the Bomb, he began his association with the Pugwash conferences in 1960. He submitted a paper to the 1961 conference, but was prevented by Soviet authorities from attending. Moreover, as his son has noted, Kapitza believed that arms control and disarmament were essential. In 1966, when Kapitza traveled to Britain to deliver a speech on Lord Rutherford, head of the Cavendish laboratory at Cambridge during the years he worked there, he made a striking allusion whose meaning was hard to miss. In 1938, when Rutherford died, Kapitza noted, "there disappeared forever the happy days of free scientific work which gave us such delight in our youth. Science has lost her freedom. . . . She has become enslaved and part of her is veiled in secrecy."[53]

The most daring of the scientists, though, remained Andrei Sakharov. Summoned to Moscow in July 1961 for a meeting with Soviet government leaders and top atomic scientists, Sakharov learned to his horror that Khrushchev planned to resume nuclear tests in the fall. Although no provision had been made for any discussion of Khrushchev's decision, Sakharov publicly volunteered his opinion that the Soviet Union had little to gain from further testing. Then he passed a brief note to Khrushchev, opposing the new tests and arguing that they would "seriously jeopardize the test ban negotiations, the cause of disarmament, and world peace." Khrushchev flew into a rage and, for half an hour or more, denounced Sakharov before the gathering. While Khrushchev spoke, recalled Sakharov, "the room was still. Everyone sat frozen, some averting their gaze, others maintaining set expressions. . . . No one looked in my direction." After the meeting, only one person came over to Sakharov to express support for his position.[54]

Despite this unpromising beginning, Sakharov continued his efforts to halt Soviet nuclear tests. In mid-August of 1961, when he and nuclear research director Yuli Khariton met again with Khrushchev, the Soviet leader asked threateningly: "Does Sakharov realize that he was wrong?" The physicist stood firm, however, and retorted that his views had not changed. Later that month, apparently in response to Sakharov's arguments, Khariton went to see Leonid Brezhnev in an unsuccessful effort to have the tests halted. Although Khariton backed away from the issue after the tests resumed that September, Sakharov persisted, especially as plans went forward for another round of tests in the fall of 1962. Meeting on the matter with Yefim Slavsky, who directed the Soviet nuclear weapons program, Sakharov secured an agreement from him to limit the new tests to one type of device. Slavsky, however, went back on this agreement, and Sakharov phoned him in a panic. "If you don't call off the test," he declared, "a lot of people are going to die for no reason." Slavsky retorted that the decision was final, whereupon Sakharov replied: "If you won't call it off, I can't work with you any more." Enraged, Slavsky shouted back: "You can go to hell if you want," and then hung up.[55]

Sakharov was determined, however, and—thanks to his crucial role in the Soviet nuclear program—still retained some credibility with Soviet officials and the ability to contact them directly. Consequently, he placed a phone call to Khrushchev and, eventually, drew the Soviet leader to the telephone. Summarizing his case, Sakharov declared: "I believe the test is pointless, and it will kill people for no reason. . . . I'm asking you to postpone tomorrow's test and to appoint a commission from the Central Committee to look into our dispute." Not feeling well, Khrushchev fobbed off Sakharov on Frol Kozlov, an influential member of the Politburo. Kozlov spoke with Sakharov the next morning and proved immovable. "The more often we conducted powerful tests," Sakharov recalled him as saying, "the sooner the imperialists would agree to a ban and the fewer overall casualties there would be." Years later, Sakharov called it "the ultimate defeat for me. A terrible crime was about to be committed, and I could do nothing to prevent it. I was overcome by my impotence, unbearable bitterness, shame, and humiliation. I put my face down on my desk and wept." This incident was "probably the most terrible lesson of my life: you can't sit on two chairs at once. I decided that I would devote myself to ending biologically harmful tests."[56]

Sakharov did not resign his position in the nuclear weapons program, however, for he had another card to play along these lines. In the summer of 1962, Viktor Adamsky, a physicist working with Sakharov who was sympathetic to his views on nuclear testing, reminded him of a proposal in 1959, brought forward by journalists and politicians, including Eisenhower, for a treaty banning atmospheric nuclear tests. This might cut through the great power impasse at Geneva on the issue of verification. Before his bitter quarrel with Slavsky, Sakharov broached the idea to that Soviet official, and he, in turn, promised to bring it to top Soviet leaders. Eventually, Slavsky did so, reportedly with some success. Naturally, Sakharov was delighted. Years later, he claimed some credit for the partial test ban treaty signed in Moscow in July 1963.[57]

In turn, the Western antinuclear movement can clearly claim some of the credit for the antinuclear activism of Soviet scientists. Explaining his decision to challenge Soviet nuclear policy, Sakharov pointed to the example of Einstein, Russell, Szilard, Pauling, Schweitzer, and other leading nuclear critics. Ironically, he even pointed to the speech Russell sent to the stormy WPC disarmament conference of July 1962. Similarly, a participant in Sakharov's scientific circle recalled that the appearance of Szilard's *Voice of the Dolphins*, with its mock trial of atomic scientists as war criminals, proved troubling to the Soviet physicist and to other concerned Soviet scientists.[58] Furthermore, the Pugwash conferences made a deep impression on Soviet participants. "We scientists have become like gypsies," Artsimovich told a journalist at the Dubrovnik meeting in the fall of 1963. "We wander from conference to conference, trying to find roads to peace, acting as voluntary advisers to our political leaders. . . . It is possible that, without trying to, we have become the most peaceful people in the world."[59]

Indeed, during the Khrushchev era, the Soviet intelligentsia, encouraged by their Western counterparts, became an important source of pressure for peace and political liberalization. In the early 1960s, particularly, antiwar books, plays, and films by Western authors and artists engendered a growing pacifist mood among Soviet writers and filmmakers. Nuclear testing, fallout, and the arms race put in a grim appearance in works like "The Icicle" (1961), one of the short stories of Andrei Sinyavsky, a Soviet author later sentenced to hard labor for slandering and subverting the Soviet state. A major controversy over what the Soviet *Literary Gazette* called the "de-heroicizing" of war broke out in 1963, with *Pravda*'s Yuri Zhukov complaining that "quite a few works" had recently portrayed war in "a depressing manner. . . . War appears in these writings as something quite unsavory, as one continuous human slaughter." Writing in *Komsomolskaya Pravda* in March 1963, a war veteran and hero of the Soviet Union assailed the film *At Your Threshold*, in which a Soviet soldier stated: "War is not a proper condition of man, it's unnatural." According to the reviewer, the producer and scriptwriter had been "imitating ugly Western models," for "war is shown to be hopeless and utterly gloomy."[60]

Despite the strictures of hard-liners, these critical appraisals of modern war did not subside. Almost a year later, on February 7, 1964, Soviet military and defense officials held a special meeting with writers and artists on the proper treatment of the military in literature and the arts. Army general A. A. Yepishev complained to the gathering about "the note of pacifism that was beginning to resound in certain books, films and paintings." There had been "excessive attention to . . . descriptions of suffering and fear, horror and confusion" and too little discussion of "the international duty of the Soviet armed forces." Marshal Rodion Malinovsky, Soviet minister of defense, called attention "to the fact that in recent times mistaken tendencies in representing the last war have appeared. Motifs of pacifism and the abstract rejection of war have made themselves felt in certain works of literature and painting and in movies." The following year, they even cropped up in the work of Major General N. Talensky, a retired Soviet military theorist who had conferred with Western peace activists at the Pugwash conferences and elsewhere. Writing in May 1965, Talensky argued that "there is no more dangerous illusion than the idea that thermonuclear war can still serve as an instrument of politics, that it is possible to achieve political aims by using nuclear weapons and still survive."[61]

With government repression blocking Soviet citizens from forming nonaligned disarmament organizations, some overseas peace groups undertook their own operations in the Soviet Union. Quaker delegations from Britain and the United States traveled to that nation, where they met with small groups of ordinary citizens, established volunteer work camps, and participated in seminars in an effort to foster ideas of peace and reconciliation. Although wary of "being used," young Friends also attended some Communist-sponsored youth festivals, at which they sought to counter pro-Soviet propaganda through the expression of a principled pacifist position.[62] Sometimes overseas activists adopted a more confrontational approach. In August 1962, when three Zengakuren leaders raised their banner in Red Square, condemning the Soviet resumption of nuclear testing, they also distributed hundreds of antinuclear leaflets—both operations interrupted by the Moscow police. In addition, they held a tense meeting with members of the Soviet Student Council and, in Leningrad, scandalized a convention of the pro-Soviet International Union of Students by speaking out against Soviet nuclear testing.[63]

That July, just a few weeks before, overseas peace activists created an even greater sensation. Only a hundred yards from Lenin's tomb, twenty-five nonaligned activists from six countries unfurled a banner reading: "We condemn Anglo-American Tests. We demand no further Soviet tests. Let all people act against all tests." Although the banner stayed up for less than a minute before plainclothes police seized it, British Committee of 100 members had greater success that week in distributing two Russian-language leaflets, "Mankind Against War" and "Against All Bombs," on the streets of Moscow. The more incendiary of the leaflets asked: "What has happened to your Revolution that your rulers should threaten the workers of other lands with these weapons? . . . We extend our hands in solidarity with the working people of Russia, over the heads of our rulers and yours. We have already taken up this struggle. It is yours, too." A news story in the *Manchester Guardian* called it "the most direct challenge to official Soviet policies and ideas to have been presented to the Soviet man in the street since freedom of speech died under Stalin."[64]

Western antinuclear activists also organized a nonviolent invasion of the Soviet Union from the seas. In the fall of 1961, to protest the resumption of Soviet nuclear testing and to present antitesting petitions from thousands of Japanese and Americans, Earle and Barbara Reynolds set out from Hiroshima for a journey to Vladivostok on board their yacht, the *Hiroshima Phoenix*. Boarded by the Soviet military ten miles off the coast of Siberia, the ship was forbidden to land; consequently, the crew members reluctantly returned to Hiroshima.[65] In October 1962, the *Everyman III*, also captained by Earle Reynolds, arrived at Leningrad on a protest mission against Soviet nuclear testing. Crew members planned to "go down the canals and rivers of the Soviet Union to Moscow itself, taking every opportunity to speak to the Soviet people about the need for unilateral disarmament." According to participants, the venture would "encourage the Soviet people to speak and act against the military policies of their government and to develop unilateralist groups in the USSR." When Soviet authorities, unenthusiastic about this prospect, began preparations to tow the vessel away, crew members grabbed leaflets and tried to leave the craft. Shoved back by Soviet soldiers lining the dockside, some crew members opened the seacocks to sink *Everyman III* in the harbor. Others leaped into the near-freezing water in an attempt to swim ashore. Eventually, the vessel was towed away, with the pacifists kept on board in captivity.[66]

The impact of these and other externally organized peace activities on Soviet citizens is difficult to assess. Sometimes, as exemplified by the ill-fated voyage of *Everyman III*, overseas activists had very little contact with the people whose resistance they sought to incite. On other occasions, they met with greater success. The short-lived antinuclear demonstration near Lenin's tomb inspired heated discussions among hundreds of local people about the demonstration and about Soviet foreign policy. The Committee of 100 claimed that it distributed its antinuclear leaflets to "many thousands of Muscovites." Even the mission of the *Everyman III* had some impact. Soviet guards joined their pacifist captives in singing songs and the Soviet pilot navigating their ship out of the harbor seemed embarrassed at his role. Indeed, despite the dangers, a surprising number of Soviet citizens expressed their sympathy. In July 1962, a village schoolteacher entered the Moskva Hotel, where nonaligned activists were staying, and presented them with his own typed peace proposals. He criticized Lenin for advocating violence, suggested a neo-Tolstoyan pacifism, and argued for a veto-free United Nations. Hotel authorities tried to chase him out, but he stood his ground and embraced Western observers.[67]

The most successful attempt to inject the nonaligned movement into Soviet life was the San Francisco to Moscow Walk for Peace. On September 15, 1961, having trekked more than 5,000 miles over a ten-month period, thirty-one peace marchers, sponsored by the Committee for Nonviolent Action, crossed the Polish border into the Soviet Union. A. J. Muste had persuaded Soviet authorities to permit this unprecedented peace and antinuclear venture, although with only eighteen days allowed to cover the 660 miles to Moscow. Making the most of their opportunity, the marchers moved at an exhausting pace—taking turns walking vast distances and sleeping in an accompanying bus, passing out leaflets to everyone within sight, and addressing frequent meetings, sometimes with from two hundred to a thousand Russians present. A marcher recalled: "Crowds turned up everywhere, men and women running across fields from threshing machines to watch us go by. In the towns the situation became uncontrollable, literally thousands of people jamming the streets of Kobrin and Bereza, hundreds in Ivatsevichy and Stelbsty and other villages that we'll never even know the names of." Everywhere they went, the marchers advocated unilateral nuclear disarmament and denounced the resumption of Soviet nuclear testing. Twice they held demonstrations directed specifically against Soviet military installations—once at a Soviet radar station, where they distributed leaflets to soldiers and to a crowd that gathered, and later in the form of a two-hour silent vigil in Red Square. When they arrived in Moscow, a leafleter recalled, "the sidewalks were crowded, salesgirls in uniforms and plasterers covered with dust came rushing out of buildings at the sight of a leaflet." By the time of their departure from the Soviet Union, the CNVA marchers had conducted the most thoroughgoing peace and disarmament campaign in that country's history. They had addressed large audiences, received extensive TV coverage, and distributed an estimated 100,000 leaflets.[68]

Overall, the response of the Soviet people was surprisingly friendly. At times, to be sure, individuals or groups became surly, but this probably reflected the presence on the scene of plainclothes police and local officials. Many a public defense of Soviet policy was clearly prepared in advance. Even so, participants pointed to "large and enthusiastic crowds" as evidence that their message had some support in Soviet life. A particularly revealing incident occurred at Moscow University. Faculty and members of the official Soviet Peace Committee tried to conclude the meeting after an hour, but the two hundred Soviet students on the scene pounded their desks and demanded that the gathering continue. When officials claimed that the room was needed for a lecture, students rose and shouted "Nonsense!" Meanwhile, ostensibly passing written questions to the marchers, students slipped them notes like: "My dear friends, do not believe . . . the words of this dirty official or his common demagogic phrases. Go your path, we are with you." Another read: "Thank you for your travel. . . . It is not for us to speak as simply as you. . . . The men's kind of thinking [here] are rather slowly changing." When the meeting finally ended, after two and a half hours, most of the crowd rose, applauded vigorously, and followed the marchers down the hall, still asking questions and talking heatedly.[69]

Although government restrictions on peace activism prevented it from playing a major role in influencing Soviet public opinion, other factors reinforced its message. Even without nuclear weapons, World War II had been a catastrophe for the Soviet Union. Furthermore, traveling exhibits and other media portrayed the terrible destruction of Hiroshima. The goal was usually to encourage hostility toward the U.S. government for dropping the Bomb, but an unintended consequence was to give viewers a chilling picture of nuclear war. Soviet citizens also gained a negative impression of the Bomb from the statements of their leaders and of visiting dignitaries, whose comments on the destructiveness of nuclear weapons frequently appeared in the Soviet press. Soviet civil defense policy, which began on a large scale in 1955, added further to popular fears of nuclear weapons. Although the official position was that, through civil defense, the nation would survive a nuclear war, the enormous mobilization behind the program—with instructions emanating from newspapers, magazines, radio, posters, films, and the schools—called attention at the same time to the dangers. Moreover, as in the United States, many people had little confidence that civil defense would work. A common joke in the Soviet Union during the early 1960s went:

Q: What should you do in case of a nuclear attack?
A: Get a shovel and a sheet, and walk slowly . . . to
   the nearest cemetery.
Q: Why slowly?
A: You mustn't start a panic.[70]

Although there seem to have been no polls of Soviet public opinion on questions of disarmament and peace, it does appear that these items had substantial popular support, and that this support, in turn, reinforced political tendencies in the same direction. Called together by the U.S. Arms Control and Disarmament Agency in 1963, a group of Western Sovietologists emphasized "the intensity of popular 'anti-war' sentiments in the Soviet Union." This "general 'peace' mood" established "a predisposition in favor of disarmament and arms control arrangements." Although they did not believe that Soviet leaders would "be induced by mass feelings to accept proposals which, in their own opinion, run counter to their national (or their own) interests," they did think that "popular sentiment" could "make itself felt" by reinforcing the position of leaders committed to similar positions. Thus, in the case of arms control and disarmament, where positive sentiment was "immeasurably stronger" than negative sentiment, public opinion would "support rather than weaken the advocacy of disarmament." Or, as another group of Sovietologists concluded a few years later, in his moves toward détente and disarmament, Khrushchev "could generally count on a popular response from the Soviet public."[71]

Other Communist Nations

Antinuclear activity also began to affect the public in other Communist nations. In East Germany, the tiny FOR group, which the regime refused to recognize, held street meetings in East Berlin protesting nuclear warfare. Rather than ban such gatherings, the regime had Communist Party activists turn up and attempt to direct them into pro-Soviet channels. Eventually, pacifists simply dissolved the meetings when the infiltrators arrived. In addition, many East Germans watched television broadcasts from West Germany, and this familiarized them to some degree with the antinuclear campaign there and elsewhere. Inspired by Bertrand Russell, one of them appealed to a friend on the party's Politburo, urging him to have the genocidal nature of nuclear weapons "officially discussed and accepted." On a visit to East Berlin, Homer Jack heard that students in the East German Christian Youth Movement opposed all nuclear weapons tests, but had "no possibility" of expressing their opposition openly.[72]

The most direct expression of antimilitary opinion in East Germany occurred after the introduction of conscription in 1962. Despite a possible penalty of imprisonment, at least three thousand young men refused induction that year. Troubled by the matter, the Protestant Church argued that conscription was unconstitutional and called for the establishment of an alternative service program for conscientious objectors. In 1964, the government relented somewhat and established construction units for such objectors—the only alternative service program in a Communist country. The high point of resistance came in 1965, when an official church conference declared that, in a world menaced by nuclear war, conscientious objection based on a Christian witness for peace should have priority over military service. This proved too much for the government to swallow. Responding to expressions of indignation from the regime, church officials retreated, claiming that they had not intended to judge the morality of military service or to question the policies of the East German government. Nevertheless, the development of the construction units attested to the remarkable degree of antiwar sentiment in East Germany. Furthermore, by bringing together substantial numbers of pacifists, these units provided a base for the further development of antimilitary opinion.[73]

The situation differed somewhat on the extremes of the world Communist movement. In Yugoslavia, where the quasi-official Yugoslav League for Peace, Independence, and Equality of Peoples took a nonaligned position, that group helped organize the Accra Assembly, sponsored a lecture in Zagreb by Canon Collins on CND, and expressed its support for the Anti-Nuclear Arms Convention of the Gandhi Peace Foundation. Insisting that "disarmament will bring immense benefit to all mankind," the Yugoslav Pugwash group held meetings at the university and at the Academy of Science, where it discussed the structure of the United Nations, "the dangers of nuclear tests," and assorted disarmament plans.[74] On the other hand, in the more forbidding climate of Maoist China, nonaligned critics of the Bomb remained relatively silent. Even the Pugwash conferences failed to mobilize a disarmament-oriented constituency. In a speech at the December 1960 Pugwash meeting, Chou Pei-Yuan—a physicist and veteran of these conferences—delivered a stinging, party-line address. Contrasting "the peace policy of the Soviet Union" with "the policy of arms expansion and war preparations of the U.S. government," Chou argued that the latter alone bore responsibility for "the danger of war." He also denounced the American scientists present, arguing that their views were "quite detrimental to the cause of world peace." Chinese scientists, he declared, "wholeheartedly support the foreign policy of peace of their government." For the next twenty-five years, Chinese scientists boycotted the Pugwash conferences.[75]

Sometimes, as in the case of the Soviet Union, overseas peace groups sought to export nonaligned peace activism to Communist nations. Having secured official approval, the San Francisco to Moscow peace marchers paraded across East Germany from August 7 to 14, 1961, carrying their banners, distributing fifteen thousand antinuclear leaflets, and talking with local people. The experience proved frustrating, however, for, as one marcher reported, "officially-sent supporters" accompanied the marchers, "constantly hammering home the 'correct' interpretation of everything" and shadowing "every meeting with the public." When the marchers defied the authorities by refusing to bypass Berlin, they were deported. Working with leaders of the West German Easter March movement, the British Committee of 100 laid plans for an international march through East Germany the following year, designed "to make it quite clear that we are against *all* nuclear weapons." But this venture apparently never got off the ground.[76]

In the following years, Western peace activists returned to East Germany. Without any authorization by the authorities, five British CND members crossed into East Berlin in May 1963 and began handing out leaflets calling for abolition of nuclear weapons, East and West. "Ordinary people accepted them with interest," one leafleter recalled, "and sometimes people came back and shook our hands to show their support." East Berlin police proved less enthusiastic, however, and after an hour the activists were arrested and deported to the West. Less flamboyant ventures faced fewer difficulties. In the spring of 1964, at the invitation of the Evangelical Academy in East Berlin, April Carter spoke before a small audience there on the Western Easter march movement. She found those present "not only very isolated from the West, but very anxious to know about the campaign and to identify with it, and to consider action within their own situation."[77]

In some other Communist nations, foreign peace activists could point to greater progress. Yugoslavia, of course, provided a very sympathetic environment. A small antinuclear delegation of Japanese *hibakusha*, as the accompanying American peace activist Barbara Reynolds recalled, was "well looked after" by the Yugoslav League for Peace, which arranged for them to address two gatherings. "Both meetings were well attended, the one in Belgrade especially so as a good-sized movie theater was completely full for the showing of our film and the presentation that followed." Even in Poland, overseas activists had some successes. Crossing that nation in 1961, the San Francisco to Moscow peace marchers distributed large numbers of antinuclear leaflets, some to Polish soldiers. The people they met seemed quite enthusiastic, talking excitedly about the possibility of unilateral disarmament, joining in the procession, presenting flowers to the marchers, and surrounding them in great crowds. In 1963, a group of activists from Britain's Youth CND, working on the reconstruction of Lublin University, organized a Hiroshima Day march through the town to a former concentration camp. Holding aloft a banner reading "Hiroshima" and adorned with the nuclear disarmament symbol, a group of forty young people from Britain, the United States, France, East Germany, and Poland began the march. It swelled to a hundred participants by the time of the concluding rally, addressed by a Youth CND activist. The event received widespread coverage in the press.[78]

The New Dimensions of the Disarmament Campaign

Although peace groups and antinuclear campaigns had never mobilized substantial support in Third World and Communist nations, the situation began to change in the late 1950s and early 1960s. As the nuclear arms race spread to the Third World, the peoples of Africa, Asia, and—to a lesser extent—Latin America became increasingly involved in resistance movements. At the Aldermaston march of April 1963, forty African and Asian nations had contingents, each marching under its country's banner.[79] Even in Communist states, where independent nuclear disarmament movements could not operate freely, a combination of nuclear crisis, courageous individuals, and rambunctious foreign movements raised the nuclear issue in an unprecedented fashion. Indeed, foreign peace groups not only proceeded to "tell it to the Russians"—as their critics had urged (albeit never done themselves)—but to substantial numbers of East Germans, Poles, Yugoslavs, and other people controlled by police state measures. Although antinuclear agitation in Communist nations remained minuscule by Western standards, it did break through the walls of silence erected by these one-party states.

The International Organization of the Nonaligned Movement, 1958–65

> The creation of an international organization, including pacifists and anti-nuclear movements, responds to an historic necessity.
>
> International Confederation for
> Disarmament and Peace, 1963

The emergence of nonaligned nuclear disarmament activities around the world led naturally to attempts at international organization. According to SANE, by the early 1960s, roughly a hundred nonaligned peace organizations operated in forty-four countries.[1] If their efforts could be coordinated or combined, critics of the Bomb would have a powerful voice in world affairs. On the other hand, despite their common demand for nuclear disarmament, nonaligned peace groups often had significant differences in approach. Some championed non-violent resistance, some a more traditional pacifism, some unilateralism (but not pacifism), and some multilateralism. In some cases, they mobilized different constituencies: students, women, the religious, or others. Furthermore, despite their broad humanitarian orientation, they had emerged as national movements and operated in different settings. At times, they even made appeals with a vaguely nationalist flavor, as when CND, calling for Britain's unilateral nuclear disarmament, publicized the slogan, "Let Britain Lead." Similar propositions—but with different countries leading—-were advanced by unilateralist groups in Canada, New Zealand, Ireland, and elsewhere. Could these and other divisions be transcended to establish a worldwide disarmament organization?

The Older Internationals

Some peace groups, of course, already operated on a global basis, most notably the pacifists. By the early 1960s, the International Fellowship of Reconciliation (FOR)—although strongest in Britain and the United States—had a membership of 41,000 in 25 countries. Of roughly comparable size, the War Resisters' International (WRI) and the Women's International League for Peace and Freedom (WILPF) maintained affiliates in 21 and 20 nations respectively.[2]

Much of their activity went into antinuclear ventures. The WILPF, for example, championed disarmament and the halting of nuclear tests during the late 1950s, issued protests against the resumption of nuclear testing in 1961, and urged restraint and the acceptance of U.N. Secretary General U Thant's proposal for immediate negotiations during the Cuban missile crisis of 1962. For the theme of its fifteenth international congress, in 1962 the WILPF chose "Total and Universal Disarmament—Now." In mid-1963, as U.S. and Soviet negotiators held another round of talks on a test ban treaty, the WILPF's executive committee issued a statement declaring that a comprehensive test ban agreement, with adequate safeguards, was technically feasible. And "even a partial ban," it noted, "would protect the world's people from the greatest hazards to their health and heredity, would inhibit the spread of nuclear weapons to many more nations, and would break the prolonged deadlock, opening the way for further negotiations on underground tests and on disarmament."[3]

Like the WILPF, the WRI threw itself into the antinuclear effort. Recognizing the great significance of the Easter marches, the WRI's 1963 world conference pledged to "encourage and aid these in every possible way." Many WRI sections cooperated closely with the broader nuclear disarmament organizations in their countries and sometimes provided the catalysts of direct action campaigns. These campaigns also drew the keen support of the WRI international office. Tony Smythe, the assistant secretary and later general secretary of the WRI, was a founder of the Committee of 100, and members of the WRI Council like A. J. Muste, Michael Randle, and Bayard Rustin were among the most prominent leaders of nonviolent resistance against preparations for nuclear war. Not surprisingly, the WRI played a key role in organizing the World Peace Brigade and the voyage of *Everyman III*. In addition, during the spring of 1962, the WRI protested the resumption of atmospheric nuclear testing by the United States and urged the Soviet Union not to retaliate by starting a new round of tests. Later that year, in the midst of the Cuban missile crisis, it urged peace groups to send letters and telegrams "appealing to the U.S.A. to withdraw immediately the blockade of Cuba, and to the Soviet Union to use the greatest possible restraint and to stop all sending of armaments to Cuba." The two governments, the WRI declared, should accept a U.N.-imposed solution to the problem.[4]

Meanwhile, the Pugwash conferences provided an increasingly important forum for physical scientists and smaller numbers of social scientists concerned with disarmament. Between September 1958 and April 1965, Rotblat, the movement's secretary-general—assisted by a continuing committee of prominent British, American, and Soviet scientists—organized an additional twelve Pugwash conferences. As their purpose was to inspire meaningful discussion among experts, conference organizers deliberately kept the gatherings small. The largest, held in London during September 1962, drew 175 participants from thirty-six countries. On other occasions, participation ranged from 25 to 74 people, drawn from up to twenty-five nations. Almost all the Pugwash gatherings dealt with aspects of disarmament. For example, the Moscow conference, held from November 27 to December 5, 1960, was organized around the theme "Disarmament and World Security." Rotblat recalled that topics for discussion at the sessions included "history of the arms race and disarmament negotiations; the dangers of the continued arms race; the current status of negotiations on the banning of nuclear tests; problems of world security systems; plans for comprehensive disarmament; political, economic and technical problems of arms limitation and disarmament"; and "the scientist's role and responsibilities." Each participant received an 800-page bound volume of the fifty-two conference papers. Perhaps more important, those in attendance—ordinarily divided by Cold War barriers—spent two afternoons conducting informal discussions in small groups, thereby enhancing interpersonal trust and communication.[5]

Behind the scenes, however, the Pugwash movement faced some thorny problems. One resulted from the role of Cyrus Eaton, the Cleveland industrialist who provided most of the funding for the first few conferences. Converted to the cause of nuclear disarmament, Eaton turned loose his powerful public relations office on its behalf, invoking the Pugwash conferences along the way. The American participants, particularly, felt embarrassed by Eaton's public statements and irked by his pressure on them to follow in his wake. "I am deeply grateful for Mr. Eaton's support," Rabinowitch confided to Russell, but the Pugwash movement was "a potentially important long-range force in human affairs, which should not be squandered on political pronouncements." Rotblat, too, found himself fighting off Eaton's attempts to influence Pugwash statements. Consequently, in the summer of 1958, Pugwash leaders began severing their ties with Eaton and funding their conferences through foundation contributions. Going even further, the U.S. group dropped the name Pugwash and adopted, in its place, Conferences on Science and World Affairs. Although the Americans suggested that the parent movement do the same, it chose to retain the name Pugwash.[6] By contrast, Bertrand Russell's increasingly controversial activities caused Pugwash leaders less embarrassment. Indeed, although Russell lost touch to some degree with the movement he founded, he still chaired the Pugwash continuing committee, sent messages of welcome to the conferences, and was consulted on policy by Rotblat.[7]

Another problem of the Pugwash movement resulted from the constraints imposed by the Soviet government on the Soviet delegation. How far could Soviet scientists go toward positions critical of Soviet policy? Szilard noted that "whenever I have conceded a point to them" at Pugwash conferences, "they responded to this as if it were an act of generosity. Their natural impulse is, in such a case, to concede a point to us—but this they are not free to do and thus they do the next best thing, which is to listen attentively and without dissent if I happen to defend certain US policies or attitudes." Furthermore, Soviet scientists did not take advantage of his occasionally critical comments about U.S. policy to use them for propaganda purposes. But was this enough? Jerome Wiesner, a U.S. physicist who attended a number of Pugwash conferences, complained to Rabinowitch in March 1959 about "the reluctance of the Soviet participants to engage in a really searching examination of issues dividing us and of technical questions involved in arms control." They were polite enough, Wiesner admitted, but "they are completely unwilling to participate in uninhibited discussion." He did not think the conferences could "make much real progress" until there were prolonged, "searching inquiries on specific issues."[8]

But the inhibitions of Soviet scientists gradually loosened. In early 1960, having secured approval from Soviet authorities, they responded enthusiastically to Rotblat's proposal to call a special conference to discuss the deadlock in Geneva on the test ban question.[9] Furthermore, although the Moscow conference at the end of the year began formally, even coolly, on the fourth day Peter Kapitza called for a blackboard and drew on it a graph illustrating the relation between armaments and military vulnerability. Later, Wiesner used the blackboard to show the correlation between levels of disarmament and measures of control. As Rotblat recalled, this technical, nonideological approach, "so familiar to the participants, transformed the whole meeting."[10] All the Soviet scientists, remarked Rabinowitch, "participated actively in the discussions during and between the formal meetings, rather than lining up behind a 'leader of the delegation,' as was the case at some of the earlier meetings." Another observer noted that E. K. Fedorov, a Soviet geophysicist and member of the Pugwash continuing committee, sat opposite Wiesner "and a great deal of communication was going on between them all the time." There was "a real conversation and meeting of minds." Kapitza proved particularly adroit at overcoming obstacles. By May 1961, the level of trust had risen to the point that U.S. and British Pugwash leaders pressed their Soviet counterparts to have the Soviet government modify its test ban proposals at Geneva.[11]

Another indication of the significance of the Pugwash conferences was the increasingly impressive nature of the delegations, especially from the nuclear powers. "The most important side of the Moscow meeting, which made it a great step forward," noted Rabinowitch, "was the outstanding list of Russian participants. It included some of the most famous Soviet scientists, several of them known for their unorthodox thinking." Moreover, roughly half of the large American and Soviet delegations was made up of advisers to their governments or of people who had served in this capacity in the past. For example, the Soviet focus on Wiesner during the Moscow conference probably reflected the fact that he was on his way to becoming the top science adviser for the incoming Kennedy administration. At subsequent meetings, high-level scientific advisers to the British government, as well as new aspirants for power, like political scientist Henry Kissinger, also made their appearance at Pugwash conferences. Rabinowitch concluded, in early 1961:

While our capacity to bring about a frank exchange of opinions in the disarmament field among competent scientists who have the trust of their governments is, as of today, our most important achievement, it is not our only achievement. We have established a wide—even if vague—mutual understanding and community of attitude, and thus we are able to provide a wide-open unofficial channel for indirect exchange of opinions between governments.[12]

External developments, however, came close to wrecking the movement. The Pugwash leadership, which had worked hard for the nuclear testing moratorium, viewed the September 1961 resumption of nuclear tests by the Soviet Union as a disaster. In addition, as Rotblat recalled, the event "cast a deep shadow" over the eighth Pugwash conference ("Disarmament and World Security"), which met from September 11 to 16, 1961, in Stowe, Vermont. Although most of the Western participants "believed that the deterioration of the political situation made it even more imperative for scientists to continue their efforts in this field," some "came with the feeling that there was no point in further talks." Furthermore, as Rotblat noted tactfully, "there was some mutual recrimination during the two plenary sessions on the first day of the conference." Privately, Rabinowitch reported that he had done his best "to prevent the 'Disarmament' conference from blowing up; and after many an anxious hour—particularly between 12:00 and 2:00 a.m.—we finally succeeded in pacifying both Topchiev and his party cell, and most of the potential Secretaries of State."[13]

Nevertheless, the movement did not disintegrate. After the initial furor at Stowe, a spirit of cooperation settled on the gathering, and its working groups dealt relatively smoothly with such issues as the elimination of fissile materials and stockpiles, the dismantling of nuclear delivery systems, and the creation of broader disarmament plans. At the largest Pugwash conference yet, held in London during September 1962, harmonious relations once more prevailed. Writing to Max Born in the aftermath of the meeting, Russell reported that "the Russians behaved exceptionally well, compromising time and time again, and at one point Topchiev announced that the Russian scientists were not in agreement amongst themselves about certain proposals and, therefore, could not vote as a delegation." The participants warned again that "a general war with nuclear weapons would be a disaster of unprecedented magnitude" and focused on "the problem of stopping nuclear tests." By the fall of 1963, Russian scientists seemed as committed to the Pugwash gatherings and their purposes as the Americans. "I can't prove it," Artsimovich told a journalist, "but without conferences like this one, it would be harder to imagine that things are going to be better."[14]

Religious organizations also had well-structured international frameworks and periodically used these to champion nuclear disarmament. Meeting in August 1959, the Central Committee of the World Council of Churches (WCC) adopted a statement calling on the nuclear powers to continue their nuclear testing moratorium and to "urgently" seek a comprehensive test ban treaty. Such a treaty would "represent the beginning of specific controls, may lead to measures of disarmament verified by international inspection and control, and will help to eliminate dreaded risks to health." In February 1960, the Executive Committee of the WCC pressed for continuing efforts toward a nuclear test ban and reaffirmed its concern for world disarmament. Meeting in New Delhi on December 5, 1961, the Assembly of the WCC adopted a dramatic appeal to all governments. "To halt the race in arms is imperative," it declared. "Complete and general disarmament is the accepted goal, and concrete steps must be taken to reach it. Meanwhile, the search for a decisive first step, such as the verified cessation of nuclear tests, should be pressed forward despite all obstacles and setbacks."[15]

The new Catholic church position provided a particularly dramatic and well-publicized critique of the Bomb. In *Mater et Magistra* (May 15, 1961), the new pope, John XXIII, continued the evolution of Catholic thought toward a condemnation of militarism. But his later encyclical, *Pacem in Terris* (April 11, 1963), begun during the harrowing days of the Cuban missile crisis, became his best-known and most radical statement. "Justice . . . right reason and humanity urgently demand that the arms race should cease; that the stockpiles which exist in various countries should be reduced equally and simultaneously . . . ; that nuclear weapons should be banned; and that a general agreement should eventually be reached about progressive disarmament and an effective method of control," he declared. "It is hardly possible to imagine that in the atomic era war could be used as an instrument of justice." Despite John's death only two months later, these ideas were reinforced by the Second Vatican Council and its final statement, *Gaudium et Spes* (1964), as well as by his successor, Paul VI. Appearing before the U.N. General Assembly on October 4,

1965, Paul called for "an oath which must change the future history of the world. No more war, war never again!" "If you wish to be brothers," he added, "let the arms fall from your hands."[16]

In fact, however, despite these striking formulations, the churches continued to exhibit no more than a limited commitment to the struggle against the Bomb. To be sure, the official Catholic peace movement, Pax Christi, began to focus on nuclear issues, as did liberal Protestant denominations. Nevertheless, as his other writings reveal, John XXIII, despite his call for disarmament, did not oppose all nuclear weapons, and neither he nor succeeding popes provided a detailed analysis of when their use would or would not be justified. *Gaudium et Spes*, a compromise between hawkish and pacifist elements within the Church, condemned the indiscriminate destruction of entire cities, but did not rule out nuclear deterrence or other aspects of a "legitimate defense." Paul VI also affirmed the right to defensive weapons, among which he apparently included the Bomb. For their part, Protestant church leaders proved rather pliant. According to the minutes of a meeting of WCC delegates with President Kennedy, held to discuss the WCC's December 1961 appeal, Bishop John Wesley Lord, vice president of the National Council of Churches, "asked the President what the Churches can do to give him the support he needs, should he ask for resumption of nuclear testing."[17] In these circumstances, world religious bodies bolstered the antinuclear movement more through their rhetoric than through their actions.

Informal Cooperation Among Newer Groups

Meanwhile, the newer nuclear disarmament organizations, formed on a national basis, forged a close relationship. British CND and SANE swapped ideas and speakers, as when SANE sponsored Canon Collins on a month-long lecture tour of thirty-five American cities and Canada. Smaller groups often leaned heavily on the larger ones. In 1964, New Zealand CND reported that "British CND has again been our main source of assistance and advice, and pamphlets and other publications have been obtained regularly from them." It also exchanged information with SANE and publications and "friendly letters" with the Canadian, Scandinavian, German, Swiss, and other nuclear disarmament groups. The process also went the other way, as when—at the behest of SANE—West Germany's Committee Against Atomic Armament pressed official negotiators to overcome the disarmament deadlock at Geneva.[18] Indeed, gestures of what a Danish leader called "international solidarity" were common. To back French antinuclear protests, British CND organized support demonstrations and sent messages of greeting. At Canadian CND's request,

Swedish antinuclear groups sent an appeal against Canada's nuclear armament to all newspapers and peace organizations in their country.[19]

Sometimes this cooperation followed functional lines. Given the ideological and personal links that existed between proponents of nonviolent civil disobedience in Britain (clustered around the Direct Action Committee and *Peace News*) and the United States (clustered around the Committee for Nonviolent Action and *Liberation*), activists in these countries took the lead in organizing joint transnational protests. The DAC and CNVA worked closely together on a number of ventures, including the Sahara project and the San Francisco to Moscow Walk for Peace.[20] The DAC's successor, the Committee of 100, continued this internationalist approach. Discussing plans for civil disobedience at Holy Loch, the committee's secretary, Michael Randle, told CNVA that the Committee realized that "if the Americans simply took the base from Scotland and put it somewhere else, the total danger to world peace would not be affected. This is why we feel it is absolutely necessary that there should be mass nonviolent action in every country which possesses nuclear weapons or where bases are situated." What was needed was "a world wide movement of resistance which will make it impossible for any government, East or West, to have nuclear bases or weapons." Subsequently, the Committee of 100 established an International Sub Committee which supported direct action projects in numerous nations. The activities of the World Peace Brigade reflected similar interaction among far-flung supporters of nonviolent resistance.[21]

Cooperation among disarmament groups also developed by constituency. Shortly before the 1960 Aldermaston march, Britain's Combined Universities CND and Youth CND, in conjunction with German and Dutch student movements, organized an international conference for students. Although delegates from forty-four organizations attended and decided to focus on disarmament, "with main emphasis on nuclear disarmament," little seems to have come of the venture. Nevertheless, organizational cooperation grew. On April 27, 1962, the Student Peace Union, the Zengakuren, and the Socialist German Student Union demonstrated simultaneously against the resumption of atmospheric nuclear testing by the United States.[22] That June, another conference, this time focused more narrowly on student peace movements, convened at the initiative of the American Friends Service Committee at Camp Sunnybrook, at Echo Lake, Pennsylvania. Delegates from Combined Universities CND and the Committee of 100 (Canada), the Student Peace Union and the FOR (United States), Youth CND and Colleges and Universities CND (Britain), Irish Universities CND, and other groups resolved to establish closer liaison among student peace organizations and proposed that the Canadian magazine *Our Generation Against Nuclear War* become their international journal. This plan, too, never reached fruition, but joint projects did continue to develop, especially among the relatively powerful student peace organizations in the United States, Canada, Britain, Denmark, Japan, and West Germany.[23]

With women's peace activism burgeoning in a number of countries, cooperation among women also began to transcend national boundaries. Ruth Gage-Colby, who coordinated international initiatives for Women Strike for Peace (WSP), announced the formation of Women's International Strike for Peace. Although this new women's peace international never quite crystallized, informal activities became common. On January 15, 1962, drawing on a broad range of international contacts, Gage-Colby sparked nuclear disarmament meetings and demonstrations in communities throughout Europe, Africa, and Asia, as well as a march of three thousand women outside the White House. Similarly, later that year, when WSP sent a delegation to meet with disarmament negotiators in Geneva, it was joined there by women activists from Austria, Britain, Canada, France, Norway, Sweden, Switzerland, West Germany, and other nations. Diana Collins, a leading organizer of women within CND and a participant at Geneva, considered it "one of the most worthwhile and encouraging efforts I have ever taken part in." In September 1962, Canada's Voice of Women hosted an International Conference of Women for Peace that drew delegates from seventeen nations. Calling for the establishment of an International Cooperation Year, the conference demanded that all governments take some concrete step in the direction of disarmament.[24]

The most dramatic of these international women's ventures occurred in 1964, when WSP organized a multinational women's rally at the Hague in opposition to the proposal for a NATO multilateral nuclear force. On May 13, despite restrictions imposed by the authorities, an estimated fifteen hundred women from fourteen NATO nations held a silent protest march outside the meeting place of the NATO council. Against a backdrop of soldiers, military police, civil police, mounted police, and police with dogs, fourteen women in summer dresses—their arms filled with tulips—presented a message of protest to the NATO ministers.[25]

Other forms of international cooperation were subtler, but no less important. As leaders of the movement met at international conferences and corresponded on key issues, their relationships deepened. Danilo Dolci was strongly influenced by Niemöller and Muste; Schweitzer leaned heavily on Cousins and Russell.[26] Often, prominent figures in the movement called on one another for messages of greeting to antinuclear rallies or for public statements on the need for disarmament. In 1963, Russell had little difficulty drawing together an all-star cast of signatories for his public appeal to halt the nuclear arms race in the Middle East. They included Born and Niemöller of West Germany, Dolci of

Italy, Pauling and Rabinowitch of the United States, Powell and Rotblat of Britain, Sartre of France, and Schweitzer of Gabon.[27] Furthermore, activists grew increasingly conscious of the movement's international dimensions thanks to the articles on activities in other lands published in their organizational newsletters, newspapers, or magazines—*Sanity* in Britain and Canada, *Voorlichtingsblad* in the Netherlands, *Atombulletin* in Switzerland, *Sane World* in the United States, *Kampagnebulletin* in Denmark, the *Banner* in Ireland, *Pläne* in West Germany, the *Bulletin* in New Zealand, and many others.[28] The symbol developed for CND's first Aldermaston march, like the march itself, swept around the world. It became not only a universal emblem for peace and disarmament, but perhaps the best-known symbol to appear in human history since the cross and the crescent.[29]

Moves Toward International Organization

In Western Europe, organizational unity began to take shape in early 1959. Initiated by the powerful British and West German antinuclear campaigns, and assisted by Holland's AAA, Sweden's AMSA, and the Swiss Movement Against Atomic Armament, a European Congress for Nuclear Disarmament met in London on January 17–18. Then it moved on to Frankfurt, where it was hosted by that city's Social Democratic administration. The gathering brought together some of Western Europe's most prominent antinuclear activists, including Russell, Collins, Rotblat, and Duff of Britain; Born, Hans Werner Richter, and Christian Mayer of West Germany; Svahnström, Alving, and Cedergren of Sweden; and Trocmé and Bourdet of France.[30] Voting to establish a European Federation Against Nuclear Arms, they soon secured the affiliation of antinuclear organizations from Austria, Belgium, Britain, Denmark, France, Ireland, Italy, the Netherlands, Norway, Sweden, Switzerland, and West Germany. Richter became the European Federation's first president, but was succeeded by Collins and, later, by an executive of three presidents: Collins, Heinz Kloppenburg (of West Germany), and Heinrich Buchbinder (of Switzerland). The federation declared that it would work to prevent nuclear proliferation, secure the renunciation of nuclear weapons, limit the use of nuclear energy to peaceful purposes, and coordinate the efforts of Europe's nuclear disarmament groups. In Richter's words, the European Federation was "politically neutral and independent."[31]

The European Federation undertook a variety of projects. Assailing proposals to equip the armed forces of Switzerland and Sweden with nuclear weapons, it dispatched letters of protest to their governments. As France geared up for nuclear testing in the Sahara, the European Federation sent a critique to de Gaulle, offered assistance to North African governments in campaigning against the tests, and pressed the Russians, Americans, and British to forgo resumption of their own testing programs. The federation also began a petition campaign to initiate a conference of the signatory powers to the Red Cross Convention for the purpose of broadening that agreement to include a ban on nuclear weapons.[32] Like its component groups, the federation was horrified by the eruption of the Cuban missile crisis, arguing that "so long as nuclear weapons and nuclear bases exist, crises of this kind will . . . threaten the people of the world with obliteration." It urged the United Nations "to mediate in the present crisis" and "to call for the dismantling of all nuclear foreign bases." Lauding disarmament proposals by the Irish, Ghanaian, and Indian governments, the European Federation gave particularly enthusiastic support to the Undén plan, a proposal by the Swedish foreign minister to establish a non-nuclear club. In a press statement of January 27, 1962, it argued that the Swedish proposal would help to bring "world-wide public opinion" to bear "on the nuclear powers, which have been led by their nuclear policies to a dead end."[33]

Despite the hopes of its founders, the European Federation was not very effective. For financial support, it could do little but fall back on the generosity of its national affiliates, and they were usually hard-pressed themselves. In addition, although some of the affiliates, like Britain's CND, were mass-based, powerful organizations, others were not. Moreover, even if they were, their vigorous campaigns within their own countries tended to keep them preoccupied. Peggy Duff, the secretary of the European Federation, recalled that although the German and Swiss groups worked hard on the Red Cross campaign, "the other organizations were far too busy on their own affairs." Finally, the European Federation was rather exclusive. It did not admit pacifist or direct actionist groups. It also remained limited to Western Europe. This cut off the European Federation from the substantial antinuclear campaigns of North America, Japan, and the Pacific, as well as from antinuclear activism elsewhere in the world. Although Collins, recognizing the federation's weakness, invited SANE to send an observer to its meetings, this was no substitute for building an effective international organization.[34]

Indeed, by 1962, the movement was leaving the European Federation behind. In late June of that year, the Accra Assembly drew together many of the leaders of nonaligned peace groups on a global basis, providing them with a surge of hope and excitement.[35] Later that summer, on "Hiroshima Day," tens of thousands of people participated in antinuclear marches, demonstrations, and memorial services in nations around the world.[36] But it was the Easter marches which provided the most striking evidence of an international breakthrough. That year, an estimated 200,000 people took part in forty-four of these "Aldermaston" marches in thirteen countries. According to Britain's *Sanity*, there had been 50,000 marchers in West Germany, 30,000 in Denmark, 20,000 in the United States, 10,000 in Canada, from 5,000 to 7,000 in Holland, 4,000 in Italy, "thousands" in Australia, and "uncountable" numbers in Britain. Washing across national boundaries, the antinuclear marches themselves become multinational. In Britain, as Duff recalled, they included "French and Germans and Italians and Scandinavians and all sorts of Africans and Asians and Japanese and Iraqis, Icelanders, Irish, Cypriots, Greeks, Americans, Australians, New Zealanders, Canadians, and South Africans." Everywhere, the new peace symbol appeared on banners and posters. In West Germany, marchers burst into a medley of British and American movement songs. In a land only recently freed from the grip of nationalist militarism, demonstrators now joined in the CND ballad, "The H-Bomb's Thunder," with its chorus:

> Men and women, stand together!
> Do not heed the men of war.
> Make your minds up now or never.
> Ban the Bomb forever more.[37]

This groundswell of support across national boundaries, combined with their close working relations of the past, convinced leaders of nuclear disarmament groups that the time had come to develop a global structure for the movement. At the Accra Assembly, delegates from nonaligned peace groups in a dozen countries, chaired by SANE's Homer Jack, met twice to discuss the idea of forming a new international. Another meeting of nonaligned leaders that July, in Moscow, heightened the determination—strongest among American, Canadian, and European groups—to fashion an international organization. Out of these gatherings came a proposal to the European Federation Against Nuclear Arms to convene a conference of nonaligned groups to explore the establishment of an international federation. Meeting in September 1962, the European Federation's executive committee approved the idea. Accordingly, the federation scheduled a conference for January 1963 in Oxford, England, sending invitations to nonaligned nuclear disarmament groups in Australia, Britain, Canada, Denmark, France, Holland, India, Ireland, Italy, Japan, New Zealand, Norway, Sweden, the United States, West Germany, and Yugoslavia. Organizations interested in participating, announced the European Federation, must be "publicly opposed to the testing, manufacture, and possession of nuclear arms by all nations."[38]

As plans for the Oxford conference went forward, nonviolent direct action groups flirted with the idea of establishing their own international. That summer, the International Sub Committee of the Committee of 100, endorsing the proposal of the Zengakuren to create "a world-wide Anti-War International," suggested holding a meeting for this purpose in Amsterdam. Nevertheless, in the face of objections from the European Federation and from the WRI—which viewed this event as competing with the forthcoming Oxford conference—the Sub Committee agreed that the Amsterdam meeting would do no more than provide "the next stage in informal international growth" of the nonviolent direct action movement.[39] Adopting this new aim, the International Sub Committee, the Dutch Committee for Peace, and the Zengakuren issued a call for the Amsterdam conference to meet from November 10 to 12. About seventy delegates and observers from Britain, Belgium, France, Holland, Japan, the United States, West Germany, and other countries attended the event, where they heard reports on antiwar activities in diverse lands, discussed how to build an independent movement in the East, and conferred on how to encourage international activities, especially nonviolent resistance. "We ask our friends in the peace movements of every country . . . to consider what they might do to promote non-violent direct action against the bomb and the danger of a third world war," they resolved, for "traditional forms of political action are proving incapable of meeting the dangers produced by power-politics." Soon thereafter, Muste and other direct action proponents made plans to meet again following the Oxford conference.[40]

From January 4 to 7, 1963, the long-awaited nonaligned conference convened at Oxford University, with delegates representing forty peace groups from eighteen countries.[41] Given the pervasive "sense of historical urgency," one participant recalled, "there was little need to discuss the desirability of setting up some kind of world organization: the question was how and what." Expected divisions among direct actionists, pacifists, unilateralists, and multilateralists failed to materialize. Instead, in plenary sessions and smaller meetings, the seventy-five delegates discussed the structure and activities of a new confederation, the meaning of nonalignment, and how to form groups in countries lacking them. Adopting a statement of principles and aims, the delegates agreed that organizations would be welcome in the new international if, "by consistent deeds and stated policies," they actively opposed the testing, manufacture, and use of nuclear weapons by any country, all nuclear bases, the membership of any country in any nuclear alliance, and the spread of nuclear weapons to additional nations. At this point, they voted unanimously to form the International Confederation for Disarmament and Peace (ICDP), a loosely structured body that would coordinate, publicize, and otherwise encourage the activities of member groups. They also elected a nineteen-member continuing committee, chaired by Kenneth Lee, secretary of the Friends Peace Committee of

Great Britain. When twenty-five organizations affiliated with the new group, the ICDP would officially begin operations.[42]

By far the most contentious issue to emerge at the Oxford conference was the admission of "observers" from the World Peace Council (WPC). As the result of a request from J. D. Bernal, the WPC president, the co-presidents of the European Federation—without consulting the nonaligned groups that had initiated the conference—invited the WPC to send "observers" to conference sessions.[43] Learning of this action in mid-December, the WRI and delegates from the United States, Canada, and India bombarded conference organizers with letters and telegrams of protest. When the conference opened, the issue remained unresolved; indeed, eleven WPC "observers" clamored for admission. Some conference delegates argued that the refusal to seat the WPC group would be both discourteous and McCarthyite. Yet a substantial majority of the delegates voted to deny admission to the WPC "observers." They argued that although they would welcome a meeting with a WPC delegation at some time in the future, a conference free of WPC participation was needed to maintain faith with the organizations that had sent them, to forge unity among nonaligned groups, to demonstrate to the public the nonaligned nature of the new organization, and to establish the basis for later discussions with the WPC.[44]

Even in the aftermath of the Oxford conference, the ICDP's relationship to the WPC remained a contentious issue. On the day after the meeting concluded, delegates of nonaligned peace groups who had attended the conference met with the representatives of the WPC, apologizing for their "discourtesy" and making clear their willingness to talk with them. At the same time, they stressed their staunch commitment to nonalignment, and this—coming on top of the conference's recent vote for exclusion—kept the atmosphere tense. Russell, who had not attended the conference, developed a very negative impression of it. In a letter to Muste, he expressed his regret at "both the shameful maneuverings of Canon Collins and the Cold War posturing of [the] Rev. Homer A. Jack."[45] Pauling, who had attended the conference and had been a fervent advocate of admitting the WPC observers, spent many months making the case publicly and privately for the utter villainy of Jack, whom he accused of wrecking the meeting. For his part, Jack declared that "the moment the World Council of Peace . . . becomes non-aligned from every turn of Soviet policy, I would eagerly favor their being admitted into the new Confederation."[46]

None of this, however, blocked the steady growth and development of the ICDP. By August 1963, when the ICDP continuing committee met at Oosterbeek, Netherlands, a sufficient number of peace groups had affiliated with the new world organization to declare it established. From January 9 to 13, 1964, representatives of affiliated groups—which now numbered thirty-one, from fifteen countries—convened in Tyringe, Sweden, for the ICDP's inaugural congress.[47] The delegates adopted a constitution underscoring their nonaligned position, decided to open an office in London, and elected leaders: Kenneth Lee (of Britain) as president, Sean MacBride (of Ireland), Joze Smole (of Yugoslavia), and Bertil Svahnström (of Sweden) as vice presidents, and Gerry Hunnius (of Canada) as secretary. The ICDP's action plan—drafted by Bourdet, Jack, and Andreas Buro (of West Germany)—called for opposition to a NATO nuclear force; support for disengagement in central Europe; creation of nuclear-free zones; renunciation of independent nuclear forces by Britain and France; normalization of relations with China and attempts to encourage that nation and France to sign the test ban treaty; and "the progressive disengagement of individual states from their military blocs." Efforts were also made at the conference to coordinate that year's Easter marches and to provide them with antinuclear themes that meshed with the ICDP's agenda. To establish "a link between the Easter marches and more positive alternatives to arms," the convention proposed that antinuclear groups promote collections for UNICEF over the Easter weekend.[48]

Addressing the ICDP delegates at Tyringe, Lee expressed his hope that the new international organization would "make us all aware of the widespread support . . . all over the world for the elimination of war" and help "spread this knowledge among the general public." In this fashion, he said, "we shall create a sense of common humanity and prepare people for allegiance to a world order which must come and is coming."[49]

Such an agenda required a powerful organization, with considerably greater strength than the ICDP ever mustered. Viewing the ICDP as McCarthyite, some nonaligned groups, like Women Strike for Peace, never joined it.[50] Another debilitating factor resided in the lingering tensions between the direct actionist, pacifist, and nonpacifist groups that comprised the organization. Complaining that the ICDP was becoming a "pacifist front," Jack argued that "what is needed is a broadly-based world organization with wide appeal and a policy based on controlled disarmament and U.N. peace-keeping machinery." By contrast, Peter Cadogan, chair of the International Sub Committee of the Committee of 100, complained that the ICDP had "done exactly nothing for the cause of international direct action," but was "mixed up with the wrong people—power-politicians posing as non-aligned."[51] Finally, the ICDP remained in desperate need of funding. Its penury might have been alleviated by a merger it nearly arranged with the International Liaison Committee of Organizations for Peace, a smaller nonaligned international with minimal activity and a more substantial treasury. But, although ILCOP did provide ICDP with some financial assistance, it rejected a merger—largely because it was already restructuring itself (into the International Peace Bureau) and because some members feared that a merger would open the door to Communist infiltration.[52]

Yet despite these difficulties the ICDP exhibited some impressive signs of growth. By 1967, fifty-six nonaligned peace groups from eighteen countries had become either full or associate members of the confederation. They included not only the three pacifist internationals, but direct action, unilateralist, multilateralist, student, and women's groups. Three of the ICDP affiliates were located in two Third World nations (India and Nigeria).[53] Initiating a variety of international projects, they worked together to block the multilateral nuclear force, to secure a nuclear nonproliferation treaty, and—of course—to organize ever larger turnouts at the yearly nuclear disarmament marches. According to British CND's *Sanity*, over the Easter 1964 weekend the turnout in Britain for the demonstration was pathetically small by past standards (a mere twenty to thirty thousand people). But this was overshadowed by the fact that an unprecedented half a million people participated in nuclear disarmament marches in twenty nations around the world.[54]

Just as important as the numbers was the rebellious spirit of internationalism that characterized the burgeoning movement. What was happening when people blithely crossed national boundaries to invade a nuclear testing site in the Sahara, to distribute antinuclear leaflets in East Germany, or to scuttle their ship in a Soviet harbor? In the spring of 1963, when the West German government banned foreign participation in the Federal Republic's Easter march, this proved more difficult to enforce than expected. Refused entry to the country at Düsseldorf airport, a contingent of fifty-four British CND members promptly staged a sit-in. West German police carried them one by one back to their plane, but they blocked the plane's take-off by refusing to fasten their seat belts. With the plane immobilized in this fashion for three days, an estimated ten thousand West German peace demonstrators gathered outside, until at last the police drove them away by assaulting them with water cannon. In addition, while the CND members were being carried onto the plane, three of the younger, more energetic activists climbed onto the roof, escaped their pursuers, and turned up at the Düsseldorf Easter march. Defying the authorities still further, one of them addressed the culminating rally.[55] Like their nervous counterparts, East and West, officials in the Federal Republic had good reason to recognize that this was no ordinary political movement.

Across the Great Divide

Aligned and Nonaligned Activists, 1958–65

> A very deep gulf separates us . . . : the difference in
> attitude toward . . . existing governmental power [and]
> toward free and unrestricted protest.
>
> Erich Fromm, 1962

The Communist-led World Peace Council (WPC), though discredited by its
Cold War partisanship, remained a substantial organization with affiliates in
many nations. Lavishly supported by Communist governments and parties, it
retained a large following not only among party members, but among Communist sympathizers. Because some of the WPC's antinuclear activities paralleled the campaigns of its nonaligned competitors, cooperation appeared to
make sense. Furthermore, some persons thought that groups trying to heal the
divisions between Communist and non-Communist countries should foster
unity between Communists and non-Communists within the peace movement.
Unity was particularly attractive to the WPC, which needed a fresh image to
reverse its decline. In addition, given the party discipline and political savvy
of many of its supporters, it might capture control of the new organizations.
And yet, by bolstering nonaligned groups, the WPC risked promoting criticism
of East bloc military measures. Similarly, working with the Communist-led and
badly tarnished WPC or, more generally, with partisans of Communism posed
substantial political risks for nonaligned peace organizations. On a more fundamental level, too, leaders of both movements faced the question: How much
did they really have in common?

The World Peace Council and Its Affiliates

Throughout the late 1950s and early 1960s, the WPC focused on the antinuclear campaign. Addressing a WPC conference in early 1961, its president,
J. D. Bernal, declared that "we are convinced . . . that disarmament, and partic-

ularly nuclear disarmament, is, and remains, the central problem." It was not a "technical" one, he insisted, and it could be solved by the expression of "the people's will for peace." In a declaration adopted later during the conference, the WPC argued that "disarmament is the hope and demand of the people. The peoples hold the key. It is for them to impose disarmament by immediate and widespread action." Thus, the WPC "solemnly appeals to men and women of the whole world to act now . . . to remove war from the life of humanity, to re-place armament by disarmament, to replace the cold war by international co-operation and peaceful co-existence."[1]

These and similar WPC injunctions helped spur Communist-led antinuclear activism in numerous nations. Stigmatized by their Soviet partisanship, WPC affiliates in countries like Denmark and Holland disintegrated.[2] But others re-mained active. In 1963, the All-India Peace Council announced a peace con-gress of a thousand delegates to "work out concrete measures to intensify the struggle for world disarmament." In France, the Movement for Peace held mass protests against that country's development of nuclear weapons, including a demonstration of ten thousand people at the Pierrelatte nuclear facility in Oc-tober 1962.[3] In Israel, Australia, and New Zealand, WPC affiliates conducted a range of peace and antinuclear activities, including protests during the Cuban missile crisis.[4] Although badly debilitated, the Canadian Peace Congress staged a "Rally for Peace and Disarmament" in 1960, organized around the theme of "Peace or Annihilation" in 1961, held a mass meeting ("Disarmament is the Only Shelter that Guarantees Survival") in 1962, and campaigned on the theme of "No Nuclear Arms for Canada" during the elections of 1963.[5] Naturally, WPC affiliates remained strongest in Communist nations. In Hungary, the Na-tional Peace Council claimed that, during the spring of 1963, it mobilized two million people for "nearly 3,000 big rallies" and "15,000 smaller meetings" as part of "disarmament month"—an extravaganza devoted to "the policy of peaceful coexistence and general and total disarmament."[6]

What distinguished the WPC and its affiliates from the nonaligned move-ment was their clear partisanship. Although Khrushchev's emphasis on peace and coexistence softened the tone of WPC pronouncements, they remained one-sided. Lamenting the failure of the 1960 summit conference to curb the nuclear arms race, the WPC charged that "responsibility for the failure . . . rests squarely upon the US government." During the Cuban crisis of 1962, it did not criticize the Soviet Union's establishment of nuclear missile bases, but only "the aggressive measures taken by [the] United States." That same year, the Canadian Peace Congress contended that "the main stumbling block to an agreement to stop the 'tests' and to begin genuine disarmament" was "the American plan for massive surprise nuclear war."[7] By contrast, the policies of

Communist states remained beyond reproach. The New Zealand Peace Council never questioned the development of Soviet nuclear weapons or the entry of China into the nuclear club. When nonaligned activists asked leaders of the East German Peace Council why they did not criticize the policies of their government, they replied that they agreed completely with its peace policy. Addressing the Sixth Hungarian Peace Congress in July 1963, the vice premier of that nation declared that the National Peace Council "enjoys the total support of our socialist state, since its aims are the same as the foreign policy of the Hungarian People's Republic."[8]

This alignment with state policy was particularly evident when, in late August 1961, the Soviet Union announced plans to break the nuclear testing moratorium. Communist organizations quickly rallied behind the Soviet decision, as did the American Communist Party, which blamed it on "ultra-reactionary war forces" in the United States.[9] On behalf of the WPC, Bernal issued an elaborate rationalization, declaring that although "lovers of peace throughout the world will deeply regret that the Soviet government has, however reluctantly, found it necessary to resume the testing of nuclear weapons," the decision "arises as a consequence of the continual attempts on one side to deal with political and negotiable proposals by threats of force." Bernal proceeded to expose this "one side" as "the N.A.T.O. powers," with their "preparations for a nuclear war." Similarly, although the Canadian Peace Congress formally endorsed "the world wide protest against any further testing of nuclear weapons," it omitted any criticism of the Soviet Union. Instead, it used the occasion to denounce "the shameless cold war hypocrisy of the U.S. government," which remained "the real source of war danger today."[10]

In Communist nations, WPC affiliates avoided even a pretense of regret at the Soviet action. Yuri Zhukov, vice chair of the Soviet Peace Committee, staunchly defended the Soviet decision, claiming that it represented "a reply to the threats of the United States and its allies to start war against us." Praising Soviet test resumption several months later, the secretary of East Germany's Peace Council called it "a great warning for such hot-heads of the west who today want to settle differences by war. The necessity of these tests is proved by the fact that we still live in peace." Liao Cheng-chih, vice chair of the China Peace Committee, argued that Soviet test resumption was "a necessary and timely warning to U.S. imperialism, which is preparing to start nuclear war. Only the imperialists and reactionaries are scared of it."[11]

WPC leaders could hardly deny their partisanship—nor did they try; they insisted instead that proponents of nonalignment missed the point. Writing in early 1962, Bernal argued that "there is a duty for all of us to assess the situation. The attitude which says: 'A plague on both your houses' is an abdication of this responsibility." Or, as he maintained later that year: "The question is not whether a peace movement in any country supports or opposes its government's policy. The question is rather whether the policy itself helps or hinders disarmament and peace." Given their Communist views, WPC leaders assumed that the practices of Communist nations promoted peace, disarmament, and, indeed, the overall betterment of humanity. Therefore, from their standpoint, rallying behind Communist state policy made perfect sense.[12]

Controversy within the WPC developed not over Communist policy, but over which Communist policy to follow. In the late 1950s and early 1960s, the conflict between the proponents of the Soviet position (emphasizing disarmament) and the Chinese position (emphasizing "national liberation struggles") grew ever more heated. At the WPC's Stockholm conference of December 1961, the Chinese delegation, backed by the Australian and the Albanian, launched a direct assault on the Soviet line. Liu Ning-yi, vice chair of the China Peace Committee, argued that "oppressed nations" must "build and strengthen their own armed forces," thus challenging "the policy of atomic blackmail on the part of American imperialism." In response, Viktor Chkhikvadse, leader of the Soviet delegation, argued that "without the prohibition of nuclear weapons the national liberation movement will be a movement for dead people."[13] Over the fierce objections of the Chinese and the Albanians, proponents of the Soviet position scheduled a conference for the following summer focused on disarmament. As might be expected, advocates of the Chinese line considered this gathering a disgrace. Denouncing the 1962 meeting in a private message to Bernal, the China Peace Committee refused to accept the gold medal awarded it by the WPC. The meeting's conclusions, it explained, "did not point out [that the] enemy of peace is United States imperialism."[14]

The division within WPC ranks widened substantially in 1963. Dispatching a stinging telegram to Bernal in May, the China Peace Committee assailed the "arbitrary restrictions" on the number of Chinese delegates to the forthcoming WPC conference, claimed that the WPC had "evaded" answering key questions it had posed, and announced that it would discontinue financial contributions because WPC actions had "become increasingly detrimental to [the] defense of world peace." That August, shortly after the signing of the partial test ban treaty by the U.S., British, and Soviet governments, Liao denounced it as "a big conspiracy in which the imperialists and their hangers-on join hands against the socialist countries, against China and against the forces of peace of the whole world." The Chinese government had "expressed its determined opposition to this dirty treaty" and "we, the Chinese people, fully support this just stand of our government." In turn, the WPC executive issued a vigorous denunciation of the Chinese position—apparently behind the back of Bernal, who protested this in a secret letter to Khrushchev, complaining that it might "fatally compromise" the WPC and "even cause it to break up."[15]

This did seem a definite possibility. At the WPC conference that opened in late November 1963, Liao delivered a blistering attack on Soviet policy and on its defenders within the WPC. "To tell the oppressed nations and peoples to disarm can only be a fraud with no other aim than to make the world peace movement abandon its task of fighting against imperialism," he charged. Although the Albanian, North Korean, Vietnamese, and Indonesian delegations, as well as most of the Japanese, endorsed the Chinese position, Soviet policy emerged victorious by a hefty majority and amid considerable rancor. According to the Chinese press agency, when Liu read out a Chinese statement at the final session, Soviet delegates "took the lead" in catcalling, desk-thumping, and yelling. In a public statement at the end of the year, Bernal sought once again to paper over "differences of opinion . . . as to the priorities of disarmament and national liberation," declaring that the WPC should focus its attention on "both these goals."[16] But, in August 1964, at the World Conference Against Atomic and Hydrogen Bombs, the leader of the Chinese delegation ridiculed the idea that "nuclear weapons rather than imperialism headed by the United States" was "the source of nuclear war" and claimed that the Soviet Union had used the test ban treaty to "oppose socialist China." When, that October, the Chinese government exploded its first atomic bomb, the basis for the stance of the China Peace Committee became clear enough. In response, the WPC—controlled by pro-Soviet elements—condemned the Chinese nuclear test for adding "to the radioactive contamination of the atmosphere" and providing the basis for "other states to step up the nuclear arms race." At the WPC's 1965 conclave, the outraged Chinese and their allies sought to take over the gathering. When this effort failed, they proceeded to harass the Russians at every turn.[17]

This Sino-Soviet rift divided the ranks of other Communist-controlled bodies, such as the World Federation of Scientific Workers,[18] and of the WPC's national affiliates. In general, the opponents of the disarmament emphasis came from the WPC's Asian and Pacific branches, although China's European ally, Albania, proved a fervent critic as well.[19] The defenders came from other regions and, particularly, from Eastern Europe, where Soviet control was strongest. Rallying behind the Soviet position, the Czechoslovak Committee of Defenders of Peace publicly charged that the China Peace Committee had "launched an offensive, not against the danger of war, but against the unity of the defenders of peace." The Bulgarians proclaimed that the WPC "cannot and will not accept such an irresponsible and adventurist line."[20] Elsewhere, as in France, Soviet leaders apparently won the backing of party officials by doing them a few favors. Some groups, however, acted on principle. The Yugoslav

League for Peace, which had refused for years even to send observers to WPC meetings, was so appalled by the Chinese position that, in 1962, it began participating with the intention of opposing it. Other affiliates found themselves badly torn by the conflict. Frank Hartley, a leader of the Australian Peace Council, told Bernal in mid-1963 that "we have passed through a difficult period because of the ideological struggle." Several months later, he reported glumly that the battle continued to rage.[21]

Improving Relations with the Nonaligned Movement

With the Communist-led peace movement externally discredited and internally divided, the leaders of the WPC sought to refurbish its strength and reputation through the establishment of closer relations with the flourishing nonaligned movement. Bernal and other WPC officials dispatched friendly letters to Pauling, Muste, Russell, and other prominent nonaligned activists, inviting them to attend WPC meetings or encouraging their cooperation with these or other Communist-led peace ventures.[22] In October 1959, Bernal also sent messages to groups such as the International FOR and SANE, asking if there were "ways in which those associated with our movement can usefully cooperate in parallel or joint activities with yourselves." Two years later, Bernal proved very cooperative when organizers of the San Francisco to Moscow Peace March sought official permission for its entry into Eastern Europe and the WPC's Soviet affiliate put the venture over the top.[23] Making the case for "cooperation among peace forces of different ideological trends," the WPC's Czech branch publicly argued that "the aims of the individual groups are neither conflicting nor do they differ from each other." Privately, however, WPC leaders took a more self-interested view of things, recognizing that, for the WPC to function with any effectiveness, it had to escape its isolation. And this could be accomplished only by attracting the support of non-Communist activists.[24]

The WPC reached a new level of cooperation with the nonaligned movement in 1961. At the initiative of British CND and SANE, an attempt was begun in 1959 to convene a "Peace Pugwash," in which leaders of the WPC, the Soviet Peace Committee, and nonaligned peace groups would meet on the basis of equality. Bernal, Canon Collins, and Homer Jack served as the planning committee, inviting an ideologically balanced group of delegates to a meeting in London from September 14 to 18. Collins explained that each participant would "come as an individual and not as a representative of any organization," although those invited were "selected on account of their high standing" in the organizations they led. Some sixty delegates from twenty countries attended the event, which proceeded in a remarkably restrained and responsible fashion. Since the Soviet Union had resumed nuclear testing only a few weeks before the conference convened, this became the center of discussions. Pointing to a prior agreement that any conference statement had to be unanimous, nonaligned leaders insisted that there would either be strong criticism of test resumption or no statement at all. For a time, a standoff ensued, with the Russians insisting that they could not sign a statement mentioning test resumption and the nonaligned saying they would sign no other. Ultimately, to the surprise of observers, the Russians (led by Ilya Ehrenburg and Alexander Korneichuk) agreed to accept a statement that—without mentioning the Soviet Union—deplored the resumption of nuclear testing, urged other nations to refrain from it, and called for a "controlled test ban."[25]

Nonaligned activists welcomed this cooperative spirit, for some, at least, desired better relations with the Communist-led movement. In a memo he sent to peace group leaders in 1959, Muste wrote that "I believe so deeply in the need of *trying* to communicate that I personally would favor an effort on the part of U.S. and West European groups . . . to agree on a proposal dealing with the problem of cooperation of peace organizations to lay before [the] WPC." In the meantime, when evaluating proposals for joint action, "we must keep our minds open but cannot ignore basic WPC attitudes."[26] Several years later, with the WPC's position clearly mellowing to reflect the new Soviet line, WSP's Dagmar Wilson argued against "excluding communists from Peace." And a few nonaligned leaders, like Pauling, not only favored working with Communists on peace efforts, but served as sponsors of WPC events. Yet Pauling's stand remained quite unusual.[27] Like Muste, most nonaligned activists were torn between a vague hope that the Communist-led peace movement might be reformed and their conviction that this was unlikely.

Attending conferences that brought the two movements together seemed a relatively easy way to improve their relationship. Some prominent Western church leaders active in the nonaligned movement—including Collins, Niemöller, Helmut Gollwitzer, Heinz Kloppenburg, and Richard Ullmann—met with clergy from Communist nations at the Christian Peace Conferences, held annually in Prague. Here, despite much talk of a common devotion to Christianity, nonaligned leaders occasionally found themselves besieged on East-West issues. Sometimes they also faced severe criticism from conservative forces at home. Nevertheless, they persisted in this experiment, and Western participation—initially scant—grew over time.[28] The London "Peace Pugwash" of September 1961 provided yet further evidence of the willingness of nonaligned leaders to meet with their Communist counterparts to discuss nuclear disarmament and other issues. Indeed, so pleased were they by the gathering that they initiated plans for a follow-up conference.[29]

Norman Cousins sparked yet another kind of meeting. Invited to the Soviet Union as part of a U.S.-Soviet cultural exchange program, Cousins gave a talk before the presidium of the Soviet Peace Committee on June 25, 1959, in Moscow. Russians and Americans both wanted peace, the SANE leader asserted, but faced some serious obstacles, including the pro-Soviet role of the American Communist Party and Soviet repression in Eastern Europe. In line with his world federalist views, Cousins called for strengthening world authority—and specifically the United Nations—as a means of securing peace. Despite the hard-hitting nature of this address, Cousins's comments on the need for private citizens' efforts to span the Cold War divide appealed to the Peace Committee, which proposed a meeting with American peace organizations. Eventually, Cousins persuaded the committee that a meeting with a more broadly based group of prominent Americans would have greater impact. Accordingly, a conference at Dartmouth College followed in October 1960. These "Dartmouth conferences"—which covered a range of issues—continued thereafter, with Cousins and Korneichuk serving as the co-chairs. When the Soviet Union announced plans to resume nuclear testing, Cousins appealed to Korneichuk "to dissuade the Soviet government from this dangerous course." Nothing materialized on this score, but the conferences continued.[30]

Given their very different orientation, nonaligned and aligned peace groups found it easier to hold meetings than to work on common projects. Although France's Communist-led Movement for Peace seemed likely to back the Sahara protest, the Direct Action Committee—fearing that its sponsorship would undermine the project's nonaligned status—decided not to approach the group. "Getting into the old typical united front attempts . . . would be the worst thing that could happen," Muste told Collins in the aftermath of the "Peace Pugwash." He surmised "that people like Professor Bernal may be looking for a 'united' world peace movement of that kind," but, personally, he would consider it "disastrous." In Muste's view, an alternative to a united but unprincipled disarmament campaign lay in strengthening the nonaligned movement and, at the same time, inviting the support of Communist-led groups for impeccably nonaligned ventures. In 1960, appealing to Soviet "peace workers," Muste and Bradford Lyttle of the Committee for Nonviolent Action explained CNVA's Omaha project and then proposed that they "similarly demand unilateral action."[31] The following September, in the midst of Soviet-American planning for the San Francisco to Moscow Peace March, Muste delivered a lengthy indictment of the Soviet resumption of nuclear testing to leaders of the Soviet Peace Committee and called for a halt to the tests. Similarly, writing to the Soviet Peace Committee's Viktor Chkhikvadze, the American FOR inquired if he and Bernal would be interested in joining it in a public statement criticizing Soviet test resumption.[32] Not surprisingly, nothing came of these proposals.

Furthermore, most nonaligned activists had little interest in attending meetings organized by the WPC. Almost invariably, nonaligned peace groups shunned the massive, carefully orchestrated conferences that the WPC staged on an annual basis. Summarizing some of the "difficulties and dangers" of such gatherings, Collins recalled that most participants "represent the Party line," and this "has sometimes been strikingly reflected." Furthermore, the Communist and pro-Communist delegates "tend to have a rather naive view of the necessities of peace-making; the communist governments desire peace, they say, therefore anything they propose must be directed towards peace, and anyone who opposes their policies must be against peace. Discussion as we understand it in the West is sometimes difficult if not absent." Finally, "communists at peace conferences . . . make the maximum use of procedural rules and democratic rights to further their purpose and an unsuspecting, often rather lazy and less dedicated, and sometimes too sentimental, Westerner" could easily be outmaneuvered. In addition, many nonaligned leaders considered the WPC's calls for peace quite hypocritical. Invited to attend the WPC's 1959 conference, Russell responded tartly: "Could you let me see any pronouncements of the World Council protesting against militaristic imperialism in East Germany, Hungary, and Tibet? The greatest contribution that could be made towards ending the Cold War would be the abandonment of militaristic imperialism by Russia and China."[33]

Even so, a substantial group of nonaligned activists accepted invitations to attend the WPC's World Congress for General Disarmament and Peace scheduled for July 1962 in Moscow. To a great extent, this reflected the extraordinary efforts of the WPC leadership to obtain their participation. When Collins insisted that if CNDers were to attend as observers, their voices would have to be heard and the Soviet press would have to print their speeches, Bernal agreed.[34] The Committee of 100 also drove a hard bargain, demanding written guarantees on a number of points, including "recognition of the fact that in our view the Russian government is as blameworthy as any other government that prepares for nuclear war and that we intend to say so." Again, Bernal agreed.[35] America's nonaligned peace groups were considerably more dubious about the Moscow gathering; ultimately, only WSP—after a bitter debate on the question—sent official delegates. Homer Jack and Erich Fromm, however, attended not as delegates or observers, but as the personal guests of Bernal.[36] Other nonaligned contingents came from Austria, Canada, Denmark, France, India, Italy, Norway, Sweden, and West Germany. Collins thought that nonaligned attendance was justified in light of the London "Peace Pugwash" and, furthermore, would either help transform the conference or expose it as "just another Communist front." The Committee of 100 planned to stage a variety of actions, including the distribution of unilateralist leaflets. American motives varied, but Jack and Fromm, at least, "had two purposes in mind: to continue to cooperate, within certain limits, with the World Council of Peace, and to correct the impression" that it "represents the entire peace movement."[37]

The result was the most diverse conference in the WPC's history. To be sure, the vast bulk of the twenty-five hundred delegates expressed the usual pro-Communist opinions and responded to a two-and-a-half-hour, belligerent address by Khrushchev with wild applause. This time, however, there were other kinds of speeches. Collins expressed his belief that both the U.S. and Soviet governments "have defied the strongly expressed wish of the rest of the world for a test ban" and that "the U.S.S.R. made a grave error" in resuming nuclear testing. Sydney Silverman, British M.P. and CND leader, criticized Khrushchev's speech for suggesting "that the Soviet Union had always been right and never made a mistake." Speaking via a recording, Russell challenged both Khrushchev and Kennedy to assert publicly that nuclear war would be worse than the victory of either ideology professed by the Cold War antagonists. Although the conference—in line with the WPC leadership's attempts at unity—produced an inoffensive final statement, eighty-one delegates from eleven countries signed a minority report, written by Kingsley Martin and Claude Bourdet. It called the Soviet Union "obstructive" for rejecting proposals for inspection of nuclear facilities, criticized the United States for "stalling on disarmament" by insisting on "an impossibly strict system of inspection," and demanded that peace movements "speak frankly and, if necessary, critically, not only about governments of which they disapprove, but also about governments they generally support."[38]

Perhaps the most sharply etched of the nonaligned messages was delivered to a conference plenary session by Homer Jack. In a half-hour speech representing the views of Norman Thomas, Fromm, and other leaders of American peace groups, Jack told a hostile, generally silent audience that "the peace movement in the United States speaks to its government." But "the peace organizations of the Soviet bloc espouse the policies of their governments, whether these governments happen to be developing greater bombs or calling for disarmament." When Jack declared that West Germany should not be allowed to rearm or have nuclear weapons, cheers filled the hall. But when he stated that West Berlin should remain free and unhindered, there were shouts of "no, no." Turning to the issue of nuclear weapons testing, Jack declared: "The World Council of Peace has raised its voice, as we have done, against the American tests. Will the World Council of Peace also join us in speaking out unequivocally against the forthcoming Soviet tests?" These remarks, he recalled, were met with "stony silence, even some hissing."[39]

Despite the sharp exchanges, the Moscow conference represented the high-water mark of cooperation between the aligned and the nonaligned peace movement. Pointing to the unprecedented diversity, Bernal called it "the beginning of a great work." At the least, it showed that WPC leaders were so eager to attract their competitors that they allowed the expression of an unprecedented array of heretical statements. Indeed, in line with Bernal's promises, nonaligned delegates were permitted to speak freely, and even the Soviet press printed abridged accounts of the addresses by Collins, Silverman, Jack, and some other nonaligned leaders. Furthermore, Ehrenburg made a strongly conciliatory speech, and even the Chinese accepted a watered-down conference report in the interest of harmony. The chair of the Polish delegation remarked hopefully that "the Moscow Congress laid the foundation for the . . . unification of all peace movements." Even Jack observed that although "the basic, pro-Soviet orientation" of the WPC had "not changed," nonaligned peace movements "should keep the door of communication open" with it. And if the WPC maintained the "policy of allowing divergent viewpoints to be heard," Americans should attend its conferences in the future.[40]

The Limits of Change

Yet the 1962 meeting also highlighted the differences between the two movements. CND participants found Khrushchev's much-vaunted speech appalling, and some simply dozed off during it. Nonaligned activists also resented the gathering's refusal to concede anything wrong with Soviet resumption of nuclear testing and the automatic condemnation of all things American. Even as he praised the Aldermaston march and U.S. peace demonstrations, the leader of the Chinese delegation portrayed these as anti-American ventures.[41] Other disconcerting behavior reflected the sectarian disdain for nonaligned disarmament activism that existed within WPC ranks. The Japanese delegation—then leaning toward the Chinese line—deliberately blocked the appearance of two *hibakusha* who had come to address the meeting on the need for ending nuclear testing and fostering international reconciliation. The intense hostility of the Japanese WPC contingent toward these teenage atomic bomb victims shocked nonaligned observers.[42]

Even more revealing was the WPC's response to events just outside the conference walls. When the conference organizers learned of Committee of 100 plans for antinuclear leafleting, they announced that leaflet distribution was forbidden beyond the meeting hall. No more awed by Soviet officials than they had been by the British variety, the Committee proceeded to distribute ten thousand unilateralist leaflets to astonished Muscovites, thereby enraging leaders of the Soviet Peace Committee. The latter were also startled by the Committee plan to stage an antinuclear demonstration. Demanding the abandonment of this venture, Soviet Peace Committee officials threatened participants with deportation. Undeterred, about twenty-five American, British, Canadian, Danish, and Norwegian delegates defied their hosts and marched to Red Square. Here they unfurled their banner protesting nuclear tests in East and West, only to have it seized and the gathering disrupted, probably by plainclothes police.[43] The final touch was a vituperative article on these antinuclear protests by Yuri Zhukov, vice chair of the Soviet Peace Committee. "A handful" of foreigners "went out of their way to get arrested or at least beaten up," stormed Zhukov. "Then they could write in the papers that peace champions were maltreated in the Soviet Union. They picked up conversations in the streets on subjects humiliating to the Soviet people and thrust provocative, slanderous leaflets on passers-by."[44]

Among others, Russell saw this clash as symptomatic of a profound division between nonaligned and pro-Communist activists. "The Soviet government evidently intended the Congress solely for their own propaganda purposes," he wrote privately. Even so, the Committee of 100 had "succeeded in putting forward forcefully the case of the nonaligned peace movement." When Zhukov sent him an effusive letter, renewing his courtship of the British leader, Russell replied sharply that he could not "recall any article in any Western newspaper which has attacked members of the Committee of 100 in quite the extreme terms which you used." Echoing remarks at the conference, Russell contended that "at the root of our present disagreement, lies a fundamental difference between the Soviet Peace Committee and independent peace organizations in the West: the Peace Committee speaks *for* its government, whereas Western peace organizations speak *to* their governments. Until this difference is recognized and resolved, any fruitful cooperation between the peace movements of East and West is unlikely."[45]

Indeed, given this difference, relations deteriorated in the aftermath of the Moscow conference. In the fall of 1962, the Soviet Peace Committee threw its weight against allowing the crew of *Everyman III* to enter the Soviet Union to demonstrate against nuclear testing.[46] Relations also grew tense at that summer's World Festival of Youth in Helsinki. Like its predecessors, this Communist-organized extravaganza brought together thousands of young people from around the world for concerts, sports events, and political forums, where they were encouraged to condemn Western "imperialism" and praise the achievements of the "Socialist camp." In late July 1962, however, a group of young activists from Danish KmA turned up, distributed seven thousand antinuclear leaflets, and held a photo exhibition in the city center. They also proposed that, at the closing event of the festival, a Hiroshima Day parade, they carry signs proclaiming "Stop All Nuclear Tests—East and West." Horrified at this prospect, festival organizers refused permission, threatening that unsanctioned signs would be "knocked out and knocked out hard." Eventually, then, some 120 nonaligned activists from fourteen countries gathered under the offending banner and, after festival organizers called the police to stop them, finally held their own vigil in a Helsinki square. Steffen Larsen, the nineteen-year-old KmA secretary, described it as "just like in Moscow."[47]

The Oxford conference of January 1963 dealt a nearly fatal blow to the relationship between the two movements. Stung by their exclusion from the meeting and, especially, by the establishment of a rival federation, the ICDP, the WPC "observers" secretly raged. "What will become of this anti-peace international?" fumed Bernal. Ehrenburg observed reproachfully: "Now they can easily form their own peace organization, which will have a similar face to ours." Bernal placed the blame for the disaster on "the small U.S. group." The Europeans, he claimed, "generally were against this new organization, with its anti-communist tendency."[48] Refusing to meet with a liaison committee appointed by the ICDP, Bernal announced that he would not talk to a delegation including Homer Jack or composed of "nonentities."[49] Thereafter, the WPC launched a bitter campaign against Jack and the ICDP. In June, the WPC's Czech affiliate charged that "some hot-headed members of pacifist organizations . . . seem to believe in their own imaginary supremacy and try to enforce their views and concepts . . . on other peace forces." These scoundrels also supported "the notorious partisans of war and armament." In August, the WPC bulletin stepped up the assault on Jack and the ICDP. Meanwhile, Bernal warned Khrushchev that groups "which are called 'unaligned' . . . are really anti-Soviet." Later that year, the top leaders of the Soviet Peace Committee publicly charged that the ICDP was controlled by "agents of the imperialists, who are working to split the ranks of the peace forces."[50]

The WPC took much the same line toward the British Committee of 100. Responding publicly to a communication that year from the WPC about disarmament, disengagement, and the halting of nuclear tests, the Committee outlined its antinuclear activities in Great Britain. Then it added: "We shall be glad to learn when you are conducting demonstrations against nuclear installations in the Warsaw pact countries," including Soviet missile bases in East Germany. Until that time, the Committee would not be "impressed by verbal protestations for disarmament." Irate, the WPC denounced "this provocative insinuation by a splinter organization which is known to be under strong influence of

Trotskyist elements." Defending its position, the WPC drew on Khrushchev's justification for Soviet test resumption. "The Soviet Union was forced to take steps to improve its own thermonuclear weapons in order to cool down certain hotheads who suggested putting an end to Russia with a single blow," the Soviet leader had argued. "The Soviet Union's strength in nuclear rockets is a decisive means of defending peace and . . . it has more than once already saved mankind from the world war which the imperialist circles of the West had been trying to unleash." Apparently convinced that this piece of Soviet propaganda effectively demolished its nonaligned critics, the Communist-led international forthrightly concluded that the WPC and its chair "fully and unreservedly endorse this statement."[51]

Yet despite the WPC's furious response to the birth of the ICDP and to other nonaligned ventures it had little alternative but to return to its courtship of independent groups. As Peggy Duff predicted in late January 1963, when the WPC campaign of defamation began, "the World Peace Council itself is in such a rocky position that it obviously cannot afford to ignore the Confederation." Furthermore, as followers of the Khrushchev line on world affairs, WPC leaders recognized that nonaligned disarmament sentiment represented a sector of public opinion with which it was necessary to remain on cordial terms. A secret meeting that year of Bernal and his pro-Soviet cohorts from Great Britain decided that the best way to handle the ICDP was to soften it up by securing the admission of friendly groups, changing its principles, and pressing for "unity."[52] Accordingly, during the ICDP's meeting at Tyringe the following year, the WPC's British affiliate, the British Peace Committee, applied to become an ICDP affiliate. And, in a public exchange, Bernal even claimed that the WPC "welcomed" the formation of the ICDP. But he still excoriated "nonalignment," a term he insisted meant "more or less the same as 'anti-communist.'"[53]

For its part, the nonaligned movement restored a measure of civility to its relations with the WPC, but henceforth steered clear of substantial participation in WPC ventures. After the bitter confrontation at Oxford in January 1963, Kenneth Lee, the ICDP president, renewed contact with the WPC and even attended its November 1963 conference as an observer. In turn, the ICDP admitted WPC observers to its Tyringe conference of January 1964 and engaged in informal meetings with them to find what it called "a basis for friendly cooperation and coexistence." Beyond the reestablishment of cordiality, however, very little of a specific nature followed. Arguing that the British Peace Committee was "not truly nonaligned," delegates at the ICDP conference rejected its application for membership. They also contended that its admission would weaken the ICDP and provide an undesirable precedent for merging the ICDP with the WPC.[54] The only concrete proposals for cooperation to come out of the gathering were to consider holding "a small conference on disengagement" to which members of the WPC would be invited and to consider cooperation on Easter marches—although "such cooperation must not harm the impact of demonstrations" and "the aim of each organization involved must be to bring pressure on its own government." In talks with the WPC, ICDP leaders emphasized that they preferred cooperation in which "both internationals kept their lines of demarcation clear."[55]

The Disintegration of the Movement in Japan

The conflict between nonaligned and pro-Communist activists also played itself out within nations. In Japan, Gensuikyo fell increasingly under Communist control during the late 1950s and early 1960s. At the 1959 World Conference, speaker after speaker denounced Western imperialism without saying a word about the Eastern variety. Furthermore, despite efforts by a small group of Western delegates and by the Japanese Socialist Party to modify the one-sided conference report, the final statement assailed Western nuclear policies but not Eastern. Similarly, the 1960 World Conference adopted an appeal contending that banning nuclear weapons could be accomplished only by a resolute struggle against world imperialism, "headed by the United States." Alienated by these developments, moderate elements, including the small Democratic Socialist Party and Zenro, a trade union federation, withdrew from Gensuikyo and, in November 1961, launched their own organization, Kakkin Kaigi (the National Council for Peace and Against Nuclear Weapons). Although the new group never developed a mass base, moderates like Kiyoshi Tanimoto did shift their allegiance to it. Moreover, their defection from Gensuikyo underscored the group's politicization.[56] Gensuikyo's slide toward Cold War alignment also disturbed nonaligned groups abroad, which stopped sending delegates or greetings to its conferences.[57]

Meanwhile, bitter factional fighting broke out within Gensuikyo. At the 1961 world conference, four major nonaligned groups—the Socialists, Sohyo (their trade union ally), the National Federation of Regional Women's Organizations, and the Japanese Council of Youth Organizations—waged a major struggle against Communist control of the organization. Nevertheless, the Communist forces successfully turned back this challenge, defending the existing leadership and putting the conference on record with yet another one-sided declaration on world affairs. They accomplished this by supplementing their solid base of Japanese Communist delegates with the votes of delegates from the WPC's foreign affiliates. "Had it not been for the support of the international delegates," Endicott confided to Bernal, Gensuikyo secretary Kaoru

Yasui "might have been unseated."[58] Even so, the situation remained volatile. At the end of the gathering, the four dissident groups released their own statement, denouncing "a section of the Gensuikyo leadership" for its autocratic methods, "political slogans," and extremist objectives, "based on a specific ideology."[59]

Ironically, one of the 1961 world conference's official resolutions quickly came back to haunt Gensuikyo's pro-Communist leaders. At the suggestion of the Soviet Peace Committee's Yuri Zhukov, the conference had voted that the first government to resume nuclear tests should "be denounced as the enemy of peace and of mankind." Naturally, then, when the Soviet Union resumed nuclear testing only two weeks later, an uproar engulfed Gensuikyo. The Communist Party quickly endorsed the Soviet action, declaring that "since the Soviet Union is a peace force, nuclear tests are a natural defensive measure." Nonaligned groups, on the other hand, demanded opposition to nuclear testing by any country. Sharply divided on the question, Gensuikyo issued a feeble statement of protest, asking the public "to examine seriously and coolly the gravity of the present situation which has forced the Soviet government to resort to this extraordinary measure." This hardly quieted the furor, and the next April, when Gensuikyo organized large rallies to protest U.S. test resumption, the Zengakuren disrupted them by chanting slogans against Soviet testing. The conflict came to a head at the August 1962 world conference, held in two separate cities. In Tokyo, nonaligned forces demanded a resolution condemning Soviet as well as U.S. nuclear tests. When this failed to pass, the Socialist and Sohyo delegates stormed out in protest. By contrast, at the conference in Hiroshima, the nonaligned forces prevailed, leading to a walkout by the Soviet, Chinese, and North Korean delegates. Meanwhile, the Zengakuren, expelled from Gensuikyo, picketed both meetings, and Kakkin Kaigi organized its own antinuclear conference.[60]

During the ensuing year, Gensuikyo disintegrated entirely. Paralyzed for a time by internal disagreements, the organization finally managed to issue a statement in February 1963, declaring its opposition to "*any* nuclear testing by *any* country." But the Communists repudiated this position, and attempts at compromise collapsed once again. Both Communists and Socialists prepared for a final showdown at that summer's world conference in Hiroshima. Shortly before the gathering convened, however, when it became apparent that the Communists had packed the meeting with thousands of additional delegates, the Socialists and Sohyo announced their withdrawal. Although this left the conference a largely Communist affair, it turned out to be the most tumultuous yet, for the gathering immediately divided over the recently signed atmospheric test ban treaty. Japanese Communists and other supporters of the Chinese position passionately denounced the treaty as a warmongering, imperialist measure. On the other hand, pro-Soviet delegates and the few remaining nonaligned activists vigorously defended it. To the consternation of observers, leftist youth groups battled, police violently attacked the Zengakuren, Chinese and Soviet delegates directed streams of invective against each other, and the Ninth World Conference descended into chaos.[61]

In the aftermath of the disastrous 1963 world conference, nonaligned groups moved toward establishing their own disarmament organization. In March 1964, they formed an interim group, which—powered largely by the Socialist Party and Sohyo—made plans for a world antinuclear convention during August of 1964 in Hiroshima and Nagasaki that would compete with Gensuikyo's. Announcing the conference, Ichiro Moritaki (chair of the Hiroshima Prefectural Council of A and H Bomb Victims' Organizations) and Kaoru Ohta (president of Sohyo) declared that a movement calling for banning the Bomb should not "approve the possession of nuclear weapons by particular countries." Furthermore, "all measures which are the stepping stones for the complete banning of nuclear weapons must be welcomed." In addition, the antinuclear campaign must be broad, "not a movement monopolized by a particular political party" for its own ends, and its internal operations must be "democratic." That August, with the support of additional groups, more than twenty thousand persons turned out for the nonaligned meeting in Hiroshima and another ten thousand for the gathering in Nagasaki.[62]

Building on this success, representatives from Japan's nonaligned peace groups voted in December to form a new organization, the Japan Congress Against Atomic and Hydrogen Bombs (Gensuikin), and formally launched it in February 1965. Along the way, they held a memorial service for the *Lucky Dragon* victims, attended by thousands, and issued a statement protesting Chinese nuclear weapons tests. In a declaration of basic principles, Gensuikin announced that it would not only seek "a complete ban on nuclear weapons" but oppose "the manufacture, stockpiling, testing, use, and dissemination of nuclear weapons by any country." Furthermore, it would "not side with any specific bloc"; instead, it would "establish broad contacts with peace movements of the world." Although Gensuikin failed to attract the support of Kakkin Kaigi, which chose to remain aloof, it nonetheless became Japan's largest nonaligned peace and disarmament organization.[63]

Meanwhile, Gensuikyo—reduced to a largely Communist constituency—grew ever more sectarian. At its 1964 world conference, the Japanese and Chinese Communists had matters well in hand, with speeches screened before delivery and delegates admitted on the basis of their pro-Peking views or barred on the basis of plans to attend rival meetings. Liu Ning-yi, head of the Chinese delegation, denounced the WPC for "taking an entirely erroneous line," condemned the test ban treaty as an "out-and-out fraud," and assailed the Soviet delegation for "double-dealing tactics." Outraged by its treatment, including the denial of its right to address the convention, the Soviet contingent led a walkout of foreign delegates, claiming that their participation had become "impossible." With Soviet bloc delegates safely out of the way, the conference settled down to issuing statements lauding the struggle against "imperialism," denouncing "schismatic meetings," and promising to "crush these intrigues."[64] When China conducted its first nuclear tests that October, Gensuikyo issued an elaborate rationalization. The following June, Gensuikyo promised that its forthcoming world conference would "rally the just anger of the people, and bring into focus the results of their struggles against the policy of aggression and nuclear war provocation by American imperialism." Although Gensuikin would be holding a rival conference, allegedly "to disrupt the movements for peace in Japan and throughout the world," Gensuikyo had "put forth the only correct policy in the movement against nuclear weapons."[65]

Assessing the results of the Communist Party's gradual takeover of Gensuikyo, most observers have concluded that it had disastrous effects on the Japanese struggle against the Bomb. Not only did it lead to the splintering of the world's largest nuclear disarmament campaign—which once seemed invincible within Japan—but, together with the later fragmentation of the movement, it discredited antinuclear activism among the masses of the Japanese people. To be sure, Gensuikyo and Gensuikin (though not Kakkin Kaigi) continued their activities. But the overall movement no longer attracted a broad cross section of the Japanese population. Instead, the two surviving organizations leaned heavily on their core constituencies for support. The Communists provided the muscle behind Gensuikyo, while the Socialists and Sohyo provided the major base for Gensuikin. Participation in the nuclear disarmament movement came to be regarded as partisan behavior, not as something for ordinary citizens. As Gensuikin admitted, the new campaign failed to build "a real movement backed by the masses from below." Consequently, although the Japanese antinuclear crusade continued, it lost much of its grassroots, popular flavor, as well as a substantial portion of its influence.[66]

Conflict in the United States

Tensions between nonaligned and aligned disarmament activists took a different form in the United States. Here the Communist Party was far weaker and, at least partly for this reason, nonaligned activists dominated the movement. America's last Communist-led peace group, the American Peace Crusade, expired in 1956. Even so, the issue surfaced in a controversy over the question of Communist participation in SANE. With no barriers to membership in this organization (or most others in American life), a noticeable number of Communists and Communist sympathizers joined SANE's local committees, particularly in the New York City area.[67] As a result, Norman Thomas wrote to Cousins on January 11, 1960, suggesting the establishment of "a better means to protect us against the interpenetration of Communists." He was particularly disturbed by the election of Henry Abrams, a veteran of Communist-oriented ventures, to SANE's Greater New York Committee. "Suppose we grant what isn't warranted by the Communists' past," declared Thomas, "namely, that they will work with us in complete good faith. Nevertheless, at a time when . . . it is necessary to insist on the possibility of patiently working with the Russian government and people," SANE would find its influence "undermined." If Communists became prominent in SANE, "the public would think us necessarily either a Communist front or completely deluded by American Communists." SANE had "to be able to speak from what is very clearly not a Communist position." Cousins responded that he was in complete agreement. "Our first concern is to win over the American people to the proposition that nuclear testing must be halted," he said. "Then there are all the specific measures involved in the building of a peace. These are highly volatile issues; and we have to be like Caesar's wife if we are to deal effectively with them."[68]

But how was SANE to handle this matter? After some discussion among SANE's leaders, Homer Jack warned that "this is obviously a divisive issue which could wreck SANE if we did nothing and could equally wreck SANE if we did the wrong thing." He suggested a national board statement saying that although SANE did not screen its members or leaders, it did not seek support from people who put allegiance to one nation above their allegiance to humanity. Thomas championed a statement reading: "In loyalty to its purpose," SANE "does not knowingly accept advocates or apologists of totalitarianism, fascist or communist. Nor does it invite to membership American citizens who apply differing standards of moral judgment: one to their own, another to a foreign land." Others, however, thought this approach mistaken. Stewart Meacham, one of SANE's Quaker leaders, argued that the best way to deal with the issue was to "be clear what we stand for and state it openly," "reject out of hand any approaches from the Communist Party," "state that we do not . . . accept members who are operating . . . under the discipline of any other organization," and "brand as smear efforts all general red-baiting attacks on SANE." With SANE's leaders bogged down for months discussing the issue, Thomas warned that the organization might "be heading for a most hurtful storm."[69]

He proved correct. On May 13, 1960, the U.S. Senate Internal Security

Subcommittee, headed by Senator Thomas Dodd, subpoenaed Abrams, then chief organizer of SANE's forthcoming rally at Madison Square Garden. Responding to questions by the subcommittee about his affiliations with Communist and Communist "front" organizations, Abrams invoked the Fifth Amendment. Cousins quickly met with Abrams and offered to defend him against the subcommittee investigation, but demanded some straight answers about his role, if any, in the Communist Party. When Abrams refused to discuss this, Cousins suspended him from his post in SANE and hurried to Washington to confer with Senator Dodd. A neighbor and friend of the senator's since their days together in the United World Federalists, Cousins assured him that SANE was not Communist controlled and had nothing to hide. Consequently, he convinced Dodd to postpone a public announcement of his subcommittee investigation until after SANE's rally on May 19. On May 25, though, in a well-publicized Senate address, Dodd called on SANE to "purge" its ranks "ruthlessly" of Communists. Although he had "no question" about the "integrity and good faith" of SANE's national leaders, Abrams was "a veteran member of the Communist party" and there was also "serious Communist infiltration at [the] chapter level." Much to the embarrassment of Cousins, Dodd claimed that he had "asked for the subcommittee's assistance in ridding" SANE "of whatever Communist infiltration does exist" and had "offered . . . to cooperate with it in every way."[70]

These events plunged SANE into the worst crisis in its history. Meeting on May 26, SANE's national board finally agreed on a statement of policy toward aligned activists: "Members of the Communist Party or individuals who are not free because of party discipline or political allegiance to apply to the misconduct of the Soviet or Chinese government the same standard by which they challenge others are barred from any voice in deciding the Committee's policies or programs." At the same time, the national board attacked the congressional investigation of SANE. "As a matter of democratic principle and practice," it declared, "we resent the intrusion of a congressional committee into the affairs of an organization which during its entire life has acted only in accordance with its declared principles." SANE was "entirely capable of carrying out its principles and guaranteeing that it will not permit their betrayal or subversion." Taking on the sensitive issue of collaboration with the Dodd committee, Cousins insisted: "SANE has turned over no names to Senator Dodd. It has received no names from Senator Dodd. We have made no commitments to Senator Dodd. No commitments have been made to us."[71]

Despite these assurances, for the rest of the year the situation remained tense and confusing. During the summer, SANE's national board agreed on the procedural steps it would take if persons committed to aligned positions remained as leaders in SANE local committees. These included inquiries about their views and activities and, if necessary, suspension. Nevertheless, when the Dodd subcommittee subpoenaed twenty-seven persons associated with Greater New York SANE, the national organization retained counsel to represent them and declared its belief that "congressional investigations of private organizations" lacked "a valid legislative purpose." SANE would not "be intimidated and will continue its policy of non-involvement with the Senate Internal Security Subcommittee . . . and similar investigatory bodies." On October 24, the national board established new criteria for SANE membership, declaring that persons who did not "apply to the actions of the Soviet Union or the Chinese government the same standards by which they challenge others are not welcome on any levels of this organization." That same day, it asked Greater New York SANE to surrender its charter, thus paving the way for a reorganization of the controversial region. After some resistance, the New York group complied, and the local chapters were required to apply for new charters—which included the new statement on membership standards—from the national organization.[72]

The SANE leadership's handling of these issues sparked a major controversy within the organization and the broader peace movement. Although only two of SANE's eighty-five national sponsors and board members resigned in protest, many members were disturbed by what they viewed as SANE's capitulation to McCarthyism. Resigning from the national board, Robert Gilmore declared that "SANE could have responded to Senator Dodd's attack with a ringing challenge to the cold war stratagem of discredit and divide, with a clear affirmation of the right of everyone to debate and dissent. . . . The fact that SANE turned down this opportunity is, to my mind, a great tragedy." By a unanimous vote, the representatives of six Long Island SANE committees declared that SANE's May 26 statement "is a setback for the cause of civil liberties" and "may lead to humiliating investigations and unfortunate personal conflicts within . . . SANE."[73] Some of the internal criticism came from the small group of Communists and the larger number of former Communists who had found a home in the organization. But much of it came from pacifists and others sensitive to violations of civil liberties, who believed that SANE's leadership had allowed congressional investigators to determine its internal procedures. Consequently, a substantial number of people withdrew from SANE in protest. They included its student section and half the chapters in the Greater New York region.[74]

In this context, Linus Pauling emerged as one of SANE's most outspoken critics. Shortly after Senator Dodd's public statement, Pauling had proposed that he become a co-chair of SANE, arguing that people upset by SANE's handling of the Abrams case would be mollified by this action. Although SANE's national board rejected this idea, it did invite Pauling to become a national sponsor of the organization. In this capacity, he objected strenuously to what he called "the McCarthy-like nature" of the implementation procedures adopted by the national board in July 1960. SANE, he insisted, had no right to question leaders or members about their beliefs. A sharp series of exchanges with Cousins ensued, followed by Pauling's resignation as a national sponsor that November.[75]

For a time, it seemed that Pauling and the other SANE dissidents might team up to establish a rival group on a "non-exclusionist" basis. In the aftermath of his resignation from SANE, Pauling began to urge the establishment of a new peace organization. "In the peace movement," he charged, "it has been not the Communists but the anti-Communists whose role has been destructive and demoralizing." At roughly the same time, former SANE chapters or breakaway groups from New York and Boston reorganized themselves on an independent basis. During the spring of 1961, they sponsored large meetings with Pauling as a featured speaker. Given the relative openness of these groups to the participation of Soviet sympathizers, some of the meetings had a pro-Soviet tone. Nevertheless, their challenge soon faded. Perhaps because he recognized the weakness and sectarianism of SANE's fledgling competitor, Pauling ultimately shied away from leading it.[76] Instead, he turned to what he called "another effort to save SANE." In a memo of June 15, 1961, to the sponsors and board of directors of SANE, Pauling again denounced its "McCarthyism" and called on it to drop its provisions for questioning leaders and members. He made no headway, though, for Cousins and other SANE leaders were determined to keep the organization on course. Meanwhile, SANE's non-exclusionist rival disintegrated.[77]

Complicating the issue of SANE's purported McCarthyism was the fact that it defended suspect individuals and their civil liberties. SANE not only offered free legal defense to those called up before the Dodd subcommittee, but worked to keep the hearings from developing in a way prejudicial to them. It also publicly and privately defended Abrams against the charge that he had attempted to have the Communist Party take over the Madison Square Garden rally. When the subcommittee subpoenaed Pauling and demanded that he produce the names of persons who had circulated his petition, SANE invited him to join its board of directors and sent a memo to all its locals, asking them to defend him. Declaring that the subcommittee's treatment of Pauling was "outrageous in its contempt for civil liberty and sinister in its implications for peace," SANE urged locals to get newspaper editors to oppose this action, to write letters to the press about it, and, if the subcommittee sought a contempt citation, to flood senators with protest letters.[78] In 1962, when the House Committee on Un-American Activities subpoenaed members of WSP, SANE denounced this move as well. "A Congressional investigation of any organization concerned with preserving the peace," declared SANE's national board, "represents an act of intimidation against the right of citizens to express their opinions on matters of human survival, and also threatens the exercise of the right of all non-governmental organizations to maintain an independent political position." Furthermore, SANE never used its new membership standards and procedures to purge anyone from its ranks.[79]

The reality was complex. SANE's leaders believed that a government body had no right to set standards for the membership or leadership of a private organization. But they also insisted that a private organization had the right and duty to set its own standards for leadership and membership. This was not a civil liberties issue, they pointed out, but a matter of organizational integrity. Responding to a protest against SANE's action, Norman Thomas suggested a "rough parallel" to workers choosing a team to represent them in collective bargaining with their bosses: "You would not knowingly have on your team of negotiators a man, however excellent he might temporarily seem, who was one of the bosses or was controlled by them." Or, as he wrote to another confidant, "I don't believe that a Communist belongs in a position of power in our Committee if it is to do the job we have in mind any more than a Roman Catholic belongs on the church board of a Methodist Church." SANE's leaders, in short, saw no contradiction between defending civil liberties and safeguarding the principles of a private organization.[80] And key figures, such as Thomas and Cousins, viewed Communists and other Soviet sympathizers as a genuine threat to SANE's principles.[81] Yet even if one granted that SANE's policies did not violate civil liberties and that the presence of Soviet sympathizers within a peace group constituted a problem, had SANE found the best solution to it?

American peace organizations differed on this point. Like SANE, other groups vehemently defended civil liberties. In 1960, the WILPF called for the abolition of the House Committee on Un-American Activities and expressed strong support for Pauling's refusal to divulge information to the Dodd subcommittee. A few years later, it filed an amicus curiae brief in defense of WSP leaders who refused to appear before congressional investigators. Similarly, the Student Peace Union (SPU) passed a strong resolution on civil liberties that called for the abolition of both the House Committee on Un-American Activities and the Senate Internal Security Subcommittee.[82] But these statements provided them with no guidance on how to deal with Soviet sympathizers. The United World Federalists had a membership policy barring Communists. Pacifist groups, by contrast, did not. Indeed, prominent pacifists criticized SANE when it adopted its new membership and leadership standards. Although pacifist organizations did not consider Communist groups a legitimate part of the peace movement and, therefore, did not join with them in sponsoring events, they felt that a clear definition of purpose was sufficient to discourage the participation of Communist sympathizers in their own activities.[83]

The largest student peace group, the SPU, adopted this position. At an SPU planning meeting in August 1960, delegates agreed that "the best way to meet the threat of possible Communist infiltration of the SPU is to discuss openly and frankly all issues as they develop, not being soft on either the U.S. or on the Soviet Union when either side transgresses what we believe to be the laws of international justice and progress toward a free and peaceful world." But "to go further than this organizationally would tend to immerse the SPU in the Cold War psychology which we are ostensibly fighting." A year later, confronting the issue of "unity in the student peace movement," the SPU national council decided that "specific examination and criticisms of the foreign policy of both the U.S. and the Soviet Union, applying the same standards for judgment in each case," were "of prime importance." Furthermore, "the struggle for peace is directly related to the struggle for a free society in which there is individual human dignity." The SPU "could not support or participate in any program of unity not consistent with these principles."[84]

Among the major U.S. peace organizations, only Women Strike for Peace was thoroughly "non-exclusionist." Indeed, its founding reflected, in part, the belief of some of its early leaders that SANE's national board had capitulated to McCarthyism. From an early date, then, WSP leaders decided to have no formal requirements for membership or even membership lists. All women willing to work "for peace" were welcome. During the investigation of WSP by the House Committee on Un-American Activities in December 1962, Dagmar Wilson astonished observers by declaring that she had no objection to Communists or anyone else working in WSP. Asked if she would "knowingly permit or welcome Nazis or Fascists," Wilson responded: "If we could only get them on our side." This approach—combined with the image WSP projected of well-meaning mothers and housewives—successfully disarmed the congressional investigators. But it did not entirely resolve the issue, for Communist sympathizers did join WSP's ranks and advance pro-Soviet positions. Even so, although WSP occasionally showed some naïveté about Communist-led groups and governments, Communist sympathizers never dominated the organization or set its overall tone. WSP remained true to its purpose, assailing all nuclear weapons and all nuclear tests.[85]

WSP's open door policy, however, remained exceptional. Surveying the American peace movement in 1963, Communist Party leader Arnold Johnson lauded WSP for its "all-inclusive character," but damned other groups for going along with "anti-Communist slanders" and "keeping Communists out of the peace movement." Contemptuously dismissing "the Jackasses" in SANE, Pauling sniped repeatedly at that organization and even convinced Bertrand Russell to sever his ties with it.[86] Actually, SANE's leaders continued to defend American peace groups against charges of Communist domination and, together with leaders of other peace organizations, worked out an exchange of visits with officials of the Soviet Peace Committee.[87] But the standoffishness of SANE and most other peace groups toward pro-Communist elements in the United States remained clear. In January 1964, the *National Guardian* publicly assailed the leadership of the American peace movement for having "emasculated" its cause through a "policy of exclusion." Responding with a stinging letter published the following month, Jack said the movement could well afford to dispense with Soviet apologists. This launched a new round of attacks on Jack and SANE by Pauling and other advocates of non-exclusion.[88] Privately, Dr. Spock, SANE's new co-chair, told Jack that he agreed with him but felt that public wrangles of this nature should be avoided. For the most part, they were, although the issue refused to die.[89]

Tensions Elsewhere

In Britain, where the Communist Party retained a more powerful presence than in the United States, the issue of relations between nonaligned and aligned activists took yet another form. In the spring of 1959, as CND continued its spectacular growth, the Communist-led British Peace Committee made some overtures to it, suggesting sending delegates to CND's coordinating body and requesting CND's support for its own "March for Life Against Nuclear Death." CND, however, rejected these proposals.[90] When, beginning that summer, major unions adopted unilateralist positions and the Labour Party started shifting in this direction, the Communist Party began to reassess its earlier opposition to CND. Finally, in May 1960, the party called on its members to join the group. As no formal barriers existed to their participation, Communists now turned up in the CND youth organization, in some local branches, and—bearing party banners—on CND marches. But, although a few Communists rose to leadership posts in CND—including Bernal, one of thirty-three people elected to CND's national council in 1961—they did not dominate it. This failure, despite repeated efforts by Bernal and other Communists to influence CND policy, reflected the high level of activity in the organization by nonaligned activists, as well as the tardiness of party members in joining the unilateralist campaign. In addition, Communist influence remained minimal, thanks to the party's staunch identification with the Soviet Union, including its nuclear weapons policy, and to the party's continued ambivalence toward CND, which seemed as likely to subvert Communists as vice versa.[91]

Relations between the direct action wing of the movement and the Communists were even worse. The Direct Action Committee "was *very* cautious about any linkage with the British Peace Committee or association with Communists for both ideological and tactical reasons," April Carter recalled. In 1958, during planning for the first Aldermaston march, members of the DAC deliberately maneuvered two Communist volunteers out of leading positions. A bit later, when a group of musicians was engaged to serve as an advance party in towns ahead of the Aldermaston march, DAC leaders grew dismayed by what they considered the pro-Soviet bias of the performers. Consequently, they selected the songs to be sung, changed some of the lyrics, and accompanied them to the events—much to the disgust of the musicians. "Perhaps we were too heavy-handed," Michael Randle remarked years later. "Nevertheless, it was crucial to establish the independent stance of the march." Given its strongly nonaligned and anarchist orientation, the Committee of 100 also looked with suspicion on the British Peace Committee and other Communist-controlled bodies. And they, in turn, had little use for the Committee of 100, especially after its antinuclear demonstration and leafleting in Moscow during the summer of 1962.[92]

In some countries, Communist-nonaligned relations were somewhat better, usually thanks to special circumstances. In Italy, where the Communist Party was probably the most liberal, independent, and popular in the world, nonaligned leaders accepted its participation (but not its dominance) in the movement.[93] A similar situation developed briefly in the Netherlands, where the Communist Party became so liberal that it broke with the Soviet Union. Therefore, when the Communist-led Peace Council offered to support the 1964 Easter march, the nonaligned Committee for Peace agreed, albeit reluctantly, and, for the first time, a clearly delineated group of Communists joined other Dutch marchers.[94] In France, the Communist Party showed fewer signs of straying from Marxist-Leninist verities, but did play a substantial role in national politics. As a result, the nonaligned movement, though guarding its autonomy, jointly demonstrated with the Communists against de Gaulle's *force de frappe*.[95] In Finland, where the government set the tone for good relations with the Soviet Union, nonaligned peace groups cooperated at times with the Communist-led Peace Committees, although they maintained their independence. Finally, in Yugoslavia, a country where official policy was deliberately balanced between East and West, the Yugoslav League for Peace became the only peace group in the world to belong to both the WPC and the ICDP.[96]

In most countries, however, relations were considerably more strained.

Alienated by efforts at the 1959 Australian Peace Congress to "whitewash every act of Russia," Marc Oliphant condemned the meeting as "a waste of time." In New Zealand, too, the CND group was quite critical of the Communist-led Peace Council, refusing to circulate a petition against the proliferation of nuclear weapons when it learned that the Peace Council had taken the lead. Reporting to the 1965 annual conference of New Zealand CND, Mary Woodward underscored the organization's "consistently non-aligned approach."[97] In Canada, where the Communist-led Canadian Peace Congress had lost most of its influence, Communist activists joined and occasionally attempted to manipulate nonaligned groups, much to the disgust of some of their leaders. Complaining about the activities of the McGill chapter of Combined Universities CND, from which Communists had effectively excluded non-Communists, Dimitri Roussopoulos wondered "what disciplinary action" the CUCND leadership could take "when one CUCND chapter threatens to discredit the whole campaign."[98]

One of the nastier confrontations occurred in West Germany. Although the government had banned the German Communist Party in 1956, its activists regrouped in the Standing Congress of All Opponents of the Nuclearization of the Federal Republic, headed by Renate Riemeck, Ulrike Meinhof, and Klaus Rainer Röhl (editor of *konkret*, a student journal financed by the East German government). Anxious to take control of the nonaligned movement, they turned out in force for a student antinuclear congress, held in January 1959 in West Berlin. Here, to their delight, they dominated the gathering and pushed through a resolution reiterating the foreign policy demands of the East German and Soviet governments. The Social Democrats, religious leaders, and others associated with the dwindling Struggle Against Atomic Death were horrified. Meanwhile, the press published stories assailing the meeting and the entire antinuclear movement. Nonaligned elements called on the Communists to withdraw the controversial Berlin resolution and on local student committees to reject cooperation with "unmistakably anti-democratic forces." When the Communists refused to retreat from their hard-line stance, the Social Democrats and other nonaligned activists withdrew from the movement in disgust. Thereafter, it had little support, except from East German youth and West German Communists. Recognizing that they now controlled a hollow shell, the Communists discarded it and moved on to champion the German Peace Union, a Communist-led political party.[99]

This bitter experience helped convince nonaligned activists of the need to limit the Communist role in antinuclear activities. In 1960, when Hans-Konrad Tempel and other pacifists formed the Easter march movement, they decided that to avoid giving Communists the opportunity to exploit it and others the impression that Communists dominated it, they would emphasize that "only individuals are taking part, not organizations." After the first march, the organizers established a central committee to handle future activities. This committee had the sole power to decide what slogans, banners, and sponsors would be included. It banned Communists from prominent positions in the movement, although it allowed them to participate in events as individuals and saw to it that the Easter march movement issued balanced appeals for nuclear disarmament. Even so, leaders of the East German government embarrassed the movement by making pronouncements suggesting that it represented their policies. At one point, the allegedly friendly government to the east even promised its support to the Easter marches. In turn, the movement leadership publicly declined the offer and recommended that East German authorities put their own house in order. Although the Easter march movement gradually evolved over the course of the 1960s into a more radical opposition force, it stayed vigorously nonaligned and free of Communist control.[100]

The Impossible Dream

Thus, despite some modest efforts at cooperation between nonaligned and aligned nuclear disarmament groups, they remained divided on the international and national levels. To some degree, this resulted from their attempts to avoid the obvious political difficulties that accompanied any close association, much less "unity." More fundamentally, however, it reflected basic differences in approach. At some points, their policies toward nuclear issues coincided— as, for example, when pro-Soviet and nonaligned groups rallied behind the atmospheric test ban treaty. But this remained a temporary, albeit confusing, phenomenon. Beneath this superficial harmony of interests yawned a chasm of differences. With one movement committed to ensuring the survival of humanity and the other to advancing the interests of Communist states, cooperation remained difficult and "unity" quite impossible.

The U.S. Atomic Energy Commission explodes an H-Bomb in the Pacific, April 1954.
Photo courtesy U.S. National Archives and Council for a Livable World.

A group of Hiroshima Maidens, after surgery in the United States, in the mid-1950s. Photo courtesy Hiroshima/Nagasaki Memorial Collection archives, Wilmington College (Ohio) Peace Resource Center.

Norman Cousins (left) and Albert Schweitzer (right) at their momentous meeting in Lambaréné, Gabon, January 1957. Photo courtesy Eleanor Cousins.

Bertrand Russell (left) and Joseph Rotblat (right), at Russell's ninetieth birthday party, 1962. Photo courtesy Pugwash Conferences on Science and World Affairs.

J.D. Bernal addresses a meeting of the World Peace Council in Berlin, July 1952, before becoming its president. Photo courtesy Bundesarchiv, Koblenz.

Top: Sheila Jones, a leader of Britain's National Council for Abolition of Nuclear Weapon Tests and, later, of CND, 1955–56. Photo courtesy Sheila Jones.

Bottom: The crew of the *Golden Rule*, in a Honolulu jail, summer 1958. Captain Albert Bigelow is fourth from left. Photo by Warren Roll, courtesy Fellowship of Reconciliation Archives.

Heinz Kloppenburg (left) and Martin Niemöller (right) at an Atomic Memorial Watch in Cologne, West Germany, August 6, 1958. Photo courtesy Bundesarchiv, Koblenz.

Top: Andrei Sakharov (left) and Igor Kurchatov (right), at the Institute of Atomic Energy, Moscow, discuss continuing the Soviet moratorium on nuclear testing, autumn 1958. Photo by D. S. Pezeverzev, courtesy Kurchatov Memorial House Museum Archive, Kurchatov Institute.

Bottom: Top U.S. policymakers converse about nuclear issues, January 1956. Left to right: George Humphrey, Dwight Eisenhower, John Foster Dulles, Dillon Anderson, Lewis Strauss, and Charles E. Wilson. Photo by National Park Service, courtesy Dwight D. Eisenhower Library.

Top: Kwame Nkrumah, Ghana's prime minister, is greeted by Eisenhower on a visit to the United States, July 1958. Photo by National Park Service, courtesy Dwight D. Eisenhower Library.

Left: Soviet premier Nikita Khrushchev, on one of his better days, September 1959. Photo by U.S. Navy, courtesy Dwight D. Eisenhower Library.

Top, opposite: Canon Collins addresses Aldermaston marchers in Trafalgar Square, London, spring 1959. Photo courtesy Bundesarchiv, Koblenz.

Bottom, opposite: The Reverend Michael Scott, speaking with Ghanaians, in preparation for the Sahara protest, fall 1959. Photo by Michael Randle, courtesy Michael Randle.

This page: Young CND activists on Britain's Aldermaston march, spring 1960. Photo courtesy CND archives.

Top: Linus Pauling leads a Walk for Disarmament, in Los Angeles, July 9, 1960. Photo courtesy Swarthmore College Peace Collection and Women Strike for Peace.

Bottom: A Hiroshima Day march, with Elsie Locke in the lead, in Christchurch, New Zealand, August 6, 1960. Photo courtesy Elsie Locke.

Top: Quakers confront the Pentagon, November 13, 1960. Photo courtesy Theodore Hetzel Collection, Swarthmore College Peace Collection.

Left: The antinuclear march from Perugia to Assisi, Italy, September 1961. Photo courtesy Commonweal Collection, University of Bradford.

Opposite: Earle and Barbara Reynolds on board the *Phoenix* in Japan, preparing to depart on a protest mission to the Soviet Union, October 1961. Photo courtesy Fellowship of Reconciliation Archives.

This page: The San Francisco to Moscow Walk for Peace enters Moscow, October 1961. Photo courtesy Swarthmore College Peace Collection and War Resisters League.

Top: Moscow residents reach eagerly for antinuclear leaflets distributed by the peace walkers, October 1961. Photo courtesy War Resisters League.

Bottom: An antinuclear demonstration organized by Combined Universities CND, with the cooperation of the Voice of Women, Ottawa, Canada, 1961 or 1962. Photo courtesy Kay Macpherson.

In a follow-up to the Sahara protest, Julius Nyerere (left), prime minister of Tanganyika (now Tanzania), talks with Bayard Rustin (right) of the War Resisters League, 1962. Photo courtesy War Resisters League.

Right: Peggy Duff, British CND secretary, on the Aldermaston march, spring 1962. Photo courtesy CND archives.

Bottom: The photo from SANE's famous "Dr. Spock Is Worried" ad, April 1962. Photo courtesy Swarthmore College Peace Collection and Peace Action.

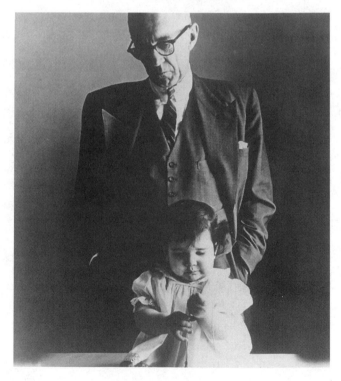

Top: Delegates to the international congress of WILPF, Asilomar, California, under surveillance by the FBI, July 1962. Photo courtesy Swarthmore College Peace Collection and Women's International League for Peace and Freedom.

Bottom: The meeting of the WPC's World Congress for General Disarmament and Peace, in Moscow, July 1962. Photo courtesy Bundesarchiv, Koblenz.

This page: The *Everyman III* and its multinational crew in Stockholm, before departing on the protest mission to Leningrad, October 1962. The banner reads: STOP NUCLEAR TESTS IN EAST AND WEST. Photo by Olle Wester, courtesy *Expressen*.

Opposite: Michael Randle, secretary of the Committee of 100, leaves Wormwood Scrubbs prison after serving twelve months for planning demonstrations at U.S. military bases, February 1963. Photo by John Hopkins, courtesy Michael Randle.

Top: An antinuclear demonstration by Action Civique Non-Violente in Lyons, France, March 31, 1963. Photo courtesy Commonweal Collection, University of Bradford.

Right: Shielded by his parliamentary immunity and bearing a banner saying GREECE, Grigoris Lambrakis makes his one-man antinuclear march from Marathon to Athens, April 1963. Shortly thereafter he was assassinated. Photo courtesy Commonweal Collection, University of Bradford.

Opposite: In the freer political climate of 1964, Greek antinuclear demonstrators—many bearing antinuclear banners and pictures of Grigoris Lambrakis—surge into Athens. Photo courtesy Commonweal Collection, University of Bradford.

Top, opposite: Dagmar Wilson, founder of Women Strike for Peace, and Kaoru Yasui, secretary of Gensuikyo, in the United States, 1963. Photo courtesy Swarthmore College Peace Collection and Women Strike for Peace.

Bottom, opposite: Pacifist leader Λ.J. Muste at a sit-in outside the Atomic Energy Commission office in New York City, August 6, 1963. He is flanked on the left by Miriam Levine (his secretary) and on the right by Judith Malina (codirector of the Living Theater). Photo courtesy War Resisters League.

This page: Women Strike for Peace demonstrators denounce the House Un-American Activities Committee, Los Angeles, 1964. Photo courtesy Swarthmore College Peace Collection and Women Strike for Peace.

New Zealand's Youth CND, "On the Beach," Tahunanui, Nelson, New Zealand, 1965.
Photo courtesy Hugh Young and Elsie Locke.

Norman Thomas, at a SANE rally against the Vietnam War, Madison Square Garden, New York City, in 1965. Photo by Diana Davies, courtesy Swarthmore College Peace Collection and Diana Davies.

Top: U.S. President John F. Kennedy with British Prime Minister Harold Macmillan, in April 1961. Photo courtesy John F. Kennedy Library.

Right: Jawaharlal Nehru, India's prime minister, visits the United States, November 1961. Photo courtesy John F. Kennedy Library.

Adlai Stevenson, U.S. Ambassador to the United Nations, at the White House in the early 1960s. Photo courtesy John F. Kennedy Library.

Kennedy and his aides share a smile with members of the Citizens Committee for a Nuclear Test Ban, August 1963. But the happiest man on the scene is clearly Norman Cousins (center). Photo courtesy Eleanor Cousins.

The honeymoon continues: SANE's Homer Jack receives a pen from U.S. President Lyndon Johnson at the signing of extension legislation for the Arms Control and Disarmament Agency, May 1965. Behind them, starting at the central pillar, are (left to right) Glenn Seaborg, J. W. Fulbright, Hubert Humphrey, Adrian Fisher, and William C. Foster. Photo courtesy Homer Jack Collection, Swarthmore College Peace Collection.

For a time, the demonstrations continue: an Easter march in Hesse, West Germany, in 1967, with banners reading SECURITY FOR ALL: DISARMAMENT! and POPE PAUL VI: NO MORE WAR! Photo courtesy Bundesarchiv, Koblenz.

Policymakers and Protest

Governments Confront the Movement, 1959–70

> Dear Lord Russell. . . . May I express my appreciation and admiration of the way you have led the struggle? . . . My old days, when I used to participate in civil disobedience . . . , came up before me, and I felt the same urge again.
>
> Jawaharlal Nehru, 1961

During the late 1950s and early 1960s, as protest against nuclear weapons burgeoned into an international movement with mass participation, high visibility, and increasing political clout, governments adapted to this phenomenon in varying ways. As before, their reaction usually reflected the degree to which nuclear disarmament activism seemed likely to advance or retard their national security objectives. If critical of the nuclear arms race, they tended to welcome, even to encourage, the popular movement against the Bomb. If committed to a national security policy based on the possession of nuclear weapons, they tended to regard the movement with suspicion and hostility. Nevertheless, although this paradigm explains a good deal about the official response to the nuclear disarmament campaign, it does not explain it all. In fact, numerous governments uninterested in nuclear disarmament cultivated the movement for reasons of expediency. Some believed that selective encouragement would help modify the arms control and disarmament policies of their enemies. Others hoped that it would still the popular clamor at home. For these reasons, even when governments found the prospect of nuclear disarmament no more appealing than in the past, they were sometimes more sophisticated in responding to the popular campaign that demanded it.

Favorable Attitudes Among Nonaligned Nations

Given their confluence of interests, antinuclear activists generally enjoyed a very cordial relationship with leaders of nonaligned and neutral countries.

Julius Nyerere of Tanzania, Jawaharlal Nehru of India, Mohammed Ayub Khan of Pakistan, Josip Broz Tito of Yugoslavia, and Kwame Nkrumah of Ghana were among the many leaders of nonaligned nations who sent messages of greeting to conferences of nuclear disarmament organizations. Attending the December 1960 meeting of the WRI, the Irish delegate reported that Ireland's antinuclear movement was "in the happy position of having the approval and encouragement" of his nation's foreign minister. In 1963, Finland's president, Urho Kekkonen, was the first signatory of a nuclear disarmament appeal circulated in his country in conjunction with a series of antinuclear marches and demonstrations.[1] Writing from Cambodia the following year, Prince Norodom Sihanouk applauded Russell's "courageous efforts to alert the peoples of the world to the mortal danger to mankind's future" and assured him of "Cambodia's wholehearted support." Similarly, Pakistan's President Khan lavished praise on the nuclear disarmament campaign and became a sponsor of the Bertrand Russell Peace Foundation. In April 1962, when Russell issued an appeal against the resumption of nuclear tests, Tito assured him that he shared his indignation and had transmitted the appeal to all members of the United Nations and to participants in the Geneva disarmament conference.[2]

Nkrumah proved particularly cooperative. The Sahara Project of 1960, based in Ghana, owed a good deal to his government's political support and unofficial financial backing. In addition, his calling of the special pan-African conference later that year to coordinate opposition to further French nuclear tests reflected his decision to carry forward the nuclear disarmament movement's goals in this broader arena. Similarly, in 1962, when Nkrumah promoted the Accra conference, "The World Without the Bomb"—providing it with the site, funding, and publicity—he acted in response to suggestions from the European Federation Against Nuclear Arms, with much of the organizing work done by the British and Ghanaian CNDs. Thereafter, efforts to set up a nonviolence training center and to provide the Accra Assembly with a permanent secretariat drew Nkrumah's backing—although, as activists soon realized, this also raised the specter of government control.[3] Meanwhile, Nkrumah formed a close relationship with Russell, encouraging him to continue mobilizing "the pressure of public opinion" behind "the imperative need to reach a settlement both on testing and disarmament." Furthermore, in response to an initiative by Russell, Nkrumah privately appealed to Gamal Abdel Nasser of Egypt to find a way "to end this frightfully dangerous arms race between Israel and Egypt which could easily lead to disaster." The nations of the Middle East, he insisted, should not "risk the certain danger of nuclear war where none is victor."[4]

Antinuclear activists also maintained excellent relations with the Indian government. Indeed, Nehru accorded an extraordinary degree of respect to nuclear disarmament leaders like Russell, with whom he engaged in a very friendly and extensive correspondence. In September 1961, shortly after the Committee of 100 began its controversial civil disobedience campaign in Great Britain, Nehru used the occasion of a press conference to express his admiration for Russell and to say that he envied the nuclear disarmament leader. The following month, noting that he would be stopping briefly in London on the way to the United States, the Indian prime minister made arrangements for a private meeting with the British philosopher. Indeed, Nehru even reported to the Indian parliament on his talks with Russell's aides, and his successor, Lal Bahadur Shastri, made a special journey to Wales to discuss foreign policy issues with the philosopher.[5] In 1962, when the Gandhi Peace Foundation convened its Anti-Nuclear Arms Convention in New Delhi, it was attended by India's prime minister, president, and vice president and by other leading Indian government officials. Addressing the concluding session of the convention, Nehru spoke of his own commitment to nonviolence. Although he rejected the call for India's unilateral disarmament, "this was said regretfully," noted an observer, "without bitterness or annoyance."[6]

The close relationship between nonaligned countries and peace organizations was also evident at the September 1961 Belgrade Conference of nonaligned nations. Accorded a privileged status at the conclave, antinuclear groups from Britain, France, Israel, Italy, the Netherlands, the United States, and other countries sent representatives. Homer Jack, representing SANE—the only nongovernmental organization from North America granted official observer status—recalled that he had "unusual access to the conference plenary sessions and heads of state themselves." He had interviews with Nehru, Nkrumah, and Sukarno, as well as briefer talks with the political leaders of Algeria, Cyprus, Burma, and Guinea. SANE also sent an official message of greetings to the gathering which was publicized in the Yugoslav press and issued as a conference document. When, only hours before the conference opened, the Soviet Union announced its resumption of nuclear tests, the press services in Belgrade immediately asked for Jack's reaction. Working with Michael Scott, who represented Britain's Committee of 100, he produced a sharp condemnation of Soviet testing. They also urged the Belgrade conference to request an emergency session of the U.N. General Assembly to demand that the Soviet Union and France adhere to the test moratorium. Although the conference did not issue as strong a critique of nuclear testing as they desired, it did call for "a special session of the General Assembly" focused on disarmament or the convening of a special U.N. disarmament conference.[7]

This general harmony of interests did not mean agreement on all tactics or issues. In the spring of 1962, when Russell proposed that nonaligned nations send protest vessels into the U.S. nuclear testing zone in the Pacific, both Nehru and Tito rejected the idea. Nehru explained to Russell that although he and his colleagues did not object "in any way" to "a privately organized venture," they did not feel it proper to "take governmental action in this matter."[8] That same year, Nehru also rejected a critique by Cousins of India's takeover of Goa and by Russell of India's behavior in its violent border clash with China. Responding to Russell's warning about a nuclear arms race in the Middle East, Lebanon's prime minister, Rashid Karamé, stated tartly that this ignored the "fundamental bases of the problem": "the establishment of Israel" and the expulsion of the Palestinians. Nevertheless, more often than not, the leaders of nonaligned nuclear disarmament groups and nonaligned states stood on the same side of the issues. In 1963, Nehru wrote, encouragingly, in the Canadian student magazine, *Our Generation Against Nuclear War*, of his conviction that "the ever-widening circle of protests that the people make is not wasted" and had "some effect even on the hardened people who control the destinies of different nations." Living "on the brink" of catastrophe, the people of the world must "carry on a crusade against nuclear war."[9]

Mixed Reactions in Soviet Bloc Countries

The Soviet Union's Warsaw Pact partners also praised nuclear disarmament activism, but in a highly selective fashion. Thanking Russell for sending him a copy of his new book, *Common Sense and Nuclear Warfare*, Poland's premier, Wladyslaw Gomulka, professed himself "at one with your opinion that finding the ways of averting the danger of war should be at present the most important task of all governments and peace-loving people." Similarly, Czechoslovakia's president, Antonin Novotny, sent his "cordial greetings" to the September 1962 Pugwash conference and expressed his confidence that it would "exert every effort to find a common road of scientists towards averting nuclear war."[10] On the other hand, the same East German authorities who fulsomely praised the West German Easter marchers strongly objected to comparable activities on their own territory. Responding to proposals from the San Francisco to Moscow peace marchers to parade through East Germany, the official Peace Council declared it would "not support any protest demonstrations in our country, for we do not see . . . what the Americans want to protest here." Although the East German government later relented and admitted the pacifist marchers, it continued to raise difficulties over their leaflets, slogans, and march route. Ultimately, it seized and deported them.[11]

This policy was in line with the regime's contention that although the armed forces of its enemies represented militarism and war, its armed forces and those of other Soviet bloc states served peace. As the Peace Council told proponents of the San Francisco to Moscow march: "We should not understand if the policy of our Government were to be put on the same level with that of the West German Government." The West German soldier "stands under the command of generals who are incorrigible war criminals, and is the myrmidon of an anti-national policy of world-wide nuclear war," noted a government booklet. By contrast, military service in East Germany "is the honorable duty of every citizen." Or, as another government pamphlet put it: "A gun is a good thing if it serves a good cause."[12]

This attitude, typical on both sides of the Cold War, often resulted in startlingly similar policies. In mid-August 1961, a group of activists from the Danish Campaign Against Nuclear Weapons traveled to Berlin to see if they could arrange to hold a nuclear disarmament demonstration in that divided city, then the focal point of international tensions. Approaching the East Berlin police, they outlined their plan to walk to the dividing line of the city from its two sectors, carrying posters and wearing shirts reading: "Negotiation: No Atom War." The Eastern police told them that since everyone in East Berlin agreed with these sentiments, a demonstration was unnecessary. Furthermore, it would be misunderstood in the West. This rebuff by the police, including their authoritarian style, reminded the Danes, as one stated, "in a very unpleasant way of the Nazi Gestapo." The West Berlin police also refused permission for the demonstration, arguing that "negotiation" was an unpopular word in West Berlin, that the populace might attack the demonstrators, and that they would not protect them. By this point, it was late in the day and, rather disgusted by the response of officials in East and West, the activists decided to return to Denmark without holding the demonstration. Before leaving, however, they distributed twenty thousand antinuclear leaflets, half in each sector of the city.[13]

Despite their professed desire for disarmament, Soviet officials also sought to keep domestic opinion from straying too far in this direction. Writing in *Pravda* in June 1963, General A. A. Yepishev argued that "authors must, whatever the circumstances, consider . . . the need for our people to defend their freedom and independence with arms in hand." The following February, before a large gathering of writers and artists, he denounced the "harmful note of pacifism" that had crept into Soviet books, films, and paintings. Following up, the president of the Soviet Academy of Arts expressed his alarm over the inattention to military-patriotic themes in the representational arts. At the same meeting, the Soviet defense minister, Marshal Rodion Malinovsky, warned of "incorrect tendencies" in literature and film, adding that "we have no right mechanically to transfer [Erich Maria] Remarque's ideas into our creative work and rob it of . . . true heroism." The government-controlled mass media created fewer problems along these lines. When the Soviet Union exploded its mammoth fifty-megaton H-Bomb on October 30, 1961, inspiring protests around the world, the Soviet press and radio withheld news of the event. As a further precaution against an adverse domestic reaction, the government jammed foreign radio broadcasts. Asked, in July 1962, why the Soviet government made no announcements within the country of its nuclear tests, Deputy Foreign Minister Valerian Zorin replied: "We do not wish to make our people nervous."[14]

Not surprisingly, the Soviet government raised significant barriers to domestic critics of its military programs. Pamphlets that advocated nonviolence were occasionally confiscated, and Soviet pacifists were barred from attending international conferences. Until 1965, Kremlin leaders deliberately prevented Peter Kapitza from traveling abroad to receive awards or to attend the Pugwash conferences. According to Khrushchev, Kapitza's refusal to work on Soviet nuclear weapons upset him greatly and triggered doubts about the physicist's loyalty. "How could a Soviet citizen say such a thing?" he wondered. In his memoirs, Khrushchev contended that the restrictions on Kapitza's right to travel had another basis. The leadership, he said, had "decided to wait a while before sending Kapitza abroad. We still hadn't accumulated enough atomic weapons. Therefore, it was essential that we keep secret from our enemies any and all information which might tip them off about how little we had." This explanation has some plausibility. Even so, it is noteworthy that Khrushchev followed it with two additional attacks on Kapitza for "refusing to work on military problems."[15]

Khrushchev's attitude toward nuclear critics was clear enough in his response to Andrei Sakharov's efforts to limit nuclear testing. In July 1961, when the Soviet physicist told a gathering of top political and scientific leaders that he opposed the decision to resume Soviet tests that fall, the action infuriated the Soviet premier. Turning red in the face and raising his voice, Khrushchev lectured this audience for half an hour or more on Sakharov's perfidy. As Sakharov recalled the tirade, Khrushchev declared:

He's moved beyond science into politics. Here he's poking his nose where it doesn't belong. . . . Leave politics to us—we're the specialists. You make your bombs and test them, and we won't interfere with you. . . . But remember, we have to conduct our policies from a position of strength. . . . That's how it is! There can't be any other policy. Our opponents don't understand any other language. . . . I'd be a jellyfish and not Chairman of the Council of Ministers if I listened to people like Sakharov!

In his memoirs, Khrushchev also recalled the incident, remarking that the scientist in Sakharov "saw his patriotic duty and performed it well, while the pacifist in him made him hesitate." The Soviet leader added: "I have nothing against pacifists—or at least I *won't* have anything against them if and when we create conditions which make war impossible. But as long as we live in a world in which we have to keep both eyes open lest the imperialists gobble us up, then pacifism is a dangerous experiment." From that point on, recalled Khrushchev, "I was somewhat on my guard with him."[16]

Although Khrushchev never departed from his view that Sakharov had failed to understand the problems of modern statecraft, he continued to show a curious respect for him. Indeed, the Soviet leader left Sakharov undisturbed in his high-status position and, as his son recalled, "often talked about him and regarded him with . . . a certain reverence." Later that year, when Khrushchev received the names of persons slated to receive important medals, he had only one question: "Is Sakharov on the list to be designated Hero of Socialist Labor?" The physicist was not, it turned out, for, among other things, he had opposed conducting nuclear tests. "This is outrageous," Khrushchev stormed. "Let there be differences of opinion. . . . It's a good thing that we can disagree, express different opinions, and debate the issues. . . . You have to talk with people like Sakharov, persuade them. There's a lot they don't understand; they live in their own world, far from the ups and downs of politics and interstate relations—where there's more dirt than there should be." Sakharov's views were "naive, but they're interesting. They come from the heart, from his wish for everyone's happiness. We have to listen to him." Accordingly, Sakharov was named a Hero of Socialist Labor for the third time.[17]

Khrushchev's successors proved less tolerant. Placing tighter controls on intellectuals, they embarked on a campaign to dampen dissent. One top nuclear official told a party conference in March 1967: "Sakharov is a good scientist. . . . But as a politician he's muddleheaded, and we'll be taking measures." A turning point came the following year, after Sakharov's controversial essay *Progress, Coexistence, and Intellectual Freedom* was published in the West. Soviet officials pressed Sakharov to disavow the work, but he refused. Consequently, that August, the authorities stripped the physicist of his security clearance and barred him from further work on Soviet weapons projects. Departing from his high-level defense post in disgrace, Sakharov obtained more humble employment at the Lebedev Institute of Physics, at a substantially lower salary. Given his immense scientific repute and his Hero of Socialist Labor awards, Soviet officials apparently did not feel able or willing to take more drastic action against him. Moreover, they may have assumed that he would mend his ways.[18]

Much of the irresolution in Soviet policy reflected the government's growing concern about public opinion. Inside the Soviet Union, the days of Stalinist terror had clearly ended, while elsewhere even Communists no longer took Soviet pronouncements at face value. With criticism of Soviet policy coming from Chinese leaders, from Western officials, and from independent peace activists, the Kremlin grew more sensitive to public relations. In the late 1950s, recalled Georgi Arbatov, then a rising figure in the party apparatus, "it became obvious that one could not simply give orders or let the KGB settle all the problems that arose. The leadership realized that far more attention should be paid to preparing positions and arguments, to improving the art of persuasion and discussion, to refining the government's own position so that it could become more attractive to the public—at home and abroad." For the first time in decades, a considerable number of intellectuals were brought into the party apparatus, where, for the most part, they bolstered the forces pressing for liberalization.[19]

To cultivate foreign opinion, Soviet officials usually worked through their chosen instrument, the World Peace Council. In early 1960, at the instigation of officials in the Foreign Ministry and the Central Committee's international department, Soviet representatives to the WPC were directed to help mobilize the international movement for a nuclear test ban. On July 8, at a press conference, Khrushchev talked publicly of the need to "raise the peoples, raise the masses for struggle against those who slow down solution of the disarmament question." The following day, WPC president J. D. Bernal called for a worldwide campaign on the dimensions of the 1950 Stockholm Appeal to convene a world disarmament conference. In the meantime, he insisted, negotiations on a test ban agreement should be brought to a satisfactory conclusion. The WPC's vast and costly international conclaves devoted to nuclear disarmament issues—including the July 1962 World Congress for General Disarmament and Peace, held in Moscow and addressed at length by Khrushchev—further attest to the seriousness with which Soviet leaders courted world opinion under WPC auspices.[20]

Even after the signing of the partial test ban treaty, Soviet leaders accorded considerable importance to WPC efforts. Writing to Bernal in September 1963, Khrushchev told him that stimulating "a new upsurge . . . of the movement is a task of great importance." Furthermore, he had dispatched "Comrades K. and V. . . . to Britain" to meet with Bernal and "discuss some urgent problems of the world peace movement." The Soviet premier was sure that this would lead to "a correct solution" to the problems Bernal, as WPC president, faced. In the meantime, he insisted that the WPC engage in "open polemics with Peking," which had taken a stand that was "inconsistent with the basic principles of the movement." On October 25, Khrushchev publicly warned against allowing the treaty with the United States to lead to the "demobilization of the forces of disarmament"—an admonition followed by "Peace Week" (November 17–24) in France. When the WPC met later that year in Warsaw, it called for new mass actions behind a comprehensive test ban, nuclear nonproliferation, and U.N. progress toward a treaty for general and complete disarmament.[21]

Although Soviet policymakers regarded the WPC as completely reliable, some also recognized its limitations. Thanks to their participation in official peace groups, members of the Central Committee's international department realized better than did most Soviet officials the significance of independent peace movements. Consequently, the Soviet government made substantial efforts to cultivate nonaligned disarmament activists. In March 1961, the KGB reported to the Central Committee that, among its propaganda targets, were "Quakers, pacifist, youth and other social organizations." That October, the Twenty-second Communist Party Congress resolved that the Soviet Union would show "understanding and support" for "all organizations and parties aiming at the prevention of war, neutralist and pacifist movements," and "bourgeois circles supporting peace and the normalization of relations between countries." Articles appeared in Soviet publications praising "the sincere pacifists, those active supporters of the radical struggle for peace and for the banning of nuclear arms," among them Russell and Pauling.[22]

Given Pauling's extraordinary prominence in the movement, as well as his advocacy of cooperation with Communist-led peace groups, he was especially popular with Soviet officials. In November 1961, he lectured at Moscow's Institute for Organic Chemistry before an audience of twelve hundred people, many of them drawn by his well-known opposition to nuclear weapons. Although Pauling's denunciation of the Soviet resumption of nuclear testing that fall greatly displeased the authorities—who refused a visa to an American peace activist seeking to deliver an antitesting petition drawn up by the American chemist to the Soviet Supreme Court—they maintained friendly relations with him. In 1970, the Soviet government awarded Pauling its Lenin Peace Prize.[23]

Soviet officials navigated the same difficult course with other nonaligned peace activists. Answering Russell's bitter protest against the Soviet Union's breaking of the nuclear test moratorium, Khrushchev devoted a seven-page letter to assuring the British leader of the Soviet Union's thorough support for "the complete and unconditional prohibition of nuclear weapons." Shortly thereafter, his wife, Nina Khrushchev, responded to another critique of nuclear testing, this time from Women Strike for Peace. Arguing that Western "threats to unleash war against the Soviet Union" had "compelled the Soviet government to carry out nuclear tests," she maintained that, nonetheless, the Soviet government stood "for disarmament and peace. Therefore, we are with you, with your movement, we are in deep sympathy with it." Even as he continued to criticize Soviet policy, Russell received deferential treatment from Soviet officials. Indeed, he marveled at how the Soviet Peace Committee's Yuri

Zhukov could move in a matter of months from flattering him in Wales, to condemning the activities of his representatives at the WPC's 1962 conference in Moscow, to sending him letters expressing warm support.[24] Even in the midst of the Cuban missile crisis, when Russell dispatched a telegram to Khrushchev pleading for restraint, the Soviet leader responded with a tactful, four-page letter. Condemning "the piratic actions of the American government" and professing the Soviet Union's peaceful intentions, Khrushchev expressed his "sincere gratitude" for Russell's concern.[25]

Unlike the true believers of the Communist-led peace movement, Soviet officials also sought to develop a friendly relationship with SANE. Meeting with Ambassador Semyon Tsarapkin in June 1959, SANE's Lenore Marshall found him—like U.S. ambassador James Wadsworth, with whom she also met—"most friendly, easy to see," and "cordial." Tsarapkin "was intensely interested in all I had to say" and remarked that a test ban treaty "should be drawn up soon." When Marshall "told him of the growing support for Sane, he was much interested." The meeting "ended on the most affectionate note": greetings to one another's children, to the American and Russian people, and finally, Tsarapkin's "special regards" to SANE. In November 1960, Anatoli Kireev, first secretary of the Soviet embassy, stopped by SANE's Washington office for a chat. According to Sandy Gottlieb, they had "met frequently in the past" and he was now "interested in our appraisal of the Kennedy administration." Gottlieb provided him with the same appraisal that had been produced for SANE's members, "namely that we can expect more disarmament planning, more vigorous negotiations, and more missiles, all at the same time." He "further suggested that a few Soviet concessions at the test ban talks in Geneva, made in the next few weeks, would help smooth the way for disarmament negotiations when Kennedy is in office." Although Kireev responded that there would be no concessions before the new president was sworn in, he promised "very serious proposals" thereafter and that the Russians would overcome Chinese belligerence.[26]

Khrushchev, too, treated SANE with respect. During early 1961, especially, letters flitted back and forth between SANE's headquarters in New York and the Soviet premier's in Moscow. Responding to SANE's antinuclear appeal to the leaders of the nuclear powers, Khrushchev dispatched a lengthy letter to Cousins and Pickett on February 8, assuring them that the Soviet government favored a test ban treaty and considered disarmament "the most important, cardinal problem which the world faces at the present time." On March 8, Cousins replied by asking for clarification of the Soviet stand on a number of items related to nuclear arms control and disarmament. In a new letter, undated, Khrushchev answered Cousins's queries at great length, stressing, among other things, that he had scrapped the idea of the inevitability of war under capitalism. Furthermore, he noted that although Cousins was a severe critic of Communism and he of capitalism, "we both recognize that neither your system nor ours can possibly win through war. You can work for peace without becoming a Communist. And we can work for peace without becoming capitalists." This was a reiteration of Khrushchev's "peaceful coexistence" policy, of course, but it also underscored the importance the Soviet leader ascribed to non-Communist peace activism.[27]

Khrushchev devoted unusual attention to another antinuclear stalwart, Leo Szilard. In September 1959, the American scientist began a lengthy correspondence with the Soviet premier,[28] which, in October 1960, resulted in an extraordinary meeting between the two men in New York City. Scheduled for fifteen minutes, their interchange lasted two hours, during which they discussed Szilard's ideas on peace, disarmament, and a settlement of the Cold War. Szilard was his usual playful, irreverent self and apparently charmed the Soviet leader. Not only did the meeting became front page news in *Pravda*, but a lengthy memorandum summarizing their conversation was sent to Russian participants in the Pugwash meetings. Szilard later received "red carpet" treatment in Moscow. Soviet officials also arranged for Szilard's whimsical *Voice of the Dolphins* to be translated into Russian and marketed in the Soviet Union. In addition, pressed by Szilard, Khrushchev agreed to back the latest of his many creative ideas—informal, ongoing meetings among highly placed Soviet and American intellectuals or, as it was soon dubbed, the "Angels Project."[29]

The Soviet government also continued to exhibit considerable respect for the Pugwash conferences. Khrushchev sent repeated, fulsome messages of greetings to these gatherings and, in 1960, when a Pugwash conference convened in Moscow, invited all participants to a reception at the Kremlin.[30] To be sure, in the early 1960s, the Soviet government expressed impatience that the Pugwash meetings did not seem to be leading to U.S.-Soviet arms control agreements. According to the U.S. ambassador, in 1961 Khrushchev complained to him that, at the latest Pugwash meeting, there had "been discussions between people who do not make decisions." Conversely, "those who do decide do not wish to talk."[31] Even so, Western observers and participants, reporting to their governments on the gatherings, were impressed by the "strong team" coming from the Soviet Union. There were top-level scientists, highly placed scientific administrators, "outstanding interpreters," and even an influential military strategist—people, they believed, who reflected the determination of Kremlin officials to make the meetings a success.[32]

Furthermore, the conferences became a conduit for high-level bargaining between the Soviet and U.S. governments. At the Moscow conference of December 1960, two U.S. participants, Jerome Wiesner and Walt Rostow, urged V. V. Kuznetsov of the Soviet Foreign Office to secure the release of two American RB-47 fliers, shot down over the Arctic that July. A few days after Kennedy's inaugural in January 1961, Khrushchev announced the release of the airmen—an action, he ingratiatingly told the U.S. ambassador, deliberately postponed to benefit Kennedy. According to George Kiastiakowsky, at the Pugwash conference of March 1963, Artsimovich "took me aside, explained that he had regular personal contact with Khrushchev, and asked me to convey forthwith the message to the White House that Khrushchev would compromise on five annual on-site inspections in the USSR." Impressed by the significance of this encounter, Kiastiakowsky flew to Washington and transmitted the message to White House officials. The Soviet government also rallied behind Artsimovich's proposal for "black boxes"—an ingenious plan for monitoring seismic activity to help verify a test ban. Endorsed by Pugwash participants in 1962, it subsequently became an important element in U.S.-Soviet arms control negotiations.[33]

Although the Soviet government certainly would have preferred to keep its courtship of foreign nuclear disarmament activists from affecting its harder-line domestic policy, this proved impossible. In May 1961, the general secretary of the German Peace Council requested guidance from the Soviet Peace Committee as to how to treat the forthcoming San Francisco to Moscow Peace March. Personally, he recommended that marchers be refused entry to East bloc countries, arguing that the latter's position on disarmament left no room for criticism and that much of the pacifist marchers' declaration was "unacceptable" because it would "mislead" the public into equating NATO's policies with those of Communist states. In response, the Soviet Peace Committee's Nikolai Tikhonov granted these points, but told the Soviet Communist Party's Central Committee that, in the event the march succeeded in the West, "it would be inexpedient . . . to deny a reception to the march participants" in Communist nations. Indeed, if visas were denied to the marchers, there was "no doubt that some persons would . . . use the march for provocative purposes"—that is, to criticize the Soviet Union.[34] Accordingly, the Soviet Peace Committee pressed the party's Central Committee to admit the marchers for six weeks, to allow them to parade through Red Square, and to provide them with appropriate facilities. On August 17, 1961, after approval from its international department, the Central Committee voted to allow the peace march to proceed through the Soviet Union for a month and to have the Soviet Peace Committee cover necessary expenses.[35] Only a few weeks later, this led to the holding of countless nuclear disarmament rallies and to the distribution of 100,000 unilateralist leaflets within previously forbidden territory.[36]

Nor was this the only way in which the cultivation of foreign peace activists and outside opinion helped to open up the Soviet Union to antinuclear agitation. To lure nonaligned delegations to the WPC's July 1962 peace congress in Moscow, Soviet authorities were forced to pay the price of allowing very critical speeches at the conference, printing reasonably accurate accounts in the Soviet press, and opening the way for further leafleting and demonstrations. To achieve some credibility at the Pugwash conferences, Kremlin officials had no choice but to send leading scientists—ultimately, even Kapitza—to develop ever closer relationships with the antinuclear scientists of the West.[37]

Even the Kremlin's chilly response to the protest voyage of *Everyman III* against Soviet nuclear testing reflected some accommodation to Western antinuclear opinion. In September 1962, the Soviet Peace Committee advised the Central Committee that it had firmly rebuffed plans for this venture. The SPC cited "the anti-Soviet nature of this project," the "hostile attitudes" of the ship's captain, Earle Reynolds, to the Soviet Union, and the tour of Barbara Reynolds with the Hiroshima peace pilgrims "for the purpose of anti-Soviet propaganda." In October, though, the SPC reported, a bit frantically, that, despite the official refusal of entry, the pacifists had not given up plans to come to the Soviet Union. Given "the inciting and anti-Soviet nature of the voyage," the SPC—backed by the KGB—recommended to the party leadership that the vessel be seized and expelled when it reached Soviet territorial waters.[38] Later that month, however, the SPC backed off somewhat, arguing that "because the voyage of the ship draws public attention in the Western European countries and in the United States," it would be "expedient" to have a conference between the crew and SPC representatives on the high seas. Going still further, the international department of the Central Committee recommended holding the meeting in Leningrad, for "this would deprive the ship's crew of the chance to claim that they were not allowed to meet the representatives of the Soviet public on Soviet territory." Eventually, then, the Central Committee decided to allow the *Everyman III* to travel to Leningrad.[39]

The Chinese government did not take these risks. As has been noted, like the Soviet government it initially championed a peace movement single-mindedly devoted to supporting the Communist position in the Cold War. At the time, this meant the Communist-led WPC. During the early 1960s, though, the Chinese and Soviet national security positions began to diverge. The Soviet government moved toward nuclear arms control agreements with the United States. China's government, by contrast, rejected any shift toward détente and insisted on developing its own nuclear weapons. Consequently, Peking officials conducted a vigorous campaign to align the WPC with their own interests.[40] Deriding the latitudinarian peace movement policies of their one-time ally, they insisted on a more militant line. "Marxist-Leninists," warned the Chinese theoretical journal *Red Flag* in 1960, "absolutely must not sink into the mire of bourgeois pacifism." In the aftermath of the WPC's relatively open Moscow Congress of July 1962, it heightened the polemics. That August, an article in the *Peking Review* asserted: "The people of the world want a peace movement which is militant, anti-imperialist and responsive to their daily needs, and not a wishy-washy pacifist talking club as some would like it to be." Thus, the Chinese government not only scorned nonaligned peace activism, but the new deference shown it by Soviet policymakers.[41]

Mixed Attitudes Among Some Western Bloc Nations

Like the Soviet government, those of a number of countries either formally or informally aligned with the United States also treated nonaligned nuclear disarmament activism with some degree of respect. In 1962, Norway's foreign minister, Halvard Lange, accepted an invitation to write an article for the WRI section's newspaper, *Pax*. That same year, New Zealand's Conservative prime minister, Keith Holyoake, told a delegation of New Zealand CND members that he would give serious consideration to the idea of a nuclear weapon–free zone in the southern hemisphere. In 1964, when CND sponsored its "Open Letter" to French President de Gaulle in protest against nuclear testing, signed by 406 organizations, Holyoake agreed to deliver it personally to the French government, a gesture much appreciated by the group.[42] Corresponding at length with Bertrand Russell in early 1963, Israeli prime minister David Ben-Gurion assured him that "many of us here in Israel have read with profound interest your books on science, philosophy, and world problems, and many more admire and esteem you for your uncompromising struggle for world peace." Although Ben-Gurion denied Russell's contention that Israel was developing nuclear weapons and stressed the danger to Israel of conventional arms, he professed his "fervent hope that you and I may live to see the success of your efforts to rid the world of the danger of atomic weapons."[43]

Nuclear disarmament groups also enjoyed a good relationship with the Conservative government of Canadian prime minister Diefenbaker. In December 1959, a delegation from the University of Toronto met with the prime minister for an hour and a half and personally delivered to him a ban-the-Bomb petition, signed by 630 faculty and 2,500 students. At the meeting, Diefenbaker talked of his government's opposition to further nuclear testing, pointed to Canada's vote in the United Nations against France's plan to test nuclear weapons, and cited the Canadian initiative for a global radiation study. "We were favorably impressed with his concern," reported David Gauthier, the delegation's leader. In turn, Diefenbaker told the press that "there is considerable merit in their viewpoint" and that his government's goal was "the complete elimination of nuclear weapons." Shortly after the formation of the Voice of Women, Diefenbaker also gave a very respectful hearing to a delegation from that group, as did External Affairs Minister Howard Green, who reportedly urged them to "continue their good work." The following year, when Diefenbaker and Green met again with VOW activists, they assured them of their earnest concern for peace and disarmament.[44]

Although some of this deferential treatment was genuine—Lange, for example, was a former pacifist leader and Green sincerely favored nuclear disarmament—much of it reflected government accommodation to political pressure. Citing a "very important and influential group of women strongly opposed to nuclear testing," the South African foreign minister told U.S. officials in 1962 that his government had a "real public opinion problem" when it came to defending U.S. tests in the atmosphere. Similarly, New Zealand External Affairs officials confided to a U.S. diplomat in 1963 that they opposed a nuclear free zone, but for "internal political reasons" had "avoided [a] public stand [on] this issue." The subject had become "politically and emotionally sensitive."[45] Even in Canada, Diefenbaker showed acute sensitivity to what he considered public opinion. As a number of Cabinet members remarked, not always favorably, the prime minister was obsessed with his mail, including petitions from the Voice of Women. In 1960, a visitor recalled, Diefenbaker reported "that his mail was running nine to one against nuclear arms for Canada" and that "this fact weighed heavily in his deliberations."[46]

Hostile Attitudes Among Some Western Bloc Nations

Other Western nations adopted a chillier approach toward nuclear disarmament activism, especially if they maintained their own nuclear weapons programs or were enthusiastic about the deployment of such weapons by their side in the Cold War. As might be expected, they took a particularly hostile view of Communist-led disarmament campaigns. Speaking in parliament, the attorney general of Australia derided participants in the Melbourne peace conference of 1959 as Communist "stooges." The West German government closed the offices of the Peace Committee—the local branch of the WPC—and prosecuted its leaders. After years of litigation, the Bonn government succeeded in sending them to prison in April 1960.[47] Nor did nonaligned peace activism necessarily fare any better. In 1967, determined to prevent a crushing electoral victory by Greece's Center Union Party and the further erosion of their influence, the

Greek armed forces seized power, established a right-wing dictatorship, and banned all of Greece's peace groups.[48]

The government of the Federal Republic of Germany proved particularly inhospitable. Crossing West Germany in 1961, the San Francisco to Moscow peace marchers found their leafleting and public meetings restricted by government pressure, culminating in their arrest for demonstrating outside the Ministry of Defense in Bonn.[49] The following year, the West German government began blocking the entry of overseas contingents who sought to participate in the Easter marches. In the spring of 1963, a dramatic confrontation emerged along the Danish border, where twenty-five hundred Danish Easter marchers were barred from entering the Federal Republic by hordes of West German soldiers armed with tanks, machine guns, water cannon, and pistols and employing newly dug trenches and snarling dogs. Faced with this startling show of force, the more intrepid of the Danes boarded buses to reach their destination, leading the police to swoop down on tourists looking suspiciously sunburned, tired, or bearded. Most returned to Denmark, where they were joined in a demonstration by hundreds of their German counterparts—the Danish government having announced, rather pointedly, that it had no objection to international disarmament gatherings on its territory! Meanwhile, West German police used force to break up the peaceful demonstration at the Düsseldorf airport, arresting forty-nine demonstrators. Those arrested included the local leader of the Easter march effort, a Protestant minister whom the authorities charged with having disturbed public peace and order.[50]

The hard line of West German policymakers toward nuclear critics even resulted in a major political scandal. In September 1962, when NATO held its West European military maneuvers, it conducted them as part of a hypothetical nuclear war. On October 10, *Der Spiegel*—a mass-market weekly magazine which had repeatedly criticized Defense Minister Strauss for authoritarianism, corruption, and his insistence that Germany should have nuclear weapons—revealed that the "war" had resulted in a disaster. Within a few days of the hypothetical Soviet attack, "large parts of England and the Federal Republic were totally destroyed," with between "ten and fifteen million dead in each country." Even for the survivors, "the chaos was unimaginable." With the publication of this ostensibly classified information, Strauss threw aside former constraints. He had West German police invade the homes of the publisher and the assistant editor in the middle of the night, tear apart their houses in a futile search for secret material, and arrest them and three journalists on the staff. Taking over the magazine's offices, the police were still occupying them a month later, supposedly searching for evidence but in practice making its publication all but impossible. Meanwhile, the magazine's editors fought back, arguing that the article had been cleared with the Defense Ministry before publication. Ultimately, this "*Der Spiegel* affair" boomeranged against Strauss and helped undermine the political fortunes of the Christian Democratic government.[51]

The government of France also exhibited little tolerance for nuclear critics. In 1959, when a SANE chapter in California petitioned the French government to halt its forthcoming nuclear tests, the French consul general denounced the action as "impudent," "cynical," "immoral, imperialistic, monopolistic, and unacceptable." The following February, as five hundred African students from French Community nations gathered to present an antitesting petition to Premier Debré, the French government had them arrested.[52] Other foreign critics received similar treatment. En route to the Paris "summit" conference in the spring of 1960, a group of British CND activists, marching under their Aldermaston banner, were arrested and deported. The following year, when the San Francisco to Moscow marchers arrived by ship at Le Havre, the authorities refused them access to French soil. Before a crowd of about four hundred French sympathizers, cheering and waving banners that called for France's nuclear disarmament, several of them leaped into the waters of the harbor. Although forced to return to Britain, they returned soon thereafter and were again refused access to France. This time, fourteen marchers leaped overboard and three managed to reach the city, where they distributed antinuclear leaflets. All, however, were imprisoned and deported by the authorities. In protest, French activists conducted their own antinuclear march across France. But they too were roughly treated. French police confiscated their banner twice, arrested them at least three times, and handled them brutally—dragging men by the ears and women by the hair.[53]

Thoroughly committed to its own nuclear weapons program, the British government also took extraordinary measures against nuclear disarmament activists. According to Alec Douglas-Home, one of Britain's prime ministers during these years, "there was no attempt at political interference with the nuclear disarmers"—"they marched . . . held their meetings," and were not "banned in any particular sense." But this claim is belied by a series of remarkable incidents. In August 1961, the British Cabinet decided to deny the Committee of 100 the right to use Trafalgar Square for a legal rally, the first rejection of a public meeting there since 1916, when permission had been refused for a demonstration against World War I. The government explained that it could not allow the gathering to serve as a "curtain-raiser" for a later nonviolent sit-down at Parliament Square.[54] That September, as plans moved forward for the Parliament Square sit-down, the government arrested and imprisoned the eighty-nine-year-old Russell, his wife, and twenty-eight other leaders of the Committee under the Defense of the Realm Act; and, on the day of the demonstration,

3,000 police took action against a nonviolent crowd of 15,000 Britons that gathered in and around Trafalgar Square. No one reached Parliament Square, declared off limits by the authorities, but the police arrested 1,314 people, including some of Britain's top cultural luminaries.[55]

This did serve as a "curtain-raiser"—for stepped-up government repression. On December 5, 1961, the head of the British Air Ministry warned Prime Minister Macmillan that Committee of 100 plans for nonviolent protests at U.S. airbases scattered about Britain raised "serious problems." Two of the bases, at Wethersfield and Brize Norton, contained U.S. planes with nuclear weapons, guarded by U.S. sentries. If demonstrators came close to the planes, the U.S. guards would be "compelled to open fire." To prevent this occurrence, he proposed mobilization of a massive British military force and the attorney general planned "serious criminal proceedings against the organizers of the demonstration." The defense minister added that, without decisive action, "it is possible that we shall have a serious incident in which an American serviceman will have shot one of the demonstrators. If this happens, it will make the political position . . . extremely difficult to hold as regards all American bases in this country."[56] The upshot was that, only days before the event, the government arrested all six staff members of the Committee of 100, charging them with violation of the Official Secrets Act. It also publicly warned that participants in the demonstration risked similar prosecution, with jail sentences of up to fourteen years. Furthermore, at the Cabinet's request, government officials approached executives of a leading bus company, suggesting that they faced comparable prosecution if they honored the company's contract to transport demonstrators. This proved convincing to the businessmen, who left large numbers of protesters stranded on the day of the event.[57]

The result was a rousing "victory" for the government. On December 9, the day of the demonstration, some 300 nonviolent activists at Wethersfeld faced what the *Times* described as "5,000 R.A.F. Regiment men, 260 R.A.F. and W.R.A.F. police, 850 civil police and special branch officers, 75 Air Ministry constabulary men, 12 R.A.F. police Alsatians, two Belvedere helicopters, and six-and-a-half miles of barbed wire fence." At Brize Norton, there were "3,000 R.A.F. men, guard dogs, barricades of newly erected wire, and three helicopters" to guard the base. The authorities arrested an estimated 860 persons at the assorted demonstrations, which the air minister assured the press had been "a flop." Convicted under the Official Secrets Act shortly thereafter, all but one of the Committee of 100 staff members received eighteen-month prison terms. The exception, a young woman sentenced to twelve months' imprisonment, grew despondent during her confinement and committed suicide. In mid-1963, the home secretary, Henry Brook, reported happily to the prime minister that Committee of 100 demonstrations at air bases seemed "played out." More-over, the police were "keeping a special watch" on Committee plans for future demonstrations. Consequently, "fresh legislative powers" did not seem neces-sary, although a need remained for "some regular means of coordinating the action required to deal with particular plans made by the Committee." Macmil-lan commented: "This seems sensible."[58]

Although the British government took a less confrontational approach to CND, it did not have much respect for it, either. "We thought they were wrong," recalled Douglas-Home. "I mean it's as simple as that. And danger-ously wrong because if the CND doctrine had really taken hold of the elec-torate . . . it would have been extremely dangerous both to ourselves and to NATO." For the most part, British officials were much too sophisticated to as-cribe the alleged errors of CND's policy to Communist control. In the spring of 1959, discussing whether the Communist Party controlled CND, Foreign Office staffers concluded that the party did not even support the nuclear disarmament group. Four years later, after the party line had shifted, the Home Office re-ported to Macmillan that although the Communist Party participated in the Al-dermaston marches, "there is little evidence that the Communists have suc-ceeded in penetrating the [nuclear disarmament] movements to any great ex-tent." CND "included good people," recalled Douglas-Home. "Canon Collins was a very sincere man. But . . . he was sincerely wrong. . . . And I'm not sure that that is [not] an even greater sin than anything else."[59]

With no meeting of minds, the government resisted other kinds of meet-ings as well. Collins repeatedly requested that Macmillan receive a deputation from CND, but the prime minister just as steadfastly refused. In 1962, the government briefly relented, but only for political reasons. That February, alarmed by plans for renewed atmospheric testing at Christmas Island, the Women's Committee of CND proposed that Macmillan meet with a delega-tion of eminent, concerned women. In this context, the minister of defense thought it would "be useful" for Macmillan to talk with them and the prime minister's own staff advised that seeing them "would prevent it being said that you were not concerned about the problems of nuclear testing." As this was a political matter, Macmillan referred it to the head of his Conservative Party, who responded that he "most strongly" urged the prime minister to receive the CND women. "The initiative about peace . . . has really captured people's imagination . . . and . . . it would give a bad impression if the Prime Minister did not meet such a very strong delegation." Furthermore, "women are natu-rally most deeply concerned with the effects, in particular the genetic effects, of tests." Consequently, after an investigation concluded that none of the women was a Communist, Macmillan met with them that March, at 10 Downing Street. The gathering was pleasant, on a high level, and provided for no resolution of the differences between these committed opponents of nuclear testing and the government.[60]

As this incident indicates, below the surface of civilized discourse lay considerable antagonism. Although Macmillan said very little about CND in his published memoirs, in reality he was stung, among other things, by the Polaris demonstrations and by the exposure of Britain's regional civil defense headquarters during the 1963 Aldermaston march. Meeting with Kennedy in late 1962, he twice spoke disparagingly of antinuclear "agitators." His attitude may also be inferred from the behavior of his usually proper wife, Dorothy, who served as his chauffeur. On one occasion, confronted by CND demonstrators, she drove her car directly at them, rolling down the window and roundly cursing them.[61] Covert operations against CND remain largely unknown,[62] but according to the CIA, the British government had CND and other nuclear disarmament groups "well infiltrated." Even the advent of Wilson's Labour government in 1964 failed to turn the tide for CND. Committed to the maintenance of good relations with the United States and regarding the CND lobby within the party as manageable and relatively unimportant—which, by this point, it was—Wilson provided it with little encouragement.[63]

By contrast, the British government gradually warmed toward the Pugwash movement. Despite the earnest efforts of the movement's organizers to maintain an unbiased, nonpolitical approach to arms control and disarmament issues, for some years British authorities viewed it with suspicion. As late as November 1960, a secret Foreign Office advisory declared that "the Pugwash Conferences are potentially dangerous to Western interests . . . since the Communists may be expected to exploit these discussions for propaganda purposes."[64] British policy, however, began to shift in December 1959. At that time, asked by Rotblat if he would join the advisory body to the British Pugwash Committee, J. D. Cockcroft of the Atomic Energy Authority contacted the Foreign Office, observing that he did not want to get involved with the Pugwash group "unless the Foreign Office thinks there is some advantage in doing so." In response, the Foreign Office urged him to accept the offer, for "we do attach importance to responsible United Kingdom scientific opinion being represented in the Pugwash movement." As it later explained, this would help prevent Pugwash "being exploited for propaganda purposes." Accordingly, Cockcroft joined and, the following spring, asked the Foreign Office if he should attend the next Pugwash conference, in Moscow. The Foreign Office responded that he should not, for it did not "wish to see the importance of the Pugwash meetings unduly inflated." But, in mid-July, noting that a "very strong Russian team" would be attending, the Foreign Office reversed course, arguing that it is "more than usually desirable that the Western delegations should include a majority of scientists of repute" who would oppose Communist "exploitation of the meeting." Indeed, it urged Cockcroft to recruit additional scientists who would be politically reliable.[65]

Thereafter, British government support for the Pugwash movement grew remarkably. The Moscow conference of late 1960, a Foreign Office official noted, "justified our present policy of encouraging participation in these meetings by reliable Western scientists and defense strategists." Future participation would "not only provide a useful insight into current thinking of individual Soviet disarmament scientists, but also help the latter to keep abreast of Western ideas as they develop." Asked by the Foreign Office to see to it that "a stronger British team was fielded" at the next conference, Cockcroft located several scientists whom he thought would provide it with "a new 'hard core.'" In addition, he noted, "we should presumably have to have Rotblat and one or two of the earlier members."[66] In May, increasingly enthusiastic about arrangements, Cockcroft inquired of the Foreign Office if the travel expenses of the British delegation could be covered from "any official or 'unofficial' fund." Adopting a more and more proprietary attitude toward the movement, A. D. Wilson of the Foreign Office "informally suggested" to one Pugwash staffer that June that "it might be wise" to sever the movement's connection with Bertrand Russell, as that "was now an embarrassment." For his part, Cockcroft conceived the idea of having the Royal Society sponsor British participation in the Pugwash conferences, noting that "this would perhaps lead to the winding up of the present Pugwash Committee."[67]

Having concluded that the Pugwash conferences could be made to serve Western interests, the British government now sought to control them. Wilson responded that "it would be most helpful if the Royal Society could be persuaded to sponsor British participation . . . and if this were to lead to the winding up of the present Pugwash Committee." One or two Pugwash old-timers might then be retained, "but the change as a whole would be a convenient way of getting over the problem of the association with the present committee of Lord Bertrand Russell." Although this plan failed to take hold, the British government did press to have specific people added to the British advisory committee. And Rotblat did not resist, provided that they were legitimate scientists and genuinely interested in arms controls. When, however, the British government suggested topics for meetings and who should be invited to them, Rotblat dug in his heels, much to the distress of the government. In October 1963, one Foreign Office official complained that the British delegation should include more people familiar with strategic issues, including government officials. But "the difficulty is to get Prof. Rotblat to pay any attention to what we think. . . . He is no doubt jealous of his independence and scientific integrity." That year, for example, neither the Foreign Office nor the Defense Ministry was "consulted about the composition of the British delegation or what they were to say." Obtaining "a new organizer for the British delegation seems to be the first need, but I do not know if there is any hope of this."[68]

Nevertheless, despite lingering irritation at the independence of the Pugwash scientists, the British government no longer doubted the value of the movement. As a Defense Ministry official reported in January 1962, Pugwash was "now a very respectable organization."[69] Later that year, the Foreign Office began prodding private companies to make financial contributions to the movement and secured a contribution from the Treasury Department. When the Home Office, still following traditional policy, advised Prince Philip that Pugwash was "a dirty word," the Foreign Office retorted that the movement now had "official blessing." Explaining the favorable attitude, Wilson pointed out that "the process of educating" Soviet experts is "bound to be of some use to us. We ourselves may pick up some useful ideas from our own scientists, with whom we keep closely in touch, and are not likely to be embarrassed by anything which they suggest. If there is ever to be a breakthrough, it is not inconceivable that the way might be prepared at a conference of this kind."[70] During 1963, the Pugwash meetings drew the intense attention of the British government, with reports on them dispatched directly to Macmillan, who read them with great interest.[71]

Even as it warmed toward the scientists, however, the British government remained determined to control public opinion. Charles Hill, the Cabinet's chief public relations operative, continued his efforts to mobilize public sentiment behind the government's H-Bomb policy. In July 1959, he reported to Macmillan that a "modest beginning has been made" toward lining up church support. A meeting had been held with the Anglican bishops of Portsmouth, Chelmsford, and Chichester at which it had been agreed to create an "informal group, comprising Conservative members of both Houses and a number of Bishops, which might meet about three or four times a year for dinner at the House." Once these meetings were "fully established and on a regular basis," Hill planned "to inject the idea that the group invite [Cabinet] Ministers to attend." For its part, the Home Office produced soothing, if irrelevant, publications that promised safety during a nuclear war. But how effective were such campaigns? "In terms of public opinion we are passing through a moderately difficult phase," Hill conceded in February 1961. "The commentators . . . are turning on us" and "there is a good deal of press 'bitchiness.'" Among other problems, "there is no progress on disarmament and the nuclear test discussions lumber along so slowly." A "success at Geneva would raise morale."

Meanwhile, "we need to do more to refute line by line the unilateralists' case."[72]

The government's sensitivity to the disarmament issue is evident in the political strategy it adopted. In June 1959, when the Labour Party announced a new policy toward nuclear weapons, including an end to British nuclear testing and the formation of a non-nuclear club, Macmillan immediately wrote to his foreign secretary, warning that "it will certainly command considerable support and we shall have to think just how to handle it." A new Conservative manifesto on nuclear weapons "must . . . deal with Disarmament and the H-Bomb," promising "not to make any further tests in the air or under water." A Conservative Party leaflet of September 1960, while defending the Bomb, did so by emphasizing peace. "By their mere existence," it argued, "nuclear weapons make war less likely because a would-be aggressor knows that even a few H-bombs falling on his country would do more damage than he could accept." Therefore, "the Aldermaston marchers want us to throw away the one weapon which can PREVENT war." A November 1960 background paper on defense policy, drafted for Cabinet members by Hill, made a similar point. In nuclear weapons, it claimed, "lies the best hope of avoiding global war."[73]

Much of the political battle, of course, hinged on a nuclear test ban. The British public had an "hysterical fear of fission products," Sir William Penney told Eisenhower's top scientific adviser in March 1960. Nor did this mood seem to change. "Whenever I talk to people about disarmament, it's always the test-ban treaty they bring me around to," noted Britain's minister of state in July 1962. "It has to do with the here and now, and they want an end to this fouling of the air they breathe." Naturally, then, the Conservatives recognized that the atmospheric test ban treaty of 1963 provided them with a political windfall, as well as yet another way to turn the tables on their critics. During the ensuing election campaign, they covered billboards with posters depicting protesters sitting down amid their disarmament symbols and including a caption which reminded viewers that, meanwhile, the British government had signed the crucial treaty.[74]

The government's best-known venture in opinion management occurred in 1965, when it blocked the television showing of *The War Game*. During the first part of that year, a rising young producer, Peter Watkins, commissioned by the BBC, made a docu-drama on life in Britain during and after a nuclear war. It was a moving, powerful film, with scenes of a firestorm, rows of bodies, badly burned survivors, and the execution of people by armed police after a food riot. Alarmed, Lord Normanbrook, BBC chair and a former Cabinet secretary, contacted the current Cabinet secretary on September 7. Because the "showing of the film on television might well have a significant effect on public attitudes towards the policy of the nuclear deterrent," he wrote, "it seems to me that the Government should have an opportunity of expressing a view about this." Consequently, the BBC held a special showing of *The War Game* on September 24 for Home Office, Defense Ministry, and other officials. After seeing the film and concluding that it would increase support for CND, they departed to consult with their Cabinet ministers. On November 5, the Cabinet secretary and other officials met with Normanbrook and, according to the latter, made it "clear" that the Home Office would "be relieved if the B.B.C. decides not to show it." Consequently, the BBC not only refused to show the film, but prevented its television broadcast anywhere in the world.[75] *The War Game* did have small private showings, and won three top film prizes: the Venice Film Festival award, the British Film Academy award, and a Hollywood Oscar. But British officials kept it off television until 1985.[76]

For the British government, as for others, the battle for public opinion was not only against its Cold War rivals.

Policymakers and Protest

The U.S. Government Confronts the Movement, 1959–70

> I spoke of the possible invitation to Dr. Schweitzer. . . .
> There were humanitarian reasons which made this desirable.
> On the other hand, he was rather undependable politically.
>
> John Foster Dulles, 1959

The attitude of the U.S. government toward the nuclear disarmament movement during these years was curiously ambivalent. On some occasions, it reacted to antinuclear groups and their leaders with considerable hostility. On others, it invited them to the White House or otherwise cultivated them. This apparent schizophrenia was less a reflection of the differing attitude toward domestic and foreign protest characteristic of Soviet policy than of the relatively widespread diffusion of power within the U.S. governing system. Congressional leaders might pillory prominent disarmament activists, even as the White House and the State Department adopted a somewhat more tolerant approach. Moreover, the FBI and CIA, although ostensibly under the control of the president, exercised some degree of independence when it came to investigation, infiltration, and harassment. In addition, the executive branch underwent a changeover in leadership, as Eisenhower's Republican administration gave way to a Democratic one in January 1961. Although the importance of this political transition should not be exaggerated, some of Kennedy's top advisers were more sympathetic to arms control and disarmament than were their predecessors. Even when they were not, they sometimes adopted a more sophisticated strategy for dealing with disarmament groups or with antinuclear opinion. Consequently, it was often difficult to tell where the U.S. government stood as it confronted the worldwide tide of protest against nuclear weapons.

Attitudes toward Communist-Led Groups

As might be expected, in their dealings with Communist-led organizations, both Eisenhower and Kennedy appointees adopted a very hostile attitude. Regarding Gensuikyo as a "communist front group," U.S. officials reported happily on its gradual disintegration.[1] In September 1961, when U.S. Ambassador Edwin Reischauer met with Gensuikyo's Kaoru Yasui, the U.S. diplomat remarked frostily that "in view of [the] strongly anti-American character of Gensuikyo's previous pronouncements," the U.S. government's "lack of reply to its past communications" was "only natural." Furthermore, he refused to deliver Gensuikyo's protest against plans for U.S. test resumption to Kennedy and informed the State Department that a presidential reply was "of course out of [the] question." Observing that Gensuikyo had acquired a reputation as "solidly pro-Communist," Reischauer hoped to "exploit this vulnerability" through a letter to the press.[2]

U.S. officials also did their best to undermine the WPC's Moscow Congress of July 1962. After discussions between Acting Secretary of State George Ball and U.S. Ambassador Llewellyn Thompson, the State Department sent policy guidance on the matter to all U.S. diplomatic posts on May 17. "To the extent feasible," read its instructions, "the U.S. government will officially ignore this Congress." But if a response seemed necessary, U.S. officials should point out that the conference was "a communist propaganda show and an attempt to disarm the people of the world psychologically in the face of a continued Soviet campaign to undermine the free world." Furthermore, they should emphasize that the sponsoring group, the WPC, was "a notorious communist-front organization" and that the invitation list was "rigged to guarantee attendance of a reliable mechanical majority favoring the Soviet viewpoint."[3]

Subsequently, U.S. officials did attack the conference on numerous occasions. Upset by the appearance of support for the conclave in Beirut, staffers at the U.S. embassy told the Lebanese Foreign Ministry of their dismay and expressed their hope that "all elements of Lebanese opinion could be fully informed of the true nature of the Congress." Meanwhile, the press officer at the U.S. Information Service in Beirut distributed background material to local editors. U.S. officials also sought to discourage Homer Jack and a delegation from Women Strike for Peace from attending the conference, but the disarmament activists ignored this advice and went anyway. Informed that Jack planned to deliver a hard-hitting critique of the WPC's partisanship, Ball told the U.S. embassy to inform him of the outcome.[4]

Investigations of Antinuclear Activism

Determined to stamp out what they considered a Communist conspiracy, U.S. police and intelligence agencies kept nonaligned nuclear disarmament activities under close scrutiny. Even before Women Strike for Peace staged its first demonstration, the FBI began investigating the group, with reports on WSP and its members soon flitting back and forth between the FBI's Washington headquarters and FBI branch offices all across the country. The forty-nine volumes of FBI records on WSP that the group later obtained under the Freedom of Information Act showed that the federal agency spied extensively on its members and their disarmament activities. Furthermore, when WSP sent its contingent to the Geneva disarmament conference in the spring of 1962, the FBI drew on the Swiss federal police and CIA agents at the U.S. embassy for similar purposes. Despite this enormous surveillance effort, by 1965 the FBI had been unable to unearth any evidence to connect WSP's Washington leadership to the Communist Party. According to the FBI's Washington office, it could discover no record of Communist activity, past or present, among WSP's leaders; furthermore, it could find no evidence that Communist groups in Washington and Maryland had urged their members to join WSP.[5]

The FBI also kept a wary eye on SANE. In the late 1950s, FBI director J. Edgar Hoover began sending memos to the White House on the dangers of a Communist takeover of the nuclear disarmament group, pointing out that it could become "a huge mass organization" with "much influence." SANE's Greater Boston Committee, he warned, was "circulating petitions in support of the Geneva Conference for abolition of the hydrogen bomb" and planning "to have these petitions presented to President Eisenhower by 'prominent citizens' sometime during Easter week." Convinced that Communists were infiltrating SANE chapters, Hoover ordered investigations of a number of them, including the controversial Greater New York Committee. These investigations were extensive and, by 1972, had produced a burgeoning FBI file. The material gathered dealt with SANE's nuclear disarmament demonstrations, its discussion of a merger with the United World Federalists, its run-in with Senator Dodd, and its decisions on how to handle the issue of Communist participation. As in the case of WSP, the FBI did not find any evidence of illegal activity or, for that matter, reason to believe that SANE was a dangerous organization—only that it could be infiltrated by Communists and FBI agents. Nevertheless, the investigations continued.[6]

The FBI busied itself with other activists as well. As Szilard set out on the antinuclear speaking tour that launched the Council for a Livable World, FBI agents trailed him from campus to campus. Meanwhile, it targeted the WILPF for lengthy investigations, including one under its COMINFIL (Communist In-filtration) program, ordered in 1962 by Hoover because "many of the programs of WILPF such as peace, disarmament, and banning nuclear testing, paralleled the Communist Party line." As part of these operations, it investigated the elderly Nobel Peace Prize winner, Emily Greene Balch, reported on the suspiciously antinuclear speeches of Ava Pauling, placed under surveillance a Chicago public meeting on fallout shelters that the WILPF cosponsored with SANE, and investigated Miami WILPF members planning a sit-down protest against the resumption of atmospheric nuclear testing. Then it forwarded the unsolicited information to the U.S. attorney general. Having spied on the international WILPF convention held in Asilomar, California, in 1962, FBI agents produced a seventeen-page secret report outlining the agenda, summarizing the speeches, naming those in attendance, and listing the WILPF's goals, particularly in the area of disarmament. Although the FBI never discovered any evidence of federal lawbreaking by this pacifist group, it pressed ahead with its investigations of what it considered the WILPF's dangerous activities.[7]

Like the FBI, the CIA regarded nuclear disarmament agitation with considerable anxiety. Planning for the president's visit to Britain in 1963, the CIA warned that "representatives of various antinuclear warfare groups . . . will probably wave 'ban the bomb' placards along the route of any scheduled motorcades to and from the airport in Great Britain, and at any other public appearances the President might make. Representatives of these groups might also try to enter Ireland and agitate for their cause during the President's visit." In an April 1963 report, the CIA maintained that the British Communist Party "continues to support and to attempt to infiltrate the Campaign for Nuclear Disarmament." And "while it has met with little success in the parent body, it does exercise some degree of influence in the youth affiliates."[8] This was a milder appraisal than the one proffered by former CIA director Allen Dulles, who—drawing on his intelligence contacts in Britain—told a gathering of the U.S. policymaking elite that year that Communists dominated the British antinuclear movement. His *Craft of Intelligence*, published at roughly the same time, listed British nuclear disarmament activism among "the tasks assigned by Moscow to Communist parties in Free World countries." Dulles explained that "such pacifist appeals are used to disguise real Soviet intentions and to soften the defenses of the Western world." Through its exposure of the British government's regional civil defense centers, he charged, "the 'ban the bomb' movement achieved a level of unusual insidiousness."[9]

In violation of its charter, the CIA also spied on domestic antinuclear groups. Initiating a mail-opening program in the mid-1950s, the CIA eventually read the private correspondence of the American Friends Service Committee, the Federation of American Scientists, and WSP, among other organizations. Within a few months of WSP's founding, the CIA began to investigate it, producing in January 1962 a short history of the group, biographical sketches of its leaders, and summaries of its many demonstrations. CIA surveillance of the disarmament group increased, and in February 1967 the intelligence agency placed an infiltrator in WSP's Washington headquarters. Once considered merely a Communist front, the group now also came under investigation as potentially "violent" and a threat to CIA installations and personnel. The CIA's infiltrator attended WSP meetings, took photographs of women demonstrators, and confiscated confidential meeting records and lists of women attending conferences. Although the CIA infiltration ended in December 1968, its surveillance of WSP continued for years thereafter. No evidence of illegal activities, plans for violence, or foreign financial assistance was ever discovered.[10]

Local and state police forces supplemented these operations. When Dr. Spock attended an Easter march conducted by Cleveland SANE, he was startled to find detectives from the "police subversive squad" taking pictures. He recalled: "It shocked me that marching for disarmament could be considered subversive." But it was.[11] The New York State police "red squad" repeatedly investigated the activities of groups like WSP and SANE. Reporting on Woodstock SANE, one police agent observed that the group had decided not to hold a Hiroshima Day parade on August 6, 1960, but had instead sponsored a forum at the Woodstock Playhouse, attended by five hundred people. He provided a full list of speakers and of people who had sent messages of support. "Any further information concerning this group," he promised, "will be forwarded by report." Another New York police agent sent the chief inspector a complete list of the names and addresses of local leaders of Greater New York SANE—a list, he noted, that "emanates from their files." He attached his memo to a copy of Senator Dodd's May 1960 speech on Communist infiltration in SANE.[12]

The attacks by Senator Dodd and his Senate Internal Security Subcommittee on nuclear disarmament organizations were particularly nasty. As his colleague, Hubert Humphrey, recalled, Dodd was a "hard-line advocate on international affairs, almost professionally anti-Communist." Consequently, his assault on national SANE in the spring of 1960 and his subcommittee's later investigation of SANE's chapter leaders were hardly surprising. As has been noted, these anti-Communist forays had very damaging effects on the disarmament group.[13] In addition, on a much smaller scale and with less publicity, the Dodd subcommittee charged that Communists had infiltrated other groups as well, including the Federation of American Scientists and the American Friends Service Committee. Dodd also issued a report claiming that the Pugwash movement was Communist-dominated. Antinuclear activists received a further drubbing in October 1960, when the Dodd subcommittee published a report listing "Organizations Favored by Communists." One group on the list, the St. Louis Committee for Nuclear Information, which had initiated the famous baby tooth study, appeared there thanks to an article in the *New World Review* (formerly *Soviet Russia Today*) that praised its work. According to Dodd, even clearly non-Communist groups had to prepare for "a concerted effort at infiltration by the Communist termites."[14]

In the latter half of 1960, Dodd and his subcommittee also conducted an investigation of Linus Pauling. Subpoenaed by the subcommittee, the Nobel Prize–winning chemist first appeared before it on June 21, when he was asked about the nuclear test ban petition he had circulated in 1957. Pauling answered all questions forthrightly and at length, until he was asked for the names of those persons who had helped him circulate the petition. Rejecting the request, he said he knew from personal experience that providing a congressional committee with names could lead to reprisals, in this case against people who had done no more than exercise their constitutional right to petition. Nevertheless, the subcommittee ordered Pauling to produce the names. When the hearings resumed on October 11, Pauling refused to comply and, consequently, it seemed that he might be cited for contempt and sentenced to prison. But, given the controversy aroused by the hearings and the possibility that the Senate might refuse to support a contempt citation, the subcommittee opted instead to discredit Pauling and the petition by focusing on what it called "Dr. Pauling's own long record of services to Communist causes and objectives." For the rest of the hearings, it paraded a long sequence of items into the record connecting Pauling with Communism. In this context, the scientist's answers hardly mattered. At the end of the hearings, the subcommittee published a lengthy report arguing that "Dr. Pauling is inextricably interwoven . . . with the entire history of the Communist 'peace movement.'"[15]

The best-publicized investigation of disarmament activism occurred in December 1962, when the House Un-American Activities Committee (HUAC) held hearings on WSP. Anxious to garner headlines, bolster its funding, and discredit yet another suspicious peace group, HUAC sought to link WSP to Communism. "The initiated Communist," explained committee chair Clyde Doyle, "knows that a Moscow call to intensify the fight for peace means that he should intensify his fight to destroy capitalism and its major bastion, the United States of America." During the hearings, the committee directed questions at fifteen subpoenaed women about their alleged Communist connections. In response, the witnesses and their supporters ridiculed such associations and talked earnestly about the need to save children from nuclear destruction. Asked if she would permit Communist Party members to occupy leading posts in WSP, Dagmar Wilson replied disarmingly that she had "absolutely no way of controlling, do not desire to control, who wishes to join . . . the efforts that the women strikers have made for peace. . . . Unless everybody in the whole world joins us in this fight, then God help us." With HUAC looking increasingly foolish in the committee room and in the press, the hearings were adjourned. Nevertheless, in 1964, it subpoenaed two WSP leaders to appear in closed session, a less dangerous forum for the committee. When they refused to testify without the presence of the public and the press, HUAC cited them for contempt of Congress.[16]

The Eisenhower Administration and Disarmament Activism

The Eisenhower administration shared some of these attitudes toward nuclear critics. Recalling Albert Schweitzer's opposition to nuclear weapons tests with bitterness, government officials evinced little interest in renewing contacts with him. At the outset of 1959, when a proposal surfaced to have Eisenhower send birthday greetings to the eighty-four-year-old physician, General Andrew Goodpaster of the White House staff vetoed the idea. Soon after that, Eisenhower had to deal with an embarrassing request from Robert Goheen, president of Princeton University, that Eisenhower join him in inviting Schweitzer to the United States to accept an honorary doctorate at that institution. Discussing the subject with Eisenhower on January 20, Dulles admitted to the president that "humanitarian reasons" made such a visit "desirable." "On the other hand," he remarked, Schweitzer was "rather undependable politically." Dulles promised Eisenhower that he would have this matter "staffed" and then report back.[17]

The staff report, prepared by John A. Calhoun, director of the State Department's Executive Secretariat, could hardly have been more hostile. It informed General Goodpaster that "as you are aware, Dr. Schweitzer's articles and speeches have been highly critical of United States nuclear test policy and closely adhere to the Communist line." As evidence for this, he cited Schweitzer's discussions with the U.S. consul general in the Congo and his criticism of Dulles for "misleading public opinion . . . about the danger of the thermonuclear bomb." Calhoun concluded that "in view of Dr. Schweitzer's dubious political attitudes, the Department does not believe that the President should join Dr. Goheen in inviting Dr. Schweitzer to visit this country."[18]

This recommendation prevailed. On March 3, in response to a request from the White House for some examples of critical statements and articles by Schweitzer, the State Department obliged by sending copies of Schweitzer's April 1957 "Declaration of Conscience," his April 1958 addresses over Norwegian radio, and the June 1958 report of the consul general. These items apparently quieted any qualms at the executive mansion. Accordingly, a draft letter to Goheen was prepared that rejected Eisenhower's participation on the basis of "articles and speeches" by Schweitzer that "have been highly critical of certain aspects of U.S. policy." Ultimately, though, the final version, dispatched by Eisenhower on March 10, avoided political issues entirely. Instead, it simply implied that a presidential invitation to "a foreign dignitary to accept an honorary degree in this country" would set a bad precedent. Although the Princeton president did send an invitation to Schweitzer, reinforced by appeals from Robert Oppenheimer and Adlai Stevenson, Schweitzer declined it. In fact, he never again visited the United States.[19]

Administration officials also regarded some leading scientific critics of nuclear weapons with suspicion. During 1960, the State Department's Charles Bohlen twice urged Szilard not to communicate directly with Khrushchev on how to deal with the arms race, going so far as to warn him that it might be a violation of the Logan Act. On behalf of the president, Secretary Herter added his warnings to Szilard, soon to depart for Moscow, that disarmament negotiations were "a most serious matter, involving the basic national security of this country."[20] In November 1960, Lewis Strauss and his successor as AEC chair, John McCone, conversed on the telephone about the fact that the AEC's General Advisory Committee had voted unanimously to give the Fermi Award to Hans Bethe. Strauss complained that Bethe had "probably done more than anyone else to hamstring the defense of the United States . . . first in opposing the hydrogen bomb and secondly in advising a moratorium on testing and continuing with that advice." In total agreement, McCone promised "to sit on the recommendation." Two days later, according to Strauss, McCone told him that he had reviewed Bethe's record and "it would make him sick" to see the physicist receive the award. He again promised to block the recommendation.[21]

The administration also looked askance at the antinuclear efforts of SANE. In the spring of 1959, as the State Department's William Elliott noted, Deputy Undersecretary of State Robert Murphy asked him to develop the kind of argument that "ought to be put into circulation throughout the official and unofficial channels in answer to the type of full-page paid advertisements in the *New York Times* and elsewhere, sponsored by Norman Thomas, Norman Cousins, and various others, including innocents like Clarence Picket [*sic*] and Eleanor Roosevelt." In response, Elliott produced a memo that argued acidly (and falsely) that "the initial stages of the type of advertisements that have been produced by . . . Norman Thomas, . . . and by Norman Cousins, the editor of the *Saturday Review of Literature* (who is omnicompetent on all issues) started by renouncing only 'testing.'" But this was not "the real objective: The real objective is to prevent the use of nuclear weapons in war, even for limited warfare," by "unilateral" action. It was "necessary, therefore, to nail down that the proponents of these paid advertisements are really inviting us to a strategic surrender in advance." If they were successful, Americans would "have to depend upon the generosity of the Soviet system to prevent us from being colonized by the population hordes of China."[22]

State Department officials showed similar distaste for overseas nuclear disarmament movements. From Britain, U.S. diplomats dispatched numerous, lengthy reports on CND's growth and development, invariably with a negative slant. Although "there is no evidence that Communists control the movement at any level," one noted, "CND propaganda" tended "to foster a kind of human despair and defeatism." In April 1960, the U.S. ambassador reported that he did not "underestimate this strong ground-swell of public awareness and disapproval of nuclear weapons" by the "extreme" CND. The organization had "gained in momentum and support among [an] influential cross section of British people" and its program had "disturbing neutralistic implications" for Britain in the Western alliance system.[23] Reporting from Ottawa in early 1960, one U.S. diplomatic official wrote reassuringly that although student antinuclear protest was burgeoning, "ban-the-bomb sentiment has not acquired sufficient momentum to threaten Canadian government policy." Fortunately, other segments of opinion had "a sounder appreciation of reality." Later that year, the U.S. consul in Vancouver warned that recent statements by Linus Pauling at a meeting sponsored by local antinuclear activists "create an unreasoned fear of radiation and of nuclear warfare which probably weakens the will to resist Communism." Indeed, "we feel that Pauling's presentation in Vancouver, combined with the increasing activity of the B.C. Committees on Radiation Hazards, tends to increase the sentiment for withdrawal from NATO and NORAD . . . as well as for Canadian neutralism."[24]

Curiously, despite the importance of budding antinuclear activism in the Soviet Union, U.S. diplomatic officials and intelligence agents remained totally unaware of it. As the physicist Herbert York has implied, their Cold War assumptions distorted their vision. Sakharov's activities and published statements "went unnoticed in the West," York recalled. "Working in the White House and the Office of the Secretary of Defense, I was then in close touch with those in the intelligence community charged with analyzing Soviet nuclear and other technological developments." But he "never heard a single suggestion that there might be people inside the Soviet nuclear establishment who were pressing for moderation. In retrospect, this seems astonishing," York conceded, "but the picture of the Soviet Union as being, in effect, a vast prison camp simply did not allow room for such an idea."[25]

Against this backdrop, Washington officials felt little inclination to cultivate overseas nuclear disarmament groups. In his lengthy policy report to Murphy, Elliott wrote scathingly of Russell and his alleged "assumption . . . that it is better to be 'red than dead.'" This policy of "surrender to the Communists," he charged, would lead to Soviet and Chinese control of large portions of the globe and "the most complete mixing of the races." Although the State Department's overall attitude toward CND and its leaders was less venomous, it was certainly not friendly. In the spring of 1960, when Canon Collins asked for a meeting of a CND delegation with Eisenhower during the president's stay in Paris, the State Department decided to reject the request. The CND leader's "respected position in the United Kingdom in the disarmament field and the well-meaning purpose implicit in his letter" rated a reply, officials decided, but it would be a negative one, citing the president's "extremely heavy schedule."[26]

The administration also adopted a cautious approach to the Pugwash movement. Although State Department officials were pleased that American delegates had blocked a putative "Soviet campaign to turn the conference to Soviet objectives," they remained fearful that "the Soviets may attempt once again to suborn the conference." On March 31, 1960, George Kistiakowsky noted in his diary, Eugene Rabinowitch stopped by to give him "a hard sell of the Pugwash conferences and a request that I assist him in raising money for more of them." Although Kistiakowsky was one of the most committed arms controllers in the Eisenhower administration, he responded that he was "not at all sure about the value of these conferences when they are on sensitive current topics . . . such as the nuclear test cessation." That May, he met with Jerome Wiesner, a scientist moving into an important advisory position in the Kennedy campaign. Wiesner urged him to support the conferences "informally because they could contribute substantially to our position on disarmament if the right people attended them instead of wild-eyed radicals"—an approach then gaining favor in the British Foreign Office. But Kistiakowsky "reserved judgment."[27] Wiesner ultimately concluded that although Kistiakowsky and the administration did not oppose attendance at the conferences, they were wary of them. He was correct. Meeting that October, State Department, CIA, and USIA officials, without seeking to discourage participation, laid plans to warn participants of potential dangers.[28]

Of all peace movement leaders, only Norman Cousins managed to develop personal ties with Eisenhower. With the departure of Strauss from the administration in 1958, an important barrier to their relationship had disappeared. Writing to the president in May 1959, Cousins offered to provide him with a draft speech discussing the role of world law in building world peace, based on Eisenhower's past statements. Eisenhower responded warmly and, at his suggestion, Cousins delivered the text of the speech to the White House.[29] Shortly thereafter, Cousins departed for a month's stay in the Soviet Union and, on his return, suggested that he meet with Eisenhower to discuss his findings. Although James Hagerty, the White House press secretary, indicated that he was "less than enthusiastic" about this prospect, Eisenhower brushed aside his reservations. Accordingly, on August 6 the two men met at the White House, where they discussed Soviet attitudes and policies at considerable length. But what did this mean for the antinuclear movement? In neither of these instances did Cousins identify himself as co-chair of SANE or even mention its activities.[30] Furthermore, in March 1960, when Cousins dispatched a moving telegram to Eisenhower, contending that his "place in human history" now hinged on "the decision confronting you on nuclear arms control," the response was perfunctory—a thirty-seven-word acknowledgment from the president's personal secretary.[31]

For Eisenhower and his circle, public opinion about nuclear fallout remained a major problem. Writing in March 1959 to the president of the National Academy of Sciences, the AEC's Willard Libby reported that "we believe that the general concern over the effects of atomic radiation is a matter of serious import." Later that month, as Kistiakowsky recalled, "public concern about the health dangers of radiation from the nuclear test fallout" became so "acute" and "charges of concealment of facts became so serious" that Eisenhower issued a public statement, assuring the public that nothing was being concealed and that the government had initiated a major study of radiation effects. In this context, the president established the Federal Radiation Council, an interagency body granted the authority to set safe radiation standards. The issue, however, continued to plague the administration. In May 1960, when Kistiakowsky presented a Council paper to the Cabinet which argued that any radiation "has some effect on living tissue," it provoked a sharp debate. Eventually, Eisenhower sent it back to the drafters for review, with the understanding that it would be published "in such form as would not scare people to death."[32]

In December 1959, with film showings of *On the Beach* scheduled to begin in the United States and fifteen other countries, administration officials grew particularly distraught. Frightened by the film's "strong emotional appeal for banning nuclear weapons," the State Department and the USIA dispatched lengthy guidelines for handling it to their posts in foreign nations. These posts were to exhibit a "matter-of-fact interest, showing no special concern." In "private discussions with government officials or opinion leaders," however, they were to emphasize the impossibility of nuclear disarmament without conventional disarmament, the limited dangers of nuclear fallout, and the utility of civil defense measures. Otherwise, the film might "mislead people and drive them to pressure for ban-the-bomb-type solutions to the nuclear weapons problem." Convinced that *On the Beach* encouraged "extreme pacifist and 'Ban the bomb' propaganda," Karl Harr of the NSC brought the issue to the administration's December 11 Cabinet meeting. At this gathering, he and other officials condemned the film and agreed on further measures to combat its influence. Although Kistiakowsky left the meeting with the belief that Harr had "an extremely limited intellect," no one, apparently, spoke up to suggest that the leaders of the U.S. government might better focus on other matters.[33]

In 1960, as the Eisenhower era drew to a close, the specter of public resistance to the Bomb continued to haunt U.S. officials. That spring, Lodge reported hopefully that the "nuclear testing issue may soon lose potency since world opinion has had years to get used to it." But other U.S. officials were less confident. According to Ambassador James Wadsworth, a top U.S. disarmament negotiator, the administration was upset by the negative public response to its statement that the U.S. government felt free to resume nuclear testing.[34] Pointing out that disarmament had "come very much to the forefront of public consciousness in Western Europe," a USIA report of April 1960 commented anxiously that, in Britain and France, the United States had "dropped to virtually a standoff with the Soviet Union" on the question of which was making more serious efforts toward general disarmament. Although now working in a private capacity, Strauss kept up his discussions on nuclear issues with government officials. Together they explored the possibility that "an intelligently directed mass hypnosis is being inflicted upon the American people using the threat of atomic warfare or fall-out as its instrument." In the past, Strauss noted, he had dismissed this idea "as a baseless conjecture" but, by December 1960, he had "come to think that it may have substance."[35]

The Kennedy Administration and Disarmament Activism

In some ways, the attitudes of the Kennedy administration showed important elements of continuity with those of its predecessor. Certainly, little seemed to change in the State Department's assessments of antinuclear groups. Reporting from India, the U.S. embassy pronounced the Gandhi Peace Foundation's Anti-Nuclear Arms Convention a "woolly affair." From Great Britain, U.S. ambassador David Bruce asked rhetorically: "How much attention should we pay to demonstrations against the Polaris base at Holy Loch, unilateralism, banning the bomb marchers," and "Bertrand Russell defeatism?" He responded: "Realistically, we must deal in terms of power," and "power, in this country, resides in its government." In June 1962, when Bruce sent the White House a protest by Russell against renewed U.S. atmospheric testing, he recommended that it "be ignored." Russell, he told the secretary of state, was "the darling of the unilateralists, not to mention the communist and fellow-travelling supporters of the CND cause."[36] U.S. diplomatic dispatches pointed hopefully to signs of CND's decline, although they warned that "it retains a stubborn and unrepentant following."[37]

Sometimes, U.S. diplomatic dispatches gave developments an undeserved Communist tinge. From Düsseldorf, in West Germany, the U.S. consul general described the Easter March committees as "dominated by neutralist, if not fellow-traveling organizations." In New Zealand, the U.S. consul reported happily that he had turned the tables on a delegation from Auckland CND, whom he described as "all died-in-the-wool fellow travelers." Reporting from Canada, U.S. officials referred to Communist participation in antinuclear demonstrations and sometimes to "Communist-infiltrated" or Communist-influenced groups. Diplomats were not entirely impervious to facts, however, and consequently, they occasionally changed their minds. Recalling their earlier dismissal of Irish CND as Communist-led, U.S. embassy officials in Dublin admitted that the group's vigorous denunciation of Soviet nuclear testing in the fall of 1961 necessitated a reassessment on this score.[38]

Indeed, most U.S. diplomats propounded a more sophisticated—albeit no more favorable—analysis. Discussing the appearance of a Sierra Leone CND in 1963, the embassy counselor merely warned that it had "all the earmarks of a trouble-maker." Reporting from Ghana, the embassy commented acidly that plans for the Accra Assembly were moving forward in a "utopian" atmosphere. In Canada, U.S. officials did not like antinuclear groups' "carping criticism of the American position on disarmament and [of] America's policy of nuclear deterrence."[39] Although they reported happily that people who demonstrated against the resumption of U.S. atmospheric nuclear testing "were for the most part considered as 'crackpots,'" and that many Canadians felt "a heartwarming sympathy" for U.S. policy, they worried that the antinuclear movement seemed to be gaining momentum. Consequently, they sought to discourage it.[40] In Montreal, the U.S. consul general developed what he called "good relations with the experienced and savvy assistant director" of the city police, who "not only agreed with us beforehand what would be done" about demonstrations, "but agreed that it would be done at his direction and not at our request." In Denmark, the embassy avoided responding to the KmA protest against resumption of U.S. atmospheric testing, for, as the first secretary noted, that "might only serve to provide the organization with grist for its publicity mill."[41]

The State Department also fretted about the insistence of otherwise friendly governments on championing nuclear disarmament. In a dispatch from Accra, the first secretary of the U.S. embassy complained that "official Ghanaian think-ing on disarmament" was characterized by "ignorance, naiveté, and one-sided-ness." He added: "Unfortunately, this outlook is shared by most Ghanaians." Keeping the Indian government in line provided the State Department with an-other major headache.[42] Even the Canadian government could no longer be trusted. According to the State Department's May 1961 briefing papers for Kennedy's trip to Ottawa, Prime Minister Diefenbaker had "demonstrated a dis-appointing indecisiveness on . . . the defense program" and an "undue sensitiv-ity to public opinion." External Affairs Secretary Green constituted even more of a problem, for he was "rigidly opposed to the resumption of nuclear tests of any kind." He had a "naive and parochial approach to some international prob-lems"—indeed, an "almost pacifist attitude." Nor, at the time, did the leader of the opposition Liberals, Lester Pearson, appear to offer much of an alternative. "Opposed to nuclear weapons for Canadian forces, he has questioned the whole course of present U.S.-Canadian defense relationships and Canada's role in NATO," warned the State Department. Consequently, he "has been encouraging to groups advocating neutralism and unilateral disarmament."[43]

Furthermore, elements within the administration took a jaundiced view of pacifist activism at home. Responding to the pacifists who had launched the civil defense protest campaign in New York City, the director of the Office of Civil and Defense Mobilization denounced them for behavior "contrary to common sense and good citizenship." The government also adopted a hard line toward the Committee for Nonviolent Action. By the summer of 1962, three members of the crew of *Everyman I*, plus two other key CNVA supporters, had been sentenced to six months in prison for the attempt to sail into the U.S. nu-clear testing area. Federal officials also planned tough legal action against CNVA's Quebec to Guantanamo peace march. What John Kennedy thought about this—if he even knew about it—remains open to speculation. But his brother Robert almost turned against the civil rights movement when he learned that one of the Freedom Riders, savagely beaten during his bus ride through the segregated South, was Albert Bigelow, captain of the *Golden Rule*. "Do you know that one of them is against the atom bomb?" Kennedy remarked with disgust. "I wonder if they have the best interest of their country at heart."[44]

Women Strike for Peace also received a chilly reception. In early 1962, when Dagmar Wilson requested that Kennedy meet with a small WSP delega-tion, McGeorge Bundy, the president's special assistant for national security affairs, ordered her sent an anonymous reply, stating that the "President regrets he will not be able to see you and members of your group." In response, the WSP secretary, noting that "it has evidently been President Kennedy's policy not to see any peace group on matters pertaining to testing" and "disarmament," expressed WSP's "continuing desire to see the President." At Bundy's suggestion, a White House aide replied curtly: "If the President should desire to meet with your group, I will let you know promptly."[45] Although Kennedy's speechwriter, Arthur Schlesinger Jr., did meet with a WSP delegation later that year, the president remained elusive, despite continued WSP attempts to see him. In May 1963, Wilson complained to Cousins: "He has given us no sign of welcome, preferring—apparently—the society of Cuban exiles, 50-mile hikers and boy scouts. . . . It is hard to support a leader . . . who retreats beyond the office doors of aides who are often defensive or hostile."[46] WSP also appealed to Jacqueline Kennedy, who as a woman and mother, presumably would be more sympathetic. But she replied that she had great confidence in her husband's policies; furthermore, "the only route to peace for us is strength." Like other encounters with the administration, this left WSP leaders feeling snubbed.[47]

Leo Szilard encountered similar rebuffs. In 1961, he moved to Washington to see if there was "a market for wisdom." U.S. officials, however, had little interest in drawing on his advice or in using his unusual access to Khrushchev. Insisting that Szilard's discussion of foreign policy matters with the Soviet leader would be harmful, the State Department's Llewellyn Thompson also warned that it was of "questionable legality." In December 1962, Szilard showed Khrushchev's enthusiastic letter on the "Angels Project" to Bundy, but the Kennedy adviser remained unimpressed. Although Kennedy officially wished the project success, William Foster, head of the Arms Control and Disarmament Agency, pulled the rug out from under it in July 1963, when he ruled that his agency's consultants would be barred from participating in "Angels" discussions. Thereafter, Szilard gave up his efforts to get the venture off the ground and to speak with Kennedy. Meanwhile, Bundy's communications with the antinuclear scientist barely hid his contempt. "Your imaginative note of November 14" was "a characteristically original suggestion," he observed, "but I doubt if it would be useful for us to conduct our relations with Chairman Khrushchev through you."[48]

Elements of Courtship

Nevertheless, the Kennedy administration proved more receptive to disarmament activists than its predecessor had. Kennedy himself met in the spring of 1962 with a delegation from the American Friends Service Committee, which urged him to undertake "unilateral initiatives" toward disarmament. The president was "friendly and gracious," they noted, and they considered the discussion "fruitful." What Kennedy thought of this encounter with leading pacifists remains unknown. But some of his advisers, at least, accorded them a certain respect. Shortly after the physicist Glenn Seaborg became AEC chair, he received a visit from Don DeVault, a friend from his graduate school days. DeVault informed Seaborg of plans by his pacifist group to hold a disarmament vigil at the AEC's Germantown headquarters. "I told him that I doubted, in terms of the facts of life and political reality," that the vigil would have much impact, Seaborg recorded in his diary. Yet the meeting "haunted me afterward. It seemed to throw into sharp relief an essential dilemma of our time. . . . The humanity in all of us cried out for release from the crushing burden of armaments and the mounting danger of nuclear holocaust." Even so, "the immediate threat of a hostile nuclear power, the Soviet Union, was there and could not be ignored by a responsible U.S. government." Seaborg hoped to resolve this dilemma through "an end to nuclear testing"; a test ban, he wrote, would provide "a means to arrest the momentum of the nuclear arms race."[49]

The Kennedy administration also adopted a more relaxed policy toward Linus Pauling. In the spring of 1962, Kennedy and his wife hosted a White House dinner for forty-nine Nobel laureates, including Pauling, an event highlighted for the press by Pauling's picketing of the mansion that day and the preceding one to protest the resumption of U.S. nuclear testing. At the dinner, Pauling recalled, the president "said to me, in a friendly way, 'Dr. Pauling—you've been around the White House for a couple of days already, haven't you?'" Jacqueline Kennedy also chided him, but without apparent rancor.[50] In fact, White House officials usually kept Pauling at arm's length, sending him very brief, perfunctory replies to his letters or telegrams, when they sent any at all. Even so, Pauling came away with a sense of access to the Kennedy administration that he had not felt in his dealings with its predecessor.[51]

In addition, the administration made some gestures toward youthful antinuclear activists. In February 1962, as placard-waving students trudged through the snow outside the White House in an attempt to dissuade Kennedy from resuming atmospheric nuclear testing, the president, with an eye to public relations, sent them a White House butler with a huge urn of coffee. (Would drinking it be a betrayal of principle? Cold and wet, they decided that it would not.) Later that day, a group of student leaders met in the White House basement with Bundy, Kennedy speechwriter Theodore Sorensen, and Wiesner. Todd Gitlin, one of the student leaders, considered this a dialogue "with the deaf" and recalled that "some of us felt the official reactions had ranged from barely concealed condescension to political dismissal." Even so, there remained a lingering sense of influence. That March, after Kennedy ordered the resumption of nuclear testing, Wiesner—a strong test ban supporter within the administration—asked the same student leaders for help. Gitlin recalled that he and another student activist "wrote a crisp, mild memo (try harder in the negotiations, and stop waving the big stick)" and "Wiesner said he took it to a meeting of the National Security Council." Although "nothing seemed to follow," students could not help but find this "heady stuff."[52]

SANE, too, was accorded a modicum of respect. In the fall of 1961, when the disarmament group asked Kennedy to send a message of greetings to its fourth annual conference, the White House—at the suggestion of the State Department—demurred. But the director of the Arms Control and Disarmament Agency did dispatch a message to the convention. Indeed, he eventually went so far as to query Homer Jack about the sincerity of Soviet officials.[53] Furthermore, in 1961 and 1962, when SANE leader Norman Thomas wrote moving letters to Kennedy that urged him not to resume U.S. nuclear testing, the president—at Schlesinger's suggestion—sent cordial responses.[54] During his first year in office, the president even adopted SANE's rhetoric about a "Peace Race," picking up the phrase through someone present at a SANE national board meeting in June 1961. Two years later, when the USIA put together a graphic arts exhibit for a showing in Moscow, it included a SANE poster condemning nuclear testing. Thus, although the White House staff pointed out that the president had never "issued a statement of specific support for SANE" and had "not committed himself to the program of SANE or to its principles," the administration did not evince overt hostility toward it either.[55]

The administration's closest association with disarmament activists emerged in connection with the Pugwash conferences. Even before the Kennedy administration took office, two of the new president's top advisers— Wiesner and Walt Rostow—joined the U.S. delegation to the November–December 1960 Pugwash conference in Moscow. As the British Foreign Office noted, this meeting "gave an opportunity for the first contact between the new Administration and the Soviet government." During the gathering, Wiesner and Rostow not only pressed Soviet officials for the release of the RB-47 fliers, but for the reduction of anti-American propaganda in the press, an end to pressure on West Berlin, and twenty on-site inspections to verify nuclear arms controls. They also engaged in what Rostow called "an extraordinarily sustained examination" of disarmament issues with their Soviet counterparts. Addressing the Pugwash participants, Rostow expressed his "hope that the remarkable channel of communication which the Pugwash movement has opened will be kept open and rapidly enlarged."[56]

Such remarks went beyond public relations. Wiesner reported to State Department and other officials that at the Moscow Pugwash conference the Soviet Union was "represented by many of its top scientists," that they talked "more freely" about arms controls than in the past, and that they were indeed "interested in the test ban talks." Ambassador Thompson thought the discussions had been "most useful" and that the Russians seemed "deeply committed" to key aspects of an arms control agreement. Debriefed by White House, State Department, and CIA officials, Rostow declared that he had "never heard such frank treatment of extremely sensitive issues" as he had from this "extraordinary collection of people." Again and again, the Russians had insisted that they were "serious about disarmament," and he was inclined to believe them. They worried about nuclear proliferation, especially to China, as well as about the fact that "the arms race would be a very expensive and unstable dead end for both of us."[57] In the following months, U.S. officials talked up the importance of the Pugwash meetings with Soviet leaders, including Khrushchev.[58] With the opening of the next Pugwash conference, in September 1961, at Stowe, Vermont, Kennedy sent it a warm message of greetings—the first from a U.S. president. He repeated the gesture in 1962 and 1963, when Pugwash conferences convened in other countries. Meanwhile, State Department officials rushed copies of papers delivered at the Pugwash meetings directly to the White House and to the secretary of state.[59]

Although neither the U.S. government nor any other dominated the Pugwash conferences, they did begin to develop what Solly Zuckerman, the British Defense Ministry's chief scientific adviser, called a "quasi-official nature." Leading U.S. government arms control and disarmament advisers participated, including not only Wiesner and Rostow, but Kistiakowsky, Bethe, Long, and Rabi. One U.S. participant at the Stowe meeting quipped: "Before, if one went to these meetings, one lost all one's 'clearances'; to come to this one, one practically needed a special pass to show you were a trusted man."[60] Between conferences, U.S. officials discussed with their British counterparts any significant breakthroughs at the meetings and the effects of the gatherings on Soviet policy, which the Americans found encouraging. In March 1963, Britain's ambassador to the United States, David Ormsby Gore, reported to London that officials at the U.S. Arms Control and Disarmament Agency "think that it may have been due in large part to the Cambridge meeting that Khrushchev decided to propose two or three on-site inspections" as the basis for a test ban treaty. Accordingly, the United States would be sending a high-level team to the next Pugwash conference, including members of the President's Science Advisory Committee. With the Soviet, British, and U.S. governments taking the Pugwash conferences seriously, they blossomed into an important forum for discussion and agreement on measures toward decelerating and halting the nuclear arms race.[61]

Yet despite its innovative approach to some forms of nuclear disarmament activism the Kennedy administration remained uneasy about most agitation against the Bomb. Regarding itself as occupying the center of the nuclear debate, it viewed antinuclear groups as representing one of the extremes. In late 1961, discussing a government booklet on civil defense measures, Sorensen complained that it would provide "ammunition for both the SANE pacifists, etc., who think we're substituting civil defense for our 'peace race' efforts, and the hard-line militarists, etc., who look upon a nuclear war as just another war." Similarly, Adam Yarmolinsky, one of McNamara's "whiz kids" at the Pentagon, defined the administration's position as a middle ground between "holocaust and surrender"; in this context, he did not consider the writings of Erich Fromm and other critics of civil defense programs "really serious in an intellectual sense."[62] Decades later, asked about antinuclear organizations, Schlesinger noted that although the administration sometimes found them politically useful, it did not identify with them. "The Kennedy administration welcomed pressure from domestic arms control groups as an offset against the pro-arms-race pressure from Congress and the military," he observed. "The administration valued these groups for political reasons rather than as a source of ideas."[63]

Kennedy was no exception. Meeting with Diefenbaker in May 1961, the president disparaged a group of Harvard faculty members who had recently spoken out against nuclear weapons as "the same individuals who had regarded the Chinese Communists as 'agrarian reformers.'" Pro-military opinion, he insisted, was a more significant challenge to his own middle-of-the-road policies. In November 1962, conversing with Adenauer, Kennedy fretted that the British Conservatives might fall from power, opening the door to a Labour Party government. According to the minutes, "he was fearful of the very leftist elements in the Labor Party, the Communists and pacifists." They "were against the concept of a firm stand in Europe, and a firm stand was in the direct interests of the US." Nor did the president give serious attention to the proposals of SANE, WSP, the Federation of American Scientists, the Student Peace Union, and other American peace organizations. As Schlesinger recalled, Kennedy "put much more stock in the advice he received from within the government . . . than he did from outside groups."[64]

Opinion Sensitivity and Management

In this context, U.S. officials spent a good deal of time fretting about the antinuclear state of public opinion. A U.S. National Intelligence Estimate of January 17, 1961, warned that "world opinion tends to recoil from nuclear weapons, submerging logical consideration of the subject in an emotional reaction of dismay." This attitude, it noted, was "cultivated although not created by Communist propaganda." Furthermore, any resumption of U.S. nuclear testing would lead "most peoples and many governments" in the non-Communist world to "fear that the East-West arms race had begun to accelerate and was once more heading towards war." In addition, "no matter how conducted, renewed US testing would also stimulate fears concerning health dangers from fallout. The US would be severely criticized in many quarters." Even U.S. allies "would find it hard to allay the anxieties of their public. The task of justification would be especially difficult in Great Britain, where the issue would be seized upon by the popular press and large segments of the Labor Party." And "in Japan, opposition would probably be so intense as to produce anti-American demonstrations and a formal protest by the government as well."[65]

The Kennedy administration took these and other warnings to heart. At an NSC meeting of May 19, 1961, the president remarked that reports from U.S. embassies around the world indicated that the public reaction to any resumption of U.S. nuclear testing would be very adverse. Consequently, he argued, unless there was a clear necessity to resume U.S. tests, action on this score probably should be postponed. That July, an opinion analysis developed for the president by USIA director Edward R. Murrow argued that resuming U.S. nuclear testing would do the United States great damage abroad. When the Soviet government resumed nuclear testing in September, the one bright spot, as Secretary of State Dean Rusk noted, was that "the Soviets are now in a highly vulnerable propaganda position." But of course, this could be reversed if the U.S. government followed the Soviet example. Worried about this possibility, the administration had Murrow launch another assessment of global reaction to the resumption of U.S. atmospheric testing in these new circumstances. Questions to be answered included: "How informed are people on nuclear weapons tests and particularly on current Soviet tests?" "If US resumes, will 'plague on both houses' feeling be counterbalanced by free world defense needs? In terms [of] local reaction, if US resumes should it resume now or later?"[66]

The results of these and other U.S. analyses of overseas opinion were not encouraging. "Most African nations," reported a U.S. diplomat, considered the prohibition of nuclear weapons "in an emotional rather than a rational way. Rational explanations of our position, therefore, are unlikely to be altogether persuasive." In Canada, Rusk told a Senate committee, the government had "a special public opinion problem on its hands," with "a considerable group of highly vocal and articulate people" pressing it "very hard" on nuclear issues.[67] Privately, the State Department lamented a growing Canadian "resistance to American influence," which had "become fuzzily connected in some quarters with potential and actual neutralism, with anti-nuclear sentiments," and "with quasi-pacifism." In Britain, too, the U.S. government recognized that—as Kennedy told Macmillan—"problems of public opinion" concerning nuclear weapons complicated policy choices and, more seriously, Anglo-American relations. Writing in February 1962, Rusk bemoaned the worldwide "emotionalism" over nuclear testing and predicted that many nations would adopt a "plague on both houses" approach. That April, he warned all U.S. diplomatic and consular posts that "considerable unfavorable public reaction [was] expected if and when" U.S. atmospheric nuclear tests began.[68]

Much of this overseas opinion problem crystallized in U.S. relations with the United Nations. In November 1961, Kennedy telephoned Ormsby Gore and asked him if the U.S. government might use Christmas Island for its nuclear tests. Given the state of world opinion, he explained, U.N. Ambassador Adlai Stevenson had raised very strong objections to conducting further tests at Eniwetok, a U.N. trust territory. Later that month, Stevenson warned Rusk that the "bulk" of U.N. General Assembly sentiment was "overwhelmingly and emotionally opposed to any test or use" of nuclear weapons, and U.S. "efforts to prevent expression of this sentiment" in U.N. resolutions had failed. In the fall of 1962, the State Department advised its posts that, in the U.N. General Assembly,

We expect to be confronted with much the same problems as last year, namely, a resolution which will include an unverified moratorium on nuclear weapons tests; a resolution calling for a denuclearized zone in Africa and perhaps elsewhere; a possible resolution calling on nuclear powers not to make nuclear weapons or know how available to non-nuclear powers and on non-nuclear powers not to acquire such weapons and possibly not to accept deployment of such weapons by others on their territory; and a resolution calling for a ban on the use of nuclear weapons or possibly a special conference to deal with this problem. . . . All of these problems pose difficulties for us in view of the emotional appeal they hold for a large part of the UN membership.[69]

The administration considered domestic public opinion less of a problem, although still a source of difficulty. Shortly after entering the White House, Kennedy commented on what he considered diminished public concern over radioactive fallout. Drawing on Murrow's analysis, Schlesinger told the president in July 1961 that "what is politically indicated abroad—i.e., demonstration of continued concern for the test ban"—had less utility at home. Even so, the administration was alert to upsurges of American concern about nuclear weapons—upsurges which created sharp uneasiness within the administration. On January 16, 1962, the day after WSP organized a picket line of three thousand women outside the White House, Kennedy was asked about it at his press conference. Flustered and remarkably inarticulate, he replied: "I saw the ladies myself. I recognized why they were here. There were a great number of them, it was in the rain. I understand what they were attempting to say. Therefore, I consider their message received." Although the administration promoted a major fallout shelter program, it recognized that this risked enhancing popular fears of nuclear war. Accordingly, the program remained subdued. As Yarmolinsky put it, the administration wanted to avoid "scaring the pants off" the public.[70]

Managing the foreign opinion problem was a direct responsibility of the USIA, which tackled it on a variety of levels. In response to a presidential order, Murrow devoted much of his efforts to putting an acceptable face on U.S. nuclear testing. Furthermore, in a May 1962 memo to all principal USIS posts, he targeted "youth and student audiences" for "increased attention." This was necessitated, among other things, by "the political role of young people in some countries and their role as pressure groups in others." Meanwhile, to provide better guidelines for opinion management, the USIA, partially financed by the Arms Control and Disarmament Agency, conducted further studies of world opinion on nuclear weapons and test ban policy. Although the surveys produced a flutter among some officials because they no longer indicated a belief that U.S. military power was overwhelmingly superior to that of the Soviet Union, the director of the State Department's intelligence branch pointed out that this was not so bad. "In Japan and Africa," he noted, "an impression of US superiority could make us the principal target for pacifist and anti-nuclear criticism. Possibly the US might aim for a middle position in opinion, neither weaker nor excessively stronger than the USSR." Upon reflection, the USIA agreed that producing "an impression closer to parity would elicit greater approval and have a more constructive influence upon other attitudes."[71]

Other government agencies also searched for ways to mitigate adverse foreign reaction. In January 1962, the U.S. consul general in Kobe advised the State Department that Earle Reynolds, who had earlier been jailed for sailing the *Phoenix* into the U.S. nuclear testing zone in the Pacific, was planning a tour of Europe and the United States by two young survivors of the Hiroshima bombing. "Although Dr. Reynolds is not himself a Communist or sympathizer and recently publicly opposed the policy statements of the pro-Soviet wing of Gensuikyo," the U.S. diplomat observed, the pacifist was not considered "politically sophisticated or knowledgeable enough to be able to detect and exclude pro-Communist candidates." By early March, however, the State Department was growing more enthusiastic about the venture. Writing to the U.S. embassy in Tokyo, Rusk explained that in view of the "youth of [the] 'peace pilgrims' and their lack of ties with Communist groups," a meeting with a high-level U.S. government official, perhaps the president "and discussion [of the] reasons for resumption of [U.S.] atmospheric testing might help to contain

Japanese criticism." The embassy, however, responded coolly that even "non-Communist moderate elements" in Japan's antinuclear movement would condemn U.S. test resumption. Furthermore, Reynolds was "completely committed to opposition to nuclear testing by any country." Consequently, Washington scrapped this plan, and the president refused requests for a meeting with the young *hibakusha*.[72]

Later that year, another effort to curry favor abroad did come to fruition. Shortly after the Gandhi Peace Foundation's Anti-Nuclear Arms Convention, the U.S. embassy in New Delhi reported that the gathering had been attended by India's most prominent political leaders. Therefore, when the Gandhi Peace Foundation announced plans to dispatch a delegation to speak with Kennedy, Ambassador Galbraith and the State Department recommended that the president meet with it. "By doing so," a State Department memo noted, "he would gain the opportunity to present our position on nuclear testing and disarmament to a group of influential Indians, who, while they would not necessarily agree with the United States position, would listen sympathetically and report U.S. views to Nehru, the Government of India, and the Indian public." Hopefully, the treatment in Washington "would contrast favorably with the reception granted the delegation which will visit Moscow"; at the least, "the Soviets would be denied a propaganda advantage."[73] On September 28, 1962, Kennedy did meet with the Indians, who urged him to work toward banning all nuclear weapons and to immediately cease atmospheric nuclear testing. The president proved affable enough, but indicated that he would not alter previous U.S. disarmament policy. In the ensuing days, the delegation met with other U.S. officials, and the story was much the same—friendly conversations without any meeting of minds.[74]

Naturally, the administration had greater control over opinion formation in the United States. Horrified by scientific studies that showed adverse health effects of fallout, the AEC had them suppressed. A 1961 study by Dr. Edward Weiss, a Public Health Service medical researcher, showed the association between radioactive fallout and the incidence of leukemia in southwest Utah. Partly because of its "potentially detrimental effects upon the government's nuclear weapons testing program," congressional researchers later concluded, the AEC refused to publish it and would not release it until 1978. Another medical study of the early 1960s, by Dr. Harold Knapp, looked at the alarming connection between fallout and radioactive iodine-131 in milk. Despite Knapp's protests, the AEC refused to release his study, except as a confidential report. It, too, was not made available to the public until 1978, when journalists finally obtained a copy under the Freedom of Information Act. In addition, as a leading scholarly specialist has noted, from the early 1950s through 1963, federal agents "harassed and coerced local doctors and public health officials into silence when local residents grew concerned about the dangers of exposure to radiation from the atomic blasts."[75]

The issue of radioactive contamination of milk propelled the entire administration into efforts to control domestic opinion. With groups like SANE and WSP emphasizing the connection between nuclear testing and children's milk, the president himself went before the press in January 1962 to counter their claims. Drinking a glass of milk before the assemblage, Kennedy announced that it offered "no hazards" from radioactive fallout. Furthermore, he said, milk was so delicious and nutritious that he had ordered it served at all White House meals. Pierre Salinger, White House press secretary, confirmed that a group of editors and publishers, lunching with the president that day, had been offered milk as an alternative to the usual wine—although he admitted that only one member of the gathering had chosen the milk.[76] Peace groups, of course, continued to question the safety of milk in the context of nuclear tests. That spring, when WSP called for a boycott of fresh milk if the U.S. government resumed atmospheric nuclear testing, it distributed thousands of leaflets in the Washington area to this effect. In response, the U.S. Public Health Service issued a warning to mothers not to participate. Attacked by the milk industry and by the government, WSP encountered serious public relations problems for the first time.[77]

Continuity and Change

Overall, then, the U.S. government only occasionally adopted a friendly approach to the nuclear disarmament movement. There were, of course, meetings and other contacts between U.S. officials and activists, many of them quite civilized. And these contacts occurred more frequently over time. But, for the most part, U.S. officials, whether of the Kennedy or Eisenhower administrations, regarded antinuclear agitation with suspicion and distrust. Driven by a traditional orientation to national security—one that relied on superiority in armaments, in this case nuclear armaments, to secure their nation's interests in the world—they almost invariably followed the internal logic of their approach. At the same time, however, their combination of cooptive ventures and efforts to counter criticism of nuclear weapons indicated how far the antinuclear movement had advanced into the realm of domestic and international politics.

Governments Change
Policies, 1958–63

The President voiced doubts that we could ever test in
Nevada again for domestic political reasons. Ambassador
Stevenson pointed up the difficulty of testing at Eniwetok.

NSC meeting minutes, 1961

For many people who lived through the period from late 1958 to early 1963, the international situation looked extraordinarily dangerous. Even in retrospect, it is easy to reach this conclusion. During this time, the 1960 Paris summit conference collapsed, nuclear arms control negotiations failed to produce an agreement, the Soviet Union, the United States, and Britain resumed atmospheric nuclear testing, the French government acquired the Bomb, and the Chinese government worked feverishly toward the same goal. Most frightening of all, missile-rattling confrontations between the Soviet Union and the United States developed over Berlin and Cuba. Yet what is missing from this tension-ridden picture is how the antinuclear movement—either directly or, through the mobilization of public opinion and government officials, indirectly—constrained the major actors and helped shape the choices they made. Even today, few have fathomed the degree to which antinuclear sentiment eased the dangerous international confrontation, slowed the nuclear arms race, and provided the basis for the unprecedented nuclear arms control agreements that were to follow.

The Hard-Liners

Some nations, admittedly, largely overcame these constraints. Ignoring a 1959 U.N. General Assembly resolution that expressed "grave concern" at France's forthcoming nuclear test and urged that nation to abandon it, de Gaulle had his government explode an atomic bomb in Algeria on February 13, 1960. "The defense of France," he insisted, must "be French."[1] Or, as he told Eisenhower: France "obviously cannot leave her life and death entirely in the hands of any other state." Furthermore, in the face of strong domestic opposition, de Gaulle subsequently pushed through legislation authorizing a French nuclear striking force. Nevertheless, though successful in securing their nuclear objectives, French officials brooded on the price their country paid in the alienation of African and other nonaligned leaders. De Gaulle, especially, keenly resented the hostility to France's nuclear status by most nations—"this coalition of alarm on the part of so many States," as he referred to it, contemptuously, in his memoirs.[2] Perhaps for this reason, he not only insisted that his government still favored nuclear disarmament—by *all* nations, he added, meaningfully—but pulled the French nuclear testing program out of Africa and shifted it to an apparently more pliant region, Polynesia, French colonial territory in the Pacific.[3]

Like the French government, the Chinese government remained thoroughly committed to developing its own nuclear weapons capability. When the Soviet Union cut off nuclear assistance in 1959, this provided an even greater spur toward independent action. In April 1960, with U.S.-Soviet test ban negotiations well under way, Premier Chou En-lai, guarding China's nuclear options, warned that his country would not be bound by any treaty they signed. Given such concerns, Chinese officials viewed the Soviet resumption of nuclear testing in the fall of 1961 with relief. The Peking government announced that it provided "a cooling dose for the hotheaded war-plotters," as well as "a powerful inspiration to all the peoples striving for peace."[4] Furthermore, both Soviet and U.S. tests, by generating debris, provided Chinese experts with design clues for their own nuclear program. Even so, official Chinese statements emphasized the deterrent value of Communist nuclear weapons and China's commitment to nuclear disarmament. According to an August 1962 article in *Renmin Ribao (People's Daily)*, when "imperialism" used nuclear weapons "to threaten the people of the world," Communist countries, "to ensure the security of the socialist camp and defend world peace, naturally must possess nuclear weapons." Because Communist nations "love peace," their "possession of nuclear weapons and the carrying out of nuclear tests . . . can only be a telling blow against the imperialist policy of . . . nuclear blackmail and therefore helps to prevent nuclear war." Indeed, "it will help force imperialism to accept some kind of agreement on the discontinuance of nuclear testing and the prohibition of nuclear weapons."[5]

Other governments also showed little sign of cutting loose from the Bomb. Anxious lest a test ban treaty strip Australia of nuclear options, Prime Minister Robert Menzies suggested in June 1961 that the British government assure his country of its willingness to either give Australia full information on how to produce the Bomb or provide it with a "supply of ready-made weapons." That September, the East German government dutifully applauded the Soviet resumption of nuclear testing as a decisive step "to put reins on the Western war-mongers."[6] Meanwhile, its West German counterpart sought to increase Bonn's control over Western nuclear policy, if possible through the establishment of a NATO nuclear force. Although West German officials denied, on occasion, that they wanted their country to develop an independent nuclear capability, powerful figures gave contrary indications. In February 1962, the secretary general of NATO reported to Kennedy that West German Defense Minister Franz Josef Strauss had told him "that if no multilateral solution to the nuclear problem were found it was unthinkable over any long period of time that the US, the UK and France should have nuclear weapons while Germany did not."[7] Even so, none of these nations moved toward developing the Bomb.

Long-Term Opponents

Similarly, numerous governments continued their long-term opposition to the Bomb, with African and Asian nations playing the leading role. In early February 1960, as France prepared for its first nuclear test in the Sahara, twenty-five African and Asian nations at the United Nations dispatched a message to the secretary general condemning the action. When French testing began, numerous nations lodged bitter protests. Expressing Ghana's "horror" at French actions, Nkrumah ordered the assets of French companies in his country frozen and, later, recalled its ambassador from France. The Moroccan government withdrew from the French-Moroccan diplomatic agreement of May 1956 and also recalled its ambassador.[8] Although French community states, then in the process of negotiating their independence from France, refrained from open protest, Egypt and the Arab League also spoke out against French nuclear tests, as did delegates from many African and Asian countries at the United Nations. Viewing France's actions as a direct affront to Africa, Nkrumah argued that if the continent had been united, French officials would never have dared "explode atomic bombs in the Sahara in spite of urgent and repeated African objections."[9]

This Afro-Asian resistance to the Bomb also flourished in less parochial circumstances. In October 1961, as the Soviet Union tested its fifty-megaton weapon, Nehru publicly denounced it as a "terrible bomb" which "will spoil not only the atmosphere but also the bodies and minds of people all over the world. Such explosions do not augur well for peace." According to a secret U.S. study, "the widespread African news and comment was universally critical of the announced Soviet [multi-megaton] test." Although African leaders often couched their critique of Soviet test resumption in terms of their opposition to "all tests," sixteen African nations, including Ghana, backed a Canadian U.N.

resolution that singled out the Soviet Union for irresponsible behavior. African nations also rallied around the idea of proclaiming their continent a nuclear weapon–free zone. First introduced at the United Nations in 1961, the idea was endorsed by the Conference of Independent African States at Addis Ababa in May 1963. By a unanimous vote, the conference agreed to coordinate efforts "to declare and accept Africa as a denuclearized zone" and to support "the banning of nuclear weapons," "thermonuclear tests," and "the manufacture of nuclear weapons."[10]

Most of these states gravitated toward the establishment of a formal bloc: the nonaligned movement. Responding to heightened U.S.-Soviet tensions in 1960, they held their first official meeting in New York City that September, during the U.N. General Assembly session. At Tito's invitation, Nehru, Nkrumah, Nasser, and Sukarno of Indonesia gathered at the Yugoslav embassy to consider how to reduce international tensions and to move the world toward disarmament. Determined to maintain Yugoslavia's independence from the superpowers, Tito had turned to other nonaligned nations in an attempt to rally them "against the bloc system." By and large, he was successful. The leaders of numerous states, many of them recently emerged from colonialism, considered their countries, in the words of a Ceylonese observer, as a "golden bridge" between East and West—a third force that would foster disarmament and end the danger of nuclear war. Given the impoverished nature of much of Africa and Asia, they often linked this vision to the idea of economic and social progress. As Nkrumah put it: "When the non-aligned nations talk of disarmament they are not merely concerned with the destructiveness and madness of the armaments race. They are thinking of the vast possibilities now denied the people of the less-developed areas for increased standards of living, the development of agriculture and industry, the planning of cities, the abolition of illiteracy and want, and the curing of disease."[11]

The nonaligned movement was formally launched the following year, in Belgrade, when, from September 1 to 6, the heads of state of twenty-five nonaligned nations hammered out their program. Although Nkrumah and Sukarno favored an anticolonialist emphasis, Nehru—deeply disturbed by the building of the Berlin Wall and by the Soviet resumption of nuclear testing—implored his colleagues to put peace first. "Imperialism, colonialism, racialism and all the rest," he insisted, were "overshadowed" by the world crisis. "Nothing is more important and has more priority than this world situation of war and peace." Supported by Tito and Nasser, Nehru ultimately prevailed. Arguing that "war has never threatened mankind with graver consequences than today," the conference declaration devoted six of twenty-seven points to disarmament. It demanded the resumption of the nuclear testing moratorium, the conclusion of a test ban agreement, and "the total prohibition of the production, possession, and utilization of nuclear and thermo-nuclear arms." In addition, the Belgrade conference voted to dispatch Sukarno and Modibo Keito (of Mali) to Washington and Nehru and Nkrumah to Moscow to press Kennedy and Khrushchev to resume negotiations for nuclear arms controls and disarmament.[12]

In the aftermath of the Belgrade conference, leaders of these nonaligned nations kept up their running attack on the Bomb. Meeting with Ghana's foreign minister about U.S. plans to resume atmospheric testing, the U.S. ambassador found him completely unsympathetic. Nuclear armaments were morally wrong, posed a mortal danger to humanity, and should be abolished, the Ghanaian leader insisted, much to the U.S. diplomat's disgust. Meanwhile, Nehru visited with Khrushchev, expressing his profound dismay at the Soviet government's resumption of nuclear testing.[13] Uncertain of the future, Nehru apparently did not rule out the possibility that if the arms race continued, India itself might some day develop nuclear weapons. Publicly, however, he struck a loftier note. Writing for a Canadian peace periodical in 1963, he declared: "Any major war will lead to nuclear war," while "any minor war, in the existing circumstances, may well lead to a major war. Thus, the only result to aim at is to put an end to war itself." And even before the necessary "change in human mentality" occurred, "we can greatly reduce the possibility of war and especially nuclear war by disarmament."[14]

The Converts

What was remarkable was that, by the early 1960s, a host of additional countries had begun to swell the ranks of the antinuclear bloc. In Sweden, the 1959 agreement among the governing Social Democrats to postpone a decision to have their country acquire nuclear weapons proved a crucial turning point. The nuclear option continued to lose favor within the party, the society, and the government until, in 1968, at the behest of the Social Democrats, Sweden's parliament passed legislation that formally renounced nuclear arms.[15] Meanwhile, the Swedish government became a leading proponent of nuclear disarmament on the international scene. In September 1961, it denounced the Soviet resumption of nuclear testing and called on the Belgrade conference to help foster renewed political and disarmament negotiations among the great powers. A few weeks later, Swedish prime minister Tage Erlander announced his "deep disappointment" that the Soviet government had exploded a fifty-megaton weapon "in spite of world-wide opinion against it." On October 26, Sweden's foreign minister, Östen Undén, unveiled a far-reaching Swedish disarmament proposal at the United Nations. Dubbed the Undén plan, it provided for the formation of a "non-nuclear club" that would facilitate the end of nuclear testing, prevent further nuclear proliferation, and establish nuclear-free zones.[16]

Other governments also spoke out sharply against nuclear weapons. The Irish government competed with the Swedish in promoting nuclear disarmament measures within the framework of the United Nations. In Finland, President Urho Kekkonen championed a massive disarmament petition and called for the establishment of the Nordic countries as a nuclear-free zone.[17] Publicly condemning U.S. resumption of underground nuclear tests in 1961 and atmospheric nuclear tests in 1962, the Japanese government assailed nuclear testing and called on Kennedy to "reconsider" his actions. As in the past, Japanese officials accompanied such statements with private assurances to the U.S. government that the protests had been made "to offset domestic political pressures." Secretly, some officials even remarked that they favored Japan's development of nuclear weapons. Nevertheless, their public protests attested to the success of disarmament groups in keeping the public policy of the Japanese government on an antinuclear course.[18] Indeed, intimidated by popular pressures, the Japanese government carefully avoided public discussions of national defense issues, canceled Eisenhower's 1960 trip to Japan amid the nationwide furor over the U.S.-Japan security treaty, and appealed to the United Nations to end the menace posed by the Bomb.[19]

A division over nuclear issues even began to pervade NATO. With Norway engulfed by antinuclear petitions and protests, that country's parliament voted in April 1961 to ban nuclear weapons from its soil in peacetime. In November, as Rusk fretted about a "serious NATO split" on a forthcoming "'ban the bomb' resolution" at the United Nations, a Danish official retorted that it would be "impossible for [the] Danish delegation to vote against any resolution aimed at abolition [of the] nuclear arms peril." Given the popular appeal of such proposals, Denmark would be compelled to vote "idealistically." Three days later, when NATO's U.N. delegates met to consider the Undén plan, most favored a negative vote or abstention, but Denmark, Norway, and Iceland pressed for a positive vote. As the Danish representative explained, his delegation had to "exercise care in taking [a] position . . . because of public opinion at home." Reporting on the meeting, the U.S. representative warned of the possibility that adopting a stand against the Swedish proposal might lead to "complete NATO disarray."[20]

During the following year, the situation worsened. In August 1962, a Norwegian diplomat notified the U.S. government that "because of the strength of Norwegian public opinion," his country would "have to vote" for a resolution at the United Nations, sponsored by India, that called for a renewed moratorium on nuclear testing. Although the U.S. government opposed the resolution, he hoped it "could find some way to be more relaxed on the moratorium question." That December, a State Department memo warned that "while the French and Germans will be sensitive to anything resembling denuclearization or disengagement in Europe, the Scandinavians and Canadians will press for greater accommodation to Soviet views." Nor, from the U.S. government standpoint, was the situation much happier with respect to nuclear deployment. Speaking to West German officials that June, Rusk complained bitterly that "the US, which is responsible for the nuclear defense of the Alliance, has had to go on its knees to plead for the deployment of its weapons." Even then, "half of the countries have said no, sometimes for trivial reasons. This has not been a pleasant experience for us."[21]

Canada, particularly, seemed to be getting out of line. Beginning in the late 1950s, the Canadian government, encouraged by the surge of antinuclear sentiment at home, gave top priority to promoting international efforts to foster disarmament and a halt to nuclear testing. Acknowledging that U.S. government response to his proposals was "chilly," External Affairs Minister Howard Green retorted that this was hardly surprising, for the United States and the Soviet Union were the nations "in a position to create all the trouble." "War would mean the end of civilization," he explained, "and Canada is caught between Russia and the United States."[22] Ottawa's increasingly antinuclear opinions became a source of serious concern to Washington as the Diefenbaker government refused to arm Canadian missiles and bombers with U.S. nuclear weapons—an action that U.S. officials considered both strategically necessary and fully justified by Canada's NATO and NORAD commitments. Unlike Green, Diefenbaker had no fundamental objection to such action. But as he plaintively told Kennedy in May 1961, Canada had experienced "an upsurge of feeling against nuclear weapons." Numerous organizations pressed him hard to refrain from the nuclear option, and his mail "was running very heavy in letters against nuclear weapons, including a very high percentage from mothers and wives." Consequently, it was "politically impossible" to accede to Washington's wishes. When the U.S. government publicly challenged him on the matter and the opposition Liberals fell into line with U.S. policy, Diefenbaker made his refusal to install nuclear weapons in Canada a centerpiece of his hard-fought 1963 re-election campaign.[23]

Other normally reliable U.S. allies were also moving in an antinuclear direction. In 1959, New Zealand's Labour government, in fulfillment of its election promise to work for cessation of nuclear testing, broke ranks with the United States and Great Britain and voted with the U.N. majority to urge France to refrain from Bomb tests in the Sahara. Even the advent of a National government the following year failed to halt the antinuclear momentum, for the new prime minister, Keith Holyoake, criticized both sides in the Cold War for resuming their tests. Writing to Macmillan, who had contacted him about proposed Western tests at Christmas Island, he explained: "Given the prevailing state of public opinion on the dangers of testing and my complete lack of knowledge regarding the military necessity, I am sure you will understand why we regard the resumption of testing . . . as a matter for deprecation." The New Zealand government also protested repeatedly to U.S. officials, noting that there existed "a great deal of public feeling in New Zealand against the resumption of atmospheric tests," and it "would be greatly exacerbated if tests were held in proximity to New Zealand-administered territory." In March 1963, following an announcement that France would shift its nuclear testing to the South Pacific, the New Zealand government dispatched a diplomatic note to the French declaring that public opinion in New Zealand had grown "greatly alarmed" by news of the French plans. Two months later, it issued a strong diplomatic protest against the establishment of a French testing site and urged France to reconsider.[24]

Meanwhile, other countries took steps to keep themselves nuclear-free. On May 1, 1963, it was announced that the presidents of Bolivia, Brazil, Chile, Ecuador, and Mexico had signed an agreement "not to manufacture, receive, store, or test nuclear arms or launching apparatus" and to work for the establishment of a "denuclearized zone" in Latin America. According to their statement, they acted in the desire to preserve "their countries from the disastrous effects of a nuclear war, and in the hope that the conclusion of a Latin American regional treaty" would encourage a similar development worldwide.[25] By mid-1963, even the Swiss government, which only five years before had trumpeted the necessity of Switzerland's acquisition of tactical nuclear weapons, had decided to abandon the idea. Although the reasons for this decision remain obscure, they apparently included the declining appeal of tactical nuclear war and the conclusion that Switzerland's traditional neutrality could best be maintained by a less provocative military posture.[26]

With national governments increasingly eager to establish their antinuclear credentials, plans to halt nuclear testing and to foster nuclear disarmament—many regarded with suspicion by Washington—garnered overwhelming support at the United Nations. In November 1959, over the objections of the U.S. and British governments, the U.N. General Assembly called on France to halt plans for nuclear testing by a vote of 51 to 16. On November 24, 1961, the General Assembly approved (by a vote of 55 to 0, with 44 abstentions) an African-sponsored resolution urging member states to "respect the continent of Africa as a denuclearized zone." On December 4, 1961, despite opposition from the West, the General Assembly approved the Undén plan by a vote of 58 to 10, with 23 abstentions. That same day, the Assembly also voted on the Irish resolution; designed to encourage nuclear nonproliferation, it sailed through by a unanimous vote. Although the U.S. government viewed the Irish formula as harmless, it took a less sanguine view of strong U.N. resolutions on nuclear issues the following year.[27]

The British Government Grows Dovish

Even the position of the nuclear-armed British government began to soften. Given the British public's skittishness about the Bomb, government officials sought to avoid policies that raised the prospect of a nuclear attack. In this context, the U.S. government's determination to establish a Polaris submarine base at Holy Loch, only thirty miles from Glasgow, created what the Cabinet called "great political difficulties." From the standpoint of "justifying" an Anglo-American agreement to "public opinion," the Cabinet noted on July 28, 1960, it was vital "to secure a satisfactory formula about the degree of our control over American submarines using the Scottish facilities." To overcome the "considerable political difficulty in securing public support in this country for these arrangements," Britain "should aim to get American agreement to full and timely consultation with us . . . and joint decision in an emergency." The Foreign Office advised the British embassy in Washington that it was "essential" to be able to "say publicly that the United Kingdom government would have full control over the launching of missiles within territorial waters."[28] But, in fact, this kind of control over the use of U.S. nuclear weapons was totally unacceptable to the U.S. government. Consequently, London officials found it difficult to develop what the foreign secretary called a formula both "satisfactory to public opinion in this country" and to the United States. Finally, on November 1, Macmillan did issue a vague statement about the missiles, claiming that there would be "the fullest possible previous consultation" before their use. But this hardly settled the issue, for the statement caused an uproar in the U.S. government and in Parliament.[29]

Like the Polaris base, the Cuban missile crisis raised the unpleasant prospect of Britain's nuclear destruction in a war started by the United States. Although, on the surface, the British government backed its U.S. partner, behind the scenes the reaction was rather different. The Lord Chancellor warned the Cabinet that "the imposition of the 'quarantine' cannot be justified as a 'pacific blockade' under international law," and the Foreign Office contested Kennedy's claim that Soviet installation of the missiles threatened the balance of power. Cabinet officials also worried that the incident would do them political damage in the House of Commons. In a cable to Kennedy on the evening of October 22, Macmillan did promise British support and sympathy. But he also expressed reservations about the legality of the blockade and his concern that it might provoke Soviet retaliation against Berlin. Seven minutes later, he cabled anxiously to the British ambassador in Washington, asking him "what it is the President is really trying to do." Macmillan added: "Since it seemed impossible to stop his actions, I did not make the effort, although . . . I was in a mind to do so. . . . I could not allow a situation . . . to develop which looks like escalating into war without trying . . . to stop it." On October 27, Macmillan proposed to Kennedy that if it would "save the Russians' face," he would be willing to scrap the Thor nuclear missiles in Great Britain in a trade-off for the Soviet missiles in Cuba.[30]

At the same time, British policymakers clung to their possession of an "independent" nuclear deterrent. On occasion, to be sure, individual officials supported the idea that it would be easier for Britain to simply accept participation in a U.S.-led nuclear program—an idea championed by Defense Secretary McNamara and other top officials in the Kennedy administration. Nevertheless, Macmillan insisted on a British Bomb. Irked by U.S. criticism of nuclear proliferation, he complained in June 1962: "We have an independent deterrent and the French are going to get one; these are facts which the Americans cannot alter. . . . I hope we can persuade Rusk, and even McNamara through him, to stop making speeches and launching plans." Meeting with Kennedy that December, Macmillan stated that Britain needed independent control of nuclear weapons "in order to remain something in the world." He conceded that "the whole thing is ridiculous," for the modest British nuclear force did not add much "to the existing nuclear strength, which is enough to blow up the world." Still, "countries which have played a great role in history must retain their dignity." Britain had to "increase or at least maintain the strength of its foreign policy, so that it could not be threatened with impunity."[31]

Even so, convinced that nuclear tests would no longer be tolerated by public opinion, British officials also believed—as they complained repeatedly during 1959—that it had become politically impossible for them to resume nuclear testing. Revealing to the Americans "that public opinion might force an agreement to discontinue tests without any control at all would be a red rag to a bull," the British embassy advised in mid-January. Nevertheless, with elections pending in the fall, as Macmillan recalled, the issue of nuclear tests "was now becoming serious for us." The government decided that summer that if no test ban agreement were reached, "it would be politically expedient, and acceptable to us on defense grounds" to seek U.S. agreement to permanent cessation of Anglo-American atmospheric testing, "combined with a moratorium on underground tests."[32] Meeting with Eisenhower on August 30, only two days after the U.S. government announced that it would only guarantee an extension of its compliance with the moratorium until the end of the year, Macmillan pressed the U.S. president "very strongly," in his words, to extend the moratorium. Eisenhower recalled that the British seemed "more concerned with world opinion" than with "the growth of Soviet military might." In addition, Macmillan "said that he might find it necessary eventually to announce that no further tests of any kind were to take place."[33]

In the aftermath of the British elections of October 1959, the Macmillan government continued to be driven by its fear of adverse public opinion. Late that month, Sir Michael Wright, Britain's chief arms control negotiator, told the U.S. ambassador that the British government was "firmly convinced it is impossible from the standpoint of British and world public opinion for [the] U.S. and British [governments] to resume testing." Although Macmillan's sweeping election victory had led U.S. officials to think that the British would be more flexible, Wright replied that "resumption of testing would cause as much difficulty in the U.K. as previously." Would not the U.S. government commit itself to a "moratorium on underground testing for one or two or three years without controls"? The tension between Britain and the United States over the resumption of nuclear testing continued into 1960. Nuclear tests had become a "genuine source of alarm" to the public, Macmillan recalled in his memoirs, and he was "particularly anxious" about the U.S. government's "apparent refusal of a moratorium."[34]

Even the August 31, 1961, announcement of Soviet test resumption failed to break the opposition of the British government to a renewed Western testing program. Delighted to turn the weight of antitesting sentiment against Moscow, Macmillan joined Kennedy in a September 3 public appeal to Khrushchev, proposing that their three nations cease all atmospheric tests without controls. Two days later, at a Cabinet meeting, Foreign Secretary Alec Douglas-Home noted that the Soviet test resumption had "given the West a considerable propaganda advantage." Moreover, since it was "unlikely" that the Soviet government would accept the Anglo-American offer, "further advantage might be derived if these governments could continue to refrain from making such tests." Macmillan liked this idea, and the Cabinet agreed that he should send a message to the U.S. government along these lines. To their dismay, however, the next day Kennedy, without consulting them, announced his plan to resume underground nuclear tests. "This hurried decision," Macmillan noted in his diary, "has taken the gilt off the gingerbread." Or, as he later complained: "We had unnecessarily helped to get the Russians 'off the hook.'"[35]

Nevertheless, as Kennedy had assured Macmillan that he would not resume *atmospheric* testing without full consultation with the British, this gave them a second line of defense. Macmillan had the British ambassador inquire whether Kennedy would agree to a statement saying that neither of their governments would resume atmospheric testing for the next six months, and after that only if obliged to do so by military necessity. Although Kennedy rejected the idea, the issue was joined again that November. The U.S. government wanted to use the British testing facilities at Christmas Island, and Douglas-Home thought that if a test was absolutely imperative, Great Britain should cooperate. But, "by acceding to the American request we expose ourselves to serious criticism," he noted. It "will come not only from uncommitted countries and the United Nations but also from India and probably, Canada, and other Commonwealth countries, as well as Japan. There will no doubt be strong protests in the United Kingdom." In these circumstances, Douglas-Home favored allowing the United States to use the island "only on very strict conditions." Even this limited concession provoked an uproar in the Cabinet, where critics argued "that it would be difficult to justify to public opinion in this country a series of atmospheric tests on the scale envisaged. . . . Ordinary people increasingly expected the government to devote their energies to securing a complete cessation of tests, at least in the atmosphere." Eventually, then, Macmillan promised to insist on the toughest of conditions for U.S. use of Christmas Island, including the criterion that each test be justifiable before "world opinion."[36]

Accordingly, British officials now gave their U.S. partners an unusually hard time of it. In a November 16 letter to Kennedy about Christmas Island, Macmillan declared that he was "concerned about the possible reactions of opinion in this country," where "public pressures" were running high against testing. "But I am much more deeply concerned about our joint position in the face of world opinion. On both these grounds, I feel that, before we take our final decision, we ought to have . . . fuller information." U.S. officials could read between the lines. As Seaborg noted, "it was evident that Macmillan meant to use our need for Christmas Island as leverage . . . to dissuade us from atmospheric testing." At the Bermuda conference of December 1961, which brought together leading officials of both countries, Douglas-Home and, especially, Macmillan warned of an unending, dangerous nuclear arms race and implored Kennedy, before deciding to resume atmospheric tests, to undertake a major new disarmament initiative. This would provide the West, Macmillan said, with "a great moral advantage." The Americans, however, were implacable and, ultimately, he acceded to their request for the use of Christmas Island, if they decided to resume testing. Even so, as Seaborg recalled, "the British prime minister had enlisted all his persuasive eloquence . . . in an effort to stay our hand."[37]

Nor did this end the conflict over Western test resumption. On January 3,

1962, the British Cabinet agreed to take steps to ready Christmas Island facilities for such tests, if both nations decided to hold them. But, as Macmillan recalled, the Cabinet "also wished for some new disarmament initiative to be taken and given wide publicity." Accordingly, on January 5, Macmillan dispatched a letter to Kennedy arguing that any announcement of test resumption would have to "be accompanied by a determined new initiative towards disarmament." Although Macmillan admitted that he needed a publicized disarmament initiative to appease domestic opinion, he now attacked the nuclear arms race in terms remarkably like those of CND. "If we do what we are now contemplating," he told Kennedy, "it would really seem to any ordinary person who reflects calmly upon it that humanity is setting out on a path at once so fantastic and so retrograde, so sophisticated and so barbarous, as to be almost incredible." "This contest will continue more or less indefinitely," he warned, and "the end may be what has nearly always been the end in these armament races—one side or the other, when it thinks it has the moment of superiority, will be tempted to put the issue to the test." Meanwhile, the Chinese, the French, and the Germans would develop nuclear weapons, which would inevitably fall into "the hands of all kinds of different characters—dictators, reactionaries, revolutionaries, madmen"—and, eventually, "the great crime will be committed." There must be "a way out of the maze in which we are set."[38]

Although Kennedy agreed to Macmillan's approach—coupling any talk of preparations for new testing with a disarmament appeal—Macmillan was still not satisfied. To be sure, he found this two-pronged strategy useful in staving off public and parliamentary criticism in February 1962. But, until the end of the month, when Kennedy notified him that he planned a television address on March 1 announcing test resumption, the British prime minister still hoped to block the action. The U.S. decision, he complained, would "shatter the hopes of millions of people across the earth." Again Macmillan asked Kennedy for a postponement, but the president would only delay his announcement until March 2—from Macmillan's standpoint, an important concession for, by that time, the House of Commons would be recessed for the weekend. Writing in his diary on March 24, Macmillan noted that there now seemed "no way of preventing the starting of the American tests at Christmas Island." Kennedy, he noted, was "under great pressure, from the Pentagon and from Congress. Here all the pressure is the other way." Fortunately, though, the U.S. president "throughout showed the greatest patience, partly because he fully understood my political position."[39]

Given British officials' resistance to nuclear testing, it was hardly surprising that they championed a test ban agreement on relatively easy terms. Behind the scenes, the British government—"primarily motivated by domestic political considerations," as it secretly admitted—succeeded in late 1958 in getting the U.S. government to disconnect a test ban from broader progress on disarmament. In February 1959, with the Geneva test ban talks snagged on the issue of international inspection and control, Macmillan wrote to Eisenhower that "perfect control is . . . quite impossible in practice"; it was only necessary to "create a control system which involves a sufficient degree of risk to a potential violator that he cannot get away undetected." Although U.S. officials made some modest compromises on a verification system, the British—striving for what Macmillan called "the agreement for which the public were looking so anxiously"—continued to advocate a more relaxed regimen. The prime minister was particularly keen on what he called "an unpoliced agreement on tests that cause fallout." He told Kennedy in mid-August 1961 that "some such move will be necessary to show that we are fully conscious of world-wide anxiety about fallout and ready to do our best to avoid it."[40]

Even after the collapse of the moratorium, London pressed hard for a test ban on terms Washington considered dangerously lax. Meeting with Kennedy in March 1962, Ormsby Gore promoted a new British plan that dropped the idea of control posts on Soviet territory. The British government felt "strongly," he said, that it was "necessary to put forward a proposal which seems reasonable both to our own and to world public opinion." In a message to Kennedy later that month, Macmillan insisted that "we cannot afford to let the hopes of the world for a nuclear test ban be dashed at Geneva without a further public effort which . . . will catch the imagination." The Russians, of course, might reject such a new proposal, "but if we can get them into this position, we should have world opinion on our side." In June, he suggested "a completely unpoliced ban, perhaps for a period of three to five years." According to Seaborg's notes, at a White House meeting of August 1, 1962, Kennedy "read a letter from Macmillan in which the prime minister said that he continued to feel that nuclear tests were not needed, that there was urgent need for a test ban, and that a test ban could be fully effective with fewer controls than the U.S. seemed to think necessary." With considerable justification, Seaborg concluded years later that "in the matters of testing and test ban negotiations, . . . the British consistently endeavored, often with success, to exercise a moderating influence on U.S. policy."[41]

Soviet Policy Wavers

Among Soviet policymakers, proponents of easing the East-West nuclear confrontation continued to hold the initiative from late 1958 to early 1960. At the Twenty-first Communist Party Congress of January 1959, Khrushchev reiterated his theme that "war is not fatally inevitable." In addition, the party adopted a new formulation arguing that war could be excluded as a possibility if the world correlation of forces favored peace. Returning from a visit to the United States, Khrushchev told the Supreme Soviet that October: "To put it bluntly, under peaceful coexistence states must meet each other halfway in the interests of peace." The West, he insisted, had already made important concessions to Communist states. In January 1960, he announced further unilateral cutbacks in the Soviet armed forces, designed to reduce them by nearly a third over the next two years. Some of this manpower cutback, of course, could be attributed to the Soviet Union's concurrent nuclear missile buildup. Furthermore, Khrushchev continued to brag about space rockets and new weapons. Nevertheless, the Soviet premier and his political allies clearly desired to reduce the cost of the Soviet armed forces and to improve relations with the United States. In addition, though their disarmament proposals continued to represent little more than Cold War propaganda, they seemed more serious about nuclear arms controls. Such goals reflected a desire to concentrate Soviet economic resources on the civilian sector, to avert what they believed would be a disastrous war, and to court world opinion through a "peace policy."[42]

Angered by these developments, conservative forces staged a counterattack. The Soviet military leadership, particularly, resented Khrushchev's cutbacks in the armed forces and the Soviet Union's emerging detente with the West. Powerful party rivals also looked askance at the weakening of Soviet defenses, as did the proponents of heavy industry and the armaments industry. In world Communist ranks, opponents of "peaceful coexistence" could count on the support of the Chinese government and its militant allies. Although Khrushchev and his supporters managed to keep the upper hand until the spring of 1960, the U-2 incident of that May undermined their influence, for they had emphasized the peaceful intentions of the Eisenhower administration. Humiliated by the U-2 flights, Khrushchev stormed about at the Paris summit conference later that month, hoping to bluff Eisenhower into a personal apology. The U.S. president, however, refused to capitulate, and, consequently, the Soviet leader's emotional gambit resulted only in destroying the meeting and undermining his authority still further. Seizing the moment, Frol Kozlov, Mikhail Suslov, and other conservatives took effective control of the Soviet party apparatus.[43]

The result was a tilt toward a harder line. Although the Kremlin continued to make ritual obeisance to disarmament, it ceased to move in this direction. Reversing Khrushchev's priorities, the Soviet government suspended earlier troop cuts, increased the military budget, built the Berlin wall, and resumed nuclear testing. As titular head of the Soviet party and state, Khrushchev presided over these measures, but without much enthusiasm. Missiles "are not cucumbers," he observed ruefully; "one can't eat them, and to repel aggression one needs no more than a certain number of them." At his meeting with Kennedy in Vienna during June 1961, Khrushchev took a hard line with the new U.S. president and again secured neither concessions nor satisfaction. Personally, he recalled in his memoirs, he felt sorry for Kennedy and "doubly sorry because what had happened did not create favorable conditions for improving relations. On the contrary, it aggravated the Cold War. This worried me. . . . We would be the ones who would have to pay for it." Publicly, Khrushchev continued to champion his "peaceful coexistence" line. Addressing party leaders in January 1961, the Soviet premier insisted that there were "two trends" observable "in the policy of the capitalist camp . . . : a bellicose-aggressive one and a more moderate sober one." Lenin himself had argued that "in the struggle to preserve peace," Communists "must" work with "sensible representatives of the bourgeoisie." In practice, though, Khrushchev drifted with the conservative tide.[44]

Whatever their conflicts over arms controls and detente, Soviet policymakers showed little inclination to use nuclear weapons. Unlike some Chinese officials of the time, Soviet leaders argued that nuclear war would be catastrophic. Therefore, they said, Soviet nuclear weapons did not exist to win such a conflict, but to deter it. The Third Party Program, adopted in 1961, contended that "the chief aim" of the party's foreign policy was "to deliver mankind from a world war of extermination," to "prevent it from breaking out." In his speeches and in his memoirs, Khrushchev argued repeatedly that in a nuclear war "the victor will be barely distinguishable from the vanquished. A war between the Soviet Union and the United States would almost certainly end in mutual defeat." Thus "war *must* be prevented because, if it breaks out in this day and age, it will bring disaster to the whole planet." Dobrynin recalled that, in 1962, shortly before he was dispatched to the United States as Soviet ambassador, Khrushchev "plainly told me that I should always bear in mind that war with the United States was inadmissable; this was above all." Commenting on his dealings with Kennedy, Khrushchev himself wrote: "I certainly was afraid of war. Who but a fool isn't? I've got no qualms about coming right out and saying we were afraid of war." Even party hard-liners like Suslov and Kozlov showed nothing but distaste for the prospect of a nuclear conflict.[45] For the most part, U.S. officials have agreed with this assessment.[46]

The Cuban missile crisis provides a revealing illustration of Soviet nuclear policy. Although Soviet emplacement of medium-range missiles proved a provocative, dangerous act, Khrushchev maintained (and many Soviet and American commentators now agree) that his intentions were defensive: to deter a U.S. invasion of Cuba and to redress a nuclear imbalance that heavily favored the United States.[47] Startled, thereafter, by the sudden mobilization of U.S. military power, Khrushchev frantically backed away from the brink. "Try to put yourself in our place," he urged Kennedy in a message of October 24, and avoid "passions" that would push humanity "toward the abyss of a world nuclear-missile war." As both sides considered their options, he ordered Soviet ships carrying the missiles to turn back. On October 26, again warning that "one should not give way to one's passions," Khrushchev assured Kennedy that Soviet leaders "are sane people." And "only lunatics or suicides, who themselves want to perish and before they die destroy the world" would launch a nuclear war. He concluded that both nations should avoid tightening the knot in the rope they held between them, thereby "dooming the world to the catastrophe of nuclear war"; instead, they should begin to relax the tension and resolve their difficulties. Specifically, Khrushchev offered to withdraw the missiles in exchange for Kennedy's promise not to invade Cuba and, later, to swap the Soviet missiles in Cuba for U.S. missiles in Turkey—offers that provided the basis for ending the crisis.[48]

The Soviet government's eagerness to avoid nuclear war played an important role in heightening the Sino-Soviet conflict. Increasingly wary of the Chinese leadership, Soviet officials continued to defer full implementation of the 1957 New Defense Technical Accord, which had provided for Soviet assistance to the Chinese nuclear program. Despite repeated promises by Moscow, the Soviet government never sent the prototype atomic bomb and other valuable nuclear information. Finally, on June 20, 1959, it formally abrogated the agreement. During the latter part of that year, Soviet nuclear specialists began their departure from China; by August 1960 they had withdrawn entirely. Viewing his Chinese partners as dangerous and unreliable, Khrushchev had reneged on them in a fashion they bitterly resented. Indeed, they sharply assailed Khrushchev's policies, as well as Soviet leadership of the world Communist movement. Even in the aftermath of the U-2 incident and the collapse of the Paris summit conference, Soviet leaders continued to reject Peking's version of Communist militancy. Indeed, the very ferocity of the Chinese attack may have pushed the Soviet government toward detente and a test ban treaty.[49]

For a "considerable time," recalled James Wadsworth, who represented the U.S. government at the Geneva test ban negotiations, "the Soviets were genuinely seeking agreement." They wanted "to bring an end to the further development of nuclear weapons by the United States, to prevent new countries from entering the restricted circle of nuclear powers, to save the . . . cost of testing, and to derive public acclaim for their initiative." Consequently, "in comparison to other East-West negotiations," the test ban talks produced "little friction and much cooperation." In March 1960, the British foreign secretary reported to his Cabinet that, at the negotiating table, the Soviet government had "come round to the view which we ourselves had urged upon the Americans." By the end of that year, seventeen articles of a draft treaty had been agreed upon.[50] Meanwhile, Khrushchev championed a test ban treaty at party meetings and, at his authorization, Soviet scientists published articles on the health hazards of nuclear testing. Admittedly, Khrushchev opposed a comprehensive verification system. "We couldn't allow the US and its allies to send their inspectors criss-crossing around the Soviet Union," he argued in his memoirs, for "they would have discovered that we were in a relatively weak position."[51] And yet, until the spring of 1960, he seemed serious enough about securing a test ban with a modest degree of verification and about continuing the testing moratorium. On January 14 of that year, he declared that the first nation to resume nuclear tests would "cover itself with shame."[52]

The conservative takeover of May 1960, however, tipped the balance against a treaty and toward the resumption of nuclear testing. Committed to developing and displaying greater military might, party conservatives had long been chilly toward a test ban, as had the military leadership, and they now spoke out more freely against it. Khrushchev, in turn, began to edge away from his former position. Meanwhile, the Soviet nuclear establishment pushed for the resumption of nuclear testing. In July 1961, Khrushchev told John J. McCloy, Kennedy's special adviser on disarmament, that Soviet military leaders and scientists were pressing him to authorize the testing of a hundred-megaton Bomb.[53] That September, only a week after Khrushchev shocked the world by announcing the resumption of Soviet nuclear testing, a member of the Soviet U.N. delegation attributed it, in part, to "great pressures on Khrushchev . . . from the military and the scientists." Chillingly, Khrushchev publicly boasted that the Soviet Union possessed both a fifty-megaton Bomb and a hundred-megaton model. "When the enemies of peace threaten us with force," he said, "they . . . will be countered with force, and more impressive force, too." More than three decades later, two leading scientists who worked on the famous fifty-megaton weapon recalled that its "unprecedented test" was "a one-time demonstration of force, part of the superpower game of mutual intimidation."[54]

Khrushchev and his allies, however, felt some embarrassment at this return to traditional behavior. Interviewed—on his own initiative—by C. L. Sulzberger of the *New York Times* a few days after announcing test resumption, the Soviet premier exhibited remarkable ambivalence: "We are making nuclear tests. . . . But what the hell do we want with tests? You cannot put a bomb in soup or make an overcoat out of it. Nevertheless, we are compelled to test." In conversations with Nehru, Khrushchev stuck to the official Soviet position but, according to the Indian leader, seemed "rather on the defensive." The ambassador from the United Arab Republic, upon protesting the Soviet test resumption, also found Soviet officials very uncomfortable and eager to change the subject. This sensitivity to foreign criticism may explain why, only two weeks after Soviet test resumption, the San Francisco to Moscow peace marchers were allowed to enter the Soviet Union and freely conduct antinuclear agitation across hundreds of miles of Soviet territory. Khrushchev's role in this remains unclear, but one Kremlinologist has argued that this unprecedented accommodation to antinuclear protest, as well as the marchers' audience with his wife, would have been impossible without the Soviet premier's approval.[55]

Still, embarrassed or not, Khrushchev and other party reformers remained reluctant, for the time being, to challenge the hard-liners. The September 1961 resumption of Soviet atmospheric nuclear testing was followed, that October, by the explosion of the fifty-megaton Soviet Bomb, spewing radioactive fallout around the world. Although the West offered an atmospheric test ban treaty in September 1961 and in August 1962, the Soviet government rejected it on both occasions. On August 5, 1962, in the aftermath of atmospheric tests conducted by the United States and Britain, the Soviet Union began a new test series, arguing that because the U.S. government had carried out the first nuclear tests in 1945, it had the right to carry out the last ones. This new test series, claimed Tass, provided a "great service to the cause of preserving peace." Although the test ban negotiations, broken off in September 1961, resumed thereafter, they produced little of apparent value. With Khrushchev unwilling or unable to press other Soviet leaders toward a compromise, arms control negotiations remained unproductive.[56]

Uncertainty in the United States

The inconsistency of Soviet foreign and military policy, combined with growing antinuclear sentiment, left the U.S. government uncertain about its own national security approach. Given its early commitment to a nuclear buildup, the Eisenhower administration constructed an unprecedented nuclear arsenal. By the time it left office, it had developed a "strategic triad" of long-range offensive nuclear forces: intercontinental ballistics missiles, submarine-launched ballistics missiles, and long-range bombers. In 1953, there were twelve hundred nuclear weapons in the U.S. stockpile; by January 1961, there were more than thirty thousand. On the other hand, like Dulles, administration officials were increasingly uneasy about "massive retaliation" and the nuclear arms race. Herbert York, who worked for the Defense Department, concluded that "defense of the population is impossible in the nuclear era" and "our only real hope for the long run lies in working out a political solution." Eisenhower seemed particularly distraught. Meeting with the president in March 1960, CIA director John McCone found him "entirely preoccupied by the horror of nuclear war." To McCone's dismay, Eisenhower never mentioned U.S. national security or "Communistic aggression," but focused on "freeing the people of the world from the dreadful fear that now hangs over them."[57]

The incoming Kennedy administration shared this uneasiness about nuclear war. Shortly after taking office, Secretary of State Rusk proposed scrapping the policy of "massive retaliation" and limiting nuclear weapons to the function of deterring a nuclear attack. At his suggestion, McNamara initiated a Defense Department study of the idea, in which the military branches were asked to consider how they might fight small wars without using nuclear weapons. In 1962, with the strong support of Rusk and McNamara, the administration approved a new policy, "flexible response," which, in Rusk's words, "raised the nuclear threshold."[58] Beginning that year, McNamara brought the idea to NATO planning meetings and—despite resistance, particularly from the West German government—won NATO's agreement to the new strategy by mid-1967. In later years, McNamara insisted that, in the early 1960s, he believed that nuclear weapons were "totally useless—except only to deter one's opponents from using them." He added: "In long private conversations with successive Presidents . . . I recommended, without qualification, that they never initiate, under any circumstances, the use of nuclear weapons. I believe they accepted my recommendation."[59]

Why did this shift occur? Kennedy administration officials have claimed that, given Soviet military advances, they considered a nuclear exchange suicidal. As Bundy put it, they believed that nuclear war would be "catastrophic to the United States." Rusk recalled that, shortly after assuming office, they received a lengthy briefing on the effects of nuclear war that proved "an awesome experience." Although he had long been aware of the power of nuclear weapons, he was "surprised nonetheless by the magnitude of destruction that a full-scale nuclear war would bring. Every aspect of life would be affected. More than one hundred million Americans would die in the first salvo." After the briefing, Kennedy had a strange expression on his face; he turned to Rusk and remarked grimly: "And we call ourselves the human race." Admittedly, some administration officials were willing to take dangerous gambles. During the Berlin crisis, Rostow insisted that "we must be prepared to increase the risk of war" on Khrushchev's "side of the line as well as facing it on ours." Even so, most policymakers, including the president, remained uneasy. According to Rusk, Kennedy "clearly understood what nuclear war meant and was appalled by it."[60]

But the prospective damage to the United States of a nuclear war does not fully explain the administration's reluctance to wage it. A late 1960 Defense Department report to the president-elect, recalled Paul Nitze, one of its drafters, contended that developing a U.S. "'win' capability" for a future nuclear war "probably was not feasible given Soviet capabilities and the political mood of the country." Furthermore, in conflicts with non-nuclear powers, the United States did not face any nuclear dangers, and yet policymakers ruled out nuclear war. "Throughout the wide range of our foreign policies in the sixties," Rusk recalled, "I was struck by the irrelevance of nuclear weapons to decision making. . . . Countries like Burma, Uruguay, and the Central African Republic aren't influenced by our nuclear bombs. They know we're not going to drop one of them, whatever the dispute. Weapons that can never be used don't translate into political influence." Why could they never be used? Reflecting on this, Rusk emphasized not only their danger, but their political stigma. "A nuclear country knows two things," he wrote: "that it would receive intolerable destruction if it attacked another nuclear power and that it would wear the mark of Cain for generations to come if it ever attacked a nonnuclear country with nuclear weapons."[61]

Even during that most dangerous of U.S.-Soviet confrontations, the Cuban missile crisis, the administration sought to minimize the risk of nuclear war. On October 16, 1962, at the first two meetings of the Executive Committee of the National Security Council (ExComm), Kennedy favored a military response to the emplacement of the Soviet missiles: an air strike against the missile sites, a general air attack, or an invasion. By contrast, his key advisers were rather dovish. "Let's not go to an air strike," Stevenson declared, "until we have explored the possibilities of a peaceful solution." At the second meeting, McNamara indicated his preference for a blockade, with Bundy and Ball expressing agreement. Rusk claimed that diplomatic action—for example, a clandestine dialogue with Castro and Khrushchev—should be explored. At the second meeting, McNamara asked the others to "consider the consequences. . . . I don't know quite what kind of world we live in after we've struck Cuba." Ball was even more emphatic. "You go in there with a surprise attack," he said, and "this isn't the *end*. This is the *beginning*." Eventually, Kennedy's advisers pulled him around from a conventional military response to a blockade.[62]

Although Kennedy's first televised address about the missiles, delivered on October 22, declared that the U.S. government would not "shrink" from the risk of "worldwide nuclear war" to remove them, the administration's subsequent handling of the crisis indicated considerable caution. In his message to Khrushchev that same night, Kennedy stressed that "the action we are taking is the minimum necessary." Furthermore, "I have not assumed that you or any other sane man would, in this nuclear age, deliberately plunge the world into war which it is crystal clear no country could win and which could only result in catastrophic consequences to the whole world." In a message to Khrushchev the following day, he declared that "we [should] both show prudence and do nothing to allow events to make the situation more difficult to control than it already is."[63] When Khrushchev suggested, in separate messages, his two proposals to end the confrontation, the administration not only formally pledged the first, but assured the Soviet leadership that it could count on the second. Consequently, although the crisis was exceptionally dangerous—largely thanks to the misunderstandings and miscalculations of the two governments—neither of them, as Bundy has written, regarded nuclear war as "remotely acceptable."[64]

The administration's caution reflected not only its desire to avoid the nuclear destruction of the United States, but its sensitivity to public opinion. As U.S. political leaders met to plot their strategy, recalled Rusk, Kennedy worried about "an adverse public reaction." He believed that "even to reveal the presence of Soviet missiles in Cuba might spark demonstrations, peace groups marching in the streets, perhaps a divisive public debate. . . . Critics would cry, 'Soviet ICBMs can already hit the United States. Why get so excited about missiles in Cuba?'" After the crisis became public, Kennedy lost his temper when a State Department press officer, calling attention to his remarks about possible "further action," touched off headlines about an imminent air attack or invasion. The president proceeded to berate the secretary of state, the assistant secretary, and the press officer, warning them, according to Sorensen, that he wanted "as little public pressure on him as possible." Foreign opinion was also a constraint. At the ExComm meeting of October 18, Rusk recalled, "I argued against a surprise attack, pointing out that world opinion would turn against us because we didn't first try diplomatic avenues." Other figures, too, opposed military action on the basis that it would not be tolerated by "world opinion." Sorensen observed that, from the ExComm perspective, one of the great advantages of the blockade was "its prudence, its avoidance of casualties and its avoidance of attacking Cuban soil"—factors that made it "more appealing to other nations than an air strike." More subtly, the choice of arguments for U.S. diplomatic messages—particularly the claim that "sane" people would not fight a nuclear war—illustrated the centrality of the ideas popularized by nuclear disarmament groups.[65]

Public opinion had less impact on the Kennedy administration's policy toward nuclear proliferation, largely because U.S. officials already viewed it with dismay. As might be expected, Washington officials—including the president—regarded with dread the prospect of China's acquiring the Bomb.[66] More surprising was the administration's chilly reaction to an independent nuclear weapons capability for major NATO allies. Believing—in Seaborg's words—that the French nuclear weapons program was "a net liability to our efforts in arms control," "an embarrassment to the West in negotiations with the Soviet Union, and a hindrance in achieving our objective of preventing further proliferation of nuclear weapons," the U.S. government took a hard line against sharing nuclear information or resources with the French. In May 1961, Kennedy secretly warned Macmillan that if their governments assisted the French nuclear program, this would increase significantly "the likelihood that the Germans would eventually wish to acquire a nuclear weapons capability." The result would be to "shake NATO to its foundations—not to mention the other serious dangers attendant on proliferation."[67] Even the British nuclear program came under hostile scrutiny, with Kennedy approving an NSC recommendation in April 1961 proclaiming the desirability of having the British "phase out of the nuclear deterrent business." This, in turn, facilitated the administration's scuttling of the Skybolt missile program, which would have left the British without a strategic weapons system had Kennedy not relented and offered them Polaris submarines. Administration officials preferred their plan for a NATO multilateral nuclear force—an arrangement designed to avert proliferation (particularly to Germany) and to keep nuclear weapons in allied nations under effective U.S. control. Among the reasons that the U.S. government wanted it seaborne was to avoid stirring up "anti-nuclear sentiment and demonstrations."[68]

By contrast, the nuclear armament of NATO nations remained a top U.S. government priority.[69] Canadian policy, particularly, alarmed U.S. officials. In November and December 1960, the U.S. embassy warned that External Affairs Minister Green's opposition to nuclear weapons "in any shape or form" and his "idée fixe on disarmament" were causing "increased difficulty" over arming Canadian military forces with U.S. nuclear weapons. In February 1962, the U.S. ambassador told Rusk that the "greatest single outstanding problem between [the] US and Canada is [the] Canadian failure [to] face up to [the] question [of] nuclear warheads." The "Diefenbaker government continues [to] procrastinate with strong elements in [the] Cabinet, particularly Foreign Minister Green, opposed to dirtying Canadian hands and reputation with nuclear weapons under any circumstances." Kennedy, particularly, pressed the Canadian government for "some forward movement in the nuclear field," which was of "great importance to the defense of Canada and the United States."[70]

The conflict came to a head in early 1963. On January 25, Diefenbaker made a speech arguing that although his government had been negotiating with Washington on nuclear defense measures, he had concluded that nuclear weapons provided "a dangerous solution" to world problems and, consequently, he would not move hastily to deploy them in Canada. Enraged by the speech, the State Department issued a public rejoinder—attacking the accuracy of the prime minister's statement and insisting that nuclear-armed forces were essential to an "effective continental defense." This startling intervention in Canada's domestic affairs was undertaken in the hope that it would help topple the minority government. And it did, much to the satisfaction of U.S. officials. According to the U.S. ambassador, Diefenbaker was now an "unscrupulous political animal at bay and we are the ones who boxed him in." Washington had "tolerated [the] essentially neurotic Canadian view of [the] world and of [the] Canadian role" for years, he claimed, but "we have now forced [the] issue."[71] Anxiously watching the ensuing election campaign—in which Diefenbaker defended his antinuclear stand and railed against U.S. government bullying—the Kennedy administration was immensely pleased by the victory of the pro-nuclear opposition.[72]

Although antinuclear opinion had a far greater impact on U.S. disarmament policy, the level of commitment was quite shallow. During the final months of the Eisenhower administration, the State Department proved incapable of developing a disarmament program, while Eisenhower's conversations about disarmament proposals, as his biographer has noted, "were exclusively concerned with propaganda advantage, or the effect of this or that proposal on the election."[73] Responding to pressure from peace groups and to a suggestion from Senator Humphrey, the Kennedy administration did establish a semiautonomous Arms Control and Disarmament Agency. Furthermore, after lengthy discussions, it developed a detailed disarmament proposal that it submitted to the U.N.'s eighteen-nation Disarmament Committee in April 1962. Even so, as Sorensen has noted, Kennedy's "initial interest in disarmament was largely for propaganda reasons—a desire to influence neutral and 'world opinion.'" This seemed vital, for as Stevenson told Rusk in March 1961, it was "crucial" that the U.S. government "appear not to be dragging its feet on disarmament at this [U.N.] Session. Appearance in these matters is fully as important as substance and . . . unless we move more quickly than we are now doing" the Soviet Union "will gain another significant propaganda victory over us." Addressing a group of congressional leaders in June, Kennedy again put the disarmament issue in the context of "propaganda."[74]

As a result, the U.S. government took a wholesale plunge into a policy of illusion. On August 17, 1961, when top U.S. policymakers met to formulate the U.S. disarmament program, the discussion clearly indicated that it was crafted largely for what one official called its "public opinion impact." Even Defense Department officials joined in assessing its "propaganda value" and its "propaganda appeal." When the acting USIA director stressed the "propaganda disadvantages" of linking conventional disarmament with nuclear disarmament, leaving Kennedy bewildered, Bundy explained that "conventional disarmament was an old tired issue, whereas nuclear disarmament was what [the] world worried about. It had more mileage." Therefore, the administration's "Program for General and Complete Disarmament"—with even the name stolen from the Soviet government's windy proposals—was hardly a serious one. As a State Department memorandum of August 1961 observed, its "primary purpose at this time . . . is to achieve Allied unity and to win out over the Soviets at the UN and around the world on the public opinion front."[75]

The major reason that, in the words of one Pentagon official, "no one in the U.S. government took the possibility of general and complete disarmament seriously," was that U.S. policymakers remained obsessed with their bitter power struggle with the Soviet Union. In the crisis atmosphere that prevailed in the summer of 1961, Seaborg recalled, government officials simply had no interest in negotiating a disarmament treaty. CIA director John McCone, Bundy acknowledged, "did not believe in stopping the nuclear arms race but in winning it."[76] Even McNamara, who ultimately concluded that the U.S. government possessed many more nuclear weapons than it needed, explained that when he assumed office, he had to "prepare for the worst plausible case." Or, as Bundy admitted, rather delicately: "Many of us did tend to believe that the superiority of our force would increase both Khrushchev's caution and his respect for our determination to act." Thus, although the deference shown by U.S. policymakers to disarmament attested to the popularity the issue had attained, winning the Cold War remained more important to them.[77]

By contrast, arms control—and, specifically, halting nuclear testing—had genuine support among U.S. government officials. From the beginning of the Geneva test ban talks, on October 31, 1958, to December 1959, proponents of a test ban held the upper hand. Admittedly, Teller, McCone (then AEC chair), and the military fought back ferociously. As Kistiakowsky recalled, "they challenged the feasibility of monitoring a treaty by inventing ever more fantastic methods of potential Soviet evasion, such as conducting tests in outer space, for instance behind the sun, or in the center of huge spherical caverns, up to thousands of feet in diameter excavated deep underground." These efforts did influence government policy and, accordingly, cast a pall on the test ban negotiations. Even so, in April 1959 Eisenhower proposed a limited nuclear test ban, requiring minimal inspection, that would prohibit atmospheric explosions of up to fifty kilometers in height. As the president wrote in his memoirs, he was "concerned by a reported increase of Free World anxiety about nuclear fallout" and also by a fear that "Macmillan might be willing to enter into a treaty with the Soviets which was not realistically enforceable." He did not mention his own belief, expressed that spring in secret meetings, that growing public concern about the arms race and fear of fallout would eventually force the U.S. government to abandon atmospheric testing unilaterally. Championing the resumption of nuclear testing, the AEC and the military promised new and important weapons developments, but Eisenhower, Herter, and Kistiakowsky refused to sanction it. Privately, Kistiakowsky told Herter that "world-wide opposition to the resumption" should be sufficient "to prolong the moratorium."[78]

Nevertheless, the stalled negotiations at Geneva played into the hands of test ban opponents. At a Cabinet meeting on December 11, 1959, Secretary of Defense Thomas Gates argued that the testing moratorium should be ended immediately. Retorting sharply, Herter asked "what impression would be created in the world if the president almost immediately upon his return from a great and very successful visit to eleven nations, which was undertaken to seek peace, should announce resumption of nuclear tests." Vice President Nixon, recognizing that Eisenhower's support was vital to his presidential ambitions, backed the secretary of state.[79] Nonetheless, Eisenhower began to waver. The opposition of Gates, McCone, and Teller made Senate approval of a test ban treaty improbable, and later that month the president expressed his nervousness on this score. Finally, on December 29, in an apparent effort to conciliate McCone, he announced that the U.S. government would not be formally bound by the moratorium after the end of the year. At the same time, as a concession to Macmillan and other opponents of testing, he declared that the U.S. government would not resume nuclear tests without prior notice and that it would continue negotiations for a treaty. Although this did not change the situation, it indicated the eroding position of testing foes.[80]

For the following year, the supporters of nuclear testing held the advantage. In the first months, to be sure, Eisenhower continued to hope that some sort of test ban agreement could be reached and to make proposals along these lines. Meeting on March 31, 1960, with Strauss, McCone reported himself "disgusted with the scientists," angry with the State Department, and dissatisfied with the president. "For political reasons," he charged, Eisenhower wanted to keep nuclear tests "from becoming an issue before November" and was "therefore postponing until after that time any resumption of testing." But, that May, when Khrushchev reacted to the U-2 incident by insulting Eisenhower and torpedoing the Paris summit conference, it convinced the president of the Soviet leader's villainy.[81] Consequently, Eisenhower—like Khrushchev—adopted a harder line. On May 24, he told the NSC that "the self-imposed moratorium cannot be continued indefinitely." Meanwhile, as Kistiakowsky recalled, "AEC and Defense went on a counteroffensive against our efforts to achieve a test ban" and stepped up their attack on the moratorium. The AEC's report for 1960 argued that continuing the moratorium entailed "risks to free world supremacy in nuclear weapons" and "a resultant threat to the free world."[82]

But the power of public opinion kept the moratorium and the test ban negotiations alive. Writing years later in his memoirs, Eisenhower maintained that "prudence demanded a resumption of testing." Even so, political considerations prevented him from giving the appropriate orders. As Herter told McCone in the summer of 1960, resuming testing not only offended Macmillan but, in the midst of a U.S. presidential campaign, represented a "political decision." Although the president was "inclined to go ahead" with the resumption of nuclear testing, he wanted to "wait until after election day" to avoid damaging Nixon's chances for election. Had Nixon won the race for president, two former AEC chairs have maintained, underground testing would have been resumed at once. But, to the dismay of the administration, he lost. Consequently, Eisenhower did no more than emphasize to Kennedy his belief that "our nation should resume needed tests without delay." This left the decision in the hands of the new president.[83]

Unlike Eisenhower, Kennedy was not inclined to resume nuclear testing. Although pressures from the outgoing president and from the Republican opposition were factors worth considering, Kennedy arrived in office publicly committed to extending the moratorium and securing a test ban. In November 1959, he had proclaimed that resuming nuclear testing would be "damaging to the American image" and that it might lead to a "long, feverish testing period" that could threaten "the very existence of human life." If the Russians resumed nuclear testing, he said, U.S. tests should be conducted underground, thus preventing "a further increase in the fallout menace." As a candidate in 1960, he declared that "no issue has more meaning for our daily lives—for the health of our children, our life expectancy, the food we eat and the very air we breathe—than the threat of radioactivity and strontium contamination." Accordingly, he pledged that if elected president, he would not be the first to resume testing in the atmosphere and would not test underground until "all reasonable opportunities" for a test ban had been exhausted. In January 1961, opening his first press conference as president, Kennedy announced that he had established a special group to prepare a new U.S. proposal for a test ban treaty. A short time later, he told a meeting of top government leaders that a test ban agreement would "have a great influence on world opinion" and also facilitate settlement of international crises.[84]

From January to August 1961, the pressures mounted to resume nuclear testing. Although Kennedy sent Arthur Dean to Geneva with the new administration proposal for a test ban treaty, the Soviet government remained uninterested. Nor did Khrushchev seem forthcoming on the subject when the two leaders met that spring in Vienna. Meanwhile, to offset the fiasco of the U.S.-sponsored invasion of Cuba, figures inside and outside the administration pressed Kennedy to resume nuclear testing. The Joint Chiefs of Staff were particularly demanding, arguing that the tests could be kept secret and, even if they were discovered, ascribed to a program of peaceful research. At a meeting of administration officials that May, McNamara strongly urged the resumption of nuclear testing, contending that it would reduce the cost of nuclear weapons and make them more effective. There was also a possibility, he said, that the government could develop an antimissile system. But Murrow observed that this would not be "very persuasive in convincing public opinion around the world of the need for U.S. resumption of tests." Moreover, Rusk remained undecided, arguing that although the government could not accept "an indefinite moratorium," there would be a "serious political reaction . . . were we to resume testing," a point conceded by McNamara. Additional pressure to test came from the Joint Committee on Atomic Energy.[85]

Nevertheless, the strength of antinuclear opinion blocked a change in policy. Nuclear test resumption was "a really tough issue," Kennedy remarked on May 4, for "the Soviets had us right on the propaganda hook." At a high-level White House meeting on May 19, he stated that U.S. embassies around the world, polled on the question of resuming nuclear testing, had all reported that the public response would be very adverse. Therefore, he said, unless a strong case could be made for test resumption, he thought the government should postpone action. A week later, writing from his post at the United Nations, Stevenson bolstered this position, arguing that the U.S. government could not "resume nuclear tests without suffering [a] severely damaging political reaction throughout [the] world." Updating a June 24 message from Murrow, Schlesinger sent Kennedy a lengthy memo that July, arguing: "Unless we persuade our allies and the uncommitted nations of the rightness of our course on the nuclear test ban issue, we stand in grave danger of losing their support."[86] The result of these and similar admonitions[87] was to keep the moratorium in place. Writing to Macmillan on August 3, Kennedy reported that he was "most reluctant to take a firm decision to resume testing." Consequently, he would send Dean back to Geneva "with instructions to make one more strenuous effort to move the Soviets." He would also address the United Nations, with a major speech focused largely or wholly on disarmament. Although he was "not very hopeful" that it would be possible to postpone tests beyond January 1, 1962, any resumption would be underground, "unless and until the Soviets resume atmospheric testing."[88]

Surprisingly, even the Soviet resumption of testing did not immediately lead to a similar policy on the part of the United States. On August 30, 1961, when

Kennedy learned of the Soviet plan, his first reaction was "unprintable," Sorensen recalled. Furthermore, at a White House meeting the next day, Rusk and others called for an immediate announcement of a decision to resume U.S. testing. But Murrow argued forcefully for delaying any statement of this kind until the U.S. government could reap the maximum propaganda advantage from Soviet flouting of world public opinion. U.S. restraint, combined with denunciations of Soviet policy, he argued, would "isolate the Communist Bloc, frighten the satellites and the uncommitted, pretty well destroy the Ban the Bomb movement in Britain, and might even induce sanity into the SANE nuclear policy group." Vice President Lyndon Johnson supported Murrow, although he warned that it would be hard to follow that tack very long. Later that day, when the president met with congressional leaders and outlined this strategy, Senator Richard Russell, chair of the Armed Services Committee, agreed that the government should "exploit" this "God-given" opportunity for its "maximum propaganda value." Accordingly, on September 3, Kennedy and Macmillan issued a public appeal to Khrushchev for an atmospheric test ban with no controls. This would "protect mankind from the increasing hazards from atmospheric pollution and . . . contribute to the reduction of international tensions," they stated. Seaborg recalled that although the offer was "a serious one," the "main expectation was that the proposal would embarrass" Khrushchev "and swing world opinion more heavily to our side." Once again, a concern about public opinion had helped stave off the resumption of U.S. nuclear testing.[89]

Within a short time, however, more traditional considerations were on the ascendant. On September 5, Kennedy decided that he could no longer postpone announcing that the U.S. government would resume underground nuclear testing. "What changed his mind," Seaborg noted, "was news of a third Soviet test." The president told Macmillan: "As their tests continued . . . it became clear to me that announcement of the decision could no longer be delayed. . . . The gravest of our dangers is that we may seem less determined than Khrushchev." Faced with the heightening pressures of the Cold War, the president had given way to orthodox assumptions about the centrality of military power among nation-states. Stevenson, though, was dismayed and complained to the president: "But we were ahead in the propaganda battle." Flaring up, Kennedy retorted: "What does that mean? I don't hear of any windows broken because of the Soviet decision." He added: "All this makes Khrushchev look pretty tough. He has had a succession of apparent victories—space, Cuba, [and] the thirteenth of August [the Berlin Wall]." He wants to encourage "the feeling that he has us on the run." "Anyway," said Kennedy, cooling down, "the decision has been made. I'm not saying it was the right decision. Who the hell knows?"[90]

But the president remained deeply concerned about public opinion. As Schlesinger recalled, "he regarded opinion as a basic constituent of power," and this led to continued U.S. efforts to embarrass the Soviet Union for testing in the atmosphere. Although Rusk felt that the administration had "dissipated" its propaganda advantage with the announcement of U.S. underground testing, Kennedy did not. In response to administration officials emphasizing the importance of "world opinion," he delivered a dramatic address on September 25 to the U.N. General Assembly. Here he excoriated Soviet nuclear tests and pointed again to the Anglo-American willingness to sign an atmospheric test ban treaty. "A nuclear disaster," he warned, would "engulf the great and the small, the rich and the poor, the committed and the uncommitted alike. Mankind must put an end to war—or war will put an end to mankind. . . . Let us call a truce to terror."[91] In October and November, the White House issued sharp statements assailing Soviet atmospheric testing, appealing to "peoples throughout the world" to reject the "Soviet campaign of fear." Meanwhile, at administration direction, the Voice of America massed transmitters for special broadcasts to the Soviet Union about the tests. These efforts had considerable impact. The U.N. General Assembly passed a resolution urging the Soviet Union not to explode its fifty-megaton Bomb and, for the first time, called for a test ban treaty along Western lines—one providing for extensive measures of verification and control.[92]

Given its sensitivity to public opinion, the administration continued to refrain from atmospheric testing. Kennedy leaned toward ordering the resumption of atmospheric tests for the same reason that he had sanctioned a renewal of underground testing: as a show of national strength. In early November 1961, pressed by the Joint Chiefs, McNamara, and the AEC for immediate resumption and angered by the Soviet fifty-megaton explosion, he ordered preparations made for such testing. But, as Schlesinger recalled, "preparation was one thing, actual testing another." Seaborg, too, found Kennedy uncharacteristically indecisive when it came to ordering the resumption of atmospheric testing.[93] For month after month, the president avoided giving the word. Nor was this surprising. Warning of dire consequences, Stevenson cautioned the president that "the political price of test resumption will be paid most directly in the United Nations and in terms of public opinion around the world." Murrow also stressed the resistance of foreign opinion, as did U.S. ambassadors overseas. Although White House and State Department officials keenly resented Macmillan's efforts to block the resumption of atmospheric testing, the British prime minister's opposition impressed Kennedy.[94]

Nor, as an elected official, could the president ignore opposition at home. Bundy's assistant, Carl Kaysen, had suggested a last "supreme effort" for a test ban before resuming atmospheric tests. In January 1962, Sorensen—Kennedy's chief domestic adviser and alter ego—made the case to the president that such a move would be good politics. On November 26, Sorensen observed, with the nation still appalled by the Soviet test series, a Gallup poll found that only 44 percent of the public favored resuming U.S. atmospheric tests, while 45 percent opposed it. Indeed, opposition to U.S. atmospheric testing had nearly doubled since the previous July. Furthermore, the "non-testers" included "more of the articulate, opinion-making citizenry who can make 'peace' a winning issue."[95] White House mail, too, ran heavily against U.S. tests. According to Adrian Fisher, deputy director of the Arms Control and Disarmament Agency, Kennedy thought "that it probably made sense . . . to resume testing. . . . But he also recognized that there were a lot of people that were going to be deeply offended by the United States resuming atmospheric testing. We had people picketing the White House, and there was a lot of excitement about it—just because the Russians do it, why do we have to do it?" As a result, when administration officials demanded atmospheric tests, Kennedy would dig in his heels and "ask: 'What are you going to learn from them? Do you really need them?' And that's the reason we didn't resume atmospheric testing."[96]

By late February 1962, however, nearly six months after the Soviet resumption of atmospheric testing and with virtually all his top advisers supporting test resumption, Kennedy was no longer willing to hold the line. Fearful that further Soviet tests, in the absence of a U.S. response, would give the Kremlin enough of a military advantage to produce dangerous diplomatic consequences, the president finally gave the go-ahead for U.S. tests in the atmosphere. On March 2, he delivered a major television address, announcing that, in the latter part of April, the U.S. government would hold atmospheric nuclear tests in the Pacific. "While we will be conducting far fewer tests than the Soviets, with far less fallout," he stated, "there will still be those in other countries who will urge us to refrain from testing at all. Perhaps they forget that this country long refrained from testing, and sought to ban all tests, while the Soviets were secretly preparing new explosions. Perhaps they forget the Soviet threats of last autumn and their arbitrary rejection of all appeals and proposals, from both the United States and the United Nations." Nevertheless, "those free peoples who value their freedom and their security . . . will, I am confident, want the United States to do whatever it must do to deter the threat of aggression." On April 25, the U.S. atmospheric test series began in the Pacific.[97]

Yet even this victory for Cold War considerations did not reflect an abandonment of concern about public opinion. In his March 2 speech, Kennedy promised to conduct no high-yield tests, thus reducing "radioactive fallout to an absolute minimum." Furthermore, he pledged to offer at the Geneva conference "a series of concrete plans for a major 'breakthrough to peace,'" including a comprehensive test ban treaty. If, in the weeks before the U.S. test series began, the Soviet government would accept such a treaty, Kennedy promised, he would cancel the tests. Behind the scenes, the administration worked even harder to appease public opinion. Rusk argued that the first explosions should take place in Nevada "to alleviate criticism that the U.S. is callous about the safety of inhabitants of the Pacific." Kennedy, though, objected to this "very vigorously," Seaborg noted, insisting that "the political cost of another mushroom cloud visible in the United States would be prohibitive."[98] Meanwhile, the State Department embarked on a worldwide effort to win support for the new U.S. position. As the atmospheric tests began that April, Sorensen recalled, "they received as little publicity as the President could 'manage.' He wanted no pictures of mushroom clouds, no eyewitness reports of each blast, and as little stimulus as possible to picketing and ban-the-bomb parades around the world." To minimize the unfavorable reaction, Kennedy also sought to end the tests as quickly as possible.[99]

Arms Control, Not Disarmament

By the early 1960s, then, the nuclear disarmament movement had emerged as a factor of some importance in world politics. Through the mobilization of public pressure, it not only helped place limits on the use of nuclear weapons, but discouraged their proliferation and development. The movement's greatest impact, however, was on nuclear testing policy. It helped hold the Soviet Union to a three-year testing moratorium, played a central role in the U.S. decision to abstain from underground testing for three years and from atmospheric testing for another eight months, and nearly drove the British out of the nuclear testing business altogether. The movement owed its relative success on this score to at least two factors. First, there was little doubt among politicians or other observers that nuclear testing alarmed the vast majority of the public. Furthermore, some policymakers considered a modicum of nuclear arms control acceptable. Key leaders among the great powers were starting to believe that, without going so far as to ban the Bomb—a policy they did not support except as propaganda—they could acquiesce to the popular demand to halt some aspects of the nuclear arms race without jeopardizing their national security. Not surprisingly, then, as antinuclear protests continued, the way lay open for the world's first nuclear arms control agreements.

The Atmospheric Test Ban Treaty
and Beyond, 1963–70

> Yesterday a shaft of light cut into the darkness. . . . For the
> first time, an agreement has been reached on bringing the
> forces of nuclear destruction under control.
>
> John F. Kennedy, 1963

Beginning in 1963, public policy showed dramatic signs of catching up with
the antinuclear movement. Starting with the atmospheric test ban treaty and
continuing through treaties to curb nuclear proliferation, ban nuclear weapons
in selected regions, and limit strategic arms, most nations of the world agreed
to support international nuclear arms control measures. In addition, many nations acted unilaterally, placing restraints on their own nuclear activities. This
remarkable shift toward checking the nuclear arms race illustrated the willingness of numerous government officials to take action on a long-neglected problem. But what accounted for that willingness? Sometimes, it resulted from
long-held concerns; at others, from a newfound understanding of the nuclear
menace, especially the menace of nuclear proliferation. To a large extent,
though, it represented the culmination of the popular campaign that nuclear
disarmament groups had mobilized against the Bomb. With the public clamor-
ing for action, the leaders of the nuclear powers recognized that nuclear arms
control measures made good politics. Furthermore, they began to realize that
antinuclear sentiment might also be employed as a political weapon against rival nations and politicians. Accordingly, public policy changed significantly,
and even erstwhile critics were pressed into service as useful allies.

Progress Toward a Test Ban Treaty

During the last half of 1962, the differences between Soviet and U.S. test ban
policy seemed to be narrowing. Within the Kennedy administration, Rusk—
stressing Soviet resistance to the inspection procedures demanded by the U.S.

government for a comprehensive test ban—began to urge a ban on atmospheric testing. By the end of August, this resulted in an offer of both kinds of treaty to Khrushchev. Although administration officials recognized that an atmospheric test ban would not necessarily halt China's development of nuclear weapons—a goal they considered increasingly important—they decided to champion it because it had a broad appeal to world opinion.[1] An atmospheric ban was also becoming increasingly acceptable to the Soviet government. Having pressed Soviet authorities that summer about the possibility of a partial test ban, Sakharov learned a few months later that there was "a great deal of interest at the top" in his proposal.[2] The Cuban missile crisis that fall also pushed Kennedy and Khrushchev toward a compromise on testing, for both men had received a firsthand education in how dangerous the nuclear situation had become.[3] In November, *Pravda* pointed to "the partisans of sanity" in the United States as a justification for "the cessation of dangerous nuclear experiments," while Gromyko noted "a saner approach" in U.S. foreign policy. At the same time, Soviet, British, and U.S. officials grew hopeful that the "black box" approach to verification, developed that fall by scientists at the Pugwash conferences, might facilitate agreement on a comprehensive test ban.[4]

With prospects for a test ban improving, Norman Cousins embarked on a potentially crucial mission. Asked by the pope to talk with Khrushchev in an effort to improve relations between the Kremlin and the Vatican, the SANE leader arranged to meet with Kennedy, in November 1962, before his departure. At the meeting, he inquired if the president wanted him to use this visit to transmit a message to the Soviet premier. Rather remarkably, the president did. Speaking at length with Cousins, Kennedy told him that he wanted to create genuinely friendly relations with the Soviet Union and that a test ban treaty provided a key means toward this end. The peace movement leader, the president explained, must help to overcome Khrushchev's suspicions and convince him of Kennedy's goodwill.[5]

In mid-December 1962, after conferring with Soviet officials in Moscow, Cousins met with Khrushchev for an intense exchange, lasting three-and-a-quarter hours. "Peace," the Soviet premier told him, "is the most important goal in the world. If we don't have peace and the nuclear bombs start to fall, what difference will it make whether we are Communists or Catholics or capitalists or Chinese or Russians or Americans? Who could tell us apart? Who will be left to tell us apart?" Cousins noted that at the end of this statement, Khrushchev's eyes had "a vacant stare." Responding to Khrushchev's questions about Kennedy, Cousins reported to the Soviet leader that the U.S. president "was extremely eager to develop the kind of relations with the Soviet Union that would help create conditions for a more peaceful and orderly world." Khrushchev expressed his desire to meet the president "more than halfway for that purpose," adding: "One thing the President and I should do right away is to conclude a treaty outlawing testing of nuclear weapons and then start to work on the problem of keeping these weapons from spreading all over the world." He was not opposed to inspection, he insisted, but to "snooping that has nothing to do with the test ban." He saw no reason, therefore, "why it shouldn't be possible for both our countries to agree on the kind of inspection that will satisfy you that we're not cheating and that will satisfy us that you're not spying."[6]

Five days later, on December 19, 1962, Khrushchev dispatched a lengthy letter to Kennedy devoted entirely to the test ban issue. The time had come, the Soviet leader argued, "to put a stop to nuclear tests once and for all, to make an end of them." Referring to a recent conversation between U.S. ambassador Dean and Vasily Kuznetsov, a Soviet foreign affairs official, during which Dean had allegedly said that two to four on-site inspections a year in the Soviet Union would be sufficient to verify a comprehensive test ban, Khrushchev offered two to three annual inspections. Because the inspection issue seemed to be the only obstacle to a test ban treaty, Khrushchev said, "we are ready to meet you halfway." Kennedy was surprised and, as Schlesinger noted, "exhilarated" by this offer—a dramatic turn by the Soviet government toward on-site inspection. Decades later, Soviet ambassador Dobrynin recalled this offer as very "psychologically difficult and innovative" and added that "many Politburo members" did not agree with it. He also maintained that it was the first direct communication between Khrushchev and Kennedy since the Cuban missile crisis two months before. "Unofficial, off-the-record talks" on a test ban treaty now began between Soviet and U.S. officials in New York.[7]

This apparent breakthrough, however, came to nothing. In mid-January, the talks began to break down. Arguing that Dean had been misunderstood, U.S. officials demanded eight to ten on-site inspections. Soviet negotiators, in turn, charged bad faith on the part of the U.S. government. Irate, Khrushchev claimed that, having secured the approval of the Soviet Council of Ministers on two to three on-site inspections to accommodate Kennedy, he could not go back and demand a higher number.[8] Moreover, behind this squabbling over the number of inspections lay the resistance to a treaty by conservatives in both societies. As Schlesinger noted, "with the intense military and partisan opposition and the senatorial battle looming ahead, it seemed impossible politically to go below eight or, at the least, seven." British officials complained, with some justice, that "it's not science but politics which holds back the President."[9] Khrushchev's influence was even shakier, particularly after the Cuban missile crisis. Party conservatives and the Chinese government both seized on his apparent capitulation to strengthen their case for a hard line toward the

United States. In this context, Khrushchev may well have thought that accommodating Kennedy once again would look like a sign of weakness. Certainly, as Rusk later remarked, "he couldn't move too far too fast."[10]

By this point, U.S. policymakers clearly wanted a treaty. In conversations with Soviet officials that January, Rusk was unusually dramatic. "A man from Mars would regard both the USSR and the United States as crazy for devoting so much to the arms race," he stated. Both countries needed to make "headway on the problem of testing." During this meeting, Rusk also raised the issue of proliferation, for this was becoming a key factor behind the administration's drive for a test ban treaty. Indeed, at a meeting of the NSC on January 22, 1963, Kennedy declared that "our primary purpose in trying to get a [test ban] treaty with Russia is to halt or delay the development of an atomic capability by the Chinese Communists."[11] Nevertheless, although appeasing world opinion had been eclipsed, in Kennedy's eyes, by containing the Chinese, it remained an important factor. Moreover, nonproliferation hinged, in part, on antinuclear sentiment. As Seaborg noted, it was unclear how Kennedy "expected a test ban negotiated between ourselves and the Soviets to affect the Chinese unless it were through the force of world opinion."[12]

Once again, the administration turned to Cousins. Asked by the Vatican to undertake another mission to Moscow, the SANE leader had again contacted the White House. In early 1963, Rusk spoke with him and, according to Cousins, "said he was concerned about the impasse in the test-ban negotiations," which he attributed to the misunderstanding over the number of on-site inspections. Rusk "thought that I might be able to bear witness to the good faith of the United States in seeking an agreement." On March 12, meeting with Kennedy for private discussions at the White House, Cousins conversed with him for an hour and twenty minutes. After reviewing the squabble over on-site inspections, Kennedy emphasized the importance of convincing Khrushchev that he was "genuinely seeking a way to end the threat of nuclear war." The president also expressed "deep gratification" at the nuclear disarmament movement's leadership in "mobilizing American public opinion in favor of a test-ban" and pointed out that "it would be of the utmost importance to mobilize American public opinion in back of a treaty." Following up, Kennedy telephoned Cousins the day before he left for Moscow, telling him to try to "get Premier Khrushchev to accept the fact of an honest misunderstanding" over the number of on-site inspections. Kennedy added: "I'm sure you can support the fact that I am acting in good faith and that I genuinely want a test-ban treaty."[13]

Meanwhile, other forces continued to push the great powers toward the test ban. In March 1963, recognizing that inspection had become the stumbling block to an accord on nuclear testing, Soviet, British, and American Pugwash scientists called on their respective governments to halt atmospheric tests. With elections looming, Macmillan recalled, he was "desperately anxious" to secure some success on this front. Sending a thirteen-page letter to Kennedy on March 16, he renewed his pressure for a test ban, claiming that it would "stop the contamination of the atmosphere," limit nuclear proliferation, and give the people of the world "a tremendous new sense of hope." That same month, a memo from USIA director Murrow made the rounds of the administration, stressing that "we know from polls and from common sense that most people think a test ban would be a good thing."[14] In addition, Kennedy and Macmillan increasingly viewed a test ban as the key to nonproliferation. At his press conference of March 21, Kennedy justified a test ban on the basis that, without it, the world might well have fifteen to twenty-five nuclear powers by the 1970s. For this reason and others, Kennedy remained keenly interested in antinuclear opinion. Only six days before, he sent Cousins a letter suggesting that he "take action to increase public support for our efforts in the field of nuclear testing and disarmament."[15]

For the time being, handling Khrushchev provided Cousins with more than enough to do. Meeting with the Soviet leader on April 12 at his country retreat, Cousins found him angry and suspicious. Although Cousins stressed Kennedy's contention that there had been an honest misunderstanding over the number of on-site inspections, Khrushchev retorted that, in an effort to accommodate Kennedy, he had worked hard to obtain the agreement of the Council of Ministers to three inspections, only to have the U.S. government suddenly demand eight. "And so once again I was made to look foolish," he complained; "but I can tell you this: it won't happen again." Cousins tried desperately to keep open the possibility of a test ban, but Khrushchev was adamant. "You don't seem to understand what the situation is here," he said. "We cannot make another offer. I cannot go back to the Council. It is now up to the United States." Indeed, he commented, Soviet hawks wanted a green light for more nuclear tests, and "I may give it to them." For Cousins, who had devoted so much of his life to halting the nuclear arms race, it was a deeply depressing moment. Nonetheless, he marshaled all his persuasive powers in an effort to bring Khrushchev around. Finally, toward the end of their six-hour conversation, the Soviet leader relented somewhat. "You can tell the President I accept his explanation of an honest misunderstanding and suggest that we get moving," he said. "But the next move is up to him."[16]

The "New Approach"

On April 22, 1963, Cousins met with Kennedy at the White House, where he reported on his meeting with Khrushchev. When Cousins emphasized the pressures on the Soviet leader to adopt a hard line, Kennedy interjected: "One of the ironic things about this entire situation is that Mr. Khrushchev and I occupy approximately the same political positions inside our governments. He would like to prevent a nuclear war but is under severe pressure from his hard-line crowd, which interprets every move in that direction as appeasement. I've got similar problems." Indeed, "the hard-liners in the Soviet Union and the United States feed on one another, each using the actions of the other to justify its own position." Inadvertently underscoring the point, the president observed that although he wanted to make a fresh start on test ban negotiations, "I don't see how we can cut down on inspections. We'd never get it through the Senate." And Soviet hard-liners, bolstered by the Chinese, they agreed, kept Khrushchev from softening his terms. When Kennedy asked him what he thought should be done, Cousins made an important suggestion. What might work, he stated, was a presidential address outlining "a breathtaking new approach toward the Russian people, calling for an end to the cold war and a fresh start in American-Russian relationships." Intrigued by the idea, Kennedy urged Cousins to send him a memorandum on the subject.[17]

Thereafter, Cousins played a central role in guiding the administration toward this "new approach." At the president's suggestion, before he left Washington he met with officials from the State Department and from the Arms Control and Disarmament Agency. On April 30, he followed up with a letter to Kennedy arguing that "the moment is now at hand for the most important single speech of your Presidency. It should be a speech which, in its breathtaking proposals for genuine peace, in its tone of friendliness for the Soviet people . . . would create a world groundswell of support." Such a speech would "head off or soften" any Khrushchev rapprochement with Communist hard-liners and, at the same time, "create a whole new context for the pursuit of peace." According to Sorensen, Kennedy particularly valued this letter, which the president passed along to him for action. Consequently, Sorensen asked Cousins to return to Washington, where they conferred on the speech, which the president thought should include some of the points made by Cousins in their meeting and in his letter. Eventually, Cousins submitted a draft of the speech, which Sorensen drew on freely as he prepared his own version, now scheduled for delivery at American University.[18]

As White House officials laid plans that spring for the president's speech, a number of additional developments smoothed the way for its delivery and acceptance. In the Soviet Union, the leading party conservative, Frol Kozlov, became fatally ill in mid-April 1963, thereby strengthening Khrushchev's influence in party affairs. Although the Soviet premier showed no sign of softening his stand on inspections, he did talk increasingly of detente with the West. This was symbolized by Soviet agreement to the installation of a "hot line" between the White House and Moscow—a direct link between U.S. and Soviet leaders first suggested by Leo Szilard.[19] Meanwhile, in the United States, an Ad Hoc Committee for a Nuclear Test Ban, put together by Cousins in the fall of 1962, swung into gear in April 1963, when fifteen organizations met to plan an integrated campaign for a treaty. Early the following month, WSP turned out two thousand supporters for a pro-treaty demonstration. On May 27, antinuclear forces made another advance when Senators Humphrey, Dodd, and thirty-two others cosponsored a Senate resolution supporting an atmospheric test ban.[20] Foreign leaders also pressed for action. That April, Pope John XXIII issued *Pacem in Terris*. In May, the new Canadian prime minister, Lester Pearson, told Kennedy that he hoped the U.S. government would "continue plugging away at [the] test ban question . . . so as to reassure public opinion that every effort [is] being made."[21]

Thus encouraged, Kennedy delivered what was probably the most remarkable speech by a U.S. president in the Cold War era. Speaking on June 10, 1963, at American University, the president focused on what he called "the most important topic on earth: world peace." He did not want "a Pax Americana enforced on the world by American weapons of war" but "peace for all men and women." He spoke of peace, he said, "because of the new face of war." In the nuclear age, "total war makes no sense" and peace had become "the necessary rational end of rational men." Americans, the president argued, should "reexamine" their attitudes toward the Soviet Union and the Cold War. "No government or social system is so evil that its people must be considered as lacking in virtue." Indeed, "we all inhabit this small planet. We all breathe the same air. We all cherish our children's future. And we are all mortal." "A fresh start," he argued, should be made on "a treaty to outlaw nuclear tests," and toward this goal he had ordered a halt to U.S. atmospheric testing and arranged with Khrushchev and Macmillan for the beginning of high-level treaty negotiations in Moscow. "Confident and unafraid," he concluded, "we labor on—not toward a strategy of annihilation but toward a strategy of peace."[22]

The Breakthrough

As Sorensen later remarked, "the 'signal' the Soviet Chairman had awaited was loud and clear." Although the American University address received surprisingly little attention in the United States,[23] it had a profound impact on the leadership of the Soviet Union. Khrushchev lauded it as the best speech by any U.S. president since Roosevelt. Despite the fact that it contained some criticism of Soviet policy, the Soviet press published it in full. Furthermore, although the Soviet government, at great expense, had been jamming Western broadcasts for fifteen years, it blocked only one paragraph of Kennedy's speech when the Voice of America relayed it to the Soviet Union. According to Seaborg, "it was as though Khrushchev had been looking for a weapon to use against Chinese criticisms of his policies toward the United States and Kennedy had provided it." Talking with British Labour Party leader Harold Wilson immediately after the address, Khrushchev praised the speech and gave him the impression that an atmospheric test ban treaty would now be acceptable. On July 2, speaking in East Berlin, the Soviet premier for the first time publicly endorsed an atmospheric test ban.[24]

The way now lay open for a long-deferred agreement. To be sure, at the last minute the U.S. Joint Chiefs of Staff declared that they could not support a test ban treaty, for it was "not in the national interest." Similarly, the Chinese Communist Party warned against Soviet "capitulation in the face of imperialist nuclear blackmail." Citing Mao, the party organ, *Renmin Ribao*, argued that nuclear war would only "hasten the complete destruction of the capitalist system." But Kennedy refused to retreat from the U.S. commitment to a treaty, while Soviet leaders announced that they could not "share the views of the Chinese leadership about creating 'a thousand times higher civilization' on the corpses of hundreds of millions of people."[25] According to a State Department dispatch, a July 10 meeting between Khrushchev and Belgium's Paul Henri Spaak "couldn't have been more relaxed, friendly, and informal. Khrushchev seemed to be in [an] excellent, cheerful, confident frame of mind, very jocular and frequently cavorting with his grandchildren or thoroughly enjoying [the] Dnieper boatride." Spaak reported to Kennedy that Khrushchev, once again, had said that an accord could be reached on an atmospheric test ban treaty.[26]

As expected, the Moscow negotiations, which began on July 15, 1963, proved productive. Averell Harriman, who headed up the U.S. delegation, had been instructed to make a comprehensive test ban treaty his primary goal, for it seemed most likely to inhibit nuclear proliferation, particularly to China. If this proved unobtainable, he was to try for an atmospheric test ban, a measure less useful in heading off proliferation but which had fewer political obstacles and great popular appeal.[27] When Khrushchev reverted to the familiar Soviet resistance to inspection, Harriman gave up on the comprehensive test ban and shifted to serious discussions of an atmospheric treaty, which proceeded smoothly. In another attempt to meet Kennedy's goal of nonproliferation, however, Harriman repeatedly raised the issue of China's nuclear program with Khrushchev, exploring whether something could be done to block it. At Kennedy's suggestion, he apparently broached the idea of a preemptive strike. But Khrushchev proved noncommittal, arguing that China's nuclear program was minor and, furthermore, that he could do nothing about it.[28] Despite these set-backs, Kennedy still wanted an agreement. Accordingly, on July 25, U.S., Soviet, and British representatives initialed an atmospheric test ban treaty—the first nuclear arms control measure in history.

As this brief description indicates, the three signatories to the treaty had somewhat different motives. The British government was certainly the one most directly driven by the force of public opinion. With elections imminent and his ruling Conservatives trailing badly in the polls, Macmillan saw a test ban treaty as a solution to his political dilemma. "Macmillan would like to find a way to recoup his political fortunes," a U.S. diplomat noted on July 9, "and some progress on a test ban agreement might help to take the wind out of the sails of the Prime Minister's political opposition." That same month, solicitous of his British counterpart, Kennedy inquired of Macmillan's secretary "if a nuclear test ban treaty would be of some assistance electorally." The secretary replied that it would. Having conferred with Harriman about prospects for the treaty on July 12, Macmillan entered in his diary: "The situation is dramatic and vital for me. If there is any chance of our agreement and a summit meeting afterwards, I will fight on in home politics. If not, I shall feel inclined to throw in my hand." Although the British government was the least important of the three parties to the Moscow negotiations, it did serve as an important source of pressure on its U.S. ally.[29]

If the Soviet government felt the impact of public concern less directly, antinuclear sentiment nonetheless influenced its policy. The treaty, to be sure, appealed to Soviet leaders because it would foster detente with the West, thereby reducing the threat of war with the United States. They also hoped that it would confirm the Soviet Union as a superpower, keep their nation from falling behind in the arms race, and inhibit the development of nuclear weapons by additional hostile countries, including West Germany. In addition, however, they liked the idea of a treaty because—as Dobrynin has revealed—it would place them on the right side of "public opinion." Moreover, it would put their Chinese rivals in a very difficult position—forcing them to choose between scrapping their Bomb project or continuing it at the price of alienating public support, particularly in Third World nations. This explains why, in the midst of the treaty negotiations, the Chinese *Renmin Ribao* complained that the treaty would be used to "create pressure of public opinion" to block China from developing nuclear weapons. It also explains why Khrushchev publicly lashed out at the Chinese for wanting "to start a war against everybody," for instigating a nuclear holocaust in which "the survivors would envy the dead." Having long worked to turn the force of antinuclear opinion against the United States, the Kremlin was beginning to mobilize it against China.[30]

This was the conclusion reached by U.S. officials. From Moscow, Harriman reported that he was piecing together "a logical theory on why Khrushchev is interested in [a] test ban." The Soviet premier's "first preoccupation is his battle" with the Chinese Communists, and he planned to "use the test ban" to "isolate them." Recalling an earlier conversation in which Yuri Zhukov of the Soviet Peace Committee depicted "world opinion" as the key to halting the Chinese Bomb project, Harriman asked him about it again. In response, Zhukov explained that "all 130 countries" should be urged to adhere to the treaty, "and then the pressure of the underdeveloped countries, particularly in Africa, would be extremely great." Harriman noted that since the Chinese "want to make headway in gaining the support of these countries in competition with the Soviet Union, such a situation . . . would obviously give Moscow a trump card to play" against the Chinese. Five days later, he argued that it had become "crystal clear" that the Soviet "objective" was "to isolate" China. Moscow wanted pressure brought to bear on the Chinese "from other countries, particularly the underdeveloped." Catching the drift of things, the *New York Times* reported that "the view in the Administration" was that Moscow supported the treaty "to further Peking's isolation and to undermine its influence in the underdeveloped countries, where anti-test sentiment runs high."[31]

In terms of their responsiveness to public opinion, U.S. officials fell somewhere between those of Britain and the Soviet Union. Although, as Seaborg noted, "restricting the proliferation of nuclear weapons" had become "the president's primary concern," it was not his only one, nor the only one among other government leaders. The treaty, administration officials believed, was not only desirable because it would freeze the U.S. nuclear advantage, reduce nuclear fallout, and improve relations with the Soviet Union, but—as Carl Kaysen, one of its negotiators, noted—because it would respond to "the wide popular feeling about nuclear tests all over the world." Reporting from Moscow on July 18, Harriman and Kaysen argued that downplaying the importance of an atmospheric treaty was "undesirable both internationally and at home." The thinking of McCone, a longtime opponent of a test ban treaty who decided to support the Moscow pact, provides a good summary of the factors weighed by U.S. officials. "By continued testing, we can improve our weapon technology and the quality and dependability of our nuclear weapons," he wrote on July 30. "On the other hand, continuation of testing would bring us up against the imponderables of world opinion, intensification of the arms race, dangers inherent in the proliferation question, and finally, fear on the part of that segment of people in the United States and, for that matter the world, whether exaggerated or not, of the consequences of radioactive fallout."[32]

Moreover, the popularity of a test ban treaty promised other important dividends. For example, many officials believed that it would undercut more thoroughgoing criticism of the Bomb. Dean wrote that the administration hoped the measure would "take the wind out of the completely irresponsible and unintelligent propaganda campaign, including the 'ban the bomb' movements, being conducted against the nuclear powers at the United Nations, in England, and elsewhere." Furthermore, like their Russian counterparts, U.S. policymakers wanted to use antinuclear opinion to inhibit the Chinese from developing the Bomb. On July 22, Rusk instructed U.S. negotiators to tell Soviet officials of the U.S government's "hope that world public opinion mobilized behind the test ban treaty would have a compelling effect" on both France and China. Four days later, he remarked that widespread acceptance of the treaty would place "powerful pressures on Peiping not to go down the nuclear path." In early August, the *New York Times* reported that U.S. officials believed "that worldwide adherence to the treaty might in the end force Communist China to do likewise to try to salvage its political position in Asia, Africa, and Latin America." And even if this strategy failed, the Chinese would be isolated.[33]

Although Kennedy, Khrushchev, and Macmillan certainly deserve a large share of credit for the treaty, the remarkable role of Norman Cousins in fostering it should not be underestimated. He had helped to launch the crucial worldwide movement—mobilizing individuals like Schweitzer and Nehru, creating organizations like SANE, and arousing worldwide public opinion—and, later, became a key figure in the diplomatic maneuvering that led directly to the nuclear test ban. As Seaborg noted, Cousins's April 1963 visit to Khrushchev "helped to make history." So, too, did his initiation of the American University address—a speech, as Schlesinger remarked, that "repudiated the self-righteous cold war rhetoric of a succession of Secretaries of State."[34] Admittedly, in an apparent effort not to embarrass the government leaders whom he served as emissary, Cousins kept his diplomatic role secret, even from the leaders of SANE. Nonetheless, his value to Kennedy and Khrushchev lay precisely in the respect he inspired in each of them as a leader of the world nuclear disarmament movement. Recognizing the extraordinary part Cousins played in these events, Kennedy presented him with one of the original signed copies of the test ban treaty.[35]

The Response to the Treaty

In the United States, the Kennedy administration embarked on a major campaign to win the backing of public opinion. Although polls showed general support among Americans for the atmospheric test ban, the president was apprehensive that ratification might be blocked in the U.S. Senate. Here, as Sorensen noted, "enough Southern Democrats might combine with Republicans to prevent the necessary two-thirds vote."[36] To offset this possibility, on July 26, the day after the treaty was initialed in Moscow, Kennedy went on the offensive with a televised address, lauding it as "an important first step—a step towards peace—a step towards reason—a step away from war." In the speech, he highlighted the fact that the treaty would end "the atmospheric tests which have so alarmed mankind." Indeed, in this public forum, he placed "freeing the world from the fears and dangers of radioactive fallout" higher on the list of benefits from the treaty than halting nuclear proliferation.[37]

In the following days, the administration began discussions with disarmament groups on generating public support. Conferring with Cousins, White House press secretary Pierre Salinger suggested that the Ad Hoc Committee for a Nuclear Test Ban be reconstituted as a citizens committee for ratification that would conduct "a whirlwind campaign for educating and mobilizing public opinion." He thought that key members of the Ad Hoc Committee, together with like-minded business leaders, should meet with the president "to form a citizens committee for test ban ratification and to decide on general strategy." As this plan moved forward, the alliance of the administration and its erstwhile critics crystallized further. On August 2, dispatched by the president, Kaysen met with leaders of United World Federalists and urged them to generate letters and "long streams of delegations to Senators." Cousins, the UWF president, had to rush away from the meeting in order to keep his appointment with Senator Humphrey, who had telephoned him at Kennedy's request so that he could hear the Democratic Whip's "appraisal and strategy on the ratification fight." Humphrey told Cousins that he was "profoundly impressed" by what he had learned from Kennedy of the emerging citizens campaign. Furthermore, he wanted pro-treaty ads placed in numerous newspapers and tapes distributed to "radio stations throughout the country." If Cousins could "get the customers" for the tapes, Humphrey said, he would "deliver" the president, the secretary of state, and other Washington luminaries. Still reeling, Cousins went off to meet with Harriman and Rusk, who gave him further advice on a "carefully coordinated" campaign.[38]

On August 7, 1963, five leaders of the newly created Citizens Committee for a Nuclear Test Ban—Cousins, James Wadsworth, Marion Folsom (a former secretary of health, education, and welfare), William Clayton (a former undersecretary of state), and Walter Reuther (president of the United Auto Workers)—held a productive meeting with Kennedy and his advisers at the White House. According to a record of the conclave, the president began by thanking Cousins for assembling the group and expressed his gratitude to members of the committee for what they were doing. Their first task, he said, was to "get the letters moving." Letters were essential, Kennedy said, "to offset the negative testimony that was certain to develop, especially when the military men had their innings. If we left it to the generals, he said, they'd be dropping bombs all over the place. . . . But it was his job to keep the bomb from being dropped—on us or anyone else." When the president expressed disappointment that the committee had not been "able to get more conservative names," Cousins handed him a full-page *Wall Street Journal* ad titled, "Why Business Leaders Want a Nuclear Test Ban Treaty." Kennedy's eyes lit up and he remarked: "Now you're talking." Most of the rest of the meeting was devoted to a discussion of mass media and organizational ventures, outlined by Cousins. They also discussed which religious leaders, scientists, and educators to approach for endorsements and who would contact them. Kennedy volunteered his help along these lines.[39]

Despite the central role of nuclear disarmament activists in organizing the Citizens Committee, they tried to keep a low profile in its subsequent efforts. Wadsworth, for example, became chair of the Citizens Committee, and Cousins was identified simply as "Editor, the *Saturday Review*." In large part, this reflected the fact that, for political reasons, White House officials did not want them to play a prominent role. "We're not sure that organizations like SANE are an asset in this phase of the campaign," Bundy remarked at the August 7 meeting. "Months ago . . . SANE performed a valuable function by sticking pins in us and forcing us to consider the problem, but we're beyond that point now. . . . The kind of persuasion we need now has to come from people who are not readily identified with causes." According to Cousins, Kennedy was glad organizations such as SANE, the American Friends Service Committee, and the United World Federalists were working for treaty ratification, but "he wanted to be sure that they did not make the test ban appear to be solely a liberal cause." Frederick Dutton, who coordinated efforts for the administration, noted that he "tried to contain" the Society of Friends, SANE, "and others who have had a major interest in a test ban," for he did "not think we pick up any support, but only suspicion, if they lobby the Hill or get out in front publicly on the treaty."[40]

Yet the administration could not dispense with them, either. As one official recalled, the White House "saw support from the grassroots as key." And it was. SANE, Americans for Democratic Action, and the United World Federalists coordinated Washington lobbying efforts, while the Federation of American Scientists handled outreach to scientists. Meanwhile, the Citizens Committee developed a Working Committee, staffed largely by persons drawn from antinuclear groups who labored full time on the ratification campaign. Cousins, who chaired the Advisory Council of the Citizens Committee, masterminded much of its work, including major advertising efforts. The Citizens Committee also distributed a taped program, praising the treaty and urging listeners to contact their senators, to four hundred radio stations. Greatly impressed by these and other activities, Kennedy expressed his "warm appreciation" to Cousins for "the fine job being done by the Committee."[41] Inevitably, well-known veterans of the antinuclear campaign moved into prominent roles. The Citizens Committee drew heavily on Dr. Spock. Cousins debated the administration's nemesis, Edward Teller, several times on television. When Albert Schweitzer sent a letter to Kennedy on August 6, praising the treaty as "one of the greatest events . . . in the history of the world," White House officials threw caution to the winds and included it in a press release.[42]

The result was a landslide victory. With public sentiment swinging ever more heavily behind the treaty, even prominent Republican senators began to jump on the bandwagon. To be sure, powerful organizations and individuals continued to oppose it, including the Air Force Association, the head of the Strategic Air Command, Admiral Radford, and Lewis Strauss. Teller told senators that "if you ratify this treaty . . . you will have given away the future safety of this country." Phyllis Schlafly, a rising star in right-wing politics, warned that it would put the United States "at the mercy of the dictators."[43] Nevertheless, by September, polls showed that public support for the treaty had reached 80 percent.[44] On September 24, the Senate voted for ratification by the overwhelming margin of 80 to 19. Naturally, the president was overjoyed at the extent of the victory. Indeed, recalled Sorensen, Kennedy had "almost a sense of discovery that he had a major new issue . . . working for him—the issue of peace." He also recognized the crucial role performed by the Citizens Committee and told Cousins that "your initiative with the group was essential."[45]

The response to the treaty was quite the reverse in China. In a statement of July 31, the Chinese government denounced it as an attempt by the nuclear powers "to consolidate their nuclear monopoly and bind the hands of all the peace-loving countries subjected to the nuclear threat." The treaty "strengthens the position of nuclear powers for nuclear blackmail and increases the danger of imperialism launching a nuclear war and a world war." Naturally, it was "unthinkable for the Chinese government to be a party to this dirty fraud." In blistering attacks on the treaty—and on the "out-and-out capitulation" of the Kremlin to "U.S. imperialist global strategy"—delivered over the ensuing months, Chinese leaders continued to argue that they favored "the complete, thorough, total and resolute prohibition and destruction of nuclear weapons." In the meantime, they argued, Communist nations (notably China) had the right and duty to develop the Bomb. "Nuclear weapons in the possession of a socialist country are always a means of defense against nuclear blackmail and nuclear war," the Chinese government insisted. "So long as the imperialists refuse to ban nuclear weapons, the greater the number of socialist countries possessing them, the better the guarantee of world peace."[46]

In the Soviet Union, the reaction was far more affirmative. The treaty seemed to enjoy substantial popularity among average people and antinuclear activists like Sakharov. Party hard-liners, on the other hand, showed little enthusiasm. Among members of the party presidium, only Khrushchev's closest allies attended the signing ceremonies.[47] Nevertheless, the critics did not voice their objections publicly. Conversely, supporters of the treaty went on the offensive, holding the Chinese up to disdain before world opinion. In a statement issued on August 3, the Soviet government argued that "only disregard of the fundamental interests of the peoples, who have long been demanding an end to nuclear explosions, could suggest the interpretation of . . . the treaty the Chinese government has sought to give." Indeed, the Chinese approach represented "connivance with those who want a global thermonuclear war and oppose negotiated settlement of international issues." On August 21, another Soviet polemic declared that "no incantations from Peking will draw the Soviet Union on to the road of madness, of irresponsible playing with the lives of hundreds of millions of people." The Chinese government was implying that "the whole world is wrong in its estimation of the significance of the test ban treaty, and . . . only the Chinese leaders have the key to wisdom."[48]

The response to the treaty was especially enthusiastic in Britain. When Macmillan reported on the newly signed agreement to the House of Commons, he received a standing ovation, not only from Conservatives but from many members of the opposition. He ranked it among the greatest of his parliamentary triumphs. A week later, on August 2, he noted happily in his diary that the latest opinion poll showed "a tremendous swing" back to the Conservatives, putting them "only 6% or so behind Labour (instead of 18%–20%)." Furthermore, he had "risen equally or even more in public favour." David Ormsby Gore, the British ambassador to the United States, told Kennedy that "the Prime Minister is in such a state of euphoria after the Test Ban agreement" that Alec Douglas-Home, his apparent successor as party leader, "doubts whether he now has any intention of resigning." Eventually, Macmillan did allow Douglas-Home to lead the Conservatives in the forthcoming elections. And, as expected, they exploited the treaty for their political benefit—a particularly useful tactic in light of the Labour Party's long-standing opposition to nuclear testing and its more recent advocacy of scrapping Britain's "independent" nuclear program. Ultimately, the Labour Party emerged victorious, but only by a narrow margin.[49]

Elsewhere, too, the treaty drew substantial support. The French government, to be sure, like the Chinese, viewed it as a hypocritical attempt by the great powers to maintain a nuclear monopoly; consequently, de Gaulle announced that it would "not divert France from equipping herself with the same sources of strength." Similarly, Albania, China's staunchest ally on the world Communist scene, denounced it as "a dangerous trap" that "corresponds only to the interests of the U.S. imperialist warmongers."[50] But, for the most part, nations around the world either grudgingly endorsed the treaty (like West Germany) or gave it their enthusiastic backing. This included the overwhelming majority of nations in the Communist, Western, and nonaligned blocs. Naturally, veterans of the antinuclear campaign were particularly enthusiastic. Delighted by the treaty, Nehru argued that it marked an end to the Cold War. By late 1980, although China, France, Cuba, Libya, North Korea, and assorted Persian Gulf states remained important holdouts, 125 nations had agreed to its provisions.[51]

In a number of ways, the atmospheric test ban treaty fulfilled the expectations of its supporters. With its signing, almost all atmospheric nuclear testing—and the resulting radioactive fallout—came to an end. As a result, the biological hazards of nuclear testing were reduced to negligible proportions. In addition, the treaty reinforced antinuclear pressures in many countries by grassroots organizations, thereby tipping the balance in some of them against the development of nuclear weapons. Finally, the treaty did serve as "a first step" toward peace, for it ushered in a period of improved relations between the Soviet bloc and Western nations. Not only did additional arms control measures follow, but so did a broad range of agreements on economic and cultural matters. Meanwhile, East-West tensions dramatically declined. Only a short time after the most dangerous confrontation of the Cold War, the Cuban missile crisis, the Soviet Union and the United States embarked on a new era of peace and detente.[52]

On the other hand, without a resolution of international conflicts, governments still gravitated toward traditional means of ensuring "national security." To obtain the support of the Joint Chiefs of Staff for the treaty, Kennedy promised them four "safeguards": a vigorous underground nuclear testing program; a readiness to resume atmospheric testing; improved nuclear detection devices; and the high-level maintenance of U.S. nuclear laboratories.[53] Consequently, although the U.S. government ended atmospheric tests, it stepped up its nuclear testing program through explosions underground. In the nineteen years from 1945 to 1963, it conducted 347 nuclear tests (215 in the atmosphere, 132 underground); in the following nineteen, it conducted 555. Much the same thing happened in the Soviet Union, where the government remained determined to overcome the U.S. nuclear advantage. From 1945 to 1963, Moscow held 209 nuclear tests (207 in the atmosphere, 2 underground); in the next nineteen years, 386. Although British nuclear testing ebbed after 1963, French testing increased substantially and Chinese testing began the following year.[54] In the context of continued international rivalry, most of the nuclear arms race simply moved underground.

Furthermore, some atmospheric nuclear testing continued. Ignoring the treaty, the French government conducted twenty-one atmospheric nuclear tests—considerably more than it conducted underground—from 1964 to 1970. Similarly, the Chinese government, which exploded its first atomic bomb on October 16, 1964, held eleven nuclear weapons tests by 1970, ten of them in the atmosphere. Assailing the first Chinese test, Rusk deplored such "atmospheric testing in the face of serious efforts made by almost all other nations to protect the atmosphere." But the Chinese government viewed this as completely hypocritical. *Renmin Ribao* retorted tartly: "So long as U.S. imperialism possesses nuclear bombs, China must have them too." Neither France nor China, of course, had signed the atmospheric test ban treaty. But this merely underscored the inability of the United States and the Soviet Union to bring all of their putative allies on board.[55]

Given popular revulsion against nuclear testing, governments continued to show some sensitivity to the issue. Asian and Latin American countries issued numerous protests against the French testing program in the South Pacific, with the governments of Australia and New Zealand raising the matter before the World Court. Chinese nuclear tests also came in for sharp criticism. These protests appear to have contributed to the end of atmospheric tests by France in 1974 and by China in 1980.[56]

U.S. and Soviet officials also remained concerned about public opinion, but not enough to sign an agreement to halt underground tests. Within the U.S. government, interest in a comprehensive test ban (CTB) treaty waned after the death of Kennedy and the succession of Lyndon Johnson to the presidency. As Seaborg—who remained AEC chair—noted, Johnson had his doubts about the partial test ban treaty and was "indifferent at best" to a comprehensive treaty, espousing it publicly "primarily to affect world opinion." Meanwhile, there developed "strong and controlling opposition to such a measure within the administration. During 1967 and 1968, especially, a CTB would have been inconsistent with a national policy to develop a new generation of offensive and defense weapons." The idea remained alive only to avoid "a setback on the public opinion front." How much interest the Soviet government had in a complete end to testing remains uncertain. According to Dobrynin, though, Khrushchev very much wanted a productive summit meeting with Kennedy "to demonstrate some success for public opinion in his country." And even after the U.S. president's death, Khrushchev spoke of a "fund of confidence" the treaty had generated which made it "possible to move further." But, in October 1964, he was at last toppled from power by his party adversaries. According to Seaborg, the departure of Kennedy and Khrushchev from the political scene closed the window of opportunity on a comprehensive test ban.[57]

Stopping the Spread of Nuclear Weapons

For a time, the threat of nuclear proliferation seemed more serious. In 1967, three years after the Chinese government set off its first atomic bomb, it exploded its first H-Bomb. Filled with enthusiasm, Chinese troops raced toward the mushroom cloud cheering "Long live Chairman Mao!"[58] Meanwhile, the Israeli government, threatened with destruction by its Arab neighbors, indicated that it was moving toward a nuclear weapons capability. In December 1965, responding to foreign reports of an Israeli nuclear project, the minister of labor declared that "Israel will not be the first to introduce nuclear weapons into the Middle East, but it will not be the second either."[59] India, too—horrified by the Chinese border attacks of 1962 and by the first Chinese nuclear explosion—began to reconsider its earlier decision not to manufacture the Bomb. Although Prime Minister Lal Bahadur Shastri, who succeeded Nehru after the latter's death in May 1964, resisted pressures for nuclear armament, he suffered a fatal heart attack in January 1966. His successor, Indira Gandhi, declared that May that India was not forever committed to forgoing nuclear weapons and ordered the upgrading of her country's nuclear facilities. Other countries were also on the brink of going nuclear.[60]

From the standpoint of the U.S. and Soviet governments, this constituted a dangerous state of affairs. Controlling nuclear proliferation became a high priority of the Johnson administration, which went so far as to consider a preemptive strike against Chinese nuclear facilities.[61] The Soviet government, too, worried about nuclear proliferation, including U.S. plans for a multilateral force (MLF), which it regarded, erroneously, as giving West Germany control over the use of nuclear weapons.[62] With most NATO nations indifferent or hostile to the MLF, in late 1964 the Johnson administration decided to stop promoting the plan and to focus its efforts, instead, on finding another means to stop the spread of nuclear weapons to "irresponsible" countries. At the time, Sweden and India were leading efforts by nonaligned nations in the U.N. General Assembly to halt nuclear proliferation and to limit the nuclear weapons capability of the nuclear powers. As might be expected, the latter had little appeal for the U.S. and Soviet governments; but the former looked quite promising.

Accordingly, in the fall of 1965 the two governments submitted draft nonproliferation treaties to the General Assembly. "Both superpowers really got behind the Nonproliferation Treaty," recalled Rusk, "because we and the Soviets basically were on the same wavelength."[63]

The non-nuclear powers, however, objected fiercely to the provisions of the U.S. and Soviet proposals, which would do little more than limit the nuclear club to its existing members. A statement issued by Alva Myrdal of Sweden observed that "the non-aligned nations . . . strongly believe that disarmament measures should be a matter of mutual renunciation." Therefore, they did not want a treaty that "would leave the present five nuclear-weapon parties free to continue to build up their arsenals." Much the same argument came from the governments of numerous NATO countries. West German foreign minister Willy Brandt argued that "the moral and political justification of a nonproliferation treaty follows only if the nuclear states regard it as a step toward restrictions of their own armaments and toward disarmament and clearly state they are willing to act accordingly." Repeatedly, critics pointed to the General Assembly's resolution of November 19, 1965, which had declared that a nonproliferation treaty "should be a step towards the achievement of general and complete disarmament and, more particularly, nuclear disarmament."[64]

Given this revolt, the scope of the emerging nonproliferation treaty was substantially broadened. The most important of the changes, Article VI, provided that each party to the treaty would "pursue negotiations in good faith at an early date on effective measures regarding cessation of the nuclear arms race and disarmament." In addition, the treaty provided that each nuclear weapon state agreed "not to transfer nuclear weapons to any non-nuclear-weapon state," while each non-nuclear weapon state pledged "not to make or acquire nuclear weapons." Furthermore, the non-nuclear weapon states agreed to accept a safeguard system, administered by the International Atomic Energy Agency, that would prevent diversion of nuclear material from reactors to weapons development. With the revised Nuclear Non-Proliferation Treaty incorporating provisions for both nonproliferation and nuclear disarmament, it swept through the U.N. General Assembly on June 12, 1968, by a vote of 95 to 4, with 21 abstentions. Although, ominously, a number of nations with nuclear ambitions refused to ratify the treaty—including Argentina, Brazil, Egypt, India, Israel, Pakistan, and South Africa—it was clearly a milestone in international efforts to halt the arms race. Johnson called it "the most important international agreement limiting nuclear arms since the nuclear age began."[65]

Rather remarkably, within a short period, more than a hundred non-nuclear nations ratified this treaty and, thereby, renounced building the Bomb. Most, of course, did not forgo a viable option, for they lacked the scientific or eco-

nomic resources to develop nuclear weapons. Still others, which had the resources, already felt some degree of security under the nuclear umbrella of the
great powers. Even so, these factors do not constitute the entire explanation for
the success of nonproliferation. Although analysts had once estimated that as
many as thirty nations might develop nuclear weapons by the 1970s, very few
of them chose to do so. Indeed, numerous countries quite capable of developing the Bomb—Sweden, Canada, Switzerland, East and West Germany, Italy,
Australia, and Japan, among others—resisted the temptation. Nor is there any
reason for them to have felt greater comfort under the nuclear umbrella of their
allies than had the British, Chinese, and French. Some, in fact, did not belong
to alliances.[66]

Clearly, other factors played key roles in limiting proliferation, notably
public opinion. By the time the Non-Proliferation Treaty cleared the United
Nations, popular opposition to nuclear weapons had already contributed to the
decisions of a number of countries, including Sweden and Japan, to forswear
the nuclear option. In January 1968, buffeted by fierce antinuclear pressures,
the Japanese prime minister formally pledged that his government would refuse
to manufacture nuclear weapons. Indeed, Tokyo's development of nuclear
weapons or rejection of the Non-Proliferation Treaty would have been political
dynamite. As a leading scholarly specialist has written: "A decision to build
nuclear bombs would have split the Japanese body politic as no other issue had
done since the termination of the war. Some observers even questioned whether
anything recognizable as a democratic system of government would have been
likely to survive." In February 1968, when a Cabinet minister did call for
Japan's nuclear armament, he was forced to resign. Moreover, although Japan
had a particularly strong antinuclear movement, every country (except France)
with a substantial nuclear disarmament campaign signed the Non-Proliferation
Treaty. Capping more than a decade of antinuclear agitation, the treaty had become difficult to resist. Even France and China, despite their refusal to sign it,
observed its key provisions.[67]

Another sign of the antinuclear tide was the negotiation of the Treaty of
Tlatelolco, which established a nuclear weapons–free zone in Latin America.
Thanks to the work of Alfonso Garcia Robles of Mexico, a leader of disarmament efforts at the United Nations, the General Assembly endorsed the treaty in
December 1967. Under its provisions, Latin American countries renounced the
right to acquire nuclear weapons and to station them on their territory. Signers
also agreed to place their nuclear facilities under the jurisdiction of the International Atomic Energy Agency and to accept enforcement measures. In turn,
nuclear powers agreed "not to contribute to acts involving a violation of the
treaty, and not to use or threaten to use nuclear weapons against the parties to

the treaty." Although twenty Latin American nations signed the treaty, which went into force in 1968, three of them (Argentina, Brazil, and Chile) did not ratify it; Cuba and Guyana refused to sign it at all. Even so, the Treaty of Tlatelolco was the first international agreement to ban nuclear weapons from an inhabited region. Together with opposition to nuclear weapons within individual nations, it helped keep Latin America out of the nuclear arms race.[68]

Other countries, too, moved to make themselves nuclear-free. In 1958, the U.S. ambassador to Japan had informed the State Department that "there is a definite possibility that one day Japan will allow us to have nuclear components in Japan (perhaps on somewhat similar terms to what we have with the UK) and will themselves have at least defensive missiles with a nuclear capability." After ten years of additional antinuclear agitation, however, these appealing possibilities ceased to exist. Giving way to enormous public pressure, Japanese prime minister Eisaku Sato announced in December 1967 that his government would not possess, manufacture, or introduce nuclear weapons into Japan. These "three non-nuclear principles," backed by an overwhelming majority of the population, quickly became a national consensus beyond which no party or government dared to venture. In November 1971, when Japan's House of Representatives voted on a resolution endorsing these principles, it passed unanimously.[69]

Canada also gradually took action to ban nuclear arms. The victory of the Liberals in Canada's 1963 parliamentary elections had led to an agreement with the U.S. government to deploy nuclear weapons in that nation. But the Liberal victory had been narrow, enabling Pearson to form no more than a minority government. Meanwhile, antinuclear sentiment remained strong. Consequently, as prime minister, Pearson drove an unexpectedly hard bargain with the U.S. government and announced that a "more acceptable non-nuclear Canadian role" would be negotiated later. Pierre Trudeau, who had been one of the fiercest critics of Pearson's pro-nuclear stand in 1963, succeeded him as prime minister in 1968. Within a short time, Trudeau announced that it was "no longer appropriate for the Canadian Armed Forces to be equipped with nuclear weapons." In the following years, he began phasing them out, leading gradually to the restoration of Canada as a nuclear-free nation.[70]

Other Arms Control Measures

By the late 1960s, nuclear arms control ventures were at high tide. Responding to an initiative of the U.N. General Assembly, the United States and the Soviet Union signed the Outer Space Treaty in 1966, banning the deployment of weapons of mass destruction in orbit or on celestial bodies. Another U.N. initiative led the two nations to begin negotiations in 1968 for the Seabed Arms Control Treaty, prohibiting the placement of weapons of mass destruction on the seabeds—a measure finally signed in 1971.[71] In addition, Johnson championed limits on strategic arms. After 1964, when the Soviet government began building an antiballistics missile (ABM) system outside Moscow, Defense Department officials began to worry that a Soviet-U.S. ABM race would be costly, ineffective, and destabilizing. McNamara carried the issue to Johnson and, although he was unable to head off pressures to build a "thin" ABM system, secured an agreement from the president to develop a sincere strategic arms limitation proposal. Johnson, increasingly beset by protest against the Vietnam War, pressed forward on this front both because of his respect for McNamara and—as a former Defense Department official recalled—"because he had come to see this issue as a way to portray himself as a man of peace and hence to overcome . . . his image as the war maker." The result was a serious U.S. proposal to the Soviet government for a freeze on offensive missiles and sharp limitations on ABM systems.[72]

This almost led to a pathbreaking strategic arms control treaty in 1968. At first, opposition to ABM systems dumbfounded Soviet policymakers, as well as Soviet scientists. When an American participant in the 1964 Pugwash conference presented his ideas on the issue, the head of the Soviet delegation said that there must have been a problem in translation, for he had heard the interpreter say that the objection was to *defensive* weapons. Eventually, though, Western Pugwash participants succeeded in convincing their Soviet counterparts that developing defensive weapons merely provided a new incentive for the other side to develop additional offensive weapons. In turn, Soviet scientists carried this message home and began changing the minds of Soviet policymakers.[73] As late as the June 1967 meeting between Soviet Premier Aleksei Kosygin and Johnson at Glassboro, New Jersey, Kremlin officials resisted the idea of a treaty to limit offensive and defensive strategic arms. On July 1, 1968, however, the Soviet government announced its agreement to enter strategic arms control negotiations. But the Soviet invasion of Czechoslovakia that August made talks politically impossible for a time. And when the administration tried to resurrect the negotiations later that year, President-elect Richard Nixon declared that he refused to be bound by them.[74]

Ultimately, though, the Nixon administration saw no alternative to strategic arms controls. With the public and Congress sour on military expenditures thanks to the Vietnam War, opponents of the administration's plan for an extensive ABM system succeeded in restricting it to two sites and in blocking new strategic weapons systems. According to Henry Kissinger, Nixon's chief national security adviser, although the administration sought to build up U.S.

strategic nuclear forces, "every new weapons program we put forward was systematically attacked or dismantled. As a result, starting in 1970 our defense department was pleading with us to negotiate a freeze" with the Soviet Union. Gerard Smith, Nixon's ACDA director who also served as his chief negotiator during the Strategic Arms Limitation Talks (SALT), later observed: "Nothing concentrated the minds of American leaders on the advantages of SALT as much as . . . congressional cuts in U.S. defense budgets. The changing popular and congressional mood about strategic arms was not lost" on the secretary of defense or on Nixon, "who felt that the SALT negotiation was perhaps the last chance for bargaining with the Soviets from a level of equality. Strategic arms control suddenly took on new seriousness and respectability."[75]

The result was the SALT I Treaty, signed with the Soviet government in 1972. It limited ABMs and, on a temporary basis, froze the number of offensive nuclear weapons. Although the treaty did not regulate qualitative improvements in weaponry, such as placing multiple warheads on a single missile, it did mark another step forward in controlling nuclear arms. The signing of the treaty also attested to how popular nuclear arms controls had become. Determined to enhance his re-election prospects, Nixon timed the agreement so that it would have a favorable impact on his 1972 presidential campaign.[76]

Using the Bomb

These same trends fed into a growing reluctance by the leaders of the nuclear powers to use the Bomb. In the mid-1960s—as "flexible response" took hold in the West—Soviet strategic doctrine began to shift away from the Kremlin's variant of massive retaliation toward admitting the possibility of a "war by stages" in Europe, in which a conventional conflict would not necessarily escalate into a nuclear one.[77] In Britain, the new Labour government also began to emphasize a conventional defense. As Denis Healey, British defense secretary, recalled, he and most of the party's defense experts in Parliament "wanted to move [NATO] away from deterrence by the nuclear tripwire, towards defense by conventional forces which would be adequate to resist anything but an all-out attack by the Warsaw powers—which, in our view, was an almost inconceivable contingency." This meshed well with U.S. policy. As Healey noted, "Washington would implicitly threaten to remove its nuclear umbrella . . . while Europe would increase its conventional contribution to the alliance, so as to raise the nuclear threshold and thus reduce America's nuclear liability."[78]

Whatever their private attitudes toward nuclear war, Johnson administration officials certainly recognized that publicly advocating it was political suicide. During the 1964 presidential campaign, when Republican candidate Barry Goldwater began talking loosely about using nuclear weapons in the quest for Cold War "victory," the Johnson administration went after him with devastating effect. McNamara spoke out on the grim consequences of nuclear war, concluding with his "doubt that any sane person would call this 'victory.'" In a major public address, Rusk declared: "No sane man could regard the incineration of most of the Northern hemisphere as a triumph for freedom." Taking up the theme in his Labor Day address, Johnson described nuclear war as a great catastrophe, with hundreds of millions dead, cities destroyed, fields in ruin, and industry demolished. "Make no mistake," he said; "there is no such thing as a conventional nuclear weapon." Bundy later claimed that although this lecture was sincere, "there was certainly politics" in it as well. Meanwhile, the Johnson campaign employed anti-Goldwater TV ads with antinuclear themes. One portrayed a little girl plucking the petals of a daisy until she dissolved into a mushroom cloud. Another showed a little girl licking an ice-cream cone as a gentle, motherly voice talked about strontium-90 and Goldwater's opposition to the atmospheric test ban treaty. If the script for Johnson's campaign sounded like it could have been written by SANE, that may have been because Johnson employed SANE's advertising firm to produce his campaign ads.[79]

The U.S. government's wariness about nuclear war is exemplified by its conduct during the Vietnam War. As Rusk put it: "Despite the enormous costs and frustrations of Vietnam, the Kennedy, Johnson, and Nixon administrations chose to fight that war with conventional means, and eventually lost the war rather than 'win' it with nuclear weapons." During the conflict, a number of U.S. officials—including military leaders and the U.S. ambassador to South Vietnam, Henry Cabot Lodge Jr.—did raise the possibility of using nuclear weapons. But, as the records of the administration's planning meetings reveal, higher-level officials refused to sanction this idea. McNamara insisted that he could not imagine a case in which nuclear weapons should be considered. Rusk also opposed the nuclear option, arguing that "many free world leaders would oppose this." Recalling the "irrelevance of nuclear weapons" in the war, Bundy—who served as a top national security adviser to two of the presidents—argued it did not result from "fear that friends of Vietnam with warheads of their own, Russians or Chinese, would use some of them in reply." Rather, he pointed to the "reaction . . . on both sides in divided Vietnam, to such attacks. . . . Could you, in that reaction, lose the war by winning it? And what would have been the reputation of the United States elsewhere—in nearby countries . . . or in the rest of the newly independent world, or in Latin America, or in the Atlantic alliance?" Even more significant, Bundy maintained, was the fact that "in the particular case of Vietnam no president could hope for understanding and support from his own countrymen if he used the bomb."[80]

Although Richard Nixon came to the presidency convinced of the utility of nuclear threats and later claimed that he "considered using nuclear weapons" on four occasions, such consideration does not appear to have gone very far. Indeed, it is not mentioned in his memoirs or in other accounts of the era. Reviewing Nixon's record on this score, Bundy maintained that "what stopped him" from even threatening to use nuclear weapons in Vietnam was "his conclusion that any use of the bomb" there "would have totally unacceptable results inside the United States, enraging the opponents of the war and setting general opinion against the new administration with such force as to make it doubtful that the government could keep up the American end of the war. . . . What the American people would not accept, the nuclear-minded president could not plausibly threaten." Similarly, as a power-hungry academic, Kissinger had long sought to make nuclear war a more acceptable option. But once in the White House, he found to his regret that nuclear nations "could not necessarily use this power to impose their will. The capacity to destroy proved difficult to translate into a plausible threat even against countries with no capacity for retaliation." Indeed, the superpowers found that the very "awesomeness of their power increased their inhibitions."[81]

Disinterest in Disarmament

In contrast to their development of arms controls and practice of nuclear restraint, the nations of the world made little progress toward disarmament. Indeed, the nuclear powers continued to expand their nuclear arsenals. In 1968, when he stepped down as defense secretary, McNamara reported that the U.S. "strategic offensive forces are immense: 1,000 Minuteman missile launchers, carefully protected belowground; 41 Polaris submarines, carrying 656 missile launchers, with the majority hidden beneath the seas at all times; and about 600 long-range bombers, approximately 40 percent of which are kept always in a high state of alert." Moreover, the Johnson administration had already moved to develop a new weapons system—multiple independently targetable reentry vehicles (MIRV), which would provide each U.S. missile with multiple warheads. Thanks to MIRV deployments, over the next few years more than 3,000 nuclear warheads were added to the U.S. strategic arsenal.[82]

Meanwhile, as Georgi Arbatov, a top Kremlin adviser of the time, has recently revealed, the Soviet government, though recognizing the dangers of the arms race, failed to challenge it in any substantial way. "No one . . . ever demanded that the Ministry of Defense or the defense industry care about disarmament," he wrote. Indeed, Leonid Brezhnev was accustomed "to granting the generals and military industrialists anything they wanted." And "they were concerned with catching up with the Americans in arms." Dobrynin drew much the same picture. "Brezhnev was fond of the military, and they of him," the Soviet ambassador recalled years later. Indeed, the Soviet leader was pathetically "proud of himself in his field marshal's uniform." Once, when Dobrynin visited him at home, Brezhnev "told me to sit with my cup of tea while he vanished. He reappeared in his grand uniform with all his medals and asked: 'How do I look?' I replied, 'Magnificent'—what else could I say?" Brezhnev was eager "to achieve strategic arms parity with the United States" and, consequently, the Soviet nuclear arsenal grew rapidly. By the end of 1969, the Soviet Union had an ICBM force virtually the same size as that of the United States.[83]

A similar sense of insecurity also paralyzed any impulses toward disarmament on the part of the other nuclear powers. Both the French and the Chinese worked feverishly to upgrade their nuclear arsenals, although the Chinese insisted that they favored an international agreement for the complete prohibition and destruction of all nuclear weapons.[84] For a time, there seemed a possibility that Britain's new Labour government might abandon the country's "independent nuclear deterrent," for the party gave the impression during the 1964 election campaign that it would scrap plans for Polaris. In fact, though, it had only committed itself to "renegotiate" the agreement with the United States. Ultimately, most of the Labour Cabinet came down on the side of acquiring the nuclear-armed submarines (albeit four rather than the original five), arguing that they would give Britain greater influence over NATO strategy and would reinforce the credibility of the U.S. nuclear deterrent. Healey claimed that "there was little chance of influencing McNamara's nuclear strategy if we had renounced nuclear weapons ourselves. . . . I did not think it was wise to entrust the future of the human race to the mathematicians in the Pentagon, who seemed to assume human characteristics only when they thought their institutional interests were at risk."[85]

Nor did nuclear disarmament have much support any longer among those who had once been its keenest advocates: the nonaligned nations of the Third World. In October 1964, at the second nonaligned summit conference in Cairo, disarmament received far less attention than at Belgrade. When the Indians proposed sending a delegation to China to protest nuclear tests then being conducted there, the conference refused to support the idea. Instead, anticolonialism emerged as the major theme, with Nkrumah arguing that "as long as oppressed classes exist, there can be no such thing as peaceful coexistence." These developments reflected the death of Nehru, the growth of Soviet-U.S. detente, and the rising militancy of African nations. In 1970, when the third nonaligned summit conference convened in Lusaka, peaceful coexistence was not on the agenda and disarmament nearly dropped from sight. For the first time, a conference declaration proposed to "safeguard international peace and security" through the development of the "military strength of each country." As a leader of the Canadian nuclear disarmament movement remarked, some years later, the new nations of the Third World "displayed, in the end, all the contradictions of national and state power. . . . They slipped into their own cycle of arms buildups."[86]

A Partial Victory

Despite these setbacks, years of worldwide agitation against the Bomb did come to fruition with a string of important antinuclear advances that began in 1963 and continued for a decade thereafter. Most of these advances took the form of internationally enforced nuclear arms control measures: an atmospheric test ban treaty; a nuclear nonproliferation treaty; treaties banning nuclear weapons from the seabed and from outer space; a nuclear-free zone treaty; and a strategic arms limitation treaty. In addition, some nations acted unilaterally by placing limits on their own nuclear activities. Perhaps most important, they refrained from waging nuclear war. Pressured by a worldwide movement and wary of public opinion, the leaders of most nations ultimately proved capable of making substantial changes in their nuclear policies. On the other hand, given their fear and suspicion of other nations, these guardians of national security rarely proved willing to dispense with nuclear weapons. As Rusk told the Joint Chiefs of Staff, "categorically," the atmospheric test ban agreement was "not a 'ban the bomb' treaty."[87]

This pattern of behavior contributes to a central irony of this story. The movement that had done so much to foster these changes desired, above all, nuclear disarmament. And this, alone, remained beyond its grasp.[88]

The Decline of the Movement, 1964–70

The Aldermaston marchers . . .
—I wonder where they're gone?
Peggy Duff, 1971

Partial victories do not necessarily invigorate social movements. The history of the world nuclear disarmament movement provides a good illustration of this point, for despite some success in limiting the testing, proliferation, and use of nuclear weapons, it declined precipitously after the early 1960s. Once-powerful organizations dwindled in size, while others disappeared entirely. The dramatic nuclear disarmament marches came to an end. Public concern about nuclear weapons sharply ebbed. Of course, even before this, a number of factors had set limits to the movement's popularity, and these continued to plague it. But as the decade wore on, new developments—both internal and external—added very substantially to the movement's problems. Thus, although the struggle against the Bomb continued to exist in a weakened form, increasingly it seemed like a relic of the past, competing unsuccessfully for public attention against the driving issues of the present.

The Ebbing of the Movement

The powerful British movement waned rapidly. Although the Committee of 100 continued for a time to stage small demonstrations at military bases and around other political issues, it formally dissolved in 1968. Meanwhile, the Bertrand Russell Peace Foundation, launched with great hopes by its namesake in 1963, was shaken by a nasty conflict between Russell and Ralph Schoenman from which it never quite recovered.[1] Only CND remained active in the struggle—organizing new demonstrations, statements, and fundraising appeals. But even this flagship of the antinuclear campaign underwent a sharp decline.

In 1964, the CND national council abandoned its yearly Aldermaston march and, facing serious financial problems, decided to cut the staff, services, and activities of the national office. Most of CND's prominent leaders dropped away, as did most of the membership. By 1971, CND had a staff of four people, debts that exceeded its annual income, and only 2,047 members. Wearers of the famous nuclear disarmament pin were greeted by the comment: "CND? I thought that died long ago."[2]

In Canada, where the British CND model had been widely emulated, events took a similar course. Beginning in late 1963, the antinuclear movement rapidly lost momentum. Prominent figures withdrew from Canadian CND and, by early 1965, most of the local branches were weak or defunct. After wrestling with the issue of the group's continued existence for several months, the national executive committee finally decided to wind up Canadian CND's operations on June 1.[3] Meanwhile, the major student nuclear disarmament group, Combined Universities CND, also did a stock-taking. According to the minutes of a January 1964 executive committee meeting, there was a discussion of "the sad state of the movement across the country." At the end of the year, CUCND stalwarts helped form a new group, the Student Union for Peace Action, and CUCND ceased to exist. Its magazine, *Our Generation Against Nuclear War*, became simply *Our Generation*. Although the Voice of Women proved more durable, it left nuclear issues largely behind as it plunged ahead with new ventures. Furthermore, by the mid-1970s, even VOW had dwindled to what two of its leaders called "a hard core."[4]

In West Germany, the once-promising movement began to break up during the late 1960s. For a time, the Campaign for Disarmament continued its remarkable growth, prospering from the tension between an increasingly radical student culture and the frozen politics of the Federal Republic. In 1968, it burgeoned still further thanks to a groundswell of opposition to emergency powers legislation being considered by the Bundestag. Accordingly, it changed its name to the Campaign for Democracy and Disarmament (Kampagne für Demokratie und Abrüstung) and, that spring—shortly after the attempted assassination of the popular student leader Rudi Dutschke—staged the largest Easter march yet. Nevertheless, the movement grew so large and all-encompassing that it lost its antinuclear focus. Indeed, the Campaign for Democracy and Disarmament soon descended into bitter factionalism and other internal disputes over its goals and strategy. Consequently, by 1970, the West German movement was disintegrating.[5]

Antinuclear movements elsewhere also underwent a sharp decline. In Denmark, nuclear disarmament marches and other activities ebbed after 1963. Voting in December 1966 to terminate its campaign, KmA closed its office in

Copenhagen, stopped publication of its journal, and destroyed its files.[6] Much the same thing happened in Norway, Sweden, and Belgium, where antinuclear campaigns dropped out of sight in the mid-1960s.[7] In the Netherlands and France, Easter marches and other antinuclear agitation persisted into the latter part of the decade, only to come to an abrupt end—as did much of the antinuclear movement—in its final years.[8] The Swiss Movement Against Atomic Armaments existed formally until 1969. In fact, however, it ceased its activities in 1967, when it held its last Easter march.[9] In Australia, CND groups expired during 1965. By that time, branches of New Zealand CND were also becoming inactive. Several years later, New Zealand CND itself collapsed, leaving its Auckland branch as the only survivor of the nationwide organization.[10]

Although the nuclear disarmament campaign held up better in the United States, it was also in trouble. After late 1963, student protest against the Bomb faded rapidly. When, in the spring of 1964, only twenty-five delegates turned out for the convention of the Student Peace Union, the organization disbanded. A few years later, the Committee for Nonviolent Action, close to collapse, was absorbed by the War Resisters League. Both SANE and Women Strike for Peace survived intact and continued to function as major peace groups, but lost momentum and support. Furthermore, both groups departed increasingly from nuclear issues. In 1969, to reflect its change of focus, SANE dropped the word "Nuclear" from its name. Cousins—who resigned from the organization in 1967—complained in the mid-1970s: "Hardly anyone talks anymore about nuclear stockpiles as the world's No. 1 problem." Indeed, "the anti-testing clamor of the Sixties now seems far off and almost unreal."[11]

In the Soviet Union, concern about the Bomb continued for a time to preoccupy prominent intellectuals. In 1967, working with the journalist Ernst Henry, Sakharov produced an article on the role of the intelligentsia in averting nuclear war. Assailing the notion that war could any longer serve as an extension of politics, the physicist argued that a nuclear showdown "would throw humanity centuries back, to the age of barbarism." When the Communist Party refused to allow publication of the article, it appeared in Roy Medvedev's *Political Diary*, a leading *samizdat* journal. "By the beginning of 1968," recalled Sakharov, "I felt a growing compulsion to speak out. . . . I was influenced by my life experience and a feeling of personal responsibility, reinforced by the part I'd played in the development of the hydrogen bomb, the special knowledge I'd gained about thermonuclear warfare, my bitter struggle to ban nuclear testing, and my familiarity with the Soviet system." Furthermore, "I shared the hopes of Einstein, Bohr, Russell, Szilard, and other Western intellectuals" that "an open society, convergence, and world government . . . might ease the tragic crisis of our age."[12]

The result was the appearance of an extraordinarily influential essay, *Progress, Coexistence, and Intellectual Freedom*, circulated in manuscript form in the Soviet Union and published in the West in July 1968. Noting that his ideas had been forged in the milieu of a "scientific-technological intelligentsia" concerned "with mankind's future," Sakharov delivered a humanistic message much like that of his overseas counterparts. Civilization, he argued, was imperiled by "a universal thermonuclear war," which "would be a means of universal suicide." "Every rational creature, finding itself on the brink of a disaster, first tries to get away from the brink." And "if mankind is to get away from the brink, it must overcome its divisions." Greeting Sakharov's 1968 manifesto in the *Bulletin of the Atomic Scientists*, Rabinowitch stated that "from the Pugwash conferences" and "many personal conversations with Russian scientists, their Western colleagues knew" that they "shared their own concerns for the future." Even so, Sakharov's essay was "the first fully spelled-out presentation of this view." Immensely impressed, Rabinowitch compared it to the Franck Report of June 1945.[13]

Nor was the impact of Sakharov's political foray limited to the West. Despite their underground status, the physicist's ideas reached a broad audience in the Soviet Union, particularly among intellectuals. Traveling in the United States, Kapitza publicly endorsed Sakharov's stand. Meanwhile, Fedor Burlatsky, a young intellectual and party reformer, delivered a paper at a Soviet sociology conference arguing that the prevention of nuclear war was "the supreme value that stood higher than national, class or other values of any state or nation." In it, he proposed that scientists from East and West work together for nuclear disarmament and peace—a plan he later discussed at length with Sakharov.[14]

Even so, nuclear disarmament gradually ceased to be a central concern of dissident Soviet intellectuals, who turned instead to championing a broad range of domestic reforms. In early 1966, leading peace-oriented physicists— Kapitza, Sakharov, Artsimovich, Igor Tamm, and Mikhail Leontovich—joining with a group of liberal artists, denounced the Communist Party's plans for the rehabilitation of Stalin. Beginning in 1965, Sakharov himself became increasingly involved with domestic political issues, particularly supporting Soviet dissidents and other victims of the regime. In this fashion, he drifted away from the nuclear weapons question. As he later remarked, he "turned from worldwide problems to the defense of individual people." Even Sakharov's *Progress, Coexistence, and Intellectual Freedom*, despite its emphasis on the need to avert a nuclear holocaust, placed a higher priority on freedom of thought, arguing that it provided "the only guarantee of the feasibility of a scientific-democratic approach to politics, economy, and culture." In March 1970,

Sakharov, Medvedev, and the mathematician Valentin Turchin addressed a letter to the Soviet leadership calling attention to a broad range of failures in the country's economic and political system. That November, Sakharov joined with two other physicists, Andrei Tverdokhlebov and Valery Chalidze, to form a Committee for Human Rights. Sakharov and other Soviet dissidents continued to call for disarmament, but without making the issue a top priority.[15]

In Japan, the movement persisted, although on a much reduced scale. Condemning Chinese and French atmospheric nuclear tests, Gensuikin also demanded the conclusion of comprehensive test ban, nonproliferation, and nuclear disarmament treaties, as well as a pledge of non-use of nuclear weapons by the nuclear powers. To block Japan's nuclearization, Gensuikin staged demonstrations in front of the Diet building in 1967, 1968, and 1969. Meanwhile, organizations of atomic bomb survivors remained active, publishing antinuclear literature and demanding relief legislation. In Hiroshima, memorial services recurred annually on August 6, stressing strongly antinuclear themes. "The major powers of the world, ever engrossed in the endless race of nuclear armament, are treading the path to man's self-destruction," warned Setsuo Yamada, Hiroshima's mayor, in 1970. Yet even in Japan fewer people heeded this message. The movement, at least, appeared factionalized, demoralized, and lacking in central direction. In 1972, a foreign observer contended that Japan's "public allergy to nuclear weapons" had come to an end.[16] He was wrong, but his mistake was understandable.

With national organizations on the wane, the international nonaligned movement also faded. Despite the potential of the International Confederation for Disarmament and Peace, including the work of British CND's Peggy Duff as general secretary after 1967, this nuclear disarmament international failed to establish itself as a powerful organization. Instead, it remained very poorly funded, thinly staffed, and—given the decline of its constituent groups just as it began operations—never able to develop much of an international campaign.[17] The Pugwash movement fared better in the late 1960s, continuing to attract an impressive array of arms control and disarmament specialists to international conferences. Nevertheless, it also experienced some loss of momentum. In 1972, Rabinowitch commented that the movement seemed to be "standing still." To some extent, he maintained, "it has become an 'establishment,' rather than a pioneering, almost revolutionary effort it had been at the beginning."[18]

The Communist-led peace movement was in considerably worse shape. At Gensuikyo's 1966 World Congress Against Atomic and Hydrogen Bombs, a furious battle erupted over the decision of the conference organizers to accept the registration of the World Federation of Democratic Youth, a Soviet-controlled group. Infuriated by this deference to the "revisionists," pro-Chinese delegates, including most foreign participants, stormed out of the meeting, declaring that they would never return. Many of the dissidents went immediately to Peking, where they were feted by leaders of the China Peace Committee, who congratulated them on their "brilliant success." That year, the Chinese also withdrew from the World Peace Council—an action that restored some measure of harmony to its meetings but did little to expand its appeal. In 1968, Soviet officials and their supporters teamed up to block any WPC resolution on the Soviet-sponsored invasion of Czechoslovakia. The contention that the invasion of Czechoslovakia posed a threat to peace, claimed the WPC, could not "be taken seriously."[19] Even a longtime WPC stalwart like James Endicott found it impossible to stomach this attitude and began to criticize Soviet foreign policy. In turn, a delegation from the Canadian Communist Party visited him and demanded that he resign as chair of the Canadian Peace Congress, which he did. Although the WPC and many of its affiliates continued to function, their credibility sank to a new low.[20]

Meanwhile, nuclear weapons ceased to provide a subject of much concern to the mass media or to the general public. Between 1964 and 1970, magazines and newspapers in the United States sharply reduced their coverage of nuclear issues, while the number of books dealing with nuclear war declined substantially. "Writers rarely write about this subject anymore, and people hardly ever talk about it," observed columnist Stewart Alsop in the late 1960s. "There has been something like a conspiracy of silence about the threat of nuclear war." According to pollsters, between 1959 and 1965 the percentage of Americans viewing nuclear war as the nation's most urgent problem fell from 64 to 16 percent. Soon the issue vanished entirely from the surveys. Opinion polls produced similar findings in Canada. In 1963, a Gallup survey had found that 18 percent of Canadians identified nuclear weapons as "Canada's chief worry." But, after surveying the worries of Canadians in late 1965, the Gallup organization reported that "no one even mentions nuclear weapons." In the early 1970s, an American sociologist contended that the atom bomb was "no longer an editorial topic for local newspapers or a conversation piece at dinner tables." It had become "a dead issue."[21]

Other societies also showed a newfound complacency about nuclear weapons. In Denmark, general concern about the nuclear issue declined during the late 1960s, and the number of newspaper and magazine articles about it fell off substantially. In Britain, 55 percent of respondents told pollsters in November 1964 that they were not worried at all about the prospect of nuclear war. That same month, only 4 percent of French respondents chose nuclear weapons as the most important problem facing France.[22] Naturally, this indifference to the nuclear arms race undermined opposition to nuclear weapons. Asked, in

June 1967, what they thought about giving up their country's atom bomb and relying on the United States for defense, only 19 percent of Britons surveyed favored the idea.[23] Between March 1964 and April 1966, support for France's *force de frappe* rose from 39 to 46 percent of French respondents, while opposition declined from 49 to 42 percent. In Japan, to be sure, one poll in 1969 found that the public opposed its country's acquisition of nuclear weapons by 62 to 16 percent and another by 72 to 14 percent. But peace movement leaders were horrified by the rising number of respondents—reaching a majority by 1972—who declared that Japan would eventually possess nuclear arms, a fatalism they viewed as paving the way for this situation. Writing in the mid-1970s, Alva Myrdal expressed her astonishment that "people all over the world have become conditioned to live on unconcerned about the steadily increasing risk" that a nuclear war "might suddenly destroy . . . our civilization."[24]

Containing the Movement

Before considering the factors that reversed the movement's fortunes, it is worth examining those that contained its advance. One was the perception that the antinuclear crusade was a Communist-directed enterprise. In the United States, especially, conservatives worked at fostering this impression. Popular columnist Fulton Lewis Jr. blithely charged that SANE was "heavily backed by some of the country's most notorious fellow travellers." Hearst columnist Jack Lotto denounced Hollywood for SANE under the headline: "Stars Aid Pro-Reds in H-Protests." Surveying the antinuclear upsurge in the United States and Britain, *Time* magazine portrayed it as part of a Communist plot.[25] In Britain, Tory denunciations of CND were supplemented, on occasion, by the well-publicized attacks of Hugh Gaitskell, the Labour Party leader who waged an unremitting campaign against unilateralism. Although conceding that Britain's nuclear disarmament did appeal to "the high-minded," Gaitskell charged that "it is popular with others for purely escapist or beatnik reasons, and with others, again, because they are fellow-travellers, if not avowed Communists." In Australia, reported Marc Oliphant, attempts to initiate public debate on disarmament were "bedevilled by the prompt branding of any meeting or rally as Communist inspired or Communist dominated, and those who take part as Red, or at least Pink. This attitude is almost universal in the press and is fostered by the government."[26]

The attack on the movement as Communist, although quite unfair, clearly had an effect. In West Germany, one activist reported, fear of being labeled Communist "causes very many people to hold themselves back . . . and to make no use of their proper rights." Hans Thirring attributed the limited influence of the Federation of Austrian Scientists, in part, to "the suspicion that scientists might be misused as 'Trojan horses' for the infiltration of the Communist version of peace and disarmament." From New Zealand, the WILPF president reported that "peace movements are not very popular here, mainly owing to the fear of Communist infiltration, which is almost a phobia."[27] In the United States, community leaders in various parts of the country remained leery about supporting antinuclear ventures thanks to their anxiety about a Communist stigma. According to Homer Jack, public apprehension about becoming mixed up with Communist enterprises did undermine SANE's appeal to moderate opinion in the United States.[28]

And yet by the early 1960s loose and unfounded charges of Communism were losing much of their effectiveness in Western nations. In the spring of 1962, only 27 percent of Britons polled expressed agreement with Gaitskell's claim that most CND supporters had Communist sympathies.[29] That October, when Irish CND distributed leaflets in Limerick, one participant recalled, "there were of course . . . the usual accusations of being communists, but these were few." In the spring of 1964, as Swiss antinuclear activists prepared for their Easter march, a group calling itself the Geneva Committee for Civic Action plastered the city with posters portraying a dove chained to a hammer and sickle. At the march, though, Swiss police interacted pleasantly with the demonstrators, with some smiling and waving to them. Even in the United States, the investigation of Women Strike for Peace by the House Committee on Un-American Activities did more to discredit the committee than the disarmament group. Headlines proclaimed: "Peace Gals Make Red Hunters Look Silly."[30] Consequently, although fears of Communist subversion helped contain the movement, they did not play a significant role in fostering its decline during the late 1960s.

Another constraint on the movement was the widespread fear of other countries, particularly in the context of the Cold War. Even if they granted the sincerity of antinuclear groups, many persons believed that they were naive, that nuclear disarmament would lead to aggression by a foreign power.[31] In the United States, fear of the Soviet Union was particularly intense. As late as December 1960, a Gallup poll found that only 50 percent of American respondents believed it "possible . . . to reach a peaceful settlement of differences with Russia." To avoid Soviet conquest, most Americans stated, they would not hesitate to wage nuclear war. Surveyed in October 1961, 81 percent of Americans declared that they would rather fight a nuclear war than live under Communism. Only 6 percent took the opposite view. Impressed by a study which suggested that people favored benign or aggressive military policies based on their image of the Soviet Union, SANE's leaders decided to make changing "public stereotypes about the Russians" SANE's major program activity in 1964.[32]

If attitudes toward the Soviet Union were somewhat less ferocious elsewhere, they were nevertheless negative enough to dampen popular enthusiasm for disarmament. Polled in March 1958, 51 percent of West German respondents said that they viewed the Soviet Union as a "serious threat." By November 1964, their number had dropped to 39 percent, but they still represented a plurality of West Germans. Cold War attitudes were also widespread in Britain. Asked in late 1962 whom they would rather have Britain side with in world affairs, Britons chose the United States over the Soviet Union by 47 to 1. Suspicious of other nations, and particularly of their Cold War antagonists, a clear plurality of Britons—46 percent—told pollsters in early 1963 that they wanted their country to be "a leading world power." Although most people preferred to be neither Red nor Dead, an intense desire to avoid the former often lowered their resistance to the latter. As Arthur Pape of Canadian CND noted, there was "a certain rationale" behind people's decision not to join this antinuclear group; "they do not think we offer them a better way to keep the peace and freedom they desire."[33]

Exhaustion and Frustration

Other factors more directly undermined the movement. By the early 1960s, veterans of the antinuclear campaign were increasingly overcome by physical and emotional fatigue. "I know I can do more than I am doing," Cousins confided to Schweitzer in October 1962, "but I confess that it is increasingly difficult to mobilize myself constantly. It is the old story, I suppose, of the adrenalin running low after having been primed constantly." The following spring, commenting on his meeting about the test ban issue with representatives of U.S. peace groups, Homer Jack reported "an accumulation of lethargy and hopelessness."[34] Exhaustion also seemed to engulf the Danish and British movements. By the early 1960s, recalled Canon Collins, CND "had had four years of arduous and enthusiastic campaigning, but . . . Great Britain remained wedded to her bomb. It was hardly surprising that older campaigners should feel tired and the younger ones dispirited." For all its differences with CND, the Committee of 100 also found itself swept by what Michael Randle called "protest weariness." In Africa, Schweitzer remained hopeful that the nuclear arms race would be halted. Even so, as Cousins recalled, his letters reflected "some fatigue. He seemed to retreat into hospital matters," arguing that it was "a great privilege . . . to be able to continue working at his profession of medicine."[35]

In part, as a number of leading activists have noted, this ebbing vitality reflected the natural tendency of movements to lose momentum. People have only so much time and energy to devote to a single cause; if it is not secured within a reasonable period, they begin to reassess their priorities. In 1963, when Vanessa Redgrave publicly resigned from the Committee of 100, she remarked that she could no longer spend her time preparing for demonstration after demonstration.[36] But in the case of the antinuclear movement, there was a deeper level of exhaustion, resulting from a steady confrontation with one of the grimmest issues of the modern world—that of nuclear holocaust. As New Zealand CND's Elsie Locke explained, "to go on living constructively and positively, people cannot dwell constantly, year after year, on the possibility of doom and destruction." Naturally, large portions of the public, alarmed by the nuclear arms race, soon slipped into what psychologists have called denial and what Robert Jay Lifton, in this context, has called "psychic numbing." One young adult stated bluntly in 1965: "If we lived in fear of the bomb we couldn't function." Leaders of the antinuclear movement pushed themselves further, but there were limits. In 1964, Cousins experienced a severe physical breakdown, a form of rheumatoid arthritis that left him bedridden and in great pain. Although doctors told him that the odds against his recovery were five hundred to one, he developed a self-treatment plan that worked. Appropriately, its central component was laughter.[37]

A related—and equally debilitating—factor was the development of a widespread sense of futility. Analyzing the collapse of nuclear disarmament movements around the world, Peggy Duff wrote: "You could blame it on frustration. They won mass support for what looked like a simple, single issue and, in the absence of any real progress, except in general awareness of the nuclear danger and one partial test ban treaty, most of them declined or died." Moreover, in Canada, the movement also felt deeply discouraged by the 1963 election victory of a party committed to that country's nuclear armament and by the arrival at the end of the year of the nuclear warheads.[38] In Britain, activists had to grapple not only with the evident failure of their Labour Party and civil disobedience strategies, but with their powerlessness during the October 1962 showdown over the Cuban missiles. Adam Roberts of *Peace News* concluded glumly that "there is very little that peace movements can do to affect the course of such a crisis," which "had the effect of paralyzing and immobilizing people."[39] Even where there were no immediate setbacks, the ongoing nuclear arms race fostered cynicism and demoralization. In Holland, the seemingly intractable nature of the nuclear issue enervated the movement. In Japan, a bar girl typified popular frustration as she complained: "All the protests of the anti-nuclear weapons movements have no more effect than chanting sutras into a horse's ear."[40]

Nor did frustration necessarily lead to productive strategies. Impatient

British activists not only bolted CND for a try at mass civil disobedience, but grew surly and turned on their leaders, blaming them for the movement's failure to halt the arms race. Irate at the lack of progress, young Britons began disrupting organized events. "We started having trouble on the Easter March . . . in 1962," recalled Duff. "After that there was trouble every year with groups labelled as 'the anarchists,'" who "picked on the CND establishment as one of the targets for their wrath." In 1963, when CND planned a Hyde Park rally, a "March Must Decide Committee" urged a boycott of the Hyde Park event in favor of its own rally. Although only thirty people attended the latter, anarchists linked arms across Whitehall to prevent the CND march from moving forward. Subsequently, enragées sought to block the paths of CND's marches, drown out speakers, and dominate the proceedings, much to the disgust of CND loyalists. "As time went on," Canon Collins recalled, "more and more groups, anarchists, Trotskyists, and so on, seemingly as hostile to the executive of CND as to nuclear weapons, . . . introduced violence and disorder." Sometimes they baited or attacked the police. Frustration and violence also overtook the movement in Holland, where young Easter marchers shocked their elders by riotous behavior in 1967 and by a brawl with police in 1968.[41]

Cooptation

Plagued by feelings of exhaustion and futility, many nuclear disarmament activists, like broad sections of the general public, were ripe for cooptation. And there did exist reasons for consolation—often sufficient to convince weary activists that they could relax their guard against the world's slide toward nuclear catastrophe. The Cuban missile crisis, though shocking in itself, convinced many people that the great powers, despite their terrifying nuclear arsenals, would not proceed to nuclear war. Indeed, a period of U.S.-Soviet rapprochement followed, punctuated by arms control and other agreements that lowered Cold War tensions. Meanwhile, in Britain, the 1964 election victory of the Labour Party raised hopes for that nation's adoption of a more dovish foreign and defense policy. Later that decade, in West Germany, the advent to power of the Social Democrats defused central European enmities and drew many young activists into mainstream politics.[42] Not even the election to the U.S. presidency of a veteran Cold Warrior like Richard Nixon stopped the trend toward accommodation among nuclear-armed nations. Consequently, much of the world was swept by a mood of detente, in which a nuclear war seemed increasingly unlikely.[43]

The most important development along these lines was the atmospheric test ban treaty of 1963. Like most of the public, peace groups around the world welcomed it. At the same time, they made it clear that such a treaty was only a beginning. In Canada, members of Combined Universities CND viewed the treaty as "an important first step, a step which the insistent activities of the peace movement had helped prepare the way for," but "only a small first step" toward nuclear disarmament. In Britain, CND's *Sanity* proclaimed a "Test Ban Victory" and went on to argue that it was "well worth celebrating." Even so, "we know very well that this is only a first step. . . . We want . . . *all* forms of nuclear testing . . . covered by the treaty. Then we want Britain to give a lead that will take the world . . . to celebrating actual disarmament."[44] Applauding the treaty for breaking through the Cold War deadlock and limiting nuclear proliferation, Bertrand Russell also warned that "the nuclear peril will not end while nuclear weapons and means of their delivery exist." In Ireland, CND's newspaper praised the treaty as reflecting "the determination of ordinary people everywhere" and urged the movement to press on "to the final abandonment and destruction of all nuclear arms and the development of the rule of law between nations."[45]

The same outlook prevailed in the United States. According to the Federation of American Scientists, the treaty represented "a first and significant step to slow the pace of the arms race and reduce the danger of nuclear war." Even so, "it is clear that the treaty is only a first step on the long road to more substantial arms control and disarmament." SANE announced that it rejoiced "at the signing and ratification" of the treaty, which "could open the door to more substantial agreements," including measures to enforce a comprehensive test ban, lessen the danger of surprise attack, develop nuclear-free zones, block the proliferation of nuclear weapons, and move toward minimal deterrence. Thus, "few if any . . . feel that SANE's work is finished."[46] Even Linus Pauling, who thought that historians might well conclude that "the formulation and signing of this treaty was the most important action taken by national governments during the whole history of the world," cautioned that it needed "to be followed by other international agreements, leading ultimately to general and complete disarmament." This carefully balanced approach reflected the movement leadership's recognition that over-optimism would undermine the antinuclear campaign. Writing to SANE's new chair, Benjamin Spock, about the treaty, Cousins warned: "One of the problems involved in winning a limited action is that it tends to obscure a war. We have reason now to celebrate. . . . But in kicking up our heels we want to be careful that the resultant dust doesn't obscure the main and remaining dangers."[47]

Yet despite these precautions much of the public and part of the movement soon believed—as Homer Jack later complained—"that peace broke out with the test ban!" In response to the signing of the treaty, support for nuclear disarmament agitation melted away rapidly in Sweden, Denmark, Austria, Holland, Belgium, Britain, Canada, New Zealand, Australia, the Soviet Union, the United States, and numerous other nations.[48] Addressing a SANE National Board meeting on the shaky state of the organization's finances, Sandy Gottlieb quipped that it was the first time he had attended a wake over a victory. In part, the dwindling support for the movement reflected the decline of the immediate danger of radioactive contamination through nuclear fallout. As Sakharov recalled: "When nuclear tests were driven underground in 1963, the biological effects of nuclear radiation ceased to alarm people. I was no exception."[49] Furthermore, the treaty seemed to herald a sharp turn toward peace and disarmament. Toronto CND reported that "after the signing of the test ban treaty, many people began to feel that it was no longer necessary to campaign for nuclear disarmament, but that the great powers would soon settle their differences and agree to disarm." With the arrival of the test ban, recalled Dr. Bernard Lown, a founder of Physicians for Social Responsibility, "it was clear to me that the nuclear war issue would fade into history, because humanity was finally understanding the dangers." Although disarmament groups continued to hammer away at the nuclear arms race, the mass media largely abandoned the issue as no longer newsworthy.[50]

Other International Crises

The antinuclear movement also lost ground because it could not cut itself off from other foreign and defense policy issues. "Ban the British Bomb was adequate in 1958," noted an internal British CND paper, "but in 1964 it has developed into an argument about the future of the V Bomber Force, of the Nassau Agreement, of the Polaris submarines and bases, and about MLF." CND would "have to say no to this and yes to that, often in great detail, in the context of the radical changes we demand in the ways in which nation-states live together." That same year, antinuclear physicist Hideki Yukawa complained about the Japanese peace movement's "exclusively anti-bomb approach," leading to "silence about small wars, conventional arms, and violence in general." In fact, however, as such comments indicate, during these years the movement was finding it impossible to ignore related issues. Repression in Greece, the admission of China to the United Nations, and Third World economic development all became important sources of concern to peace activists and their organizations.[51] Dutch, Swedish, and American peace groups turned increasingly to addressing the problems of Third World nations,[52] as did the Pugwash movement, which devoted three of the six conferences it held between 1965 and 1970 to economic development issues. By 1970, even Eugene Rabinowitch—long a mainstay of the antinuclear movement—was arguing that "confrontation between rapidly advancing 'developed' world and stagnant 'undeveloped' world . . . is as much a threat for the peaceful future of mankind as is the confrontation of nuclear superpowers."[53]

Unlike the WPC and its affiliates, the nonaligned movement assailed the August 1968 Warsaw Pact invasion of Czechoslovakia. Outraged by the military crushing of the "Prague spring," peace groups led protest demonstrations around the world. Meeting two days after the invasion began for the ICDP's biannual conference, delegates immediately condemned it and pressed ahead with further protest activities. On behalf of the War Resisters' International, Hugh Brock, April Carter, and Michael Randle organized simultaneous leafleting and protests in Warsaw, Sofia, Budapest, and Moscow.[54] Opposition to the invasion was widespread in the Soviet Union, particularly among the intelligentsia. Long discussions about the event occurred in private homes, and as Sakharov later revealed, "many persons" refused "to attend the innumerable official meetings held in support of the intervention." On August 25, Pavel Litvinov and Larisa Bogoraz led a small group of dissidents to Red Square for a public protest. Bearing signs reading "Hands Off Czechoslovakia," they sat by Lobnoe Mesto, a place of execution in Czarist Russia, for a brief time before the arrival of KGB agents, who beat them, tore up their signs, and arrested them. Only minutes later, cars carrying Alexander Dubček and other Czech leaders brought by force to Moscow, sped across Red Square.[55]

By far the greatest international preoccupation, however, was the Vietnam War. Commenting on the movement's decline, Homer Jack recalled that, with the war's escalation in 1965, "the attention of American and European activists soon was transferred from next steps in disarmament to massive efforts to end the war in Southeast Asia." Peggy Duff, too, concluded that, around the world, "the war in Vietnam superseded the Bomb in public interest and concern." For many participants in the antinuclear campaign, as for the general public, the war in Southeast Asia "seemed a more immediate danger" than did nuclear war. It also drew on the same feelings of moral revulsion, triggered this time by the spectacle of a great power using the latest technology to destroy a small peasant nation. Thomas Merton, a Trappist monk and influential theologian, while utterly rejecting nuclear war, had clung to the Catholic Church's traditional "just war" theory. Nevertheless, shocked by the brutality of the Vietnam conflict, he eventually concluded that it had become impossible to distinguish morally between nuclear holocaust and this kind of "conventional" war. "The war in Vietnam is a bell tolling for the whole world," he wrote, warning that "violent death may spread over the entire earth."[56] Millions of people reached a similar conclusion.

In Britain, as Randle noted, activism shifted "away from the Bomb and towards the issue of the Vietnam War." As early as August 5, 1964, CND issued "an urgent call" to political, union, church, youth, and other organizations to "take immediate action in demanding an end to the war in Vietnam." With the Johnson administration's escalation of the war in 1965, CND and the Committee of 100 organized and supported a variety of protest activities. In addition, CND staged large demonstrations against the war in 1966 and 1967.[57] Nevertheless, the momentum in the antiwar struggle shifted for a time to the Vietnam Solidarity Campaign, an organization that identified with Vietnam's Communist revolutionaries and dismissed CND, now merely one of many groups opposing the war, as "passé and irrelevant." CND gravitated toward the more moderate British Campaign for Peace in Vietnam—which favored British dissociation from U.S. policy and the right of the Vietnamese to settle their own affairs—and provided the group with officers and office space. Like CND, pacifists took an early stand against the war, pressed the prime minister to dissociate himself from U.S. policy, and distributed antiwar leaflets to U.S. troops. In this fashion, as a number of CND leaders remarked, the Vietnam War diverted the attention of the antinuclear movement and, ultimately, weakened it.[58]

Much the same pattern developed in Japan. Appalled by the Vietnam War, especially the U.S. use of "napalm bombs and other weapons of mass destruction," Gensuikin declared in the spring of 1965 that it felt compelled to address the issue. The war, it argued, was "interlaced significantly with other problems of the world," including the nuclear arms race; indeed, the Vietnam conflict threatened "to explode into a worldwide nuclear war." Accordingly, that year Gensuikin made the war the centerpiece of its World Conference Against Atomic and Hydrogen Bombs. It also joined with unions, women's organizations, the Zengakuren, the Socialist and Communist parties, and other citizens' groups to form the Japan Peace for Vietnam Committee, better known as Beheiran. Taking a nonaligned stand, Beheiran grew rapidly, organizing enormous antiwar demonstrations. In 1970, it rallied almost 800,000 people against the war and in defense of Japan's "peace constitution." Although this represented an unprecedented outpouring of the Japanese peace constituency, Beheiran's exclusive focus on the Vietnam War had the effect of marginalizing the nuclear issue and those organizations still dealing with it.[59]

In Canada, the Vietnam War quickly supplanted nuclear war as the movement's top concern. Even as it tottered toward collapse in 1965, Canadian CND petitioned and protested against the conflict. It also produced a new leaflet with the nuclear arms issue downgraded to point number two; point one was "Vietnam." Later that year, the final issue of CND's newsletter reported that its plans for creating "a broader organization" had been stalled, for "the Vietnam crisis monopolizes all efforts at the moment."[60] Operating independently, Combined Universities CND sponsored a December 1964 demonstration calling for withdrawal of all foreign troops from Vietnam and for a Canadian initiative to bring the war to an end. Thereafter, its successor, the Student Union for Peace Action, threw itself into teach-ins and other antiwar ventures.[61] Meanwhile, the Voice of Women made ending the Vietnam War its major priority. It exposed the U.S. use of nerve gas, defoliants, pellet bombs, and napalm in the war, aided civilians in Vietnam and American draft resisters in Canada, and implored the Canadian government to adopt "an independent, peacemaker role." It also sponsored an exchange of visits with Vietnamese women, taking the latter on an antiwar speaking tour of Canada.[62]

Naturally, the Vietnam War had particular resonance in the United States. Even before Johnson began dispatching a million U.S. combat troops to that country, American peace groups sharply criticized U.S. policy. In September 1963, rejecting U.S. support for the Diem dictatorship, SANE argued that unless a more democratic, less repressive regime could be established, the U.S. government should abandon its military and economic role in that nation. Later that fall, SPU and SDS organized antiwar picketing, charging that the U.S. government was sacrificing "the needs of the Vietnamese people to America's Cold War interests." The following year, in New York City, the War Resisters League, the FOR, and the Socialist Party sponsored the first substantial antiwar demonstration.[63] With the escalation of the war in 1965, these and other groups began the whirlwind of protests against the Vietnam War that, ultimately, convulsed the nation. Typical of WSP's many fervent antiwar activities was a Mothers' March on Capitol Hill to Stop the Killing. Even the Federation of American Scientists came out strongly against the war, contending that it was "damaging to the interests of our nation, of the people of Vietnam, and of mankind."[64] Naturally, the obsession of these groups with the war undermined their antinuclear programs, which in most cases virtually disappeared. Furthermore, groups like WSP and SANE underwent a decline, losing ground to the broad coalitions that, increasingly, directed antiwar protests or to newer, more youthful, and sometimes more militant organizations.[65]

In other nations that sent troops to Vietnam, the war also became a source of enormous controversy, with the same debilitating effects on antinuclear activism. In Australia, the Victorian CND dissolved into the Vietnam Day Committee and the Sydney CND became the Vietnam Action Committee. Australia's revulsion against the war led to startlingly vigorous and widespread peace protests in that country, including a turnout of 120,000 people for an antiwar demonstration in May 1970. It also broke the momentum of the antinuclear struggle, which faded from sight.[66] In New Zealand, CND issued an antiwar statement in August 1964. At the same time, however, it warned members that "we are a Campaign for NUCLEAR Disarmament, and must not lose punch by spreading ourselves too wide." But, in fact, CND proved unable to resist the challenge of the war's escalation. At CND's 1965 Easter march, noted the group's *Bulletin*, "Vietnam was inevitably the issue in everyone's mind." CND held marches, vigils, and other protests against the war and formally affiliated with the Joint Council on Vietnam, which coordinated strategy for New Zealand's emerging antiwar movement. That August, CND reported that "the continuing crisis in Vietnam has overshadowed . . . the [antinuclear] work of the Campaign." Within a short time, the Vietnam crisis swallowed it almost completely.[67]

Even in nations not directly involved in the conflict, the trend was much the same. Some of Denmark's leading nuclear disarmament activists played key roles in protests against the Vietnam War. In Finland, the Committee of 100 organized its country's first antiwar teach-ins. In Italy, CND staged a demonstration against the war as part of the October 1965 "International Days of Protest" and also waged an antiwar petition campaign.[68] Peace and disarmament groups in Austria, Ireland, and the Netherlands moved quickly to condemn the Vietnam War, as did the West German Campaign for Disarmament, which as early as its 1965 Easter march called Vietnam "the most dangerous focus of crisis in the world."[69] In Sweden, Bertil Svahnström, chair of the Campaign Against Nuclear Weapons, announced the formation in August 1965 of a Committee for Peace in Vietnam, on which he served as international secretary. Initiated by the Swedish Peace and Arbitration Society, the new group brought together most Swedish peace organizations, as well as political parties and other citizens groups, in a massive antiwar campaign.[70] In France, all the major elements of the antinuclear movement threw their energies into the struggle against the war in Vietnam. The French Movement Against Atomic Armament sponsored antiwar marches and helped form the Indochina Solidarity Front. To reflect its broadened concerns, in 1968 it renamed itself the Movement for Disarmament, Peace, and Liberty. Meanwhile, abandoned by activists, antinuclear activities declined precipitously.[71]

The nonaligned movement's international organizations followed a roughly similar trajectory. Increasingly obsessed with the Vietnam crisis, the WILPF sponsored antiwar advertisements signed by women from around the world, sent a fact-finding commission to North and South Vietnam, and demanded free elections and the withdrawal of U.S. troops.[72] Turmoil over the war spilled over into Pugwash conferences during 1965 and 1966. Pressed for action by Russell and other stalwarts, Rotblat drew on contacts with the French, Ho Chi Minh, and others to arrange a secret meeting in Paris in an unsuccessful attempt by Pugwashers to bring the conflict to an end.[73] Meanwhile, the ICDP swung into action, coordinating worldwide protests against the war. It mobilized well-known intellectuals and other prominent figures, sent a religious delegation to Hanoi, and played a key role in organizing the 1967 Stockholm conference on Vietnam. Although the ICDP, like the other nonaligned internationals, survived as an organization, it left the nuclear issue behind as it single-mindedly devoted itself to halting the Vietnam conflict.[74]

From the standpoint of the Communist-led peace movement, opposing the Vietnam War—what the China Peace Committee termed "U.S. imperialist policies of war and aggression"—was never in question. Around the world, WPC affiliates excoriated U.S. war policy and lauded that of the Vietnamese Communists.[75] "Like all peace-loving forces," wrote Nikolai Tikhonov, chair of the Soviet Peace Committee, his organization actively supported "the Week of Solidarity with the Struggle of the Vietnamese People for Freedom and Independence and Against American Aggressors." In the context of the Indochina War, resolved Gensuikyo's 1964 World Conference Against Atomic and Hydrogen Bombs, "the most urgent task of the movement and a sacred duty imposed on all of us is to deal a decisive blow on American imperialism." Writing to Alexander Korneichuk of the Soviet Peace Committee in 1966, Bernal argued that the conflict in Vietnam "has come to include all questions of peace and war in the world, and it should be rightly our central and immediate object to bring it to an end in conditions satisfactory to the heroic Vietnamese people." But what would happen, then, to "the larger and longer aims of the movement"? The focus on "the aggressive nature of American imperialism," Bernal noted, "inevitably makes difficult and perhaps temporarily impossible all attempts at arms limitation and disarmament." Consequently, although the U.S. government's Vietnam policy—by substantiating charges of U.S. imperialism—gave a new lease on life to the Communist-led peace movement, antinuclear activities were jettisoned.[76]

Misunderstanding the Problem

The ruthless military interventionism of the great powers, coupled with their intractable commitment to nuclear weapons, led many antinuclear activists to conclude that they faced a deeply rooted, systemic problem. And this, in turn, suggested that championing nuclear disarmament was too shallow, that something more fundamental was necessary before the Bomb could be banned. Typically, Peggy Duff concluded that "the simple moral issue to which the campaigns clung as the source of all evil was a symptom rather than a cause. The invention and development of nuclear weapons coincided with and was fed by a similar escalation in the cold war." In Duff's view, an effective movement had to come to grips with the fact that "the bombs were the children of the blocs, that the blocs were the offspring of the cold war, and that the cold war was sustained and nourished by political systems" in East and West.[77] But what were the systems?

In the Soviet Union, nonaligned peace activists eventually concluded that the system was the one that regularly harassed them: dictatorship. "Arms control discussions," Sakharov concluded,

> can produce decisive results only when they are joined to the resolution of broader and more complicated problems of military-political and ideological confrontation, including questions of human rights. . . . As long as a country has no civil liberty, no freedom of information, and no independent press, then there exists no effective body of public opinion to control the conduct of the government and its functionaries. Such a situation is not just a misfortune for citizens unprotected against tyranny and lawlessness; it is a menace to international security.

Not surprisingly, then, Sakharov and other Soviet peace proponents increasingly championed the defense of human rights, for as he put it, "in the final analysis it is impossible to achieve international security and trust without first overcoming the closed nature of Soviet society."[78] According to another prominent Soviet dissident, Pavel Litvinov, all Soviet human rights activists regarded nuclear weapons with dismay. But they emphasized human rights because they came to believe that a victory in this realm was essential if war and nuclear weapons were to be curbed.[79]

In Western democracies, a portion of the antinuclear constituency also developed a systemic analysis and, like Soviet activists, condemned a system close at hand—in this case, capitalism. Confronted by a savage war on a poor peasant nation, accompanied by long-term racism and endemic poverty, many of America's student activists responded by turning sharply leftward. Increasingly, SDS and other youthful peace groups argued that these ills reflected a vicious American imperialism, driven by the greed of U.S. corporations. For the first time, many activists began to identify with Third World revolutionaries.[80] The same process of radicalization occurred in Canada, where the Student Union for Peace Action emerged along roughly the same lines as SDS. One Canadian New Leftist recalled, with satisfaction: "The war in Vietnam . . . shocked the peace movement out of its woolly aspirations for 'international peace' and forced it to come to terms with the operations of American corporate capitalism."[81] Indeed, in Canada, Britain, West Germany, Switzerland, Sweden, New Zealand, and other Western nations, a youthful New Left burst onto the scene in the late 1960s with a militantly anticapitalist, antimperialist, and occasionally violent message.[82] Moreover, although this swing to the Left developed largely among the restless young, it affected others as well. In the context of the Vietnam War, even Bertrand Russell dropped his calls for U.S.-Soviet detente and adopted a sharply anticapitalist analysis, championing Third World revolution and excoriating the worldwide machinations of "US imperialism."[83]

This "revolutionary" emphasis had a debilitating effect on the movement. Having agreed to participate in Russell's War Crimes Tribunal of 1967, the Italian pacifist Danilo Dolci became disgruntled by its one-sided, anti-American tone and, eventually, withdrew from it. In Britain, the growing sectarianism of the British New Left and of the campaign against the Vietnam War—which disintegrated repeatedly into violent confrontations with the police—repelled numerous peace activists, including the Marxist E. P. Thompson. American pacifists found themselves whipsawed between partisans of revolutionary solidarity and defenders of their traditional nonviolence.[84] In West Germany, the Easter marches became infused with such a "revolutionary" flavor that more moderate elements withdrew from them in disgust, leading to their collapse. Much the same thing happened in Austria, where radicals seized control of the 1968 Easter march and, thereby, ensured that it would be the nation's last. At the same time, the excitement and romantic appeal of revolution pulled youthful idealists away from the difficult, more humdrum, tasks of the antinuclear movement. As a historian of the British nuclear disarmament campaign has observed, with talk of revolution in the air, "CND and the whole edifice of established Labour Movement politics seemed somewhat dull, unadventurous and passé." In France, as Claude Bourdet has noted, MCAA branches became "greenhouses" of the near revolution of May 1968. After the student rebellion collapsed, many of them never started up again.[85]

Other kinds of radical thinking also upstaged or confused the struggle against the Bomb. In Britain, Committee of 100 activists turned toward empowering the poor through the development of squatters' movements. In France, MCAA branches popularized new ideas of social transformation: ecology, autogestion, and feminism.[86] Moreover, as the emerging women's movement turned into a worldwide liberation struggle, it began to redefine the issue of violence, replacing the antinuclear movement's emphasis on global militarism with a focus on domestic and sexual violence. Activists in the women's movement also condemned the maternalist emphasis of women's antinuclear groups and showed little interest in joining them. Two former leaders of Canada's Voice of Women recalled plaintively: "With . . . the emphasis on the liberation of women in the late sixties, the young intellectuals were effectively occupied in discovering themselves and the facts of their oppression. To raise one's consciousness as a woman became to them more urgent than peace . . . or disarmament." Even if this judgment is too harsh, the women's liberation movement certainly raised new and difficult issues for the antinuclear campaign to confront, most notably by insisting that another deeply rooted system—patriarchy—was responsible for the arms race.[87]

Consequently, in the West, as in the East, many activists moved beyond emphasizing the dangers of the Bomb to developing systemic analyses. Proceeding down these lines, they became the major reformers and social critics of their time. But their systemic critiques, although laying the groundwork for an attack on an array of other important problems, failed to contribute much to the campaign for nuclear disarmament. Quite the contrary, when it came to the nuclear menace, their systemic analyses often proved either futile or debilitating. Nor, in retrospect, should this surprise us. In their desperate efforts to cope with the multiple crises of the 1960s, many activists had either lost sight of or failed to comprehend the driving force of the nuclear arms race—the pathology of the international system. And, inevitably, this misreading of the problem weakened their attempts to generate a solution.

Reflections on Decline

Curiously, then, the struggle against the Bomb dwindled just as its most important victories were being won. Under enormous pressure from an aroused citizenry, nuclear war had been averted and important arms control measures had been put into place. But, despite these advances—in part, because of them—the movement could not be sustained. In early 1968, when Shinzo Hamai died suddenly, a tape recording of his last Peace Declaration as Hiroshima's mayor, played at his funeral, repeated the familiar refrain: "War in the nuclear age is no longer a means of self-defense. It is nothing less than an act of suicide."[88] By this time, however, the words had a distant quality—the echo of a fast-receding and only dimly understood past. Caught up by more immediately pressing issues, activists and citizens alike turned their attention elsewhere. Indeed, by the end of the decade, the nuclear arms race and the movement that had opposed it so vigorously had both dropped largely out of sight.

The Ambiguous Victory

No social advance rolls in on the wheels of
inevitability. It comes through the tireless
efforts . . . of dedicated individuals.

Martin Luther King Jr.

Beginning in 1954 and cresting in the late 1950s and early 1960s, a mass
movement against nuclear weapons swept across broad portions of the globe.
In some nations, this was the largest protest campaign to appear for decades; in
others, for centuries. Although the movement was strongest in North America,
Western Europe, Japan, and Australasia—where peace and disarmament groups
had previously established themselves—it mustered support in most nations of
the world. Indeed, the nuclear disarmament movement became genuinely international, mobilizing as many as half a million people simultaneously for
street demonstrations and other popular manifestations against the Bomb in
dozens of nations. Sometimes, indeed, it became transnational, as nuclear protesters surged forth from country to country, usually to the dismay of their governments. Western activists even broke through the "iron curtain" and brought
the antinuclear campaign to Communist nations. Given the severe limitations
on independent political activity in Communist lands, mass movements comparable to CND and SANE could not develop there. Even so, the antinuclear
campaign won converts in high places, particularly among Soviet scientists and
other intellectuals, who pressed the Soviet government to halt key aspects of
the nuclear arms race.

Although the movement and, particularly, its critique of the Bomb, had a
broad popular appeal, some groups clearly found it more attractive than did
others. In non-Communist nations, conservative and right-wing constituencies
often remained wary, apparently because their militant opposition to Communism overpowered their distaste for the Bomb. Liberal and left-wing constituencies, by contrast, found the antinuclear campaign considerably more at-

tractive. Less convinced of the total villainy of the "enemy" and more devoted to humanitarian causes, they constituted the political backbone of the antinuclear campaign. Given these kinds of political preferences, disarmament activists naturally had their greatest impact on Labor, Socialist, and Social Democratic parties, as well as on the Democratic Party in the United States. Only on occasion, and then usually driven by expediency, did more conservative parties show any sympathy for the antinuclear cause.

The movement also galvanized specific social groups. More than any other social action campaign to come along for decades, the struggle for nuclear disarmament tapped the impatience of the young, especially college students with avant garde politics. Its vision of a world saved from nuclear holocaust touched their moral idealism, while its activities—marches, demonstrations, and sit-ins—seemed a welcome relief from the humdrum politics of the early Cold War era. Furthermore, the movement had a strong appeal to intellectuals and other members of the educated middle class. Scientists, given their familiarity with the new weaponry and their sense of responsibility for it, played a central part in the antinuclear campaign. But other intellectuals were also prominent. In an age when working class–based politics was on the wane, absorbed into an apparent consensus by the mass media and the promise of middle-class prosperity, intellectuals were themselves becoming an agency of social change. Economically comfortable but politically restless, they provided the new movement with a respectable, articulate component.

In addition, the movement drew very substantial support from women, particularly those with college educations. Deeply concerned about the future of their children and often excluded from mainstream politics, they found in the struggle against the Bomb an appropriate vehicle for social and political activism. On the leadership level, too, women like Pat Arrowsmith, April Carter, Peggy Duff, Sheila Jones, Elsie Locke, Kay Macpherson, Antoinette Pirie, Inga Thorsson, Helen Tucker, Dagmar Wilson, and Mary Woodward played very significant roles in the antinuclear campaign. But, for the most part, they were eclipsed as movement leaders by Claude Bourdet, Canon Collins, Norman Cousins, Martin Niemöller, Linus Pauling, Bertrand Russell, Albert Schweitzer, Norman Thomas, and other men. Most of these men, to be sure, were famous before becoming spokespersons for nuclear disarmament.[1] On the other hand, the fact that such talented women, in the years prior to their movement work, did not attain comparable eminence says a great deal about the discrimination against women in the political and intellectual life of their time. Not surprisingly, then, the movement not only attracted the services of very energetic, capable women, but often became a launching pad for their entry into politics and the professions.

The key to the movement's mass appeal lay in its emphasis on the Bomb as a threat to human survival. Although traditional scholarship has argued that most people avoided confronting the full horror of nuclear devastation by focusing on nuclear testing,[2] in fact both the movement and the public were deeply concerned about the prospect of wholesale nuclear annihilation. Ending nuclear testing was merely a starting point in a larger crusade to save humanity from destruction—useful along these lines because such tests were dangers in themselves and because halting them would stop the nuclear arms race. This was why movements and policymakers alike referred to the atmospheric test ban treaty as "a first step." Nor, as we have seen, was it the last step in the continuing efforts of antinuclear groups, the public, and some government officials to control nuclear weapons.

On the other hand, although the movement wanted nothing less than to ban the Bomb, it adopted a rather pragmatic approach, at least compared to pacifist organizations, with their unyielding opposition to weapons and war. SANE and WSP, for example, championed multilateral treaties for arms control and disarmament—exactly the position adopted by the great powers, at least on paper. Even CND-style groups, though unilateralist, advocated nuclear disarmament by the lesser powers—a program that, if adopted, would have left the U.S. and Soviet governments with their nuclear arsenals intact and other nations with their full potential for waging conventional war. These relatively moderate positions enabled antinuclear groups to appeal to a broad, nonpacifist constituency, horrified by the Bomb but unwilling to promote a thoroughgoing rejection of military force. At the same time, the movement could (and did) draw on substantial numbers of pacifists and other uncompromising critics of war.

Nuclear disarmament groups also achieved a broad appeal by stressing the dangers of nuclear weapons rather than the pathology of the international system. This focus is particularly striking when set against the previous round of protest against the Bomb, which had emphasized the necessity of building "One World."[3] Furthermore, many of the movement's most prominent leaders—including Cousins, Bourdet, Einstein, Pauling, Rotblat, Sakharov, and Szilard—had no use for the nation-state system. "Peace will not be secure until there is an effective world government," Russell wrote to a supporter in 1962, "but I should not like to see world government added to our program," for "some of our supporters might consider [it] irrelevant." Addressing a Pugwash conference in late 1960, Rotblat observed: "Everyone agrees that some sort of world government is the only basis for a stable world, but it is also abundantly clear that this will not materialize for a very long time. . . . It should, however, be possible to start with something less ambitious."[4] Banning the Bomb, of course, seemed less ambitious and, accordingly, politically more feasible.

And, in fact, having found an effective vantage point, the movement made substantial headway within the intermediate institutions of civil society. In a relatively short time, it brought the nuclear issue to the fore within unions, professional groups, religious bodies, political parties, and other mass organizations. Moreover, the movement's unusual size, unorthodox tactics, and train of celebrities made it a leading news item in the mass communications media, heightening popular awareness of the nuclear arms race. Brought face to face with the nuclear danger, much of the public came to regard the Bomb with suspicion and fear. As Peggy Duff recalled, the movement created "throughout the world an awareness that nuclear war meant annihilation."[5] Undoubtedly, portions of the public would have reached this conclusion without the catalyst of a movement. Indeed, in certain ways, the movement mirrored public opinion. Even so, without the spur of organized agitation, opposition to the Bomb might well have remained a silent undercurrent, overridden by the conventional wisdom that the greater a nation's military strength, the greater its security. Certainly, government officials took the movement seriously enough. Some praised and courted it, while others turned angrily on antinuclear agitators, whom they blamed, with considerable justification, for shattering public complacency and instigating serious challenges to their nuclear policies.

Furthermore, these challenges had considerable effect. Aroused world public opinion contributed substantially to the nuclear testing moratorium of 1958, to the reluctance of the great powers to resume nuclear testing thereafter, to the atmospheric test ban treaty of 1963, to the nuclear nonproliferation treaty of 1968, to the first strategic nuclear arms controls, and to other nuclear arms control measures. It also helped block the deployment of nuclear weapons in some nations and the development of nuclear weapons in others. Finally, it helped convince the leaders of the nuclear powers that the waging of nuclear war had become politically impossible. Other factors, of course, also fed into government decisions on nuclear policy. But to leave out of the decision-making process the factor of world public opinion—and behind it the widespread agitation of the nuclear disarmament movement—is to miss a vital part of the story.[6]

Another indication that the movement influenced public policy can be seen in the functional division among government officials over nuclear issues. Individual beliefs, of course, played a role in shaping the decisions of policymakers. Even so, the pattern of choice is revealing. In the United States, for example, the enthusiasts for nuclear arms control were administrators with constituencies mobilized by the movement: presidents (the only elected national security officials and, thus, the administrators most responsive to domestic opinion), secretaries of state and U.N. ambassadors (sensitive to the upsurge of foreign opinion), and White House science advisers (the most attuned to the scientists' movement). Conversely, opponents of nuclear arms controls came from the Defense Department, the Joint Chiefs of Staff, and the Atomic Energy Commission (those with a military or weapons laboratory constituency). This lineup changed slightly in 1961, when a veteran of the scientists' movement became chair of the AEC, but not enough to alter its overall contours.

Not surprisingly, some activists and policymakers have emphasized the influence of disarmament campaigns and of the pressure they brought to bear on nuclear policy. The credit for the atmospheric test ban treaty, contended Irish CND's newspaper, belonged to "the marchers, the letter-writers, the petitioners, in dozens of countries and on every continent." According to Sheila Jones, CND regarded the test ban treaty as "one of its important victories." Looking back on the atmospheric test ban, AEC Chair Glenn Seaborg reached a similar conclusion. Thanks to "popular concern about nuclear testing," he maintained, "persistent pressure was brought to bear on the nuclear powers by influential leaders and movements throughout the world." Although usually inclined to emphasize the internal dynamics of policymaking, McGeorge Bundy wrote in 1988 that he agreed with Seaborg that "what produced the treaty was steadily growing worldwide concern over the radioactive fallout from testing." The atmospheric test ban, he maintained, "was achieved primarily by world opinion."[7]

Some government participants were even more specific in apportioning responsibility. Recalling his years as White House science adviser, Jerome Wiesner gave the major credit for moving Kennedy toward the 1963 treaty to the WSP, SANE, and Linus Pauling. Sir Solly Zuckerman, the top science adviser to the British Defense Ministry, emphasized the contributions of the Pugwash movement. At a meeting in September 1990, he declared that "Pugwash played a significant part in bringing to public awareness, and in particular, to educating our political and military masters, that nuclear bombs were not just more powerful agents of destruction than conventional weapons. Pugwash told them . . . that nuclear weapons had vastly more destructive power than anything that had been known before, and that their use would entail widespread lethal and enduring radiation hazards." He added: "I was serving as an official in the days when the Partial Test Ban Treaty was concluded," and "I can say here and now, that the pressure brought to bear by Pugwash at that time on us officials . . . played a real part in pushing us along" toward its successful conclusion.[8]

Curiously, however, most activists and policymakers—as well as virtually all historians—have failed to recognize the efficacy of the movement. Stuart Hall, a prominent New Leftist and leader of the British CND during its early years, told an interviewer in 1978 that the influence of CND was "ENORMOUS. . . . Politically it was *very* influential." But, paradoxically, the Bomb was "the *one* thing we couldn't do anything about!" April Carter, too, has argued that Britain's "strong grass-roots movement ultimately had very little effect in terms of government policy." Despite his intense disagreement with disarmament activists on other matters, Sir Alec Douglas-Home, Britain's former foreign secretary and prime minister, advanced a similar interpretation. Asked if he repudiated the notion that CND was "a major influence" on the atmospheric test ban treaty, he responded: "Absolutely, yes." He explained: "The reason we were able to get on to the nuclear test ban treaty in the atmosphere was that all of us, including the Russians, were afraid of the fall-out and the effect on unborn babies, and all that kind of thing. And they didn't need the CND to emphasize that."[9]

How should we account for this dismissal of the movement's efficacy? For policymakers, any concession to their critics is an embarrassment. Irate at those who have forced them into a corner, they do not want to hand them a "victory." Furthermore, their "weakness," if known, will embolden peace protesters and the "enemy" (who, they assume, is only impressed by "strength"). Consequently, they tend to hide their deference to public pressure and to portray any policy shifts as consistent with their own beliefs. The effectiveness of this cover-up is enhanced by the fact that policymakers are rarely influenced directly by peace or disarmament groups, but by the intermediate institutions, including public opinion, they have aroused. Peace protesters, in turn, are loathe to grant much to policymakers. They want to avoid being deceived by official dissimulation. Furthermore, they have a tendency to underrate the significance of the policy shift. Accustomed to serving as sharp critics of government policy, they find it difficult to reverse gears and applaud government behavior. Moreover, accepting a policy change at face value might encourage complacency and, thus, undermine "the cause," which is driven by dissatisfaction. Consequently, both policymakers and protesters cover up indications that they have developed a relationship.

However chilly this relationship might have been in the 1950s, by the early 1960s—as policymakers inched toward nuclear arms controls—it was growing warmer. How else can one explain Khrushchev's willingness to admit nuclear disarmament demonstrators to the Soviet Union, his courtship of figures like Russell and organizations like SANE, or his lengthy meetings with Szilard and Cousins? How else can one explain the Western governments' escalating enthusiasm for the Pugwash conferences, or the Kennedy and Johnson administrations' rhetoric about a sane nuclear policy? Kennedy not only employed Cousins to serve as his test ban intermediary with Khrushchev, but followed his advice by delivering the crucial American University address. Subsequently, when Kennedy sought to mobilize public opinion behind ratification of the test ban, he had Cousins head up the operation and even publicized the plaudits of Albert Schweitzer—a far cry from the Eisenhower administration's earlier rejection of the missionary as a follower of "the Communist line." Similarly, the British government, which had once regarded Rotblat with suspicion, honored him in 1964 with a CBE—Commander of the British Empire—for his work on the Pugwash conferences.[10]

As should be apparent, this growing courtship of movement leaders was limited largely to men. The fact that government officials did not similarly employ or cultivate the nuclear disarmament campaign's women leaders should hardly come as a surprise, given the nearly universal exclusion of women from politics and, particularly, from the realm of national security policy. Furthermore, the relative indifference by policymakers, nearly all of them male, to the advice of prominent women activists may have been reinforced by the movement's emphasis on women protesters as politically unsophisticated wives and mothers. The "feminine mystique" was certainly useful in charming reporters and overcoming charges of subversive activities. But it did nothing to ensure that women leaders were taken seriously in the national security apparatus, where top officials engaged in male bonding of a locker-room type.[11] Nor, given the widespread prejudice against women, does it seem likely that a more feminist approach would have afforded them greater influence. Consequently, women's nuclear disarmament activism, so impressive at the grassroots level, rarely accorded women access to the higher echelons of government power.[12]

Of course, a key reason for the perception that the movement did not change policy lies in the ambiguous nature of its victory: it had helped secure nuclear arms controls, but not disarmament. As Seaborg noted, "arms control is different from disarmament. It does not seek to abolish nuclear arms. . . . Instead it seeks to defuse the nuclear arms competition in various ways, such as by bringing about more moderate and stable levels of nuclear arms, by eliminating the more provocative and threatening weapons or deployments, and by preventing dangerous, further stages in the arms race." Rhetoric to the contrary, from the standpoint of the leaders of the great powers, this was about as far as they wanted to go. As Sweden's Alva Myrdal reported in 1972, she and many others participating in U.N. disarmament efforts found "hardly any tangible results" of their work, a consequence of the fact "that the superpowers have not seriously tried to achieve disarmament." Or, as she wrote a few years later, "although seemingly they struggle against each other, they are in a kind of conspiracy, dividing between them the responsibility for saying nyet or no." Through their "secret and undeclared collusion," disarmament agreements have been prevented. "And so the gaming and the arms race continue."[13]

As a result, the nuclear disarmament campaign of the 1950s and 1960s left

an ambiguous legacy. Thanks to nuclear arms controls and to the growing atmosphere of nuclear restraint, the world appeared a safer place in the early
1970s than it had seemed two decades before. In 1953, the editors of the *Bulletin of the Atomic Scientists* had set the hands of their Doomsday Clock at two
minutes to midnight. By 1972, the clock's hands stood at twelve minutes to
midnight, the most optimistic setting in its history.[14] Even so, as Myrdal noted,
there was remarkably little sign of disarmament. Speaking in 1974 before the
United Nations, U.S. Senator Stuart Symington reported that the U.S. stockpile of nuclear weapons had reached the equivalent of the destructive power of
615,385 Hiroshima bombs. When Soviet nuclear capabilities were included,
the figure for the nuclear explosive force of the two superpowers soared to over
a million times the atomic bomb that had annihilated Hiroshima.[15] Moreover,
Britain, France, and China also had nuclear weapons, and several additional
countries were in the process of building them.

The "Great Mystery"

Decades later, brooding on the stormy world of international relations in which
he had once played a leading part, Dean Rusk penned some startling comments. "Looking back over my eighty years," he wrote, "I am confronted by a
great mystery and cannot begin to suggest an answer. I am convinced that the
peoples of the Soviet Union, and indeed, people everywhere—Europe, China,
Africa, the United States—prefer peace to war. How is it that this universal
yearning for peace at the grass roots is not translated into better relations
among governments?"[16] This formulation, of course, is somewhat overdrawn,
for—as we have seen—the "universal yearning" at the grass roots did translate
into "better relations," both in terms of nuclear arms controls and an emerging
U.S.-Soviet detente. Even so, there is a recognizable core of truth to Rusk's
observation, for—during these years—the great powers neither ended the Cold
War nor moved to embrace nuclear disarmament.

Others noted a disjuncture between peaceful desires and their roles as government officials. Gerard Smith recalled that when he worked for the AEC and
the State Department in the 1950s and 1960s, "I could not reconcile my understanding of Christian belief about justifiable use of force and my knowledge of
the blast, heat and radiation effects of nuclear explosions. I finally gave up the
effort, suspended judgment and kept my conscience quiet with the conclusion
that there was no alternative." Like Smith, Seaborg pointed to "a personal
dilemma in which I frequently found myself while AEC chairman. At all times,
then and since, I have strongly believed that judicious arms control agreements,
most especially a comprehensive test ban treaty, are essential to secure a tol-

erable future for humankind. Yet, in my official position, I felt obligated on occasion to point out the technical need for certain types of tests. This was especially true when . . . it was national policy to develop major new weapons."
Seaborg considered this "a clear instance of the old Washington adage, 'Where
you stand is where you sit.'"[17]

This same divorce between personal values and the role of the national security manager is evident among officials at the summit of power. For example,
take their curious response to the atmospheric test ban treaty. When he learned
that the treaty had been accepted at Moscow, Macmillan burst into tears. A similar phenomenon occurred during the final negotiation of the treaty. Attending a
track meet with Khrushchev at Moscow Stadium, Harriman noted that when
in the closing ceremonies Soviet and American athletes paraded around the
track arm-in-arm and the crowd burst into a tremendous ovation, tears sprang
into Khrushchev's eyes. If Kennedy responded to the treaty in the same fashion, there is no record of it. Nor was he a sentimental man. But, according to
Sorensen, "no other single accomplishment in the White House ever gave him
greater satisfaction." Of course, it can be argued that all three national leaders
felt delighted by what they considered a diplomatic and political triumph.[18] But
it was a particular kind of triumph—a triumph over Cold War divisions, a triumph of reconciliation in the face of murderous international conflict. Their
emotional response to the treaty provides one further indication of how deeply,
under "normal" conditions, government leaders were locked into a stance of
suspicion, fear, and enmity, even though, on a personal level, they yearned to
be free of it.

These observations—and, most tellingly, the stubborn clinging by nation-
states to their nuclear arsenals—suggest that the failure to secure nuclear disarmament was rooted in the structure of international relations. In a world of
competing nation-states, with no higher level of sovereignty to resolve their
disputes, nations gravitated naturally toward military force as the best guarantee of their "national security." In 1959, assessing the stalemate in disarmament
negotiations, Rabinowitch concluded that conflict among nations led governments to believe "that the main interest of one state or society is to weaken, if
not to destroy, the other. This kind of 'national aim' has been traditional in all
human history. Antique and modern states and empires have been built up by
pursuing such aims, and have been destroyed when they failed in the power
contest." Similarly, Salvador de Madariaga, who had once supervised disarmament efforts for the League of Nations, argued that same year: "Loyalty to
the world community . . . is not strong enough to counterbalance, integrate, and
sublimate nationalism; and, therefore, the nations of the world have to follow a
policy of sheer power. . . . Such a situation inevitably leads to armaments."[19]

Structures, of course, can be modified to accommodate new realities, given sufficient determination. The carnage of World Wars I and II had led to the creation of international institutions, most notably the League of Nations and the United Nations. But these new institutions remained remarkably weak, largely because of the unwillingness of nation-states to relinquish much of their sovereignty. Similarly, the menace of global annihilation, coupled with a mass mobilization against it, encouraged world statesmen to flirt with the idea of internationally imposed nuclear disarmament. But, in this case as well, they resisted taking the plunge. Cousins complained to Schweitzer: "The heart of the problem . . . is that the statesmen are aware of the nature of nuclear force but find it difficult to face up to the implications. . . . Instead, they allow themselves to be governed by the same old conditioned reflexes produced by the long centuries of struggle between nation and nation." Writing in 1963, Rabinowitch thought it "unlikely that any American administration, or any Soviet government, will reverse the customary national priorities. Perhaps we must undergo some shocking experience, such as an abortive nuclear attack . . . to demonstrate how close we live to the abyss."[20]

Nor was the reluctance to challenge the traditional prerogatives of the nation-state limited to policymakers. As the British historian Arnold Toynbee observed in 1968: "Nationalism is today about ninety per cent of the real religion of about ninety per cent of the human race." And it was "nationalism, fanatically inflamed and simultaneously armed with the atomic weapon," that "is threatening today to stampede mankind into committing mass suicide." To Toynbee, a religious man and a supporter of CND, nationalism was "an avatar of the devil," "an expression of demoniac, and therefore self-destructive, collective self-centeredness in the peoples of each of the 125 sovereign national states among which mankind has now partitioned itself."[21] Even if one considers Toynbee's contention overdrawn, it is difficult to deny the appeal of nationalism to much of the world's population. People might fear the Bomb; but they also feared national subordination, conquest, or defeat.

The structure of international relations, undergirded by nationalist sentiments, placed the world nuclear disarmament movement in an exceptionally difficult position. All it wanted, the movement argued, was to ban the Bomb. But, as policymakers and portions of the public well understood, banning the Bomb would have substantial effects on national security policies. Under great popular pressure, policymakers might limit nuclear testing, regulate the arms race, or draw back from nuclear war. But, for the most part, they were not about to give up their nuclear weapons or, for that matter, reform the international system. By focusing on weapons rather than on international relations, nuclear disarmament groups seemed to avoid the sticky issue of "national security." But they could not avoid it entirely. Ultimately, a competitive international system, plagued with fear and international rivalry, placed constraints on their progress, halting them far short of the nuclear disarmament they desired.

Yet if the movement's campaign for nuclear disarmament foundered on the fierce hostilities of the international order, its accomplishments were still quite substantial. In the face of bitter opposition from many government leaders, it had helped to end atmospheric nuclear testing, secure the world's first nuclear arms control agreements, and lessen the possibilities of nuclear war. Furthermore, it unleashed a new wave of dynamic social forces—most notably movements among students, women, and intellectuals—as agencies of social change. Even as they put aside nuclear concerns, they took up other issues of great moment, including the Vietnam War, environmental protection, women's liberation, and assorted campaigns for social justice. Often they drew on the movement's innovative techniques, including mass marches and nonviolent resistance. Meanwhile, many of the nuclear disarmament organizations, though dwindling, survived over the ensuing decades. And, in the late 1970s and early 1980s, when the international system again threatened to send the world careening toward nuclear catastrophe, they became the core of a new mass movement. As millions of people poured into the streets of Sydney and New York, Amsterdam and Moscow, Budapest and London, bearing the nuclear disarmament symbol, it became the largest grassroots movement in world history—one which exemplified, through its global nature, the gradual emergence of a world community.

Today, as we look back on more than half a century of nuclear threat and counter-threat—and particularly on the terrible nuclear explosions and confrontations of the 1950s and 1960s—it is time to face up to what happened and why. Many writers repeat the hoary argument, advanced again and again by government officials, that, paradoxically, nuclear weapons have provided the key to our survival. Despite their confident assertion of this proposition, it remains no more than a hypothesis that can be neither proven nor disproven. But, having explored the growth and influence of the popular campaign against nuclear weapons, we can posit an alternative explanation for our good fortune. It suggests that, even in the midst of a murderous system of international relations, humane considerations can have an impact—indeed, that they helped to curb the nuclear arms race and to avert its most disastrous consequences. More specifically, it suggests the remarkable degree to which our survival, physical and moral, has resulted from the activities of those men and women who worked to free humanity from the menace of nuclear annihilation.

Reference Matter

Notes

For complete authors' names, titles, and publication data on works cited in short form in these Notes, consult the Bibliography. The following abbreviations are used:

AE	Atomic Energy
AEA	Atomic Energy Authority
AEC	Atomic Energy Commission
AS	Administration Series
BAS	*Bulletin of the Atomic Scientists*
CDSP	*Current Digest of the Soviet Press*
CND	Campaign for Nuclear Disarmament
CNVA	Committee for Nonviolent Action
CPC	Country Project Correspondence, 1952–63
CPF	Country Project Files
DOS	Department of State
FAS	Federation of American Scientists
FO	Foreign Office
FOR	Fellowship of Reconciliation
FRUS	*Foreign Relations of the United States*
ICDP	International Confederation for Disarmament and Peace
NSF	National Security Files
NYT	*New York Times*
OR	Office of Research
OSANSA	Office of the Special Assistant for National Security Affairs

OSS	Office of the Staff Secretary
PC	Pugwash Conferences
PM	Prime Minister's
PN	*Peace News*
POBR	Public Opinion Barometer Reports, 1955–62
POF	President's Office Files
RA	Bertrand Russell Archive
RR	Research Reports, 1960–63
SANE	National Committee for a Sane Nuclear Policy
SCPC	Swarthmore College Peace Collection
SecState	Secretary of State
SPU	Student Peace Union
USIA	United States Information Agency
WHCF	White House Central Files
WILPF	Women's International League for Peace and Freedom
WPC	World Peace Council
WPF	World Project Files, 1953–63
WRI	War Resisters' International
WSP	Women Strike for Peace

Preface Epigraph: Camus, *Actuelles, III*, p. 182.

Book Epigraph: This chorus comes from what British CND literature referred to as the "Marching Song" for its first Aldermaston March. In later years, CND identified the song more fully as "The H-Bomb's Thunder," written by John Brunner. It was sung to the tune of "Miner's Life Guard." "Songs for the Aldermaston March" (1958), Reel 13, CND (Britain) Records, London-Warwick; "Sanity Songsheet," enclosure in *Sanity* [Britain], Good Friday / Saturday 1963.

Chapter 1

Epigraph: "Russell-Einstein Manifesto of July 9, 1955," in Nathan and Norden, eds., *Einstein on Peace*, p. 632.

1. This first surge of public activity and its decline are the subject of volume 1 of this trilogy: Wittner, *One World or None*.

2. Divine, *Blowing on the Wind*, p. 4; Hewlett and Holl, *Atoms*, pp. 172–75.

3. According to standards later developed by the U.S. government, the Marshall Islanders received twenty-five times the permissible lifetime dose of radiation. In 1977, Congress enacted legislation providing compensation of $150 million for the illnesses and deaths among the Marshallese caused by the U.S. nuclear testing program. Winkler, *Life Under a Cloud*, pp. 93–94; Hacker, *Elements of Controversy*, pp. 227–28; Ball, *Justice Downwind*, pp. 174–75.

4. The AEC disclaimed responsibility for Kuboyama's death, pointing out that he died of hepatitis contracted from a blood transfusion during his hospital treatment for radiation exposure. Yet, at least indirectly, his death resulted from the Bikini Bomb test. The State Department awarded his widow $2,777.78. Divine, *Blowing on the Wind*, pp. 4–7; Mazuzan

and Walker, *Controlling the Atom*, p. 42; Lapp, *Voyage*, passim; Hacker, *Elements of Controversy*, p. 158.

5. "The H-Bomb and World Opinion," *BAS* 10 (May 1954): 163–64; Hewlett and Holl, *Atoms*, p. 177; Pfau, *No Sacrifice Too Great*, p. 166.

6. Mazuzan and Walker, *Controlling the Atom*, pp. 43–46; Divine, *Blowing on the Wind*, p. 75; Hewlett and Holl, *Atoms*, pp. 340–41, 345–46; Weart, *Nuclear Fear*, p. 201.

7. Dulles referred to "massive retaliatory power" in his speech, but the press dubbed the policy "massive retaliation," which it assumed, correctly, meant reliance upon the waging of nuclear war. *FRUS, 1952–1954*, 2: 593; J. F. Dulles, "Evolution of Foreign Policy," p. 108; *FRUS, 1955–1957*, 19: 60–61.

8. Holloway, *Soviet Union*, pp. 32–33, 84, 164; Dinerstein, *War and the Soviet Union*, p. 66.

9. Ståhle, *Internationella Kvinnoförbundet*, p. 28; Frank J. Gordon, "A Brief History of the Women's International League for Peace and Freedom" (1981), p. 5, WILPF (International Office) Records.

10. John R. Minor, "Political Machinery for Peace," *BAS* 11 (Mar. 1955): 85; *PN*, Sept. 24, 1954.

11. Muelder, "Pacifism," pp. 159–60; Ormrod, "Churches," p. 199; Hiebert, *Impact of Atomic Energy*, pp. 242–44.

12. Flannery, ed., *Pattern for Peace*, pp. 234–37, 270–73; Divine, *Blowing on the Wind*, p. 59; Hanson, *Catholic Church*, p. 282; Vaillancourt, "Cinq papes modernes," p. 53.

13. Russell, *Final Years*, pp. 88–89; R. Clark, *Life of Bertrand Russell*, pp. 536–38.

14. Joliot-Curie to Russell, Jan. 31, 1955, Class 600, RA 1; Goldsmith, *Frédéric Joliot-Curie*, pp. 191–93; Wooster, "Some Recollections," p. 28.

15. Russell to Joliot-Curie, Feb. 4, 1955, Class 600, RA 1; R. Clark, *Life of Bertrand Russell*, p. 539.

16. Russell to Einstein, Feb. 11, 1955, and Einstein to Russell, Feb. 16, 1955, Class 710, RA 1; Nathan and Norden, eds., *Einstein on Peace*, pp. 623–26.

17. Russell to Niels Bohr, Mar. 8, 1955, Russell to Otto Hahn, Apr. 5, 1955, Russell to Einstein, Apr. 5, 1955, and Joliot-Curie to Russell, May 13, 1955, Class 600, RA 1; R. Clark, *Life of Bertrand Russell*, p. 541; Biquard, *Frédéric Joliot-Curie*, p. 112.

18. The five were Niels Bohr, Otto Hahn, Manne Siegbahn, Harold Urey, and Lord Adrian. Bohr to Russell, Apr. 20, 1955, Hahn to Russell, Apr. 23, 1955, Siegbahn to Russell, June 30, 1955, and Urey to Russell, July 7, 1955, Class 600, RA 1; Russell, *Final Years*, pp. 92–93; R. Clark, *Life of Bertrand Russell*, p. 542.

19. Russell, *Final Years*, pp. 91–92; Einstein to Russell, Apr. 11, 1955, Class 710, RA 1; Nathan and Norden, eds., *Einstein on Peace*, p. 631.

20. Russell to Cecil F. Powell, May 7, 1955, Joliot-Curie to Russell, May 13, June 7, 1955, and Russell to Joliot-Curie, June 17, 1955, Class 600, RA 1; R. Clark, *Life of Bertrand Russell*, p. 541; Goldsmith, *Frédéric Joliot-Curie*, pp. 193–95.

21. Joliot-Curie to Russell, July 4, 1955, Class 600, RA 1; Russell, *Final Years*, pp. 92, 95; Biquard, *Frédéric Joliot-Curie*, p. 112.

22. Although Max Born had endorsed the statement, Russell inadvertently left his name off the list of signers. Linus Pauling, a distinguished American chemist, also endorsed the statement, but too late to be included on the original list of signatories. Russell, *Final Years*, pp. 95–97, 124–29; Rotblat, *Scientists*, p. 2.

23. Nathan and Norden, eds., *Einstein on Peace*, pp. 632–36; R. Clark, *Life of Bertrand Russell*, p. 543; Rotblat, *Scientists*, p. 2.

24. Born, ed., *Born-Einstein Letters*, pp. 200–201; Born to Russell, Jan. 21, Mar. 23, 1955, Class 600, RA 1.

25. Hahn, *My Life*, p. 220; Born to Russell, Apr. 1955, Class 600, RA 1; "Scientists Appeal for Abolition of War," *BAS* 11 (Sept. 1955): 237.

26. "Fifty-two Nobel Laureates," in Weinberg and Weinberg, eds., *Instead of Violence*, pp. 101–2; Born to Russell, Aug. 8, 1955, Class 600, RA 1; Born to Russell, Nov. 3, 1955, Born-Russell Correspondence.

27. Suzuki, "Japanese Attitudes," p. 114; Totten and Kawakami, "Gensuikyo," p. 834; Yasumasa Tanaka, "Japanese Attitudes Toward Nuclear Arms," *Public Opinion Quarterly* 34 (1970): 29; Mendel, *Japanese People*, pp. 151–60; Herbert Passin, "Japan and the H-Bomb," *BAS* 11 (Oct. 1955): 289–92.

28. Suzuki, "Declining Role of Ideology," p. 124; Committee for the Compilation of Materials, *Hiroshima and Nagasaki*, pp. 575–77; S. Tsurumi, *An Intellectual History*, pp. 99–100; Koschmann, "Postwar Democracy," p. 2.

29. Tano Jodai to Gertrude Baer, Mar. 25, 1954, Reel 79, and Tano Jodai, "The Death of Mr. Kuboyama" (Oct. 15, 1954), Reel 80, WILPF (International) Records; David Wurfel, "The Japanese F.O.R. Today," *Fellowship* 21 (July 1955): 10–11; Tano Jodai, "Japan Appeals to World Opinion," *Pax et Libertas* 21 (Apr. 1955): 3.

30. "Statement by the Science Council of Japan at Their 17th General Assembly," *Atomic Scientists' Journal* 4 (Jan. 1955): 161; Allison to SecState, Aug. 6, 1954, 711.5611/8-654, DOS Records. See also *PN*, Oct. 29, 1954.

31. Kamata and Salaff, "Atomic Bomb," pp. 47–48; Koschmann, "Postwar Democracy," p. 3; Oe, *Hiroshima Notes*, p. 11.

32. Committee for the Compilation of Materials, *Hiroshima and Nagasaki*, pp. xl, 605; *Meaning of Survival*, p. 114; Shinzo Hamai, "Peace Declaration" (Aug. 6, 1954), Folder 333, WRI Records, Amsterdam.

33. *Meaning of Survival*, pp. 117, 122; Kaoru Yasui to Dear Friend, June 17, 1955, Folder 333, WRI Records, Amsterdam; Committee for the Compilation of Materials, *Hiroshima and Nagasaki*, pp. 577–78; Hersey, *Hiroshima*, p. 97.

34. Totten and Kawakami, "Gensuikyo," pp. 833–39; Koschmann, "Postwar Democracy," pp. 10–11; Stockwin, *Japanese Socialist Party*, pp. 88–89.

35. "Japanese Opinion on Problems of Atomic Energy and Nuclear Weapons" (Mar. 12, 1956), p. 6, and "Japanese Reactions to U.S. Nuclear Tests" (Aug. 28, 1956), p. 1, Box 1, POBR, OR, USIA Records.

36. Kaoru Yasui, "Invitation to the 2nd World Conference Against Atomic and Hydrogen Bombs" (Apr. 1, 1956), Class 640, RA 1; Signe Hojer, "Japan United Against Nuclear Weapons," *Pax et Libertas* 22 (Dec. 1956): 8–9. See also *PN*, Aug. 31, 1956.

37. Boyer, *By the Bomb's Early Light*, p. 352; Divine, *Blowing on the Wind*, p. 18; Weart, *Nuclear Fear*, pp. 183–84; "Minutes of Meeting Held at Home of Mrs. Gellhorn on November 28, 1956," Box 1, Committee for Environmental Information Records; "The Nuclear Weapons Test Ban," *BAS* 12 (Sept. 1956): 268.

38. A Brooklyn pacifist reported glumly in March 1954: "Few people today seem interested in studying the problems of world peace, partly because it seems safer not to be interested in such matters, lest we be considered 'subversive.'" Wittner, *Rebels Against War*, pp. 215–20; Alonso, *Peace as a Women's Issue*, pp. 159–85; Mary S. McDowell to Dear Friend, Mar. 15, 1954, Rustin Papers.

39. John Swomley, "Nuclear Weapons Tests" (1957), Box 24a, and "Stop the H-Bomb Tests!" Box 28, FOR (United States) Records; Brittain, *Rebel Passion*, pp. 67–68; *NYT*, May 7, 1956.

40. Fellowship of Reconciliation, *A Sane Man's Guide*; Fellowship of Reconciliation, *How to Hide from an H-Bomb*.

41. Stein and Conners, "Civil Defense Protests," p. 81; War Resisters League, *History of*

the War Resisters League, p. 7; Garrison, "Our Skirts," pp. 201–10; Day, *Loaves and Fishes*, pp. 160–61; *Catholic Worker*, July–Aug. 1955; "International Civil Defense Demonstration, June 15, 1955," Box 4, FOR (United States) Records.

42. Szilard to Chester Bowles, May 24, 1955, Box 4, and Szilard to Archibald Alexander, Oct. 10, 1956, Box 74, Szilard Papers; *NYT*, Feb. 6, 1955; Leo Szilard, "The First Step to Peace," *BAS* 11 (Mar. 1955): 104; Leo Szilard, "Draft of a Letter to the Editor of *The New York Times* (Summer 1956)," in Hawkins, Greb, and Szilard, eds., *Toward a Livable World*, pp. 145–47.

43. "Scientists' Group Urges Worldwide Ban on Further Nuclear Tests" (June 8, 1956), Box 53, FAS Records; "The Nuclear Weapons Test Ban," p. 268; *NYT*, Oct. 25, 1956.

44. "FAS Position," *F.A.S. Newsletter*, Oct. 22, 1956; Gilpin, *American Scientists*, pp. 135–48, 154–56; Higinbotham to Maurice Shapiro, Aug. 1, 1955, Box 37, FAS Records.

45. The rise and decline of the world government movement are covered, *inter alia*, in Wittner, *One World or None*, and Wooley, *Alternatives to Anarchy*, pp. 3–82.

46. Yavenditti, "Hiroshima Maidens," pp. 21–39; Hersey, *Hiroshima*, pp. 142–44; Lifton, *Death in Life*, pp. 337–38; *Meaning of Survival*, p. 117; Cousins, "Maidens Are Coming"; Tadao Watanabe, "Testimonial of Gratitude" (Nov. 7, 1956), Cousins Papers, Beverly Hills.

47. Cousins, *Present Tense*, p. 266.

48. Hiebert, *Impact of Atomic Energy*, pp. 268, 271; *NYT*, Apr. 16, 1954; Jack, *Nuclear Politics*, p. 20; Lee, "In the Valley," p. 63.

49. Hazel Gaudet Erskine, "The Polls: Atomic Weapons and Nuclear Energy," *Public Opinion Quarterly* 27 (Summer 1963): 157–59; Gallup, ed., *Gallup Poll*, pp. 1230–31.

50. Kramer, Kalick, and Milburn, "Attitudes Toward Nuclear Weapons," p. 13; Gallup, ed., *Gallup Poll*, p. 1353.

51. In the 1954 survey, the college-educated were the most hawkish, whereas those with a grade school education were the most dovish. Kramer, Kalick, and Milburn, "Attitudes Toward Nuclear Weapons," pp. 13–14; Gallup, ed., *Gallup Poll*, pp. 1229, 1452.

52. Stevenson, Address Before the American Society of Newspaper Editors, Apr. 21, 1956, in W. Johnson, ed., *Papers*, 6: 118; Hewlett and Holl, *Atoms*, pp. 338–39; Stevenson to J. Robert Oppenheimer, Aug. 6, 1956, Box 69, Oppenheimer Papers.

53. Martin, *Adlai Stevenson*, pp. 365–80; Adlai E. Stevenson, Nationwide Television Address of Oct. 15, 1956, in W. Johnson, ed., *Papers*, 6: 282–86.

54. *NYT*, Oct. 17, 1956; Divine, *Blowing on the Wind*, pp. 96–109; *Newsweek* 48 (Oct. 29, 1956): 27. For the overwhelmingly positive mail generated by Stevenson's position on testing, see Boxes 460–62, Stevenson Papers.

55. Willard Wirtz, who played a major role in preparing the Democrat's statements on the test ban, later remarked that Stevenson "knew it would not be a political plus" but believed it "had to be said." McKeever, *Adlai Stevenson*, pp. 380–81.

56. Martin, *Adlai Stevenson*, pp. 206–7, 235, 367; Stevenson, Address Before the American Society of Newspaper Editors, Apr. 21, 1956, in W. Johnson, ed., *Papers*, 6: 118.

57. Divine, *Blowing on the Wind*, pp. 93–94; Sullivan, *Nuclear Democracy*, p. 9; Hewlett and Holl, *Atoms*, p. 368.

58. Stevenson thanked Cousins for his "splendid contribution on the hydrogen bomb." Stevenson to Cousins, June 25, 1956, in W. Johnson, ed., *Papers*, 6: 162; Cousins to Chloe Fox, July 18, 1956, and Stevenson to Cousins, July 30, 1956, Box 427, and Stevenson to Cousins, Dec. 15, 1956, Box 476, Stevenson Papers; Stevenson to Cousins, Aug. 26, 1956, Cousins to Willard Wirtz, Sept. 25, 1956, and Cousins, undated draft of speech, Box 263, Cousins Papers, Los Angeles; *NYT*, Oct. 24, 1956.

59. Adlai Stevenson, Address to UWF Dinner, Nov. 18, 1964, Cousins Papers, Beverly Hills.

60. Gilbert McAllister to Russell, July 23, 1954, and Usborne to Russell, July 29, 1954, Class 570, RA 1.

61. Russell, "The Danger to Mankind," *BAS* 10 (Jan. 1954): 8–9; Russell to Ianthe Carswell, Apr. 17, 1956, Class 630, RA 1.

62. Ingram, *Fifty Years*, p. 23; "British FOR Asks End of H-Bomb Tests," *Fellowship* 22 (Sept. 1956): 28; *PN*, May 21, 1954, Mar. 9, 1956; "Proceedings of the London Yearly Meeting, 1955," p. 81, and "Proceedings of the London Yearly Meeting, 1956," pp. 34, 40, London Yearly Meeting Records; "News from the National Sections," *Pax et Libertas* 21 (Apr. 1955): 19.

63. *PN*, July 1, 1955.

64. H. Brock, *Century of Total War*, pp. 21–33; Olwen Battersby et al., "Operation Gandhi," Reel 5, FOR (Britain) Records; Randle, "Pacifism, War Resistance," pp. 28–30; *Sanity* [Britain], Good Friday 1962, p. 2; R. Taylor, *Against the Bomb*, pp. 116–21; Randle to the author, Oct. 4, 1994.

65. Ormrod, "Churches," p. 199; Groom, *British Thinking*, pp. 199–201; *PN*, Oct. 15, 1954, Mar. 25, 1955, Jan. 27, 1956.

66. *PN*, May 7, 1954; *NYT*, Mar. 28, 1954.

67. "H-Bomb and World Opinion," pp. 166–67; Divine, *Blowing on the Wind*, p. 21; Morrison, *I Renounce War*, pp. 89–90; Clement R. Attlee, "The Political Problem," *BAS* 10 (Oct. 1954): 327–28.

68. Driver, *Disarmers*, pp. 28–29; Acland, "No Defense Against Nuclear Attack," pp. 27–40; *PN*, May 6, 1955; Myers, "British Peace Politics," p. 62. For a somewhat different view, see Pierre, *Nuclear Politics*, p. 102.

69. Although the petition presented to Churchill at the end of the year contained 375,000 signatures, most authorities say the number of signers reached half a million. Myers, "British Peace Politics," pp. 62–63; Soper to Bertrand Russell, May 24, 1954, Class 600, RA 1; Parkin, *Middle Class Radicalism*, p. 111; Ceadel, "Britain's Nuclear Disarmers," pp. 220–21; Donald Soper et al. to Churchill, Dec. 31, 1954, PREM 11/1052, PM Records.

70. R. Taylor, *Against the Bomb*, pp. 5–8; Liddington, *Long Road to Greenham*, pp. 178–84.

71. Gallup, ed., *Gallup International Public Opinion Polls: Great Britain*, pp. 325, 348–49, 357; "State of Opinion on Projected NATO Atomic Defense Plans and on the Banning of Nuclear Weapons" (Mar. 28, 1955), p. 2, Box 4, POBR, OR, USIA Records.

72. Gallup, ed., *Gallup International Public Opinion Polls: Great Britain*, pp. 363, 389; "Western European Press Reactions to Announcement of 1956 Nuclear Tests" (Jan. 25, 1956), p. 1, Box 7, Intelligence Bulletins, and "A Note on Public Reactions to U.S. Atomic Weapons Tests" (June 22, 1956), p. 1, Box 4, POBR, OR, USIA Records.

73. "State of Opinion on Projected NATO Atomic Defense Plans and on the Banning of Nuclear Weapons" (Mar. 28, 1955), p. 5, and "Pre-Conference State of Opinion on Some Atomic Issues" (July 13, 1955), p. 2, Box 4, POBR, OR, USIA Records; Gallup, ed., *Gallup Poll*, p. 1227.

74. Cioc, *Pax Atomica*, pp. 21–25; *PN*, Oct. 15, 1954; "How I Became a Pacifist—as told by Dr. Martin Niemöller" (n.d.), Box 16, Series B, Sayre Papers; Born to Einstein, Nov. 28, 1954, in Born, ed., *Born-Einstein Letters*, p. 230.

75. Kelleher, *Germany*, pp. 35–38; Weart, *Nuclear Fear*, p. 216; Rupp, *Ausserparlamentarische Opposition*, p. 72.

76. "Trends in West German Attitudes on the Use of Atomic Weapons in Western Defense" (Oct. 10, 1955), p. 4, Box 4, and "Some Current West German Public Opinion Trends on Atomic Issues" (May 17, 1957), p. 1, Box 5, POBR, OR, USIA Records.

77. Deutsch and Edinger, *Germany*, pp. 26–27; "State of Opinion on Projected NATO

Atomic Defense Plans and on the Banning of Nuclear Weapons" (Mar. 28, 1955), p. 3, Box 4, POBR, OR, USIA Records.

78. Opposition to such a ban stood at only 5 percent. Noelle and Neumann, eds., *Germans*, p. 396; "State of Opinion on Projected NATO Atomic Defense Plans and on the Banning of Nuclear Weapons" (Mar. 28, 1955), p. 5, and "Pre-Conference State of Opinion on Some Atomic Issues" (July 13, 1955), p. 2, Box 4, POBR, OR, USIA Records.

79. Scheinman, *Atomic Energy Policy*, pp. 110–11; Caldwell, "French Socialists' Attitudes," p. 78; "Western European Press Reactions to Announcement of 1956 Nuclear Tests" (Jan. 25, 1956), p. 7, Box 7, Intelligence Bulletins, OR, USIA Records.

80. "A Note on Public Reactions to U.S. Atomic Weapons Tests" (June 22, 1956), pp. 1–2, Box 4, POBR, OR, USIA Records; Merritt and Puchala, eds., *Western European Perspectives*, pp. 387–88.

81. The data on French attitudes toward the use of nuclear weapons are relatively scarce because the U.S. government concluded that the subject was "too sensitive to explore in France" at the time of the 1955 survey. Merritt and Puchala, eds., *Western European Perspectives*, p. 381; "State of Opinion on Projected NATO Atomic Defense Plans and on the Banning of Nuclear Weapons" (Mar. 28, 1955), p. 2, Box 4, POBR, OR, USIA Records.

82. "State of Opinion on Projected NATO Atomic Defense Plans and on the Banning of Nuclear Weapons" (Mar. 28, 1955), p. 5, and "Pre-Conference State of Opinion on Some Atomic Issues" (July 13, 1955), p. 2, Box 4, POBR, OR, USIA Records; Gallup, ed., *Gallup International Public Opinion Poll: France*, p. 200.

83. "Current Public Opinion in Italy About Select International Issues" (Oct. 1, 1956), pp. 23–24, Box 9, Intelligence Bulletins, OR, USIA Records; Francis T. Williamson to DOS, May 4, 1954, 711.5611/5-454, DOS Records.

84. "A Note on Public Reactions to U.S. Atomic Weapons Tests" (June 22, 1956), p. 1, "State of Opinion on Projected NATO Atomic Defense Plans and on the Banning of Nuclear Weapons" (Mar. 28, 1955), pp. 2, 4–5, and "Pre-Conference State of Opinion on Some Atomic Issues" (July 13, 1955), p. 2, Box 4, POBR, OR, USIA Records; Merritt and Puchala, eds., *Western European Perspectives*, pp. 381–83, 387–88, 393, 395.

85. Gallup, ed., *Gallup Poll*, p. 1254; *PN*, Oct. 5, 1956; "A Note on Norwegian and Danish Views of Atomic Energy for Peace" (Mar. 7, 1956), p. 2, Box 4, POBR, OR, USIA Records.

86. *PN*, June 8, 1956; Rudling, *Kampen mot Atomvapen*, p. 27.

87. Abbott to SecState, Apr. 7, 1954, 711.5611/4-754, DOS Records; Rudling, *Kampen mot Atomvapen*, p. 81; Ståhle, *Internationella Kvinnoförbundet*, p. 29.

88. Fehrm, "Sweden," pp. 214–15; Rudling, *Kampen mot Atomvapen*, pp. 12–27; Ahlmark, *Den svenska atomvapendebatten*, pp. 21–22; Andrén, *Power-Balance*, pp. 174–75; Myrdal, *Game of Disarmament*, p. 86; Erlander, *Tage Erlander*, p. 84; Wigforss et al., *Nej! till svenska atomvapen*, pp. 1–7.

89. The Dutch Association of Scientific Workers, with some six hundred members, was politically nonaligned and had previously withdrawn from the World Federation of Scientific Workers. H. A. Tolhoek to Rotblat, July 12, 1955, enclosure in Rotblat to Russell, July 14, 1955, Class 600, RA 1; Saar Boorlage, "The Problem of Nuclear Disarmament in the Netherlands," *Youth Against the Bomb* (June 1960), p. 5, Box 28, Series B, SANE Records; "Comité 'Stopzetting Atoombomproeven' wendt zich tot de Nederlandse regering," *Voorlichtingsblad* 1.9/10 (ca. Jan. 1960).

90. Everts and Walraven, *Vredesbeweging*, p. 41; "A Note on Public Reactions to U.S. Atomic Weapons Tests" (June 22, 1956), pp. 1–2, Box 4, POBR, OR, USIA Records.

91. "Western European Press Reactions to Announcement of 1956 Nuclear Tests" (Jan. 25, 1956), p. 11, Box 7, Intelligence Bulletins, and "A Note on West European Attitudes To-

ward Banning Atomic Tests and the Production of Atomic Weapons" (Mar. 26, 1957), p. 2, Box 5, POBR, OR, USIA Records.

92. "Pre-Conference State of Opinion on Some Atomic Issues" (July 13, 1955), p. 2, Box 4, POBR, OR, USIA Records.

93. Roy M. Melbourne to DOS, Apr. 25, 1955, 711.5611/4-2558, DOS Records; *PN*, Dec. 24, 1954; Brassel and Tanner, "Zur Geschichte der Friedensbewegung," pp. 62–64; Heiniger, "Die schweizerische Antiatombewegung," pp. 50–53.

94. "Swiss Churchmen Seek Ban on Atom Blasts," *Fellowship* 22 (Mar. 1956): 27.

95. Sakharov, *Memoirs*, pp. 170–73, 179; Holloway, *Stalin and the Bomb*, p. 317; Klose, *Russia and the Russians*, p. 146; Romanov, "Answers to the Questions," p. 559.

96. Holloway, *Stalin and the Bomb*, p. 363; Adamsky, "Becoming a Citizen," pp. 21–22, 28–29, 32–33; personal interview with Sergei Kapitza, June 28, 1990.

97. Orlov, *Dangerous Thoughts*, p. 139; Sagdeev, *Making of a Soviet Scientist*, p. 53; Holloway, *Stalin and the Bomb*, pp. 294, 319, 366–67; Adamsky, "Becoming a Citizen," pp. 30, 32–34; Gilpin, *American Scientists*, p. 151.

98. N. Khrushchev, *Khrushchev Remembers: The Last Testament*, pp. 64–65. For another illustration of Kapitza's cheekiness, see Kapitza to Khrushchev, Aug. 23, 1956, in "Peter Kapitsa: The Scientist Who Talked Back to Stalin," *BAS* 56 (Apr. 1990): 33.

99. Kapitza's son has confirmed that the Soviet physicist grew critical of nuclear weapons during these years. Kapitza, "The Task of All Progressive Humanity (Polemic with Bertrand Russell)," in Kapitza, *Experiment, Theory, Practice*, pp. 338–41; personal interview with Sergei Kapitza, June 28, 1990.

100. Igor Kurchatov et al., "Opasnosti atomnoi voiny i predlozhenie prezidenta Eizenkhauera" (The danger of atomic war and President Eisenhower's proposal), ca. late March 1954, enclosure in V. Malyshev to Nikita Khrushchev, Apr. 1, 1954, l. 38ff., d. 126, op. 30, f. 5, Central Committee of the Communist Party of the Soviet Union Records, cited in Smirnov and Zubok, "Nuclear Weapons after Stalin's Death," pp. 14–15.

101. Donald W. Smith to DOS, Apr. 15, 1954, and enclosed clipping from the *Daily Telegraph* (Sydney), Apr. 9, 1954, 711.5611/4-1554, DOS Records; *PN*, June 25, 1954.

102. David Purnell, "Australian Quakers and Peace, 1900–1963," Australian Quaker Peace Committee Records; "News from the National Sections," *Pax et Libertas* 21 (Apr. 1955): 18; Bertrand Russell, *Man's Peril* (1955), Reel 54, WILPF (International) Records.

103. *Peacemaker*, Apr. 1955; Siracusa, "Peace Movements," pp. 2–3; "Australian Section," *Pax et Libertas* 22 (Dec. 1956): 9.

104. Wellington to DOS, Mar. 30, 1954, 711.5611/3-3054, DOS Records; Clements, *Back from the Brink*, pp. 38–39, 98–99; Locke, *Peace People*, p. 160.

105. "War, the Bomb and Nuclear Weapon Tests" (1984), FOR (India) Records; *PN*, Apr. 22, 1955.

106. *PN*, Sept. 28, 1956; Divine, *Blowing on the Wind*, p. 27.

107. Divine, *Blowing on the Wind*, p. 19; Weart, *Nuclear Fear*, p. 201; Erskine, "The Polls: Atomic Weapons," p. 183; Gallup, ed., *Gallup Poll*, p. 1322.

108. Gallup, ed., *Gallup Poll*, p. 1254; "A Note on Norwegian and Danish Views on Atomic Energy for Peace" (Mar. 7, 1956), p. 2, Box 4, POBR, OR, USIA Records.

109. "Pre-Conference State of Opinion on Some Atomic Issues" (July 13, 1955), p. 2, and "State of Opinion on Projected NATO Atomic Defense Plans and on the Banning of Nuclear Weapons" (Mar. 28, 1955), pp. 3–4, Box 4, and "Japanese Opinion on Problems of Atomic Energy and Nuclear Weapons" (Mar. 12, 1956), p. 6, Box 1, POBR, OR, USIA Records.

110. "Japanese Opinion on Problems of Atomic Energy and Nuclear Weapons" (Mar. 12, 1956), p. 6, Box 1, POBR, OR, USIA Records.

111. "Current Trends in Attitudes Toward the US and the USSR" (July 8, 1957), p. 8, Box 5, "Japanese Reactions to U.S. Nuclear Tests" (Aug. 28, 1956), p. 3, Box 1, and "Some Indications of the Present Standing of the U.S. vs. the U.S.S.R. in Finnish Public Opinion" (Oct. 31, 1956), Box 4, POBR, OR, USIA Records.

112. Majorities or pluralities in all of these countries disapproved of Soviet nuclear testing. "A Note on Public Reactions to U.S. Atomic Weapons Tests" (June 22, 1956), pp. 1–2, Box 4, POBR, OR, USIA Records.

Chapter 2

Epigraph: Quoted in Homer Jack, "What Is Happening at the Geneva Disarmament Talks?" (Apr. 29, 1962), Box 52, Series IVB, Jack Papers.

1. In 1992, the Stockholm International Peace Research Institute estimated that by the end of 1958 there had been 196 nuclear explosions by the United States, 90 by the Soviet Union, and 21 by Britain. At least 165 of them occurred during the years 1957 and 1958. Ferm, "Nuclear Explosions, 1945–91," p. 118.

2. Between 1954 and 1956, Schweitzer's standing rose from tenth to fourth. Brabazon, *Albert Schweitzer*, pp. 17–417; Gallup, ed., *Gallup Poll*, pp. 1296, 1386–87, 1462.

3. Cousins, *Dr. Schweitzer*, pp. 11–18, 167; Jack, ed., *On Nuclear War and Peace*, pp. 3–8.

4. Cousins, *Dr. Schweitzer*, pp. 130, 165–73; Cousins to Jawaharlal Nehru, Feb. 13, 1957, in Cousins, *Albert Schweitzer's Mission*, pp. 158–59.

5. Cousins, *Dr. Schweitzer*, pp. 173–75; Schweitzer to Cousins, Feb. 23, Apr. 22, 1957, in Cousins, *Albert Schweitzer's Mission*, pp. 164–66, 174–75.

6. Schweitzer, "A Declaration of Conscience," pp. 17–20.

7. Hewlett and Holl, *Atoms*, p. 390; Nordness to USIA, May 9, 1957, Phillips to USIA, May 8, 1957, "18.14 Weapons—Test Moratorium, a. General, 1957" Folder, AE Lot File, and Willis to SecState, Apr. 24, 1958, 957.40/4-2458, DOS Records; *PN*, July 12, 1957; Rudling, *Kampen mot Atomvapen*, p. 35.

8. Cousins to Schweitzer, May 20, 1957, in Cousins, *Albert Schweitzer's Mission*, p. 193; Cousins to Jawaharlal Nehru, Nov. 18, 1957, Box 269, Cousins Papers, Los Angeles. For abridged versions in peace and disarmament publications, see Albert Schweitzer, "An Appeal to Mankind," *Fellowship* 23 (June 1957): 23–24; Albert Schweitzer, "Appeal to End Nuclear Tests," *BAS* 13 (June 1957): 204–5.

9. "Schweitzer, Albert (1)" and "Schweitzer, Albert (2)" folders, Box 2786, Alpha File, WHCF, Eisenhower Records; Jack, ed., *On Nuclear War and Peace*, p. 13.

10. Hewlett and Holl, *Atoms*, p. 390; *Daily News* (New York), Apr. 25, 1957.

11. Martin, *Adlai Stevenson*, pp. 414–15; Schweitzer to Cousins, Nov. 11, 1957, Apr. 14, Aug. 24, 1958, in Cousins, *Albert Schweitzer's Mission*, pp. 200–201, 208–10, 223–24; Brabazon, *Albert Schweitzer*, p. 440.

12. Schweitzer, *Peace or Atomic War?*; Schweitzer to Cousins, May 17, Aug. 24, 1958, in Cousins, *Albert Schweitzer's Mission*, pp. 215, 224.

13. Schweitzer retained this third place standing in 1959 and 1960. Cousins to Schweitzer, Nov. 24, 1958, in Cousins, *Albert Schweitzer's Mission*, p. 236; Anderson to Cousins, Oct. 12, 1958, Box 271, Cousins Papers, Los Angeles; Gallup, ed., *Gallup Poll*, pp. 1584, 1647, 1696.

14. Rotblat, *Scientists*, p. 1; "Memorandum I" (Spring 1954), "Memorandum II" (Summer 1954), "American Response" (Oct. 1, 1954), "European Response" (Oct. 1, 1954), and Rotblat to Rabinowitch, Oct. 29, 1954, Box 1, Rabinowitch Papers, Chicago.

15. Rotblat, *Scientists*, p. 1; Patrick Armstrong to Russell, May 13, 1955, with enclosures, Class 570, RA 1; Russell, *Final Years*, pp. 98–99; personal interview with Joseph Rotblat, July 12, 1990; Eugene Rabinowitch, "Pugwash—History and Outlook," *BAS* 13 (Sept. 1957): 243; R. Clark, *Life of Bertrand Russell*, pp. 543–44.

16. Russell to Rotblat, Sept. 10, 1955, Class 600, RA 1; Rabinowitch, "Pugwash," p. 243; Rotblat, *Scientists*, pp. 2–3; Rotblat, "Movements of Scientists," p. 134.

17. Rotblat, *Scientists*, pp. 3–4; Rotblat, "Movements of Scientists," pp. 133–34; Eaton to Russell, July 13, 1955, Class 600, and Powell to Russell, Feb. 18, 1956, and Eaton to Russell, Dec. 3, 1956, Class 625, RA 1; personal interview with Joseph Rotblat, July 12, 1990.

18. A total of sixty-four persons were invited to the conference, but many declined to attend because of other commitments, a common situation among eminent scientists. Rabinowitch, "Pugwash," pp. 244–48; Rotblat, *Scientists*, pp. 4–5.

19. Grodzins and Rabinowitch, eds., *Atomic Age*, p. 537; Rotblat, *Scientists*, p. 6; Rabinowitch to Russell, Aug. 14, 1957, Class 625, RA 1.

20. Rotblat, *Scientists*, pp. 4–5, 141–47; Hawkins, Greb, and Szilard, eds., *Toward a Livable World*, p. 153, and Szilard, "Draft of a Letter to the *Bulletin of the Atomic Scientists* (August 15, 1957)," in *Toward a Livable World*, pp. 164–65; Leo Szilard, "To Stop or Not to Stop," *BAS* 16 (Mar. 1960): 82.

21. Rotblat, *Scientists*, p. 7; Minutes of the meeting of the Pugwash Continuing Committee, Dec. 18–20, 1957, and Powell to Russell, July 22, 1957, Class 625, RA 1; *NYT*, July 10, 1957; Rabinowitch, "Pugwash," pp. 243–48.

22. Personal interview with Joseph Rotblat, July 12, 1990; Minutes of the meeting of the Pugwash Continuing Committee, Dec. 18–20, 1957, Class 625, RA 1; Rotblat, *Scientists*, pp. 7–8, 13–14, 37–41; Rotblat, "Movements of Scientists," pp. 134–35.

23. Rotblat to Russell, Nov. 27, 1957, Class 625, RA 1; Rotblat, *Scientists*, pp. 8–10, 46, 50; Rotblat, "Movements of Scientists," pp. 135–38; personal interview with Joseph Rotblat, July 12, 1990.

24. Pauling's background is discussed in Wittner, *One World or None*, pp. 60–61, 208–9, 272–73, 292, 315, 400; Robert J. Paradowski, "About the Author," in Pauling, *No More War!* pp. i–vi.

25. For background on the St. Louis antinuclear movement, which included scientists from the campus and women's group leaders in the community, see Sullivan, *Nuclear Democracy*, pp. 6–19.

26. Pauling, *No More War!* pp. 189–92; Commoner to Pauling, May 24, 1957, Pauling Papers; *NYT*, June 4, 1957; Pauling to Eisenhower, June 4, 1957, OF 108-A(3), WHCF, Eisenhower Records.

27. Schweitzer to Pauling, Dec. 29, 1957, Pauling Papers.

28. Pauling to Eisenhower, June 4, 1957, OF 108-A(3), WHCF, Eisenhower Records; Divine, *Blowing on the Wind*, pp. 127–28, 182–83; Daniel M. Singer to Sigmund P. Harris, July 18, 1960, Box 38, 1972 Addendum, FAS Records; Rabinowitch to Pauling, May 18, 1957, Pauling Papers.

29. Pauling, *No More War!* pp. 193–97; Commoner to Pauling, Oct. 11, 1957, Pauling to Norman Cousins, Mar. 25, 1958, Pauling to Hammarskjold, July 3, 1958, and Pauling to Alfred C. Williams, Jan. 16, 1959, Pauling Papers.

30. Helen C. Allison, "Outspoken Scientist," *BAS* 16 (Dec. 1960): 390; Divine, *Blowing on the Wind*, pp. 182–86; Pauling, *No More War!* p. 84.

31. Weart, *Nuclear Fear*, p. 203; Allison, "Outspoken Scientist," p. 390; Carlson, *Genes, Radiation, and Society*, pp. 378–79; Weisskopf, *Privilege*, p. 213.

32. Homer Jack, "What Is Happening at the Geneva Disarmament Talks?" (Apr. 29, 1962), Box 52, Series IVB, Jack Papers; Schweitzer to Cousins, May 17, 1958, in Cousins,

Albert Schweitzer's Mission, p. 216; Hanson, *Catholic Church*, p. 282; Zahn, *War, Conscience, and Dissent*, pp. 91–93.

33. Hiebert, *Impact of Atomic Energy*, p. 245; Lee, "In the Valley," p. 217; Flannery, ed., *Pattern for Peace*, p. 296; Straus, "Peace, Culture, and Education," p. 202.

Chapter 3

Epigraph: Sung by London medical students after the first Aldermaston march, this was performed to the tune of "John Brown's Body." Driver, *Disarmers*, p. 61.

1. One sign of how Japan's past experience continued to weigh upon the present was the furor aroused in Japan by former President Harry Truman's public comment in February 1958 that he had "not the slightest" regret that he had ordered use of the atomic bomb during World War II. *FRUS, 1955–1957*, 19: 443; Lifton, *Death in Life*, pp. 333–35.

2. *PN*, Mar. 1, 1957; Kagawa to Friends in Christ, May 28, 1957, Box 33, Series B, Sayre Papers.

3. The Japanese comprised the third largest national group. "Japanese Physicists Address Their British Colleagues," *BAS* 13 (May 1957): 178; R. W. Selby to H. C. Hainsworth, Jan. 21, 1958, FO 371/135572, FO Records.

4. A *New York Times* account reported the number of students at thirty-five thousand, but this may be a typographical error, for a leading Japanese scholar has placed the number at 350,000. *PN*, Feb. 8, 1957; Bamba, "Peace Movement," p. 40; *NYT*, May 18, 1957.

5. Free, *Six Allies*, pp. 50–51; Harlan B. Clark to SecState, Feb. 25, 1958, 711.5611/2-2558, DOS Records.

6. John Swomley, "Memo on Japan Council Against A and H Bombs" (1957), Box 24A, FOR (United States) Records; Kaoru Yasui to Bertrand Russell, Sept. 5, 1957, Sept. 25, 1958, Class 640, RA 1; "Walk for Peace," *Fellowship* 25 (Jan. 1, 1959): 21; *PN*, Sept. 6, 1957.

7. MacArthur to SecState, May 4, 1957, 711.5611/5-257, DOS Records; "Japan Public Opinion Survey: Part I" (June 1957), pp. 19–20, Box 61, CPF, OR, USIA Records. See also *NYT*, May 19, 1957.

8. Mendel, *Japanese People*, pp. 161, 166; Suzuki, "Japanese Attitudes," p. 103.

9. Harlan B. Clark to DOS, Feb. 25, 1958, 711.5611/2-2558, and U.S. Embassy (Tokyo) to SecState, Apr. 2, 1958, 711.5611/4-258, DOS Records; A. L. Mayall to H. C. Hainsworth, Mar. 18, 1958, FO 371/135573, FO Records; Hazel Gaudet Erskine, "The Polls: Atomic Weapons and Nuclear Energy," *Public Opinion Quarterly* 27 (Summer 1963): 164.

10. "Japan Public Opinion Survey: Part I" (June 1957), p. 22, Box 61, CPF, OR, USIA Records; Douglas H. Mendel Jr., "Japanese Views of the American Alliance," *Public Opinion Quarterly* 23 (Fall 1959): 340; Suzuki, "Japanese Attitudes," p. 103.

11. Gallup, ed., *Gallup Poll*, p. 1562; "World Poll II—Group Breakdowns," Box 3, WPF, OR, USIA Records.

12. Groom, *British Thinking*, p. 201; *PN*, Apr. 5, 1957; R. Taylor, *Against the Bomb*, pp. 11–12.

13. Divine, *Blowing on the Wind*, pp. 123–25; Hewlett and Holl, *Atoms*, p. 389; Robert Davies to Bertrand Russell, May 13, 1957, Class 630, RA 1.

14. Rotblat, "Movements of Scientists," p. 123; personal interview with Joseph Rotblat, July 12, 1990; Hugh Brock to Linus Pauling, Nov. 27, 1957, Pauling Papers; *PN*, Sept. 13, 1957.

15. Gallup, ed., *Gallup International Public Opinion Polls: Great Britain*, pp. 409, 411, 429, 446–47. See also Whitney to USIA, Feb. 4, 1958, Box 7, CPC, OR, USIA Records.

16. R. Taylor, *Against the Bomb*, pp. 7–18; Ianthe Carswell to Russell, Mar. 25, Apr.

23, 1957, Class 630, RA 1; personal interview with Sheila Jones, July 10, 1990; *NYT*, May 13, 1957; Hinton, *Protests and Visions*, p. 157; Liddington, *Long Road to Greenham*, p. 186.

17. H. Brock, *Century of Total War*, pp. 34–36; *PN*, Apr. 2, 1957; Randle, "Pacifism, War Resistance," p. 31; Driver, *Disarmers*, pp. 35–36; "Brief History of the Direct Action Committee Against Nuclear War" (June 22, 1961), Direct Action Committee Against Nuclear War Records; oral history interview with Pat Arrowsmith, Reel 3; Randle to the author, Oct. 4, 1994.

18. Carter, *Peace Movements*, p. 46; Driver, *Disarmers*, pp. 34–35; *PN*, May 10, 1957.

19. In May 1957, polls found that the British supported nuclear retaliation for a nuclear attack upon West European cities, but overwhelmingly opposed first use of nuclear weapons for defense against a conventional attack. Gallup, ed., *Gallup International Public Opinion Polls: Great Britain*, pp. 436, 442; "Current Trends on Western European Defense Issues and the Role of Atomic Weapons" (July 25, 1957), pp. 14–16, Box 5, POBR, OR, USIA Records.

20. Kennan claimed that he felt "horror and remorse" over "all the stir" his lectures created. *PN*, May 10, 17, June 7, 1957; R. Taylor, *Against the Bomb*, p. 19; Kennan to J. Robert Oppenheimer, Dec. 17, 1957, Box 43, Oppenheimer Papers.

21. Duff, *Left, Left, Left*, p. 119; *PN*, July 26, Sept. 27, 1957; Free, *Six Allies*, pp. 58–59, 76–77, 182; Carter, *Peace Movements*, pp. 46–47; R. Taylor, "Labour Party," pp. 102–6; Bevan, "Naked to the Conference Table."

22. Despite its heartfelt sentiments, Priestley's article was not spontaneous. Peggy Duff of the NCANWT began a chain of events that led the editor of the *New Statesman* to ask Priestley, one of his regular contributors, to write the piece. Priestley, "Britain and the Nuclear Bombs"; R. Clark, *Life of Bertrand Russell*, pp. 556–57.

23. Collins, *Faith Under Fire*, pp. 302–6; Duff, *Left, Left, Left*, pp. 119–21; Peggy Duff to Trevor Thomas, Dec. 9, 1957, Box 8, Series B, SANE Records; Duff to Russell, Dec. 26, 1957, Jan. 24, 1958, Class 630, RA 1; Minutes of the CND Executive Committee meetings of Jan. 21, 28, 1958, Reel 1, CND (Britain) Records, London-Warwick.

24. Of the thirty-three sponsors of the NCANWT, twenty-eight became sponsors of CND, and all but one of the NCANWT's 115 local groups joined the new organization. Goss suggested calling the new group the Campaign for a Sane Nuclear Policy. Priestley favored the League Against Atomic Warfare, and Kingsley Martin proposed the Council for Nuclear Disarmament. The name, like the new movement, was an amalgam. Minutes of the CND Executive Committee meeting of Feb. 15, 1958, Reel 1, CND (Britain) Records, London-Warwick; Driver, *Disarmers*, p. 44; R. Clark, *Life of Bertrand Russell*, p. 558.

25. Duff to Russell, Dec. 4, 19, 30, 1957, Class 630, RA 1; Driver, *Disarmers*, pp. 51–52; Collins, *Faith Under Fire*, pp. 296, 307–8.

26. The police set their dogs on the relatively respectable crowd, and one member of the House of Lords was rather badly mauled—an embarrassment that led to ending the practice of unleashing police dogs upon political demonstrations. Despite the extraordinary nature of the public meeting, the press largely ignored it, covering, instead, the disturbance at 10 Downing Street. A. Taylor, *A Personal History*, p. 228; Collins, *Faith Under Fire*, pp. 308–9; R. Taylor, *Against the Bomb*, pp. 27–28.

27. Duff to Russell, Feb. 20, 1958, and Russell to Duff, Feb. 24, 1958, Class 630, RA 1.

28. Duff, *Left, Left, Left*, pp. 122–24; R. Taylor, *Against the Bomb*, pp. 24–28; Russell to Rabinowitch, Mar. 14, 1958, Class 625, RA 1; Bertrand Russell, "Only World Government Can Prevent the War Nobody Can Win," *BAS* 14 (Sept. 1958): 259–61.

29. "There can be no harm in trying morality for a change," Taylor argued, pointing to the fact that after Britain renounced the slave trade in 1806, other countries followed its example. Executive Committee Report with Amendments, CND National Conference, Mar. 7–8, 1959, pp. 3–5, Reel 4, and Minutes of CND Executive Committee meetings of Feb. 27,

Apr. 14, June 29, July 24, Nov. 17, and Dec. 15, 1958, Reel 1, CND (Britain) Records, London-Warwick; personal interview with Joseph Rotblat, July 12, 1990; R. Taylor, "Labour Party," pp. 100–101; A. Taylor, *A Personal History*, pp. 225–29; Sisman, *A. J. P. Taylor*, pp. 276–77.

30. April Carter to the author, Mar. 7, 1994; Collins, *Faith Under Fire*, p. 297; Duff, *Left, Left, Left*, p. 115; Randle, "Non-Violent Direct Action," p. 134; "Walk for Peace," *Fellowship* 25 (Jan. 1, 1959): 22; oral history interview with Pat Arrowsmith, Reel 3.

31. Driver, *Disarmers*, pp. 54–55; M. Jones, "Aldermaston 1958"; Pat Arrowsmith to Rustin, Apr. 2, 1958, Rustin Papers; Carter, *Peace Movements*, p. 48; Randle, "Pacifism, War Resistance," p. 30; Minutes of CND Executive Committee meeting of Apr. 14, 1958, Reel 1, CND (Britain) Records, London-Warwick.

32. Collins, *Faith Under Fire*, pp. 325–27; Minutes of CND Executive Committee meetings of June 1, 1958 and Oct. 25, 1959, Reel 1, CND (Britain) Records, London-Warwick; R. Taylor, *Against the Bomb*, p. 23.

33. At the North Pickenham construction site, some workers physically assaulted DAC activists; others, however, defended them. "Brief History of the Direct Action Committee Against Nuclear War" (June 22, 1961), p. 1, Direct Action Committee Against Nuclear War Records; Carter to Arlo Tatum, May 8, 1958, Folder 273, WRI Records, Amsterdam; Randle, Carter, and Arrowsmith to Linus Pauling, Nov. 14, 1958, Pauling Papers; oral history interview with Pat Arrowsmith, Reels 3 and 4; *PN*, Oct. 3, Dec. 12, 1958.

34. A statement that year by pacifist groups and others in Britain's traditional peace movement declared that "it is war itself rather than any particular weapon . . . which is the evil confronting mankind." Nevertheless, condemning nuclear weapons as "instruments of mass murder" and "of mass suicide," it urged the British government to renounce them. Collins, *Faith Under Fire*, pp. 267–68; *PN*, Feb. 28, Mar. 7, July 18, 1958; Minutes of the Annual General Meeting, Peace Pledge Union, Apr. 19–20, 1958, Box 4, Peace Pledge Union Records; Morrison to Brittain, Apr. 11, 1958, Hugh Brock to Brittain, Apr. 14, 1958, "Peace News 1958" Folder, and Morrison to Brittain, Apr. 21, June 3, 1958, "Morrison, Sybil" Folder, Brittain Papers; Brittain, *Rebel Passion*, p. 69; R. Taylor and C. Pritchard, *Protest Makers*, pp. 23–24; "Weapons of Mass Destruction" (1958), Box 4, National Peace Council Records.

35. An informal survey of Aldermaston marchers during the 1959 march found that more than 40 percent were under twenty-one. R. Taylor, *Against the Bomb*, p. 32; R. Taylor and C. Pritchard, *Protest Makers*, p. 23; Minnion and Bolsover, eds., *CND Story*, p. 27.

36. Personal interviews with E. P. Thompson and Dorothy Thompson, Nov. 1, 1989; R. Taylor, *Against the Bomb*, pp. 331–35.

37. At the Lambeth conference of 1958, the Anglican bishops retreated from their earlier critique of nuclear war. Asked about the prospect that "the whole of humanity" would be destroyed in a nuclear conflagration, the archbishop of Canterbury replied serenely: "But they've all got to die sometime, and it shouldn't be all that dreadful if they all died at the same moment." R. Taylor, *Against the Bomb*, pp. 39–40; *PN*, Sept. 5, 1958; Ormrod, "Churches," p. 199; Norman, "Churches," p. 270.

38. R. Taylor, *Against the Bomb*, pp. 37–41; Parkin, *Middle Class Radicalism*, p. 63; "Proceedings of the London Yearly Meeting, 1958," pp. 12, 33, London Yearly Meeting Records.

39. One study of CND supporters found that in the 1959 general election, 54 percent voted Labour, 2 percent Conservative, 2 percent Liberal, 1 percent Communist, and 1 percent other parties. Some 40 percent were not eligible to vote or chose not to do so. Coburn Kidd to DOS, Mar. 3, 1958, 741.00/3-358, DOS Records; R. Taylor, *Against the Bomb*, pp. 283–86; R. Taylor and C. Pritchard, *Protest Makers*, pp. 24–25.

40. Between November 1957 and November 1958, the percentage of Britons believing nuclear testing harmful to future generations rose from 43 to 54 percent. Gallup, ed., *Gallup International Public Opinion Polls: Great Britain*, pp. 450, 453–54, 463, 482, 484; "West European Attitude Trends and Defense Morale in the Wake of the Lebanese and Quemoy Crises" (Jan. 1959), pp. 12–13, Box 5, POBR, OR, USIA Records; Erskine, "The Polls: Atomic Weapons," p. 164.

41. Gallup, ed., *Gallup International Public Opinion Polls: Great Britain*, pp. 450, 460–61, 476.

42. Pickett to Linus Pauling, Mar. 27, 1958, and Russell Johnson to Pauling, Dec. 30, 1957, Pauling Papers; Hiebert, *Impact of Atomic Energy*, pp. 271–74; "Opposition to H-Bomb Continues to Grow," *Fellowship* 23 (July 1957): 27; "Members Bring 10,000 Signatures in Appeal to the President" (July 25, 1957), Box 32, WILPF (United States) Records.

43. John Swomley, "Nuclear Weapons Tests" (July 1957), and Charles Walker to Key People, Feb. 7, 1958, Box 24a, and Minutes of the meeting of the FOR Executive Committee, Nov. 18, 1957, Box 4, FOR (United States) Records; "FOR Joins in H-Bomb Vigil," *Fellowship* 23 (Nov. 1957): 26.

44. Paul Doty to Clinton Anderson, June 14, 1957, Box 126, Anderson Papers; "Nuclear Test Ban, U.N. Control of Space Research, and U.N. Police Force—First Steps Toward Peace," *BAS* 14 (Mar. 1958): 125.

45. Szilard, "Draft of a Letter to the *Bulletin of the Atomic Scientists* (August 15, 1957)," in Hawkins, Greb, and Szilard, eds., *Toward a Livable World*, p. 161; Muller to Szilard, Sept. 9, 1957, Box 13, Szilard Papers.

46. Weart, *Nuclear Fear*, pp. 203–4; Alice Kimball Smith, "The Recognition of Responsibility," *Our Generation Against Nuclear War* 1 (Autumn 1961): 46; "Opposition to H-Bomb," p. 26.

47. Lawrence Scott, "Memo One—Shared Thinking" (Apr. 30, 1957), and Lawrence Scott to those interested in the formation of a Committee to Stop H-Bomb Tests, May 13, 1957, Box 4, Series B, and "A Short History of SANE" (1960), Box 1, Series A, SANE Records; "Seven Years for a Sane Nuclear Policy," *Sane World*, Apr. 15, 1964, p. 1.

48. Clarence Pickett and Norman Cousins to Dear Sir, July 3, 1957, Thomas to Steering Committee, June 24, 1957, and Jack to Steering Committee, n.d., Reel 61, Thomas Papers; "A Short History of SANE" (1960), Box 1, Series A, SANE Records; Jack, *Nuclear Politics*, pp. 30–31. For an early instance of a nuclear critic appealing for sanity, see the 1946 classic: Swing, *In the Name of Sanity*.

49. In addition to Cousins, Fromm, Jack, Pickett, and Thomas, they included Roger Baldwin (founder of the American Civil Liberties Union), John C. Bennett (dean, Union Theological Seminary), Harrison Brown (atomic scientist), Paul Doty (chair, Federation of American Scientists), Harry Emerson Fosdick (minister), Clark Eichelberger (director, American Association for the United Nations), Robert Gilmore (executive secretary, AFSC, New York), Oscar Hammerstein II (playwright), Donald Harrington (minister), John Hersey (novelist), Lenore Marshall (poet), Lewis Mumford (writer), Robert Nathan (chair, Americans for Democratic Action), James G. Patton (president, National Farmers Union), Eleanor Roosevelt (political commentator), Elmo Roper (pollster), James T. Shotwell (president emeritus, Carnegie Endowment for International Peace), and Paul Tillich (theologian). "Seven Years for a Sane Nuclear Policy," p. 1; *NYT*, Nov. 15, 1957.

50. *NYT*, Nov. 15, 1957.

51. "Seven Years for a Sane Nuclear Policy," p. 1; Arno G. Huth, "Response to the First Statement issued by the National Committee for a Sane Nuclear Policy, November 15 to December 31, 1957" (Jan. 1958), and Robert Gilmore to Cousins, Feb. 20, 1958, Box 4, Series B, SANE Records; Thomas to Cousins, June 19, 1958, Reel 61, Thomas Papers.

52. Gottlieb, "National Committee for a SANE Nuclear Policy," pp. 155–56; Donald Keys to J. David Bowen, Aug. 29, 1958, Box 7, Series B, SANE Records.

53. Cousins, *Improbable Triumvirate*, p. 132; Chatfield, *American Peace Movement*, p. 105; Katz, *Ban the Bomb*, p. 31; Cousins to Schweitzer, May 9, 1958, in Cousins, *Albert Schweitzer's Mission*, pp. 212–13; *Congressional Record*, 85th Cong., 2d Sess., June 4, 1958, vol. 104, p. 10,097.

54. "Seven Years for a Sane Nuclear Policy," p. 1; Pickett to Helen Beardsley, Nov. 7, 1957, Box 7, Series B, SANE Records.

55. See, for example, Wittner, *One World or None*, pp. 50, 56, 66–72, 77, 308, 317.

56. Thomas to Dulles, Apr. 1, July 1, 1953, Box 67, J. F. Dulles Papers, Princeton; Cousins to Schweitzer, Dec. 30, 1957, in Cousins, *Albert Schweitzer's Mission*, p. 204; Cousins to Peter Charlton, June 18, 1958, Box 2, Series B, SANE Records. See also Thomas to Cousins, Sept. 25, 1958, Reel 61, Thomas Papers; Cousins to Robert Jungk, July 17, 1958, Box 2, and Erich Fromm, "Memorandum" (n.d.), Box 4, Series B, SANE Records.

57. For an alternative view—that SANE and other critics of the arms race were irrationally obsessed with nuclear testing—see Divine, *Blowing on the Wind*, p. 323; Weart, *Nuclear Fear*, pp. 212–13.

58. Lawrence Scott, "Memo One—Shared Thinking" (Apr. 30, 1957), Box 4, Series B, SANE Records; War Resisters League, *A WRL History of Protest*, n.p.; Bigelow, *Voyage*, p. 24; *NYT*, Aug. 7, 1957; Robinson, *Abraham Went Out*, pp. 163–64.

59. *NYT*, Aug. 7, 1957; Bigelow, *Voyage*, pp. 42–46; George Willoughby et al. to Dwight Eisenhower, Jan. 8, 1958, and "Summary Information on a Voyage to Eniwetok" (1958), AEC Records.

60. Bigelow, *Voyage*, pp. 115–248; *NYT*, Oct. 8, 1993; *PN*, May 16, June 20, July 11, 1958; Reynolds, *Forbidden Voyage*; Cousins, "Earle Reynolds and His Phoenix."

61. Bigelow, *Voyage*, p. 159; Reynolds, *Forbidden Voyage*, pp. 180, 281.

62. Norman Cousins to Robert Pickus, Jan. 28, 1958, and SANE to the President et al., Box 4, and Donald Keys to Barbara Reynolds, July 1959, Box 29, Series B, SANE Records.

63. Lawrence Scott to Cousins, Feb. 28, 1958, Box 4, Series B, SANE Records; Cousins, "Men of the Golden Rule"; Cousins, "Earle Reynolds and His Phoenix."

64. War Resisters League, *A WRL History of Protest*, n.p.; A. J. Muste to Stuart Morris, Jan. 17, 1958, Folder 403, WRI Records, Amsterdam; "An Appeal to the Soviet Peoples and Government" (May 1958), Box 15, Muste Papers.

65. "Six Reasons Why We Ask You to Stop Work on Missile Site Construction" (Aug. 1958), "Non-violent Action against the Cheyenne, Wyoming Missile Base, Report #2" (Aug. 1958), "Statement by Kenneth and Ellanor Calkins" (Aug. 1958), and "Cheyenne Anti-Missile Base Non-Violent Action Project" (Aug. 1958), Box 2, Muste Papers.

66. Lawrence Scott to George Willoughby et al., Aug. 28, 1958, and Bradford Lyttle to Lyle Tatum, Oct. 17, 1958, Box 2, Muste Papers; Robinson, *Abraham Went Out*, p. 164.

67. According to Muste's son, after his retirement as executive secretary of the FOR and his wife's death in 1954, Muste "became much more of an activist and began . . . engaging more frequently in civil disobedience." "Westtown Consultation on Direct Action" (Sept. 17–18, 1958) and Willoughby to Muste, Oct. 1, 1959, Box 15, Muste Papers; Robinson, *Abraham Went Out*, pp. 164–65; John M. Muste to the author, June 9, 1992.

68. Arno G. Huth, "Response to the First Statement issued by the National Committee for a Sane Nuclear Policy, November 15 to December 31, 1957" (Jan. 1958), Box 4, Series B, SANE Records; *NYT*, Apr. 9, May 26, 1958; Bigelow, *Voyage*, p. 163; *Denver Post*, Aug. 29, 1958, clipping in Box 2, Muste Papers; "How Sane the SANE?"

69. At the time, it had more than a thousand such letters requiring response. That same year, the chair of the Congressional Joint Committee on Atomic Energy also received a large

quantity of mail calling for an end to nuclear weapons tests. Morse Salisbury to James Hagerty, June 21, 1957, OF 108-A, WHCF, Eisenhower Records; "Political—Debate over H-Bomb Tests" Folder, Box 126, Anderson Papers.

70. Divine, *Blowing on the Wind*, pp. 161–62; Weart, *Nuclear Fear*, pp. 217–18; Winkler, *Life Under a Cloud*, p. 101; Hiebert, *Impact of Atomic Energy*, pp. 256–57, 264–65, 268–69.

71. Stevenson had been in communication with Cousins about this trip since early March; therefore, he may have known even during its planning stage that Schweitzer was preparing to condemn nuclear testing. Stevenson, "Why I Raised the H-Bomb Question; Davis, *Politics of Honor*, pp. 389–91; Stevenson to Cousins, Mar. 5, 1957, in W. Johnson, ed., *Papers*, 6: 488.

72. Hewlett and Holl, *Atoms*, p. 391; Weart, *Nuclear Fear*, p. 212; Morse to Gertrude Faust, Mar. 13, 1958, Box 20, Committee for Environmental Information Records; *NYT*, May 18, 1958.

73. From April 1954 to May 1958, support for a unilateral halt to U.S. nuclear testing rose from 20 to 29 percent; meanwhile, opposition fell from 71 to 60 percent. Hazel Gaudet Erskine, "The Polls: Defense, Peace, and Space," *Public Opinion Quarterly* 25 (Fall 1961): 480.

74. Ibid.; Gallup, ed., *Gallup Poll*, pp. 1487–88, 1541. Slightly different figures are provided in Eugene J. Rosi, "Mass and Attentive Opinion on Nuclear Weapons Tests and Fallout, 1954–1963," *Public Opinion Quarterly* 29 (Summer 1965): 283.

75. The historian Robert Divine has argued that "Sputnik ended the first phase of the quest for a test ban. As the American people and their leaders agreed on the need to regain the strategic lead from the Russians, they were deaf to pleas for a halt to testing." But his evidence is not convincing. For example, he compares a poll showing majority support for *multilateral* action to halt nuclear testing in 1957 to one showing majority opposition to *unilateral* action in 1958. In fact, throughout 1957 and 1958, most Americans supported a multilateral test ban. Divine, *Blowing on the Wind*, pp. 173, 205.

76. Rosi, "Mass and Attentive Opinion," p. 287; Gallup, ed., *Gallup Poll*, pp. 1488, 1553. Both Divine and historian Allan Winkler depict "fear of fallout" as the major factor motivating critics of the Bomb. Divine, *Blowing on the Wind*, p. 139; Winkler, *Life Under a Cloud*, pp. 84–108.

77. Evan, "An International Public Opinion Poll," pp. 234–46.

78. "Is There a Pacifist Revival?" *Liberation* 3 (May 1958): 3; "The Only Realism" (1958), Box 28a, FOR (United States) Records.

79. This was a key point made by the Peace Pledge Union's Sybil Morrison in her critique of pacifist support for CND. Morrison to Vera Brittain, Apr. 11, 1958, "Peace News 1958" Folder, and Apr. 21, 1958, "Morrison, Sybil" Folder, Brittain Papers.

80. See, for example, Grenville Clark and Louis Sohn's landmark study, *World Peace Through World Law*, published in 1958. It urged the strengthening of the United Nations to the degree necessary to maintain world order and included a comprehensive plan for disarmament.

81. By June 1958, the UWF's membership stood at 12,866, down from 13,208 in September 1957. The PPU's membership in early 1958 was little more than 7,000. Minutes of the National Executive Committee meeting, United World Federalists, June 16, 1958, Box 55, Cousins Papers, Los Angeles; Minutes of the Annual General Meeting, Peace Pledge Union, Apr. 19–20, 1958, Box 4, Peace Pledge Union Records.

82. See, for example, Russell, "Only World Government"; Cousins to Kiyoichi Tsuchioka, Sept. 24, 1958, Box 180, Cousins Papers, Los Angeles. Aside from Cousins (honorary president of UWF), Oscar Hammerstein II (vice president of UWF) and Walter Reuther (vice president of UWF) were also SANE luminaries.

83. The DAC's Pat Arrowsmith had previously been active in the Crusade for World Government. Patrick Armstrong to Russell, May 29, 1957, Class 570, RA 1; Harrington to Cousins, Aug. 12, 1958, Box 189, Cousins Papers, Los Angeles; oral history interview with Pat Arrowsmith, Reel 3.

Chapter 4

Epigraph: Anti-Atoombom-Actie, "Oproep" (1957), Portfeuille No. 18, Publications Pacifistes et Internationales.

1. Cioc, *Pax Atomica*, pp. 35, 42–43, 75; Mushaben, "Cycles," p. 27; Edward Page Jr. to DOS, Nov. 22, 1957, 762A.00/11-2257, DOS Records.

2. C. F. von Weizsäcker, "Should Germany Have Atomic Arms?" *BAS* 13 (Oct. 1957): 283–85; Heisenberg, *Inner Exile*, pp. 141–42; "Declaration of the German Nuclear Physicists," *BAS* 13 (June 1957): 228; Cioc, *Pax Atomica*, pp. 43, 75–76.

3. Cioc, *Pax Atomica*, pp. 44, 78–80; Rupp, *Ausserparlamentarische Opposition*, pp. 82–88; Kitzinger, *German Electoral Politics*, p. 88; von Weizsäcker, "Should Germany Have Atomic Arms?" pp. 285–86; Hahn, *My Life*, pp. 224–26.

4. Von Weizsäcker wrote privately, soon thereafter, that preventing Germany from making its own nuclear weapons "was the most important political aim" of the Göttingen declaration. "Now nobody here is very likely to start his own production." Hahn, *My Life*, p. 226; von Weizsäcker, *Politics of Peril*, p. 203; von Weizsäcker to Leo Szilard, Sept. 16, 1957, Box 20, Szilard Papers.

5. Kelleher, *Germany*, p. 112; *NYT*, May 19, 1957; Cioc, *Pax Atomica*, pp. 41–42; Noelle and Neumann, eds., *Germans*, p. 441; "Some Current West German Public Opinion Trends on Atomic Issues" (May 17, 1957), pp. 1–2, Box 5, POBR, OR, USIA Records.

6. In fact, the administration's decision to "go nuclear" had been made in October 1956 and the formal program, MC-70, had been adopted in April 1957. Kitzinger, *German Electoral Politics*, p. 89; Cioc, *Pax Atomica*, pp. 44–45; Boutwell, *German Nuclear Dilemma*, p. 20.

7. Kitzinger, *German Electoral Politics*, pp. 89–90, 140–42, 346–47; Trimble to Sec-State, Aug. 19, 1957, 762A.00/8-1957, and Edward Page Jr. to SecState, Sept. 5, 1957, 762A.00/9-557, DOS Records; Dülffer, "Movement," p. 426.

8. On the other hand, the Free Democratic vote dropped from 9.5 to 7.7 percent. Bruce to SecState, June 28, 1957, 762A.00/6-2857, Elim O'Shaughnessy to DOS, July 5, 1957, 762A.00/7-557, Bruce to SecState, Sept. 16, 1957, 762A.00/9-1657, and Bruce to SecState, Sept. 26, 1957, 762A.00/9-2657, DOS Records; Cioc, *Pax Atomica*, pp. 45–46.

9. Opposition stood at 64 percent. That same month, another West German poll found that 70 percent of respondents opposed nuclear missile sites in the Federal Republic. Noelle and Neumann, eds., *Germans*, p. 441; Lynch to SecState, Dec. 19, 1957, 762A.00/12-1957, DOS Records.

10. Trimble to SecState, Nov. 6, 1957, 762A.00/11-657, Harry Schwartz to DOS, Dec. 20, 1957, 762A.00/12-2057, and Bruce to SecState, Mar. 26, 1958, 762A.00/3-2658, and Apr. 12, 1958, 762A.00/4-1258, DOS Records; Boutwell, *German Nuclear Dilemma*, pp. 21–23; Kelleher, *Germany*, p. 113.

11. Rupp, *Ausserparlamentarische Opposition*, pp. 130–43, 162–91, 289–96; Maney to SecState, Mar. 31, 1958, 762A.00/3-3158, Sandalls to SecState, Apr. 17, 1958, 762A.00/4-1758, Page to SecState, Apr. 23, 1958, 762A.00/4-2358, and Warren Blumberg to DOS, June 11, 1958, 762A.00/6-1158, DOS Records; *PN*, May 2, 1958; Cioc, *Pax Atomica*, pp. 119–22, 126; Theodor Michaltscheff, "The Struggle for Peace in the German Federal Republic," *War Resistance* 2.12 (1965): 14–15.

12. Noelle and Neumann, eds., *Germans*, p. 354; Cioc, *Pax Atomica*, pp. 126–28; Otto, "Kampagne 'Kampf dem Atomtod,'" p. 215; Rupp, *Ausserparlamentarische Opposition*, pp. 162–72, 191–92; Maney to SecState, Mar. 29, 1958, 762A.00/3-2958, and Gufler to SecState, May 3, 1958, 762A.00/5-358, DOS Records.

13. Cioc, *Pax Atomica*, pp. 118–20; Rupp, *Ausserparlamentarische Opposition*, pp. 130–35, 173–80; Carter, *Peace Movements*, p. 59; Dülffer, "Movement," pp. 427–28, 431–32. For the role of pacifists, see Heinz Kloppenburg, "IFOR German Branch: Report for 1958," Box 14, Series B, Sayre Papers; Hans Konrad Tempel, "Atomic Disarmament in the Federal Republic of Germany" (1962), pp. 1–2, Folder 249, WRI Records, Amsterdam; *PN*, May 2, 1958.

14. Noelle and Neumann, eds., *Germans*, p. 441; Gufler to Sec State, May 6, 1958, 762A.00/5-658, and Lewis to DOS, May 19, 1958, 762A.5611/5-1958, DOS Records; Kelleher, *Germany*, p. 113; Rupp, *Ausserparlamentarische Opposition*, pp. 194–202.

15. Gufler to SecState, Apr. 1, 1958, 762A.00/4-158, Trimble to SecState, May 9, 1958, 762A.00/5-958, William R. Taylor to DOS, June 4, 1958, 762A.00/6-458, and Raymond P. Ludden to DOS, June 6, 1958, 762A.00/6-658, DOS Records.

16. Cioc, *Pax Atomica*, pp. 95–111, 115; Scharrer, "War and Peace," pp. 275–76; Hiebert, *Impact of Atomic Energy*, pp. 253–56; Warren Blumberg to DOS, June 11, 1958, 762A.00/6-1158, DOS Records.

17. Cioc, *Pax Atomica*, pp. 118, 122–25; Hiebert, *Impact of Atomic Energy*, p. 222; *PN*, Oct. 24, 1958; Born to Bertrand Russell, Mar. 18, Apr. 15, 1958, Class 710, RA 1.

18. Deutsch and Edinger, *Germany*, p. 208; Boutwell, *German Nuclear Dilemma*, pp. 27, 29; Scharrer, "War and Peace," pp. 283–84; Blancke to SecState, Mar. 24, 1958, 762A.00/3-2458, and Bruce to SecState, July 8, 1958, 762A.00/7-858, DOS Records; Rupp, *Ausserparlamentarische Opposition*, pp. 224–25.

19. The SPD vote increased from 34.5 percent, in 1954, to 39.5 percent. The Free Democrats, however, lost ground. Cioc, *Pax Atomica*, pp. 126, 129–33; Edward S. Maney to DOS, May 28, 1958, 762A.00/5-2858, and Bruce to SecState, July 8, 1958, 762A.00/7-858, and July 9, 1958, 762A.00/7-958, DOS Records.

20. Blancke to SecState, Nov. 24, 1958, 762A.00/11-2458, and Gufler to SecState, Dec. 8, 1958, 762A.00/12-858, DOS Records; Kelleher, *Germany*, pp. 56–57.

21. Cioc, *Pax Atomica*, pp. 138–39; Warren Blumberg to DOS, Nov. 21, 1958, 762A.00/11-2158, DOS Records; Boutwell, "Politics," p. 75; Ansgar Skriver to Bertrand Russell, Oct. 18, 1958, Class 320, RA 2; Skriver to Russell, Nov. 14, 1958, Class 640, RA 1; *PN*, Mar. 6, 1959.

22. Michaltscheff, "Struggle for Peace," pp. 13–19; Kelleher, *Germany*, p. 114; "The Work of Action Reconciliation / Peace through Reconciliation" (1988), pp. 1–3, Aktion Sühnezeichen / Friedensdienste Records.

23. Gallup, ed., *Gallup Poll*, p. 1562; Hazel Gaudet Erskine, "The Polls: Atomic Weapons and Nuclear Energy," *Public Opinion Quarterly* 27 (Summer 1963): 164; "Current Trends in U.S. Versus Soviet Standing in Western Europe" (Feb. 1959), p. 13, Box 5, POBR, OR, USIA Records; *PN*, Nov. 21, 1958.

24. *NYT*, May 19, 1957; *New York Herald Tribune*, Nov. 17, 1957; Gallup, ed., *Gallup Poll*, p. 1555.

25. Birnbaum, "Swedish Experience," pp. 70–71; Reiss, *Without the Bomb*, pp. 50–51; Fehrm, "Sweden," p. 215; Ahlmark, *Den svenska atomvapendebatten*, p. 24.

26. Roy Haverkamp to DOS, June 17, 1957, 711.5611/6-1757, and June 18, 1957, 758.5611/6-1857, and William Owen to DOS, Dec. 3, 1958, 758.5611/12-358, DOS Records; Rudling, *Kampen mot Atomvapen*, pp. 29–30, 42.

27. Ståhle, *Internationella Kvinnoförbundet*, pp. 29–30; Rudling, *Kampen mot Atom-*

vapen, pp. 32–33; Larson, "Etiska argument," pp. 156–67; Andersson and Lindkvist, "Peace Movement in Sweden," pp. 11–12.

28. Fogelström, *Kampen för fred*, pp. 255–56; Santi, *100 Years*, p. 43.

29. Fogelström, *Kampen för fred*, pp. 257–61; Lindkvist, "Mobilization Peaks and Declines," p. 158; "The Fellowship in Sweden" (August 1959), Box 42, Series B, Sayre Papers; Rudling, *Kampen mot Atomvapen*, pp. 39, 42; Erlander, *Tage Erlander*, p. 85; Larson, "Etiska argument," p. 167; Fogelström and Morell, *I stället för atombomb*, p. 65.

30. *PN*, May 31, 1957, May 23, 1958; Erskine, "The Polls: Atomic Weapons," p. 187; Peterson to SecState, Nov. 25, 1957, 759.5611/11-2557, DOS Records.

31. Willis to SecState, Apr. 24, 1958, 957.40/4-2458, DOS Records; *PN*, July 12, 1957; "Norway's Political and Economic Situation," *Pax et Libertas* 23 (Oct.–Dec. 1958): 4–5.

32. Erskine, "The Polls: Atomic Weapons," p. 187; Norwegian Gallup Institute survey of Nov. 1957, p. 70, Box 83, CPF, and "World Poll II—Group Breakdowns," Box 3, WPF, OR, USIA Records.

33. *PN*, May 30, 1958; Brassel and Tanner, "Zur Geschichte der Friedensbewegung," pp. 64–65; Adrian B. Colquitt to DOS, June 18, 1958, 754.5611/6-1858, Taylor to SecState, July 14, 1958, 754.5611/7-1458, and Colquitt to DOS, Aug. 6, 1958, 754.5611/8-658, DOS Records.

34. Adrian B. Colquitt to DOS, June 18, 1958, 754.5611/6-1858, DOS Records; Heiniger, "Die schweizerische Antiatombewegung," pp. 53–65, 81–111; Ackermann, "Resistance," pp. 249–50; "Karl Barth Says No to Nuclear Weapons," *Fellowship* 25 (May 1, 1959): 3–4.

35. Heiniger, "Die schweizerische Antiatombewegung," pp. 66–70; Amherd, "Die Friedensbewegung," pp. 107–8; Adrian B. Colquitt to DOS, June 18, 1958, 754.5611/6-1858, Aug. 6, 1958, 754.5611/8-658, and Oct. 8, 1958, 754.5611/10-858, DOS Records; Ackermann, "Resistance," pp. 243–44, 247–49.

36. Ackermann, "Resistance," pp. 250–51; Carter, *Peace Movements*, p. 61.

37. *PN*, Feb. 22, 1957; Saar Boorlage, "The Problem of Nuclear Disarmament in the Netherlands," *Youth Against the Bomb* (June 1960), p. 5, Box 28, and F. Boerwinkel, K. May, and G. A. de Bock, Telegram (1958?), Box 4, Series B, SANE Records; "Kerk en Vrede," *Fellowship* 23 (Nov. 1957): 20–21.

38. Young to SecState, Nov. 21, 1957, 756.5611/11-2157, DOS Records; *PN*, Nov. 22, 1957; Verkuil, *De grote illusie*, pp. 53–55.

39. *PN*, Mar. 6, 1959; Carter, *Peace Movements*, p. 75; Anti-Atoombom-Actie, "Oproep" (1957), Portefeuille No. 18, Publications Pacifistes et Internationales; Everts and Walraven, *Vredesbeweging*, p. 42; Saar Boorlage, "The Problem of Nuclear Disarmament in the Netherlands," *Youth Against the Bomb* (June 1960), p. 5, Box 28, Series B, SANE Records.

40. Erskine, "The Polls: Atomic Weapons," p. 187; *New York Herald Tribune*, Nov. 17, 1957; *PN*, June 28, 1957; Everts and Walraven, *Vredesbeweging*, p. 41; Verkuil, *De grote illusie*, pp. 44–46.

41. Maurice Cosyn to Trevor Thomas, Jan. 22, 1958, Cosyn to Donald Keys, Nov. 29, 1958, "Comme Hiroshima et Nagasaki L'Organisation des Nations Unies est Menacée de Destruction," and R. Verbist and Charles VanHerbruggen to SANE, Nov. 6, 1958, Box 7, Series B, SANE Records; *PN*, Nov. 21, 1958.

42. Another poll found that, in April 1958, residents of Brussels supported the cessation of U.S. nuclear weapons tests by 68 to 30 percent. Erskine, "The Polls: Atomic Weapons," pp. 164, 187; Gallup, ed., *Gallup Poll*, p. 1555.

43. "Ireland and the Hydrogen Bomb," *Pax*, Aug. 1957, pp. 7–8; Connor Farrington,

"The Aldermaston March," *Pax*, Spring 1958, pp. 15–18; "Committee for Nuclear Disarmament," *Pax*, Spring 1958, p. 4; Helen Chenevix, "Irish Campaign for Nuclear Disarmament," *Pax*, Summer–Autumn 1958, pp. 2–3; "Irish Nuclear Disarmament Campaign," *Pax*, Winter–Spring 1958–59, pp. 9–10.

44. Gallup, ed., *Gallup International Public Opinion Polls: France*, pp. 213, 232; Erskine, "The Polls: Atomic Weapons," p. 187; "Current Trends in U.S. Versus Soviet Standing in Western Europe" (Feb. 1959), p. 13, Box 5, POBR, OR, USIA Records.

45. Gallup, ed., *Gallup Poll*, p. 1562.

46. See, for example, Bernard Boudouresques, "Naissance d'une opposition: 1945–1965," *Alternatives Non Violentes*, no. 46 (Dec. 1982): 8–9; Max Isenbergh to DOS, Apr. 24, 1958, 751.5611/4-2458, DOS Records.

47. For the absorption in resistance to the Algerian war of people who would later become leaders of the French antinuclear movement, see "Report from Josephine Noble on FOR General Assembly" (Mar. 7, 1957), Mouvement International de la Réconciliation Records; Brittain, *Rebel Passion*, p. 155; Hill, "André Trocmé," p. 961.

48. Ira Morris to John Collins, Nov. 24, 1958, and Ira Morris, "Formation of a French anti-nuclear warfare organization," Box 10, Series B, SANE Records.

49. Born in Italy, Lanza del Vasto—a poet, musician, and author—had spent a year in India, during which he became a coworker of Gandhi. In response to the Indian leader's suggestion that he start a nonviolence center in Europe, del Vasto founded the Community of the Ark in France just after World War II. It later spread to Spain, Morocco, Latin America, Canada, and other parts of the world. *Liberté*, Apr. 18, 1958, and Jean Lasserre, "Marcoule—Atomic Center—France—11 April 1958" (Apr. 1958), Box 8, Trocmé Papers; *PN*, Apr. 18, 1958; "French Pacifists in Atomic 'Sitdown,'" *Fellowship* 24 (June 1, 1958): 3; "Lanza del Vasto Dies," *Fellowship* 47 (Mar. 1981): 19.

50. *PN*, July 11, 1958; Lanza del Vasto, "French Satyagraha against Atom Plant," *Sarvodaya* 8 (Aug. 1958): 94.

51. Theodore B. Olson to USIA, June 17, 1957, "18.14 Weapons—Test Moratorium, a. General, 1957" Folder, AE Lot File, DOS Records; Gallup, ed., *Gallup Poll*, p. 1555.

52. *New York Herald Tribune*, Nov. 17, 1957; Erskine, "The Polls: Atomic Weapons," p. 187; "Current Trends in U.S. Versus Soviet Standing in Western Europe" (Feb. 1959), p. 13, Box 5, POBR, OR, USIA Records.

53. Erskine, "The Polls: Atomic Weapons," pp. 164, 187; "World Poll II—Group Breakdowns," Box 3, WPF, OR, USIA Records.

54. "Public Opinion in Spain—A Survey of Madrid and Cadiz: II. Attitudes Toward American Troops and Bases" (Mar. 1958), p. 6, and "Public Opinion in Spain—A Survey of Madrid and Cadiz: I. Comparative Standing of the U.S. versus the U.S.S.R." (Mar. 1958), p. 7, Box 5, POBR, OR, USIA Records.

55. *PN*, Mar. 1, 1957; Summy and Saunders, "Disarmament," pp. 28–29; Tame and Robotham, *Maralinga*, p. 104; Erskine, "The Polls: Atomic Weapons," p. 187.

56. Summy and Saunders, "Disarmament," p. 29; Rotblat, *Pugwash*, p. 85; Cockburn and Ellyard, *Oliphant*, pp. 225–28.

57. Redner and Redner, *Anatomy of the World*, pp. 271–72; Saunders and Summy, *Australian Peace Movement*, p. 33; Frank A. Waring to DOS, July 11, 1958, 711.5611/7-1158, DOS Records.

58. In this poll, conducted in major cities of non-Communist nations, 37 percent of Melbourne respondents indicated their belief that the United States should stop its nuclear testing; 56 percent disagreed. Gallup, ed., *Gallup Poll*, p. 1555.

59. *New York Herald Tribune*, Nov. 17, 1957; Erskine, "The Polls: Atomic Weapons," p. 164.

60. Lincoln Efford, "Notes on Some Activities of the Peace Union and No More War Movement in New Zealand" (Mar. 1957), Folder 355, WRI Records, Amsterdam.

61. Jean Sammons to Evelyn Peat, Oct. 29, 1958, Reel 80, WILPF (International) Records; *PN*, June 14, 1957; Lincoln Efford to Arlo Tatum, June 3, 1957, Folder 355, WRI Records, Amsterdam; Locke, *Peace People*, pp. 160–62; Clements, *Back from the Brink*, p. 41.

62. Mary Woodward, untitled statement (1963), Box 14, Canadian CND Records; "Notes on the history of the NZ Campaign for Nuclear Disarmament," Locke Papers; Jean Sammons to Evelyn Peat, Oct. 29, 1958, Reel 80, WILPF (International) Records; Leon Crutcher to DOS, Sept. 17, 1959, 744.5611/9-1759, and S. D. Berger to DOS, Mar. 5, 1958, 711.5611/3-558, DOS Records; Locke, *Peace People*, p. 162; Blamires, *War Tests the Church*, p. 75.

63. Isabel Showler to James Finlay, July 29, 1957, Box 1, FOR (Canada) Records, Toronto; Peggy Duff to Bertrand Russell, Feb. 25, 1958, Class 630, RA 1.

64. Mildred Fahrni and Edna Barnett, "Canadian F.O.R. Report" (1958), Box 1, FOR (Canada) Records, Toronto; *PN*, Aug. 15, Oct. 17, 1958.

65. *PN*, Feb. 15, 1957; Brittain, *Rebel Passion*, pp. 102–3; Nevin and Kathleen Sayre, "South American Journey 1958" (1958), Box 1, International FOR Records.

66. Erskine, "The Polls: Atomic Weapons," pp. 164, 185, 187; *New York Herald Tribune*, Nov. 17, 1957; "World Poll II—Group Breakdowns" (1957), Box 3, WPF, OR, USIA Records; Gallup, ed., *Gallup Poll*, p. 1555.

67. *NYT*, May 19, 1957, Feb. 3, 1958; *PN*, May 24, 1957. See also S. Narayanaswamy to Donald Keys, Nov. 7, 1958, Box 11, Series B, SANE Records; Free, *Six Allies*, p. 17.

68. Gallup, ed., *Gallup Poll*, pp. 1555, 1562.

69. Donald Dumont to DOS, Aug. 8, 1958, 751.5611/8-858, DOS Records.

70. Eugene Rabinowitch, "After Pugwash: The Soviet Reaction," *BAS* 13 (Nov. 1957): 314–15; Z. Medvedev, *Soviet Science*, p. 63; personal interview with Sergei Kapitza, June 28, 1990; Evangelista, "Soviet Scientists and Nuclear Testing," p. 18; Eugene Rabinowitch, "A. V. Topchiev, 1907–1962," *BAS* 19 (Mar. 1963): 8–9.

71. Sakharov's article was published in 1958 and reprinted in a Russian-language anthology of Soviet writings on the subject in 1959. The first English-language version appeared in 1960. A. V. Topchiev to Leo Szilard, Dec. 14, 1957, Box 19, Szilard Papers; Sakharov, *Memoirs*, pp. 200–204; Evangelista, "Soviet Scientists and Nuclear Testing," p. 17; Sakharov, "Radioactive Carbon."

72. This statement was also signed by M. O. Auezov, a well-known Kazakh writer. Takibayev, "Ahead of Time," pp. 633–34.

73. Sakharov, *Memoirs*, pp. 207–9; Sakharov, *Sakharov Speaks*, pp. 10, 32; *NYT*, Sept. 10, 1973, Dec. 16, 1989.

74. N. Khrushchev, *Khrushchev Remembers: The Last Testament*, pp. 69–70.

75. Sagdeev, *Making of a Soviet Scientist*, p. 66. For Kurchatov's concern at that time, see Chapter 1.

76. For the theory that Sakharov's position was influenced by a disastrous explosion, in 1957, at a Soviet nuclear waste dump, see Z. Medvedev, *Soviet Science*, pp. 93–97; Klose, *Russia and the Russians*, pp. 147–51. Sakharov, however, does not mention this incident in his writings.

77. Sakharov, *Sakharov Speaks*, p. 32; Sakharov, *Memoirs*, p. 201; Sakharov, *My Country and the World*, p. 4.

78. Recalling Sakharov's insistence upon the dangers of nuclear testing, Teller wrote in exasperation: "How could a scientist of Sakharov's ability confuse popular exaggeration with fact? How did he come to place so much emphasis on statements made by Schweitzer and Pauling?" Teller, "Two Stories," pp. 114–15.

Chapter 5

Epigraph: Gufler to SecState, Apr. 14, 1958, 762A.00/4-1458, DOS Records.

1. John Swomley, "Nuclear Weapons Tests" (July 1957), Box 24a, FOR (United States) Records; Santi, *100 Years*, p. 42; "Bulletin of Information No. 18: Report on the 1958 Conference" (Feb. 1959), Box 12, International Peace Bureau Records, SCPC.

2. Trevor Thomas to Peggy Duff, Dec. 30, 1957, Box 8, Collins to Cousins, June 9, 1958, Box 4, Cousins to Ira Morris, Dec. 18, 1958, Box 10, and Collins to Donald Keys, Nov. 19, 1958, Box 8, Series B, SANE Records; Cousins to Russell, June 13, 1958, Class 410, RA 1; Collins, *Faith Under Fire*, pp. 310–11.

3. Oral history interview with Pat Arrowsmith, Reel 4; Lawrence Scott to Vera Brittain et al., Jan. 2, 1958, and Hugh Brock to Scott, Feb. 28, Mar. 13, 1958, Folder 404, WRI Records, Amsterdam; *Pax*, Spring 1958, p. 11; Carter, *Peace Movements*, p. 40.

4. Hiebert, *Impact of Atomic Energy*, p. 219; *NYT*, Apr. 5, Aug. 1, 1958; Divine, *Blowing on the Wind*, p. 203.

5. Adrian B. Colquitt to DOS, Aug. 6, 1958, 754.5611/8-658, DOS Records; Peggy Duff to Russell, May 28, 1958, Class 630, RA 1; Minutes of CND Executive Committee Meeting of June 1, 1958, Reel 1, CND (Britain) Records, London-Warwick; *PN*, July 4, Aug. 8, 15, 1958.

6. Collins, *Faith Under Fire*, pp. 310–11; Hans Werner Richter to André Trocmé, Nov. 19, 1958, Box 8, Trocmé Papers; Christian Mayer to Donald Keys, Nov. 26, 1958, Box 10, Series B, SANE Records.

7. Joliot-Curie, "The World-wide Movement," p. 38; Jean Laffitte to Paul Robeson, Mar. 18, 1955, Box 12, Robeson Papers; Biquard, *Frédéric Joliot-Curie*, pp. 108–9.

8. Bloomfield, Clemens, and Griffiths, *Khrushchev*, pp. 31–32; Committee for the Compilation of Materials, *Hiroshima and Nagasaki*, p. 577; Rotblat, "Movements of Scientists," p. 129.

9. Joliot-Curie to Linus Pauling, June 20, 1957, Pauling Papers; Weart, *Scientists in Power*, p. 270.

10. *PN*, Apr. 26, Aug. 23, 1957; Rotblat, "Movements of Scientists," p. 130; Biquard, *Frédéric Joliot-Curie*, pp. 120–21; Bernal, *World Without War*, p. 222.

11. "Stop the Tests, Outlaw the H-Bomb" (Apr. 4, 1954), Canadian Peace Congress Records, SCPC; "The Canadian Peace Congress, 1948 to 1978," Canadian Peace Congress Records, Toronto.

12. Peristerakis, "To Elliniko Kinima Eirinis," pp. 90–91; Andreas Zakkas to Linus Pauling, June 21, 1957, Pauling Papers; Greek Committee for International Detente and Peace, *32 Years of Struggle*, p. 2. For similar activities in the Netherlands, see Everts and Walraven, *Vredesbeweging*, p. 41.

13. Theodor Michaltscheff, "The Struggle for Peace in the German Federal Republic," *War Resistance* 2.12 (1965): 16; Abbot to SecState, Apr. 7, 1954, 711.5611/4-754, DOS Records; Overstreet and Windmiller, *Communism in India*, pp. 425–27.

14. Communist motives for launching and sustaining the WPC are discussed at greater length in Shulman, *Stalin's Foreign Policy Reappraised*; Wittner, *One World or None*, pp. 177–86. The Soviet government's increasing interest in a nuclear arms control agreement is taken up in Chapter 8.

15. Klein, "Impact of Peace Movements," pp. 5–6, 8; Ilukhina, "Fate of Pacifism," pp. 5–6; "Resolution of the CPSU Central Committee Secretariat: About the participation of the Soviet delegation in the session of the World Peace Council in Colombo (June 1957)," *Protocol* 42 (May 24, 1957), l. 5, d. 66, op. 15, f. 4, Central Committee of the Communist Party of the Soviet Union Records.

16. Lewis and Xue, *China Builds the Bomb*, p. 40; Kuo, "Ban Atomic Weapons!"; Turski and Zdanowski, *Peace Movement*, p. 67; Schlaga, "Peace Movement," pp. 133–34.

17. *NYT*, Nov. 26, 1956, Oct. 23, 1966; Endicott, *James G. Endicott*, p. 326; H. Johnson, *Searching for Light*, pp. 368–70; Turski and Zdanowski, *Peace Movement*, p. 70.

18. James Endicott, too, resisted the implications of Khrushchev's denunciation of Stalin. When the Soviet government asked all Stalin Peace Prize winners to exchange their medals for Lenin Peace Prizes, he pointedly refused to return his. "Message to the Fourteenth Congress of the French Communist Party," in Biquard, *Frédéric Joliot-Curie*, pp. 172–74; Endicott, *James G. Endicott*, pp. 306–8.

19. Werskey, *Visible College*, p. 318. See, for example, Bernal, *World Without War*, p. 24.

20. Endicott, *James G. Endicott*, pp. 331–35.

21. W. R. T. Gore to Bertrand Russell, Mar. 12, 1958, Class 630, RA 1; R. Taylor, "Marxist Left," pp. 163, 165.

22. Joliot-Curie to Russell, Feb. 26, Mar. 26, 1958, Class 630, RA 1.

23. Yasui to Trevor Thomas, Apr. 23, 1958, Box 11, and Bernal and F. Vigne to General Secretary, SANE, Dec. 5, 1958, Box 7, Series B, SANE Records.

24. Max Isenbergh to DOS, Apr. 24, 1958, 751.5611/4-2458, Abbot to SecState, Apr. 7, 1954, 711.5611/4-754, and Gufler to SecState, Apr. 25, 1958, 762A.00/4-2558, DOS Records.

25. Parkin, *Middle Class Radicalism*, pp. 77–81; R. Taylor, "Marxist Left," pp. 163–65; N. Young, *An Infantile Disorder?* p. 154; E. P. Thompson, "Protest and Revise," *END Journal*, no. 37 (1989): 37.

26. See, for example, Kaoru Yasui to Bertrand Russell, June 10, 1957, Class 640, RA 1.

27. Scalapino, *Japanese Communist Movement*, p. 117; Homer Jack, "The 1964 Hiroshima Conference and the Japanese Peace Movement," p. 2, Box 410, Cousins Papers, Los Angeles; Homer Jack, "The Tokyo Conference and Beyond," *BAS* 14 (Feb. 1958): 91–92.

28. The conference resolutions called for severing ties between Japan, South Korea, and Taiwan and normalizing relations with the People's Republic of China. They also praised the Soviet Union for suspending nuclear tests and denounced U.S. and British policies in the Middle East as a threat to world peace. *Japan Times*, Aug. 31, 1958; André Trocmé, "Fourth International Conference Against A- and H-Bombs," *Fellowship* 24 (Nov. 1, 1958): 29–30; Scalapino, *Japanese Communist Movement*, p. 118.

29. Hiebert, *Impact of Atomic Energy*, pp. 248–51; Hall, "Church and the Independent Peace Movement," pp. 195–96; Werner-Christoph Schmauch, "The Christian Peace Conference," and Carl Soule, "Christian Peace Conference of 1964," Christian Peace Conference Records.

30. Pauling to the author, Jan. 25, 1988; Pauling to Charles Sadron, Mar. 7, 1958, and Pauling to Kaoru Yasui, June 24, 1958, Pauling Papers; Pauling and Ikeda, *A Lifelong Quest*, p. 97.

31. Santi, *100 Years*, p. 41; *PN*, Jan. 20, 1956; "The Fellowship in Sweden" (Aug. 1959), Box 42, Series B, Sayre Papers; Lindkvist, "Mobilization Peaks and Declines," p. 158; Minutes of CND Executive Committee meeting of July 11, 1958, Reel 1, CND (Britain) Records, London-Warwick.

32. Ackermann, "Resistance," p. 242; Leon Crutcher to DOS, Sept. 17, 1959, 744.5611/9-1759, DOS Records; Mary Woodward, untitled statement (1963), Box 14, Canadian CND Records.

33. McReynolds, "Pacifists," p. 60; Donald Keys to F. Vigne, Dec. 19, 1958, Box 7, Series B, SANE Records; Jack to Muste, Oct. 8, 1958, Box 7, Muste Papers.

34. R. Clark, *Life of Bertrand Russell*, p. 546; Russell to Joliot-Curie, Mar. 8, 29, 1958, Class 630, RA 1.

35. Russell to Lord Halsbury, July 4, 1958, and Russell to F. Vigne, July 4, 1958, Class 630, RA 1; *NYT*, July 10, 1958; Minutes of CND Executive Committee meeting of July 11, 1958, Reel 1, CND (Britain) Records, London-Warwick.

36. Grace M. Beaton to Japan Preparatory Committee for World Conference Against Atomic and Hydrogen Bombs, July 15, 1955, Arlo Tatum to Kaoru Yasui, July 9, 1956, and Arlo Tatum to Reginald Reynolds, July 25, 1957, Folder 333, WRI Records, Amsterdam.

37. Peggy Duff to Donald Keys, July 30, 1959, Box 21, Series B, SANE Records; Jack, *Nuclear Politics*, p. 32; Homer Jack, "Some Hard Lessons," *Fellowship* 23 (Nov. 1957): 9–10; Jack to Earle Reynolds, Mar. 13, 1962, Box 306, Cousins Papers, Los Angeles.

38. Arlo Tatum to Kaoru Yasui, Jan. 22, 1958, Folder 333, WRI Records, Amsterdam; A. J. Muste to Yasui, Feb. 11, 1958, Box 11, Series B, SANE Records.

39. Trevor Thomas to Kaoru Yasui, May 8, 1958, Box 11, Series B, SANE Records; A. J. Muste, "Comment on Madame Nehru's Material on Relations with World Peace Congress" (May 13, 1959), Box 7, Muste Papers; Trocmé, "Fourth International Conference," pp. 29–30.

40. Klehr and Haynes, *American Communist Movement*, pp. 145–47; Roussopoulos, *From Protest to Resistance*, p. 125; Arlo Tatum to A. J. Muste, Nov. 21, 1956, Folder 403, WRI Records, Amsterdam; Lindkvist, "Mobilization Peaks and Declines," p. 157; Zariski, "Italian Socialist Party," p. 377.

41. Endicott, *James G. Endicott*, pp. 326–28; B. Roberts, "Women's Peace Activism," pp. 294–95; Roussopoulos, *From Protest to Resistance*, p. 125; Locke, *Peace People*, pp. 154–56.

42. See, for example, Overstreet and Windmiller, *Communism in India*, pp. 428–29.

43. N. Young, "Why Peace Movements Fail," p. 12.

44. See, for example, Wittner, *One World or None*, pp. 319–23.

45. Kleidman, *Organizing for Peace*, pp. 110, 127; Thompson, "Protest and Revise," pp. 36–38; personal interview with E. P. Thompson, Nov. 1, 1989; R. Taylor, *Against the Bomb*, pp. 331–34; Bess, *Realism*, pp. 105–8.

46. Endicott, *James G. Endicott*, pp. 328–29; Peterson, "Cold War and Denmark," p. 194; Carter, *Peace Movements*, pp. 62–63.

47. K. Tsurumi, *Social Change*, pp. 309–10, 329–34.

48. N. Young, "Why Peace Movements Fail," p. 12.

49. See, for example, "National Board Resolutions Re: Civil Liberties," Box 4, and WILPF, "Internal Security" (1956), Box 32, WILPF (United States) Records; "The F.O.R. and Civil Liberties, 1953" (May 1953), Box 4, FOR (United States) Records; Alonso, *Peace as a Women's Issue*, pp. 170–72; Wittner, *Rebels Against War*, pp. 215–17.

50. Ianthe Carswell to Russell, Mar. 25, 1957, Class 630, RA 1.

51. A Swedish scholar provides a somewhat different interpretation, arguing that "some persons left the AMSA voluntarily so that it could not be accused of communism." Leon Crutcher to DOS, Sept. 17, 1959, 744.5611/9-1759, DOS Records; Russell to Lady Tyrrell, May 7, 1958, Class 630, RA 1; Fogelström, *Kampen för Fred*, pp. 257–58; Lindkvist, "Mobilization Peaks and Declines," p. 158.

52. Bacon, *One Woman's Passion*, pp. 261–69; Alonso, *Peace as a Women's Issue*, pp. 170–85.

53. Cousins to Thomas, June 13, 1958, Reel 61, Thomas Papers.

54. Thomas to Cousins, June 19, 1958, Reel 61, Thomas Papers; Lewy, *Cause That Failed*, p. 226.

Chapter 6

Epigraph: Macmillan to the Chancellor of the Duchy of Lancaster, Mar. 24, 1958, PREM 11/2778, PM Records.

1. "The H-Bomb and World Opinion," *BAS* 10 (May 1954): 165; *NYT*, Apr. 3, 5, 13, 1954; *PN*, Apr. 9, Dec. 31, 1954.

2. Myrdal, *Game of Disarmament*, p. 85; Homer A. Jack, "The Asian-African Conference," *BAS* 11 (June 1955): 221–22.

3. Jack, "Asian-African Conference," p. 222; *Meaning of Survival*, pp. 134–35; Tito to Russell, May 26, 1958, Class 625, RA 1; Rotblat, *Scientists*, p. 41.

4. Nevertheless, the WPC continued its activities in that city under another name. Nehru to Cousins, June 6, 1957, in Cousins, *Albert Schweitzer's Mission*, p. 197; Santi, *100 Years*, p. 39.

5. Peggy Duff to Bertrand Russell, July 3, 1958, Class 630, RA 1; Adrian B. Colquitt to DOS, Aug. 6, 1958, 754.5611/8-658, DOS Records; *PN*, July 4, 11, Aug. 8, 15, 1958; Ackermann, "Resistance," pp. 244–45.

6. In turn, nuclear disarmament leaders recognized Nehru's importance as a proponent of peace and disarmament. In April 1955, Einstein expressed his "sincere appreciation" for the Indian prime minister's "untiring constructive efforts in the field of international relations." Menon to Russell, Jan. 3, Mar. 11, 1955, Class 600, RA 1; Einstein to Nehru, Apr. 6, 1955, Box 7, Szilard Papers.

7. Russell, *Final Years*, pp. 99–100; Nehru to Russell, Apr. 21, 1958, Class 650, RA 1.

8. Nehru to Cousins, Feb. 19, Mar. 16, June 6, 1957, in Cousins, *Albert Schweitzer's Mission*, pp. 159–71, 197–98.

9. "H-Bomb and World Opinion," p. 167; Holloway, *Soviet Union*, pp. 31–32; *NYT*, Mar. 21, 1954; Smirnov and Zubok, "Nuclear Weapons after Stalin's Death," pp. 14–15; Holloway, *Stalin and the Bomb*, pp. 336–39.

10. Iu. V. Aksiutin and O. V. Volobuev, *XX s"ezd KPSS: novatsii i dogmy* (Moscow: Politizdat, 1991), p. 60, and Andrei Malenkov, *O moiem otsi Georgii Malenkov* (Moscow: NTS Teknoekos, 1992), p. 115, cited in Smirnov and Zubok, "Nuclear Weapons after Stalin's Death," p. 15; Holloway, *Stalin and the Bomb*, p. 338.

11. L. A. Openkin, "Na istoricheskom pereput'e," *Voprosy istorii KPSS* 1 (1990): 116, cited in Smirnov and Zubok, "Nuclear Weapons after Stalin's Death," p. 15.

12. W. N. Walmsley Jr. to DOS, Apr. 15, 1955, 711.5611/4-1558, DOS Records; Holloway, *Stalin and the Bomb*, pp. 335, 339, 369; *FRUS, 1955–1957*, 20: 380, 396; Bloomfield, Clemens, and Griffiths, *Khrushchev*, p. 12; Dinerstein, *War and the Soviet Union*, pp. 66–67, 78–79.

13. Burlatsky, *Khrushchev*, p. 199; N. Khrushchev, *Khrushchev Remembers: The Last Testament*, p. 71; N. Khrushchev, *Khrushchev Remembers: The Glasnost Tapes*, p. 192; Richter, *Khrushchev's Double Bind*, pp. 56–57; Holloway, *Soviet Union*, pp. 32–35, 42.

14. Bloomfield, Clemens, and Griffiths, *Khrushchev*, pp. 5–6, 21–25, 33–34, 68–71, 82–85; Holloway, *Stalin and the Bomb*, pp. 340–41; Richter, *Khrushchev's Double Bind*, pp. 70–71; Dobrynin, *In Confidence*, p. 147.

15. "Talk with the American Correspondent," p. 100; Halperin, "Chinese Attitudes," pp. 137–47; N. Khrushchev, *Khrushchev Remembers: The Glasnost Tapes*, p. 148; N. Khrushchev, *Khrushchev Remembers*, p. 470; Lewis and Xue, *China Builds the Bomb*, pp. 6–34, 38–39, 229.

16. Mushaben, "Swords to Plowshares," p. 125; *NYT*, Apr. 5, 1954; Lewis and Xue, *China Builds the Bomb*, pp. 40, 261; Scalapino, *Japanese Communist Movement*, p. 118.

17. Bernard Gufler to SecState, Apr. 29, 1957, 762A.00/4-2957, Apr. 16, 1958, 762A.00/4-1658, DOS Records; Cioc, *Pax Atomica*, p. 204.

18. Molotov was still arguing years later that "pacifist ideas are pernicious." Telephone interview with Pavel Litvinov, Oct. 7, 1990; Smirnov and Zubok, "Nuclear Weapons after Stalin's Death," p. 15; *Krasnaya zvezda* [Red star], Mar. 22, 1957, in *CDSP* 9 (June 5, 1957): 27; Resis, ed., *Molotov Remembers*, pp. 388–89.

19. Sakharov, *Memoirs*, pp. 194–95. For another chilling incident recalled by Sakharov, this time involving a top KGB official, see *Memoirs*, p. 160.

20. Second quarterly report (Zarubin), July 16, 1954, p. 62, and third quarterly report, Oct. 8, 1954, p. 27, pap. 14, por. 14, op. 38, fond: Ref. po SShA, and P. Fedosimov, "International Movement for a Cessation of Testing of Hydrogen Weapons (brief information)," Jan. 22, 1955, no. 194/112-USA, pap. 289, por. 31, op. 39, fond: Ref. po SShA, Soviet Ministry of Foreign Affairs Records, cited in Evangelista, "Soviet Scientists and Nuclear Testing," pp. 4–6; Jönsson, *Soviet Bargaining*, p. 153.

21. A similar argument was made that year by party ideologist Mikhail Suslov. Holloway, *Soviet Union*, pp. 75–76; Scott and Scott, *Soviet Military Doctrine*, pp. 20–21; Richter, *Khrushchev's Double Bind*, p. 87.

22. N. Khrushchev, *Khrushchev Remembers: The Last Testament*, pp. 59–60; Sakharov, *Memoirs*, p. 204; Richter, *Khrushchev's Double Bind*, p. 117; Goldsmith, *Frédéric Joliot-Curie*, pp. 224–25.

23. For a discussion of Soviet policy toward nonaligned activism and its leadership during Stalin's time, see Wittner, *One World or None*, pp. 291–95.

24. Patrick Armstrong to Russell, Apr. 18, 1958, Class 570, RA 1; Pauling and Ikeda, *A Lifelong Quest*, p. 80.

25. Blumberg and Owens, *Energy and Conflict*, pp. 181–83; Cousins to L. D. Kislova, Nov. 24, 1958, Box 208, Cousins Papers, Los Angeles.

26. Harrison Brown to Pierre Auger et al., Mar. 16, 1948, and Brown to George C. Marshall, Mar. 15, 1948, Box 16, Emergency Committee of Atomic Scientists Records; Leo Szilard to Dean Rusk, ca. Dec. 1949, Box 16, Szilard Papers.

27. Z. Medvedev, *Soviet Science*, p. 62; Evangelista, "Soviet Scientists and Nuclear Testing," p. 18; Leo Szilard to Charles Bohlen, June 16, 1960, Box 19, Szilard Papers; Rotblat, *Scientists*, p. 7.

28. According to Herbert York, a U.S. atomic scientist and former national security official, at the first Pugwash conference, in July 1957, Vladimir Pavlichenko, the secretary and interpreter for the Soviet delgation, was "the KGB's point man in this area." York maintained that John Whitman was "the CIA representative on the U.S. delegation." Rotblat, too, believed that Pavlichenko was a KGB agent, who added the party line to statements made by Topchiev and others. Personal interview with Sergei Kapitza, June 28, 1990; York, *Making Weapons, Talking Peace*, pp. 246–47; personal interview with Joseph Rotblat, July 11, 1994.

29. "On the conduct of a broad international conference of scientists for the cessation of tests of atomic and hydrogen weaponry," Central Committee Presidium to comrades Aristov et al., July 4, 1957, order from protocol no. 103, No. p103/XIX, TsK, and Andrei Gromyko to Central Committee, July 20, 1957, item 24: "On the Call for an international conference of scientists for the cessation of nuclear tests," Secretariat session of Aug. 2, 1957, from protocol no. 45, 20th convocation, CPSU Central Committee, Central Committee of the Communist Party of the Soviet Union Records, cited in Evangelista, "Soviet Scientists and Nuclear Testing," pp. 18–21.

30. Khrushchev to Eaton, May 31, 1958, Class 625, RA 1.

31. N. Khrushchev, *Khrushchev Remembers: The Last Testament*, pp. 65, 69–70; Sakharov, *Memoirs*, p. 208.

32. Sakharov, *Memoirs*, p. 209; "On the letter from the American scientist L. Pauling," item 18, commission session of Apr. 7, 1958, from protocol no. 7, Commission on questions of ideology, culture, and international party contacts, 20th convocation, CPSU Central Committee, and Ponomarev to Central Committee, Aug. 7, 1958, p. 2, microfilm roll 3340, Central Committee of the Communist Party of the Soviet Union Records, cited in Evangelista, "Soviet Scientists and Nuclear Testing," pp. 21–22, 27–28.

33. See, for example, "About an invitation to the USSR for the delegation of Hungarian champions of peace," protocol 41 (May 21, 1957), d. 65, op. 15, f. 4, and "About an invitation to the USSR for the delegation of Latin American champions of peace—the participants in the World Peace Council session in Colombo," protocol 43 (June 11, 1957), l. 143, d. 67, op. 15, f. 4, Central Committee of the Communist Party of the Soviet Union Records.

34. *Izvestia*, Jan. 1, 1958, in *CDSP* 10 (Feb. 12, 1958): 16; *Pravda*, June 29, 1954, in *CDSP* 6 (Aug. 11, 1954): 17; *Pravda*, May 12, 1955, in *CDSP* 7 (June 22, 1955): 14.

35. *FRUS, 1955–1957*, 4: 150–54. For additional indications of British and French interest in obtaining atomic weapons from the United States, see *FRUS, 1955–1957*, 4: 124–31 and 27: 31, 133, 135–37, 189.

36. Australian prime minister Robert Menzies praised Britain's Bomb tests—which produced a wave of cancer among Australian troops and the aborigines—as "one further proof . . . that scientific development in the British Commonwealth is at an extremely high level." Redner and Redner, *Anatomy of the World*, pp. 159–61; Tame and Robotham, *Maralinga*, pp. 138–96; Clements, *Back from the Brink*, p. 34.

37. Pierre, *Nuclear Politics*, pp. 87–94, 176, 178; *Manchester Guardian*, Jan. 2, 1985.

38. Scheinman, *Atomic Energy Policy*, pp. 171–91, 216–18; Goldschmidt, *Atomic Adventure*, pp. 98–99; Seaborg, *Stemming the Tide*, pp. 74–75.

39. Kelleher, *Germany*, pp. 9, 28; *FRUS, 1955–1957*, 20: 737–38; Central Intelligence Agency, "West German Defense Minister Strauss" (July 1961), Reel 2, *CIA Research Reports*. For other material pointing to the likelihood of West Germany becoming an independent nuclear power, see *FRUS, 1955–1957*, 27: 189; Healey, *Time of My Life*, p. 314; Bruce to SecState, Feb. 28, 1958, 762A.5611/2-2858, DOS Records.

40. Hewlett and Holl, *Atoms*, p. 214; *FRUS, 1952–1954*, 13: 1474; Churchill to Eisenhower, Apr. 16, 1956, Box 14, DDE Diary Series, Eisenhower Papers; *NYT*, Mar. 2, 1955.

41. *FRUS, 1955–1957*, 19: 500 and 20: 475; Bundy, *Danger and Survival*, p. 377; Blechman and Fisher, *Silent Partner*, p. 70.

42. Macmillan, *Riding the Storm*, p. 297; *FRUS, 1955–1957*, 20: 661 and 4: 169.

43. *FRUS, 1955–1957*, 20: 201 and 26: 249–50, 291–95.

44. Ibid., 27: 422–23; Bruce H. Millen to SecState, June 13, 1957, 757.00/6-1357, and Frances E. Willis to SecState, Apr. 25, 1958, 757.00/4-2558, DOS Records; Seaborg, ed., *Journal*, 1: 132.

45. J. V. Martin Jr., "Japanese Diplomatic Note on Pacific Nuclear Tests" (May 4, 1956), 711.5611/5-456, and MacArthur to SecState, Feb. 21, 1958, 711.5611/2-2158, DOS Records; *FRUS, 1955–1957*, 23: 495–96.

46. Churchill to Eisenhower, Mar. 29, 1954, in Boyle, ed., *Churchill-Eisenhower Correspondence*, p. 131; "H-Bomb and World Opinion," p. 166; "Extract from record of a Meeting between the Secretary of State and Mr. Dulles in Washington on Tuesday, January 31, 1956," Minutes of White House meeting of Feb. 1, 1956, AB 6/1817, AEA Records; *FRUS, 1955–1957*, 27: 740–41. See also *FRUS, 1955–1957*, 27: 630–33, 646–49.

47. Writing in his diary on December 1, 1957, the prime minister referred to antinuclear activists as "all the pro-Russians and all the pacifists and all the sentimentalists." Macmillan, *Riding the Storm*, pp. 297–99; Horne, *Macmillan*, p. 52. Macmillan's diary remains

closed to researchers, although a friendly biographer, Alistair Horne, was permitted to read and quote it.

48. John Swomley, "Nuclear Weapons Tests: The Position of the Fellowship of Reconciliation" (July 1957), Box 24a, FOR (United States) Records; *PN*, Mar. 8, 1957; Scalapino, *Japanese Communist Movement*, p. 118.

49. Nolting to SecState, Apr. 9, 1958, 711.5611/4-958, and Frances E. Willis to SecState, Apr. 29, 1958, 957.40/4-2958, DOS Records.

50. "Statement made in House of Commons on July 11, 1955 by The Hon. L. B. Pearson, M.P.," enclosure in Frederic Hudd to Russell, July 22, 1955, Class 650, RA 1.

51. G. E. Crombie to J. B. Johnston, Mar. 26, 1958, Canadian government note of Feb. 28, 1958, enclosure in U.K. High Commissioner in Canada to Commonwealth Relations Office, Mar. 5, 1958, Commonwealth Relations Office to U.K. High Commissioner in Canada, Jan. 21, 1958, AB 6/2110, AEA Records.

52. Canadian government note of Feb. 28, 1958, enclosure in U.K. High Commissioner in Canada to Commonwealth Relations Office, Mar. 5, 1958, Commonwealth Relations Office to U.K. High Commissioner in Canada, Jan. 21, 1958, AB 6/2110, AEA Records.

53. "Please don't repeat what I have just said to the scientists," he added. Cioc, *Pax Atomica*, pp. 77–78.

54. Raymond P. Ludden to DOS, Apr. 24, 1957, 762A.00/4-2457, DOS Records; Hahn, *My Life*, pp. 224–25; Max Born to Bertrand Russell, May 7, 1957, Class 710, RA 1; Lewis Strauss, "Memorandum for the Files of Lewis L. Strauss" (May 29, 1957), Box 26A, AEC Series, Strauss Papers.

55. *FRUS, 1955–1957*, 26: 291–95; Lewis L. Strauss, "Memorandum for the Files of Lewis L. Strauss" (May 29, 1957), Box 26A, AEC Series, Strauss Papers; Schweitzer to Cousins, Dec. 4, 1958, in Cousins, *Albert Schweitzer's Mission*, p. 237.

56. Page to SecState, May 7, 1958, 762A.00/5-758, DOS Records; Cioc, *Pax Atomica*, p. 78; *FRUS, 1955–1957*, 20: 661–62.

57. Personal interviews with Joseph Rotblat, July 12, 1990, July 11, 1994; Secretary of State for Commonwealth Relations to Prime Minister, Dec. 17, 1957, PREM 11/2159, PM Records; Executive Committee Report with Amendments, CND National Conference, Mar. 7–8, 1959, Reel 4, CND (Britain) Records, London-Warwick.

58. Macmillan to Russell, May 1, 1958, Class 650, RA 1; *Times* (London), May 2, 1958.

59. H. C. Hainsworth to R. N. Quirk, Jan. 2, 1958, Commonwealth Relations Office to U.K. High Commissioner in Canada, Jan. 21, 1958, AB 6/2110, AEA Records.

60. Cockcroft to William Strath, Feb. 10, 1958, Cockcroft to Thomson, Feb. 18, 1958, Thomson to Cockcroft, Feb. 21, 1958, H. C. Hainsworth to J.C.A. Roper, Mar. 11, 1958, and Hainsworth to P. L. Carter, May 9, 1958, AB 6/2110, AEA Records.

61. H. C. Hainsworth to P. L. Carter, May 9, 1958, AB 6/2110, AEA Records; D. P. Reilly to F. F. Turnbull, July 25, 1962, FO 371/163160, FO Records.

62. Gill Brown's minutes of Feb. 18 and Mar. 3, 1958, and Ian Harvey, "Anti H-Bomb Campaign" (Mar. 3, 1958), FO 371/135536, FO Records.

63. Butler to Macmillan, Feb. 21, 1958, Macmillan's minute of Feb. 21, 1958, P. de Z., "Note" (Feb. 26, 1958), and Plowden to Butler, Mar. 11, 1958, PREM 11/2542, PM Records.

64. Pat Arrowsmith to Minister of Supply, Mar. 17, 1958, AB 16/2660, AEA Records; Plowden to Macmillan, Mar. 19, 1958, and Macmillan's minute of Mar. 19, 1958, PREM 11/2542, PM Records.

65. The statement misrepresented CND's position, for the organization did not advocate unilateral action by the United States or by the Soviet Union, but by Britain. A. K. Rawlinson to F. A. Bishop, Mar. 24, 1958, Bishop to Rawlinson, Mar. 24, 1958, and D.E.H. Peirson to Pat Arrowsmith, Mar. 25, 1958, AB 16/2660, AEA Records.

66. He added that at the Trafalgar Square sendoff, "the speeches were moderate in tone" and that at Aldermaston, there was "no embarrassment or trouble . . . caused to the Atomic Energy Establishment or its staff." Butler to Macmillan, Apr. 16, 1958, PREM 11/2542, PM Records.

67. Plowden to Macmillan, Apr. 16, 1958, and Macmillan's minute of Apr. 17, 1958, PREM 11/2542, PM Records; H. T. Morgan's minute of June 24, 1958, FO 371/135541, FO Records.

68. B. Birnberg to FO, Oct. 8, 1958, and Gill Brown's minute of Oct. 16, 1958, FO 371/132700, FO Records; Macmillan, *Riding the Storm*, p. 478.

69. Another U.S. official observed: "We [in the State Department] understand that the Japanese de marche . . . is intended as a sop to the opposition parties in the Diet and is primarily for domestic consumption." *FRUS, 1952–1954*, 14: 1776, 1780; Howard L. Parsons, "Nuclear Tests in the Pacific" (May 3, 1956), 711.5611/5-356, and Noel Hemmendinger to William Sebald, May 4, 1956, 711.5611/5-456, DOS Records.

70. J. V. Martin Jr., "Japanese Diplomatic Note on Pacific Nuclear Tests" (May 4, 1956), 711.5611/5-456, John Foster Dulles to American Embassy, Tokyo, May 8, 1956, 711.5611/5-856, and MacArthur to SecState, Sept. 19, 1957, 711.5611/9-1957, DOS Records.

71. *FRUS, 1955–1957*, 23: 495–96; MacArthur to SecState, Feb. 21, 1958, 711.5611/2-2158, and Harlan B. Clark to DOS, Feb. 25, 1958, 711.5611/2-2558, DOS Records.

72. Wellington to DOS, Mar. 30, 1954, 711.5611/3-3054, Elbridge Durbrow to DOS, Apr. 27, 1954, 711.5611/4-2754, and Dennis to USIA, Apr. 28, 1954, 711.5611/4-2854, DOS Records. See also *FRUS, 1955–1957*, 9: 605.

73. *FRUS, 1955–1957*, 4: 17–18; Burgess to SecState, Feb. 7, 1958, 711.5611/2-758, DOS Records.

74. Raymond P. Ludden to SecState, July 1, 1957, 762A.00/7-157, Blancke to SecState, Aug. 2, 1957, 762A.00/8-257, William F. Gray to DOS, Aug. 29, 1957, 762A.00/8-2957, Trimble to SecState, Nov. 6, 1957, 762A.00/11-657, and Maney to SecState, Sept. 19, 1958, 762A.00/9-1958, DOS Records.

75. Raymond P. Ludden to DOS, May 22, 1958, 762A.00/5-2258, and Trimble to DOS, May 13, 1958, 762A.00/5-1358, DOS Records.

76. *FRUS, 1955–1957*, 20: 614; Bruce to SecState, Apr. 12, 1958, 762A.00/4-1258, and Trimble to DOS, May 13, 1958, 762A.00/5-1358, DOS Records. See also Blechman and Fisher, *Silent Partner*, p. 84; *NYT*, May 19, 1957.

77. Cioc, *Pax Atomica*, pp. 80–86, 205; Blancke to SecState, Aug. 2, 1957, 762A.00/8-257, and Wells to SecState, Aug. 28, 1957, 762A.00/8-2857, DOS Records.

78. *Manchester Guardian*, Jan. 2, 1985; Adamthwaite, "Nations Shall Speak," pp. 411–13; British Cabinet meeting of Feb. 22, 1956, 16(3), CAB 128, Cabinet Records.

79. Reginald Butler to Macmillan, Mar. 15, 1957, Macmillan's minute of Apr. 13, 1957, P. de Z. to Macmillan, Apr. 25, 1957, and Macmillan's minute of Apr. 26, 1957, PREM 11/2555, PM Records. For the British government's fear of upsetting the public with a film on British nuclear tests, see British Cabinet meeting of Jan. 22, 1958, 8(8), CAB 128, Cabinet Records.

80. The Windscale disaster led to the sealing off of two atomic piles and the discarding of two million liters of contaminated milk by neighboring farmers. The original report showed that radioactive milk, up to three times above the official danger level, had been released for human consumption, and that the government had allowed contaminated lamb to be sold for a month after the incident. It also revealed that the fire had produced a radioactive cloud with more than six hundred times the iodine content of the later Three Mile Island nuclear disaster in the United States. This embarrassed the Macmillan government, for a variety of reasons. *Manchester Guardian*, Jan. 10, 1988; Horne, *Macmillan*, pp. 53–55.

81. Butler's minute of Feb. 7, 1958, and Douglas-Home to Macmillan, Apr. 24, 1958, PREM 11/2549, PM Records.

82. Personal interview with Joseph Rotblat, July 11, 1994; *Guardian*, Aug. 20, 1994; Adamthwaite, "Nations Shall Speak," pp. 412–14.

83. Churchill's parliamentary statements of Mar. 10, 1955, PREM 11/1056, PM Records; British Cabinet meeting of Mar. 12, 1957, 17(4), CAB 128, Cabinet Records; *NYT*, May 18, 1957.

84. *FRUS, 1955–1957*, 20: 201 and 27: 631–33; "Extract from record of a Meeting between the Secretary of State and Mr. Dulles in Washington at 2:30 p.m. on Tuesday, January 31, 1956," AB 6/1817, AEA Records.

85. *FRUS, 1955–1957*, 27: 646–50; Minutes of White House meeting of Feb. 1, 1956, AB 6/1817, AEA Records.

86. *FRUS, 1955–1957*, 27: 740–42 and 4: 226–29.

87. "What's Back of the 'Fall-Out' Scare," *U.S. News and World Report 42* (June 7, 1957), pp. 25–27.

88. Butler to Macmillan, Feb. 21, 1958, PREM 11/2542, PM Records; Gill Brown's minute of Mar. 3, 1958, and [Illegible]'s minute of Mar. 3, 1958, FO 371/135536, FO Records. See also R.W.J. Hooper's and Sir P. Dean's minutes of Mar. 4, 1958, FO 371/135536, FO Records.

89. Macmillan to Plowden, Mar. 16, 1958, PREM 11/2778, Butler to Macmillan, Mar. 22, 1958, and Macmillan's minute of Mar. 22, 1958, PREM 11/2542, PM Records.

90. Macmillan to Chancellor of the Duchy of Lancaster, Mar. 24, 1958, PREM 11/2778, PM Records.

91. Chancellor of the Duchy of Lancaster to Macmillan, Apr. 2, 1958, with Macmillan's handwritten approval, PREM 11/3484, PM Records.

92. Chancellor of the Duchy of Lancaster to Macmillan, Apr. 22, 1958, and P. de Z. to B. M. Shedden, Apr. 25, 1958, PREM 11/2778, PM Records.

93. Chancellor of the Duchy of Lancaster to Macmillan, May 7, 1958, PREM 11/2778, PM Records.

94. Ibid.

95. See the letters and responses in the folder FO 371/132700, FO Records.

96. See the correspondence in the folder PREM 11/2553, PM Records.

97. Hill to Prime Minister, Aug. 13, 1958, PREM 11/3396, PM Records.

Chapter 7

Epigraph: "'Face the Nation' as broadcast over the CBS Television Network, May 4, 1958," Box 806, Anderson Papers.

1. Ambrose, *Eisenhower*, 2: 171; Gaddis, *Strategies of Containment*, pp. 127–63; Weigley, *American Way*, pp. 399–404.

2. At a meeting with British officials in early 1953, Dulles argued that "it was wrong to attach the stigma of immorality to any particular weapon." *FRUS, 1952–1954*, 2: 447, 533, and 5: 511–12; "Memorandum of Conversation" (Mar. 6, 1953), 711.5611/3-653, DOS Records.

3. Wilson to Lewis Strauss, Nov. 3, 1954, 711.5611/11-354, DOS Records; Ferrell, ed., *Diary of James C. Hagerty*, p. 211; *FRUS, 1955–1957*, 19: 302, 313.

4. According to the minutes of a meeting with the JCS on March 30, 1956, Eisenhower said that he would use nuclear weapons "in any war with the Soviets." Two months later, he told military leaders that "it was fatuous to think that the U.S. and USSR would be locked into a life and death struggle without using such weapons." Bundy, *Danger and Survival*, p. 377; *FRUS, 1955–1957*, 19: 281, 312.

5. *FRUS, 1955–1957*, 19: 511–12.

6. Ambrose, *Eisenhower*, 2: 51; Bundy, *Danger and Survival*, pp. 244–45; *FRUS, 1952–1954*, 15: 1636–40, 1653–55, 1700, 1704–9. See also Eisenhower, *Mandate for Change*, pp. 180, 248.

7. Radford suggested helpfully that "we could use atomic weapons on the Vietminh if this seemed the best means of smashing them and cleaning up Indochina." The president preferred to offer some atomic bombs to the French for that purpose. *FRUS, 1952–1954*, 13: 1271, 1447, 1591, 1703–4, 1714.

8. Democratic Party leaders exhibited considerably greater caution. Ambrose, *Eisenhower*, 2: 238–39.

9. *FRUS, 1955–1957*, 20: 2–4, 136.

10. *FRUS, 1952–1954*, 2: 900, 1175; "Memorandum of Conversation" (Jan. 7, 1954), Box 4, AS, Eisenhower Papers; *FRUS, 1955–1957*, 23: 92.

11. Divine, *Blowing on the Wind*, p. 11; Strauss, *Men and Decisions*, p. 350; Strauss to David Lawrence, Apr. 30, 1956, Box 113, AEC Series, Strauss Papers.

12. According to Strauss, shortly after he was sworn in as AEC chair, the president took him aside and told him: "My chief concern and your first assignment is to find some new approach to the *dis*arming of atomic energy." Four years later, when Eisenhower reminded him of this, Strauss was able to fob the president off with vague talk of "looking at a lot of ideas." *FRUS, 1952–1954*, 2: 1342–43; Strauss, *Men and Decisions*, p. 336; Hughes, *Ordeal of Power*, p. 203.

13. *FRUS, 1952–1954*, 2: 1379–80; Ferrell, ed., *Diary of James C. Hagerty*, p. 42.

14. *FRUS, 1952–1954*, 2: 1383–85, 1419–20, 1425 28.

15. *FRUS, 1955–1957*, 19: 85–86. See also 19: 29–30.

16. Ibid., 19: 194, 527, and 20: 324; Strauss to Eisenhower, July 23, 1957, Box 5, AS, Eisenhower Papers.

17. J. W. Hanes Jr., "Memorandum for the Secretary" (Apr. 23, 1956), Box 4, General Correspondence and Memoranda Series, J. F. Dulles Papers, Abilene; Strauss to Murray Snyder, Oct. 4, 1956, Box 3, Hughes Papers.

18. Hughes, *Ordeal of Power*, pp. 191–95; Bundy, *Danger and Survival*, pp. 329–30.

19. Strauss to Emmet Hughes, Oct. 15, 1956, Box 3, Hughes Papers; Gloria to Strauss, Oct. 18, 1956, Box 26E, and Strauss, "Memorandum for Files of Lewis L. Strauss" (Oct. 15, 1956), Box 14, AEC Series, Strauss Papers.

20. Strauss, "Memorandum for the Files of Lewis L. Strauss" (Oct. 21, 1956), Box 14, AEC Series, Strauss Papers; Hewlett and Holl, *Atoms*, pp. 371–72; Divine, *Blowing on the Wind*, p. 102.

21. Paul F. Foster, "Memorandum to LLS" (June 20, 1955), with handwritten comments by Everett Holles and John MacKenzie, Box 83, AEC Series, Strauss Papers.

22. Hewlett and Holl, *Atoms*, p. 304; P. J. Farley, "Memorandum for the Files" (Dec. 28, 1955), "18.14 Weapons-Test Moratorium, a. General, 1957" Folder, AE Lot File, DOS Records; Libby to Strauss, Jan 12, 16, 1956, and Strauss to Libby, Jan. 13, 16, 1956, Box 60, AEC Series, Strauss Papers.

23. Strauss, "Draft" (Apr. 17, 1956), Strauss to Pius XII, Apr. 17, Aug. 6, 1956, and Angelo Dell'Acqua to Strauss, Apr. 27, 1956, Box 83, AEC Series, Strauss Papers.

24. Eisenhower to Schweitzer, Jan. 13, 1955, PPF 1326, WHCF, Eisenhower Records; Dulles to American Consul (Leopoldville), Jan. 10, 1955, Box 97, J. F. Dulles Papers, Princeton; "Minutes: 63rd Meeting of AEC Advisory Committee on Biology and Medicine" (June 18, 1957), AEC Records.

25. Libby to Schweitzer, Apr. 25, 1957, in Libby, "An Open Letter"; McKnight to USIA, May 8, 1957, "18.14 Weapons-Test Moratorium, a. General" Folder, AE Lot File, DOS Records.

26. Holles to Libby, Apr. 26, 1957, Box 60, AEC Series, Strauss Papers.

27. Gerard Smith to Paul Foster, Aug. 7, 1957, and John L. McGruder to Strauss, Aug. 13, 1957, Box 100, AEC Series, Strauss Papers; Brabazon, *Albert Schweitzer*, pp. 440–41.

28. Frances E. Willis to SecState, Apr. 24, 1958, 957.40/4-2458, and Willis to SecState, Apr. 25, 1958, 757.00/4-2558, DOS Records; "Atomic Energy Commission Meeting 1366" (Apr. 29, 1958), AEC Records.

29. Dulles to American Embassy (Oslo), May 2, 1958, 957.40/4-2958, Frances E. Willis to SecState, May 12, 1958, 957.40/5-1258, and George Spiegel to Cal Potts, May 13, 1958, "18.14 Weapons-Test Moratorium, C. Other World Opinion" Folder, AE Lot File, DOS Records.

30. Hoover to Strauss, May 14, June 2, 9, 1958, Box 100, AEC Series, Strauss Papers.

31. Green to SecState, May 27, 1958, and Herter to Green, May 28, 1958, 711.5611/5-2758, DOS Records.

32. Green to DOS, June 19, 1958, 711.5611/6-1958, DOS Records.

33. Strauss to Rabinowitch, Apr. 30, 1953, and Lewis L. Strauss, "Memorandum for the Files of Lewis L. Strauss" (Apr. 25, 1957), Box 12, AEC Series, Strauss Papers.

34. Eisenhower to Strauss, Nov. 25, 1957, Box 5, AS, Eisenhower Papers; J.C.A. Roper to H. C. Hainsworth, Feb. 27, 1958, AB 6/2110, AEA Records; Lewis L. Strauss, "Memorandum for the Files of Lewis L. Strauss" (Dec. 5, 1958), Box 67, AEC Series, Strauss Papers.

35. Subsequently, both Oliphant and Peierls were knighted by the British government. Schwartz, "F.B.I. and Dr. Einstein," pp. 168–73; Theoharis and Cox, *Boss*, pp. 278–79; Robert E. Hoey to DOS, July 8, 1960, 600.0012/7-860, DOS Records; Peierls, *Bird of Passage*, p. 324.

36. Pfau, *No Sacrifice Too Great*, pp. 157, 173; U.S. Atomic Energy Commission, *In the Matter of J. Robert Oppenheimer*, p. 1019; Hewlett and Holl, *Atoms*, pp. 41–71, 81, 100; Eisenhower, *Mandate for Change*, pp. 312–13.

37. Hermann J. Muller, "Chronology Relating to the Paper . . . for the International Conference on the Peaceful Uses of Atomic Energy" (Oct. 4, 1955), Muller Papers; Paul W. McDaniel to Muller, July 22, 1955, AEC Records; Hewlett and Holl, *Atoms*, pp. 266–68; Carlson, *Genes, Radiation, and Society*, pp. 356–58, 360; Everett Holles to Strauss, Sept. 20, 1955, Box 70, AEC Series, Strauss Papers.

38. Hermann J. Muller, "Chronology Relating to the Paper . . . for the International Conference on the Peaceful Uses of Atomic Energy" (Oct. 4, 1955), Muller Papers; Hewlett and Holl, *Atoms*, p. 268; Paul W. McDaniel to Harry S. Traynor, Sept. 26, 1955, AEC Records.

39. Carlson, *Genes, Radiation, and Society*, pp. 364–66; Hewlett and Holl, *Atoms*, p. 268; Libby to Strauss, Oct. 27, 1955, Box 60, AEC Series, Strauss Papers; Strauss, *Men and Decisions*, p. 414.

40. Personal interview with Ralph E. Lapp, June 28, 1987; Oliver Townsend, "Memorandum to the Files" (Aug. 28, 1952), Box 58, AEC Series, Strauss Papers.

41. A typed copy of a letter from Lapp to a friend, located in Strauss's files, has two tiny photographs of the original attached to it. Strauss to Bryan LaPlante, Oct. 30, 1952, and Lapp to Art, June 18, 1955, and attachments, Box 58, AEC Series, Strauss Papers.

42. J. A. Waters to Strauss, June 10, 1955, Anderson to Strauss, June 23, 1955, "Notes on Dr. Ralph Lapp," enclosure in Everett Holles to Strauss, Sept. 21, 1955, and Holles to Strauss, June 30, 1955, Box 58, AEC Series, Strauss Papers.

43. Dupkin to Strauss, June 23, Nov. 7, 1955, Box 58, AEC Series, Strauss Papers.

44. Strauss to Libby, Oct. 10, 1956, Box 60, and Lewis L. Strauss, "Memorandum for the Files of Lewis L. Strauss" (Apr. 25, 1957), Box 12, AEC Series, Strauss Papers.

45. Bryan F. LaPlante, "Memorandum for the Chairman" (May 28, 1957), LaPlante to

Strauss, June 5, 1957, and Dupkin to Strauss, July 17, 1956, Box 58, AEC Series, Strauss Papers.

46. "Roadblocks to a World Traveler"; Linus Pauling, "The Department of State and the Structure of Proteins," "Affidavit by Linus Pauling" (Sept. 3, 1954), R. B. Shipley to Pauling, Oct. 1, 1954, and Charles E. Saltzman to Pauling, Nov. 19, 1954, Pauling Papers.

47. U.S. Representative Francis Walter, chair of the House Committee on Un-American Activities, promptly accused Pauling of spreading Communist propaganda. Bryan F. LaPlante to K. D. Nichols, Sept. 28, 1954, Box 80, AEC Series, Strauss Papers; *Public Papers: Eisenhower, 1957*, p. 429; Divine, *Blowing on the Wind*, p. 141.

48. Strauss to Kenneth S. Pitzer, June 4, 1957, Box 26G, Everett Holles to Strauss, June 4, 1957, Box 80, and Lewis L. Strauss, "Memo or provided to President for his press conference on 6/5/57," Box 26E, AEC Series, Strauss Papers; Mazuzan and Walker, *Controlling the Atom*, p. 48.

49. Strauss to Libby, June 5, 1957, Box 60, AEC Series, Strauss Papers; Everett Holles to James Hagerty, June 12, 1957, Strauss to Andrew Goodpaster, June 28, 1957, and Adams to Pauling, June 29, 1957, OF 108-A, WHCF, Eisenhower Records.

50. Strauss might have wanted to do still more to destroy Pauling's reputation, but as he explained when the Hearst press offered to make available to him its Pauling files, he was "not judgement proof"—an apparent reference to the fact that Pauling sometimes took his political detractors to court and won. Hewlett and Holl, *Atoms*, p. 451; Strauss to Meade Alcorn, Sept. 3, 1957, Box 26G, Virginia H. Walker to Strauss, Sept. 6, 1957, and John L. McGruder, "Memorandum for the Telephone File" (May 8, 1958), Box 80, AEC Series, Strauss Papers.

51. Teller and Latter, "The Compelling Need for Nuclear Tests," pp. 64, 66.

52. Hoover to Robert Cutler, June 19, 1957, with enclosure: "Communist Exploitation of Radiation 'Fall-Out' Controversy" (June 12, 1957), pp. 21–23, Box 3, Federal Bureau of Investigation, *Communist Propaganda in the United States: Part VIII: Campaigns*, pp. 53–54, Box 2, FBI Series, OSANSA, White House Office Records; Pauling to Elizabeth Anne Newton, June 7, 1960, Pauling Papers.

53. Since Hoover offered no evidence of illegal activity by the WILPF, the attorney general took no action. Morse Salisbury to Lewis L. Strauss, July 29, 1957, with handwritten comments by Everett Holles and Strauss, Box 113, AEC Series, Strauss Papers; Dion, "FBI Surveillance," pp. 6–8, 16; Garrison, "Our Skirts," p. 208.

54. Hoover to Robert Cutler, Nov. 4, 1957, and enclosures, Box 3, FBI Series, OSANSA, White House Office Records; Chauncey Robbins, "Memorandum for the Staff Secretary, the White House" (Nov. 21, 1957), OF 108-A(4), WHCF, Eisenhower Records.

55. Hoover to Robert Cutler, Jan. 30, 1958, Box 1, FBI Series, OSANSA, White House Office Records; Robinson, *Abraham Went Out*, p. 101.

56. Clarence Pickett to Thomas Stephens, May 5, 1954, GF 155-B, WHCF, Eisenhower Records.

57. This later backfired on the White House, for the U.S. senators from Massachusetts did not want to alienate their Quaker constituents. Democratic Senator John F. Kennedy finally worked out provisions for the petitions to be accepted, a fact that irked Republican Senator Leverett Saltonstall, who desired the credit for it. Consequently, the White House staff prepared a bogus, backdated letter to bolster Saltonstall's claim to having made the arrangement. Bigelow, *Voyage*, p. 41; Maxwell Rabb, "Memorandum for Mr. Hagerty" (Jan. 14, 1958) and attached notes, Box 1215, General File, WHCF, Eisenhower Records.

58. "Atomic Energy Commission Meeting No. 1334" (Feb. 12, 1958), AEC Records; CINCPAC to SecState, Feb. 14, 1958, 711.5611/2-1458, Dulles to American Embassy (Tokyo), Mar. 6, 1958, 711.5611/3-658, Mar. 27, 1958, 711.5611/3-1158, Apr. 2, 1958, 711.5611/4-258, Arleigh Burke to Christian Herter, Mar. 14, 1958, 711.5611/3-1458, Dulles

to Strauss, Apr. 11, 1958, 711.5611/4-1158, and DIO COMFOURTEEN to SecState, Apr. 25, 1958, 711.5611/4-2558, DOS Records.

59. Bigelow, *Voyage*, pp. 115–248; Reynolds, *Forbidden Voyage*, p. 281; "'Face the Nation' as broadcast over the CBS Television Network, May 4, 1958," Box 806, Anderson Papers; *NYT*, May 5, 1958.

60. "Atomic Energy Commission Meeting 1369" (May 6, 1958), "Atomic Energy Commission Meeting 1371" (May 9, 1958), and "Meeting Between Chairman Strauss and Members of National Committee for Non-Violent Action Against Nuclear Tests" (May 13, 1958), AEC Records; Hewlett and Holl, *Atoms*, pp. 484–85; Strauss, *Men and Decisions*, p. 413.

61. Eisenhower to Cousins, Mar. 22, 1951, Cousins Papers, Beverly Hills; Cousins to Eisenhower, Aug. 4, 1952, Box 269, Cousins Papers, Los Angeles.

62. Eisenhower to Cousins, Aug. 6, 1956, Cousins to Eisenhower, Aug. 22, 1956, and attached note, and anonymous note, Box 7, Name Series, Eisenhower Papers.

63. Cousins to Eisenhower, Jan. 23, 1957, acw [Ann C. Whitman] to Barbara, n.d., and Bernard Shanley to Cousins, Feb. 25, 1957, PPF 1326, WHCF, Eisenhower Records.

64. Cousins to Eisenhower, June 7, 1957, Strauss to Eisenhower, June 18, 1957, and Eisenhower to Cousins, June 21, 1957, Box 7, Name Series, Eisenhower Papers.

65. Cousins to Eisenhower, June 27, 1957, Eisenhower to Cousins, July 9, 1957, Box 7, Name Series, Eisenhower to Strauss, July 2, 1957, and Strauss to Eisenhower, July 3, 1957, Box 5, AS, Eisenhower Papers.

66. Cousins to Eisenhower, July 15, 1957 and hand-written notation, and Ann Whitman to Strauss, July 20, 1957, OF 108-A, WHCF, Eisenhower Records; Strauss to Whitman, July 23, 1957, Box 5, AS, Eisenhower Papers.

67. The president eventually suggested that the group submit a memorandum and meet with Gerard Smith, the special assistant to the secretary of state, to discuss it. Thomas to Eisenhower, July 12, 1957, A.C.W. Note, Fisher Howe to Miss Bernau, July 19, 1957, and Eisenhower to Thomas, July 23, 1957, OF 137, WHCF, Eisenhower Records.

68. Cousins to Eisenhower, Nov. 13, 1957, Box 269, Cousins Papers, Los Angeles; Robert Gray to Thomas, Jan. 17, 1958, and Thomas to Lewis Strauss, Feb. 10, 1958, Box 114, AEC Series, Strauss Papers.

69. Boxes 29–32, Series G, SANE Records; Lasky to Strauss, Apr. 23, 1958, and Bonnie Crosby to Lasky, Apr. 28, 1958, Box 88, AEC Series, Strauss Papers.

70. Divine, *Blowing on the Wind*, pp. 20–21. See also *FRUS, 1955–1957*, 19: 398.

71. W. K. Scott to General Paul T. Carroll, Apr. 9, 1954, OF 108-A, WHCF, Eisenhower Records; Elbridge Durbrow to DOS, Apr. 27, 1954, 711.5611/4-2754, DOS Records.

72. John Foster Dulles, "Memorandum" (Jan. 19, 1958), Box 15, Chronological Series, J. F. Dulles Papers, Abilene; "United States Reply to Letter from Lord Russell" (Feb. 6, 1958), Box 142, J. F. Dulles Papers, Princeton.

73. M. Gordon Knox to DOS, May 7, 1958, 711.5611/5-758, and Belton O. Bryan to SecState, Mar. 6, 1958, 741.00/3-658, DOS Records. See also Whitney to SecState, May 22, 1958, 741.00/5-2258, DOS Records.

74. Dulles agreed that an SPD victory "would not be good." *FRUS, 1955–1957*, 26: 137, 4: 127.

75. Ibid., 26: 244, 291.

76. Ibid., 20: 719; Dulles to James B. Conant, Sept. 29, 1957, Box 113, J. F. Dulles Papers, Princeton; Bruce to SecState, Sept. 26, 1957, 762A.00/9-2657, DOS Records.

77. Bruce to SecState, Mar. 26, 1958, 762A.00/3-2658, Sandalls to DOS, Apr. 23, 1958, 762A.00/4-2358, and William R. Taylor to DOS, June 4, 1958, 762A.00/6-458, DOS Records. Heinemann was elected president of West Germany in 1969 and served in this capacity until his retirement in 1974.

78. *FRUS, 1952–1954*, 14: 1644–49.

79. Ferrell, ed., *Diary of James C. Hagerty*, p. 40; Central Intelligence Agency, "Memorandum for the Record" (Apr. 28, 1954), enclosure in Frank G. Wisner to Strauss, Apr. 29, 1954, Box 28, Strauss Papers.

80. In October of that year, he convinced CIA Director Richard Helms to conduct yet another fruitless investigation of the subject. Strauss to Edward R. Trapnell, May 16, 1966, Box 26G, Strauss to Helms, Oct. 6, 1966, and Helms to Strauss, Oct. 10, 1966, Box 15, AEC Series, Strauss Papers.

81. *NYT*, Apr. 21, 1957; Kaoru Yasui to John F. Kennedy, Sept. 19, 1961, in *No More Hiroshimas!* 8 (Oct. 1961): 9; Robert L. Burns to L. Arthur Minnich, June 23, 1956, and enclosures, OF 108-A, and John C. Bugher to Jane Nishiwaki, June 1, 1954, Box 9, Subject Series, Confidential File, WHCF, Eisenhower Records.

82. Strauss to Albert L. Latter, Aug. 30, 1957, Box 26G, AEC Series, Strauss Papers; MacArthur to SecState, May 28, 1958, and Herter to American Embassy (Tokyo), May 28, 1958, 711.5611/5-2858, DOS Records.

83. *FRUS, 1955–1957*, 19: 37; Hewlett and Holl, *Atoms*, p. 362; Paul F. Foster, "Memorandum for the Chairman" (Mar. 8, 1955), and Lewis Strauss to Foster, Mar. 8, 1955, Box 113, AEC Series, Strauss Papers.

84. Gordon Dean Diary, May 27, 1953, Broudy Papers; *FRUS, 1952–1954*, 2: 532–33, 1171–74.

85. That December, Eisenhower again expressed his concern about how to discuss U.S. nuclear policy "without at the same time scaring our allies to death." "The Human Effects of Nuclear Weapons Development" (Nov. 21, 1956), Box 4, AS, Eisenhower Papers; *FRUS, 1955–1957*, 19: 372, 415–18, 568, 707–8.

86. A. J. Goodpaster, "Memorandum of Conference with the President" (Mar. 21, 1956), Box 13, DDE Diary Series, Eisenhower Papers; Divine, *Blowing on the Wind*, pp. 76, 213.

87. To mask U.S. government sponsorship, the USIA farmed out many of its opinion surveys to local polling organizations. Streibert to Lewis Nixon, Oct. 26, 1955, Box 5, and Leo Crespi to Morton Fosberg, Jan. 7, 1955, Box 6, CPC, OR, USIA Records.

88. "Atomic Energy Commission Meeting No. 1047" (Dec. 8, 1954), AEC Records; Hewlett and Holl, *Atoms*, pp. 280–86; Percival Brundage, "Memorandum for Colonel Andrew J. Goodpaster, Jr." (Feb. 3, 1955), OF 108-A(2), Eisenhower Records; Divine, *Blowing on the Wind*, p. 37.

89. *FRUS, 1955–1957*, 20: 73–74, 90–91; Hewlett and Holl, *Atoms*, pp. 291–95.

90. Ball, *Justice Downwind*, pp. 59, 86, 89, 92, 95, 126, 164; *NYT*, Jan. 8, Feb. 23, 1979, Dec. 3, 14, 1989; *Washington Post*, Apr. 19, 1979. See also Gallagher, *American Ground Zero*.

91. Government reports, kept secret until 1979 show that the dead sheep had a concentration of radioactivity in their thyroid glands of from 250 to 1,000 times the maximum concentration permissible in humans. "Atomic Energy Commission Meeting No. 866" (May 22, 1953), and "Atomic Energy Commission Meeting No. 875" (June 10, 1953), AEC Records; Hewlett and Holl, *Atoms*, pp. 150–59; Ball, *Justice Downwind*, pp. 43–48, 205–10; Weart, *Nuclear Fear*, p. 185; *NYT*, Feb. 15, 23, Apr. 20, 1979.

92. Ball, *Justice Downwind*, pp. 72–75; "Atomic Energy Commission Meeting No. 1062" (Feb. 23, 1955), AEC Records; Hewlett and Holl, *Atoms*, pp. 289–90; Divine, *Blowing on the Wind*, p. 44.

93. In the case of *Irene Allen et al. v. United States* (1984), a U.S. district court ruled that, through negligence, the U.S. government's operatives at the Nevada test site were responsible for the deaths and injuries of ten plaintiffs. The court went on to declare that because the AEC had failed in its duty to alert citizens to the radiation dangers, "many people

were exposed to more radiation, and greater risk, than ever needed to be." Ball, *Justice Downwind*, pp. 129–30, 155–58.

94. "Memorandum in Support of Defendants' Motion for Summary Judgment" (Nov. 12, 1985), *Alice P. Broudy v. United States of America*, Broudy Papers; Ball, *Justice Downwind*, p. 204; Hewlett and Holl, *Atoms*, p. 456; *NYT*, Dec. 16, 1993.

95. Divine, *Blowing on the Wind*, pp. 44, 163; "What's Back of the 'Fall-Out' Scare," pp. 26–27; Ball, *Justice Downwind*, p. 77; Federal Civil Defense Administration, *Facts About Fallout* (1955), Series B, SANE Records; Weart, *Nuclear Fear*, p. 222.

96. Weart, *Nuclear Fear*, p. 201; Divine, *Blowing on the Wind*, p. 43; Strauss to Virginius Dabney, May 7, 1958, Box 113, AEC Series, Strauss Papers; Edwin Plowden to F. A. Bishop, June 18, 1958, PREM 11/2553, PM Records.

97. "Chairman Strauss's Statement on Pacific Tests," *BAS* 10 (May 1954): 163–64; Eisenhower, *Waging Peace*, p. 474; Strauss, *Men and Decisions*, p. 411.

98. Divine, *Blowing on the Wind*, pp. 30–31; Gilpin, *American Scientists*, p. 182.

99. Ralph K. White to Morton Fosberg, Dec. 8, 1954, Jan. 13, 1955, Henry Loomis to Lewis Strauss, Jan. 6, 1955, "Major Reasons for Including Each Item in Present Four-Nation Questionnaire" (Jan. 13, 1955), and Loomis to Joseph B. Phillips, Apr. 21, 1955, Box 6, and Dulles to American Embassy (London), June 10, 1955, Box 7, CPC, and White to Walter Lampshire, June 10, 1955, Box 1, Area Project Correspondence, 1954–63, OR, USIA Records.

100. Hewlett and Holl, *Atoms*, p. 285; *FRUS, 1955–1957*, 9: 521, 563.

101. *FRUS, 1955–1957*, 9: 505–6, 517–18, 530–31, 542, 597–98; "U.S. and Free World Standing in the Philippines, and Reactions to Related Issues" (Sept. 1959), p. 23, Box 1, POBR, OR, USIA Records.

102. Weart, *Nuclear Fear*, pp. 156–58, 162–63; Hewlett and Holl, *Atoms*, pp. 59–60, 72; Winkler, *Life Under a Cloud*, pp. 145–46.

103. *FRUS, 1955–1957*, 9: 512, 516, 520, 538, 540, 542, 547–48.

104. Weart, *Nuclear Fear*, pp. 168–73, 210–11; Winkler, *Life Under a Cloud*, pp. 140, 143.

105. Strauss did have some interest in "clean" weapons. He told an NSC meeting in late 1957 that although he had "no intention of eliminating 'dirty' weapons," a "'clean' weapon" would be helpful in some circumstances. For example, "if the United States was preparing to land large forces in some foreign area, we would want to use 'clean' weapons of high yield to prepare this area for such a U.S. landing." "Statement by Lewis L. Strauss, Chairman, U.S. Atomic Energy Commission" (July 19, 1956), Box 9, Speech File, Strauss Papers; Anderson, *Outsider*, pp. 202–3; *FRUS, 1955–1957*, 20: 761.

106. Mary Vance Trent to Ellsworth R. Mosman, Feb. 12, 1954, 711.5611/2-1254, and Dennis A. Flinn to Max Bishop, Aug. 4, 1955, 711.5611/8-455, DOS Records.

107. Max W. Bishop to Mr. Hoover et al., Aug. 9, 1955, 711.5611/8-455, DOS Records; Barker, *Hiroshima Maidens*, p. 80; Norman Cousins, untitled essay, Box 270, Cousins Papers, Los Angeles.

108. Flinn to Bishop, Aug. 4, 1955, 711.5611/8-455, DOS Records; Barker, *Hiroshima Maidens*, pp. 80–82; Norman Cousins, untitled essay, Box 270, Cousins Papers, Los Angeles.

109. Flinn to Bishop, Aug. 4, 1955, 711.5611/8-455, DOS Records; Tokyo to SecState, May 12, 1955, and Ralph J. Blake to DOS, n.d., in Hersey, *Hiroshima*, pp. 146–47; Norman Cousins, untitled essay, Box 270, Cousins Papers, Los Angeles.

110. The report claimed that the occasional pacifist comments of the Maidens (e.g. "I abhor war") buttressed Communist-led peace activities. The closest it came to identifying anyone associated with the project as a *bona fide* Red occurred when it noted that an intelligence agent considered one of the accompanying physicians "a possible Communist." This sort of thing did not impress U.S. Air Force officials, who, having studied the intelligence

data on the physician and having failed to find "any derogatory information" on the other passengers, decided to provide transportation for the group to the United States. Flinn to Bishop, Aug. 4, 1955, and Bishop to Mr. Hoover et al., Aug. 9, 1955, 711.5611/8-455, DOS Records.

111. The State Department did, however, help to derail a similar program, suggested by ministers and community leaders in Mobile, Alabama, for the "maidens" of Nagasaki. Norman Cousins, untitled essay, Box 270, and Adams to Cousins, Nov. 15, 1956, Box 269, Cousins Papers, Los Angeles; Barker, *Hiroshima Maidens*, pp. 96–97, 118–19, 143.

Chapter 8

Epigraph: A. J. Goodpaster, "Memorandum of Conference with the President, August 12, 1958" (Aug. 14, 1958), Box 3, Alpha Subseries, Subject Series, OSS, White House Office Records.

1. Kohl, *French Nuclear Diplomacy*, pp. 5–10, 15; W. F. Libby, "Memorandum for the Chairman" (Nov. 18, 1955), Box 60, AEC Series, Strauss Papers; Scheinman, *Atomic Energy Policy*, pp. xvi, 193–94; de Gaulle, *Memoirs*, pp. 201–2, 204–9, 213–15; Divine, *Blowing on the Wind*, p. 228.

2. Lewis and Xue, *China Builds the Bomb*, pp. 41–42, 61–63, 68, 70; Drifte, "China," pp. 45–46.

3. Lewis and Xue, *China Builds the Bomb*, pp. 69–70; N. Khrushchev, *Khrushchev Remembers: The Last Testament*, pp. 254–55.

4. *FRUS, 1955–1957*, 27: 736–37, 743–47, 749–51; Horne, *Macmillan*, pp. 45–50; Pierre, *Nuclear Politics*, pp. 95–96, 140; Macmillan, *Riding the Storm*, p. 296.

5. According to the U.S. ambassador, at a meeting in March 1957 Macmillan expressed "his concern at [the] possibility [that] Soviet [Union] might at some time decide to talk seriously on disarmament. He speculated on dangers which would result from any appreciable disarmament." Macmillan, *Riding the Storm*, pp. 292, 460–61; *FRUS, 1955–1957*, 20: 456.

6. British Cabinet meeting of Apr. 10, 1956, 27(2), and British Cabinet meeting of Apr. 15, 1957, 34(4), CAB 128, Cabinet Records; *FRUS, 1955–1957*, 20: 632–33; Ambrose, *Eisenhower*, 2: 404; Macmillan, *Riding the Storm*, p. 332.

7. British Cabinet meeting of July 20, 1956, 51(6) CAB 128, Cabinet Records; Gerard Smith to Mr. Murphy, July 26, 1956, "18.14 Weapons—Test Moratorium, a. General, 1956" Folder, AE Lot File, DOS Records.

8. Foreign Secretary and Minister of Defense, "Limitation of Nuclear Tests" (Sept. 1956), AB 6/1817, AEA Records; British Cabinet meeting of Oct. 25, 1956, 74(6), CAB 128, Cabinet Records.

9. Macmillan, *Riding the Storm*, pp. 289–90, 296–98, 305–6, 308.

10. Wright, *Disarm and Verify*, p. 135; "UK/US Discussions at the White House, June 9th, [1958]," FO 371/135540, and Macmillan to Foreign Secretary, July 8, 1958, FO 371/135550, FO Records.

11. Macmillan to Eisenhower, enclosure in Hood to Burke Elbrick, Mar. 27, 1958, 711.5611/3-2758, and John Foster Dulles to Macmillan, Apr. 10, 1958, 711.5611/4-1058, DOS Records; British Cabinet meeting of Apr. 1, 1958, 28(1), CAB 128, Cabinet Records; FO to British Embassy (Washington), Apr. 5, 1958, FO 371/135538, FO Records.

12. Lewis L. Strauss, "Memorandum for the Files of Lewis L. Strauss" (Aug. 20, 1958), Box 67, AEC Series, Strauss Papers; Macmillan to Eisenhower, Aug. 20, 1958, FO 371/135551, FO Records; Ambrose, *Eisenhower*, 2: 478.

13. *PN*, Apr. 26, June 21, 1957; *NYT*, May 20, 1957; Divine, *Blowing on the Wind*, p. 75.

14. Jacobson and Stein, *Diplomats, Scientists*, p. 21; Sharma, ed., *Indian Atom*, p. 78; *NYT*, May 18, 19, 20, 1957, Feb. 3, 1958.

15. Reiss, *Without the Bomb*, pp. 50–55; Quester, "Sweden," pp. 52–53; Erlander, *Tage Erlander*, pp. 77–79, 83–84, 86–93; Ahlmark, *Den svenska atomvapendebatten*, pp. 15–16, 18.

16. Divine, *Blowing on the Wind*, pp. 75, 119–20; Jacobson and Stein, *Diplomats, Scientists*, pp. 20–21; Hewlett and Holl, *Atoms*, p. 389; *NYT*, Apr. 22, 1958.

17. Howard L. Parsons, "Nuclear Tests in the Pacific" (May 3, 1956), 711.5611/5-356, J. V. Martin Jr., "Japanese Diplomatic Note on Pacific Nuclear Tests" (May 4, 1956), 711.5611/5-456, John Foster Dulles to American Embassy (Tokyo), May 8, 1956, 711.5611/5-856, MacArthur to SecState, Feb. 21, 1958, 711.5611/2-2158, and Harlan B. Clark to DOS, Feb. 25, 1958, 711.5611/2-2558, DOS Records; *FRUS, 1955–1957*, 23: 495–96.

18. Pempel, "Japan's Nuclear Allergy," p. 169; *Meaning of Survival*, pp. 125, 130; *FRUS, 1955–1957*, 23: 395.

19. *FRUS, 1955–1957*, 20: 279, 23: 285; Pempel, "Japan's Nuclear Allergy," p. 169.

20. U.S. officials reluctantly concluded that the Japanese government would not "consent to the deployment of US nuclear weapons in Japan in the foreseeable future." *FRUS, 1958–1960*, 18: 78–79, 83, 115.

21. Passin, "Nuclear Arms and Japan," pp. 78–79, 85, 100; Hersey, *Hiroshima*, p. 97; *Meaning of Survival*, pp. 129–30.

22. Clements, *Back from the Brink*, pp. 36–43, 101.

23. Einhorn, *National Security*, pp. 56–58; *FRUS, 1955–1957*, 4: 214–15; Bjol, *Hvem bestemmer*, p. 288; Hayden Raynor to DOS, Feb. 27, 1958, 711.5611/2-2758, DOS Records.

24. Grepstad, "Norway," pp. 1–2; *FRUS, 1955–1957*, 27: 528–29; Boel, *Socialdemokratiets atomvåbenpolitik*, pp. 4–6.

25. The British government had previously agreed to installation of the missiles. *FRUS, 1955–1957*, 4: 240; Pierre, *Nuclear Politics*, p. 140.

26. *FRUS, 1955–1957*, 4: 240, 244–47, 249–51; Burgess to SecState, Feb. 7, 1958, 711.5611/2-758, DOS Records.

27. Nolting to SecState, Apr. 3, 1958, 711.5611/4-358, and P. Jandrey, "Memorandum of Conversation" (Apr. 24, 1958), "18.4 Weapons—Test Moratorium, d. Position of US-UK-France" Folder, AE Lot File, DOS Records.

28. Holloway, *Soviet Union*, pp. 32–35, 84–85; Holloway, *Stalin and the Bomb*, pp. 343–44; Scott and Scott, *Soviet Military Doctrine*, pp. 20–21; *Pravda*, Sept. 1, 1956, in *CDSP* 8 (Oct. 10, 1956): 17; N. Khrushchev, *Khrushchev Remembers: The Last Testament*, p. 53.

29. Bloomfield, Clemens, and Griffiths, *Khrushchev*, pp. 164–65; *Istoricheskii arkhiv* 4 (1993): 5, 36–37, in Smirnov and Zubok, "Nuclear Weapons after Stalin's Death," p. 17; Richter, *Khrushchev's Double Bind*, p. 103; Resis, ed., *Molotov Remembers*, pp. 354–55, 388–89.

30. Lewis and Xue, *China Builds the Bomb*, pp. 60–61, 63–64; N. Khrushchev, *Khrushchev Remembers: The Last Testament*, pp. 254–55, 268–69.

31. *FRUS, 1955–1957*, 20: 394, 468, 480–81, 502, 535.

32. Ibid., 27: 774; Hewlett and Holl, *Atoms*, pp. 397–98; *FRUS, 1955–1957*, 20: 732–33.

33. At the time, Stassen, too, believed that Soviet negotiators were very serious about an agreement with the United States and, therefore, that it was within grasp. Bloomfield, Clemens, and Griffiths, *Khrushchev*, pp. 153–55, 157, 159, 174; Appleby, "Eisenhower and Arms Control," p. 28; Hewlett and Holl, *Atoms*, pp. 387–88.

34. *FRUS, 1955–1957*, 20: 675–76, 706, 732.

35. Dobrynin, *In Confidence*, pp. 37–39; *FRUS, 1955–57*, 20: 327, 379–83, 734; Kistiakowsky, *A Scientist*, p. xliv; Bloomfield, Clemens, and Griffiths, *Khrushchev*, pp. 90–91, 96, 175.

36. Weart, *Nuclear Fear*, p. 146; *Krasnaya zvezda*, Sept. 3, 1957, in *CDSP* 9 (Oct. 9, 1957): 17–18; Holloway, *Soviet Union*, pp. 84–85; Divine, *Blowing on the Wind*, p. 120; Bloomfield, Clemens, and Griffiths, *Khrushchev*, p. 97.

37. Bloomfield, Clemens, and Griffiths, *Khrushchev*, p. 91. For Khrushchev's own linkage between the Soviet missile program, the space satellite program, and his public demand to "put an end to the 'cold war,' stop the arms race, ban atomic and hydrogen weapons, and free mankind from the threat of another world war," see his speech of January 22, 1958, in *Pravda* and *Izvestia*, Jan. 26, 1958, in *CDSP* 10 (Mar. 5, 1958): 15–17. His later reflections on the connection between Soviet military confidence and disarmament can be seen in N. Khrushchev, *Khrushchev Remembers: The Glasnost Tapes*, pp. 71–72.

38. Khrushchev's letter announcing Soviet intentions to Eisenhower and Macmillan resembles the wording suggested by this memo. G. Saksin to Andrei Gromyko, Jan. 25, 1958, "Problems of disarmament, on a halt to testing of atomic and hydrogen weapons, 29 January–29 October 1958, folder 194/III-USA, pap. 92, por. 36, op. 44, Fond: Ref. po SShA, Department of American Countries, Russian Foreign Ministry Archives, Moscow, cited in Evangelista, "Soviet Scientists and Nuclear Testing," p. 15; *Pravda*, Apr. 6, 1958, in *CDSP* 10 (May 14, 1958): 26.

39. Zhores Medvedev, one of those arguing that military experts opposed the Soviet test suspension, has also suggested the possibility that the decision "was in some way related" to a recent nuclear disaster in the Urals area. "It was probably necessary to shut down plutonium-producing plants temporarily, and this was a good excuse for Khrushchev's unexpected move." This hypothesis, though, has never been substantiated. Nor, if it is correct, is it clear why military experts would have opposed test suspension. Sakharov, *Memoirs*, pp. 206–7; David Ormsby Gore to Selwyn Lloyd, Feb. 10, 1959, FO 371/140436, FO Records; Z. Medvedev, *Soviet Science*, p. 96.

40. Secretary of State Dulles conceded that the Russians had scored "a certain propaganda victory." The Western conviction that Moscow's move was totally cynical grew when the Soviet government resumed nuclear testing on September 30, 1958, after the U.S. government finally agreed to join the Russians in stopping tests. Nevertheless, upon completing its tests, the Soviet government stuck to the moratorium for the next three years. Divine, *Blowing on the Wind*, pp. 201, 233–34.

41. Ambrose, *Eisenhower*, 2: 243; *FRUS, 1955–1957*, 20: 273, 298.

42. Radford and others returned to the attack later in the meeting, with Radford predicting hopefully that "the use of these nuclear weapons would become accepted throughout the world just as soon as people could lay their hands upon them." *FRUS, 1955–1957*, 19: 204–6, 211, 307.

43. Patterson, "President Eisenhower," p. 5; Cook, *Declassified Eisenhower*, pp. 154, 164–67; *FRUS, 1955–1957*, 20: 323; Eisenhower to Richard L. Simon, Apr. 4, 1956, "Apr. '56 Miscellaneous (5)" Folder, Box 14, DDE Diary Series, Eisenhower Papers.

44. Lewis L. Strauss, "Memorandum for the Files of Lewis L. Strauss" (Apr. 7, 1958), Box 67, AEC Series, Strauss Papers. See also *FRUS, 1955–1957*, 19: 526.

45. *FRUS, 1955–1957*, 19: 499–503.

46. Ibid., 27: 734–37; Ambrose, *Eisenhower*, 2: 405; Bundy, *Danger and Survival*, p. 488; Seaborg, *Stemming the Tide*, pp. 77–78; *FRUS, 1955–1957*, 4: 214–15.

47. *FRUS, 1955–1957*, 4: 215. Exactly what Dulles meant by this is unclear, for the subsequent portion of the document remains classified by order of the NSC.

48. Ibid., pp. 254–55; Seaborg, *Stemming the Tide*, pp. 77–78.

49. *FRUS, 1955–1957*, 20: 279, 404, 483, 542–43, 546, and 27: 735; A. J. Goodpaster, "Memorandum of a Conference with the President, September 11, 1956" (Sept. 14, 1956), Box 17, DDE Diary Series, Eisenhower Papers.

50. *FRUS, 1955–1957*, 27: 178, 766; Ambrose, *Eisenhower*, 2: 479; Baum, "Two's Company"; de Gaulle, *Memoirs*, pp. 207–9, 213–15.

51. Hewlett and Holl, *Atoms*, pp. 223, 274–75; Dulles to Eisenhower, Apr. 6, 1954, Box 26D, AEC Series, Strauss Papers; *FRUS, 1952–1954*, 2: 1452–56, 1465–72; Charles E. Wilson to SecState, June 4, 1954, 711.5611/6-454, DOS Records.

52. Lodge, *As It Was*, p. 71; *FRUS, 1955–1957*, 4: 16; Minutes of the Cabinet meeting of Mar. 25, 1955, Box 5, Cabinet Series, Eisenhower Papers.

53. *FRUS, 1955–1957*, 20: 133, 245, 258; "U.S. Goals at Geneva" (July 1, 1955), Box 89, J. F. Dulles Papers, Princeton; Harold Stassen, "Memorandum for the President" (Sept. 16, 1955), Box 34, AS, Eisenhower Papers.

54. Conceding Dulles's point, Stassen now backed off from his earlier call for candor and remarked that he did not want "the President or the Secretary of State getting up and saying publicly that nuclear weapons should not be banned. . . . Nuclear bombs cannot be banned, but we should not make a positive declaration to that effect." He cited a debate over banning the Bomb at the British Labour Party's recent convention. *FRUS, 1955–1957*, 20: 141, 150, 220.

55. In a memo to Stassen that same day, Dulles said that if U.S. proposals did not, among other things, call for eventual reductions in nuclear weapons, they "are likely to persuade many that the U.S. is not seriously interested in disarmament." As a result, Stassen's plan "would not be sufficient to maintain for us our leadership in the free world coalition and to secure the essential support of world public opinion." *FRUS, 1955–1957*, 20: 287–88, 294–98, 302.

56. Divine, *Blowing on the Wind*, pp. 66–69, 86, 111; *FRUS, 1955–1957*, 20: 406–8, 427. See also Patterson, "President Eisenhower," p. 6; Eisenhower to Lewis Strauss, Aug. 30, 1956, Box 17, DDE Diary Series, Eisenhower Papers; *FRUS, 1955–1957*, 20: 538.

57. Responding to Lodge's warnings about loss of support at the United Nations, Strauss declared: "Continuation of our experiments is so important . . . that, in my view, we should fight to be able to continue even should we stand *alone*." *FRUS, 1955–1957*, 20: 278, 287, 424–25; Lewis L. Strauss, "Memorandum for the Files of Lewis L. Strauss" (May 25, 1957), Box 26E, and Strauss to Lodge, Sept. 19, 1957, Box 61, AEC Series, Strauss Papers.

58. *FRUS, 1955–1957*, 20: 419–21, 524; Hewlett and Holl, *Atoms*, p. 397; *FRUS, 1955–1957*, 23: 395–96; Dulles to Stassen, Sept. 27, 1957, Box 12, AS, Eisenhower Papers. See also *FRUS, 1955–1957*, 20: 483–85.

59. A. J. Goodpaster, "Memorandum of Conference with the President" (June 24, 1957), Box 25, DDE Diary Series, Eisenhower Papers; *FRUS, 1955–1957*, 20: 649, 666, 739–40; Hewlett and Holl, *Atoms*, pp. 400–401; Divine, *Blowing on the Wind*, pp. 148–49, 177–78.

60. Killian, *Sputnik*, p. 152; York, *Making Weapons, Talking Peace*, p. 117; Hewlett and Holl, *Atoms*, p. 464.

61. Killian, *Sputnik*, pp. 153–54; Hewlett and Holl, *Atoms*, p. 470; personal interview with Ronald Spiers, Oct. 28, 1992.

62. Lewis L. Strauss, "Memorandum for the Files of Lewis L. Strauss" (Mar. 24, 1958), Box 67, AEC Series, Strauss Papers; Pfau, *No Sacrifice Too Great*, pp. 213–14.

63. Ambrose, *Eisenhower*, 2: 449–51; A. J. Goodpaster, "Memorandum of Conference with the President, Mar. 24, 1958" (Mar. 28, 1958), Box 31, DDE Diary Series, Eisenhower Papers.

64. Personal interview with Ronald Spiers, Oct. 28, 1992; Hewlett and Holl, *Atoms*, p. 479; Dulles to Macmillan, Apr. 10, 1958, 711.5611/4-1058, DOS Records.

65. Ambrose, *Eisenhower*, 2: 452–53; Strauss, *Men and Decisions*, p. 424; Hewlett and Holl, *Atoms*, p. 489; Anderson, *Outsider*, pp. 200–201.

66. Ambrose, *Eisenhower*, 2: 453; Lewis L. Strauss, "Memorandum for the Files of Lewis L. Strauss" (Apr. 28, 1958), Box 67, AEC Series, Strauss Papers; John Foster Dulles, "Memorandum for the President" (Apr. 30, 1958), Box 6, White House Memoranda Series, J. F. Dulles Papers, Abilene; "Telephone Call Chronology, May 1, 1958," Box 33, DDE Diary Series, Eisenhower Papers.

67. "UK/US Discussions at the White House, June 9th [1958]," FO 371/135540, and Washington (Embassy) to FO, July 4, 1958, FO 371/135550, FO Records; James J. Wadsworth to Dulles, June 24, 1958, "18.14 Weapons—Test Moratorium, d. Position of US-UK-France" Folder, AE Lot File, DOS Records.

68. In a letter to Macmillan, Dulles argued that "our standing in the world is at a point where there is real danger to us in being adjudged militaristic. That danger can have consequences as serious as the foregoing of some nuclear weapons knowledge." The U.S. government could not afford "to take further serious risks in relation to world opinion." Berding, *Dulles*, pp. 143–44; Dulles to Macmillan, Aug. 20, 1958, FO 371/135551, FO Records.

69. A. J. Goodpaster, "Memorandum of Conference with the President, August 12, 1958" (Aug. 14, 1958), Box 3, Alpha Subseries, Subject Series, OSS, White House Office Records; A. J. Goodpaster, "Memorandum of Conference with the President, August 18, 1958" (Aug. 18, 1958), Box 35, DDE Diary Series, Eisenhower Papers.

70. Lewis L. Strauss, "Memorandum for the Files of Lewis L. Strauss" (Aug. 20, 1958), Box 67, AEC Series, Strauss Papers; Hewlett and Holl, *Atoms*, pp. 545–46; "Memorandum of Conversation" (Aug. 21, 1958), Box 12, International Series, Eisenhower Papers.

71. *NYT*, Aug. 23, 1958; Divine, *Blowing on the Wind*, pp. 228–29, 231–33, 238–39; Hacker, *Elements of Controversy*, pp. 196–97.

72. Dulles to Adenauer, June 30, 1958, Box 125, J. F. Dulles Papers, Princeton; *FRUS, 1955–1957*, 4: 198–99, 20: 734.

Chapter 9

Epigraph: "Magna Carta of the Nuclear Age," in *Sanity* [Britain], Easter Sunday 1963, p. 2.

1. Executive Committee Report with Amendments, CND National Conference, Mar. 7–8, 1959, Reel 4, CND (Britain) Records, London-Warwick; Antoinette Pirie to Linus Pauling, Oct. 25, 1959, Pauling Papers; *PN*, May 20, Nov. 25, 1960.

2. During one base demonstration, two workers announced that they were quitting on principle. At the Bristol Aircraft Corporation, workers drew up a plan for conversion to civilian production. "Brief History of the Direct Action Committee Against Nuclear War" (June 22, 1961), Direct Action Committee Against Nuclear War Records; Carter, "Direct Action," pp. 50–52; Randle, "Non-Violent Direct Action," pp. 134–36; *PN*, Dec. 18, 1959, Jan. 8, Apr. 18, Sept. 9, 1960; *NYT*, Jan. 3, 1960; oral history interview with Pat Arrowsmith, Reels 5, 6.

3. Collins, *Faith Under Fire*, p. 310.

4. Minnion and Bolsover, eds., *CND Story*, p. 25; Minutes of CND Executive Committee meeting of Feb. 6, 1959, Reel 1, CND (Britain) Records, London-Warwick; Collins, *Faith Under Fire*, pp. 311–12, 315.

5. The U.S. ambassador, who estimated attendance at eighty thousand, was struck by the culminating rally's "enormous size, diverse support, vigorous spirit, and dramatic cumulative force." Collins, *Faith Under Fire*, pp. 313, 316–17; R. Taylor, *Against the Bomb*, pp. 49, 57; Carter, *Peace Movements*, p. 48; *PN*, Apr. 22, 1960; *NYT*, Apr. 19, 1960; Vera Brit-

tain, *The Meaning of Aldermaston* (1960), pp. 3–4, Peace Pledge Union Records; Whitney to SecState, Apr. 20, 1960, 600.0012/4-2060, DOS Records.

6. M. Gordon Knox to SecState, May 13, 1959, 741.00/5-1359, DOS Records; Pierre, *Nuclear Politics*, p. 180; *PN*, July 17, Aug. 28, 1959; Peggy Duff to Donald Keys, July 30, 1959, Box 21, Series B, SANE Records.

7. Parkin, *Middle Class Radicalism*, pp. 113–26; *PN*, May 13, July 15, 1960; P. Williams, *Hugh Gaitskell*, pp. 575–76; R. Taylor, "Labour Party," p. 112.

8. Campaign for Nuclear Disarmament, "Annual Report, April 1960/March '61," p. 3, Reel 4, CND (Britain) Records, London-Warwick; R. Taylor, "Labour Party," pp. 112–14; Driver, *Disarmers*, p. 95.

9. Driver, *Disarmers*, pp. 95–97; P. Williams, *Hugh Gaitskell*, pp. 622–53.

10. Campaign for Nuclear Disarmament, "Annual Report, April 1960/March '61," p. 3, Reel 4, CND (Britain) Records, London-Warwick; *Let Britain Lead* (1961), CND (Britain) Records, SCPC; *PN*, Oct. 6, 1961.

11. Parkin, *Middle Class Radicalism*, pp. 126–39; R. Taylor, "Labour Party," pp. 115–19; Duff, *Left, Left, Left*, pp. 191–93, 196–97; Healey, *Time of My Life*, pp. 241–42; Bruce to SecState, Feb. 16, 1962, Reel 9, *National Security Files*.

12. Randle, "Non-Violent Direct Action," pp. 146–47, 150; Peggy Duff to Russell, Jan. 7, 22, 1959, Class 630, RA 1; Collins, *Faith Under Fire*, pp. 328–30.

13. CND did organize support demonstrations, however. Minutes of CND Executive Committee meeting of Jan. 2, 1959, Reel 1, "Decisions of National Conference, 1959," Reel 4, CND (Britain) Records, London-Warwick; Duff, *Left, Left, Left*, p. 169; *PN*, Dec. 25, 1959.

14. Duff, *Left, Left, Left*, pp. 130–31; Russell to Avner Falk, Dec. 3, 1961, Class 640, RA 1; R. Clark, *Life of Bertrand Russell*, pp. 568–69.

15. Schoenman, "Bertrand Russell," p. 241; Driver, *Disarmers*, pp. 106–12; R. Clark, *Life of Bertrand Russell*, pp. 572–73; Russell to Henry Moore, Sept. 16, 1960, Class 630, RA 1.

16. Collins, *Faith Under Fire*, pp. 319–24; "Chairman's Report," Reel 3, Russell to CND, Oct. 31, 1960, "The Resignation of Earl Russell" (Nov. 5, 1960), Reel 2, and Minutes of CND Executive Committee meeting of Nov. 5, 1960, Reel 1, CND (Britain) Records, London-Warwick; Collins to Russell, Sept. 25, 1960, Russell and Michael Scott, "Press Statement" (Sept. 30, 1960), Russell and Collins, untitled and undated statement, Michael Scott to CND Executive and Branches, Oct. 19, 1960, Russell, untitled statement (Oct. 31, 1960), and James Mitchell to Russell, Oct. 25, 1960, Class 630, RA 1; Duff, *Left, Left, Left*, pp. 171–74.

17. R. Clark, *Life of Bertrand Russell*, pp. 584–86; Schoenman, "Bertrand Russell," pp. 246–47; Schoenman, "Mass Resistance," p. 109; "A Call to Action," Committee of 100 Records; Michael Randle to Dear Sir, Feb. 22, 1961, Class 630, RA 1; *PN*, Feb. 24, 1961.

18. "Parliament Square Assembly" (Apr. 1961) and "Bertrand Russell calls for vast movement of protest" (Aug. 1961), Committee of 100 Records; "Committee of 100 Announces Non-Violent Civil Disobedience, Saturday, 29 April," Randle Papers; Duff, *Left, Left, Left*, p. 179; *PN*, May 5, 1961.

19. *PN*, May 26, June 2, 1961; Randle, "Non-Violent Direct Action," p. 135; Pat Arrowsmith to Vera Brittain, June 8, 1961, "Direct Action Committee Against Nuclear War" Folder, Brittain Papers; oral history interview with Pat Arrowsmith, Reel 6.

20. April Carter to Michael Randle, Sept. 28, 1960, Randle Papers; Hugh Brock to A. J. Muste, Oct. 24, 1961, Box 8, CNVA Records; Driver, *Disarmers*, pp. 106–7; April Carter to the author, Mar. 7, 1994; Randle to the author, Oct. 4, 1994; oral history interview with Pat Arrowsmith, Reel 6; "Final Statement by the D.A.C." (June 22, 1961), Direct Action Committee Against Nuclear War Records.

21. Russell's sentence was reduced to a week, which he spent reading in the prison hospital. Michael Randle to CNVA, July 14, 1961, Box 5, CNVA Records; "Statement Made by Lord Russell at Bow Street" (Sept. 12, 1961), Committee of 100 Records; Russell, *Final Years*, pp. 152–57; Randle, "Non-Violent Direct Action," p. 137; Collins, *Faith Under Fire*, p. 331; R. Clark, *Life of Bertrand Russell*, pp. 590–92; *Manchester Guardian*, Sept. 18, 19, 1961.

22. "Statement to be delivered to the U.S.S.R. Embassy on Tuesday, Oct. 22nd, 1961," Class 640, RA 1; *NYT*, Oct. 31, 1961; "Danger Radioactive," Randle Papers; "Statement by Bertrand Russell on Parliament Square Demonstrations 24 March 1962," Pauling Papers.

23. Schoenman, "Bertrand Russell," p. 247; Ralph Schoenman to Pauling, Mar. 30, 1962, Pauling Papers; *PN*, Dec. 1, 1961, Jan. 19, 1962; International Sub Committee, National Committee of 100, "Bulletin" (Summer 1962), Committee of 100 Records; Minutes of the National Committee of 100 meeting, Sept. 29–30, 1962, Class 630, RA 2.

24. The Committee of 100 had called for fifty thousand participants. The police made 860 arrests at the December 9 demonstrations, and sent 129 to prison. "Mass Resistance, Wethersfield—Ruislip, 9th December 1961," Randle Papers; Randle, "Non-Violent Direct Action," pp. 138–39; Carter, *Peace Movements*, pp. 50–51; Randle to the author, Oct. 4, 1994; R. Clark, *Life of Bertrand Russell*, pp. 592–93; *Times* (London), Dec. 11, 1961.

25. R. Clark, *Life of Bertrand Russell*, pp. 595–99; Russell to Kennedy, Oct. 23, 24, 1962, Russell to Khrushchev, Oct. 23, 24, 26, 1962, Russell to Macmillan, Oct. 23, 1962, Russell to Castro, Oct. 26, 1962, and "Press Statement" (Oct. 23, 1962), RA 1; Pat Arrowsmith to Russell, Nov. 6, 1962, Class 630, RA 2; Randle, "Non-Violent Direct Action," p. 141.

26. Randle, "Non-Violent Direct Action," pp. 138–41; Carter, *Peace Movements*, p. 50; Hinton, *Protests and Visions*, p. 169; *PN*, Apr. 6, 20, July 20, 1962; April Carter to the author, Mar. 7, 1994.

27. Brian Richardson to Russell, Apr. 6, 1961, "Summary of Working Group Discussion on 6th April About Easter Sit-down" (Apr. 8, 1961), and Tony Smythe to the Working Committee, Committee of 100, Apr. 11, 1961, Class 630, RA 1.

28. Peggy Denny to Russell, Dec. 22, 1961, Class 630, RA 1; April Carter to the author, Mar. 7, 1994; Carter, *Peace Movements*, p. 51; Brandon, *Burning Question*, pp. 52–53.

29. Russell to Michael Randle, Apr. 10, 1961, and "Press statement" (Dec. 14, 1961), Class 630, RA 1.

30. Russell, *Final Years*, pp. 159–60, 162, 166; R. Clark, *Life of Bertrand Russell*, pp. 603–4; Russell to the Secretary, Committee of 100, Jan. 8, 1963, Class 630, RA 1; Carter, *Peace Movements*, pp. 51–52.

31. R. Taylor, *Against the Bomb*, p. 68; Collins, *Faith Under Fire*, pp. 327, 332–33.

32. Carter, *Peace Movements*, p. 53; "Campaign for Nuclear Disarmament," CND (Britain) Records, SCPC; Campaign for Nuclear Disarmament, "Annual Report, April 1960/March '61," pp. 4, 6–7, Reel 4, CND (Britain) Records, London-Warwick.

33. When five thousand nuclear disarmament demonstrators turned out in Glasgow in February 1961, the *Scotsman* called it "one of the biggest protest gestures Scotland has seen since the Labour troubles of 30 years ago." "And in Belfast," *Pax*, Oct. 1961; *PN*, Feb. 24, 1961.

34. R. Taylor, *Against the Bomb*, pp. 72, 79, 89–91, 102–3; *Sanity* [Britain], Easter Sunday 1963, p. 3, Apr. 1963, p. 1, Mar. 1964.

35. R. Taylor, "Labour Party," pp. 117–19; Collins to Russell, Mar. 28, May 19, 1961, Class 630, RA 1.

36. Minutes of the CND Executive Committee meeting of Sept. 3, 1961, Reel 1, CND (Britain) Records, London-Warwick; Duff, *Left, Left, Left*, p. 191; *International Bulletin*, Sept. 1962; R. Taylor, *Against the Bomb*, p. 78.

37. Minutes of the CND National Council meeting of Oct. 27, 1962, Reel 1, CND (Britain) Records, London-Warwick; R. Taylor, *Against the Bomb*, pp. 88–89; *Sanity* [Britain], Nov. 1962, p. 1.

38. *PN*, Sept. 21, 1962; Duff, *Left, Left, Left*, pp. 201–2; Carter, *Peace Movements*, p. 49; "After Cuba—Steps Towards Peace," Reel 2, CND (Britain) Records, London-Warwick.

39. According to CND, twenty to thirty thousand people attended the rally, leading the *Guardian* to headline its story on the event: "CND Still Very Much Alive." *Sanity* [Britain], Apr. 1964.

40. It was more in line with an older, middle-class, "high-minded" tradition of antislavery, Corn Law, and League of Nations campaigns.

41. Parkin, *Middle Class Radicalism*, pp. 16–187; Driver, *Disarmers*, pp. 59–60; *PN*, Oct. 30, 1959; Duff, *Left, Left, Left*, p. 160; Pete Snedden, "To Our International Contacts" (1965), Folder 305, WRI Records, Amsterdam.

42. Parkin, *Middle Class Radicalism*, pp. 87–89; Duff, *Left, Left, Left*, p. 128; Bess, *Realism*, pp. 111–13; Thompson, "A Psessay in Ephology," pp. 2–8.

43. Ormrod, "Churches," pp. 199–201, 207–10; Parkin, *Middle Class Radicalism*, pp. 60–63, 67–68, 73–77; Minutes of the CND Executive Committee meetings of June 30, July 2, 1961, Reel 1, CND (Britain) Records, London-Warwick; *PN*, May 13, 1960. For the important role of the Friends Peace Committee in CND, see "Proceedings of the London Yearly Meeting, 1960," p. 21, "Proceedings of the London Yearly Meeting, 1961," pp. 158–59, "Proceedings of the London Yearly Meeting, 1962," p. 110, and "Proceedings of the London Yearly Meeting, 1964," p. 117, London Yearly Meeting Records.

44. Carter, *Peace Movements*, p. 54; *Sanity* [Britain], July 1963, p. 2; Eglin, "Women and Peace," pp. 236–39; Minutes of the CND Executive Committee meeting of July 29, 1962, Reel 1, CND (Britain) Records, London-Warwick; *PN*, Jan. 12, 1962, May 8, 1964; Driver, *Disarmers*, p. 127; Liddington, *Long Road to Greenham*, pp. 192–93. For a discussion of "maternalist" and other kinds of women's antimilitarism, see Pierson, "Did Your Mother Wear Army Boots?"

45. Duff, *Left, Left, Left*, pp. 162–63; Pete Snedden, "To Our International Contacts" (1965), Folder 305, WRI Records, Amsterdam; *Sanity* [Britain], July 1963, p. 2; "Majority Report of the Executive Committee" (Nov. 1964), Reel 1, CND (Britain) Records, London-Warwick; Parkin, *Middle Class Radicalism*, pp. 146–48, 157–61, 166.

46. Snyder, *Politics*, pp. 60–61, 84; Gallup, ed., *Gallup International Public Opinion Polls: Great Britain*, p. 604; *Sanity* [Britain], Nov. 1961, p. 3.

47. *Manchester Guardian*, Sept. 27, 1961; Minutes of the CND Executive Committee meeting of Nov. 18, 1962, Reel 1, CND (Britain) Records, London-Warwick; personal interview with E. P. Thompson, Nov. 1, 1989; Driver, *Disarmers*, pp. 148–54.

48. Duff, *Left, Left, Left*, pp. 203–4; Randle to the author, Oct. 4, 1994.

49. Duff, *Left, Left, Left*, pp. 203–4; Russell, *Common Sense and Nuclear Warfare*, p. 65; Russell, *Has Man a Future?*, pp. 73, 77–86; Findley R. Rea to Russell, June 3, 1960, Class 630, RA 1; *Sanity* [Britain], Dec. 1961, p. 2; Boserup and Iverson, "Demonstrations," p. 347.

50. R. Taylor, *Against the Bomb*, p. 28; Philip Noel-Baker to Russell, June 16, 1959, Class 640, Patrick Armstrong to Russell, Sept. 23, 1959, Russell to Armstrong, Sept. 26, 1959, Class 570, and Collins to Russell, Jan. 22, 1960, Class 630, RA 1.

51. See, for example, the comments along these lines made by Canon Collins and A. J. P. Taylor in Collins, *Faith Under Fire*, p. 337; *Sanity* [Britain], Mar. 1964.

52. Gallup, ed., *Gallup International Public Opinion Polls: Great Britain*, pp. 450, 460–61, 476, 499, 553–54, 558, 562, 567, 584, 604, 614, 650, 663, 668, 686.

53. Ibid., pp. 572, 733.

54. In the United States, by contrast, 81 percent preferred to fight a nuclear war. Driver, *Disarmers*, pp. 235–36; *Sanity* [Britain], Good Friday / Saturday 1963, p. 10; Gallup, ed., *Gallup International Public Opinion Polls: Great Britain*, pp. 492, 553, 1741.

55. Gallup, ed., *Gallup International Public Opinion Polls: Great Britain*, pp. 514, 600, 623, 626, 663.

56. Ibid., p. 699; Gallup, ed., *Gallup Poll*, p. 1562; Hutchison to USIA, Sept. 12, 1962, Reel 9, *National Security Files*; "West European Public Opinion on Disarmament" (July 1963), p. 3, Box 15, RR, OR, USIA Records; *Sanity* [Britain], Easter 1964.

57. Carter, *Peace Movements*, p. 57; "Majority Report of the Executive Committee" (Nov. 1964), Reel 1, CND (Britain) Records, London-Warwick; personal interview with Sheila Jones, July 10, 1990.

58. Donald Keys to Dennis Knight, Mar. 26, 1959, and Mary Van Stolk to Keys, Mar. 31, 1959, Box 19, Series B, SANE Records; Mary Van Stolk to Bertrand Russell, Oct. 28, 1960, Class 640, RA 1; "History of the Edmonton Committee on the Control of Radiation Hazards" (Sept. 22, 1960), Box 8, Canadian CND Records, Hamilton.

59. "History of the Edmonton Committee on the Control of Radiation Hazards" (Sept. 22, 1960), Box 8, and "Prominent Canadians Form Committee on Radiation Hazards & Nuclear Policy," Box 1, Canadian CND Records, Hamilton; Mary Van Stolk to Pauling, Sept. 25, 1959, Pauling Papers; Jan Van Stolk to Norman Cousins, Sept. 16, 1959, Box 19, Series B, SANE Records.

60. Edmonton Committee for the Control of Radiation Hazards, "Monthly Newsletter," and National Committee for the Control of Radiation Hazards, "Monthly Newsletter" (Nov. 1960), Box 26, Committee for Environmental Information Records; Moffatt, *History*, pp. 88–90.

61. Hugh Keenleyside to John Diefenbaker, Mar. 30, 1961, and F. C. Hunnius to Keenleyside, Apr. 21, 1961, "Everyone wants PEACE but . . . what can YOU do?" Box 2, Canadian CND Records, Hamilton; "Statement by the Executive of the Canadian Committee for the Control of Radiation Hazards" (1961), enclosure in F. C. Hunnius to Bertrand Russell, Feb. 17, 1962, and David Gauthier to Russell, Mar. 6, 1961, Class 640, RA 1; Abraham Feinberg to Canon Collins, Feb. 3, 1961, Box 35, Series B, SANE Records; Hunnius, "Will Canada Lead?" p. 112.

62. "Draft Program and Organization Questions" (Jan. 11, 1963), and "What is the Canadian Campaign for Nuclear Disarmament?" Box 1, Canadian CND Records, Hamilton; "The Annual Conference of the C.C.N.D.," *SOS*, no. 13 (Apr. 1962).

63. Roussopoulos, ed., *New Left*, p. 8; Kostash, *Long Way*, pp. xxii–xxiii; "Provisional Policy Statement" (1960), enclosure in Elka Cohen to Bertrand Russell, Nov. 16, 1960, Class 640, RA 1; "End the Arms Race or End the Human Race," Box 1, Combined Universities CND-Student Union for Peace Action Records; "Support the Combined Universities Campaign for Nuclear Disarmament," Combined Universities CND Records; Roussopoulos, *From Protest to Resistance*, p. 127.

64. *Information Bulletin*, Sept. 27, 1961, p. 1, Folder 188, WRI Records, Amsterdam; Hunnius, "Will Canada Lead?" p. 112; Roussopoulos to Howard Adelman, Jan. 14, 1961, Box 1, Combined Universities CND-Student Union for Peace Action Records; Roussopoulos, *From Protest to Resistance*, p. 128.

65. Bertrand Russell, "Preface to First Issue," *Our Generation Against Nuclear War* 1 (Autumn 1961): 3; Elvin S. Shapiro to Russell, Jan. 8, 1962, Class 640, RA 1.

66. "Voice of Women—Some Questions and Answers," "Statement by Annual Meeting, Voice of Women, June 16–17, 1961," Voice of Women Records; Macpherson and Sears, "Voice of Women," pp. 71–72; Macpherson, *When in Doubt*, pp. 89–94; Moffatt, *History*, pp. 114–17.

67. Macpherson and Sears, "Voice of Women," pp. 73, 82–83; Macpherson, *When in Doubt*, pp. 93–96, 99, 139; Thérèse Casgrain to VOW members, Oct. 17, 1962, Box 310, Cousins Papers, Los Angeles; Helen Tucker, "Voice of Women: And the Conference for International Cooperation Year," *Our Generation Against Nuclear War* 1 (Summer 1962): 26–29; Casgrain, *Woman*, pp. 157–62; Trofimenkoff, "Thérèse Casgrain."

68. J. M. McNamee and A. Friend to Friend, n.d., Box 5, Combined Universities CND-Student Union for Peace Action Records; *PN*, Mar. 23, 1962; Gary Moffatt to Neil Haworth, July 1963, Box 7, CNVA Records; Roussopoulos, *From Protest to Resistance*, p. 131.

69. "Address of Jacques Larue-Langlois" (Oct. 25, 1963), Box 1, Canadian CND Records, Hamilton; Richard H. Courtenaye to DOS, Oct. 16, 1963, POL 21 CAN, 1963 Series, DOS Records.

70. Mildred Fahrni to Tony Smythe, Aug. 10, 1960, Folder 188, WRI Records, Amsterdam; Brittain, *Rebel Passion*, pp. 186–87; Regehr and Rosenblum, "Canadian Peace Movement," p. 226; Kostash, *Long Way*, pp. xxii–xxiii.

71. John C. McDonald, "Neutrals for Peace," *Canadian World Federalist*, no. 9 (Jan.–Feb. 1963): 14; Brock Chisholm, "Disarmament and World Government," *SOS*, no. 14 (May 1962): 1; B. G. Whitmore to Linus Pauling, Aug. 22, 1960, Pauling Papers; "Why Don't We Get Together?" *Canadian World Federalist*, no. 6 (Apr.–May 1962): 20–21.

72. "Across the Nation," *SOS*, no. 14 (May 1962): 2; *PN*, Apr. 27, 1962; *Sanity* [Britain], Easter Sunday 1962, pp. 1, 3, 8; Robert H. Frowick to DOS, Apr. 26, 1962, 711.5611/4-2662, DOS Records.

73. Diefenbaker, *One Canada*, 3: 129; "Statement on Cuba Crisis," *International Bulletin*, Jan. 1963; Macpherson, *When in Doubt*, p. 98; *Sanity* [Britain], Dec. 1962, p. 2.

74. Epstein, "Canada," pp. 176–78; Lyon, *Canada*, pp. 89–90, 103; Ghent, "Did He Fall?" pp. 246–69; Pearson, *Mike*, 3: 69–75; Gordon, "Liberal Leadership," p. 200; Diefenbaker, *One Canada*, 3: 7, 13–15.

75. *Sanity* [Britain], Apr. 1963, p. 2; *PN*, Mar. 15, 1963; Minutes of the Canadian CND Board of Directors' Meeting of Apr. 20–21, 1963, Box 1, Canadian CND Records, Hamilton.

76. Lyon, *Canada*, pp. 140–41, 158; Macpherson and Sears, "Voice of Women," pp. 75–76; "Press Release, Thursday, March 18, 1963," Box 2, Canadian CND Records, Hamilton.

77. "Fate had it," Trudeau argued, "that the final thrust came from the Pentagon and obliged Mr. Pearson to betray his party's platform as well as the ideal with which he had always identified himself. Power presented itself to Mr. Pearson; he had nothing to lose except honor. He lost it. And his whole party lost it with him." Lyon, *Canada*, pp. 211–13; Paul and Laulicht, *In Your Opinion*, p. 3; Gordon, "Liberal Leadership," pp. 200–201.

78. Girard, *Canada*, pp. 66–79; Giangrande, *Nuclear North*, p. 185.

79. Roussopoulos, *From Protest to Resistance*, p. 128; Minutes of the Canadian CND's Board of Directors' meetings of Apr. 20–21, Oct. 25–27, 1963, and "Summary of Possible Policy Positions for the CCND" (Oct. 23, 1963), Box 1, Canadian CND Records, Hamilton; Ian Gentles to Harold Applebaum, Nov. 29, 1963, Box 15, 1971 Series, Spock Papers; *PN*, Apr. 10, 1964.

80. Arthur Pape to Linus Pauling, June 25, 1964, Pauling Papers; Roussopoulos, *From Protest to Resistance*, p. 131; *PN*, July 3, 1964; Kostash, *Long Way*, p. 4.

81. Regehr and Rosenblum, "Canadian Peace Movement," p. 226; Macpherson and Sears, "Voice of Women," pp. 76–77; Macpherson, *When in Doubt*, pp. 101–7; Casgrain, *Woman*, pp. 164–65; B. Roberts, "Women's Peace Activism," pp. 297–99.

82. The ratio of support to opposition went from 61:31 (December 1961), to 54:32 (December 1962), to 49:32 (June 1963). Gallup, ed., *Gallup Poll*, p. 1744; Paul and Laulicht, *In Your Opinion*, p. 57.

83. Paul and Laulicht, *In Your Opinion*, pp. 19, 24, 58, 83, 85, 93, 101.

84. Brian and Veronica Maltby to Bertrand Russell, Mar. 8, 1962, Class 640, RA 1; Maltbys to Linus Pauling, Mar. 8, 1962, Pauling Papers.

85. Summy and Saunders, "Disarmament," pp. 30–31; *Sanity* [Britain], Aug. 1963, p. 3, May 1964; Gordon and Osmond, "An Overview," pp. 22–23; *Weekend News* (Perth), Nov. 17, 1962, Reel 13, CND (Britain) Records, London-Warwick.

86. *Weekend News* (Perth), Nov. 17, 1962, Reel 13, CND (Britain) Records, London-Warwick; Saunders and Summy, "One Hundred Years," pp. 61–62; *Peacemaker*, May–June, July, Sept.–Oct. 1962, Aug. 1963; Queensland CND, "Voice of CND" (Apr. 1963), Box 11, Canadian CND Records, Hamilton.

87. Summy, "Australian Peace Council," pp. 243–54; Summy and Saunders, "Disarmament," pp. 27, 29–30; *Peacemaker*, Dec. 1959; Gilbert and Jordan, "Traditions of Dissent," pp. 354–55; Forrester, *Fifteen Years*, pp. 30–45, 49.

88. Redner and Redner, *Anatomy of the World*, p. 274; "Proceedings of the Tenth Pugwash Conference on Science and World Affairs, London, September 3–7, 1962," pp. 59–60, PC Records, London; Brittain, *Rebel Passion*, pp. 189–90; Tom Wardle to Homer Jack, July 21, 1961, Box 17, Series III, Jack Papers; *Peacemaker*, July 1962.

89. *PN*, Mar. 30, 1962, Nov. 13, 1964; Sybil Cookson to Bertrand Russell, Dec. 31, 1964, Class 320, RA 2; *Bulletin* [New Zealand], Mar. 1965.

90. Saunders and Summy, "One Hundred Years," p. 62; *International Bulletin*, Aug. 1962, p. 7; *Sanity* [Britain], Apr. 1963, p. 3; "Seven Ways to Sanity," *Peace Action* 3 (May 1962): 3; "Aldermaston Support in Victoria," *Peace Action* 3 (May 1962): 4.

91. *Sanity* [Britain], Oct. 1962, p. 6; *International Bulletin*, Sept. 1962, p. 17; *Peace Information Bulletin*, Apr. 1963; Donald W. Lamm to DOS, Aug. 17, 1962, 711.5611/8-1762, DOS Records.

92. A. D. Brand to Bertrand Russell, Apr. 3, 1963, Class 640, RA 1; *Sanity* [Britain], May 1963, p. 3; *PN*, Apr. 26, 1963; Saunders and Summy, "One Hundred Years," p. 72.

93. Albinski, *Politics*, p. 102; "News from the Peace Front," *Fellowship* 27 (Oct. 15, 1961): 3.

94. Sharp, "Militarism," p. 197; Albinski, *Politics*, pp. 26–29; Summy and Saunders, "Disarmament," p. 29; Siracusa, "Peace Movements," p. 3; "What Sort of Base in Australia?" *Bulletin* [New Zealand], May 1963.

95. In Britain, 84 percent favored and 9 percent opposed abolition of nuclear weapons. Albinski, *Politics*, p. 27; "Some Worldwide Attitudes Toward Disarmament and Nuclear Issues" (July 1963), pp. 2, 6, Box 16, RR, OR, USIA Records.

96. Mary Woodward, untitled statement (1963), Box 14, Canadian CND Records, Hamilton; "New Zealand Movement for Nuclear Disarmament—Bulletin 3—July 1959," Box 27, Series B, SANE Records; "Notes on the history of the NZ Campaign for Nuclear Disarmament," Locke Papers; Locke, *Peace People*, pp. 164–66, 186; Clements, *Back from the Brink*, pp. 100–101; "The New Zealand Campaign for Nuclear Disarmament" (1963), Class 630, RA 2; Mary Woodward, *The Bomb: A New Zealand View* (1963), CND (New Zealand) Records.

97. Clements, *Back from the Brink*, pp. 100–101; Locke, *Peace People*, pp. 164, 170; *International Bulletin*, Aug. 1962, pp. 6–7; *PN*, Apr. 27, 1962.

98. Locke gives somewhat smaller figures. *Sanity* [Britain], May 1963, p. 2; *Bulletin* [New Zealand], May 1963; Locke, *Peace People*, p. 170.

99. Alec Stafford to F. C. Hunnius, Nov. 10, 1961, Box 14, Canadian CND Records, Hamilton; *International Bulletin*, Sept. 1962; Phyllis Andrews to Bertrand Russell, July 3, 1963, Class 640, RA 1; *Bulletin* [New Zealand], Nov. 1964.

100. *International Bulletin*, Jan. 1963; *Sanity* [Britain], Dec. 1962, p. 2; Locke, *Peace People*, p. 170.

101. It was the largest petition in New Zealand since the women's franchise of 1893. *Bulletin* [New Zealand], Mar. 1963; *Sanity* [Britain], Aug. 1963, p. 3; S. Burton to Bertrand Russell, June 19, 1963, "Petition to the Honourable Speaker," Class 630, RA 2; Clements, *Back from the Brink*, p. 53; Locke, *Peace People*, p. 180.

102. *Bulletin* [New Zealand], Aug. 1962, July 1963, Sept., Nov. 1964, Mar. 1965; Locke, *Peace People*, pp. 174–76; Reports from New Zealand CND National Committee to the annual conference, Aug. 22–23, 1964, Aug. 21–22, 1965, Folder 356, WRI Records, Amsterdam; "CND historical summary," Locke Papers.

103. Clements, *Back from the Brink*, p. 101; *PN*, Apr. 13, 1962; New Zealand Section, WILPF, Statement of Feb. 17, 1963, and Jean Smith to Louise Sanasen, Aug. 9, 1965, Reel 80, WILPF (International) Records; Evelyn Peat, "National Sections in Action," *Pax et Libertas* 26 (July–Sept. 1961): 11–12.

104. Brittain, *Rebel Passion*, p. 194; Stowell to the editor, Feb. 22, 1964, New Zealand CND to all Branches (ca. Apr. 1964), and *Guardian*, Aug. 12, 1964, CND (New Zealand) Records; *PN*, July 17, 1964; *Bulletin* [New Zealand], Sept. 1964; Elsie Locke to the author, Apr. 4, 1996; Mary Woodward to the author, Apr. 9, 1996.

105. Mary Woodward, untitled statement (1963), Box 14, Canadian CND Records, Hamilton; Report from New Zealand CND National Committee to the annual conference, Aug. 22–23, 1964, Folder 356, WRI Records, Amsterdam; Locke, *Peace People*, pp. 168, 186; Clements, *Back from the Brink*, pp. 100–101.

106. *Bulletin* [New Zealand], Nov. 1963, Sept., Nov. 1964; Report from New Zealand CND National Committee to the annual conference, Aug. 22–23, 1964, Folder 356, WRI Records, Amsterdam; Elsie Locke to the author, Apr. 4, 1996; Locke, *Peace People*, pp. 176–77; Pamela Creegan to Bertrand Russell, Dec. 1962, Class 640, RA 1.

107. *Bulletin* [New Zealand], Aug. 1962; A. C. Barrington to Tony Smythe, June 1962, Folder 355, WRI Records, Amsterdam; Ray Wynn to Elizabeth Tapper, July 10, 1962, Reel 80, WILPF (International) Records.

108. Clements, *Back from the Brink*, pp. 51–59; Locke, *Peace People*, p. 182; *Bulletin* [New Zealand], Mar., Nov., 1964; Report from New Zealand CND National Committee to the annual conference, Aug. 21–22, 1965, Folder 356, WRI Records, Amsterdam.

109. Report from New Zealand CND National Committee to the annual conference, Aug. 22–23, 1964, Folder 356, WRI Records, Amsterdam.

Chapter 10

Epigraph: "Kampagnen mod Atomvåben: Påskemarchen 1961," Aldrig mere Krig Records.

1. Villum Hansen to Alexander Langsdorf, Feb. 5, 1959, and Hansen to Commoner, Nov. 24, 1959, Box 26, Committee for Environmental Information Records; *Sane World*, Mar. 15, 1962.

2. *PN*, Aug. 14, 1959, May 3, 1963; Hagbard Jonassen to Tony Smythe, Sept. 3, 1961, Jonassen to WRI, Feb. 2, 1962, and "Aldrig Mere Krig, 1960–63," Folder 196, WRI Records, Amsterdam; Jorgensen, *Atomvåbnenes rolle*, p. 66; Bjol, *Hvem bestemmer*, p. 214.

3. Jorgensen, *Atomvåbnenes rolle*, pp. 65–66, 167; "Aldrig Mere Krig, 1960–63," Folder 196, WRI Records, Amsterdam; Krasner, *Political Influence*, p. 2.

4. *PN*, Apr. 7, 1961, Apr. 27, 1962; Jorgensen, *Atomvåbnenes rolle*, pp. 77, 169; Steffen Larsen to Bertrand Russell, Mar. 24, 1962, Class 640, RA 1; Hagbard Jonassen to Arlo Tatum, Mar. 28, 1961, and Jonassen to Tony Smythe, Apr. 23, 1962, Folder 196, WRI Records, Amsterdam.

5. *NYT*, Sept. 1, Oct. 26, 1961; Hagbard Jonassen to Tony Smythe, Sept. 3, 1961, Folder 196, WRI Records, Amsterdam; Bjol, *Hvem bestemmer*, p. 216; Jorgensen, *Atomvåbnenes rolle*, pp. 66, 77.

6. *Sanity* [Britain], Apr. 1963, p. 3, May 1963, p. 3; *PN*, Apr. 26, 1963; Steffen Larsen to International Contacts, 1963, Folder 197, WRI Records, Amsterdam; Larsen to International Contacts, Sept. 6, 1963, Kampagnen mod Atomvåben Records.

7. *Peace Information Bulletin*, Apr. 1963; Steffen Larsen to Friend, Sept. 28, 1962, Box 12, Canadian CND Records, Hamilton; Jorgensen, *Atomvåbnenes rolle*, p. 77; "Appel" (1963), Folder 197, WRI Records, Amsterdam.

8. *PN*, June 26, Sept. 18, 1964; Steffen Larsen to International Contacts, July 17, Sept. 1964, and Larsen, "General Election 1964" (Sept. 25, 1964), Folder 197, WRI Records, Amsterdam; Jorgensen, *Atomvåbnenes rolle*, pp. 87, 170.

9. *PN*, May 3, 1963; Jorgensen, *Atomvåbnenes rolle*, pp. 168–69; Bjol, *Hvem bestemmer*, pp. 215–16; Steffen Larsen to International Contacts, Oct. 18, 1963, Box 12, Canadian CND Records, Hamilton.

10. Boserup and Iverson, "Demonstrations," pp. 343–44; Steffen Larsen to Friends, Dec. 11, 1962, Box 6, CNVA Records.

11. Jorgensen, *Atomvåbnenes rolle*, pp. 96–99, 121, 169–70; Bjol, *Hvem bestemmer*, pp. 216–18; "Danes Hold Great Peace March," *Youth Against the Bomb*, Dec. 1960, p. 3, CND (Britain) Records, SCPC; Boserup and Iverson, "Demonstrations," pp. 329–31; Marian and Hans Sinn to Tony Smythe, Dec. 7, 1963, Folder 189, WRI Records, Amsterdam; Steffen Larsen to Gail Paradise, Oct. 28, 1963, Box 6, SPU Records; Jens Maigård to Bertrand Russell, ca. Oct. 1960, Class 640, RA 1.

12. Jorgensen, *Atomvåbnenes rolle*, p. 170; Boel, *Socialdemokratiets atomvåbenpolitik*, p. 60; *PN*, June 16, 1961; Hagbard Jonassen to Arlo Tatum, Mar. 28, 1961, Folder 196, WRI Records, Amsterdam.

13. A January 1961 Gallup poll found that only 18 percent of Danes favored arming NATO's European nations with nuclear weapons. Jorgensen, *Atomvåbnenes rolle*, pp. 117–18; Hagbard Jonassen to Tony Smythe, Apr. 23, 1962, Folder 196, and Steffen Larsen, "General Election 1964" (Sept. 25, 1964), Folder 197, WRI Records, Amsterdam; Einhorn, *National Security*, p. 83; Jenkins, "Who Are These Marchers?" p. 52; Boel, *Socialdemokratiets atomvåbenpolitik*, p. 53.

14. "Atomprotestkampanjen," pp. 231–32; *PN*, Aug. 30, 1963; Grepstad, "Norway," p. 5; Nilson, "Peace Movement in Norway," pp. 36–37; *Sanity* [Britain], Feb. 1962, p. 4.

15. "Atomprotestkampanjen," p. 232; Ragnar Kvam to Toronto Committee for Survival, Mar. 1962, Box 2, Canadian CND Records, Hamilton; *PN*, Apr. 21, May 19, Sept. 29, Nov. 17, 1961, Aug. 30, 1963; Carter, *Peace Movements*, p. 75; Niels Mathiesen, "The Peace Movement in Norway" (1962), Folder 63, WRI Records, Amsterdam.

16. "Proceedings of the Tenth Pugwash Conference on Science and World Affairs, London, September 3–7, 1962," p. 84, PC Records, London; Evelyn Peat, "National Sections in Action," *Pax et Libertas* 26 (July–Sept. 1961): 12; *Fredsbladet* 10 (Nov.–Dec. 1962): 6, 8; Anne-Marit Sletten Duve to Dagmar Wilson, Apr. 20, 1962, Box 6, Series I, WSP Records, SCPC; Naeve, ed., *Changeover*, pp. 213–14.

17. Niels Mathiesen, "The Peace Movement in Norway" (1962), Folder 63, Mathiesen to Tony Smythe, Nov. 8, 1962, Folder 363, and Marian and Hans Sinn to Smythe, Dec. 7, 1963, Folder 189, WRI Records, Amsterdam; Anne-Marit Sletten Duve to Dagmar Wilson, Box 6, Series I, WSP Records, SCPC.

18. *PN*, May 10, Aug. 30, 1963; Grepstad, "Norway," pp. 5–6; *Sanity* [Britain], Apr. 1963, p. 3; *Sanity* [Canada], Apr.–May 1963; "News Release No. 21" (Mar. 2, 1964), Box 5, WRI Records, SCPC.

19. "Norwegian Students to World Statesmen," *Pax et Libertas* 27 (Apr.–June 1962): 9; *PN*, Jan. 5, 1962; Norwegian Section of WISP to Kennedy, n.d., Box 6, Series I, WSP Records, SCPC; Ruge, "Are You a Member?"

20. "Proceedings of the Tenth Pugwash Conference on Science and World Affairs, London, September 3–7, 1962," p. 84, PC Records, London; Katrine Förland to Linus Pauling, Dec. 28, 1961, Pauling Papers; Galtung, "Foreign Policy Opinion," pp. 229–30.

21. Pharo, "Cold War," p. 166; *PN*, Oct. 7, 28, 1960, Aug. 30, 1963; Carter *Peace Movements*, p. 63; "Resolution on Foreign Policy and Security Policy," enclosure in A. G. Ronhovde to DOS, May 27, 1963, POL 12 NOR, DOS Records.

22. "Till dem som stött AMSA!" and "50 svenskar deltog i Holbækmarschen," *Mot svensk atombomb* 2.2 (1960); *PN*, Aug. 14, 1959; Wiberg, *Provstopp nu!* p. 8; Svahnström to Linus Pauling, Dec. 17, 1959, Pauling Papers.

23. Fogelström, *Kampen för fred*, p. 265; Svahnström to Bertrand Russell, Aug. 9, 1961, and [Illegible] to Russell, Nov. 16, 1961, "Fackeltåg mot Atomvapen" (1961), Class 640, RA 1.

24. Fogelström, *Kampen för fred*, pp. 269–71; *International Bulletin*, Sept. 1962, Jan. 1963; *Peace Information Bulletin*, Apr. 1963; Tom Alberts, "Information Bulletin from the Campaign for Nuclear Disarmament" (1963), Folder 387, WRI Records, Amsterdam.

25. "News Release No. 21" (Mar. 2, 1964), Box 5, WRI Records, SCPC; Svahnström to Bertrand Russell, Mar. 3, 1964, Class 640, RA 1; Svahnström to Russell, July 22, 1964, Class 320, RA 2.

26. Fogelström, *Kampen för fred*, pp. 254–65, 268; Ståhle, *Internationella Kvinnoförbundet*, p. 31; Autobiographical notes by Bertil Svahnström (1963), Folder 387, WRI Records, Amsterdam.

27. Lindkvist, "Mobilization Peaks and Declines," pp. 158–59; Ståhle, *Internationella Kvinnoförbundet*, p. 31; "Preliminary Reactions to the Soviet 50-Megaton Threat and the Multi-Megaton Tests" (Oct. 27, 1961), p. 2, Box 6, RR, OR, USIA Records.

28. Andersson and Lindkvist, "Peace Movement in Sweden," p. 12; Bertil Sandén to Bertrand Russell, May 18, 1962, Class 640, RA 1; Nordal Åkerman to Linus Pauling, May 27, 1963, Pauling Papers.

29. "Preliminary Reactions to the Soviet 50-Megaton Threat and the Multi-Megaton Tests" (Oct. 27, 1961), p. 2, Box 6, RR, OR, USIA Records; *Sanity* [Britain], Oct. 1962, p. 6.

30. Rudling, *Kampen mot Atomvapen*, pp. 45, 48–52, 55–67, 73–78; G. Alonzo Stanford to DOS, July 27, 1959, 758.5611/7-2759, DOS Records; Andersson and Lindkvist, "Peace Movement in Sweden," pp. 29–30.

31. Fogelström, *Kampen för fred*, p. 261; Andrén, *Power-Balance*, p. 180; Andersson and Lindkvist, "Peace Movement in Sweden," pp. 29–30.

32. Quester, "Sweden," p. 53; Bertil Svahnström to Linus Pauling, Mar. 14, 1960, Pauling Papers; Fogelström, *Kampen för fred*, p. 262.

33. William M. Owen to DOS, Apr. 23, 1959, 758.5611/4-2359, and Bonbright to SecState, Nov. 13, 1959, 758.5611/11-1359, DOS Records; Erlander, *Tage Erlander*, pp. 94–98; Myrdal, *Game of Disarmament*, pp. xxiii, 86–87, 172.

34. *Peacemaker*, May 1961; *PN*, Oct. 27, 1961, Mar. 27, 1964. For the background to the unusual relationship between the Peace Union and the Peace Committee, see Wittner, *One World or None*, p. 224.

35. Despite the generational break, the Committee of 100 did operate for a time out of the offices of the Peace Union. Marian and Hans Sinn to Tony Smythe, Dec. 7, 1963, Folder 189, WRI Records, Amsterdam; Taipale, "Peace Movement in Finland," pp. 20, 23–26, 30.

36. Cioc, *Pax Atomica*, pp. 111–15, 151–76; Scharrer, "War and Peace," pp. 276–77; Kelleher, *Germany*, pp. 114–16; Boutwell, *German Nuclear Dilemma*, pp. 32–36.

37. Otto, "Ostermarsch der Atomwaffengegner," pp. 162–65; Otto, *Vom Ostermarsch*

zur APO, pp. 70–73; *NYT*, Apr. 19, 1960; *PN*, Apr. 29, 1960; Tempel to Bertrand Russell, July 7, 1960, Class 630, RA 1; Tempel, "Atomic Disarmament in the Federal Republic of Germany" (1962), p. 2, Folder 249, WRI Records, Amsterdam.

38. *PN*, Apr. 7, 1961, Apr. 27, 1962, Apr. 26, 1963, Apr. 10, 1964; *Sanity* [Britain], May 1962, pp. 1–2, Apr., May 1964; Klaus Vlack to Bertrand Russell, Mar. 21, 1965, Class 640, RA 1; Otto, "Ostermarsch der Atomwaffengegner," p. 166.

39. *Sanity* [Britain], Easter Sunday 1962, pp. 1, 3, 8; "Ostermärsche der Atomwaffengegner: Auch 1963," Portfeuille No. 2, Publications Pacifistes et Internationales; "Aufruf zum Ostermarsch der Atomwaffengegner 1962" (1962), Folder 247, WRI Records, Amsterdam.

40. Otto, *Vom Ostermarsch zur APO*, pp. 85–89, 96–102, 118–19, 122–23; Otto, "Ostermarsch der Atomwaffengegner," pp. 166–72; "Ostermarsch der Atomwaffengegner 1966" (1966), Folder 247, WRI Records, Amsterdam.

41. *Sanity* [Britain], Feb. 1962, p. 4; J. Owen Zurhellen Jr. to SecState, Sept. 20, 1961, 711.5611/9-2061, DOS Records; *International Bulletin*, Sept. 1962, Jan. 1963.

42. Hans-Konrad Tempel, "Atomic Disarmament in the Federal Republic of Germany" (1962), p. 2, Folder 249, and H. G. Friedrich, "The Peace Movement in West Germany" (1962), Folder 63, WRI Records, Amsterdam; *PN*, Dec. 9, 1960; Alois Stoff to Bertrand Russell, Jan. 25, 1962, Class 640, RA 1; Otto, *Vom Ostermarsch zur APO*, pp. 113–18.

43. Rotblat, "Movements of Scientists," p. 124; Cioc, *Pax Atomica*, p. 87; Born to Bertrand Russell, Oct. 7, 1959, Class 710, RA 1; "Proceedings of the Tenth Pugwash Conference on Science and World Affairs, London, September 3–7, 1962," pp. 69–71, PC Records, London.

44. Theodor Michaltscheff, "The Struggle for Peace in the German Federal Republic," *War Resistance* 2.12 (1965): 18; H. G. Friedrich, "The Peace Movement in West Germany" (1962), Folder 63, WRI Records, Amsterdam; Otto, *Vom Ostermarsch zur APO*, pp. 133–38; Andrew Trasler, "Official Attitudes to the Easter Marches," *War Resistance* 2.10 (1964): 13–14.

45. The 1967 appeal was also signed by 1,507 teachers, 486 university faculty members and scientists, 1,378 trade union officials, 891 artists, and 577 writers and publishers. Otto, *Vom Ostermarsch zur APO*, pp. 100–101, 139–40; Carter, *Peace Movements*, p. 60; Otto, "Ostermarsch der Atomwaffengegner," pp. 165–66, 168–70.

46. Tempel held the top post until 1964, when he resigned in accord with his belief that offices should be rotated. Alois Stoff, "Ostermarsch Information" (Mar. 27, 1961), Class 640, RA 1; Heinz Kloppenburg, "Report to IFOR Regional Committees" (July 1962), Box 15, Series B, Sayre Papers; "Change of Speaker" (1964), Folder 249, WRI Records, Amsterdam.

47. Otto, *Vom Ostermarsch zur APO*, pp. 125–32; Trasler, "Official Attitudes," pp. 13–14; *PN*, Sept. 2, 1960, May 22, 1964; Alois Stoff, "Ostermarsch Information" (Mar. 27, 1961), Class 640, RA 1.

48. Carter, *Peace Movements*, pp. 60–61; Otto, *Vom Ostermarsch zur APO*, pp. 140–44; Extract from Gerard Daechsel to Housmans / Peace News, Apr. 3, 1961, Reel 13, CND (Britain) Records, London-Warwick; Tempel to Russell, Feb. 18, 1962, Class 640, RA 1.

49. Otto, "Ostermarsch der Atomwaffengegner," pp. 170–72.

50. Noelle and Neumann, eds., *Germans*, p. 271; Merritt and Puchala, eds., *Western European Perspectives*, p. 357; Den Oudsten, "Database on International Security."

51. "West European Attitudes Toward Disarmament" (Aug. 1961), p. 11, Box 5, POBR, and "West European Public Opinion on Disarmament" (July 1963), p. 3, Box 15, RR, OR, USIA Records; Merritt and Puchala, eds., *Western European Perspectives*, p. 397.

52. *PN*, Mar. 6, 1959; Saar Boorlage, "The Problem of Nuclear Disarmament in the Netherlands," *Youth Against the Bomb* (June 1960), pp. 5–6, Box 28, Series B, SANE

Records; "Comité 'Stopzetting Atoombomproeven' wendt zich tot de Nederlandse regering," *Voorlichtingsblad* 1.9/10 (ca. Jan. 1960): n.p.

53. "Dutch Pacifists Gird for Elections," *Fellowship* 25 (Mar. 1, 1959): 2; Verkuil, *De grote illusie*, p. 44; *PN*, Mar. 20, 1959.

54. Verkuil, *De grote illusie*, pp. 46–49; Everts and Walraven, *Vredesbeweging*, pp. 42–43; "Report to the I.F.o.R. Council" (Aug. 1961), Box 36, Series B, Sayre Papers; "Anti Atoombom Mars: Nieuwjaarsdag 1961," Class 640, RA 1; *PN*, Apr. 7, Dec. 29, 1961, Apr. 27, 1962, Apr. 26, 1963; *Sanity* [Britain], May 1963, p. 3.

55. *Sane World*, Mar. 15, 1962; *Sanity* [Britain], Feb. 1962, p. 4; *Banner*, ca. Aug. 1963.

56. Verkuil, *De grote illusie*, pp. 47–48; Everts and Walraven, *Vredesbeweging*, pp. 42–43; "Oproep!" (1962), "Verklaring van de Ban de Bom-Groep" (June 30, 1962), Portefeuille No. 18, Publications Pacifistes et Internationales.

57. "Proceedings of the Tenth Pugwash Conference on Science and World Affairs, London, September 3–7, 1962," pp. 78–80, PC Records, London.

58. Everts, "Peace Movement and Public Opinion," p. 11; Everts, "Continuity and Change," p. 20.

59. Verkuil, *De grote illusie*, pp. 50–57; J. B. Th. Hugenholtz, "Netherlands Reformed Church on Nuclear Armament" (Dec. 1962), Box 36, Series B, Sayre Papers; Everts and Walraven, *Vredesbeweging*, pp. 44–45. For a fuller discussion of *Pacem in Terris* and of the Catholic church's overall shift on nuclear issues, see Chapter 13.

60. *PN*, Apr. 22, 1960, Mar. 29, May 17, 1963, Mar. 13, 20, 1964; Jean van Lierde, "Rapport de la section Belge" (1963), Folder 177, WRI Records, Amsterdam; Lubelski-Bernard, "Les mouvements de la paix," p. 384; *Sanity* [Britain], Good Friday / Saturday 1963, p. 12; "News from the Peace Front," *Fellowship* 29 (Apr. 15, 1963): 3.

61. *PN*, Nov. 17, 1961, May 18, 1962; Lubelski-Bernard, "Les mouvements de la paix," pp. 383–84; MacArthur to SecState, Mar. 27, 1962, 600.0012/3-2762, and J. J. Crowley to DOS, May 11, 1962, 600.0012/5-1162, DOS Records; "Peace Demonstrations in Continuous Eruption," *Fellowship* 28 (June 1, 1962): 2.

62. *PN*, May 15, 1959, Apr. 6, 1962; *International Bulletin*, Sept. 1962; *Sane World*, Nov. 1, 1962; Heiniger, "Die schweizerische Antiatombewegung," pp. 71–80, 112–17; Amherd, "Die Friedensbewegung," pp. 125–26, 134–43; Bindschedler, "Switzerland," p. 221.

63. Brassel and Tanner, "Zur Geschichte der Friedensbewegung," pp. 69–70; Heiniger, "Die schweizerische Antiatombewegung," pp. 122–28; *PN*, May 31, 1963.

64. Kobe to Linus Pauling, May 30, 1963, Pauling Papers; Heiniger, "Die schweizerische Antiatombewegung," pp. 160–65; *PN*, Apr. 6, 1962; Brassel and Tanner, "Zur Geschichte der Friedensbewegung," p. 78; *International Bulletin*, Sept. 1962.

65. *Combat*, Feb. 8, 1960; Heineger, "Die schweizerische Antiatombewegung," pp. 118–19.

66. *Atombulletin*, Mar. 1963; Florangela Castiglione to Bertrand Russell, Mar. 9, 1963, Class 640, RA 1; *PN*, Apr. 26, 1963, Apr. 10, 1964; *Sanity* [Britain], Apr. 1964.

67. Brassel and Tanner, "Zur Geschichte der Friedensbewegung," pp. 65–69; Heiniger, "Die schweizerische Antiatombewegung," pp. 1–10, 129–65.

68. Gerhard Jordan, "State Treaty, Neutrality and Peace in Austria," *Disarmament Campaigns*, June 1985, p. 10; Fellner, "Hans Thirring," pp. 386–87; "Proceedings of the Tenth Pugwash Conference on Science and World Affairs, London, September 3–7, 1962," pp. 61–63, PC Records, London.

69. Jordan, "Peace Activities," p. 1; *PN*, Dec. 7, 1962, Jan. 18, 1963.

70. *Sanity* [Britain], Feb. 1963, p. 2, Apr. 1963, p. 3, May 1963, p. 3; Jungk to J. D. Bernal, May 13, 1963, Box 60, Bernal Papers; Gerry Hunnius to Dan and Charles, Feb. 20, 1963, and Hunnius to Tony Smythe, Mar. 18, 1963, Folder 188, WRI Records, Amsterdam;

Peace Information Bulletin, Apr. 1963; *PN*, Apr. 26, 1963, Dec. 11, 1964; Jordan, "Peace Activities," pp. 1–2.

71. A. Farrington to Bertrand Russell, June 17, 1962, Class 630, RA 1; "With the Irish from Aldermaston to London," *Pax*, Summer 1960, pp. 15–19; Edward Prince to DOS, Sept. 29, 1961, 600.0012/9-2961, DOS Records; B. de Courcy Ireland, "The Irish Campaign for Nuclear Disarmament," *Pax*, Spring 1961, pp. 3–4; *You Believe in the Deterrent?*, Box 13, Canadian CND Records, Hamilton.

72. Betty de Courcy Ireland, "Civil Defense and Nuclear Disarmament," *Pax*, Autumn 1962, pp. 4–5; *International Bulletin*, Aug., Sept. 1962, Jan. 1963; "News Release No. 8" (Oct. 25, 1962), Box 5, WRI Records, SCPC; "Limerick Active Against the Bomb," *Banner*, June 1963.

73. "Garden Fete," *Pax*, Autumn 1960; Marguerite Lovell to Members and Friends, Mar. 1962, Ireland Miscellaneous Peace Material; "Pacifism is Breaking Out," *Pax*, Spring 1962, p. 1; "Ireland and the Cuban Crisis," *Banner*, June 1963.

74. "Pacifists at the Cross-roads," *Pax*, Spring 1961, p. 2; "Garden Fete," *Pax*, Autumn 1960; *Pax*, Autumn 1961; "Editorial," *Pax*, Spring 1961, p. 1.

75. "Nuclear Testing Resolution at Church of Ireland Synod," *Pax*, Autumn 1962, pp. 9–10; "Dublin Greets Peace Conference," *Banner*, June 1963; "Selling 'The Banner,'" *Banner*, ca. Aug. 1963; "Looking at Irish Politics," *Banner*, ca. Aug. 1963.

76. Peader O'Donnell, "Somewhere out the Road in History," *Banner*, June 1963; B. de Courcy Ireland, "The Irish Campaign for Nuclear Disarmament," *Pax*, Spring 1961, p. 4; *PN*, Jan. 26, 1962; *International Bulletin*, Jan. 1963; "Young Dublin Against Bomb," *Banner*, ca. Aug. 1963.

77. *PN*, Aug. 28, 1958; "Proceedings of the Tenth Pugwash Conference on Science and World Affairs, London, September 3–7, 1962," pp. 66–67, PC Records, London; Kohl, *French Nuclear Diplomacy*, p. 106.

78. "News from the Peace Front," *Fellowship* 26 (Apr. 1, 1960): 3; *PN*, Mar. 11, 1960; Brittain, *Rebel Passion*, p. 148.

79. *Combat*, Apr. 14, 15, 18, 1960; Max Isenbergh to DOS, Apr. 2, 1960, 751.5611/4-260, DOS Records.

80. Ira Morris, "Formation of a French anti-nuclear warfare organization," Morris to L. John Collins, Nov. 24, 1958, and Morris to Cousins, Dec. 9, 1958, Box 10, Series B, SANE Records; Trocmé to Dear Sir, Dec. 4, 1958, Box 10, Trocmé Papers; *PN*, June 12, 1959.

81. Ira Morris, "First Public Meeting of the Nuclear Disarmament Campaign in France," Box 22, Series B, SANE Records; "French Anti-Nuclear Group Holds First Public Meeting," *Fellowship* 25 (July 15, 1959): 2.

82. Minutes of the French Federation Against Atomic Armament meetings of June 5, Sept. 17, 1959, and "Appel National" (Nov. 1959), Box 10, and Trocmé and Kastler to the President, French Republic, July 14, 1959, "Fédération Française contre l'armement atomique," Box 8, Trocmé Papers; Bernard Boudouresques, "Naissance d'une opposition: 1945–1965," *Alternatives Non Violentes*, no. 46 (Dec. 1982): 11–12; *L'homme devant l'atome*, June 1960, pp. 2–7.

83. *L'homme devant l'atome*, June 1960, pp. 7–15; Boudouresques, "Naissance," p. 12; *PN*, Apr. 5, 1963.

84. Kastler to Bourdet, Oct. 12, 1959, and Kastler to Trocmé, Oct. 19, 1959, Box 10, Trocmé Papers; Carter, "Sahara Protest Team," pp. 151–53.

85. For the absorption of the peace constituency in the Algerian controversy, see Evelyn Peat, "National Sections in Action," *Pax et Libertas* 26 (July–Sept. 1961): 11; Defrasne, *Le Pacifisme*, p. 120; Philip F. Palmedo, "The Debate on the 'Force de Frappe' Takes Shape," *BAS* 20 (June 1964): 29–30; Schalk, *War and the Ivory Tower*, pp. 61–111.

86. Bourdet to the author, June 25, 1993.

87. Report of the International Sub Committee, Committee of 100, Sept. 22, 1962, Class 630, RA 2; Gervis, "France's Ban-the-Bombers," p. 91; "News Release No. 9" (Nov. 23, 1962), Box 5, WRI Records, SCPC.

88. *PN*, Apr. 12, June 7, 1963; "News Release No. 14" (June 18, 1963), Box 5, WRI Records, SCPC; *Combat*, Jan. 6, 1966.

89. Bourdet, "Désarmement Nucléaire," p. 4; Gervis, "France's Ban-the-Bombers," pp. 91–92; Moch, *Non à la force de frappe*; *PN*, Apr. 5, 1963; *Sanity* [Britain], Apr. 1963, p. 2; "Qu'est-ce que la guerre nucléaire?" Union Pacifiste de France Records.

90. "M.C.A.A.," Class 640, RA 1; *PN*, Nov. 22, 29, 1963; "News Release No. 17" (Nov. 20, 1963), Box 5, WRI Records, SCPC; *Sanity* [Britain], Dec. 1963, p. 2.

91. *PN*, May 1, 1964; Boudouresques, "Naissance," p. 12; Howorth, *France*, pp. 28–29; "The Anti-Armament March from Frontignan to Montpellier, 24th April" (1966), Folder 209, WRI Records, Amsterdam; Claude Bourdet to Cher Ami, Feb. 1967, and Bourdet to Madame, Monsieur, Feb. 1968, Bourdet correspondence, Mendès-France Papers.

92. Bourdet, "Rebirth," p. 194; Bourdet to the author, June 25, 1993; "Le Troisième Congrès du M.C.A.A.," *Alerte Atomique*, no. 13 (Feb.–Mar. 1967): 13.

93. Kohl, *French Nuclear Diplomacy*, pp. 104–5, 170; Ira Morris to L. John Collins, Nov. 24, 1958, Box 10, Series B, SANE Records; Bourdet, "Désarmement Nucléaire," p. 3; Caldwell, "French Socialists' Attitudes," pp. 121–22; "Preliminary Reactions to the Soviet 50-Megaton Threat and the Multi-Megaton Tests" (Oct. 27, 1961), p. 5, Box 6, RR, OR, USIA Records.

94. Gallup, ed., *Gallup International Public Opinion Polls: France*, pp. 262, 276, 325, 359, 387–88, 417.

95. Merritt and Puchala, eds., *Western European Perspectives*, p. 389; Gallup, ed., *Gallup International Public Opinion Polls: France*, pp. 388, 534, 601, 680; Caldwell, "French Socialists' Attitudes," p. 151.

96. "West European Attitudes Toward Disarmament" (Aug. 1961), p. 4, Box 5, POBR, and "West European Public Opinion on Disarmament" (July 1963), pp. 3–4, Box 15, RR, OR, USIA Records.

97. Kohl, *French Nuclear Diplomacy*, pp. 116–19, 169–70; Caldwell, "French Socialists' Attitudes," pp. 115–20, 126–32, 155–56; *Combat*, May 22, July 6, July 20, 1966; Bourdet, "Désarmement Nucléaire," pp. 6–7; "An Interview with Claude Bourdet," *END Bulletin* 6 (Autumn 1981): 6.

98. "Marcia Perugia-Assisi per la frateilanza dei popoli" (1961), and Franco Perna to John Nevin Sayre, Oct. 19, 1961, Box 32, Series B, Sayre Papers; Aldo Capitini, "Sulla lettera di Salboroli che mi riguarda" (July 26, 1962), Folder 323, and Mario Tassoni, "The Peace Movement in Italy," Folder 63, WRI Records, Amsterdam; "La marcia Perugia-Assisi e dopo" (1961), Marcucci Papers; *L'Unita*, Sept. 25, 1961.

99. *NYT*, Oct. 26, 1961; *Sanity* [Britain], Feb. 1962, p. 4; *PN*, Apr. 27, 1962.

100. Balducci, "Peace Movement," pp. 214–15; Reinhardt to SecState, Apr. 27, 1962, 711.5611/4-2762, DOS Records; Jean and Hildegard Goss-Mayr, "Report on Work in Italy, April 16 to May 10, 1963," Box 32, Series B, Sayre Papers; Brittain, *Rebel Passion*, pp. 180–81.

101. Aldo Capitini, "Problemi del metodo nonviolento" (Aug. 20, 1962), and "Lettera Circolare Mensile di Coordimento del Movimento Nonviolento per la Pace" (Nov. 1962), Folder 323, WRI Records, Amsterdam.

102. "The Peace Movement in Italy," *Fellowship* 29 (Mar. 1, 1963): 31–32; Aldo Capitini to the Committee of 100, Mar. 8, 1962, and *Paese Sera*, Nov. 19–20, 1962, Class 640, and Tommaso Fiore to Bertrand Russell, Jan. 23, 1963, Class 630, RA 1; *Il Domani*, Feb.

1962, Marcucci Papers; Mario Tassoni, "The Peace Movement in Italy" (1962), Folder 63, WRI Records, Amsterdam; *PN*, Apr. 13, Nov. 23, 1962.

103. *PN*, Apr. 13, Nov. 30, 1962, May 10, 1963; Jean and Hildegard Goss-Mayr, "Report on Work in Italy, April 16 to May 10, 1963," Box 32, Series B, Sayre Papers; Musto, *Catholic Peace Tradition*, pp. 195–96.

104. The original USIA data differs slightly from the final figures. Den Oudsten, "Database on International Security"; "International Survey XX-14: Italy" (July 1962), p. 5, and "International Survey XX-15 Italy" (Feb. 1963), Box 56, CPF, OR, USIA Records.

105. Only 34 percent opposed banning the Bomb in these circumstances. "West European Attitudes Toward Disarmament" (Aug. 1961), p. 11, Box 5, POBR, and "West European Public Opinion on Disarmament" (July 1963), pp. 3–4, Box 15, RR, OR, USIA Records; Merritt and Puchala, eds., *Western European Perspectives*, pp. 389, 391, 397–98.

106. De Andreis, "Nuclear Debate," pp. 195–97; Zariski, "Italian Socialist Party," pp. 372–81; De Grand, *Italian Left*, pp. 131–39; Kogan, *Political History*, pp. 173–94.

107. Blackmer, "Continuity and Change," pp. 56–63; Tarrow, "Communism," pp. 631–32; Barkan, *Visions of Emancipation*, pp. 16–17, 39, 115; De Grand, *Italian Left*, pp. 139–42, 167.

108. "Peace Movement in Italy," pp. 31–32; Myers, "Dilemmas," pp. 88, 90; Marco Pannella to A. J. Muste, June 6, 1963, Box 5, CNVA Records; Carter, *Peace Movements*, pp. 75–76.

109. Woodhouse, *Struggle for Greece*, p. 288; Greek Committee for International Detente and Peace, *32 Years of Struggle*, p. 2; Peristerakis, "To Elliniko Kinima Eirinis," pp. 91–95.

110. Peristerakis, "To Elliniko Kinima Eirinis," pp. 102, 233–34; *PN*, June 29, 1962, Sept. 20, 1963; Peristerakis to Bertrand Russell, ca. Feb. 1963, Feb. 28, 1963, Class 320, RA 2; Peristerakis and Nikos Constantopoulos to Linus Pauling, Mar. 12, 1963, Pauling Papers.

111. Peristerakis, "To Elliniko Kinima Eirinis," pp. 154–65; Duff, *Left, Left, Left*, pp. 245–46; Marion Sarafis, "Background to the Greek Anti-Nuclear Movement," *END Bulletin*, no. 7 (Winter 1981–82): 16; Bertrand Russell Youth League for Nuclear Disarmament and Peace, "Declaration" (1964), Folder 306, WRI Records, Amsterdam; Bertrand Russell, "Statement Concerning Deportation of My Secretary From Greece" (Apr. 21, 1963), Class 640, RA 1; *Sanity* [Britain], Good Friday / Saturday 1963, p. 12, May 1963, p. 3, July 1963, p. 7; *PN*, Apr. 26, Sept. 20, 1963.

112. The Lambrakis affair is portrayed in the film *Z*. "Outline of Events in Greece," Class 320, RA 2; *Sanity* [Britain], July 1963, p. 7; Duff, *Left, Left, Left*, pp. 247–53.

113. Peristerakis, "To Elliniko Kinima Eirinis," pp. 233–34; M. Kyrkos, "The Fourth Marathon March," Box 6, CNVA Records; *PN*, Sept. 20, 1963.

114. Andreas Theophilou to the Secretary, WRI, May 18, 1963, Folder 306, WRI Records, Amsterdam; Peristerakis, "To Elliniko Kinima Eirinis," pp. 211–18; *PN*, Aug. 16, 1963.

115. *Sanity* [Britain], July 1963, p. 7; Iatrides, "American Attitudes," p. 70; Zaharopoulos, "Monarchy," pp. 205–6; Meynaud, *Rapport*, pp. 7–18.

116. Peristerakis, "To Elliniko Kinima Eirinis," pp. 208–11; *PN*, May 22, 1964; M. Nikolaides to Friends, Feb. 4, 1966, Folder 307, WRI Records, Amsterdam; Duff, *Left, Left, Left*, p. 254.

Chapter 11

Epigraph: WSP press release of June 11, 1962, Box 2, WSP Records, Madison.

1. This crisis, which pivoted around the issue of Communist domination, is discussed in Chapter 14.

2. Yasui to Bertrand Russell, Sept. 5, 1959, Jan. 12, 1960, and "News Release" (Apr. 25, 1962), Class 640, RA 1; "Call to Int'l Action," *No More Hiroshimas!* 8 (Oct. 1961): 5, 11.

3. Brittain, *Rebel Passion*, p. 211; Paul M. Sekiya, "The Report on the Japanese Fellowship of Reconciliation" (Jan. 1965), FOR (Japan) Records; Evelyn Peat, "National Sections in Action," *Pax et Libertas* 26 (July–Sept. 1961): 11; Yasaburo Shimonaka to Bertrand Russell, Nov. 10, 1959, Class 640, RA 1.

4. "Proceedings of the Tenth Pugwash Conference on Science and World Affairs, London, September 3–7, 1962," pp. 72–77, PC Records, London; Edwin Reischauer to DOS, May 14, 1962, 600.001/5-1462, DOS Records; *PN*, June 21, 1963.

5. Koschmann, "Postwar Democracy," pp. 15–16; *Meaning of Survival*, p. 147.

6. "Internationalization of Our Anti-War Movement—Zengakuren" (Nov. 1962), Reel 13, CND (Britain) Records, London-Warwick; "The Resolution Adopted by 20th National Congress of Zengakuren, July 5–8, Tokyo" (1963), Folder 337, WRI Records, Amsterdam; *Sanity* [Britain], Oct. 1962, p. 6; *PN*, Oct. 5, 1962, Mar. 1, 1963.

7. Miyata, "Education for Peace," pp. 16–19; Mendel, "Public Views," pp. 155, 160; Edwin Reischauer to SecState, Nov. 4, 1961, 711.5611/11-461, DOS Records; "Preliminary Reactions to the Soviet 50-Megaton Threat and the Multi-Megaton Tests" (Oct. 27, 1961), pp. 8–9, Box 6, RR, OR, USIA Records.

8. Doshisha University president Shinobu Tabata, like many other Japanese, argued that Japan should scrap the Security Treaty and adopt a policy of disarmament and permanent neutrality. Stockwin, *Japanese Socialist Party*, p. 86; *Meaning of Survival*, p. 142; K. Tsurumi, *Social Change*, pp. 336–37; Kurino and Kodama, "A Study," pp. 122–23; Ueda, "Tabata Shinobu," pp. 242–43.

9. Pempel, "Japan's Nuclear Allergy," p. 169; *PN*, June 21, 1963, Nov. 20, 1964; *Sanity* [Britain], Apr. 1963, p. 3; "Protest at U.S. Bases in Japan," *Banner*, ca. Aug. 1963.

10. *Meaning of Survival*, pp. 142, 144; K. Tsurumi, *Social Change*, p. 336.

11. "Some Worldwide Attitudes Toward Disarmament and Nuclear Issues" (July 1963), pp. 2, 6, Box 16, RR, OR, USIA Records; Reiss, *Without the Bomb*, p. 118; Passin, "Nuclear Arms and Japan," pp. 68–72, 83; Mendel, "Public Views," p. 165.

12. Mendel, "Public Views," pp. 162, 164, 166; Yasumasa Tanaka, "Japanese Attitudes Toward Nuclear Arms," *Public Opinion Quarterly* 34 (1970): 27; Pempel, "Japan's Nuclear Allergy," p. 173; Ishida, "Beyond the Traditional Concepts," p. 142.

13. Mendel, "Public Views," p. 160; Stockwin, *Japanese Socialist Party*, pp. 82, 87, 161; Totten and Kawakami, "Gensuikyo," p. 840; *Meaning of Survival*, p. 142; *NYT*, Oct. 26, 1961.

14. Homer Jack, "SANE Comment," *Sane World*, Dec. 15, 1962; Homer Jack, Donald Keys, and Harold Applebaum, "The Future of SANE" (Mar. 4, 1963), Box 410, Cousins Papers, Los Angeles; "Seven Years for a Sane Nuclear Policy," *Sane World*, Apr. 15, 1964; Gottlieb, "National Committee," p. 156; "A Short History of SANE" (1960), Box 1, Series A, SANE Records.

15. Allen, *Mark It*, p. 375; Maxine Gomberg to Cousins, Dec. 11, 1959, Box 210, Cousins Papers, Los Angeles; *New York Post*, May 19, 1961; personal interview with Homer Jack, June 12, 1988; "Seven Years for a Sane Nuclear Policy."

16. Clarence Pickett and Norman Cousins to Eisenhower, Aug. 22, 1958, GF-155B, WHCF, Eisenhower Records; "Seven Years for a Sane Nuclear Policy," p. 1; *NYT*, Oct. 31, 1958; *PN*, Nov. 21, 1958.

17. "Seven Years for a Sane Nuclear Policy," p. 1; Cousins to Adlai Stevenson, Oct. 13, 1959, Cousins Papers, Beverly Hills; Cousins to Thomas, Mar. 25, 1960, Reel 38, Thomas Papers.

18. Pickett to Thomas, June 10, 1959, and Fromm to Thomas, June 4, 1959, Reel 36,

and Thomas to Cousins and Pickett, June 2, 1959, Reel 61, Thomas Papers; personal interview with Thomas, Oct. 4, 1966.

19. "Seven Years for a Sane Nuclear Policy"; "Sane Tasks Ahead," *Sane World*, Oct. 15, 1963; Jack, "SANE Comment"; Thomas to Homer Jack, Jan. 4, 1960, Box 16, Series III, Jack Papers.

20. "Seven Years for a Sane Nuclear Policy"; *International Bulletin*, Sept. 1962; *New York Herald Tribune*, Aug. 7, 1960; *NYT*, Aug. 7, 1960.

21. "Seven Years for a Sane Nuclear Policy"; Spock to Homer Jack, Feb. 28, 1962, Box 10, 1971 Series, Spock Papers; Bloom, *Doctor Spock*, pp. 242–45; Spock and Morgan, *Spock on Spock*, pp. 167–69.

22. Thomas to Jack, Sept. 5, 1961, Box 17, Series III, Jack Papers; Cousins to Dmitry Muravyev, Oct. 23, 1961, Cousins Papers, Beverly Hills; "National SANE Criticizes Resumption of Soviet Nuclear Tests" (Aug. 5, 1962), Box 306, Cousins Papers, Los Angeles; "Seven Years for a Sane Nuclear Policy."

23. "Seven Years for a Sane Nuclear Policy"; Jack, *Nuclear Politics*, pp. 37–38; Homer Jack, "The International Work of the National Committee for a Sane Nuclear Policy" (Dec. 27, 1963), Box 60, Series B, SANE Records.

24. "National SANE Urges U.S.-U.S.S.R. Steps Away from Brink" (Oct. 24, 1962) and "National SANE Urges No Military Invasion of Cuba" (Oct. 27, 1962), Box 36, Series B, SANE Records; "The U.S.-Cuban Crisis" (Oct. 24, 1962), Box 306, Cousins Papers, Los Angeles; "Crisis Strengthens War Group," *Sane World*, Nov. 1, 1962.

25. Personal interview with Homer Jack, June 12, 1988; Homer Jack et al., "The Future of SANE" (Mar. 4, 1963), Box 410, Cousins Papers, Los Angeles; Cousins to Cyrus Eaton, Jan. 27, 1960, Cousins Papers, Beverly Hills; Bloom, *Doctor Spock*, p. 248; "Seven Years for a Sane Nuclear Policy."

26. "Call to Nonviolent Action Against Missiles at the Omaha, Nebraska ICBM Base" (1959), and Muste to Margaret C. McCulloch, Aug. 5, 1959, Box 7, Muste Papers; W. Young, *Visible Witness*, pp. 5–17; "What is CNVA" (1962), author's possession.

27. Bradford Lyttle, "Polaris as a Symbol For a Nonviolent Action Project" (1959), Box 15, Muste Papers; Deming, "Peacemakers," pp. 471–72; War Resisters League, *A WRL History of Protest*, n.p.; "What is CNVA" (1962), author's possession.

28. Muste to Henry Hitt Crane, Aug. 4, 1959, Box 7, Muste to Norman Whitney, July 27, 1960, Box 1, and Muste to Max Fitch, Sept. 27, 1960, Box 14, Muste Papers; Deming, "Peacemakers," p. 472.

29. Ross Flanagan, "Public Demonstrations and Peace" (July 8, 1960), and Albert Bigelow to Bradford Lyttle, May 27, 1960, Box 1, and Lawrence Scott to members of CNVA, Jan. 1, 1961, Box 14, Muste Papers; Bigelow to CNVA, June 15, 1960, Box 5, CNVA Records.

30. See, for example, "Another Conscience Speaks at Omaha"; Edwin Guerard to Bertrand Russell, Mar. 3, 1961, Class 630, RA 1.

31. P. Brock, *Twentieth Century Pacifism*, p. 253; "San Francisco to Moscow Walk for Peace" (1960), "What is CNVA" (1962), and "The Continuing Cuban Crisis: Policy Statement of the Quebec-Washington-Guantanamo Walk for Peace" (1963), author's possession.

32. "Everyman II Enters Nuclear Test Zone," *Fellowship* 28 (July 15, 1962): 1; *PN*, July 13, 1962; A. J. Muste to L. John Collins, July 24, 1962, Box 22, Muste Papers; War Resisters League, *A WRL History of Protest*, n.p.

33. Garrison, "Our Skirts," pp. 211–17; Stein and Conners, "Civil Defense Protests," pp. 81–83; Hentoff, *Peace Agitator*, pp. 4–5; Muste to André Trocmé, May 4, 1960, Box 10, Muste Papers; "Protest," pp. 33–34.

34. The colleges and universities included Cornell, Oberlin, Princeton, Rochester, Rut-

gers, and Syracuse. At New York City's High School of Music and Art, a hundred students wore armbands to protest the drill, and twenty were suspended for refusing to remove them. Garrison, "Our Skirts," pp. 217–18; "2,000 New Yorkers Protest Civil Defense Drill," *Fellowship* 27 (May 15, 1961): 1–2.

35. Amy Swerdlow, one of WSP's early leaders and its foremost historian, has written that "the number fifty thousand became part of the founding legend of WSP. It was an estimate, according to the organizers, based on reports from the sixty cities. . . . To verify this figure I tallied the highest numbers I could find reported by the strike organizers or local papers for each city, and even with this generous method . . . I could arrive at a total no higher than twelve thousand strikers." Swerdlow, *Women Strike for Peace*, p. 247.

36. Although, ironically, the idea for a "strike" was suggested to the organizers by a man—the ubiquitous Lawrence Scott of the American Friends Service Committee—this was the last time WSP's Washington organizers included men in their planning meetings or looked to them for leadership. Swerdlow, *Women Strike for Peace*, pp. 17–18.

37. WSP deliberately remained a very loosely structured, participatory, "nonorganized" group, without membership, dues, or elections. Swerdlow tactfully refers to "thousands" of participants and contends that locals numbered "over one hundred." Swerdlow, *Women Strike for Peace*, pp. 3, 15–26, 46–50, 70–80; WSP press release of June 4, 1962, Box 2, WSP Records, Madison; "Women Strike for Peace" (Jan. 1, 1962), Box 1, Series I, WSP Records, SCPC.

38. WSP press releases of June 11, 1962, and Jan. 25, 1963, Box 2, WSP Records, Madison; Kay Johnson to Khrushchev, May 14, 1962, Box 2, Series I, WSP Records, SCPC; Swerdlow, *Women Strike for Peace*, pp. 80–85, 193–96; Winkler, *Life Under a Cloud*, p. 102; Alonso, *Peace as a Women's Issue*, p. 207.

39. Swerdlow, *Women Strike for Peace*, pp. 86–90, 122, 127–28, 205–14; "Women Strike for Peace—A short history of activities during 1963 and 1964" (1964), Box 1, Series I, WSP Records, SCPC; Alonso, *Peace as a Women's Issue*, p. 209; Stoll, "Women Strike for Peace," p. 147.

40. WSP leader Ruth Gage-Colby claimed that WSP members were motivated by a "concern for their children and by a love and understanding of life, which by the nature of things are known best to women." "Women Strike for Peace" (Jan. 1, 1962), "Women Strike for Peace—A short history of activities during 1963 and 1964" (1964), Box 1, Series I, WSP Records, SCPC; Swerdlow, *Women Strike for Peace*, pp. 52–69; Dagmar Wilson, "Statement by Women Strike for Peace on the Occasion of the Mothers' Lobby for a Test Ban" (May 7, 1963), Box 2, WSP Records, Madison; Speech by Gage-Colby at Moscow Conference, July 1962, 82.403, Deutscher Friedensrat Records.

41. Rupp and Taylor, *Survival in the Doldrums*; Garrison, "Our Skirts"; Solomon and Fishman, "Youth and Peace," p. 57; Swerdlow, *Women Strike for Peace*, p. 67.

42. Putney and Middleton, "Student Acceptance or Rejection of War," pp. 658, 665; Gallup, ed., *Gallup Poll*, pp. 1745, 1753.

43. Although the organization eventually acquired a more diverse constituency, pacifists and members of the Young People's Socialist League continued to play key roles. Ken Calkins, "The Student Peace Union," *Fellowship* 26 (Mar. 1, 1960): 5; Altbach, "American Peace Movement," p. 65; "Coordinator's Report—The Student Peace Union as of Nov. 1, 1959," Box 1, SPU Records, Madison; Philip Altbach to member of the SPU Advisory Council, Feb. 6, 1962, Class 640, RA 1; personal interview with Dorothy Tristman, July 27, 1994.

44. A. J. Muste suggested the idea of "unilateral initiatives" to the August 1960 gathering, which voted to endorse it. Minutes of the SPU national planning meeting of Aug. 27–28, 1960, "Program Statement of the 1961 National Convention of the Student Peace Union," Box 1, SPU Records, Madison; "Student Peace Union" (1961), Box 1, SPU Records, SCPC.

45. Altbach, "American Peace Movement," p. 65; Parker, "National Student Peace Union," p. 150; Altbach to Kunizo Takasaka, June 26, 1963, Box 6, SPU Records, Madison.

46. SPU formally adopted CND's nuclear disarmament symbol as its own at the SPU national meeting of August 27, 1960, in Nyack. Proponents argued that "like the cross and fish in early Christianity, it is simple and easily remembered. It can also be drawn or painted quickly." Chatfield, *American Peace Movement*, p. 107; Minutes of the SPU national planning meeting of Aug. 27–28, 1960, Box 1, SPU Records, Madison.

47. Philip Altbach, "Students on the March," *Fellowship* 28 (July 1, 1962): 7–8; "Student Peace Groups," p. 179; Parker, "National Student Peace Union," pp. 151–52; "Student Peace Union" (1961), Box 1, SPU Records, SCPC; Minutes of the SPU National Council Meeting of Dec. 27–29, 1961, Box 1, SPU Records, Madison.

48. "SANE Attacks Fallout," *Bulletin* [United States], Oct. 1962, p. 3; "Nuclear Testing: Statement by SPU National Steering Committee" (Oct. 3, 1961), Box 3, and Minutes of the SPU national convention, Apr. 27–29, 1962, Box 1, SPU Records, Madison; "'Even the Fruits of Victory Would be Ashes in our Mouth'—Kennedy" (Oct. 1962), Box 2, SPU Records, SCPC.

49. Gitlin, *Sixties*, pp. 86–93; "Student Peace Groups"; Sale, *SDS*, p. 51.

50. "Washington Action" (1962), Box 2, SPU Records, SCPC; Altbach, "Students on the March," pp. 6–8; Isserman, *If I Had a Hammer*, pp. 197–98; *Sane World*, Mar. 1, 1962; Gitlin, *Sixties*, pp. 93–94.

51. In April 1962, the SPU's two national co-chairs, its national secretary, and its three field secretaries were all male, and men constituted a substantial majority of those elected to its national council. Females were better represented at the grassroots level. Philip Altbach to Bertrand Russell, Apr. 15, 1962, Class 640, RA 1; Minutes of the SPU national convention, Apr. 27–29, 1962, Box 1, SPU Records, Madison.

52. Putney and Middleton, "Student Acceptance or Rejection of War," pp. 655–58, 662; Solomon and Fishman, "Youth and Peace," pp. 55–68; Unger, *Movement*, pp. 47–50.

53. John Swomley, "A Program for Nuclear Pacifism" (Sept. 15, 1959), Box 24a, FOR (United States) Records; "Soviets Resume Nuclear Weapons Tests: U.S. Follows," *Fellowship* 27 (Sept. 15, 1961): 1; personal interview with A. J. Muste, June 2, 1966; *New York Herald Tribune*, Aug. 7, 1960; War Resisters League, *A WRL History of Protest*, n.p.

54. Gail Paradise to Charlie Walker, Oct. 7, 1963, Box 6, SPU Records, Madison; K. Williams, "American Friends Service Committee," p. 155.

55. Stoll, "Women's International League," pp. 153–54; Peat, "National Sections," p. 12; "Statement of Mrs. Annalee Stewart, Women's International League for Peace and Freedom" (July 7, 1960), Box 32, WILPF (United States) Records.

56. Clarence Pickett, for example, who served as co-chair of SANE until 1963, had led the AFSC, while Homer Jack, SANE's executive director, was a member of the FOR. A. J. Muste, chair of CNVA, had worked for the FOR.

57. "The Doors Open Again" (Nov. 1960), Box 28a, FOR (United States) Records; personal interview with Jim Peck, Apr. 21, 1966; Alonso, *Peace as a Women's Issue*, pp. 206–7; Peat, "National Sections," p. 12; Bussey and Tims, *Women's International League*, pp. 244–45; Bacon, *One Woman's Passion*, pp. 280–84.

58. "Scientists Warn That French A-Bomb Test Makes Test Ban Urgent" (FAS press release of Feb. 13, 1960) and "Scientists Urge U.S. to Adopt 'No First Strike' Policy" (FAS press release of Feb. 24, 1963), Box 408, Cousins Papers, Los Angeles; "Scientists Appraise Atmospheric Tests," *BAS* 18 (Apr. 1962): 33.

59. Rabinowitch to Linus Pauling, Nov. 14, 1961, Pauling Papers; Eugene Rabinowitch, "Test Ban Now," *BAS* 19 (Apr. 1963): 2; Eugene Rabinowitch, "The Fearful Choice," *BAS* 16 (May 1960): 189; Eugene Rabinowitch, "New Year's Thoughts 1963," *BAS* 19 (Jan. 1963): 2.

60. Comments by Bethe on CBS Reports, Mar. 31, 1960, Box 40, Szilard Papers; Gilpin, *American Scientists*, p. 159; personal interview with Ralph Lapp, June 28, 1987.

61. Khrushchev responded that no one would have time to shave if war occurred. Seaborg, *Kennedy, Khrushchev*, pp. 61–62; Leo Szilard, "To Stop or Not to Stop," *BAS* 16 (Mar. 1960): 82–84, 108; Leo Szilard, "How to Live with the Bomb and Survive," *BAS* 16 (Feb. 1960): 59–73; Szilard to Eisenhower, Oct. 13, 1960, Box 7, and Szilard to Kennedy, May 10, June 6, 1961, Box 11, Szilard Papers; Bernstein, "Introduction," pp. liii–lx.

62. Pauling to Schweitzer, Mar. 28, 1960, Pauling to Kennedy, Oct. 18, 1961, Mar. 1, 1962, and Pauling to Khrushchev, Oct. 18, 1961, Pauling Papers; Linus Pauling, "The Danger of Nuclear Holocaust," *Frontier*, Oct. 1961, pp. 1–4, enclosure in Pauling to the author, Jan. 25, 1988; *NYT*, Oct. 31, 1961; Hagar, *Force of Nature*, p. 532.

63. Shortly after Kennedy's inauguration, Pauling had written to tell him that "you are our great hope for peace." Pauling to Ralph Schoenman, May 10, 1962, and Kay Halle to Pauling, Feb. 3, 1961, Pauling Papers; Sorensen, *Kennedy*, p. 384; Pauling and Ikeda, *A Lifelong Quest*, pp. 69, 74.

64. Pauling received the prize for 1962. Pauling to Bethe, June 28, Sept. 26, 1963, Pauling to Bertrand Bussell, May 10, 1962, Oct. 8, 1963, Joseph Rotblat to Pauling, May 16, 1962, and Pauling to Harry Kalven Jr., June 28, 1963, Pauling Papers; Hagar, *Force of Nature*, pp. 525–27.

65. Boulding, "Peace Research Movement," pp. 40–41; A. J. Muste to Francis Jude, Nov. 4, 1960, Box 2, Muste Papers; DeBenedetti, "Peace Opposition," p. 19; Keys, "American Peace Movement," p. 297.

66. Osgood, *An Alternative*; Melman, *Peace Race*; Conroy, "Conference on Peace Research," pp. 385–86. The Conference on Peace Research in History later evolved into the Peace History Society.

67. Emery Reves, one of the best-known advocates of world government, adopted an especially sectarian stance, writing a slashing attack against disarmament for *Look* magazine. Keys, "New Federalists," p. 38; Donald Keys to Cousins, ca. June 1962, Box 306, Cousins Papers, Los Angeles; Reves, "Why Waste Time?"

68. Donald Keys to Bertram F. Willcox, Mar. 2, 1959, and Sanford Gottlieb to Keys, Nov. 9, 1960, Series B, SANE Records; *Sane World*, June 15, 1962.

69. Personal interview with Homer Jack, June 12, 1988; "SANE Comment," *Sane World*, Nov. 1, 1963; "Study Committee Proposes UWF-SANE Consolidation," *Federalist* 10 (Mar. 1964): 1–2; "Terminate Consolidation Negotiations," *Federalist* 11 (June 1965): 2; Keys to Leonora Somers, June 21, 1965, Box 69, Series B, SANE Records.

70. Thomas to Gottlieb, Oct. 16, 1961, Reel 61, Thomas Papers; Chatfield, *American Peace Movement*, p. 110; Keys, "American Peace Movement," pp. 298–99; Alfred Hassler, "The Fellowship of Reconciliation and Turn Toward Peace" (1962), Box 24a, FOR (United States) Records; "Turn Toward Peace," Box 8, SPU Records, SCPC.

71. *NYT*, Sept. 1, 1961; "Groups Protest Nuclear Tests by U.S., USSR," *Fellowship* 27 (Sept. 15, 1961): 2; Brittain, *Rebel Passion*, p. 99.

72. "The Peacemakers," *Sane World*, Dec. 1, 1962; *International Bulletin*, Jan. 1963; "Emergency Rally for Peaceful Solutions of the Cuban Crisis" (1962), Box 36, Series B, SANE Records.

73. The *Christian Science Monitor* estimated that fifty thousand people participated in peace walks or other demonstrations over the Easter weekend, but this seems an exaggeration. DeBenedetti, *Peace Reform*, p. 167; *Christian Science Monitor*, Apr. 3, 1961.

74. *Sanity* [Britain], Easter Sunday 1962, pp. 1, 3, 8, May 1963, p. 3; *International Bulletin* (Aug. 1962), p. 6; "Crisis Strengthens War Group"; "Peace Demonstrations: Evaluation with Recommendations," Box 410, Cousins Papers, Los Angeles; *PN*, Sept. 13, 1963.

75. Jack, *Nuclear Politics*, pp. 27–28; Lee, "In the Valley," pp. 65–66, 69–71, 225; Cousins to Schweitzer, Oct. 1, 1962, in Cousins, *Albert Schweitzer's Mission*, pp. 282–83.

76. Key members of the commissions setting its foreign and defense policies came from the Defense Department. Musto, *Catholic Peace Tradition*, pp. 252, 260; "A Dialogue with Eileen Egan," Pax Christi International Records, Antwerp; McNeal, *American Catholic Peace Movement*, pp. 172–77, 191–93, 229–30; McNeal, *Harder Than War*, pp. 92–104.

77. By contrast, Catholics constituted the predominant group among the counter-demonstrators, who carried picket signs reading "Pacifism Leads to Communism" and "They're Not *Red*, They're YELLOW." Solomon and Fishman, "Youth and Peace," pp. 58, 68, 70.

78. Keys, "American Peace Movement," p. 304; Weart, *Nuclear Fear*, pp. 213, 217–18; Winkler, *Life Under a Cloud*, pp. 101–2.

79. Hagar, *Force of Nature*, p. 485; "Fallout Shelters"; Jack, *Nuclear Politics*, p. 37; "Opinion," p. 30.

80. Kissinger was a member of the U.S. delegation to the conference. American Legion folder, June–July 1959, Box 192, Cousins Papers, Los Angeles; *Christian Science Monitor*, Jan. 31, 1961; Divine, *Blowing on the Wind*, p. 230; Minute by E. J. W. Barnes of Sept. 6, 1962, FO 371/163162, FO Records.

81. Teller explained that evolution depended upon mutation. Teller to Alvin Weinberg, Sept. 12, 1961, Box 18, Szilard Papers; Teller, with Allen Brown, "Fallout Scare"; Hagar, *Force of Nature*, p. 484.

82. One leading public opinion analyst, Eugene Rosi, provides figures even more opposed to renewed testing. Divine, *Blowing on the Wind*, p. 291; Gallup, ed., *Gallup Poll*, pp. 1726, 1743, 1753, 1759; Helen Gaudet Erskine, "The Polls: Atomic Weapons and Nuclear Energy," *Public Opinion Quarterly* 27 (Summer 1963): 185–86; Eugene Rosi, "Mass and Attentive Opinion on Nuclear Weapons Tests and Fallout, 1954–1963," *Public Opinion Quarterly* 29 (Summer 1965): 283.

83. Solberg, *Hubert Humphrey*, p. 217; Rosi, "Mass and Attentive Opinion," p. 283; Schlesinger, *A Thousand Days*, p. 913.

84. Another study reports the figures as 91 percent in 1961 and 96 percent in 1963. Gallup, ed., *Gallup Poll*, pp. 1726, 1734, 1808; Lumsden, "Nuclear Weapons," p. 104.

85. Gallup, ed., *Gallup Poll*, p. 1741.

86. Ibid., pp. 1691, 1839, 2088.

87. Jacobson and Stein, *Diplomats, Scientists*, pp. 169–70; Divine, *Blowing on the Wind*, pp. 268–69, 289, 291; "HHH letters" Folder, Cousins Papers, Beverly Hills; Humphrey, *Education*, p. 227.

88. "Other Summit Conferences"; *NYT*, Oct. 10, 1960; Sorensen, *Kennedy*, pp. 610–13; Powaski, *March to Armageddon*, p. 72.

89. *Washington Post*, Aug. 10, 1962; Gitlin, *Sixties*, p. 97; Sanford Gottlieb, "The Peace Candidates and the 1962 Elections" (Nov. 13, 1962), Sanford Gottlieb, "Political Action for Peace" (Nov. 13, 1962), Peter Irons et al., "Peace and Politics, 1962," pp. 30–33, and Jerome Grossman, "Comments on an Independent Candidacy" (Jan. 1963), Box 47, Series B, SANE Records; *International Bulletin*, Jan. 1963.

90. The Council for a Livable World claimed that, in its first thirty years of operations, it helped elect eighty U.S. senators. Bernstein, "Introduction," pp. liii–liv, lx–lxiii; Leo Szilard, "Are We on the Road to War?" *BAS* 18 (Apr. 1962): 23–30; Szilard and Allan Forbes Jr. to Marjorie V. Edwards, Sept. 27, 1962, and Szilard to Edwards, Mar. 25, 1963, Council for a Livable World Records; Sanford Gottlieb, "Memo on Conversation with Leo Szilard" (Aug. 1, 1962), Box 51, Series B, SANE Records; Lanouette, *Genius*, pp. 460–61.

91. Gar Alperovitz to Joel A. Huberman, Nov. 4, 1961, Box 4, Szilard Papers; Solberg,

Hubert Humphrey, p. 217; Humphrey to Dean Rusk, July 6, 1961, 711.5611/7-661, DOS Records; Leo Szilard to Marjorie V. Edwards, Mar. 25, 1963, Council for a Livable World Records; Gottlieb to Robert Schwartz, Jan. 11, 1965, Box 69, Series B, SANE Records; *NYT*, May 28, 1963.

Chapter 12

Epigraph: Kaunda, then a leader of the United National Independence Party of Northern Rhodesia, explained in a British Committee of 100 leaflet: "While $100,000,000 an hour are spent on arms, two out of three human beings live below subsistence level. Our cause is one." "Declaration" (1961), Folder 275, WRI Records, Amsterdam.

1. See, for example, Walker, "Nonviolence in Africa," pp. 186–88; Mazrui, *Political Values*, pp. 108–10; Hope and Young, *Struggle for Humanity*, pp. 109–44; Camara, *Revolution through Peace*; Aram, "Peace in Nagaland."

2. In the mid-1960s, the WRI had affiliates in three Third World countries and the WILPF in four. War Resisters League, *Peace Calendar, 1967*; Bussey and Tims, *Women's International League*, p. 245.

3. April Carter to Alfred Williams, June 17, 1959, Box 21, Series B, SANE Records; *PN*, June 12, Aug. 14, 1959; Carter, "Sahara Protest Team," pp. 126–27; *Peacemaker*, May 1961.

4. Carter, "Sahara Protest Team," p. 128; *Peacemaker*, May 1961; John P. Meagher to DOS, Oct. 16, 1959, 751.5611/10-1659, DOS Records; Donald Harrington to Norman Thomas, Aug. 29, 1958, Reel 35, Thomas Papers.

5. Direct Action Committee Against Nuclear War, "Protest Against French Atomic Tests in Sahara" (Sept. 29, 1959), Box 19, Series B, SANE Records; George Willoughby to Rustin, Nov. 5, 1959, Rustin Papers; Carter, "Sahara Protest Team," pp. 128–30; Randle, "Non-Violent Direct Action," p. 136; Randle to the author, Oct. 4, 1994; *PN*, Nov. 13, 27, 1959; Robinson, *Abraham Went Out*, p. 171.

6. "Text of cablegram to Bayard Rustin 11/14/59 prepared by A. J. Muste and Stanley Levison," Muste to Rustin and Bill Sutherland, Nov. 15, 1959, and Jim Peck to Rustin, Nov. 16, 1959, Rustin Papers; Carter, "Sahara Protest Team," pp. 143–44.

7. Carter, "Sahara Protest Team," pp. 126–27, 132–39; *PN*, Dec. 18, 25, 1959, Jan. 1, 22, 1960; Robinson, *Abraham Went Out*, pp. 171–72; A. J. Muste, "Africa Against the Bomb (II)," *Liberation* 4 (Feb. 1960): 11–14.

8. Carter, "Sahara Protest Team," pp. 137, 139–40; *PN*, Dec. 25, 1959, Feb. 5, 12, 19, Mar. 4, 1960; *Combat*, Jan. 26, Feb. 13–14, 1960.

9. *Peacemaker*, May 1961; Carter, "Sahara Protest Team," pp. 140–41; "Conference on Positive Action for Peace and Security in Africa to be Held in Accra April 7th–9th," Box 18, Series B, SANE Records; Randle, "Non-Violent Direct Action," p. 136; Robinson, *Abraham Went Out*, pp. 173–75.

10. Although Ghana CND continued to exist, by late 1961 Gbedemah was in hiding. Muste to André Trocmé, Apr. 18, 1960, Sutherland to Muste, June 27, 1960, and Muste to Christopher Farley, Sept. 8, 1960, Box 17, and Muste to Randle, Apr. 25, 1961, Box 25, Muste Papers; Carter, "Sahara Protest Team," pp. 141–43; Homer Jack to Heinrich Buchbinder, Dec. 13, 1961, Box 33, Series B, SANE Records.

11. Sutherland to Rustin, Jan. 20, 1959, and Kaunda to Sutherland, Feb. 1959, Box 31, Muste Papers; "Declaration" (1961), Folder 275, WRI Records, Amsterdam; Mazrui, *Political Values*, p. 107.

12. Rustin to Muste, Feb. 22, 1962, Box 31, Muste Papers; Robinson, *Abraham Went Out*, p. 177.

13. Rustin to Muste, Feb. 22, 1962, Box 31, Muste Papers; Minutes of the European Regional Council of the World Peace Brigade meeting of Dec. 2, 1962, Folder 435, WRI Records, Amsterdam; Tatum, "World Peace Brigade," pp. 129–31; Robinson, *Abraham Went Out*, pp. 176–78; Walker, "Nonviolence in Africa," pp. 190–210.

14. Randle to Muste, Mar. 13, 1963, Box 36, Muste Papers; Robinson, *Abraham Went Out*, pp. 178–80; Walker, "Nonviolence in Africa," pp. 189, 207–9; Mazrui, *Political Values*, pp. 113–14.

15. Halvor O. Ekern to DOS, Jan. 3, 1963, 600.0012/1-363, DOS Records.

16. *PN*, Aug. 14, 1959; Eve Hall to Bertrand Russell, Feb. 28, 1962, Class 640, RA 1; Theodore Kloppenburg to Tony Smythe, Sept. 28, 1961, Folder 372, WRI Records, Amsterdam; Brittain, *Rebel Passion*, pp. 196, 199.

17. P. D. vander Puije to John F. Kennedy, Jan. 19, 1962, 711.5611/1-1962, DOS Records; Duff, *Left, Left, Left*, pp. 235–36; Nkrumah, *Africa Must Unite*, p. 199; "The World Without the Bomb Accra Assembly," Pauling Papers; Jack, "Disarmament Talk in Accra"; C. S. Burchill, "The World Without the Bomb," *Canadian World Federalist*, no. 8 (Nov.–Dec. 1962): 16–17.

18. *Bulletin* [New Zealand], July 1963; *Sanity* [Britain], May 1963, p. 3; Boaten to Homer Jack, May 14, 1963, Box 53, Series B, SANE Records; Minutes of the Council meeting of the ICDP, June 24–27, 1964, ICDP Records.

19. "The Role and Trend of Public Opinion in Africa: 1960" (Jan. 30, 1961), p. 11, Box 4, and "The Role and Trend of Public Opinion in Africa—1961" (Feb. 16, 1962), pp. 4–6, Box 7, RR, OR, USIA Records. See also "Reaction to the Presidential Announcement on Nuclear Testing" (Mar. 6, 1962), p. i, Box 7, RR, OR, USIA Records.

20. *PN*, Aug. 7, 1959; "Preliminary Reactions to the Soviet 50-Megaton Threat and the Multi-Megaton Tests" (Oct. 27, 1961), p. 21, Box 6, "Reaction to the Presidential Announcement on Nuclear Testing" (Mar. 6, 1962), p. i, Box 7, and "Some Worldwide Attitudes Toward Disarmament and Nuclear Issues" (July 1963), p. 2, Box 16, RR, OR, USIA Records.

21. Altan Zeki Ünver to Paulings, May 22, 1961, Pauling Papers; Abidine Dino to Bertrand Russell, Sept. 20, 1964, Class 320, RA 2; *PN*, Aug. 7, 1964; "Final Communique of the Conference for the Denuclearization of the Mediterranean" (July 1964), Class 320, RA 2.

22. "Bulletin No. 7" (Apr. 1958) and "Bulletin No. 8" (Apr. 1959), Israel WRI Records; Bing, *Israeli Pacifist*, pp. 89–122; Evelyn Peat, "National Sections in Action," *Pax et Libertas* 26 (July–Sept. 1961): 11.

23. "The Atom Bomb in Israel," *New Outlook* 4 (Feb. 1961): 14–17; *Ma'ariv*, Feb. 17, 1961; "Preliminary Reactions to the Soviet 50-Megaton Threat and the Multi-Megaton Tests" (Oct. 27, 1961), p. 15, Box 6, RR, OR, USIA Records.

24. Avner Falk to Bertrand Russell, Nov. 8, 1961, Class 640, RA 1; Barbour to SecState, Dec. 14, 1961, 711.5611/12-1461, Apr. 30, 1962, 711.5611/4-3062, DOS Records.

25. Flapan, "Israel's Attitude," pp. 276–77; "On Nuclear Weapons in the Middle East," *New Outlook* 5 (May 1962): 12; Simha Flapan, "For an Atom-Bomb Free Middle East," *New Outlook* 5 (May 1962): 13; *PN*, June 22, 1962.

26. Yehuda Ben-Moshe to Bertrand Russell, Sept. 30, 1964, Oct. 20, 1966, and Israel Loeff to Ralph Schoenman, May 9, 1963, Class 320, RA 2; "An Appeal for Nuclear Disarmament," *New Outlook* 8 (Mar. 1965): 21.

27. Hillel Schenker, "Back to the Past," *New Outlook* 30 (Oct. 1987): 12–13; "From the Editors," *New Outlook* 1 (July 1957): 3–4; Eliezer Livne, "There Is No Absolute Weapon," *New Outlook* 5 (Feb. 1962): 9–12; Victor Cigielman, "Rockets Now—What Next?" *New Outlook* 5 (Sept. 1962): 5–8; S. Zalman Abramov, "Denuclearizing the Arab-Israeli Region,"

New Outlook 5 (Nov.–Dec. 1962): 45–49; Gavriel Stein, "Technological Considerations and Nuclear Development in Israel," *New Outlook* 7 (Feb. 1964): 34–38, 58; Flapan, "For an Atom-Bomb Free Middle East," p. 15.

28. *PN*, Oct. 12, 1962; *Sane World*, May 1, 1962.

29. *Jerusalem Post*, May 17, 1963; Simon Shereshevsky to Russell, Mar. 29, 1963, Russell to Shereshevsky, Apr. 18, 1963, and Russell to Max Born, May 20, 1963, Class 640, RA 1; Hodes, *Martin Buber*, pp. 158–59; Friedman, *Martin Buber's Life*, p. 325; *Sanity* [Britain], Apr. 1964.

30. Flapan, "Israel's Attitude," p. 277; *Sanity* [Britain], Mar. 1963, p. 10; Twersky, "Is Silence Golden?" pp. 40–41.

31. *PN*, July 22, 1960; Christopher Farley to Peter Cadogan, Dec. 11, 1962, Class 630, RA 2; Marie-Therese and Bengt Danielsson and Giff Johnson, "Polynesia—France's Sugar-Coated Nuclear Fortress," *WIN* 18 (Aug. 1, 1982): 15.

32. "U.S. and Free World Standing in the Philippines, and Reactions to Related Issues" (Sept. 1959), p. 23, Box 1, POBR, "Preliminary Reactions to the Soviet 50-Megaton Threat and the Multi-Megaton Tests" (Oct. 27, 1961), p. 10, Box 6, and "Reaction to the Presidential Announcement on Nuclear Testing" (Mar. 6, 1962), p. i, Box 7, RR, OR, USIA Records.

33. "The Role and Trend of Public Opinion in South Asia: 1960" (Jan. 30, 1961), p. 7, Box 4, and "Some Worldwide Attitudes Toward Disarmament and Nuclear Issues" (July 1963), p. 2, Box 16, RR, OR, USIA Records.

34. Hazel Gaudet Erskine, "The Polls: Atomic Weapons and Nuclear Energy," *Public Opinion Quarterly* 27 (Summer 1963): 186; Mohammed Elias to Bertrand Russell, May 21, 1962, Class 640, RA 1; B.E.L. Timmons to DOS, July 6, 1962, 711.5611/7-662, DOS Records.

35. K. K. Chandy, "The Fellowship of Reconciliation in India" (1980), p. 5, FOR (India) Records; Peat, "National Sections in Action," p. 11.

36. Desai, "Intervention in Riots"; P. Brock, *Twentieth-Century Pacifism*, pp. 216–20; personal interview with Dhirendra Sharma, Oct. 11, 1995; Dhadda to Homer Jack, Dec. 6, 1961, and Jack to Dhadda, Dec. 12, 1961, Box 17, Series III, Jack Papers.

37. G. Ramachandran to Muste, May 17, 1962, Box 30, Muste Papers; Harold Snyder, "Gandhism and Indian Attitudes Toward the Arms Race" (Aug. 1962), and *Statement Issued by the Anti-Nuclear-Arms Convention* (June 1962), Gandhi Peace Foundation Records.

38. *Statement Issued by the Anti-Nuclear-Arms Convention* (June 1962), and Harold Snyder, "Gandhism and Indian Attitudes Toward the Arms Race" (Aug. 1962), Gandhi Peace Foundation Records; R. R. Diwaker to Bertrand Russell, Sept. 23, 1962, Class 640, RA 1; "Gandhi Peace Foundation Urges President Kennedy Immediate Cessation of Nuclear Tests" (Oct. 17, 1962), Box 5, WRI Records, SCPC; Hume, "Chakravarti Rajagopalachari," p. 788.

39. P. Brock, *Twentieth-Century Pacifism*, pp. 220–21; James Bristol, "India Revisited—Nonviolence Reassessed," *Fellowship* 29 (May 1, 1963): 3–8; Gupta, "Indian Dilemma," p. 56; Crabb, *Elephants and the Grass*, pp. 210–11.

40. Singh to Bertrand Russell, Jan. 28, 1962, Class 640, RA 1; "News from the Peace Front," *Fellowship* 29 (Oct. 1, 1963): 4.

41. *Peace Information Bulletin*, Apr. 1963; *Sanity* [Britain], Apr. 1963, p. 3; Siddharaj Dhadda to Bertrand Russell, Apr. 12, 1963, Class 320, RA 2; Shankarrao Deo to Russell, June 24, 1963, Class 640, RA 1; Max Maxwell, "Delhi-Peking Walk 'An Experiment,'" *Friend* 121 (Mar. 15, 1963): 320.

42. K. K. Chandy, "The Fellowship of Reconciliation in India" (1980), p. 5, undated clipping from *New Zealand Christian Pacifist*, FOR (India) Records.

43. Gupta, "Indian Dilemma," pp. 55–67; R. Jones, "India," pp. 105–8; "Some Worldwide Attitudes Toward Disarmament and Nuclear Issues" (July 1963), p. 2, Box 16, RR, OR, USIA Records.

44. Bertrand Russell, "Message to the People of Chile and Latin America" (Nov. 8, 1963), Class 640, RA 1; "The Role and Trend of Public Opinion in Latin America" (Jan. 31, 1961), p. 6, Box 4, RR, OR, USIA Records.

45. Edward Shimabuko et al. to Bertrand Russell, Oct. 25, 1962, Sergio de Souza Brasil Silva to Russell, Mar. 9, 1963, and Allende to Russell, Aug. 22, 1964, Class 640, RA 1; Hoyt to SecState, Nov. 3, 1961, 711.5611/11-361, DOS Records.

46. "Preliminary Reactions to the Soviet 50-Megaton Threat and the Multi-Megaton Tests" (Oct. 27, 1961), pp. 11–12, Box 6, and "The Role and Trend of Public Opinion in Latin America: 1961" (Feb. 16, 1962), pp. 6–7, 19, Box 7, RR, OR, USIA Records.

47. "Reaction to the Presidential Announcement on Nuclear Testing" (Mar. 6, 1962), p. i, Box 7, and "Some Worldwide Attitudes Toward Disarmament and Nuclear Issues" (July 1963), p. 2, Box 16, RR, OR, USIA Records.

48. Topchiev claimed that the Soviet Union "was compelled to resume nuclear testing" by the aggressive actions of the U.S. government. "Proceedings of Sixth Pugwash Conference, Moscow, USSR, November 27–December 5, 1960," pp. 6–9, and "Papers and Reports of the Ninth Pugwash Conference on Science and World Affairs, August 25–30, 1962," pp. 86–89, PC Records, London.

49. "Excerpt from a Television Interview with Mike Wallace (February 27, 1961)," in Hawkins, Greb, and Szilard, eds., Toward a Livable World, p. 338; Feld, "Artsimovich," p. 84; Long, "A Renaissance Man," pp. 86–87; personal interview with Joseph Rotblat, July 11, 1994. See also Otto Frisch, "Notes on the Pugwash Conference, Moscow, Nov. 26 to Dec. 5, 1960," AB 16/2748, AEA Records.

50. Solly Zuckerman, "Conference on Science and World Affairs (8th Pugwash Meeting), Vermont, September 11–16, 1961," AB 16/2748, AEA Records; B. T. Price, "The 11th Pugwash Conference on Science and World Affairs, 20th–25th September, 1963" (Oct. 16, 1963), FO 371/171190, FO Records.

51. Smirnov, "This Man," pp. 609–11; Jönsson, Soviet Bargaining, pp. 151, 168–69; S. Kapitza, "Scope of His Personality," p. 103; personal interview with Sergei Kapitza, June 28, 1990. See also Sagdeev, Making of a Soviet Scientist, pp. 64–65, 104.

52. McElheny, "Kapitsa to Visit England," p. 744; NYT, Apr. 15, 1962.

53. Rotblat, Pugwash, p. 108; Eugene Rabinowitch to V. Poremsky, Jan. 21, 1970, Box 2, Rabinowitch Papers, Albany; personal interview with Sergei Kapitza, June 28, 1990; McElheny, "Kapitsa's Visit to England," p. 727.

54. Sakharov, Memoirs, pp. 215–17. See also Sakharov, Sakharov Speaks, pp. 32–33; Sakharov, Alarm and Hope, p. xii.

55. Sakharov, Memoirs, pp. 218–19, 226–28. See also Sakharov, Sakharov Speaks, pp. 33–34.

56. Adamsky, "Becoming a Citizen," p. 24; Sakharov, Memoirs, pp. 228–29. See also NYT, Sept. 10, 1973; Sakharov, Sakharov Speaks, pp. 12, 34.

57. Sakharov, Memoirs, pp. 230–32; NYT, Sept. 10, 1973; Sakharov, Sakharov Speaks, pp. 13, 34.

58. Sakharov, Memoirs, pp. 201, 281; Sakharov, Sakharov Speaks, pp. 32, 107; Sakharov, My Country and the World, p. 4; Adamsky, "Becoming a Citizen," p. 37.

59. Graham, Science in Russia, pp. 167–68; Lang, An Inquiry, p. 154.

60. Bloomfield, Clemens, and Griffiths, Khrushchev, p. 179; Friedberg, A Decade of Euphoria, pp. 306–10; Tertz, Fantastic Stories, pp. 39–40; S. Borzenko, "No, It Was Not Like That!" Komsomolskaya Pravda, Mar. 31, 1963, in CDSP 15 (May 8, 1963): 19–20.

61. *Krasnaya zvezda*, Feb. 9, 1964, in *CDSP* 16 (Feb. 26, 1964): 3–5; Holloway, *Soviet Union*, pp. 164–65; Homer Jack, "The Moscow Conference for General Disarmament and Peace" (July 23, 1962), p. 11, Box 52, Series B, SANE Records.

62. Scott, *Quakers in Russia*, pp. 278–84; Miller, *No Cloak, No Dagger*, pp. 12–19; "Proceedings of the London Yearly Meeting, 1959," pp. 4–5, London Yearly Meeting Records; Abrams, "Moscow World Youth Forum."

63. *PN*, Aug. 10, 1962; David Komatsu, "Japanese Students Arrested in Moscow," *Bulletin* [United States], Oct. 1962, p. 2.

64. Homer Jack, "The Moscow Conference for General Disarmament and Peace" (July 23, 1962), pp. 10–11, Box 52, Series B, SANE Records; Jack, "'Peace' Talk," p. 965; "Against All Bombs," enclosure in Ken Weller to Bertrand Russell, July 20, 1962, Class 630, RA 1; *Manchester Guardian*, July 12, 1962.

65. *Meaning of Survival*, p. 157; Earle Reynolds et al., "Press Statement" (Oct. 29, 1961), in Naeve, ed., *Friends of the Hibakusha*, p. 154; *Peacemaker*, Jan.–Feb. 1962.

66. "London to Leningrad Voyage Against Tests" (July 22, 1962), Folder 435, WRI Records, Amsterdam; International Sub Committee, National Committee of 100, "Bulletin," No. 1 (Summer 1962), p. 3, Committee of 100 Records; *Sanity* [Britain], Nov. 1962, p. 6; *Peacemaker*, Nov.–Dec. 1962.

67. Homer Jack, "The Moscow Conference for General Disarmament and Peace" (July 23, 1962), p. 10, Box 52, Series B, SANE Records; International Sub Committee, National Committee of 100, "Bulletin," No. 1 (Summer 1962), p. 2, Committee of 100 Records; *Peacemaker*, Nov.–Dec. 1962; *Sanity* [Britain], Nov. 1962, p. 8.

68. "Statement of A. J. Muste to Soviet Peace Committee in Moscow" (Sept. 8, 1961), Box 4, Series IV, CNVA Records; "Peace Walkers Demonstrate in Moscow, Talk with Mrs. K.," *Fellowship* 27 (Oct. 15, 1961): 1; Jerry Lehmann, "The Walkers and the Muscovites," *Fellowship* 28 (May 1, 1962): 13–16; *Peacemaker*, Nov.–Dec. 1961.

69. "Peace Walkers Demonstrate"; Lehmann, "The Walkers," pp. 14–16; *Peacemaker*, Nov.–Dec. 1961; *PN*, Oct. 6, 13, 1961; Naeve, ed., *Changeover*, pp. 197–99.

70. Weart, *Nuclear Fear*, pp. 136, 238–40.

71. Dallin et al., *Soviet Union*, pp. 79–81; Bloomfield, Clemens, and Griffiths, *Khrushchev*, p. 179.

72. "Unofficial FOR Shows Strength in East Germany," *Fellowship* 25 (Mar. 15, 1959): 3; Homer A. Jack, "West/East Berlin Diary" (Jan. 1963), Box 54, Series B, SANE Records; Ruth L. Hidden-Mottek to Russell, Jan. 3, 1963, Class 640, RA 1.

73. "A History of the Peace Movement," p. 32; Klein, "East Germany," pp. 1–2; Sandford, *Sword and the Plowshare*, pp. 27–31; Allen, *Germany East*, pp. 94–96.

74. *International Bulletin*, Aug., Sept., 1962; "Proceedings of the Tenth Pugwash Conference on Science and World Affairs, London, September 3–7, 1962," pp. 81–82, PC Records, London.

75. "Proceedings of Sixth Pugwash Conference, Moscow, USSR, November 27–December 5, 1960," pp. 515–22, PC Records, London; personal interview with Joseph Rotblat, July 11, 1994; Eugene Rabinowitch, "Thoughts on the Pugwash Meeting in Moscow" (Jan. 25, 1961), pp. 3–4, Box 49, Rabi Papers.

76. "Peace Marchers Enter East Germany," *Fellowship* 27 (Aug. 15, 1961): 2; *PN*, Aug. 25, Sept. 1, 15, 1961; Peter Cadogan to Bertrand Russell, May 15, 1962, Class 630, RA 1.

77. *Sanity* [Britain], May 1963, p. 3; *Sanity* [Canada], June 1963; April Carter, untitled statement on visit to East Berlin, Folder 273, WRI Records, Amsterdam.

78. Naeve, ed., *Friends of the Hibakusha*, p. 206; *PN*, Sept. 15, 1961; *Sanity* [Britain], Sept. 1963, p. 4.

79. *Sanity* [Britain], Good Friday / Saturday 1963, p. 2.

Chapter 13

Epigraph: "Principles and Aims of the International Confederation for Disarmament and Peace," *Fellowship* 29 (Mar. 1, 1963): 10.

1. Weinberg and Weinberg, eds., *Instead of Violence*, p. 4.

2. The WILPF sections were located in Australia, Austria, Britain, Canada, Denmark, Finland, France, Germany, India, Israel, Italy, Japan, Lebanon, Netherlands, New Zealand, Nigeria, Norway, Sweden, Switzerland, and the United States. Smaller WILPF groups existed in Ghana and South Korea. Brittain, *Rebel Passion*, p. 73; Hentoff, *Peace Agitator*, p. 102; War Resisters League, *Peace Calendar, 1967*, n.p.; Bussey and Tims, *Women's International League*, p. 245.

3. Bussey and Tims, *Women's International League*, pp. 222–23, 227, 229–30, 238–39, 242–43.

4. Randle to the author, Oct. 4, 1994; "War Resisters' International 11th Triennial Conference" (July 1963), 226.1080, Deutscher Friedensrat Records; WRI News Release No. 2 (May 1962) and WRI News Release No. 8 (Oct. 25, 1962), Box 5, WRI Records, SCPC.

5. Rotblat, "Movements of Scientists," pp. 136–37; Rotblat, *Scientists*, pp. 41–50; personal interview with Joseph Rotblat, July 11, 1994.

6. Pugwash leaders also desired to distance themselves from Eaton because of his occasional pro-Soviet pronouncements and his receipt of the Lenin Peace Prize. Personal interviews with Joseph Rotblat, July 12, 1990, July 11, 1994; Rotblat, *Scientists*, pp. 9–10, 41; Rabinowitch to Russell, Sept. 28, 1959, Class 625, RA 1; Frederick Seitz to Rabinowitch, Sept. 13, 1960, Box 9, Rabinowitch Papers, Chicago; R. Clark, *Life of Bertrand Russell*, p. 546; Homer Jack to L. John Collins, Feb. 20, 1961, Box 35, Series B, SANE Records.

7. Rotblat to Russell, May 9, 1961, Class 625, RA 1; "Proceedings of Sixth Pugwash Conference, Moscow, USSR, November 27–December 5, 1960," p. 12, PC Records, London.

8. Szilard to I. I. Rabi, Oct. 24, 1960, Box 7, Rabi Papers; Wiesner to Rabinowitch, Mar. 10, 1959, Box 9, Rabinowitch Papers, Chicago.

9. Evangelista, "Soviet Scientists and Nuclear Testing," pp. 29–30; Rotblat to Russell, Mar. 25, 1960, Class 625, RA 1.

10. Rotblat, *Scientists*, p. 46; Wayland Young, "The Sixth International Pugwash Conference of Scientists," Class 625, RA 1.

11. Eugene Rabinowitch, "Thoughts on the Pugwash Meeting in Moscow" (Jan. 25, 1961), Box 49, Rabi Papers; Wayland Young, "The Sixth International Pugwash Conference of Scientists, Moscow," FO 371/149403, FO Records; Rotblat to Russell, May 9, 1961, Class 625, RA 1.

12. To help ensure a well-connected delegation from the United States at Moscow, the American Pugwash committee proposed a delay in the conference date, and the Soviet Pugwash Committee agreed to it. Eugene Rabinowitch, "Thoughts on the Pugwash Meeting in Moscow" (Jan. 25, 1961), Box 49, and Eugene Rabinowitch, Bentley Glass, and Harrison Brown to A. V. Topchiev, Aug. 3, 1960, Box 26, Rabi Papers; Wayland Young, "The Sixth International Pugwash Conference of Scientists," Class 625, RA 1; Rotblat, *Scientists*, pp. 44–45, 49.

13. Personal interview with Joseph Rotblat, July 11, 1994; Rotblat, *Scientists*, pp. 49–50; Rabinowitch to I. I. Rabi, Sept. 25, 1961, Box 49, Rabi Papers.

14. Rotblat, *Scientists*, p. 50; Russell to Born, Sept. 17, 1962, Born-Russell Correspondence; "Tenth Pugwash Conference on Science and World Affairs, Final Report of the Statement Committee" (1962), Box 148, Office of Science and Technology, Executive Office of the President Records; Lang, *An Inquiry*, p. 159.

15. Hiebert, *Impact of Atomic Energy*, pp. 247–48; "An Appeal to All Governments and

Peoples" (Dec. 5, 1961), enclosure in "Memorandum of Conversation" (Mar. 13, 1962), 600.0012/3-1362, DOS Records.

16. Musto, *Catholic Peace Tradition*, pp. 187–93; Hanson, *Catholic Church*, pp. 283, 353; John XXIII, *Pacem in Terris*, pp. 39, 43; Vaillancourt, "Cinq papes modernes," pp. 54–56; "Address of Pope Paul VI," pp. 7–8.

17. Bernard Lalande, "The Development of Pax Christi International from 1945–1965," p. 5, Pax Christi International Records, Antwerp; Hanson, *Catholic Church*, p. 283; McNeal, *American Catholic Peace Movement*, pp. 202–6, 215; "Memorandum of Conversation" (Mar. 13, 1962), 600.0012/3-1362, DOS Records.

18. At the beginning of 1964, Homer Jack produced a lengthy list of SANE's international activities, many designed "to maintain a relationship with sister disarmament and peace organizations in other parts of the world," and proposed an international budget for the year. *Sane World*, Mar. 1, 1963; Report from New Zealand CND National Committee to the annual conference, Aug. 22–23, 1964, Folder 356, WRI Records, Amsterdam; F. G. U. Glass to Donald Keys, Nov. 3, 1958, Box 10, and Homer Jack, "The International Work of the National Committee for a Sane Nuclear Policy" (Jan. 2, 1964), Box 60, Series B, SANE Records.

19. Steffen Larsen to Bertrand Russell, Apr. 16, 1962, Class 640, RA 1; Minutes of the CND Executive Committee meeting of Nov. 14, 1963, Reel 1, CND (Britain) Records, London-Warwick; *Sanity* [Canada], April–May 1963.

20. Carter, *Peace Movements*, p. 73; Randle to the author, Oct. 17, 1990, Oct. 4, 1994; April Carter to Barry Marks, Jan. 16, 1961, Reel 13, CND (Britain) Records, London-Warwick.

21. Michael Randle to CNVA, July 14, 1961, Box 5, CNVA Records; Peter Cadogan to Max Maxwell, Nov. 19, 1963, Box 25, Muste Papers. See also Committee of 100, "L'Homme contre la guerre" (Summer 1962), 66.323, Deutscher Friedensrat Records.

22. Campaign for Nuclear Disarmament, "Annual Report, April 1960/March '61," Reel 4, and "Internationalization of Our Anti-War Movement—Zengakuren" (Nov. 1962), Reel 13, CND (Britain) Records, London-Warwick; International Conference on Nuclear Disarmament for Students and Youth "Bulletin," no. 1 (Nov. 1960), 397.2141, Deutscher Friedensrat Records; Philip Altbach to Bertrand Russell, Apr. 15, 1962, Class 640, RA 1.

23. "Conferences: Sunnybrook," *International Bulletin* (Aug. 1962), p. 12; "International Declaration on the Student Peace Movement, Camp Sunnybrook," *Our Generation Against Nuclear War* 1 (Summer 1962): 56–59; Susan Bricker to Gail Paradise, July 22, 1963, and Paradise to Charlie Walker, Oct. 7, 1963, Box 6, SPU Records, Madison.

24. Speech by Gage-Colby at the Moscow Conference, July 1962, 82.403, Deutscher Friedensrat Records; Swerdlow, *Women Strike for Peace*, pp. 188–89, 192–98; Macpherson, *When in Doubt*, pp. 94–95; *International Bulletin*, Sept. 1962, p. 6.

25. Swerdlow, *Women Strike for Peace*, pp. 205–12; *Sanity* [Canada], June 1964.

26. Bess, *Realism*, p. 198; Jack, *Nuclear Politics*, p. 35; Schweitzer to Russell, Sept. 2, 1961, Oct. 24, 1962, Class 710, and Schweitzer to Russell, May 29, 1963, Class 640, RA 1; Schweitzer to Cousins, Nov. 24, Dec. 4, 1958, Mar. 3, 1959, Oct. 10, 30, 1961, Oct. 22, 31, Nov. 11, 1962, in Jack, ed., *On Nuclear War and Peace*, pp. 112–29.

27. Hugh Keenleyside to Norman Thomas, Feb. 12, 1960, and Schweitzer to Thomas, Mar. 1, 1960 (?), Reel 61, Thomas Papers; Russell to Rabinowitch, May 20, 1963, and Rabinowitch to Russell, June 8, 1963, Box 2, Rabinowitch Papers, Albany; Born to Russell, May 25, 1963, Class 640, RA 1; Bertrand Russell, "Stop M.E. Nuclear Race!" *New Outlook* 7 (Feb. 1964): 2–3.

28. For a list of eighty-six peace periodicals published in 1963 by new groups or by affiliates of pacifist bodies, or independently produced, see "Associated Periodicals," *Peace Information Bulletin*, Apr. 1963, pp. 12–13.

29. Duff, *Left, Left, Left*, p. 117.

30. "European Congress for Nuclear Disarmament: Chairman's Opening Remarks," Box 21, Series B, SANE Records; Collins to Russell, Jan. 21, 1959, Class 630, RA 1; Collins, *Faith Under Fire*, p. 311; Duff, *Left, Left, Left*, pp. 226–28; Carter, *Peace Movements*, p. 75.

31. Richter to Harold Bing, Oct. 14, 1959, Folder 200, WRI Records, Amsterdam; Collins, *Faith Under Fire*, p. 311; European Federation Against Nuclear Arms, "Crisis on Cuba" (Oct. 24, 1962), Box 36, and "European Federation Against Nuclear Arms" (Oct. 13, 1959), Box 21, Series B, SANE Records.

32. L. John Collins to Lord Simon of Wythenshawe, Sept. 30, 1959, and Hans Werner Richter and Collins to Bertrand Russell, Aug. 6, 1959, Class 630, RA 1; Minutes of CND Executive Committee meeting of Oct. 25, 1959, Reel 1, CND (Britain) Records, London-Warwick; "European Federation Against Nuclear Arms" (Oct. 13, 1959), Box 21, and Hajo Schedlich to SANE, July 13, 1959, Box 22, Series B, SANE Records.

33. European Federation Against Nuclear Arms, "Crisis on Cuba" (Oct. 24, 1962), Box 36, Series B, SANE Records; "Nuclear Disarmament," *Pax*, Autumn 1960, p. 12; *Sanity* [Britain], Feb. 1962, p. 1; Dimitrios Roussopoulos, "Internationalizing the Nuclear Disarmament Movement," *Our Generation Against Nuclear War* 1 (Winter 1962): 19–22.

34. Collins to Lord Simon of Wythenshawe, May 3, 1960, Class 630, RA 1; Collins, *Faith Under Fire*, pp. 337–38; Duff, *Left, Left, Left*, pp. 228–29; Carter *Peace Movements*, p. 76; Collins to Norman Cousins, Box 19, Series B, SANE Records.

35. See, for example, K. C. Woodsworth, "The Accra Assembly: The World Without the Bomb," *Our Generation Against Nuclear War* 1 (Summer 1962): 41–51; Stuart Hall, "Further Observations on Accra," *Our Generation Against Nuclear War* 1 (Summer 1962): 51–53.

36. "Thousands Observe Hiroshima Day," *Fellowship* 28 (Aug. 15, 1962): 2; Locke, *Peace People*, p. 168.

37. *International Bulletin*, Aug. 1962, pp. 1, 5; *Sanity* [Britain], Easter Sunday 1962, pp. 1, 3, 8, May 1962, pp. 1–2; Duff, *Left, Left, Left*, pp. 132–33; "Songs for the Aldermaston March," Reel 13, CND (Britain) Records, London-Warwick.

38. Duff, *Left, Left, Left*, pp. 237, 240; Carter, *Peace Movements*, p. 76; Homer Jack, "Preface to Fourth Issue," *Our Generation Against Nuclear War* 1 (Summer 1962): 4; Jack to Peggy Duff, July 26, 1962, Box 41, Series B, SANE Records; *Sanity* [Britain], Dec. 1962, p. 2.

39. "Internationalization of Our Anti-War Movement—Zengakuren," Reel 13, CND (Britain) Records, London-Warwick; International Sub Committee, National Committee of 100, "Bulletin," No. 1 (Summer 1962), p. 2, Committee of 100 Records; Peter Cadogan, "The International Anti-War Conference—10th/12th November 1962" (Oct. 13, 1962), Folder 63, and Peter Cadogan to Tony Smythe, Oct. 2, 1962, Folder 275, WRI Records, Amsterdam; "Report of the International Sub Committee—Cambridge 22nd Sept., 1962," Class 630, RA 2.

40. "Amsterdam Conference, 10–12 November 1962," Folder 63, WRI Records, Amsterdam; *PN*, Nov. 16, 1962; Muste to Bertrand Russell, Dec. 10, 1962, Muste to Hugh Brock, Dec. 11, 1962, Box 35, and Russell to Muste, Jan. 6, 1963, Box 37, Muste Papers.

41. I have adopted the figures used by Homer Jack, a participant from the United States, and by a report in British CND's *Sanity*. Another U.S. participant contended that the delegates represented forty-four organizations from eighteen nations. Homer A. Jack, "Oxford Conference: Organizing the Non-Aligned," *BAS* 19 (June 1963): 38; *Sanity* [Britain], Feb. 1963, p. 5; Alfred Hassler, "The World's Newest Peace Group," *Fellowship* 29 (Mar. 1, 1963): 11.

42. Jack, "Oxford Conference," pp. 38–39; Hassler, "The World's Newest Peace

Group," pp. 13–14, 25; Dimitrios Roussopoulos, "International Confederation for Disarmament and Peace," *Our Generation Against Nuclear War* 2 (Winter/Spring 1963): 55–59; *Sanity* [Britain], Feb. 1963, pp. 4–5.

43. On November 10, 1962, during a discussion of the Oxford conference, Bernal asked Canon Collins if the WPC might send observers. Taken with the idea, Collins secured the agreement of the CND National Council to ask the European Federation to issue the invitations. When he later met with the other European Federation presidents, Collins apparently failed to discuss the issue adequately with them. Minutes of the CND National Council meeting of Nov. 10, 1962, Reel 1, CND (Britain) Records, London-Warwick; *Sanity* [Britain], Apr. 1963, p. 2; Alfred Hassler to Linus Pauling, Sept. 10, 1963, Pauling Papers.

44. Tony Smythe to Peggy Duff, Dec. 14, 1962, Folder 273, WRI Records, Amsterdam; "The Oxford Conference and Observers from the World Council of Peace" (Mar. 1963), Box 60, and Robert Gilmore to Peggy Duff, Dec. 13, 1962, Box 41, Series B, SANE Records; Hassler, "The World's Newest Peace Group," pp. 14–15; Jack, "Oxford Conference," p. 39; *PN*, Jan. 11, 1963.

45. *Sanity* [Britain], Feb. 1964, pp. 4–5; *PN*, Jan. 11, 18, 1963; Russell to Muste, Jan. 26, 1963, Box 37, Muste Papers.

46. Pauling to L. John Collins, Jan. 22, 1963, Collins to M. S. Arnoni, June 17, 1963, Pauling to Heinz Kraschutzki, July 8, 1963, and Alfred Hassler to Linus and Ava Helen Pauling, Sept. 10, 1963, Pauling Papers; Jack to David Boulton, Mar. 22, 1963, Box 65, Bernal Papers.

47. The ICDP affiliates were the International FOR, the WRI, and the Accra Assembly (all international bodies); Victorian CND (Australia); Canadian CND and Combined Universities CND (Canada); the Komiteen for Oplysning om Atomfaren (Denmark); Action Civique Nonviolente and the MCAA (France); the Arbeitsgemeinschaft Deutscher Friedensverbände and the Kampagne für Abrüstung (Federal Republic of Germany); the Sarva Seva Sangh (India); the Irish Pacifist Movement (Ireland); the Comitato per il Disarmo Atomico and the Consulta per la Pace (Italy); the Comite voor de Vrede and Anti-Atoombom Actie (Netherlands); CND (New Zealand); the Folkereisning mot Krig (Norway); KmA (Sweden); CND, Colleges and Universities CND, the Committee of 100, the Campaign Caravan Workshops, the Friends Peace Committee, Youth CND (Britain); the FOR, SANE, the Student Peace Union, and the War Resisters League (United States); and the Yugoslav League for Peace, Independence, and Equality of Peoples (Yugoslavia). Six of the affiliated groups did not send delegates. "International Confederation for Disarmament and Peace Now Functioning," *Fellowship* 29 (Sept. 15, 1963): 1; ICDP, "Report of the Inaugural Congress held at Tyringe, Sweden, Jan. 9–13, 1964," pp. 11–12, ICDP Records; *Sanity* [Britain], Feb. 1964, p. 5.

48. *Sanity* [Britain], Feb. 1964, pp. 4–5; ICDP, "Report of the Inaugural Congress held at Tyringe, Sweden, Jan. 9–13, 1964," pp. 12, 38, 41, ICDP Records; "A Report on the Confederation for Peace," *Our Generation Against Nuclear War* 3 (ca. 1964): 5–7.

49. ICDP, "Report of the Inaugural Congress held at Tyringe, Sweden, Jan. 9–13, 1964," p. 9, ICDP Records.

50. For WSP's assumptions about the ICDP, see Dagmar Wilson to Ruth Gage-Colby, Jan. 4, 1962 (actually 1963), Box 2, Series I, WSP Records, SCPC; Swerdlow, *Women Strike for Peace*, pp. 207–8.

51. Jack to Gerry Hunnius, Feb. 17, 1964, Folder 151, and Cadogan to Philip Seed, July 28, 1964, Folder 275, WRI Records, Amsterdam. For other signs of tensions along these lines, see Tony Smythe to Hans and Marian Sinn, May 7, 1964, Folder 189, and Devi Prasad to A. J. Muste, May 13, 1963, and Muste to Prasad, June 13, 1963, Folder 403, WRI Records, Amsterdam.

52. Kenneth Lee to Devi Prasad, June 9, 1965, Folder 151, WRI Records, Amsterdam; Minutes of the ICDP Administrative Committee meeting of Nov. 9, 1963, and ICDP, "Report of the Inaugural Congress held at Tyringe, Sweden, Jan. 9–13, 1964," pp. 6–7, ICDP Records; Booth, *International Peace Bureau*, pp. 6–7; Minutes of the meeting of the Executive Committee and members of the International Peace Bureau, Jan. 13, 1964, Box 12, and "Exchange of Periodicals and International Information Service" (May 22, 1964), Box 1, International Peace Bureau Records, SCPC; "General Background" (Summer 1970), p. 2, International Peace Bureau Records, Geneva; Santi, *100 Years*, pp. 44–48.

53. For the forty-one regular member and fifteen associate member organizations, see "The International Confederation for Disarmament and Peace," enclosure in Peggy Duff to Dear Friend, Oct. 1967, Reel 3, CND (Britain) Records, London-Warwick.

54. *PN*, Aug. 7, 1964; Minutes of the meeting of the ICDP Council, Sept. 5–8, 1965, ICDP Records; *Sanity* [Britain], Apr. 1964.

55. *Sanity* [Britain], Easter Sunday 1963, p. 3, May 1963, p. 3.

Chapter 14

Epigraph: Fromm to J. D. Bernal, Jan. 22, 1962, Box 52, Series B, SANE Records.

1. Speech by Bernal to the WPC New Delhi conference, Mar. 24–28, 1961, "Declaration on Disarmament" (1961), 227.1083, Deutscher Friedensrat Records.

2. Krasner, *Political Influence*, p. 2; *Peace Courier*, July–Aug. 1989, p. 13.

3. Romesh Chandra to Dear Friends, Oct. 1963, Class 640, RA 1; Donald Edgar to DOS, Nov. 9, 1959, 751.5611/11-959, DOS Records; *PN*, Nov. 23, 1962.

4. "The Israel Peace Movement Calls for a Cesssation of the Arms Race" (Mar. 17, 1960), 397.2143, Deutscher Friedensrat Records; "Speeches at the 7th World Conference (2)," *No More Hiroshimas!* 8 (Oct. 1961): 8; Flora Gould to WSP, Nov. 1, 1962, Box 6, Series I, WSP Records, SCPC; Frank J. Hartley and Victor James to Dear Friends, Nov. 9, 1962, Box 36, Series B, SANE Records.

5. "The Canadian Peace Congress, 1948 to 1978," Canadian Peace Congress Records, Toronto; Eva Sanderson to Bertrand Russell, Feb. 19, 1962, Class 640, RA 1; "No Nuclear Arms for Canada" (1963), *Peace Newsletter*, June 1963, Canadian Peace Congress Records, SCPC.

6. *To Our Friends: Peace Movement in Hungary* (Aug. 1963), pp. 6–7, Hungary Miscellaneous Peace Material.

7. "Declaration of the Presidential Committee of the World Council of Peace" (May 29, 1960), Box 18, and WPC to Dear Friends, Oct. 24, 1962, Box 36, Series B, SANE Records; *Peace Letter*, May 28, 1962, Box 10, Canadian CND Records, Hamilton.

8. Locke, *Peace People*, p. 176; Homer Jack, "Work for Peace Assayed in East, West Berlin," *Sane World*, Feb. 15, 1963; *To Our Friends: Peace Movement in Hungary* (Aug. 1963), pp. 12–13, Hungary Miscellaneous Peace Material. See also Yuri Zhukov, "1963—Peace," *Information Bulletin* [Soviet Union], no. 1 (1963).

9. "Preliminary Reactions to the Soviet 50-Megaton Threat and the Multi-Megaton Tests" (Oct. 27, 1961), p. 1, Box 6, RR, OR, USIA Records; *NYT*, Sept. 1, 1961.

10. The South African Peace Council was an exception to the rule, announcing that it deplored the Soviet action. "Statement by Professor J. D. Bernal, F.R.S." (Aug. 31, 1961), 297.1593, Deutscher Friedensrat Records; Canadian Peace Congress press release of Sept. 1, 1961, Box 10, Canadian CND Records, Hamilton; "South African Peace Council—Statement on Nuclear Tests" (1961), "South Africans for Peace" Folder, AD 2186, African National Congress Records.

11. Yuri Zhukov, "Conversation with a Distant Friend," *Pravda*, July 24, 1962, WPC Records; Kurt Hälker to Astrid Wollnick, Dec. 27, 1961, 297.1593, Deutscher Friedensrat Records; "A Timely Warning," p. 7.

12. J. D. Bernal, "Disarmament" (1962), "Opening Speech by Professor Bernal" (July 1962), 82.402, Deutscher Friedensrat Records.

13. *Peace Letter*, July 9–11, 1960, 397.2144, Deutscher Friedensrat Records; Forrester, *Fifteen Years*, pp. 48–49; "Speech Delivered . . . by Liu Ning-yi, Vice Chairman of the China Peace Committee" (Dec. 18, 1961), WPC Records; Endicott, *James G. Endicott*, pp. 334–35.

14. Homer Jack to Erich Fromm et al., Mar. 9, 1962, Box 43, Series B, SANE Records; China Peace Committee to Bernal, Aug. 31, 1962, Box 62, Bernal Papers.

15. Sinopeace to Bernal, May 13, 1963, Box 60, and Bernal to Khrushchev, Aug. 21, 1963, Box 61, Bernal Papers; Liao, "Thoroughly Expose the Reactionary Nature."

16. "Speech by Liao Cheng-chih, Leader of the Chinese Delegation" (Nov. 28, 1963), WPC Records; *NYT*, Nov. 29, Dec. 2–5, 1963; "New Year Statement by Professor J. D. Bernal" (Dec. 30, 1963), Box 39, Muste Papers.

17. Lewis and Xue, *China Builds the Bomb*, p. 195; Statement by J. D. Bernal (Oct. 27, 1964), Box 60, Bernal Papers; *NYT*, July 13, 1965; *Observer*, July 18, 1965, Class 640, RA 1.

18. See, for example, Powell, "Nuclear Weapons," pp. 3–4.

19. "Peking Rally Backs Tokyo Conference," pp. 8–9; "Smash the Test Ban Treaty Fraud!"; Willis Airey to Bernal, Sept. 2, 1963, Box 61, Bernal Papers; *Sane World*, Mar. 15, 1962; *NYT*, Dec. 2, 3, 1963, July 13, 1965.

20. *Izvestia*, July 7, 1964, in *CDSP* 16 (July 29, 1964): 21; James G. Endicott to Dear Friends, Aug. 10, 1963, Box 10, Canadian CND Records, Hamilton; *Information*, Nov. 1964, pp. 14–17, Czechoslovak Peace Committee Records; *NYT*, Dec. 2, 1963.

21. Wall, *French Communism*, p. 218; Homer Jack to Erich Fromm et al., Mar. 9, 1962, Box 43, Series B, SANE Records; Hartley to Bernal, June 27, Sept. 4, 1963, Box 60, Bernal Papers.

22. Pierre Biquard to Pauling, Mar. 13, 1959, and Bernal to Pauling, Mar. 25, 1960, Nov. 23, 1961, Pauling Papers; Bernal to Muste, Dec. 5, 1961, Box 39, Muste Papers; Eugénie Cotton to Russell, Apr. 21, 1959, Class 630, and Flora Gould to Russell, Nov. 1, 1963, Class 640, RA 1.

23. Bernal to General Secretary, SANE, Oct. 5, 1959, Box 22, Series B, SANE Records; Bernal to Howard Schomer, Oct. 6, 1959, Box 39, and Muste to Colin Bell, May 15, 1963, Box 36, Muste Papers; Pis'mo SKZM s informatsiei o peregovorakh s A. J. Muste ot organizatorov pochoda, June 15, 1961, l. 125–26, d. 1060, op. 16, f. 4, Central Committee of the Communist Party of the Soviet Union Records.

24. *Information*, June 1963, pp. 4–5, Czechoslovakia Miscellaneous Peace Material; "Chairman's Report for Meeting of [WPC] Presidential Committee" (Jan. 23, 1960), 397.2143, Deutscher Friedensrat Records; A. L. Walker to Baron Allard, Apr. 8, 1963, Box 60, Bernal Papers.

25. Homer Jack, "Peace Pugwash in London," Box 43, Series B, SANE Records; Collins to A. J. Muste, June 21, 1961, and Muste to Harold Fay, Sept. 20, 1961, Box 34, Muste Papers; Roussopoulos, "International Peace Action," pp. 144–45.

26. A. J. Muste, "Comment on . . . Relations with World Peace Congress" (May 13, 1959), Box 7, Muste Papers.

27. Wilson to Ruth Gage-Colby, Jan. 4, 1962 (actually 1963), Box 2, Series I, WSP Records, SCPC; Pauling to the author, Dec. 15, 1987; Pauling to George A. Feri, June 18, 1962, Pauling Papers; *Peace Letter*, Oct. 10, 1963, Canadian Peace Congress Records, SCPC.

28. Werner-Christoph Schmauch, "The Christian Peace Conference" (ca. 1963), and Carl Soule, "Christian Peace Conference of 1964" (Dec. 1963), Christian Peace Conference

Records; Dale Aukerman, "The All-Christian Peace Assembly in Prague," *Fellowship* 27 (Sept. 1, 1961): 30–31; Miller, *No Cloak, No Dagger*, p. 9.

29. Muste to L. John Collins, Sept. 20, 1961, Box 34, Muste Papers; Homer Jack to Norman Thomas, Jan. 23, 1962, Reel 62, Thomas Papers; Jack to Erich Fromm et al., Mar. 9, 1962, Box 43, Series B, SANE Records.

30. Cousins, "An Address in Moscow," pp. 10–12, 27–28; *NYT*, July 20, 1959; Warner and Shuman, *Citizen Diplomats*, pp. 167–72.

31. Carter, "Sahara Protest Team," p. 153; Muste to Collins, Sept. 20, 1961, Box 34, and Lyttle and Muste to Alexandr Nesmeyanov, Apr. 1, 1960, Box 14, Muste Papers.

32. "Statement of A. J. Muste to Soviet Peace Committee in Moscow" (Sept. 8, 1961), Box 4, Series IV, CNVA Records; Alfred Hassler to Chkhikvadze, Oct. 25, 1961, Box 1, Series B, Sayre Papers.

33. Collins, *Faith Under Fire*, p. 290; Russell to Eugénie Cotton, Apr. 24, 1959, Class 630, RA 1. See also Stewart Meacham to A. J. Muste, May 29, 1959, Box 7, Muste Papers; Erich Fromm to J. D. Bernal, Jan. 22, 1962, Box 52, Series B, SANE Records.

34. *Sanity* [Britain], June 1962, p. 3, Aug. 1962, p. 3; Minutes of the CND National Council meeting of June 3, 1962, Reel 1, CND (Britain) Records, London-Warwick.

35. Peter Cadogan to Colin Sweet, May 15, 1962, Ivor Montagu to Cadogan, May 24, 1962, and Cadogan to Bertrand Russell, May 24, 1962 and n.d., Class 630, RA 1; Cadogan to Tony Smythe, May 23, 30, 1962, Folder 275, WRI Records, Amsterdam.

36. Homer A. Jack, "The Moscow Conference for General Disarmament and Peace" (July 23, 1962), pp. 1–3, Donald Keys, "The Moscow Conference of the World Council of Peace," Box 52, and Jack to Fromm et al., Mar. 9, 1962, Box 43, Series B, SANE Records; *NYT*, June 9, July 3, 1962; Frances Herring to Dagmar Wilson, May 8, 1962, Ruth Gage-Colby to Wilson, May 10, 1962, Gage-Colby to Herring, May 30, 1962, Wilson to Samuel Belk, June 25, 1962, and Herring to Carol Urner et al., July 17, 1962, Box 2, Series I, WSP Records, SCPC.

37. Fromm also thought that his attendance might help him secure the freedom of Heinz Brandt, a West German union leader apparently kidnapped by East German agents. Collins to Jack, May 7, 31, 1962, and Homer A. Jack, "The Moscow Conference for General Disarmament and Peace" (July 23, 1962), p. 7, Box 52, Series B, SANE Records; Peter Cadogan to Bertrand Russell, May 15, 1962, Class 630, RA 1; Fromm to Norman Cousins, May 30, 1962, Cousins Papers, Beverly Hills.

38. Homer A. Jack, "The Moscow Conference for General Disarmament and Peace" (July 23, 1962), pp. 4–6, 9, Box 52, Series B, SANE Records; *Sanity* [Britain], Aug. 1962, p. 3; Jack, "'Peace' Talk"; *NYT*, July 11, 15, 1962; Bertrand Russell, "Message to the Conference on Disarmament in Moscow, July, 1962," Class 640, RA 1; "Minority Statement . . . at the Moscow Congress," Reel 3, CND (Britain) Records, London-Warwick.

39. Despite this tough speech, Jack and SANE were publicly denounced in the United States by Freedom House, which charged that his conference attendance had furthered "the Soviet cause." *NYT*, July 13, 1962; *New York Herald Tribune*, July 13, 1962; Jack, *Nuclear Politics*, p. 39; *New York Post*, Sept. 2, 1962.

40. "Opening Speech by Professor Bernal" (July 1962), 82.402, Deutscher Friedensrat Records; Collins, *Faith Under Fire*, p. 343; *Sanity* [Britain], Aug. 1962, p. 3; Turski and Zdanowski, *Peace Movement*, p. 85; "Hopeful Signs in Moscow-Dominated Peace Conference," *Fellowship* 28 (Aug. 15, 1962): 1; Jack, "'Peace' Talk," p. 965; Homer A. Jack, "The Moscow Conference for General Disarmament and Peace" (July 23, 1962), p. 12, Box 52, Series B, SANE Records.

41. *Sanity* [Britain], Aug. 1962, p. 3; K. B. Jenkins to DOS, July 20, 1962, 600.0012/7-2062, DOS Records; "Hopeful Signs," p. 1; Mao, "Way to General Disarmament," p. 11.

42. These young, homesick "Peace Pilgrims" had just completed a world tour in which they presented the official Hiroshima Appeal. At the Moscow conference, however, the Japanese delegation snubbed them as "imperialist agents," barred their addressing the meeting, and refused to release interpreters for their use. Naeve, ed., *Friends of the Hibakusha*, pp. 207–15, 222; *PN*, Aug. 24, 1962.

43. Roussopoulos, *From Protest to Resistance*, p. 62; Duff, *Left, Left, Left*, pp. 238–39; Homer A. Jack, "The Moscow Conference for General Disarmament and Peace" (July 23, 1962), pp. 10–11, Box 52, Series B, SANE Records; Zhukov to Bertrand Russell, Sept. 27, 1962, Class 630, RA 1; International Sub Committee of the Committee of 100, "Bulletin" (Summer 1962), Committee of 100 Records.

44. International Sub Committee of the Committee of 100, "Bulletin" (Summer 1962), Committee of 100 Records; Bertrand Russell to A. J. Muste, Sept. 21, 1962, Box 37, Muste Papers; Official Tass summary and translation from *Pravda*, July 18, 1962, Class 630, RA 1.

45. Russell to David Fottes, July 18, 1962, Zhukov to Russell, Aug. 13, 1962, and Russell to Zhukov, Oct. 24, 1962, Class 630, RA 1.

46. M. Kotov to Central Committee of the Communist Party of the Soviet Union, Sept. 18, Oct. 11, 1962, l. 100–101, 110–11, d. 250, op. 18, f. 4, Central Committee of the Communist Party of the Soviet Union Records; A. J. Muste to Linus Pauling, Oct. 8, 1962, Pauling Papers.

47. "Helsinki Festival," *International Bulletin*, Sept. 1962; Norm Uphoff, "Test Protest Barred at Helsinki," *Bulletin* [United States] (Oct. 1962), pp. 4, 10; *Sanity* [Britain], Oct. 1962, p. 6; Larsen to Gerry Hunnius, Aug. 24, 1962, Box 12, Canadian CND Records, Hamilton. For earlier conflict at a Communist-organized "youth" gathering, see Abrams, "Moscow World Youth Forum."

48. "Stenographic notes of meeting of W.C.P. observers group" (ca. Jan. 6, 1963), Box 65, Bernal Papers.

49. *Sanity* [Britain], Feb. 1963, p. 4; A. L. Walker to J. Stuart Innerst, Jan. 17, 1963, Box 65, Bernal Papers; David Boulton, "Alignment and Non-Alignment," *Our Generation Against Nuclear War* 2 (ca. spring 1963): 71.

50. Peggy Duff to A. J. Muste, Jan. 29, 1963, Box 18, Muste Papers; *Information*, June 1963, p. 6, Czechoslovakia Miscellaneous Peace Material; Bulletin of the WPC, Aug. 14, 1963, WPC Records; Bernal to Khrushchev, Aug. 21, 1963, Box 61, Bernal Papers; *Sanity* [Britain], Dec. 1963, p. 5.

51. *PN*, June 14, 1963; WRI, "News Release No. 14" (June 18, 1963), Box 5, WRI Records, SCPC.

52. Duff to A. J. Muste, Jan. 29, 1963, Box 18, Muste Papers; Bourdet, "Désarmement nucléaire," p. 5; "Meeting with Prof., Bill, Ivor & Co.," Box 65, Bernal Papers.

53. In a conciliatory approach to the WRI, the East German Peace Council asked plaintively: "Why should we fight the government of the German Democratic Republic when it again and again makes proposals for . . . general disarmament and for the maintenance and protection of peace in Europe?" It failed to see any benefit "in introducing into the peace movement a differentiation between 'uncommitted' and 'committed' peace organizations as certain people did at Oxford." *Sanity* [Britain], Feb. 1964, pp. 4–5; Boulton, "Alignment and Non-Alignment," pp. 67–69; Peace Council of the German Democratic Republic to WRI, July 24, 1963, 226.1080, Deutscher Friedensrat Records.

54. Donald Keys to Benjamin Spock, scrawled on Keys to Walter Diehl and O. P. Paliwal, Feb. 8, 1965, Box 18, 1971 Series, Spock Papers; ICDP, "Report of the Inaugural Congress held at Tyringe, Sweden, Jan. 9–13, 1964," pp. 7, 20–21, 27, ICDP Records; *Sanity* [Britain], Feb. 1964, pp. 4–5.

55. In early 1966, Bernal reported to Korneichuk that nonaligned peace groups "are still

very hesitant in identifying themselves with us in any organizational way." ICDP, "Report of the Inaugural Congress held at Tyringe, Sweden, Jan. 9–13, 1964," p. 75, ICDP Records; Bernal to Korneichuk, Apr. 20, 1966, Box 61, Bernal Papers.

56. *PN*, Aug. 28, 1959; *Manchester Guardian*, Aug. 20, 21, 1959; Scalapino, *Japanese Communist Movement*, p. 118; Fujiko Isono, "Anti-Nuclear Movement in Japan—Recent Trend," *Pax et Libertas* 26 (Oct.–Dec. 1961): 4–5; Totten and Kawakami, "Gensuikyo," p. 836; Earle Reynolds, "My Personal Relations with Gensuikyo," pp. 2–3, 7, Japan Council Against Atomic and Hydrogen Bombs Records.

57. The WRI's general secretary explained that Gensuikyo "has now taken sides in the Cold War and the reports of the last Conference made it clear that the majority of the delegates were on the side of the Soviet Union, including even praise for their armed forces." Minutes of CND Executive Committee meeting of Sept. 3, 1959, Reel 1, CND (Britain) Records, London-Warwick; Norman Cousins to Steve Allen, June 9, 1960, Cousins Papers, Beverly Hills; Harold Bing to Yasui, Jan. 13, 1961, and Arlo Tatum to Yasui, Apr. 11, 1961, Folder 333, WRI Records, Amsterdam.

58. The stacked nature of the committees also faciliated the Communist victory. Totten and Kawakami, "Gensuikyo," p. 836; Scalapino, *Japanese Communist Movement*, pp. 118–20; Endicott to Bernal, Aug. 25, 1961, Box 60, Bernal Papers; Isono, "Anti-Nuclear Movement," p. 5.

59. Stockwin, *Japanese Socialist Party*, p. 100; *Peacemaker*, Nov.–Dec. 1961.

60. Totten and Kawakami, "Gensuikyo," pp. 836–37; *International Bulletin*, Sept. 1962; Stockwin, *Japanese Socialist Party*, pp. 100–102; "Gensuikyo's Statement on the Soviet Decision," *No More Hiroshimas!* 8 (Oct. 1961): 2; Scalapino, *Japanese Communist Movement*, pp. 120–27; *PN*, Aug. 24, 1962; *Sanity* [Britain], Oct. 1962, p. 6.

61. After Zhukov denounced the Chinese and their supporters as madmen, Chu Tzu-chi, a leader of the China Peace Committee, returned to the rostrum to shout: "The Soviet Union is incapable, and always will be, of achieving a single one of the things that China has achieved." Totten and Kawakami, "Gensuikyo," p. 838; *Meaning of Survival*, pp. 163, 166–67; *PN*, June 21, Aug. 2, 23, 1963; Oe, *Hiroshima Notes*, pp. 36, 43–47, 57; "Salute the Victory of the Hiroshima Conference"; Scalapino, *Japanese Communist Movement*, pp. 156–61.

62. *Meaning of Survival*, pp. 169–70; *PN*, Aug. 7, 21, 1964; "A Summing Up of . . . the Japan Congress Against Atomic and Hydrogen Bombs" (Apr. 3, 1970), p. 3, "Information," no. 1 (May 20, 1965), p. 1, Japan Congress Against Atomic and Hydrogen Bombs Records, SCPC; Moritaki and Ota to Friends, June 10, 1964, and enclosure, "The Banning A- and H-Bombs Movement in Japan" (June 10, 1964), Folder 333, WRI Records, Amsterdam.

63. "A Summing Up of . . . the Japan Congress Against Atomic and Hydrogen Bombs" (Apr. 3, 1970), pp. 3–6, "Information," no. 1 (May 20, 1965), pp. 2–5, Japan Congress Against Atomic and Hydrogen Bombs Records, SCPC; "What Is Gensuikin?" Japan Congress Against Atomic and Hydrogen Bombs Records, Tokyo; *Meaning of Survival*, pp. 176, 186.

64. Scalapino, *Japanese Communist Movement*, pp. 233–34; Homer Jack, "The 1964 Hiroshima Conference and the Japanese Peace Movement," p. 3, Box 410, Cousins Papers, Los Angeles; *NYT*, Aug. 2, 1964.

65. "Let Us Go Forward, Holding Aloft the Banner for the Total Prohibition of Nuclear Weapons," *No More Hiroshimas!* 11 (Nov. 1964): 8; Yushin Hosoi et al. to WRI, June 10, 1965, Folder 333, WRI Records, Amsterdam.

66. Hook, "Ban the Bomb Movement," p. 35; Bamba, "Peace Movement," p. 40; Lifton, *Death in Life*, p. 292; "A Summing Up of . . . the Japan Congress Against Atomic and Hydrogen Bombs" (Apr. 3, 1970), p. 12, Japan Congress Against Atomic and Hydrogen Bombs Records, SCPC.

67. Glazer, "Peace Movement," p. 292; Isserman, *If I Had a Hammer*, pp. 180, 184; Clarence Pickett to Norman Cousins, Mar. 25, 1960, Box 231, Cousins Papers, Los Angeles; Norman Thomas to Pickett et al., Mar. 23, 1960, Reel 61, Thomas Papers.

68. Thomas to Cousins, Jan. 11, 1960, Cousins to Thomas, Jan. 25, 1960, and Cousins to Donald Keys, Jan. 25, 1960, Reel 61, Thomas Papers.

69. Jack to Thomas et al., Jan. 27, 1960, Norman Thomas, "Suggested formulation for a statement" (ca. late Jan. 1960), and Thomas to Clarence Pickett et al., Mar. 23, 1960, Box 231, Cousins Papers, Los Angeles; Meacham to Thomas, Apr. 20, 1960, Reel 61, Thomas Papers.

70. Cousins to Edmund C. Berkeley, June 30, 1960, Box 20, Series B, SANE Records; Cousins to Editor of the *New York Journal-American*, ca. late May 1960, Box 231, and Cousins to Irv Nebenzahl, June 22, 1960, Box 230, Cousins Papers, Los Angeles; Lewy, *Cause That Failed*, pp. 227–28; U.S. Senate, Internal Security Subcommittee, *Communist Infiltration*, pp. 1–27, 35–40; *NYT*, May 26, 1960.

71. "Standards for SANE Leadership" (May 26, 1960) and "Statement of Policy, May 27, 1960," Box 230, Cousins Papers, Los Angeles; Norman Cousins, Letter to the Editors, *Liberation* 5 (Dec. 1960): 3.

72. Homer Jack to members of the National Board, n.d., Box 230, Cousins Papers, Los Angeles; Jack to National Sponsors, Nov. 23, 1960, Reel 61, Thomas Papers; Lewy, *Cause That Failed*, pp. 230–33.

73. Homer Jack to L. John Collins, Feb. 20, 1961, Box 35, Gilmore to Friends, June 27, 1960, Box 18, and "Resolution Adopted by Executive Committee of the Long Island Committee for a Sane Nuclear Policy" (July 25, 1960), Box 24, Series B, SANE Records.

74. Sanford Gottlieb to Cousins, Oct. 18, 1960, Box 253, and Stewart Meacham to Cousins, July 12, 1960, Box 231, Cousins Papers, Los Angeles; A. J. Muste to Meacham, Feb. 13, 1962, Box 6, Muste Papers; Meacham to Cousins, Sept. 14, 1960, Box 18, and Muste to Cousins, Sept. 24, 1960, Box 20, Series B, SANE Records; Keys, "American Peace Movement," p. 297; Lewy, *Cause That Failed*, pp. 232–33.

75. Cousins to Pauling, Aug. 4, 28, 1961, Box 253, Cousins Papers, Los Angeles; Pauling to Cousins, Aug. 11, 20, 1960, and Cousins to Pauling, Aug. 17, Sept. 2, 1960, Cousins Papers, Beverly Hills; Pauling to Nolan Kerschner, Nov. 8, 1960, Pauling Papers.

76. Pauling to Nicholas Cheronis, Mar. 8, 1961, Pauling to Dr. Strout, May 31, 1961, Edmund C. Berkeley to Pauling, Apr. 18, 1961, Pauling to Homer Page, May 16, 1961, Pauling to Chester Carlson, July 24, 1961, and Pauling to Corliss Lamont, Aug. 14, 1961, Pauling Papers; Gabriel Kolko to Norman Thomas, May 6, 1961, Reel 61, Thomas Papers.

77. Pauling remained the great hope for SANE's critics. Abrams told him that "you are the real leader of the peace movement in this country." Pauling to the sponsors and directors of SANE, June 15, 1961, Donald Harrington to Pauling, Aug. 2, 1961, and Abrams to Pauling, Oct. 23, 1962, Pauling Papers; Victor Reuther to Pauling, June 22, 1961, Pauling to Cousins, Sept. 26, 1961, and Cousins to Pauling, Oct. 2, 1961, Box 253, Cousins Papers, Los Angeles.

78. Norman Cousins and Clarence Pickett to local committee chairs, Sept. 12, 1960, Norman Thomas to the Editor, *New York Journal-American*, n.d., and Thomas to David Martin, May 31, 1960, Reel 61, Thomas Papers; Minutes of the SANE Administrative Committee meeting of Aug. 30, 1960, Box 230, Cousins Papers, Los Angeles; E. I. Meyerding to all local committees, July 20, 1960, Pauling Papers.

79. What SANE would have done about the suspect individuals and chapters had they not resigned from the organization remains unknown. Statement by the National Executive Committee of SANE, Dec. 7, 1962, Box 306, Cousins to Pauling, Sept. 6, Oct. 2, 1961, and Pauling to Cousins, Sept. 26, Oct. 27, 1961, Box 253, Cousins Papers, Los Angeles.

80. Cousins to Linus Pauling, Aug. 17, Sept. 2, 1960, Cousins Papers, Beverly Hills; Thomas to Muste, June 14, 1960, Thomas to Hugh Wolfe, May 18, 1960, and Thomas to John Darr Jr., Sept. 14, 1960, Reel 61, Thomas Papers; Donald Harrington to Pauling, Aug. 2, 1961, Pauling Papers.

81. Thomas rested his case on the Communist record. He contended that "it is no answer to say that as yet the Communists or Party-liners in our organization have done nothing we didn't approve of. We are entitled to judge the present and the future by the past and I have had plenty of experience of initial cooperation ending in an effort to capture the organization or control its policy by fair means or foul." In another exchange that spring, he declared: "I know what the Communists did to the North American Committee to Aid Spanish Democracy and the League Against War and Fascism. I grant that circumstances are now somewhat different and I should not anticipate any such extreme calamity. But short of that a lot of harm can be done to the cause." Cousins shared his views. Thomas to Muste, June 14, 1960, and Thomas to Stewart Meacham, Apr. 22, 1960, Reel 61, Thomas Papers; Cousins to Linus Pauling, June 21, 1961, Box 253, Cousins Papers, Los Angeles.

82. "Annual Meeting, June 18–22, 1960," Box 14, WILPF (United States) Records; Bacon, *One Woman's Passion*, p. 300; Philip Altbach, "Students on the March," *Fellowship* 28 (July 1, 1962): 8.

83. Keys, "American Peace Movement," pp. 300–303; Robert Gilmore to Friends, June 27, 1960, Box 18, Series B, SANE Records; Stewart Meacham to Norman Cousins, July 12, 1960, Box 231, Cousins Papers, Los Angeles; A. J. Muste, "The Crisis in SANE" (1960), Box 9, Muste Papers; David McReynolds to *NYT*, Aug. 8, 1960, Box 13, Series B, War Resisters League Records.

84. Minutes of the SPU national planning meeting of Aug. 27–28, 1960, Box 1, SPU Records, Madison; "SPU Statement on Unity in the Student Peace Movement" (Sept. 2, 1961), Box 1, SPU Records, SCPC. See also Michael Parker, "Political Tendencies in the Peace Movement" (1961), Box 1, SPU Records, Madison; Isserman, *If I Had a Hammer*, p. 196.

85. Swerdlow, *Women Strike for Peace*, pp. 1, 6, 46–47, 51, 98–99, 117–19, 122–23, 198–203, 219, 224; Alonso, *Peace as a Women's Issue*, pp. 202–9; Speech by Ruth Gage-Colby at Moscow Conference, July 1962, 82.403, Deutscher Friedensrat Records.

86. A. Johnson, "American Peace Movement," pp. 6–9, 14; Pauling to J. D. Bernal, Apr. 19, 1963, Box 86, Bernal Papers; Russell to SANE, Mar. 27, 1962, Class 640, RA 1; Pauling to Russell, May 10, 1962, Pauling Papers.

87. Norman Thomas to Allen Dulles, June 25, 1963, Box 110, A. Dulles Papers; Homer Jack to N. S. Tikhonov, Oct. 30, 1962, Reel 62, Thomas Papers; Homer Jack, "The International Work of the National Committee for a Sane Nuclear Policy" (Jan. 2, 1964), Box 60, Series B, SANE Records; Sanford Gottlieb, "Conversing with Russians," *BAS* 21 (Jan. 1965): 35–36.

88. "It's Time for a Broad U.S. Peace Movement"; Anne Eaton to Benjamin Spock, Mar. 3, 1964, and Jack to Spock, Mar. 25, 1964, Box 16, 1971 Series, Spock Papers; Pauling to H. Stuart Hughes, Mar. 12, 1964, Pauling Papers.

89. Spock to Jack, Mar. 18, 27, 1964, Box 16, 1971 Series, Spock Papers; Donald Keys to Robert Pickus, Apr. 29, 1965, Box 69, Series B, SANE Records.

90. Minutes of the CND Executive Committee meetings of Apr. 11, 12, May 24, 1959, Reel 1, CND (Britain) Records, London-Warwick.

91. A survey of 1963 Aldermaston marchers found that only 4 percent planned to vote Communist. Parkin, *Middle Class Radicalism*, pp. 82–87; R. Taylor, "Marxist Left," pp. 165–67; Myers, "British Peace Politics," pp. 219–24; Duff, *Left, Left, Left*, pp. 127–28; "Campaign for Nuclear Disarmament" (May 1961), Reel 1, CND (Britain) Records, Lon-

don-Warwick; "Meeting with Prof., Bill, Ivor & Co.," Box 65, Bernal Papers; telephone interview with Nigel Young, Oct. 12, 1993; *Sanity* [Britain], July 1963, p. 2.

92. Carter to the author, Mar. 7, 1994; oral history interview with Pat Arrowsmith, Reel 3; Randle to the author, Oct. 4, 1994.

93. Blackmer, "Continuity and Change," pp. 56–63; Aldo Capitini, "Sulla lettera di Salboroli che mi riguarda" (July 26, 1962), Folder 323, and Mario Tassoni, "The Peace Movement in Italy" (1962), Folder 63, WRI Records, Amsterdam; Myers, "Dilemmas," pp. 88, 90.

94. Verkuil, *De grote illusie*, pp. 48–49; Everts and Walraven, *Vredesbeweging*, p. 43; *PN*, Apr. 10, 1964.

95. Howorth, *France*, pp. 28–29; *PN*, May 1, 1964; Bourdet, "Désarmement nucléaire," p. 3; Randal Angiel's notes on an interview with Claude Bourdet, June 9, 1994, author's possession.

96. *PN*, Oct. 27, 1961; Taipale, "Peace Movement in Finland," p. 30; "Session of the World Council of Peace" and "Congress of the International Confederation for Disarmament and Peace," *Information Bulletin* [Yugoslavia] 13 (Jan. 1964): 4–6.

97. Cockburn and Ellyard, *Oliphant*, p. 228; Mora Cotton to Elizabeth Tapper, July 18, 1961, Reel 80, WILPF (International) Records; "Notes on the history of the NZ Campaign for Nuclear Disarmament," Locke Papers.

98. Avakumovic, *Communist Party*, p. 247; Roussopoulos to Michael Rowan, Feb. 13, 1961, Box 1, Combined Universities CND–Student Union for Peace Action Records.

99. Years later, Meinhof became a leader of the Red Brigades, a terrorist group. *PN*, Apr. 5, 1963; Cioc, *Pax Atomica*, pp. 116–17, 134–38; Rupp, *Ausserparlamentarische Opposition*, pp. 250–61; Hubert Stubenrauch, "The Peace Movement in Germany," *War Resistance* 2.4 (1963): 8.

100. Otto, *Vom Ostermarsch zur APO*, pp. 72, 98; Otto, "Ostermarsch der Atomwaffengegner," pp. 163, 168, 172; *PN*, Apr. 5, 1963; Andrew Trasler, "Official Attitudes to the Easter Marches," *War Resistance* 2.10 (1964): 14.

Chapter 15

Epigraph: He added: "Unfortunately, Prime Ministers cannot indulge in this kind of thing." Nehru to Russell, Sept. 19, 1961, Class 650, RA 1.

1. Norman Thomas to Nyerere, May 24, 1960, Reel 61, Thomas Papers; "Proceedings of the Tenth Pugwash Conference on Science and World Affairs, London, September 3–7, 1962," pp. 28–31, PC Records, London; *Pax*, Spring 1961; *Sanity* [Britain], Apr. 1963, p. 3.

2. Sihanouk to Russell, Mar. 17, 1964, Khan to Russell, July 1964, and Tito to Russell, Apr. 27, 1962, Class 650, RA 1.

3. Carter, *Peace Movements*, pp. 73–74. For a more detailed treatment of these ventures, see Chapter 12.

4. Nkrumah to Russell, June 14, 1960, Apr. 28, May 30, June 29, 1962, Apr. 24, 1963 (with enclosure: Nkrumah to Nasser, Apr. 24, 1963), July 2, 1963, and Russell to Nkrumah, May 9, 1962, Class 650, RA 1.

5. In turn, Russell had a very favorable opinion of Nehru. "The friends of humanity throughout the world have come to look to you for a kind of wisdom which is lacking in the nations that lead in the realm of destructive armaments," he wrote. "Those of us who will not yield to despair hope that in this dangerous time you may find means of saving the world from criminal, suicidal madness." Nehru to Russell, June 6, 1960, Sept. 19, Oct. 12, 1961, and Russell to Nehru, May 19, 1960, Class 650, RA 1; R. Clark, *Life of Bertrand Russell*, p. 608.

6. By contrast, Nehru kept his distance from the World Peace Council. Harold Snyder, "Gandhism and Indian Attitudes Toward the Arms Race" (Aug. 1962), Gandhi Peace Foundation Records; Nehru to J. D. Bernal, June 1, 1962, 82.403, Deutscher Friedensrat Records.

7. Homer A. Jack to Members of SANE's National Board, Sponsors, and local SANE Committees, Sept. 7, 1961, Box 34, Series B, SANE Records. See also Michael Scott to the President, Conference of Uncommitted Nations, Belgrade, Sept. 1, 1961, Reel 9, *National Security Files.*

8. Tito to Russell, Apr. 27, 1962, and Nehru to Russell, May 16, 1962, Class 650, RA 1.

9. Nehru to Cousins, Jan. 21, 1962, Cousins Papers, Beverly Hills; Nehru to Russell, Dec. 4, 1962, and Karamé to Russell, May 13, 1963, Class 650, RA 1; Jawaharlal Nehru, "Preface to Sixth Issue," *Our Generation Against Nuclear War* 2 (Winter/Spring 1963): 3.

10. Gomulka to Russell, Jan. 24, 1959, Class 650, RA 1; "Proceedings of the Tenth Pugwash Conference on Science and World Affairs, London, September 3–7, 1962," p. 30, PC Records, London.

11. Andrew Trasler, "Official Attitudes to the Easter Marches," *War Resistance* 2.10 (1964): 14; Willmann to Stuart Morris, June 1, 1961, and Bradford Lyttle to Tadeus Strozalkowsky and Mikhail Kotov, Aug. 9, 1961, 200.968, Deutscher Friedensrat Records; *PN*, Sept. 1, 1961.

12. Willmann to Stuart Morris, June 1, 1961, 200.968, Deutscher Friedensrat Records; Hilda Morris, "Militarism in East Germany," *War Resistance* 2.10 (1964): 15.

13. Hagbard Jonassen to Tony Smythe, Sept. 3, 1961, Folder 196, WRI Records, Amsterdam.

14. Friedberg, *A Decade of Euphoria*, pp. 310–11; *Krasnaya zvezda*, Feb. 9, 1964, in *CDSP* 16 (Feb. 26, 1964): 3–5; *NYT*, Oct. 31, 1961; Lang, *An Inquiry*, p. 65.

15. Brittain, *Rebel Passion*, p. 182; Eugene Rabinowitch to V. Poremsky, Jan. 21, 1970, Box 2, Rabinowitch Papers, Albany; Boag, Rubinin, and Shoenberg, eds., *Kapitza*, p. 75; N. Khrushchev, *Khrushchev Remembers: The Last Testament*, pp. 65–68.

16. Sakharov, *Memoirs*, pp. 215–17; N. Khrushchev, *Khrushchev Remembers: The Last Testament*, pp. 68–71. See also Sakharov, *Sakharov Speaks*, pp. 32–33.

17. Sakharov, on the other hand, took a rather dim view of Khrushchev's alleged respect for democracy and dissent. S. Khrushchev, *Khrushchev on Khrushchev*, pp. 341–42; Altshuler, "Next to Sakharov," p. 50.

18. Graham, *Science in Russia*, pp. 168–70; Sakharov, *Memoirs*, pp. 275, 581; Sakharov, *Alarm and Hope*, p. xi; *NYT*, Dec. 16, 1989; Adamsky, "Becoming a Citizen," pp. 31, 42.

19. Arbatov, *System*, pp. 82–83.

20. V. Kuznetsov and V. Tereshkin to Central Committee, Feb. 10, 1960, "On the strengthening of the public campaign for conclusion of an agreement on halting tests of nuclear weaponry," session of Feb. 18, 1960, materials to protocol no. 43, 20th convocation, ed. khr. 482, op. 1, f. 11, Commission on questions of ideology, culture, and international party contacts, Central Committee of the Communist Party of the Soviet Union Records, cited in Evangelista, "Soviet Scientists and Nuclear Testing," pp. 24–25; Freers to SecState, July 13, 1960, 600.0012/7-1360, DOS Records. The WPC's 1962 conference and others are discussed in Chapter 14.

21. Khrushchev to Bernal, Sept. 6, 1963, Box 61, Bernal Papers; Bloomfield, Clemens, and Griffiths, *Khrushchev*, pp. 198–99.

22. Personal interview with Victor Malkov, Dec. 4, 1994; KGB to Central Committee, Communist Party of the Soviet Union, Mar. 10, 1961, St.-199/10c, Oct. 3, d. 85, op. 13, f. 4, Central Committee of the Communist Party of the Soviet Union Records, cited in Zubok, "Spy vs. Spy," p. 24; Ribkin, "On the Nature," p. 106.

23. Telephone interview with Pavel Litvinov, Oct. 7, 1990; Graham, *Science and Philosophy*, p. 317; M. Menshikov to Pauling, Oct. 5, 1961, Pauling Papers; "Questions of disarmament, 4 January–23 August 1962," 194/III, pap. 143, por. 40, op. 48, Department of the USA, Russian Foreign Ministry Archives, Moscow, cited in Evangelista, "Soviet Scientists and Nuclear Testing," p. 22; Hagar, *Force of Nature*, p. 533; Pauling and Ikeda, *A Lifelong Quest*, p. 80.

24. Khrushchev to Russell, Oct. 1961, Class 650, RA 1; Nina Khrushcheva to Dagmar Wilson, Nov. 14, 1961, Box 2, Series I, WSP Records, SCPC; Russell to A. J. Muste, Sept. 21, 1962, Pauling Papers.

25. On October 26, in a key letter to Kennedy during the missile crisis, Khrushchev commented approvingly on Russell's "concern for the fate of the world." Russell to Khrushchev, Oct. 23, 1962, and Khrushchev to Russell, Oct. 24, 1962, Class 650, RA 1; Khrushchev to Kennedy, Oct. 26, 1962, in *Department of State Bulletin* 69 (Nov. 19, 1973): 645.

26. Marshall to Robert Gilmore, June 29, 1959, quoted in Gilmore to Norman Cousins et al., n.d., Reel 61, Thomas Papers; Gottlieb to Homer Jack, Nov. 16, 1960, Box 230, Cousins Papers, Los Angeles.

27. Encouraged by Khrushchev's apparent flexibility, Cousins drafted a "peace" appeal for the Soviet premier to mail to Eisenhower. Apparently, though, Khrushchev never sent it. Khrushchev to Cousins and Pickett, Feb. 8, 1961, Box 41, Series B, SANE Records; Cousins to Khrushchev, Mar. 8, 1961, and Khrushchev to Cousins, n.d., in Cousins, *Albert Schweitzer's Mission*, pp. 258–66; Draft of Khrushchev to Eisenhower, enclosure in Cousins to Cyrus Eaton, Sept. 27, 1960, Cousins Papers, Beverly Hills. See also "Soviets Answer SANE," *BAS* 17 (Sept. 1961): 295–96.

28. See, for example, Szilard to Khrushchev, Sept. 6, 1959, June 27, Aug. 16, 30, Sept. 12, 30, Nov. 24, Dec. 2, 20, 1960, Sept. 20, Oct. 4, 1961, Oct. 9, Nov. 4, 15, 19, 25, 1962, July 15, 1963, Box 11, Szilard Papers; Khrushchev to Szilard, Aug. 30, 1960, Nov. 4, 1962, in Hawkins, Greb, and Szilard, eds., *Toward a Livable World*, pp. 269, 305–6.

29. Bernstein, "Introduction," pp. lvii–lviii; "'Conversation with K on October 5, 1960' (Recorded October 9, 1960)," in Hawkins, Greb, and Szilard, eds., *Toward a Livable World*, pp. 279–87 and 254–57; Leo Szilard to Whom it *does* concern, Sept. 8, 1960, Box 41, Szilard Papers; Bess, *Realism*, pp. 74–76.

30. Although the reception was canceled because of Khrushchev's illness, some of the participants were later invited to meet with him. "Proceedings of Sixth Pugwash Conference, Moscow, USSR, November 27–December 5, 1960," pp. 10–11, and "Proceedings of the Tenth Pugwash Conference on Science and World Affairs, London, September 3–7, 1962," pp. 26–27, PC Records, London; "Messages Received at Stowe," *BAS* 17 (Nov. 1961): 385; Evangelista, "Soviet Scientists and Nuclear Testing," pp. 40–41; Rotblat, *Scientists*, p. 45.

31. B. T. Price to A. D. Wilson, May 11, 1962, FO 371/163160, FO Records; Thompson to SecState, Mar. 10, 1961, 600.0012/3-1061, DOS Records.

32. Solly Zuckerman, "Conference on Science and World Affairs (8th Pugwash Meeting), Vermont, September 11–16, 1961," AB 16/2748, AEA Records; B. T. Price, "The 11th Pugwash Conference on Science and World Affairs, 20th–25th September, 1963" (Oct. 16, 1963), FO 371/171190, FO Records.

33. Schlesinger, *A Thousand Days*, pp. 301–2, Kistiakowsky, *A Scientist*, pp. 423–24; Evangelista, "Soviet Scientists and Nuclear Testing," pp. 36–37.

34. Willmann to Soviet Committee for the Defense of Peace, May 3, 1961, l. 114–15, Zapiska predsedatelya Sovetskogo Komiteta Zashchity Mira N. A. Tichonova v TsK KPSS, May 17, 1961, l. 107–8, d. 1060, op. 16, f. 4, Central Committee of the Communist Party of the Soviet Union Records.

35. Pis'mo SKZM s informatsiei o peregovorakh s A. J. Muste ot organizatorov pochoda, June 15, 1961, l. 125–26, Zapiska v TsK KPSS Zam. zaveduyushchego Mezhdunarodnym Otdelom TsK KPSS G. Shumeiko, Aug. 12, 1961, l. 100–101, Postanovlenie secretariata TsK KPSS, #193, n. 8, Aug. 17, 1961, l. 99, d. 1060, op. 16, f. 4, Central Committee of the Communist Party of the Soviet Union Records.

36. In early September, Soviet officials suddenly announced that the march across Soviet territory would be cut back to eighteen days. March leaders believed this change of policy resulted from their civil disobedience in East Germany—a practice which led to their expulsion from that country and probably chilled the enthusiasm of their prospective Soviet hosts. Even so, what is remarkable in these circumstances is that Soviet authorities admitted the marchers at all. Naeve, ed., *Changeover*, pp. 201, 203.

37. For fuller discussions of these incidents and of the San Francisco to Moscow march, see Chapters 12 and 14.

38. Soviet Peace Committee to Central Commmittee of the Communist Party of the Soviet Union, Sept. 18, Oct. 11, 1962, l. 100–101, 110–11, d. 250, op. 18, f. 4, Central Committee of the Communist Party of the Soviet Union Records.

39. Soviet Peace Committee to Central Committee of the Communist Party of the Soviet Union, Oct. 15, 1962, l. 99, V. Tereshkin to the Central Committee of the Communist Party of the Soviet Union, Oct. 15, 1962, l. 98, and Resolution of the Central Committee of the Communist Party of the Soviet Union, Oct. 17, 1962 (Protocol 45, Point 5), l. 96, d. 250, op. 18, f. 4, Central Committee of the Communist Party of the Soviet Union Records.

40. The battle between Soviet-led and Chinese-led forces for control of the WPC is discussed in Chapter 14.

41. Clemens, "Sino-Soviet Dispute," p. 214; "Peking Rally Backs Tokyo Conference," p. 7.

42. Niels Mathiesen, "The Peace Movement in Norway" (1962), Folder 63, and "Report from New Zealand Campaign for Nuclear Disarmament . . . August 21–22, 1965," Folder 356, WRI Records, Amsterdam; Locke, *Peace People*, p. 180.

43. Ben-Gurion to Russell, May 6, 30, 1963, and Russell to Ben-Gurion, May 17, 1963, Class 650, RA 1.

44. British Embassy (Ottawa) to Commonwealth Relations Office, Dec. 30, 1959, FO 371/149390, FO Records; Macpherson and Sears, "Voice of Women," p. 72; Ghent, "Canadian-American Relations," p. 113; Naeve, ed., *Changeover*, p. 207.

45. According to another U.S. diplomatic report, New Zealand's secretary of external affairs told the U.S. ambassador "his personal opinion that nuclear tests were not nearly as harmful as alarmists would have them, but said that the pressure of public opinion and press opinion would probably force the government to protest any confirmed French decision to test nuclear bombs in its Pacific territories. . . . This is an election year." Satterthwaite to SecState, Mar. 2, 1962, 711.5611/3-262, Raymond A. Valliere to DOS, Jan. 17, 1963, 751.5611/1-1763, and Akers to SecState, May 28, 1963, POL 7 US/HARRIMAN, 1963 Series, DOS Records.

46. Lyon, *Canada*, pp. 89–90; Ghent, "Canadian-American Relations," pp. 75–76, 83, 203–4.

47. Gilbert and Jordan, "Traditions of Dissent," p. 355; Rudolf Deku et al. to Dear Sir, dear Madam, Oct. 18, 1959, 396.2137, Deutscher Friedensrat Records; Theodor Michaltscheff, "The Struggle for Peace in the German Federal Republic," *War Resistance* 2.12 (1965): 16.

48. Rousseas, *Death of a Democracy*; Frangos and Schwab, eds., *Greece Under the Junta*, pp. 15–30; Greek Committee for International Detente and Peace, *32 Years of Struggle*, p. 3.

49. *PN*, Oct. 20, 1961; "Peace Walkers Demonstrate in Moscow, Talk with Mrs. K.," *Fellowship* 27 (Oct. 15, 1961): 1.

50. *PN*, Aug. 24, 1962; *Sanity* [Britain], Good Friday / Saturday 1963, p. 4, May 1963, p. 3; Steffen Larsen to international contacts, 1963, Folder 197, WRI Records, Amsterdam; Edmund H. Kellogg to DOS, Apr. 30, 1963, POL 25 W GER, 1963 Series, DOS Records.

51. Brandon, *Burning Question*, pp. 50–51; Ardagh, *Germany*, p. 314.

52. Romain Gary to Joseph Sutherland, Dec. 7, 1959, *Los Angeles Times*, Dec. 12, 1959, Box 22, Series B, SANE Records; Carter, "Sahara Protest Team," p. 140.

53. *PN*, May 6, 27, 1960, June 16, 23, 30, July 14, 1961.

54. Oral history interview with Alec Douglas-Home, p. 6; R. A. Butler, "Demonstration in Trafalgar Square by Nuclear Disarmers" (July 31, 1961), C. (61) 125, CAB 129, and British Cabinet Meeting of Aug. 1, 1961, C.C. (61) 46, CAB 128, Cabinet Records; G. Lord, Minutes of meeting with Committee of 100 representatives, Aug. 24, 1961, PREM 11/3387, PM Records; "Press Statement issued by Committee of 100" (1961), Class 630, RA 1.

55. Those arrested included John Osborne, Vanessa Redgrave, and Shelagh Delany. *Daily Mirror*, Sept. 13, 1961, *Daily Telegraph*, Sept. 18, 1961, Randle Papers; *Guardian*, Sept. 18, 19, 1961.

56. Julian Amery to Prime Minister, Dec. 5, 1961, R. E. M. B. to Prime Minister, Dec. 6, 1961, and Minister of Defense to Prime Minister, Dec. 6, 1961, PREM 11/4284, PM Records.

57. Randle, "Non-Violent Direct Action," pp. 138–39; British Cabinet Meeting of Dec. 7, 1961, C.C. (61) 68, CAB 128, Cabinet Records; Illegible to Prime Minister, Dec. 8, 1961, PREM 11/4284, PM Records; *Daily Express*, Dec. 8, 1961, Randle Papers; Michael Randle to the Editor, *Independent*, Jan. 16, 1994.

58. *Times* (London), Dec. 11, 1961; Randle, "Non-Violent Direct Action," pp. 140–41; Brook to Prime Minister, June 6, 1963, and Macmillan's minute of June 10, 1963, PREM 11/4284, PM Records.

59. Oral history interview with Alec Douglas-Home, pp. 3, 5; Minute by G. Brown, n.d., by J.E.T. Egg of Apr. 7, 1959, by T. Barker of Apr. 7, 1959, and by G. Brown of Apr. 8, 1959, FO 371/140482, FO Records; "The Development of the Nuclear Disarmament Movement," enclosure in C. Cunningham to P. Woodfield, Apr. 17, 1963, PREM 11/4285, PM Records.

60. Minutes of CND Executive Committee meeting of May 24, 1959, Reel 1, CND (Britain) Records, London-Warwick; Diana Collins to Macmillan, Feb. 1, 1962, P. J. Woodfield to Macmillan, Feb. 9, 1962, Iain Macleod to Woodfield, Feb. 14, 1962, Woodfield to Macleod, Feb. 15, 1962, Woodfield to Macmillan, Mar. 13, 1962, and "Note for the Record" (Mar. 15, 1962), PREM 11/4290, PM Records; *Guardian*, Mar. 5, 1962; *Independent*, Jan. 9, 1994.

61. Macmillan, *At the End*; Diefenbaker, *One Canada*, 3: 102; L. Thompson, "Memorandum of Conversation" (Dec. 19, 1962), 741.5611/12-1962, DOS Records; Horne, *Macmillan*, pp. 166, 467.

62. PREM 11/2778, the folder from the Prime Minister's Records containing the documentation on the government's early campaign to counter CND, is followed, sequentially, by four others that are marked "closed for the next 100 years." This extraordinary conjunction suggests that these carefully guarded materials may reveal some nasty practices.

63. Central Intelligence Agency, "Security Conditions in Western Europe During President Kennedy's Visit (23 June–3 July 1963)," p. 2, Reel 1, *CIA Research Reports*; R. Taylor, "Labour Party," p. 120.

64. Rotblat, "Movements of Scientists," p. 136; FO to certain of Her Majesty's Representatives, Nov. 23, 1960, FO 371/163160, FO Records.

65. Cockcroft to Patrick Dean, Dec. 4, 1959, Apr. 20, 1960, Dean to Cockcroft, Dec. 11, 1959, Apr. 29, July 14, 1960, and Cockcroft to Rotblat, Dec. 18, 1959, AB 16/2748, AEA Records.

66. J. O. Wright to A. R. Isserlis, Jan. 6, 1961, FO 371/149403, FO Records; Cockcroft to Solly Zuckerman, Feb. 10, 1961, AB 6/2627, AEA Records.

67. Cockcroft to Hugh Stephenson, May 16, June 26, 1961, and Wilson to Solly Zuckerman, June 16, 1961, AB 16/2748, AEA Records.

68. Wilson to Cockcroft, July 12, 1961, AB 16/2748, and Cockcroft to Howard Florey, Aug. 3, 1961, AB 6/2627, AEA Records; personal interview with Joseph Rotblat, July 11, 1994; Minute by A.D.F. Pemberton-Piggott of Oct. 25, 1963, FO 371/171190, FO Records.

69. B. T. Price to D. M. Cleary, Jan. 26, 1962, FO 371/163160, FO Records. See also Minute by A. D. Wilson of Feb. 9, 1962, by T. C. Barker of Feb. 26, 1962, FO 371/163160, and Minute by D. E. Tatham of July 8, 1963, FO 371/171190, FO Records.

70. Minute by R.F.G. Sarell of Mar. 5, 1962, Wilson to Cockcroft, June 5, 1962, Solly Zuckerman to Wilson, June 7, 1962, and R. McC. Andrew to A. H. Hewin, July 5, 1962, FO 371/163160, and Wilson to F. F. Turnbull, Aug. 10, 1962, FO 371/163161, FO Records.

71. See Folder FO 371/17189, FO Records.

72. Chancellor of the Duchy of Lancaster to Macmillan, July 29, 1959, PREM 11/2778, and Hill to Macmillan, Feb. 17, 1961, PREM 11/3396, PM Records; Brandon, *Burning Question*, pp. 127–28.

73. Macmillan to Foreign Secretary, June 25, Aug. 24, 1959, PREM 11/2840, and "Defence" (Sept. 1960) and Hill to Cabinet members, Nov. 22, 1960, PREM 11/3074, PM Records.

74. Kistiakowsky, *A Scientist*, p. 290; Lang, *An Inquiry*, p. 63; Randle to the author, Oct. 4, 1994.

75. In answer to protests, the BBC insisted that there was "no outside pressure." Goodwin, "Low Conspiracy?" pp. 18–20; *Times* (London), Nov. 14, 18, 27, 1965; Adamthwaite, "Nations Shall Speak," p. 402; H. Forrest to General Manager, BBC, Mar. 25, 1968, Reel 3, CND (Britain) Records, London-Warwick; BBC to the National Peace Council, Dec. 15, 1965, "National Peace Council" Folder, Brittain Papers.

76. As a result, when Watkins received an award as the best television director of the year, it came two decades after the film's production. "The War Game: CND Group Showings," Reel 3, CND (Britain) Records, London-Warwick; Brandon, *Burning Question*, pp. 58–59.

Chapter 16

Epigraph: J. F. Dulles, "Memorandum of Conversation with the President" (Jan. 20, 1959), Box 7, White House Memoranda Series, J. F. Dulles Papers, Abilene.

1. MacArthur to SecState, Feb. 12, 1960, 711.5611/2-1260, DOS Records; "Donnybrook at Hiroshima" (Aug. 21, 1963), Box 17, RR, OR, USIA Records.

2. Reischauer to SecState, Sept. 22, 1961, 711.5611/9-2261, DOS Records. Gensuikyo later published its letter as Yasui to Kennedy, Sept. 19, 1961, in *No More Hiroshimas!* 8 (Oct. 1961): 9.

3. Ball to American Embassy (Moscow), May 7, 1962, 600.0012/5-762, Thompson to SecState, May 10, 1962, 600.0012/5-1062, and DOS to All American Diplomatic Posts, May 17, 1962, 711.5611/5-1762, DOS Records.

4. The State Department also requested careful monitoring of Sino-Soviet disagreements about Communist-led peace activism. Meyer to DOS, June 6, 1962, 600.0012/6-662, Ball to

American Embassy (Moscow), 600.0012/6-1962, and DOS to All American Diplomatic Posts, June 15, 1962, 600.0012/6-1562, DOS Records; Dagmar Wilson to Samuel E. Belk, June 25, 1962, Box 2, Series I, WSP Records, SCPC.

5. Halperin et al., *Lawless State*, p. 146; Swerdlow, *Women Strike for Peace*, pp. 101–2.

6. Hoover to Gordon Gray, Nov. 9, 1959, Box 1, and Hoover to Gray, Mar. 26, 1959, Box 2, FBI Series, OSANSA, White House Office Records; Lewy, *Cause That Failed*, p. 226; "The SANE File," Box 29, Series G, SANE Records.

7. Lanouette, *Genius*, pp. 450–52; Alonso, *Peace as a Women's Issue*, p. 185; Dion, "FBI Surveillance," pp. 1, 5, 8–9, 13. See also Bacon, *One Woman's Passion*, p. 290.

8. Central Intelligence Agency, "Security Conditions in Western Europe During President Kennedy's Visit (23 June–3 July 1963)," Reel 1, Central Intelligence Agency, "The British Communist Party" (Apr. 12, 1963), Reel 4, *CIA Research Reports*.

9. Norman Thomas to Dulles, June 25, 1963, and Dulles to Thomas, June 28, 1963, Box 110, A. Dulles Papers; A. Dulles, *Craft of Intelligence*, p. 227.

10. When the CIA's operations against domestic groups became public in the mid-1970s, WSP instituted a lawsuit against the CIA, charging surveillance, infiltration, and mail-opening. The CIA offered an out-of-court financial settlement, which WSP accepted. U.S. Senate, Select Committee to Study Governmental Operations with Respect to Intelligence Activities, *Final Report*, 5: 573–74; Swerdlow, *Women Strike for Peace*, pp. 123–24; Halperin et al., *Lawless State*, pp. 146–47; Adams, *Peacework*, p. 14.

11. Spock and Morgan, *Spock on Spock*, p. 170. See also Swerdlow, *Women Strike for Peace*, p. 102.

12. Halperin et al., *Lawless State*, p. 146; S.N.R. to District Inspector, District "C," Bureau of Criminal Investigation, Aug. 15, 1960, and Sgt. J.N.D. to Chief Inspector, Commanding, Bureau of Criminal Investigation, July 11, 1960, Case 2016, Box 30, Non-Criminal Investigation Case Files, New York State Division of State Police Records.

13. Humphrey, *Education*, p. 253. The Dodd-SANE confrontation and its effects are discussed in Chapter 14.

14. Sullivan, *Nuclear Democracy*, p. 53; Rotblat, "Movements of Scientists," p. 132; personal interview with Joseph Rotblat, July 11, 1994.

15. Kalven, "Congressional Testing of Linus Pauling: The Legal Framework"; Kalven, "Congressional Testing of Linus Pauling: Sourwine," pp. 484–91; Hagar, *Force of Nature*, pp. 512–22; U.S. Senate, Internal Security Subcommittee of the Committee on the Judiciary, *Testimony of Dr. Linus Pauling*, Parts I and II; U.S. Senate, Internal Security Subcommittee of the Committee on the Judiciary, *Report on the Hearings of Dr. Linus Pauling*, p. 6.

16. Federal courts threw out the contempt citation. Swerdlow, *Women Strike for Peace*, pp. 97–123; WSP press releases of Dec. 11, 12, 1962, Box 2, WSP Records, Madison; U.S. House of Representatives, Committee on Un-American Activities, *Communist Activities*; "Women Strike for Peace—A short history of activities during 1963 and 1964" (1964), Box 1, Series I, WSP Records, SCPC.

17. Penciled notation on Percival Brundage to Ann Whitman, Jan. 4, 1959, PPF 1326, WHCF, Eisenhower Records; John Foster Dulles, "Memorandum of Conversation with the President" (Jan. 20, 1959), Box 7, White House Memoranda Series, J. F. Dulles Papers, Abilene.

18. John A. Calhoun, "Memorandum for Brig. Gen. A. J. Goodpaster" (Feb. 27, 1959), Box 3, Name Series, Confidential File, WHCF, Eisenhower Records.

19. John A. Calhoun, "Memorandum for Brig. Gen A. J. Goodpaster" (Mar. 4, 1959), Wilton B. Persons, "Suggested Reply," and Eisenhower to Goheen, Mar. 10, 1959, Box 3, Name Series, Confidential File, WHCF, Eisenhower Records; Brabazon, *Albert Schweitzer*, p. 443.

20. Bohlen to Szilard, June 14, July 12, 1960, and Herter to Szilard, Nov. 10, 1960, Box 19, Szilard Papers.

21. Lewis L. Strauss, "Mcmorandum for the Files of Lewis L. Strauss" (Nov. 1, 1960), Box 39, and Lewis L. Strauss, "Memorandum for the Files" (Nov. 3, 1960), Box 67, AEC Series, Strauss Papers.

22. Elliott sent copies of this lengthy memo to the secretary of state, the vice president, and to White House officials, among others. Elliott to Robert Murphy, June 3, 1959, 711.5611/6-359, DOS Records.

23. Albert E. Irving to DOS, Jan. 20, 1960, 600.0012/1-2060, and Whitney to SecState, Apr. 20, 1960, 600.0012/4-2060, DOS Records.

24. P. Wesley Kriebel to DOS, Jan. 6, 1960, 600.0012/1-660, and Robert Tepper to DOS, Dec. 12, 1960, 600.0012/12-1260, DOS Records.

25. York, *Making Weapons, Talking Peace*, pp. 327–28.

26. Elliott to Murphy, June 3, 1959, 711.5611/6-359, and John A. Calhoun, "Memorandum for Brig. Gen. A. J. Goodpaster" (Apr. 29, 1960), 600.0012/4-2660, DOS Records.

27. William J. Gehron to Mr. Fleischer, June 1, 1959, "3. Conferences and Meetings, 27. Pugwash Conference, 1957–1961" Folder, AE Lot File, DOS Records; Kistiakowsky, *A Scientist*, pp. 292, 322.

28. Victor Weisskopf to I. I. Rabi, July 6, 1960, Box 8, Rabi Papers; Walter G. Whitman to Mr. Farley, Oct. 18, 1960, "3. Conferences and Meetings, 27. Pugwash Conference, 1957–1961" Folder, AE Lot File, DOS Records.

29. Eisenhower did not use the speech. Cousins to Eisenhower, May 22, 1959, and Eisenhower to Cousins, May 30, June 10, 1959, Cousins Papers, Beverly Hills.

30. Ann [Whitman] to Thomas E., ca. late July 1959, OF 225, WHCF, Eisenhower Records; John S. D. Eisenhower, "Memorandum of Conference with the President" (Aug. 6, 1959), Box 43, DDE Diary Series, Eisenhower Papers.

31. Cousins did have another pleasant visit with Eisenhower, at the latter's request, that fall. Cousins to Eisenhower, Mar. 27, 1960, and Ann C. Whitman to Cousins, Mar. 29, 1960, OF 108-A, WHCF, Eisenhower Records; Cousins to Albert Schweitzer, Oct. 4, 1960, in Cousins, *Albert Schweitzer's Mission*, pp. 246–51.

32. Libby to Detlov W. Bronk, Mar. 12, 1959, Box 63, Office of Science and Technology, Executive Office of the President Records; Kistiakowsky, *A Scientist*, pp. 27, 249; Minutes of the Cabinet meeting of May 12, 1960, Box 16, Cabinet Series, Eisenhower Papers.

33. Robert Gray, "'On the Beach'—Joint USIA-State Information Guidance for Missions Abroad" (Dec. 7, 1959), "Memorandum for the Vice President" (Dec. 10, 1959), and Minutes of Cabinet Meeting of Dec. 11, 1959, Box 15, Cabinet Series, Eisenhower Papers; Kistiakowsky, *A Scientist*, p. 195.

34. Lodge to SecState, May 12, 1960, 600.0012/5-1260, DOS Records; United Kingdom Delegation (Geneva) to FO, Jan. 10, 1960, FO 371/149272, FO Records.

35. "West European Climate of Opinion on the Eve of the Paris Summit Conference: General Standing of the U.S. vs. the U.S.S.R." (Apr. 1960), p. 22, Box 5, POBR, OR, USIA Records; Strauss to Helen Hedges, Dec. 7, 1960, Box 26G, AEC Series, Strauss Papers.

36. American Embassy (New Delhi) to DOS, June 29, 1962, 600.0012/6-2962, and Bruce to DOS, May 25, 1962, 600.0012/5-2562, DOS Records; Bruce to SecState, July 17, 1961, and Bruce to McGeorge Bundy, June 7, 1962, Reel 9, *National Security Files*.

37. Bruce to SecState, Sept. 8, 1961, 600.0012/9-861, and Frazier Meade to DOS, 600.0012/4-2562, DOS Records; Albert E. Irving to DOS, Apr. 12, 1963, Reel 10, *National Security Files*.

38. Edmund H. Kellogg to DOS, May 31, 1963, POL 13 W GER, 1963 Series, James P. Parker to DOS, May 9, 1962, 711.5611/5-962, Robert H. Frowick to DOS, Apr. 26, 1962,

711.5611/4-2662, Jerome Gaspard to DOS, Mar. 23, 1962, 711.5611/3-2362, and Edward P. Prince to DOS, Sept. 29, 1961, 600.0012/9-2961, DOS Records.

39. Halvor O. Ekern to SecState, Jan. 3, 1963, 600.0012/1-363, J. B. Engle to DOS, May 18, 1962, 600.0012/5-1862, and Robert B. Memminger to DOS, Mar. 30, 1961, 600.0012/3-3061, DOS Records.

40. Jerome Gaspard to DOS, Mar. 31, 1962, 711.5611/3-3162, May 8, 1962, 711.5611/5-862, and Frederick T. Rope to DOS, Apr. 3, 1962, 711.5611/4-362, DOS Records.

41. Jerome Gaspard to DOS, May 8, 1962, 711.5611/5-862, and Vincent P. Wilber to DOS, Mar. 6, 1962, 711.5611/3-662, DOS Records.

42. James B. Engle to DOS, May 8, 1962, 600.0012/5-862, and Chester Bowles to American Embassy (New Delhi), Sept. 29, 1961, 600.0012/9-1861, DOS Records; Schoenbaum, *Waging Peace and War*, p. 373.

43. Wright, *Disarm and Verify*, p. 132; "Diefenbaker, John George" (May 1961), "Green, Howard (Charles)" (May 1961), and "Pearson, Lester Bowles ('Mike')" (May 1961), Box 113, POF, Kennedy Papers.

44. Frank B. Ellis to Mary Sharmat, Apr. 24, 1961, Box 8, Series B, War Resisters League Records; A. J. Muste to L. John Collins, July 24, 1962, Box 22, Muste Papers; Office of the Coordinator of Cuban Affairs (Miami), to DOS, Dec. 4, 1963, POL 21 CAN, 1963 Series, DOS Records; Branch, *Parting the Waters*, p. 475.

45. Anonymous to Wilson, Apr. 6, 1962, Kay Johnson to Kenneth O'Donnell, Apr. 22, 1962, and O'Donnell to Johnson, Apr. 25, 1962, Box 660, Subject File, WHCF, Kennedy Papers.

46. Swerdlow, *Women Strike for Peace*, p. 122; Dagmar Wilson to Bundy, June 10, 1963, "PC 1, 5-1-63—7-10-63" Folder, Subject File, WHCF, Kennedy Papers; Wilson to Cousins, May 27, 1963, Box 408, Cousins Papers, Los Angeles.

47. Jacqueline Kennedy to Wilson, Nov. 13, 1961, Wilson to Kennedy, Nov. 27, 1961, and Ruth Gage-Colby to Wilson, May 10, 1962, Box 2, Series I, WSP Records, SCPC; Anne Eaton to Pierre Salinger, Mar. 26, 1963, "PC 1, 3-11-63—4-30-63" Folder, Subject File, WHCF, Kennedy Papers.

48. Bernstein, "Introduction," pp. lviii–lx; Thompson to Szilard, Nov. 27, 1961, Box 19, and Bundy to Szilard, Nov. 21, 1963, Box 20, Szilard Papers; Lanouette, *Genius*, p. 438; Bess, *Realism*, pp. 75–77.

49. Seaborg had once been a member of the Franck Committee, the Met Lab group that, during World War II, had urged President Truman not to use the atomic bomb. His views on arms control and disarmament differed sharply from those of his predecessors, Lewis Strauss and John McCone. "Quakers Visit President: Urge Unilateral Initiatives," *Fellowship* 28 (May 15, 1962): 1; Seaborg, *Kennedy, Khrushchev*, p. 62.

50. Pauling to Albert Schweitzer, May 8, 1962, and Pauling to Bertrand Russell, May 10, 1962, Pauling Papers; Hagar, *Force of Nature*, pp. 537–38.

51. "Pauling, Linus (Dr.)" Folder, Name File, WHCF, Kennedy Papers; Pauling and Ikeda, *A Lifelong Quest*, p. 70; Pauling to the author, Dec. 15, 1987.

52. Isserman, *If I Had a Hammer*, pp. 197–98; Gitlin, *Sixties*, pp. 94–95.

53. Foster to Jack, Oct. 12, 1961, 600.0012/10-1261, and L. D. Battle, "Memorandum for Mr. Frederick L. Holborn" (Oct. 26, 1961), 600.0012/10-2661, DOS Records; Holborn to Sanford Gottlieb, Oct. 27, 1961, "PC 1 Disarmament, Aug. 1, 1961 thru Oct. 30, 1961" Folder, Box 660, Subject File, WHCF, Kennedy Papers; personal interview with Homer Jack, June 12, 1988.

54. Thomas to Kennedy, Sept. 8, Oct. 26, 1961, Jan. 8, 1962, Schlesinger, "Memorandum for Mr. Fred Holborn" (Sept. 18, 1961), and Kennedy to Thomas, Sept. 21, Nov. 14,

1961, "PC 1 Disarmament, 12-1-61—3-20-62" Folder, Subject File, WHCF, Kennedy Papers.

55. Gottlieb, "National Committee," p. 157; "Seven Years for a Sane Nuclear Policy," *Sane World*, Apr. 15, 1964; Frederick L. Holborn to Kenneth A. Jonnson, Feb. 14, 1962, "PC 1 Disarmament, Feb. 1, 1962 thru Mar. 31, 1962" Folder, Box 660, Subject File, WHCF, Kennedy Papers.

56. Rotblat, *Scientists*, p. 46; Schlesinger, *A Thousand Days*, pp. 301–2; A. D. Wilson to C. J. Hayes, Apr. 26, 1962, FO 371/163160, FO Records; "Transcript of W. W. Rostow's Report on Pugwash Meeting in Moscow" (Dec. 9, 1960), "3. Conferences and Meetings, 27. Pugwash Conference, 1957–1961" Folder, AE Lot File, DOS Records; "Proceedings of Sixth Pugwash Conference, Moscow, USSR, November 27–December 5, 1960," p. 799, PC Records, London.

57. E. D. Sohm, "Memorandum of Conversation" (Dec. 6, 1960), Thompson to Sec-State, Dec. 6, 1960, and "Transcript of W. W. Rostow's Report on Pugwash Meeting in Moscow" (Dec. 9, 1960), "3. Conferences and Meetings, 27. Pugwash Conference, 1957–1961" Folder, AE Lot File, DOS Records.

58. Edmund Gullion, "Memorandum of Conversation" (Jan. 25, 1961), 600.0012/1-2561, and Thompson to SecState, Mar. 10, 1961, 600.0012/3-1061, DOS Records.

59. Rotblat, *Scientists*, pp. 47–48, 56–57; "Messages Received at Stowe," *BAS* 17 (Nov. 1961): 385; "Proceedings of the Tenth Pugwash Conference on Science and World Affairs, London, September 3–7, 1962," pp. 27–28, PC Records, London; Bruce to SecState, Sept. 6, 1962, 600.0012/9-662, DOS Records.

60. Solly Zuckerman, "Conference on Science and World Affairs (8th Pugwash Meeting) Vermont, September 11–16, 1961," AB 16/2748, AEA Records; B. T. Price, "The 11th Pugwash Conference on Science and World Affairs" (Oct. 16, 1963), FO 371/171190, FO Records.

61. In late 1963, the outgoing U.S. ambassador to the Soviet Union reported happily that "through the Pugwash and other meetings of this type," Americans had "done a great deal to educate the Soviets in the realities of disarmament problems." David Ormsby Gore to FO, Mar. 5, 20, 1963, FO 371/171189, FO Records; Rotblat, "Movements of Scientists," p. 139; *FRUS, 1961–1963*, 7: 904. See also Wiesner, *Where Science and Politics Meet*, p. 169; J. D. Cockcroft to I. I. Rabi, Nov. 2, 1961, Box 49, Rabi Papers.

62. Conversely, Todd Gitlin, listening to Yarmolinsky in the summer of 1962, had a revelation that "men such as this were not going to be persuaded to be sensible. . . . They were going to have to be dislodged." Theodore Sorensen, "Memorandum to the President" (Nov. 23, 1961), and Yarmolinsky to Norman Podhoretz, Feb. 15, 1962, "Civil Defense" Folder, Sorensen Papers; Gitlin, *Sixties*, p. 96.

63. Schlesinger to the author, Mar. 8, 1995.

64. One of the Quakers who met with Kennedy in the spring of 1962 came away with the impression that "the President, while desirous of peace, is not going to give dynamic leadership to strengthen the forces and climate for peace." *FRUS, 1961–1963*, 13: 127, 1158; Schlesinger to the author, Mar. 8, 1995; George Willoughby to Friends International Center, Geneva, May 17, 1962, in Naeve, ed., *Friends of the Hibakusha*, p. 191.

65. *FRUS, 1961–1963*, 7: 2–4.

66. Seaborg, ed., *Journal*, 1: 282; Arthur Schlesinger Jr. to Kennedy, July 21, 1961, FO 371/157076, FO Records; Rusk to Adlai Stevenson, Sept. 2, 1961, 600.0012/9-261, and Murrow to DOS and USIA posts, Nov. 2, 1961, 711.5611/11-261, DOS Records.

67. Solly Zuckerman to Harold Macmillan, Dec. 15, 1961, PREM 11/3246, PM Records; Robinson McIlvaine to DOS, Mar. 23, 1962, 600.0012/3-2362, DOS Records; Ghent, "Canadian-American Relations," p. 112.

68. "Scope Paper" (May 2, 1961), Box 113, POF, and Kennedy to Macmillan, July 10,

1963, "National Security Council Meetings, 1963, No. 515, 7/9/63" Folder, NSF, Kennedy Papers; Rusk to USUN, Feb. 23, 1962, 711.5611/2-2162, and Rusk to All American Diplomatic and Consular Posts, Apr. 4, 1962, 711.5611/4-462, DOS Records.

69. Ormsby Gore to FO, Nov. 4, 1961, PREM 11/3246, PM Records; Stevenson to SecState, Nov. 22, 1961, 600.0012/11-2261, and DOS to U.S. Diplomatic and Consular Posts, Sept. 7, 1962, 600.0012/9-762, DOS Records.

70. Seaborg, ed., *Journal*, 1: 26; Schlesinger to Kennedy, July 21, 1961, FO 371/157076, FO Records; Swerdlow, *Women Strike for Peace*, pp. 192–93; Winkler, *Life Under a Cloud*, pp. 126–28.

71. Sperber, *Murrow*, p. 673; Murrow to All Principal USIS Posts, May 23, 1962, Box 5, CPC, Donald M. Wilson, "Memorandum for the President" (July 10, 1963), Box 8, and Thomas L. Hughes to Murrow, Sept. 24, 1963, and unsigned to Hughes, n.d., Box 6, WPF, OR, USIA Records.

72. Chalker to DOS, Jan. 23, 1962, 711.5611/1-2362, Rusk to U.S. Embassy (Tokyo), Mar. 6, 1962, 711.5611/2-2062, and Leonhart to SecState, Mar. 8, 1962, 711.5611/3-862, DOS Records; Naeve, ed., *Friends of the Hibakusha*, pp. 181–83.

73. American Embassy (New Delhi) to DOS, June 29, 1962, 600.0012/6-2962, and "Memorandum to Mr. McGeorge Bundy," 600.0012/9-1062, DOS Records.

74. "Indian Group," p. 626; "Memorandum of Conversation" (Oct. 3, 1962), 600.0012/10-362, and Ball to USUN, Oct. 5, 1962, 711.5611/10-562, DOS Records.

75. Ball, *Justice Downwind*, pp. 109–10, 198; Hacker, *Elements of Controversy*, pp. 222–24, 228–30.

76. Jeanne S. Bagby, "Cold War Cassandras," in Naeve, ed., *Friends of the Hibakusha*, pp. 98–99; *NYT*, Jan. 24, 1962.

77. Bagby, "Cold War Cassandras," p. 100; Swerdlow, *Women Strike for Peace*, p. 84.

Chapter 17

Epigraph: The NSC meeting occurred on November 2, 1961. *FRUS, 1961–1963*, 2: 220.

1. Divine, *Blowing on the Wind*, p. 288; *PN*, Nov. 27, 1959; Kohl, *French Nuclear Diplomacy*, p. 93.

2. De Gaulle to Eisenhower, May 25, 1959, in Bundy, *Danger and Survival*, p. 478; Goldschmidt, *Atomic Adventure*, pp. 121–23; "Aspects Politiques des Problèmes posés par l'armement Nucléaire Français" (Dec. 17, 1958), Box 8, Mendès-France Papers; de Gaulle, *Memoirs*, p. 215.

3. The Algerian independence struggle, of course, also made a change of test site imperative. "Points discussed with General de Gaulle at Rambouillet on March 12 and 13, 1960," PREM 11/3162, PM Records; Macmillan, *Pointing the Way*, pp. 181–82.

4. Lewis and Xue, *China Builds the Bomb*, pp. 64–65; Jönsson, *Soviet Bargaining*, pp. 81–132; Seaborg, *Kennedy, Khrushchev*, p. 23; "China Supports Soviet Decision."

5. Lewis and Xue, *China Builds the Bomb*, p. 140; "Vital Questions for the Peace Movement," p. 9.

6. Menzies to Harold Macmillan, June 29, 1961, PREM 11/3202, PM Records; *NYT*, Sept. 1, 1961.

7. Sommer, "Objectives of Germany," pp. 43–45; Robert Creel, "Memorandum of Conversation" (Mar. 21, 1963), Reel 4, *National Security Files*; Foy Kohler, "Memorandum of Conversation" (Feb. 6, 1962), 600.0012/2-662, DOS Records. See also *FRUS, 1961–1963*, 13: 417, 428; Nitze, *From Hiroshima to Glasnost*, p. 210.

8. *PN*, Feb. 12, 19, 1960; *NYT*, Feb. 14, 1960; *Combat*, Apr. 4, 1960.

9. Carter, "Sahara Protest Team," pp. 140, 144; *NYT*, Feb. 14, 1960; *Combat*, Mar. 13, 1960; Nkrumah, *Africa Must Unite*, p. 203.

10. "Preliminary Reactions to the Soviet 50-Megaton Threat and the Multi-Megaton Tests" (Oct. 27, 1961), pp. 18, 22–25, Box 6, RR, OR, USIA Records; Myrdal, *Game of Disarmament*, p. 202; Crabb, *Elephants and the Grass*, pp. 109–10.

11. Beker, *Disarmament Without Order*, pp. 60–61; Crabb, *Elephants and the Grass*, pp. 80–81, 102, 108–9; Nkrumah, *Africa Must Unite*, p. 199.

12. Jack, "What Happened at Belgrade," pp. 1141–42; Mortimer, *Third World Coalition*, p. 14; Kimche, *Afro-Asian Movement*, pp. 96–97; Beker, *Disarmament Without Order*, pp. 61–62; *Documents on American Foreign Relations: 1961*, pp. 466–71.

13. Russell to SecState, Mar. 3, 1962, 711.5611/3-362, DOS Records; British Embassy (Delhi) to Commonwealth Relations Office, Sept. 15, 1961, PREM 11/3392, PM Records.

14. Jain, "India," pp. 90–91; Jawaharlal Nehru, "Preface to Sixth Issue," *Our Generation Against Nuclear War* 2 (Winter/Spring 1963): 3–4.

15. Erlander, *Tage Erlander*, pp. 98–101; Reiss, *Without the Bomb*, pp. 57–65; Birnbaum, "Sweden's Nuclear Policy," pp. 298–305; Fehrm, "Sweden," pp. 216–19.

16. Reiss, *Without the Bomb*, pp. 65–67; Parsons to SecState, Sept. 1, 1961, Reel 9, *National Security Files*; *NYT*, Oct. 31, 1961; Andrén, *Power-Balance*, pp. 175–82; Myrdal, *Game of Disarmament*, p. 194; Wiberg, *Provstopp nu!*, p. 9.

17. Kurt Westerholm to Bertrand Russell, Mar. 4, 1964, Class 650, RA 1; Myrdal, *Game of Disarmament*, p. 199. For a comparison of the Swedish and Irish proposals, see Myrdal, *Game of Disarmament*, pp. 166–67.

18. Walter P. McConaughy, "Memorandum of Conversation" (Sept. 12, 1961), 711.5611/9-1261, Edwin Reischauer to SecState, Nov. 4, 1961, 711.5611/11-461, Mar. 1, 1962, 711.5611/3-162, Apr. 9, 1962, 711.5611/4-962, J. A. Yager, "Memorandum of Conversation" (May 31, 1962), 711.5611/5-3162, and John Goodyear to DOS, June 21, 1962, 794.5611/6-2162, DOS Records; Hayato Ikeda to Kennedy, Mar. 2, 1962, "Japan-General 1962" Folder, Box 120, POF, Kennedy Papers.

19. Mendel, "Public Views," p. 176; Reiss, *Without the Bomb*, p. 117.

20. *PN*, Aug. 30, 1963; *FRUS, 1961–1963*, 7: 231; Blair to SecState, Nov. 24, 1961, 600.0012/11-2461, and Plimpton to SecState, Nov. 27, 1961, 600.0012/11-2761, DOS Records.

21. Yost to SecState, Aug. 7, 1962, 600.0012/8-762, DOS Records; *FRUS, 1961–1963*, 13: 421, 456–57.

22. Rusk fumed about Canada's "neutralist tendencies." Lyon, *Canada*, pp. 223–28; British Embassy (Ottawa) to Commonwealth Relations Office, Dec. 30, 1959, FO 371/149390, FO Records; Ghent, "Canadian-American Relations," p. 84; Charles Kiselyak to DOS, Nov. 3, 1960, 600.0012/11-360, DOS Records; *FRUS, 1961–1963*, 13: 1152.

23. Green, too, remarked that his government's position on nuclear weapons resulted "primarily" from the political imperatives "of domestic public opinion." Lyon, *Canada*, pp. 89–90; *FRUS, 1961–1963*, 13: 1150–51, 1157, 1161, 1164; Ghent, "Canadian-American Relations," pp. 57–69, 74–75, 81–83, 203–8, 225–26; Richard Wigglesworth to DOS, July 25, 1960, 742.5611/7-2560, Livingston Merchant to SecState, Mar. 8, 1962, 711.5611/3-862, and Merchant to DOS, Apr. 30, 1962, 600.0012/4-3062, DOS Records.

24. Holyoake, noted the U.S. ambassador, was "deeply concerned" with Pacific testing, for he "had just returned from his electorate where he had been subjected [to] grueling questions on [the] subject." Clements, *Back from the Brink*, pp. 44–46, 50–51; Holyoake to Macmillan, Nov. 14, 1961, PREM 11/3246, PM Records; "Memorandum of Conversation" (Jan. 11, 1962), 711.5611/1-1162, U.S. Embassy (Wellington) to DOS, Mar. 1, 1962, 711.5611/3-162, and Akers to SecState, Feb. 15, 1962, 711.5611/2-1562, DOS Records.

25. *PN*, May 31, 1963; *Bulletin* [New Zealand], July 1963.

26. Raymond F. Courtney, "Memorandum of Conversation" (Feb. 15, 1960), 711.5611/2-1560, and Henry B. Cox to DOS, July 26, 1963, POL 2-1 SWITZ, 1963 Series, DOS Records; A. Roberts, *Nations in Arms*, pp. 52–54, 224.

27. *PN*, Nov. 27, 1959; *Peace Information Bulletin*, Apr. 1963; Myrdal, *Game of Disarmament*, pp. 166–67; DOS to U.S. Diplomatic and Consular Posts, Sept. 7, 1962, 600.0012/9-762, and Harlan Cleveland to SecState, Oct. 8, 1962, 600.0012/10-862, DOS Records; *FRUS, 1961–1963*, 7: 596.

28. British Cabinet meetings of June 23, 1960, C.C. (60) 37 and July 28, 1960, C.C. (60) 48, CAB 128, Cabinet Records; FO to British embassy (Washington), Aug. 18, 1960, PREM 11/2941, PM Records.

29. The British government could not easily back off from siting the U.S. base at Holy Loch, for that was the price Eisenhower had demanded for providing the British government with the Skybolt missile. British Cabinet meeting of Sept. 15, 1960, C.C. (60) 50, CAB 128, Cabinet Records; P. E. Ramsbotham, "Polaris Base Agreement" (Nov. 2, 1960), and S. K. C. to Phelps, Nov. 3, 1960, PREM 11/2941, PM Records; L. Thompson, "Memorandum of Conversation" (Dec. 19, 1962), 741.5611/12-1962, DOS Records.

30. *Times* (London), Jan. 1, 1993; *Daily Telegraph*, Jan. 1, 1993; *Guardian*, Jan. 2, 1993; *Independent*, Jan. 2, 1993; Macmillan, *At the End*, pp. 214–15, 431.

31. W. W. Rostow, "Memorandum of Conversation" (Mar. 2, 1963), Reel 10, *National Security Files*; Horne, *Macmillan*, p. 330; *FRUS, 1961–1963*, 13: 1103–5, 1109–11.

32. FO to British Embassy (Paris), Jan. 14, 1959, and British Embassy (Washington) to FO, Jan. 1, 1959, FO 371/140433, FO Records; Macmillan, *Pointing the Way*, p. 86; Kistiakowsky, *A Scientist*, p. 36; British Cabinet Defense Committee meeting of July 7, 1959, C. (59) 23, CAB 129, Cabinet Records.

33. Macmillan, *Pointing the Way*, p. 86; Eisenhower, *Waging Peace*, pp. 422–23.

34. Edward Gardner, "Memorandum for Chairman McCone" (Oct. 27, 1959), Box 6, McCone Papers; Kistiakowsky, *A Scientist*, pp. 133–34; Macmillan, *Pointing the Way*, p. 179.

35. Macmillan, *Pointing the Way*, pp. 396–97; British Cabinet meeting of Sept. 5, 1961, C.C. (61) 49, CAB 128, Cabinet Records.

36. Macmillan, *Pointing the Way*, pp. 397, 405; Alec Douglas-Home, "Use of Christmas Island for United States Nuclear Tests" (Nov. 10, 1961), C. (61) 179, CAB 129, and British Cabinet meeting of Nov. 14, 1961, C.C. (61) 62, CAB 128, Cabinet Records.

37. Macmillan to Kennedy, Nov. 16, 1961, PREM 11/3246, PM Records; Macmillan, *Pointing the Way*, p. 409; Seaborg, *Kennedy, Khrushchev*, pp. 118, 126–31; *FRUS, 1961–1963*, 7: 272–81.

38. British Cabinet meeting of Jan. 3, 1962, C.C. (62) 36, CAB 128, Cabinet Records; Macmillan, *At the End*, pp. 153–58, 161; *Independent*, Jan. 2, 1993; Schlesinger, *A Thousand Days*, pp. 492–93.

39. Sorensen, *Kennedy*, pp. 622–23; Macmillan, *At the End*, pp. 164–67, 173–74; Schlesinger, *A Thousand Days*, p. 496; Horne, *Macmillan*, p. 504.

40. John Foster Dulles, "Memorandum of Conversation with Mr. Selwyn Lloyd" (Oct. 19, 1958), Box 1, General Correspondence and Memoranda Series, J. F. Dulles Papers, Abilene; Wright, *Disarm and Verify*, p. 130; Macmillan, *Riding the Storm*, p. 592; Macmillan, *Pointing the Way*, pp. 185–86, 190–91; *FRUS, 1961–1963*, 7: 139.

41. *FRUS, 1961–1963*, 7: 365–66, 393, 471; Macmillan, *At the End*, p. 170; Seaborg, *Kennedy, Khrushchev*, pp. 114, 167. For a similar analysis, from the British side, see Wright, *Disarm and Verify*, pp. 136–37.

42. Scott and Scott, *Soviet Military Doctrine*, pp. 23–24; Richter, *Khrushchev's Double Bind*, p. 105; S. Khrushchev, *Khrushchev on Khrushchev*, pp. 21–22; Bloomfield, Clemens,

and Griffiths, *Khrushchev*, pp. 106–7, 117–19, 167, 179, 204; Holloway, *Soviet Union*, pp. 35, 58, 180; Clemens, "Sino-Soviet Dispute," pp. 219–20.

43. Bloomfield, Clemens, and Griffiths, *Khrushchev*, pp. 120, 168–69, 177, 189, 235–38; Jönsson, *Soviet Bargaining*, pp. 155–69; Burlatsky, *Khrushchev*, pp. 155–57; Dobrynin, *In Confidence*, pp. 41–42; Richter, *Khrushchev's Double Bind*, pp. 126–27, 130–31.

44. Bloomfield, Clemens, and Griffiths, *Khrushchev*, p. 174; Clemens, "Sino-Soviet Dispute," p. 213; Jönsson, *Soviet Bargaining*, pp. 170–90; Richter, *Khrushchev's Double Bind*, pp. 126, 131, 144–46; N. Khrushchev, *Khrushchev Remembers: The Last Testament*, pp. 499–500.

45. Clemens, "Sino-Soviet Dispute," pp. 210–11; Scott and Scott, *Soviet Military Doctrine*, p. 33; Holloway, *Soviet Union*, p. 42; N. Khrushchev, *Khrushchev Remembers: The Last Testament*, pp. 492, 528–30; Dobrynin, *In Confidence*, p. 51; Richter, *Khrushchev's Double Bind*, p. 135.

46. James Wadsworth, a leading U.S. disarmament negotiator, noted that Soviet officials had an "ingrained feeling that some 'madmen' in Washington might launch a war against them." Bundy, too, argued years later that "there is no evidence that the Soviet government has ever come close to using even one of its warheads." Wadsworth, *Price of Peace*, p. 16; Bundy, *Danger and Survival*, p. 587.

47. N. Khrushchev, *Khrushchev Remembers*, pp. 493–96; N. Khrushchev, *Khrushchev Remembers: The Last Testament*, p. 511; N. Khrushchev, *Khrushchev Remembers: The Glasnost Tapes*, pp. 171–72, 176; Dobrynin, *In Confidence*, p. 73; Burlatsky, *Khrushchev*, pp. 173–76; Bundy, *Danger and Survival*, pp. 415–19; Richter, *Khrushchev's Double Bind*, pp. 149–50.

48. Khrushchev to Kennedy, Oct. 24, 26, 1962, in *Department of State Bulletin* 69 (Nov. 19, 1973): 638–39, 643–45; Dobrynin, *In Confidence*, pp. 86–89; Bundy, *Danger and Survival*, p. 441.

49. Drifte, "China," p. 46; "A Comment on the Soviet Government's Statement of August 3," pp. 28–29; Lewis and Xue, *China Builds the Bomb*, pp. 61, 64–65, 72; N. Khrushchev, *Khrushchev Remembers: The Last Testament*, pp. 268–69; Richter, *Khrushchev's Double Bind*, p. 137; Bloomfield, Clemens, and Griffiths, *Khrushchev*, pp. 136–37, 274–75; Arbatov, *System*, p. 95.

50. Wadsworth, *Price of Peace*, pp. 63–65, 73; British Cabinet meeting of Mar. 22, 1960, C.C. (60) 19, CAB 128, Cabinet Records.

51. In 1962, the State Department's principal adviser on Soviet affairs argued that Khrushchev resisted inspection because he desired "to conceal his relative weakness." Jönsson, *Soviet Bargaining*, p. 149; Lebedinsky, ed., *Soviet Scientists*; N. Khrushchev, *Khrushchev Remembers: The Last Testament*, pp. 410–12, 536; *FRUS, 1961–1963*, 7: 498.

52. Jönsson, *Soviet Bargaining*, pp. 150–51; Cousins, *Improbable Triumvirate*, p. 169.

53. Jönsson, *Soviet Bargaining*, pp. 149–51, 166–69; personal interview with Sergei Kapitza, June 28, 1990; Seaborg, *Kennedy, Khrushchev*, p. 74.

54. Bloomfield, Clemens, and Griffiths, *Khrushchev*, pp. 160–61; Robert E. Matteson, "Memorandum of Conversation" (Sept. 8, 1961), 611.61/9-861, DOS Records; Adamsky and Smirnov, "Moscow's Biggest Bomb," pp. 19–20.

55. Jönsson, *Soviet Bargaining*, pp. 172–73; T. N. Kaul to Harold Macmillan, Sept. 13, 1961, and F. Roberts to FO, Sept. 6, 1961, PREM 11/3392, PM Records.

56. Bloomfield, Clemens, and Griffiths, *Khrushchev*, p. 153; *Sane World*, Sept. 1, 1962; Dean, *Test Ban*, pp. 40–42.

57. York, *Making Weapons, Talking Peace*, pp. 194, 198; Gaddis, *Strategies of Containment*, p. 174; Kistiakowsky, *A Scientist*, pp. 382–83; John A. McCone, "Notes for the Files of John A. McCone" (Mar. 10, 1960), Box 5, McCone Papers.

58. Rusk, *As I Saw It*, pp. 246–48; Cohen, *Dean Rusk*, pp. 195–96; Schoenbaum, *Waging Peace and War*, pp. 328–30; McNamara, "Military Role," p. 63.

59. McNamara, "Military Role," pp. 63–64, 79; *FRUS, 1961–1963*, 13: 370–71, 450–53; Healey, *Time of My Life*, pp. 306, 310; Kissinger, *White House Years*, pp. 96–97. See also Rusk, *As I Saw It*, p. 248; McNamara, *In Retrospect*, p. 345.

60. Bundy, *Danger and Survival*, p. 379; Rusk, *As I Saw It*, pp. 246–47; Walt W. Rostow, "Memorandum to the President" (June 26, 1961), Reel 5, *National Security Files*.

61. Nitze, *From Hiroshima to Glasnost*, p. 246; Rusk, *As I Saw It*, pp. 249–50, 344.

62. M. White, "Exorcizing the Myths," pp. 1–8; Rusk, *As I Saw It*, pp. 229–34; Bundy, *Danger and Survival*, pp. 412–13; John A. McCone, "Memorandum for the File" (Oct. 23, 1962), in McAuliffe, ed., *CIA Documents*, p. 291.

63. "Soviet Threat to the Americas," p. 716; Kennedy to Khrushchev, October 22, 23, 1962, in *Department of State Bulletin* 69 (Nov. 19, 1973): 635–37.

64. Bundy, *Danger and Survival*, pp. 432, 453; Rusk, *As I Saw It*, pp. 238–41, 366; *NYT*, Oct. 14, 1992.

65. Rusk, *As I Saw It*, pp. 231–32; Sorensen, *Kennedy*, pp. 681–82, 688, 712; John A. McCone, "Memorandum for the File" (Oct. 19, 1962), and John A. McCone, "Memorandum for USIB Members" (Oct. 19, 1962), in McAuliffe, ed., *CIA Documents*, pp. 169, 193–94.

66. Rusk to Paris, Aug. 28, 1962, 711.5611/8-2562, DOS Records; William C. Burdett, "Memorandum of Conversation" (Dec. 4, 1962), Reel 1, *National Security Files*; I. I. Rabi to William C. Foster, Sept. 12, 1962, Box 12, Rabi Papers.

67. Seaborg, *Kennedy, Khrushchev*, p. 111; Bundy, *Danger and Survival*, pp. 485–86, 498; Kennedy to Macmillan, May 8, 1961, PREM 11/3328, PM Records; Athens to SecState, May 4, 1962, 711.5611/5-462, and John F. Kennedy, "Memorandum for Secretary of State, Secretary of Defense" (May 25, 1962), 600.0012/5-2562, DOS Records.

68. Rusk and McNamara made this argument in a July 1962 memo. Rusk to Seaborg, Oct. 18, 1961, 711.5611/10-1861, DOS Records; Healey, *Time of My Life*, pp. 244–45; "Memorandum of Conversation" (Sept. 13, 1962), Reel 9, *National Security Files*; *FRUS, 1961–1963*, 13: 108, 378, 432–33, 477, 1073; Harold Watkinson to Macmillan, Dec. 15, 1961, PREM 11/3247, PM Records.

69. For the Kennedy administration's sharp distinction between nuclear proliferation and U.S. government–controlled "multilateral arrangements" for nuclear weapons, see Rusk to Paris, Apr. 28, 1962, 711.5611/8-2562, DOS Records.

70. Willis Armstrong to SecState, Nov. 29, 1960, 600.0012/11-2960, U.S. Embassy (Ottawa) to DOS, Dec. 6, 1960, 600.0012/12-660, and Livingston Merchant to SecState, Feb. 26, 1962, 600.0012/2-2662, DOS Records; *FRUS, 1961–1963*, 13: 1162, 1171.

71. As Rusk later phrased it, Diefenbaker had "attempted to renege on his defense commitments to the United States." Ghent, "Did He Fall?" pp. 259–70; William R. Tyler to Under Secretary, Jan. 29, 1963, 742.5611/1-2963, DOS Records; *FRUS, 1961–1963*, 13: 1193–99, 1217.

72. Even before the election victory, the U.S. ambassador reported hopefully that Canadians were "on the road to . . . understanding better and accepting to a greater extent their dependence on us." Ghent, "Canadian-American Relations," p. 267; William H. Brubeck, "Memorandum for Mr. McGeorge Bundy" (Apr. 5, 1963), "Canada Security, 1963" Folder, Box 113, POF, Kennedy Papers; Sorensen, *Kennedy*, p. 576; W. Walton Butterworth to George McGhee, Mar. 19, 1963, POL CAN-US, 1963 Series, DOS Records.

73. Kistiakowsky, *A Scientist*, pp. 86–87, 180; Ambrose, *Eisenhower*, 2: 591.

74. Keys, "American Peace Movement," p. 304; Schlesinger, *A Thousand Days*, pp. 472–79; Sorensen, *Kennedy*, pp. 518–19; Stevenson to SecState, Mar. 7, 1961, 600.0012/3-761, DOS Records; *FRUS, 1961–1963*, 7: 92–93.

75. Freeman Dyson, a physicist who worked at the ACDA, recalled that "the old hands all knew that . . . the disarmament negotiations were nothing but an exercise in propaganda." *FRUS, 1961–1963*, 7: 144–45; Dean, *Test Ban*, pp. 25–27; Seaborg, *Kennedy, Khrushchev*, p. 96; Dyson, *Disturbing the Universe*, p. 133.

76. Morton H. Halperin, "Arms Control: A Twenty-Five-Year Perspective," *F.A.S. Public Interest Report* 36 (June 1983): 4; Seaborg, *Kennedy, Khrushchev*, p. 96; Bundy, *Danger and Survival*, p. 420.

77. Arthur Dean, the administration's chief disarmament negotiator, wrote a few years later that, among all governments of the world, "national security"—and not "disarmament"—was "the first priority." McNamara, *Essence of Security*, p. 58; Bundy, *Danger and Survival*, p. 379; Dean, *Test Ban*, pp. 65–67.

78. Kistiakowsky, *A Scientist*, pp. 5–6, 53; Hewlett and Holl, *Atoms*, pp. 554–55; David Ormsby Gore to Selwyn Lloyd, Feb. 10, 1959, FO 371/140436, FO Records; Eisenhower, *Waging Peace*, pp. 352, 479; Divine, *Blowing on the Wind*, pp. 256–60, 281, 284–85.

79. A short time later, Nixon told Lewis Strauss that he disliked the moratorium, but found himself in a difficult position, "in view of the stand that the President was taking." Kistiakowsky, *A Scientist*, p. 195; Lewis L. Strauss, "Memorandum for the Files of Lewis L. Strauss" (Mar. 31, 1960), Box 62, AEC Series, Strauss Papers.

80. Kistiakowsky, *A Scientist*, p. 204; Macmillan, *Pointing the Way*, pp. 105, 109; Divine, *Blowing on the Wind*, p. 295; Eisenhower, *Waging Peace*, p. 480.

81. According to Macmillan, Eisenhower concluded that the Soviet premier "was a real S.O.B." Divine, *Blowing on the Wind*, pp. 296–99; Kistiakowsky, *A Scientist*, pp. 282, 287; Lewis L. Strauss, "Memorandum for the Files of Lewis L. Strauss" (Mar. 31, 1960), Box 62, AEC Series, Strauss Papers; Macmillan, *Pointing the Way*, pp. 207–8.

82. Kistiakowsky, *A Scientist*, pp. 314, 335, 343; Divine, *Blowing on the Wind*, pp. 315–16; Seaborg, *Kennedy, Khrushchev*, p. 33.

83. Eisenhower, *Waging Peace*, p. 481; "Telephone Calls, July 1, 1960," Box 13, Herter Papers; Jacobson and Stein, *Diplomats, Scientists*, p. 263; Strauss, *Men and Decisions*, p. 426; Seaborg, *Kennedy, Khrushchev*, p. 25.

84. Seaborg, *Kennedy, Khrushchev*, p. 32; Sorensen, *Kennedy*, p. 617; Sullivan, *Nuclear Democracy*, p. 37; Seaborg, ed., *Journal*, 1: 71.

85. Sorensen, *Kennedy*, pp. 617–18; *FRUS, 1961–1963*, 7: 21–27, 54–55, 73, 76, 116–24; Harold Caccia to A. D. Wilson, May 12, 1961, FO 371/157117, FO Records; Roswell Gilpatric to John J. McCloy, Apr. 28, 1961, 711.5611/4-2861, and Woodruff Wallner to Harland Cleveland, May 24, 1961, 711.5611/5-2461, DOS Records; Arthur Schlesinger Jr., "Journal," p. 48, enclosure in Schlesinger to the author, Mar. 8, 1995.

86. *FRUS, 1961–1963*, 7: 59, 81–83; Seaborg, *Kennedy, Khrushchev*, p. 65; Arthur Schlesinger Jr., "Memorandum for the President" (July 20, 1961), "Nuclear Test Ban, 7/1/61–8/6/61" Folder, Sorensen Papers.

87. For other statements emphasizing world abhorrence of U.S. test resumption, see *FRUS, 1961–1963*, 7: 46; Harlan Cleveland to SecState, May 22, 1961, 711.5611/5-2261, May 31, 1961, 711.5611/5-3161, DOS Records; John Kenneth Galbraith, "Memorandum for the President" (June 12, 1961), "Test Ban, 6/4/61–7/31/61" Folder, Schlesinger Papers.

88. In early August, Sorensen recalled, Kennedy "decided to order preparations for underground tests but not actually to resume them until it was absolutely clear—not only to him but to the world—that he had done everything possible to obtain a treaty." At an NSC meeting, he said that "we should clearly resume testing fairly soon, but the UN problem is a serious one." Kennedy to Macmillan, Aug. 3, 1961, FO 371/157076, FO Records; McGeorge Bundy, "Memorandum of decision, July 27, 1961, test ban scenario" (July 28, 1961), 600.0012/7-2861, DOS Records; Sorensen, *Kennedy*, p. 618; *FRUS, 1961–1963*, 7: 137.

89. Seaborg, *Kennedy, Khrushchev*, pp. 81–86; Sorensen, *Kennedy*, pp. 619–20; *FRUS, 1961–1963*, 7: 149–56; Sperber, *Murrow*, p. 660; Rusk, *As I Saw It*, p. 254; *Public Papers: John F. Kennedy, 1961*, p. 587.

90. A variant on this exchange occurred a few days earlier, when Harlan Cleveland of the State Department suggested bringing the issue of Soviet testing to the U.N. Security Council for the purpose of mobilizing world opinion. In response, McCloy, exploded: "World opinion? I don't believe in world opinion. The only thing that matters is power. What we have to do now is to show that we are a powerful nation." Seaborg, *Kennedy, Khrushchev*, p. 88; Kennedy to Macmillan, Sept. 5, 1961, 711.5611/9-561, DOS Records; Schlesinger, *A Thousand Days*, pp. 481–83.

91. The Republican opposition scorned this approach. Soviet tests "should bring all the woolly-heads to their senses," Nixon declared, "but . . . a substantial number of them still contend that we should be primarily concerned with propaganda and let the Communists gain the advantage." Dean Rusk, "Memorandum for the President" (Sept. 14, 1961), "State, 8/61–9/61" Folder, POF, Kennedy Papers; Schlesinger, *A Thousand Days*, pp. 482–85; *Public Papers: John F. Kennedy, 1961*, pp. 621–22; Nixon to Lewis Strauss, Sept. 12, 1961, Box 106, AEC Series, Strauss Papers.

92. *Public Papers: John F. Kennedy, 1961*, p. 675; Seaborg, *Kennedy, Khrushchev*, p. 117; Kennedy to Norman Cousins, Nov. 8, 1961, Cousins Papers, Beverly Hills; Schlesinger, *A Thousand Days*, p. 486.

93. Oral history interview with Theodore Sorensen, pp. 76–78; *FRUS, 1961–1963*, 7: 213–14; Schlesinger, *A Thousand Days*, pp. 486–89, 495; Seaborg, *Kennedy, Khrushchev*, pp. 124–25.

94. Adlai Stevenson, "Memorandum for the President" (Feb. 21, 1962), "Nuclear Testing, 1962–1963" Folder, POF, Kennedy Papers; *FRUS, 1961–1963*, 7: 221; Reischauer to SecState, Feb. 13, 1962, 711.5611/2-1362, DOS Records; McGeorge Bundy, "Memorandum for the President" (Oct. 27, 1961), Reel 9, *National Security Files*; Schlesinger, *A Thousand Days*, pp. 493–94; Arthur Schlesinger Jr. to the author, Mar. 8, 1995.

95. Schlesinger took the same approach in a December 1961 memo to Kennedy. Theodore C. Sorensen, "Memorandum for the President" (Jan. 25, 1962), "Nuclear Test Ban" Folder, Sorensen Papers; *FRUS, 1961–1963*, 7: 282–85.

96. Frederick G. Dutton to Hubert H. Humphrey, July 2, 1962, 700.5611/6-2162, DOS Records; oral history interview with Adrian Fisher, p. 10.

97. Schlesinger, *A Thousand Days*, pp. 495–97; *FRUS, 1961–1963*, 7: 331–37; *Public Papers: John F. Kennedy, 1962*, pp. 186–92; Seaborg, *Kennedy, Khrushchev*, pp. 137, 150–51.

98. According to a participant in a White House staff meeting in late 1961, Bundy said that the administration wanted to avoid tests in Nevada because "everyone would squawk about fall-out in their milk." *Public Papers: John F. Kennedy, 1962*, pp. 186–92; Seaborg, *Kennedy, Khrushchev*, pp. 136–37; *FRUS, 1961–1963*, 7: 259, 321.

99. Rusk to All American Diplomatic Posts, Feb. 28, 1962, 711.5611/2-2862, DOS Records; Rusk to All American Diplomatic Posts, Apr. 20, 1962, Reel 9, *National Security Files*; Sorensen, *Kennedy*, p. 624; *FRUS, 1961–1963*, 7: 440–42.

Chapter 18

Epigraph: *Public Papers: John F. Kennedy, 1963*, pp. 601–2.

1. Seaborg, *Kennedy, Khrushchev*, pp. 164–66, 171; Rusk, *As I Saw It*, p. 255; Macmillan, *At the End*, pp. 177–78; Schlesinger, *A Thousand Days*, p. 894; oral history interview with Adrian Fisher, pp. 13–15; *FRUS, 1961–1963*, 5: 502, 512, 520–21, 523–24, 586.

2. Sakharov, *Memoirs*, pp. 230–31; Adamsky, "Becoming a Citizen," pp. 38–39; *NYT*, Sept. 10, 1973. See also R. E. Matteson, "Memorandum of Conversation" (Nov. 19, 1962), 600.0012/11-1962, DOS Records.

3. On October 28, the two leaders exchanged messages concerning the importance of arms control and disarmament. Schlesinger, *A Thousand Days*, p. 893; Sorensen, *Kennedy*, pp. 725–26; Seaborg, *Kennedy, Khrushchev*, pp. 176, 300; *FRUS, 1961–1963*, 7: 592.

4. Jönsson, *Soviet Bargaining*, p. 201; A. D. Wilson to Michael Wright, Nov. 22, 1962, FO 371/163164, FO Records; oral history interview with Theodore Sorensen, p. 80; *FRUS, 1961–1963*, 7: 576–77, 580–81, 585–86.

5. Cousins, *Improbable Triumvirate*, pp. 20–29; Norman Cousins, "Jan. 4 Memo to JFK," and "Memorandum on NC mission to Rome and Moscow written by NC at the request of Father Morlion," Cousins Papers, Beverly Hills.

6. Norman Cousins, "Jan. 4 Memo to JFK," Cousins Papers, Beverly Hills; Cousins, *Improbable Triumvirate*, pp. 32–35, 45, 53–54.

7. Although the degree to which Cousins's mission affected Soviet policy remains unclear, Kennedy was impressed by it. Writing to Cousins that January, he praised it as a "most interesting and fruitful journey," with results that "so far have been promising." *FRUS, 1961–1963*, 7: 623–24, 627; Seaborg, *Kennedy, Khrushchev*, pp. 178–79; Schlesinger, *A Thousand Days*, pp. 895–96; Sorensen, *Kennedy*, p. 728; Dobrynin, *In Confidence*, p. 100; Cousins, *Improbable Triumvirate*, p. 73; Kennedy to Cousins, Jan. 31, 1963, Cousins Papers, Beverly Hills.

8. *FRUS, 1961–1963*, 7: 624; Sorensen, *Kennedy*, p. 728; Schlesinger, *A Thousand Days*, p. 896; Robert Brandin, "Memorandum of Conversation" (Mar. 21, 1963), Reel 4, *National Security Files*.

9. Wiesner and other scientific advisers thought that five inspections would have sufficed; McNamara would have settled for six. Schlesinger, *A Thousand Days*, p. 897; Macmillan, *At the End*, pp. 455–56; *FRUS, 1961–1963*, 7: 532.

10. *FRUS, 1961–1963*, 7: 553; Bloomfield, Clemens, and Griffiths, *Khrushchev*, p. 281; "A Comment on the Soviet Government's Statement of August 21," pp. 56–57; Seaborg, *Kennedy, Khrushchev*, p. 299; Schlesinger, *A Thousand Days*, p. 897; Rusk, *As I Saw It*, p. 255.

11. On February 8, he went even further, telling a meeting of top U.S. officials that "the whole reason for having a test ban is related to the Chinese situation." Yet this was an exaggeration. John G. Guthrie, "Memorandum of Conversation" (Jan. 10, 1963), 600.0012/1-1063, DOS Records; "Remarks of President Kennedy to the National Security Council Meeting of January 22, 1963," and "National Security Council Meetings, 1963, No. 508, 1/22/63" Folder, Box 314, NSF, Kennedy Papers; *FRUS, 1961–1963*, 7: 542, 629, 646.

12. Seaborg, *Kennedy, Khrushchev*, p. 181.

13. Cousins, *Improbable Triumvirate*, pp. 78–80; Norman Cousins, "Private discussion with the President" (Mar. 12, 1963), Cousins Papers, Beverly Hills; Sorensen, *Kennedy*, p. 728.

14. Personal interview with Joseph Rotblat, July 12, 1990; oral history interview with Adrian Fisher, p. 22; *FRUS, 1961–1963*, 7: 655–56; Macmillan, *At the End*, pp. 460–61, 465; Sperber, *Murrow*, p. 673.

15. Seaborg, *Kennedy, Khrushchev*, pp. 198–99; Horne, *Macmillan*, p. 507; Kennedy to Cousins, Mar. 15, 1963, Cousins Papers, Beverly Hills.

16. Cousins, *Improbable Triumvirate*, pp. 92–101; "Memorandum on NC missions to Rome and Moscow written by NC at the request of Father Morlion," Cousins Papers, Beverly Hills.

17. Cousins, *Improbable Triumvirate*, pp. 113–17; Norman Cousins, "April 22, 1963," Cousins Papers, Beverly Hills.

18. Although Sorensen mentions taking material for the speech "from Cousins, Bundy, Kaysen, my brother Tom and others," including Kennedy, the speech clearly bore Cousins's imprint. One of its most striking formulations—the need to "make the world safe for diversity"—had appeared almost five years earlier in a letter he wrote. Cousins, *Improbable Triumvirate*, pp. 120–23; Cousins to Kennedy, Apr. 30, 1963, and Cousins to Sorensen, June 1, 1963, "Nuclear Test Ban" Folder, Box 36, Sorensen Papers; oral history interview with Theodore Sorensen, pp. 71–73; Sorensen, *Kennedy*, pp. 729–32; Cousins to L. D. Kislova, Nov. 24, 1958, Box 208, Cousins Papers, Los Angeles.

19. Jönsson, *Soviet Bargaining*, pp. 193–98; Bloomfield, Clemens, and Griffiths, *Khrushchev*, pp. 240, 281; Richter, *Khrushchev's Double Bind*, p. 162; *NYT*, June 6, 1963; Szilard to Khrushchev, Sept. 30, 1960, and "Conversation with K on October 5, 1960" (Oct. 9, 1960), in Hawkins, Greb, and Szilard, eds., *Toward a Livable World*, pp. 277, 284–85.

20. Getting the hawkish Dodd on board raised hopes for ratification of a test ban treaty by the Senate. Knopf, "Domestic Politics," pp. 286–87; *NYT*, May 8, 1963; Seaborg, *Kennedy, Khrushchev*, p. 227; Humphrey, *Education*, p. 253; Schlesinger, *A Thousand Days*, pp. 899–900.

21. *FRUS, 1961–1963*, 13: 1202.

22. *Public Papers: John F. Kennedy, 1963*, pp. 459–64.

23. Nor was all the attention favorable. Republican members of Congress charged that it was "a soft line that can accomplish nothing," "a shot from the hip," and "a dreadful mistake." Sorensen, *Kennedy*, p. 733.

24. *FRUS, 1961–1963*, 7: 762, 862; oral history interview with Benjamin Read, p. 8; Sorensen, *Kennedy*, p. 733; Seaborg, *Kennedy, Khrushchev*, pp. 217, 227; Schlesinger, *A Thousand Days*, p. 904; Dean, *Test Ban*, pp. 91–92.

25. The Joint Chiefs of Staff had begun to express resistance that April, but their opposition came to a head on July 9. *FRUS, 1961–1963*, 7: 679, 683–85, 720–24, 783–84; Seaborg, *Kennedy, Khrushchev*, pp. 220–23, 228–29; Rusk, *As I Saw It*, pp. 255–56; "U.S. Nuclear Fraud Exposed"; Schlesinger, *A Thousand Days*, p. 905. For an inside view of the heated dispute between the Chinese and Soviet parties over nuclear policy, see Arbatov, *System*, pp. 97–100.

26. McKillop to SecState, July 10, 11, 1963, POL 7 US/Harriman, 1963 Series, DOS Records.

27. National Security Council, "Instructions for Honorable W. Averell Harriman" (July 10, 1963), "National Security Council Meetings, 1963, No. 515, 7/9/63" Folder, NSF, Kennedy Papers; Rusk to Foster and Harriman, June 28, 1963, Box 539, and Kennedy to Khrushchev, July 15, 1963, Box 541, Harriman Papers; Seaborg, *Kennedy, Khrushchev*, pp. 227, 229, 241.

28. Administration officials differ on the preemptive strike. Seaborg claims that Kennedy had Harriman "feel out Khrushchev on the subject of launching a joint preemptive strike on China's nuclear facilities." Bundy says that "there had been talk in Washington about the possibility of preemptive action," but it was "not serious planning or real intent." Historical scholarship supports Seaborg's account. *FRUS, 1961–1963*, 7: 799–801; Seaborg, *Kennedy, Khrushchev*, pp. 238–39, 241–42; oral history interview with Benjamin Read, pp. 24–25; William H. Sullivan, "Points to Be Explored with the Russians" (July 9, 1963), Box 540, Harriman Papers; Schlesinger, *A Thousand Days*, p. 908; Foy Kohler to SecState, July 27, 1963, POL 7 US/Harriman, 1963 Series, DOS Records; Seaborg, ed., *Journal*, 1: 9; Bundy, *Danger and Survival*, p. 532; Chang, *Friends and Enemies*, pp. 229–49.

29. Allen Davies, "Memorandum of Conversation" (July 9, 1963), POL 7 US/Harriman, 1963 Series, DOS Records; Horne, *Macmillan*, pp. 516–19, 523–24. See also Macmillan, *At the End*, p. 483; *FRUS, 1961–1963*, 7: 814.

30. Bloomfield, Clemens, and Griffiths, *Khrushchev*, pp. 206, 248; Dobrynin, *In Confidence*, pp. 99–100; Seaborg, *Kennedy, Khrushchev*, pp. 244–45; *NYT*, July 20, 1963; *FRUS, 1961–1963*, 7: 817.

31. Harriman to SecState, July 18, 23, 1963, Box 540, and John J. de Martino to Benjamin Read, Oct. 2, 1964, Box 539, Harriman Papers; *NYT*, Aug. 2, 1963. See also Seaborg, *Kennedy, Khrushchev*, p. 249; Schlesinger, *A Thousand Days*, p. 915.

32. Seaborg, *Kennedy, Khrushchev*, p. 227; Schlesinger, *A Thousand Days*, pp. 910–11; *FRUS, 1961–1963*, 13: 884–85; Kaysen to Willy Brandt, July 5, 1963, Box 539, Harriman Papers; *FRUS, 1961–1963*, 7: 807, 864.

33. "If the response to this treaty can serve to increase their isolation," Kennedy noted in remarks originally slated for a speech on July 26, "then the outlook is not altogether gloomy." Personal interview with Ronald Spiers, Oct. 28, 1992; Dean, *Test Ban*, p. 83; *FRUS, 1961–1963*, 7: 832; *NYT*, Aug. 2, 1963; Chang, *Friends and Enemies*, pp. 247–48. See also Sorensen, *Kennedy*, p. 736.

34. Schlesinger argues that "left to itself, the Department of State would not have persevered with the [test ban] issue, nor would it ever have proposed an American University speech." He gives the credit for the initiative, however, to Kennedy. Seaborg, *Kennedy, Khrushchev*, p. 207; Schlesinger, *A Thousand Days*, p. 909.

35. Personal interview with Homer Jack, June 12, 1988; Katz, *Ban the Bomb*, p. 84.

36. Sorensen, *Kennedy*, pp. 736–37; Schlesinger, *A Thousand Days*, pp. 909–10; oral history interview with Theodore Sorensen, p. 82; oral history interview with Benjamin Read, p. 17.

37. *Public Papers: John F. Kennedy, 1963*, pp. 601–6.

38. Cousins, *Improbable Triumvirate*, pp. 127–28; Norman Cousins, "August 2, 1963," Cousins Papers, Beverly Hills.

39. Cousins, *Improbable Triumvirate*, pp. 130–32; "Group of Prominent Americans Pledge Support for Test Ban Treaty in Meeting with President Kennedy," "Disarmament—Nuclear Test Ban Part II" Folder, POF, Kennedy Papers; Norman Cousins, "August 7, 1963," Cousins Papers, Beverly Hills; Sorensen, *Kennedy*, p. 739.

40. Norman Cousins, "August 7, 1963," Cousins Papers, Beverly Hills; "Citizens Committee for a Nuclear Test Ban" Folder, Box 55, Series B, SANE Records; Cousins, *Improbable Triumvirate*, p. 135; Frederick G. Dutton, "Memorandum to Mr. Sorensen" (Aug. 16, 1963), Box 100, POF, Kennedy Papers.

41. Knopf, "Domestic Politics," pp. 288–96; "SANE ACTION" (Aug. 8, 1963), Box 410, Cousins Papers, Los Angeles; Cousins to Kennedy, Aug. 26, 1963, Cousins Papers, Beverly Hills; McGeorge Bundy to Cousins, Aug. 30, 1963, "RS 2/" Folder, Box 889, Subject File, WHCF, Kennedy Papers.

42. Frederick G. Dutton, "Memorandum to Mr. Sorensen" (Aug. 16, 1963), Box 100, POF, Kennedy Papers; Warner and Shuman, *Citizen Diplomats*, p. 179; Schweitzer to Kennedy, Aug. 6, 1963, in Jack, ed., *On Nuclear War and Peace*, pp. 152–53; Marshall and Poling, *Schweitzer*, p. 288.

43. Seaborg, *Kennedy, Khrushchev*, pp. 268–69, 276; oral history interview with Mike Mansfield, p. 31; Schlesinger, *A Thousand Days*, p. 911; Sorensen, *Kennedy*, p. 739.

44. This figure is used by Schlesinger. A Gallup poll indicated that, of those Americans who had heard of the treaty, 63 percent favored it, 17 percent opposed it, and 20 percent had no opinion. Schlesinger, *A Thousand Days*, p. 913; Gallup, ed., *Gallup Poll*, p. 1837.

45. Cousins, who attended a victory luncheon with White House staffers and members of Congress, reported that there were also "many references" made to the importance of Schweitzer's role. Schlesinger, *A Thousand Days*, p. 913; oral history interview with Theodore Sorensen, p. 85; Kennedy to Cousins, Oct. 7, 1963, "COUSINS, I-P" Folder,

WHCF, Kennedy Papers; Cousins to Schweitzer, Oct. 4, 1963, in Cousins, *Albert Schweitzer's Mission*, pp. 299–300.

46. Similarly, Kuo Mo-jo, chair of the China Peace Committee, maintained that the treaty was a "great fraud worked out by imperialists in league with modern revisionists." "Statement of the Chinese Government"; "Statement by the Spokesman of the Chinese Government"; "A Comment on the Soviet Government's Statement of August 21"; *Chicago Tribune*, Aug. 2, 1963.

47. Schlesinger, *A Thousand Days*, p. 909; *NYT*, Sept. 10, 1973; Jönsson, *Soviet Bargaining*, pp. 203–6; Dean, *Test Ban*, p. 61; Seaborg, *Kennedy, Khrushchev*, p. 299.

48. "Statement of the Soviet Government of August 3, 1963," pp. 170, 179; "Statement of the Soviet Government of August 21, 1963," pp. 185, 203.

49. Macmillan, *At the End*, p. 434; Horne, *Macmillan*, p. 528; Ormsby-Gore to Kennedy, Aug. 2, 1963, Box 31, POF, Kennedy Papers; Pierre, *Nuclear Politics*, pp. 251–53.

50. Schlesinger, *A Thousand Days*, pp. 913–14; "For the Total Banning and Destruction of Nuclear Weapons," p. 19; "Albanian Government's Statement," p. 13.

51. *FRUS, 1961–1963*, 7: 870–76; Brandt, *People and Politics*, p. 111; Pandey, *Nehru*, p. 392; Seaborg, *Kennedy, Khrushchev*, p. 285.

52. Kistiakowsky, *A Scientist*, p. 424; Seaborg, *Kennedy, Khrushchev*, pp. 286, 289–91; Sorensen, *Kennedy*, pp. 740–46; Rusk, *As I Saw It*, p. 259; Dobrynin, *In Confidence*, p. 106.

53. Although the U.S. military remained the central force behind this approach, others were in complete agreement. Rusk recalled that "on every point I supported the chiefs. From the viewpoint of foreign policy, I felt that we needed these safeguards and underground tests." Seaborg, *Kennedy, Khrushchev*, pp. 269–71, 286–88; Sorensen, *Kennedy*, pp. 738–39; Schlesinger, *A Thousand Days*, pp. 911–13; Rusk, *As I Saw It*, pp. 258–59.

54. These figures include the hundreds of nuclear tests the U.S. government kept secret until its revelations of 1993 and 1994 and include the small number of so-called "peaceful nuclear explosions." "Known Nuclear Tests Worldwide, 1945–1994," *BAS* 51 (May/June 1995): 71; Seaborg, *Kennedy, Khrushchev*, p. 288.

55. "Known Nuclear Tests," p. 71; Lewis and Xue, *China Builds the Bomb*, pp. 1–2; *FRUS, 1961–1963*, 13: 222–23.

56. Clements, *Back from the Brink*, pp. 53–59; *Combat*, May 5, 7, 8, 1966; Sharp, "Militarism," p. 188; Ferm, "Nuclear Explosions," p. 119; "Known Nuclear Tests," p. 71.

57. Seaborg, *Stemming the Tide*, pp. 6, 214–15, 238, 243, 456–57; Seaborg, *Kennedy, Khrushchev*, pp. 300–301; Dobrynin, *In Confidence*, pp. 111–12.

58. Lewis and Xue, *China Builds the Bomb*, pp. 202–6.

59. Although the Israeli government adopted a policy of refusing to confirm or deny that it possessed nuclear weapons, foreign analysts have agreed that Israel probably developed a nuclear weapons capability in the late 1960s or early 1970s. Egypt, Libya, and other Arab states also sought to obtain the Bomb. Reiss, *Without the Bomb*, pp. 143–72; Bundy, *Danger and Survival*, pp. 506–7; Rosen, "Nuclearization," p. 178.

60. In 1967, Zulfikar Ali Bhutto, an emerging leader in Pakistani politics, declared that since India was "determined to proceed with her plans to detonate a nuclear bomb," Pakistan "must therefore embark upon a similar program." A few years later, as prime minister, Bhutto ordered the beginning of his country's own nuclear venture, arguing that, to attain nuclear parity, the Pakistani people would "even eat grass." Jain, "India," pp. 91–93; R. Jones, "India," pp. 105–11; Seaborg, *Stemming the Tide*, pp. 117–18, 254; Edwards, "Canada's Nuclear Industry," pp. 134–35.

61. According to Rusk, though, the idea of a preemptive strike "never got anywhere when it reached the top levels of policy." Rusk, *As I Saw It*, p. 340; Seaborg, *Stemming the Tide*, pp. 7, 59, 111–12, 201; Chang, *Friends and Enemies*, p. 250.

62. Rusk, *As I Saw It*, p. 341; Dean, *Test Ban*, pp. 121–22; Seaborg, *Stemming the Tide*, p. 131.

63. L. Johnson, *Vantage Point*, p. 477; Rusk, *As I Saw It*, pp. 341–42; Seaborg, "Introduction," in Seaborg, ed., *Journal*, 1: 9–10; Myrdal, *Game of Disarmament*, p. 168.

64. Seaborg, *Stemming the Tide*, pp. 161–62, 217, 356–57, 366–68; Myrdal, *Game of Disarmament*, p. 168; Beker, *Disarmament Without Order*, pp. 115, 119; Barton and Weiler, eds., *International Arms Control*, p. 88.

65. Seaborg, *Stemming the Tide*, pp. 369, 377; Rusk, *As I Saw It*, pp. 342–44; Jack, *Nuclear Politics*, p. 46; Beker, *Disarmament Without Order*, p. 114.

66. Myrdal, *Game of Disarmament*, pp. 86, 171–72; Carter, *Peace Movements*, p. 78; Bindschedler, "Switzerland," pp. 222–25; Myrdal, "Dynamics," pp. 221–22.

67. Reiss, *Without the Bomb*, pp. 117–18, 134–36; *Guardian*, Aug. 5, 1995; Drifte, "China," p. 47.

68. Myrdal, *Game of Disarmament*, pp. 200–202; Seaborg, *Stemming the Tide*, p. 341; Powaski, *March to Armageddon*, p. 121; Rusk, *As I Saw It*, p. 353.

69. Whether or not U.S. naval vessels carrying nuclear arms have entered Japanese ports has been a source of great contention in Japan. However, even if this facet of the nuclear ban has not been enforced, neither the Japanese nor the U.S. government has dared to admit it. *FRUS, 1958–1960*, 18: 27; Akaha, "Japan's Three Nonnuclear Principles," p. 75; Reiss, *Without the Bomb*, pp. 118–19; Suzuki, "Declining Role of Ideology," pp. 124–25; *Meaning of Survival*, pp. 234, 279; Pempel, "Japan's Nuclear Allergy," p. 170.

70. Ghent, "Canadian-American Relations," pp. 274–75, 278–79; Epstein, "Canada," pp. 178–79; Regehr, "Canada and the U.S. Nuclear Arsenal," p. 110.

71. Barton and Weiler, eds., *International Arms Control*, pp. 97–101; Rusk, *As I Saw It*, pp. 345–48.

72. Rusk, *As I Saw It*, pp. 348–50; York, *Making Weapons, Talking Peace*, pp. 222–25; Morton H. Halperin, "Arms Control: A Twenty-Five-Year Perspective," *F.A.S. Public Interest Report* 36 (June 1983): 5–6; L. Johnson, *Vantage Point*, pp. 479–81.

73. York, *Making Weapons, Talking Peace*, pp. 222–23; Weisskopf, *Privilege*, p. 215; Evangelista, "Soviet Scientists as Arms Control Advisors," pp. 11–36; Feld, "Artsimovich," pp. 84–85; personal interview with Sergei Kapitza, June 28, 1990; personal interview with Joseph Rotblat, July 12, 1990; Peierls, *Bird of Passage*, p. 285.

74. L. Johnson, *Vantage Point*, pp. 483–90; Rusk, *As I Saw It*, pp. 349–51; Seaborg, "Introduction," in Seaborg, ed., *Journal*, 1: 14–15.

75. Nitze, *From Hiroshima to Glasnost*, pp. 294–95, 304; Kissinger, *White House Years*, pp. 204–10; Primack and von Hippel, *Advice and Dissent*, pp. 62–72, 178–92; "Kissinger's Critique," p. 17; Smith, *Doubletalk*, pp. 29–30.

76. Seaborg, *Stemming the Tide*, pp. 440–41, 452; Myrdal, *Game of Disarmament*, p. 106; Winkler, *Life Under a Cloud*, p. 184; Barton and Weiler, eds., *International Arms Control*, pp. 92, 197–207.

77. Soviet officials also believed that a great-power war had to be avoided. Dobrynin recalled that when he met with Leonid Brezhnev and asked for instructions as to how to deal with the United States, the Soviet leader "would invariably answer, 'What instructions do you need? . . . Let there be peace; that's the main thing.'" McNamara, "Military Role," p. 66; Scott and Scott, *Soviet Military Doctrine*, pp. 45–49; Richter, *Khrushchev's Double Bind*, p. 177; Dobrynin, *In Confidence*, pp. 130–31.

78. Healey, *Time of My Life*, pp. 245, 308.

79. The firm was Doyle, Dane, and Bernbach, a company connected to SANE through William Bernbach's service on SANE's board. Given these kinds of appeals, as well as Goldwater's genuine hawkishness, SANE activists rallied behind Johnson, much to his pleasure.

T. White, *Making of the President*, pp. 353–58, 384, 387; McNamara, *In Retrospect*, pp. 149–50; *NYT*, Aug. 3, 1964; Katz, *Ban the Bomb*, pp. 72, 91; Bundy, *Danger and Survival*, pp. 537–38; Bloom, *Doctor Spock*, pp. 252–53.

80. Rusk, *As I Saw It*, pp. 457, 499; Cohen, *Dean Rusk*, p. 238; *Pentagon Papers*, 2: 322, 3: 65, 175, 238; McNamara, *In Retrospect*, pp. 109, 111, 147, 160–61, 173–74, 194, 245, 253, 275; Bundy, *Danger and Survival*, pp. 536–37.

81. Rosenblatt, *Witness*, pp. 78–79; Bundy, *Danger and Survival*, pp. 538–41; Kissinger, *Nuclear Weapons*; Kissinger, *White House Years*, pp. 66–67.

82. McNamara, *Essence of Security*, p. 54; Powaski, *March to Armageddon*, pp. 115–16.

83. McNamara recognized that "the Soviet build-up is in part a reaction to our own build-up since the beginning of the 1960s." Arbatov, *System*, pp. 174–75, 180; Dobrynin, *In Confidence*, pp. 130, 154; Powaski, *March to Armageddon*, p. 114; McNamara, *Essence of Security*, p. 60.

84. Drifte, "China," pp. 46–47; Clemens, "Sino-Soviet Dispute," pp. 220–21.

85. Healey, *Time of My Life*, pp. 245, 302–4, 307; Pierre, *Nuclear Politics*, pp. 251–92; R. Taylor, "Labour Party," p. 120.

86. Kimche, *Afro-Asian Movement*, pp. 114–17; Beker, *Disarmament Without Order*, pp. 63–65; Willetts, *Non-Aligned Movement*, pp. 24–25; Dimitri Roussopoulos, "The Politics of the Peace Movement," *Our Generation* 15 (Fall 1982): 3. See also Walker, "Nonviolence in Africa," p. 188; Hope and Young, *Struggle for Humanity*, pp. 223–57.

87. *FRUS, 1961–1963*, 7: 877.

88. For a discussion of the differences between arms control and disarmament, see Morgenthau, *Politics Among Nations*, pp. 373–96.

Chapter 19

Epigraph: Dedication in Duff, *Left, Left, Left.*

1. Randle, "Non-Violent Direct Action," p. 142; Russell, *Final Years*, pp. 215–317; Bertrand Russell, "Private Memorandum concerning Ralph Schoenman" (Dec. 8. 1969), in R. Clark, *Life of Bertrand Russell*, pp. 640–51.

2. Minutes of the CND Executive Committee meeting of Sept. 5, 1970, Reel 1, CND (Britain) Records, London-Warwick; R. Taylor, *Against the Bomb*, pp. 108–12; *PN*, July 10, 1964; Minnion and Bolsover, eds., *CND Story*, p. 150; Cox, *Overkill*, pp. 220–21.

3. Schmitz, *Anti-Nuclear Protest*, p. 8; M. J. Coldwell to K. C. Woodsworth, Nov. 14, 1963, Box 2, and Minutes of the Canadian CND Executive Committee meetings of Jan. 26, Feb. 20, and Apr. 13, 1965, Box 1, Canadian CND Records, Hamilton; Moffatt, *History*, pp. 93, 97.

4. Minutes of the Combined Universities CND meeting of Jan. 28, 1964, Box 1, Combined Universities CND–Student Union for Peace Action Records; "Editorial Statement," *Our Generation* 3:4 and 4:1 (n.d.): 3–5; Macpherson and Sears, "Voice of Women," p. 89.

5. Otto, *Vom Ostermarsch zur APO*, pp. 145–77; Merkl, "Pacifism," p. 87; Mushaben, "Cycles," pp. 29–30.

6. Bjol, *Hvem bestemmer*, pp. 216–17; Boel, *Socialdemokratiets atomvåbenpolitik*, p. 16; Jorgensen, *Atomvåbnenes rolle*, pp. 90–91.

7. Nilson, "Peace Movement," p. 37; Lumsden, "Nuclear Weapons," p. 108; Erik Alfsen, "De förste år av Nei til atomvåpen" (1986), p. 1, Nei til Atomvåpen Records; Lindkvist, "Mobilization Peaks and Declines," p. 159; Lubelski-Bernard, "Les mouvements de la paix," p. 384.

8. Verkuil, *De grote illuse*, pp. 49–50; Everts, "Reviving Unilateralism," p. 42; Claude Bourdet to Cher Ami, Feb. 1967, and Bourdet to Madame, Monsieur, Feb. 1968, Bourdet correspondence, Mendès-France Papers; Toulat, *La bombe*.

9. Brassel and Tanner, "Zur Geschichte der Friedensbewegung," p. 70; Heiniger, "Die schweizerische Antiatombewegung," pp. 160–72.

10. Summy and Saunders, "Disarmament," p. 32; Report from the New Zealand CND National Committee to the annual conference, Aug. 21–22, 1965, Folder 356, WRI Records, Amsterdam; Locke, *Peace People*, p. 186.

11. Unger, *Movement*, p. 83; Chatfield, *American Peace Movement*, p. 114; Wittner, *Rebels Against War*, p. 280; Boyer, "From Activism to Apathy," pp. 825–26, 837.

12. Sakharov, *Sakharov Speaks*, pp. 15–16, 36–38; Sakharov and Henry, "Scientists and the Danger"; Klose, *Russia and the Russians*, pp. 156–58; Sakharov, *Memoirs*, p. 281.

13. Sakharov, *Sakharov Speaks*, pp. 55–114; Sakharov, *Alarm and Hope*, p. xi; *NYT*, July 22, 1968, Dec. 16, 1989; Eugene Rabinowitch, "The Sakharov Manifesto," *BAS* 24 (Nov. 1968): 2–3.

14. Sakharov, *Sakharov Speaks*, p. 15; Burlatsky, *Khrushchev*, pp. 257–58, 260, 262; Adamsky, "Becoming a Citizen," p. 42; Eugene Rabinowitch to V. Poremsky, Jan. 21, 1970, Box 2, Rabinowitch Papers, Albany.

15. The Sakharov-Medvedev-Turchin letter urged "the renunciation of weapons of mass destruction as a matter of principle," but focused on other issues. *NYT*, July 22, 1968, Dec. 16, 1989; Z. Medvedev, *Soviet Science*, p. 107; Klose, *Russia and the Russians*, p. 156; Sakharov, *Memoirs*, pp. 267–80; Sakharov, *Sakharov Speaks*, pp. 24–25, 44, 132; Sakharov, "An Autobiographical Note," pp. 178–79.

16. "A Summing Up of . . . the Japan Congress Against Atomic and Hydrogen Bombs" (Apr. 3, 1970), pp. 7–8, Japan Congress Against Atomic and Hydrogen Bombs Records, SCPC; Committee for the Compilation of Materials, *Hiroshima and Nagasaki*, p. 582; *Meaning of Survival*, pp. 176–83; Setsuo Yamada, "Peace Declaration" (Aug. 6, 1970), Folder 333, WRI Records, Amsterdam; Passin, "Nuclear Arms," p. 67.

17. Carter, *Peace Movements*, p. 77; Claude Bourdet to the author, June 25, 1993; Minutes of the ICDP Council meeting of June 24–27, 1964, ICDP Records; Peggy Duff to Dear Friend, Oct. 1967, Reel 3, CND (Britain) Records, London-Warwick.

18. Rotblat, "Movements of Scientists," p. 137; Rabinowitch to Edwin D. Fowle, June 7, 1972, Box 1, Rabinowitch Papers, Albany.

19. Scalapino, *Japanese Communist Movement*, pp. 278–79; Endicott, *James G. Endicott*, pp. 343, 348; "Statement on the Proposed Non-Aligned Conference" (Dec. 1968), WPC Records.

20. Even Linus Pauling, invited personally by J. D. Bernal to join the WPC, declined to do so. Endicott, *James G. Endicott*, pp. 348, 351–52; Penner, *Canadian Communism*, p. 227; Bernal to Pauling, May 27, 1966, and Pauling to Bernal, June 6, 1966, Box 86, Bernal Papers.

21. Paarlberg, "Forgetting," p. 136; Boyer, "From Activism to Apathy," pp. 825–26; Lowther, "Decline of Public Concern," pp. 77, 79; Lyon, *Canada*, p. 78.

22. Boel, *Socialdemokratiets atomvåbenpolitik*, p. 15; Gallup, ed., *Gallup International Public Opinion Polls: Great Britain*, p. 781; Gallup, ed., *Gallup International Public Opinion Polls: France*, p. 444.

23. In September 1965, 60 percent of British respondents considered it either important or very important to "keep Britain strong in nuclear arms." Gallup, ed., *Gallup International Public Opinion Polls: Great Britain*, pp. 827, 930.

24. Gallup, ed., *Gallup International Public Opinion Polls: France*, pp. 417, 521; Asada, "Japanese Perceptions," pp. 213–14; Myrdal, *Game of Disarmament*, pp. 318–19.

25. In an April 1958 story, *Time* identified Pauling as a "longtime supporter of Commu-

nist-line fronts," claimed that a burgeoning movement against nuclear weapons was "customary before U.S. nuclear tests but rarely before U.S.S.R. nuclear tests," and that CND believed "that nuclear disarmament will probably bring Communist domination, but that domination is preferable to the . . . prospect of nuclear war." Its view of SANE was no more charitable. *Cincinnati Enquirer*, Apr. 21, 1960, Box 9, Muste Papers; Allen, *Mark It*, p. 406; "How Sane the SANE?" pp. 13–14.

26. *PN*, May 18, 1962; Hugh Gaitskell, "Memorandum on the Deterrent" (Apr. 13, 1960), in P. Williams, ed., *Diary*, pp. 635–41; "Proceedings of the Tenth Pugwash Conference on Science and World Affairs, London, September 3–7, 1962," pp. 59–60, PC Records, London.

27. Naeve, ed., *Changeover*, p. 210; "Proceedings of the Tenth Pugwash Conference on Science and World Affairs, London, September 3–7, 1962," p. 61, PC Records, London; Ray Wynn to Elizabeth Tapper, May 12, 1962, Reel 80, WILPF (International) Records.

28. Roy Kepler to Norman Cousins, June 15, 1957, Box 1, and Joan V. Cobb to Trevor Thomas, Jan. 15, 1958, Box 8, Series B, SANE Records; personal interview with Homer Jack, June 12, 1988.

29. According to pollsters, 40 percent expressed disagreement. Gallup, ed., *Gallup International Public Opinion Polls: Great Britain*, p. 632. See also Snyder, *Politics*, p. 84.

30. In Canada, when a Vancouver city council member charged that the Communist Party was behind the local Committee on Radiation Hazards, the local newspaper retorted that his remarks were "ill-considered" and "intemperate," and that members of the committee had a broad range of political backgrounds. "Limerick Active Against the Bomb," *Banner*, June 1963; *PN*, Apr. 10, 1964; Swerdlow, *Women Strike for Peace*, pp. 97–123; Hayden Raynor to DOS, May 3, 1961, 600.0012/5-361, DOS Records.

31. See, for example, Loring Fiske to SANE, Nov. 22, 1957, Box 10, and Francis K. McCune to Norman Cousins and Clarence Pickett, June 16, 1958, Box 4, Series B, SANE Records; Divine, *Blowing on the Wind*, pp. 260, 268.

32. Gallup, ed., *Gallup Poll*, pp. 1699, 1741; *Sanity* [Britain], Jan. 1964, p. 2.

33. Blechman and Fisher, *Silent Partner*, p. 203; Gallup, ed., *Gallup International Public Opinion Polls: Great Britain*, pp. 659, 684; Arthur Pape, "Working Paper #3 for CCND Policy Committee" (ca. 1964), Box 2, Canadian CND Records, Hamilton.

34. Cousins to Schweitzer, Oct. 1, 1962, in Cousins, *Albert Schweitzer's Mission*, p. 283; Jack to Norman Thomas, Mar. 8, 1963, Reel 62, Thomas Papers.

35. Jorgensen, *Atomvåbnenes rolle*, p. 85; personal interview with Sheila Jones, July 10, 1990; Collins, *Faith Under Fire*, p. 344; Randle to the author, Oct. 4, 1994; Cousins, *Albert Schweitzer's Mission*, p. 300.

36. N. Young, "Why Peace Movements Fail," pp. 13–14; April Carter to the author, Mar. 7, 1994; A. Taylor, *A Personal History*, p. 230; Brandon, *Burning Question*, p. 52; Frazier Meade to DOS, Jan. 16, 1963, 600.0012/1-1663, DOS Records.

37. Locke, *Peace People*, p. 186; Weart, *Nuclear Fear*, pp. 264, 266–67; Lifton, *Death in Life*, pp. 500–510; Warner and Shuman, *Citizen Diplomats*, p. 160.

38. Duff, *Left, Left, Left*, p. 267; Moffatt, *History*, pp. 94–95; Combined Universities CND National Secretariat to All CUCND Executive Committees and National Members, Aug. 6, 1963, Box 1, Combined Universities CND–Student Union for Peace Action Records.

39. Duff, *Left, Left, Left*, p. 163; April Carter to the author, Mar. 7, 1994; Sheila Jones to the author, Aug. 25, 1995; Shelley, "Pacifism, War Resistance," p. 37.

40. Everts, "Reviving Unilateralism," p. 42; Lifton, *Death in Life*, p. 299.

41. Duff, *Left, Left, Left*, pp. 215–16; *PN*, May 11, 1962, Apr. 19, 1963; *Sanity* [Britain], May 1963, p. 8; Collins, *Faith Under Fire*, pp. 333–34; Verkuil, *De grote illusie*, p. 49.

42. Eugene Rabinowitch, "New Year's Thoughts 1964," *BAS* 20 (Jan. 1964): 2; April Carter to the author, Mar. 7, 1994; Sheila Jones to the author, Aug. 25, 1995; "Minority Re-

port of the Executive Committee" (Nov. 1964), Reel 1, CND (Britain) Records, London-Warwick; Merkl, "Pacifism," pp. 87–88.

43. Everts, "Reviving Unilateralism," pp. 42–43; Meyer, "Peace Protest," p. 14; Lumsden, "Nuclear Weapons," p. 119; "Notes on the history of the NZ Campaign for Nuclear Disarmament," Locke Papers.

44. CND organized a demonstration in Trafalgar Square to celebrate the signing of the treaty. Combined Universities CND National Secretariat to All CUCND Executive Committees and National Members, Aug. 6, 1963, Box 1, Combined Universities CND–Student Union for Peace Action Records; *Sanity* [Britain], Aug. 1963, p. 1; Minutes of the CND Executive Committee meeting of July 23, 1963, Reel 1, CND (Britain) Records, London-Warwick.

45. Bertrand Russell, "Statement on the Test Ban Treaty for the Soviet Embassy Press Agency" (Aug. 15, 1963), Class 650, RA 1; "Test Ban Treaty—Victory But Don't Relax Yet," *Banner*, ca. Aug. 1963. See also Grossi, "From Contempt to Credibility," p. 6.

46. "FAS: For Further Arms Control," *BAS* 19 (Nov. 1963): 46; "SANE Tasks Ahead," *Sane World*, Oct. 15, 1963; Homer Jack, "Where Do We Go From Here?" Box 53, Series B, SANE Records.

47. Pauling to Joseph Mayer, Oct. 18, 1963, Pauling Papers; Cousins to Spock, Sept. 26, 1963, Box 14, 1971 Series, Spock Papers.

48. Personal interview with Homer Jack, June 12, 1988; Andersson and Lindkvist, "Peace Movement," p. 12; *END Journal*, Feb.–Mar. 1984, p. 14; George Breuer, "Limits to Unilateralism," *END Journal*, Apr.–May 1983, p. 26; ter Veer, "New Peace Movements," p. 10; Everts and Walraven, *Vredesbeweging*, p. 43; Lubelski-Bernard, "Les mouvements de la paix," pp. 384–85; Duff, *Left, Left, Left*, p. 224; Summy and Saunders, "Disarmament," pp. 31–32; Dimitri Roussopoulos, "The Politics of the Peace Movement," *Our Generation* 15 (Fall 1982): 4; Moffatt, *History*, p. 95; Carter, *Peace Movements*, p. 41.

49. Minutes of the SANE National Board meeting of Sept. 16, 1963, Box 410, Cousins Papers, Los Angeles; Boyer, "From Activism to Apathy," pp. 830–31; Seaborg, *Stemming the Tide*, p. 205; Sakharov, *Memoirs*, p. 204.

50. "T.C.N.D. Bulletin" (June 12, 1965), "Toronto Campaign for Nuclear Disarmament" Folder, Box 7, Radical Organizations Archive; Warner and Shuman, *Citizen Diplomats*, p. 36; Locke, *Peace People*, pp. 185–86.

51. "Majority Report of the Executive Committee" (Nov. 1964), Reel 1, CND (Britain) Records, London-Warwick; *PN*, Aug. 21, 1964; R. Taylor, *Against the Bomb*, pp. 266–69; Macpherson and Sears, "Voice of Women," p. 81.

52. Everts and Walraven, *Vredesbeweging*, p. 46; Lindkvist, "Mobilization Peaks and Declines," p. 159; Student Peace Union, "Statement on Foreign Policy" (1964), Box 1, SPU Records, Madison.

53. Joseph Rotblat to Bertrand Russell, Feb. 23, 1966, Class 625, RA 1; Rotblat, "Movements of Scientists," p. 137; Rabinowitch to Hans Thirring, Sept. 30, 1970, Box 3, Rabinowitch Papers, Albany.

54. Duff, *Left, Left, Left*, p. 244; Roussopoulos, *From Protest to Resistance*, p. 62; Brock to Vera Brittain, Sept. 25, 1968, "Brock, Hugh" Folder, Brittain Papers; Randle to the author, Oct. 4, 1994.

55. Ilukhina and Pavlova, "Totalitarianism," p. 3; Dobrynin, *In Confidence*, p. 183; Sagdeev, *Making of a Soviet Scientist*, pp. 131–32; Sakharov, *Memoirs*, pp. 290–91.

56. Jack, *Nuclear Politics*, p. 45; Duff, *Left, Left, Left*, p. 268; Peggy Duff, "What You Don't Know About the Arms Race," *Our Generation* 13: 1 (1979): 8; McNeal, *American Catholic Peace Movement*, pp. 141–42.

57. Randle to the author, Oct. 4, 1994; "CND Statement on Vietnam Crisis" (Aug. 5,

1964), Folder 273, WRI Records, Amsterdam; Minutes of the CND Executive Committee meetings of May 15, Sept. 11, and Oct. 16, 1965, Reel 1, CND (Britain) Records, London-Warwick; Andrew Papworth to Vera Brittain, Oct. 28, 1965, "Committee of 100" Folder, Brittain Papers; "Easter '67," Class 630, RA 2; Cox, *Overkill*, pp. 217–18.

58. Cox, *Overkill*, pp. 215, 218–19; R. Taylor, "Marxist Left," pp. 168–69; Sybil Morrison to Prime Minister, Feb. 19, 1965, "Morrison, Sybil" Folder, Brittain Papers; Shelley, "Pacifism, War Resistance," pp. 40–41; Duff, *Left, Left, Left*, p. 207; personal interview with Sheila Jones, July 10, 1990.

59. "Invitation to the Twentieth Anniversary World Conference Against A- & H-Bombs" (May 20, 1965), Japan Congress Against Atomic and Hydrogen Bombs Records, SCPC; Bamba, "Peace Movement," p. 41; Y. Tsurumi, "Beheiran"; Bamba and Howes, "Conclusion," pp. 270–71.

60. Minutes of the Canadian CND Executive Committee meeting of Apr. 13, 1965, Box 1, Canadian CND Records, Hamilton; Canadian CND Newsletter, no. 3 (Sept. 22, 1965) and 4 (Dec. 15, 1965), Folder 188, WRI Records, Amsterdam.

61. Lana Lockyer to War Resisters League, Dec. 15, 1964, Box 2, Combined Universities CND–Student Union for Peace Action Records; Kostash, *Long Way*, pp. 45–54; Regehr and Rosenblum, "Canadian Peace Movement," p. 226.

62. Macpherson, *When in Doubt*, pp. 118–28; Macpherson and Sears, "Voice of Women," pp. 79–80, 84–86; Kay Macpherson and Sara Good, "Canadian Voice of Women for Peace," *Peace Magazine* 3 (Oct./Nov. 1987): 26; "Vietnamese Women Visit Canada" (July 1969), Voice of Women Records.

63. "U.S. Must Change South Vietnam Policy," *Sane World*, Nov. 1, 1963, p. 1; Philip Altbach to Advisory Council Members, Oct. 5, 1963, Class 640, RA 1; Gail Paradise to Charlie Walker, Oct. 7, 1963, Box 6, SPU Records, Madison; David McReynolds to Dear Friend, Dec. 5, 1964, Box 35, War Resisters League Records; Zaroulis and Sullivan, *Who Spoke Up?* p. 26.

64. A postcard poll on issuing the FAS statement revealed 685 members in favor, 244 against. Of those against, 217 said the war was not an FAS issue. Only about 20 claimed they supported U.S. policy. "World Protests on Vietnam War," *Pax et Libertas* 30 (Jan.–Mar. 1965): 15; Donald Keys to Norman Thomas, July 7, 1965, Box 70, Series B, SANE Records; McNeal, *American Catholic Peace Movement*, pp. 234–36; Swerdlow, *Women Strike for Peace*, pp. 129–42, 159–86; Federation of American Scientists, "On the War in Vietnam" (Mar. 5, 1967), Box 49, and W. A. Higinbotham to Dan Singer, Mar. 18, 1967, Box 38, 1972 Series, FAS Records.

65. Personal interview with Homer Jack, June 12, 1988; Swerdlow, *Women Strike for Peace*, pp. 129–30, 164; "Preliminary Mobilization Memorandum," National Mobilization Committee to End the War in Vietnam Records; DeBenedetti and Chatfield, *An American Ordeal*, pp. 114–274, 320, 350.

66. Summy and Saunders, "Disarmament," p. 32; Gilbert and Jordan, "Traditions of Dissent," pp. 355–57; Gordon and Osmond, "An Overview," p. 23.

67. *Bulletin* [New Zealand], Sept. 1964, May 1965; Locke, *Peace People*, pp. 192–93; Clements, *Back from the Brink*, pp. 102–6; "Report from New Zealand Campaign for Nuclear Disarmament" (Aug. 21–22, 1965), Folder 356, WRI Records, Amsterdam.

68. Bjol, *Hvem bestemmer*, p. 217; Taipale, "Peace Movement in Finland," p. 27; Giovanni Maciocia to Eric Weinburger, Oct. 23, Dec. 2, 1965, Box 7, CNVA Records.

69. Breuer, "Limits to Unilateralism," p. 26; News Release No. 34 (Dec. 29, 1964), Box 5, WRI Records, SCPC; Everts and Walraven, *Vredesbeweging*, p. 44; "Frieden für Vietnam" (1965), Folder 247, WRI Records, Amsterdam.

70. Bertil Svahnström, "Swedish Vietnam Committee Formed" (Aug. 23, 1965), Folder 388, and "Vietnam Peace Project" (1966), Folder 387, WRI Records, Amsterdam; Andersson and Lindkvist, "Peace Movement," p. 12.

71. Howorth, *France*, p. 29; "Pourquoi cette Marche?" (1966), Folder 209, WRI Records, Amsterdam; Bourdet, "Rebirth," p. 194; Bourdet, "Désarmement nucléaire," p. 8.

72. Frank J. Gordon, "A Brief History of the Women's International League for Peace and Freedom" (1981), p. 5, WILPF (International Office) Records; Foster, *Women for All Seasons*, pp. 8–9.

73. Rotblat, *Scientists*, pp. 64, 68–69; Rotblat to Russell, Aug. 5, 1965, Class 625, RA 1; personal interview with Joseph Rotblat, July 11, 1994.

74. "Vietnam: A Call for Action Now" (May 5, 1965), Minutes of the ICDP Council meeting, Sept. 5–8, 1965, Minutes of the ICDP Executive meeting, Jan. 27, 1966, ICDP Records; Peggy Duff to Dear Friend, Oct. 1967, Reel 3, CND (Great Britain) Records, London-Warwick; Duff, *Left, Left, Left*, pp. 243–44; Kenneth Lee to Devi Prasad, Dec. 6, 1968, Folder 151, WRI Records, Amsterdam; personal interview with Homer Jack, June 12, 1988.

75. Li Chu-wen to Bertrand Russell, Sept. 21, 1965, Class 640, RA 1. See, for example, "End U.S. Aggression Now!" *No More Hiroshimas!* 12 (Apr. 1965); Turski and Zdanowski, *Peace Movement*, p. 78; "Canadian Peace Congress, 1948 to 1978," Canadian Peace Congress Records, Toronto.

76. Tikhonov to Russell, July 1964, Class 650, RA 1; Japan Council against A & H Bombs, *Documentary Photographs*, pp. 26–27; Bernal to Korneichuk, Apr. 20, 1966, Box 61, Bernal Papers.

77. Duff, *Left, Left, Left*, p. 267.

78. Sakharov, *Alarm and Hope*, pp. 117, 172–73. See also pp. 4–5, 11, 104–5; Sakharov, *My Country and the World*, pp. 63–64.

79. Telephone interview with Pavel Litvinov, Oct. 7, 1990. See also Orlov, *Dangerous Thoughts*, p. 195.

80. Gitlin, *Sixties*, pp. 261–408; Sale, *SDS*, pp. 344–657; N. Young, *An Infantile Disorder?* pp. 174–79.

81. "Student Union for Peace Action," Student Union for Peace Action Records; Roussopoulos, *From Protest to Resistance*, pp. 129–30; Kostash, *Long Way*, pp. xxiv–xxv, 3–6, 28.

82. N. Young, *An Infantile Disorder?* pp. 158–59; Otto, *Vom Ostermarsch zur APO*, pp. 158, 173–76; Mushaben, "Cycles," pp. 29–30; Brassel and Tanner, "Zur Geschichte der Friedensbewegung," p. 71; Lindkvist, "Mobilization Peaks and Declines," p. 159; Clements, *Back from the Brink*, pp. 103–4.

83. R. Clark, *Life of Bertrand Russell*, 602–3, 614–15; Schoenman, "Bertrand Russell," pp. 243–45.

84. Bess, *Realism*, pp. 116–18, 201–2; H. Clark, "Nonviolent Resistance," p. 58; N. Young, *An Infantile Disorder?* p. 159; Bacon, *One Woman's Passion*, pp. 318–19.

85. Otto, "Ostermarsch der Atomwaffengegner," pp. 172–73; Jordan, "Peace Activities," p. 1; R. Taylor, "Labour Party," p. 121; Bourdet, "Désarmement nucléaire," pp. 7–8.

86. Shelley, "Pacifism, War Resistance," p. 40; N. Young, *An Infantile Disorder?* p. 158; Howorth, *France*, pp. 29–30.

87. Liddington, *Long Road to Greenham*, pp. 198–203; Macpherson and Sears, "Voice of Women," pp. 83–84; Swerdlow, *Women Strike for Peace*, pp. 227–31, 238–39, 241.

88. *Meaning of Survival*, p. 196.

Conclusion

Epigraph: Larson and Micheels-Cyrus, *Seeds of Peace*, p. 224.

1. Some women supporters of the nuclear disarmament campaign (e.g. Eleanor Roosevelt, Vera Brittain, and Coretta Scott King) were already famous, but did not play central roles in it or devote most of their energies to it.

2. See, for example, the work of the historian Robert Divine, who was discussing the behavior of Americans. Divine, *Blowing on the Wind*, p. 323.

3. See, for example, Wittner, *One World or None*.

4. Szilard, too, commented that "talking about world government doesn't seem to be very useful," for "these things are rather far in the future" and the Bomb has a "much, much greater urgency." Russell to Ken Weller, July 21, 1962, Class 630, RA 1; "Proceedings of Sixth Pugwash Conference, Moscow, USSR, November 27–December 5, 1960," p. 670, PC Records, London; "Disarmament: Doctor Szilard interviews Dr. Teller" (n.d.), CBS reports, Box 40, Szilard Papers.

5. Duff, *Left, Left, Left*, p. 158.

6. Of course, it could be argued that some officials used the antinuclear state of public opinion to justify their own opposition to more hawkish alternatives. But, even if they did, this still means that such opinion—and behind it the movement—played a crucial role.

7. *Banner*, ca. Aug. 1963; Sheila Jones to the author, Aug. 25, 1995; Seaborg, *Kennedy, Khrushchev*, pp. 286–87; Bundy, *Danger and Survival*, pp. 460–61.

8. Rabinowitch, too, argued that the Pugwash conferences "contributed, more or less directly, to developments such as the test ban or the non-proliferation treaty." Hamilton, "M.I.T.," p. 1476; Zuckerman, "Opening Address," p. 5; Rabinowitch to Murray Todd, June 4, 1970, Box 3, Rabinowitch Papers, Albany.

9. In 1963, Homer Jack remarked that "American peace organizations ought to be fairly modest in accepting any credit for signing of the test ban treaty." A quarter-century later, he said much the same thing. Cousins, he insisted, "did more for the test ban than did all of SANE!" R. Taylor and C. Pritchard, *Protest Makers*, p. 109; Carter, *Peace Movements*, p. 77; oral history interview with Alec Douglas-Home, pp. 2–3; Homer A. Jack, "Where Do We Go From Here?" Box 53, Series B, SANE Records; personal interview with Homer Jack, June 12, 1988.

10. Personal interview with Joseph Rotblat, July 11, 1994.

11. For some joking on the subject of nuclear weapons and virginity between Macmillan and Kennedy in late 1962 and between Rusk and Dobrynin in mid-1963, see L. Thompson, "Memorandum of Conversation" (Dec. 19, 1962), 741.5611/12-1962, DOS Records; *FRUS, 1961–1963*, 7: 704–5.

12. In Sweden, of course, the antinuclear stand of Inga Thorsson and the Social Democratic Women's Organization weighed heavily against Sweden's development of nuclear weapons. This exception, though, proves the rule, for it indicates that where women had a substantial role in politics, as in Sweden, their leaders helped formulate public policy.

13. Seaborg, *Stemming the Tide*, p. 449; Myrdal, *Game of Disarmament*, pp. xiii, 110, 293–94.

14. In 1963, after the signing of the atmospheric test ban treaty, the *Bulletin*'s editors gave it this setting. But, in 1968, dismayed by nuclear proliferation, they pushed it forward to seven minutes to midnight. Seaborg, *Kennedy, Khrushchev*, facing p. 145.

15. Myrdal, *Game of Disarmament*, p. 178.

16. Rusk, *As I Saw It*, p. 367.

17. Smith, *Doubletalk*, p. 13; Seaborg, *Stemming the Tide*, p. 236.

18. Describing Macmillan's reaction, Schlesinger pointed to the treaty's additional value

in offsetting the political damage caused the Tory government by a major sex scandal. Macmillan, *At the End*, p. 487; Seaborg, *Kennedy, Khrushchev*, p. 250; Sorensen, *Kennedy*, p. 740; Schlesinger, *A Thousand Days*, p. 908.

19. Eugene Rabinowitch, "First Things First," *BAS* 15 (Nov. 1959): 361; De Madariaga, "Disarmament?" p. 72.

20. Cousins to Albert Schweitzer, Oct. 2, 1961, in Cousins, *Albert Schweitzer's Mission*, p. 269; Grodzins and Rabinowitch, eds., *Atomic Age*, p. 167.

21. Toynbee, "Holy See and the Work of Peace," p. 35.

Bibliography

Manuscript Sources

African National Congress Records, University of the Witwatersrand, Johannesburg, South Africa

Aktion Sühnezeichen / Friedensdienste Records, Office, Berlin, Germany

Aldrig mere Krig Records, Swarthmore College Peace Collection, Swarthmore, Pa. (hereafter SCPC)

Clinton P. Anderson Papers, Library of Congress, Washington, D.C.

Atomic Energy Authority Records, Public Record Office, Kew, Britain

Atomic Energy Commission Records, Department of Energy Archives, Washington, D.C.

Australian Quaker Peace Committee Records, Office, Victoria, Australia

J. Desmond Bernal Papers, University Library, Cambridge University, Cambridge, Britain

Max Born–Bertrand Russell Correspondence, Mills Memorial Library, McMaster University, Hamilton, Ontario, Canada

Vera Brittain Papers, Mills Memorial Library, McMaster University, Hamilton, Ontario, Canada

Alice Pat Broudy Papers, Broudy Home, Monarch Beach, Calif.

Cabinet Defense Committee Records, Public Record Office, Kew, Britain

Cabinet Records, Public Record Office, Kew, Britain

Campaign for Nuclear Disarmament (Britain) Records, British Library of Political and Economic Science, London School of Economics and Political Science, University of London, London, Campaign for Nuclear Disarmament Office, London, and Modern Record Center, University of Warwick Library, Warwick, Britain (microfilm); SCPC

Campaign for Nuclear Disarmament (New Zealand) Records, SCPC

Canadian Campaign for Nuclear Disarmament Records, Mills Memorial Library, McMaster University, Hamilton, Ontario, Canada; SCPC

Canadian Peace Congress Records, Office, Toronto, Ontario, Canada; SCPC

Central Committee of the Communist Party of the Soviet Union Records, Storage Center for Contemporary Documentation (Tsentr Khraneniia Sovremennoi Dokumentatsii), Moscow, Russia

Christian Peace Conference Records, SCPC
Combined Universities Campaign for Nuclear Disarmament Records, SCPC
Combined Universities Campaign for Nuclear Disarmament–Student Union for Peace Action
    Records, Mills Memorial Library, McMaster University, Hamilton, Ontario, Canada
Committee for Environmental Information Records, Western Historical Manuscript
    Collection, Thomas Jefferson Library, University of Missouri, St. Louis, Mo.
Committee for Nonviolent Action Records, SCPC
Committee of 100 Records, SCPC
Council for a Livable World Records, SCPC
Norman Cousins Papers, Cousins Home, Beverly Hills, Calif.; University Research Library,
    University of California, Los Angeles, Calif.
Czechoslovakia Miscellaneous Peace Material, SCPC
Czechoslovak Peace Committee Records, SCPC
Department of State Records, National Archives, College Park, Md., Washington, D.C.
        Atomic Energy Lot File (#57D688)
        Central Decimal File
Deutscher Friedensrat Records, Federal Archives (Bundesarchiv), Berlin, Germany
Direct Action Committee Against Nuclear War Records, SCPC
Allen W. Dulles Papers, Seeley Mudd Library, Princeton University, Princeton, N.J.
John Foster Dulles Papers, Dwight D. Eisenhower Library, Abilene, Kans.; Seeley Mudd Li-
    brary, Princeton University, Princeton, N.J.
Dwight D. Eisenhower Papers as President of the United States (Ann Whitman File), Dwight
    D. Eisenhower Library, Abilene, Kans.
Dwight D. Eisenhower Records as President, White House Central Files, Dwight D. Eisen-
    hower Library, Abilene, Kans.
        Alphabetical File
        Confidential File
        General File
        Official File
        President's Personal File
Emergency Committee of Atomic Scientists Records, Joseph Regenstein Library, University
    of Chicago, Chicago, Ill.
Federation of American Scientists Records, Joseph Regenstein Library, University of
    Chicago, Chicago, Ill.
Fellowship of Reconciliation (Britain) Records, British Library of Political and Economic
    Science, London, Britain (microfilm)
Fellowship of Reconciliation (Canada) Records, SCPC; United Church Archives, Victoria
    University, University of Toronto, Toronto, Ontario, Canada
Fellowship of Reconciliation (India) Records, Office, Kottayam, India
Fellowship of Reconciliation (Japan) Records, SCPC
Fellowship of Reconciliation (United States) Records, SCPC
Foreign Office Records, Public Record Office, Kew, Britain
Gandhi Peace Foundation Records, SCPC
Averell W. Harriman Papers, Library of Congress, Washington, D.C.
Christian Herter Papers, Dwight D. Eisenhower Library, Abilene, Kans.
Emmet John Hughes Papers, Seeley Mudd Library, Princeton University, Princeton, N.J.
Hungary Miscellaneous Peace Material, SCPC
International Confederation for Disarmament and Peace Records, SCPC
International Fellowship of Reconciliation Records, SCPC
International Peace Bureau Records, Office, Geneva, Switzerland; SCPC

Ireland Miscellaneous Peace Material, SCPC
Israel War Resisters International Records, SCPC
Homer A. Jack Papers, SCPC
Japan Congress Against Atomic and Hydrogen Bombs Records, Office, Tokyo, Japan; SCPC
Japan Council Against Atomic and Hydrogen Bombs Records, SCPC
Kampagnen mod Atomvåben Records, SCPC
John F. Kennedy Papers, John F. Kennedy Library, Boston, Mass.
      National Security Files
      White House Central Files (Subject File and Name File)
Elsie Locke Papers, Locke Home, Christchurch, New Zealand
London Yearly Meeting Records, Library, Friends House, London, Britain
Edmondo Marcucci Papers, SCPC
John A. McCone Papers, Dwight D. Eisenhower Library, Abilene, Kans.
Pierre Mendès-France Papers, Institute Pierre Mendès-France, Ecole Polytechnique, Paris, France
Mouvement International de la Réconciliation Records, SCPC
Hermann J. Muller Papers, Lilly Library, Indiana University, Bloomington, Ind.
A. J. Muste Papers, SCPC
National Committee for a Sane Nuclear Policy Records, SCPC
National Mobilization Committee to End the War in Vietnam Records, SCPC
National Peace Council Records, SCPC
Nei til Atomvåpen Records, Office, Oslo, Norway
Non-Criminal Investigation Case Files, New York State Division of State Police Records, New York State Archives, Albany, N.Y.
Office of Science and Technology, Executive Office of the President Records, National Archives, Washington, D.C.
J. Robert Oppenheimer Papers, Library of Congress, Washington, D.C.
Linus and Ava Helen Pauling Papers, Kerr Library, Oregon State University, Corvallis, Ore.
Pax Christi International Records, Office, Antwerp, Belgium; SCPC
Peace Pledge Union Records, SCPC
Prime Minister's Records, Public Record Office, Kew, Britain
Publications Pacifistes et Internationales Parus Après 1940, Library, Peace Palace, The Hague, Netherlands
Pugwash Conferences Records, Office, London, Britain; SCPC
Isidor I. Rabi Papers, Library of Congress, Washington, D.C.
Eugene I. Rabinowitch Papers, Joseph Regenstein Library, University of Chicago, Chicago, Ill.; University Library, State University of New York, Albany, N.Y.
Radical Organizations Archive, Mills Memorial Library, McMaster University, Hamilton, Ontario, Canada
Michael Randle Papers, Randle Home, Bradford, Britain
Paul Robeson Papers, Schomburg Center for Research in Black Culture, New York Public Library, New York, N.Y.
Bertrand Russell Archives 1 and 2, Mills Memorial Library, McMaster University, Hamilton, Ontario, Canada
Bayard Rustin Papers, Library of Congress, Washington, D.C.
John Nevin Sayre Papers, SCPC
Arthur M. Schlesinger Jr. Papers, John F. Kennedy Library, Boston, Mass.
Theodore Sorensen Papers, John F. Kennedy Library, Boston, Mass.
Benjamin Spock Papers, George Arents Research Library, Syracuse University, Syracuse, N.Y.

Adlai E. Stevenson Papers, Seeley Mudd Library, Princeton University, Princeton, N.J.
Lewis L. Strauss Papers, Herbert Hoover Library, West Branch, Iowa
Student Peace Union Records, SCPC; State Historical Society of Wisconsin, Madison, Wisc.
Student Union for Peace Action Records, SCPC
Leo Szilard Papers, Central University Library, University of California, San Diego, Calif.
Norman M. Thomas Papers, New York Public Library, New York, N.Y. (microfilm)
André and Magda Trocmé Papers, SCPC
Union Pacifiste de France Records, SCPC
United States Information Agency Records, Washington National Records Center, Suitland, Md.
Voice of Women Records, SCPC
War Resisters' International Records, International Institute for Social History (International Instituut voor Sociale Geschiedenis), Amsterdam, Netherlands; SCPC
War Resisters League Records, SCPC
White House Office Records, Dwight D. Eisenhower Library, Abilene, Kans.
    Office of the Special Assistant for National Security Affairs
    Office of the Staff Secretary
Women Strike for Peace Records, SCPC; State Historical Society of Wisconsin, Madison, Wisc.
Women's International League for Peace and Freedom (International) Records, SCPC (microfilm)
Women's International League for Peace and Freedom (International Office) Records, Office, Geneva, Switzerland
Women's International League for Peace and Freedom (United States) Records, SCPC
World Peace Council Records, SCPC

Interviews

Personal Interviews
    Ruzanna Ilukhina, May 22, 1991
    Homer Jack, June 12, 1988
    Sheila Jones, July 10, 1990
    Sergei Kapitza, June 28, 1990
    Bruce Kent, July 10, 1990
    Betty Goetz Lall, December 5, 1989
    Ralph E. Lapp, June 28, 1987
    Pavel Litvinov, October 7, 1990
    Victor Malkov, December 4, 1994
    A. J. Muste, June 2, 1966
    James Peck, April 21, 1966
    Joseph Rotblat, July 12, 1990, July 11, 1994
    Dhirendra Sharma, October 11, 1995
    Ronald I. Spiers, October 28, 1992
    Norman M. Thomas, October 4, 1966
    Dorothy Thompson, November 1, 1989
    E. P. Thompson, November 1, 1989
    Dorothy Tristman, July 27, 1994
    Nigel Young, October 12, 1993

Oral History Interviews
  American Institute of Physics, Niels Bohr Library, New York, N.Y.
    Hans A. Bethe, October 27–28, 1966, May 8–9, 1972
  Imperial War Museum, London, Britain
    Pat Arrowsmith, ca. 1992
  John F. Kennedy Library, Boston, Mass.
    Chester Bowles, February 2, 1965
    William O. Douglas, November 9, 1967
    Adrian Fisher, May 13, 1964
    Mike Mansfield, June 23, 1964
    Benjamin H. Read, October 17, 1969
    Theodore Sorensen, April 15, 1964
  Colin Pritchard, Southampton, Britain
    Alec Douglas-Home, March 17, 1965

Peace Movement Periodicals

Alerte Atomique (Mouvement Contre L'Armement Atomique, Paris)
Alternatives Non Violentes (Mouvement pour une Alternative Non-Violente, Montrond, France)
Atombulletin (Schweizerische Bewegung gegen die atomare Aufrüstung, Zurich)
Atomic Scientists' Journal (Atomic Scientists' Association, London)
The Banner (Irish Campaign for Nuclear Disarmament, Dublin)
Bulletin (New Zealand Campaign for Nuclear Disarmament, Christchurch)
Bulletin (Student Peace Union, Chicago)
Bulletin of the Atomic Scientists (Independent, Chicago)
Canadian World Federalist (World Federalists of Canada, Ottawa)
Catholic Worker (Catholic Worker, New York City)
Disarmament Campaigns (International Peace Communication and Co-ordination Center, the Hague)
END Bulletin (European Nuclear Disarmament, London)
END Journal (European Nuclear Disarmament, London)
F.A.S. Newsletter (Federation of American Scientists, Washington, D.C.)
F.A.S. Public Interest Report (Federation of American Scientists, Washington, D.C.)
Federalist (United World Federalists, Washington, D.C.)
Fellowship (Fellowship of Reconciliation, Nyack, N.Y.)
Fredsbladet (Kristent Fredslag, Oslo)
The Friend (Independent, London)
Gensuikin News (Japan Congress Against Atomic and Hydrogen Bombs, Tokyo)
L'homme devant l'atome (Fédération française contre l'armement atomique, Paris)
Information Bulletin (Soviet Peace Committee, Moscow)
Information Bulletin (Yugoslav League for Peace, Independence, and Equality of Peoples, Belgrade)
International Bulletin (European Federation Against Nuclear Arms, London)
Liberation (Independent, New York City)
Mot svensk atombomb (Aktionsgruppen mot svensk atomvapen, Stockholm)
New Outlook (Independent, Tel Aviv)
No More Hiroshimas! (Japan Council Against Atomic and Hydrogen Bombs, Tokyo)
Our Generation (Independent, Montreal)

Our Generation Against Nuclear War (Combined Universities Campaign for Nuclear Disarmament, Montreal)
Pax (Irish Pacifist Movement, Dublin)
Pax et Libertas (Women's International League for Peace and Freedom, Geneva)
Peace Action (New South Wales Peace Committee, Sydney, Australia)
Peace Courier (World Peace Council, Helsinki)
Peace Information Bulletin (International Confederation for Disarmament and Peace, Geneva)
Peace Magazine (Canadian Disarmament Information Service, Toronto)
Peacemaker (Federal Pacifist Council, Melbourne)
Peace News (Peace Pledge Union, later Independent, London)
Sane World (National Committee for a Sane Nuclear Policy, New York City)
Sanity (Campaign for Nuclear Disarmament, London)
Sanity (Canadian Campaign for Nuclear Disarmament, Toronto)
Sarvodaya (Independent, Tanjore, India)
SOS (Independent, later Canadian Campaign for Nuclear Disarmament, Toronto)
Voorlichtingsblad (Anti-Atoombom-Actie, Haarlem, Netherlands)
War Resistance (War Resisters' International, Brussels)
War Resister (War Resisters' International, Enfield, Britain)
WIN (War Resisters League, New York City)
WRL News (War Resisters League, New York City)

Other Sources

Abrams, Irwin. "The Moscow World Youth Forum of 1961." *Quaker History* 84 (Fall 1995): 131–51.
Ackermann, E. E. "The Resistance to Atomic Rearmament in Switzerland." *Contemporary Issues* 10 (Aug.–Sept. 1960): 241–54.
Acland, Sir Richard. "No Defense Against Nuclear Attack," pp. 27–40 in Charles W. Lomas and Michael Taylor, eds., *The Rhetoric of the British Peace Movement*. New York: Random House, 1971.
Adams, Judith Porter. *Peacework: Oral Histories of Women Peace Activists*. Boston: Twayne, 1991.
Adamsky, Viktor. "Becoming a Citizen," pp. 21–43 in P. N. Lebedev Physics Institute, *Andrei Sakharov: Facets of a Life*. Gif-sur-Yvette: Editions Frontières, 1991.
Adamsky, Viktor, and Yuri Smirnov. "Moscow's Biggest Bomb: The 50-Megaton Test of October 1961." Cold War International History Project *Bulletin*, no. 4 (Fall 1994): 3, 19–21.
Adamthwaite, Anthony. "'Nations Shall Speak Peace Unto Nations': The BBC's Response to Peace and Defense Issues, 1945–1961," pp. 397–416 in Maurice Vaïsse, ed., *Le Pacifisme en Europe des années 1920 aux années 1950*. Brussels: Bruylant, 1993.
"Address of Pope Paul VI to the General Assembly of the United Nations." *Catholic Mind* 63 (Nov. 1965): 4–11.
Ahlmark, Per. *Den svenska atomvapendebatten*. Stockholm: Aldus/Bonniers, 1965.
Akaha, Tsuneo. "Japan's Three Nonnuclear Principles: A Coming Demise?" *Peace and Change* 11 (Spring 1985): 75–89.
"Albanian Government's Statement." *Peking Review* 6 (Aug. 23, 1963): 13–15.
Albinski, Henry S. *Politics and Foreign Policy in Australia: The Impact of Vietnam and Conscription*. Durham, N.C.: Duke University Press, 1970.
Allen, Bruce. *Germany East: Dissent and Opposition*. Montreal: Black Rose Books, 1989.

Allen, Steve. *Mark It and Strike It*. New York: Holt, Rinehart & Winston, 1960.

Alonso, Harriet Hyman. *Peace as a Women's Issue: A History of the U.S. Movement for World Peace and Women's Rights*. Syracuse: Syracuse University Press, 1993.

Altbach, Philip G. "The American Peace Movement, 1900–1962." Manuscript, 1963.

Altshuler, L. V. "Next to Sakharov," pp. 44–52 in P. N. Lebedev Physics Institute, *Andrei Sakharov: Facets of a Life*. Gif-sur-Yvette: Editions Frontières, 1991.

Ambrose, Stephen E. *Eisenhower*. 2 vols. New York: Simon & Schuster, 1983, 1984.

Amherd, Leander. "Die Friedensbewegung in der Schweiz (1945 bis 1980)." Lizentiatsarbeit, Historical Institute, University of Bern, 1984.

Anderson, Clinton P. *Outsider in the Senate*. New York: World Publishing, 1970.

Andersson, Jan, and Kent Lindkvist, "The Peace Movement in Sweden," pp. 5–32 in Werner Kaltefleiter and Robert L. Pfaltzgraff, eds., *The Peace Movements in Europe and the United States*. London: Croom Helm, 1985.

Andrén, Nils. *Power-Balance and Non-Alignment: A Perspective on Swedish Foreign Policy*. Stockholm: Almqvist & Wiksell, 1967.

"Another Conscience Speaks at Omaha." *Christian Century* 76 (July 29, 1959): 868–69.

Appleby, Charles A., Jr. "Eisenhower and Arms Control: A Balance of Risks." Paper presented at the Society for Historians of American Foreign Relations Conference, Annapolis, Md., June 26, 1987.

Aram, M. "Peace in Nagaland," pp. 208–19 in A. Paul Hare and Herbert H. Blumberg, eds., *Liberation without Violence*. London: Rex Collings, 1977.

Arbatov, Georgi. *The System: An Insider's Life in Soviet Politics*. New York: Random House, 1992.

Ardagh, John. *Germany and the Germans*. New York: Harper & Row, 1987.

Asada, Sadao. "Japanese Perceptions of the A-Bomb Decision, 1945–1980," pp. 199–219 in Joe C. Dixon, ed., *The American Military in the Far East*. Washington, D.C.: U.S. Government Printing Office, 1980.

"Atomprotestkampanjen," pp. 229–33 in Hans Fredrik Dahl et al., eds., *Pax Leksikon*. Oslo: Pax forlag, 1978.

Avakumovic, Ivan. *The Communist Party in Canada: A History*. Toronto: McClelland & Stewart, 1975.

Bacon, Margaret Hope. *One Woman's Passion for Peace and Freedom: The Life of Mildred Scott Olmsted*. Syracuse: Syracuse University Press, 1993.

Balducci, Ernesto. "Peace Movement in Italy," pp. 214–18 in Ervin Laszlo and Jong Youl Yoo, eds., *World Encyclopedia of Peace*, vol. 2. Oxford: Pergamon Press, 1986.

Ball, Howard. *Justice Downwind: America's Atomic Testing Program in the 1950s*. New York: Oxford University Press, 1986.

Bamba, Nobuya. "Peace Movement at a Standstill: Roots of the Crisis." *Bulletin of Peace Proposals* 13 (1982): 39–42.

Bamba, Nobuya, and John F. Howes, "Conclusion: Japanese Society and the Pacifist," pp. 251–71 in Nobuya Bamba and John F. Howes, eds., *Pacifism in Japan: The Christian and Socialist Tradition*. Vancouver: University of British Columbia Press, 1978.

Barkan, Joanne. *Visions of Emancipation: The Italian Workers Movement Since 1945*. New York: Praeger, 1984.

Barker, Rodney. *The Hiroshima Maidens: A Story of Courage, Compassion, and Survival*. New York: Viking, 1985.

Barton, John H., and Lawrence D. Weiler. eds. *International Arms Control: Issues and Agreements*. Stanford: Stanford University Press, 1976.

Baum, Keith W. "Two's Company, Three's a Crowd: The Eisenhower Administration, France, and Nuclear Weapons." *Presidential Studies Quarterly* 20 (Spring 1990): 315–28.

Beker, Avi. *Disarmament Without Order: The Politics of Disarmament at the United Nations.* Westport, Conn.: Greenwood Press, 1985.

Berding, Andrew H. *Dulles on Diplomacy.* Princeton: D. Van Nostrand, 1965.

Bernal, J. D. *World Without War.* London: Routledge & Kegan Paul, 1958.

Bernstein, Barton J. "Introduction," pp. xvii–lxxiv in Helen Hawkins, G. Allen Greb, and Gertrud Weiss Szilard, eds., *Toward a Livable World: Leo Szilard and the Crusade for Nuclear Arms Control.* Cambridge, Mass.: MIT Press, 1987.

Bess, Michael. *Realism, Utopia, and the Mushroom Cloud: Four Activist Intellectuals and Their Strategies for Peace, 1945–1989.* Chicago: University of Chicago Press, 1993.

Bevan, Aneurin. "Naked to the Conference Table," pp. 41–53 in Charles W. Lomas and Michael Taylor, eds., *The Rhetoric of the British Peace Movement.* New York: Random House, 1971.

Bigelow, Albert. *The Voyage of the Golden Rule: An Experiment with Truth.* Garden City, N.Y.: Doubleday, 1959.

Bindschedler, Rudolf L. "Switzerland," pp. 221–26 in Jozef Goldblat, ed., *Non-Proliferation: The Why and the Wherefore.* London: Taylor & Francis, 1985.

Bing, Anthony G. *Israeli Pacifist: The Life of Joseph Abileah.* Syracuse: Syracuse University Press, 1990.

Biquard, Pierre. *Frédéric Joliot-Curie.* New York: Paul S. Eriksson, 1966.

Birnbaum, Karl E. "Sweden's Nuclear Policy." *International Journal* 20 (Summer 1965): 297–311.

———. "The Swedish Experience," pp. 68–75 in Alastair Buchan, ed., *A World of Nuclear Powers?* Englewood Cliffs, N.J.: Prentice-Hall, 1966.

Bjol, Erling. *Hvem bestemmer: Studier i den udenrigspolitiske beslutningsproces.* Copenhagen: Juris og Okonomforbundets Forlag, 1983.

Blackmer, Donald L. M. "Continuity and Change in Postwar Italian Communism," pp. 21–68 in Donald L. M. Blackmer and Sidney Tarrow, eds., *Communism in Italy and France.* Princeton: Princeton University Press, 1975.

Blamires, Edgar Percy. *War Tests the Church.* London: Fellowship of Reconciliation, 1958.

Blechman, Barry M., and Cathleen S. Fisher. *The Silent Partner: West Germany and Arms Control.* Cambridge, Mass.: Ballinger, 1988.

Bloom, Lynn Z. *Doctor Spock: Biography of a Conservative Radical.* Indianapolis: Bobbs-Merrill, 1972.

Bloomfield, Lincoln, Walter D. Clemens Jr., and Franklyn Griffiths. *Khrushchev and the Arms Race: Soviet Interests in Arms Control and Disarmament, 1954–1964.* Cambridge, Mass.: MIT Press, 1966.

Blumberg, Stanley A., and Gwinn Owens. *Energy and Conflict: The Life and Times of Edward Teller.* New York: G. P. Putnam's Sons, 1976.

Boag, J. W., P. E. Rubinin, and D. Shoenberg, eds. *Kapitza in Cambridge and Moscow: Life and Letters of a Russian Physicist.* Amsterdam: North-Holland, 1990.

Boel, Erik. *Socialdemokratiets atomvåbenpolitik: Denmarks atomvåbenfri status.* Aarhus: Aarhus Universitet, 1986.

Booth, Arthur. *The International Peace Bureau.* Geneva: International Peace Bureau, 1977.

Born, Max, ed. *The Born-Einstein Letters.* New York: Macmillan, 1971.

Boserup, Anders, and Claus Iverson. "Demonstrations as a Source of Change: A Study of British and Danish Easter Marchers." *Journal of Peace Research* 3: 4 (1966): 328–47.

Boulding, Kenneth E. "The Peace Research Movement in the U.S.," pp. 40–51 in Ted Dunn, ed., *Alternatives to War and Violence.* London: James Clarke, 1963.

Bourdet, Claude. "Désarmement nucléaire en France." Manuscript, 1990, author's possession.

————. "The Rebirth of a Peace Movement," pp. 190–201 in Jolyon Howorth and Patricia Chilton, eds., *Defense and Dissent in Contemporary France*. London: Croom Helm, 1984.

————. "The Way to European Independence." *New Reasoner*, no. 5 (Summer 1958), pp. 12–24.

Boutwell, Jeffrey. *The German Nuclear Dilemma*. Ithaca: Cornell University Press, 1990.

————. "Politics and the Peace Movement in West Germany." *International Security* 7 (Spring 1983): 72–92.

Bowles, Chester. *Promises to Keep: My Years in Public Life, 1941–1969*. New York: Harper & Row, 1971.

Boyer, Paul. *By the Bomb's Early Light*. New York: Pantheon Books, 1985.

————. "From Activism to Apathy: The American People and Nuclear Weapons, 1963–1980." *Journal of American History* 70 (Mar. 1984): 821–44.

Boyle, Peter G., ed. *The Churchill-Eisenhower Correspondence, 1953–1955*. Chapel Hill: University of North Carolina Press, 1990.

Brabazon, James. *Albert Schweitzer: A Biography*. New York: G. P. Putnam's Sons, 1975.

Branch, Taylor. *Parting the Waters: America in the King Years, 1954–63*. New York: Simon & Schuster, 1989.

Brandon, Ruth. *The Burning Question: The Anti-Nuclear Movement Since 1945*. London: Heinemann, 1987.

Brandt, Willy. *People and Politics: The Years 1960–1975*. Boston: Little, Brown, 1978.

Brassel, Ruedi, and Jakob Tanner. "Zur Geschichte der Friedensbewegung in der Schweiz," pp. 17–90 in Thomas Bein, Ruedi Brassel, and Martin Leuenberger, eds., *Handbuch Frieden Schweiz*. Basel: Z-Verlag, 1986.

Brittain, Vera. *The Rebel Passion: A Short History of Some Pioneer Peace-makers*. London: George Allen & Unwin, 1964.

Brock, Hugh. *The Century of Total War*. London: Peace News, n.d.

Brock, Peter. *Twentieth-Century Pacifism*. New York: Van Nostrand Reinhold, 1970.

Bundy, McGeorge. *Danger and Survival*. New York: Random House, 1988.

Burlatsky, Fedor. *Khrushchev and the First Russian Spring: The Era of Khrushchev Through the Eyes of His Advisor*. New York: Charles Scribner's Sons, 1991.

Bussey, Gertrude, and Margaret Tims. *Women's International League for Peace and Freedom, 1915–1965: A Record of Fifty Years' Work*. London: George Allen & Unwin, 1965.

Caldwell, Bill S., III. "The French Socialists' Attitudes Toward the Use of Nuclear Weapons, 1945–1978." Ph.D. diss., University of Georgia, 1980.

Camara, Helder. *Revolution through Peace*. New York: Harper Colophon, 1972.

Camus, Albert. *Actuelles, III: Chroniques algériennes, 1939–1958*. Paris: Gallimard, 1958.

Capitini, Aldo. *Le tecniche della nonviolenza*. Milan: Feltrinelli, 1968.

Carlson, Elof Axel. *Genes, Radiation, and Society: The Life and Work of H. J. Muller*. Ithaca: Cornell University Press, 1981.

Carter, April. "Direct Action Against Nuclear War," pp. 49–52 in John Minnion and Philip Bolsover, eds., *The CND Story*. London: Allison & Busby, 1983.

————. *Peace Movements: International Protest and World Politics Since 1945*. London: Longman, 1992.

————. "The Sahara Protest Team," pp. 126–56 in A. Paul Hare and Herbert H. Blumberg, eds., *Liberation without Violence*. London: Rex Collings, 1977.

Casgrain, Thérèse F. *A Woman in a Man's World*. Toronto: McClelland & Stewart, 1972.

Ceadel, Martin. "Britain's Nuclear Disarmers," pp. 218–44 in Walter Laqueur and Robert Hunter, eds., *European Peace Movements and the Future of the Western Alliance*. New Brunswick, N.J.: Transaction Books, 1985.

Chang, Gordon R. *Friends and Enemies: The United States, China, and the Soviet Union, 1948–1972*. Stanford: Stanford University Press, 1990.

Chatfield, Charles. *The American Peace Movement: Ideals and Activism*. New York: Twayne Publishers, 1992.

"China Backs Soviet Decision on Nuclear Tests." *Peking Review* 5 (Aug. 3, 1962): 14.

"China Supports Soviet Decision to Conduct Nuclear Tests." *Peking Review* 4 (Sept. 8, 1961): 6.

CIA Research Reports: Europe, 1946–1976. Frederick, Md.: University Publications of America, 1982. Microfilm.

Cioc, Mark. *Pax Atomica: The Nuclear Defense Debate in West Germany During the Adenauer Era*. New York: Columbia University Press, 1988.

Clark, Grenville, and Louis B. Sohn. *World Peace Through World Law*. Cambridge, Mass.: Harvard University Press, 1958.

Clark, Howard. "Nonviolent Resistance and Social Defense," pp. 49–69 in Gail Chester and Andrew Rigby, eds., *Articles of Peace*. Bridport, Dorset: Prism Press, 1986.

Clark, Ronald W. *The Life of Bertrand Russell*. London: Jonathan Cape and Weidenfeld & Nicolson, 1975.

Clemens, Walter D., Jr. "The Sino-Soviet Dispute: Dogma and Dialectics on Disarmament." *International Affairs* 41 (Apr. 1965): 204–22.

Clements, Kevin. *Back from the Brink: The Creation of a Nuclear-Free New Zealand*. Wellington: Allen & Unwin / Port Nicholson Press, 1988.

Cockburn, Stewart, and David Ellyard. *Oliphant*. Adelaide: Axiom Books, 1981.

Cohen, Warren I. *Dean Rusk*. Totowa, N.J.: Cooper Square Publishers, 1980.

Collins, L. John. *Faith Under Fire*. London: Leslie Frewin Publishers, 1966.

"A Comment on the Soviet Government's Statement of August 3" (Aug. 15, 1963), pp. 9–32 in *People of the World, Unite, For the Complete, Thorough, Total and Resolute Prohibition and Destruction of Nuclear Weapons*. Peking: Foreign Languages Press, 1963.

"A Comment on the Soviet Government's Statement of August 21" (Sept. 1, 1963), pp. 33–61 in *People of the World, Unite, For the Complete, Thorough, Total and Resolute Prohibition and Destruction of Nuclear Weapons*. Peking: Foreign Languages Press, 1963.

Committee for the Compilation of Materials on Damage Caused by the Atomic Bombs in Hiroshima and Nagasaki. *Hiroshima and Nagasaki: The Physical, Medical, and Social Effects of the Atomic Bombings*. New York: Basic Books, 1981.

Congressional Record.

Conroy, F. Hilary. "The Conference on Peace Research in History: A Memoir." *Journal of Peace Research* 3: 4 (1969): 385–88.

Cook, Blanche Wiesen. *The Declassified Eisenhower: A Divided Legacy of Peace and Political Warfare*. Garden City, N.Y.: Doubleday, 1981.

Cousins, Norman. "An Address in Moscow." *Saturday Review* 42 (July 25, 1959): 10–12, 27–29.

———. *Albert Schweitzer's Mission: Healing and Peace*. New York: W. W. Norton, 1985.

———. *Dr. Schweitzer of Lambaréné*. New York: Harper & Brothers, 1960.

———. "Earle Reynolds and His Phoenix." *Saturday Review* 41 (Oct. 11, 1958): 26–27.

———. *The Improbable Triumvirate: John F. Kennedy, Pope John, Nikita Khrushchev*. New York: W. W. Norton, 1972.

———. "The Maidens are Coming." *Saturday Review* 38 (Apr. 9, 1955): 24–25.

———. "The Men of the Golden Rule." *Saturday Review* 41 (May 17, 1958): 24.

———. *Present Tense: An American Editor's Odyssey*. New York: McGraw-Hill, 1967.

Cox, John. *Overkill: The Story of Modern Weapons*. Harmondsworth, Eng.: Penguin Books, 1981.

Crabb, Cecil V., Jr. *The Elephants and the Grass: A Study of Nonalignment.* New York: Frederick A. Praeger, 1965.

Crane, Ernest. *I Can Do No Other: A Biography of Ormond Burton.* Auckland: Hodder & Stoughton, 1986.

Dallin, Alexander, et al. *The Soviet Union and Disarmament.* New York: Frederick A. Praeger, 1964.

Davis, Kenneth S. *The Politics of Honor: A Biography of Adlai E. Stevenson.* New York: G. P. Putnam's Sons, 1967.

Day, Dorothy. *Loaves and Fishes.* New York: Harper & Row, 1963.

Dean, Arthur H. *Test Ban and Disarmament: The Path of Negotiation.* New York: Harper & Row, 1966.

De Andreis, Marco. "The Nuclear Debate in Italy." *Survival* 28 (May–June 1986): 195–207.

DeBenedetti, Charles. "The Peace Opposition in Cold War America, 1955–1965." Paper presented at the Organization of American Historians convention, Detroit, Apr. 3, 1981.

————. *The Peace Reform in American History.* Bloomington: Indiana University Press, 1980.

DeBenedetti, Charles, and Charles Chatfield. *An American Ordeal: The Antiwar Movement of the Vietnam Era.* Syracuse: Syracuse University Press, 1990.

Defrasne, Jean. *Le Pacifisme.* Paris: Presses Universitaires de France, 1983.

de Gaulle, Charles. *Memoirs of Hope: Renewal and Endeavor.* New York: Simon & Schuster, 1971.

De Grand, Alexander. *The Italian Left in the Twentieth Century.* Bloomington: Indiana University Press, 1989.

de Madariaga, Salvador. "Disarmament? The Problem Lies Deeper." *New York Times Magazine* (Oct. 11, 1959): 17, 72–75.

Deming, Barbara. "The Peacemakers." *Nation* 191 (Dec. 17, 1960): 471–75.

den Oudsten, Eymert. "Database on International Security," 1988. Manuscript, author's possession.

Desai, Narayan. "Intervention in Riots in India," pp. 74–91 in A. Paul Hare and Herbert H. Blumberg, eds., *Liberation without Violence.* London: Rex Collings, 1977.

Deutsch, Karl W., and Lewis J. Edinger. *Germany Rejoins the Powers: Mass Opinion, Interest Groups, and Elites in Contemporary German Foreign Policy.* Stanford: Stanford University Press, 1959.

Diefenbaker, John G. *One Canada: Memoirs of the Right Honourable John G. Diefenbaker: Vol. III, The Tumultuous Years.* Toronto: Macmillan, 1977.

Dinerstein, Herbert S. *War and the Soviet Union.* New York: Frederick A. Praeger, 1959.

Dion, Susan. "The FBI Surveillance of the Women's International League for Peace and Freedom, 1945–1963." *Journal for Peace and Justice Studies* 3: 1 (1991): 1–21.

Divine, Robert A. *Blowing on the Wind: The Nuclear Test Ban Debate, 1954–1960.* New York: Oxford University Press, 1978.

Dobrynin, Anatoly. *In Confidence.* New York: Times Books, 1995.

Documents on American Foreign Relations: 1961. New York: Harper & Brothers, 1962.

"Down With U.S. Nuclear War Plots, Destroy All Nuclear Arms." *Peking Review* 6 (Aug. 9, 1963): 17–18.

"Down With U.S. Nuclear War Threats!" *Peking Review* 5 (Aug. 10, 1962): 16–17.

Drifte, Reinhard. "China," pp. 45–55 in Jozef Goldblat, ed., *Non-Proliferation: The Why and the Wherefore.* London: Taylor & Francis, 1985.

Driver, Christopher. *The Disarmers: A Study in Protest.* London: Hodder & Stoughton, 1964.

Duff, Peggy. *Left, Left, Left.* London: Allison & Busby, 1971.

Dülffer, Jost. "The Movement Against Rearmament 1951–55 and the Movement Against Nuclear Armament 1957–59 in the Federal Republic: A Comparison," pp. 417–34 in Maurice Vaïsse, ed., *Le Pacifisme en Europe des années 1920 aux années 1950*. Brussels: Bruylant, 1993.

Dulles, Allen. *The Craft of Intelligence*. New York: Harper & Row, 1963.

Dulles, John Foster. "The Evolution of Foreign Policy." *Department of State Bulletin* 30 (Jan. 25, 1954): 107–10.

Dyson, Freeman. *Disturbing the Universe*. New York: Harper & Row, 1979.

Edwards, Gordon. "Canada's Nuclear Industry and the Myth of the Peaceful Atom," pp. 122–70 in Ernie Regehr and Simon Rosenblum, eds., *Canada and the Nuclear Arms Race*. Toronto: James Lorimer, 1983.

Eglin, Josephine. "Women and Peace: From the Suffragists to the Greenham Women," pp. 221–59 in Richard Taylor and Nigel Young, eds., *Campaigns for Peace: British Peace Movements in the Twentieth Century*. Manchester: Manchester University Press, 1987.

Einhorn, Eric S. *National Security and Domestic Politics in Post-War Denmark: Some Principal Issues, 1945–1961*. Odense: Odense University Press, 1975.

Eisenhower, Dwight D. *Mandate for Change, 1953–1956*. Garden City, N.Y.: Doubleday, 1963.

———. *Waging Peace, 1956–1961*. Garden City, N.Y.: Doubleday, 1965.

Endicott, Stephen. *James G. Endicott: Rebel Out of China*. Toronto: University of Toronto Press, 1980.

Epstein, William. "Canada," pp. 171–84 in Jozef Goldblat, ed., *Non-Proliferation: The Why and the Wherefore*. London: Taylor & Francis, 1985.

Erlander, Tage. *Tage Erlander, 1955–1960*. Stockholm: Tidens Förlag, 1976.

Evan, William M. "An International Public Opinion Poll on Disarmament and 'Inspection by the People': A Study of Attitudes toward Supranationalism," pp. 231–50 in Seymour Melman, ed., *Inspection for Disarmament*. New York: Columbia University Press, 1958.

Evangelista, Matthew. "Soviet Scientists and Nuclear Testing, 1954–1963." Paper presented at the Conference on New Evidence on Cold War History, Moscow, Russia, Jan. 1993.

———. "Soviet Scientists as Arms Control Advisors: The Case of ABM." Paper presented at the Fourth World Congress for Soviet and East European Studies, Harrogate, Britain, July 21–26, 1990.

Everts, Philip P. "Continuity and Change in Public Attitudes on Questions of Security." Paper presented at the Joint Meetings of the World Association for Public Opinion Research and the American Association of Public Opinion Research, Toronto, May 20–23, 1988.

———. "The Peace Movement and Public Opinion: Prospects for the Nineties." Paper presented at the Convention of the International Studies Association, London, Mar. 28–Apr. 1, 1989.

———. "Reviving Unilateralism: Report on a Campaign for Nuclear Disarmament in the Netherlands." *Bulletin of Peace Proposals* 11: 1 (1980): 40–56.

Everts, Philip P., and G. Walraven. *Vredesbeweging*. Utrecht: Spectrum, 1984.

"Fallout Shelters." *Life* 51 (Sept. 15, 1961): 95–108.

Fehrm, Martin. "Sweden," pp. 213–20 in Jozef Goldblat, ed., *Non-Proliferation: The Why and the Wherefore*. London: Taylor & Francis, 1985.

Feld, Bernard. "Artsimovich and the Pugwash Movement," pp. 84–86 in *Reminiscences about Academician Lev Artsimovich*. Moscow: Nauka, 1985.

Fellner, Fritz. "Hans Thirring," pp. 386–87 in Helmut Donat and Karl Holl, eds., *Die Friedensbewegung: Organisierter Pazifismus in Deutschland, Österreich und in der Schweiz*. Düsseldorf: ECON Taschenbuch Verlag, 1983.

Fellowship of Reconciliation. *How to Hide from an H-Bomb*. New York: Fellowship of Reconciliation, 1956.

―――. *A Sane Man's Guide to Civil Defense*. New York: Fellowship of Reconciliation, 1955.

Ferm, Ragnild. "Nuclear Explosions, 1945–91," pp. 117–19 in *World Armaments and Disarmament: SIPRI Yearbook 1992*. Oxford: Oxford University Press, 1992.

Ferrell, Robert H., ed. *The Diary of James C. Haggerty: Eisenhower in Mid-Course, 1954–1955*. Bloomington: Indiana University Press, 1983.

Flannery, Harry W., ed. *Pattern for Peace: Catholic Statements on International Order*. Westminster, Md.: Newman Press, 1962.

Flapan, Simha. "Israel's Attitude Towards the NPT," pp. 271–90 in Bhupendra Jasani, ed., *Nuclear Proliferation Problems*. Cambridge, Mass.: MIT Press, 1974.

Fogelström, Per Anders. *Kampen för fred*. Stockholm: Bonniers, 1971.

Fogelström, Per Anders, and Roland Morell. *I stället för atombomb*. Stockholm: Bonniers, 1958.

"For the Total Banning and Destruction of Nuclear Weapons." *Peking Review* 6 (Aug. 9, 1963): 19–20.

Forrester, J. P. *Fifteen Years of Peace Fronts*. Sydney: McHugh Printery, 1964.

Foster, Catherine. *Women for All Seasons: The Story of the Women's International League for Peace and Freedom*. Athens: University of Georgia Press, 1989.

Frangos, George, and Peter Schwab, eds. *Greece Under the Junta*. New York: Facts on File, 1973.

Free, Lloyd A. *Six Allies and a Neutral*. Glencoe, Ill.: Free Press, 1958.

Friedberg, Maurice. *A Decade of Euphoria: Western Literature in Post-Stalin Russia, 1954–1964*. Bloomington: Indiana University Press, 1977.

Friedman, Maurice. *Martin Buber's Life and Work: The Later Years, 1945–1965*. New York: E. P. Dutton, 1983.

Gaddis, John Lewis. *Strategies of Containment: A Critical Appraisal of Postwar American National Security Policy*. New York: Oxford University Press, 1982.

Gallagher, Carole. *American Ground Zero: The Secret Nuclear War*. Cambridge, Mass.: MIT Press, 1993.

Gallup, George H., ed. *The Gallup International Public Opinion Polls: France 1939, 1944–1975*. New York: Random House, 1976.

―――. *The Gallup International Public Opinion Polls: Great Britain 1937–1975*. New York: Random House, 1976.

―――. *The Gallup Poll: Public Opinion, 1935–1971*. 3 vols. New York: Random House, 1972.

Galtung, Johan. "Foreign Policy Opinion as a Function of Social Position." *Journal of Peace Research* 1: 3–4 (1964): 206–31.

Garrison, Dee. "'Our Skirts Gave Them Courage': The Civil Defense Protest Movement in New York City, 1955–1961," pp. 201–26 in Joannne Meyerowitz, ed., *Not June Cleaver: Women and Gender in Postwar America, 1945–1960*. Philadelphia: Temple University Press, 1994.

Gervis, Stephanie. "France's Ban-the-Bombers." *Nation* 197 (Aug. 24, 1963): 91–93.

Ghent, Jocelyn Maynard. "Canadian-American Relations and the Nuclear Weapons Controversy, 1958–1963." Ph.D. diss., University of Illinois, Urbana-Champaign, 1976.

―――. "Did He Fall or Was He Pushed? The Kennedy Administration and the Collapse of the Diefenbaker Government." *International History Review* 1 (Apr. 1979): 246–70.

Giangrande, Carole. *The Nuclear North: The People, the Regions, and the Arms Race*. Toronto: Anansi, 1983.

Gilbert, Alan D., and Ann-Mari Jordan. "Traditions of Dissent," pp. 338–65 in M. McKernan and M. Browne, eds., *Australia: Two Centuries of War and Peace*. Canberra: Australian War Memorial and Allen & Unwin, 1988.

Gilpin, Robert. *American Scientists and Nuclear Weapons Policy*. Princeton: Princeton University Press, 1962.

Girard, Charlotte S. M. *Canada in World Affairs, 1963–1965*. Toronto: Canadian Institute of International Affairs, n.d.

Gitlin, Todd. *The Sixties: Years of Hope, Days of Rage*. New York: Bantam, 1987.

Glazer, Nathan. "The Peace Movement in America—1961." *Commentary* 31 (Apr. 1961): 288–96.

Goldschmidt, Bertrand. *The Atomic Adventure*. Oxford: Pergamon Press, 1964.

Goldsmith, Maurice. *Frédéric Joliot-Curie*. London: Lawrence & Wishart, 1976.

Goodwin, Peter. "Low Conspiracy? Government Interference in the BBC." Manuscript, author's possession.

Gordon, Richard, and Warren Osmond. "An Overview of the Australian New Left," pp. 3–39 in Richard Gordon, ed., *The Australian New Left: Critical Essays and Strategy*. Melbourne: William Heinemann, 1970.

Gordon, Walter. "The Liberal Leadership and Nuclear Weapons," pp. 199–203 in Ernie Regehr and Simon Rosenblum, eds., *Canada and the Nuclear Arms Race*. Toronto: James Lorimer, 1983.

Gottlieb, Sanford. "National Committee for a SANE Nuclear Policy." *New University Thought* 2 (Spring 1962): 155–57.

Graham, Loren R. *Science and Philosophy in the Soviet Union*. New York: Alfred A. Knopf, 1972.

———. *Science in Russia and the Soviet Union: A Short History*. Cambridge: Cambridge University Press, 1993.

Greek Committee for International Detente and Peace. *32 Years of Struggle*. Athens: Greek Committee for International Detente and Peace, 1987.

Grepstad, Jon. "Norway and the Struggle for Nuclear Disarmament." Paper presented at the 1981 World Conference Against Atomic and Hydrogen Bombs, Tokyo, Hiroshima, and Nagasaki, Aug. 3–9, 1981.

Grodzins, Morton, and Eugene Rabinowitch, eds. *The Atomic Age: Scientists in World Affairs*. New York: Basic Books, 1963.

Groom, A. J. R. *British Thinking About Nuclear Weapons*. London: Frances Pinter, 1974.

Grossi, Verdiana. "From Contempt to Credibility: The Peace Movement in Switzerland, 1945–1992." Paper presented at the International Peace Research Association convention, Malta, Nov. 2, 1994.

Gupta, Sisir. "The Indian Dilemma," pp. 55–67 in Alastair Buchan, ed., *A World of Nuclear Powers?* Englewood Cliffs, N.J.: Prentice-Hall, 1966.

Hacker, Barton C. *Elements of Controversy: The Atomic Energy Commission and Radiation Safety in Nuclear Weapons Testing, 1947–1974*. Berkeley: University of California Press, 1994.

Hagar, Thomas. *Force of Nature: The Life of Linus Pauling*. New York: Simon & Schuster, 1995.

Hahn, Otto. *My Life: The Autobiography of a Scientist*. New York: Herder & Herder, 1970.

Hall, B. Welling. "The Church and the Independent Peace Movement in Eastern Europe." *Journal of Peace Research* 23 (June 1986): 193–208.

Halperin, Morton H. "Chinese Attitudes toward the Use and Control of Nuclear Weapons," pp. 135–57 in Tang Tsou, ed., *China's Policies in Asia and America's Alternatives*. Chicago: University of Chicago Press, 1968.

Halperin, Morton H., et al. *The Lawless State: The Crimes of the U.S. Intelligence Agencies.* New York: Penguin Books, 1976.

Hamilton, Andrew. "M.I.T.: March 4 Revisited Amid Political Turmoil." *Science* 167 (Mar. 13, 1970): 1475–76.

Hanson, Eric O. *The Catholic Church in World Politics.* Princeton: Princeton University Press, 1987.

Hawkins, Helen S., G. Allen Greb, and Gertrud Weiss Szilard, eds. *Toward a Livable World: Leo Szilard and the Crusade for Nuclear Arms Control.* Cambridge, Mass.: MIT Press, 1987.

Healey, Denis. *The Time of My Life.* London: Michael Joseph, 1989.

Heiniger, Markus. "Die schweizerische Antiatombewegung, 1958–1963: Eine Analyse der politischen Kultur." Lizentiatsarbeit, Historical Seminar, University of Zurich, 1980.

Heisenberg, Elisabeth. *Inner Exile.* Boston: Birkhäuser, 1984.

Hentoff, Nat. *Peace Agitator: The Story of A. J. Muste.* New York: Macmillan, 1963.

Hersey, John. *Hiroshima.* New York: Vintage Books, 1989.

Hewlett, Richard G., and Jack M. Holl. *Atoms for Peace and War: Eisenhower and the Atomic Energy Commission.* Berkeley: University of California Press, 1989.

Hiebert, Erwin N. *The Impact of Atomic Energy.* Newton, Kans.: Faith and Life Press, 1961.

Hill, Albert S. "André Trocmé," pp. 959–61 in Harold Josephson, ed., *Biographical Dictionary of Modern Peace Leaders.* Westport, Conn.: Greenwood Press, 1985.

Hinton, James. *Protests and Visions: Peace Politics in Twentieth-Century Britain.* London: Hutchinson Radius, 1989.

"A History of the Peace Movement." *Labour Focus on Eastern Europe* 8: 1 (1985): 32–33.

Hodes, Aubrey. *Martin Buber: An Intimate Portrait.* New York: Viking Press, 1971.

Holloway, David. "The Scientist and the Tyrant." *New York Review of Books* 37 (Mar. 1, 1990): 23–25.

———. *The Soviet Union and the Arms Race.* New Haven: Yale University Press, 1983.

———. *Stalin and the Bomb: The Soviet Union and Atomic Energy, 1939–1956.* New Haven: Yale University Press, 1994.

Hook, Glenn D. "The Ban the Bomb Movement in Japan: Whither Alternative Security?" *Social Alternatives* 3 (Mar. 1983): 35–39.

Hope, Marjorie, and James Young. *The Struggle for Humanity: Agents of Nonviolent Change in a Violent World.* Maryknoll, N.Y.: Orbis Books, 1977.

Horne, Alistair. *Macmillan, 1957–1986.* London: Macmillan, 1989.

"How Sane the SANE?" *Time* 71 (Apr. 21, 1958): 13–14.

Howorth, Jolyon. *France: The Politics of Peace.* London: Merlin Press, 1984.

Hughes, Emmet J. *The Ordeal of Power: A Political Memoir of the Eisenhower Years.* New York: Atheneum, 1963.

Hume, John C., Jr. "Chakravati Rajagopalachari," pp. 786–89 in Harold Josephson, ed., *Biographical Dictionary of Modern Peace Leaders.* Westport, Conn.: Greenwood Press, 1985.

Humphrey, Hubert H. *The Education of a Public Man: My Life and Politics.* Garden City, N.Y.: Doubleday, 1976.

Hunnius, F. C. "Will Canada Lead?" *New University Thought* 2 (Spring 1962): 111–14.

Iatrides, John O. "American Attitudes Toward the Political System of Postwar Greece," pp. 49–73 in Theodore A. Couloumbis and John O. Iatrides, eds., *Greek-American Relations: A Critical Review.* New York: Pella, 1980.

Ilukhina, Ruzanna. "The Fate of Pacifism in Russia." Manuscript, 1991, author's possession.

Ilukhina, Ruzanna, and Tatiana Pavlova. "Totalitarianism and Free Thinking: The Role of Independent Peace and Pacifist Ideas in the USSR in the Ending of the Cold War." Paper presented at the International Congress of Historical Sciences, Montreal, Sept. 1, 1995.

"Indian Group Calls for Cessation of Nuclear Testing in Atmosphere." *Department of State Bulletin* 47 (Oct. 22, 1962): 626.

Ingram, Kenneth. *Fifty Years of the National Peace Council, 1908–1958.* London: National Peace Council, 1958.

Ishida, Takeshi. "Beyond the Traditional Concepts of Peace in Different Cultures." *Journal of Peace Research* 6 (1969): 133–45.

Isserman, Maurice. *If I Had a Hammer: The Death of the Old Left and the Birth of the New Left.* New York: Basic Books, 1987.

"It's Time for a Broad U.S. Peace Movement." *National Guardian* 16 (Jan. 9, 1964): 1–2.

Jack, Homer A. "Disarmament Talk in Accra." *Christian Century* 79 (Aug. 1, 1962): 936–37.

———. *Nuclear Politics After Hiroshima/Nagasaki: Unitarian Universalist and Other Responses.* Swarthmore: 1987 Minns Lectures, 1987.

———. "'Peace' Talk in Moscow." *Christian Century* 79 (Aug. 8, 1962): 964–65.

———. "What Happened at Belgrade." *Christian Century* 78 (Sept. 27, 1961): 1141–43.

———, ed. *On Nuclear War and Peace.* Elgin, Ill.: Brethren Press, 1988.

Jacobson, Harold K., and Eric Stein. *Diplomats, Scientists, and Politicians: The United States and the Nuclear Test Ban Negotiations.* Ann Arbor: University of Michigan Press, 1966.

Jain, Girilal. "India," pp. 89–99 in Jozef Goldblat, ed., *Non-Proliferation: The Why and the Wherefore.* London: Taylor & Francis, 1985.

Japan Council against A and H Bombs. *Documentary Photographs, 1945–1985: For a World Free of Nuclear Weapons.* Tokyo: Japan Council against A and H Bombs, 1986.

Jenkins, Robin. "Who Are These Marchers?" *Journal of Peace Research* 4: 1 (1967): 46–60.

John XXIII. *Pacem in Terris.* Glen Rock, N.J.: Paulist Press, 1963.

Johnson, Arnold. "The American Peace Movement." *Political Affairs* 42 (Mar. 1963): 1–14.

Johnson, Hewlett. *Searching for Light: An Autobiography.* London: Michael Joseph, 1968.

Johnson, Lyndon Baines. *The Vantage Point: Perspectives on the Presidency, 1963–1969.* New York: Holt, Rinehart & Winston, 1971.

Johnson, Walter, ed. *The Papers of Adlai E. Stevenson.* Boston: Little, Brown, 1976.

Joliot-Curie, Frédéric. "The World-wide Movement against the Atomic Peril." *Scientific World* 2: 4 (1958): 36–39.

Jones, Mervyn. "Aldermaston 1958," pp. 42–45 in John Minnion and Philip Bolsover, eds., *The CND Story.* London: Allison & Busby, 1983.

Jones, Rodney W. "India," pp. 101–23 in Jozef Goldblat, ed., *Non-Proliferation: The Why and the Wherefore.* London: Taylor & Francis, 1985.

Jönsson, Christer. *Soviet Bargaining Behavior: The Nuclear Test Ban Case.* New York: Columbia University Press, 1979.

Jordan, Gerhard. "Peace Activities in Austria Since 1945." Paper presented at the American-European Consultation on Peace Research in History, Stadtschlaining, Austria, Aug. 1986.

Jorgensen, Klaus. *Atomvåbnenes rolle i dansk politik med saerligt henblik på Kampagnen mod Atomvåben 1960–68.* Odense: Odense University Press, 1973.

Kalven, Harry, Jr. "Congressional Testing of Linus Pauling: The Legal Framework," pp. 466–78 in Morton Grodzins and Eugene Rabinowitch, eds., *The Atomic Age: Scientists in World Affairs.* New York: Basic Books, 1963.

———. "Congressional Testing of Linus Pauling: Sourwine in an Old Bottle," pp. 479–93 in Morton Grodzins and Eugene Rabinowitch, eds., *The Atomic Age: Scientists in World Affairs.* New York: Basic Books, 1963.

Kamata, Sadao, and Stephen Salaff. "The Atomic Bomb and the Citizens of Nagasaki." *Bulletin of Concerned Asian Scholars* 14 (Apr.–June 1982): 38–50.

Kapitza, Peter L. *Experiment, Theory, Practice: Articles and Addresses.* Dordrect, Holland: D. Reidel, 1980.

Kapitza, Sergei P. "The Scope of His Personality," pp. 99–104 in *Reminiscences about Academician Lev Artsimovich.* Moscow: Nauka, 1985.

Katz, Milton S. *Ban the Bomb: A History of SANE.* New York: Greenwood Press, 1986.

Kelleher, Catherine McArdle. *Germany and the Politics of Nuclear Weapons.* New York: Columbia University Press, 1975.

Kendrick, Alexander. *Prime Time: The Life of Edward R. Murrow.* Boston: Little, Brown, 1969.

Keys, Donald F. "The American Peace Movement," pp. 295–306 in Elton B. McNeil, ed., *The Nature of Human Conflict.* Englewood Cliffs, N.J.: Prentice-Hall, 1965.

———. "The New Federalists." *Worldview* 16 (Mar. 1973): 37–41.

Khrushchev, Nikita. *Khrushchev Remembers.* Boston: Little, Brown, 1970.

———. *Khrushchev Remembers: The Glasnost Tapes.* Boston: Little, Brown, 1990.

———. *Khrushchev Remembers: The Last Testament.* Boston: Little, Brown, 1974.

Khrushchev, Sergei. *Khrushchev on Khrushchev.* Boston: Little, Brown, 1990.

Killian, James R., Jr. *Sputnik, Scientists, and Eisenhower.* Cambridge, Mass.: MIT Press, 1977.

Kimche, David. *The Afro-Asian Movement: Ideology and Foreign Policy of the Third World.* Jerusalem: Israel Universities Press, 1973.

Kissinger, Henry A. *Nuclear Weapons and Foreign Policy.* New York: Harper & Brothers, 1957.

———. *White House Years.* Boston: Little, Brown, 1979.

"Kissinger's Critique." *Economist* 270 (Feb. 3, 1979): 17–22.

Kistiakowsky, George B. *A Scientist at the White House.* Cambridge, Mass.: Harvard University Press, 1976.

Kitzinger, U. W. *German Electoral Politics: A Study of the 1957 Campaign.* Oxford: Clarendon Press, 1960.

Klehr, Harvey, and John Earl Haynes. *The American Communist Movement: Storming Heaven Itself.* New York: Twayne Publishers, 1992.

Kleidman, Robert. *Organizing for Peace: Neutrality, the Test Ban, and the Freeze.* Syracuse: Syracuse University Press, 1993.

Klein, Fritz. "East Germany and Eastern Europe." Paper presented at the International Congress of Historical Sciences, Montreal, Sept. 1, 1995.

———. "Impact of Peace Movements on the End of the Cold War." Paper presented at the American Historical Association convention, Washington, D.C., Dec. 30, 1992.

Klose, Kevin. *Russia and the Russians: Inside the Closed Society.* New York: W. W. Norton, 1984.

Knopf, Jeffrey William. "Domestic Politics, Citizen Activism, and U.S. Nuclear Arms Control Policy." Ph.D. diss., Stanford University, 1991.

Kogan, Norman. *A Political History of Postwar Italy.* New York: Frederick A. Praeger, 1966.

Kohl, Wilfrid L. *French Nuclear Diplomacy.* Princeton: Princeton University Press, 1971.

Koschmann, J. Victor. "Postwar Democracy and Japanese Ban-the-Bomb Movements." Manuscript, author's possession.

Kostash, Myrna. *Long Way From Home.* Toronto: James Lorimer, 1980.

Kramer, Bernard M., S. Michael Kalick, and Michael Milburn. "Attitudes Toward Nuclear Weapons and Nuclear War: 1945–1982." *Journal of Social Issues* 39 (Spring 1983): 7–24.

Krasner, Michael A. *The Political Influence of the New Danish Peace Movement, 1979–1986.* Aarhus, Denmark: Institute of Political Science, University of Aarhus, 1986.

Kuo Mo-jo. "Ban Atomic Weapons!" *People's China*, no. 6 (Mar. 16, 1955): 3–5.

Kurino, Ohtori, and Katsuya Kodama. "A Study on the Japanese Peace Movement," pp. 119–27 in Katsuya Kodama and Unto Vesa, eds., *Towards a Comparative Analysis of Peace Movements*. Hants, Eng.: Dartmouth Publishing, 1990.

Lang, Daniel. *An Inquiry into Enoughness: Of Bombs and Men and Staying Alive*. New York: McGraw-Hill, 1965.

Lanouette, William, with Bela Silard. *Genius in the Shadows: A Biography of Leo Szilard*. New York: Charles Scribner's Sons, 1992.

Lapp, Ralph E. *The Voyage of the Lucky Dragon*. New York: Harper & Row, 1958.

Larson, Ellen. "Etiska argument i den svenska freds- och försvarsdebatten under åren 1957–1970," *Acta Universitatis Upsaliensis*, no. 2 (1973): 156–94.

Larson, Jeanne, and Madge Micheels-Cyrus. *Seeds of Peace*. Philadelphia: New Society Publishers, 1987.

Lebedinsky, A. V., ed. *Soviet Scientists on the Danger of Nuclear Tests*. Moscow: Foreign Languages Publishing House, 1960.

Lee, Matthew C. "In the Valley of the Shadow of Death: American Churches and the Bomb, 1945–1970." Ph.D. diss., University of California, Los Angeles, 1991.

Lewis, John Wilson, and Xue Litae. *China Builds the Bomb*. Stanford: Stanford University Press, 1988.

Lewy, Guenter. *The Cause That Failed: Communism in American Political Life*. New York: Oxford University Press, 1990.

Liao Cheng-chih. "Thoroughly Expose the Reactionary Nature of the Tripartite Treaty." *Peking Review* 6 (Aug. 9, 1963): 12–16.

Libby, Willard F. "An Open Letter to Dr. Schweitzer." *Saturday Review* 40 (May 25, 1957): 8–9, 36–37.

Liddington, Jill. *The Long Road to Greenham: Feminism and Anti-Militarism in Britain since 1820*. London: Virago Press, 1989.

Lifton, Robert J. *Death in Life: Survivors of Hiroshima*. New York: Simon & Schuster, 1967.

Lindkvist, Kent. "Mobilization Peaks and Declines of the Swedish Peace Movement," pp. 147–67 in Katsuya Kodama and Unto Vesa, eds., *Towards a Comparative Analysis of Peace Movements*. Hants, Eng.: Dartmouth Publishing, 1990.

Locke, Elsie. *Peace People: A History of Peace Activities in New Zealand*. Christchurch: Hazard Press, 1992.

Lodge, Henry Cabot. *As It Was: An Inside View of Politics and Power in the '50s and '60s*. New York: W. W. Norton, 1976.

Long, Franklin. "A Renaissance Man," pp. 86–87 in *Reminiscences about Academician Lev Artsimovich*. Moscow: Nauka, 1985.

Lowther, Mary P. "The Decline of Public Concern Over the Atom Bomb." *Kansas Journal of Sociology* 9 (Spring 1973): 77–88.

Lubelski-Bernard, Nadine. "Les mouvements de la paix en Belgique (1945–1960)," pp. 373–95 in Maurice Vaïsse, ed., *Le Pacifisme en Europe des années 1920 aux années 1950*. Brussels: Bruylant, 1993.

Lumsden, Malvern. "Nuclear Weapons and the New Peace Movement," pp. 101–26 in *World Armaments and Disarmament: SIPRI Yearbook 1983*. New York: International Publications Service, 1982.

Lyon, Peyton V. *Canada in World Affairs, 1961–1963*. Toronto: Oxford University Press, 1968.

Macmillan, Harold. *At the End of the Day, 1961–1963*. New York: Harper & Row, 1973.

———. *Pointing the Way, 1959–1961*. New York: Harper & Row, 1972.

———. *Riding the Storm, 1956–1959*. London: Macmillan, 1971.

Macpherson, Kay. *When in Doubt, Do Both: The Times of My Life.* Toronto: University of Toronto Press, 1994.

Macpherson, Kay, and Meg Sears. "The Voice of Women: A History," pp. 71–89 in Gwen Matheson, ed., *Women in the Canadian Mosaic.* Toronto: Peter Martin, 1976.

"Man Against Machine." *Newsweek* 60 (July 2, 1962): 51.

Mao Tun. "The Way to General Disarmament and World Peace." *Peking Review* 5 (July 20, 1962): 5–13.

Marshall, George, and David Poling. *Schweitzer.* Garden City, N.Y.: Doubleday, 1971.

Martin, John Bartlow. *Adlai Stevenson and the World.* Garden City, N.Y.: Doubleday, 1977.

Mazrui, Ali A. *Political Values and the Educated Class in Africa.* London: Heinemann, 1978.

Mazuzan, George T., and J. Samuel Walker. *Controlling the Atom: The Beginnings of Nuclear Regulation, 1946–1962.* Berkeley: University of California Press, 1984.

McAuliffe, Mary S., ed. *CIA Documents on the Cuban Missile Crisis.* Washington, D.C.: Central Intelligence Agency, 1992.

McElheny, Victor K. "Kapitsa to Visit England." *Science* 152 (May 6, 1966): 744.

———. "Kapitsa's Visit to England." *Science* 153 (Aug. 12, 1966): 725–27.

McKeever, Porter. *Adlai Stevenson: His Life and Legacy.* New York: William Morrow, 1989.

McNamara, Robert. *The Essence of Security.* New York: Harper & Row, 1968.

———. *In Retrospect: The Tragedy and Lessons of Vietnam.* New York: Times Books, 1995.

———. "The Military Role of Nuclear Weapons: Perceptions and Misperceptions." *Foreign Affairs* 62 (Fall 1983): 59–80.

McNeal, Patricia F. *The American Catholic Peace Movement, 1928–1972.* New York: Arno Press, 1978.

———. *Harder than War: Catholic Peacemaking in Twentieth-Century America.* New Brunswick, N.J.: Rutgers University Press, 1992.

McReynolds, David. "Pacifists and the Vietnam Antiwar Movement," pp. 53–70 in Melvin Small and William D. Hoover, eds., *Give Peace a Chance: Exploring the Vietnam Antiwar Movement.* Syracuse: Syracuse University Press, 1992.

The Meaning of Survival: Hiroshima's 36 Year Commitment to Peace. Hiroshima: *Chugoku Shimbun* and the Hiroshima International Cultural Foundation, 1983.

Medvedev, Roy. *Khrushchev.* Oxford: Basil Blackwell, 1982.

Medvedev, Roy, and Zhores A. Medvedev. *Khrushchev: The Years in Power.* New York: Columbia University Press, 1976.

Medvedev, Zhores A. *Soviet Science.* New York: W. W. Norton, 1978.

Melman, Seymour. *The Peace Race.* New York: George Braziller, 1962.

Mendel, Douglas, Jr. *The Japanese People and Foreign Policy.* Berkeley: University of California Press, 1961.

———. "Public Views of the Japanese Defense System," pp. 149–80 in James H. Buck, ed., *The Modern Japanese Military System.* Beverly Hills, Calif.: Sage, 1975.

Merkl, Peter H. "Pacifism in West Germany." *School of Advanced International Studies Review*, no. 4 (Summer 1982): 81–91.

Merritt, Anna J., and Richard L. Merritt, eds. *Public Opinion in Semisovereign Germany: The HICOG Surveys, 1949–1955.* Urbana: University of Illinois Press, 1980.

Merritt, Richard L., and Donald J. Puchala, eds. *Western European Perspectives on International Affairs: Public Opinion Studies and Evaluations.* New York: Frederick A. Praeger, 1968.

"Messages Exchanged by President Kennedy and Chairman Khrushchev During the Cuban Missile Crisis of October 1962." *Department of State Bulletin* 69 (Nov. 19, 1973): 635–55.

Meyer, David S. "Peace Protest and Policy: Explaining the Rise and Decline (and Rise and

Decline) of Antinuclear Movements in Post-War America." Paper presented at American Political Science Association convention, Washington, D.C., Aug. 1991.

Meyer, Robert S. *Peace Organizations Past and Present*. Jefferson, N.C.: McFarland, 1988.

Meynaud, Jean. *Rapport Sur L'Abolition de la Démocratie en Grèce*. Montreal: Etudes de Science Politique, 1967.

Miller, John. *No Cloak, No Dagger: Recent Quaker Experience in East-West Encounters*. London: East-West Relations Committee, Society of Friends, 1965.

Minnion, John, and Philip Bolsover, eds. *The CND Story*. London: Allison & Busby, 1983.

Miyata, Mitsuo. "Education for Peace," *Internationales Jahrbuch für Geschichts- und Geographie-Unterricht* 14 (1972/73): 3–21.

Moch, Jules. *Non à la force de frappe*. Paris: Robert Laffont, 1963.

Moffatt, Gary. *History of the Canadian Peace Movement Until 1969*. St. Catherines: Grapevine Press, 1969.

Morgenthau, Hans J. *Politics Among Nations: The Struggle for Power and Peace*. New York: Alfred A. Knopf, 1967.

Morrison, Sybil. *I Renounce War: The Story of the Peace Pledge Union*. London: Sheppard Press, 1962.

Mortimer, Robert A. *The Third World Coalition in International Politics*. New York: Praeger Publishers, 1980.

Muelder, Walter G. "Pacifism and the World Council of Churches," pp. 153–68 in Thomas A. Shannon, ed., *War or Peace? The Search for New Answers*. Maryknoll, N.Y.: Orbis Books, 1980.

Mushaben, Joyce Marie. "Cycles of Peace Protest in West Germany: Experiences from Three Decades." *West European Politics* 8 (Jan. 1985): 24–40.

————. "Swords to Plowshares: The Church, the State and the East German Peace Movement." *Studies in Comparative Communism* 17 (Summer 1984): 123–35.

Musto, Ronald G. *The Catholic Peace Tradition*. Maryknoll, N.Y.: Orbis, 1986.

Myers, Frank Earle. "British Peace Politics: The Campaign for Nuclear Disarmament and the Committee of 100, 1957–1962." Ph.D. diss., Columbia University, 1965.

————. "Dilemmas in the British Peace Movement Since World War II." *Journal of Peace Research* 10: 1–2 (1973): 81–90.

Myrdal, Alva. "Dynamics of European Nuclear Disarmament," pp. 209–76 in Ken Coates, ed., *The Dynamics of European Nuclear Disarmament*. Nottingham: Spokesman, 1981.

————. *The Game of Disarmament: How the United States and Russia Run the Arms Race*. New York: Pantheon, 1976.

Naeve, Virginia, ed. *Changeover: The Drive for Peace*. Denver: Alan Swallow, 1963.

————, ed. *Friends of the Hibakusha*. Denver: Alan Swallow, 1964.

Nathan, Otto, and Heinz Norden, eds. *Einstein on Peace*. New York: Schocken Books, 1968.

National Security Files: Western Europe, 1961–1963. Frederick, Md.: University Publications of America, 1992. Microfilm.

Nilson, Sten Sparre. "The Peace Movement in Norway," pp. 33–48 in Werner Kaltefleiter and Robert L. Pfaltzgraff, eds., *The Peace Movements in Europe and the United States*. London: Croom Helm, 1985.

Nitze, Paul H. *From Hiroshima to Glasnost: At the Center of Decision, A Memoir*. New York: Grove Weidenfeld, 1989.

Nkrumah, Kwame. *Africa Must Unite*. New York: Frederick A. Praeger, 1963.

Noelle, Elisabeth, and Erich Peter Neumann, eds. *The Germans: Public Opinion Polls, 1947–1966*. Allensbach: Verlag für Demoskopie, 1967.

Norman, Edward. "The Churches and the Peace Movement: The British Experience," pp.

260–72 in Walter Laqueur and Robert Hunter, eds., *European Peace Movements and the Future of the Western Alliance*. New Brunswick, N.J.: Transaction Books, 1985.

Oe, Kenzaburo. *Hiroshima Notes*. Tokyo: YMCA Press, 1981.

"Opinion." *Time* 78 (Sept. 15, 1961): 30–31.

Orlov, Yuri. *Dangerous Thoughts: Memoirs of a Russian Life*. New York: William Morrow, 1991.

Ormrod, David. "The Churches and the Nuclear Arms Race," pp. 189–220 in Richard Taylor and Nigel Young, eds., *Campaigns for Peace: British Peace Movements in the Twentieth Century*. Manchester: Manchester University Press, 1987.

Osgood, Charles E. *An Alternative to War or Surrender*. Urbana: University of Illinois Press, 1962.

"The Other Summit Conferences." *Nation* 190 (June 4, 1960): 482.

Otto, Karl A. "Kampagne 'Kampf demn Atomtod,'" pp. 214–15 in Helmut Donat and Karl Holl, eds., *Die Friedensbewegung: Organisierter Pazifismus in Deutschland, Österreich und in der Schweiz*. Düsseldorf: ECON Taschenbuch Verlag, 1983.

———. "'Ostermarsch der Atomwaffengegner': Die Friedensbewegung der 60er Jahre." *Geschichtsdidaktik* 7: 2 (1982): 161–92.

———. *Vom Ostermarsch zur APO: Geschichte der ausserparlamentarischen Opposition in der Bundesrepublik, 1960–1970*. Frankfurt: Campus, 1977.

Overstreet, Gene D., and Marshall Windmiller. *Communism in India*. Berkeley: University of California Press, 1960.

Paarlberg, Rob. "Forgetting About the Unthinkable." *Foreign Policy* 10 (1973): 132–40.

Pandey, B. N. *Nehru*. New York: Stein & Day, 1976.

Parker, Michael. "National Student Peace Union." *New University Thought* 2 (Spring 1962): 150–52.

Parkin, Frank. *Middle Class Radicalism: The Social Bases of the British Campaign for Nuclear Disarmament*. Manchester: Manchester University Press, 1968.

Parry, Albert. *Peter Kapitsa on Life and Science*. New York: Macmillan, 1968.

Passin, Herbert. "Nuclear Arms and Japan," pp. 67–132 in William H. Overholt, ed., *Asia's Nuclear Future*. Boulder: Westview Press, 1977.

Patterson, David S. "President Eisenhower and Arms Control." *Peace and Change* 11: 3–4 (1986): 3–24.

Paul, John, and Jerome Laulicht. *In Your Opinion*. Clarkson, Ont.: Canadian Peace Research Institute, 1963.

Pauling, Linus. *No More War!* New York: Dodd, Mead, 1983.

Pauling, Linus, and Daisaku Ikeda. *A Lifelong Quest for Peace*. Boston: Jones & Bartlett, 1992.

Pearson, Lester B. *Mike: The Memoirs of the Right Honorable Lester B. Pearson. Vol. III: 1957–1968*. Chicago: Quadrangle Books, 1975.

Peierls, Rudolf. *Bird of Passage: Recollections of a Physicist*. Princeton: Princeton University Press, 1985.

"Peking Rally Backs Tokyo Conference." *Peking Review* 5 (Aug. 31, 1962): 7–9.

Pempel, T. J. "Japan's Nuclear Allergy." *Current History* 68 (Apr. 1975): 169–73, 183.

Penner, Norman. *Canadian Communism: The Stalin Years and Beyond*. Toronto: Methuen, 1988.

The Pentagon Papers: The Senator Gravel Edition. 5 vols. Boston: Beacon Press, 1975.

Peristerakis, Michalis N. "To Elliniko Kinima Eirinis." Ph.D. diss., Panteios University, Athens, 1988.

Peterson, Nikolaj. "The Cold War and Denmark." *Scandinavian Journal of History* 10: 3 (1985): 191–209.

Pfau, Richard. *No Sacrifice Too Great: The Life of Lewis L. Strauss*. Charlottesville: University Press of Virginia, 1984.

Pharo, Helge. "The Cold War in Norwegian and International Historical Research." *Scandinavian Journal of History* 10: 3 (1985): 163–89.

Pierre, Andrew J. *Nuclear Politics: The British Experience with an Independent Strategic Force, 1939–1970*. London: Oxford University Press, 1972.

Pierson, Ruth Roach. "'Did Your Mother Wear Army Boots?': Feminist Theory and Women's Relation to War, Peace and Revolution," pp. 205–27 in Sharon Macdonald, Pat Holden, and Shirley Ardener, eds., *Images of Women in Peace and War*. London: Macmillan Education, 1987.

Powaski, Ronald E. *March to Armageddon: The United States and the Nuclear Arms Race, 1939 to the Present*. New York: Oxford University Press, 1989.

Powell, C. F. "Nuclear Weapons and the Federation." *Scientific World* 8: 1 (1964): 3–4.

Priestley, J. B. "Britain and the Nuclear Bombs." *New Statesman* 54 (Nov. 2, 1957): 554–56.

Primack, Joel, and Frank von Hippel. *Advice and Dissent: Scientists in the Political Arena*. New York: Basic Books, 1974.

"Protest." *New Yorker* 36 (May 14, 1960): 33–35.

Public Papers of the Presidents of the United States: Dwight D. Eisenhower, 1957. Washington, D.C.: U.S. Government Printing Office, 1958.

Public Papers of the Presidents of the United States: Dwight D. Eisenhower, 1960–61. Washington, D.C.: U.S. Government Printing Office, 1961.

Public Papers of the Presidents of the United States: John F. Kennedy, 1961. Washington, D.C.: U.S. Government Printing Office, 1962.

Public Papers of the Presidents of the United States: John F. Kennedy, 1962. Washington, D.C.: U.S. Government Printing Office, 1963.

Public Papers of the Presidents of the United States: John F. Kennedy, 1963. Washington, D.C.: U.S. Government Printing Office, 1964.

Puchala, Donald J. *Western European Attitudes on International Problems, 1952–1961: A Summary of USIA Public Opinion Surveys in France, West Germany, Great Britain and Italy*. New Haven: Yale University Political Science Research Library, 1964.

Putney, Snell, and Russell Middleton. "Some Factors Associated with Student Acceptance or Rejection of War." *American Sociological Review* 27 (Oct. 1962): 655–67.

Quester, George H. "Sweden and the Nuclear Non-Proliferation Treaty." *Cooperation and Conflict* 5: 1 (1970): 52–64.

Randle, Michael. "Non-Violent Direct Action in the 1950s and 1960s," pp. 131–61 in Richard Taylor and Nigel Young, eds., *Campaigns for Peace: British Peace Movements in the Twentieth Century*. Manchester: Manchester University Press, 1987.

———. "Pacifism, War Resistance, and the Struggle Against Nuclear Weapons: Part I," pp. 27–36 in Gail Chester and Andrew Rigby, eds., *Articles of Peace*. Bridport, Dorset: Prism Press, 1986.

Redner, Harry, and Jill Redner. *Anatomy of the World: The Impact of the Atom on Australia and the World*. Melbourne: Fontana/Collins, 1983.

Regehr, Ernie. "Canada and the U.S. Nuclear Arsenal," pp. 101–21 in Ernie Regehr and Simon Rosenblum, eds., *Canada and the Nuclear Arms Race*. Toronto: James Lorimer, 1983.

Regehr, Ernie, and Simon Rosenblum, "The Canadian Peace Movement," pp. 225–30 in Ernie Regehr and Simon Rosenblum, eds., *Canada and the Nuclear Arms Race*. Toronto: James Lorimer, 1983.

Reiss, Mitchell. *Without the Bomb: The Politics of Nuclear Nonproliferation*. New York: Columbia University Press, 1988.

Resis, Albert, ed. *Molotov Remembers*. Chicago: Ivan R. Dee, 1993.

Reves, Emery. "Why Waste Time Discussing Disarmament?" *Look* 25 (Mar. 28, 1961): 67–70, 72.

Reynolds, Earle. *The Forbidden Voyage*. New York: David McKay, 1961.

Ribkin, Ye. I. "On the Nature of World Nuclear Rocket War," pp. 101–15 in William R. Kintner and Harriet Fast Scott, eds., *The Nuclear Revolution in Soviet Military Affairs*. Norman: University of Oklahoma Press, 1968.

Richter, James G. *Khrushchev's Double Bind: International Pressures and Domestic Coalition Politics*. Baltimore: Johns Hopkins University Press, 1994.

"Roadblocks to a World Traveler." *Chemical and Engineering News* 33 (Nov. 28, 1955): 5156–57.

Roberts, Adam. *Nations in Arms: The Theory and Practice of Territorial Defense*. London: Macmillan, 1986.

Roberts, Barbara. "Women's Peace Activism in Canada," pp. 276–308 in Linda Kealey and Joan Sangster, eds., *Beyond the Vote: Canadian Women and Politics*. Toronto: University of Toronto Press, 1989.

Robinson, Jo Ann. *Abraham Went Out: A Biography of A. J. Muste*. Philadelphia: Temple University Press, 1981.

Romanov, Yu. A. "Answers to the Questions of American Television Correspondents," pp. 556–62 in P. N. Lebedev Physics Institute, *Andrei Sakharov: Facets of a Life*. Gif-sur-Yvette: Editions Frontières, 1991.

Rosen, Steven J. "Nuclearization and Stability in the Middle East," pp. 157–84 in Onkar Marwah and Ann Schulz, eds., *Nuclear Proliferation and the Near-Nuclear Countries*. Cambridge, Mass.: Ballinger, 1975.

Rosenblatt, Roger. *Witness: The World Since Hiroshima*. Boston: Little, Brown, 1985.

Rotblat, Joseph. "Movements of Scientists Against the Arms Race," pp. 115–57 in Joseph Rotblat, ed., *Scientists, the Arms Race and Disarmament: A UNESCO/Pugwash Symposium*. London: Taylor & Francis, 1982.

———. *Pugwash—the First Ten Years*. New York: Humanities Press, 1968.

———. *Scientists in the Quest for Peace: A History of the Pugwash Conferences*. Cambridge, Mass.: MIT Press, 1972.

Rousseas, Stephen. *The Death of a Democracy: Greece and the American Conscience*. New York: Grove Press, 1968.

Roussopoulos, Dimitrios I. *From Protest to Resistance and the International War System*. Montreal: Black Rose Books, 1986.

———. "International Peace Action." *New University Thought* 2 (Spring 1962): 142–45.

———, ed. *The New Left in Canada*. Montreal: Black Rose Books, 1970.

Rudling, Anna. *Kampen mot Atomvapen*. Stockholm: Tidens Förlag, 1975.

Ruge, Mari Holmboe. "Are You a Member of a Peace Organization?" *Journal of Peace Research* 3: 4 (1966): 389–94.

Rupp, Hans K. *Ausserparlamentarische Opposition in der Ära Adenauer: Der Kampf gegen die Atombewaffnung in den fünfziger Jahren*. Cologne: Pahl-Rugenstein, 1970.

Rupp, Leila J., and Verta Taylor. *Survival in the Doldrums: The American Women's Rights Movement, 1945 to the 1960s*. New York: Oxford University Press, 1987.

Rusk, Dean. *As I Saw It*. New York: Penguin Books, 1990.

Russell, Bertrand. *Common Sense and Nuclear Warfare*. London: George Allen & Unwin, 1959.

———. *The Final Years: 1944–1969*. Vol. 3 of *The Autobiography of Bertrand Russell*. New York: Bantam Books, 1970.

———. *Has Man a Future?* New York: Simon & Schuster, 1962.

Sagdeev, Roald Z. *The Making of a Soviet Scientist.* New York: John Wiley, 1994.

Sakharov, Andrei D. *Alarm and Hope.* New York: Alfred A. Knopf, 1978.

————. "An Autobiographical Note," pp. 175–79 in Edward D. Lozansky, ed., *Andrei Sakharov and Peace.* New York: Avon Books, 1985.

————. *Memoirs.* New York: Alfred A. Knopf, 1990.

————. *My Country and the World.* New York: Alfred A. Knopf, 1975.

————. "Radioactive Carbon in Nuclear Explosions and Nonthreshold Biological Effects," pp. 39–49 in A. V. Lebedinsky, ed., *Soviet Scientists on the Danger of Nuclear Tests.* Moscow: Foreign Languages Publishing House, 1960.

————. *Sakharov Speaks.* New York: Alfred A. Knopf, 1974.

Sakharov, Andrei D., and Ernst Henry. "Scientists and the Danger of Nuclear War," pp. 228–34 in Stephen Cohen, ed., *An End to Silence: Uncensored Opinion in the Soviet Union.* New York: W. W. Norton, 1982.

Sale, Kirkpatrick. *SDS.* New York: Vintage, 1974.

"Salute the Victory of the Hiroshima Conference." *Peking Review* 6 (Aug. 30, 1963): 13–15.

Sandford, John. *The Sword and the Ploughshare: Autonomous Peace Initiatives in East Germany.* London: Merlin Press and European Nuclear Disarmament, 1983.

Santi, Rainer. *100 Years of Peace Making.* Geneva: International Peace Bureau, 1991.

Saunders, Malcolm, and Ralph Summy. *The Australian Peace Movement: A Short History.* Canberra: Peace Research Centre, Australian National University, 1986.

————. "One Hundred Years of an Australian Peace Movement, 1885–1984: Part II: From the Second World War to Vietnam and Beyond." *Peace and Change* 10 (Fall/Winter 1984): 57–75.

Scalapino, Robert A. *The Japanese Communist Movement, 1920–1966.* Berkeley: University of California Press, 1967.

Schalk, David L. *War and the Ivory Tower: Algeria and Vietnam.* New York: Oxford University Press, 1991.

Scharrer, Siegfried. "War and Peace and the German Church," pp. 273–317 in Walter Laqueur and Robert Hunter, eds., *European Peace Movements and the Future of the Western Alliance.* New Brunswick, N.J.: Transaction Books, 1985.

Scheinman, Lawrence. *Atomic Energy Policy in France Under the Fourth Republic.* Princeton: Princeton University Press, 1965.

Schlaga, Rüdiger. "Peace Movement as a Party's Tool? The Peace Council of the German Democratic Republic," pp. 129–46 in Katsuya Kodama and Unto Vesa, eds., *Towards a Comparative Analysis of Peace Movements.* Hants, Eng.: Dartmouth Publishing, 1990.

Schlesinger, Arthur M., Jr. *A Thousand Days: John F. Kennedy in the White House.* Boston: Houghton Mifflin, 1965.

Schmitz, Gerald. *Anti-Nuclear Protest and the Peace Movement.* Ottawa: Library of Parliament, 1983.

Schoenbaum, Thomas J. *Waging Peace and War: Dean Rusk in the Truman, Kennedy, and Johnson Years.* New York: Simon & Schuster, 1988.

Schoenman, Ralph. "Bertrand Russell and the Peace Movement," pp. 227–52 in George Nakhnikian, ed., *Bertrand Russell's Philosophy.* London: Duckworth, 1974.

————. "Mass Resistance in Mass Society," pp. 106–10 in David Boulton, ed., *Voices From the Crowd: Against the H-Bomb.* Philadelphia: Dufour Editions, 1964.

Schwartz, Richard Alan. "The F.B.I. and Dr. Einstein." *Nation* 237 (Sept. 3–10, 1983): 168–73.

Schweitzer, Albert. "A Declaration of Conscience." *Saturday Review* 40 (May 18, 1957): 17–20.

————. *Peace or Atomic War?* New York: Henry Holt, 1958.

Scott, Harriet Fast, and William F. Scott. *Soviet Military Doctrine: Continuity, Formulation, and Dissemination*. Boulder: Westview Press, 1988.

Scott, Richenda C. *Quakers in Russia*. London: Michael Joseph, 1964.

Seaborg, Glenn T. *Journal of Glenn T. Seaborg*. Vol. 1. Berkeley: Lawrence Berkeley Laboratory, University of California, 1989.

————. *Kennedy, Khrushchev, and the Test Ban*. Berkeley: University of California Press, 1981.

————. *Stemming the Tide: Arms Control in the Johnson Years*. Lexington, Mass.: Lexington Books, 1987.

Sharma, Dhirendra, ed. *The Indian Atom: Power and Proliferation*. New Delhi: Philosophy and Social Action, 1986.

Sharp, Rachel. "Militarism and Nuclear Issues in the Pacific," pp. 176–204 in Rachel Sharp, ed., *Apocalypse No: An Australian Guide to the Arms Race and the Peace Movement*. Sydney: Pluto Press, 1984.

Shelley, Diana. "Pacifism, War Resistance, and the Struggle Against Nuclear Weapons: Part II," pp. 36–48 in Gail Chester and Andrew Rigby, eds., *Articles of Peace*. Bridport, Dorset: Prism Press, 1986.

Shulman, Marshall D. *Stalin's Foreign Policy Reappraised*. New York: Atheneum, 1966.

Siracusa, Joseph M. "Peace Movements in Australia and New Zealand and the Cold War." Paper presented at the International Peace Research Association convention, Malta, Oct. 30–Nov. 4, 1994.

Sisman, Adam. *A. J. P. Taylor: A Biography*. London: Sinclair-Stevenson, 1994.

"Smash the Test Ban Treaty Fraud!" *Peking Review* 6 (Aug. 9, 1963): 36–38.

Smirnov, Yuri N., and Vladislav Zubok. "Nuclear Weapons after Stalin's Death: Moscow Enters the H-Bomb Age." Cold War International History Project *Bulletin*, no. 4 (Fall 1994): 1, 14–18.

Smith, Gerard. *Doubletalk: The Story of the First Strategic Arms Limitation Talks*. Garden City, N.Y.: Doubleday, 1980.

Snyder, William P. *The Politics of British Defense Policy, 1945–1962*. Columbus: Ohio State University Press, 1964.

Solberg, Carl. *Hubert Humphrey: A Biography*. New York: W. W. Norton, 1984.

Solomon, Frederic, and Jacob R. Fishman. "Youth and Peace: A Psychosocial Study of Student Peace Demonstrators in Washington, D.C." *Journal of Social Issues* 20 (July 1964): 54–73.

Sommer, Theo. "The Objectives of Germany," pp. 39–54 in Alastair Buchan, ed., *A World of Nuclear Powers?* Englewood Cliffs, N.J.: Prentice-Hall, 1966.

Sorensen, Theodore C. *Kennedy*. New York: Harper & Row, 1965.

"The Soviet Threat to the Americas." *Department of State Bulletin* 47 (Nov. 12, 1962): 715–20.

Sperber, A. M. *Murrow: His Life and Times*. New York: Freundlich Books, 1986.

Spock, Benjamin, and Mary Morgan. *Spock on Spock*. New York: Pantheon, 1989.

Ståhle, Elisabeth. *Internationella Kvinnoförbundet för Fred och Frihet*. Stockholm: IKFF, 1988.

"Statement by the Spokesman of the Chinese Government—A Comment on the Soviet Government's Statement of August 6" (Aug. 15, 1963). *Peking Review* 6 (Aug. 16, 1963): 7–15.

"Statement of the Chinese Government Advocating the Complete, Thorough, Total and Resolute Prohibition and Destruction of Nuclear Weapons" (July 31, 1963). *Peking Review* 6 (Aug. 2, 1963): 7–8.

"Statement of the Soviet Government of August 3, 1963," pp. 167–80 in *People of the World,*

Unite, For the Complete, Thorough, Total and Resolute Prohibition and Destruction of Nuclear Weapons. Peking: Foreign Languages Press, 1963.

"Statement of the Soviet Government of August 21, 1963," pp. 181–208 in *People of the World, Unite, For the Complete, Thorough, and Resolute Prohibition and Destruction of Nuclear Weapons.* Peking: Foreign Languages Press, 1963.

Stein, Robert, and Carolyn Conners. "Civil Defense Protests in New York." *New University Thought* 1 (Spring 1961): 81–83.

Stevenson, Adlai E. "Why I Raised the H-Bomb Question." *Look* 21 (Feb. 5, 1957): 23–25.

Stockwin, J. A. A. *The Japanese Socialist Party and Neutralism.* Carlton: Melbourne University Press, 1968.

Stoll, Louise. "Women Strike for Peace." *New University Thought* 2 (Spring 1962): 146–47.

———. "Women's International League for Peace and Freedom." *New University Thought* 2 (Spring 1962): 152–54.

Straus, Virginia. "Peace, Culture, and Education: A Buddhist Response to the Global Ethic." *Buddhist-Christian Studies* 15 (1995): 199–211.

Strauss, Lewis L. *Men and Decisions.* Garden City, N.Y.: Doubleday, 1962.

"Student Peace Groups." *New University Thought* 1 (Spring 1961): 75–80.

Sullivan, William Cuyler, Jr. *Nuclear Democracy: A History of the Greater St. Louis Citizens' Committee for Nuclear Information, 1957–1967.* St. Louis: Washington University, 1982.

Summy, Ralph. "The Australian Peace Council and the Anticommunist Milieu, 1949–1965," pp. 233–64 in Charles Chatfield and Peter van den Dungen, eds., *Peace Movements and Political Cultures.* Knoxville: University of Tennessee Press, 1988.

———. "Militancy and the Australian Peace Movement, 1960–67." *Politics* 5 (Nov. 1970): 148–62.

Summy, Ralph, and Malcolm Saunders. "Disarmament and the Australian Peace Movement: A Brief History." *World Review* 26 (Dec. 1987): 15–52.

Suzuki, Sunao. "The Declining Role of Ideology in Citizens' Movements." *Japan Quarterly* 23 (Apr.–June 1976): 121–26.

———. "Japanese Attitudes Toward Nuclear Issues," in Japan Peace Research Group, ed., *Peace Research in Japan* (1974–75): 99–117.

Swerdlow, Amy. "Ladies' Day at the Capitol: Women Strike for Peace Versus HUAC." *Feminist Studies* 8 (Fall 1982): 493–520.

———. *Women Strike for Peace: Traditional Motherhood and Radical Politics in the 1960s.* Chicago: University of Chicago Press, 1993.

Swing, Raymond Gram. *In the Name of Sanity.* New York: Harper & Brothers, 1946.

Taipale, Ilkka. "The Peace Movement in Finland," pp. 17–49 in Kimmo Kiljunen, Folke Sundman, and Ilkka Taipale, eds., *Finnish Peace Making.* Helsinki: Peace Union of Finland, 1987.

Takibayev, Zh. S. "Ahead of Time," pp. 631–35 in P. N. Lebedev Physics Institute, *Andrei Sakharov: Facets of a Life.* Gif-sur-Yvette: Editions Frontières, 1991.

"Talk with the American Correspondent Anna Louise Strong," pp. 97–101 in *Selected Works of Mao Tse-tung,* vol. 4. Peking: Foreign Languages Press, 1969.

Tame, Adrian, and F. P. J. Robotham. *Maralinga: British A-Bomb, Australian Legacy.* Sydney: Fontana/Collins, 1982.

Tarrow, Sidney. "Communism in Italy and France: Adaptation and Change," pp. 575–640 in Donald L. M. Blackmer and Sidney Tarrow, eds., *Communism in Italy and France.* Princeton: Princeton University Press, 1975.

Tatum, Arlo De Vere. "World Peace Brigade," pp. 129–34 in Ted Dunn, ed., *Alternatives to War and Violence.* London: Clarke, 1963.

Taylor, A. J. P. *A Personal History*. London: Hamish Hamilton, 1983.

Taylor, Richard. *Against the Bomb: The British Peace Movement, 1958–1965*. Oxford: Clarendon Press, 1988.

————. "The Labour Party and CND: 1957 to 1984," pp. 100–130 in Richard Taylor and Nigel Young, eds., *Campaigns for Peace: British Peace Movements in the Twentieth Century*. Manchester: Manchester University Press, 1987.

————. "The Marxist Left and the Peace Movement in Britain Since 1945," in Richard Taylor and Nigel Young, eds., *Campaigns for Peace: British Peace Movements in the Twentieth Century*. Manchester: Manchester University Press, 1987.

Taylor, Richard, and Colin Pritchard. *The Protest Makers*. Oxford: Pergamon Press, 1980.

Teller, Edward. "Two Stories," pp. 107–18 in Edward D. Lozansky, ed., *Andrei Sakharov and Peace*. New York: Avon, 1985.

Teller, Edward, and Albert Latter. "The Compelling Need for Nuclear Tests." *Life* 44 (Feb. 10, 1958): 64–66, 69–72.

Teller, Edward, with Allen Brown. "The Fallout Scare." *Saturday Evening Post* 235 (Feb. 10, 1962): 34–36.

Tertz, Abram. *Fantastic Stories*. New York: Grosset & Dunlap, 1967.

ter Veer, Ben. "The New Peace Movements in Western Europe." *International Peace Research Newsletter* 21: 3 (1983): 10–16.

Theoharis, Athan G., and John Stuart Cox. *The Boss: J. Edgar Hoover and the Great American Inquisition*. Philadelphia: Temple University Press, 1988.

Thomas, Norman M. *The Prerequisites for Peace*. New York: W. W. Norton, 1959.

Thompson, E. P. "A Psessay in Ephology." *New Reasoner* (Autumn 1959): 1–8.

"A Timely Warning to the War-Maniacs." *Peking Review* 4 (Sept. 8, 1961): 6–7.

Totten, George O., and Tamio Kawakami. "Gensuikyo and the Peace Movement in Japan." *Asian Survey* 4 (May 1964): 833–41.

Toulat, Jean. *La bombe ou la vie*. Paris: Fayard, 1969.

Toynbee, Arnold J. "The Holy See and the Work of Peace: An Historian's View," pp. 27–42 in Francis Sweeney, ed., *The Vatican and World Peace*. Gerrards Cross, Eng.: Colin Smythe, 1970.

Trofimenkoff, Susan Mann. "Thérèse Casgrain and the CCF in Quebec," pp. 139–68 in Linda Kealey and Joan Sangster, eds., *Beyond the Vote: Canadian Women and Politics*. Toronto: University of Toronto Press, 1989.

Tsurumi, Kazuko. *Social Change and the Individual: Japan Before and After Defeat in World War II*. Princeton: Princeton University Press, 1970.

Tsurumi, Shunsuke. *An Intellectual History of Wartime Japan, 1931–1945*. London: Routledge & Kegan Paul, 1986.

Tsurumi, Yoshiyuki. "Beheiren." *Japan Quarterly* 16 (Oct.–Dec. 1969): 444–48.

Turski, Marian, and Henryk Zdanowski. *The Peace Movement: People and Facts*. N.p., Poland: Interpress Publishers, 1976.

Twersky, David. "Is Silence Golden? Vanunu and Nuclear Israel." *Tikkun* 3 (Jan.–Feb. 1988): 39–43.

Ueda, Katsumi. "Tabata Shinobu: Defender of the Peace Constitution," pp. 221–49 in Nobuya Bamba and John F. Howes, eds., *Pacifism in Japan: The Christian and Socialist Tradition*. Vancouver: University of British Columbia Press, 1978.

Unger, Irwin. *The Movement: A History of the American New Left, 1959–1972*. New York: Dodd, Mead, 1974.

Unnithan, T. K., and Yogendra Singh. *Sociology of Non-Violence and Peace: Some Behavioural and Attitudinal Dimensions*. New Delhi: Research Council for Cultural Studies, 1969.

U.S. Atomic Energy Commission. *In the Matter of J. Robert Oppenheimer*. Cambridge, Mass.: MIT Press, 1971.

U.S. Department of State. *Foreign Relations of the United States. 1952–1963*. Washington, D.C.: U.S. Government Printing Office, 1984–1995.

U.S. House of Representatives, Committee on Un-American Activities. *Communist Activities in the Peace Movement (Women Strike for Peace and Certain Other Groups)*. 87th Cong., 2d sess. Washington, D.C.: U.S. Government Printing Office, 1963.

"U.S. Nuclear Fraud Exposed." *Peking Review* 6 (July 26, 1963): 47–49.

U.S. Senate, Internal Security Subcommittee of the Committee on the Judiciary. *Communist Infiltration in the Nuclear Test Ban Movement*. 86th Cong., 2d sess. Washington, D.C.: U.S. Government Printing Office, 1960.

———. *Report on the Hearings of Dr. Linus Pauling*. 87th Cong., 1st sess. Washington, D.C.: U.S. Government Printing Office, 1961.

———. *Testimony of Dr. Linus Pauling*. Part I. 86th Cong., 2d sess. Washington, D.C.: U.S. Government Printing Office, 1960.

———. *Testimony of Dr. Linus Pauling*. Part II. 86th Cong., 2d sess. Washington, D.C.: U.S. Government Printing Office, 1960.

U.S. Senate, Select Committee to Study Governmental Operations with Respect to Intelligence Activities. *Final Report: Book III, Supplementary Detailed Staff Reports on Intelligence Activities and the Rights of Americans*. 94th Cong., 2d sess. Washington, D.C.: U.S. Government Printing Office, 1976.

Vaillancourt, Jean-Guy. "Cinq papes modernes, le concile Vatican II et la paix mondiale." *Sociologie et sociétés* 22 (Oct. 1990): 49–64.

Verkuil, I. D. *De grote illusie: De Nederlandse vredesbeweging na 1945*. Utrecht: HES, 1988.

"Vital Questions for the Peace Movement." *Peking Review* 5 (Aug. 17, 1962): 8–10.

von Weizsäcker, Carl Friedrich. *The Politics of Peril*. New York: Seabury Press, 1978.

Wadsworth, James J. *The Price of Peace*. New York: Frederick A. Praeger, 1962.

Walker, Charles C. "Nonviolence in Africa," pp. 186–212 in Severyn T. Bruyn and Paul M. Rayman, eds., *Nonviolent Action and Social Change*. New York: Irvington, 1979.

Wall, Irwin M. *French Communism in the Era of Stalin: The Quest for Unity and Integration*. Westport, Conn.: Greenwood Press, 1983.

Warner, Gale, and Michael Shuman. *Citizen Diplomats*. New York: Continuum Publishing, 1987.

War Resisters League. *History of the War Resisters League*. New York: War Resisters League, 1980.

———. *Peace Calendar, 1967*. New York: War Resisters League, 1966.

———. *A WRL History of Protest Against Nuclear Testing*. New York: War Resisters League, 1986.

Weart, Spencer R. *Nuclear Fear: A History of Images*. Cambridge, Mass.: Harvard University Press, 1988.

———. *Scientists in Power*. Cambridge, Mass.: Harvard University Press, 1979.

Weinberg, Arthur, and Lila Weinberg, eds. *Instead of Violence*. Boston: Beacon Press, 1965.

Weigley, Russell F. *The American Way of War: A History of United States Military Strategy and Policy*. Bloomington: Indiana University Press, 1977.

Weisskopf, Victor F. *The Privilege of Being a Physicist*. New York: W. H. Freeman, 1989.

Werskey, Gary. *The Visible College*. London: Allen Lane, 1978.

"What's Back of the 'Fall-Out' Scare." *U.S. News & World Report* 42 (June 7, 1957): 25–28.

"Where Is Heaven?" *Nation* 194 (Apr. 21, 1962): 342.

White, Mark J. "Exorcizing the Myths: The Kennedys and the Cuban Missile Crisis." Paper presented at the Society for Historians of American Foreign Relations conference, Vassar College, Poughkeepsie, N.Y., June 21, 1992.

White, Theodore H. *The Making of the President 1964.* New York: New American Library, 1965.

Wiberg, Ingrid Segerstedt. *Provstopp nu!* Stockholm: Fredsårsdelegationen Skriftserie, 1986.

Wiesner, Jerome B. *Where Science and Politics Meet.* New York: McGraw-Hill, 1965.

Wigforss, Ernst, et al. *Nej! till svenska atomvapen.* Stockholm: Tidens Förlag, 1959.

Willetts, Peter. *The Non-Aligned Movement.* London: Frances Pinter, 1978.

Williams, Kale. "American Friends Service Committee." *New University Thought* 2 (Spring 1962): 154–55.

Williams, Philip M. *The Diary of Hugh Gaitskell, 1945–1956.* London: Jonathan Cape, 1983.

————. *Hugh Gaitskell: A Political Biography.* London: Jonathan Cape, 1979.

Winkler, Allan M. *Life Under a Cloud: American Anxiety About the Atom.* New York: Oxford University Press, 1993.

Wittner, Lawrence S. *One World or None: A History of the World Nuclear Disarmament Movement Through 1953.* Vol. 1 of *The Struggle Against the Bomb.* Stanford: Stanford University Press, 1993.

————. *Rebels Against War: The American Peace Movement, 1933–1983.* Philadelphia: Temple University Press, 1984.

Woodhouse, Christopher M. *The Struggle for Greece, 1941–1949.* London: Hart-Davis, Mac-Gibbon, 1976.

Wooley, Wesley T. *Alternatives to Anarchy: American Supranationalism since World War II.* Bloomington: Indiana University Press, 1988.

Wooster, W. A. "Some Recollections of the W.F.S.W." *Scientific World,* Anniversary number (1966): 26–29.

Wright, Michael. *Disarm and Verify.* New York: Frederick A. Praeger, 1964.

Yavenditti, Michael J. "The Hiroshima Maidens and American Benevolence in the 1950s." *Mid-America* 64 (Apr.–July 1982): 21–39.

York, Herbert F. *Making Weapons, Talking Peace: A Physicist's Odyssey from Hiroshima to Geneva.* New York: Basic Books, 1987.

Young, Nigel. *An Infantile Disorder? The Crisis and Decline of the New Left.* London: Routledge & Kegan Paul, 1977.

————. "Why Peace Movements Fail: A Historical and Social Overview." *Social Alternatives* 4 (Mar. 1984): 9–16.

Young, Wilmer J. *Visible Witness: A Testimony for Radical Peace Action.* Wallingford, Pa.: Pendle Hill, 1961.

Zaharopoulos, George. "The Monarchy and Politics in Modern Greece," pp. 190–208 in John T. A. Koumoulides, ed., *Greece in Transition: Essays in the History of Modern Greece.* London: Zeno, 1977.

Zahn, Gordon C. *War, Conscience, and Dissent.* New York: Hawthorn Books, 1967.

Zariski, Raphael. "The Italian Socialist Party: A Case Study in Factional Conflict." *American Political Science Review* 56 (June 1962): 372–90.

Zaroulis, Nancy, and Gerald Sullivan. *Who Spoke Up? American Protest Against the War in Vietnam, 1963–1975.* Garden City, N.Y.: Doubleday, 1984.

Zubok, Vladislav M. "Spy vs. Spy: The KGB vs. the CIA, 1960–1962." Cold War International History Project *Bulletin,* no. 4 (Fall 1994): 22–33.

Zuckerman, Solly. "Opening Address," pp. 4–5 in Joseph Rotblat, ed., *Towards a Secure World in the 21st Century.* London: British Pugwash Trust, 1991.

Index

In this index "f" after a number indicates a separate reference on the next page, and "ff" indicates separate references on the next two pages. A continuous discussion over two or more pages is indicated by a span of numbers. *Passim* is used for a cluster of references in close but not consecutive sequence.

Library of Congress Cataloging-in-Publication Data

Wittner, Lawrence S.
    The struggle against the bomb / Lawrence S. Wittner.
        p.   cm. — (Stanford nuclear age series)
    Includes bibliographical references and index.
    Contents: v. 2. Resisting the bomb: A history of the nuclear disarmament movement,
    1954–1970
    ISBN 0-8047-2918-2(v.2)(cl.) : ISBN 0-8047-3169-1(pbk.)
        1. Nuclear disarmament—History. 2. Antinuclear movement—History.   I. Title.
    II. Series.
JX1974.7.W575   1997
327.1'74'09—dc20   92-28026
                                                                                        CIP

⊗ This book is printed on acid-free paper